JEREMIAH 37–52

VOLUME 21C

THE ANCHOR BIBLE is a fresh approach to the world's greatest classic. Its object is to make the Bible accessible to the modern reader; its method is to arrive at the meaning of biblical literature through exact translation and extended exposition, and to reconstruct the ancient setting of the biblical story, as well as the circumstances of its transcription and the characteristics of its transcribers.

THE ANCHOR BIBLE is a project of international and interfaith scope: Protestant, Catholic, and Jewish scholars from many countries contribute individual volumes. The project is not sponsored by any ecclesiastical organization and is not intended to reflect any particular theological doctrine. Prepared under our joint supervision, THE ANCHOR BIBLE is an effort to make available all the significant historical and linguistic knowledge which bears on the interpretation of the biblical record.

THE ANCHOR BIBLE is aimed at the general reader with no special formal training in biblical studies; yet it is written with the most exacting standards of scholarship, reflecting the highest technical accomplishment.

This project marks the beginning of a new era of cooperation among scholars in biblical research, thus forming a common body of knowledge to be shared by all.

William Foxwell Albright
David Noel Freedman
GENERAL EDITORS

THE ANCHOR BIBLE

JEREMIAH
37–52

◆

A New Translation
with Introduction and Commentary

JACK R. LUNDBOM

THE ANCHOR BIBLE
Doubleday
New York   London   Toronto   Sydney   Auckland

THE ANCHOR BIBLE
PUBLISHED BY DOUBLEDAY
a division of Random House, Inc.
1745 Broadway, New York, New York 10019

THE ANCHOR BIBLE, DOUBLEDAY, and the portrayal of an
anchor with the letters A and B are trademarks of
Doubleday, a division of Random House, Inc.

Library of Congress Cataloging-in-Publication Data

Bible. O.T. Jeremiah XXXVII–LII. English. Lundbom. 2004.
    Jeremiah 37–52: a new translation with introduction and commentary
    By Jack R. Lundbom.—1st ed.
        p. cm. — (The Anchor Bible; v. 21C)
    Includes bibliographical references and indexes.
        1. Bible. O.T. Jeremiah XXXVII–LII—Commentaries. I. Lundbom,
    Jack R. II. Title. III. Series: Bible. English. Anchor Bible. 1964; v. 21C.
    BS192.2.A1 1964.G3 vol. 21C
    [BS1523]
    220.7'7 s—dc21
    [224'. 2077]

                                                        97–35473
                                                        CIP

ISBN 0-385-51160-4

First Edition

10 9 8 7 6 5 4 3 2 1

To David and Jeanie

CONTENTS

◆

Preface   xiii

JEREMIAH 37–52: A TRANSLATION   1

TRANSLATION, NOTES, AND COMMENTS   47

V. Behold the Man! (37:1–40:6)   49
  A. Jeremiah's Word Rendered Cheap (37:1–16)   49
    1. A Nation the Shadow of Its King (37:1–2)   49
    2. Jeremiah Asked by Zedekiah to Mediate (37:3–11)   49
    3. Jeremiah Imprisoned on Charge of Desertion (37:12–16)   49
  B. Another Request, Another Answer (37:17–21)   62
  C. Jeremiah again in the Pit (38:1–6)   64
  D. Ebed-melech to the Rescue (38:7–13)   69
  E. One Final Request, One Final Answer (38:14–28)   73
  F. Mercy and No Mercy (39:1–14)   80
    1. Jerusalem Taken, Zedekiah Captured (39:1–10)   80
    2. Jeremiah Spared by Nebuchadrezzar (39:11–14)   80
  G. Grace to the Humble (39:15–40:6)   96
    1. Ebed-melech to Be Rescued (39:15–18)   96
    2. The Whole Land before Jeremiah (40:1–6)   96
VI. Turn and Take Your Journey—to Egypt! (40:7–44:30)   106
  A. Buildup and Breakdown at Mizpah (40:7–41:18)   106
    1. Resettlement under Gedaliah (40:7–12)   106
    2. The Plot against Gedaliah (40:13–16)   106
    3. The Murder of Gedaliah (41:1–3)   107
    4. Arrivals from the North (41:4–6)   107
    5. Another Round of Violence (41:7–10)   107
    6. Rescue at the Pool of Gibeon (41:11–15)   108
    7. On to Geruth Chimham! (41:16–18)   108
  B. Jeremiah's Word again Rendered Cheap (42:1–22)   125
    1. Remnant Asks Jeremiah to Mediate (42:1–6)   125
    2. Yahweh Answers the Remnant (42:7–22)   125

C. Exile to Egypt (43:1–13)   138
  1. Remnant Rejects Yahweh's Word! (43:1–4)   138
  2. On to Tahpanhes! (43:5–7)   138
  3. But Nebuchadrezzar Will Come to Egypt! (43:8–13)   138
D. Final Prophecies in Egypt (44:1–30)   151
  1. Once Again: Queen of Heaven Worship (44:1–25)   151
  2. Whose Word Will Be Confirmed—Mine or Theirs? (44:26–30)   153
VII. Baruch's Colophon (45:1–5)   171
VIII. Oracles to the Foreign Nations (46:1–51:64)   181
  A. Superscription to the Foreign Nation Oracles (46:1)   181
  B. What about Egypt? (46:2–28)   184
    1. Pride Cometh before the Fall (46:2–12)   184
      a) Hasty Advance, Hasty Retreat (46:2–6)   184
      b) Egypt Rises like the Nile! (46:7–8)   195
      c) Rise Up, O Horses! (46:9–10)   198
      d) Rise Up and Get Balm! (46:11–12)   202
    2. Pharaoh Is All Talk (46:13–17)   205
    3. Invasion, Destruction, and Exile for Egypt (46:18–26)   213
      a) Daughter Egypt Better Start Packing (46:18–19)   213
      b) A Horsefly from the North on Heifer Egypt (46:20–21)   216
      c) An Enemy More Numerous than Locusts (46:22–23)   220
      d) Egypt Given Over to a People from the North (46:24–26)   223
    4. But Jacob Will Return Home (46:27–28)   227
  C. A Day for Yahweh against the Philistines (47:1–7)   229
  D. What about Moab? (48:1–47)   242
    1. Devastation for the Whole of Moab (48:1–10)   242
      a) Moab the Renowned Is No More (48:1–2)   242
      b) Moab's Cry Is Heard (48:3–7a)   250
      c) Exile and Wandering Ahead for Moab (48:7b–10)   256
    2. Look at Moab Settled into His Lees! (48:11–13) 263
    3. The Talk Now and the Talk Later (48:14–24)   269
      a) Warriors Are We! (48:14–17a)   269
      b) How the Mighty Scepter Is Broken! (48:17b–18)   273
      c) What Has Happened? (48:19–24)   276
    4. The Horn of Moab Is Cut Off (48:25–27)   282
    5. Go Live in a Rock! (48:28)   285
    6. We Have Heard of the Pride of Moab (48:29–31)   286
    7. Gladness and Rejoicing Are No More (48:32–34)   290

8. Lament the End of Moab! (48:35–38a)   296

9. Moab like a Broken Jar (48:38b–39)   300

10. Eagles Above and Traps Below (48:40–44)   302

    a) Look Out for the Eagle! (48:40–41)   302

    b) Scare, Pit, and Snare Are before You! (48:42–43)   304

    c) One of Them Will Get You! (48:44)   305

11. In the Shadow of Heshbon They Stop (48:45–47)   307

E. What about the Ammonites? (49:1–6)   312

    1. So Why Has Milcom Inherited Gad? (49:1–2)   312

    2. Scream, Rabbah's Daughters! (49:3–6)   318

F. What about Edom? (49:7–22)   324

    1. Is There No Longer Wisdom in Teman? (49:7–11)   324

    2. Yahweh to Bring the Eagle Down! (49:12–18)   333

    3. As a Lion, as an Eagle against Edom (49:19–22)   341

G. What about Damascus? (49:23–27)   347

H. What about Kedar? (49:28–33)   351

    1. Curtains for the People of the East! (49:28–30)   351

    2. A Desert Nation to the Winds (49:31–33)   356

I. Elam too Shall Be Scattered (49:34–39)   359

J. And What about Babylon? (50:1–51:58)   364

    1. Babylon Is Taken (50:1–3)   364

    2. Israel and Judah Will Ask the Way to Zion (50:4–5)   372

    3. My People Became Lost Sheep (50:6–7)   376

    4. Wander from the Midst of Babylon! (50:8–10)   380

    5. Babylon Facing Yahweh's Fury (50:11–13)   385

    6. Babylon Facing Yahweh's Vengeance (50:14–15)   389

    7. Cut Off the Sower from Babylon (50:16)   393

    8. Israel Back in Its Pasture (50:17–20)   394

    9. Shattered Is the Hammer of the Whole Land! (50:21–28)   398

    10. Curtains for Arrogant Babylon! (50:29–30)   408

    11. A Day for Mr. Arrogance As Well! (50:31–32)   411

    12. Their Redeemer Is Strong! (50:33–34)   414

    13. A Sword upon Chaldeans! (50:35–38a)   417

    14. A Land of Images with New Inhabitants (50:38b–40)   422

    15. A People from the North against Babylon! (50:41–43)   426

    16. As a Lion from the Jordan against Babylon! (50:44–46)   428

    17. I Am Rousing a Destroying Wind (51:1–5)   430

    18. A Golden Cup Was Babylon (51:6–10)   436

   19. You Who Dwell by Many Waters (51:11–14)   443

   20. Yahweh the God of Creation! (51:15–19)   449

   21. You Were a Club for Me, Weapons of War (51:20–24)   451

   22. From Destroying Mountain to Burned-Out Mountain (51:25–26) 457

   23. Sanctify the Nations against Her! (51:27–33)   460

   24. Bel No Longer King in Babylon (51:34–45)   469

   25. Look! A Reckoning for Babylon and Its Images (51:46–51)   481

   26. Look Again! A Reckoning for Babylon and Its Images (51:52–57) 489

   27. The Walls of Grand Babylon Demolished! (51:58)   497

  K. Seriah's Colophon (51:59–64)   501

IX. Postscript (52:1–34)   511

  A. Zedekiah Meets the King and Goes to Prison (52:1–11)   511

    1. Summary of Zedekiah's Reign (52:1–3)   511

    2. Capture of Jerusalem and Zedekiah (52:4–11)   511

  B. Jerusalem: Destruction, Remnant, Looting, and Death (52:12–27) 517

    1. Destruction, yet a Remnant (52:12–16)   517

    2. Temple Treasures Go to Babylon (52:17–23)   517

    3. Death to Jerusalem's Great and Small (52:24–27)   518

  C. Deportation Summary (52:28–30)   532

  D. Jehoiachin Leaves Prison For The King's Table (52:31–34)   534

APPENDIXES

Appendix IV   545

  Conversion Tables of Weights, Measures, and Distances   545

    a) Shekels to Grams and Ounces   545

    b) Cubits to Inches, Feet, Meters, and Yards   545

    c) Centimeters to Inches   546

    d) Feet to Meters   546

    e) Meters to Feet   546

    f) Miles to Kilometers   547

    g) Kilometers to Miles   547

    h) Roman Miles to English Miles and Kilometers   548

    i) Dunams to Acres   548

Appendix V   549

  Haplography in Jeremiah 21–52   549

    Summary for Jeremiah 21–52   563

    Combined Summary for Jeremiah 1–52   563

Appendix VI   564
    MT and LXX Compared on Names with Titles in Jeremiah 1–52   564
        A. MT and LXX on "Yahweh of Hosts"   564
        B. MT and LXX on "Jeremiah" + Title   566
        C. MT and LXX on "Nebuchadrezzar (king of Babylon)"   566
Appendix VII   568
    Section Markings in Jeremiah 1–52   568
Appendix VIII   577
    Table of Archaeological Periods in Palestine   577
Appendix IX   578
    Names of Months in the Jewish Calendar   578
Appendix X   579
    Jeremiah Chronology   579
Appendix XI   582
    Assigned Dates to Texts in the Book of Jeremiah   582
        Josiah's Reign (627–609 B.C.)   582
        Jehoiakim's Early Reign (609–604 B.C.)   583
        Around Jerusalem's Capture in 597 B.C.   583
        After Jerusalem's Capture and First Judahite Exile in 597 B.C. 584
        Zedekiah's Early Reign (597–594 B.C.)   584
        Around the Fall of Jerusalem in 586 B.C.   584
        After the Fall of Jerusalem and Second Judahite Exile in 586 B.C. 584
        Mizpah Sojourn (586–582 B.C.)   585
        Geruth Chimham Sojourn (after 582 B.C.)   585
        Among Judahite Exiles in Egypt (after 582 B.C.)   585
        After Nebuchadrezzar's Death (562 B.C.)   585
        After Cyrus Captures Babylonia (539 B.C.)   585
Appendix XII   586
    Glossary of Rhetorical Terms   586

INDEXES

Index of Authors   595
Index of Scripture   603

ILLUSTRATIONS FROM THE DEAD SEA SCROLLS

◆

4QJeremiah^a Fragments   539

4QJeremiah^b Fragments   540

4QJeremiah^{d,e} Fragments   540

4QJeremiah^c Fragments   541

PREFACE

◆

Jeremiah 37–52 brings to completion my three-volume *Jeremiah* commentary for the Anchor Bible. The publication of two concluding volumes instead of one resulted in a decision to include the Bibliography Supplement and Abbreviations Supplement in *Jeremiah 21–36*, and the Appendixes in the present volume.

The Appendixes at the end of this volume consist of one giving conversion tables for weights, measures, and distances (Appendix IV); one listing arguable cases of LXX and MT haplography in chaps. 21–52 (Appendix V), supplementing the earlier list of arguable haplographies in chaps. 1–20 contained in Appendix III of *Jeremiah 1–20*; one providing comparisons between the MT and LXX on selected names with and without titles appearing in the entire book (Appendix VI); one on section markings (*setumah* and *petuḥah*) in the entire book as they appear in M^L, M^A, and M^P, also in the Qumran fragments (Appendix VII); one on the archaeological periods in ancient Palestine (Appendix VIII); one on months of the Jewish calendar (Appendix IX); one giving a Jeremiah chronology and important dates against which the prophet's ministry may be viewed (Appendix X); one on dates assigned to prophetic utterances and narrated events in the book (Appendix XI); and one giving a glossary of rhetorical terms used throughout the commentary (Appendix XII).

In *Jeremiah 1–20* I list over 50 arguable cases of LXX loss by haplography, a number I thought at the time to be unusually large. I imagined things would be different in chaps. 21–52, where, in appreciably more prose one might expect to find MT expansion, e.g., divine and human names provided with titles, clichés filled out, homiletical material embellished, and the like. But the reverse proved to be true. In Jeremiah 21–52 one will find listed in Appendix V some 278 arguable losses in LXX due to haplography (MT haplographies number 32), all but 40 of which went undetected in the work of Janzen (1973). Added to the number in chaps. 1–20, we have a total of 330 arguable LXX haplographies in the book of Jeremiah (MT haplographies total 39), an extraordinary number by any measure. Virtually all the losses are due to homoeoarcton or homoeoteleuton (a handful are due to consonants appearing in succession), which means that by a well-established and perfectly objective text-critical method a considerable number of differences between the two texts can be explained. A count of Hebrew words arguably missing in the LXX's Hebrew *Vorlage* due to haplography turns up the number 1,715, which is 7.8% of the total Hebrew word count in the book of Jeremiah (21,835 words). Graf (p. xliii) estimated that the LXX lacked 2,700 words of the Hebrew MT, which means that haplography can account for well over half this total (64%). The count of

Hebrew words arguably lost in the MT by haplography is 39.[1] The LXX losses, which for me came quite unexpected, are nothing short of phenomenal, and it is not too much to say that the MT-LXX problem—and I refer here only to the difference in length between the two texts, not the different ordering of materials after 25:13a—must be viewed quite differently from the way that most scholars view it today, whereby the LXX is given consistent preference. The Qumran fragments have no real bearing on this question (*pace* Holladay II 3), except to say that 4QJer[b] having affinities to LXX 10:1–10 points now to the probability that the shorter LXX text was translated from a shorter Hebrew *Vorlage*, not the result of a large-scale abridgment of the Hebrew, as some earlier scholars imagined (Janzen 1973: 128).

Albright (1959: 341) stated over 40 years ago that the Qumran evidence shows quite clearly that ancient scrolls suffered far more from omissions by copyists than from additions. The evidence from Jeremiah bears out the truth of this statement, and as a result turns much Jeremiah scholarship on its head—at least the older and residual source-critical scholarship that finds in the text only expansion, expansion, and more expansion, said to derive from dittography, conflation, interpretive glosses, and words quarried from elsewhere in the Hebrew Bible. This expansionist bias survives in the commentaries of Holladay and especially McKane (in his "rolling corpus" theory), both of which show a consistent preference for shorter LXX readings. *Biblia Hebraica*, despite two learned Jeremiah editors (Kittel and Rudolph), fails to cite a number of LXX omissions, does not always get the variations between the MT and LXX right, and has a definite bias in favor of an expanded MT. I hope these shortcomings will be remedied in the new *BHQ*. It now seems quite clear that in the received text of Jeremiah what we have is not so much proto-MT expansion by busy scribes in Babylon, but proto-LXX loss by careless and inattentive scribes in Egypt. Or to put it another way, the LXX translator(s) of Jeremiah had the misfortune of working from a "bad Hebrew Bible." Its text was shorter and defective. We can only be glad that more Jeremiah passages were not quoted by writers of the NT, for whom the LXX Bible was normative.

The photos of Qumran Cave IV fragments of Jeremiah are reproduced with the kind permission of Prof. Emanuel Tov of the Hebrew University in Jerusalem.

—Jack R. Lundbom
Clare Hall, Cambridge, 2003

---

[1] In 9 of the 39 MT haplographies, the loss was of just one letter, and these were not counted as words in the present tally of 39 words.

JEREMIAH 37–52:
A TRANSLATION

◆

V. BEHOLD THE MAN! (37:1–40:6)

A. Jeremiah's Word Rendered Cheap (37:1–16)

1. A Nation the Shadow of Its King (37:1–2)

37 [1]And Zedekiah son of Josiah, whom Nebuchadrezzar, king of Babylon, made king in the land of Judah, reigned as king in place of Coniah son of Jehoiakim. [2]But he did not listen, he and his servants and the people of the land, to the words of Yahweh that he spoke through Jeremiah the prophet.

2. Jeremiah Asked by Zedekiah to Mediate (37:3–11)

37 [3]King Zedekiah sent Jehucal son of Shelemiah and Zephaniah son of Maaseiah, the priest, to Jeremiah the prophet saying: 'Pray would you on our behalf to Yahweh our God.' [4]Now Jeremiah was coming and going amidst the people, and they had not put him in the prison house. [5]The army of Pharaoh had gone out from Egypt, and the Chaldeans who were besieging Jerusalem heard a report of them and withdrew from Jerusalem. [6]And the word of Yahweh came to Jeremiah the prophet:

[7]Thus said Yahweh, God of Israel:
Thus you shall say to the king of Judah who sent you to me to inquire of me: Look, the army of Pharaoh that went out to help you will return to its own land, Egypt. [8]And the Chaldeans shall return and fight against this city and take it, and they shall burn it with fire.

[9]Thus said Yahweh:
Do not deceive yourselves saying, The Chaldeans will surely go away from us; indeed they will not go away! [10]Even if you should strike down the entire army of the Chaldeans who are fighting you and there remained among them only wounded men, each man in his tent, they would rise up and burn this city with fire.

[11]So it happened when the army of the Chaldeans withdrew from Jerusalem because of the army of Pharaoh.

3. Jeremiah Imprisoned on Charge of Desertion (37:12–16)

37 [12]And Jeremiah set out from Jerusalem to go to the land of Benjamin for an apportioning from there amidst the people. [13]And he came into the Benjamin Gate, and there was a guard officer whose name was Irijah son of Shelemiah, son of Hananiah, and he laid hold of Jeremiah the prophet saying, 'To the Chaldeans you are deserting!' [14]And Jeremiah said, 'A lie! I am not deserting to the Chaldeans.' But he did not listen to him, and Irijah laid hold of Jeremiah and brought him to the princes. [15]And the princes were furious with Jeremiah, and they beat him and put him in the stockhouse, the house of Jonathan the

scribe, for they had made it a prison house. [16]Indeed Jeremiah went to the Pit House, yes, to the cells! And Jeremiah dwelt there many days.

B. Another Request, Another Answer (37:17–21)

37 [17]Then King Zedekiah sent and brought him, and the king asked him in his house secretly, and said, 'Is there a word from Yahweh?' And Jeremiah said, 'There is!' And he said, 'Into the hand of the king of Babylon you will be given.' [18]Then Jeremiah said to King Zedekiah, 'How have I sinned against you and against your servants and against this people that you have put me in the prison house? [19]And where are your prophets who prophesied to you saying, "The king of Babylon will not come against you and against this land?" [20]Now do hear, my lord the king, do let my petition be laid before you. Return me not to the house of Jonathan the scribe so I will not die there.' [21]So King Zedekiah commanded and they committed Jeremiah into the court of the guard and gave him a pita bread daily from the bakers' street until all the bread was consumed from the city. And Jeremiah dwelt in the court of the guard.

C. Jeremiah Again in the Pit (38:1–6)

38 [1]Now Shephatiah son of Mattan heard, also Gedaliah son of Pashhur and Jucal son of Shelemiah and Pashhur son of Malchiah, the words that Jeremiah continued to speak to all the people:
 [2]Thus said Yahweh:
 Whoever stays in this city shall die by sword, by famine, and by pestilence, and whoever goes out to the Chaldeans shall live; and his life will be his booty, and he shall live.

 [3]Thus said Yahweh:
 This city shall surely be given into the hand of the army of the king of Babylon, and he shall take it.
[4]So the princes said to the king, 'Kindly have this man put to death, seeing that he continues to weaken the hands of the fighting men who are left in this city—and the hands of all the people—by speaking to them words such as these; indeed this man is not seeking the welfare of this people, rather evil!' [5]And King Zedekiah said, 'Look, he is in your hand, for there is not anything the king can do with you.' [6]And they took Jeremiah and cast him into the pit of Malchiah the king's son, which was in the court of the guard. And they let Jeremiah down with ropes. And in the pit there was no water, only mud. And Jeremiah sank in the mud.

D. Ebed-melech to the Rescue (38:7–13)

38 [7]But Ebed-melech the Cushite, a eunuch man, heard—since he was in the king's house—that they had put Jeremiah into the pit. Now the king was sitting

in the Benjamin Gate. [8]So Ebed-melech went out from the king's house and spoke to the king: [9]'My lord the king, these men have done evil in all that they did to Jeremiah the prophet, in that they cast him into the pit, and he's as good as dead where he is, because of the famine.' For there was no longer bread in the city. [10]Then the king commanded Ebed-melech the Cushite: 'Take in hand from here thirty men and bring up Jeremiah the prophet from the pit, before he dies. [11]So Ebed-melech took the men in hand and went into the house of the king, to the lower storeroom, and took from there worn rags and worn clothes and sent them down to Jeremiah into the pit by ropes. [12]And Ebed-melech the Cushite said to Jeremiah, 'Now put these worn rags and clothes under your armpits rather than under the ropes.' And Jeremiah did so. [13]So they pulled Jeremiah with ropes and brought him up from the pit. And Jeremiah dwelt in the court of the guard.

E. One Final Request, One Final Answer (38:14–28)

38 [14]And King Zedekiah sent and brought Jeremiah the prophet to him, to the third entrance that was in the house of Yahweh. And the king said to Jeremiah, 'I am going to ask you something; do not keep anything hidden from me.' [15]And Jeremiah said to Zedekiah, 'If I tell you, will you not surely put me to death? And if I give you advice, you will not listen to me.' [16]Then King Zedekiah swore secretly to Jeremiah: 'As Yahweh lives who made this life of ours, I will not put you to death nor give you into the hand of these men who seek your life.' [17]And Jeremiah said to Zedekiah:

Thus said Yahweh, God of hosts, God of Israel:

If you will only go out to the princes of the king of Babylon, then you yourself will live and this city will not be burned with fire; yes, you and your house will live! [18]But if you will not go out to the princes of the king of Babylon, then this city will be given into the hand of the Chaldeans and they will burn it with fire. As for you, you shall not escape from their hand.

[19]Then King Zedekiah said to Jeremiah: 'I am afraid of the Judahites who have deserted to the Chaldeans, lest they give me over into their hand, and they abuse me.' [20]And Jeremiah said, 'They will not give you over.' Obey now the voice of Yahweh according to what I am saying to you, that it may go well with you, and you yourself will live. [21]But if you refuse to go out, this is the word that Yahweh has shown me: [22]'And there they were, all the women who remained in the house of the king of Judah, being brought out to the princes of the king of Babylon, yes, there they were saying:

They misled you and overcame you
　　your trusted men
Your feet are sunk in the muck
　　they have drawn back

[23]And all your wives and your children are being brought out to the Chaldeans, and you, you are not escaping from their hand. Indeed by the hand of the king of Babylon you are being seized, and this city will be burned with fire.' [24]Then

Zedekiah said to Jeremiah, 'Do not let anyone know of these words, and you shall not die.' [25]And if the princes hear that I have spoken with you, and they come to you and say to you, "Now tell us what you spoke to the king; do not keep it hidden from us and we will not put you to death, also what the king spoke to you," [26]then you shall say to them, "I laid my request before the king so that he would not send me back to the house of Jonathan to die there."' [27]Then all the princes came to Jeremiah and asked him, and he told them in accordance with all these words that the king commanded. So they ceased to speak with him, for the conversation had not been heard. [28]And Jeremiah dwelt in the court of the guard until the day that Jerusalem was taken. And he was there when Jerusalem was taken.

F. Mercy and No Mercy (39:1–14)

1. Jerusalem Taken, Zedekiah Captured (39:1–10)

39 [1]In the ninth year of Zedekiah, king of Judah, in the tenth month, Nebuchadrezzar, king of Babylon, came—also all his army—to Jerusalem and they besieged it. [2]In the eleventh year of Zedekiah, in the fourth month, on the ninth of the month, the city was breached. [3]And all the princes of the king of Babylon entered and sat in the Middle Gate: Nergalsharezer the Samgar, Nebusarsechim the Rab-saris, Nergalsharezer the Rab-mag, and all the remaining princes of the king of Babylon. [4]And it happened when Zedekiah, king of Judah, saw them, also all the fighting men, that they fled. And they went out by night from the city in the direction of the king's garden, through the gate between the double walls; and he went out in the direction of the Arabah. [5]But the army of the Chaldeans pursued after them and overtook Zedekiah in the desert regions of Jericho. And they got hold of him, and brought him up to Nebuchadrezzar, king of Babylon, at Riblah in the land of Hamath, and he spoke judgments to him. [6]And the king of Babylon slaughtered Zedekiah's sons at Riblah before his eyes, and all the nobles of Judah the king of Babylon slaughtered. [7]Then the eyes of Zedekiah he blinded, and he bound him in bronze chains to bring him to Babylon. [8]And the house of the king and the house of the people the Chaldeans burned with fire, and the walls of Jerusalem they broke down. [9]And the rest of the people who were left in the city, and the deserters who had deserted to him, and the rest of the people who were left Nebuzaradan the Rab-tabahim exiled to Babylon. [10]But some of the poor people who were without anything Nebuzaradan the Rab-tabahim left in the land of Judah, and he gave to them vineyards and fields in that day.

2. Jeremiah Spared by Nebuchadrezzar (39:11–14)

39 [11]And Nebuchadrezzar, king of Babylon, commanded concerning Jeremiah through Nebuzaradan the Rab-tabahim: [12]Get hold of him and keep your eyes upon him, and do not do anything bad to him, but whatever he says to you do

thus with him. [13]So Nebuzaradan the Rab-tabahim sent, also Nebushazban the Rab-saris, Nergalsharezer the Rab-mag, and all the chief officers of the king of Babylon. [14]And they sent and got hold of Jeremiah from the court of the guard, and gave him to Gedaliah son of Ahikam, son of Shaphan, to bring him out to the house. So he dwelt amidst the people.

G. Grace to the Humble (39:15–40:6)

1. Ebed-melech to Be Rescued (39:15–18)

39 [15]And to Jeremiah came the word of Yahweh when he was confined in the court of the guard: [16]Go and you shall say to Ebed-melech, the Cushite:
Thus said Yahweh of hosts, God of Israel:
Look I am bringing my words to this city for evil and not for good, and they shall come to pass before you in that day.

[17]But I will rescue you in that day—oracle of Yahweh—and you will not be given into the hand of the men before whom you are in dread.

[18]For I will surely see to your escape, and by the sword you will not fall, and your life will be your booty because you trusted in me—oracle of Yahweh.

2. The Whole Land before Jeremiah (40:1–6)

40 [1]The word that came to Jeremiah from Yahweh after Nebuzaradan the Rab-tabahim let him go from Ramah when he got hold of him (for he was bound in chains amidst all the exiles of Jerusalem and Judah who were being exiled to Babylon). [2]And the Rab-tabahim got hold of Jeremiah and said to him, 'Yahweh your God spoke this evil toward this place. [3]So Yahweh brought it about and did according to what he spoke. Indeed you sinned before Yahweh and did not obey his voice, so this thing happened to you. [4]But now, look, I have released you today from the chains that are on your hands. If it seems good in your eyes to go with me to Babylon, come, and I will keep my eye upon you; but if it seems bad in your eyes to go with me to Babylon, stay back. See, the whole land is before you; wherever it seems good and right in your eyes to go, go!' [5]And still he did not turn. 'Either turn to Gedaliah son of Ahikam, son of Shaphan, whom the king of Babylon appointed in the cities of Judah, and dwell with him amidst the people, or wherever it seems right in your eyes to go, go.' Then the Rab-tabahim gave him an allowance and a present, and let him go. [6]Jeremiah then went to Gedaliah son of Ahikam at Mizpah. And he dwelt with him amidst the people who were left in the land.

VI. TURN AND TAKE YOUR JOURNEY—TO EGYPT! (40:7–44:30)

A. Buildup and Breakdown at Mizpah (40:7–41:18)

1. Resettlement under Gedaliah (40:7–12)

40 ⁷Then all the princes of the troops who were in the field—they and their men—heard that the king of Babylon had appointed Gedaliah son of Ahikam in the land, and that he had appointed to be with him men, and women, and small children, and some of the poor of the land from those who had not been exiled to Babylon. ⁸So they went to Gedaliah at Mizpah: Ishmael son of Nethaniah, Johanan and Jonathan sons of Kareah, Seraiah son of Tanhumeth, the sons of Ephai the Netophathite, and Jezaniah son of the Maacathite, they and their men. ⁹And Gedaliah son of Ahikam, son of Shaphan, swore to them and to their men, saying: 'Do not be afraid of serving the Chaldeans; dwell in the land and serve the king of Babylon, that it may go well with you. ¹⁰As for me, look I am dwelling in Mizpah to stand before the Chaldeans who will come to us. As for you, gather wine, summer fruit, and oil, and put into your jars, and dwell in your cities that you have seized.' ¹¹Even all the Judahites who were in Moab, and among the Ammonites, and in Edom, and who were in all the other lands heard that the king of Babylon had given a remnant to Judah and that he had appointed over them Gedaliah son of Ahikam, son of Shaphan. ¹²So all the Judahites returned from all the places where they had been dispersed and came to the land of Judah, to Gedaliah at Mizpah. And they gathered wine and summer fruit in great quantity.

2. The Plot against Gedaliah (40:13–16)

40 ¹³Then Johanan son of Kareah and all the princes of the troops who were in the field came to Gedaliah at Mizpah, ¹⁴and they said to him, 'Do you indeed know that Baalis, king of the Ammonites, has sent Ishmael son of Nethaniah to strike you down?' But Gedaliah son of Ahikam did not believe them. ¹⁵Then Johanan son of Kareah said to Gedaliah in secret at Mizpah: 'Do let me go and strike down Ishmael son of Nethaniah, and no one will know. Why should he strike a person down and all the Judahites who are gathered about you be scattered, and the remnant of Judah perish?' ¹⁶But Gedaliah son of Ahikam said to Johanan son of Kareah, 'Do not do this thing, for you are speaking a lie about Ishmael.'

3. The Murder of Gedaliah (41:1–3)

41 ¹And it happened in the seventh month, Ishmael son of Nethaniah, son of Elishama, of royal descent and one of the chief officers of the king, came with

ten men to Gedaliah son of Ahikam at Mizpah, and they ate food together there at Mizpah. [2]Then Ishmael son of Nethaniah got up, also the ten men who were with him, and they struck down Gedaliah son of Ahikam, son of Shaphan, with the sword. So he killed him, whom the king of Babylon had appointed in the land. [3]And all the Judahites who were with him, that is, Gedaliah, at Mizpah, and the Chaldeans who were found there, that is, the fighting men, Ishmael struck down.

4. Arrivals from the North (41:4–6)

41 [4]And it happened on the day after the killing of Gedaliah, when no one knew, [5]that men came from Shechem, from Shiloh, and from Samaria—80 men, beards shaven, clothes torn, and self-inflicted slashes—with cereal offering and frankincense in their hand to bring to the house of Yahweh. [6]And Ishmael son of Nethaniah went out from Mizpah to meet them, weeping as he was walking. And it happened as he met them that he said to them, 'Come to Gedaliah son of Ahikam.'

5. Another Round of Violence (41:7–10)

[7]And it happened as they came into the midst of the city that Ishmael son of Nethaniah—he, and the men who were with him—slaughtered them and cast them into the midst of the cistern. [8]But ten men were found with them who said to Ishmael, 'Don't kill us, for we have hidden stores in the field—wheat, barley, oil, and honey.' So he held back, and did not kill them amidst their brothers. [9]Now the cistern into which Ishmael cast all the corpses of the men whom he struck down because of Gedaliah—it was the one that King Asa made on account of Baasha, king of Israel. Ishmael son of Nethaniah filled it with the slain. [10]Then Ishmael took captive the entire remnant of the people who were in Mizpah—the daughters of the king, and all the other people who remained in Mizpah, over whom Nebuzaradan the Rab-tabahim had appointed Gedaliah son of Ahikam. And Ishmael son of Nethaniah took them captive and went to cross over to the Ammonites.

6. Rescue at the Pool of Gibeon (41:11–15)

41 [11]Then Johanan son of Kareah and all the princes of the troops who were with him heard all the evil that Ishmael son of Nethaniah had done, [12]and they took all the men and went to fight with Ishmael son of Nethaniah, and they found him by the great pool that was in Gibeon. [13]And it happened as all the people who were with Ishmael saw Johanan son of Kareah and all the princes of the troops who were with him that they were glad. [14]So all the people whom Ishmael had taken captive from Mizpah turned about, and returning they went over to Johanan son of Kareah. [15]And Ishmael son of Nethaniah escaped with eight men from before Johanan, and went over to the Ammonites.

7. On to Geruth Chimham! (41:16–18)

41 [16]Then Johanan son of Kareah and all the princes of the troops who were with him took the entire remnant of the people whom he recovered from Ishmael son of Nethaniah, from Mizpah, after he struck down Gedaliah son of Ahikam: men, fighting men, and women, and small children, and eunuchs, whom he brought back from Gibeon. [17]And they went and dwelt at Geruth Chimham, which is near Bethlehem, going to enter Egypt [18]because of the Chaldeans, for they were afraid of them, for Ishmael son of Nethaniah had struck down Gedaliah son of Ahikam, whom the king of Babylon had appointed in the land.

B. Jeremiah's Word Again Rendered Cheap (42:1–22)

1. Remnant Asks Jeremiah to Mediate (42:1–6)

42 [1]Then all the princes of the troops, including Johanan son of Kareah and Jezaniah son of Hoshaiah, and all the people from the least to the greatest, came forward [2]and said to Jeremiah the prophet, 'Do let our request be laid before you, and pray on our behalf to Yahweh your God, on behalf of this entire remnant, for we remain a few from many, as your eyes now see us. [3]And let Yahweh your God tell us the way in which we should go and the thing that we should do.' [4]And Jeremiah the prophet said to them, 'I hear. Look I will pray to Yahweh your God according to your word; and the entire word that Yahweh answers you I will tell you; I will not hold back from you a word.' [5]Then they, they said to Jeremiah, 'Yahweh be a true and faithful witness against us if not according to the entire word that Yahweh your God sends you for us, we so do. [6]If for good or if for evil, the voice of Yahweh our God to whom we are sending you we will obey, in order that it may go well with us. Indeed we will obey the voice of Yahweh our God!'

2. Yahweh Answers the Remnant (42:7–22)

42 [7]And it happened at the end of ten days that the word of Yahweh came to Jeremiah. [8]So he announced to Johanan son of Kareah and to all the princes of the troops who were with him, and to all the people from the least to the greatest, [9]and said to them:

Thus said Yahweh, God of Israel, to whom you sent me to lay your request before him:

[10]If you will indeed dwell in this land, then I will build you up and not overthrow you, and I will plant you and not uproot you, for I have repented concerning the evil that I did to you. [11]Do not be afraid because of the king of Babylon, of whom you are now afraid.

Do not be afraid because of him—oracle of Yahweh—for I am with you to save you and rescue you from his hand. ¹²And I will grant you mercies, and he will be merciful with you and let you return to your soil.

¹³But if you are saying, 'We will not dwell in this land,' not obeying the voice of Yahweh your God, ¹⁴saying: 'No! Indeed we will enter the land of Egypt to the end that we will not see war, and the sound of the trumpet we will not hear, and for food we will not hunger, and there we will dwell,' ¹⁵well now, therefore, hear the word of Yahweh, Remnant of Judah:

Thus said Yahweh of hosts, God of Israel:

If you then have definitely set your faces to enter Egypt and you enter to sojourn there, ¹⁶then it will happen: the sword of which you are now afraid shall overtake you there in the land of Egypt; and the famine about which you are now worrying shall follow you hard there in Egypt; and there you shall die. ¹⁷So shall all the persons become who set their faces to enter Egypt to sojourn there; they shall die by sword, by famine, and by pestilence; they shall not have a survivor or fugitive because of the evil that I am bringing upon them.

¹⁸For thus said Yahweh of hosts, God of Israel:

Just as my anger and my wrath were poured out upon the inhabitants of Jerusalem, so my wrath will be poured out upon you when you enter Egypt. And you shall be a curse, and a desolation, and a swearword, and a reproach, and you shall not see this place again.

¹⁹Yahweh has spoken concerning you, Remnant of Judah, Do not enter Egypt! Know for sure that I have warned you today. ²⁰Indeed you led yourselves astray, for you, you sent me to Yahweh your God saying, 'Pray on our behalf to Yahweh our God, and according to all that Yahweh our God says, so tell us and we will do.' ²¹And I told you today, and you have not obeyed the voice of Yahweh your God regarding all that he sent me to you. ²²Now then, know for sure that by sword, by famine, and by pestilence you shall die in the place where you wish to enter to sojourn.

C. Exile to Egypt (43:1–13)

1. Remnant Rejects Yahweh's Word! (43:1–4)

43 ¹And it happened when Jeremiah had finished speaking to all the people all the words of Yahweh their God, that is, all these words with which Yahweh their God had sent him to them. ²Then said Azariah son of Hoshaiah, with Johanan son of Kareah and all the insolent men saying to Jeremiah, 'You are telling a lie! Yahweh our God did not send you saying, You shall not enter Egypt to sojourn there. ³Indeed, Baruch son of Neriah has incited you against us in order to give us into the hand of the Chaldeans, to kill us or exile us to Babylon.' ⁴So Johanan son of Kareah and all the princes of the

troops and all the people did not obey the voice of Yahweh to dwell in the land of Judah.

2. On to Tahpanhes! (43:5–7)

43 [5]Then Johanan son of Kareah and all the princes of the troops took the entire remnant of Judah that had returned from all the nations where they were dispersed to sojourn in the land of Judah—[6]men and women and small children, and daughters of the king, yes every person whom Nebuzaradan the Rabtabahim had left behind with Gedaliah son of Ahikam, son of Shaphan, including Jeremiah the prophet and Baruch son of Neriah. [7]And they came to the land of Egypt, for they did not obey the voice of Yahweh. And they came as far as Tahpanhes.

3. But Nebuchadrezzar Will Come to Egypt! (43:8–13)

43 [8]And the word of Yahweh came to Jeremiah in Tahpanhes: [9]Take in your hand large stones, and you shall hide them with mortar in the pavement that is at the entrance of the house of Pharaoh in Tahpanhes, before the eyes of the Judahite men. [10]And you shall say to them:

Thus said Yahweh of hosts, God of Israel:

Look I am sending for and will take Nebuchadrezzar, king of Babylon, my servant, and I will set his throne over these stones that I have hidden, and he will spread his pavilion over them. [11]And he shall come and strike down the land of Egypt: Whoever is to death—to death, and whoever is to captivity—to captivity, and whoever is to the sword—to the sword. [12]And I will kindle a fire in the houses of the gods of Egypt, and he shall burn them and take them captive, and wrap up the land of Egypt as the shepherd wraps himself up with his garment; then he shall leave from there in peace. [13]Also, he shall break the obelisks of Beth-shemesh (that is in the land of Egypt), and the houses of the gods of Egypt he will burn with fire.

D. Final Prophecies in Egypt (44:1–30)

1. Once Again: Queen of Heaven Worship (44:1–25)

44 [1]The word that came to Jeremiah for all the Judahites who were dwelling in the land of Egypt, those who were dwelling in Migdol, and in Tahpanhes, and in Memphis, and in the land of Pathros:

[2]Thus said Yahweh of hosts, God of Israel:

You, you have seen all the evil that I brought upon Jerusalem and upon all the cities of Judah. And look they are a ruin this day and there is no one dwelling in them [3]because of their evil that they did to provoke me to anger, to go to burn incense, to serve other gods that they have not known—they, you, and your fathers. [4]And I sent to you all my servants the prophets—

constantly I sent—saying, kindly do not do this abominable thing that I hate. [5]But they did not listen; they did not bend their ear to turn from their evil not to burn incense to other gods. [6]So my wrath was poured out, and my anger, and it burned in the cities of Judah and in the streets of Jerusalem, and they became a ruin, a desolation, as at this day.

[7]Now then, thus said Yahweh, God of hosts, God of Israel:
Why are you doing a great evil to yourselves, to cut off for you man and woman, child and infant from the midst of Judah so a remnant is not left for you, [8]to provoke me to anger with the works of your hands, to burn incense to other gods in the land of Egypt to which you are coming to sojourn, so as to cut off for you, so that you become a swearword and a reproach among all the nations of the earth? [9]Have you forgotten the evils of your fathers, and the evils of the kings of Judah and the evils of their wives, and your evils and the evils of your wives, which they did in the land of Judah and in the streets of Jerusalem? [10]They are not crushed even to this day. And they are not afraid. And they walk not in my law and in my statutes, which I set before you and before your fathers.

[11]Therefore thus said Yahweh of hosts, God of Israel:
Look I am setting my face against you for evil and to cut off all Judah. [12]And I will take the remnant of Judah who have set their faces to enter the land of Egypt to sojourn there, and they shall all be consumed in the land of Egypt; they shall fall by the sword, by famine they shall be consumed; from the least to the greatest, by sword and by famine they shall die; and they shall become a curse, a desolation, and a swearword, and a reproach. [13]Yes, I will reckon with those who dwell in the land of Egypt as I reckoned with Jerusalem—by sword, by famine, and by pestilence. [14]And there shall not be a fugitive or survivor for the remnant of Judah who have come to sojourn there in the land of Egypt, then to return to the land of Judah where they carry their great desire to return to dwell; but they shall not return— except fugitives.

[15]Then they answered Jeremiah—all the men who knew that their wives were burning incense to other gods, and all the wives who were standing by, a large assembly, and all the people who were dwelling in the land of Egypt, in Pathros: [16]"The word that you have spoken to us in the name of Yahweh, we will not listen to you. [17]For we fully intend to do everything that has gone forth from our mouth, to burn incense to the Queen of Heaven and pour out drink offerings to her, just as we did—we and our fathers, our kings and our princes—in the cities of Judah and in the streets of Jerusalem; then we ate our fill of bread and were well-off, and evil we did not see. [18]But from the time we left off burning incense to the Queen of Heaven and pouring out drink offerings to her we have lacked everything, and by sword and by famine we have been consumed. [19]And when we are burning incense to the Queen of Heaven and pouring out

drink offerings to her, is it against the will of our husbands that we make for her cakes to portray her, and pour out drink offerings to her?'

²⁰Then Jeremiah said to all the people—against the men and against the women, and against all the people who were answering him a word: ²¹'Indeed, the incense that you burned in the cities of Judah and in the streets of Jerusalem, you and your fathers, your kings and your princes, and the people of the land—them Yahweh remembers. Now did it enter his mind? ²²So Yahweh could no longer bear because of your evil doings, because of the abominations that you did, and your land became a ruin, and a desolation, and a swearword, without inhabitant, as at this day. ²³Because you burned incense and because you sinned against Yahweh, and did not obey the voice of Yahweh, and in his law and in his statutes and in his testimonies you did not walk, therefore this evil has met you, as at this day.

²⁴Then Jeremiah said to all the people and to all the women: Hear the word of Yahweh all Judah who are in the land of Egypt:
    ²⁵Thus said Yahweh of hosts, God of Israel:
    You and your wives, yes, you have spoken with your mouth, and with your hands you have carried it out, saying, 'We fully intend to perform our vows that we vowed to burn incense to the Queen of Heaven and to pour out drink offerings to her.' Well then, confirm fully your vows and perform fully your vows!

2. Whose Word Will Be Confirmed—Mine or Theirs? (44:26–30)

²⁶Therefore hear the word of Yahweh all Judah who are dwelling in the land of Egypt:
    Look I, I have sworn by my great name—said Yahweh—that my name will no longer be called on the mouth of any person of Judah who now says, 'As the Lord Yahweh lives,' in all the land of Egypt.

²⁷Look I am watching over them for evil and not for good, and every person of Judah who is in the land of Egypt will be consumed by sword and by famine, until they are ended. ²⁸And those escaping the sword shall return from the land of Egypt to the land of Judah—a few people. Then all the remnant of Judah who came to the land of Egypt to sojourn shall know whose word will be confirmed—mine or theirs. ²⁹And this is the sign to you—oracle of Yahweh—that I am reckoning against you in this place so that you may know that my words will be fully confirmed against you for evil.

³⁰Thus said Yahweh:
    Look I am giving Pharaoh Hophra, king of Egypt, into the hand of his enemies, into the hand of those who seek his life, just as I gave Zedekiah, king

of Judah, into the hand of Nebuchadrezzar, king of Babylon, his enemy and the one who sought his life.

VII. BARUCH'S COLOPHON (45:1–5)

45 ¹The word that Jeremiah the prophet spoke to Baruch son of Neriah when he had written these words on a scroll from the dictation of Jeremiah, in the fourth year of Jehoiakim son of Josiah, king of Judah: ²Thus said Yahweh, God of Israel, concerning you, Baruch. ³You have said, 'Woe now to me, for Yahweh has added sorrow to my pain. I am weary with my groaning and rest I cannot find.' ⁴Thus you shall say to him:

Thus said Yahweh:

Look, what I have built up I am overthrowing, and what I have planted I am uprooting, and that is the whole earth. ⁵And you, you are seeking for yourself great things? Do not seek.

For look I am bringing evil upon all flesh—oracle of Yahweh—but I will give you your life for booty in all the places where you go.

VIII. ORACLES TO THE FOREIGN NATIONS (46:1–51:64)

A. Superscription to the Foreign Nation Oracles (46:1)

46 ¹What came as the word of Yahweh to Jeremiah the prophet concerning the nations.

B. What about Egypt? (46:2–28)

1. Pride Cometh before the Fall (46:2–12)

a) Hasty Advance, Hasty Retreat (46:2–6)

46 ²For Egypt: Concerning the army of Pharaoh Neco, king of Egypt, which was by the River Euphrates at Carchemish, and which Nebuchadrezzar, king of Babylon, struck down in the fourth year of Jehoiakim son of Josiah, king of Judah.

> ³Ready buckler and shield!
> and advance to battle!
> ⁴Harness the horses!
> and rise up, O horsemen!

Stand ready with helmets!
   Polish lances!
     Put on scale armor!

[5]'So why have I seen . . . ?'
   They are terrified!
     drawing back!
Their warriors are beaten
   and a flight they are fleeing
They do not turn back
   terror on every side!
     —oracle of Yahweh.

[6]The swift cannot flee
   the warrior cannot escape
Up north on the bank of River Euphrates
   they have stumbled, and they have fallen!

b) Egypt Rises like the Nile! (46:7–8)

46 [7]Who is this that rises like the Nile
   like the great river, its waters swell?

[8]Egypt rises like the Nile
   and like the great river, the waters are swollen
For he said, 'I will rise
I will cover the earth
   I will destroy city and inhabitants in it.'

c) Rise Up, O Horses! (46:9–10)

46 [9]Rise up, O horses!
   and go like mad, O chariots!
     and let the warriors move on out!
Cush and Put holding the buckler
   and Ludim holding, bending the bow

[10]That day is for the Lord Yahweh of hosts
   a day of vengeance, to avenge himself on his foes
The sword will consume and be sated
   and it will drink its fill of their blood
Indeed a feast for the Lord Yahweh of hosts
   in a land of the north by River Euphrates.

d) Rise Up and Get Balm! (46:11–12)

46 [11]Rise up to Gilead and get balm
   virgin daughter Egypt!

In vain you keep doing it
  a healing scar there is not for you

[12]Nations have heard of your disgrace
  your cry has filled the earth
Indeed warrior on warrior they stumbled
  together the two of them fell.

2. Pharaoh Is All Talk (46:13–17)

46 [13]The word that Yahweh spoke to Jeremiah the prophet about the coming of
Nebuchadrezzar, king of Babylon, to strike down the land of Egypt.
  [14]Declare in Egypt, and proclaim in Migdol
    and proclaim in Memphis, and in Tahpanhes say:
  'Stand ready, and prepare yourself
    for the sword has consumed those around you'

[15]So why is your mighty bull lying flat?
  it stands not, because Yahweh shoved it
    [16]he kept on; stumbling, yes, it fell

Each person to his fellow, indeed, they said:
  'Arise, and let us go back to our people
and to the land of our birth
  before the oppressive sword'

[17]Call the name of Pharaoh
  king of Egypt:
    'Loud Noise, Who Lets the Deadline Pass.'

3. Invasion, Destruction, and Exile for Egypt (46:18–26)

a) Daughter Egypt Better Start Packing (46:18–19)

46 [18]'As I live'—oracle of the King
  Yahweh of hosts is his name
Indeed like Tabor among the mountains
  and like Carmel by the sea, he will come

[19]Exile baggage prepare for yourself
  sitting daughter Egypt!
Indeed Memphis shall become a desolation
  and burned without inhabitant.

b) A Horsefly from the North on Heifer Egypt (46:20–21)

46 ²⁰A beautiful, beautiful heifer was Egypt
  a horsefly from the north came, came
²¹Even her hired hands in her midst
  were like stall heifers

Indeed even they, they turned back
  they fled together, they did not stand
Indeed the day of their disaster came upon them
  the time of their reckoning.

c) An Enemy More Numerous than Locusts (46:22–23)

46 ²²Her sound is like a snake going
  indeed with strength they are coming
  yes, with axes they came against her
like those cutting wood

²³They cut down her forest—oracle of Yahweh—
  indeed it was not searched out!
  indeed they were more numerous than locusts
yes, of them there was no number.

d) Egypt Given Over to a People from the North (46:24–26)

46 ²⁴Daughter Egypt has been greatly shamed
  she is given into the hand of a people from the north.

²⁵Yahweh of hosts, God of Israel, said:
Look I will make a reckoning to Amon of Thebes, and upon Pharaoh, and
upon Egypt, and upon her gods, and upon her kings, and upon Pharaoh,
and upon those trusting in him. ²⁶And I will give them into the hand of
those who seek their life, and into the hand of Nebuchadrezzar, king of
Babylon, and into the hand of his servants.

But afterward she shall dwell as in the days of old—oracle of Yahweh.

4. But Jacob Will Return Home (46:27–28)

46 ²⁷But you, do not you be afraid, Jacob my servant
  and do not you be broken, Israel
For look I will save you from afar
  and your offspring from the land of their captivity
Jacob will return and be undisturbed
  yes, be at ease and none will frighten

²⁸You, do not you be afraid, Jacob my servant
  —oracle of Yahweh—
    for I am with you
For I will make a full end of all the nations
    among which I have dispersed you
But of you I will not make a full end
    Yes, I will correct you justly
        but I will by no means leave you unpunished.

C. A Day for Yahweh against the Philistines (47:1–7)

47 ¹What came as the word of Yahweh to Jeremiah the prophet, to the Philistines before Pharaoh struck down Gaza.
  ²Thus said Yahweh:
Look, waters are rising from the north
    and have become an overflowing torrent
They will overflow the land in its entirety
    the city and those living in it
The people cry out
    everyone living in the land wails

³At the sound of the stamping hoofs of his stallions
    at the clatter of his chariotry, the rumbling of its wheels
Fathers do not turn to children
    for weakness of hands
⁴Because of the day that has come to devastate
    everyone of the Philistines
To cut off for Tyre and for Sidon
    every survivor, helper

For Yahweh is devastating the Philistines
    remnant of the island of Caphtor
⁵Baldness has come to Gaza
    Ashkelon is silenced
    remnant of their strength
How long will you slash yourselves?

⁶Woe! sword of Yahweh!
    how much longer before you are idle?
Gather yourself into your sheath
    rest and be silent

⁷But how can you be idle?
    when Yahweh has commanded it
toward Ashkelon and toward the seacoast
    there he has assigned it.

D. What about Moab? (48:1–47)

1. Devastation for the Whole of Moab (48:1–10)

a) Moab the Renowned Is No More (48:1–2)

48 ¹For Moab.
   Thus said Yahweh of hosts, God of Israel:
   Woe to Nebo, for it is devastated
      Kiriathaim is very shamed, is captured
      The Height is very shamed and shattered
   ²The Praise of Moab is no more

   In Heshbon they planned evil against her:
      'Come, and let us cut her off from being a nation'
   Even Madmen, you shall be muted
      after you the sword shall go.

b) Moab's Cry Is Heard (48:3–7a)

48 ³The sound of a scream from Horonaim:
      'Destruction and a great shatter!'
      ⁴Moab is shattered
   Her young ones make heard a cry

   ⁵Yes, at the Luhith ascent
      weeping on weeping goes up
   Yes, on the Horonaim descent
      a distressful, shattering scream they hear

   ⁶Flee, deliver your own lives
      and be like Aroer in the desert.

⁷ᵃFor because of your trust in your works and in your treasures, even you, you shall be captured.

c) Exile and Wandering Ahead for Moab (48:7b–10)

48 ⁷ᵇChemosh shall go out into exile
      his priests and his princes together
   ⁸The devastator shall come to every city
      and the city shall not escape

   The valley shall perish
      and the tableland be wrecked
         —as Yahweh said.

   ⁹Make a rosette for Moab
      for ruined she shall go out

Her cities shall become a desolation
  without an inhabitant in them.

[10]Cursed be he who does the work of Yahweh half-heartedly
  and cursed be he who holds back his sword from blood.

2. Look at Moab Settled into His Lees! (48:11–13)

48 [11]Moab has been at ease from his youth
  and settled is he into his lees
He has not been poured from container to container
  and into exile he has not gone
Therefore his flavor has remained in him
  and his fragrance has not changed.

[12]Look, hereafter, days are coming—oracle of Yahweh—when I shall send to him decanters and they will decant him; and his containers they will pour out and his jars they will smash. [13]Then Moab shall be ashamed of Chemosh just as the house of Israel was ashamed of Bethel, their trust.

3. The Talk Now and the Talk Later (48:14–24)

a) Warriors Are We! (48:14–17a)

48 [14]How can you say, 'Warriors are we
  and valiant men for war'?
[15]The devastator of Moab and her cities has come up
  and the best of his young men have gone down to the slaughter
    —oracle of the King, Yahweh of hosts is his name

[16]The disaster of Moab is near to come
  his trouble hastens apace
[17a]Give consolation to him, all you round about him
  and all you who know his name.

b) How the Mighty Scepter Is Broken! (48:17b–18)

48 [17b]Say, 'How the mighty scepter is broken
  the most glorious staff!'
[18]Come down from glory and sit in thirst
  sitting daughter Dibon
For the devastator of Moab has come up against you
  he has destroyed your fortresses.

c) What Has Happened? (48:19–24)

48 ¹⁹To the way, stand and watch
   sitting one of Aroer!
Ask him who flees and her who escapes
   say: 'What has happened?'

²⁰Moab is very shamed
   indeed she is shattered
     wail and cry out!
Declare by the Arnon:
   'Indeed Moab is devastated.'

²¹Judgment has come to the tableland—to Holon, and to Jahzah, and upon Mephaath, ²²and upon Dibon, and upon Nebo, and upon Beth-diblathaim, ²³and upon Kiriathaim, and upon Beth-gamul, and upon Beth-meon, ²⁴and upon Kerioth, and upon Bozrah, and upon all the cities of the land of Moab, those far and those near.

4. The Horn of Moab Is Cut Off (48:25–27)

48 ²⁵The horn of Moab is cut off
   his arm is broken
    —oracle of Yahweh.

²⁶Make him drunk, because against Yahweh he made himself great. Then Moab shall splash in his vomit and become a joke—even he. ²⁷Then surely the joke is for you, Israel, if among thieves he has been found. For more than all your words against him, you will shake your head!

5. Go Live in a Rock! (48:28)

48 ²⁸Abandon the cities
   and go live in a rock
     sitting ones of Moab!
Become like a dove that nests
   in the sides of an open gorge.

6. We Have Heard of the Pride of Moab (48:29–31)

48 ²⁹We have heard of the pride of Moab
   great haughtiness
His loftiness and his pride and his arrogance
   and the highness of his heart

³⁰I, I know—oracle of Yahweh—his insolence
   his boastings are not right

what they do is not right
³¹Therefore over Moab I will wail
  for all of Moab I will cry out
    for the men of Kirheres I will moan.

7. Gladness and Rejoicing Are No More (48:32–34)

48 ³²More than the weeping of Jazer I weep for you
  O vine of Sibmah!
Your branches extended over the sea
  as far as the sea
    Jazer they reached
Upon your summer fruit and upon your vintage
  the devastator has fallen

³³Gladness and rejoicing are taken away
  from the garden land, from the land of Moab
And wine from the presses I made cease
  no one treads a shout
    the shout is not a shout!
³⁴—the cry from Heshbon as far as Elealeh, as far as Jahaz; they raised their voice from Zoar as far as Horonaim, as far as Eglath-shelishiyah. Indeed, even the waters of Nimrim are a desolation.

8. Lament the End of Moab! (48:35–38a)

48 ³⁵I have made cease for Moab—oracle of Yahweh
  the one who brings up to the high place
    and the one who burns incense to his gods
³⁶Therefore my heart for Moab moans like flutes
  and my heart toward the men of Kirheres moans like flutes
    therefore the rest of what one has made—they are lost!

³⁷For every head is shaved
  and every beard cut off
On all hands are slashes
  and on (all) loins sackcloth
^{38a}On all the roofs of Moab and in her squares
  —everywhere rites of mourning.

9. Moab like a Broken Jar (48:38b–39)

48 ^{38b}For I have broken Moab
  like a jar in which no one takes delight
    —oracle of Yahweh

[39]'How it is shattered!' wail
   'How Moab has turned the back ashamedly!'
So Moab shall become a joke and a terror
   to all those round about it.

10. Eagles Above and Traps Below (48:40–44)
a) Look Out for the Eagle! (48:40–41)

48 [40]For thus said Yahweh:
Look, as the eagle he flies
   and he spreads his wings toward Moab
[41]The towns are taken
   and seized are the strongholds
And the heart of the warriors of Moab shall be in that day
   as the heart of a woman much distressed.

b) Scare, Pit, and Snare Are before You! (48:42–43)

48 [42]Moab shall be exterminated from being a people
   for against Yahweh he made himself great
[43]Scare, and pit, and snare
   are against you, sitting one of Moab
      —oracle of Yahweh.

c) One of Them Will Get You! (48:44)

48 [44]The one who flees from the scare
   shall fall into the pit
And the one who comes up from the pit
   shall be taken in the snare
For I will bring to her, to Moab
   the year of their reckoning
      —oracle of Yahweh.

11. In the Shadow of Heshbon They Stop (48:45–47)

48 [45]In the shadow of Heshbon they stopped
   those fleeing without strength
Indeed a fire went forth from Heshbon
   a flame from within Sihon

And it consumed the temples of Moab
   and the crown of the uproarious sons

[46]Woe to you, Moab
   the people of Chemosh has perished
Indeed your sons are taken captive
   and your daughters into captivity.

⁴⁷But I will restore the fortunes of Moab in the days afterward—oracle of Yahweh.
Thus far the judgment on Moab.

E. What about the Ammonites? (49:1–6)

1. So Why Has Milcom Inherited Gad? (49:1–2)

49 ¹For the Ammonites.
　Thus said Yahweh:
　Has Israel no sons?
　　Has he no inheritor?
　So why has Milcom inherited Gad
　　and his people live in his cities?

　²Look, hereafter, days are coming—oracle of Yahweh:
I will make Rabbah of the Ammonites hear
　the shout of battle
and she shall become a desolate tell
　her daughters burned with fire.
Then Israel shall inherit those who inherited him—said Yahweh.

2. Scream, Rabbah's Daughters! (49:3–6)

49 ³Wail, Heshbon, for Ai is devastated
　scream, Rabbah's daughters!
Put on sackcloth, beat your chests
　and run back and forth in the stone enclosures

For Milcom into exile shall go
　his priests and his princes together

⁴How you boast in valleys
　your flowing valley
　　turnable daughter!
The one trusting in her treasures:
　'Who will come to me?'

⁵Look I am bringing terror against you
　—oracle of the Lord Yahweh of hosts—
　from everyone on every side of you
And you shall be dispersed, each one before him
　and none will gather him who flees.

⁶But afterward I will surely restore the fortunes of the Ammonites
　—oracle of Yahweh.

F. What about Edom? (49:7–22)

1. Is There No Longer Wisdom in Teman? (49:7–11)

49 ⁷For Edom.

Thus said Yahweh of hosts:
Is there no longer wisdom in Teman?
counsel has perished from people of understanding
their wisdom stinks!
⁸Flee! Be gone! Go deep to dwell
dwellers of Dedan
For Esau's disaster I have brought upon him
at the time I reckoned with him

⁹If grape-pickers came to you
they would surely leave gleanings
If thieves in the night
they would destroy but enough for themselves

¹⁰But I, I have stripped Esau
I have uncovered his hiding places
so the hidden one he cannot be
His offspring is devastated
also his brothers and his neighbors
and he is no more
¹¹Abandon your orphans
I, I will keep alive
As for your widows
put your trust upon me.

2. Yahweh to Bring the Eagle Down! (49:12–18)

49 ¹²For thus said Yahweh:
Look, those for whom there is no judgment to drink the cup must surely drink. Are you then one who will surely go free? You will not go free, for you will surely drink!

¹³For by myself I have sworn—oracle of Yahweh—that a desolation, a reproach, a ruin, and a swearword Bozrah shall become, and all her cities shall become eternal ruins.

¹⁴I have heard a message from Yahweh
and an envoy is sent among the nations:
'Gather together and go against her!
Up! To the battle!'

[15]For look! I have made you small among the nations
  despised among humankind

[16]Your horror!
   the arrogance of your heart
      has deceived you
Inhabitant in the clefts of the rock
   occupier of the top of the hill
For as the eagle, you make high your nest
   from there I will bring you down!
      —oracle of Yahweh.

[17]So Edom shall become a desolation; everyone passing by it will be horrified and will hiss at all her blows, [18]just like the overthrow of Sodom and Gomorrah and her neighbors—said Yahweh. No person shall inhabit there, and no human shall sojourn in her.

3. As a Lion, as an Eagle against Edom (49:19–22)

49 [19]Look, as a lion goes up
   from the pride of the Jordan to perennial pasture
Indeed I will in a moment chase him from her
   and who is the young man I will appoint over her?
Indeed who is like me?
   and who will summon me?
      and who is this, a shepherd that can stand before me?

[20]Therefore hear the counsel of Yahweh that he counseled toward Edom, and his plans that he planned toward the inhabitants of Teman:
   Surely they shall drag them away—the little ones of the flock
      surely their pasture shall be horrified over them
   [21]At the sound of their fall the land quakes—a scream
      at the Red Sea its sound is heard!

[22]Look, as the eagle he goes up and flies
   and spreads his wings over Bozrah
The heart of the warriors of Edom shall be in that day
   as the heart of a woman greatly distressed.

G. What about Damascus? (49:23–27)

49 [23]Concerning Damascus.
   Hamath is shamed, also Arpad
      for an evil report they have heard

They rock
  anxiety in the sea
    they cannot keep quiet

²⁴Damascus went limp
  she turned to flee
    but panic grabbed hold of her
Distress and pangs seized her
  like a woman in labor
²⁵How she is utterly forsaken
  city of praise
    town of my joy!

²⁶Therefore her young men shall fall in her open squares
  and all the men of war shall be silent in that day
    —oracle of Yahweh of hosts
²⁷And I will kindle a fire in the wall of Damascus
  and it will consume the citadels of Ben-hadad.

H. What about Kedar? (49:28–33)

1. Curtains for the People of the East! (49:28–30)

49 ²⁸To Kedar and to the kings of Hazor whom Nebuchadrezzar, king of Babylon, struck down.
  Thus said Yahweh:
  Up! advance to Kedar!
    Devastate the people of the east!
²⁹Their tents and their flocks they shall take away
  their curtains and all their gear

  Their camels they shall carry off for themselves
    and they shall call out upon them: 'Terror on every side!'
³⁰Flee! Wander all about! Go deep to dwell!
  dwellers of Hazor
    —oracle of Yahweh.
For Nebuchadrezzar, king of Babylon, has counseled against you a counsel
and planned against you a plan.

2. A Desert Nation to the Winds (49:31–33)

49 ³¹Up! advance to a nation at ease
  who dwells in security

—oracle of Yahweh
No doors and no bars for it
   they dwell alone

[32]And their camels shall be for booty
   and their noisy cattle for spoil

For I will scatter them to every wind
   those who crop the hair at the temples
And from every one of its sides
   I will bring their disaster
     —oracle of Yahweh.

[33]Hazor shall become a den of jackals
   a desolation forever
No person shall inhabit there
   and no human shall sojourn in her.

I. Elam Too Shall Be Scattered (49:34–39)

49 [34]What came as the word of Yahweh to Jeremiah the prophet concerning Elam in the beginning of the reign of Zedekiah, king of Judah:
   [35]Thus said Yahweh of hosts:
Look I am shattering the bow of Elam
   the first line of their strength.
[36]And I will bring to Elam four winds
   from the four corners of the heavens
And I will scatter them to all these winds, and there shall be no nation to
   which the dispersed of Elam do not come.

[37]And I will break Elam before their enemies
   before those who seek their life
And I will bring evil upon them
   my burning anger
     —oracle of Yahweh.

And I will send after them the sword
   until I have made an end of them
[38]And I will set my throne in Elam
   and I will banish from there king and princes
     —oracle of Yahweh.

[39]But it will happen in the days afterward, I will surely restore the fortunes
   of Elam—oracle of Yahweh.

J. And What about Babylon? (50:1–51:58)

1. Babylon Is Taken (50:1–3)

50 ¹The word that Yahweh spoke to Babylon, to the land of the Chaldeans, through Jeremiah the prophet.
>²Declare among the nations and make heard
>>set up a flag! make heard!
>>>keep it not hidden, say:
>Babylon is taken
>>Bel is very ashamed
>>>Merodach is shattered
>Her images are very ashamed
>>her idols are shattered

>³For a nation from the north has come up upon her
>>it, it will make her land a desolation
>and an inhabitant will not be in her
>>from human to beast
>>>they are wandering, they are gone.

2. Israel and Judah Will Ask the Way to Zion (50:4–5)

50 ⁴In those days and at that time—oracle of Yahweh—the children of Israel shall come, they and the children of Judah together.

>Weeping continually they shall go
>>and Yahweh their God they shall seek
>⁵'Zion,' they will ask
>>their faces in this direction
>'Come!' And they attach themselves to Yahweh!
>>The eternal covenant will not be forgotten!

3. My People Became Lost Sheep (50:6–7)

50 ⁶My people became lost sheep
>>their shepherds let them wander off
>>>mountains led them astray
>From mountain to hill they went
>>they forgot their resting place

>⁷All who found them consumed them
>>and their foes said, 'We are not guilty'
>inasmuch as they sinned against Yahweh

The Righteous Pasture
and Hope of Their Fathers—Yahweh.

4. Wander from the Midst of Babylon! (50:8–10)

50 [8]Wander from the midst of Babylon
    from the land of the Chaldeans, go out
        and become like he-goats before the sheep

[9]For look, I am the one rousing
    and bringing up against Babylon
an assembly of great nations
    from the land of the north
And they shall line up against her
    from there she shall be taken

Its arrows are like those of a successful warrior
    who does not return empty
[10]Yes, the Chaldeans have become spoil
    all who despoil her shall be sated
        —oracle of Yahweh.

5. Babylon Facing Yahweh's Fury (50:11–13)

50 [11]How glad you are! How you exult!
    plunderers of my heritage
How you frisk like a threshing heifer
    and neigh like stallions

[12]Your mother is greatly shamed
    she who bore you is disgraced
Look, the last of nations
    a wilderness of drought and a desert!

[13]At Yahweh's fury she shall not be inhabited
    and she shall become a desolation—all of her
All passing by Babylon shall be horrified
    and shall hiss over all her blows.

6. Babylon Facing Yahweh's Vengeance (50:14–15)

50 [14]Line up against Babylon round about
    all who bend the bow

Shoot at her
  spare not an arrow
    (for against Yahweh she has sinned)

¹⁵Shout against her round about
  she has given her hand
Her towers have fallen
  her walls are overthrown.

For this is the vengeance of Yahweh. Take vengeance against her; as she has done, do to her!

7. Cut Off the Sower from Babylon (50:16)

50 ¹⁶Cut off the one sowing from Babylon
  and the one handling the sickle at harvest time
Before the oppressive sword
  each to his people they turn
    and each to his land they flee.

8. Israel Back in Its Pasture (50:17–20)

50 ¹⁷Israel is a dispersed sheep
  lions have isolated.

First the king of Assyria consumed him, and lastly Nebuchadrezzar, the king of Babylon, has gnawed his bones.

¹⁸Therefore thus said Yahweh of hosts, God of Israel:
Look I will make a reckoning to the king of Babylon and to his land, as I made a reckoning to the king of Assyria. ¹⁹And I will restore Israel to his pasture, and he shall graze on Carmel and the Bashan, and on the mountains of Ephraim and Gilead his appetite shall be sated.

²⁰In those days and at that time—oracle of Yahweh—the iniquity of Israel shall be sought out and there shall be none, also the sins of Judah, and they shall not be found. For I will forgive those whom I leave remaining.

9. Shattered Is the Hammer of the Whole Land! (50:21–28)

50 ²¹Against the land, Merathaim
  go up against her
And to the inhabitants of Pekod
  slay and devote to destruction the last of them

—oracle of Yahweh—
(and do according to all that I have commanded you).

²²The sound of war in the land
  yes, a great shatter!

²³How he is cut off and shattered
  the hammer of the whole land!
How she has become a desolation
  Babylon among the nations!

²⁴You set a trap for yourself
      and even you were captured, Babylon!
      and you, you did not know
You were found, and even you were seized
    for with Yahweh you ventured into a struggle

²⁵Yahweh opened his armory
  and brought out the weapons of his wrath
For Lord Yahweh of hosts had this work
  in the land of the Chaldeans

²⁶Come against her from every side
  open her granaries
Pile her up like heaps and devote her to destruction
  let there not be for her a remnant!

²⁷Slay all her bulls
  let them go down to slaughter
Woe to them for their day has come
  the time of their reckoning.

²⁸The sound of escapees and fugitives from the land of Babylon to declare in Zion: the vengeance of Yahweh our God, the vengeance of his temple.

10. Curtains for Arrogant Babylon! (50:29–30)

50 ²⁹Summon to Babylon a multitude
  all who bend the bow
Encamp against her round about
  let there not be for her an escape

Repay her according to her deed
  according to all that she has done, do to her

For to Yahweh she acted arrogantly
   to the Holy One of Israel

[30]Therefore her young men shall fall in her open squares
   and all her men of war shall be silent in that day
      —oracle of Yahweh.

11. A Day for Mr. Arrogance As Well! (50:31–32)

50 [31]Look, I am against you, Arrogance
   —oracle of Lord Yahweh of hosts
For your day has come
   the time I reckon with you

[32]Arrogance shall stumble and fall
   and there will not be one to pick him up
And I will kindle a fire in his cities
   and it will consume everything round about him.

12. Their Redeemer Is Strong! (50:33–34)

[33]Thus said Yahweh of hosts:
Oppressed are the children of Israel
   and the children of Judah together
All their captors hold them strongly
   they refuse to let them go

[34]Their Redeemer is strong
   Yahweh of hosts is his name
He'll pleadingly plead their plea
   so as to give the earth rest
      and give unrest to the inhabitants of Babylon.

13. A Sword upon Chaldeans! (50:35–38a)

50 [35]A sword upon Chaldeans—oracle of Yahweh—
   and to the inhabitants of Babylon
      and to her princes and to her wise men
[36]A sword to the diviners, that they become foolish
   a sword to her warriors, that they be broken

[37]A sword to his horses and to his chariots
   and to all the mixed races who are in her midst
      that they become women
A sword to her treasures, that they become booty
   [38a]a drought to her waters, that they be dried up.

14. A Land of Images with New Inhabitants (50:38b–40)

50 ³⁸ᵇIndeed it is a land of images
   and with terrors they are going mad!

³⁹Therefore desert beasts with island beasts shall inhabit, and daughter ostriches shall inhabit her. And she shall not again be inhabited for all time, and she shall not be settled for generation after generation. ⁴⁰Just like God's overthrow of Sodom and Gomorrah and her neighbors—oracle of Yahweh. No person shall inhabit there, and no son of man shall sojourn in her.

15. A People from the North against Babylon! (50:41–43)

50 ⁴¹Look! a people comes
   from the north
A great nation and many kings are roused
   from remote parts of the earth

⁴²Bow and sword they seize
   cruel are they, they have no mercy
Their sound makes a roar like the sea
   on horses they ride
Lined up like one man for battle
   against you, daughter Babylon!

⁴³The king of Babylon has heard the report of them
   his hands are weakened
Distress seizes him
   pain like a woman in labor.

16. As a Lion from the Jordan against Babylon! (50:44–46)

50 ⁴⁴Look, as a lion goes up
   from the pride of the Jordan to perennial pasture
Indeed I will in a moment chase them from her
   and who is the young man I will appoint over her?
Indeed who is like me?
   and who will summon me?
      and who is this one, a shepherd that can stand before me?

⁴⁵Therefore hear the counsel of Yahweh that he counseled toward Babylon, and his plans that he planned toward the land of the Chaldeans:
   Surely they shall drag them away—the little ones of the flock
      surely the pasture shall be horrified over them
   ⁴⁶At the sound 'Babylon is captured!' the land quakes
      and a cry among the nations is heard.

17. I Am Rousing a Destroying Wind (51:1–5)

51 [1]Thus said Yahweh:
Look I am rousing against Babylon
    and against the inhabitants of Leb-qamai
        a destroying wind
[2]And I will send to Babylon
    strangers who will scatter her
        and empty her land
Because they were against her round about
    in the day of evil

[3]God will bend, will bend
    the bender his bow
        and God will rise in his scale armor!
Spare not her young men
    devote to destruction all her host!
[4]The slain have fallen in the land of the Chaldeans
    and those pierced in her streets

[5]But Israel is not widowed, nor Judah
    before his God, before Yahweh of hosts
But their land is filled with guilt
    before the Holy One of Israel.

18. A Golden Cup Was Babylon (51:6–10)

51 [6]Flee from the midst of Babylon
    and deliver each his own life
        be not silenced in her iniquity
For this is Yahweh's time of vengeance
    a requital he is repaying her

[7]A golden cup was Babylon
    in the hand of Yahweh
        making drunk all the earth
From her wine drank the nations
    therefore went mad the nations

[8]Suddenly Babylon is fallen and shattered
    wail madly over her!
Get balm for her pain
    perhaps she can be treated

[9]We treated Babylon, but she could not be treated
    forsake her, and let us go each to his land

For her judgment reaches to the heavens
and is lifted up to the clouds

[10]Yahweh has brought forth our vindication
come, and let us recount in Zion
the work of Yahweh our God.

19. You Who Dwell by Many Waters (51:11–14)

51 [11]Sharpen the arrows!
fill the quivers!
Yahweh has roused the spirit of the kings of Media, for his purpose against Babylon is to destroy it; for this is the vengeance of Yahweh, the vengeance of his temple.
[12]To the walls of Babylon!
set up a flag!
strengthen the watch!
station watchmen!
prepare men in ambush!
For Yahweh both planned and did what he said to the inhabitants of Babylon.

[13]You who dwell by many waters
by manifold treasures
Your end has come
your cutoff measure
[14]Yahweh of hosts has sworn by himself:
Surely I have filled you
humanity like the locust
and they shall raise a shout over you.

20. Yahweh the God of Creation! (51:15–19)

51 [15]The Maker of the earth by his strength
the Establisher of the world by his wisdom
and by his understanding he stretched out the heavens

[16]When he utters his voice—a roar in heavens' waters
clouds come up from the ends of the earth
Lightning bolts for rain he made
and he brought forth the wind from his storehouses

[17]Every human is stupid without knowledge
every smith is very shamed because of the idol
For his cast image is a lie
and no breath is in them

¹⁸They are nothing—a laughable work!
   at the time of their reckoning they shall perish

¹⁹Not like these is the Portion of Jacob
   for the one forming everything is he
And Israel is his tribal heritage
   Yahweh of hosts is his name!

21. You Were a Club for Me, Weapons of War (51:20–24)

51 ²⁰You were a club for me
   weapons of war:

And with you I smashed nations and with you I destroyed kingdoms
   ²¹and with you I smashed horse and its rider
     and with you I smashed chariot and its rider

     ²²and with you I smashed man and woman
       and with you I smashed old and young
     and with you I smashed young man and maiden

    ²³and with you I smashed shepherd and his flock
  and with you I smashed farmer and his team
and with you I smashed governors and commanders.

²⁴But I will repay to Babylon and to all the inhabitants of Chaldea all their evil that they did in Zion before your eyes—oracle of Yahweh.

22. From Destroying Mountain to Burned-Out Mountain (51:25–26)

51 ²⁵Look, I am against you, O Destroying Mountain
   —oracle of Yahweh—
     the one destroying all the land!
So I will stretch out my hand against you
   and I will roll you down from the cliffs
     and make you a burned-out mountain.

²⁶They shall not take from you stone for a corner or stone for foundations; indeed eternal desolations you shall be—oracle of Yahweh.

23. Sanctify the Nations against Her! (51:27–33)

51 ²⁷Set up a flag in the land
   blow the trumpet in the nations

Sanctify the nations against her
  summon the kingdoms against her
    —Ararat, Minni, and Ashkenaz

Appoint the marshal against her
  bring up the horse like a bristling locust
[28]Sanctify the nations against her
  —the kings of Media
her governors and all her commanders
  and all land under his rule

[29]Thus the land quakes and writhes
  for it rises up against Babylon
    —the plans of Yahweh to make the land of Babylon
    a desolation without inhabitant

[30]The warriors of Babylon cease to fight
  they sit in the strongholds
Their strength is sapped
  they have become women!
They have set her dwellings on fire
  her bars are broken

[31]Runner runs to meet runner
  and herald to meet herald
To herald the news to the king of Babylon
  that his city is taken from every side
[32]also the fords have been seized
  and the marshes they have burned with fire
    and the men of war are terrified.

[33]For thus said Yahweh of hosts, God of Israel:
Daughter Babylon is like a threshing floor at the time one treads her. Just a
little while, and the harvest time will come upon her.

24. Bel No Longer King in Babylon (51:34–45)

51 [34]He consumed me, he shook me up
  Nebuchadrezzar, king of Babylon
    he set me down an empty jar
Like a monster he swallowed me
  he filled his belly with my delicacies
    he rinsed me out
[35]'My violated flesh be upon Babylon'
  let the inhabitant of Zion say

'My blood be upon the inhabitants of Chaldea,'
    let Jerusalem say

³⁶Therefore thus said Yahweh:
Look I have pled your plea
    and I have avenged your avenging
I have drained her sea
    and I have dried up her fountain
³⁷And Babylon will become heaps
    a den of jackals
a desolation and an object of hissing
    without inhabitant

³⁸Together like lions they roar
    they growl like lion cubs
³⁹When they are heated I will set out their drinks
    and make them drunk so they become silly
They shall sleep an eternal sleep
    and not waken—oracle of Yahweh
⁴⁰I will bring them down like lambs to the slaughter
    like rams with he-goats

⁴¹How Sheshak is taken
    and the praise of all the land occupied!
How she has become a desolation
    Babylon among the nations!
⁴²The sea has come up upon Babylon
    with its roaring heaps she is covered
⁴³Her cities have become a desolation
    a land of drought and desert
        (a land in which any person shall not dwell
    and a human shall not pass through)

⁴⁴So I have reckoned with Bel in Babylon
    and taken out what he swallowed from his mouth
And nations will not stream to him any longer
    even the wall of Babylon has fallen!
⁴⁵'Go out from her midst, my people!
    and deliver each his own life
        from the burning anger of Yahweh!'

25. Look! A Reckoning for Babylon and Its Images (51:46–51)

51 ⁴⁶Now lest your heart be weakened and you become afraid at the rumor heard in the land, as the rumor comes in this year and after it the rumor in the next year, and violence is in the land, and ruler is against ruler:

⁴⁷Look, hereafter, days are coming
  when I will reckon with the images of Babylon
And all her land shall be shamed
  and all her slain shall fall in her midst

⁴⁸They shall cry for joy concerning Babylon
  sky and land
    and all that is in them
For from the north they shall come to her
  the devastators!—oracle of Yahweh.

⁴⁹Yes, Babylon is to fall, O slain of Israel!
Yes, to Babylon fell the slain of all the land!

⁵⁰You who have escaped from the sword:
  Go, don't just stand there!
Remember Yahweh from afar
  and let Jerusalem come to your mind

⁵¹We are shamed, for we have heard the reproach
  disgrace covers our faces
For strangers have come
  against the holy places of Yahweh's house.

26. Look Again! A Reckoning for Babylon and Its Images (51:52–57)

51 ⁵²Look, hereafter, days are coming
  —oracle of Yahweh—
when I will reckon with her images
  and in all her land the slain shall groan

⁵³If Babylon should climb to the sky
  and if she should make inaccessible her fortified height
From me devastators shall come to her
  —oracle of Yahweh.

⁵⁴The sound of a cry from Babylon
  and a great shatter from the land of the Chaldeans
⁵⁵For Yahweh is devastating Babylon
  and killing in her a great sound

Yes, their waves roar like many waters
  their crashing sound is uttered
⁵⁶For it has come upon her
  upon Babylon—the devastator!

And her warriors have been taken
  their bows shattered
For a God of requital is Yahweh
  he will surely repay.

[57]And I will make drunk her princes and her wise men, her governors and
her commanders, and her warriors. And they shall sleep an eternal sleep,
and not waken—oracle of the King, Yahweh of hosts is his name!

27. The Walls of Grand Babylon Demolished! (51:58)

51 [58]Thus said Yahweh of hosts:
The walls of grand Babylon
  shall be totally demolished!
And her high gates
  with fire they shall burn

So peoples labor for nothing
  and nations for fire, so they tire themselves.

K. Seraiah's Colophon (51:59–64)

51 [59]The word that Jeremiah the prophet commanded Seraiah son of Neriah,
son of Mahseiah, when he went with Zedekiah, king of Judah, to Babylon in
the fourth year of his reign. Now Seraiah was caravan prince. [60]And Jeremiah
wrote all the evil that would come to Babylon in one scroll, all these words that
are written toward Babylon. [61]And Jeremiah said to Seraiah: 'When you come
to Babylon, then you shall see to it that you read aloud all these words. [62]And
you shall say:

> Yahweh, you, yourself have spoken toward this place, to cut it off without
> there being an inhabitant in it, from human to beast; indeed eternal deso-
> lations it shall be.

[63]And when you have finished reading this scroll aloud, you shall tie a stone
to it, and you shall throw it into the middle of the Euphrates. [64]Then you
shall say:

> Even so shall Babylon sink and not rise, because of the evil that I am bring-
> ing upon it.'

so they tire themselves

Thus far the legacy of Jeremiah.

IX. POSTSCRIPT (52:1–34)

A. Zedekiah Meets the King and Goes to Prison (52:1–11)

1. Summary of Zedekiah's Reign (52:1–3)

52 ¹Zedekiah was twenty-one years old when he became king, and he reigned eleven years in Jerusalem. His mother's name was Hamutal daughter of Jeremiah from Libnah. ²And he did what was evil in the eyes of Yahweh, just like everything that Jehoiakim had done. ³Indeed, concerning the anger of Yahweh—it came against Jerusalem and Judah until he cast them away from his presence. So Zedekiah rebelled against the king of Babylon.

2. Capture of Jerusalem and Zedekiah (52:4–11)

⁴And it happened in the ninth year of his reign, in the tenth month, on the tenth of the month,Nebuchadrezzar, king of Babylon, came—he and all his army—against Jerusalem. And they encamped against it and built a siege wall against it all around. ⁵So the city came under siege until the eleventh year of King Zedekiah. ⁶In the fourth month, on the ninth of the month, the famine in the city became severe, and there was not any bread for the people of the land. ⁷Then the city was breached, and all the fighting men fled, and they went out from the city by night in the direction of the gate between the double walls, which was by the king's garden, though the Chaldeans were against the city all around. So they went in the direction of the Arabah. ⁸But the army of the Chaldeans pursued after the king and overtook Zedekiah in the desert regions of Jericho. And all his army was scattered from him. ⁹So they captured the king and brought him up to the king of Babylon at Riblah in the land of Hamath, and he spoke judgments against him. ¹⁰And the king of Babylon slaughtered Zedekiah's sons before his eyes, and also all the princes of Judah he slaughtered at Riblah. ¹¹Then the eyes of Zedekiah he blinded, and he bound him in bronze chains. And the king of Babylon brought him to Babylon and put him in the detention house until the day of his death.

B. Jerusalem: Destruction, Remnant, Looting, and Death (52:12–27)

1. Destruction, yet a Remnant (52:12–16)

¹²In the fifth month, on the tenth of the month (it was the nineteenth year of King Nebuchadrezzar, king of Babylon), Nebuzaradan the Rab-tabahim came. He stood before the king of Babylon in Jerusalem. ¹³And he burned the house of Yahweh, and the house of the king, and all the houses of Jerusalem, yes,

every great house he burned with fire. [14]And all the walls of Jerusalem round about, the entire army of the Chaldeans who were with the Rab-tabahim broke down. [15]But some of the poor people, and the rest of the people who were left in the city, and the deserters who had deserted to the king of Babylon, and the rest of the craftsmen, Nebuzaradan the Rab-tabahim exiled. [16]And some of the poor of the land Nebuzaradan the Rab-tabahim left for vinedressers and for plowmen.

2. Temple Treasures Go to Babylon (52:17–23)

[17]And the bronze pillars that belonged to Yahweh's house, the stands and the bronze sea that were in Yahweh's house, the Chaldeans broke in pieces, and they carried away all their bronze to Babylon. [18]And the pots, the shovels, the snuffers, the sprinkling bowls, the incense dishes, and all the vessels of bronze with which they served, they took. [19]And the small bowls, the fire pans, the sprinkling bowls, the pots, the lampstands, the incense dishes, and the libation bowls—whatever was gold for gold, and whatever was silver for silver, the Rab-tabahim took. [20]The two pillars, the one sea and the twelve bronze bulls that were underneath the sea, and the stands that King Solomon made for Yahweh's house—there was no weight to the bronze from all these vessels. [21]Regarding the pillars: eighteen cubits high the one pillar, and a thread of twelve cubits would encircle it; its thickness four fingers—it was hollow. [22]And a capital of bronze was above it, and the height of the one capital five cubits; also lattice-work and pomegranates were above the capital round about—all of it bronze. And likewise for the second pillar and pomegranates. [23]So there were ninety-six pomegranates to a side; all the pomegranates: one hundred above the lattice-work round about.

3. Death to Jerusalem's Great and Small (52:24–27)

[24]And the Rab-tabahim took Seraiah the head priest, Zephaniah the associate priest, and the three keepers of the threshold, [25]and from the city he took one eunuch who was an overseer of the fighting men, seven men from those seeing the king's face who were found in the city, the scribe of the prince of the army who conscripted the people of the land, and sixty men from the people of the land who were found amidst the city. [26]And Nebuzaradan the Rab-tabahim took them and brought them to the king of Babylon at Riblah. [27]And the king of Babylon beat them and put them to death at Riblah in the land of Hamath. So Judah went into exile from its land.

C. Deportation Summary (52:28–30)

52 [28]This is the people that Nebuchadrezzar exiled in the seventh year: 3,023 Judahites. [29]In the eighteenth year of Nebuchadrezzar, from Jerusalem: 832

persons. [30]In the twenty-third year of Nebuchadrezzar, Nebuzaradan the Rab-tabahim exiled 745 Judahite persons. Total persons: 4,600.

D. Jehoiakim Leaves Prison for the King's Table (52:31–34)

52 [31]And it happened in the thirty-seventh year of the exile of Jehoiachin, king of Judah, in the twelfth month, on the twenty-fifth of the month, Evil-merodach, king of Babylon, in the year he became king, lifted up the head of Jehoiachin, king of Judah, and brought him out from the prison house. [32]And he spoke good things to him, and he put his seat above the seat of the kings who were with him in Babylon. [33]So he changed his prison clothes and ate food in his presence regularly all the days of his life. [34]On his allowance: a regular allowance was given to him from the king of Babylon, a day's portion each day, until the day of his death, all the days of his life.

TRANSLATION, NOTES, AND COMMENTS

◆

V. BEHOLD THE MAN! (37:1–40:6)

♦

A. JEREMIAH'S WORD RENDERED CHEAP (37:1–16)

1. A Nation the Shadow of Its King (37:1–2)

37 ¹And Zedekiah son of Josiah, whom Nebuchadrezzar, king of Babylon, made king in the land of Judah, reigned as king in place of Coniah son of Jehoiakim. ²But he did not listen, he and his servants and the people of the land, to the words of Yahweh that he spoke through Jeremiah the prophet.

2. Jeremiah Asked by Zedekiah to Mediate (37:3–11)

37 ³King Zedekiah sent Jehucal son of Shelemiah and Zephaniah son of Maaseiah, the priest, to Jeremiah the prophet saying: 'Pray would you on our behalf to Yahweh our God.' ⁴Now Jeremiah was coming and going amidst the people, and they had not put him in the prison house. ⁵The army of Pharaoh had gone out from Egypt, and the Chaldeans who were besieging Jerusalem heard a report of them and withdrew from Jerusalem. ⁶And the word of Yahweh came to Jeremiah the prophet:

⁷Thus said Yahweh, God of Israel:

Thus you shall say to the king of Judah who sent you to me to inquire of me: Look, the army of Pharaoh that went out to help you will return to its own land, Egypt. ⁸And the Chaldeans shall return and fight against this city and take it, and they shall burn it with fire.

⁹Thus said Yahweh:

Do not deceive yourselves saying, The Chaldeans will surely go away from us; indeed they will not go away! ¹⁰Even if you should strike down the entire army of the Chaldeans who are fighting you and there remained among them only wounded men, each man in his tent, they would rise up and burn this city with fire.

¹¹So it happened when the army of the Chaldeans withdrew from Jerusalem because of the army of Pharaoh.

3. Jeremiah Imprisoned on Charge of Desertion (37:12–16)

37 ¹²And Jeremiah set out from Jerusalem to go to the land of Benjamin for an apportioning from there amidst the people. ¹³And he came into the

Benjamin Gate, and there was a guard officer whose name was Irijah son of Shelemiah, son of Hananiah, and he laid hold of Jeremiah the prophet saying, 'To the Chaldeans you are deserting!' [14]And Jeremiah said, 'A lie! I am not deserting to the Chaldeans.' But he did not listen to him, and Irijah laid hold of Jeremiah and brought him to the princes. [15]And the princes were furious with Jeremiah, and they beat him and put him in the stockhouse, the house of Jonathan the scribe, for they had made it a prison house. [16]Indeed Jeremiah went to the Pit House, yes, to the cells! And Jeremiah dwelt there many days.

RHETORIC AND COMPOSITION

MT 37:1–16 = LXX 44:1–16. Chapters 37–44 contain what some have called the *via dolorosa* prose of the Jeremiah book, describing as they do Jeremiah's suffering before and after the collapse of the nation from the vantage point of one who had observed it at close range. Zimmerli (1984: 356) refers to the "passion narrative of the prophet." These designations apply particularly to chaps. 37–38, which report Jeremiah's imprisonments prior to Jerusalem's capture. This prose is widely—but not universally—attributed to Jeremiah's friend and colleague Baruch (Giesebrecht, xxi; Mowinckel 1946: 61–62; Eissfeldt 1965: 354–55; Holladay), who at the end adds a personal word about his own suffering (LXX: 51:31–35; MT: chap. 45). Mowinckel attached importance to the location of chap. 45 after giving up earlier ideas about Source B prose being anonymous (Mowinckel 1914: 30), a fact that goes unnoticed in Eissfeldt and some of the commentaries (e.g., Holladay II: 286; Keown et al., 209). This prose is assigned to Baruch also because of the wealth of detail it contains: personal names, place-names, and precise locations, to say nothing of reported conversations and dates attached to various events. Peake and Hyatt note a particular abundance of intimate detail in chap. 38, but actually it is present in all of the chapters.

Wanke (1971) and particularly Pohlmann (1978) date the material too late for it to emanate from Baruch, and Carroll's rejection of a Baruch "passion narrative" is based on his view that Jeremiah's suffering is incidental compared to the accent being placed in the narrative on the divine word. That the divine word controls the march of events is obvious enough (37:2), but this no more precludes human suffering—which is manifestly present in these chapters—than it does in the NT Gospels, where the term "passion narrative" originated. Zimmerli embellished the term only to say that Jeremiah's sufferings were intended to reflect "the much greater suffering of Yahweh himself" (1984: 357–58). McKane (p. 943) brackets out portions of narrative as being historically incredible, e.g., Zedekiah's intercession request in 37:3, because he reduces theology to politics: Jeremiah must at every point be pro-Babylonian. Jeremianic authorship of the Foreign Nation Oracles is rejected by McKane for the same reason, which represents a complete misunderstanding of Hebrew prophecy generally, and of Jeremiah's prophecy in particular. Theology is assuredly in politics, but theology is just as certainly above and beyond all things political. Reductionism of this kind also flattens out real-life complexities, substituting in their place contrived and overly-complex literary redactions.

The prose of 37–44 is an intact sequential composition in the main, but consists of narrative segments many of which have their own integrity and are ordered in a fashion not corresponding to the march of events. For example, 37:3–5 begins *in medias res*: the siege of Jerusalem began earlier, and we are now at the point where the Babylonians have withdrawn because of an Egyptian advance. The beginning of the siege is reported finally in 39:1. Also, in 37:21 Jeremiah is incarcerated in the court of the guard, where bread is given him daily until the city falls, but then chap. 38 goes back to report an event occurring earlier (v 1), concluding again with a summary statement that Jeremiah lived in the court of the guard until Jerusalem was taken (v 28). The fall of Jerusalem, Jeremiah's release by Nebuzaradan, and Jeremiah's assignment to Gedaliah are all reported in 39:1–14, after which follows in 39:15–18 another event that took place when Jeremiah was confined to the court of the guard. This is followed in 40:1–6 by a second release of Jeremiah from chains at Ramah, where it is stated again in conclusion that Jeremiah was entrusted to the care of Gedaliah. The two accounts of Jeremiah's imprisonment and release during the siege (37:12–21; 38:1–13), and the two accounts of his later freeing by the Babylonians (39:11–14; 40:1–6), were taken by earlier source critics to be double reportings of single events (Skinner 1926: 256–60). They are still understood in this fashion by some commentators, e.g., Bright and Jones, but such an interpretation is now considered unlikely, not only because the accounts in question can be explained as successive events, but more importantly, because there are too many differences in detail for them to be doublets, whether oral or literary (Seitz 1985: 86; Holladay II, 282). Subsequent narrative reporting the Mizpah and Geruth Chimham sojourns, and the escape to Egypt, follows more or less in chronological order, only here events are compressed (e.g., the Mizpah sojourn), making impossible a historically precise reconstruction. The mention of Gedaliah's murder as having occurred in "the seventh month" (41:1), which is taken from 2 Kgs 25:25, has no reference to a year in either place (see Notes).

This prose is similar to that in chaps. 11–20: undated, and combining narrative with oracle(s). Only the segments having parallels in 2 Kings contain documentation: two dates on the beginning of the siege and the fall of Jerusalem (39:1–2); and a reference to Gedaliah's murder in "the seventh month" (41:1; cf. 2 Kgs 25:1–2, 25). The structure of the material has been created largely—but not exclusively—by stereotyped opening and closing phrases, giving it a rhetorical character that will facilitate its presentation to an audience that must listen to it being spoken aloud.

In 37:1–40:6 are narrative segments closing with what I would call "ballast lines," i.e., weighty sentences, formulaic in nature, which bring each segment to a recognizable end. These sentences and the segments they delimit have been recognized by Kremers (1953: 122–27), Wanke (1971: 93–95), and

Abrego (1983a: 8; 1983b: 65), although none agrees exactly with the others on delimitation or on how far the larger structure extends. The key observation is that every closing line but one predicates "Jeremiah" by the verb *yšb*, "dwell," e.g., in 37:16 the line is "And Jeremiah dwelt (*wayyēšeb*) there many days." I agree with Wanke that 38:6, "And Jeremiah sank in the mud," is a closing line that delimits 38:1–6 as a segment. But against Wanke, I begin the larger structure at 37:1—taking vv 1–2 as Introduction, and the first segment as vv 3–16—and end it with the last *wayyēšeb* ("and he dwelt") line in 40:6. Wanke's analysis cannot be followed in chaps. 40–43, because after 40:6 his form-critical units inadequately describe the material and are largely unsupported by section markings.

A major break in the narrative occurs at 40:6 (see Rhetoric and Composition for 39:1–14), after which rhetorically significant vocabulary identifying segments to the end of chap. 44 is different (see Rhetoric and Composition for 40:7–12). The structure of 37:1–40:6 is then the following:

Superscription	37:1–2
Oracles for Zedekiah and Imprisonment for Jeremiah	37:3–16
And Jeremiah dwelt there many days *wayyēšeb*	
Oracle for Zedekiah and Jeremiah's Release from Prison	37:17–21
And Jeremiah dwelt in the court of the guard *wayyēšeb*	
Oracles to the People and Imprisonment for Jeremiah	38:1–6
And Jeremiah sank in the mud *wayyiṭbaʿ . . . baṭṭîṭ*	
Intervention by Ebed-melech and Jeremiah's Release from Prison	38:7–13
And Jeremiah dwelt in the court of the guard *wayyēšeb*	
Oracle to Zedekiah and No Imprisonment for Jeremiah	38:14–28
And Jeremiah dwelt in the court of the guard until the day	
that Jerusalem was taken *wayyēšeb*	
Capture of Jerusalem and Release for Jeremiah	39:1–14
So he dwelt amidst the people *wayyēšeb*	
Oracles to Ebed-melech and Release for Jeremiah	39:15–40:6
And he dwelt with him amidst the people who	
were left in the land *wayyēšeb*	

The present narrative segment (37:1–16) is delimited at the top end by a *setumah* in M^L and a *petuḥah* in M^A and M^P prior to v 1, which is also the chapter division. The lower end is marked by a *petuḥah* in M^L (only) after v 16, which is a conclusion, not a dependent clause introducing v 17 (*pace* AV and RSV, but changed in NRSV). A *petuḥah* after v 2 in M^P (only) sets off the superscription from the narrative reporting Zedekiah's request for mediation. A *setumah* in M^A, M^L, and M^P after v 11 points to this verse being a conclusion, but T takes vv 11–12 together, a reading that is adopted in all modern Versions since the AV, and by most commentators (Giesebrecht, Volz, Weiser, Rudolph, Thompson, Holladay, McKane). Verse 11 actually can be read either way, and may double as a conclusion and a beginning, which is what happens in Deut 13:1[Eng 12:32] and 28:69[Eng 29:1] (Lundbom 1996a: 306–8, 312–13). If v 11 is a statement of closure, then together with v 5 it frames the oracle:

The army of Pharaoh had gone out from Egypt, and *the Chaldeans* who were   v 5
besieging Jerusalem heard a report of them and *withdrew from Jerusalem*

So it happened when the army of *the Chaldeans withdrew from Jerusalem*   v 11
before *the army of Pharaoh*

If this division be accepted, it nevertheless remains the case that v 12 follows in sequence, and the incident involving Jeremiah and Irijah can be taken as having occurred during the break in the siege. Other section markings exist prior to the superscription in 37:6 (a *petuḥah* in M^A, M^L, and M^P), and prior to the messenger formula in 37:9 (a *setumah* in M^L; a *petuḥah* in M^A and M^P). Section markings seem to follow messenger formulas or places in the text where Yahweh begins speaking in the first person (see Rhetoric and Composition for 22:28–30).

The present narrative segment divides into three: 1) a superscription to chaps. 37–38 (vv 1–2); 2) a report of Zedekiah asking for Jeremiah's mediation on behalf of the nation, with two oracles of reply (vv 3–11); and 3) a report of Jeremiah's imprisonment on the charge of desertion (vv 12–16). The whole of vv 1–16 is crafted into a key word chiasmus:

Zedekiah . . . *did not listen (lō' šāma')* to the words of Yahweh (*'el-dibrê yhwh*)   v 2
Jeremiah not yet put in *the prison house (bêt hakkĕlî'* [Kt])   v 4
  The Chaldeans . . . *withdrew (yē'ālû) from Jerusalem*   v 5
    Word of Yahweh (*dĕbar-yhwh*) comes to Zedekiah   v 6
  When the Chaldeans *withdrew (bĕhē'ālôt) from Jerusalem*   v 11
Irijah *did not listen (lō' šāma')* to Jeremiah   v 14
Jeremiah put in *the prison house (lĕbêt hakkele')*   v 15

The two oracles in the second portion of narrative have balancing conclusions:

I   . . . *and they shall burn it with fire*   *ûśĕrāpūhā bā'ēš*   v 8
II   *they would . . . burn this city with fire*   *wĕśārĕpû 'et-hā'îr hazz'ōt bā'ēš*   v 10

Other prose dated during the final siege of Jerusalem is in 21:1–10, and in chaps. 32 and 34.

NOTES

37:1. *And Zedekiah son of Josiah, whom Nebuchadrezzar, king of Babylon, made king in the land of Judah, reigned as king in place of Coniah son of Jehoiakim.* On Nebuchadrezzar's capture of Jerusalem in 597 B.C. and Jehoiachin's exile to Babylon, see Note for 29:1. This statement documenting a change in kingship seems at first glance to be lifted from the Deuteronomic History; however, both it and v 2 are as different from 2 Kgs 24:17–20 as they are similar. The similarities are largely formal, which could be accounted for if vv 1–2 emanate from Baruch, a Deuteronomic scribe. The unusual feature is the expression "reigned as king" (*yimlāk-melek*), from which the cognate accusative *melek* is usually deleted (even in AV) with T and the LXX. However, the expression (with a perfect verb) occurs in 23:5. This is unlikely MT dittography (*pace* Ehrlich 1912: 336; Rudolph; Bright; Janzen 1973: 142, 155 n. 7; Holladay; Keown et al.), better explained as an LXX omission due to haplography (homoeoteleuton: *mlk . . . mlk*). Cognate accusatives are common in Jeremiah (see Note on 22:16). Kimḥi says the meaning here is not that Zedekiah followed Jehoiachin as king, but that he reigned in his stead, since Jehoiachin's three-month tenure did not reckon him as a king (cf. 1:3). If this be the case, it gives to *taḥat* ("in place of, instead of") a nuance it does not have in the accession statements of Kings. Jeremiah, it is true, did not envision the Davidic line as being carried on through Jehoiachin (22:30; 36:30); nevertheless, Jehoiachin is called "king of Judah" when he is elevated by Evil-merodach (52:31–34; 2 Kgs 25:27–30), and it is through him—not Zedekiah—that the Messianic line is traced (Matt 1:11–12).

Nebuchadrezzar, king of Babylon. The LXX lacks "king of Babylon," as it does in 35:11 [LXX 42:11]. But these are rarities; more often the LXX omits "Nebuchadrezzar" (see Note on 21:2).

Coniah son of Jehoiakim. "Coniah" is a shortened form of "Jehoiachin" (see Note for 22:24). The LXX omits "Coniah son (of)," with the result that Zedekiah is said to reign in place of Jehoiakim. As explained above, this has contextual support from 36:30. Peake takes the LXX reading as an attempt to bridge the gap between chaps. 36 and 37: In 36 Jehoiakim is the ruling monarch; here in 37 it is Zedekiah. But a better explanation (D. N. Freedman) is that the *Vorlage* to the LXX, at some earlier point, contained the full name "Jehoiachin" (G^A has *iechoniou uiou*), and that subsequently *yĕhôyāqîn ben* was lost due to haplography (homoeoarcton: *y . . . y*).

2. *But he did not listen, he and his servants and the people of the land, to the words of Yahweh that he spoke through Jeremiah the prophet.* The form is again Deuteronomic, but not the content. Zedekiah does not do what is evil in Yahweh's sight as Jehoiakim did (2 Kgs 24:19), but along with everyone else, he fails to listen to Yahweh's words as spoken through Jeremiah. This description of covenant disregard, which recurs in Baruch prose (25:3; 36:31; 44:5, 16), is picked up by the Chronicler (2 Chr 36:12) and repeated in 1 Esd 1:47. By casting blame on Zedekiah and his servants, the superscription is seen as introducing only chaps. 37 and 38, since in chap. 39 the captured king and his servants are turning a deaf ear to no one. The "people of the land," i.e., people generally (see Note for 1:18), must here be a Judahite population as yet undefeated by Nebuchadrezzar. In the prose of chaps. 42–44, which reports a post-586 B.C. Judahite remnant still resisting Yahweh's word, the key verb is not "listen," *šmʿ*, but "obey," *šmʿ b* (see Rhetoric and Composition for 42:1–22).

and his servants. Hebrew *waʿăbādāyw.* "Servants" of the king are important royal officials (see Note for 21:7).

Jeremiah the prophet. The LXX lacks "the prophet," as it does also in vv 3, 6, 13, and throughout much of the book (see Note for 25:2 and Appendix VI B).

3. *King Zedekiah sent Jehucal son of Shelemiah and Zephaniah son of Maaseiah, the priest, to Jeremiah the prophet saying: 'Pray would you on our behalf to Yahweh our God.'* Troop movement out of Egypt has forced a Babylonian withdrawal from Jerusalem (v 5), and the king now wants intercession to the end that the siege be abandoned for good. Will Yahweh respond favorably? When Zedekiah sent his earlier embassy (21:2), the word coming back was unfavorable. Zedekiah also received an unfavorable word at some other point during the siege (34:1–7). Zedekiah may also be testing the prophet and the word he is delivering. The first embassy was sent in the hope of securing a withdrawal, and although Yahweh's answer promised nothing of the kind, the Babylonians now have withdrawn, and Zedekiah might think his earlier instincts right and Jeremiah's prophetic word wrong. But the beleaguered king may also fear the worst. The language is urgent and emphatic: "Pray would you on our behalf" (*hitpallel-nā' ba'ădēnû*). Hezekiah implored Isaiah to make an urgent prayer (*tĕpillâ*) on Judah's behalf when Jerusalem was threatened by the Assyrians (Isa 37:4 = 2 Kgs 19:4). The intercessory prayer here is no different from the request in 21:2 for a divine oracle (Thelle 1998). Both embassies request intercession, and both receive their answers by divine oracle.

Jehucal son of Shelemiah. One of Zedekiah's princes, who in 38:1 (where his name is spelled "Jucal") calls along with others for Jeremiah's death. The name "Jehucal" in its variant spellings has turned up on an Arad ostracon, a Lachish bulla, and other contemporary artifacts. "Shelemiah" has been found on seals from Arad, Jerusalem, and elsewhere. On both names, see Appendix I.

Zephaniah son of Maaseiah, the priest. Hebrew *wĕ'et-ṣĕpanyāhû ben-ma'ăśēyâ hakkōhēn.* The NJV translates "Zephaniah son of the priest Maaseiah." Grammatically, the title can apply to either father or son, but since the reference here is to Zephaniah, the title belongs to him. The NEB and REB have it correctly: "the priest Zephaniah son of Maaseiah." As it turns out, both individuals are high-ranking priests. Zephaniah is associate to the high priest (52:24), sent by Zedekiah with Pashhur son of Malchiah on an earlier embassy to request Jeremiah's intercession (21:1). Maaseiah is one of three "keepers of the threshold" in the Temple (35:4). On the names "Zephaniah" and "Maaseiah," see Appendix I. Zephaniah appears to have been kindly disposed to the prophet, which is a change from Jehoiakim's reign, when the priests were among the most hostile to Jeremiah (20:1–2; 26:7–11). A letter from Babylon criticized Zephaniah for being soft on Jeremiah when the prophet was preaching a long exile (29:24–32). Zephaniah was also not part of the accusing group in 38:1, though his companion Jehucal was. One wonders, then, if in the present situation Zedekiah was not employing a "good cop / bad cop" strategy, sending on the embassy one person critical of Jeremiah, which would be Jehucal, and one person kindly disposed toward him, which would be Zephaniah? This would preclude any collusion between the two and make more likely a truthful reporting of what the prophet had said. The earlier team of Pashhur and Zephaniah appears to have been another matchup in which loyalties toward the prophet were divided (see Note for 21:1).

Pray would you on our behalf to Yahweh our God. In 21:2 the embassy says, "Seek (*dĕrāš*) Yahweh would you on our behalf," which means the same. Jeremiah earlier was told by Yahweh not to pray on behalf of the people (7:16; 11:14; 14:11); however, bans such as these were not for all time. In 21:1–2 and 42:1–3 intercessions are made, and Yahweh answers. The LXX omits "our God," which it often does (Janzen 1973: 80–81).

4. *Now Jeremiah was coming and going amidst the people, and they had not put him in the prison house.* This anticipates the harsh imprisonment awaiting the prophet in the house of Jonathan the scribe (v 15), not the assignment after his release to the court of the guard (v 21), where contact with people was permitted, though on a limited basis (32:1–15; 39:15–18).

amidst the people. Hebrew *bĕtôk hā'ām*. The LXX has "within the city" (*tēs poleōs*). Aquila supports the reading of MT (*en mesō tou laou*).

the prison house. Hebrew *bêt hakkĕlî'* (Kt); Q has the spelling *hakkĕlû'* (cf. 52:31). In v 15 and 2 Kgs 25:27 is the more usual *(hak)kele'*, which appears to be the general term for prison. The Akk word for prison house is *bît kīli* (CAD 8: 360–61).

5. *The army of Pharaoh had gone out from Egypt, and the Chaldeans who were besieging Jerusalem heard a report of them and withdrew from Jerusalem.* The Pharaoh now, following the death of Psammetichus II, was the ambitious but incompetent Apries (= Hophra of 44:30), who ascended the throne in 589 B.C. (see Note on 39:1). At the beginning of his reign, Judah dispatched an embassy to Egypt for the purpose of soliciting aid in fighting the Babylonians (Ezek 17:15). This embassy is possibly corroborated in the Lachish Letters (Freedy and Redford 1970: 481; Bright 1981: 330; Lipschits 1998: 472), where Letter #3 (lines 13–18) makes the following reference to a Judahite commander visiting Egypt:

> And to your servant it has been reported that the general of the army, Coniah, son of Elnathan, has gone down to enter Egypt, and he has sent to fetch from here Hodaviah, the son of Ahijah, and his men.
> (Di Vito, *ABD* 4: 127; cf. Torczyner 1938: 45–73; *ANET*[3] 322)

The original translator, Torczyner, imagined that the embassy was carried out in connection with the flight of Uriah of Kiriath-jearim to Egypt (26:20–23), but this view did not meet with acceptance (Albright 1941b: 22 n. 22; D. W. Thomas 1946; 1961). The consensus now is that it fits rather into Zedekiah's last years, and represents an effort to secure Egyptian help in fighting the Babylonians.

who were besieging Jerusalem. Hebrew *haṣṣārîm 'al-yĕrûšālayim*. Syntax is awkward and the LXX omits, but the words are nevertheless present in Aq, Theod, T, and Vg. The omission can be attributed to haplography (homoeoteleuton: *m . . . m*, or *ym . . . ym* if "Jerusalem" had the dual ending *-ayim*, as it always does in the Dead Sea Scrolls and the Qere of MT).

and withdrew from Jerusalem. Fried and Freedman (2001: 2260) date the lifting of the siege between December 29, 588 and February 24, 587 B.C.

7. *Thus said Yahweh, God of Israel.* The LXX omits "God of Israel," as it commonly does (Janzen 1973: 75–76).

Thus you shall say. Hebrew *kōh tō'mĕrû.* The plural verb indicates that Jeremiah is giving the messengers the following word to relay to the king. A singular verb in the LXX (*epeis*) has Yahweh telling Jeremiah to speak directly to the king. The LXX adjusts the subsequent pronouns accordingly. McKane (following Duhm) favors the LXX reading, assuming that the oracle following had no original connection with the embassy of v 3, and that MT is a patchwork connecting v 3 with v 7. Such a view is contrived (see Rhetoric and Composition), and should be rejected. Read the MT.

Look, the army of Pharaoh that went out to help you will return to its own land, Egypt. Ezekiel makes the same prediction about Apries' ill-fated adventurism against the Babylonians (Ezek 17:15–17), which is supplemented by oracles in Ezek 29:1–12; 30:20–26; and 31:1–18 (Freedy and Redford 1970: 470–72). Egypt as a worthless ally is given classic expression in Isa 30:1–7, the point being repeated in Jer 2:18–19, 36 and painfully remembered in Lam 4:17.

Look. On the common beginning of the Jeremiah oracle with *hinnēh,* see Note for 1:9.

8. *And the Chaldeans shall return.* There is a play in vv 7–8 on *šûb* ("return"): Pharaoh's army will return (*šāb*) to Egypt, whereas the Chaldeans will return (*šābû*) to besiege Jerusalem. The prediction of Nebuchadnezzar's return to resume the siege and take the city is made also in 34:21–22.

9–10. *The Chaldeans will surely go away from us; indeed they will not go away! Even if you should strike down the entire army of the Chaldeans . . . and there remained among them only wounded men, each man in his tent, they would rise up and burn this city with fire.* Good hyperbole (Hayes 1963: 84); also a *correctio,* on which see Note for 7:19. Compare 2 Sam 5:6 and Lev 26:36–37. The point of this hyperbole, in which Yahweh hypothesizes a Judahite victory with both armies at the point of exhaustion, is that Jerusalem will be destroyed even without Babylonian military might.

indeed they will not go away. Translating *kî* as an asseverative, "indeed," which makes an emphatic counterpart for the people's "surely go away."

wounded men. Hebrew *mĕduqqārîm* is lit. "those pierced (by the sword)," who will soon be dead (51:4; Lam 4:9). Here the not-yet dead are pressed into service to do the impossible.

each man in his tent. Cornill imagines just one survivor to a tent. The LXX has "each in his place" (*ekastos en tō topō autou*), which allows for stricken soldiers lying on the battlefield (Streane).

12. *And Jeremiah set out from Jerusalem to go to the land of Benjamin for an apportioning from there amidst the people.* A relative has perhaps died, and Jeremiah must take care of a land apportionment in connection with his right of redemption (J. Pedersen 1964 I–II: 84–85), a transaction that was settled finally when Jeremiah's cousin came to him in the court of the guard (32:6–15). According to Fried and Freedman (2001: 2261), this redistribution was occasioned by the laws of the Jubilee, since the tenth year of Zedekiah was a Jubilee

year (see Note for 34:8–9). The words "from there" (*miššām*) means "from Anathoth," where the adjudication was to have taken place. The T has: "to divide
the inheritance which belonged to him there." The verb is an H-stem infinitive
of *hlq* with elision of the *hē'* (GKC §53q), more commonly seen in the Qal and
Piel with the meaning "to divide (land)" (Josh 13:7; 14:5; 18:2, 10; Mic 2:4).
The LXX has *tou agorasai ekeithen* ("to buy from that place"), which gives
similar meaning. Aquila, Theod, Symm, and Vg have comparable renderings.

the land of Benjamin. Hebrew *'ereṣ binyāmīn.* The territory just north of Jerusalem, in which lay Jeremiah's home village of Anathoth (1:1). See further
Note for 6:1. A few MSS have *'el-'ereṣ* (T: *lĕ'ereṣ*), which reads more smoothly.
The preposition *'el* ("to") could have been lost in the MT by haplography (homoeoarcton: *'aleph . . . 'aleph*).

amidst the people. I.e., people in Anathoth.

13. *And he came into the Benjamin Gate.* Hebrew *wayĕhî-hû' bĕša'ar binyāmīn.* Mentioned again in 38:7 and in Zech 14:10, this northern city gate
leading to Benjamin and Anathoth has been variously identified with the
Ephraim Gate (2 Kgs 14:13; Neh 8:16; Graf; Cheyne), the Muster Gate (Neh
3:31; *ABD* 1: 673), the People's Gate (17:19; see Note there), the Sheep Gate in
the northeast (Neh 3:32; Avi-Yonah 1954: 241), and other gates, and is probably
to be distinguished from the Upper Benjamin Gate of 20:2. Jerusalem's city
gates, then as now, were fortified complexes with multiple chambers, so one
does not simply pass through them, but rather comes "into" them.

a guard officer whose name was Irijah son of Shelemiah, son of Hananiah. Hebrew *ba'al pĕqīdut* (lit. "master of the watch") denotes an officer in charge of
the gatekeepers and watchmen in the city, or else those stationed at the principal gates. Akkadian *bēl piqitti* is a representative of the king or temple official
(AHw 1: 120). A double patronym suggests that this individual was well known.
The LXX goes its own way with *anthrōpos par' ō kateluen* ("a man with whom
he lodged"). On the names "Shelemiah" and "Hananiah," see Appendix I.

To the Chaldeans you are deserting! The verb *npl*, "fall," means here "to fall
into the hands of (the enemy)," i.e., desert, or surrender. Others had been or
later on would be deserting (38:19; 39:9; 52:15); in fact, Jeremiah was advocat-
ing as much (6:1; 21:9), admitting also on occasion of wanting himself to run
away (9:1[Eng 9:2]; 12:5). If it were known that Jeremiah was involved in a
land deal, that might have even strengthened suspicions that Jeremiah was de-
fecting, and could have led to his being detained at the gate of the city. In antiquity, an enemy would sometimes spare the land of prominent persons in
order to sow dissension among a conquered people, since the common folk
would then suspect that such persons were in collaboration with them. Reuven
Yaron, in a public lecture given at the Law School of the University of California, Berkeley (June 6, 1977), pointed out how Pericles, in 431 B.C., offered to
give up land for public use to rid himself of the suspicion that he was collaborating with the enemy.

14. *And Jeremiah said, 'A lie! I am not deserting to the Chaldeans.' But he did
not listen to him.* As we have said, appearances may have indicated otherwise,

but Jeremiah's denial means that the arresting official, who may well have known Jeremiah, either did not believe him—which is what had been happening to the prophet all along—or else simply wanted a pretext for making the arrest.

A lie! Hebrew *šeqer.* See 2 Kgs 9:12.

the princes. Royal and nonroyal figures in Zedekiah's government, largely upper-level civil and military officials. See further on *śārîm* ("princes") in Note for 24:1.

15. *And the princes were furious with Jeremiah.* The verb *qṣp* is strong, meaning "to be furious, enraged." Zedekiah's princes show themselves hostile to the prophet again in 38:4–6 and 24–27, which is a change from Jehoiakim's reign when the princes were his friends, supporting him and giving him cover when needed (26:10–16, 24; 36:11–19). Graf (p. 452) suggested that Jehoiakim's princes were taken to Babylon in the exile of 597 B.C., being replaced in Zedekiah's reign with new princes of low rank. This finds support in Jeremiah's vision of the good and bad figs in chap. 24.

and they beat him. Hebrew *wĕhikkû ʾōtô.* The verb *nkh* can mean either "beat (savagely)" or "beat to kill"; here, as in 52:27, a severe beating is indicated. Persecution and plots were nothing new to the prophet; they occurred earlier (see Note on 18:18).

in the stockhouse. Hebrew *bêt hāʾēsûr.* Jeremiah is now apparently put again in the stocks; cf. 20:2. The LXX omits the term, but it appears in Aq, Theod, Symm, T, and Vg, arguing for its retention. The omission can be attributed to haplography (whole-word: *byt . . . byt*). Multiple terms for prison here and in the next verse make for clarification and emphasis. It is unnecessary in the present verse to assume MT expansion resulting from conflation (*pace* Janzen 1973: 22; Holladay; McKane).

the house of Jonathan the scribe, for they had made it a prison house. A private residence being used as a prison conforms to ANE practice generally. Prisons in antiquity were located in royal palaces, temples, and houses or special quarters of important individuals (Oppenheim 1967: #3, 73; #11, 82; #46, 105–6; Riemschneider 1977; Frymer 1977; cf. *bīt kīli* in CAD 8: 361). Sasson (1977: 105) says that at Mari such did not differ significantly from other dwellings. Imprisonment in the ANE was not a means of punishment per se; it was for detaining individuals until a decision could be made on what to do with them, whether to free them, put them to death, or leave them simply to die, in which case bloodguilt would be avoided. In an old Hittite text, a certain Aškaliya, an influential person from the city of Hurmu, wanted to kill a potter by the name of Išpudaš-Inara, and so had him thrown into prison. When it became known that the individual was imprisoned, someone—very likely the king—moved to free him, though the text does not state this explicitly. The text does suggest that the person was imprisoned outside the king's purview, perhaps in another city, or locked up in a room of his enemy, Aškaliya. The more likely possibility is that the fellow was being held in the house of his enemy until the time of trial, which would indicate that houses in Old Hittite cities were holding places for persons suspected of crime (Riemschneider 1977: 118–19). In the case here, we know nothing about Jonathan the scribe, but since a prison was located in his house, he must have been a scribe of some standing. Bright calls him "the royal secretary."

16. *Indeed Jeremiah went to the Pit House.* The initial *kî* is best read as an asseverative, i.e., "Indeed." Some commentators get a comparable reading from the LXX's "And Jeremiah came" (*kai ēlthen Ieremias*). The AV and RSV render as "When," beginning an awkward dependent clause. This is remedied in the NRSV, although for some reason the final "Jeremiah" in the verse continues to be untranslated. The Hebrew reads: "And *Jeremiah* dwelt there many days."

to the Pit House, yes, to the cells! Hebrew *ʾel-bêt habbôr wĕʾel-haḥănūyôt*. The two terms in apposition are for emphasis. The narrator wants to say: "Jeremiah went to the Pit House, yes, to the wretched cells!" Jonathan's Pit House was so named because it had a below-ground *bôr* ("pit, cistern"), which if it were in good repair could be used to store water or grain (see Note on 2:13). The pit into which Jeremiah was cast in the court of the guard was a near-empty water cistern, where he sank in the mud (38:6). Hebrew *ḥānût* is a *hapax legomenon* in the OT, taken usually to mean "(vaulted) cells" (cf. KB³). These cells were likely cramped spaces equipped with stocks. Abarbanel says it was the worst kind of prison. And we can figure as much, since Jeremiah after his release petitioned the king not to send him back there, lest he die (v 20). The Neo-Sumerian Nungal-Hymn describes the Nippur temple prison as a miserable dungeon (Frymer 1977: 82). A portion reads:

Its people, like sparrows dropped from the claws of an owl, peer towards
    its opening as towards the rising sun
Brother wishes destruction upon brother; their sense is deranged
A youth does not know his acquaintances; they walk around like strangers
A man does not recognize his acquaintances; their appearance is altered
That house: its core is laden with the groanings of tears and laments. . . .

And Jeremiah dwelt there many days. Here real suffering of the prophet was experienced, and were Jeremiah being made out as a hero, which he is not, we would find out something more about that suffering. The LXX omits "Jeremiah," which could be more haplography (homoeoarcton: *y . . . y*).

MESSAGE AND AUDIENCE

This major narrative collection begins by introducing King Zedekiah in familiar Deuteronomic style, stating that he reigned in place of Coniah (= Jehoiachin) son of Jehoiakim, who it will be remembered was carried off with the queen mother and other prominent citizens to Babylon in 597 B.C. The audience is also reminded that Judah's last monarch owed his kingship to Nebuchadrezzar, king of Babylon. The introduction continues with a broad judgment on Zedekiah, his servants, and the population at large, faulting them not in usual fashion for continuing the evil of former kingships, which they did continue, but for not heeding Yahweh's words as they came via Jeremiah the prophet.

What follows is a report of an embassy sent by King Zedekiah to Jeremiah, requesting that he pray to Yahweh on the nation's behalf. Jehucal, one of Zedekiah's princes, and Zephaniah, the associate priest, were the ones sent. The request is polite, but urgent. The narrator informs us that Jeremiah is still moving freely in the city, not yet having been put into the prison house. Then we learn why the request for intercession has been made. A siege by the Babylonians had begun, but troop movement out of Egypt forced a withdrawal. The king's request was doubtless that Yahweh be pleased to end the siege for good. Jeremiah presumably brought the king's request to Yahweh, and what follows is the answer that came back.

A first oracle states that Egypt's army will return home. Bad news! Worse still, the Chaldeans will return to Jerusalem, take it, and burn it with fire. On the heels of this oracle comes another. The king and others should not deceive themselves, thinking the Chaldeans will go away. They will not go away. To drive the point home, Yahweh says that even in the unlikely case that Judah should happen to defeat the entire Chaldean army, their mortally wounded soldiers would still rise up and burn the city. Will the audience now understand that Yahweh's purpose regarding Jerusalem is sure?

The narrative segment concludes by reporting an incident that took place while the siege was lifted. Jeremiah was on his way out of the city, headed presumably for Anathoth to attend to a land transaction. When he came into the Benjamin Gate, he was spotted by a guard officer named Irijah, who arrested him and accused him of deserting to the Babylonians. The Babylonians were gone, but this fellow seems to think they will return. Jeremiah denounced the charge as a lie, saying he was not deserting. But Irijah did not believe him, arrested the prophet, and brought him to the princes, before whom the charge was repeated. They were understandably angry, but why such naked rage? Surely this was the buildup of much more, and so they proceeded to beat Jeremiah and put him in Jonathan's Pit House, an unspeakable dungeon of darkness, cramped quarters, and God only knows what else. There, we are told, Jeremiah dwelt many days! One day, two days, but why many days?

Audiences hearing this narrative following the report in chap. 36 of Jehoiakim's scroll-burning will perhaps discern that Judah's two last kings treated as so much rubbish Yahweh's words spoken by the prophet Jeremiah. There is also a subtle irony in that the scroll-burning becomes a portent of the burning of all Jerusalem. Both of the present oracles end with the prediction that Jerusalem will be set afire. The juxtaposition of narratives may also point up the fact that whereas in chap. 36 it was only the king who did not listen (v 25), here in chap. 37 it is everyone.

This segment, as part of an original narrative collection that included only 37:1–40:6, can be dated anytime after the fall of Jerusalem in 586 B.C. The expanded collection of 37:1–44:30 will have to date from the sojourn period in Egypt, which is sometime after 582 B.C.

B. ANOTHER REQUEST, ANOTHER ANSWER
(37:17–21)

37 [17]Then King Zedekiah sent and brought him, and the king asked him in his house secretly, and said, 'Is there a word from Yahweh?' And Jeremiah said, 'There is!' And he said, 'Into the hand of the king of Babylon you will be given.' [18]Then Jeremiah said to King Zedekiah, 'How have I sinned against you and against your servants and against this people that you have put me in the prison house? [19]And where[1] are your prophets who prophesied to you saying, "The king of Babylon will not come against you and against this land?" [20]Now do hear, my lord the king, do let my petition be laid before you. Return me not to the house of Jonathan the scribe so I will not die there.' [21]So King Zedekiah commanded and they committed Jeremiah into the court of the guard and gave him a pita bread daily from the bakers' street until all the bread was consumed from the city. And Jeremiah dwelt in the court of the guard.

RHETORIC AND COMPOSITION

MT 37:17–21 = LXX 44:17–21. The present narrative segment is delimited at the top by a *petuḥah* in M[L] before v 17, but only in that codex. The segment ends with the closing phrase of v 21, "And Jeremiah dwelt in the court of the guard" (see Rhetoric and Composition for 37:1–16). None of the three major medieval codices has a section here; nevertheless, after v 21 is a chapter division. The M[L] (only) has a *setumah* after v 17, the purpose of which is not altogether clear. It may simply separate Jeremiah's word of Yahweh to the king from the dialogue that follows.

NOTES

37:17. *Then King Zedekiah sent and brought him, and the king asked him in his house secretly, and said, 'Is there a word from Yahweh?'* Jeremiah is summoned from prison presumably because the Babylonians are back and have resumed the siege (Cheyne; Volz; Weiser; Rudolph). A resumption of the siege would seem to be indicated also by Jeremiah's questioning the king about the favorable predictions of other prophets (v 19), which are now rendered false. The summons is done secretly, because if the king makes it known he will inflame all the more the princes who imprisoned Jeremiah. Here we begin to see a weak king at the mercy of his princes, unable in a crisis to do much of anything that will help the situation (cf. 38:5).

Into the hand of the king of Babylon you will be given. The prediction also in 32:4 and 34:3.

---

[1]Reading the Q *wĕʾayê*.

18. *How have I sinned against you and against your servants and against this people that you have put me in the prison house?* Compare later Dan 6:22. The MT has *nětattem*, "you (plural) have put me," which faults the king along with others for the imprisonment (v 15); the singular verb of the LXX and Vg makes Zedekiah solely responsible (cf. 32:3).

your servants. I.e., royal officials of the king; see 37:2 and Note for 21:7.

19. *And where are your prophets who prophesied to you saying, "The king of Babylon will not come against you and against this land?"* Hananiah was one such prophet (28:2–4, 11), and he is dead. Others are still around. Earlier, Jeremiah's enemies put to him the question: "Where is the word of Yahweh? Let it come!" (17:15). For other rhetorical questions of "Where . . . ?" type, see 2:28 and 13:20. The LXX omits "against you and" (*'ălêkem wě*), which Janzen (1973: 118) recognizes as being attributable to haplography (homoeoarcton: *'l* . . . *'l*).

And where? Reading the Q: *wě'ayyēh* (2:28), although the Kt: *wě'ayyô* ("And where is it?") is more vigorous, asking for the (fulfillment of the) word spoken by these other prophets (Kimḥi).

20. *Now do hear, my lord the king, do let my petition be laid before you.* Hebrew *těḥinnātî* ("my petition") is a plea for grace / favor (*ḥnn* in TDOT 5: 25–26). The verb is *tippāl*, lit. "let it fall." The expression occurs elsewhere in 36:7; 38:26; and 42:2, 9. Volz (p. 339) sees in this exchange "the helpless, pleading prophet and the helpless, pleading king." The imprecative *nā'*, however, indicates emphasis (and forcefulness) more than politeness, although the latter cannot be excluded here since Jeremiah is addressing the king. But something more is required than the usual "please!"

Jonathan the scribe. See Note on 37:15.

21 *So King Zedekiah commanded and they committed Jeremiah into the court of the guard.* The "court of the guard" (*ḥăṣar hammaṭṭārâ*) was in the royal palace (32:2; Neh 3:25), a place where Jeremiah could be detained but still be permitted a measure of freedom (32:1–15; 38:1–3). He was probably safer here than anywhere else (Calvin). Rudolph says that Zedekiah's committing of Jeremiah to the court of the guard shows that he was himself a man of good will, but one who could not prevail against his ministers and other fanatics.

and they committed . . . and gave him. Hebrew *wayyapqîdû . . . wěnātōn lô*. The H-stem imperfect with *waw consecutive* is followed here by an infinitive absolute (Volz; cf. GKC §113z).

a pita bread. Hebrew *kikkār-leḥem* (lit. "a round bread") is a soft flat bread, round in shape, which even today continues to be the common bread in Jerusalem and throughout the Middle East. It is basic subsistence, and not infrequently in the OT is a symbol of poverty (1 Sam 2:36; Prov 6:26).

bakers' street. In ancient times—also in medieval Europe and today in the souks (marketplaces) of the Middle East—certain streets or quarters of the city carry the name of the shops or craftsmen who cluster there. These "streets" (*ḥûṣôt*) are referred to in 1 Kgs 20:34.

until all the bread was consumed from the city. On the famine at the end of the siege, see 52:6.

MESSAGE AND AUDIENCE

The Babylonians had returned to Jerusalem to resume the siege, and this narrative segment tells how Zedekiah, wanting a fresh word from Yahweh, was compelled to fetch Jeremiah from prison to ask him for such. No messengers are named, but undoubtedly some were sent. Once the prophet is present in the palace, Zedekiah asks him privately if there is a word from Yahweh. The answer is immediate: "There is! The king will be handed over to the Babylonians." This same word was given to the king before (21:7). Jeremiah then follows with a rebuke, asking how he has wronged the king and others to be dropped into the miserable pit he has been in. Moreover, where are the sunshine prophets who said the Babylonians would not return? The king knows that Hananiah is dead; other prophets are either in hiding or are surprisingly quiet. The king is surprisingly quiet. Jeremiah then implores the king not to return him to Jonathan's house, lest he die there. The king honors the request, having the good sense to commit Jeremiah to the court of the guard and see that he is given a pita bread daily while the supply lasts. So Jeremiah resides now in the court of the guard.

This segment is a sequel to the one immediately preceding, and when the two are heard in tandem, it becomes clear that Jeremiah's real enemies are the princes, not the king, and that power is in fact divided between the two. The princes threw Jeremiah into prison; the king got him out. But the audience knows that in the interim the Babylonians returned, which undoubtedly changed things. In any event, the prophet's imprisonment was followed by a release, indicating that Yahweh's promise of rescue to Jeremiah had been fulfilled, at least up till now. This segment can be dated along with the others in 37:1–40:6 to the period just after the fall of Jerusalem.

C. JEREMIAH AGAIN IN THE PIT (38:1–6)

38 ¹Now Shephatiah son of Mattan heard, also Gedaliah son of Pashhur and Jucal son of Shelemiah and Pashhur son of Malchiah, the words that Jeremiah continued to speak to all the people:
²Thus said Yahweh:
Whoever stays in this city shall die by sword, by famine, and by pestilence, and whoever goes out to the Chaldeans shall live;[1] and his life will be his booty, and he shall live.

³Thus said Yahweh:
This city shall surely be given into the hand of the army of the king of Babylon, and he shall take it.

---

[1] Reading the Kt yĕḥāyâ ("he shall live"); the Q has wĕḥāyâ ("then he shall live"); cf. 21:9.

⁴So the princes said to the king, 'Kindly have this man put to death, seeing that he continues to weaken the hands of the fighting men who are left in this city—and the hands of all the people—by speaking to them words such as these; indeed this man is not seeking the welfare of this people, rather evil!' ⁵And King Zedekiah said, 'Look, he is in your hand, for there is not anything the king can do with you.'² ⁶And they took Jeremiah and cast him into the pit of Malchiah the king's son, which was in the court of the guard. And they let Jeremiah down with ropes. And in the pit there was no water, only mud. And Jeremiah sank in the mud.

RHETORIC AND COMPOSITION

MT 38:1–6 = LXX 45:1–6. The present narrative segment is delimited by the closing phrases in 37:21 and 38:6, the former being, "And Jeremiah dwelt in the court of the guard," and the latter, "And Jeremiah sank in the mud" (see Rhetoric and Composition for 37:1–16). The upper limit is also the chapter division. The conclusion is confirmed by a *setumah* in M^A and M^L, and a *petuḥah* in M^P, after v 6, although one MS in the Cambridge Genizah Collection (A 14.4) has no section there. The M^L has a *setumah* and the M^P a *petuḥah* before v 2, which sets off the narrative from the first oracle. The M^A has no section there, nor does A 14.4 in the Cambridge Genizah Collection. All three medieval codices, M^A, M^L, and M^P, as well as Cambridge Genizah MS A 14.4, have sections after v 2, which separate the two oracles. In M^A, M^L, and M^P the section is a *setumah*.

The oracles begin similarly with the phrase "(in) this city":

I   Whoever stays *in this city* shall die by sword . . .   *bāʿîr hazzōʾt*   v 2
II *This city* shall surely be given into the hand . . .   *hāʿîr hazzōʾt*   v 3

For other versions of these two oracles, see 21:8–10.

NOTES

38:1. *Shephatiah son of Mattan.* This individual is not otherwise known. He is probably one of the king's princes (v 4). The name Shephatiah (= "Yahweh has judged") with the spelling *šĕpaṭyāhu* appears on bullae from Tell Beit Mirsim and on four contemporary seals, one of which has turned up at Lachish (see Appendix I).

Gedaliah son of Pashhur. This individual is also unknown, although the suggestion has been made that he might be the son of Pashhur, the priest, who put Jeremiah in the stocks (20:1–3). More likely he is one of Zedekiah's princes. On the names "Gedaliah" and "Pashhur," see Appendix I.

Jucal son of Shelemiah. The same individual mentioned in 37:3, where Zedekiah sends him to request intercession from Jeremiah. There his name is

---

²Repointing MT *ʾetkem* ("you") to *ʾittĕkem* ("with you").

spelled "Jehucal" (see Note there). Over time the intervocalic *hē*' was lost; thus the shortened form.

Pashhur son of Malchiah. Zedekiah sent this individual to request an earlier intercession from Jeremiah (see Note on 21:1). On the name "Malchiah" (= "Yah[weh] is my King"), which has turned up on the Arad ostraca and on numerous seals and seal impressions from Tell Beit Mirsim and elsewhere, see Appendix I. The LXX lacks the name and patronym, but they are present in Aq and Theod. "Malchiah" in Jeremiah's time would have been spelled *mlkyhw*, as in v 6 (the spelling *-yh* for the personal name of God is a postexilic phenomenon). Assuming that the name was written *-yhw* in the *Vorlage* to the LXX, we have then another loss due to haplography (homoeoteleuton: *yhw . . . yh*[*w*]). See also Janzen 1973: 119.

the words that Jeremiah continued to speak to all the people. In the court of the guard Jeremiah enjoys a measure of freedom and has opportunities for contact with people of the city. Even in his imprisonment the word he is under obligation to preach is getting out (cf. 2 Tim 2:9). The Piel participle *mĕdabbēr* ("continued to speak"), here as elsewhere, may indicate repeated and intensified action (Blayney; Cheyne; cf. GKC §52f), which would account for the strong reaction that follows. But the Piel is the normal form of the verb *dbr*. Another Piel participle in v 4, *mĕrappē*' ("continues to weaken"), definitely indicates intensified action.

2. *Whoever stays in this city shall die by sword, by famine, and by pestilence, and whoever goes out to the Chaldeans shall live; and his life will be his booty, and he shall live.* Virtually a repeat of an earlier oracle (21:9), but no reason with Duhm and others to delete in the present context (Weiser; Bright; Holladay; Jones). People visiting Jeremiah now in the court of the guard hear these words again (cf. 21:8–10).

by sword, by famine, and by pestilence. On this stereotypical phrase, which occurs often in Jeremiah with or without "pestilence," see Note on 5:12. Here the LXX lacks "and by pestilence," which happens in 21:9 and elsewhere, but not always. Sometimes the entire triad is translated (Janzen 1973: 43–44). There is no clear pattern pointing to "pestilence" as an MT expansion term (*pace* Holladay; McKane), and here in the present verse, Aq, Theod, and Symm all translate—the two former with *kai en thanatō* ("and by death"), and the latter with *kai en loimō* ("and by pestilence"). The LXX omission in this case could be attributed to haplography (homoeoarcton: *w . . . w*).

and his life will be his booty. For variations on this pithy remark, see 21:9; 39:18; and 45:5.

3. *This city shall surely be given into the hand of the army of the king of Babylon, and he shall take it.* This is another version of what appears in 21:10. The prediction of Jerusalem falling to Nebuchadnezzar also occurs elsewhere, e.g., in 21:10; 32:3, 28; 34:2, 22; 37:8; and 38:18, 23.

4. *So the princes said to the king, 'Kindly have this man put to death.'* With polite sarcasm, the princes now press strongly for Jeremiah's death. In Jehoiakim's reign it was the prophets and priests calling for the same (26:11), with the

princes supporting Jeremiah and providing him with safekeeping (see Note for 37:15). It is easy to condemn these upper-level civil and military officials, hell-bent as they are on defending the city and closed to Yahweh's word as it comes through Jeremiah, but a more realistic appraisal views their action as precisely what one might expect in wartime. From a political point of view, Jeremiah is guilty of treason. Jones (pp. 459–60) remarks, "Who cannot have sympathy with those who bear responsibility for the safety of the realm? Once military resistance has begun, it is all or nothing . . . Jeremiah is doing what no citizen can be allowed to do. He is undermining morale, and this is for evil, not for good."

seeing that. Hebrew *kî-ʿal-kēn.* On this expression, see also 29:28 and Gen 18:5.

he continues to weaken the hands of the fighting men who are left in this city. Jeremiah himself lamented in similar fashion over the news of an enemy approaching Jerusalem (see Note on 6:24). The expression "to weaken you[r] hands" (*lrpt tdyk[m]*) has turned up in the Lachish Letters in connection with the present conflict (6:6; de Vaux 1939: 197–98; Albright 1938: 15–16; 1941b: 22; ANET³ 322; cf. Torczyner 1938: 102–19), where it seems that words being spoken in Jerusalem are adversely affecting the morale out near Lachish. Who the individuals were speaking such words we do not know. If they were princes in Jerusalem (so Albright's reconstruction of 6:5), they certainly are not the princes here. Another view is that the letter is referring to a prophet (so Torczyner's reconstruction of 6:5), with Uriah of Kiriath-jearim and Jeremiah cited as possible candidates. Neither identification has been taken seriously. On Torczyner's discredited theory connecting the prophet of the Letters with Uriah of Kiriath-jearim, see Note for 26:20. Letter #3 mentions a prophet saying "Beware!" but his identity is not known (D. W. Thomas 1946; 1961), and the term "prophet" is no longer conjectured on the much-effaced Letter #6. These uncertainties notwithstanding, the crisis reflected in the Lachish Letters is definitely the same crisis that is reflected here (see Note on 37:5).

he continues to weaken. Hebrew *hûʾ-mĕrappēʾ.* The verb is *rph* ("make slack, weaken"), not *rpʾ* ("heal"), with the Piel participle having intensive force (cf. v 1: *mĕdabbēr,* "continued to speak"). On ל״ה verbs adopting characteristics of verbs ל״א, see GKC §75rr. Several MSS have *mĕrappeh.*

5. *Look, he is in your hand, for there is not anything the king can do with you.* "In your hand" = "in your power." Zedekiah's words in the LXX are reduced to "Look, he is in your hand," after which the narrator continues, "For the king was unable to do anything against them (*pros autous*)." The king is helpless in the present situation. He knows full well the danger of a loss of morale; at the same time he does not himself want to put the prophet to death (26:15; Ps 105:15; cf. Haddad 1982: 59). So the decision is left with the princes. In the NT, compare the actions of Pilate when faced with what to do with Jesus (Matt 27:24).

6. *And they took Jeremiah and cast him into the pit of Malchiah the king's son.* To say that the princes "cast" (*šlḥ* in the H-stem) Jeremiah into the pit is to describe the action emotionally, unless, as Cogan (1968: 133) argues, *šlḥ* here

simply means "to abandon" (cf. Ps 71:9; Ezek 16:5). They did, after all, lower Jeremiah down by ropes. Leaving him in the pit will accomplish the same purpose as killing him, with the one difference that the princes are then spared the charge of shedding innocent blood (see Note for 37:15). The princes probably do not want to kill Jeremiah any more than the king does (Rice 1975: 96). The LXX omits "And they took Jeremiah," which can be attributed to haplography (homoeoarcton: *wy . . . wy*). The words are translated in Aq, Theod, and Symm.

the pit. Hebrew *habbôr.* On the unusual grammar of a determinative preceding a proper name, see GKC §127f. D. N. Freedman suggests the loss of a second *bwr* after the term having the determinative, so the reading would have been: *'el-habbôr bôr malkîyyāhû* ("to the pit, the pit of the king"). This loss could be explained by haplography (whole-word: *bwr . . . bwr*). The pit is a bottle-shaped water cistern (see Note on 2:13), from which escape is impossible (for a drawing, see P. J. King 1993: 155). Jeremiah's earlier prison was a pit inside the house (37:16). This pit is in the open court of the guard, probably supplied with a cover.

Malchiah the king's son. Malchiah was not a son of Zedekiah, who was no more than 32 at the time (Hyatt; cf. 2 Kgs 24:18). If he was the father of Pashhur, mentioned in v 1, he could be roughly the same age as the king. Or he could be a son of Jehoiakim, possibly even Josiah. Kings having large harems possessed many sons. Some have argued that "the king's son" is a nonroyal title, but this view is still subject to debate (see Note for 36:26).

with ropes. And. This LXX omission can also be attributed to haplography (homoeoarcton: *b . . . b*, or homoeoteleuton: *w . . . w*), although "with ropes" is again omitted by LXX in v 11. Here in this verse, "with ropes" is translated by Aq and Symm (*en schoiniois*).

And in the pit there was no water, only mud. Water cisterns nearly empty have wet mud in the bottom (Ps 40:3[Eng 40:2]). A cistern of this description is what we might expect in July, the month the city was taken (39:2). The water had been used up, and under normal circumstances the cistern would not begin to fill up again until the winter rains came, which would be about November.

And Jeremiah sank in the mud. The LXX abbreviates: "And he was in the mud." Aquila and Symm both contain "Jeremiah." This experience may figure in Jeremiah's later vision of Zedekiah being taunted by the women of Jerusalem as they are led away captive, where they will be singing of the king's feet being sunk "in the muck" (v 22: *babbōṣ*).

MESSAGE AND AUDIENCE

This narrative segment reports how four of the king's princes, all mentioned by name, had been listening in on what Jeremiah was telling people who visited him in the court of the guard. Two brief oracles, or excerpts from oracles, are then given. Oracle I repeats Jeremiah's new twist on the "two ways" teaching of Deut 30:15–20: those who stay in the city will die; those who desert will live.

Oracle II states without embellishment that the city will indeed fall to the king of Babylon.

The princes can no longer countenance such treasonous talk, and they petition the king to have Jeremiah put to death. The man is a liability to those risking their lives to save the city, not to mention the troubled souls everywhere, limp with fear that the war effort might not succeed. Anyone speaking as Jeremiah does is surely not seeking the well-being of Jerusalem. Zedekiah can do nothing, and so he turns the prophet over to the princes. Not wanting to kill him outright, the princes cast him into Malchiah's pit in the court of the guard, letting him down with ropes. Thankfully, the pit is without water, but there is enough slime at the bottom for Jeremiah to sink in, which is what happens.

The present segment follows in sequence from the prior one, reporting for the prophet a reversal of fortunes after Zedekiah released him from Jonathan's infamous Pit House. The larger sequence of events is now imprisonment, release, and imprisonment again. Like the other narrative segments in 37:1–40:6, this one can be dated to the period just after the fall of Jerusalem.

D. EBED-MELECH TO THE RESCUE (38:7–13)

38 ⁷But Ebed-melech the Cushite, a eunuch man, heard—since he was in the king's house—that they had put Jeremiah into the pit. Now the king was sitting in the Benjamin Gate. ⁸So Ebed-melech went out from the king's house and spoke to the king: ⁹"My lord the king, these men have done evil in all that they did to Jeremiah the prophet, in that they cast him[1] into the pit, and he's as good as dead where he is, because of the famine.' For there was no longer bread in the city. ¹⁰Then the king commanded Ebed-melech the Cushite: 'Take in hand from here thirty men and bring up Jeremiah the prophet from the pit, before he dies. ¹¹So Ebed-melech took the men in hand and went into the house of the king, to the lower storeroom, and took from there worn rags[2] and worn clothes and sent them down to Jeremiah into the pit by ropes. ¹²And Ebed-melech the Cushite said to Jeremiah, 'Now put these worn rags and clothes under your armpits rather than under the ropes.' And Jeremiah did so. ¹³So they pulled Jeremiah with ropes and brought him up from the pit. And Jeremiah dwelt in the court of the guard.

RHETORIC AND COMPOSITION

MT 38:7–13 = LXX 45:7–13. This narrative segment, like the others in 37:1–40:6, is delimited by the closing line of the preceding segment, and its own closing line of v 13: "And Jeremiah dwelt in the court of the guard" (see Rhetoric

---

[1] Heb lacks "him."

[2] Reading the Q *sĕḥābôt* ("rags"), which lacks the definite article.

and Composition for 37:1–16). The upper limit of the segment is marked also by a *setumah* in M^A and M^L, and a *petuḥah* in M^P, prior to v 7. At bottom is a *setumah* in M^A and M^L, and a *petuḥah* in M^P, after v 13.

NOTES

38:7–8. *Ebed-melech the Cushite.* Ebed-melech means "servant of the king," and T translates it as such, not as a personal name. Rashi, following T and later Midrash, identifies the individual with Baruch. Kimḥi, however, takes the term as a proper name, which doubtless it is. Duhm notes that *melek* is without the article, suggesting a personal name (compare *ʿebed-hammelek* in 2 Kgs 22:12). The LXX translates as a personal name (*Abdemelech*). Ebed-melech was a Cushite (= Ethiopian; see Note on 13:23), one of many black-skinned people who came north in antiquity—also in later times—for military and domestic service (2 Sam 18:21–32). A Cushite army fought unsuccessfully against Asa of Judah at Mareshah, in the Shephelah (2 Chr 14:8–14[Eng 14:9–15]). Kings of antiquity commonly employed foreigners—very often prisoners of war—in their governments as security against ambitious nobles or other would-be ursurpers, receiving from them a greater loyalty than from native subjects. Gelb (1973: 92–93) points out how prisoners of war, particularly, were made royal bodyguards, citing David's personal militia of Cherethites, Pelethites, and Gittites who remained loyal to him during the rebellion of Absalom (2 Sam 15:18). Ethiopian slaves were common in pre-Islamic Arabia, being plentiful at Mecca before the Hijra (Muhammad's flight to Mecca in A.D. 622); some even rose to high positions, e.g., a number formed the nucleus of the Aḥābish, or Meccan militia (*EncIs* 1: 24). In the present narrative, the point being made is that it was a foreigner who intervened to save the life of Jeremiah, which carries with it the more weighty theological affirmation that Yahweh acts to deliver his chosen ones by people from outside the community (Jones). This biblical truth finds restatement in the book of Ruth, in the kindly acts of Cyrus the Persian (Isa 44:28; 45:1–8; Ezra 1), and in Jesus' parable of the Good Samaritan (Luke 10:29–37). If Yahweh can press into service foreigners to punish his chosen people, which he does (25:9), he can also save by the same.

eunuch man. Hebrew *ʾîš sārîs.* The LXX lacks the term, which may be MT expansion for clarification (cf. Janzen 1973: 73). Although eunuchs were often high-ranking officials in government and in the military (see Note on 52:25), Ebed-melech is a palace eunuch performing domestic service (Kimḥi). The suggestion has been made (Hitzig; Cornill) that he was keeper of the harem, which is a possibility. The king's harem is heard from—albeit in a vision—later in the chapter (vv 22–23), and eunuchs are numbered with women and children in the wandering band of post-586 B.C. survivors (41:16). Ebed-melech knows the palace and has access to its lower storeroom (v 11).

since he was in the king's house. I.e., he was there presently, where he apparently overheard what had happened to Jeremiah. He may have resided elsewhere. The phrase is parenthetical.

Now the king was sitting in the Benjamin Gate. So Ebed-melech went out from the king's house and spoke to the king. The Benjamin Gate was in the northern wall of the city, although its exact location is unknown (see Note for 37:13). The king was doubtless in the gate to hear complaints and render judgments (Volz; cf. 2 Sam 15:2–6), which gives Ebed-melech the perfect opportunity to lay before him the injustice done to Jeremiah.

9. *My lord the king, these men have done evil in all that they did to Jeremiah the prophet, in that they cast him into the pit.* The LXX omits the polite "My lord the king," and follows with a reading that lays blame on the king. It has: "You have acted wickedly in what you have done to kill this man facing hunger." Peake and Cornill judge the MT reading to be better, with which I concur. Theodotion supports MT. There is no reason for Ebed-melech to fault the king; in fact, such a thing would not happen in ancient Near Eastern culture, particularly in public (Haddad 1982: 61). Zedekiah has consistently tried to avoid punitive action against Jeremiah, and Ebed-melech can achieve his purpose perfectly well by politely and urgently calling the king's attention to an injustice perpetrated by one party against another.

and he's as good as dead where he is, because of the famine. Hebrew *wayyāmāt* ("and he's as good as dead") is an imperfect with *waw consecutive*, which usually translates as past tense, although here the verb may also express a consequence: "so that he dies" (GKC §111 l). Some emend to get a future, since Jeremiah is not yet dead. However, the MT reading—preserved in T ("he is like a dead man")—is more vigorous. The point is that Jeremiah will be dead if left much longer in the pit. Ebed-melech is speaking with a sense of urgency (Volz). On the famine at the end of the siege, see 52:6.

where he is. Hebrew *taḥtāyw* is lit. "in his place." Compare Exod 16:29 and 2 Sam 2:23.

For there was no longer bread in the city. On one of the Arad ostraca (1:5), *mēʿôd* means "from what is left over" (Aharoni 1981: 12–13). Cornill thinks the narrator is now speaking, not Ebed-melech, who just finished saying that the city is experiencing famine. In Ebed-melech's mouth, the words are a redundancy. Whether the narrator is speaking, or whether it is Ebed-melech, the words do not render superfluous the rescue operation since a freed Jeremiah will die from hunger anyway (*pace* Peake; Bright; Carroll). The end is not yet. In situations such as this one the natural thing to do is preserve life as long as is humanly possible. Once out of the pit, Jeremiah at least has a chance of survival; in the pit he does not. That is the point being made.

10. *Take in hand from here thirty men and bring up Jeremiah the prophet from the pit, before he dies.* These are men who happen at the moment to be in the vicinity of the Benjamin Gate. Their involvement in the current crisis will make for a dramatic public event. With thirty men coming to the court of the guard to rescue Jeremiah, the four angry princes may just as well stay in their quarters, for their action against the prophet has now been effectively neutralized. Substituting "three" for "thirty," suggested by Hitzig and Graf and accepted

by nearly all commentators and modern Versions since (but not the NIV and NJB; cf. AV), ranks as one of the least supportable emendations in the entire book of Jeremiah and betrays a painfully unimaginative reading of the text. The LXX, T, and Vg all read "thirty," with only one Heb MS reading "three." It is not a question of whether three men could have done the job. They certainly could have, even though something is to be said for the view that these men are weakened due to a lack of food (Rashi; Kimḥi) and from having to fight in defense of the city. What is being depicted here is an effort by the king, once the opportunity has presented itself, to effectively counter an action by the princes, who forced his hand and ursurped his power. Throughout chaps. 37–38, Zedekiah is portrayed as playing a game with the royal house, where integrity counts for nothing and appearances are everything, and for the moment, at least, the king has the upper hand.

in hand. Hebrew bĕyādĕkā, lit. "in your hand." Ebed-melech is being empowered by the king to carry out his order. If the men resist, he is to make them go (Kimḥi).

11. in hand. Hebrew bĕyādô, "in his hand," which is lacking in the LXX.

to the lower storeroom. Hebrew ʾel-taḥat hāʾôṣār. The AV follows T, which has "under the treasury." Compare also NJV, NIV, and REB. An ʾôṣār can house treasures, weapons, grain, wine, and oil, and apparently old rags. Ebed-melech knows his way around the palace and has access to this storeroom. Many commentators and some modern Versions (RSV; NRSV; NEB [but not REB]; JB; NJB) emend ʾel-taḥat with Ehrlich (1912: 340) to meltāḥat, "wardrobe" (2 Kgs 10:22). This may or may not bring us to the right room, but requires too much alteration of the Hebrew. Read the MT.

worn rags and worn clothes. Hebrew bĕlôyē hassĕḥābôt ûbĕlôyē mĕlāḥîm. The precise meaning of these terms is not known; all three occur only here and in the next verse. Some sort of rags are indicated (shb means "to drag"), which doubtless includes old, worn, and tattered clothes.

12. Now put these worn rags and clothes under your armpits rather than under the ropes. Reading mittaḥat as "rather than under," which is what the sense requires. The particle min can mean "in preference to, rather than" (8:3; Hos 6:6; cf. BDB, 582). Presumably Jeremiah could have put the rags under the rope passing across his back. Cushioning such as this was not used when Jeremiah went into the pit. The abbreviated LXX reading, tauta thes hypokatō tōn schoiniōn ("Put these under the ropes"), is not right. The rags do not go under the ropes—the very thing Ebed-melech wants to make clear to Jeremiah—but under the armpits.

armpits. Hebrew ʾaṣṣilôt yādeykā (lit. "joints of the hand / arm") is here probably "armpits" (Rashi; Calvin; KB³). The term yād signifies the forearm (including the hand), which could make "elbows" a proper translation, but this requires a different picture of Jeremiah coming out of the mud.

13. So they pulled Jeremiah with ropes and brought him up from the pit. For this kindness and trust shown in Yahweh, Ebed-melech was given an oracle assuring his own rescue (39:15–18).

And Jeremiah dwelt in the court of the guard. The nervous and offended princes will be heard from again before this drama is over (vv 24–27), but Jeremiah's return to the court of the guard shows that they are the ones now rendered powerless.

MESSAGE AND AUDIENCE

This narrative segment introduces a foreigner in the royal house who intervened between strident princes who had left Jeremiah to die in a mud-bottom pit and a weak king who probably did not want this to happen, but could do nothing to prevent it. Ebed-melech, an Ethiopian eunuch, got word in the royal palace of what had happened to Jeremiah, and having learned that the king was deciding cases at the Benjamin Gate decided that this was the time to lay an injustice before him. So he went over to speak with him. Ebed-melech told the king of the evil these men had done. Jeremiah, he said, is a dead man down there, particularly with the famine gripping the city. Bread was now gone. The king then ordered Ebed-melech to take thirty men at hand and go rescue Jeremiah before he died. Ebed-melech did just that, going first to the palace storeroom, where he got some old rags. Arriving at the pit, he lowered the rags to Jeremiah, telling him to place them under his armpits. Those standing around, not manning the ropes, were doubtless shouting out other advice. Jeremiah did as told and was brought up from the pit. It was a dramatic moment, with cheers likely coming from those looking on. The princes were not there; if they were, they could do nothing. It was still crisis time, but Jeremiah was at least returned to the court of the guard.

This narrative segment is a sequel to the prior one, and the two will be heard in tandem just as the segments in 37:12–16 and 17–21 were, conveying again Jeremiah's imprisonment by angry princes and a rescue authorized by the king. The segment, along with the others in 37:1–40:6, can date from sometime after 586 B.C. A post-586 audience will doubtless see in the present rescue a fulfillment of Yahweh's promise to Jeremiah that his life would be preserved, but they will be sobered in knowing that rescue came this time from a foreigner, not by some courageous or faithful Judahite.

Soon after, Ebed-melech was given a salvation oracle by Jeremiah (39:15–18). And like Baruch the scribe, Ebed-melech went on subsequently to enjoy an even greater reputation, e.g., in the pseudepigraphical *Paraleipomena Jeremiou (ParJer)*, a popular legend written by a Palestinian Jew ca. A.D. 136, and linked to the Bar Kochba revolt (Licht 1963; Kraft and Purintun 1972).

E. ONE FINAL REQUEST, ONE FINAL ANSWER (38:14–28)

38 [14]And King Zedekiah sent and brought Jeremiah the prophet to him, to the third entrance that was in the house of Yahweh. And the king said to

Jeremiah, 'I am going to ask you something; do not keep anything hidden from me.' [15]And Jeremiah said to Zedekiah, 'If I tell you, will you not surely put me to death? And if I give you advice, you will not listen to me.' [16]Then King Zedekiah swore secretly to Jeremiah: 'As Yahweh lives who made this life of ours, I will not put you to death nor give you into the hand of these men who seek your life.' [17]And Jeremiah said to Zedekiah:

Thus said Yahweh, God of hosts, God of Israel:

If you will only go out to the princes of the king of Babylon, then you yourself will live and this city will not be burned with fire; yes, you and your house will live! [18]But if you will not go out to the princes of the king of Babylon, then this city will be given into the hand of the Chaldeans and they will burn it with fire. As for you, you shall not escape from their hand.

[19]Then King Zedekiah said to Jeremiah: 'I am afraid of the Judahites who have deserted to the Chaldeans, lest they give me over into their hand, and they abuse me.' [20]And Jeremiah said, 'They will not give you over.' Obey now the voice of Yahweh according to what I am saying to you, that it may go well with you, and you yourself will live. [21]But if you refuse to go out, this is the word that Yahweh has shown me: [22]'And there they were, all the women who remained in the house of the king of Judah, being brought out to the princes of the king of Babylon, yes, there they were saying:

They misled you and overcame you
    your trusted men
Your feet are sunk in the muck
    they have drawn back

[23]And all your wives and your children are being brought out to the Chaldeans, and you, you are not escaping from their hand. Indeed by the hand of the king of Babylon you are being seized, and this city will be burned with fire.'[1] [24]Then Zedekiah said to Jeremiah, 'Do not let anyone know of these words, and you shall not die.' [25]And if the princes hear that I have spoken with you, and they come to you and say to you, "Now tell us what you spoke to the king; do not keep it hidden from us and we will not put you to death, also what the king spoke to you," [26]then you shall say to them, "I laid my request before the king so that he would not send me back to the house of Jonathan to die there."' [27]Then all the princes came to Jeremiah and asked him, and he told them in accordance with all these words that the king commanded. So they ceased to speak with him, for the conversation had not been heard. [28]And Jeremiah dwelt in the court of the guard until the day that Jerusalem was taken. And he was there when Jerusalem was taken.

---

[1]Repointing MT *tiśrōp* ("you will burn") to an N-stem *tiśśārēp* ("it will be burned") with T and LXX.

RHETORIC AND COMPOSITION

MT 38:14–28 = LXX 45:14–28. The present narrative segment is not a variant of 37:17–21, as some have suggested, but the report of a separate and independent event (Volz). Delimitation is made primarily on the basis of the closing statement in v 13, "And Jeremiah dwelt in the court of the guard," and its own closing statement in v 28, "And Jeremiah dwelt in the court of the guard until the day that Jerusalem was taken" (see Rhetoric and Composition for 37:1–16). Corroborating these limits at the top end are a *setumah* in M^A and M^L, and a *petuḥah* in M^P, prior to v 14, and at the bottom end by a *setumah* in M^A and M^P, and a *petuḥah* in M^L, after v 28, which is also the chapter division.

There is debate over whether the final words of v 28b, "And he was there when Jerusalem was taken," ends the present segment or introduces the segment following. Some commentators and modern Versions take the phrase as introducing 39:1 (Keown et al. with emendation; NIV); others as introducing 39:3, where vv 1–2 are judged a later intrusion (Giesebrecht; Duhm; Peake; Cornill; Volz; Weiser; Rudolph; Bright; Jones; RSV; JB [but not NJB]; NJV; NSB), while still others omit all or part of the line with the LXX and S (Thompson; NEB; REB). Taking the line as introducing 39:1 or 39:3 means disregarding the section markings after these verses, which are present in all three medieval codices: M^A, M^L, and M^P. The decision here has been to take the words as a supplemental conclusion to the present segment, which follows T and the Jewish tradition, also the AV and NJB. The *setumah* then in the middle of v 28 (in M^L only) can be seen as marking the original end to the segment.

Other sections in M^A, M^L, and M^P, and in one Cairo Genizah MS (A 14.5), are the following:

after 38:16	a *setumah* in M^A and M^L; a *petuḥah* in M^P
in the middle 38:17	a *setumah* in M^A only
after 38:17	a section in Genizah MS A 14.5
after 38:18	a *setumah* in M^A and M^L; a *petuḥah* in M^P
after 38:19	a *petuḥah* in M^L only
after 38:23	a *setumah* in M^A and M^P; a *petuḥah* in M^L; no section in A 14.5
after 38:26	a *petuḥah* in M^A and M^L; a *setumah* in M^P
after 38:27	a *petuḥah* in M^L only

The majority of these sections mark conclusions of direct speech, and in the case of v 27, a conclusion to the dialogue. The reasons for a *setumah* in M^A in the middle of 38:17, and a section in the Cairo Geniza MS after 38:17, are unclear.

The narrative taken as a whole, in particular the sequence of speakers, is nicely structured:

Narrative Opening	v 14
Zedekiah speaks to Jeremiah	vv 15–16
Jeremiah speaks to Zedekiah	vv 17–18
Zedekiah speaks to Jeremiah	v 19

Jeremiah speaks to Zedekiah	vv 20–23
Zedekiah speaks to Jeremiah	vv 24–26
Narrative Conclusion + Addendum	vv 27–28

Verse 22 contains a double bicolon of poetry in Qina meter (3:2), taken variously as a taunt song or a lament. Budde (1883) thought it was an old lament containing stock phrases derived from professional mourning women. Jahnow (1923: 124–31) compared it with David's lament over Abner in 2 Sam 3:33–34. It lacks the tone of David's lament, and since it is addressed directly to the king, and points up the desertion of trusted friends when the king needed them most, I think it has to be a taunt song in Qina rhythm (Giesebrecht; Volz; Skinner 1926: 258). The narrative resumes in the next verse, with v 22 giving no evidence of being a later insertion (*pace* Duhm; Volz).

NOTES

38:14. *King Zedekiah sent and brought.* Predication with these same verbs occurs in 37:17.

the third entrance that was in the house of Yahweh. The location of this entrance (*mābô'*) is not known, although Haupt (1902: 585–86) suggested a southern entrance to the Temple area from the court of the royal palace, called "the king's outer entrance" in 2 Kgs 16:18 (cf. 11:19; Jer 26:10). It was a private place, in any case, which is what the situation called for.

I am going to ask you something; do not keep anything hidden from me. Jeremiah's answer in v 15 indicates that the king is seeking advice; yet in 50:2 the expression "keep (it) not hidden" (*'al-tĕkaḥēdû*) refers to a divine word, and the word Jeremiah goes on to give Zedekiah in the present instance is bona fide revelation (vv 17–18). See Note on 50:2.

15. *And if I give you advice, you will not listen to me.* This is an unusual statement, in that Jeremiah does not imagine himself delivering the king a divine word, but rather giving him advice (Heb *'î'āṣĕkā*). Advice (*'ēṣâ*) more commonly comes from wise men (18:18) and counselors to the king (e.g., Ahithophel in 2 Samuel 15–17). But McKane (1995: 149) says counsel can be embodied in prophetic utterance, which may be correct, since Jeremiah goes on to give the king a divine oracle.

16. *secretly.* Hebrew *bassēter*. The LXX omits, although it does translate the term in 37:17. Here the term is superfluous (Cornill: "a useless addition"), as they are already at a secret location.

As Yahweh lives who made this life of ours. On expanded oaths, see Note for 16:14–15.

these men who seek your life. I.e., the princes. The LXX omits "who seek your life," but the words are translated in Aq and Symm.

17–18. *Yahweh, God of hosts, God of Israel.* The LXX omits "of hosts, God of Israel" as it does elsewhere (see Appendix VI).

If you will only go out to the princes of the king of Babylon, then you yourself will live and this city will not be burned with fire; . . . But if you will not go out to the princes of the king of Babylon, then this city will be given into the hand of the Chaldeans and they will burn it with fire. As for you, you shall not escape from their hand*. A repetition of the prophecy in 21:8–9 (Weiser). See also Deut 30:15–20. For other prophecies on the destruction of Jerusalem, see Note on 38:3.

the princes of the king of Babylon. These are royal and nonroyal appointees, serving the king of Babylon as upper-level civil and military officials (39:3). On the translation of "princes" for *śārîm*, see Note for 24:1. Nebuchadnezzar was in Riblah at the time (see Note for 39:1), so any surrender would have to be to his princes. The words are absent in the LXX, but present in Aq and Symm.

from their hand. The LXX omits, but Aq has the term.

19. *I am afraid of the Judahites who have deserted . . . lest . . . they abuse me*. It is a singular indignity to suffer abuse from your own people, but this wartime sport was common in antiquity.

20. *Obey now the voice of Yahweh . . . that it may go well with you, and you . . . will live*. The stereotypical language of Deuteronomy, where fidelity to the covenant is said to bring life and well-being. On the phrase, *wĕyîṭab lĕkā / lākem* ("that it may go well with you"), see Note for 7:23.

21. *this is the word that Yahweh has shown me*. Here the divine word comes in a vision. On the mixing of visual and auditory elements in Jeremiah's prophetic experience, see 2:31 and 23:18.

22. *And there they were . . . yes, there they were*. Hebrew *wĕhinnēh*, occurring twice here, requires something more than the usual "Look!" or "Behold!" Calvin says the repeated particle is to lead Zedekiah to the very scene itself.

all the women who remained in the house of the king of Judah. These are palace women left behind when Jehoiachin went to Babylon (Kimḥi; Cheyne; Rudolph), who then became concubines in the harem of Zedekiah. Zedekiah's own wives are mentioned in v 23.

yes, there they were saying. The women are the speakers (*'ōmĕrôt*).

They misled you and overcame you, your trusted men. Perhaps because they belonged to former kings, these women very quickly show disloyalty to Zedekiah. The line repeats almost verbatim in Obad 7, although there the context is different. Obadiah taunts Edom about the deceit of trusted allies. For the parallel to Obad 7, see Raabe 1996: 30; for parallels between Jer 49:7–10, 14–16 and Obad 1–8, see Rhetoric and Composition for 49:7–11. The language here is Jeremianic, as one can see from a comparison with 20:10: *ykl* ("to overcome"), and *'ĕnôš šĕlômî* ("my trusted friends"). See also the poetry in 13:21, which anticipates Jerusalem's earlier surrender in 597 B.C.

your trusted men. Hebrew *'anšê šĕlōmekā* is lit. "men of your peace." Compare "my trusted friend(s)" (*'ĕnôš šĕlômî*) in 20:10. Rashi thinks these are the false prophets, but more likely they are military and government officials, perhaps the king's army, who deserted him in the end (2 Kgs 25:5). The line is ironic: trusted men are seen to be untrustworthy.

Your feet are sunk in the muck. Hebrew *bōṣ* is a *hapax legomenon* in the OT, but cognates in Aram (*biṣṣā'*, "marsh"), Akk (*baṣu, baṣṣu*, "sand"), and Ar (*baḍḍat*, "waterlogged ground"), make the meaning secure (KB³). Rashi says the term means "mire." A likely allusion to Jeremiah's own experience in the pit (v 6), but with two important differences: 1) the usage here is metaphorical; and 2) no one will rescue Zedekiah, whereas Jeremiah had help from Ebed-melech, the king himself, and a rescue team of thirty men.

they have drawn back. Hebrew *nāsōgû 'āḥôr.* For the same expression, see 46:5. This second line is an added irony: According to the law (Exod 23:5), even the fallen animal of one's enemy is to be helped up, but here, trusted subordinates abandon the king in his hour of greatest need.

23. *And all your wives and your children are being brought out to the Chaldeans.* Prisoners, including women and children, are portrayed in procession on reliefs of Shalmaneser III (859–825 B.C.); cf. *ANEP²* 124 #358 (lower register); and 127 #365 (lower register). Another Assyrian relief shows women and children being taken away in oxcarts; see *ANEP²* 128 #367.

this city will be burned with fire. The LXX lacks "with fire."

24. *Do not let anyone know of these words, and you shall not die.* The phrase *'îš 'al-yēdaʿ* ("Do not let anyone know") occurs also in 36:19. A veiled threat like one from the princes to Jeremiah in the following verse, but with the difference that the present words also give reassurance.

25. *and we will not put you to death.* A veiled threat (Peake) whether empty or otherwise. The princes are saying that if Jeremiah refuses to tell them, they will kill him.

26. *I laid my request before the king.* Hebrew *mappîl-'ănî tĕḥinnātî lipnê hammelek.* On the expression "to lay one's request before," see Note for 37:20.

the house of Jonathan. See Note for 37:15.

27. *Then all the princes came to Jeremiah and asked him, and he told them in accordance with all these words that the king commanded.* The oft-discussed point whether Jeremiah is guilty here of telling an untruth is a bit sterile. Assuming the princes did ask Jeremiah to tell them everything the king said, and everything he said to the king—where is it written that one has to comply with such a request, particularly when the individuals making it are known to be evil intentioned? The fact that the king provided Jeremiah with an answer he could give the princes, which did have a basis in fact, and that Jeremiah gave this answer when asked should elicit censure from no one.

for the conversation had not been heard. The LXX has the expanded reading "because the word of the Lord was not heard," which puts to rest any doubts about the ethical nature of the conversation between Jeremiah and the king. Aquila and Symm support the reading of MT.

And he was there when Jerusalem was taken. The formulaic closing states that Jeremiah remained in the court of the guard until the city was captured. This statement goes somewhat further, saying that he was there at the time of capture, and even after (Hebrew *ka'ăšer* means "after" in Judg 16:22). Ehrlich (1912: 342) emends the verb to *wayĕḥî,* with the line then stating that even with Jerusalem's capture, Jeremiah remained alive. But this emendation is not necessary.

MESSAGE AND AUDIENCE

This narrative segment reports Zedekiah's final attempt to wring some hope out of Jeremiah, bringing him this time to a Temple location where privacy could be assured. His request is for an unabridged word. Jeremiah is wary, wanting to know if the king will not then put him to death. The king has been dismissive of Yahweh's word before, why should he listen now? But the king swears an oath in Yahweh's name that he will not put Jeremiah to death, nor will he turn him over to those wishing to do so. The princes remain a threat. Jeremiah then complies with an oracle from Yahweh, one the king has heard before. If the king surrenders to the Babylonians, his life and the city will be spared. If he does not, the city will be captured and set ablaze, and the king will not escape.

Zedekiah does not reject the word, but admits to being afraid of surrender. The princes of Babylon could turn him over to Judahites who have already deserted, and they could physically abuse him. But Jeremiah says this will not happen, and he repeats his word in the familiar language of Deuteronomy: if the king obeys Yahweh's voice, it will go well with him, and he will live. If he does not, Yahweh has given Jeremiah a vision of Zedekiah's harem being brought out to the princes of Babylon, singing as they go a taunt song about how the king's trusted men have deceived him. The line about the king's feet being sunk in the mud is a vivid reminder to both of them that Jeremiah's feet were in the mud earlier. But Jeremiah was pulled free. Will this happen to Zedekiah? Apparently not, for Zedekiah's wives and children are also seen in the procession, and Zedekiah is not with them. He has been seized, Jeremiah says, and the city is being burned with fire.

The king hears all this with remarkable calm. He simply tells Jeremiah not to repeat the words to anyone, and he will not die. Should the princes hear that the two have been in conversation, and demand from Jeremiah a report of what transpired, he is to say that he petitioned the king not to be sent back to Jonathan's prison, where he would die. A reasonable request, expanding on a portion of the conversation but not a complete report. The princes do corner him and demand a debriefing, and Jeremiah tells them what the king instructed him to say. Happily, they leave him alone, as they had not overheard what was said. The narrative ends by saying that Jeremiah remained in the court of the guard until the city was taken, and a supplement states that he was also there when the city was taken.

This narrative segment concludes the running account of Jeremiah's suffering during the final siege of Jerusalem, also his encounters with and various rescues by the beleaguered Zedekiah. It prepares the audience to hear about the subsequent capture of the city, its destruction by fire, and Zedekiah's capture, which follow in chap. 39. The date of this segment, like the others in 37:1–40:6, is sometime after the fall of Jerusalem in 586 B.C.

F. Mercy and No Mercy (39:1–14)

1. Jerusalem Taken, Zedekiah Captured (39:1–10)

39 [1]In the ninth year of Zedekiah, king of Judah, in the tenth month, Nebuchadrezzar, king of Babylon, came—also all his army—to Jerusalem and they besieged it. [2]In the eleventh year of Zedekiah, in the fourth month, on the ninth of the month, the city was breached. [3]And all the princes of the king of Babylon entered and sat in the Middle Gate: Nergalsharezer the Samgar, Nebusarsechim the Rab-saris, Nergalsharezer the Rab-mag, and all the remaining princes of the king of Babylon. [4]And it happened when Zedekiah, king of Judah, saw them, also all the fighting men, that they fled. And they went out by night from the city in the direction of the king's garden, through the gate between the double walls; and he went out in the direction of the Arabah. [5]But the army of the Chaldeans pursued after them and overtook Zedekiah in the desert regions of Jericho. And they got hold of him, and brought him up to Nebuchadrezzar, king of Babylon, at Riblah in the land of Hamath, and he spoke judgments to him. [6]And the king of Babylon slaughtered Zedekiah's sons at Riblah before his eyes, and all the nobles of Judah the king of Babylon slaughtered. [7]Then the eyes of Zedekiah he blinded, and he bound him in bronze chains to bring him to Babylon. [8]And the house of the king and the house of the people the Chaldeans burned with fire, and the walls of Jerusalem they broke down. [9]And the rest of the people who were left in the city, and the deserters who had deserted to him, and the rest of the people who were left Nebuzaradan the Rab-tabahim exiled to Babylon. [10]But some of the poor people who were without anything Nebuzaradan the Rab-tabahim left in the land of Judah, and he gave to them vineyards and fields in that day.

2. Jeremiah Spared by Nebuchadrezzar (39:11–14)

39 [11]And Nebuchadrezzar, king of Babylon, commanded concerning Jeremiah through Nebuzaradan the Rab-tabahim: [12]Get hold of him and keep your eyes upon him, and do not do anything bad to him, but whatever he says to you do thus with him. [13]So Nebuzaradan the Rab-tabahim sent, also Nebushazban the Rab-saris, Nergalsharezer the Rab-mag, and all the chief officers of the king of Babylon. [14]And they sent and got hold of Jeremiah from the court of the guard, and gave him to Gedaliah son of Ahikam, son of Shaphan, to bring him out to the house. So he dwelt amidst the people.

RHETORIC AND COMPOSITION

MT 39:1–14 = LXX 46:1–3, 14. With chap. 39 comes a break of some sort in the larger collection of chaps. 37–44. Cornill said chap. 39 had nothing to do with chap. 38, which is a slight exaggeration; nevertheless, 39:1–10 does interrupt Jeremiah's personal drama to report Jerusalem's fall and Zedekiah's capture, and the verses themselves are little different from what is written in 52:4–16 and 2 Kgs 25:1–12. Also, Graf and Rudolph proposed that the superscription of 1:1–3, since it ends with the capture of Jerusalem, introduced a book containing only chaps. 1–39. I supported this view in *Jeremiah 1–20* but now propose a minor revision. A narrative compilation in which each segment has a closing ballast line begins at 37:1 and ends at 40:6 (see Rhetoric and Composition for 37:1–16), which precludes—in the present text, at least—a major break between chaps. 38 and 39 or between chaps. 39 and 40. It appears that 39:1–40:6 had a closure function in some earlier Jeremiah book comparable to the closure function now exercised by chap. 52 in the present book. We note the following story-line parallels in the two passages:

Jer 39:1–40:6	Jer 52:1–34
Jerusalem's fall, Zedekiah's capture, death of prominent citizens, and exile for others	Jerusalem's fall, Zedekiah's capture, death of prominent citizens, and exile for others
39:1–10	52:1–11, 24–30
Jeremiah released from prison and given a food allowance (*'ărūḥâ*)	Jehoiachin released from prison and given a food allowance (*'ărūḥâ*)
39:11–14; 40:1–6	52:31–34

The LXX omits vv 4–13 of the present segment, which most scholars—but not all—attribute to haplography (homoeoarcton: *wy . . . wy* or two-word: *melek bābel . . . melek bābel*). This is doubtless true. Arguments by Jones supporting the shorter LXX text are unconvincing. Janzen (1973: 118) agrees that the LXX most likely suffers from haplography, but still wants to give this text preference because vv 4–10 "surely are secondary," a judgment surviving from Giesebrecht. Holladay says the same. Actually, the alleged secondary nature of vv 4–10 and the LXX omission of vv 4–13 have nothing to do with each other. Once again, the longer MT is a better text and likely the original. The LXX omission of vv 4–13 is preserved in Theod, with portions existing also in Aq and Symm (Field 1875: 688–90; Swete 1899: 334–35).

The question of borrowing has been raised for the present verses because of the two parallels to vv 1–10 occurring elsewhere in the Bible. Some commentators (Montgomery 1951: 559; Hyatt; Bright) think the narrator may have borrowed from the Deuteronomic Historian, although all three passages, when compared to the others, have additions and omissions. Verse 3 of the present passage exists nowhere else. While the borrowing question has consumed a century or more of Jeremianic scholarship, it is best left to one side. We know scarcely more about borrowing than Giesebrecht, Duhm, and others did a century ago. What is clear is that 37–40:6 and 52 each have their own distinct literary structure (see Rhetoric and Composition for 37:1–16 and 52:1–11), so if the present verses contain any borrowed material, it has been well-integrated into the context where it now appears.

The present narrative segment reports 1) Jerusalem's fall and Zedekiah's capture (vv 1–10); and 2) Jeremiah's release as authorized by the Babylonian king (vv 11–14). Delimitation is based first on the existence of closing lines in 37:1–40:6, which in the present segment is "So he dwelt amidst the people" in v 14 (see Rhetoric and Composition for 37:1–16). The upper limit is marked additionally by a *petuḥah* in M^L, and a *setumah* in M^A and M^P, before v 1, which is also the chapter division. There is uncertainty about the final words of 38:28b, which I take with T and Jewish tradition to conclude the prior segment, probably being a later add-on (see Rhetoric and Composition for 38:14–28). The lower limit of the segment is marked additionally by a *setumah* in M^A and M^L, and a *petuḥah* in M^P, after v 14. Another *setumah* occurs in M^L and M^P after v 1, the purpose of which is unclear.

In the first portion of narrative, a repetition of the verb *lqḥ* ("to grab hold") points up the contrasting actions of the Babylonians toward Zedekiah on the one hand, and Jeremiah on the other:

> And [the Chaldeans] got hold of (wayyiqḥû) [Zedekiah] and brought him up to Nebuchadrezzar, king of Babylon . . . and he spoke judgments to him.
>
> (v 5)

> And Nebuchadrezzar, king of Babylon, commanded concerning Jeremiah. . . . Get hold of him (qāḥennû) and keep your eyes upon him, and do not do anything bad to him, but whatever he says to you do thus with him.
>
> (vv 11–12)

This contrast appears to be intentional as the verb in 52:9 is *tpś* ("capture"), not *lqḥ* ("get hold of").

NOTES

39:1. *In the ninth year of Zedekiah, king of Judah, in the tenth month, Nebuchadrezzar, king of Babylon, came—also all his army—to Jerusalem and they besieged it.* "The tenth (day) of the month" is added in 52:4; 2 Kgs 25:1; and Ezek 24:1. Although precise dates are calculated for the beginning of the siege and the fall of Jerusalem, a one-year discrepancy results from conflicting reckonings in the Bible and attempted correlations between the biblical reckonings and reckonings in the Babylonian Chronicle. In addition, there is uncertainty as to whether a Babylonian calendar was in use in Judah at the time (since ca. 604 B.C.), or being used by biblical narrators writing later, where the New Year begins in March/April (= Nisan reckoning). On the names of months in the Jewish calendar, see Appendix IX. Some believe that the older Israelite calendar, where the New Year begins in September/October (= Tishri reckoning), remained in effect up until Jerusalem's fall. A lower chronology (Montgomery 1951: 560; Tadmor 1956: 230; Cogan and Tadmor 1988: 323) begins the siege of Jerusalem in Tebet (January) 587. A higher chronology (Bright 1965: 242; 1981: 329–30; Malamat 1968: 151; J. Gray 1970: 764; Fried and Freedman 2001: 2269) begins it a year earlier, in Tebet 588. Thiele (1956: 23), however, says the siege begins in January 588 regardless of what calendar is used, and that evidence from the Babylonian Chronicle makes this date final. The 588 date is the one followed here. On Assyrian and Babylonian siege warfare, see Eph'al (1984) and Note for 6:6.

In the ninth year of Zedekiah. Hebrew *baššānâ hattěšî'ît lěṣidqîyyāhû*. In Lachish Letter #20 is found the fragmented reading *btš'yt* . . . *[y]hu*, which might possibly be "in the ninth (year) . . . [of Zedeki]ah" (Tufnell 1953: 339; cf. Ginsberg 1940: 12; Diringer 1943: 93–94). Letter #20 was found atop the tell in ruins dating subsequent to the first destruction of Lachish in 598 B.C., which puts it in the reign of Zedekiah.

In the ninth year . . . in the tenth month. G^BS have only "in the ninth month," which may conflate year and month, or be a mistaken citation from 2 Kgs 25:3, where both MT and LXX have "(on) the ninth of the month" (*pace* RSV and NRSV, which expand without notation to "on the ninth day of the fourth month"; cf. Jer 52:6 and v 1 above). Compare defective Gk readings in 52:4.

Nebuchadrezzar . . . came . . . to Jerusalem. The implication here is that Nebuchadrezzar came to Jerusalem with his army. In 52:4 and 2 Kgs 25:1 the point is made explicitly: "he and his army came." But other indications are that he remained at his headquarters in Riblah (v 5), attending to unrest in western Syria and threats of interference from Egypt, leaving the siege of Jerusalem to subordinates (38:17–22; 39:3; cf. Josephus, *Ant* x 135; Calvin; Montgomery 1951: 560; Bright; Gray 1970: 764; Cogan and Tadmor 1988: 322–23). A threat of interference from Egypt was ever present, especially now, with the accession in 589 B.C. of the ambitious Pharaoh Apries (= Hophra of 44:30), who, in classical sources is reported to have embarked on an ill-fated naval expedition against Sidon and Tyre (Herodotus ii 161; Diodorus Sic. i 68; cf. Gray 1970: 763). The Wadi-Brisa Inscription (Weissbach 1906; Rogers 1926: 365–66; *ANET*³ 307) states too that Nebuchadrezzar at some point was dealing with an enemy in western Syria, yet another indication that the siege of Jerusalem was only one matter occupying his attention. It could be that Nebuchadrezzar came with his army to Jerusalem, and then once the siege had begun, turned things over to subordinates and returned to Riblah. This is the view of Josephus (*Ant* x 131–35), who has him setting up the siege but not present when the city fell.

Nebuchadrezzar. The same spelling as in 52:4; compare the spelling "Nebuchadnezzar" in 2 Kgs 25:1, and see Note on 21:2.

and they besieged it. Expanded to include a prior encampment in 52:4 and 2 Kgs 25:1. For a symbolic acting out of this siege, see Ezekiel 4. The beginning of the siege of Jerusalem was marked in later Jewish tradition by a fast on the tenth of Tebet, the tenth month (Zech 8:19; cf. Milgrom, "Fasting and Fast Days" in *EncJud* 6: 1191).

2. *In the eleventh year of Zedekiah, in the fourth month, on the ninth of the month, the city was breached.* The unthinkable happened (Lam 4:12). The lower chronology dates Jerusalem's fall on 9 Tammuz (July); 586; the higher chronology on 9 Tammuz (July), 587. Malamat (1968; 1975: 143; 1979: 218; 1990: 74), following the Tishri (= fall) calendar and adopting here the lower chronology, has the siege lasting two and a half years. The chronology of Thiele (1956) yields a similar result. This time frame is reasonable, though it stretches the biblical reckoning of a siege from Zedekiah's ninth to eleventh years, and creates a clear conflict with Josephus (*Ant* x 116), who says the siege lasted eighteen months. Yet Shalmaneser V besieged Samaria for three years (2 Kgs 17:5). The chronological problem is real and cannot be settled with certainty. We know, too, that the siege was broken for a time when the Egyptians made their advance northward (37:5, 11). On the famine at the time of surrender, see 52:6 and 2 Kgs 25:3. The breach of the city was marked in later Jewish tradition by a fast on the seventeenth of Tammuz, the fourth month (Zech 8:19; cf. Milgrom, "Fasting and Fast Days" in *EncJud* 6: 1191).

3. *And all the princes of the king of Babylon entered and sat in the Middle Gate.* The city gate is where judgment takes place (Köhler 1956a: 149–75), and now instead of Judah's elders occupying the benches, it is ranking officers of the Babylonian army. Jeremiah said this would happen (1:15; 21:4). Nebuchadrezzar is not present, which probably means he is at Riblah (see v. 1).

in the Middle Gate. Hebrew *bĕša'ar hattāwek*. Mentioned in the OT only here, this gate has been located either on the city's northern wall (Duhm; Paton 1906; Malamat 1968: 155), perhaps being the Fish Gate (Neh 3:1–3; 12:39; cf. Zeph 1:10; 2 Chr 33:14), or in the center of the city (Blayney; Cheyne; Rudolph). Kimḥi, citing the Jerusalem Talmud (Erubin 5:1), says the "Middle Gate" was one of seven names given to the eastern gate of the Temple. However, in 1978, Avigad discovered a segment of city wall under the Justinian Cardo (the Broad Wall), and a gate in the immediate vicinity, which he took to be the Middle Gate referred to here (Avigad 1983: 59; 1985: 472; Bieberstein and Bloedhorn 1994 II: 253, 306). This gate was situated in the middle of the northern defense wall, and its remains can be seen at the "Israelite Tower" in the Jewish Quarter of the Old City. The Babylonians doubtless entered Jerusalem from the north, as all attackers did, since this was the city's highest elevation and the only side unprotected by ravines (Paton 1906: 3; Avigad 1983: 59). They then took their seats in the Middle Gate, which would have been close to where the breach was made.

Nergalsharezer the Samgar, Nebusarsechim the Rab-saris, Nergalsharezer the Rab-mag. Difficulty in rendering these Babylonian names shows up already in the Versions, which betray uncertainty about components and a general unawareness that names are followed by titles. What we have are three names with titles (Bogaert 1990: 317), the same number—but not all the same persons—as in v 13. If one were to read MT's hyphenated *samgar-nebu* as a separate name, which is possible (= Akk *Sinmagir-Nabu*), the names and individuals would then be four: Nergal-sharezer, Samgar-nebu, Sarsechim the Rab-saris, and

Nergal-sharezer the Rab-mag (compare RSV, NJV, and NJB). But a contemporary cuneiform text suggests that *samgar* is a title for Nergal-sharezer (see below), leaving *nebu* a component of the following name. The *samgar-nebu* of MT is then incorrect.

Nergalsharezer the Samgar. Nergalsharezer is a Hebraicized form of Akk Nergal-šar-uṣur (Neriglissar). This individual, or else Nergalsharezer the Rab-mag cited here and in v 13, is likely the one who later seized the throne from Nebuchadrezzar's successor, Amelmarduk, and reigned from 560 to 556 B.C. (Bright 1965: 243; 1981: 352–53). Hebrew *samgar* (= Akk *simmagir* [*sin-magir*]) is the title of a high official, or else a place-name (CAD 15: 272–73; AHw 2: 1045). The consensus now is that *samgar* belongs with the prior name, which in Akk yields either Nergal-sar-user, the Sin-magir (high official), or Nergal-sar-user from Sin-magir (Bewer 1925–26). An individual so designated has come to light in "The Court of Nebuchadnezzar" document (*ANET³* 308), where also the Nebuzaradan mentioned in vv 9–14 is listed. Some commentators (Giesebrecht; Rudolph; Bright; Holladay; Jones; McKane) suggest that the two Nergalsharezers are only one person, but that view is to be rejected. These are two individuals with the same name (Kimḥi), cited here with different titles in order to distinguish one from the other.

Nebusarsechim the Rab-saris. The now-expanded name of Nebusarsechim has support in LXX's *Nabousachar.* The component in MT is "Nebu" (as in Nebuchadrezzar), not "Nebo," as appears in Isa 46:1. Both are equivalent to Akk *Nabû* (= god). The *Rab-saris* ("chief of the eunuchs") is another title for a high state official.

Nergalsharezer the Rab-mag. The term *rab-mag* is a Hebraicized form of Akk *rab mugi*, the title of a high military official (*mugu* in CAD 10/2: 171; AHw 2: 667; KB³); its meaning, at least here, is not "chief astrologer/soothsayer" (*pace* BDB, 550; NJB). The term has turned up in an economic memorandum from the Sippar temple records (BM 49656: 3), where at Nabopolassar's accession reference is made to "the accountant of the *rab mungu*" (Wiseman 1956: 94).

4. *And it happened when Zedekiah, king of Judah, saw them, also all the fighting men, that they fled.* Whether the king and his soldiers actually saw the Babylonian officials sitting in the Middle Gate is unclear. The text seems to indicate that these individuals were seen inside the city. Josephus (*Ant* x 136) says that Zedekiah and his entourage fled after learning that the Babylonian commanders had entered the Temple. In any case, the decision was reached quickly to make an escape.

fighting men. Hebrew *'anšê hammilḥāmâ.* I.e., soldiers; see also 38:4.

that they fled. The verb is an imperfect with *waw consecutive*, thus past tense.

And they went out by night from the city in the direction of the garden of the king, through the gate between the double walls. With the enemy entering the city from the north, the king and his entourage had to make their escape to the south. But acccording to 52:7 and 2 Kgs 25:4, the Chaldeans had surrounded the city.

by night. If penetration of the city was during daylight hours, as seems likely, since the king and his soldiers are said to have seen the enemy, then a wait in some concealed place was necessary until the city could be exited under the cover of darkness. But Josephus (*Ant* x 136) reports that the city was taken about midnight. For an acted parable, anticipating both royalty and people preparing for exile by day and fleeing the city by night, see Ezek 12:1–12. Then, as now, flights of this sort commonly occur at night (cf. Ezek 12:4).

in the direction of the king's garden, through the gate between the double walls. The king's garden and the gate between the double walls were at the south end of the City of David, but precisely where we do not know. The general area was the Gihon Spring and the King's Pool (= Pool of Shelah), which provided water for the garden. Although various gates have been suggested, e.g., the Fountain Gate (Neh 2:14; 3:15), and the Dung Gate, the opening may have been unnamed (*pace* NEB and REB). It could have been a secret exit prepared for an eventuality such as the present one. Kimḥi says it was a secret gate, unknown to the Chaldeans. The double-wall construction resulted from a second wall built by Hezekiah to protect Jerusalem against Assyrian attack, a stretch of which was known to have existed in this area (Isa 22:9–11; 2 Chr 32:3–5; cf. Avigad 1983: 56–60). The king then fled from the southeast corner of the city, heading east in the direction of Jericho and the Dead Sea.

and he went out in the direction of the Arabah. I.e., the king went out, although there were doubtless others who went with him. The T, some MSS, and the Vrs have "they went" plural (cf. 52:7). The route of flight would be the expected one, down the Adummim to the Jordan Valley, where the king could then cross the Jordan and seek sanctuary in Ammonite country (cf. 40:14; 41:15), or else turn south in the direction of caves west of the Dead Sea, where fugitives in all periods have sought refuge. King David used both escape routes, hiding from Saul in a cave near En-Gedi (1 Samuel 24), and crossing the Jordan into Ammonite country when his son Absalom was in pursuit (2 Sam 15:23–16:14; 17:22–29). The Ascent of Adummim (*maʿălēh ʾădummîm*), as it is called in the Bible, was an ancient trade route and Judah's northern boundary in the early settlement period. Modern Arabic preserves the ancient name in Wadi Talʿat ed-Damm ("The Ascent of Blood"), which is south of the modern road opposite Wadi Qelt (Wilkinson 1975: 14–18). The ascent began in the Jordan Valley, then through mountainous wilderness to Jerusalem, and ended at the En-rogel Spring in the Kidron Valley. Here one is close to where Zedekiah exited the city (Josh 15:5–7; 18:16–18). Josephus (*Ant* x 136) rightly states that the escape was "through the wilderness." Heading downward, the ancient road probably followed the same course as the Roman road—and at the upper end, the modern road, going from Jerusalem via Bethany down to Wadi Qelt, and then following Wadi Qelt to Jericho. On the Jerusalem–Jericho Road, see Wilkinson 1975 and Dorsey 1991: 204–6; on the Ascent of Adummim, see Baly (1974: 185–86); Noth (1966b: 90); and Aharoni (1979: 59–60).

the Arabah. Hebrew *hāʿărābâ*. The Arabah is used broadly in the OT to refer to the rift valley extending from the Sea of Galilee in the north to the Gulf of Aqaba in the south (Deut 1:1; 2:8; 3:17; 4:49). It includes the Jordan Valley, through which the Jordan River flows, the semidesert areas on both sides of the Dead Sea, and the Wadi el-ʿArabah extending from the Dead Sea to the Gulf of Aqaba. The term also had localized meaning, referring as it does here to the semidesert region south of Jericho (v 5). Without the definite article, the term can mean simply "desert," as in 2:6.

5–7. Ezekiel's acted parable follows the same story line as here: capture of the king, flight of the king's companions, death to all but a select few who are permitted an escape, exile of the king to Babylon, and the king's inability to see Babylon when he gets there (Ezek 12:13–16).

5. *But the army of the Chaldeans pursued after them and overtook Zedekiah in the desert regions of Jericho.* Compare the chase envisioned in 16:16. In 52:8 and 2 Kgs 25:5, it is said additionally that Zedekiah's army scattered at this point, and a few MSS and the S add the words here.

after them . . . Zedekiah. The plural "them" is followed by "Zedekiah" singular, the reverse of what happened in v 4. The Chaldeans are pursuing the king and his party. G. R. Driver (1960: 122), however, argues that the Hebrew may contain an abbreviation: *hm* for *hmlk* ("the king"), which would bring the present reading into line with 52:8 (*ʾaḥărê hammelek*).

the desert regions of Jericho. Hebrew *ʿarĕbōt yĕrēḥô*. The semidesert area of the Arabah south of Jericho (Josh 4:13; 5:10), not the densely forested area east and north (*pace* McKane, 1364).

And they got hold of him, and brought him up to Nebuchadrezzar, king of Babylon, at Riblah in the land of Hamath, and he spoke judgments to him. Zedekiah had been told repeatedly that he would not manage an escape from his enemies, but would be captured (34:3, 21; 37:17; 38:18, 23).

Riblah in the land of Hamath. An ancient city in central Syria on the Orontes River, situated also on an important highway from Mesopotamia to Egypt. Modern Ribleh and its nearby ruins lie in Lebanon's Bacca Valley, about 58 kilometers northeast of Baalbeck and 32 kilometers southwest of the Syrian city of Homs. Riblah is roughly 80 kilometers south of Hama (= Hamath), in Syria. The ancient city was an important military and administrative center where, together with nearby Kadesh, many wars were fought. That the Assyrians used it as a military base we know from Nimrud Letter #70 (ca. 740 B.C.), which mentions Rablē (Saggs 1963: 79–80). The base was later taken over by the Egyptians. At Riblah Jehoahaz was brought before Pharaoh Neco in 609 B.C., put in chains, and taken away to Egypt (2 Kgs 23:33). At the present time, Riblah is headquarters for Nebuchadrezzar while he is besieging Jerusalem and dealing with enemies in western Syria (cf. Wadi Brisa Inscription cited in v 1). Zedekiah is thus brought before the Babylonian king there.

in the land of Hamath. Corrupted in the LXX of 52:9 to *Deblatha*, and lacking altogether in 2 Kgs 25:6. But see 2 Kgs 23:33. On the city of Hamath, see Note for 49:23.

and he spoke judgments to him. Hebrew *wayĕdabbēr ʾittô mišpāṭîm*. In 1:16 and 4:12 Yahweh promised to utter judgments (*dbr mšpṭym*) against an unfaithful

Judah. Here Zedekiah is not pleading his case before the Babylonian king (*pace* NEB, but corrected in REB), but hearing sentences meted out to an unfaithful vassal. They are more than one: death for his sons (and Judah's nobles); and for himself a blinding, enchainment, and exile to Babylon. The plural *mišpāṭîm* corresponds to Jeremianic usage elsewhere (1:16; 4:12; 12:1; cf. 52:9). See also Ezek 5:8, 10, 15. 2 Kings 25:6 reads "and they spoke a judgment (*mišpāṭ*) against him" (*pace* RSV), which has Zedekiah's captors making a single accusation against Zedekiah to Nebuchadrezzar. It would doubtless be damning, but not a sentence per se. Zedekiah stands guilty. Having sworn a loyalty oath to the Babylonian king (Ezek 17:16, 18; 2 Chr 36:13; Josephus, *Ant* x 101), he is now judged for breaking that oath.

6. *And the king of Babylon slaughtered Zedekiah's sons at Riblah before his eyes, and all the nobles of Judah the king of Babylon slaughtered.* A good example of syntactic chiasmus in prose, serving to highlight the king's role in the killings. Others doubtless carried out the bloody deed (2 Kgs 25:7: "they slaughtered"). The reading here is supported by Jer 52:10, only without the "king of Babylon" repetition. Things followed a different course in 597 B.C., when Nebuchadrezzar exiled unharmed royalty and prominent citizens to Babylon. But then King Jehoiachin and the queen mother surrendered. A punishment similar to the one here was promised Pashhur the priest, who would see friends being killed (20:4), and to exiles in Babylon, who would look on when Nebuchadrezzar put to death the (false) prophets Ahab son of Kolaiah and Zedekiah son of Maaseiah (29:21). The detail here of nobles being slaughtered is lacking in 2 Kgs 25:7, but it was predicted (Jer 34:18–20). For princes who were shamefully killed in Jerusalem, see Lam 5:12.

slaughtered. Hebrew *šāḥaṭ*. Milgrom (1991: 715) says this is the Priestly writer's exclusive verb for animal slaughter. In 41:7 it refers again to human slaughter, as it does here.

7. *Then the eyes of Zedekiah he blinded.* The verb is ʿwr in the Piel. Zedekiah's eyes get the emphasis, coming as they do at the beginning of the sentence, perhaps because the king had been told: "And your eyes shall see the eyes of the king of Babylon" (34:3; cf. 32:4). A cruel punishment it is, as the killing of his sons would be the last thing Zedekiah would see before being blinded. Blinding was a common punishment in antiquity for slaves, both captured and rebellious; however, often just one eye, so the slave could work (Gelb 1973: 87; Cogan and Tadmor 1988: 318; cf. Judg 16:21; 1 Sam 11:2). Herodotus (iv 2) reports the Scythians blinding slaves and prisoners of war. Shalmaneser I (ca. 1265–1235 B.C.) deported 14,000 blinded Hanigalbatians to Assyria (Machinist 1982: 18), and in the Treaty between Ashurnirari V of Assyria and Matiʾilu of Arpad, one of the curses for breaking the treaty is blinding (ANET³ vi, 533). For a bas-relief showing an Assyrian king putting out the eyes of a prisoner, kneeling with hands tied and a ring through his lip, see Maspero 1900: 546. One of the Sefire Inscriptions (I A), dated ca. 750 B.C., contains three penalties for breaking a loyalty oath, providing an even more striking parallel to what is happening here:

As this wax is consumed by fire, thus Arpad [and its dependencies] shall
be consumed . . .
As [this][1] man of wax is blinded, thus Matti'el shall be blinded . . .
[As] this calf is cut up, thus Matti'el and his nobles shall be cut up.

$$(ANET^3\ 660;\ CS\ II\ 214;\ cf.\ Deist\ 1971)$$

Ezekiel gave a cryptic word concerning this last king of Judah: "and I will bring
him to Babylon . . . yet he shall not see it; and he shall die there" (Ezek 12:13).

bronze chains. Hebrew *nĕḥuštayim*, a dual of *nĕḥōšet* ("bronze"), means
"bronze chains." Samson was put in bronze chains after being blinded by the
Philistines (Judg 16:21). These were to shackle the prisoner's feet (Kimḥi),
probably not both the hands and feet, as Holladay suggests, although we later
learn that Jeremiah's hands were chained when he was with an exile-bound
group at Ramah (40:4). A seventh-century relief from Ashurbanipal's palace
shows Egyptian prisoners being led away from Thebes with tied hands and
chained feet ($ANEP^2$ 5 #10; cf. 250; Yadin 1963: 462), which corresponds to
David's depiction in his lament over Abner (2 Sam 3:34):

| Your hands were not bound | *yādekā lō'-'ăsûrôt* |
| and your feet not thrust into bronze chains | *wĕragleykā lō'-linḥuštayim huggāšû* |

Cogan and Tadmor (1988: 318) think the present usage is archaic, since in the
late Iron Age chains were made of iron (cf. Pss 105:18; 149:8). But could not
some bronze chains still be around?

to bring him to Babylon. This was predicted explicitly in 32:5, also indirectly
in 34:4–5. In 52:11 it says that Nebuchadrezzar did in fact bring Zedekiah to
Babylon, continuing: "and [he] put him in the detention house until the day of
his death," which balances the "until the day of his death" statement regarding
Jehoiachin (see Rhetoric and Composition for 52:1–11). This supplement is
not present in 2 Kgs 25:7.

8. *And the house of the king and the house of the people the Chaldeans burned
with fire, and the walls of Jerusalem they broke down.* In 52:13 and 2 Kgs 25:9
Nebuzaradan is said to have arrived in Jerusalem one month after its capture,
at which time he burned all the city's buildings. Walls were brought down by
the army working alongside Nebuzaradan, rendering the city no longer a city.
In antiquity, walls were necessary for a city worthy of the name. Jeremiah had
warned repeatedly that Jerusalem and its gates would be burned with fire
(17:27; 21:10; 32:29; 34:2, 22; 37:8, 10; 38:17–18, 23), also the house of the king
(6:5; 17:27; 21:14; 22:7), but nowhere is he reported as saying that the city walls
would be razed. He said only that an appointed enemy would come against them
(1:15; cf. Isa 2:5; 5:5). Nevertheless, Jerusalem's fallen walls were sorely lamented (Lam 2:2, 5–9; Pss 80:13[Eng 80:12] and 89:41[Eng 89:40]). With the
destruction of Jerusalem, the larger Israelite nation was now effectively at an

---

[1]The $ANET^3$ translation has "As a man of wax. . . ." But the wax figurine was actually present
when the curse was being recited.

end. Tiglath-pileser III and Shalmaneser V reduced to ruins the cities of Northern Israel, with Samaria the capital falling in 722 B.C. (2 Kgs 15:29; 17:1–6; Bright 1981: 274–75), and Sennacherib destroyed 46 of Judah's fortified cities in his campaign of 701 B.C. (ANET³ 288; CS II 303; cf. 2 Kgs 18:13), many of which were never rebuilt. Of those that were rebuilt, archaeological evidence points to a destruction of Lachish, Tell Beit Mirsim, Beth-shemesh, Gezer, Beth-zur, Khirbet Rabud (likely Debir), Gibeah, Ramat Raḥel, Arad, Tel Malḥata, Tel Masos, and En-Gedi in or around 586 B.C. (cf. Malamat 1979: 217). Judah, then, like its sister-state Israel in the north, was left a veritable ruin. Later Jewish tradition marked the destruction of the Temple by a fast on the ninth of Ab, the fifth month (Zech 7:3, 5; 8:19; cf. Milgrom, "Fasting and Fast Days" in EncJud 6: 1191).

the house of the king and the house of the people. In 52:13 and 2 Kgs 25:9 it says "the house of Yahweh, and the house of the king, and all the houses of Jerusalem, yes, every great house." What then is the "house of the people" here? The AV (following S) has "houses [plural] of the people," which may be a harmonization attempt with "all the houses of Jerusalem." But T has "house of the people." Kimḥi translates the singular as a collective, saying it means "houses of the people." This may be the right answer, as "house of the king" could also be a collective, referring to more than one royal building. In 33:4 is remembered the destruction of "the houses of this city and the houses of the kings of Judah." The expression could then be merismus: "house of king and people," i.e., all houses. Landsberger (1949) notes that "House of the People" later became a popular designation for the synagogue inveighed against by the Talmud, and in the Mandaean scriptures was identified with the Temple, suggesting to him that the term may here be a postexilic interpolation meaning Temple. The argument is not very convincing. It is striking that the burning of the Temple goes unmentioned. Yet, the destruction of Israel's first sanctuary at Shiloh goes unmentioned in 1 Samuel 4 (see Note for 7:12). On the burning of the Temple and of private houses in Jerusalem, see Note for 52:13.

9. The narrative here—also in 52:15 and 2 Kgs 25:11—proceeds to name those who were exiled. The economy in reporting such an unblessed event is not to be wondered at. No mention is made of the violence, indignity, and death—within the city and without—once the Babylonians had become masters of Jerusalem, to say nothing of the trauma experienced by those being exiled. We get but a glimpse of the unspeakable horrors characterizing the time in the Lamentations (Lam 1:4, 7, 11, 19; 2:11–12, 19–22; 4:4–5, 7–10, 14–15; and 5:11–14).

the deserters who had deserted. The verb is *npl*, "to fall," which here as elsewhere in the chapters means "fall into the hands of." These individuals could be either deserters or persons taken prisoner. The former is more likely. Kimḥi says they are those who defected before the fall of the city. Jeremiah advised desertion (21:9; 38:2), and was himself accused of the same (37:13).

and the rest of the people who were left. A catchall category, perhaps referring to those rounded up outside of Jerusalem (Calvin). In 2 Kgs 25:11 the phrase is "and the rest of the multitude" (*wĕ'ēt yeter hehāmôn*); in 52:15 it is "the rest of the craftsmen" (*wĕ'ēt yeter hā'āmôn*), which must refer to craftsmen not taken in the exile of 597 B.C. (29:2; 2 Kgs 24:14, 16). See Note for 52:15.

Nebuzaradan the Rab-tabahim. Hebrew *rab-ṭabbāḥîm* means "chief of the cooks / butchers," the same title, basically, given to the Egyptian Potiphar: *śar haṭṭabbāḥîm* (Gen 37:36; 39:1). The present individual is known from Akkadian texts as Nabu-zer-iddina(m), Nebuchadrezzar's chief baker / cook ("The Court of Nebuchadnezzar," *ANET*³ 307; Kuhrt 1995: 605–7). He is chief steward, responsible for food distribution and organizing the exile, as he is doing here and in 40:1, 5. He also carries out executions (T: "the chief of the killers"). The latter gives the title an ominous tone, as he is Nebuchadrezzar's "hatchet man." Aḥmad al-Djazzar Pasha (ca. 1722–1804), legendary eighteenth-century military and political figure in southern Syria, also onetime governor of Beirut, was nicknamed "the butcher" (*al-djazzar*) because of his ferocity in fighting the Bedouin and successfully defending Acre against Napoleon (*EncIs* Supp 5–6: 268–69). In the latter war he is reported to have threatened death to any soldier contemplating surrender to the enemy. During the Second World War, Klaus Barbie, "the Butcher of Lyons," tortured victims and presided over an estimated 5,000 executions during the German occupation of France (1942–1944).

exiled to Babylon. According to 52:29, the number carried off in this second exile was only 832 persons, a significantly smaller number than in the first exile of 597 B.C.

10. *But some of the poor people who were without anything Nebuzaradan the Rab-tabahim left in the land of Judah, and he gave to them vineyards and fields in that day*. A fulfillment of the prophecy in 27:11. The meek literally do inherit the land (Ps 37:11; Matt 5:5). This redistribution and subsequent kindness to Jeremiah (vv 11–15) could be used to support Lambert's suggestion that the "king of justice" in the British Museum cuneiform tablet is indeed Nebuchadrezzar (see Note for 2:34).

vineyards and fields. Hebrew *kĕrāmîm wîgēbîm*. The term *yĕgēbîm* is an OT *hapax legomenon* of uncertain meaning. "Fields" is from the T, with other Vrs preferring "cisterns" (G^OL and Theod: *hydreumata*; Vg: *cisternas* = Heb *gēbîm*). Rashi says "fields to till." In 52:16 and 2 Kgs 25:12 the equally rare *yōgĕbîm* is usually rendered "plowmen" or the like. De Geus (1975: 73) plausibly suggests "irrigated terraces" for *yĕgēbîm* and "terrace workers / owners" for *yōgĕbîm* in 52:16 and 2 Kgs 25:12.

in that day. This expression is future-oriented in Jeremiah, referring to the coming day of Yahweh (see Notes for 4:9 and 46:10). Usually "that day" is one of judgment (4:9; 25:33; 39:16; 48:41; 49:22, 26; and 50:30), but here, as in vv 17–18, it is a day of kind deliverance.

11. *Nebuchadrezzar . . . commanded concerning Jeremiah through Nebuzaradan*. It is remarkable that Nebuchadrezzar should have knowledge about Jeremiah, though he could have learned something about Judah's internal affairs in 597, when he took the city and brought the king, queen mother, and a number of leading citizens to Babylon. He could also have learned about Jeremiah from

recent deserters (Holladay). Intelligence of this sort goes on in all wars; also, acts of kindness to select individuals, after a war is over, help pacify the conquered enemy.

12. *and keep your eyes upon him.* I.e., look after him. Hebrew *wĕ'êneykā śîm 'ālāyw*. The idiom "to keep the eyes upon someone (for good / bad)" occurs also in 24:6; 40:4; and in Amos 9:4.

but whatever he says to you. Hebrew *kî 'im* can simply be read as *kî*, meaning "but" (M^L and M^A do not point *'m*).

13–14. *So Nebuzaradan the Rab-tabahim sent, also Nebushazban the Rab-saris, Nergalsharezer the Rab-mag, and all the chief officers of the king of Babylon. And they sent.* . . . The double occurrence of "sent"—first a singular, then a plural—makes for awkward English. The Hebrew predicates with a singular verb its primary subject, "Nebuzaradan the Rab-tabahim," after which other subjects are added, and the narrative carries on with a plural verb. The same construction occurs in vv 1 and 4. In the present instance there may also be a chain of command: Nebuzaradan first sends word to his chief officers, then the officers send others to do the fetching. The person or persons who actually go after the prophet are not mentioned.

13. *Nebushazban the Rab-saris, Nergalsharezer the Rab-mag.* Nebushazban the Rab-saris was not one of those who came and sat in the Middle Gate, unless we identify him with Nebusarsechim the Rab-saris, whose name in v 3 required reconstruction. If Nebuchadrezzar has only one Rab-saris ("chief of the eunuchs"), then the two names must refer to the same individual. Otherwise the person here is another Rab-saris. Nergalsharezer the Rab-mag was at the Gate. See further Note on v 3.

14. *and gave him to Gedaliah son of Ahikam, son of Shaphan.* As one can see from the double patronym, Gedaliah belongs to the well-known Shaphan scribal family, with whom Jeremiah had a long-standing friendship. Shaphan was there when the Temple law-book was found in the reign of Josiah (2 Kgs 22:3–14), and Ahikam, Gedaliah's father, provided protection for Jeremiah after his trial in 609 B.C. (26:24). Other sons of Shaphan figured prominently in Baruch's reading of the Jeremiah scroll in 604 B.C. (36:10), and in carrying Jeremiah's letter to Babylon following the exile of 597 B.C. (29:3). "Gedaliah" was a common name in Judah, belonging to another individual in the book (38:1), and known outside the Bible from the Arad ostraca and from seals and bullae found in Jerusalem, Lachish, Tell Beit Mirsim, and elsewhere (see Appendix I). The seal impression found at Lachish in 1935 may actually derive from the Gedaliah here. It was attached to a papyrus sent to Lachish, and reads *lgdlyhw 'šr 'lhbyt*, "belonging to Gedaliah, the one who is over the house" (G. E. Wright 1938a: 11–12; Diringer 1941: 103; Tufnell 1953: 348 #173). Wright says the expression "one who is over the House" is a title designating a high royal official (Gen 43:16; 1 Kgs 18:3; Isa 22:15).

to bring him out to the house. The translation of T. The verb is *yṣ'* in the H-stem, meaning "to bring out" (so also the LXX, although omitting "to the house"). Gedaliah, once he has received Jeremiah, is to bring him to his house

(Kimḥi). Jeremiah does not go to his own house (AV: "to carry him home"). The fact that "house" has the article (*habbāyit*) indicates that it is a prominent house. In light of the seal impression just mentioned, we can probably assume that this was Gedaliah's house at Mizpah (40:6).

MESSAGE AND AUDIENCE

In reporting the fall of Jerusalem, this narrative fragment brings to a culmination all that has gone before. In the narrative immediately preceding, Jeremiah tells Zedekiah and other city residents that waiting out the siege simply will not work, and that the only hope is surrender; otherwise the city will fall. For this message he suffers much. But brought to a culmination even more in this narrative is a life committed to divine service, an accumulation of preaching to nations of the world about rooting up and breaking down, and a word of God that does not return void. Yahweh has proven true to the same covenant that the people have violated, and the day of reckoning said to come, has come. A tragic narration, really, spoken in few words but vindicating Yahweh's word and the messenger of that word. In the long term, this word will be a word of truth for all generations to come.

The narrative begins, as do narratives of the Deuteronomic History, by giving the date when Nebuchadrezzar's army began its siege of Jerusalem. It does not say the king was in Syria attending to other concerns. What matters is that the Babylonians came to subdue Jerusalem—now a second time in a decade. The siege itself is not described. The next date given is when the city was broken open, and no sooner did this happen, but officers of the king of Babylon entered and seated themselves in the Middle Gate. From there judgments against the city were meted out. What these were we are not told. Three of the Babylonian officers are named with their titles, but many more were present.

Then follows the flight of a beaten Zedekiah, his family, and some of his princes. At the sight of the enemy, they headed in a southerly direction. If it was daylight, they waited in a secret place until an escape was possible under the cover of darkness. By nightfall they had slipped out a gate between the city's double walls, and headed in the direction of the Arabah. But the enemy learned of their escape, also their escape route, and overtook the king in the desert wasteland south of Jericho. Once caught, Zedekiah was marched north by his captors to Riblah, where he saw Nebuchadrezzar face to face. The Babylonian king wasted no time in sentencing his unfaithful vassal. The first punishment was having to see his own sons slaughtered in cold blood, and after them the princes who were with him. Then Zedekiah was blinded, chained at the feet in heavy bronze, and made to take the long road to Babylon. Will the audience have any pity on Zedekiah and the other victims? Yes and no.

Some weeks later, the king's house and houses of the people were set ablaze, and the walls of the city came crashing down. Nebuzaradan presided over this final indignity, after which his attention was turned to organizing the exile. Captured people, deserters, residents of Jerusalem, and others from outside the city were rounded up and readied for the trip. But before commencing the march, Nebuzaradan, in his capacity as chief steward, gave to the poorest of the poor not going to Babylon vineyards and fields. For them the day of Yahweh was both darkness and light.

The narrative goes on to say that Nebuchadrezzar himself gave Nebuzaradan orders concerning Jeremiah. Nebuzaradan was to locate him, look after him, and do with him as Jeremiah wished. So he and his commanding officers, some of whom sat earlier in the Middle Gate preparing another agenda, sent for Jeremiah. Arriving hungry and thirsty from the court of the guard, the prophet was entrusted to his friend Gedaliah and brought to Gedaliah's house at Mizpah. Jeremiah then, like the poorest of the poor, was shown favor on a day remembered otherwise as a day of unspeakable judgment. The narrator, who is likely Baruch, also bears silent witness to the fulfillment of divine promises made to Jeremiah, that he would be rescued at a time when others would not.

This narrative, like the others in 37:1–40:6, dates from after Jerusalem's destruction in 586 B.C., but perhaps not long after, since the names and titles of Babylonian officers, together with other details, are remembered and reported. It will be climactic when heard in tandem with earlier narrative segments reporting Jerusalem under siege (chaps. 37–38), but will not be complete until supplemented by the promise of life to Ebed-melech and the report about Nebuzaradan releasing Jeremiah at Ramah and laying before him the whole land for a choice as to where he might go (39:15–40:6).

O Jerusalem, Jerusalem
An old city you were
Perched atop a Canaanite mountain
When Egypt's peaks were not yet old

Melchizedek, your priestly king
Blessed the good Abraham
With bread and wine
By God Most High
When Chedor-laomer got his due
And Lot perhaps more than his due

They knew of you in Egypt
Before Moses crossed the Sea
Five centuries before David
When Pharaohs and city-kings up north
Called you Urushalim
City of Abdi-Hiba

Then David took you as a bride
To be his own

And Yahweh too took rest in you
After arduous journey
Through desolate wilderness
Into Canaan, promised, as yet unsettled

But it was left to Solomon
To dress you like the queen you were
In beautiful cedar and stone
Ivory, silver, and gold
So nations would come to visit you
And visit you they did—yes, they did!

But your beauty was not all you thought
You romanticized the good King David
But forgot Yahweh your God
And so your high city walls
And tunneled water from Gihon
Were protection only for a time

Micah said you'd be plowed like a field
But the people more gladly heard Isaiah
Who said the Assyrians wouldn't take you
And they didn't
But the good Hezekiah they cooped up tight
Like a bird in a cage

O Inviolable One, or so you thought
Until Jeremiah thundered in your ears
A word so clear, so powerful
That you could not stand it
When he said you would fall
You waxed hostile and ugly

But you fell, yes you did!
And strangers took seat in your Middle Gate
Burned up your cedar forests
Broke down your stone mountains
And the people who were your flesh and blood
They left for dead or carted away

O Jerusalem, Jerusalem
City of glory, city of shame
The whole world knows both
And cannot forget you.

G. GRACE TO THE HUMBLE (39:15–40:6)

1. Ebed-melech to Be Rescued (39:15–18)

39 [15]And to Jeremiah came the word of Yahweh when he was confined in the court of the guard: [16]Go and you shall say to Ebed-melech, the Cushite:
Thus said Yahweh of hosts, God of Israel:
Look I am bringing[1] my words to this city for evil and not for good, and they shall come to pass before you in that day.

[17]But I will rescue you in that day—oracle of Yahweh—and you will not be given into the hand of the men before whom you are in dread.

[18]For I will surely see to your escape, and by the sword you will not fall, and your life will be your booty because you trusted in me—oracle of Yahweh.

2. The Whole Land before Jeremiah (40:1–6)

40 [1]The word that came to Jeremiah from Yahweh after Nebuzaradan the Rab-tabahim let him go from Ramah when he got hold of him (for he was bound in chains amidst all the exiles of Jerusalem and Judah who were being exiled to Babylon). [2]And the Rab-tabahim got hold of Jeremiah and said to him, 'Yahweh your God spoke this evil toward this place. [3]So Yahweh brought it about and did according to what he spoke. Indeed you sinned before Yahweh and did not obey his voice, so this thing[2] happened to you. [4]But now, look, I have released you today from the chains that are on your hands.[3] If it seems good in your eyes to go with me to Babylon, come, and I will keep my eye upon you; but if it seems bad in your eyes to go with me to Babylon, stay back. See, the whole land is before you; wherever it seems good and right in your eyes to go, go!' [5]And still he did not turn. 'Either turn to Gedaliah son of Ahikam, son of Shaphan, whom the king of Babylon appointed in the cities of Judah, and dwell with him amidst the people, or wherever it seems right in your eyes to go, go.' Then the Rab-tabahim gave him an allowance and a present, and let him go. [6]Jeremiah then went to Gedaliah son of Ahikam at Mizpah. And he dwelt with him amidst the people who were left in the land.

---

[1]Reading the Q *mēbî*; Kt lacks *'aleph* before *'et* (see Notes).
[2]Reading the Q, also with numerous MSS and the Talmud (Blayney), which supplies *dābār* with the article.
[3]Reading "your hands" plural with many MSS, the LXX, S, and Vg; MT *yādekā* is probably a dual (KB[3]).

RHETORIC AND COMPOSITION

MT 39:15–18; 40:1–6 = LXX 46:15–18; 47:1–6. The present segment contains: 1) a report of three salvation oracles given to Ebed-melech (39:15–18); and 2) a report of Jeremiah's second release by Nebuzaradan at Ramah (40:1–6). The segment is delimited primarily by the formal closing statements in 39:14 and 40:6, the latter being "And he dwelt with him amidst the people who were left in the land" (see Rhetoric and Composition for 37:1–16). Delimitation at the top end is confirmed by a *setumah* in M^A and M^L, and a *petuḥah* in M^P, before 39:15. At the bottom end confirmation is by a *setumah* in M^L, and a *petuḥah* in M^A and M^P, after 40:6. Separating the two segment portions is a *setumah* in M^L and M^P, and a *petuḥah* in M^A, after v 18, which is also the chapter division.

The two segment portions have balancing superscriptions, the first of which inverts the normal word order of the second:

I   *And to Jeremiah came the word of Yahweh . . .*   39:15
II *The word that came to Jeremiah from Yahweh . . .*   40:1

Ebed-melech's salvation oracles, which invite comparison with the salvation oracles given to Baruch (chap. 45), are out of chronological sequence. The superscription says they were given while Jeremiah was in the court of the guard, which is when the siege of Jerusalem was still in progress. Some commentators, wanting to remedy this chronological infelicity, relocate the verses to the end of chap. 38 (Cornill; Bright; Holladay), which is unnecessary. The prose in chaps. 21–45 is more out of chronological sequence than in sequence. Some commentators (Duhm; Cornill; Hyatt; Carroll) have also judged the present verses to be legend, having little or no historical value. But Peake early on (p. 179) called Duhm's view an "ingenious romance rest[ing] on no solid foundation," and he dismissed in similar fashion Cornill's view that the verses contained insignificant content. The views of Hyatt and Carroll make no advance over those of Duhm and Cornill. There is no basis whatsoever for calling this "legend." The present verses have as much claim to historical credibility as any other prose in chaps. 37–44. On the unlikelihood that the release here is a variant of the Jerusalem release (39:11–14), see the discussion on doublets in Rhetoric and Composition for 37:1–16. Rice (1975: 98) says the location of this segment is intentional, contrasting as it does a king who acted without faith and lost his life, with a servant who acted in faith and had his life preserved.

The three oracles to Ebed-melech are linked together by these key words:

I   *and they shall come to pass . . . in that day*   *wĕhāyû . . . bayyôm hahû'*   v 16
II   *. . . in that day*   *bayyôm-hahû'*   v 17
III *and . . . will be*   *wĕhāyĕtâ*   v 18

The phrase of v 16 is lacking in the LXX, but this is likely due to haplography (see Notes).

The narrative of Jeremiah's release in 40:1–6, except for v 6, was similarly judged as legendary by Duhm and Cornill, largely because of theological pronouncements by a foreigner in vv 2–3. But as Giesebrecht pointed out, theological judgments on the fall of Jerusalem are no indication of legend.

The narrative in 40:1–6 is bound together by an inclusio (cf. Abrego 1983a: 16; 1983b: 91):

amidst all the exiles . . . to Babylon . . . Nebuzaradan the Rab-tabahim let him go   v 1
bĕtôk kol-gālût . . . bābelâ . . . šallaḥ ʾōtô nĕbûzarʾădān rab-ṭabbāḥîm

the Rab-tabahim . . . let him go . . . amidst the people . . . in the land   vv 5b–6
rab-ṭabbāḥîm . . . yĕšallĕḥēhû . . . bĕtôk hāʿām . . . bāʾāreṣ

NOTES

39:15. *And to Jeremiah came the word of Yahweh.* A variation of the superscription in 40:1, with inverted syntax ("to Jeremiah" comes at the beginning). For other examples of this superscription type in the Jeremiah book, see Notes for 7:1 and 21:1.

when he was confined in the court of the guard. The LXX omits "when he was confined," which can be attributed to haplography (homoeoarcton: *b* . . . *b*). The words appear in Aq and Theod. This confinement was subsequent to Ebed-melech's rescue of Jeremiah from the pit (38:13).

16. *Go and you shall say to Ebed-melech, the Cushite.* Jeremiah's confinement in the court of the guard did not preclude him from having interaction with other people, as Bright and Thompson imagine. While there, Jeremiah had contact with people from both inside and outside the palace area (38:1). We also need not imagine with Carroll that Jeremiah had to go to the king's house to find Ebed-melech. The two could have met in the court of the guard (Cheyne).

Go and you shall say. Hebrew *hālôk wĕʾāmartâ.* A common verbal pairing in the Jeremiah prose (see Note for 28:13).

Ebed-melech, the Cushite. See Note for 38:7–8.

Yahweh of hosts, God of Israel. The LXX omits "of hosts," as elsewhere (see Appendix VI).

Look I am bringing my words to this city for evil and not for good. A foil for the good word to come; see also 1:14–19 and 45:4–5.

Look I am bringing. Hebrew *hinĕnî mēbî.* For this expression in the mouth of Yahweh, see elsewhere 5:15; 11:11; 19:3, 15; 31:8; 35:17; 45:5; and 49:5. The construction *hinĕnî* + participle is frequent in both poetry and prose, commonly beginning the Jeremianic oracle (see Note for 1:15). On "Look, I am bringing evil" in Jeremiah, see Note for 6:19. The Kt omission of the *ʾaleph* in the participle occurs also in 19:15 (cf. GKC §74k). The loss could be due to haplography.

for evil and not for good. Hebrew *lĕrāʿâ wĕlōʾ lĕṭôbâ* can also be rendered "for bad and not for good"; cf. 40:4. The same expression occurs in 21:10 and 44:27.

and they shall come to pass before you in that day. Ebed-melech will see with his own eyes the prophecy regarding Jerusalem fulfilled (Rashi; Kimḥi). The words are lacking in the LXX, and the *Tendenz* again with commentators has been to take "in that day" as a dittography from the beginning of v 17 (Peake; Cornill; Rudolph), or simply to omit the words on the *lectio brevior praeferenda est* principle (McKane). But what we likely have is another LXX haplography (homoeoarcton: *wh . . . wh*).

in that day. The term is future-oriented in Jeremiah, with the coming day now imminent. The day bringing judgment for Jerusalem will bring deliverance for Ebed-melech (v 17). On the Day of Yahweh, see Notes for 4:9 and 46:10.

17. *But I will rescue you.* Hebrew *wĕhiṣṣaltîkā*. Ebed-melech is promised rescue just as Jeremiah was (1:19; 15:20).

and you will not be given into the hand of the men before whom you are in dread. Jeremiah was given a similar promise by Zedekiah (38:16). The precise opposite was promised to Jehoiachin (22:25), where those giving him cause for dread (*yāgôr*) were the Babylonians. Rashi thinks Ebed-melech is also afraid of the Babylonians (they wield the sword in v 18), but Kimḥi and others believe it is the princes, of whom Jeremiah was afraid. When Ebed-melech rescued Jeremiah from the pit, he effectively undid an effort by the princes to do away with the prophet. Bright points out too that it was very bold of Ebed-melech, a palace servant, to charge the princes with a crime before the king (38:9). But Carroll may be right in saying that the princes will have fled or been killed on "that day," in which case it could not be them, but would have to be the new masters of Jerusalem, viz., the Babylonians.

18. *I will surely see to your escape.* The verb *mlṭ* in the Piel, when used transitively, means "save someone, allow to escape." When used intransitively, as in the word to Zedekiah (38:18), the meaning is "escape, save oneself" (KB³). The distinction has theological significance. Yahweh told Zedekiah that if he disobeyed the prophetic word he would not stand a chance in attempting his own escape. But Yahweh will assuredly see to Ebed-melech's escape, because he has trusted in Yahweh.

and your life will be your booty. For variations on this pithy remark, see 21:9; 38:2; and 45:5.

because you trusted in me. Trust is a precious commodity, and when placed in Yahweh, it brings blessing and makes the difference between salvation and damnation (see Note for 17:7). Trust placed in various deceptions (13:25; 28:15; 29:31), fortified cities (5:17), (false) individuals (9:3[Eng 9:4]; 17:5), unreliable allies (2:37), and even the Temple (7:4), becomes a mistaken trust.

40:1. *The word that came to Jeremiah from Yahweh.* On this superscription, see Notes for 7:1 and 21:1. Exactly why it appears here is unclear, since no oracle or oracles follow. Cornill's view that it cannot be original is largely beside the point because one is still left to explain its function now. The uneconomical view of Cheyne that a prophecy has been lost or moved to another place is scarcely more help. It could be that the superscription is meant to introduce oracles in the whole of chaps. 40–42 (Rashi), or chaps. 40–43 (Giesebrecht), in which case it has a more general function than usual. A better explanation is that the superscription introduces a divine word spoken to Jeremiah through Nebuzaradan (vv 2–3). Jones rightly points out that people other than Jeremiah are used to express the divine will. Josiah, for example, is faulted by the Chronicler for not having listened to words of Neco that came from the mouth of God (2 Chr 35:22).

after Nebuzaradan the Rab-tabahim let him go from Ramah when he got hold of him (for he was bound in chains amidst all the exiles of Jerusalem and Judah who were being exiled to Babylon). When Nebuzaradan and the Babylonian officials "got hold" (*lqḥ*) of Jeremiah in Jerusalem, it was for the purpose of releasing him and turning him over to Gedaliah (39:11–14). Now Nebuzaradan or subordinates are said to have "got hold" (*lqḥ*) of the prophet again, and we are told parenthetically that he was sitting enchained in Ramah awaiting exile to Babylon along with other prisoners. The Hebrew does not say that Jeremiah was brought to Ramah in chains, which is what the LXX says, due to its lack of "(and) he was bound" (LXX: "when he had taken him in chains . . ."). But the omitted words of the LXX appear in Aq and Symm. The LXX reading is reflected in the translations of NEB, REB, and NJV; but the T breaks after "when he got hold of him," which is correct. What follows is a parenthetical statement expanding upon Jeremiah's remand in or around Ramah. If Jeremiah arrived at Gedaliah's house in Mizpah, where he was to go (39:14), his capture and enchainment would not have occurred in Jerusalem, but rather somewhere between Mizpah and Ramah, which lie close to one another.

let him go. The meaning of *šlḥ* in the Piel, occurring again in v 5. This is the great Exodus word in Exod 4:21, 23; 5:1; et passim. Jeremiah's release doubtless had an impact on others who were not released, but were kept enchained for the trip to Babylon.

he was bound in chains. Hebrew *wĕhû'-'āsûr ba'ăziqqîm*. The LXX, as we just mentioned, lacks "(and) he was bound." On the pointing of the Kt *ba'ăziqqîm*, see §GKC 35d. According to v 4, the chains were on Jeremiah's hands. On the more usual custom of chaining prisoners' feet and binding their hands, see Note for 39:7.

Nebuzaradan the Rab-tabahim. Nebuchadrezzar's first-in-command; see Note for 39:9.

Ramah. A town just north of Jerusalem, usually identified with modern er-Ram, seven kilometers north of the city (E. Robinson 1874 I: 576), or else Ramallah, 12 kilometers north (*ABD* 5: 613). Ramah gained prominence in the period of the Judges, when Deborah and Samuel were associated with the place (Judg 4:5; 1 Sam 1:19; 7:17). More recently, Rachel has been heard weeping at Ramah for her children "because they are not" (Jer 31:15). Ramah, situated on the road leading north, is presently a holding place for exile-bound prisoners.

Jerusalem and. The LXX omits, which can be due to haplography (homoeo-arcton: *y . . . y*).

2–3. And the Rab-tabahim got hold of Jeremiah and said to him. The prefixed *lamed* on *lĕyirmĕyāhû* ("of Jeremiah") is unusual; the LXX simply has "him." This time, like the first (39:12–14), Nebuzaradan the Rab-tabahim "got hold" (*lqḥ*) of Jeremiah with good intention.

Yahweh your God spoke this evil toward this place. So Yahweh brought it about and did according to what he spoke. Indeed you sinned before Yahweh and did not obey his voice, so this thing happened to you. Here we have the unusual circumstance of Jeremiah being instructed by a Babylonian official in his own theology (Peake). Might a foreigner have spoken thus to Jeremiah, or is this simply a speech crafted by Baruch or someone else, corresponding little or not at all to what was actually said by Nebuzaradan to Jeremiah? Volz doubts that Nebuzaradan could have spoken such a judgment. Thiel (1981: 58) calls the language "Deuteronomistic," although it is precisely what one encounters elsewhere in the Jeremiah prose. The speech does have an interesting parallel, however, in the message sent earlier by the Rab-shakeh of Assyria to King Hezekiah (2 Kgs 18:19–25 = Isa 36:4–10), where Yahweh's name is heard on the lips of a foreigner, and Hezekiah is instructed on a reform he himself carried out. This individual, like the present Rab-tabahim, speaks as if he were a prophet (Calvin), claiming direct revelation from Yahweh and a mandate from Yahweh to go up against the land of Judah. Here in the present case it is unnecessary to ask whether Nebuzaradan had a proper understanding of Judah's sin or the covenant relationship. In a world of multiple religions, national gods, and universal beliefs that the actions of peoples and nations could passionately anger the gods, the statement of Nebuzaradan is eminently reasonable.

The shorter LXX reading in v 3 is not the result of multiple MT conflations (*pace* Janzen 1973: 22), but rather multiple LXX haplographies: 1) *wayyābē'*, "So he brought it about" (homoeoarcton: *wy . . . wy*); 2) *ka'ăšer dibbēr*, "according to what he spoke" (homoeoarcton: *k . . . k*); and 3) *wĕhāyâ lākem haddābār hazzeh*, "So this thing happened to you" (homoeoarcton: *w . . . w*). The second omission has been reckoned as an MT plus by Stipp (1997: 194) because the phrase is not reproduced by the LXX in 27:13 or 39:12. This last omission is countered by readings in Aq and Theod.

4–5. These verses are also abbreviated in the LXX. The omission of *wĕ'attâ* ("But now") can be due to haplography (homoeoteleuton: *h . . . h*). Omitted also is "today," which admits no obvious explanation but is better retained. Theodotion has the term. The main omission is "but if it seems bad in your eyes to go with me to Babylon, stay back. See, the whole land is before you; wherever it seems good and right in your eyes to go, go." This betrays a corrupt text, the result of which is an abbreviated LXX reading (it is not MT dittography, as Volz suggests). The LXX retains the following imperative, *lēk* ("go!"), and combines it with the imperative *wĕšūbâ* ("and [re]turn") in v 5, to read: "Go and return to Gedaliah . . ." (*apotreche kai anastrepson pros Godolian . . .*). The LXX omission of *wĕ'ôdennû lō'-yāšûb* ("And still he did not turn") can be attributed to haplography (homoeoarcton: *w . . . w*), however see below.

I will keep my eye upon you. The explicit command of Nebuchadrezzar (cf. 39:12). For the idiom "to keep one's eye upon someone," see Note for 39:12.

See, the whole land is before you; wherever it seems good and right in your eyes to go, go. The words "See, the whole land is before you" are echoes out of Israel's past. Abraham said these words to Lot at their parting of the ways (Gen 13:9); Yahweh said them to the aged Moses on the heights of Moab (Deut 34:1); and Yahweh promised the same to landless Israelites in the wilderness (Deut 1:8). All have parallels to the present situation: Nebuzaradan's words are parting words; they are spoken to someone well advanced in life, if not yet ready to die; and with the words go actual possession of the land, not just a look at it.

5. *And still he did not turn.* Hebrew *wĕʿôdennû lōʾ-yāšûb*. This phrase has been a problem for translators ancient and modern. The LXX, T, and Vg omit, and many modern commentators (Giesebrecht, Peake, Cornill, Rudolph, and Bright) take the text to be corrupt. The omission in the LXX is likely due to haplography (homoeoarcton: *w . . . w*), with the Hebrew being eminently readable. The noun with verbal suffix, *ʿôdennû*, occurs often in the OT, and its adverbial meaning, "still he," is not really in doubt (KB³; cf. GKC §100 o). Compare 33:1: "when he was still (*ʿôdennû*) confined in the court of the guard"; Gen 18:22: "and Abraham was still (*ʿôdennû*) standing before Yahweh"; Num 11:33: "the meat was still (*ʿôdennû*) between their teeth." See additionally 1 Sam 13:7 and 1 Kgs 12:2. This overly brief sentence, interrupting the speech of Nebuzaradan, speaks volumes. Jeremiah has been given the option of going with Nebuzaradan to Babylon where he will be well-cared for, or to go anywhere he chooses in the land of Judah. But being offered every possibility is like having no possibilities, so we see this newly freed man standing before Nebuzaradan, not turning, not moving, probably not speaking. McKane and others think *lōʾ-yāšûb* means "He did not return (an answer)." The phenomenon is well known not only among people, but among animals, birds, and fish newly released from captivity. For a brief moment they do not move; they do not know where to go. There is a certain irony here in the case of Jeremiah, who, in his earlier preaching so often had to tell other frightened souls to "get a move on" (4:6: "Set up a flag, to Zion take refuge! don't just stand there"; 8:14: "Why are we just sitting? Gather together! and let us enter the fortified cities"; and particularly 51:50: "You who have escaped from the sword: Go, don't just stand there!"). Now he himself is unable to move.

Either turn to Gedaliah son of Ahikam . . . or wherever it seems right in your eyes to go, go. Nebuzaradan resumes his speech to Jeremiah, giving him the options for staying in Judah. On the long form of the imperative *šūbâ* ("turn!" or "return!") before *ʾaleph*, see GKC §72s. "Return!" may actually be the correct rendering here if Jeremiah had already been at Gedaliah's house before the arrest leading to the present confinement. Holladay notes that Jeremiah was "given (*ntn*) to Gedaliah" in 39:14, and now is being "returned (*šûb*) to Gedaliah." Jeremiah decided finally to go to Gedaliah (v 6). According to Josephus (*Ant* x 158), Jeremiah urged Nebuzaradan before departing to release

Baruch, which he presumably did. Jeremiah and Baruch are together later at Geruth Chimham, near Bethlehem, where they are accused of collaborating to dissuade the group from going to Egypt (43:3). On Josephus's treatment of Jeremiah's release by Nebuzaradan and the Gedaliah governorship recorded in chaps. 40–41 and 2 Kgs 25:22–25, see Begg 1994.

cities of Judah. The LXX has *en gē*, "in the land," perhaps assuming that Judah had no cities remaining (Carroll; cf. 34:22). But Mizpah remained (see below), and there may have been others. The MT is supported by T ("cities of the house of Judah"), also Aq and Symm (*en tais polesin Iouda*).

and dwell with him amidst the people. Here the LXX adds "in the land of Judah."

an allowance and a present. Hebrew *'ărūḥâ ûmaś'ēt*. The allowance included food (52:34), although *maś'ēt* can also be food (Gen 43:34). The LXX reduces this phrase to a single term, *dōra* ("gifts"), but T ("gifts . . . and presents"), Symm (*estiatorian kai lēmma*, "an allowance of food and a gift"), and Vg (*cibaria et munuscula*, "rations and a small present") reflect the two terms of MT.

6. *Gedaliah son of Ahikam.* The LXX lacks "son of Ahikam," which is common—though not universal—in the LXX (Janzen 1973: 149). The patronym is included in v 5. On the seal impression from Lachish reading, "belonging to Gedaliah, the one who is over the house," see Note on 39:14.

Mizpah. Occurring nearly always with the article (*hammiṣpâ* = "the watch-tower"), this Mizpah is the important Benjaminite town where Samuel judged (1 Sam 7:15–16) and Saul was elected king (1 Sam 10:17–24). Now it is the capital of a Neo-Babylonian province. The OT knows also a "Mizpah / Mizpeh" in Gilead (Judg 10:17; 11:29), a "Mizpeh of Moab" (1 Sam 22:3), and "the Mizpeh" in Judah's Shephelah district (Josh 15:38). For nearly a century, Benjaminite Mizpah was believed to be Nebi Samwil, an imposing tell ca. five miles north of Jerusalem (E. Robinson 1874 I: 460), but now identification is commonly made with Tell en-Naṣbeh, an eight-acre site eight miles north of Jerusalem on the Nablus Road, excavated by William Badè between 1926 and 1935 (McCown 1947; Muilenburg 1947a; 1955; idem, "Mizpah" in *IDB* K–Q, 407–9). On the Albright-Muilenburg debate over Nebi Samwil and Tell en-Naṣbeh, argued on the basis of topography, geography, and details provided here in Jeremiah 40–41, see G. E. Wright 1947: 76–77. Holladay in his commentary continues to favor Nebi Samwil, repeating the Albright arguments in support of the site. But the Muilenburg argument that Mizpah has to be on the main north–south road favors Tell en-Naṣbeh. Excavations at Tell en-Naṣbeh (*lmlk* jar handles) show that Mizpah was probably the northern limit of Judah in the seventh century B.C. (McCown 1947: 160; Stager 1975: 247). According to 2 Kgs 23:8, Josiah's kingdom extended "from Geba to Beersheba," Geba (modern Jeba) being a neighboring town to Mizpah, six miles north-northeast of Jerusalem (1 Kgs 15:22; cf. Lance 1971: 332). The Tell en-Naṣbeh excavations have been subsequently reevaluated by J. Zorn (1993; 1997; *OEANE* 4: 101–3; *NEAEHL* 3: 1098–1102), who revises the stratigraphy and redates, with the result that a Babylonian stratum (Zorn's Stratum 2) is now identified. There was not a destruction at the end of Iron II (ca. 586 B.C.), which correlates with the narrative here that Mizpah became a Babylonian provincial center after Jerusalem was destroyed. This particular conclusion had been reached earlier (G. E. Wright 1947: 70). The Iron II town was protected by a casemate wall, and many buildings, with modifications, continued in use after 586 B.C. Fragments of contemporary dwellings and agricultural areas were also uncovered outside the town wall. In the Babylonian period newer, different, and more spacious dwellings replaced buildings that preceded.

MESSAGE AND AUDIENCE

This narrative segment is an epilogue of sorts: the promise of rescue to Ebed-melech and the report of Jeremiah's second release at Ramah, reducing the shock of Jerusalem's fall and completing Jeremiah's release that first took place at the court of the guard. Baruch, if he is the narrator, has appended the promise of rescue to Ebed-melech for perhaps the same reason he appended the promise of his own rescue in chap. 45. For post-586 B.C. audiences in both Mizpah and Babylon, Jeremiah's release at Ramah concludes on an upbeat note a first edition of the present narrative collection, just as Jehoiachin's release will later conclude on an upbeat note chap. 52 and the final Jeremiah book.

Ebed-melech's rescue is announced in three divine oracles. Ebed-melech with his own eyes will see fulfilled on the day of Yahweh the judgment prophecy against Jerusalem, but he himself will be rescued on that day. Ebed-melech will not fall into the hands of those he fears; his rescue is assured because he trusted in Yahweh.

In the second portion of the present narrative segment, the audience is told about a most unusual word from Yahweh that came to Jeremiah after his release at Ramah. It came via the Rab-tabahim, who spoke like a prophet—a Yahweh prophet, no less—telling him that Yahweh had decreed this evil against Jerusalem because the nation failed to obey his voice. Not news, particularly, to Jeremiah, but surely a different message from the one Zedekiah must have heard from Nebuchadrezzar at Riblah! In any case, Nebuzaradan released Jeremiah from his chains, and gave him the option of coming to Babylon where he would be looked after, or else of staying back. The whole land was laid out before Jeremiah; he could go anywhere. But Jeremiah stood motionless. Nebuzaradan then told him either to go to Gedaliah, where he may already have been before his arrest, or to a place of his own choosing. As a parting gesture, Nebuzaradan gave Jeremiah an allowance of food and a present, and let him go. Jeremiah then went to Gedaliah at Mizpah, the new provincial center, and resided with the people there.

The audience may not have missed the language and symbolism of the moment. For Jeremiah this was an "exodus" and gift of the land all in one, which contained unmistakable implications for the nation in future days. The only hope now for the covenant people was a new Exodus from Babylon and a return to the land. The latter had already been symbolized in Jeremiah's purchase of the field in Anathoth (chap. 32). The audience would also have seen in Jeremiah's release a further fulfillment of Yahweh's promise that the prophet's life would be spared.

When this passage is heard in tandem with what precedes, Ebed-melech's trust in Yahweh will be contrasted with a lack of the same on the part of Zedekiah. Because of this, Ebed-melech's life will be spared. The oracles to Ebed-melech date to the time of Jeremiah's final confinement in the court of the guard. This report of their delivery, together with the report of Jeremiah's release at Ramah, can be dated sometime after the fall of Jerusalem in 586 B.C.

Ebed-melech, together with Baruch, lived on in the pseudepigraphical work, *Paraleipomena Jeremiou (ParJer)*, on which see Message and Audience for 38:7–13. In this work, the two confidants of Jeremiah are reported as having buried the prophet after he was stoned.

VI. Turn and Take Your Journey— to Egypt! (40:7–44:30)

◆

A. Buildup and Breakdown at Mizpah (40:7–41:18)

1. Resettlement under Gedaliah (40:7–12)

40 ⁷Then all the princes of the troops who were in the field—they and their men—heard that the king of Babylon had appointed Gedaliah son of Ahikam in the land, and that he had appointed to be with him men, and women, and small children, and some of the poor of the land from those who had not been exiled to Babylon. ⁸So they went to Gedaliah at Mizpah: Ishmael son of Nethaniah, Johanan and Jonathan sons of Kareah, Seraiah son of Tanhumeth, the sons of Ephai¹ the Netophathite, and Jezaniah son of the Maacathite, they and their men. ⁹And Gedaliah son of Ahikam, son of Shaphan, swore to them and to their men, saying: 'Do not be afraid of serving the Chaldeans; dwell in the land and serve the king of Babylon, that it may go well with you. ¹⁰As for me, look I am dwelling in Mizpah to stand before the Chaldeans who will come to us. As for you, gather wine, summer fruit, and oil, and put into your jars, and dwell in your cities that you have seized.' ¹¹Even all the Judahites who were in Moab, and among the Ammonites, and in Edom, and who were in all the other lands heard that the king of Babylon had given a remnant to Judah and that he had appointed over them Gedaliah son of Ahikam, son of Shaphan. ¹²So all the Judahites returned from all the places where they had been dispersed and came to the land of Judah, to Gedaliah at Mizpah. And they gathered wine and summer fruit in great quantity.

2. The Plot against Gedaliah (40:13–16)

40 ¹³Then Johanan son of Kareah and all the princes of the troops who were in the field came to Gedaliah at Mizpah, ¹⁴and they said to him, 'Do you indeed know that Baalis, king of the Ammonites, has sent Ishmael son of Nethaniah to strike you down?' But Gedaliah son of Ahikam did not believe them. ¹⁵Then Johanan son of Kareah said to Gedaliah in secret at

---

¹Reading the Q with S and T; Kt spelling is "Ophai," which is followed by LXX and Vg.

Mizpah: 'Do let me go and strike down Ishmael son of Nethaniah, and no one will know. Why should he strike a person down and all the Judahites who are gathered about you be scattered, and the remnant of Judah perish?' [16]But Gedaliah son of Ahikam said to Johanan son of Kareah, 'Do not do[2] this thing, for you are speaking a lie about Ishmael.'

3. The Murder of Gedaliah (41:1–3)

41 [1]And it happened in the seventh month, Ishmael son of Nethaniah, son of Elishama, of royal descent and one of the chief officers of the king, came with ten men to Gedaliah son of Ahikam at Mizpah, and they ate food together there at Mizpah. [2]Then Ishmael son of Nethaniah got up, also the ten men who were with him, and they struck down Gedaliah son of Ahikam, son of Shaphan, with the sword. So he killed him, whom the king of Babylon had appointed in the land. [3]And all the Judahites who were with him, that is, Gedaliah, at Mizpah, and the Chaldeans who were found there, that is, the fighting men, Ishmael struck down.

4. Arrivals from the North (41:4–6)

41 [4]And it happened on the day after the killing of Gedaliah, when no one knew, [5]that men came from Shechem, from Shiloh, and from Samaria— 80 men, beards shaven, clothes torn, and self-inflicted slashes—with cereal offering and frankincense in their hand to bring to the house of Yahweh. [6]And Ishmael son of Nethaniah went out from Mizpah to meet them, weeping as he was walking. And it happened as he met them that he said to them, 'Come to Gedaliah son of Ahikam.'

5. Another Round of Violence (41:7–10)

[7]And it happened as they came into the midst of the city that Ishmael son of Nethaniah—he, and the men who were with him—slaughtered them and cast them[3] into the midst of the cistern. [8]But ten men were found with them who said to Ishmael, 'Don't kill us, for we have hidden stores in the field—wheat, barley, oil, and honey. So he held back, and did not kill them amidst their brothers. [9]Now the cistern into which Ishmael cast all the corpses of the men whom he struck down because of Gedaliah—it was the one that King Asa made on account of Baasha, king of Israel. Ishmael son of Nethaniah filled it with the slain. [10]Then Ishmael took captive the entire remnant of the people who were in Mizpah—the daughters of the king, and all the other people who remained in Mizpah, over whom Nebuzaradan the Rab-tabahim had appointed Gedaliah son of Ahikam. And

---

[2]The short form of the Kt, *ta'aś*, often occurs with the preposition *'al*. The Q is *ta'ăśēh*. On the spellings, see GKC §75hh.

[3]Supplying with G[VL] and S "and he cast them," which is lacking in MT; cf. v 9.

Ishmael son of Nethaniah took them captive and went to cross over to the Ammonites.

6. Rescue at the Pool of Gibeon (41:11–15)

41 ¹¹Then Johanan son of Kareah and all the princes of the troops who were with him heard all the evil that Ishmael son of Nethaniah had done, ¹²and they took all the men and went to fight with Ishmael son of Nethaniah, and they found him by the great pool that was in Gibeon. ¹³And it happened as all the people who were with Ishmael saw Johanan son of Kareah and all the princes of the troops who were with him that they were glad. ¹⁴So all the people whom Ishmael had taken captive from Mizpah turned about, and returning they went over to Johanan son of Kareah. ¹⁵And Ishmael son of Nethaniah escaped with eight men from before Johanan, and went over to the Ammonites.

7. On to Geruth Chimham! (41:16–18)

41 ¹⁶Then Johanan son of Kareah and all the princes of the troops who were with him took the entire remnant of the people whom he recovered from Ishmael son of Nethaniah, from Mizpah, after he struck down Gedaliah son of Ahikam: men, fighting men, and women, and small children, and eunuchs, whom he brought back from Gibeon. ¹⁷And they went and dwelt at Geruth Chimham,[4] which is near Bethlehem, going to enter Egypt ¹⁸because of the Chaldeans, for they were afraid of them, for Ishmael son of Nethaniah had struck down Gedaliah son of Ahikam, whom the king of Babylon had appointed in the land.

RHETORIC AND COMPOSITION

MT 40:7–41:18 = LXX 47:7–48:18. The narrative continues in segments, only now the repeated phrases come at the beginning. Seven segments are clustered in 40:7–41:18, where the key phrases are *wĕkol-śārê haḥăyālîm* ("Then / and all the princes of the troops"), and *wayĕhî* ("And it happened"). These same phrases—along with another—give structure to the segments in chap. 42. The key phrases here:

I	*Then . . . all the princes of the troops . . .*	*wa . . . kol-śārê haḥăyālîm*	40:7
II	*. . . and all the princes of the troops . . .*	*wĕkol-śārê haḥăyālîm*	40:13
III	*And it happened . . .*	*wayĕhî*	41:1
IV	*And it happened . . .*	*wayĕhî*	41:4
V	*And it happened . . .*	*wayĕhî*	41:7
VI	*. . . and all the princes of the troops . . .*	*wĕkol-śārê haḥăyālîm*	41:11
VII	*. . . and all the princes of the troops . . .*	*wĕkol-śārê haḥăyālîm*	41:16

---

[4]Reading with many MSS and the Q; Kt unclear.

The middle segment (IV) also ends with an "And it happened" statement (v 6b), which could be significant. Some commentators (Rudolph; Weiser; Hyatt; Carroll; Jones) have already delimited 40:7–41:18 as a unit, perhaps because the verses cover Gedaliah's governorship at Mizpah. Bright takes the verses as part of a larger segment, 40:7–43:7, which was delimited by Duhm. Although abbreviated versions of 40:7–9 and 41:1–3 occur in 2 Kgs 25:23–25, Thiel (1981: 61) finds nothing in 40:7–41:18 indicating "Deuteronomic" redactional work, a conclusion reached earlier by Hyatt.

The Hebrew here is awkward in places, e.g., unusual syntax, uncommon use of *'el* to mean "by" or "about," verbs doubled up, synonyms juxtaposed, elliptical and parenthetical expressions, in addition to which there are numerous differences between MT and LXX. Many of the latter are minor, e.g., the LXX omission of names and patronyms, changing of pronouns, changing from singular to plural, and vice versa. With few exceptions, the LXX preserves a shorter text than MT, which is usual. The majority of LXX omissions can be attributed to haplography, but for those that cannot be, *a priori* decisions in favor of the shorter LXX text (e.g., McKane p. 996) will not do. It is not simply a question of LXX abridgment, which in some cases cannot be ruled out, but more often of a longer MT reading due to prolix Hebrew style or a poorly preserved Hebrew *Vorlage* to the LXX.

The present narrative is full of detail, and what textual infelicities there are bear little or not at all on the question of Baruch authorship, which has been argued for 40:7–41:18 by Duhm, Volz, Bright, Holladay, and others. Holladay says this narrative has all the marks of an eyewitness account, which it does. Hyatt and Jones, following N. Schmidt (*EncBib* 2: 2386), judge 40:7–41:18 to be from a source other than Baruch, with Hyatt noting that the verses make no mention of Jeremiah. Baruch's work is limited by Hyatt to chaps. 1–39, for which 1:1–3 is an introduction. The nonmention of Jeremiah is cited often by commentators, although few assign it the importance Carroll and McKane do. That Jeremiah does not figure in these verses is of no importance, really, unless one assumes a narrative where mention of the prophet must be made at every turn. Nothing is said of Jeremiah in the report of Jerusalem's fall (39:1–10). The present verses are a setup for chap. 42, where Jeremiah's mediation must be sought following the Gedaliah tragedy and events that occurred in its aftermath.

The narrative proceeds chronologically, although events have been compressed as in chap. 1. At 40:13 is likely a four-year interval following the joyful harvest of 40:12 (see Note for 41:1), which allows time for a rebuilding phase at Mizpah, for Gedaliah to be the "one over the house" (see Note on 39:14), and for Gedaliah's murder to be correlated with Nebuzaradan's return to Judah in 582 B.C. (52:30; see Note for 41:1).

The present cluster is tied together by the following inclusio:

40:7   . . . *the king of Babylon had appointed Gedaliah son of Ahikam in the land . . .*

41:18   . . . *Gedaliah son of Ahikam, whom the king of Babylon had appointed in the land.*

This cluster is delimited additionally by a *setumah* in M^L, and a *petuḥah* in M^A and M^P, before 40:7, and by a *petuḥah* in M^A and M^P, and a *setumah* in M^L, after 41:18. All the segments but one, 41:1–3, have corroborating section markings. But *BHS* breaks after 41:3, and is followed by the RSV, JB, NAB, NJV, NIV, and NSB. The seven segments and their corroborating sections are the following:

40:7–12 M^L and M^P have a *petuḥah* and M^A a *setumah* after 40:12
40:13–16 M^L has a *setumah* and M^A and M^P a *petuḥah* after 40:16; also chapter division
41:1–3   No section after 41:3
41:4–6 M^L only has a *setumah* after 41:6
41:7–10 M^A and M^L have a *setumah* and M^P a *petuḥah* after 41:10
41:11–15 M^A, M^L, and M^P all have a *setumah* after 41:15.
41:16–18 M^A and M^P have a *petuḥah* and M^L a *setumah* after 41:18.

NOTES

40:7. Most modern Versions translate with Vg and AV as a dependent clause: "(Now) when all the princes of the troops . . . ," but the verse reads better as an independent sentence (NJV; NSB).

the princes of the troops. Hebrew *śārê haḥăyālîm*; cf. *śar haṣṣābā* ("prince of the army") in 52:25. These are probably former officers of Judah's army that managed to avoid capture by the Babylonians. On the translation of "princes" for *śārîm*, see Note for 24:1.

in the field. Hebrew *baśśādeh.* This is usually taken to mean "in the open country" (Deut 22:25), but Kimḥi says the meaning here is "in the villages" (cf. v 10b). We are talking in any case about the hill country north of Jerusalem, where Babylonian penetration was minimal, community life was least disrupted, and a new social and political reality is now developing with indigenous leaders taking control of inhabitable towns and villages (Lipschits 1998: 474).

the king of Babylon had appointed Gedaliah. Some modern Versions (RSV; NEB; JB; NIV) here and in 41:18 follow the AV in translating *pqd* as "made governor."

and that he had appointed to be with him men, and women, and small children, and some of the poor of the land from those who had not been exiled to Babylon. The H-stem of *pqd* can also mean "hand over to" or "commit into the care of," which occurs in one of the Arad Inscriptions (24:15) where a certain Malchiah is instructed to hand over 50 [men] to the care of one Elisha (Aharoni 1981: 46–49). On the frequency of *pqd* in Jeremiah, see Note for 5:9. The LXX omits "and small children, and some of the poor of the land from those," which is more loss by haplography (homoeoteleuton: *m . . . m*), not MT expansion (*pace* Janzen 1973: 53; Holladay). Theodotion has the omitted words; Aq and Symm have *kai ta nēpia . . .* ("and the young children . . ."). Many of the modern Versions (RSV; NEB; NJV; NIV; NRSV; REB) take "men, and women, and small children" as constituting "the poor of the land," but in T the poor are a separate category (*ûmiddalat* = "*and* some of the poor"). This latter reading, which is found in Calvin, the AV, and other modern Versions (JB; NAB; NJB), is the correct one. There were the poor, and others besides the poor left in the land (41:10, 16; 43:6).

8. *Ishmael son of Nethaniah.* A man of royal descent (41:1) who will emerge as the chief rival to Gedaliah for control of the nascent Mizpah community. The names "Ishmael" and "Nethaniah" occur elsewhere in the Bible (Gen 16:15–16; Jer 36:14), and are attested on extrabiblical seals, bullae, ostraca, and inscriptions (see Appendix I).

Johanan and Jonathan sons of Kareah. Johanan will emerge as the other prominent leader in the narrative to follow. "And Jonathan" is lacking in a few MSS, the LXX, T Codex Reuchlinianus (T^f), and 2 Kgs 25:23, all of which can be due to haplography (homoeoteleuton: *n . . . n*), according to Rudolph (cf. *BHS*). "Jonathan" is translated in the AV, but omitted in the RSV, JB (but restored in NJB), NAB, and NRSV. There is scant basis for treating the name as a false doublet of Johanan (*pace* Cornill; Volz), or for assuming MT conflation (*pace* Janzen 1973: 17; Holladay). In the subsequent narrative Jonathan is not mentioned, but that may simply result from being eclipsed by his more prominent brother, who, before the narrative is concluded, will have eclipsed everyone else as well. "Jonathan" is a familiar biblical name (1 Samuel 14). "Kareah" (*qārēaḥ*), vocalized Korah (*qōraḥ*), is well known in the Bible because of the Levitical Temple singers (Psalms 42, 44–49; 2 Chr 20:19), and is attested also outside the Bible (see "Johanan ben Kareah" in Appendix I).

Seraiah son of Tanhumeth. Mentioned in 2 Kgs 25:23, but someone not heard of again in the subsequent narrative. For "Seraiah," see Note on 51:59 and Appendix I. "Tanhumeth" occurs as "Tanhum" on the Arad ostraca, on a bulla from Tell Beit Mirsim, and elsewhere (see Appendix I).

the sons of Ephai the Netophathite. This is the only reference in the OT to these individuals, although their omission in 2 Kgs 25:23 may result from scribal error, since in that listing Seraiah son of Tanhumeth becomes "the Netophathite." The name "Ephai" has shown up on two seventh-century tomb inscriptions from Khirbet el-Qom (see Appendix I). Netophah was in the general vicinity of Bethlehem (Neh 7:26; 1 Chr 2:54), located earlier at Beit Nettif, east of Bethlehem (Cornill; Peake), but now commonly identified with Khirbet badd faluh, halfway between Bethlehem and Tekoa (Alt 1932: 12; Kob 1932: 52–54; Rudolph; Holladay). Nearby the latter site is a spring called ʿAin en-Natuf, which preserves the biblical name ("Netophah" in *IDB* K–Q, 541). According to Neh 12:28 and 1 Chr 9:16, Netophathites inhabited more than one village.

Jezaniah son of the Maacathite. I.e., Jezaniah the Maacathite (see Note for 41:11). In 2 Kgs 25:23 the name is spelled "Jaazaniah." This fellow, of whom there is also no subsequent mention in the narrative, was a foreigner like Doeg the Edomite (1 Sam 21:7) or Uriah the Hittite (2 Sam 11:3), now resident in Judah. The Maacathites inhabited the mountainous and heavily wooded north Transjordan area between Gilead and Mt. Hermon. Along with the Geshurites, who lived to the south, they were not driven out by the Israelites after Moses' conquest of Og, king of Bashan (Deut 3:14; Josh 12:5; 13:11, 13; cf. Mazar 1961: 16–17). Early Israelite tradition reckoned Maacah to be a son of Nahor, Abraham's brother, by a concubine, Reumah (Gen 22:24). Currently, Maacath is a district of Syria. An onyx seal with a fighting cock and inscribed, "Belonging to Jaazaniah, servant of the king," was found in a sixth-century B.C. tomb at Tell en-Naṣbeh. In the view of Badè, the excavator, it very likely belonged to the Jezaniah mentioned here (Badè 1933; 1934: 75–77; fig. 13; McCown 1947: 8–9, 118, 163; pl. 57, ##4 and 5; *ANEP*^{2} 85 #277). The Jaazaniah of this seal may, like Ishmael, have belonged to Jerusalem's royal house, although May (1939: 146–47) argued that "servant of the king" meant that Jaazaniah was proclaiming himself a servant of the exiled Jehoiachin, which would have met with Babylonian approval. Others individuals named "Jaazaniah / Jezaniah" are mentioned in the book of Jeremiah (35:3; 42:1 MT), and the name is attested on the Lachish and Arad ostraca and on other contemporary seals and bullae (see Appendix I).

9. *And Gedaliah . . . swore to them and to their men.* An oath may have been necessary if the men feared betrayal to the Babylonians; thus far they have evaded capture, but Gedaliah could turn them in.

'*Do not be afraid of serving the Chaldeans; dwell in the land and serve the king of Babylon, that it may go well with you.*' This advice, in the familiar language of Deuteronomy, is essentially what Jeremiah gave to Judahites in Babylon after their exile of 597 B.C. (29:5–7). On the phrase "that it may go well with you," see Note for 7:23. The LXX's *tōn paidōn* ("the servants") supports the reading of 2 Kgs 25:24, "Do not be afraid of the Chaldean servants (*mēʿabdê hakkaśdîm*)," which reduces the Chaldean officials, like King Nebuchadrezzar, to instruments in the hand of Yahweh (cf. 25:9; 27:6; 43:10). Readings of Aq (*mē phobeisthe tou douleuein tois Chaldaiois*) and Symm (*mē phobeisthe douleuein tois Chaldaiois*) support the MT.

10. *As for me, look I am dwelling in Mizpah to stand before the Chaldeans who will come to us.* After "I am dwelling," the LXX adds *enantion hymōn* ("before you"), and instead of "who will come to us" has "who will come against you." The latter reading, which finds support in Aq and Symm (*pros hymas*), implies that Gedaliah anticipates having to mediate between these battle-ready princes and the Babylonian occupational forces. The expression "to stand before" (*laʿămōd lipnê*) means "to be in the service of" (see Note for 15:19). Gedaliah's role as governor is to serve the Babylonians and represent his own people before them.

As for you, gather wine, summer fruit, and oil, and put into your jars. Jerusalem fell in the fourth month (July), and now in the fifth or sixth month (August or September) grapes, figs, olives, pomegranates, dates, and mulberries have been harvested or are ready to harvest (see Note on 8:20). The Babylonians left some vineyards and orchards intact (Lipschits 1998: 475). The question here is whether the people are being told to harvest fruit in the field, which is the usual interpretation, or to gather someone else's harvest that has been processed and is now stored away, in which case their vessels will then be filled with wine (*yayin*), not grapes, summer fruit that is already dried, and olive oil (*šemen*), not olives (cf. Josh 7:11). One can "gather" in a literal sense summer fruit (48:32; Mic 7:1), but can one "gather" wine and oil? Cheyne argued that *yayin* originally meant cluster of grapes, as its Arabic cognate does (cf. KB³), but there is still the problem of *šemen*, which can only mean (olive) oil. McKane says that the reference here is not to harvesting per se, but to the appropriation of produce already harvested and stored by people who have since been displaced. He notes that T has "fig cake" (*dbl*) instead of "summer fruit" (*qayiṣ*), which makes all three fruits of a processed nature. He may be right. We see hidden stores of wheat, barley, oil, and honey being surrendered to Ishmael in 41:8. But "gather" (*'sp*) could also mean "harvest" in a broad sense. Jeremiah is seen elsewhere to expand the harvesting imagery to include people (5:10; 8:13). Also, the joy commonly perceived as being hidden behind the words of v 12 points to a better than usual ingathering from orchards and vineyards, not the "thieving" operation McKane envisions. See also Duhm's comment on v 12 below.

'*and dwell in your cities that you have seized.*' The Babylonians did not reduce every city to rubble, and of those that remained some have now reverted to local rule. Duhm and Volz take the perfect verb *tĕpaśtem* as a *futurum exactum*: "you will have seized" (GKC §106 o), which puts the possession of the cities in the future. Cheyne believes the cities are not yet taken because the leaders with their men are still in the open country. We are probably talking, in any case, about cities north of Jerusalem, which archaeological excavations show to have largely escaped Babylonian destruction (Lipschits 1998: 474–75). The LXX has "in the cities" for MT's "in your cities."

11–12. We learn here that people fled to neighboring Transjordan countries when Babylon invaded Judah. Now they are returning to join the community at Mizpah. This return could be taken as a fulfillment of earlier prophecy— both judgment and restoration (8:3; 16:14–15; 23:3, 7–8; 24:9; 29:14, 18; 32:37)—but if so, that fulfillment will be short-lived.

and who were in all the other lands. Hebrew *wa'ăšer bĕkol-hā'ărāṣôt*. The expression *bĕkol-hā'ărāṣôt* must be read "in all the *other* lands"; compare *kol-hā'ām*, "all the *other* people," in 41:10. The LXX has *kai hoi en pasē tē gē* ("and those in all the land"), the reference of which appears to be (greater) Judah. Aquila has *kai en pasais tais gaiais* ("and in all the countries"). Read the MT.

So all the Judahites returned from all the places where they had been dispersed. The LXX omits, but this can be attributed to haplography (homoeoarcton: *wy . . . wy*). Variations of the phrase "from all the places / lands where they had been dispersed" occur twelve times in Jeremiah (8:3; 16:15; 23:3, 8; 24:9; 29:14, 18; 30:11 [*pûṣ*]; 32:37; 40:12; 43:5; and 46:28), of which five, says Janzen (1973: 53), are omitted in the LXX. But Janzen incorrectly states that the entire sentence occurs twelve times; in fact, only part of the sentence does, and the phraseology varies (e.g., the verb in 30:11 is *pûṣ*, not *ndḥ*).

And they gathered wine and summer fruit in great quantity. Duhm comments: "Es war ein gutes Jahr; die Anfang liess sich für die neue Kolonie gut

an, Jer muss seine Freude daran gehabt haben [It was a good year; the beginning started well for the new colony, and Jeremiah must have had joy in it]."
Was this another early but short-lived fulfillment of prophecy (cf. 32:15)?

great quantity. Hebrew *harbēh mĕʾōd.* The expression is a superlative: it was
a grand harvest.

14. *'Do you indeed know that Baalis, king of the Ammonites, has sent Ishmael
son of Nethaniah to strike you down?'* The Ammonites were present at the Jerusalem conference in 594–593 B.C., when the talk was rebellion against Babylon
(27:3), and it is possible that the Baalis mentioned here was king of Ammon at
the time; otherwise it was his predecessor, ʿAmminadab II (Tell Sīrān Bottle Inscription dated to ca. 600 B.C.; see the Cross "Ammonite King List" in Herr
1985: 171, revised from Cross 1973b; Stern 2001: 238–40; *CS II* 139). The
planned rebellion, in any case, came to nothing, and Baalis may now want to
settle the score with those who opposed it. Jeremiah spoke out against the plan
(27:2–11), and perhaps it was opposed also by Gedaliah, now the Babylonian
appointee at Mizpah. Thus the plot against Gedaliah by Baalis, who, according to Josephus (*Ant* x 160), had designs of his own to rule Judah. Ammonite
opposition to the Babylonians continued. Nebuchadnezzar threatened Ammon (Ezek 21:23–32[Eng 21:18–27]) when he returned to the area in 588 B.C.,
going instead to attack Judah. And when Edom made common cause with the
Babylonians in destroying the Jerusalem Temple (Obad 9–14; Ezek 25:12–14;
35:15; Ps 137:7), there is no indication that Ammon joined in. Finally, when
Zedekiah was caught near Jericho, it is quite possible he was heading for safe
haven in Ammon, as Ishmael will now do shortly (41:15). Ammon, therefore,
will be solidly opposed to a Babylonian presence in the area, and it is not hard
to imagine why Baalis might sponsor this plot against Gedaliah. According to
Josephus (*Ant* x 181–82), Nebuchadnezzar marched against Ammon in 582
B.C. and brought the nation into subjection. This would have been punishment for its disloyalty in 594 B.C., and the role it is now playing in disrupting
community life at Mizpah. An Ammonite bulla discovered in 1984 at Tell el-
ʿUmeiri, about eight miles southwest of Amman, names this Ammonite king as
"Baʿalyišaʿ" or "Baʿalyašaʿ" (D. N. Freedman: "Baal has saved"; cf. Herr 1985;
Younker 1985; *ABD* 1: 195; *OEANE* 1: 104). Herr dates the bulla to ca. 600 B.C.

has sent. The LXX adds *pros se* ("to you"), which Holladay says may reflect
the omission of *ʾēleykā* in MT. If so, the loss could be attributed to haplography
(homoeoarcton: *ʾaleph . . . ʾaleph*).

to strike you down. I.e., to take your life. Hebrew *lĕhakkōtĕkā nāpeš.* This
forceful idiom, not easily rendered into English, occurs again in v 15. See also
Gen 37:21 and GKC §117 ll.

But Gedaliah son of Ahikam did not believe them. Gedaliah is often portrayed as a high-minded person who, although somewhat naïve, was nevertheless above rumor. But such a view is predicated on the questionable
assumption that Johanan, the other main player in the narrative and the one
being contrasted with Ishmael, was an upstanding person. In actual fact, Johanan was himself a man of dubious character. This can be seen in the proposal

he now makes to kill Ishmael secretly. Gedaliah cannot condone that, nor should anyone. As the narrative goes on to state, Johanan was as insolent as all the rest, and subsequently accused Jeremiah of lying and collaborating with Baruch when, in fact, the prophet had reported to him a word from Yahweh (43:2–3). Gedaliah—although later events proved him dreadfully wrong—acts reasonably in the present situation by not believing Johanan, who is spokesman for the group claiming a plot by Ishmael. Johanan in his charge against Ishmael could have been acting with just as much self-interest as Ishmael.

15. *and no one will know.* Can Gedaliah believe such a thing? Someone will surely find out, and then Gedaliah will be in deep trouble for permitting such a thing to happen.

'*Why should he strike a person down and all the Judahites who are gathered about you be scattered, and the remnant of Judah perish?*' A rhetorical question, the answer to which is "No reason at all that he should!" For a similar question beginning with *lāmmâ* ("Why?"), see Gen 27:45.

16. '*Do not do this thing, for you are speaking a lie about Ishmael.*' Gedaliah was right about not allowing Johanan to murder Ishmael in secret, but was proven wrong in disbelieving Johanan about the plot on his life. Hebrew *šeqer* ("lie") occurs often in Jeremiah (see Note on 5:2).

41:1. *And it happened in the seventh month.* This would be September–October (= Tishri), but of what year we know not. Most likely the narrative has telescoped Gedaliah's reign into two or three months: Jerusalem falls in July (39:2), summer fruits are harvested in August–September (40:12), and now in September–October, just after Gedaliah is murdered, pilgrims arrive from the north to mark the Feast of Booths (41:4–5; cf. Exod 23:16b; Deut 16:13–15). The telescoping is greater yet in 2 Kgs 25:24–25, but with less detail, it is less obvious. Jones says of the event to be reported: "The narrator understands that this is three months after the fall of Jerusalem (cf. 39:2)," which may be going too far, but there are scholars who nevertheless accept this chronology (Volz; Rudolph; Holladay; Begg 1994: 31). Others (Grätz 1870; 1875: 415; Hyatt; Boadt; Hayes and Hooker 1988: 98) take the Gedaliah plot and murder to have occurred three or four years later, which makes considerably more sense, since the murder can then be correlated with Nebuzardan's return to Judah in 582 B.C., at which time he took more exiles to Babylon (52:30). The "seventh month" then is not in the same year as the "fourth month" of 39:2. If the *via dolorosa* prose originally concluded at 40:6, as I have argued, then the chronological scheme in the expanded version (chaps. 37–44) is secondary.

Ishmael son of Nethaniah, son of Elishama, of royal descent and one of the chief officers of the king. Here is given a fuller description of the individual introduced in 40:8, now shown to be a rival who wants to do away with Gedaliah. The added information, given also in 2 Kgs 25:25, helps us understand why. Ishmael was a member of Jerusalem's royal house, in the Davidic line, who entertained ambitions of his own about ruling Judah's remnant community. He probably resented Gedaliah's appointment, in that Gedaliah was from the Shaphan scribal family and not in the Davidic line (Peake; Lipschits 1998:

482). Boadt rightly notes the tension existing between the Shaphan family and the royal family in Jehoiakim's time (chaps. 26 and 36; see also Note for 36:12). A contemporary seal impression of unknown provenance has turned up with the inscription "Belonging to Ishmael, the king's son," which may possibly derive from the individual named here (Barkay 1993). Malamat (1999: 37) thinks that Ishmael was a descendant of Naamah, the Ammonite wife of King David, which would further document Ishmael's Ammonite connections. Another seal impression turned up over a century ago with the inscription "Belonging to Elishama, the king's son" (Torrey 1923: 108; Avigad 1997: 53 #11). In Torrey's view, "son of the king" means just what it says: a person of royal descent. If the Elishama here is Ishmael's grandfather (and not a more distant relative; cf. 2 Sam 5:16; 1 Chr 3:8), then an identification is possible with Elishama, the scribe who held a high position in Jehoiakim's government, but who does not appear to have come from a scribal family (36:12, 20). See the genealogy in 1 Chr 2:34–41. The struggle about to unfold, in any case, is between an heir to the royal line of Elishama (i.e., Ishmael son of Nethaniah), and an heir to the nonroyal line of Shaphan (i.e., Gedaliah son of Ahikam). The name "Elishama," besides having turned up on bullae from Judahite sites (Appendix I: "Ishmael ben Nethaniah ben Elishama"; also Avigad 1997: 76–77 ##81–83; 93 #138; 127 #262; 173 #408), has been found on a seal and many bullae of Ammonite origin (A. Levin 1996; Avigad 1997: 326–27 #871; 339–40 ##911–15; 344 #926). For discussion of the title "the king's son," see Note for 36:26.

and one of the chief officers of the king. Hebrew *wĕrabbê hammelek.* The LXX and 2 Kgs 25:25 omit, but both are attributable to haplography (homoeoarcton: *w . . . w*). See Barthélemy 1986: 741–43. On *rab* meaning "chief officer," see Note for 39:3.

and they ate food together there at Mizpah. The expression *yō'kĕlû . . . leḥem* ("they ate bread / food"), here as elsewhere, means sharing a substantial meal (52:33; Gen 43:25, 32). Presumably Ishmael and his men had come to Mizpah at Gedaliah's invitation. Oriental hospitality obligates one to care for and treat generously guests in one's palace, house, or tent (Gen 19:7–8; Judg 19:23), for which reason plots such as the present one are easily carried off, particularly if the feasting leads to weariness and drunkenness. Josephus, in fact, embellishes his report of the incident by saying that Gedaliah entertained Ishmael and his company with a lavish banquet, at the end of which he fell into a drunken sleep (Ant x 168–69; Begg 1994: 32–33). In this condition he was then murdered. Judith, one might remember from the story bearing her name, murders a weary and drunken Holofernes after he hosts a lavish banquet in her honor (Jdt 12:10–13:10).

at Mizpah. The LXX omits. Giesebrecht says the term is superfluous, but from a stylistic point of view probably original (cf. the repetition of "Egypt" in 42:16).

2. *Then Ishmael son of Nethaniah got up, also the ten men who were with him, and they struck down Gedaliah son of Ahikam, son of Shaphan, with the sword. So he killed him.* The LXX lacks "son of Ahikam, son of Shaphan, with the sword. So he killed him," yielding an impoverished reading which is doubtless

the victim of more haplography (homoeoteleuton: *w . . . w*). Both Holladay and McKane obscure matters by dividing the omission in two, and then in each case going with the shorter LXX reading. Volz notes the LXX omission of *wayyāmet 'ōtô* ("So he killed him"), also a plural instead of a singular verb in G[OL] and the other Vrs, but says the MT is nevertheless good. Later Jewish tradition marked the murder of Gedaliah by a fast on the third of Tishri, the seventh month (Zech 7:5; 8:19; cf. Milgrom, "Fasting and Fast Days" in *EncJud* 6: 1191).

the ten men who were with him. Hebrew *'ittô* ("with him") here and in v 7 means "being under the orders of"; cf. 26:22; 1 Sam 22:6; 2 Sam 1:11; 17:12 (Aharoni 1981: 48). Eleven bravos proved to be more than a match for perhaps a larger number of men caught unaware (Cheyne). The other princes and their men are not present, reappearing only later to chase Ishmael (v 11). Carroll's view that Johanan's absence and reappearance points to a "lack of realism in the story" is contrived.

3. *And all the Judahites who were with him, that is, Gedaliah, at Mizpah, and the Chaldeans who were found there, that is, the fighting men, Ishmael struck down.* This appears to be a slight exaggeration (Hyatt; Bright; McKane), since not everyone at Mizpah was killed. The reading in 2 Kgs 25:25 without "all" is better. According to v 10, a remnant survived. A killing of Chaldean soldiers would be sure to have reverberations back in Babylon, and was, no doubt, added reason for the return of Babylonian forces in 582 B.C.

that is, Gedaliah. The LXX omits, which can be attributed to haplography (homoeoteleuton: *w . . . w*), although the LXX and 2 Kgs 25:25 abbreviate the verse. Giesebrecht, Duhm, Cornill, Holladay, and McKane take the words as an MT plus (McKane: "in the interests of explicitness").

that is, the fighting men. Another parenthetical remark lacking in the LXX and 2 Kgs 25:25. This may be an MT plus, specifying the Chaldeans as soldiers of the occupation. See also v 16.

4. *on the day after the killing.* Hebrew *bayyôm haššēnî lĕhāmît* is lit. "on the second day of the killing." The NJV has "second day after," but most commentators and modern Versions take the expression to mean the next day.

when no one knew. Is this meant to echo Ishmael's words in 40:15: "and no one will know"? The meaning here is probably that no one outside Mizpah had yet heard the news, least of all the pilgrims sighted on the Shechem–Jerusalem road, whom Ishmael will lure into the city. Josephus (*Ant* x 170) says that no one of the 80 men had yet heard what happened to Gedaliah.

5. *from Shechem, from Shiloh, and from Samaria.* Cities north of Mizpah, all prominent in the old Northern Kingdom. Shechem and Samaria were onetime capitals of Northern Israel. Shiloh was the site of Israel's first sanctuary, and home to the boy Samuel (see Note for 7:12). More recently these cities may have come under the influence of Jerusalem as a result of Josiah's Reform (2 Kgs 23:19–20; 2 Chr 34:6–7). The LXX has "Salem" for "Shiloh" (Aq and Symm: "Salom"), which cannot be right.

beards shaven, clothes torn, and self-inflicted slashes. Common signs of mourning (16:6; 47:5; 48:37). Shaven beards and body mutilations show nonadherence to the prohibitions in Lev 19:27–28; 21:5; and Deut 14:1. And yet, shaving oneself bald as an expression of grief was widely practiced, anticipated, and even brought on by Yahweh himself (Amos 8:10; Isa 22:12; Mic 1:16; Ezek 7:18). Calvin notes the legal prohibition against slashing and its association with Baal worship, yet he excuses the men for carrying out the practice. On shaven beards and self-imposed baldness, see Note for 7:29.

cereal offering and frankincense. Destruction of the Temple put an end to animal sacrifices (D. Jones 1963), but cereal and frankincense offerings continued to be made by Jewish worshipers, as we see here. These two offerings, which are commonly associated in the OT (17:26; 41:5; Isa 43:23; 66:3), were made in Jerusalem after the return from exile (Neh 13:5, 9). And after the Egyptians destroyed the Yahu temple in the Jewish colony at Elephantine, in 410 B.C., surviving letters between the priests at Elephantine and the Persian governor of Judah reveal that cereal offerings, frankincense, and burnt offerings (= animal sacrifices) were not offered during the three years following the temple's destruction, for which reason the priests were petitioning the governor to permit a rebuilding so the offerings could be resumed (AP 30.21–26; 31.21–26; *ANET*³ 491–92). The request was granted, except that animal sacrifices were not reinstated, only cereal and frankincense offerings (AP 32–33; Milgrom 1991: 629–30). On the "cereal offering" (*minḥâ*), see Note for 14:12; on "frankincense" (*lĕbônâ*), see Note for 6:20.

the house of Yahweh. I.e., the site of Yahweh's house in Jerusalem. In the postexilic period the Feast of Booths was celebrated on the Temple site before the building itself was rebuilt (Ezra 3:1–6). The Talmud states that sacrifices can be made even when there is no Temple (Megillah 10a), also that incense can be made on the site of the altar when there is no altar (Zebaḥim 59a).

6. *And Ishmael son of Nethaniah went out from Mizpah to meet them.* The pilgrims were simply passing by; therefore Ishmael had to go out to invite them into the city. Josephus (*Ant* x 170), stating that the pilgrims came bearing gifts for Gedaliah, implies that their destination was Mizpah. Muilenburg, in his argument for Mizpah being Tell en-Naṣbeh, makes much of the point that Mizpah has to lie on the Shechem–Jerusalem road (see Note for 40:6). Nebi Samwil does not.

weeping as he was walking. Hebrew *hōlēk hālōk ûbōkeh.* On constructions with *hlk* as expressing continued action, see GKC §113u. On the infinitive absolute following the participle, see 23:17 and GKC §113r. Ishmael is pretending to grieve along with the pilgrims (Kimḥi, Calvin, and others), which apparently the LXX did not understand (Giesebrecht). The LXX has "and they [i.e., the pilgrims] were walking and weeping" (*autoi eporeuonto kai eklaion*). Note also the LXX omission of the infinitive absolute in the construction *'ōmĕrîm 'āmôr* ("continually saying") in 23:17.

And it happened as he met them. The LXX omits: haplography (homoeoarcton: *wy . . . wy*).

'Come to Gedaliah son of Ahikam.' The deception continues, but Ishmael's tears convey that something is wrong. Bright's "Welcome in the name of Ge-

daliah ben Ahikam!" is the invitation of a composed individual pretending that everything in Mizpah is fine, which it is not the right picture.

7. *And it happened as they came into the midst of the city that Ishmael son of Nethaniah—he, and the men who were with him—slaughtered them and cast them into the midst of the cistern.* Ishmael and his men were armed and the pilgrims were not; nevertheless, the number of victims (70) suggests a more savage butchery than what took place earlier. Why Ishmael should kill unwary passersby is hard to understand. Calvin, Giesebrecht, Rudolph, and others suggest robbery as a motive, which is possible, since 10 were spared after surrendering hidden stores of food. In Calvin's view the wicked become hardened; whereas at first they may fear to murder innocents, once they begin, it becomes easy and they hasten to do more of the same. It is also possible that Ishmael is trying to conceal his earlier crime, which is typical of criminal behavior. When the pilgrims become aware of Gedaliah's murder, they will spread the word, so Ishmael may at this point still be trying to conceal his ambitions rather than reveal them. But if he is afraid of the word getting out, why does he spare the 10? The LXX omits "he and the men who were with him."

into the midst of the city . . . into the midst of the cistern. The repetition of *tôk* ("midst") is consistent with the style, so the second occurrence need not be omitted with the LXX (*pace* Cornill; Bright; Holladay; McKane; and others). In v 8 is another repetition of *tôk*.

the cistern. Hebrew *habbôr*. The definite article suggests the same cistern into which the other bodies were cast. Jeremiah was left in a cistern to die (38:6). On ancient cisterns, see Note for 2:13.

8. *hidden stores in the field.* Hebrew *maṭmōnîm baśśādeh*. The 10 men have a cache of food in some field, most likely in a storage pit. Was it back in one of the northern cities from which they had come, or at a location nearer to Mizpah? Gibeon had an abundance of storage pits, as Pritchard's excavations have shown, and perhaps Ishmael's short detour there after leaving Mizpah was to pick up this cache of food. But there were doubtless other cisterns in the immediate area.

honey. Hebrew *děbaš* could be "date honey," not honey from bees (P. J. King 1993: 151).

amidst their brothers. Hebrew *bětôk 'ăḥêhem*. A third occurrence of *tôk*, adding to the two in v 7. The traveling group consisted only of men (v 5).

9. *Now the cistern into which Ishmael cast all the corpses of the men whom he struck down because of Gedaliah . . .* Hebrew *běyad-gědalyāhû* ("because of Gedaliah") is difficult, the meaning presumably being that Ishmael murdered the pilgrims because of his earlier murder of Gedaliah (NJV: "in the affair of Gedaliah"). Kimḥi says that since Ishmael killed Gedaliah he killed these others too, i.e., the latter evil came about because of the former. Most commentators and some modern Versions (RSV; JB; NAB; REB; NSB) emend and add the following *hû'* ("it") to get the reading of the LXX, which is, "a great pit it was" (*phrear mega touto estin*). But even emendation does not yield a smooth reading of the Hebrew. Also, the "great pit" of 1 Macc 7:19, to which reference

is often made, is less than decisive. The term *bĕyad* (lit. "by the hand of") can be translated "because of," as the AV has done. This meaning is now attested for Ug *byd* (Rin 1963: 32–33; Dahood 1963: 301–2). Compare Isa 64:6[Eng 64:7]: "and you dispersed us because of (*bĕyad*) our iniquities"; also Job 8:4: "then he will expel them because of (*bĕyad*) their transgression."

the corpses of the men. The LXX omits; perhaps an explanatory gloss (Holladay).

it was the one that King Asa made on account of Baasha, king of Israel. The OT makes no reference to this pit, but does report Asa's fortification of Mizpah against Baasha (1 Kgs 15:22).

Ishmael . . . filled it with the slain. The unconventional syntax in the Hebrew is to emphasize that Ishmael literally *filled* the pit with bodies of the slain.

10. *Then Ishmael took captive the entire remnant of the people who were in Mizpah.* The LXX's *apestrepsen* ("he turned back") translates *šûb* instead of *šbh*, its meaning presumably being that Ishmael prevented a traumatized remnant from fleeing Mizpah once they had learned of the murders. Aquila has *echmalōteusen* ("he took captive"), which supports MT. Bright points out that Jeremiah would have been among these captives since he later appears with them at Geruth Chimham (42:1–6). Baruch would also have been in the group (43:3, 6).

the daughters of the king. These are either daughters of Judah's last kings or else princesses not exiled to Babylon, but entrusted to the care of Gedaliah (43:6). Peake thinks they may have been related to Ishmael, which is possible.

and all the other people who remained in Mizpah. Cornill takes this repetition in the verse, which the LXX omits, as a needless MT addition. However, *kol-hā'ām* appears here to mean "all the *other* people," which makes sense in the context because "the daughters of the king" have just been singled out for special mention. Compare *bĕkol-hā'ărāṣôt* meaning "in all the *other* lands" in 40:11. The omission could be due to haplography (homoeoarcton: *'aleph . . . 'aleph*), although one then has to decide what to do with the preceding *waw*.

Nebuzaradan. The LXX omits, as it sometimes does with names, patronyms, and titles. See Janzen 1973: 150–51.

And Ishmael son of Nethaniah took them captive. The LXX omits. Cornill takes as another needless repetition; however, this loss can be attributed to haplography (homoeoarcton *wy . . . wy*).

and went to cross over to the Ammonites. According to Josephus (*Ant* x 160), Ishmael fled to Ammon earlier when Jerusalem was under siege. Since he was in league with the Ammonite king, Ammon would be the natural place to seek safe haven.

11. *Johanan . . . and all the princes of the troops . . . heard all the evil that Ishmael . . . had done.* It is not just Johanan and his men who hear what happened in Mizpah, but the other princes—Jonathan, Johanan's brother, Seraiah son of Tanhumeth, the sons of Ephai the Netophathite, and Jezaniah the Maacathite—together with their men (40:8). These individuals, all of fighting capability, were away from Mizpah when the killings took place, which goes some way in explaining why Ishmael chose the time he did to execute his plot.

News of the carnage now reaches these princes where they are, also word that Ishmael has fled and taken with him an unwilling and frightened band of fellow travelers.

12. *all the men.* The LXX has "their men," but T, Aq, and Symm have "all the men."

the great pool that was in Gibeon. Hebrew *mayim rabbîm* is lit. "great / many waters," taken here to mean "pool of great waters" by Rashi and Kimḥi (T: "pool of many waters"). This is the pool around which the young men of Abner and young men of Joab played a dangerous game years earlier (2 Sam 2:12–17). On Gibeon and the excavations carried out at modern el-Jib by James Pritchard, see Note for 28:1. Pritchard (1956; 1959) discovered this pool, also the extensive water system of which it was a part (for a picture, see *ANEP*[2] 367 #879). The presence of Ishmael and his captives at Gibeon has figured in the debate over Mizpah's location. If the site is Tell en-Naṣbeh, as is widely assumed, Gibeon is then some three miles to the southwest, not exactly in a direct line to Ammon where Ishmael is headed, but also not much of a detour, given the short distance between the two sites. From Gibeon Ishmael could have proceeded to Ammon in the usual way, going south and east to Jerusalem, then down the Ascent of Adummim to the Jordan Valley (see Note for 39:4). But if Mizpah is identified with Nebi Samwil, the escape route—assuming no detour—would be north and east, following a course to Ramah, Jebaʿ, and down the Wadi es-Sweinit to the Jordan Valley (Albright's view; cf. Muilenburg 1947a: 33–34), otherwise past Bethel to Michmash, and down the Wadi Qelt to the Jordan Valley (Holladay). All three escape routes are possible, the one being advocated here involving a slight detour if Ishmael goes to Gibeon to collect the cache of food—a collection he must make before going to Ammon. Or a circuitous route may have been chosen to throw off enemy pursuit (Hyatt; Jones).

13–14. *that they were glad. So all the people whom Ishmael had taken captive from Mizpah turned about.* The LXX omits, which is most likely more loss due to haplography (homoeoarcton: *wyš . . . wyš*). The people were glad to see a group sufficient in size to overpower Ishmael and his men. As it turned out, Ishmael made his escape with only eight men (v 15).

14. *and returning they went over to Johanan son of Kareah.* Taking the first of two verbs with Volz as an auxiliary (see again v 17). The LXX omission of "and they went over" is likely more haplography (homoeoteleuton: *w . . . w*).

15. *And Ishmael son of Nethaniah escaped with eight men from before Johanan.* Ishmael had ten men earlier (41:1), which means he lost two in the fighting or else because of desertion. The LXX omits "from before Johanan," but it is present in T. Giesebrecht takes the phrase as being original.

16. *son of Nethaniah, from Mizpah, after he struck down Gedaliah son of Ahikam.* Another LXX omission again present in T, but which Giesebrecht and others delete as secondary. But the prose here is prolix, which means the words are probably better retained.

men, fighting men. Hebrew *gĕbārîm* can mean "strong men" or simply "men" (see Note for 17:5), whereas *ʾanšê hammilḥāmâ* are definitely "fighting men," i.e., soldiers. The LXX (*dunatous andras en polemo*, "mighty men in war"), Vg (*fortes viros ad praelium*, "strong men for battle"), and AV ("even mighty men of war") all combine the two Hebrew terms into a single expression describing "soldiers," which is what the T accomplishes in its translation: "the mighty men, the men who made war." Modern scholars read two separate terms in the Hebrew, with virtually everyone following Hitzig in taking *'anšê hammilḥāmâ* as an erroneous gloss on *gěbārîm*. According to this view, *gěbārîm* originally meant simply "men," being a correlative term to "women" coming next in the list (cf. 40:7; 43:6; 44:20). It may be noted that *'anšê hammilḥāmâ* is parenthetical in v 3, where the LXX and 2 Kgs 25:25 do not have the term. The upshot of all this is that no soldiers were originally among the captives (Peake; Bright), which is reasonable. But the MT has both soldiers and male civilians in the group. The modern Versions divide over interpretation: some translate only "soldiers," or the like (RSV; NAB; NIV; NRSV; NSB); some translate only "men" (Moffatt; AmT; JB); and some translate "men" and "soldiers" (NEB; REB; NJV). The NJB takes the second term as a clarification of the first: "men—fighting men."

and small children. Hebrew *wěṭap.* The LXX has *kai ta loipa* ("and those remaining"); Aq and Symm have *kai ton ochlon* ("and the multitude"). Compare 43:6, where the LXX has *kai ta nēpia*, "and the small children" (Rahlfs). Read the MT.

and eunuchs. These are no doubt actual eunuchs, like Ebed-melech (38:7), who are caring for "the king's daughters" (Cornill; Rudolph). One wonders if Ebed-melech might not have been among them (cf. 39:17–18).

17. *Geruth Chimham, which is near Bethlehem.* Geruth Chimham is probably a village, the name of which derived from the Chimham who had the honor of escorting David across the Jordan on his return to Jerusalem after the rebellion of Absalom (2 Sam 19:38–41[Eng 19:37–40]). Chimham was of the house of Barzillai, a wealthy Gileadite (1 Sam 19:33[Eng 19:32]). Either from Barzillai or from the king, Chimham could have received a portion of land from David's patrimony in Bethlehem (1 Kgs 2:7; cf. *ABD* 2: 995). The term *gērût* ("Geruth") is a *hapax legomenon* in the OT, but probably means "lodging place(s)" or "khan(s)," as indicated by Symm (*tais paroikiais*) and Vg (*peregrinantes*). The narrative portrays Geruth Chimham as a temporary stopping place. Aquila reads "the sheepfolds (*tois phragmois*) of Chimham," which has similar meaning.

going to enter Egypt. Hebrew *lāleket lābô' miṣrāyim.* Another instance where the first verb is auxiliary to the second (Volz). See earlier v 14. The LXX omits "to enter."

MESSAGE AND AUDIENCE

The audience hears in this narrative cluster about Gedaliah's governorship in Mizpah and the sojourn there, its happy beginning, and tragic end. Things began with leaders of scattered detachments from Judah's defeated army hearing about Nebuchadnezzar's appointment of Gedaliah over those remaining in Judah, and paying a visit to Gedaliah at the new provincial center in Mizpah. The Mizpah community was mixed: men, women, small children, and a company of poor folk. The princes too were a mixed assemblage: Ishmael from the Judaean royal family, the sons of Ephai from the Bethlehem area, and Jezaniah the Maacathite, a Syrian expatriate in Judah who perhaps also belonged to the Judaean royal house, or who claimed to. If there was any bad blood or dissension among those assembled, we are given no hint of it. Gedaliah's word to the group, supported by an oath to allay fears about potential double-dealing, is a simple one. He is the appointee in Mizpah who will mediate between the Babylonians and remaining Judahites in the land. So far as the princes and their men are concerned, they are to bring in the harvest graciously left to them, store it, and live peaceably in cities they have seized. Word of Gedaliah's appointment had also reached Judahites residing in Moab, Ammon, Edom, and elsewhere, and they have now come to join the Mizpah community. The whole company proceeds then to gather summer fruits in great quantity. It seems as if Jeremiah's words about people returning to the land and the land yielding a rich harvest are being wonderfully fulfilled.

At a later time, however, most likely a few years later, Johanan and the other princes come again to Gedaliah, this time to inform him of an Ammonite-sponsored plot to take the governor's life. The man to watch is Ishmael, who is said to have been put up to this mischief by King Baalis. But Gedaliah does not believe them. Did Ishmael appear to be a schemer when they first met? Or is Johanan the good person many make him out to be? What does become clear is that Johanan is not above carrying out some mischief of his own, proposing as he does to Gedaliah that he put Ishmael away secretly. No one will know, he says. Will the audience believe this? There can be little quarrel with Johanan's point about Ishmael's plot not being allowed to happen, for the fragile community at Mizpah can scarcely survive should Gedaliah be killed. People would be scattered to the four winds. Gedaliah wisely rejects Johanan's proposal, but is the rumor about Ishmael an outright lie? Gedaliah has no suspicions about Ishmael, which may show naïveté on his part, or else cunning on the part of Ishmael. It is probably some of both.

In the seventh month of that same year, Ishmael came with 10 men to Gedaliah at Mizpah, probably at the latter's invitation, and they ate a meal together. It was doubtless a meal of some substance since this was, after all, the governor's residence. The narrator now tells us more about just who Ishmael is. He is a descendent of Elishama, a royal figure who was one of the chief officers of the king. Details of the meal are not reported; instead we are told simply that Ishmael with his men got up from the table and put Gedaliah to the sword, and are reminded too that the one killed was an appointee of the king of Babylon. The slaughter claimed other lives, perhaps those present with Gedaliah at the table. Parenthetically we are told, perhaps by a later editor, that the slain Chaldeans were soldiers of the occupation. There is bound to be a day of reckoning for this act of violent madness.

In the next segment we learn that on the day after Gedaliah's murder, when word had not yet reached anyone outside the city, a band of 80 pilgrims from the northern cities of Samaria, Shechem, and Shiloh were sighted on the road, headed for Jerusalem. In hand were cereal offerings and frankincense to offer on the Temple site, and the shaven beards, torn clothes, and self-inflicted slashes indicated that the pilgrims were in a state of mourning, which was not usual for celebrating the Feast of Booths. The pilgrims should have been joyful, singing as they walked. Ishmael went out to meet them, but the cunning old fox feigned grief by weeping as he walked. When he met the pilgrims, he invited them to come and see Gedaliah son of Ahikam.

They did so, and no sooner had they come into the city but another ruthless slaughter began, with Ishmael and his partners in crime then casting bodies one by one into the midst of the cistern, where, more than likely, other bodies lay at the bottom. Ten of the pilgrims managed to bargain for their lives by surrendering stores of food they had hidden in the field—wheat, barley, oil, and honey. So Ishmael stopped the bloodletting, and did not kill them. Parenthetically we are then told that this cistern was one King Asa had dug on account of the ambitious Baasha, king of Israel. After Ishmael filled the cistern with the slain, he gathered up the dwindling remnant—and there was one, thankfully, which included women of Judah's royal house—and took them captive on a journey that would lead finally into Ammonite country.

Word by now had reached Johanan and the other princes about the massacre at Mizpah, and the chase was on to catch Ishmael before he left the country. The audience by now is able to understand how these murders were pulled off: Ishmael had taken advantage of the absence of the other princes and their men, who, had they been in Mizpah, could have prevented what happened. The pursuers found Ishmael and his fellow travelers at the great pool of Gibeon. The captives were overjoyed, and with all haste came to join those who made possible their freedom. Ishmael managed to escape with 8 of his men, returning to Ammon, not as a hero, but as a bigtime loser.

The final segment of the cluster reports that Johanan and the other princes took with them the rescued group and went to Geruth Chimham, near Bethlehem, the plan being that they would stay there briefly and then head for Egypt. The fear now was reprisal for the deaths of Gedaliah and the Babylonian soldiers. One man's wicked deed put them all under suspicion.

This narrative cluster is a setup for what is to follow, which is the need now to request from Jeremiah a divine oracle telling the group what to do next. Its chief link with what precedes is to report further on the remnant that survived Jerusalem's destruction and the demise of the nation. Also, in the present cluster are suggestions of prophecy being fulfilled—prophecies of a return to the land and the land once more yielding an abundant harvest. As things turned out, the harvest—although grand—was simply a "firstfruits," if it was anything. Hopes of restoration in the land were short-lived, and many years would actually have to pass before these prophecies would have real fulfillment. A delay along similar lines occurred when the covenant people left Egypt on their way to the Promised Land.

This narrative may certainly derive from Baruch, the scribe now accompanying Jeremiah and an eyewitness to everything that has occurred. The date of the composition can be put any time after 582 B.C., when the sojourn in Mizpah has ended and the journey to Geruth Chimham has already taken place.

B. JEREMIAH'S WORD AGAIN RENDERED CHEAP (42:1–22)

1. Remnant Asks Jeremiah to Mediate (42:1–6)

42 [1]Then all the princes of the troops, including Johanan son of Kareah and Jezaniah son of Hoshaiah, and all the people from the least to the greatest, came forward [2]and said to Jeremiah the prophet, 'Do let our request be laid before you, and pray on our behalf to Yahweh your God, on behalf of this entire remnant, for we remain a few from many, as your eyes now see us. [3]And let Yahweh your God tell us the way in which we should go and the thing that we should do.' [4]And Jeremiah the prophet said to them, 'I hear. Look I will pray to Yahweh your God according to your word; and the entire word that Yahweh answers you I will tell you; I will not hold back from you a word.' [5]Then they, they said to Jeremiah, 'Yahweh be a true and faithful witness against us if not according to the entire word that Yahweh your God sends you for us, we so do. [6]If for good or if for evil, the voice of Yahweh our God to whom we are sending you we will obey, in order that it may go well with us. Indeed we will obey the voice of Yahweh our God!'

2. Yahweh Answers the Remnant (42:7–22)

42 [7]And it happened at the end of ten days that the word of Yahweh came to Jeremiah. [8]So he announced to Johanan son of Kareah and to all the princes of the troops who were with him, and to all the people from the least to the greatest, [9]and said to them:

Thus said Yahweh, God of Israel, to whom you sent me to lay your request before him:

[10]If you will indeed dwell in this land, then I will build you up and not overthrow you, and I will plant you and not uproot you, for I have repented concerning the evil that I did to you. [11]Do not be afraid because of the king of Babylon, of whom you are now afraid.

Do not be afraid because of him—oracle of Yahweh—for I am with you to save you and rescue you from his hand. [12]And I will grant you mercies, and he will be merciful with you and let you return to your soil.
[13]But if you are saying, 'We will not dwell in this land,' not obeying the voice of Yahweh your God, [14]saying: 'No! Indeed we will enter the land of Egypt to the end that we will not see war, and the sound of the trumpet we will not hear, and for food we will not hunger, and there we will dwell,' [15]well now, therefore, hear the word of Yahweh, Remnant of Judah:
Thus said Yahweh of hosts, God of Israel:
If you then have definitely set your faces to enter Egypt and you enter to sojourn there, [16]then it will happen: the sword of which you are now afraid shall overtake you there in the land of Egypt; and the famine about which you are now worrying shall follow you hard there in Egypt; and there you shall die. [17]So shall all the persons become who set their faces to enter Egypt to sojourn there; they shall die by sword, by famine, and by pestilence; they shall not have a survivor or fugitive because of the evil that I am bringing upon them.

[18]For thus said Yahweh of hosts, God of Israel:
Just as my anger and my wrath were poured out upon the inhabitants of Jerusalem, so my wrath will be poured out upon you when you enter Egypt. And you shall be a curse, and a desolation, and a swearword, and a reproach, and you shall not see this place again.
[19]Yahweh has spoken concerning you, Remnant of Judah, Do not enter Egypt! Know for sure that I have warned you today. [20]Indeed you led yourselves astray,[1] for you, you sent me to Yahweh your God saying, 'Pray on our behalf to Yahweh our God, and according to all that Yahweh our God says, so tell us and we will do.' [21]And I told you today, and you have not obeyed the voice of Yahweh your God regarding all that he sent me to you. [22]Now then, know for sure that by sword, by famine, and by pestilence you shall die in the place where you wish to enter to sojourn.

RHETORIC AND COMPOSITION

MT 42:1–22 = LXX 49:1–22. Narrative segments in this chapter begin and end with stereotypical phrases: "Then / and (to) all the princes of the troops," along with "And it happened," carrying over from 40:7–41:18 as beginning phrases, and ending phrases about "obeying / not obeying the voice of Yahweh." The phrases "And it happened / came" and "they did not obey the voice of Yahweh" structure narrative segments also in chap. 43, embodying a theology that dominates the narrative on through to the end of chap. 44. Here in

---

[1]Reading the Q *hit'êtem* ("you led astray"); the Kt cannot be read.

chap. 42 are two narrative segments: 1) vv 1–6; and 2) vv 7–22, where the key phrases are the following:

I	*Then . . . all the princes of the troops . . .*	*wa . . . kol-śárê haḥăyālîm*	v 1
	. . . the voice of Yahweh . . . we will obey . . .	*běqôl yhwh . . . nišmaʿ*	v 6
	we will obey the voice of Yahweh . . .	*nišmaʿ běqôl yhwh*	

II	*And it happened . . .*	*wayěhî*	v 7
	. . . and to all the princes of the troops . . .	*wě'el kol-śárê haḥăyālîm*	v 8
	. . . and you have not obeyed the voice of Yahweh . . .	*wělō' šěmaʿtem běqôl yhwh*	v 21

This division in a basically continuous narrative is supported by the section markings. There is a *petuḥah* in M^A and M^P, and a *setumah* in M^L, before v 1, which is also the chapter division. A *setumah* in M^L and M^P, and a *petuḥah* in M^A, after v 6 mark the end of the first segment and the beginning of the second. There also appears to be a section in 2QJer after v 6. The end of the second segment is marked by a *setumah* in M^A, M^L, and M^P after v 22, which is also the chapter division. An additional *setumah* after v 17 in M^L (only) separates Oracles III and IV in the second segment.

Most commentators reckon vv 1–6 to be a unit, with a lesser number (Giesebrecht; Duhm; Cornill; S. R. Driver; Thompson) taking vv 7–22 as a second unit. Others (Rudolph; Weiser; Bright; Holladay) follow Volz in transposing vv 19–22 after 43:1–3, which puts Jeremiah's charge that the people are disingenuous after the people's rejection of the oracles. This transposition is unnecessary, as the narrative reads perfectly well "as is." The present sequence simply requires that at v 20 (not v 19) Jeremiah has come to realize that the people are not accepting what they have been told. Moreover, the transposition requires adding a "Then Jeremiah replied" at the beginning of v 19, for which there is no textual support. The JB adopted the rearrangement, but it was abandoned in the NJB. Jones takes 42:1–43:7 as one unbroken composition, which has possible support in the abridgment of the verses in 2 Kgs 25:26; however, a unit this long leaves hanging Jeremiah's Tahpanhes oracle in 43:8–13.

As in 40:7–41:18, so also here are numerous variations between MT and LXX, although many are minor, e.g., the LXX omission of patronyms, titles ("the prophet" in v 4; "of hosts" in vv 15 and 18), pronouns, particles ("on our behalf" in v 2; "all" in v 4); changes of names ("Azariah" for Jezaniah" in v 1), and plurals to singulars; and different readings of Hebrew verbs (*yšb* instead of *šwb* in v 10). More significant are LXX omissions—small and large—that can be attributed to haplography. In v 17 is also a LXX plus, which may be an MT loss due to haplography. Holladay and McKane follow Duhm (and Janzen) in supporting the shorter LXX text at almost every turn; others generally favor the LXX, but do from time to time express a preference for the longer readings in MT. Repetitions should most often be retained when the LXX omits them, and the number of arguable LXX omissions due to haplography speaks against *a priori* approval of the shorter LXX text (see Appendix V). At the very least, these probable haplographies should cut back on conjectural restorations of an imagined LXX *Vorlage*, dittographies said to exist in MT, and alleged MT expansions thought to have been quarried from other readings in the book. The strongest case for MT expansion is omitted patronyms and titles in the LXX (Janzen 1973: 69–116, 139–72), although even here some abridgment may occur.

Volz and Weiser scan vv 10–12 as poetry, but most commentators take the verses to be prose. The narrator here is most likely Baruch, who, being an eye-witness to the events, is responsible for reporting them in such rich detail (Volz). There is no (late) "Deuteronomic" editing in the chapter, as Duhm, Cornill, Hyatt, Thiel, and McKane maintain. Duhm and McKane claim that vv 15–18 destroy the connection between v 14 and v 19, and are therefore secondary; Thiel (1981: 66) attributes vv 19–22 to a later "Deuteronomic supplementer." Neither view is convincing.

The first segment of the narrative (vv 1–6) records a dialogue between Jeremiah and the people, where Jeremiah's speech occupies the center position (Begg 1994: 42):

Princes and people	vv 2–3
Jeremiah	vv 4
Princes and people	vv 5–6

The second segment begins with a brief third-person narrative (vv 7–9a), after which come four oracles (vv 9b–11a; vv 11b–12; vv 15b–17; v 18), interspersed twice with words spoken by Jeremiah (vv 13–15a; vv 19–22). Jeremiah's words framing Oracles III and IV (vv 15a–19a) and his concluding words to the group (vv 19b–22) are both tied together by the inclusio (Abrego 1983a: 20; 1983b: 111):

. . . *hear the word of Yahweh,*	. . . *šimʿû dĕbar-yhwh*	v 15a
Remnant of Judah:	*šĕʾērît yĕhûdâ*	
Yahweh has spoken concerning you,	*dibber yhwh ʿălêkem*	v 19a
Remnant of Judah:	*šĕʾērît yĕhûdâ*	
Know for sure . . .	*yādōaʿ tēdĕʿû*	v 19b
. . . know for sure . . .	*yādōaʿ tēdĕʿû*	v 22

The LXX lacks "Remnant of Judah" in v 15a, and "know for sure" in v 22, both of which should be retained (see Notes).

NOTES

42:1–6. This request for Jeremiah's intercession and a response that the people keep Yahweh's commandments has turned up in the Qumran *Apocryphon of Jeremiah* (4Q385^b ii; Dimant 1994), although in that document the band of survivors had already gone to Tahpanhes. The directive to exiles in Egypt that they keep Yahweh's commandments is recorded also in 2 Macc 2:1–3.

1–2. *came forward and said.* Hebrew *wayyiggĕšû . . . wayyō'mĕrû.* Volz takes the two verbs as expressing a single idea; see again vv 8–9; also 41:14, 17.

1. *Johanan son of Kareah and Jezaniah son of Hoshaiah.* Johanan son of Kareah continues as spokesman for the traveling group, and with him now at the head of the delegation calling on Jeremiah is one Jezaniah son of Hoshaiah, who is not Jezaniah the Maacathite of 40:8, but—assuming the text is correct—a brother of Azariah son of Hoshaiah, who is mentioned in 43:2. Here and in 43:2 the LXX has "Azarias son of Massaiou," leading numerous commentators (Giesebrecht; Duhm; Cornill; Volz; Rudolph; Weiser; Bright; Holladay; McKane) and some modern Versions (RSV; NEB; JB; NAB; NSB) to replace "Jezaniah" with "Azariah" in the present verse. This results in one son of Hoshaiah, not two. The solution is not wholly satisfactory, since the LXX patronym *Maasaiou* does not translate "Hoshaiah." Both T and Vg have "Jezaniah son of Hoshaiah," which is adopted by the AV, NJV, and NIV, and on balance is the better of the two readings. The LXX appears to have eclipsed Johanan son of Kareah's brother Jonathan in 40:8 (see Note there). Also omitted in the LXX is the patronym "son of Kareah," which occurs again in v 8 and elsewhere (cf. Janzen 1973: 150). The name "Jezaniah / Jaazaniah" appears also in 35:3 and 40:8, and is attested on the Lachish and Arad ostraca, and on contemporary seals and bullae; "Hoshaiah" is attested on the Lachish and Horvat Uza ostraca, and on seals, bullae, and other contemporary documents (see Appendix I).

from the least to the greatest. On this phrase, which occurs again in v 8, see Note for 6:13.

2. *Do let our request be laid before you, and pray on our behalf to Yahweh your God.* Hebrew *tĕḥinnâ* ("request, supplication") is a "plea for favor / grace," occurring frequently in the Psalms (Pss 6:10[Eng 6:9]; 28:2, 6; 31:23[Eng 31:22]; 55:2[Eng 55:1]; 116:1; 119:70; 130:2; 140:7[Eng 140:6]; 143:1) where, with great joy, the psalmist learns that Yahweh has given a positive response. On the expression "to lay one's request before," see Note for 37:20. The group here is looking for a favorable word from Yahweh, which gives a first hint of their wanting divine approval for going on to Egypt. Jeremiah not long before was asked to make divine intercession by King Zedekiah, who wanted Jerusalem spared, but the response was negative (21:2; 37:3). Because the retractable people of Jerusalem never tired of asking Jeremiah to pray for their welfare, Yahweh finally had to tell the prophet not to make intercession (14:11; cf. 7:16; 11:14). Indeed, Jeremiah himself became disillusioned about his role as intercessor after having spoken good for people, who then returned the favor by digging a pit to take his life (18:20). Here he will learn again that intercession is wasted on a people who promise to obey Yahweh's word and then end up not obeying it (42:20–21).

on our behalf . . . on behalf of. The LXX lacks the first "on our behalf," but Giesebrecht retains, saying it has rhetorical effect. Aquila (*peri hēmōn*), Symm (*hyper hēmōn*), and T all have the words. Arguments for a conflate text (Janzen 1973: 17) or an MT insertion (McKane) should be rejected.

for we remain a few from many. The group was probably small, but the conclusion should not be drawn that their departure from Mizpah left Judah devoid of inhabitants. Others doubtless remained in the country (Lipschits 1998: 483); in 52:30 it is reported that 745 Judahites were exiled to Babylon in 582 B.C. The idea of a few people going to Egypt in hopes of expanding there (cf. v 14) would be an interesting appeal to the Exodus tradition (Exod 1:7, 20; Deut 26:5), but this will not happen (vv 15–17), because the Exodus experience will be reversed (Alonso-Schökel 1981: 249). For Jeremiah, the future of the covenant people lies with the exiles in Babylon (24:5–7); they are the ones that will be built up (29:6), and from Babylon the new Exodus will take place (29:10–14). On the covenant people returning to Egypt even though they were never to return, see Deut 17:16 and 28:68 (cf. Hos 8:13).

3. *'And let Yahweh your God tell us the way in which we should go and the thing that we should do.'* The request is sufficiently ambiguous, making one wonder again if the decision to go to Egypt has not already been made (cf. 41:17). If it has, the question may simply be which route to take (Cheyne). Or are the people and their leaders open to any destination, including a location in Judah? Jewish interpretation is divided over this question (Rosenberg, 326). Other commentators split over whether the request is sincere (Cheyne; Peake; Hyatt) or disingenuous (Calvin; Streane). Calvin cites the common human tendency to seek advice after one has already made up one's mind what to do. Streane compares with Ahab's disingenuous behavior in 1 Kings 22.

as your eyes now see us. I.e., as you yourself now see (us). The LXX lacks the pronoun "us." Calvin says this remark and the earlier one about the group being small is meant to evoke pity.

4. *I hear.* Hebrew *šāmaʿtî.* Hayward's (1987: 159) translation of T is similarly cryptic: "I have heard (you)."

Look I will pray to Yahweh your God. Volz notes that Jeremiah says "Yahweh *your* God" to the people, and then in v 5 the people say "Yahweh *your* God" to him. The pronoun usage is not fortuitous (*pace* Bright: "interesting but probably not significant"), pointing up distance if not outright tension between people and prophet. Something similar occurred in the wilderness when, after Aaron fashioned his golden calf, Yahweh said to Moses: "Go down; for *your* people whom *you* brought up from the land of Egypt have behaved corruptly," to which Moses replies: "Why, O Yahweh, does your anger burn hot against *your* people whom *you* brought forth from the land of Egypt?" (Exod 32:7, 11). Similarly in the NT, the elder brother in Jesus' parable of the Lost (Prodigal) Son says to his father after hearing about his younger brother's return and the party going on: "But when this son of *yours* came . . ." (Luke 15:30; cf. Hultgren 2000: 81–82). The vigor of the exchange is lost in the LXX, which has "our God" (*Theon hēmōn*). But see the reported words of the people in v 20.

'the entire word that Yahweh answers you I will tell you; I will not hold back from you a word.' W. Janzen (1981: 99) thinks that Jeremiah may be giving here more assurance than is asked of him, although the possibility that a prophet

might withhold all or part of the divine word is a real one (see Note for 50:2). Calvin says Jeremiah is regarding the people with suspicion.

that Yahweh answers you. The LXX omits "you" (*'etkem*), which can be due to haplography (homoeoarcton: *'aleph . . . 'aleph*). Emending MT to "your God" (Volz; Rudolph) is not necessary.

5. *Then they, they said*. The Hebrew emphasizes by adding the independent pronoun.

'*Yahweh be a true and faithful witness against us.*' Calvin says the people swear an oath because they think Jeremiah suspects them of being insincere. That they were (vv 19–21). In the NT compare Peter's denial of Jesus with an oath (Matt 26:72–74 et passim). On being a true and faithful witness, see Prov 14:5, 25.

the entire word that Yahweh your God sends you for us, we so do. Alonso-Schökel (1981: 248) points out the similarity to a confession made by the people in Exod 19:8 and 24:3, 7.

6. *the voice of Yahweh our God . . . we will obey, in order that it may go well with us. Indeed we will obey the voice of Yahweh our God!* Obedience is what Yahweh asked of the Wilderness generation, according to 7:23, where the phrase "that it may go well with you" refers here as it does in Deuteronomy to reaping the copious benefits that accrue from living in fidelity to covenant demands. Gedaliah, too, told the people it would go well with them if they stayed in the land and served the king of Babylon (40:9). Here the discourse normalizes after the alienating pronouns of vv 4–5; it is now "the voice of Yahweh *our* God . . . we will obey . . . we will obey the voice of Yahweh *our* God."

in order that. Or "to the end that." Hebrew *lĕma'an 'ăšer* expresses purpose (H. G. Mitchell 1879: 23; GKC §165b); the conjunction *'ăšer* alone has this meaning in v 14.

we are sending. The Kt *'ănû* is postbiblical Hebrew for "we," found in the Bible only here (GKC §32d); Q has the usual *'ănaḥnû*.

7. *And it happened at the end of ten days that the word of Yahweh came to Jeremiah*. This remarkable statement is the only one of its kind in Scripture (Abarbanel), although we really do not know whether such a wait was that much out of the ordinary. It could be that Jeremiah often waited days for answers to his intercessons. Some time elapsed between Jeremiah's rebuff by Hananiah and his return to give Hananiah a judgmental word from Yahweh (28:12), and twice we are told that Jeremiah waited—how long we do not know—for Yahweh's word after being told it would come (18:1–5; 32:6–8), but none of these situations fits the one here. Skinner (1926: 336–37) suggested that the ten-day wait was so that Jeremiah might attain certainty of the message he was delivering, but this is doubtful. Certainty is required for every proclamation of Yahweh's word. Jones says that since it is the Lord's message, not Jeremiah's, it comes in the Lord's time.

that the word of Yahweh came to Jeremiah. On this third-person superscriptional form, see Note for 28:12.

8–9. *So he announced . . . and said*. A double verb construction as in vv 1–2 (see there).

8. *who were with him*. The LXX lacks these words, although it translates them in 41:11 and 16. How they could be an MT gloss (so Janzen 1973: 54; Holladay) is unclear.

9. *and said to them*. 2QJer has אלוהימה for MT אליהם, which Baillet (1962: 63) says is a "curious mistake of the scribe."

God of Israel, to whom you sent me to lay your request before him. The LXX omits, which can be attributed to haplography (homoeoarcton: *'aleph . . . 'aleph*). Theodotion has the words. This is not an MT pastiche of additions from elsewhere (*pace* Duhm; Janzen 1973: 54; Holladay; McKane).

your request. Hebrew *tĕḥinnatkem*. 2QJer has the plural with full suffix, *tḥnwtykmh*, "your requests" (= Vg *preces vestras*; Baillet 1962: 63).

10. *If you will indeed dwell in this land*. Hebrew *'im-šôb tēšĕbû bā'āreṣ hazzō't*. The MT reading is difficult because it appears to combine the infinitive of *šûb* ("to return") with a conjugated form of *yšb* ("to dwell"). The Versions render the first verb as an infinitive of *yšb*, which gives the meaning "if you will indeed dwell in this land." This is the sense required, and virtually all commentators and all modern Versions go with this translation, or something similar. But Holladay says the MT reading is the *lectio difficilior*, and he cites other examples where Jeremiah combines different but similar roots in unconventional ways (8:13; 48:9). One should note also that *šûb* ("return") occurs in a context similar to the present one in v 12. But because of considerable interplay and confusion in the Hebrew Bible among the three roots, *šûb, yšb, and šbh*, D. N. Freedman suggests that *šôb* is here a byform of the verb *yšb*, and does in fact mean "dwell" (compare *wĕšabtî* in Ps 23:6, which can only mean "And I will dwell," but is derived from *šûb*, not *yšb*; D. N. Freedman 1976: 162–63). The MT reading can then stand. The point is that the traveling group should abandon their hell-bent trek to Egypt and dwell in Judah.

then I will build you up and not overthrow you, and I will plant you and not uproot you. The object *'etkem* ("you") after the first verb in each pair does double-duty for the second verb; cf. 24:6. The perfect *ûbānîtî* with *waw consecutive* has future meaning: "then I will build up" (Giesebrecht). On these four verbs, which are paired elsewhere in Jeremiah, see Note for 1:10. Here the accent is on building and planting, as it is in 24:6; 29:5, 28; 31:28; and elsewhere (see Note for 24:6).

for I have repented concerning the evil that I did to you. The verb is *nḥm* meaning "regret, be sorry for, repent." For its use with reference to Yahweh, see Note for 15:6. Yahweh presently is truly sorry for the evil done to his covenant people, but he may also be saying that he is no longer thinking evil because judgment has been carried out (Peake). Now is the time to begin things anew. So if an "I am sorry" is implied, it could mean "I should never have done what I did" (see "When God Repents" in Andersen and Freedman 1989: 639–79 [= D. N. Freedman 1997 I: 409–46]), or "It pained me to do what unfortunately was necessary." In either case, divine grace is still not guaranteed; building and planting are conditional on people remaining in the land.

The following oracles, together with Jeremiah's interpretive comment, state that disobedience will only lead to another round of evil from the divine hand. Jeremiah knows too—despite personal experience to the contrary—that mediation can bring about Yahweh's repentance (cf. Exod 32:11–14; Amos 7:3, 6), and since he is now engaged in just such an activity, the people must be warned what will happen if they disobey.

11. *Do not be afraid because of him . . . for I am with you to save you and rescue you from his hand.* Years earlier Yahweh reassured Jeremiah with these words (1:8, 19; 15:20). More recently, Jeremiah has been convinced that Nebuchadnezzar is Yahweh's appointee to maintain order in the world, and that all nations must surrender to him (27:5–7; Skinner 1926: 338). Gedaliah, too, at the beginning of his governorship told assembled leaders and their men not to be afraid of serving the Babylonians (40:9). But now with the murder of Gedaliah, Babylonian soldiers, and other innocents at Mizpah, there is new reason for fear (cf. 41:17–18). Even though the individuals in this group were not responsible for those murders, the Babylonians could well "exact vengeance without too nice a discrimination between the guilty and the innocent" (Peake). On the great "I am with you" promise in Scripture," see Note on 1:8.

you. 2QJer has the long form *'tmh* for MT *'tm.*

12. *And I will grant you mercies, and he will be merciful with you.* Yahweh says he will grant mercies to these frightened souls, and that the king of Babylon will do likewise. Instead of "he will be merciful," the LXX, S, and Vg have "I will be merciful," which continues Yahweh's gracious predisposition and also makes for an inelegant redundancy. The MT reading is better, and should be adopted (Calvin; Berridge 1970: 207). For a similar joining of first and third person, see 43:10, 12.

and let you return to your soil. Hebrew *wĕhēšîb 'etkem 'el-'admatkem.* The Versions (except T) have Yahweh continuing to say what he himself will do; however, they divide in reading *šûb* or *yšb.* The LXX (*epistrepsō hymas,* "I will return you") translates the H-stem of *šûb,* but S and Vg (*habitare vos faciam,* "I shall make your dwelling") translate the H-stem of *yšb.* Aquila too has *kathisō hymas* ("I will settle you"). Modern commentators similarly divide over which verb to read (see v 10), but generally interpret the phrase as stating what the king of Babylon will do. Some commentators (Blayney; Giesebrecht; Duhm; Peake; Cornill; Streane; Volz; McKane) repoint to *wĕhōšîb* ("and he will settle / let dwell"), which gets around a perceived problem of people returning to a land they are still in. Others (Cheyne; Rudolph; Weiser; Bright; Thompson; Holladay; Keown et al.) stay with "let you return," which Rudolph says makes good sense. In either case, Yahweh promises positive action by the king of Babylon in restoring the Judahite community to what it was before the Mizpah massacre. As it turned out, the promise was wasted on a people determined to go to Egypt, and when Nebuzaradan did come to Judah, he took another 745 people to Babylon (52:30).

13–15a. These intervening words of Jeremiah anticipate the protasis of the following oracle, "If you then have definitely set your faces to enter Egypt and you enter to sojourn there . . ." (v 15b). In the whole of vv 10–19a is more preaching on the "two ways," familiar from Deut 30:15–20 and found elsewhere in Jer 21:8–9; 26:3–6; and 38:17–18 (see further Note on 6:16).

13. *not obeying the voice of Yahweh your God.* Set forth also as a covenant condition in Deut 8:18–20; 28:15, 45, 62.

14. *saying: 'No!'* Hebrew *lēʾmōr lōʾ*. The LXX omits. In MT these words make an awkward reading because of the repetition of *lēʾmōr* ("saying") from v 13, although a second *lēʾmōr* may have been deemed necessary to mark the resumption of an interrupted quotation. Giesebrecht thinks the LXX translator did not correctly understand *lōʾ* as meaning "No!"

'No! Indeed we will enter the land of Egypt to the end that we will not see war, and the sound of the trumpet we will not hear, and for food we will not hunger, and there we will dwell.' An echo of the cry made by the Wilderness generation, where death in Egypt was thought preferable to war and hunger in an unsettled wasteland (Exod 16:2–3; Num 14:2–3). Alonso-Schökel (1981) views the present situation against the background of the Exodus tradition, although it is not clear that Jeremiah here is an "anti-Moses" figure.

to the end that. On *ʾăšer* expressing purpose in final clauses, see GKC §165b and compare *lĕmaʿan ʾăšer* in v 6.

15. *Remnant of Judah.* Lacking in the LXX, which can be attributed to haplography (homoeoteleuton: *h . . . h*). The words are present in Aq and Theod. The term and its repetition in v 19 aid in framing the two concluding oracles (see Rhetoric and Composition). The view of Duhm, Holladay, and McKane that MT has quarried the term from v 19 and added it here is to be rejected.

If you then have definitely set your faces to enter Egypt. "To set the face" (with either *ntn* or *śym / śwm*) is an idiom expressing determination (21:10; 44:11–12; Ezek 15:7 [2×]; 14:8; Lev 20:5), attested also in Ugaritic and Akkadian texts (Layton 1986). Compare Akk *šakānu* with *panu* (CAD 17/1: 138–40). Berridge (1970: 204) says the idiom appears in none of the Deuteronomic writings, only in the Holiness Code and Ezekiel. See in the NT Luke 9:51: "he [Jesus] set his face to go to Jeruslem."

16. *then it will happen.* Hebrew *wĕhāyĕtâ*. On this feminine form, see GKC §112y.

sword . . . famine. See Note for 5:12.

and there you shall die. Jeremiah's emphatic answer to the people's "and *there* we will dwell" in v 14 (Volz).

17. *So shall all the persons become.* The LXX adds *kai pantes hoi allogeneis* ("and all the foreigners" = *wĕkōl-hazzārîm*), which could have been lost in MT through haplography (homoeoteleuton: *ym . . . ym*). With the phrase would be an explicit mention of foreigners in the traveling band, people perhaps such as Jezaniah son of the Maacathite (see Note on 40:8).

by sword, by famine, and by pestilence. The LXX omits "and by pestilence," which could be due to haplography (homoeoarcton: *w . . . w*). The term is represented in Theod (*kai en thanatō*) and Symm ([*kai*] *en loimō*). But Giesebrecht says the LXX omission of this term is usual (see again v 22). For discussion and support of the LXX reading, see Janzen 1973: 43–44.

they shall not have a survivor or fugitive. See 44:14, although there the judgment is mitigated.

the evil that I am bringing upon them. For this Jeremianic expression, see Note on 6:19.

18. *Just as my anger and my wrath were poured out upon the inhabitants of Jerusalem, so my wrath will be poured out upon you when you enter Egypt.* On the *ka'ăšer . . . kēn* ("Just . . . so") construction, see Note for 2:26. This, in a nutshell, is the basic message to the end of chap. 44. The people see going to Egypt as their salvation, but Yahweh says they will meet the same fate as those previously inhabiting Jerusalem.

my anger and my wrath. Hebrew *'appî waḥămātî.* On this stereotyped expression in Jeremiah, see Note for 21:5. Compound subjects can take a singular verb (GKC §146f). The LXX has only one term, *ho thumos mou*, and if its *Vorlage* lacked *waḥămātî* ("and my wrath"), this loss could be attributed to haplography (homoeoteleuton: *y . . . y*).

And you shall be a curse, and a desolation, and a swearword, and a reproach. These terms all appear in strings of curse words in Jeremiah (see Note for 24:9).

a curse. Hebrew *'ālâ.* On this term, see Note for 29:18.

a desolation. Hebrew *šammâ.* A very common term in Jeremiah (see Note for 24:9).

a swearword. Hebrew *qĕlālâ.* On this term, see Note for 24:9.

a reproach. Hebrew *ḥerpâ.* Another very common term in Jeremiah (see Note for 24:9).

19. *Yahweh has spoken concerning you, Remnant of Judah, Do not enter Egypt!* The T, Symm, and Vg read *dbr* as a noun, "word," which is what appears in v 15a. If the Hebrew were pointed *dĕbar-yhwh* ("the word of Yahweh") rather than *dibber yhwh* ("Yahweh has spoken"), we would get the reading: "The word of Yahweh against you, Remnant of Judah: 'Do not enter Egypt!'" Despite wide support for this reading, the initial words are not introductory, nor is "Do not enter Egypt" a supplemental divine word. The entire sentence — including "Do not enter Egypt" — is Jeremiah speaking (Holladay; NAB; NJV; NRSV; NSB), summarizing what has just been said in the oracles of vv 15b–18 (see Rhetoric and Composition). The MT pointing, therefore, is correct.

Know for sure. Hebrew *yādōa' tēdĕ'û.* This expression, repeating in v 22, comes also from the mouth of Jeremiah when he makes his defense before the court (26:15).

that I have warned you today. This LXX omission is likely due to haplography (whole word plus: *ky h . . . ky h*), as Janzen (1973: 118) and Holladay both recognize. Aquila has the words.

20. *Indeed you led yourselves astray.* Hebrew *hit'êtem bĕnapšôtêkem* (Q) is lit. "you caused error in yourselves." The Vg: *decepistis animas vestras,* "you deceived your own souls." The people and their leaders deceived themselves

when they asked Jeremiah to mediate, for now it turns out that they were of no mind to obey Yahweh's word, even though they emphatically said they were (v 6). The Q reading, incidentally, indicates that the Kt is a misspelling due to metathesis (*taw* and *yod* inverted). Some editions of *BHS* leave out the *yod* in the Q, but it is present in the marginal readings of both M^L and M^A.

for you, you sent me. Hebrew *kî-'attem šĕlaḥtem*. The independent pronoun is for emphasis. See also the emphatic *wĕhēmmâ*, "as for them," in v 5. It was the people, after all, who sent Jeremiah to intercede with Yahweh in the first place.

to Yahweh your God. The LXX omits, and some take as an MT plus (Cornill; Janzen 1973: 54; Holladay; McKane). D. N. Freedman suggests LXX haplography due to a repetition of the letters *'aleph* and *lamed*: *'l . . . 'l . . . l'. . . .* In the same verse the LXX lacks a second "our God," and misreads a third "our God" after "Yahweh."

our God . . . so tell us. The LXX's *peri hēmōn* appears to misread *'ĕlōhênû* ("our God") as *'ēlênû* ("concerning us"), after which an omitted *kēn haggedlānû* ("so tell us") can be attributed to haplography (homoeoteleuton: *nw . . . nw*). The LXX, once again, is not the better text (*pace* McKane).

21. *And I told you today.* Hebrew *wā'aggid lākem hayyôm.* Omitted in the LXX, probably due to haplography (homoeoarcton: *w . . . w*).

and you have not obeyed the voice of Yahweh your God regarding all that he sent me to you. The very thing the people promised *not* to do (v 13). See again 43:4, 7; and 44:23. The problem of disobedience is an ancient one (7:24–26; Num 14:22).

your God regarding all. Omitted in the LXX, probably due to haplography (homoeoarcton: *'aleph . . . 'aleph*). Janzen (1973: 67, 80) and Holladay take the MT as another "pastiche expansion."

22. *know for sure that.* Hebrew *yādōa' tēdĕ'û kî.* Omitted in the LXX, but structurally necessary (see Rhetoric and Composition).

by sword, by famine, and by pestilence. On this triad, see v 17 and Note for 5:12. The LXX again lacks "and by pestilence," but it is present in Aq, Theod, and Symm.

you wish to enter to sojourn. The verb *ḥpṣ* means "to take pleasure in, delight in" (6:10; 9:23[Eng 9:24]), but with the connotation of intention or purpose it is somewhat like the English, "What is your pleasure?" The people's pleasure at this point is to go to Egypt.

MESSAGE AND AUDIENCE

The first segment of narrative reports to its audience what happened next to the anxious band of travelers who left Mizpah and have now taken up temporary residence at Geruth Chimham. It has already been told that they were of a mind to go to Egypt (41:17), and while nothing is said here of that plan, it is nevertheless in the background as the people express their desire to see what Yahweh has in mind. The company led by Johanan son of Kareah and one

Jezaniah son of Hoshaiah approaches Jeremiah and asks him to intercede with Yahweh on their behalf. Jeremiah has done this often enough before. The request now is for Yahweh's favor regarding the journey they have undertaken. Citing their diminishing numbers, the people ask that Jeremiah's God tell them which way to go and what they should do. Jeremiah hears them, and says he will pray to Yahweh, who, by the way, is not just his God but theirs, and he will bring back to them Yahweh's word in its entirety. He will not hold back a thing good or bad. The people respond with a great show of faith, taking an oath that they will accept Yahweh's word in full. They, too, know that this word could be for good or ill, but so be it; their promise is to obey the voice of Yahweh their God, confident that in so doing it will go well with them. This promise is repeated a second time.

The second segment reports Yahweh's answer in four oracles, added to which are comments interspersed from the prophet. It took ten days for an answer to come, and when it came Jeremiah returned to the people and their leaders to report it to them. The first oracle promised conditional salvation. If this people will return from the journey they are currently on, and will dwell in Judah, Yahweh will build them up. Yahweh is no longer of a mind to bring evil on his people or his land. The people must not be afraid of the king of Babylon, even though Yahweh knows they are afraid. A companion oracle then reiterates this promise of salvation. It is the same basic word that was given to the prophet at his call and commissioning. The people need not be afraid; Yahweh will rescue them from the one they fear and will show them mercy, allowing them to return to their land. Jeremiah saw it happen in his own life. The same can happen again. The people wanted a favorable word from Yahweh; now they have received it.

Jeremiah then intervenes with a word of his own, anticipating the remaining oracles that set forth conditional judgment. If the people will not dwell in the land, which in this case adds up to disobeying the voice of Yahweh, and are determined to enter Egypt in the hopes that war and famine will not follow them there, they must then hear this word from Yahweh. Yahweh's word, make no mistake about it, is coming here in all its fullness; the prophet is not holding back a word. The oracle states that if the people are determined to go to Egypt, the sword and famine they hope to escape will in fact overtake them. In Egypt they will die. This point is restated, with the unwelcome addition that the group, now but a remnant, will end up without a survivor. A final oracle states that the group will be a victim of Yahweh's wrath just as Jerusalem's inhabitants were, and their sorry end will live on only as curses and reproaches in the mouths of those who do survive, and they will never see this land again.

Jeremiah concludes with some words of his own. He says Yahweh has now spoken to this remnant telling them not to enter Egypt. Jeremiah has given them fair warning. Then comes some body language from the people that they will not accept what they have heard. Is it in their eyes? Is it a stony silence conveying more than words? However the message was conveyed, Jeremiah's final words (vv 20–22) are to people who, for all practical purposes, have rejected Yahweh's word. The prophet accuses them of outright deceit. They asked for intercession and promised to do what Yahweh told them. But now they say they will not do it. What this people really wanted was divine approval for a plan already made. Jeremiah can only say that they shall meet a sorry end in the land where they are going. This narrative, probably also from Baruch, can be dated anytime after 582 B.C.

C. EXILE TO EGYPT (43:1–13)

1. Remnant Rejects Yahweh's Word! (43:1–4)

43 ¹And it happened when Jeremiah had finished speaking to all the people all the words of Yahweh their God, that is, all these words with which Yahweh their God had sent him to them. ²Then said Azariah son of Hoshaiah, with Johanan son of Kareah and all the insolent men saying to Jeremiah, 'You are telling a lie! Yahweh our God did not send you saying, You shall not enter Egypt to sojourn there. ³Indeed, Baruch son of Neriah has incited you against us in order to give us into the hand of the Chaldeans, to kill us or exile us to Babylon.' ⁴So Johanan son of Kareah and all the princes of the troops and all the people did not obey the voice of Yahweh to dwell in the land of Judah.

2. On to Tahpanhes! (43:5–7)

43 ⁵Then Johanan son of Kareah and all the princes of the troops took the entire remnant of Judah that had returned from all the nations where they were dispersed to sojourn in the land of Judah—⁶men and women and small children, and daughters of the king, yes, every person whom Nebuzaradan the Rab-tabahim had left behind with Gedaliah son of Ahikam, son of Shaphan, including Jeremiah the prophet and Baruch son of Neriah. ⁷And they came to the land of Egypt, for they did not obey the voice of Yahweh. And they came as far as Tahpanhes.

3. But Nebuchadrezzar Will Come to Egypt! (43:8–13)

43 ⁸And the word of Yahweh came to Jeremiah in Tahpanhes: ⁹Take in your hand large stones, and you shall hide them with mortar in the pavement that is at the entrance of the house of Pharaoh in Tahpanhes, before the eyes of the Judahite men. ¹⁰And you shall say to them:
  Thus said Yahweh of hosts, God of Israel:
  Look I am sending for and will take Nebuchadrezzar, king of Babylon, my servant, and I will set his throne over these stones that I have hidden, and he will spread his pavilion over them. ¹¹And he shall

come[1] and strike down the land of Egypt: Whoever is to death—to death, and whoever is to captivity—to captivity, and whoever is to the sword—to the sword. [12]And I will kindle a fire in the houses of the gods of Egypt, and he shall burn them and take them captive, and wrap up the land of Egypt as the shepherd wraps himself up with his garment; then he shall leave from there in peace. [13]Also, he shall break the obelisks of Beth-shemesh (that is in the land of Egypt), and the houses of the gods of Egypt he will burn with fire.

RHETORIC AND COMPOSITION

MT 43:1–13 = LXX 50:1–13. The present chapter contains three narrative segments: vv 1–4; vv 5–7; and vv 8–13, which derive their structure from the same stereotypical phrases that provide the structure for the narrative segments of chap. 42 (see Rhetoric and Composition for 42:1–22):

I	*And it happened . . .*	*wayĕhî*	v 1
	And . . . did not obey the voice of Yahweh . . .	*wĕlō'-šāma' . . . bĕqôl yhwh*	v 4
II	*. . . and all the princes of the troops . . .*	*wĕkol-śárê haḥăyālîm*	v 5
	. . . they did not obey the voice of Yahweh . . .	*lō' šāmĕ'û bĕqôl yhwh*	v 7
III	*And it came . . .*	*wayĕhî*	v 8
	. . . .		

Section markings corroborate this breakdown, except that the major medieval codices do not have a section after v 4. But in 4QJer[b[d]] the scribe did leave an interval after this verse, which could be a section (Tov 1997: 204). One may also note that there is no section in any of the medieval codices after v 3, where many commentators divide. The beginning of the unit is marked by a *setumah* in M[A], M[L], and M[P] before v 1, which is the chapter division. After v 7 is a *setumah* in M[A], M[L], and M[P], but apparently not in 4QJer[b[d]] (Tov 1997: 204). In 4QJer[b[d]] is also an interval after v 9, which could be a section before the words of introduction to the oracle. The end of the unit is marked by a *setumah* in M[L], and a *petuḥah* in M[A] and M[P], after v 13. Duhm and others take v 13 as a later addition, which it may be since the prediction it contains appears to have been fulfilled years later (see Notes). All three medieval codices have in addition a *setumah* after v 1, which sets off the word of introduction (v 1) from the people's response to Jeremiah's oracles (vv 2–4). Portions of this chapter are represented in the Qumran scrolls: 43:3–9 (Tov: 43:2–10) in 4QJer[b[d]], and 43:8–11 in 2QJer. The former follows closely the text of the LXX; the latter reflects the textual tradition of MT.

These segments like those preceding have numerous textual variations between MT and LXX, most of which are again quite minor. The LXX has pronoun

---

[1]Reading the Q *ûbā'* with T; Kt *ûbā'â* ("it [fem.] shall come") may refer to the "camp" according to Kimḥi (*maḥăneh* seems to be both masculine and feminine).

changes, misreadings of the Hebrew, and numerous omissions—patronyms, titles, particles, and phrases, some of which are likely due to haplography. Duhm, Cornill, Holladay, and McKane express consistent preference for the LXX, whereas Giesebrecht evaluates more positively the MT, and he is followed in this respect by Volz, Rudolph, and Weiser. The MT, though more prolix, is much the better text, and deserves in most cases preference over the LXX, also in vv 2–10 over 4QJer[b][d], which reflects the shorter text of LXX.

The entire chapter is prose (*pace* Volz, who scans vv 10b–12 as poetry), which commentators have generally attributed to Baruch. That Baruch has authored this prose gains in plausibility with the group's having moved to Egypt. Baruch is the one person of known scribal capability in the group (v 3), and the likely person to record what was happening. Verses 8–13 are said by Duhm to be "a historically worthless Midrash," but commentators since, with the exception of McKane, reject with Giesebrecht this radical assessment. McKane claims vv 8–13 do not go well with vv 1–7, but that is because he takes vv 8–13 as a judgment against Egypt, not against Jews residing in Egypt—a dubious distinction, to say the least, which McKane then accommodates to his notion that Jeremiah cannot be a prophet to other nations. As it happens, vv 1–7 and vv 8–13 go perfectly well together; their alleged lack of coherence (so Duhm and McKane) is purely contrived.

NOTES

43:1. *And it happened.* The *wayĕhî* may also be rendered "And the following happened," since the verse (concluded by a section marking) is not a dependent clause, but an independent sentence introducing the response to Jeremiah's oracles in vv 2–4.

to all the people. Hebrew *'el-kol-hā'ām*. The LXX lacks *kol* ("all"), which could be due to haplography (homoeoteleuton: *l . . . l*). Aquila and Symm reflect MT with *panta ton laon*.

2. *Then said Azariah son of Hoshaiah, with Johanan son of Kareah and all the insolent men saying to Jeremiah, 'You are telling a lie! Yahweh our God did not send you saying, You shall not enter Egypt to sojourn there.'* Jeremiah has been traveling with Johanan ever since the latter assumed control over the Mizpah remnant at Gibeon, and only a few days ago Johanan was one of those asking Jeremiah to intercede on the remnant's behalf, which he did. Now Johanan and the others, having received an answer not to their liking, are openly hostile, accusing Jeremiah of speaking a lie (*šeqer*)—a serious charge, one that Jeremiah leveled at the Jerusalem prophets he considered false (23:14, 26, 32; 27:10, 14, 16; 28:15; 29:23, 31). The charge is also made that Yahweh had not "sent" (*šlḥ*) Jeremiah, which again, Jeremiah had said about other prophets (23:21, 32; 27:15; 28:15). At his trial in 609 B.C., Jeremiah said he had been sent by Yahweh, and those present accepted his testimony (26:12–16). Where had Johanan and the others been in the years prior to Jerusalem's fall? Did they not know this man Jeremiah, and his reputation for being a true prophet of Yah-

weh? Calvin finds it incredible that Johanan and the others could dismiss what the prophet has told them. In his view, Johanan was a wise, prudent, and upright man, better than Gedaliah. Calvin, it seems, has not discerned this man's true character. Johanan may have been better than Ishmael, but not much, for he too was not above murder on the sly, which marks Ishmael for being the evil man he was (see Note on 40:14). We recall also various hidden subtleties in the narrative reporting the request for intercession, also in Jeremiah's response, which point to tension already between Jeremiah and members of the group, e.g., the ambiguity in how the request was worded (v 3); the "your God" language in the exchange between prophet and people (vv 4–5); Jeremiah's need to specify that he will deliver Yahweh's word in its entirety (v 4); the people's need to swear an oath in support of their claim that they will obey Yahweh (v 5); and above all, Jeremiah's anticipation of a negative response by the leaders, one of whom was Johanan, and others who were with them (vv 19b–22).

Azariah son of Hoshaiah. Probably a brother to Jezaniah son of Hoshaiah, who earlier acted as spokesman for the group together with Johanan son of Kareah (see Note for 42:1). "Azariah" is a common name in the period, having turned up in a number of extrabiblical contexts (see Appendix I).

Johanan son of Kareah. See Note on 40:8.

with all the insolent men saying to Jeremiah. The LXX lacks "the insolent ones" (*hazzēdîm*), which may be due to haplography (homoeoteleuton: *ym . . . ym*). The word should be retained (Giesebrecht; Rudolph). Baruch, assuming that he is the narrator, may in using this term be responding not only to Jeremiah's discreditation as a true Yahweh prophet but also to the slander following (v 3). The plural participle *'ōmĕrîm*, though common enough in the poetry and prose, makes for a redundancy after the earlier "Then (he) said," for which reason some modern Versions (RSV, NJV, NIV, NJB, NSB) do not translate it. Some commentators following Giesebrecht emend to *wĕhammōrîm*, "and (the) rebellious," which gives the embellished reading, "arrogant and rebellious men." But this is little more than a guess, and not particularly convincing with the lack of any textual support. This emended reading was adopted by JB, but abandoned in NJB. The LXX and Vg have both verbs, and both verbs were translated by the AV. Since the participle predicates "arrogant men," it could be that these individuals, being distinguished by the narrator from Johanan and Azariah, are voicing their rejection loudly and repeatedly in the background (like backbenchers in the English Parliament), for which reason a second verb is deemed necessary. But then something more vigorous than "saying" would be required. The NAB translates: "and all the insolent men shouted to Jeremiah."

You are telling a lie. Hebrew *šeqer 'attâ mĕdabbēr*. The LXX lacks "You are telling," which gives nevertheless an acceptable reading since *šeqer* ("a lie") can stand alone (37:14; cf. Ehrlich 1912: 348). But the omission could also be due to haplography (homoeoteleuton: *r . . . r*).

Yahweh our God did not send you saying. The LXX lacks "our God" as elsewhere, but here it follows with *pros hēmas*, "to us" (= Heb *'ēlênû*), which could be a misreading of *'ĕlōhênû* ("our God"), or else an indication that *'ēlênû* was present in its *Vorlage*. If *'ēlênû* was present in the LXX's *Vorlage*, then the lack of "our God" could be another loss due to haplography (homoeoarcton: *'l . . . 'l*). It is also possible that *'ēlênû* was lost in MT due to haplography (homoeoteleuton: *ynw . . . ynw*), since the sense requires "to us."

3. *'Indeed, Baruch son of Neriah has incited you against us in order to give us into the hand of the Chaldeans, to kill us or exile us to Babylon.'* Here we learn for the first time that Baruch is present in the traveling party; later in v 6 we are told that Baruch arrived in Egypt with Jeremiah and the others. At first glance, it is surprising to see Baruch targeted by the group over an intercession request that did not go its way. The charge of treasonous collaboration with the Babylonians is a weighty one, but since it is baseless it cannot be taken that seriously. We need not wonder then, as some commentators do, how a mere amanuensis to Jeremiah could be so assertive, or imagine with Duhm and Hyatt that Baruch's influence over the prophet must be increasing now that Jeremiah is an aged man. It is lame for the people to suggest that Baruch somehow managed to impede Jeremiah's delivery of the divine word, although Baruch belonged to an important profession and did descend from one of Jerusalem's leading scribal families. Also, by blaming Baruch the people will seemingly preempt the charge that they have rejected Yahweh and the prophet delivering Yahweh's word to them. But Baruch in writing the narrative had the last word, even if Johanan and others did get their way.

Baruch son of Neriah. 4QJer[b[d]] appears to lack "son of Neriah" (Tov 1997: 203–4), which is present in the LXX.

in order to. Hebrew *lĕma'an* can express definite purpose in final clauses (H. G. Mitchell 1879: 24; GKC §165b). See also 44:29.

4. Jeremiah does not answer this reckless charge; the narrative simply resumes, stating that the people and their leaders disobeyed Yahweh by not remaining in Judah.

Johanan son of Kareah. 4QJer[b(d)] lacks "son of Kareah," which is also lacking in the LXX. Both texts omit the patronym again in v 5.

5. *the entire remnant of Judah that had returned from all the nations where they were dispersed to sojourn in the land of Judah.* This expansive statement—allowing even for exaggeration—must simply refer to those who returned to Mizpah from neighboring countries after learning that Gedaliah had been appointed governor (40:11–12), and who now make up the company of which Johanan is the leader. The LXX has a shorter reading, omitting "from all the nations where they were dispersed."[2] 4QJer[b[d]] has a gap at this point, which Janzen (1973: 182–83) said could be filled with the text of LXX, but not the text of MT. Tov (1997: 203), however, fills the gap with text from the MT up until "to sojourn in the land of Judah," which he takes to be the omission. Giese-

---

[2]*BHS* has its "a—a" omission wrong, failing to include *niddĕḥû-šām*, "they were dispersed [there]."

brecht, Volz, Weiser, and Rudolph all went earlier with MT, which is the better reading (*pace* Duhm; Janzen 1973: 53 #141; Holladay; McKane).

to sojourn in the land of Judah. The LXX has "to settle in the land" (*katoikein en tē gē*), which probably assumes that "Judah" is the land in question. Janzen (1973: 182–83) read "land of Egypt" in a damaged 4QJer[b(d)], which made no sense (returnees came from other nations to Judah, not to Egypt). This is because he read only a single *mem* in line 4, which he took to be the final letter of *miṣrayim*, "Egypt." But Tov (1997: 203) more recently has read two letters in the line, *šin, mem*, which rules out "Egypt," and produces *šām* ("there") in the verse. There is also a perceived problem in the reference to people "sojourning" (*gwr*) in Judah. It is more usual to speak of "sojourning" in Egypt (42:15, 17, 22; 43:2, 5; 44:8, 12, 14, 28). However, sojourning in Judah is possible. It was possible earlier for the Rechabites (35:7), and of late it describes precisely what the company here has been doing. The MT reading is then acceptable and the one that should be retained.

6. *men and women and small children, and daughters of the king*. Enumerations of a similar nature occur in 40:7 and 41:16. Hebrew *gĕbārîm* here means "(able-bodied) men," which the LXX translates as *tous dunatous andras* ("the mighty men"); cf. 41:16. "Daughters of the king" (*bĕnôt hammelek*) may denote "princesses" more generally (see Note for 41:10). When Petrie arrived to excavate ancient Tahpanhes in 1886, he was told that the large building in ruins there was known as *Kasr el Bint el Yehudi*, "The Palace of the Jew's Daughter."

yes, every person whom Nebuzaradan the Rab-tabahim had left behind with Gedaliah son of Ahikam, son of Shaphan, including Jeremiah the prophet and Baruch son of Neriah. Another inclusive statement like the one in v 5. Here, allowing once again for exaggeration, reference must be to those people entrusted to Gedaliah's care at Mizpah, not everyone remaining in Judah after Nebuzaradan had returned home.

Nebuzaradan the Rab-tabahim. 4QJer[b(d)] omits "the Rab-tabahim," as does the LXX, and spells the name *nbwzrdn* ("Nebuzardan"), which more closely corresponds to LXX's *Nabouzardan*.

Ahikam, son of Shaphan. 4QJer[b(d)] lacks "son of Shaphan," as does the LXX.

7. *the land of Egypt*. The LXX lacks "land," but the word is present in Symm and 4QJer[b(d)].

And they came as far as Tahpanhes. 4QJer[b(d)] omits *'ad* ("as far as"), which gives the reading preferred by Calvin: "(and) they entered Tahpanhes."

Tahpanhes. Hebrew *taḥpanḥēs*. The etymology of the name is uncertain; it may mean "Fort of the Negro" (Copher 1975: 15; cf. KB[3]). The spelling lacks a *nun* in 4QJer[b(d)], but Tov (1997: 205) says this is probably a scribal error (in v 9 it has an "n"; the LXX spelling is *Taphnas*). Tahpanhes, cited earlier in 2:16 and present in Ezek 30:18 with a different spelling, was a frontier town located in Egypt's eastern Delta on the caravan route leading to Palestine and points north. Bordering on Sinai, the ancient town is now commonly identified with Tell Defneh, a desert site near Lake Menzaleh, about twelve miles west of the present-day Suez Canal. Tell Defneh preserves the Greek name, *Daphne / Daphnai* (of

Pelusium), which is mentioned by Herodotus (ii 30; cf. Petrie 1888: 47; Alt 1943). Excavation of the site was carried out in 1886 by Petrie (1888: 47–96 + plates; 1892: 50–63), who uncovered the ruins of a fortified residence built originally for Psammetichus I (664–610 B.C.). The excavation also turned up an abundance of Greek pottery and other Greek artifacts, from which it may be concluded that Greek mercenaries manned the fort during the reigns of Psammetichus I, Neco II, Psammetichus II, and Apries / Hophra (664–570 B.C.). This corroborates Herodotus's report that Psammetichus I gave Greeks sanctuary in Egypt, after which he employed them as mercenaries in his army (see Note for 46:9). Petrie believed that the population during this period was mixed, but was mostly Greek. With the accession of Amasis (570–526 B.C.), the town was emptied of Greeks, and Egyptians were brought in to man the fort. These were later replaced by Persians. The group now arriving may have had to wait at this town until Egyptian officials decided on their entrance into the country, but later we hear about Jews living here as well as in certain other parts of the country (44:1). According to the pseudepigraphical *Lives of the Prophets* (2:1–2; *OTP II*: 386), Jeremiah was stoned to death at Tahpanhes and buried there.

8. *And the word of Yahweh came to Jeremiah in Tahpanhes.* On this superscription in third-person form, see Note for 28:12.

9. *Take in your hand large stones, and you shall hide them with mortar in the pavement that is at the entrance of the house of Pharaoh in Tahpanhes, before the eyes of the Judahite men.* This is another of the many symbolic acts carried out by Jeremiah over the years, on which see § Introduction: Prophetic Symbolism: Act and Being; also Note for 13:1. Although it is unclear precisely where in front of Pharaoh's house Jeremiah was to hide these stones, the interpretation of the action given in the oracle following is clear enough. Some years earlier, at the village of Parah near Jeremiah's home, the prophet hid a loincloth in a rock to dramatize Judah's loss of pride for abandoning the covenant. The action here symbolizes a coming judgment upon Egypt, but the main point is that this newly-arrived remnant from Judah, which is still a rebellious bunch, will share in that judgment even though it came to Egypt to find refuge.

Take in your hand large stones. Hebrew *qaḥ bĕyādĕkā 'ăbānîm gĕdōlôt*. The imperatives *qaḥ* and *qĕḥû* ("Take!") occur commonly in divine commands to the prophet: "*Take* the loincloth that you bought . . . *and take* from there the loincloth" (13:4, 6); "*Take* this wrath-filled cup of the wine" (25:15); "*Take* wives and beget sons and daughters . . . *and take* wives for your sons, and your daughters give to husbands" (29:6); "*Take* these deeds" (32:14); and "*Take* for yourself a writing-scroll . . . once again *take* for yourself another roll" (36:2, 28). The stones here are large because they must support the throne of the Babylonian king (v 10).

and you shall hide them with mortar in the pavement that is at the entrance of the house of Pharaoh in Tahpanhes. The fortified residence uncovered here does not appear to have been occupied during the reign of Apries, which is when Johanan and his company arrive from Judah, and it is doubtful whether it was a palace per se. The ruin seems rather to have been a government build-ing manned by soldiers and other officials whose job it was to guard Egypt's northern frontier. The capital of Egypt at the time was at Saïs in the western Delta. At Elephantine, which guarded the southern frontier, was a "house of the king" (*byt mlk'*) dating to the Persian period, as we know from the Elephan-tine papyri (AP 2.12, 14, 16). This too was a governmental building, since the king lived neither here nor at nearby Syene. Petrie found in front of the Tah-panhes fortress, to the northwest, an extensive brick pavement he thought was probably used as a public square and a place to transact business. He believed this pavement was what is described in the present verse (Petrie 1888: 50–51; 1892: 54). For pictures of the reconstructed fortress and the pavement, see Pet-rie 1892 and Maspero 1900: 496.

with mortar in the pavement that. Perhaps lacking in the LXX (so *BHS*), in which case the omission could be due to haplography (homoeoarcton: *b* . . . *b*). But the LXX may have misunderstood the Hebrew since it translates *bĕ-petaḥ* ("at the entrance") with a double expression, *en prothurois en pulē* ("in the entrance, at the gate"). The readings of Aq and Theod (*en tō kruphiō*), also Symm (*en apokruphois*), appear to translate Heb *ballāṭ* (omitting the *mem*), meaning "in secret." Cornill, who accepts the idea of secrecy, imagines an ac-tion occurring at night (cf. Ezek 12:7). But this cannot be right. The act is a public one, and doubtless occurred in broad daylight.

with mortar in the pavement. Hebrew *bammeleṭ bammalbēn*. The first term, *meleṭ*, is a *hapax legomenon* in the OT, but sufficiently clarified by Ar *milāṭ*, which means "(clay) mortar" (Rashi; Kimḥi; G. R. Driver 1937–38: 122; Kelso 1948: 35 #86). It does not mean "clay pavement" or the like (*pace* Rudolph; Bright; Holladay; cf. KB³), which wrongly assumes a glossing by *malbēn* follow-ing. The stones are not hidden *in* mortar, but *with* mortar (mortar being the binding agent). Streane has it right. He says the command is to "lay [the stones] with mortar in the pavement (or square)." McKane too has the proper sense. The meaning of *malbēn* is similarly uncertain, but "pavement" or "brick terrace" in the present context is widely accepted (cf. KB³). Akkadian *nalbanu* means "brickwork" (G. R. Driver 1937–38: 122) or "brick mold" (*CAD* 11/1: 199–200). A brick terrace is precisely what Petrie found in front of the entrance to the fort.

the house of Pharaoh. Lacking in 4QJer^b(d), but present in the LXX. Janzen (1973: 183) says the loss is probably by haplography (homoeoarcton: *b* . . . *b*). But just prior in the text is a lacuna (Tov 1997: 205 says 23 letter-spaces), mak-ing reconstruction of the line difficult.

before the eyes of the Judahite men. Symbolic acts require witnesses (19:10); in fact, that is the purpose in carrying them out. This one is per-formed in a foreign country, like Seraiah's symbolic act on the banks of the Euphrates some years earlier (51:61–64; cf. Amesz 1997). The witnesses here, as there, will be only Jews, and maybe just a small company (Rudolph; Hyatt). For the expression *lĕ'ênê*, "before the eyes of," see also 19:10; 28:1, 5, 11; 32:12. We need not wonder how such a theatrical performance escaped the notice of local authorities. It is a good guess that they did not even know it was happening.

10. *Look I am sending for and will take.* Hebrew *hinĕnî šōlēaḥ wĕlāqaḥtî.* The doubling of verbs is common in Jeremiah, occurring elsewhere in the present chapters (41:14, 17; 42:1–2; 43:12). "Look I" is the common beginning to the Jeremiah oracle (see Note on 1:15).

Nebuchadrezzar, king of Babylon, my servant. On this unusual expression, which occurs two other times in 25:9 and 27:6, see Note for 25:9. In all three texts the LXX lacks "my servant." 2QJer has the spelling "Nebuchadnezzar"; 4QJer[b][d] spells with a *resh,* which agrees with MT.

and I will set his throne over these stones that I have hidden. The throne of Nebuchadrezzar symbolizes his rule and execution of judgments; see 1:15–16 and 49:38. The LXX has *kai thēsei,* "and he will set up," but Aq *thēsō,* "I will set up." Read the MT.

that I have hidden. Here Yahweh speaks as if he is the one carrying out the symbolic action. Was not Jeremiah commanded to hide the stones? The LXX therefore reads *katekrupsas,* "you hid." But Aq and Symm have *katekrupsa,* "I hid," and both Volz and Rudolph think the first person can stand. Yahweh is identifying Jeremiah's actions as his own (Calvin).

and he will spread his pavilion over them. Hebrew *wĕnāṭâ ʾet-šaprîrô* [Q] *ʿālêhem.* Here we have a shift to the third person, the subject now being the Babylonian king. Such shifts are not to be wondered at. A shift from the divine "I" to the royal "he" occurred in 42:12, and it will happen again in 43:12. There is uncertainty regarding *šaprîrô* (Q), a *hapax legomenon* in the OT but generally agreed to carry the same or similar meaning as its cognate noun, *šiprâ,* "beauty" (Job 26:13; KB[3]). Kimḥi makes the connection and comes up with the rendering, "(his) beautiful tent." Rashi earlier translated the term as "(his) tent"; Calvin the same. The Versions give no help. Commentators and most modern Versions (AV; RSV; NEB; JB; NAB; NJV; NIV) render *šaprîrô* as "his canopy, (royal) tent, pavilion." The one other meaning sometimes proposed is "(royal) carpet," which would lie under the throne (Giesebrecht; Streane; NSB: "tronmatta"). The verb is *nṭh,* "to spread," which Jeremiah uses in 10:20 for spreading a tent. Blayney, however, believed the term signified nothing more than "beautiful, elegant, splendid," and so he translated, "and he shall spread forth his splendor over them." Reference here would be to the splendor attached to the king's regal estate: his throne, pavilion, carpet, colorful robes, and the like. Interjecting the idea of royal splendor makes for irony, in that a foreign ruler is portrayed in colorful majesty amidst a people—natives and expatriates—who, because of his coming have been or will be reduced to ragged beggars. The contrasting imagery has a parallel in Jeremiah's symbolic act of hiding the loincloth, where the ruined garment after retrieval was contrasted to an Israel Yahweh intended for himself as a "glorious decoration" (13:11).

11. *he shall come and strike down the land of Egypt.* Again a doubling of verbs (see v 10). The judgment will be upon Egypt, but the point being made in the

oracle is that it will fall upon the Judahite immigrants who have entered Egypt to seek refuge. Ezekiel, too, fully expected a Babylonian invasion of Egypt (Ezekiel 29–32). For references in the ancient sources to Nebuchadnezzar invading Egypt in 582 and 568 B.C., see Note for 46:13. If an invasion did occur in 582, and the Judahite immigrants arrived about this time (see Note for 41:1), the present prophecy would have been fulfilled very quickly. Tahpanhes, a border town, would have been one of the first to be captured (cf. Ezek 30:18).

Whoever is to death — to death, and whoever is to captivity — to captivity, and whoever is to the sword — to the sword. An echo of Jeremiah's ironic words in 15:2, although this enumeration lacks "and whoever is to famine — to famine." Hebrew *māwet* ("death") can also mean "pestilence" (so T; RSV; JB; NJV; REB), which leads to death (cf. 18:21). Captivity here must be taken seriously if there is any truth in the report of Josephus (*Ant* x 181–82) that Nebuchadnezzar invaded Egypt in 582 B.C. and took resident Jews to Babylon. Josephus also states that the Egyptian king was killed by Nebuchadnezzar, but this is not borne out by other known events (Bright 1981: 352 n. 25).

12. *And I will kindle a fire in the houses of the gods of Egypt, and he shall burn them and take them captive.* On the shift from the divine "I" to the royal "he," see above v 10. Yahweh will act; so will Nebuchadnezzar. There is no reason to emend with LXX, S, and Vg to "and he shall kindle," even though virtually all commentators and many of the modern Versions (RSV; NEB; JB; NAB; NIV; NSB) do just that. Aquila and Symm have *ekkausō pur* ("I will kindle a fire"); a first-person reading exists also in T. Although appeal can be made to third-person usage of *yṣt* in Jeremiah (32:29; 51:30, and 58 — all plural), the more common usage, as Blayney points out, is "I will kindle" with Yahweh as subject (17:27; 21:14; 49:27; 50:32; cf. Amos 1:14). The first person is preferred by the AV and NJV, and is the better reading.

and he shall burn them and take them captive. The houses (= temples) of Egypt's gods shall be burned and the gods taken away (cf. NEB; REB; NIV; NSB). The (idols of) gods are not burned (*pace* JB; NAB; NJB). Assyrian documents from Sargon II (721–705 B.C.) and Esarhaddon (680–669 B.C.) boast of images taken from conquered people (*ANET*³ 286, 291 d iv). Nebuchadnezzar burned the Temple in Jerusalem, and subsequent rulers in the ancient Near East — not to mention marauding bands — burned temples in other places. In the document entitled "Nabonidus' Rise to Power" (*ANET*³ 311 x), reference is made to Manda-hordes destroying the temples of Marduk, one of which is said to have lain in ruins for 54 years. Cyrus, upon entering Babylon (539 B.C.), reported finding Marduk sanctuaries in other cities ruined and their images in far distant places. The latter he proceeded to restore (*ANET*³ 316). Calvin notes too how Xerxes burned and destroyed temples on campaigns into Greece and Asia (cf. Herodotus viii 32–35, 53–55). One of the Elephantine papyri reports the Egyptian despoliation of a Jewish temple at Elephantine in 410 B.C. (see Note on 41:5), mentioning also earlier temple razings by Cambyses when he ravaged Egypt (525 B.C.). The Bible too reports images of gods being carried away captive (48:7; Amos 5:26–27; Isa 46:2).

and wrap up the land of Egypt as the shepherd wraps himself up with his gar-ment. For the Jeremianic comparison using *ka'ăšer*, see Note for 7:14. Nebu-chadnezzar will wrap himself (*'ātâ*) with the subjugated peoples of Egypt, i.e., he will have dominion over them as easily as a shepherd wraps himself (*ya'ṭeh*) in his cloak. Rashi, Kimḥi, Calvin, and Blayney imagine a plundering, which is indicated in T ("and they shall empty the land") and supported by Ezek 29:19–20. The other Versions, except the LXX, contain a "wrapping" metaphor (Aq: *kai anabaleitai*; Symm: *kai peribalomenos*; Theod: *kai peribalei*; and Vg: *et amicietur*). The LXX imagines another sort of cleaning; it translates: "and he shall delouse (*phtheiriei*) Egypt as a shepherd delouses (*phtheirizei*) his cloak," where the idea seems to be that the king of Babylon will pick off Egypt's unde-sirables as a shepherd cleans his lice-infested cloak. This could mean an attack on escapees from Babylonian-conquered lands, specifically the Judahite arriv-als led by Johanan son of Kareah. Giesebrecht thought the LXX translator probably did not understand the Heb verb *'ṭh*, but scholarly opinion changed following an article by von Gall (1904) in which it was argued that there were two Hebrew verbs, one *'ṭh* meaning "wrap oneself up," and another *'ṭh* mean-ing "delouse." The LXX simply read the latter. A swing in support of the LXX followed, by scholars (Cornill; Ehrlich 1912: 349; Volz; Condamin; Rudolph; Weiser; Bright; Thompson; Boadt; Holladay; and Keown et al.) and in the modern Versions (Moffatt; AmT; RSV; NEB; JB; NAB; NRSV; REB; NSB). But the NJV and NIV stayed with the Versions and interpretations by medieval Jewish commentators, as the AV had done earlier. The LXX rendering, though having an edge with more vivid imagery, is nevertheless on shaky etymological ground. Ancient Hebrew may have had a homonymous verb meaning "to seize, grasp," as Arabic does (*'ṭh* II KB[3]; cf. Isa 22:17), but "delouse" remains entirely conjectural. Jones and McKane have legitimate doubts about the LXX reading, which is best abandoned (NJB gave up the reading of JB).

then he shall leave from there in peace. I.e., he shall leave Egypt with the same ease that marked his coming. If reference is to the king making off with plunder (Blayney), then no voices will be raised up in protest. There appears to be exaggeration here, perhaps even hyperbole.

13. *Also, he shall break the obelisks of Beth-shemesh (that is in the land of Egypt), and the houses of the gods of Egypt he will burn with fire*. Bracketing out "that is in the land of Egypt," which appears to be a gloss (see below), we have a nice syntactic chiasmus. Destroying symbols of sun worship will serve the in-terests of Yahwism, which stood firmly opposed to the same during the years of Israelite nationhood. The Josianic Reform sought to root out sun worship in Jerusalem (2 Kgs 23:5, 11; cf. Jer 8:2), and one notes also a seemingly inten-tional avoidance of the term for "sun," *šemeš*, in the P account of Creation (Gen 1:16; but see Jer 31:35). Whether Nebuchadnezzar did any damage to the temples and obelisks of Beth-shemesh (= Heliopolis) is not known. If he did, a blow would have been struck at the very heart of Egypt, not simply at a border town. Classical sources (Diodorus Sic. i 46; Strabo, *Geog.* xvii 1.27–28) report that when Cambyses conquered Egypt in 525 B.C. he did burn the tem-

ples and mutilate the obelisks of Heliopolis. In subsequent years all but a few of these obelisks were toppled or carted off to other cities, first to Alexandria, then to Rome and other cities in Europe and America.

obelisks of Beth-shemesh. Beth-shemesh (lit. "House of the Sun," as in T) is cited elsewhere in the OT by its Hebrew name *'ôn*, "On" (Gen 41:45, 50; 46:20; corrupted to *'āwen*, "Nothingness," in Ezek 30:17). The Egyptian name was *Ounû* (lit. "Pillared City"), but the city is better known today as "Heliopolis" (Gk: "City of the Sun"; cf. *'îr haheres* in Isa 19:18). Heliopolis was an ancient city, identified now with Tell el-Ḥiṣn-Maṭarîyah, a site five miles east of the Nile in a northern suburb of Cairo. The city's importance was entirely religious, not political, dedicated to the worship of the sun-god Re, or Atum-Re. Herodotus (ii 59) knew of its temple and the annual festival held there in honor of the sun. Heliopolis enjoyed a revival during the Saïte period, or Twenty-Sixth Dynasty (664–525 B.C.), during which time its priests gained a reputation for intellectual and scientific pursuits (Strabo, *Geog.* xvii 1.29). Pythagoras reportedly studied there in the sixth century B.C. (Habachi 1977: 39).

Heliopolis was known also for its many obelisks, two of which stood on either side of the entrance to its Temple of the Sun. These are referred to here as *maṣṣēbôt*, the term used in the OT for stone pillars of Patriarchal times and the early monarchy deemed legitimate as worship symbols (Gen 28:18, 22; 31:13) or tomb memorials (Gen 35:20; 2 Sam 18:18), but which were later placed under a ban because of their association with Baal worship (Hos 3:4; Deut 12:3; 16:22; 2 Kgs 3:2; cf. Jer 2:27; 3:9), and as a result destroyed (2 Kgs 10:27; 23:14; cf. Hos 10:1–2). Egypt's obelisks were slender, four-sided shafts of solid rock gently tapering upward to a pyramidal top. These pyramidions, as they were called, were usually of limestone or granite and of varying heights, the most impressive being the colossal shafts of red Aswan (= Syene) granite over 100 feet tall and weighing in excess of 200 tons. Obelisks were customarily placed in pairs at entrances to temples and tombs, those flanking temple entrances being comparable to the Jachin and Boaz pillars on either side of the entrance to Solomon's Temple (see Note for 52:17). Most of the upright monoliths at Heliopolis were already ancient in Jeremiah's time, and the city's reputation as an obelisk center was well established. The oldest known obelisks there were a pair erected by Sesostris I for his new temple ca. 1942 B.C., one of which is still standing. The other was reported by an Arab traveler in the twelfth century A.D. to be lying on the ground in two pieces (Habachi 1977: 48–49); it is no longer extant. When Petrie excavated Tell Ḥiṣn in 1912, all he found were about two dozen obelisk fragments near the standing obelisk (Petrie and Mackay 1915: 5–6; Porter and Moss 1934: 60; Saleh 1981: 39–41). The obelisks of Heliopolis were erected by Thutmosis III (ca. 1490–1436 B.C.), Sethos I (ca. 1305–1290 B.C.), Ramses II (ca. 1290–1224 B.C.); and Psammetichus II (594–589 B.C.). A small, red, granite obelisk, not quite twenty feet in height, was erected not at Heliopolis but probably at the capital city of Saïs by Apries (Hophra), the reigning pharaoh when Jeremiah and fellow Judahites were in the country. It stands presently in the Piazza della Minerva in Rome.

The obelisks of Heliopolis, like those of other Egyptian cities, found their way to new locations once the city diminished in importance, and their removal and re-erection makes for facinating reading. Two obelisks of Heliopolis, set up in 1468 B.C. by Thutmosis III, were brought to Alexandria by Caesar Augustus before the Christian era. Known as "Cleopatra's Needles," one found its way to London in 1878, where it was erected on an embankment along the Thames (Budge 1926: 51–75; Habachi 1977: 164–76); the other went in 1879 to Central Park in New York City, where it stands today behind the Metropolitan Museum of Art (J. A. Wilson 1964: 57–60; Habachi 1977: 176–82). Another obelisk begun by Sethos I but finished by Ramses II, which originally graced the sun temple of Heliopolis, was removed by Caesar Augustus from Egypt in 10 B.C. and re-erected in the Circus Maximus at Rome. Today this collosal pillar, 32.77 meters in height and weighing an estimated 235 tons, stands in Rome's Piazza del Popolo. On it is an inscription calling Sethos I "the one who fills Heliopolis with obelisks that their rays may illuminate the Temple of Re" (Habachi 1977: 118–19). Three more Heliopolis obelisks erected by Ramses II were moved by the Caesars to Rome; one also to Florence. The ones in Rome are at the Piazza della Rotunda, the garden of the Villa Celimontana, and the Viale delle Terme di Diocleziano. The one in Florence is in the Boboli Gardens. One of two obelisks erected by Psammetichus II at Heliopolis now stands at Monte Citorio in Rome. And more from other Egyptian cities can be seen today in Constantinople (Istanbul), Paris, Cairo, and elsewhere. On the obelisks of Egypt and their removal to cities in Europe and America, see J. E. Alexander 1879; Gorringe 1882; and Habachi 1977.

(that is in the land of Egypt). Doubtless a gloss (Giesebrecht), distinguishing this Beth-shemesh from places having the same name in Israel, particularly the Beth-shemesh in the northeast Shephelah, 24 kilometers west of Jerusalem (1 Samuel 6). The LXX has *tous en On* ("those in On").

and the houses of the gods of Egypt he will burn with fire. A specific reference to the temples of Beth-shemesh; the similar statement in v 12 is more general.

MESSAGE AND AUDIENCE

The first narrative segment reports the response of people and their leaders to oracles brought them by Jeremiah. Their reaction is open hostility, and Baruch expresses a bit of his own in reporting the exchange that took place. Azariah son of Hoshaiah and Johanan son of Kareah, with other insolent men chiming in loudly, accuse Jeremiah of telling a lie. Yahweh could scarcely have sent the prophet with a message not to enter Egypt, and the one getting the brunt of this naked rage is none other than Baruch, who is accused of a treasonous scheme to remand the whole company to the Babylonians to be killed or exiled. Will the audience believe this? Baruch then reports that the whole lot has willfully disobeyed the voice of Yahweh to remain in Judah. The second segment reports briefly the journey southward to Egypt. The whole company that came together at Mizpah under Gedaliah, including Jeremiah and Baruch, made the journey, going as far as the border town of Tahpanhes.

The final segment reports a symbolic prophecy given to Jeremiah for delivery at Tahpanhes. The prophet is to take in hand good-sized stones and bury them with mortar in the brick pavement in front of the entrance to Pharaoh's house. He is to do it in full view of the men of Judah. In the word accompanying the symbolic act Yahweh says he is summoning Nebuchadrezzar, his servant, who will set his throne and all his kingly splendor over the stones in the pavement. The Babylonian king shall strike a blow against Egypt, and Yahweh says, as he did to people in Jerusalem earlier, that the hapless residents in the land will have their choice of escape. They can choose death, perhaps by pestilence, go into captivity, or fall by the sword. Yahweh says further that he will kindle a fire in the temples of Egypt, burning them and carrying off their gods into captivity. Indeed, he will wrap the land of Egypt as a shepherd wraps himself in his cloak, leaving behind the dead and a ruined land with the same ease that marked his coming. Then, or perhaps later at the hand of a subsequent conquerer, the obelisks of Beth-shemesh will be broken and the temples of this celebrated city burned with fire.

The audience is not told that Jeremiah carried out this action, but perhaps it knows that he did as instructed. This narrative, like the others of which it is a part, can be dated anytime after 582 B.C.

D. FINAL PROPHECIES IN EGYPT (44:1–30)

1. Once Again: Queen of Heaven Worship (44:1–25)

44 [1]The word that came to Jeremiah for all the Judahites who were dwelling in the land of Egypt, those who were dwelling in Migdol, and in Tahpanhes, and in Memphis, and in the land of Pathros:

[2]Thus said Yahweh of hosts, God of Israel:

You, you have seen all the evil that I brought upon Jerusalem and upon all the cities of Judah. And look they are a ruin this day and there is no one dwelling in them [3]because of their evil that they did to provoke me to anger, to go to burn incense, to serve other gods that they have not known—they, you, and your fathers. [4]And I sent to you all my servants the prophets—constantly I sent—saying, kindly do not do this abominable thing that I hate. [5]But they did not listen; they did not bend their ear to turn from their evil not to burn incense to other gods. [6]So my wrath was poured out, and my anger, and it burned in the cities of Judah and in the streets of Jerusalem, and they became a ruin, a desolation, as at this day.

[7]Now then, thus said Yahweh, God of hosts, God of Israel:
Why are you doing a great evil to yourselves, to cut off for you man and woman, child and infant from the midst of Judah so a remnant is not left for you, [8]to provoke me to anger with the works of your hands, to burn incense to other gods in the land of Egypt to which you are coming to sojourn, so as to cut off for you, so that you become a swearword and a reproach among all the nations of the earth? [9]Have you forgotten the evils of your fathers, and the evils of the kings of Judah and the evils of their wives, and your evils and the evils of your wives, which they did in the land of Judah and in the streets of Jerusalem? [10]They are not crushed even to this day. And they are not afraid. And they walk not in my law and in my statutes, which I set before you and before your fathers.

[11]Therefore thus said Yahweh of hosts, God of Israel:
Look I am setting my face against you for evil and to cut off all Judah. [12]And I will take the remnant of Judah who have set their faces to enter the land of Egypt to sojourn there, and they shall all be consumed in the land of Egypt; they shall fall by the sword, by famine they shall be consumed; from the least to the greatest, by sword and by famine they shall die; and they shall become a curse, a desolation, and a swearword, and a reproach. [13]Yes, I will reckon with those who dwell in the land of Egypt as I reckoned with Jerusalem—by sword, by famine, and by pestilence. [14]And there shall not be a fugitive or survivor for the remnant of Judah who have come to sojourn there in the land of Egypt, then to return to the land of Judah where they carry their great desire to return to dwell; but they shall not return— except fugitives.

[15]Then they answered Jeremiah—all the men who knew that their wives were burning incense to other gods, and all the wives who were standing by, a large assembly, and all the people who were dwelling in the land of Egypt, in Pathros: [16]"The word that you have spoken to us in the name of Yahweh, we will not listen to you. [17]For we fully intend to do everything that has gone forth from our mouth, to burn incense to the Queen of Heaven and pour out drink offerings to her, just as we did—we and our fathers, our kings and our princes—in the cities of Judah and in the streets of Jerusalem; then we ate our fill of bread and were well-off, and evil we did not see. [18]But from the time we left off burning incense to the Queen of Heaven and pouring out drink offerings to her, we have lacked everything, and by sword and by famine we have been consumed. [19]And when we are burning incense to the Queen of Heaven and pouring out drink offerings to her, is it against the will of our husbands that we make for her cakes to portray her, and pour out drink offerings to her?'

²⁰Then Jeremiah said to all the people—against the men and against the women, and against all the people who were answering him a word: ²¹'Indeed, the incense that you burned in the cities of Judah and in the streets of Jerusalem, you and your fathers, your kings and your princes, and the people of the land—them Yahweh remembers. Now did it enter his mind? ²²So Yahweh could no longer bear because of your evil doings, because of the abominations that you did, and your land became a ruin, and a desolation, and a swearword, without inhabitant, as at this day. ²³Because you burned incense and because you sinned against Yahweh, and did not obey the voice of Yahweh, and in his law and in his statutes and in his testimonies you did not walk, therefore this evil has met you, as at this day.

²⁴Then Jeremiah said to all the people and to all the women: Hear the word of Yahweh all Judah who are in the land of Egypt:
    ²⁵Thus said Yahweh of hosts, God of Israel:
    You and your wives, yes, you have spoken with your mouth, and with your hands you have carried it out, saying, 'We fully intend to perform our vows that we vowed to burn incense to the Queen of Heaven and to pour out drink offerings to her.' Well then, confirm fully your vows and perform fully your vows!

2. Whose Word Will Be Confirmed—Mine or Theirs? (44:26–30)

²⁶Therefore hear the word of Yahweh all Judah who are dwelling in the land of Egypt:
    Look I, I have sworn by my great name—said Yahweh—that my name will no longer be called on the mouth of any person of Judah who now says, 'As the Lord Yahweh lives,' in all the land of Egypt.

²⁷Look I am watching over them for evil and not for good, and every person of Judah who is in the land of Egypt will be consumed by sword and by famine, until they are ended. ²⁸And those escaping the sword shall return from the land of Egypt to the land of Judah—a few people. Then all the remnant of Judah who came to the land of Egypt to sojourn shall know whose word will be confirmed—mine or theirs. ²⁹And this is the sign to you—oracle of Yahweh—that I am reckoning against you in this place so that you may know that my words will be fully confirmed against you for evil.

³⁰Thus said Yahweh:
    Look I am giving Pharaoh Hophra, king of Egypt, into the hand of his enemies, into the hand of those who seek his life, just as I gave Zedekiah, king of Judah, into the hand of Nebuchadrezzar, king of Babylon, his enemy and the one who sought his life.

RHETORIC AND COMPOSITION

MT 44:1–30 = LXX 51:1–30. This chapter concluding the *via dolorosa* prose divides into two segments: 1) vv 1–25, which are four oracles with intervening narrative; and 2) vv 26–30, which are three final oracles. Both segments are preceded by superscriptions (vv 1, 26a).

The structure of the chapter, supported by section markings (ס = *setumah*; פ = *petuḥah*), is the following:

			פ M^A, ס M^L, פ M^P
I	Superscription	v 1	ס M^L
	Oracle I	vv 2–6	ס M^A, M^L, M^P
	Oracle II	vv 7–10	ס M^A, M^L, M^P
	Oracle III	vv 11–14	פ M^A, ס M^L, M^P
	Narrative I: men and women speaking	vv 15–19	ס M^A, פ M^L, ס M^P
	Narrative II: Jeremiah speaking	vv 20–23	ס M^A, M^L, פ M^P
	Narrative III: Jeremiah speaking	v 24	ס M^L
	Oracle IV	v 25	ס M^A, פ M^L, ס M^P
II	Superscription	v 26a	
	Oracle I	v 26b	
	Oracle II	vv 27–29	פ M^A, ס M^L, פ M^P
	Oracle III	v 30	ס M^A, M^L, M^P

The reconstructed 2QJer, according to Baillet (1962: 64), does not have a *setumah* after v 1. Section markings, as one can see, support the breakdown above with two exceptions: 1) there is no section after the superscription in v 26a; and 2) there is no section after the oracle in v 26b. That v 26a is a superscription is clear from a comparison with the superscription of v 1, which varies only slightly in wording and is expanded by containing the names of three cities where Judahites are living. The reasons for delimiting v 26b as a separate oracle are that it begins with *hinĕnî* ("Look I"), as does the oracle in vv 27–29, and that it has its own messenger formula, *'āmar yhwh* ("said Yahweh").

The two segments are further structured by repetitions and balancing key words:

I	Superscription			v 1
	Oracle I	*And look they. . . . this day*	*wĕhinnām . . . hayyôm*	
			hazzeh	v 2
		. . . as at this day	*kayyôm hazzeh*	v 6
	Oracle II	. . . .		v 7
		. . . even to this day	*'ad hayyôm hazzeh*	v 10
	Oracle III	*Look I . . .*	*hinĕnî*	v 11
		. . . .		
	Narrative I	*Then they answered . . .*	*wayya'ănu*	v 15
	Narrative II	*Then Jeremiah said . . .*	*wayyō'mer yirmĕyāhû*	v 20
		. . . as at this day	*kĕhayyôm hazzeh*	v 22

	. . . *as at this day*	*kayyôm hazzeh*	v 23
Narrative III	*Then Jeremiah said . . .*	*wayyō'mer yirmĕyāhû*	v 24
Oracle IV	. . . .		
	. . . *confirm fully*	*hâqēm tāqîmĕnâ*	v 25b
II Superscription			v 26a
Oracle I	*Look I . . .*	*hinĕnî*	v 26b
	. . . .		
Oracle II	*Look I . . .*	*hinĕnî*	v 27
	. . . *whose word will be confirmed*	*dĕbar-mî yāqûm*	v 28
	. . . *my words will be fully confirmed*	*qôm yāqûmû dĕbāray*	v 29
Oracle III	*Look I . . .*	*hinĕnî*	v 30
	. . . .		

This chapter has the same claim to Baruch authorship as other chapters in the collection. Baruch is with the arrivals in Egypt, and thus the natural one to both observe and record the events occurring there. Variations between the MT and LXX are much the same as in prior chapters, with Holladay (following Janzen) and McKane going in almost every case with the shorter LXX text, and other commentators dividing between MT and LXX readings (for a summary, see McKane, 1083). In this chapter are twelve arguable cases of LXX loss due to haplography, adding to the mounting evidence in support of the longer MT, which in my judgment is consistently the better text when all variant readings are analyzed. It is simply not the case, as Janzen (1973: 108) states, that "the majority of G shorter readings in this chapter . . . [are] shown to be superior." Jeremiah prose is laden with repetitions, and these are not the result of dittography, nor do they come about because scribes expanded existing readings by quarrying words and phrases from other places in the book. The two rhetorical questions in vv 7–9 of Oracle II have an abundance of *accumulatio* and stereotyped phraseology that does not occur in any other oracle, but simply reflects the rhetorical prose scattered throughout the book. We have here in Baruch's concluding prose a vigorous discourse, something akin to the music of an organist who ends a grand performance by pulling out all the stops.

Oracles I, II, and III in the first segment progress from past evil, to present evil, to evil planned for the future. Yahweh brought the past evil and will bring the evil of the future. Judahites in Egypt are doing the present evil to themselves:

I	Past evil brought on Judahites in Jerusalem and Judah	vv 2–6
II	Judahites now in Egypt doing evil to themselves	vv 7–10
III	Coming evil on all Judahites living in Egypt	vv 11–14

In Narrative II of the first segment (vv 20–23) is a chiastic structure noted already by Boys (1825: 42), which clears up a well-known pronoun problem:

Indeed, *the incense* that you burned in the cities of Judah and in the streets of Jerusalem *you and your fathers, your kings and your princes, and the people of the
land—them* Yahweh remembers
Now *did it enter* his mind?   v 21

The pronoun *'ōtām* ("them") refers to "you and your fathers, your kings and
your princes, and the people of the land," and the singular verb *taʿăleh* ("did it
enter") refers back to "the incense."

In Oracle IV of the first segment (v 25), a syntactic chiasmus clarifies an unusual gender shift:

you have spoken (feminine) / with your mouth
and with your hands / you have carried it out (masculine)

Another syntactic chiasmus appears in v 12 (see Notes).
Catchwords connecting to Baruch's colophon in chap. 45 are the following:

44:27 *Look I . . . for evil   hinĕnî . . . lĕrāʿâ* 45:5 *you are seeking . . . do not seek*
44:30 *those who seek . . . the one who   . . . look I . . . evil   hinĕnî . . . rāʿâ*
       sought

In the MT, where Baruch's colophon is left intact and the Foreign Nation
Oracles are relocated to the end of the book, a thematic link exists between the
via dolorosa prose ending in Egypt (44:30) and the Egypt oracles beginning the
Foreign Nation Collection (chap. 46).

NOTES

44:1. *The word that came to Jeremiah for all the Judahites who were dwelling in
the land of Egypt, those who were dwelling in Migdol, and in Tahpanhes, and
in Memphis, and in the land of Pathros.* On this superscription, which occurs
most often in the abbreviated form, "The word that came to Jeremiah from
Yahweh," see Notes for 7:1 and 21:1. In the form in which it appears here,
compare 25:1. This final word on record from the prophet is not addressed
simply to new arrivals at the border town of Tahpanhes, but to "all the Judahites" resident in Egypt. The other key term here is *hayyōšĕbîm*, "(those) who
were dwelling." Judahites have been living in Egypt from before the destruction of Jerusalem (24:8), and have spread throughout the country. Tahpanhes
and Memphis are mentioned in 2:16, and all three cities are put on war alert
in the oracle against Egypt in 46:14. Skinner (1926: 341) says the present
chapter reads like a letter to Jews in these localities, but a face-to-face meeting
is more likely, particularly in light of the spirited dialogue taking place over
Queen of Heaven worship. Where such an encounter might have taken place
is not known, nor is it known whether Jeremiah traveled to one or more of
these areas. The "land of Pathros" is in the far south, known otherwise as Upper Egypt.

Migdol. An Egyptian frontier town north and east of Tahpanhes, on the coastal road from Asia into Egypt. The ancient location had been put at either Tell es-Sêrnut or Tell el-Ḥêr, but more recently Israeli archaeologists from Ben Gurion University have excavated a 25–acre site one kilometer north of Tell el-Ḥêr, known as T. 21, which they believe to be Migdol of the Saïte period, i.e., the seventh and sixth centuries B.C. (Oren 1984; Stern 2001: 223–24). Quantities of local Egyptian and imported Greek pottery from the period were found there, indicating that the fort—like the one at Tahpanhes—was manned by Greek mercenaries. Migdol of the Hellenistic and Roman periods (*Magdolas* of Herodotus) is thought to be Tell el-Ḥêr, replacing the earlier site after its destruction by Cambyses in 525 B.C. Tell el-Ḥêr, having no pre-Persian remains, would then be the Migdol of the Elephantine papyri (Porten 1968: 42, 90). Ezekiel uses the expression "from Migdol to Syene" (Ezek 29:10; 30:6), which compares to "from Dan to Beersheba" in Israel On Migdol, see further Note on 46:14.

Tahpanhes. The border town to which Johanan son of Kareah and his company came. See Note on 43:7.

Memphis. The old capital of Egypt south of modern Cairo. It is not the present capital, which is farther west, at Saïs. "In Memphis" is lacking in the LXX, but present in 2QJer. The LXX omission is likely due to haplography (homoeoarcton: *wb . . . wb*), not MT expansion quarried from 2:16 or 46:14 (*pace* Janzen 1973: 57; Holladay; and McKane).

the land of Pathros. This is "Pathrusim" according to the Table of Nations (Gen 10:14; cf. 1 Chr 1:12); in Egyptian it is *Patoris*, and in Akk *Paturisi*, both of which mean "the South Land." Pathros is Upper Egypt, the district south of Thebes. See also Isa 11:11; Ezek 29:14; 30:14.

2. *You, you have seen all the evil that I brought upon Jerusalem and upon all the cities of Judah.* The emphatic pronoun at the beginning may be to people in the audience who actually witnessed the destruction in Judah. See also the emphatic pronouns concluding v 3.

And look they are a ruin this day. The term "ruin" (*horbâ*), occurring also in vv 6 and 22, is a common curse word in Jeremiah (see Note for 25:9), included often in stereotyped curse-word strings (see Note for 24:9).

this day. Lacking in the LXX, but present in 2QJer. The omission is likely attributed to haplography (homoeoteleuton: *h . . . h*). A variation of the same expression occurs at the end of v 6, which the LXX translates. The repetition has rhetorical value (see Rhetoric and Composition), arguing against its deletion here (*pace* Janzen 1973: 57; Holladay; McKane). Giesebrecht, Volz, Rudolph, Weiser, Bright, and others retain.

and there is no one dwelling in them. This phrase is said by Baillet to be lacking in 2QJer, but Janzen (1973: 57) reconstructs the damaged fragment to support LXX's *apo enoikōn* ("without inhabitant"). The readings then are essentially the same.

3. *to provoke me to anger, to go to burn incense, to serve other gods.* The fivefold repetition of *lĕ* ("to") makes for alliteration. The LXX lacks "to serve"

(la'ăbōd), leading some commentators (Giesebrecht, Duhm, Bright, Holladay, McKane) to delete, but the omission can be attributed to haplography (homoeoarcton: *l . . . l*). The term is present in 2QJer, also in Aq (*douleuein*), Symm, and Theod (*latreuein*). "Provoking (Yahweh) to anger" (Piel and H-stem of *k's*) occurs in Deut 32:16, 21, and again in Jer 44:8 (see Note for 7:18). On burning incense to other gods, see 19:13 and Note for 1:16.

that they have not known—they, you, and your fathers. See Deut 13:7[Eng 13:6]. The LXX has "you have not known," which anticipates the shift to a second person in v 4. It also omits "they, you, and your fathers," which is probably due to haplography (homoeoteleuton: *m . . . m*). The words are present in Aq and Theod.

4. *And I sent to you all my servants the prophets—constantly I sent.* On the rhetorical idiom of a repeated verb used together with *škm*, see Note for 7:13. The expression "I sent to you all my servants the prophets" is discussed in Note for 7:25.

kindly do not do this abominable thing that I hate. The imprecative *nā'* ("kindly") is here a rebuke. "This abominable thing" (*děbar-hattō'ēbâ hazzō't*) is the burning of incense to other gods. "The abominations" of v 22 refer to this practice along with other things that Yahweh finds detestable (see Note for 2:7).

5. *But they did not listen; they did not bend their ear.* Hearing or not hearing is all important in ancient Israelite religion (so Deuteronomy). In the Baruch prose the recurring theme is that people did not listen to or obey Yahweh's word (or voice) as it came via the prophets (3:13; 9:12[Eng 9:13]; 11:8; 13:11; 19:15; 25:3; 34:17; 35:14–16, 18; 36:31; 37:2; 40:3; 42:21; 43:4, 7; 44:5, 16, 23).

6. *So my wrath was poured out, and my anger, and it burned in the cities of Judah and in the streets of Jerusalem, and they became a ruin, a desolation, as at this day.* A fulfillment of the prophecy given in 7:20. See also 33:10. A similar prophecy was made to the Egypt-bound group in 42:18. For a list of land and city curses in Jeremiah, see Note for 48:9.

in the cities of Judah and in the streets of Jerusalem. On this phrase, see Note for 11:6.

a ruin, a desolation. Hebrew *lěḥorbâ lišmāmâ.* Common terms in the curseword strings of Jeremiah (see Note for 24:9).

as at this day. Hebrew *kayyôm hazzeh.* This phrase, familiar from Deuteronomy, occurs elsewhere in Jeremianic prose (see Note for 11:5).

7. *Now then.* Hebrew *wě'attâ.* A rhetorical particle signaling a discourse shift from past time to present time (see Note for 2:18). This oracle and the next combine with the prior oracle to form an argument *a minori ad maius*, i.e., If Yahweh did not spare Jerusalem and the cities of Judah, *how much more* will he not spare Egyptian cities in which Judahites are now living (v 13)? On arguments from the lesser to the greater, see Note for 3:1 and §Introduction: Rhetoric and Preaching: Argumentation.

Yahweh, God of hosts, God of Israel. Here the LXX translates *sěbā'ôt* ("of hosts") with *pantokratōr*, as it does occasionally (see Appendix VI). In v 11 it omits "of hosts."

Why are you doing a great evil to yourselves? Evil is commonly perceived as a force coming from outside, as in Oracles I and III, where it is brought by Yahweh. Here, however, Jeremiah says that the people are bringing it upon themselves (cf. 26:19b; 42:20).

child and infant. War claims the lives of innocent children and infants (6:11; Lam 2:11–12).

8. *to burn incense to other gods in the land of Egypt to which you are coming to sojourn.* A letter has turned up in a sixth-century tomb in Saqqara written by a Phonecian woman from Tahpanhes to another woman in Memphis. In it the Phonecian woman says after greeting her friend and inquiring about her welfare: "I wish you blessings from Baal-Zaphon and from all the gods of Tahpanhes" (Beyerlin 1978: 253–54).

the works of your hands. I.e., idols. See Note for 48:7a.

so as to cut off for you. Hebrew *lĕmaʿan hakrît lākem.* As in the previous verse, the activity of the people is seen to be self-destructive.

so that you become a swearword and a reproach among all the nations of the earth? What happened in Judah (44:22) will also happen in Egypt (42:18; 44:12). "Swearword" (*qĕlālâ*) and "reproach" (*ḥerpâ*) are stock curse words in Jeremiah (see again v 12, and Note for 24:9).

9. *Have you forgotten the evils of your fathers . . . ?* An initial silence to this rhetorical question will give way to a spirited response (vv 15–19) once the indictment and judgment fall upon the men and their wives. The "evils of the fathers" is a recurring theme in Jeremiah (2:5; 3:25; 7:25–26; 9:13[Eng 9:14]; 11:7–8, 10; 14:20; 16:11–12, 19; 19:4–5; 23:27; 34:14; 44:3, 9, 21).

and the evils of the kings of Judah and the evils of their wives. The Heb has *nāšāyw* ("his wives"), which refers to the wives of each king (Kimhi; Hitzig; Weiser). The wives of Solomon, for example, were great patrons of idolatry and burned incense to other gods (1 Kgs 11:4, 8). The LXX has "your (plural) princes," which may have been influenced by the collocation of "kings" and "princes" in vv 17 and 21, also the second person pronouns in the present verse. But this reading has no advantage over the reading of MT; in fact, it is inferior, pairing as it does "kings of Judah" with "your princes" (rather than "their princes"). The LXX reading should therefore be rejected (*pace* Blayney; Graf; Cheyne; Giesebrecht; Duhm; Peake; Cornill; Volz; and others). The Versions ancient and modern all read the MT, except Moffatt, AmT, and NJB.

and your evils. The LXX omits; probably more haplography (two-word: *wʾt rʿt . . . wʾt rʿt*).

10. *They are not crushed.* Hebrew *dukkĕʾû* is a Pual of *dkʾ*, meaning here "to be crushed in spirit, humbled" (Rashi; Kimhi). See Isa 19:10; 57:15; Ps 143:3. The verb gave the Versions difficulty. The LXX (*ouk epausanto*) and T have "they have not ceased," i.e., they have not ceased from their evil; Aq, Symm (*ouk ekatharisthēsan*), and Vg (*non sunt mundati*) have "they are not cleansed (from their evil)." Theodotion (*ouk etapeinōthēsan,* "they have not been humbled") supports MT. Yahweh turns now to address an unspecified audience,

expressing incredulity that generations can continue in their evil and be unaffected by the adversity it brings about. Compare Amos 4:6–11.

And they are not afraid. Hebrew *wĕlō᾽ yārĕ᾽û.* The LXX omits, which can be attributed to haplography (whole-word: *wl᾽ . . . wl᾽*). Janzen (1973: 25, 118) considers haplography a possible explanation. Theodotion translates with *kai ouk ephobēthēsan;* most all modern commentators also translate. There is no good reason here to posit secondary MT expansion (*pace* Holladay; McKane).

And they walk not in my law and in my statutes, which I set before you and before your fathers. In the Shiloh Oracle as reported in 26:4, failure to walk in Yahweh's law (*tôrâ*) will bring about the destruction of Jerusalem and its Temple. The accusation made here repeats with little change in v 23; 9:12[Eng 9:13]; and 32:23. On "walking" as a metaphor for conduct or behavior in the OT, see Notes for 6:16 and 23:14. "Statutes" (*huqqōt*) are the legal provisions in Deuteronomy (Deut 4:1, 8; 6:1–2; 8:11; 11:32; et passim). The LXX lacks "in my law and," which is doubtless more loss by haplography (homoeoarcton: *b . . . b*, or homoeoteleuton: *w . . . w*, with the sequence *wb* repeating), and should not be omitted (*pace* Janzen 1973: 57; Holladay; and McKane). The term "in my law" appears in Aq, Theod, T, and the other Vrs.

11–12. The LXX text here is considerably reduced. The MT and LXX read as follows:

MT	LXX	
Therefore thus said Yahweh	Therefore thus said the Lord	v 11
lākēn kōh-᾽āmar yhwh	*dia touto outōs eipen kurios*	
of hosts, God of Israel		
ṣĕbā᾽ôt ᾽ĕlōhê yiśrā᾽ēl		
Look I am setting my face	Look I have set my face	
hinĕnî śām pānay	*idou egō ephistēmi to prosōpon mou*	
against you for evil and to cut off all Judah.	. . . . to set free all . . .	v 12
bākem lĕrāʿâ ûlĕhakrît ᾽et-kol-yĕhûdâ	. . . . *tou apolesai pantas . . .*	
And I will take the remnant of Judah	. . . . the remnant . . .	
wĕlāqaḥtî ᾽et-šĕ᾽ērît yĕhûdâ	. . . . *tous kataloipous . . .*	
who have set their faces to enter		
᾽ăšer-śāmû pĕnêhem lābô᾽		
the land of Egypt to sojourn there,		
᾽ereṣ-miṣrayim lāgûr šām		
and they shall all be consumed		
wĕtammû kōl		

in the land of Egypt; *bĕ'ereṣ miṣrayim*	. . . who are in Egypt . . . *tous en aigyptō*
they shall fall by the sword *yippōlû baḥereb*	and they shall fall by the sword *kai pesountai en romphaia*
by famine they shall be consumed; *bārā'āb yittammû*	and by famine they shall be forsaken *kai en limo ekleipsousin*
from the least to the greatest, *miqqāṭōn wĕ'ad-gādōl*	from small to great *apo mikrou heōs megalou*
by sword and by famine they shall die; *baḥereb ûbārā'āb yāmūtû*	
and they shall become a curse, *wĕhāyû lĕ'ālâ*	and they shall become a reproach, *kai esontai eis oneidismon*
a desolation, and a swearword, and a reproach. *lĕšammâ wĕliqlālâ ûlĕḥerpâ*	and a destruction, and a curse . . . *kai eis apōleian kai eis kataran*

The LXX here is not shorter because of a haplographic loss in its *Vorlage*. The translation before us was perhaps made from a scroll that had suffered physical damage of some sort, and a reading as good as possible was arrived at. It cannot be claimed that the LXX, simply because of its brevity, is the superior reading (*pace* Janzen 1973: 58; Holladay; McKane). The reading of Theod follows MT. In v 12 is an abundance of *accumulato*, which, however, is lost on McKane (p. 1073), who says that the MT "is grossly overloaded," containing verses that "have been laboriously and indiscriminately expanded." See §Introduction: Rhetoric and Preaching: Accumulation.

11. *I am setting my face against you for evil . . . who have set their faces to enter the land of Egypt.* On "to set the face" as an expression of determination, see Note for 42:15. There appears to be a wordplay here with a double occurrence of the idiom: the people's determination to go to Egypt is matched by Yahweh's determination to bring judgment upon them (Bright; Layton 1986: 178). Psalm 34:17[Eng 34:16] says: "The face of Yahweh is against doers of evil."

to cut off all Judah. I.e., the people of Judah in Egypt (vv 14, 28).

12. *from the least to the greatest.* For this Jeremianic expression, see Note on 6:13.

and they shall become a curse, a desolation, and a swearword, and a reproach. The LXX has only three terms, and it is unclear which one has been omitted. On this string of curse words, some of which occur in vv 8 and 22, see Note for 24:9.

13. *Yes, I will reckon with those who dwell in the land of Egypt as I reckoned with Jerusalem.* For the comparison using *ka'ăšer*, see v 30 and Note on 7:14.

The construction as a whole is similar to one in 50:18. Judahites have come to Egypt in hopes of finding refuge, but Yahweh says the judgment meted out in Jerusalem will follow them there. On the verb *pqd* ("pay a visit, reckon") in Jeremiah, see v 29 and Note for 5:9.

by sword, by famine, and by pestilence. 2QJer has "and by famine." The LXX omits *ûbaddāber*, "and by pestilence," which can be more loss due to haplography (homoeoarcton: *w . . . w*). The Versions have the term. For a discussion of this triad and the occasional omission of "and by pestilence," see Note on 42:17.

14. *And there shall not be a fugitive or survivor for the remnant of Judah who have come to sojourn there in the land of Egypt, then to return to the land of Judah where they carry their great desire to return to dwell; but they shall not return—except fugitives.* The unwelcome word in 22:27, "to the land where they will carry their great desire to return, there they shall not return," goes out to exile-bound Jehoiachin and the queen mother. The wishful thinking in Jerusalem—fostered by the false prophets (27:16; 28:3–4)—was that Jehoiachin and the exiles would return quickly from Babylon. The people here—perhaps residents in Egypt for some time, not more-recent arrivals—entertain what Calvin calls a foolish hope that one day they will return. The T calls it a deception. But the judgment—in its present form, at least—does admit exceptions ("except fugitives"). See also v 28. Since it is stated at the outset that no "fugitive" (*pālîṭ*) will survive the Egypt sojourn (see 42:17), the concluding words must be a later mitigating gloss. The LXX omits "to dwell there."

15. *Then they answered Jeremiah.* The whole company—men and women both—answer the prophet, and the defense following is likewise broadly made. Queen of Heaven worship is a family affair (7:18).

their wives were burning incense to other gods. On this practice, see Note for 19:13.

a large assembly. Perhaps a special festival honoring the Queen of Heaven (Cheyne; Duhm).

and all the people who were dwelling in the land of Egypt, in Pathros. "In Pathros" stands in apposition to "in the land of Egypt" (cf. v 1), which is to say that those answering Jeremiah are people from Pathros. Nothing is said about an exchange taking place in Pathros, which is in Upper Egypt (v 1). Jeremiah could be meeting the Pathros people at Tahpanhes or some other nearby location.

16. *'The word that you have spoken to us in the name of Yahweh, we will not listen to you.* An outright rejection of Yahweh and his word, making one wonder if the cult here is as syncretistic as in the Persian period, when people at Elephantine were worshiping Anat-Yahu (Boadt). Yet Jeremiah had problems in Jerusalem when speaking in Yahweh's name (20:8–9; 26:8–9). On people's refusal to listen to Yahweh's word as a dominant theme in the Baruch prose, see v 5.

17. *For we fully intend to do everything that has gone forth from our mouth.* Compare 2:25b. Husbands and wives have vowed together to burn incense and pour out drink offerings to the Queen of Heaven, and they fully intend to

carry out their vows (v 25). On vowing to Yahweh, see Num 30:2, 12; Deut 23:24[Eng 23:23]; and Ps 66:13–14.

Queen of Heaven. A goddess associated directly or indirectly with Assyro-Babylonian Ishtar, known throughout Palestine and the surrounding region as Ashtart (Gk Astarte), to whom the people are burning incense, pouring out drink offerings, and making cakes (see Note on 7:18). For the many figurines of this goddess that have turned up from excavations in Judah and neighboring countries, see Kletter 1996 and Stern 2001. The number from Judah alone currently stands at 822, over 400 of which are from Jerusalem (Kletter 1996: 45; Stern 2001: 206). Here, as elsewhere, the Queen of Heaven had become a consort to the male deity, who in Judah was either Yahweh or Baal. Survival of this cult in Egypt is confirmed by an Aramaic papyrus found at Hermopolis in the Egyptian Delta (Herm W 4:1), dated to the fifth century B.C. (Porten and Greenfield 1968: 216; Porten 1974: 159), which sends greetings "to the temple of Bethel and to the temple of the Queen of Heaven (*lbyt mlkt šmyn*)." See further Milik (1967: 560, 583); Fitzmyer (1980: 10); and Delcor (1982: 112–14). For MT *mĕleket* as a corrupted form of *malkat* ("queen"), see Note on 7:18.

we and our fathers, our kings and our princes. Compare the enumerations in vv 9 and 21.

in the cities of Judah and in the streets of Jerusalem. The more common stereotypical phrase in Jeremiah, repeated in v 21. See also 7:17 and Note for 11:6. In v 9 it is "in the land of Judah and in the streets of Jerusalem."

then we ate our fill of bread and were well-off, and evil we did not see. "And (we) were well-off" is *wannihyeh ṭôbîm* (cf. NJV). This nostalgia for the "good old days" is a distant memory, hearkening back most likely to Manasseh's long and peaceful reign (Weiser). The reigns of Jehoiakim and Zedekiah could not be so characterized. Compare the wistful yearnings of the Wilderness generation in Num 11:4–6. Hosea, too, notes that people in his time went after false gods because they credited them with supplying their bread and water (Hos 2:7[Eng 2:5]).

18. *But from the time we left off burning incense to the Queen of Heaven and pouring out drink offerings to her, we have lacked everything, and by sword and by famine we have been consumed*. A different slant on things, to say the least! Crenshaw (1971: 31) calls it "historical pragmatism." This cessation must have taken place during the reform years of Josiah, with the privation resulting from Josiah's tragic death and the inglorious years under Jehoiakim and Zedekiah. These years saw a punitive visit by Pharaoh Neco, a rampage of Chaldeans, Syrians, Moabites, Ammonites, and Edomites through the land, and two invasions by Nebuchadnezzar and his Babylonian army, the last one of which brought down the nation (Peake; Streane; Skinner 1926: 343; Condamin; Holladay). The suggestion by Morton Smith (1975: 15) that reference here is to the suspension of all cults other than Yahweh's during the final siege of Jerusalem is doubtful, despite the parallel drawn to the cessation of sacrifices during the Roman siege of Jerusalem in A.D. 70.

and pouring out drink offerings to her. The LXX omission can be attributed to haplography (homoeoteleuton: *ym . . . ym*). Janzen (1973: 118) also suggests haplography, but his explanation of a skip from *whsk* to *ḥsrnw* is unconvincing. Symm has the words (*kai spendousai autē spondas*).

19. Here the women are speaking, as reference is made subsequently to the consent required of husbands for vows they have taken (Num 30:6–15). Bright proposes changing the participle *mĕqaṭṭĕrîm* ("are burning incense") to a feminine, but that may be unnecessary (GKC §145u). The G^L inserts at the beginning of the verse: "And the women said," which Rudolph and Holladay say was lost in MT by haplography (homoeoarcton: *w . . . w*, or homoeoteleuton: *w . . . w*). Speaker changes, however, can occur without there being any notation in the text (see 6:4–5; Gordis 1949: 177).

cakes. Bread or sweet cakes (see Note for 7:18). Milgrom (1991: 188, 412) says these are cereal offerings, basically. On the association of cereal offerings and incense, see Note for 41:5.

to portray her. I.e., to make an image of her. Hebrew *lĕhaʿăṣibâ*, where a third feminine singular suffix is to be read despite the lack of a *mappiq* in the final *hēʾ* (cf. GKC §58g). The LXX and S omit the term, but it is translated in Symm (*tō gluptō autēs*). There is no good reason to delete (*pace* Kuenen 1894: 198–99; Duhm; Cornill; Holladay; McKane; G. Greenberg 2001: 236–37). A hoard of decorated clay molds has been found in the kitchen of the royal palace at Mari, one of which portrays a nude female goddess. The suggestion has therefore been made that molds were used to produce an image of the goddess on the cakes (Rast 1977: 171–76; for a picture, see Malamat 1971: 21). Rast also cites a mold found in Palestine, in some sort of cultic structure at Taanach, which portrays a goddess thought to be Ashtart (Gk Astarte; see further Note for 7:18). Image-making on bread and cakes has its modern parallels. Rast notes the practice of impressing bread used for the Christian Eucharist with liturgical symbols. The monks of Saint Catherine's Mount Sinai Monastery bake bread for their rituals with imprinted forms of the Virgin Mary and Saint Catherine (see *National Geographic* 125:1 [January, 1964], 88–89). A century ago cakes of the Virgin and child were reportedly baked at Christmas in northern England, where the practice was said to be a vestige of Roman Catholicism in the country (Carr 1908).

20. *Then Jeremiah said to all the people—against the men and against the women, and against all the people who were answering him a word.* The response is made also to the women who spoke up in v 19. The Heb term for "men" is *gĕbārîm*, on which see Note for 41:16.

21. The beginning of this rhetorical question picks up stereotypical language from v 17. The issue here is not the burning of incense; it is the burning of incense to *other gods* (1:16; 19:13).

Indeed, the incense . . . ? Reading the *lōʾ* as an asseverative and completing the question with "Now did it enter his mind?"

the people of the land. I.e., the people generally (see Note on 1:18).

them Yahweh remembers. I.e., all the people of Jerusalem who burned incense to other gods (see Rhetoric and Composition for a chiasmus in the verse). The object "them" (*'ōtām*), which heads the clause for emphasis and which the LXX omits, is not the "other gods" (*pace* Kimḥi).

Now did it enter his mind? Of course not. For the expression, "enter (Yahweh's) mind," see also 3:16 and 7:31.

22. *So Yahweh could no longer bear.* The imperfect verb has a *waw consecutive* attached to the negative; thus past tense.

because of your evil doings. On this stereotyped phrase, see Note for 21:12.

and your land became a ruin, and a desolation, and a swearword, without inhabitant, as at this day. On this string of curse words, some of which occur in vv 8 and 12, see Note for 24:9. Hebrew *ḥorbâ* ("ruin"), occurring also in vv 6 and 22, is a common Jeremiah curse word (see Note for 25:9).

without inhabitant. Lacking in the LXX, but translated by Aq and Theod.

as at this day. On the expression here and in v 23, see Note for 11:5.

23. *Because you burned incense and because you sinned against Yahweh, and did not obey the voice of Yahweh, and in his law and in his statutes and in his testimonies you did not walk, therefore this evil has met you, as at this day.* This is Jeremiah's reading of the evil times. Hebrew *mippĕnê 'ăšer* simply means "because" (cf. Exod 19:18; KB³). On the disregard of Yahweh's "law, statutes, (and testimonies)," see above v 10. The LXX lacks "as at this day," but the repetition from v 22 has rhetorical value and should be taken as genuine (Giesebrecht).

therefore this evil has met you, as at this day. See Deut 31:29, also Jeremiah's prayer to Yahweh after buying the field in Anathoth (32:23).

24. *Then Jeremiah said to all the people and to all the women.* Here the women seem to be singled out for special mention (Bright: "particularly the women"), but this is not a warrant for deleting "to all the people and" (*pace* Volz; Rudolph; Holladay), for which there is no textual support. The decision to delete is influenced in part by the LXX reading in v 25, which addresses the women only. The words in question—save "all"—are present in the LXX (*tō laō kai*). Giesebrecht retains, and Boadt correctly notes that not all the blame can be put on the women. It is clear from prior verses, also from 7:18, that Queen of Heaven worship was a family affair.

all Judah who are in the land of Egypt. Lacking in the LXX, and probably due to haplography (homoeoarcton: *k . . . k*). Duhm and others delete, but the words are present in Theod.

25. *You and your wives, yes, you have spoken with your mouth, and with your hands you have carried it out.* "Mouth" and "hands" are not simply a rhetorical contrast, but form part of a technical expression for making and carrying out vows (Duhm; cf. v 17). The expression occurs in 1 Kgs 8:15 and 24 with reference to Yahweh fulfilling a promise he has made.

You and your wives. The LXX has "You women" (*hymeis gunaikes*), which may be guided by the feminine plural verb, *wattĕdabbērĕnâ* ("and you have spoken"), coming next. However, all the suffixes and the following verb, *millē'tem* ("you have carried it out") are masculine plural, which speaks against emending MT, as virtually all commentators do. Kimḥi (following T) reads the MT, and so does the Vg (*vos et uxores vestrae*). The men and their wives both continue as addressees, the alternation of feminine and masculine verbs most likely being intentional. We see this alternation elsewhere in Jeremiah (see Note for 48:20). The syntax is chiastic (see Rhetoric and Composition). In Amos 8:13 a feminine plural verb predicates masculine and feminine subjects.

Well then, confirm fully your vows and perform fully your vows! "Well then," or something like it, is required to make the transition to this final irony, which is an example of *epitrope* (see Note on 7:21). The emphatic construction also echoes what the people were just quoted as saying. Kimḥi says the verb forms are feminine because God is addressing women who usually perform this worship. On the pointing of *tāqîmĕnâ*, see KB³; GKC §72k. A few MSS have *niskêkem* ("your drink offerings") for the final *nidrêkem* ("your vows"), giving the reading: "and perform fully your drink offerings" (cf. JB [but not NJB]; NRSV; NSB)

26. *Look I, I have sworn by my great name.* Yahweh alone can swear by his own name (see Note for 49:13). On the divine self-asseveration, *ḥay-'ānî* ("As I live"), see Note for 22:24.

my name will no longer be called on the mouth of any person of Judah who now says, 'As the Lord Yahweh lives,' in all the land of Egypt. This is Yahweh's answer to those making vows to other gods, a problem that existed earlier in Judah (5:2, 7; 7:9; 12:16), where oaths made in Yahweh's name were therefore banned (4:1–2). Another interpretation here is that oaths in Yahweh's name will no longer be heard because there will be no Jews left in Egypt to swear them (Kimḥi; Calvin; cf. v 27).

27. *Look I am watching over them for evil and not for good.* See 21:10. Yahweh "watches over" (*šqd*) both his word (1:12) and his covenant people (31:28).

and every person of Judah who is in the land of Egypt will be consumed by sword and by famine, until they are ended. Impassioned rhetoric. That such a thing did not happen is evident from the following verse (Kimḥi). On the expression, "until they are ended" (*'ad-kĕlôtām*), see 9:15[Eng 9:16] and 49:37. A discussion on Yahweh making a "full end" is found in Note for 5:10.

28. *And those escaping the sword shall return from the land of Egypt to the land of Judah—a few people.* An intervening word of hope intentionally placed at the center of the oracle. For this mode of composition in Jeremiah and elsewhere, see Rhetoric and Composition for 20:7–10. Talk of a remnant softens not only the impact of v 27, but also v 29. See in addition the end of v 14.

from the land of Egypt. Lacking in the LXX.

a few people. Hebrew *mĕtê mispār*. Literally, "males of (a small) number." For this use of *mispār*, see Isa 21:17 and Ezek 12:16.

Then all the remnant of Judah who came to the land of Egypt to sojourn shall know whose word will be confirmed—mine or theirs. Two opposing words await confirmation: a word of well-being spoken by devotees of other gods, which we have just heard, and Yahweh's word of judgment, which is the controlling theme of the oracle. Confirmation is not being awaited on the return to Judah. The sign in v 29 also points to forthcoming evil. Some time needs to elapse before it will become clear which word is true and which word will come to pass (28:8–9; cf. Deut 18:21–22).

mine or theirs. Lacking in the LXX, doubtless due to haplography (homoeoteleuton: *m . . . m*). The words should not be deleted (*pace* Cornill; Holladay; McKane). The T, Aq (*par' emou ē par' autōn*), Theod (*ho emos ē ho autōn*), and Vg (*meus an illorum*) all support MT.

29. *And this is the sign to you . . . that I am reckoning against you in this place*. The sign is the prophetic word here given, which shall be confirmed on the day evil comes. Because this was said to be the only instance of Yahweh giving a "sign" (*'ôt*) in the preaching of Jeremiah, Cornill (following Hitzig) argued that the verse (along with v 30) was unoriginal. In Isaiah's preaching, signs appear frequently (Isa 7:10–17; 8:18; 19:20; 20:3; 37:30; 38:7). However, despite a lack of the term "sign" in Jeremiah's almond rod vision (1:11–12), what we have still is a sign to the prophet-designate that his word of call awaits a later fulfillment (see Note for 1:12). Jeremiah also spoke affirmatively about Yahweh's "signs and wonders" (*'ōtôt ûmōpětîm*) in the prayer following his purchase of the field (32:20–21), which was itself another sign that houses, fields, and vineyards would once again be bought in the land (32:15). On the verb *pqd*, which means "reckon, pay a visit (for the purpose of punishment)," see Note for 5:9.

in this place so that you may know that my words will be fully confirmed against you. The LXX omits, which is rightly taken by Giesebrecht, Duhm, and Janzen (1973: 118) to be a loss attributable to haplography (whole-word: *'lykm . . . 'lykm*). Holladay does not note the omission, and McKane predictably goes with the shorter LXX reading (MT is "secondary embellishment"). The words are present in Aq and Theod.

so that. On *lěma'an* expressing definite purpose in final clauses, see Note for 43:3.

30. *Look I am giving Pharaoh Hophra, king of Egypt, into the hand of his enemies, into the hand of those who seek his life, just as I gave Zedekiah, king of Judah, into the hand of Nebuchadrezzar, king of Babylon, his enemy and the one who sought his life*. Hophra, the biblical name for Apries, was Pharaoh of Egypt from 589 to 570 b.c. In T he is simply called "the Broken One" (*pr'* = "to break"), a disparaging epithet and near-equivalent to Hophra (cf. 46:17). Hayward (1987: 167 n. 2) notes that in 46:2 T calls Neco "Pharaoh the Lame One" (*nkh* = "to be lame"). According to Josephus (*Against Apion* i 133; *Ant* x 181–82), Nebuchadnezzar invaded Egypt after subduing the Syrians, Moabites, and Ammonites in his twenty-third year, i.e., 582 b.c. He is then said to have killed the reigning Egyptian king and taken Judahites in Egypt captive to Babylon. The killing of the Egyptian king is widely discounted (Hophra ruled from 589–570 b.c.), but invasion and exile could have occurred, since in this same year the Babylonians returned to Jerusalem and exiled more Judahites to Babylon (52:30). Classical sources (Herodotus ii 169; Diodorus Sic. i 68) report that Apries (Hophra) met his end after being captured by Amasis, who gave him over to enemies who strangled him. This could fulfill the present prophecy,

which does not say that Hophra will fall to Nebuchadnezzar, but simply to "his enemies." There is no reason, then, to judge this a *vaticinium ex eventu* (*pace* Cornill; Hyatt; McKane). Nebuchadnezzar did invade Egypt in his thirty-seventh year, i.e., 568 B.C., but then Amasis was king (see Note for 46:13). The comparison made here between Hophra and Zedekiah is striking, since the two struck an ill-advised alliance during Judah's last days (37:5; cf. Hyatt).

Pharaoh Hophra. The LXX omits "Pharaoh," but not due to haplography (*pace* Janzen 1973: 118). Aquila and Theod have only *Ophrēn* (Hophra), suggesting MT expansion.

into the hand of his enemies. On this phrase, see Note for 12:7.

just as I gave Zedekiah. See comparison with *ka'ăšer* in v 13.

MESSAGE AND AUDIENCE

Jeremiah's last recorded words are to a broad audience of Jewish expatriates living throughout Egypt. In the first oracle, people are reminded of the evil visited upon Jerusalem and the cities of Judah, which is now a matter of record. The people are told why this happened, and for any who may have heard Jeremiah's preaching in Jerusalem, the explanation is nothing new. Yahweh was provoked by the worship of gods the covenant people had not known. Infidelity had been building for generations. Yahweh sent prophets to say that he hated this abomination, but the people did not listen and did not turn from their evil way. So Yahweh's wrath was poured out, the result of which was the ruin of Jerusalem and all Judah.

The second oracle moves into the present, addressing the expatriates in Egypt. These people are on the same ruinous course, and Yahweh begins by asking why they are doing it. They are cutting off for themselves a remnant, with the result that they too will become a curse among the nations. A second rhetorical question betrays mounting audience resistance. Has this people forgotten the evils of Jerusalem and Judah (7:18–20)? Some of the very men and women standing there were party to this evil. But no one is greatly moved. No one is afraid. Yahweh ends by citing a disregard of covenant law obligating them and prior generations. Is not the covenant what this ruin of a nation is all about?

Oracle III promises a future judgment for Judahites living in Egypt, effectively cutting off the remnant that came there to survive. Death shall come as it did in Judah: by sword, famine, and pestilence. Once again, they will become a shameful curse. Another comparison is made to the horror of Jerusalem. There will be no fugitives or survivors to return to Judah, as many hope to do. Later it is said that some fugitives will return, but the outlook still is exceedingly grim.

What follows is a response from the Pathros contingent in the far south. The men, beside whom stand the wives busy with incense burning, along with others make a substantial gathering. They all give Jeremiah an unqualified rejection, saying that they fully intend to carry out vows made to the Queen of Heaven, burn incense, and pour drink offerings to her, just as they and earlier generations did in Jerusalem and the cities of Judah. In their view, times were considerably better when this worship was carried out; things actually got bad, they say, when the practice was discontinued, after which they lacked everything and became victims of sword and famine. The women conclude by asking rhetorically if the good prophet thinks they are making the cakes and pouring out drink offerings without the consent of their husbands.

Jeremiah is unmoved. From him comes Yahweh's point of view, and the impassioned rhetoric continues unabated. Does this people think that what occurred on Jerusalem's streets and in Judah's cities—by people whom Yahweh remembers—even entered the divine mind? Jeremiah then repeats what was stated in Yahweh's oracle about judgment coming to the covenant people because of their rank infidelity.

Oracle IV answers the Pathros delegation, the women in particular, although it is directed also to other Judahites living in Egypt. If the people are determined to vow and act on vows to the Queen of Heaven, there is little more that can be said. Yahweh tells them to go ahead, then, and do what they are set on doing!

The three final oracles are addressed to all Judahites in Egypt. In the first, Yahweh swears that his own name will no longer be heard on the lips of any person now swearing Yahweh oaths in Egypt. The people cannot have it both ways. If they are going to worship the Queen of Heaven, then oaths in Yahweh's name cannot be taken. In the second oracle, Yahweh says once again to this broad audience that he is planning evil for them; sword and famine will meet them until they are finished. It remains to be seen whose word will be confirmed, Yahweh's or the people's. The oracle closes by stating that the present word is a sign of the evil to come. This oracle of judgment, like the earlier one, is provided at some later time with a word of hope (v 28a). A few will survive the judgment and return to the land of Judah. The final oracle is a judgment on Hophra, king of Egypt. Yahweh says that he will come to an inglorious end by falling into the hands of enemies, just as Zedekiah, king of Judah, did.

When this narrative is heard in tandem with the narrative in chap. 43, the issue there about people disobeying Yahweh by coming to Egypt will here be reaffirmed and supplemented by another disobedience, i.e., the worshiping of other gods, specifically the Queen of Heaven. The oracles here will also reinforce the oracle and symbolic action of 43:9–13, which promise judgment on Egypt and those Judahites living in Egypt. The link from 43:13 to the present oracles is a mention in 43:13 of obelisks to the sun at Heliopolis. The present oracles polemicize against the worship of all heavenly bodies.

The present preaching and accompanying narrative can be dated any time after 582 B.C., with an *ad quem* of 570 B.C., when Hophra's reign ended.

The situation depicted here is well portrayed in the words of a twentieth-century hymn by John E. Bowers (b. 1923):

> The prophets spoke in days of old
>   to those[1] of stubborn will
> Their message lives and is retold
>   where hearts are stubborn still.
>   (*HAMNS*, 1983 #513)

---

[1] Text has "men."

VII. BARUCH'S COLOPHON (45:1–5)

◆

45 ¹The word that Jeremiah the prophet spoke to Baruch son of Neriah when he had written these words on a scroll from the dictation of Jeremiah, in the fourth year of Jehoiakim son of Josiah, king of Judah: ²Thus said Yahweh, God of Israel, concerning you, Baruch. ³You have said, 'Woe now to me, for Yahweh has added sorrow to my pain. I am weary with my groaning and rest I cannot find.' ⁴Thus you shall say to him:

Thus said Yahweh:
Look, what I have built up I am overthrowing, and what I have planted I am uprooting, and that is the whole earth. ⁵And you, you are seeking for yourself great things? Do not seek.

For look I am bringing evil upon all flesh—oracle of Yahweh—but I will give you your life for booty in all the places where you go.

RHETORIC AND COMPOSITION

MT 45 = LXX 51:31–35. The present verses are delimited at the top end by a *setumah* in M^L, M^A, and M^P prior to v 1, and at the bottom end by a *setumah* in M^L and M^P, and a *petuḥah* in M^A, after v 5. The unit, then, is coterminous with MT chap. 45. The M^L also has *setumah*s after vv 1 and 3, which set off Baruch's lament from the superscription preceding and the oracles following; M^A and M^P do not have these section markings.

The verses are familiar Jeremiah prose containing: 1) a superscription stating that what follows is a word Jeremiah spoke to Baruch at the time Baruch wrote a scroll from Jeremiah's dictation in Jehoiakim's fourth year (v 1); 2) an expanded messenger formula introducing the word for Baruch from Yahweh (v 2); 3) a recounting by Jeremiah to Baruch of a lament Baruch made earlier, to which the present divine word is an answer (vv 2–3); and 4) two oracles, constituting the divine word given earlier to Jeremiah, prefaced by a directive that Jeremiah deliver them to Baruch (vv 4–5).

The verses, then, feature a lament (or "confession") by Baruch (Giesebrecht; Cornill; Volz; Hyatt; Zimmerli 1984: 357) and two oracles from Yahweh mixing judgment and salvation. Duhm and Rudolph call the latter Baruch's "word of consolation." Judgment is upon the nation; salvation is for Baruch. Jeremiah received the same message—judgment for the nation, salvation for himself—in the oracles accompanying his commissioning (see Rhetoric and Composition for 1:13–19).

Taken in its entirety, chap. 45 is reducible neither to a lament nor to a salvation oracle (*pace* Graupner 1991: 164 n. 18), even though both elements, as we noted, are present. Based on content and location in the book, the verses are seen to function as a colophon—more precisely, an expanded colophon—which puts them form-critically with colophons similarly written in 36:1–8 and 51:59–64 (Lundbom 1986b). The scribe of record in the present colophon, also the one in 36:1–8, is Baruch son of Neriah. The scribe of record in the colophon of 51:59–64 is Seraiah son of Neriah, Baruch's brother. Both belong to the scribal family of Mahseiah (32:12; 51:59), on which see Note for 51:59.

Evaluated according to colophon criteria set forth by Leichty (1964), the present expanded colophon contains the following basic elements:

1. name of the scribe (with patronym) making the copy: "Baruch son of Neriah"
2. source for the copy: "these words [written] on a scroll from the dictation of Jeremiah" (= 1:5–20:18; cf. 36:4, 32)
3. date: the fourth year of Jehoiakim
4. reason for making the copy: Yahweh commanded it (36:27–28)
5. curse and blessing: the whole land will be destroyed, but Baruch will escape with his life
6. catchword: "sorrow" (45:4; cf. 20:18).

Earlier I cited only five of the ten Leichty criteria as having been met here, not including the catchword "sorrow." This catchword at one time linked the colophon to the concluding poem of the First Edition, 20:14–18 (Rietzschel 1966: 128; Lundbom 1986b: 99–101, 107; §Introduction: The First Edition of the Book of Jeremiah). The phrases providing the linkage:

20:18	to see hard times *and sorrow*	*wĕyāgôn*
45:3	for Yahweh has added *sorrow* to my pain	*yāgôn*

Now with six of the Leichty criteria being met, the claim is strengthened that this prose was intended to perform a colophon function. Also, we note the obvious but nevertheless important fact that relocation, when it occurred, was to another end position, viz., a completed book of what is now 51 chapters. In the LXX it still occupies this position, another indication that this prose was meant in a final stage of redaction to function as a scribal colophon.

In its earlier position as a conclusion to chap. 20, the colophon was also linked by other key words to the call narrative in chap. 1 (Muilenburg 1970a: 236):

45:4	1:9–10
Look ...	*Look* ...
what I have built up	*to uproot*
I am overthrowing	*... and to overthrow*

and what I have planted   *to build up*
I am uprooting   *and to plant*

The two oracles begin characteristically with *hinnēh*, "Look," and *hinĕnî*, "Look I" (Wanke 1971: 134), providing a link to the oracles of commissioning in 1:15–16, 18–19:

	45:4–5				1:15, 18		
I	*Look....*	*hinnēh...*	v 4	I	*...look I...*	*...hinĕnî...*	v 15
II	*...look I*	*...hinĕnî...*	v 5	II	*...look...*	*...hinnēh...*	v 18

The colophon in its relocated position—following 51:30 in the LXX and following 44:30 in the MT—is not a conclusion to the *via dolorosa* prose (MT chaps. 37–44). It is an independent passage of earlier date linked to this prose only by catchwords. Yet it does manage to juxtapose Baruch's suffering and the suffering of Jeremiah. The colophon also does not mean to link up chap. 36 or chaps. 43–44 with the Foreign Nation Oracles (*pace* Thiel 1981: 84–85; Seitz 1989: 22), although in the case of the latter, catchwords do make a connection. Its primary function in the relocated position is to conclude an expanded Jeremiah book, indirectly presenting, in the words of Mowinckel (1946: 61–62), the author to his audience. Muilenburg (1970b: 57), too, took chap. 45 to be a one-time conclusion to the Jeremiah book.

Catchwords connecting chap. 45 to chap. 44:

45:5 *you are seeking ... do not seek*   44:27 *Look I ... for evil   hinĕnî... lĕrāʿâ*
      ... look I ... evil   hinĕnî...   44:30 *those who seek ... the one who sought*
rāʿâ

Catchwords connecting chap. 45 to chap. 46 (in MT):

45:1 *in the fourth year of Jehoiakim*   46:2 *in the fourth year of Jehoiakim*

NOTES

45:1. *The word that Jeremiah the prophet spoke to Baruch son of Neriah. . . .* A superscription similar to the one in 51:59, stating that what follows is a word spoken by Jeremiah to his scribal colleague and friend. There is no dialogue here; Jeremiah is the speaker and Baruch the one listening. Baruch's earlier lament is being relayed back to him. The word of Yahweh comes to Baruch via Jeremiah, who received it earlier. On the difficult "Thus you shall say to him" in v 4, see below.

Baruch son of Neriah. For background on this scribe featured prominently in the book of Jeremiah, his relation to Seraiah son of Neriah (51:59–64), and the seal impressions that have turned up with his name on them, see Note for 36:4.

when he had written these words on a scroll from the dictation of Jeremiah. The translation of *bĕkotbô* as "when he had written" follows the AV, which puts Jeremiah's word to Baruch after the scroll-writing was completed. It is possible that this word could have been spoken while Jeremiah was dictating and Baruch was writing, since the process doubtless took time, and pauses in the work would have allowed for conversation between the two. However, the narrative is better read as a culmination of discussions that took place earlier, one in which Baruch made his lament to Jeremiah, and another when Jeremiah sought mediation with Yahweh on Baruch's behalf. The lament could have been made during the scroll-writing, but mediation requires more time: Jeremiah must bring the complaint to Yahweh, wait for an answer, and then convey the answer back to Baruch.

these words. Usually taken to mean the words on the first scroll of 605 (36:1–8), otherwise the words on the replacement scroll written after the first scroll was destroyed (36:32). Kimḥi says "these words" are words recorded at the beginning of the book, up until the fourth year of Jehoiakim. In my view, the words at some point were those contained in the First Edition of 1–20 (§Introduction: The First Edition of the Book of Jeremiah), then upon relocation of the colophon, made to include all the oracles and narrative in a book of 51 chapters (Lundbom 1986b: 99–101).

from the dictation of Jeremiah. Hebrew *mippî yirmĕyāhû* is lit. "from the mouth of Jeremiah." On these dictations, see 36:4 and 32.

in the fourth year of Jehoiakim. I.e., 605 B.C., when Yahweh instructed Jeremiah to prepare his first scroll (36:1). In this year Jeremiah also delivered his Egypt poems against the background of the Battle of Carchemish (46:2–12), and preached against Judah and the nations in light of this pivotal Babylonian victory (25:1–38). Some scholars (Giesebrecht; Duhm; Skinner 1926: 346) doubt the 605 date here, imagining that Baruch's lament and Yahweh's response had to be post-586 B.C. But this view has been sufficiently refuted (Cornill; Volz; Weiser 1954; Muilenburg 1970a: 235). The catastrophe of vv 4–5 lies in the future. Also, chap. 45 does not follow chronologically the post-586 events of chaps. 37–44. A date of 605 is then right for the passage.

2. *Thus said Yahweh, God of Israel, concerning you, Baruch.* The LXX lacks "God of Israel," as elsewhere (cf. Janzen 1973: 75–78). This oracle is to an individual. Pashhur the priest received a divine oracle (20:4–6), and so did Ebed-melech, the Ethiopian (39:15–18). The oracle to the latter was a mix of judgment and salvation, which is what we have here (Weiser 1954).

3. *You have said.* The LXX has *hoti eipas*, "because you have said," leading some scholars to restore a *kî* thought to have been lost by haplography (Duhm; Rudolph; Weiser; Bright; Wanke 1971: 133; Carroll). A *kaph* could have been lost, but what about the *yod*? A dependent clause yields good sense only because the LXX later omits "Thus you shall say to him" (v 4). Bright: "Because you have said . . . this is what Yahweh has said." However, the directive at the beginning of v 4 can remain (see below), which makes a dependent clause here unnecessary.

Woe now to me. Hebrew *'ôy-nâ' lî.* The same lament occurs in 4:31, and twice more without the emphatic *nā'* in 10:19 and 15:10 where Jeremiah makes it. On the terms *ʾôy* and *hôy* in Jeremiah, and their use both as laments and prophetic invectives, see Note for 22:13. The LXX has *oimmoi oimmoi*, "woe (is me), woe (is me)," which achieves emphasis in another way. The T follows MT, which could, nevertheless, be a victim here of whole-word haplography. Aquila and Symm have *ouai dē moi* ("woe now to me!").

For Yahweh has added sorrow to my pain. Hebrew *kî-yāsap yhwh yāgôn ʿal-makʾōbî*. One disaster is heaped upon another. The term *yāgôn* ("sorrow, grief") occurs frequently in the Psalms (see Note for 20:18). Grief swept in earlier upon Jeremiah (8:18; 20:18), and now it comes to Baruch. Muilenburg (1970a: 235) says: "As [Baruch] had written the terrible words of judgment upon the royal house and the people of Judah, line after line, he must have been torn with anxiety and sorrow." Doubtless with him, as with Jeremiah, personal sorrow was intermixed with sorrow over a nation—his very own—that had lost its way and was headed for ruin (cf. 8:21). Baruch's "pain" (*makʾōb*) is also one the whole nation experienced (30:15). Later on, pain becomes redemptive in the Suffering Servant figure (Isa 53:3–4), that "man of pains" (*ʾîš makʾōbôt*) who is made to bear "our pains" (*makʾōbēnû*).

I am weary with my groaning and rest I cannot find. A syntactic chiasmus. "I am weary with my groaning" (*yāgaʿtî bĕʾanḥātî*), could be a quote from Ps 6:7[Eng 6:6]. The LXX has: "I lay down to sleep (*ekoimēthēn*) in groaning." Giesebrecht says *mĕnûḥâ* ("rest") here is not calmness, but a solid resting place. The distinction appears overdrawn, as both meanings apply. Baruch would be a strange sort of person if he did not experience personal unease over events at Carchemish, combined with a doom message for Judah. At the same time, both he and Jeremiah may well have lacked a secure resting place while Jehoiakim was king, although they may have found such a place after disappearing from public view (cf. 36:19, 26). The T interprets "and rest I cannot find" to mean "I have found no prophecy" (= the spirit of prophecy has not rested upon me; cf. Num 11:26), an interpretation surviving in Jewish tradition, but rejected roundly by Calvin.

4. *Thus you shall say to him.* The phrase is difficult, since a cursory reading would seem to indicate that Yahweh is addressing Jeremiah, whereas up to this point (vv 2–3) Jeremiah has been addressing Baruch. The superscription (v 1) indicates that Jeremiah is addressing Baruch throughout. Many commentators (Giesebrecht; Peake; Cornill; Streane; Volz; Rudolph; Bright; McKane) thus omit the phrase, which is an economical solution even though there is no textual basis for doing so. Janzen (1973: 134) too takes the phrase as expansion, but does not consider it a clarifying gloss. If we are going to retain the phrase and render it sensibly, we must either presume an ellipsis or else imagine that words have fallen out of the text. What we need is a prior "And Yahweh said to me" (cf. 1:7, 9, 12, 14; 13:6; 14:11, 14; et passim) so the narrative would read: "And Yahweh said to me, 'Thus you shall say to him.'" Jeremiah then continues as speaker and sense is made of the narrative as a whole. Jeremiah is simply reporting what Yahweh said to him earlier. The following sequence of events should therefore be assumed:

Baruch makes his lament to Jeremiah
Jeremiah brings the lament before Yahweh
Yahweh responds by giving Jeremiah two oracles for Baruch
Jeremiah later tells Baruch that Yahweh has a word for him (v 2)
Jeremiah first repeats back to Baruch his earlier lament (v 3)
Jeremiah then says that Yahweh instructed him to tell Baruch the
    following (v 4a)
Jeremiah proceeds to give Baruch the two oracles from Yahweh (vv 4b–5)

Our present narrative is truncated not only because earlier events have gone
unreported, but because time lapses have been compressed, particularly the
lapse occurring between the prophet's attempt at mediation and Yahweh's return with an answer. In narratives elsewhere in the book, time lapses are clearly
indicated (28:12; 42:7). Compare too the smooth-flowing narratives in 36:1–8
and 39:15–18. If *wayyō'mer yhwh 'ēlay* ("And Yahweh said to me") did at one
time exist in the present text, which can be no more than a conjecture, its loss
could be due to haplography (homoeoteleuton: *y . . . y*). Note the probable
loss of "And the word of Yahweh came to me" in 3:1.

*what I have built up I am overthrowing, and what I have planted I am uproot-
ing.* These verbs from Jeremiah's call (1:10) and elsewhere (12:14–17; 18:7–9;
24:6; 31:28, 38–40; 42:10) define the prophet's message: Yahweh is creator
and destroyer. The LXX adds the first person pronoun *egō* to all four verbs. The
Vg too has an emphatic *ego* for "overthrowing" and "uprooting": *ego destruo
. . . ego evello.* Zimmerli (1984: 357) says about the answer: "The suffering of
the prophet and his companion is only to be understood as the pale reflection
of the comprehensive suffering of Yahweh."

and that is the whole earth. Hebrew *wĕ'et-kol-hā'āreṣ hî'*. The T interprets
kol-hā'āreṣ to mean "the whole land of Israel." Many MSS and K^{OR} add *lî* ("to
me") at the end, which, when combined with *hî'* ("that, it"), gives the embellished T reading: "it is mine," or "which belongs to me." According to this interpretation, Yahweh is saying that all Israel belongs to him. But considering
that the whole earth is undergoing vast transformation and mighty empires are
being broken down and built up (1:10), "the whole earth" may be a better
translation. Hebrew *hā'āreṣ* can mean either "the earth" or "the land," and
both belong to Yahweh. The broader interpretation is supported by 27:5–7,
where it says that Yahweh, who made the earth (*hā'āreṣ*), is giving Judah and
the lands (*hā'ărāṣôt*) around it into the hand of Nebuchadnezzar. The present
phrase is lacking in the LXX, leading a number of commentators (Giesebrecht;
Duhm; Peake; Cornill; Condamin; Hyatt; Bright; Holladay; Jones; McKane)
to omit as a gloss. But the phrase should be retained; its loss is probably due to
haplography (homoeoarcton: *w't . . . w't*). The phrase is translated in Aq and
Symm.

5. *And you, you are seeking for yourself great things? Do not seek.* A question
without the *hē'* interrogative (H. G. Mitchell 1908; Rudolph; cf. GKC §150a).
Yahweh's words are a reprimand. Should Baruch be seeking great things for

himself when the whole world is in upheaval and the nation of Judah is tumbling toward ruin? What then are the "great things" (*gĕdōlôt*)? The usual answer is that they are Baruch's personal ambitions, perhaps to hold a government
office such as his brother Seraiah has (51:59), or to become a prophet like his
master (Rashi, following T). But de Boer (1973) says that *gĕdōlôt* ("great things")
is not used in the OT to indicate personal ambition, but denotes rather the
hidden, wondrous, and miraculous works of God (33:3; Deut 10:21; 2 Kgs 8:4;
Pss 71:19; 106:21; 131:1; et passim). In his view, Baruch has called upon the
miracle-working God to act on behalf of himself and the nation, to alter their
fate (cf. 21:2), a plea that God now rejects. This explanation must be rejected,
however. First, there is no hint whatsoever that Baruch made his plea with the
nation in mind. The great things were "for himself" (*lĕkā*), no one else. Second, the very point of Oracle II is that Yahweh *will do* a miraculous work, viz.,
save Baruch. So the "great things" must refer to his personal ambition, regardless
of what the term signifies elsewhere in the OT. We know from thirteenth- and
fourteenth-century B.C. Egyptian documents that scribes held high aspirations
within the profession (see in ANET³ 431–34: "In Praise of Learned Scribes,"
and "The Satire on the Trades"), which one might expect of individuals coming from noble families (Gadd 1956: 23; Lambert 1957: 6–7; Rainey 1969: 127–
28). Also "great things," being a general term, can certainly admit to a broader
interpretation than de Boer allows. Baruch has in mind something great for
himself, and Yahweh now rejects all his ambitions because of the destructive
work he is carrying out. Yet the irony, as Muilenburg (1970a) points out, is that
Baruch goes on to become a bigger-than-life figure in the later intertestamental
literature, e.g., his name is given to an apocryphal book, and he figures prominently in other noncanonical books (see Message and Audience).

For look I am bringing evil upon all flesh. On the Jeremianic expression, "I
am bringing evil," see Note for 6:19. "All flesh" (*kol-bāśār*) means all people
(Gen 6:12, 13), not just all Israelites (*pace* Duhm).

but I will give you your life for booty in all the places where you go. This is the
saving word for Baruch, given later to Ebed-melech (39:18) and any who would
surrender to the Babylonians during the final siege of Jerusalem (21:9; 38:2).
But the salvation is reduced in scope, making the promise seem almost like
another rebuke. Hebrew *šālāl* is booty taken in war (RSV and NRSV: "prize of
war"). A soldier's dream, at war's end, is to return home with quantities of
booty. But here things will be different. Judah's war is a lost cause, and its defenders—along with others—will be lucky to escape with their lives (T substitutes "escape" for "booty"; cf. JB, NIV, REB). The NEB paraphrases: "but you
shall save your life and nothing more." Jeremiah's only promise for the future
was his life (1:8, 19; 15:20–21), and Weiser points out that "the disciple is not
above the master" (Matt 10:24; Luke 6:40). This having been said, the promise
of one's life ought not be trivialized. People in all times and places have been
grateful to escape with their lives when everything else was lost. When all is
said and done, the gift of one's life is to be taken as a blessing from a kind and
merciful God.

in all the places where you go. This could point toward exile (Holladay), although before and after Jerusalem's fall Baruch will experience some shifting about in dangerous situations within Judah.

MESSAGE AND AUDIENCE

Baruch in this expanded colophon is indirectly presenting himself—initially to an audience hearing the First Edition of the book of Jeremiah (1–20), later to an audience hearing a larger Jeremiah book read (1–51). It states at the beginning that Jeremiah spoke the word here to Baruch after Baruch wrote the first scroll of Jeremiah's prophecies from dictation. The audience will likely know that Baruch is Jeremiah's scribe, friend, and confidant.

The messenger formula indicates that the present word is a divine word to Baruch. Jeremiah begins by repeating a lament Baruch made to him earlier. Baruch said he was under a near-curse because Yahweh had added sorrow to his pain. He was weary with groaning, unable to find rest. Jeremiah can relate to this; he too has been there. Jeremiah then says that Yahweh instructed him to relate to Baruch two brief oracles, which he presumably did. In the first, Yahweh says that what he built up he is bringing down, and what he planted he is uprooting—the entire earth. Is Baruch asking for great things? He should not so ask. The timing could not be worse. In the second oracle Yahweh says that he is bringing evil on everyone; nevertheless, Baruch will get his own life as war booty in every place where he goes. Sounds as if life will be a bit unsettled. This word deflates a lifetime of dreams, but at the same time offers hope if the good scribe has the ears to hear it. What might a pre-586 B.C. audience make of such preaching? Do they know that they too could have their lives as war booty if they would surrender to the king of Babylon? And do they know that Ebed-melech, the Ethiopian, because he trusted Yahweh, also has his future locked up?

Baruch and Ebed-melech both live on in tradition as confidants of Jeremiah and the ones who bury him, finally, after he is stoned, in the pseudepigraphical work, *Paraleipomena Jeremiou* (Kraft and Purintun 1972). The notoriety denied Baruch during his lifetime is more than compensated for in later Jewish literature and tradition, where he appears bigger than life (Muilenburg 1970a: 237–38). An apocryphal letter is attributed to him (second century B.C. with additions) as well as several apocalpyses (Grintz, *EncJud* 4: 266–67; for texts see Tov 1975b and Charlesworth *OTP I*: 615–79). J. E. Wright (1996), noting Baruch's notoriety in subsequent literature, calls him "the ideal sage."

The date given for this word to Baruch is the fourth year of Jehoiakim, i.e., 605 B.C. A public reading of the colophon would have to come later, but how much later we cannot say. It would have been heard when the First Edition was read publicly, and then heard again when a larger Jeremiah book had been compiled and read publicly. To these audiences Baruch's survival would be a matter of record. The accent now would be on Baruch's association with Jeremiah, the one who preserved the prophet's legacy and walked the same path of suffering that his master did.

Dietrich Bonhoeffer cited the present passage often—in his preaching at Finkenwalde and in his *Letters and Papers from Prison*. In his reflections on the baptism of Dietrich Bethge, in May 1944, he noted how fragmentary life was now compared with the life his parents had known. He said:

> We realize more clearly than formerly that the world lies under the wrath and grace of God. We read in Jer. 45: "Thus says the Lord: Behold, what I have built I am breaking down, and what I have planted I am plucking up. . . . And do you seek great things for yourself? Seek them not; for, behold, I am bringing evil upon all flesh; . . . but I will give your life as a prize of war in all places to which you may go." If we can save our souls unscathed out of the wreckage of our material possessions, let us be satisfied with that. If the Creator destroys his own handiwork, what right have we to lament the destruction of ours? It will be the task of our generation, not to "seek great things," but to save and preserve our souls out of the chaos, and to realize that it is the only thing we can carry as a "prize" from the burning building.
> (Bonhoeffer 1971: 297)

Bonhoeffer was not himself saved, but his disciple, Ebehard Bethge, was. It was Bethge, after all, who became the "Baruch" of the Bonhoeffer legacy both during the war and in the years following.

Writing two months later from Tegel Prison, on July 21, 1944, Bonhoeffer told Bethge that

> it is only by living completely in this world that one learns to have faith. One must completely abandon any attempt to make something of oneself, whether it be a saint, or a converted sinner, or a churchman. . . . By this-worldliness I mean living unreservedly in life's duties, problems, successes and failures, experiences and perplexities. In so doing we throw ourselves completely into the arms of God, taking seriously, not our own sufferings, but those of God in the world—watching with Christ in Gethsemane. That, I think, is faith; that is *metanoia*; and that is how one becomes a man and a Christian (cf. Jer. 45!). (Bonhoeffer 1971: 369–70)

The Swedish hymnwriter, Nils Frykman (1842–1911), penned these lines after overcoming his own sense of despondency one evening along a road in rural Sweden:

> Why should I be anxious, I have such a Friend
> Who bears in his heart all my woe
> This Friend is the Savior, on him I depend
> His love is eternal I know

His mercy, I know, is sufficient for me
And therein my soul finds its peace
He chastens with love, ever patient is he
O Savior, your mercy I laud.
    (tr. Aaron Markuson, *CovH* 1996 #431)

VIII. ORACLES TO THE FOREIGN NATIONS (46:1–51:64)

◆

A. SUPERSCRIPTION TO THE FOREIGN NATION ORACLES (46:1)

46 ¹What came as the word of Yahweh to Jeremiah the prophet concerning the nations.

RHETORIC AND COMPOSITION

MT 46:1 = LXX 0. This superscription introduces the entire Foreign Nation Collection of oracles in chaps. 46–51. It is lacking in the LXX, where the collection comes after 25:13a. An abbreviated "which Jeremiah prophesied against all the nations" occurs in MT 25:13b, which in Rahlfs's edition of the LXX is placed at the end of the Foreign Nation Collection, i.e., at the beginning of chap. 32. Ziegler in his edition omits it from the text. The upper limit of the present unit is marked by a section before v 1—*setumahs* in M^L and M^P, a *petuḥah* in M^A—at which point a chapter division also occurs. The lower limit is set by the superscription beginning "For Egypt," in v 2.

The placement of Foreign Nation Oracles in the LXX after 25:13a is generally thought to be the more original (§Introduction: MT and LXX; also Tov 1985: 217; Lundbom 1986b; and Gosse 1986; 1990 refuting Seitz 1989). This has Baruch's colophon ending a book of 51 chapters (LXX 51:31–35 = MT 45), and assumes that the placement in MT 46–51 is a relocation, in which the colophon of Seraiah ben Neriah, Baruch's brother, ends a book of comparable length (MT 51:59–64 = LXX 28:59–64; Lundbom 1986b). Foreign Nation Collections come at the center of Isaiah (chaps. 13–23) and Ezekiel (chaps. 25–32).

In LXX the Foreign Nation Oracles appear in a different sequence: Elam, Egypt, Babylon, Philistia, Edom, Ammon, Kedar-Hazor, Damascus, and Moab. This order has no apparent significance, so honors here are given to MT, where the superpowers Egypt and Babylon appear first and last, respectively, and the list as a whole corresponds more or less to the lineup of nations in 25:19–26. The placement of Egypt first is explainable in that, except for Baruch's colophon in chap. 45, continuity is created with chaps. 43–44, which report Jeremiah's sojourn in Egypt and judgments against Judahites living there. Babylon's placement last is climactic. Duhm, Janzen (1973: 115–16), and Carroll argue that the LXX sequence is more original. Holladay and McKane argue in support of the MT sequence. The matter is difficult to decide. I find evidence only for an independent Babylon collection (MT 50–51), it being apparent that Seraiah's colophon originally concluded only the Babylon oracles—as it still does in the LXX (Lundbom 1986b: 103). A scroll (or scrolls) of 51 chapters was completed in the early exile—in two main editions in Egypt and Babylon. The former concluded with a colophon by Baruch (LXX) and the latter with a colophon by Seraiah (MT).

Anonymity and a late date assigned to the Jeremiah Foreign Nation Oracles belong to late eighteenth- and nineteenth-century German literary criticism, where, already in Eichhorn (1790) and deWette (1807), sections were denied to the prophet (Lundbom 1975:3–4 [= 1997: 6–7]). Budde (1878; 1906: 20–21) judged the Babylon oracles to be nongenuine, with Schwally (1888) a decade later denying Jeremianic authorship for the entire Foreign Nation corpus. Schwally's radical assessment is reflected in Duhm and Volz, surviving also little changed in the more recent commentaries of Carroll and McKane, despite the fact that many early scholars (Hitzig, Graf, Giesebrecht, Cornill, Peake) and an even greater number since have claimed at least some of these oracles for Jeremiah. Mowinckel (1914: 65–66), for example, thought Jeremiah was concerned about foreign nations when their future was tied up with Judah's, e.g., in the oracles of chaps. 25, 27, and 43. He also conceded the Egypt oracles (chap. 46) and perhaps those against Philistia (chap. 47) to Jeremiah. The assessment of Giesebrecht regarding the latter was similar. Scholars since have claimed for Jeremiah a portion of the oracles in chaps. 46–49, and perhaps by the same margin have denied Jeremianic authorship for most of chaps. 50–51; see Condamin; Rudolph; Weiser; Hyatt (1956: 277–84); Eissfeldt (1961; 1965: 362–64); Bright (pp. 307–8, 359–60); Boadt; and Jones. Childs (1959: 194–95) points out that chaps. 46–49 are characterized by explicit plays on vocabulary and motifs in chaps. 4–6. Eissfeldt in his authentic Jeremiah core included the Babylon oracle of 50:17–20, and Holladay (II: 401) has brought things almost full circle by attributing no less than 82 verses or portions of verses in the Babylon oracles to the prophet. And this is to say nothing of Cassuto's (1973c) sharp critique of Schwally, whose wholesale deletions of the Foreign Nation material in chap. 25 were necessary to bring that text into line with his point of view regarding chaps. 46–51.

A change in perspective came with form criticism. We now realize that early Israelite prophecy and prophecy known from elsewhere in the ANE included oracles against enemy nations, which means that the Foreign Nation Oracles, beginning with Amos and continuing through to Jeremiah and Ezekiel, must be placed in a larger context. According to J. H. Hayes (1968: 81–82), Foreign Nation Oracles originated in contexts of war. Within Israel, war oracles against other nations are heard from Samuel (1 Sam 15:2–3), men of God prophesying to Ahab (1 Kgs 20:13–14, 28), and Elisha (2 Kgs 3:16–19 et passim). Later come foreign nation oracles from Amos, Isaiah, Jeremiah, Ezekiel, and other prophets of greater reputation. According to Hayes, every prophetic book in the OT, except

Hosea, contains oracles against non-Israelite nations. Among neighboring peoples, prophetic-type individuals were giving oracles in the second millennium B.C. for and against other nations, e.g., Balaam son of Beor (Numbers 23–24), prophets known from the Mari Letters (*ANET*[3] 629–30; Malamat 1966: 214–19, citing ARM XIII 23), and prophets of the Egyptian execration texts (Bentzen 1950). Esarhaddon of Assyria was encouraged by prophetic oracle to do battle with enemies (*ANET*[3] 605), the scene perhaps being similar to the prophetic frenzy occurring before Ahab and Jehoshaphat in 1 Kings 22.

Although it is often stated that Jeremiah's Foreign Nation poetry is of exceptional quality, it is also claimed that the same is stereotypical (Budde 1878: 458–59), lacking in great ideas that stir the mind and grip one's inner being. My own view is that the poetry is vivid, rich in imagery, and replete with irony, and probably no more stereotypical than other poetry in the book. Oracles here make effective use of repetition, and in them are many of the same rhetorical structures that one finds in the Judah oracles. They also teem with the vocabulary and phraseology of the Judah oracles, and if these do not emanate from Jeremiah, they must come from an imitator—which is what some scholars have had to conclude. So far as great ideas are concerned, the Foreign Nation Oracles lack the specificity of the Judah oracles, e.g., there are neither arguments detailing wrongdoing nor calls for repentance; the prophet has no personal involvement in the sin, guilt, and suffering of these nations, so of confessions personal and corporate one hears nothing. How could it be otherwise? There are also no arguments with false prophets, escapes from personal enemies, or run-ins with officials of Temple and state, details of which fill or lurk in the shadows of the oracles and confessions in chaps. 1–20. The prophet does not know other nations in the way he knows his own. Nor are any of these nations under judgment for covenant violation, as they have no covenant with Yahweh and can only be cited for unspecified wickedness (25:31), hubris (50:31–32), and the worship of idols (50:38; 51:47, 52).

From within the book of Jeremiah is evidence aplenty that Jeremiah has been assigned by Yahweh an expanded mission of prophet to the nations. The point is made twice in the prophet's call (1:5, 10), where "nations" (*goyîm*) means all nations including the prophet's own. Compare also 9:24–25[Eng 9:25–26]; 10:25; 16:19–20; 18:7–10; 25:1–38; 28:8; 36:2; and 51:20. It must be said, however, that Jeremiah's judgment upon the nations does not automatically translate into salvation for Judah, much less reflect the narrow nationalism that is the hallmark of false prophecy. In the long term, these oracles spell salvation for a covenant people that has been duly chastened (cf. Deut 32:34–42), but in the short term they pronounce judgment on everyone, as the sweep of nations in Amos 1:2–2:16 does. If Yahweh judges nations with whom he has no covenant, *a fortiori* he will judge a people with whom he does have a covenant and who willfully disobeys it. But as 25:15–29 makes clear, judgment comes first to Jerusalem and the cities of Judah; then to the nations round about. The main point then in the present oracles is that Yahweh, at the end of the day, is Lord and Judge of all nations.

NOTES

46:1. *What came as the word of Yahweh to Jeremiah the prophet concerning the* *nations.* A superscription similar to those in 1:2; 14:1; 47:1; and 49:34, introducing all of chaps. 46–51.

concerning the nations. Many MSS and the G^{OL} add *kol,* i.e., "concerning all the nations," which is the reading in 25:13. The loss in MT could be explained by haplography (homoeoteleuton: *l . . . l*). The term "nations" basically means "foreign nations" (= Gentiles), although one will note that 46:27–28 (= 30:10–11) is a word of salvation to Israel.

MESSAGE AND AUDIENCE

The audience here, which is Judah and not the foreign nations, is being told first of all that Yahweh's call designating Jeremiah "prophet to the nations" has been fulfilled. The audience is also being readied for a collection of prophecies that, with only a few exceptions, have to do with the fortunes of other nations. This audience doubtless knows Judah's humiliations at the hands of other nations in 609, 597, 586, and perhaps 582, and may now derive comfort from the fact that these agents of Yahweh's inglorious work have already, or will in the future, get theirs. When all the nations have been chastened, the question will be one of remnants, and which of them will have a future.

B. WHAT ABOUT EGYPT? (46:2–28)

1. Pride Cometh before the Fall (46:2–12)

a) Hasty Advance, Hasty Retreat (46:2–6)

46 ²For Egypt: Concerning the army of Pharaoh Neco, king of Egypt, which was by the River Euphrates at Carchemish, and which Nebuchadrezzar, king of Babylon, struck down in the fourth year of Jehoiakim son of Josiah, king of Judah.

³Ready buckler and shield!
   and advance to battle!
⁴Harness the horses!
   and rise up, O horsemen!
Stand ready with helmets!
   Polish lances!
      Put on scale armor!

⁵"So why have I seen . . . ?'
   They are terrified!

drawing back!
Their warriors are beaten
  and a flight they are fleeing
They do not turn back
  terror on every side!
  —oracle of Yahweh.

⁶The swift cannot flee
  the warrior cannot escape
Up north on the bank of River Euphrates
  they have stumbled, and they have fallen!

RHETORIC AND COMPOSITION

MT 46:2–6 = LXX 26:2–6. The Egypt oracles divide in two on the basis of the superscriptions in vv 2 and 13. The collection has a stereotyped closing in v 26b. Supporting the two groupings, vv 2–12 and vv 13–26, is a *petuḥah* in M^L at the end of v 12 and a *setumah* at the end of v 26. The M^P has a *setumah* at the end of v 12 and a *petuḥah* at the end of v 26. The M^A in both places has a *petuḥah*. The superscription in v 2 presents the entire collection of Egypt oracles ("For Egypt"), giving also a historical context for the oracle(s) in vv 3–12 following.

Scholars generally take vv 3–12 as a single oracle, there being only one messenger formula in v 5 and no concluding section marking before v 12. But there is also general agreement about a division into stanzas, the first of which is vv 3–6. How the remaining verses divide up is answered differently. Some scholars, e.g., Weiser, Rudolph, J. G. Snaith (1971: 23), and Jones, propose three stanzas: 3–6, 7–10, and 11–12, which have the repeated verbs "stumble" and "fall" ending Stanzas I (v 6bβ) and III (v 12b), and another obvious repetition, "north . . . River Euphrates," ending Stanzas I (v 6bα) and II (v 10c). The one problem with this otherwise convincing breakdown is that the phrase "Rise up, O horses" in v 9, which is parallel formally (a summons to battle) and rhetorically (a repeated "rise up") to recognized beginnings in vv 3–4 and v 11, is unaccounted for. But this can be remedied by isolating vv 7–8 as a unit, and making v 9 a new beginning. Christensen (1975: 215–17) and Watson (1984: 381) in separate analyses do precisely this, although each views the larger whole differently. Verses 7–8, in any case, should be taken as a self-standing question and answer on the hubris of Egypt, and the whole of vv 3–12 made divisible into four units. My own preference is to take each unit as a separate poem rather than as a stanza within a larger poem, the reason being that each can stand alone, and nothing requires a reading of the whole. In fact, it is difficult to read all the units in sequence. McKane (p. 1121) discusses the "stop-start-stop" effect in the verses, and whether a composition taking in all the verses has coherence. I believe that four poems have been combined and were perhaps intended to be recited as a group, which means the distinction is not great. Other poems in Jeremiah show evidence of grouping on the basis of recurring formal and rhetorical features, e.g., 6:1–7 and 8–12; 11:18–20; and 12:1–3.

Key words in the four poems are the following:

I	*buckler*	*māgēn*	v 3
	horses . . . and rise up . . .	*hassûsîm . . . waʿălû*	v 4
	Their warriors	*gibbôrêhem*	v 5
	the warrior	*haggibbôr*	v 6
	Up north . . . River Euphrates	*ṣāpônâ . . . nĕhar-pĕrāt*	
	they have stumbled, and they have fallen	*kāšĕlû wĕnāpālû*	

II	*. . . . . .rises*	*yaʿăleh*	v 7
	. . . . .rises	*yaʿăleh*	v 8
	. . . I will rise . . . the earth	*ʾaʿăleh . . . ʾereṣ*	

III	*Rise up, O horses*	*ʿălû hassûsîm*	v 9
	. . . . .warriors	*haggibbôrîm*	
	. . . . .buckler	*māgēn*	
	the north . . . River Euphrates	*ṣāpôn . . . nĕhar-pĕrāt*	v 10

IV	*Rise up . . . .*	*ʿălî*	v 11
	. . . . .the earth	*hāʾāreṣ*	v 12
	. . . warrior on warrior they stumbled	*gibbôr bĕgibbôr kāšālû*	
	. . . fell . . .	*nāpĕlû*	

The poems having greatest continuity are I and III (similar beginnings and endings), I and IV (similar endings), and III and IV (same beginnings). The continuity—or contrast—in II and IV consists of Egypt's boast in v 8 that her expansion will cover "the earth," and "the earth" in v 12 hearing Egypt's cry of defeat (Holladay). There is another *bĕʾereṣ* in v 10, usually translated "in the land / country," but this does not appear to be a significant key word. All four poems contain the verb *ʿlh*, "rise (up)," it being the prominent verb in II. Key words function here as elsewhere to link poems together (i.e., catchwords).

The Egypt oracles have been highly acclaimed poetry. Blayney says they have "a very animated style" and "great poetic energy and liveliness of colouring." Bright, too, says their vividness and poetic quality is "unexcelled by anything in the book." These oracles are widely—though not universally—attributed to Jeremiah, with even Giesebrecht conceding a possible genuine nucleus in 46:2–12. Poetic and rhetorical features familiar from the Judah oracles, e.g., chiasmus, double meanings, assonance, repeated roots, heightened vocabulary, change of speaker, and irony, mark the verses as Jeremianic (Holladay 1962a: 44–47; van der Westhuizen 1991–92: 85).

The present verses contain a prose superscription (v 2), followed by an oracle in poetry (vv 3–6). The superscription picks up "River Euphrates" from vv 6 and 10. Mention of "Nebuchadrezzar, king of Babylon" recurs in the superscription of v 13 and again in v 26 at the end of the collection. The oracle contains a summons to battle in vv 3–4 (Bach 1962: 51; Christensen 1975: 217), after which in vv 5–6 is depicted the rout of the Egyptian army. There is no account of the battle itself (J. G. Snaith 1971: 22). The summons to battle—using plural imperatives—could be to both armies, but better sense and better poetry are the result if the addressee is only the Egyptians. This makes for irony in the words commanding readiness, and accounts for the surprised "So why have I seen . . . ?" beginning v 5. Holladay's proposal that the summons goes out to the Babylonian army eliminates both the irony and the surprise.

This surprised "So why have I seen . . . ?" which is an interjection presumably by the prophet, has given rise to suggestions that the poem or this portion of it might be a vision. Fohrer (1972: 148) calls v 5 a "vision report," and de Jong (1981: 369) speaks too of a vision in v 5a. Lindblom (1965: 143) called the same a "literary vision" with both visual and auditory elements, citing as other examples 4:13; 6:22–26; and 31:15. Volz, noting the combination of oracle and vision, said the speaker was nevertheless a poet, not a visionary. A messenger formula at the end of the verse would seem to indicate a bona fide prophetic oracle (Rudolph), which it doubtless is. Everson (1974: 333–34) and Holladay call the same a mocking song taunting Egypt, which would not conflict with it also being a prophetic oracle.

The oracle divides into three stanzas: vv 3–4, v 5, and v 6, which recognizes the discourse shift at the beginning of v 5 and the messenger formula concluding the verse. Stanza I consists of two bicolons and a tricolon. Stanza II reverses, with a tricolon and two bicolons. Watson (1984: 380) takes "So why have I seen . . . ?" as a monocolon, which is possible but not necessary. Stanza III consists of two bicolons. Yahweh is presumably speaker of the oracle, except for Jeremiah's intrusive "So why have I seen . . . ?" beginning v 5.

Stanza I contains a string of seven imperatives creating asyndeton, on which see Note for 4:5. Stanza II has this nice chiasmus:

II	*Their warriors . . . they are fleeing . . .*	*gibbôrêhem . . . nāsû*	v 5b
	he cannot flee . . . the warrior . . .	*yānûs . . . haggibbôr*	v 6a

In the MT are catchwords linking chap. 45 to the beginning of the Foreign Nation Collection:

46:2 *in the fourth year of Jehoiakim*   45:1 *in the fourth year of Jehoiakim*

NOTES

46:2. *For Egypt.* Hebrew *lěmiṣrayim.* A short introduction similar to those in the king and prophet collections (21:11; 23:9), also the oracle collections against Moab (48:1), Ammon (49:1), Edom (49:7), Damascus (49:23), and Kedar-Hazor (49:28), the last-mentioned being expanded as here. Jeremiah prophesied judgment against Egypt and Jews living in Egypt in 9:25[Eng 9:26];

25:19; 43:8–13; and 44:26–30. Other prophecies against Egypt appear in Isaiah 19–20 and Ezekiel 29–32.

Concerning the army of Pharaoh Neco, king of Egypt, which was by the River Euphrates at Carchemish, and which Nebuchadrezzar, king of Babylon, struck down in the fourth year of Jehoiakim son of Josiah, king of Judah. The Battle of Carchemish, fought between Babylon and Egypt in 605 B.C. (= the fourth year of Jehoiakim), was a decisive Babylonian victory over the army of Pharaoh Neco II; cf. 2 Kgs 24:7. The battle is reported in the Babylonian Chronicle (BM 21946: obv. 1–7; Wiseman 1956: 23–27, 66–69; 1985: 12–17; cf. D. N. Freedman 1956: 52–53; Malamat 1956: 249), also in Josephus (*Ant* x 84–86; *Against Apion* i 128–44). After Nineveh's fall to the Babylonians and the Medes in 612 B.C., and the Assyrian's subsequent defeat at Haran in 610, Pharaoh Neco (610–594 B.C.) ventured northward in 609 to aid the Assyrians in one last attempt to retake Haran. On the way, he killed Josiah, who tried to stop him. The larger mission having failed, Neco proceeded to take control of Carchemish, held it briefly, only to lose it now to the Babylonians. The Chronicle tells us that the Egyptians sustained another crushing defeat farther south at Hamath, which Malamat says must be Riblah "in the land of Hamath," where Nebuchadnezzar then set up headquarters (39:5; 52:9, 27). As a result of these victories, Nebuchadnezzar gained undisputed control over the western portion of the Assyrian Empire, which included Syria and Palestine. A year later in 604, Nebuchadnezzar was down in the Philistine plain, where he destroyed Ashkelon and Ekron. By 601–600 B.C. Neco was fighting Nebuchadnezzar on the border of his own country.

the River Euphrates. Hebrew *nĕhar-pĕrāt.* LXX: *potamō euphratē.* The Euphrates is sometimes named in the OT (Gen 2:14; 15:18) and sometimes called simply "(the) River," *nāhār* (Jer 2:18; Num 22:5; Josh 24:3, 14). See also Deut 11:24. This river, which is the largest in western Asia, originates in the Armenian highlands, passes Carchemish, and then begins a southeasterly flow, emptying finally, together with the Tigris, into the Persian Gulf. Along this river, forming part of the Fertile Crescent from Babylon to Egypt, traders caravanned and ancient armies marched. See T. Jacobsen, "Euphrates," in *IDB* E–J: 180–81.

Carchemish. This ancient Hittite city, most recently a provincial capital in the Assyrian Empire, survives as a huge, 230-acre mound on the west bank of the Upper Euphrates, northeast of Aleppo, on the Syrian–Turkish border. The present-day Syrian village of Jerablus lies to the southwest; to the northwest is a more recent Turkish village named Kargamis (*OEANE* 1: 423). Carchemish was excavated by the British Museum in three campaigns: 1878–81, 1914, and 1920 (see Hogarth 1914; Woolley 1921; Woolley and Barnett 1978). One of the more spectacular sites to be uncovered there was "House D" in the outer town, where evidence turned up of an Egyptian presence in the city prior to its destruction by Nebuchadnezzar (Woolley 1921: 125–28 + pls. 19, 22, and 23). Found among the burned ruins, particularly in the doorways but also in two of the rooms, were hundreds of bronze and iron arrow heads, many javelin heads, a sword, a bronze shield, and human bones. Some objects were Hittite, but many were of Egyptian origin or showed Egyptian influence, e.g., bowls and flasks with Egyptian inscriptions, bronze statuettes of Egyptian deities, and most importantly, seals and seal impressions of Psammetichus I and Neco II.

Nebuchadrezzar, king of Babylon. On the spelling, Nebuchadrezzar, see Note on 21:2. At the time of the Battle of Carchemish, Nebuchadrezzar was not yet king, simply crown prince. A few months later he succeeded his father, Nabopolassar, as king of Babylon.

the fourth year of Jehoiakim son of Josiah. I.e., 605 B.C. The LXX omits "son of Josiah," which may be an MT plus (Janzen 1973: 69–75, 144), although LXX has it in 51:31 [= MT 45:1]. This date should not be relocated to v 1 (*pace* Rudolph), nor should it be taken as applying to all the oracles up to 49:33 simply because the Elam oracle in 49:34 is given a date in the reign of Zedekiah. Intervening superscriptions in 46:13 and 47:1, both with historical references, speak against this. The "fourth year of Jehoiakim" is nevertheless an important year, and is associated with Jeremiah's oracles against the foreign nations in chap. 25 (see v 1). Nebuchadnezzar came to power in this year (cf. 25:1), and in Jerusalem it was the year when Jeremiah dictated a first scroll of oracles to Baruch (chap. 36), giving then also to Baruch a personal word that became Baruch's colophon to the scroll (chap. 45). A slight discrepancy in chronology, however, exists in connection with this date. According to the Babylonian Chronicle, the Battle of Carchemish took place in 605 B.C. This would translate into the third year of Jehoiakim if we assume a Tishri [autumn] reckoning of the new year, the battle occurring as it did before the death of Nabopolassar on Ab 8 (Malamat 1956: 250). Bright (1981: 326 n. 45) also notes a one-year discrepancy in the regnal years of both Jehoiakim and Nebuchadnezzar in 2 Kgs 24:12; 25:8; and Jer 52:28–29. But Clines (1972: 28) says that the "fourth year of Jehoiakim" can be reconciled with the Chronicle by assuming a Nisan (spring) new year, which leads him to conclude that a Nisan reckoning of regnal years was probably used in the closing decades of the Kingdom of Judah. Tadmor (1956: 229) reckons the fourth year of Jehoiakim as Nebuchadnezzar's accession year, and the fifth year of Jehoiakim as Nebuchadnezzar's first year of rule.

3. *Ready buckler and shield!* Hebrew *'irkû* ("Ready!") means lit. "position (for battle)." Here begins a series of seven imperatives issued by Yahweh to Egyptian charioteers, calvary, and foot-soldiers facing Nebuchadnezzar and the military might of Babylon. The repeated *û* endings are euphonic. See the description of the Babylonian army coming against Judah in 6:23, later turned around for use against Babylon (50:42; cf. 50:14). Kimhi says the commands here can go to either army. If they go to the Egyptians, the words are sarcastic (*Mezudath David*). Its army, after all, is soon to be routed. Also, the prophet's surprise comment in v 5a makes sense only if the Egyptians are being addressed, which is the usual interpretation (*pace* Christensen and Holladay). Commentators take the speaking voices in vv 3–4 to be the excited soldiers urging one another on (Volz), as in 6:4–6, or else officers barking out commands to

their troops (Bright, Carroll). But the speaker is first and foremost Yahweh, who could be imitating the soldiers or their commanders. Whether this "summons to battle" is a formal feature of the oracle, as proposed by Bach (1962: 51–66) and Christensen (1975: 217), is unclear, yet one does note similar calls in 46:9; 50:14, 21, 29–30; and 51:3, 11a, and others of a general nature elsewhere.

buckler and shield. Hebrew *māgēn wĕṣinnâ.* The *māgēn* ("buckler") is a small round shield (T: "round") held in one hand, largely to protect the face. Foot-soldiers carried them, and so did the cavalry and chariot soldiers. A ninth-century stone relief from Tell Halaf (= ancient Guzana, east of Haran in northern Syria, near the Turkish border) depicts a cavalry man astride a prancing horse with a round shield; for a picture, see *ANEP²* 50 #164; cf. 268. The third man in a three-man chariot held two bucklers, one to protect the driver and the other to protect the archer (Erman 1894: 547). Egyptian bucklers could also be rounded at the top and rectangular at the bottom. A model of forty Egyptian soldiers in formation, each holding a shoulder-to-knee length cone-shaped buckler in the left hand, is pictured in *ANEP²* 55 #180; cf. 270. For discussion on bucklers and shields used by soldiers in ancient Egypt, with drawings of foot soldiers and charioteers, see Erman 1894: 524–47. Assyrian bucklers—*ergo* those used by the Babylonians—were typically round. Assyrian troops with round shields attacking Lachish appear on the Lachish relief; for pictures, see Ussishkin 1982: 81, 106. The army of Uzziah was equipped with bucklers (2 Chr 26:14). Hebrew *ṣinnâ* is the large rectangular shield that protects the entire body, commonly used in siege warfare to protect the archers, but other soldiers as well. We can deduce its larger size from the descriptions given in 1 Kgs 10:16–17 and 2 Chr 9:15–16 (the RSV translates *ṣinnâ* as "large shield[s]"). A shield-bearer would stand at the side of a foot soldier and protect him with this large shield. For discussion and a description of shield types, also pictures of Assyrian soldiers with bucklers and shields, see J. W. Wevers, "Weapons and Implements of War" in *IDB* R–Z: 824; Yadin 1963: 13–15, 299, 418–19; and Gonen 1975: 60–67.

Shields in Egypt and elsewhere were typically constructed of a wood wicker (= plaited twigs or reeds) or metal frame, and covered with leather. The wooden shield of Tutankhamun was covered with antelope skin. The leather was then rubbed with oil (2 Sam 1:21; Isa 21:5), probably to keep the leather from cracking, although Rashi says it was so that spears would glide off them. Yadin (1963: 202–3) has pictures of the manufacture of shields in Egypt. A workman in one is seen stretching a piece of leather over a wooden block. In another, from a Theban tomb, workmen are making shields, chariot wheels, and coverings for quivers. Metal shields were rare because of their excessive weight; also they were not as strong as shields made from wood. However, a circular bronze shield (possibly of Greek origin) did turn up at Carchemish, presumably from the battle described here (Woolley 1921: 128 + pl. 24). On shields from Neco's army found at Carchemish, see also Wiseman 1985: 15–16.

4. *Harness the horses!* Hebrew *'isrû* means "tie, bind," here "harness," the horses to chariots; cf. Exod 14:6. Isaiah says that Egypt's vaunted horse-and-

chariot force is as nothing when Yahweh fights against it (Isa 31:1–3). In the Theban tomb picture of workmen making war implements is a completed chariot frame with parts of the harness hanging from its shafts (see Yadin 1963: 202). For pictures of horses harnessed to Assyrian chariots, see Yadin 1963: 452, 454–55.

and rise up, O horsemen! The verb ʿǎlû here doubtless means "rise up (onto the horses)," i.e., mount them. In v 9 the same verb calls for the horses to "rise up," i.e., rear up.

Stand ready with helmets! Bright: "Fall in—with helmets," which is carried over into the NAB and NJV. The verb yṣb in the Hithpael means "to station oneself." S. R. Driver translates: "stand forth with (your) helmets." This same verb followed by maddûaʿ ("so why?") occurs also in vv 14b–15a. Helmets in the ANE were round or cone-shaped, usually made of metal (Yadin 1963: 15; Gonen 1975: 69–71) but sometimes of leather. The mighty Goliath wore a helmet of bronze (1 Sam 17:5). Reliefs in the British Museum of Assyrian troops attacking Lachish (701 B.C.) show them wearing cone-shaped helmets; for pictures, see Ussishkin 1982: 79, 95. The crest of an Assyrian helmet from this battle turned up in the Lachish excavations; for a picture, see *ANEP*[2] 54 #175. For a picture of a lancer wearing a spiked, cone-shaped helmet from Arslan Tash, see *ANEP*[2] 53 #174. Inside a gold helmet taken from a tomb at Ur were found fragments of cloth and wool stuffing, indicating that it probably was fitted with a quilted cap to make the wearer more comfortable (see *ANEP*[2] 49 #160; cf. 268). Soldiers in Uzziah's army were equipped with helmets (2 Chr 26:14).

Polish lances! Hebrew mirqû hārĕmāḥîm. Some commentators (Duhm, Cornill, Peake, Rudolph) are worried about the sequence here, saying that a directive to polish lances is too late if the battle is about to commence. The LXX has *probalete ta dorata* ("throw the lances"), leading some (Cornill; Ehrlich 1912: 352–53; Rudolph; Holladay) to propose emendations. They are unnecessary. McKane allows for poetic license, saying that this can be a last-minute burnishing of the spears. Compare the polishing of arrows in 51:11. But here, as elsewhere in poetry, actions need not follow in logical progression and are to be taken as a whole (see Note on 1:15). Calvin sees these directives as a setup. Jeremiah enumerates the complete armor so that victory, according to human reckoning, is already theirs. But all the Egyptian weaponry counts for nothing, since force and arms are of no importance to God (cf. Isa 31:1–3).

lances. Hebrew rĕmāḥîm. These are spears with a long shaft and a pointed head, mentioned in Judg 5:8 (with "buckler"); 1 Kgs 18:28; and elsewhere. Joel 4:10[Eng 3:10] says, "Beat your pruning hooks into lances." Lances exceeding body height are held in the right hand by the 40 Egyptian soldiers pictured in *ANEP*[2] 55 #180.

Put on scale armor! The verb is lbš, "to put on (a garment), wear." KB[3] lists siryôn as "scale armor," cognate with Akk sari(j)am, "coat of mail." Some MSS have the spelling širyôn, as in 1 Sam 17:5, 38, where the armor of Goliath is described. Goliath apparently wore a full coat of armor, for its weight was said to be "five thousand shekels of bronze," not including the bronze protecting his legs. A fragment of a coat of mail from Nuzi (mid–second millennium B.C.) survives with substantial bronze plates that were laced together with thongs; for a picture, see ANEP² 49 #161; cf. 268. Metal scales gradually replaced the heavier plates, and coats of mail were reduced to waist-length so as to be less burdensome. A neck-to-waist coat of mail, made of metal scales strung together, is displayed in the fine Scythian collection of the Hermitage in St. Petersburg. However, some archers in the armies of Ashurnasirpal II and Shalmaneser III wore armored coats reaching down to their ankles. Coats of mail typically were made of thick cloth or leather, to which hundreds of small metal scales, joined together, were attached. A Theban tomb painting depicts a bronze coat of mail consisting of some 450 scales, having also a leather collar for protecting the neck. At the end of the Assyrian period, we see the earliest-known cavalry wearing scale armor — in depictions of Assurbanipal in the seventh century. For further discussion of body armor and coats of mail used in Egypt and Assyria, also pictures and drawings of soldiers in scale armor, see Erman (1894: 545); Yadin (1963: 14–15, 196–97, 354, 418–19); and Gonen (1975: 77–80). The Babylonians also fought in scale armor (51:3).

5. 'So why have I seen . . . ?' Hebrew maddûaʿ ("So why?") is a particle expressing wonder (Calvin), followed here by the verb "I have seen." The two words appear together (with an object) in 30:6. The lack of an object here has given rise to modifications of the MT, the three most common being: 1) a substitution of "what" for "why" (Volz; Rudolph; Weiser; Bright; Thompson; Carroll; JB; NAB; NIV; NSB); 2) the addition of an object—"it" or "them" (Peake; Streane; Jones; Keown et al.; RSV; NJB); or 3) an omission of "I have seen" with the LXX, making possible a connection with the following verb, where the reading then becomes "Why are they terrified?" or the like (Giesebrecht; Duhm; Cornill; Holladay; McKane). T has "why have I seen them broken?" and is followed by NEB, NJV, and NRSV. The NEB and REB are more paraphrastic yet. The verb "I have seen" should not be omitted with LXX (so even Janzen 1973: 108–9), if for no other reason because of an occurrence of the same two-word combination in 30:6. My suggestion is to take the statement as unfinished, which in classical rhetoric was called aposiopesis (ad Herennium iv 30). A good example of this figure is in Exod 32:32 (Crown 1963). Here Yahweh has been the speaker in vv 3–4, and now Jeremiah brings in his own voice, anticipating what both of them see as being a complete rout of the Egyptian army. But Yahweh does not let him finish, going on himself to tell of the rout. Another interruption by Yahweh in a "so why?" construction occurs in 8:19. See also Jeremiah's unfinished "so they may find out . . ." in 10:18. Elsewhere multiple imperatives are followed by maddûaʿ in vv 14–15 (Kegler 1980: 274), and somewhat differently in 30:6.

They are terrified! The plural adjective ḥattîm (cf. 1 Sam 2:4) can also mean "shattered, dismayed." Jeremiah uses the cognate verb, ḥtt, in 1:17 and elsewhere. The subject of the verb has no antecedent, which is not uncommon in Hebrew discourse, but reference has to be to the Egyptians (Rashi; Kimḥi).

drawing back! Hebrew nĕsōgîm ʾāḥôr. See the same expression in 38:22.

Their warriors are beaten. The verb *yukkattû* (H-stem passive) is strong, meaning "beaten to pieces" (Mic 1:7; Isa 24:12). First fright, then retreat, now crushing defeat.

and a flight they are fleeing. Hebrew *mānôs nāsû.* For this "cognate accusative" construction, where an object is added to a verb of the same stem, see Note on 22:16. Jeremiah's double occurrence of a verbal root in succession is a signature construction; see Note on 11:18. The noun *mānôs* can also mean "refuge" (16:19), which here would require the elliptical translation: "and (for) refuge they are fleeing." But the omission of prepositions is frequent in poetry, reflecting an earlier stage of the language when case endings were still used. The battle, in any case, has turned into a complete rout, as the Egyptians are now running for their lives.

They do not turn back. I.e., to look behind (RSV; NEB; JB; NIV; NSB). Hebrew *lōʾ hipnû.* Kimḥi says they do not turn their faces toward their pursuers, but flee with all haste. Cheyne adds that they look not back with the object of rallying scattered forces. The Babylonian Chronicle says that a remnant of the Egyptian army escaped to Hamath, but (so quickly) without weapons that they were totally defeated (BM 21946: obv. 5–6; Wiseman 1956: 66–69). Jeremiah seems to be making a playful contrast in the verse on "turning (back)," as he did often in the early chapters with the verb *šûb.* Here, using different verbs, he is saying: The Egyptians have turned back (*sûg*) in battle, but now being in flight do not turn back (*pnh*). The verb *pnh* in the H-stem occurs often in Jeremiah's Foreign Nation Oracles (see also 46:21; 47:3; 48:39; 49:24; and 50:16). Years ago Ruben (1899: 461) made the suggestion that here and in vv 9 and 12 we have echoes of Nahum:

Jer 46:5:	*and they do not turn back*	*wĕlōʾ hipnû*
Nah 2:9[Eng 2:8]:	*but none turns back*	*wĕʾên mapneh*
Jer 46:9:	*and go like mad, O chariots!*	*wĕhithōlĕlû hārekeb*
Nah 2:5[Eng 2:4]:	*the chariots go like mad*	*yithôlĕlû hārekeb*
Jer 46:12:	*nations . . . your disgrace*	*gôyim qĕlônēk*
Nah 3:5:	*nations . . . your disgrace*	*gôyim . . . qĕlônēk*

terror on every side! Hebrew *māgôr missābîb.* A signature term of Jeremiah's (see 49:29 and Note on 6:25), here summing up the mounting chaos in the Egyptian camp. A connection is also made to the next verse, which states that the most able soldiers cannot escape. Why? Terror surrounds them on every side. The Babylonian Chronicle says that the defeat of the remnant at Hamath was so complete that not one of the Egyptians escaped to his own country (BM 21946: obv. 7; Wiseman 1956: 68–69). Holladay's judgment that *missābîb* ("on every side") is a gloss is without basis.

6. *The swift cannot flee, the warrior cannot escape.* The negative *ʾal* with the imperfect describes something that cannot happen (GKC §107p). The swift (*haqqal*) cannot run at all (because of fear or injury), or more likely, he cannot

run away fast enough (Kimḥi; Cheyne). In either case, he cannot escape, which is what the parallel colon states. The swiftness of the Babylonian horses, noted in 4:13 and Hab 1:8–9, may have something to do with it. Hebrew *hag-gibbôr* ("the warrior") can also be translated "the strong" (Bright), which would then complement "the swift." In Amos 2:14–16, said by Duhm to be influential here, there is a pronounced emphasis on the swift and the strong. Andersen and Freedman (1989: 340) find there three types of individuals: the swift, the strong, and the warrior (v 14).

Up north on the bank of River Euphrates. For *yad* meaning "bank" or "border," see Exod 2:5; Num 13:29; and Deut 2:37 (Joüon 1933). Hebrew *'al-yad* normally means "by the side of." The LXX lacks "river" (causing many to delete), yet it includes the term in vv 2 and 10. On the term *nāhār* ("river"), see v 2. "The north" here as elsewhere carries overtones of judgment; see Note on 1:14.

they have stumbled, and they have fallen! Hebrew *kāšĕlû wĕnāpālû*. The verbs are a standard pair in the OT, appearing together again in vv 12 and 16, and elsewhere in 6:15; 50:32; Ps 27:2; Isa 8:15; 31:3 (an Egypt oracle); and Dan 11:19. Both verbs are common in Jeremiah, *kšl* ("stumble") occurring 11 times (6:15, 21; 8:12; 18:15, 23; 20:11; 31:9; 46:6, 12, 16; 50:32), and *npl* (of people "falling") no less than 32 times. "Falling," it should be noted, does not always mean "to fall by the sword," i.e., to be killed, but can mean "to surrender / desert to the enemy," as in 21:9; 37:13, 14; 38:19; and 39:9. Thus people who "fall"—some of them, at least—end up being captives (38:19; 39:9).

MESSAGE AND AUDIENCE

Yahweh begins this oracle by issuing rapid-fire battle orders, much as if he were commander-in-chief of the army. We know not what army this is, but soldiers hold bucklers and shields, they ride on horses and in chariots, and they wear helmets, carry lances, and are fitted in scale armor. Might this be the Egyptian army? Or the Babylonian? Whoever they are, the call goes out to prepare for battle. The next voice to be heard is the prophet's own. He interjects, "So why have I seen . . . ?" but is cut off in mid-sentence, with Yahweh now reporting what both have observed. It was no battle at all, or if it was one, it quickly turned into a rout. Soldiers suffered panic attacks, drew back, and were as well as beaten. When put to flight they did not look back. Their situation was hopeless. Terror was on every side! The swift could not run away; the mighty could not escape. The oracle closes with mention of the northern Euphrates, which must be where this mighty army has stumbled and fallen.

The audience now knows the battle site, and doubtless has independent knowledge of who was defeated. The oracle is about the Egyptians. But why did Yahweh encourage them? They performed so poorly. The same wonderment was expressed by Jeremiah. Yahweh it seems was being ironic, his directives being no more than a foil to prepare a pro-Egyptian audience in Jerusalem for an Egyptian victory. The audience may remember the ironic tone of Yahweh's initial word through Micaiah (1 Kgs 22:15), which feigned victory but was followed by a sober word predicting the exact opposite. The king of Israel was not fooled, however, and perhaps this pro-Egyptian audience was not fooled either. In any case, its expectations were dashed. The defeat was decisive and total. Some in the Jerusalem audience may actually have been happy with the outcome, seeing the Egyptian defeat as Neco's rightly deserved punishment for having killed Josiah four years earlier (J. G. Snaith 1971: 28). The primary audience is made up of Judahites living in Jerusalem (Calvin), although Egypt as a secondary audience need not be ruled out. For those hearing this oracle, there are echoes, surely, of earlier oracles spoken by Amos (2:14–16), Isaiah (31:1–3), and Nahum (2:4–9[Eng 2:3–8]; 3:5). Later audiences, however, require a superscription telling what battle and where, between whom, and when.

This oracle when heard in tandem with the poem following (vv 7–8) sets up the question of v 7: "Who is this that rises like the Nile, like the great river, its waters swell?" It is now recognized that Yahweh, by encouraging the Egyptians to seize the battle before them, only adds to the hubris already theirs, an elevated self-appraisal that has to be brought down and is brought down in vv 5–6, and in the poems remaining. The superscription is doubtless correct in placing this oracle at the time of the Battle of Carchemish, in 605 B.C. Whether it was spoken before or after the battle cannot be determined.

b) Egypt Rises like the Nile! (46:7–8)

46 ⁷Who is this that rises like the Nile
   like the great river, its waters swell?

⁸Egypt rises like the Nile
   and like the great river, the waters are swollen
For he said, 'I will rise
   I will cover the earth
   I will destroy city and inhabitants in it.'

RHETORIC AND COMPOSITION

MT 46:7–8 = LXX 26:7–8. These verses are delimited as a separate poem (see Rhetoric and Composition for 46:2–6). That v 7 begins a new discourse is indicated by a return to the theme of hubris, which began—with greater subtlety—the oracle in vv 3–4 (Duhm; Rudolph; Weiser). This poem also connects with the end of that oracle, bringing in the Nile to balance the Euphrates (v 6; cf. 2:18).

The poetry consist of two bicolons and a tricolon breaking into two stanzas. The whole has nice repetition, one example being the verb *ʿlh* ("rise") occurring in the first colon of each line:

I   *Who . . . . . . .rises like the Nile*   v 7
     like the great river, its waters swell?

II   *Egypt rises like the Nile*   v 8
    and like the great river, the waters are swollen
    For he said, 'I will rise . . . .

    . . . .

The speaker of the poem can be either Yahweh or Jeremiah, as there is no messenger formula and no indication of a divine "I." Since Yahweh is speaker of the prior oracle, except for the first colon in v 5, perhaps the speaker here is Jeremiah. Speakers in the following oracle (vv 9–10) appear to alternate. The voice of Pharaoh or a personified Egypt is introduced in v 8b.

    On catchwords linking the poem cluster in 46:3–12, see Rhetoric and Composition for 46:2–6.

NOTES

46:7. *Who is this that rises like the Nile, like the great river, its waters swell?* Reading the imperfect *ya'ăleh* here and in 8a as a present, "(it) rises," and taking the *waw* on *wayyō'mer* in 8b as a *waw consecutive*, "for he said" (Duhm). This poem begins again with irony, asking the identity of the one who is harboring expansionist pretensions. Holladay notes that behind the rhetorical question, "Who is this that rises like the Nile?" is an awareness that the Nile also sinks (cf. Amos 8:8; 9:5). The rise and fall of the Nile is an annual occurrence, providing fertility for the land on either side. But the sinking to be described will occur at a river much farther north (46:2). For other passages where water and sea imagery carry overtones of judgment, see Note on 47:2.

    Who is this? Hebrew *mî-zeh*. The expression occurs also in 49:19.

    The Nile. Hebrew *yĕ'ōr* means simply "river" or "canal," usually—but not always—in Egypt. In Gen 41:1–3 and Isa 19:6–8, reference is to the Nile, as here. Hebrew *šîḥôr* denotes the Nile in 2:18.

    like the great river. Reading *nĕhārôt* (lit. "rivers") here and in v 8 as a plural of amplification (Volz; cf. GKC §124e).

    its waters swell? The verb *g'š* means "heave, swell, surge (noisily)," the Hithpael occurring one other time in Jeremiah to describe turbulent waves (5:22). Some imagine here the primeval waters of the deep that bring chaos and disorder (May 1955: 16; Bright; Boadt; Holladay). While allusions to ANE mythical imagery are doubtless in the background, deriving with the historical allusions even more from Mesopotamia than from Egypt (Huddlestun 1995: 360–63), the metaphor nevertheless aptly describes the expansionistic aims of Pharaoh Neco. Compare 47:2; also Isa 8:6–8.

    8. *Egypt rises like the Nile, and like the great river, the waters are swollen.* Egypt is now named, and McKane (p. 1115) is mistaken to call the repetition in 8a "the product of an unimaginative, pedestrian explicitness which destroys the literary effect of v. 7." Similar judgments were made by Cornill, Volz, Rudolph, and Weiser, who, following the lead of Schwally (1888: 192 n. 1), went beyond the LXX omission of 8aβ to delete all of 8a. The omission of 8aβ in the LXX, which appears to be "and like the great river, the waters are swollen," is likely due to haplography (homoeoarcton: *w . . . w*). The LXX reading has little to commend it, and should be rejected in favor of the reading of MT. One must also recognize among earlier critical scholars a definite bias against textual repetition, although curiously enough, variations could also be emended away to make correspondences more exact! Here the repetition with its variations makes for good poetry, with the answering of one's own rhetorical question called *hypophora* by the classical rhetoricians; cf. 30:15; 31:20; Song 3:6–7; 8:5; and Note on 49:7.

the waters are swollen. Hebrew *yitgōᶜăšû māyim.* Taking *māyim* as definite without the article, and the Hithpolel verb as a passive (GKC §67 l). On the Hithpolel meaning "to heave," see Note for 25:16. Many scholars (Blayney; Giesebrecht; Ehrlich 1912: 353; Bright; Keown et al.) argue that an original suffix on *māyim* ("waters") was lost by haplography from the following *wy*, which is possible. The T, S, and other Vrs have "its waters." On the other hand, variations in poetry this repetitive are perhaps better preserved than eliminated.

For he said, 'I will rise, I will cover the earth.' Reading a *waw consecutive* on *wayyō'mer* ("For he said"), which can also be translated "For he thought" (see Note on 3:7). The NSB has "Han tänker" ("He thinks"). A past tense suggests that the boast was made before the Battle of Carchemish, perhaps while Neco was still in Egypt or on his way north. The H-stem imperfect *'aᶜăleh* should probably be repointed to a Qal: *'eᶜĕleh,* "I will rise (up)" (cf. Isa 14:13–14; Ezek 38:11), although this could be another internal H-stem (see Note for 2:26) intending to magnify the arrogance of the boast: "I will indeed rise up." We are undoubtedly hearing a boast ascribed to Neco (so T), even though the subject in 8a is Egypt. Otherwise it is a personified Egypt speaking (van der Westhuizen 1991–92: 90; NIV without textual support emends to "she said," and the REB has an interpretive "says Egypt").

'I will destroy city and inhabitants in it.' The LXX omits "city and." Retain with MT, taking "city" as a collective (T: "cities"), i.e., meaning no city in particular. Neco's activities in north Syria, before his defeat at Carchemish, were not simply defensive. In 606 B.C. the Egyptian army besieged and captured the city of Kimuḫu, south of Carchemish, and in the year following, crossed the Euphrates and defeated the Babylonian army at Quramati, forcing it to withdraw (BM 22047: rev. 24–26; Wiseman 1956: 66–67; D. N. Freedman 1956: 52).

I will destroy. On the pointing of *'ōbîdâ,* see GKC §68i.

MESSAGE AND AUDIENCE

This poem taken by itself is a rhetorical question answered by the one posing it, supplemented by an ascribed quotation giving the answer substance. The audience will perhaps know at the outset that the someone rising like the Nile is likely to be Egypt, its godlike Pharaoh, or both. Egypt or Neco is then heard making the grand boast that it intends to rise and cover the earth, and in so doing to destroy cities and the people inhabiting them.

Heard in tandem with the oracle preceding, the question comes close to being one the audience itself may have been asking after hearing about a crushing defeat on the Upper Euphrates. It already imagines that this is Egypt, so when the answer is supplied, it nods knowingly. This poem also facilitates for its audience a return to the beginning of the prior oracle, repeating with irony the hubris underlying Egypt's military aspirations. If Jeremiah is the speaker, then he is complementing what Yahweh said earlier. Yahweh assailed Egypt's hubris indirectly; Jeremiah brings it into the open.

The date of this poem can be the same as the prior oracle, 605 B.C. The background is Nebuchadnezzar's imminent or accomplished defeat of Neco at Carchemish.

c) Rise Up, O Horses! (46:9–10)

46 ⁹Rise up, O horses!
  and go like mad, O chariots!
    and let the warriors move on out!
  Cush and Put holding the buckler
    and Ludim holding, bending the bow

¹⁰That day is for the Lord Yahweh of hosts
  a day of vengeance, to avenge himself on his foes
The sword will consume and be sated
  and it will drink its fill of their blood
Indeed a feast for the Lord Yahweh of hosts
  in a land of the north by River Euphrates.

RHETORIC AND COMPOSITION

MT 46:9–10 = LXX 26:9–10. This appears to be another divine oracle, even though as in vv 3–6 there is no messenger formula. For a delimitation of these verses in the larger grouping of vv 3–12, see Rhetoric and Composition for 46:2–6. The structure here is basically the same as vv 3–6: multiple imperatives summoning an army to begin battle; then a description of the army's defeat. Of the battle itself there is no mention. J. G. Snaith (1971: 22–23) discerns another sudden transition at midpoint, as in v 5a, with the difference that here the defeat is credited to Lord Yahweh of Hosts who brought it about.

The oracle divides nicely into two stanzas. Stanza I (v 9) is the summons to battle (Bach 1962: 52; Christensen 1975: 217), not a summons to flight as imagined by Holladay and Brueggemann. It consists of a tricolon and a bicolon. Yahweh is the speaker on the analogy of Yahweh being the speaker in Stanza I of the first oracle (vv 3–4). Here, as there, Yahweh appears to be imitating battlefield discourse. Some commentators (Calvin; Cornill; Peake;

Streane; Volz; Weiser) who assume that v 9 continues v 8 have Pharaoh as the speaker. But v 9 begins a new poem where the speaker is again Yahweh. Stanza II (v 10) describes Egypt's defeat in three bicolons of poetry, not prose, as printed in NJV. Here Jeremiah can be the speaker, since Yahweh's judgment is being described by another. Volz says the poet here is a spectator.

Stanza II begins lines 1 and 3 with the divine name and epithet, making an inclusio:

II   That day is *for the Lord Yahweh of hosts*   v 10a

. . . .

Indeed a feast *for the Lord Yahweh of hosts*   v 10c

. . . .

The LXX has a different and somewhat diminished repetition: "the Lord our God" (*kuriō tō theō ēmōn*) in line 1, and "the Lord of Hosts" (*tō kuriō sabaōth*) in line 3.

For the key words (= catchwords) linking this poem to others in the larger grouping of vv 3–12, see Rhetoric and Composition for 46:2–6. There is an additional linkage to the next poem in vv 11–12 with a repetition of *kî* ("indeed, for"), which begins each final bicolon:

Indeed (*kî*) a feast for the Lord Yahweh of hosts   v 10
Indeed (*kî*) warrior on warrior they stumbled   v 12

The same particle links a cluster of poems at the end of the Egypt collection (46:18–23). On the rhetorical uses of the particle *kî* in the OT, see Muilenburg 1961a.

NOTES

46:9. *Rise up, O horses!* The command is given here for horses to rear up and charge into battle. The tone is ironic, as in vv 3–4, since the army is known to be headed for defeat. This army is not departing from Egypt (so Streane), but about to engage the Babylonians at Carchemish, as in vv 3–4. Compare Nah 3:2–3. A ninth-century basalt inscription from Tell Halaf shows a rider astride a horse reared up; for a picture, see *ANEP*[2] 50 #164. Modern bikers and motorcyclists sometimes rear off with their front wheel in the air (called "pop-a-wheelie").

and go like mad, O chariots! Hebrew *wĕhithōlĕlû hārekeb*. On the Hithpolel of *hll*, "go mad / act madly," see Note for 25:16. The singular *rekeb* is another collective, i.e., "chariots." There is an echo here of Nah 2:5, on which see Note for 46:5. In Israel, King Jehu was known for his reckless chariot driving (2 Kgs 9:20).

and let the warriors move on out! Reading the imperfect *wĕyēṣĕ'û* as a jussive: "let them move on out," which is the rendering of the AV, RSV, NJV, NRSV, REB, and NJB. The LXX has an imperative, *exelthate* ("go out!"), which is read by commentators opting for consistency in the three colons. But the variation in the Hebrew makes for good—arguably better—poetry.

Cush and Put holding the buckler, and Ludim holding, bending the bow. Cush, Put, and Lud(im) are personified mercenary contingents in the Egyptian army, referred to again in v 21 as "hired soldiers"; cf. Nah 3:9; Ezek 30:5; and 38:5 (just Cush and Put). In Ezek 27:10 Lud and Put are mercenaries in Tyre's army. In the Table of Nations in Genesis 10, Cush and Put are sons of Ham (Gen 10:6), brothers to Egypt (Gen 10:6). Lud is a son of Shem (Gen 10:22), and Ludim, as spelled here, a son of Egypt (Gen 10:13).

Cush. Hebrew *kûš.* The biblical name for Ethiopia, a country south of Egypt inhabited by non-Egyptians (= present-day Ethiopia and Sudan). On Cush and the Cushites, see Note for 13:23. Cushites arrayed for battle (2050–1800 B.C.) are pictured in *IDB* E–J: 176. These people carried bows four cubits long, according to Herodotus (vii 69), and used arrows pointed with sharpened stones. Here, allowing for economy in the poetry, Cushites are depicted as holders of the bucklers.

Put. Hebrew *pûṭ.* Probably to be identified with Libya to the west of Egypt, based on the translation of Put in the LXX (*Libues*) and the Vg (*Libyes*), also what can be concluded from Old Persian inscriptions. The identification of Put (*Phoutēs*) with Libya was also made by Josephus (*Ant* i 132–34), and this is now the generally accepted view of modern scholars (Blayney; Giesebrecht; Duhm; Simons 1954: 178–84; 1959: 75–76; Holladay; cf. KB³; T. O. Lambdin, "Put," *IDB* K–Q: 971). "Libya" was used to translate Put in the AV. Other commentators (Cheyne; Peake; Rudolph; Bright; McKane; Carroll; Jones), however, have argued for an identification with Punt in the Egyptian texts (= Somalia, on the east coast of Africa), but Lambdin says this should be given up. One objection to the Libyan identification is the mention of both "Put" (*Pûṭ*) and the "Libyans" (*Lûbîm*) in Nah 3:9. But the LXX translates the two names with only one, i.e., "Libyans" (*Libues*). Lambdin also points out that while LXX translations of this name vary considerably in Jeremiah and Ezekiel, except for Ezek 30:5 (which has problems in both MT and LXX), Put is always translated Libyans.

the buckler. Hebrew *māgēn* is a small, usually round shield held in the hand. A circular bronze shield of Greek design found at Carchemish may have belonged to a mercenary soldier; see Note on 46:3.

and Ludim holding, bending the bow. Or "treading the bow." Hebrew *wělûdîm tōpěśê dōrěkê qāšet.* The composite bow required both the foot and the hand to set the arrow. See 50:14, 29; 51:3; and Note on 9:2[3]. For a picture of two Assyrian archers stringing a composite bow, one stabilizing the bow with his knee, see Yadin 1963: 453. There is thus scant justification for omitting *tōpěśê* ("holding") with the LXX, as most commentators and some modern translations (JB; NAB; NIV; NRSV; NSB) do, judging it a "careless repetition" from the prior colon. Aquila, Symm, T, and Vg translate both verbs (cf. AV; NEB; NJV). The bowmen of Lud (*lûd*) are referred to also in Isa 66:19.

Ludim. Hebrew *lûdîm* could be the plural of Lud, i.e., "the Ludites," or the name "Ludim" of Gen 10:13 = 1 Chr 1:11. Two peoples are usually suggested here: African Libyans or the Lydians of Asia Minor. The latter occur as *Luddu* in the Assyrian texts. If Put is identified with Libya, it is doubtful—though not impossible—that Lud might also be so identified. But reading Libyans here requires an emendation from *lûdîm* to *lûbîm*, which some scholars make (Duhm; Cornill; McKane). The LXX and Vg both have Lydia (*Ludoi; Lydii*), which is probably what is meant. In the Table of Nations, Ludim is set in the context of peoples who have settled in Asia Minor or the Greek islands, e.g., the Casluhim, from whence came the Philistines and the Caphtorim (Gen 10:13–14 = 1 Chr 1:11–12; cf. Jer 47:4 and Amos 9:7). Lydians also better suit Lud in Isa 66:19. During the reign of Psammetichus I (664–610 B.C.), Egypt received help resisting Assyria from Gyges, king of Lydia, which may correlate with what Herodotus (ii 152) says about sanctuary being given to Ionian and Carian pirates by Psammetichus, who then used these individuals as mercenaries in his army (Bright 1981: 313; CAH 3/2: 711). In any event, Greek influence was present in Egypt in the late seventh century B.C., and at the time Greeks were doubtless fighting in the Egyptian army (Gardiner 1961: 355–57; CAH 3/3: 32–47). Greek pottery is attested in all the eastern Mediterranean countries and in Egypt during the seventh century B.C., pointing to a penetration of Greek traders and mercenaries in the region (Stern 2001: 217–27). The bronze shield from Carchemish, as we just mentioned, appears to be of Greek design and origin. See further Mellink, "Lud, Ludim" in *IDB* K–Q: 178–79.

10. *That day is for the Lord Yahweh of hosts, a day of vengeance, to avenge himself on his foes.* Holy war ideology is full blown here (Bach 1962; Christensen 1975: 217–18; J. G. Snaith 1971: 25), particularly with the epithet "Yahweh of hosts" (= Yahweh of the army), which is to say, Egypt's day on the battlefield will bring not vengeance from the Babylonians, but from Yahweh, who is the prime mover in events taking place on the bank of River Euphrates. A "day of Yahweh" comes not only for Israel (see Note on 4:9), but for other nations as well (46:21; 47:4; 48:41; 49:22, 26; 50:27, 30, 31; Isa 2:12; 13:6, 9).

a day of vengeance, to avenge himself on his foes. Hebrew *yôm nĕqāmâ lĕhinnāqēm miṣṣārāyw.* Vengeance belongs to Yahweh, according to the *locus classicus* in Deut 32:34–42, where also is present the idea that Yahweh is the avenger of nations, including Israel. Mendenhall (1973: 95–98) prefers translating *nqm* as "punitive vindication" when God is subject. See also Peels 1995: 124–27, and Note on 5:9. But the question here is whether Yahweh might not actually be avenging the death of Josiah brought about by Neco a few years earlier. Kimḥi and Calvin thought so. A different view is presented in 2 Chr 35:20–24, but in later texts Yahweh is clearly said to avenge evil done to Israel (50:15, 28; 51:6, 11, 36; Isa 34:8; 63:4).

Lord Yahweh of hosts . . . Lord Yahweh of hosts. Hebrew *'adōnāy yhwh ṣĕbā'ôt.* The LXX omits the first "of hosts," but translates the second with *sabaōth,* the only time it does so in the entire book of Jeremiah. See Appendix VI. This expanded form of the divine name occurs again in 50:25.

to avenge himself on his foes. See Isa 1:24. The foes here may not only be Egypt with its mercenary forces, but Jehoiakim and the pro-Egyptian party in Jerusalem (de Jong 1981: 375–76).

The sword will consume and be sated. The LXX adds *(tou) kuriou* ("of the Lord") after "sword," perhaps to distinguish this weapon as the one belonging to Yahweh (the enemy), not the mercenary soldiers of v 9 (McKane; Sharp 1997: 491). On the consuming sword of Yahweh, see 12:12; 47:6; 49:37; Deut 32:41–42; Judg 7:20; Isa 27:1; 31:8; 34:5–6; 66:16; and Zech 13:7.

and it will drink its fill of their blood. Compare Isa 34:5–7. The verb here is *wĕrāwĕtâ*, which can mean "drink to drunkenness" (Rashi), although this is not its usual sense in the OT.

Indeed. Reading the Heb *kî* as an asseverative.

feast. Hebrew *zebaḥ*. Or "sacrifice." See 25:34; Isa 34:5–7; Zeph 1:7; and particularly Ezek 39:17–20, where slaughtered foes on the day of Yahweh will be like so many rams, lambs, goats, and bulls—all animals that are offered in Jewish sacrificial worship. Josiah, in fact, is said in his reform to have "sacrificed" *(yizbaḥ)* the priests of the high places on their altars (2 Kgs 23:20).

in a land of the north. Hebrew *bĕ'ereṣ ṣāpôn.* On the phrase "from a land of the north," see Note for 16:14–15. Reference here is to Carchemish.

River Euphrates. See Note on 46:6.

MESSAGE AND AUDIENCE

This oracle begins with Yahweh again giving battle orders, this time to the horses, chariots, and warriors of a ready army. With Cush and Put holding the buckler, and Lud preparing to set the arrow in its bow, we can imagine that this is none other than the army of mighty Egypt. The summons to readiness has an ironic sound, and if this goes undetected by the Jerusalem audience, it will scarcely be missed when Jeremiah speaks his own word about the day belonging to Lord Yahweh of hosts, a day on which he will avenge himself on his foes. Yahweh's sword will be sated with the fat of victims, and drunk with their blood—a veritable feast there will be up north by the River Euphrates. Neither Egypt nor Babylon is mentioned, but it will be clear to anyone in 605 B.C. that Yahweh is giving victory at Carchemish to Nebuchadnezzar and his army, and Egypt, as happened long ago, is the foe on whom vengeance is taken. Whether this is vengeance for the death of Josiah, the audience itself is left to decide. And one wonders, too, how Jehoiakim and the pro-Egyptian party in Jerusalem are likely to have responded.

d) Rise Up and Get Balm! (46:11–12)

46 [11]Rise up to Gilead and get balm
    virgin daughter Egypt!
In vain you keep doing it[1]
    a healing scar there is not for you

---

[1]Reading the Q, *hirbêt* ("you keep doing"); the Kt is the archaic feminine spelling; cf. 2:20, 33; et passim.

^{12}Nations have heard of your disgrace
　　your cry has filled the earth
Indeed warrior on warrior they stumbled
　　together the two of them fell.

RHETORIC AND COMPOSITION

MT 46:11–12 = LXX 26:11–12. This poem is the last of four in a group comprising vv 3–12. Delimitation from the oracle preceding is determined solely by formal and rhetorical criteria (see Rhetoric and Composition for 46:2–6). Closure—to the poem and also the group of poems—is indicated by a *petuḥah* in M^L and M^A, and a *setumah* in M^P, at the end of v 12, after which a prose superscription in v 13 introduces the next oracle. If one is to assign the poem a genre, it would best be the lament (Dobbs-Allsopp 1993: 133), although biting irony precludes it from being a true lament.

The poem consists of two stanzas. Stanza I (v 11) is two bicolons (*BHS*), not a tricolon and a bicolon (*pace* Holladay). Stanza II (v 12) is also two bicolons. The prophet himself is likely the speaker. Stanza II has a nice syntactic chiasmus in the first bicolon:

II　Nations have heard / of your disgrace　　　　　　　　　　　　v 12
　　　your cry / has filled the earth

Linkage to the prior poem is made by a repetition of *kî* ("indeed") beginning each final bicolon:

Indeed (*kî*) a feast for the Lord Yahweh of hosts　　　　　　　v 10
Indeed (*kî*) warrior on warrior they stumbled　　　　　　　　v 12

For more key words (= catchwords) linking this poem to others in the group, see Rhetoric and Composition for 46:2–6.

Catchwords connecting to the next oracle in 46:14–17 are these:

v 12 *stumbled . . . fell*　　　　　　　　v 16 *stumbling . . . it fell*

NOTES

46:11. *Rise up to Gilead and get balm, virgin daughter Egypt!* The widely-noted irony here (Chotzner 1883: 14: "sarcasm"; Rudolph; Weiser), is called *epitrope*, which is feigned support for an action known to bring harm or to be of no avail (see Note on 7:21). Egypt is told to get balm from Gilead even though, as we soon learn, there is no chance she will be healed. Babylon is told the same in 51:8. Gilead may still be under Egyptian control (J. G. Snaith 1971: 17), with trade in balm and other commodities currently going on. Nevertheless, Jeremiah is speaking metaphorically, and his point is that Egypt should not even bother going, although she has in the past and may still be doing so.

Rise up to Gilead. Or "Go up to Gilead." Hebrew *ʿălî gilʿād.* "Gilead" is not a vocative, as "horses" is with the same verb in v 9. In 49:28 we have *ʿălû ʾel-* ("go up to"), but in 22:20 it is *ʿălî* without *ʾel,* as here.

balm. Hebrew *ṣārî.* Identified in the OT with Gilead (see Note on 8:22).

virgin daughter Egypt! The term "daughter Egypt" appears in vv 19 and 24. On the various "daughter" metaphors, see Kartveit 2001 and Note for 4:11. There is added irony in the prophet's use of *bĕtûlat,* "virgin" (Calvin); in 18:13 it is "virgin Israel"; cf. Amos 5:2 ("virgin Israel"); Isa 23:12 ("virgin daughter Sidon"); 47:1 ("virgin daughter Babylon").

In vain you keep doing it. Hebrew *laššāwʾ hirbêt* (Q). The H-stem of *rbh* can take an object and mean "to multiply" (30:19), or, when followed by *lĕ* and the infinitive of another verb can mean "to do (something) continually" (1 Sam 1:12; 2 Sam 14:11; cf. BDB; KB³). Here—and particularly in v 16—the verb appears to stand alone. While it is possible that an object may have fallen out of the text, a perfectly good reading can be had if coordination is made with a *preceding* verb, which here would be two verbs: *ʿălî* ("rise up") and *qĕḥî* ("get") in 11a. Jeremiah then says: "In vain you continue (or have continued) to go up to Gilead to get balm." The following *rĕpuʾôt* ("healing") is not the object of *hirbêt,* which is the reading of MT, LXX, T, and the modern translations (e.g., RSV: "In vain you have used many medicines"). As one can tell from a comparison with 30:13, *rĕpuʾôt* belongs with the following colon (*pace* BHS). Hebrew *laššāwʾ* ("in vain") is a common Jeremianic expression (2:30; 4:30; 6:29; 18:15). There is now added indignity in that Egyptian knowledge of medicine was much celebrated in antiquity, e.g., Homer (*Odyssey* iv 228–32); also Herodotus (ii 84), who noted that medical practice was so widespread in Egypt that doctors had even become specialists. The testimony of classical authors is corroborated by the sixteenth-century B.C. Ebers Papyrus (Bryan 1931), and by other surviving medical and surgical papyri from Egypt.

a healing scar there is not for you. This colon occurs verbatim in 30:13b, supporting a break in the line before *rĕpuʾôt* ("healing"). For a discussion of these terms and the incurable wound as a curse in ancient society, see Note on 30:13. There will thus be no healing for Egypt, just as there was none for Zion. At the time of Jerusalem's fall in 586 B.C., Ezekiel said in an oracle that Yahweh would wound the Pharaoh of Egypt and simultaneously strengthen the king of Babylon (Ezek 30:20–26).

12. *Nations have heard of your disgrace.* Hebrew *qĕlônēk* ("your disgrace") is not a common Jeremiah word, occuring only one other time in 13:26. In Nah 3:5 Yahweh says he will let the nations look upon the disgrace (*qālôn*) of Nineveh. For other echoes of Nahum in Jeremiah's Egypt oracles, see Note on 46:5. Some commentators, e.g., Duhm, Cornill, Bright, Carroll, and Mc-Kane, emend in view of the LXX reading, *phōnēn sou,* "your noise" (= *qōlēk*), which is unnecessary despite a more exact parallelism with "your cry" in the next colon (Peake; Volz; Weiser; Holladay). Other Versions, including T, support MT whose reading is adopted in all the modern Versions except NEB and REB.

your cry has filled the earth. Hyperbole. Hebrew *ṣĕwāḥâ* is more properly a wail (14:2; Isa 24:11). Dobbs-Allsopp (1993: 133) says that Daughter Egypt is lamenting the destruction of her country, a commonplace in the city-lament genre. Compare 47:2.

Indeed warrior on warrior they stumbled. I.e., they stumbled (*kāšālû*) one over the other in fleeing the enemy (Rashi and Kimhi; cf. Lev 26:37).

together the two of them fell. The T assumes that both are killed, but such is not required (see Note on 46:6 regarding "falling," also the standard word pair "stumble . . . fall").

MESSAGE AND AUDIENCE

The opening "rise up" in this poem is neither a call for horsemen to mount horses and enter battle nor one to the horses that they themselves rear up and make their charge, but for a bloodied Egypt to go up to Gilead and get balm. If Egypt ever was a virgin, she is not one now. Daughter Egypt has gone for balm before, many times in fact, but she is told here that doing so now is for nought because no healing scar will cover her wound. O that she could have such a scar, which would show not only her wound but also that she emerged a survivor! Instead she is told that nations have heard of her disgrace, and her loud cry that has filled the earth. Her crack warriors stumbled over one another fleeing the enemy, with both of them falling to the ground.

This poem appears to have been composed after Egypt's defeat at Carchemish in 605 B.C., at which time the talk in Jerusalem and elsewhere was about wounds, remedies, disgrace, and cries of defeat. The end of the poem looks back on an army defeated miserably by the Babylonians.

When this oracle is heard in tandem with others that have preceded, the repetition of "rise up" will be but another twist for the audience to absorb. Now it is the "virgin daughter Egypt" (the irony has not abated), who is told to rise up and get balm from Gilead. But alas, it will do no good, which makes the defeat alluded to earlier one now of finality. This oracle appropriately closes the cluster by putting Egypt's shame and loud screams before all nations of the earth, a final act of poetic justice for one who boasted earlier of dominating these nations.

2. Pharaoh Is All Talk (46:13–17)

46 [13]The word that Yahweh spoke to Jeremiah the prophet about the coming of Nebuchadrezzar, king of Babylon, to strike down the land of Egypt.
[14]Declare in Egypt, and proclaim in Migdol
and proclaim in Memphis, and in Tahpanhes say:
'Stand ready, and prepare yourself
for the sword has consumed those around you

[15]So why is your mighty bull lying flat?
   it stands not, because Yahweh shoved it
      [16]he kept on; stumbling, yes, it fell

Each person to his fellow, indeed, they said:
   'Arise, and let us go back to our people
and to the land of our birth
   before the oppressive sword'

[17]Call the name[1] of Pharaoh
   king of Egypt:
      'Loud Noise, Who Lets the Deadline Pass.'

RHETORIC AND COMPOSITION

MT 46:13–17 = LXX 26:13–17. This unit is delimited at the top by the superscription in v 13, before which is a *petuḥah* in M[L] and M[A], and a *setumah* in M[P]. The next section in M[L] and M[A] comes after v 19, but the judgment here is that an oracle is concluded in v 17, where many modern Versions (RSV, NRSV, NJV, NIV, REB, NSB) make a break. Pharaoh's disparaging name is climactic, with vv 18–19 being a separate oracle predicting Egyptian defeat and exile. This latter oracle belongs structurally to a three-oracle cluster comprising vv 18–23 (see Rhetoric and Composition for 46:18–19). Most commentators take all of vv 14–24 as a single poem, although some (Volz; Rudolph; Weiser; Bright) divide between vv 19 and 20, making two parts or stanzas. Christensen (1975: 218, 220) envisages three stanzas: 14–17, 18–19, and 20–24, the breakdown adopted by Keown et al.

The superscription places all the poetry through v 24 in the context of punitive campaigns carried out by Nebuchadnezzar against Egypt—on the Egyptian frontier and within Egypt itself—subsequent to the Battle of Carchemish. The Babylonian army is the "foe from the north" mentioned in vv 20 and 24. The prose oracle in vv 25–26 recounts unambiguously the bad news for Egypt, making an inclusio of sorts with the superscription (cf. Carroll, 772). The present oracle in vv 14–17 does not speak directly about Egypt being invaded (Memphis's destruction comes in v 19), suggesting a date after Carchemish and before an Egyptian defeat on its own soil (cf. 43:8–13; 44:26–30).

The oracle—although again without a messenger formula—divides into four stanzas. Stanza I (v 14) and Stanza III (v 16bc) are double bicolons; Stanza II (vv 15–16a) and Stanza IV (v 17) tricolons. Holladay makes IV a bicolon by deleting "king of Egypt," for which there is no textual support. Stanzas I and III balance each other with a repetition of "sword" in the final colon. Stanza I has this repetition of verbs:

---

[1]Revocalizing MT *qorʾû šām* ("they called there") to *qirʾû šēm* ("call the name") with LXX and Vg.

I	Declare . . . *and proclaim* . . .	. . . *wĕhašmî ͑û*	v 14a
	and proclaim . . . . say	*wĕhašmî ͑û*.	

Cornill (p. 451) calls such repetition in immediate succession unbearable ("unerträglich"), but in fact it is good poetry, good rhetoric, and very Jeremianic. The same verb is repeated in different fashion at the beginning of another oracle (50:2). The second bicolon of this stanza is a syntactic chiasmus, which, in usual Jeremianic fashion, has the verbs at the extremes (Lundbom 1975: 64 [= 1997: 85]):

I	*and proclaim / in Memphis*	*wĕhašmî ͑û / bĕnōp*
	and in Tahpanhes / say	*ûbĕtaḥpanḥēs / ͑imrû*

Both of these structures support the MT over against omissions in the LXX (see Notes).

Stanzas alternate speaker and bring in additional voices, a common feature of the Jeremianic oracle. Yahweh is the speaker of Stanza I, beginning with imperatives to a multiple audience; cf. 4:5; 5:1; 46:3–4; 49:14. In 14a he addresses messengers selected to carry his message; in v 14b comes the message itself. Then Jeremiah interjects with *maddûa ͑* ("So why?") in Stanza II (Yahweh is referred to in the third person), countering resistance from those not wanting to hear the divine message. Structurally we have an oracle much like the one in vv 3–6, as was noted already by Rudolph:

I	Yahweh addressing a multiple audience with imperatives	v 14 / vv 3–4
	Key words: *hityaṣṣēb* ("Stand ready!") / *hityaṣṣĕbû* ("Stand ready!")	
II	Jeremiah's interjection expressing incredulity	v 15 / v 5
	Key words: *maddûa ͑* ("So why?") / *maddûa ͑* ("So why?")	

Kegler (1980: 274) discerns a fuller form-critical structure taking in v 16 of the present oracle and vv 5b–6 of the earlier oracle, but that assumes a destruction account in v 16, which is supported by one reading of the verse that remains questionable and does not follow the line of interpretation taken here. In Stanza III mercenaries and other expatriates in Egypt are heard discussing their return home, and in Stanza IV they give a "parting shot" on leaving the country. In the LXX these foreigners continue speaking into v 17. But if the MT of v 17 is to be read, then we have the following correspondence between III and IV:

III	*Each person to his fellow, indeed, they said:*	v 16b
	Direct speech of the expatriates	
IV	*They called there, Pharaoh, king of Egypt:*	v 17
	Direct speech of the expatriates	

Catchwords connecting to the prior oracle in 46:11–12:

v 16 *stumbling . . . it fell*	v 12 *stumbled . . . fell*

Catchwords connecting to the following oracle in vv 18–19:

v 14 *Memphis*   v 19 *Memphis*

NOTES

46:13. *The word that Yahweh spoke to Jeremiah the prophet.* A superscription beginning like those in 45:1; 50:1; and 51:59. The LXX lacks "the word" and "the prophet"; T has "the word of prophecy." Aquila has "the word" (*ho logos*).

the coming of Nebuchadrezzar, king of Babylon, to strike down the land of Egypt. A general statement placing the prophecies of vv 14–26 in the context of Nebuchadrezzar's battle with Neco in 601–600 B.C. on the Egyptian frontier, and one or more subsequent invasions by the Babylonian king into Egypt itself (Rashi; Kimḥi; Blayney; Giesebrecht). These follow Carchemish, which is cited in 46:2. Jeremiah fully expected Babylon to invade Egypt (43:8–13; 44:30), as did Ezekiel (Ezekiel 29–32). Josephus (*Against Apion* i 133; *Ant* x 181–82) reports that Nebuchadrezzar in his twenty-third year, i.e., 582 B.C., occupied Syria, made war on the Moabites and Ammonites (see Notes on 48:6 and 49:2), and then invaded Egypt, killing the Egyptian king and appointing another, after which the Jews living in Egypt were exiled to Babylon. The killing of the Egyptian king is widely discounted, but if an invasion did occur in this year, an exile of Jews living in Egypt could have taken place. In this year there was a third deportation from Judah (Jer 52:30). Ezekiel 29:17 dates a prophecy against Egypt in Jehoiachin's 27th year, i.e., 571/0 B.C., at which time the siege on Tyre had been given up. According to some Babylonian text fragments (BM 33041, 33053), Nebuchadrezzar, in his 37th year, i.e., 568 B.C., invaded Egypt in the reign of Pharaoh Amasis (Wiseman 1956: 94–95; ANET[3] 308; cf; Bright 1981: 352; Elat 1991: 31). It is generally agreed that Nebuchadrezzar did not conquer Egypt on this visit (Hyatt; Gardiner 1961: 362; Stager 1996: 71), but probably did invade the country as Jeremiah and Ezekiel said he would, inflicting indignities commensurate with an invasion. On Egyptian exiles living in Babylon during the sixth century B.C., see Note for 46:19.

Nebuchadrezzar. The LXX omits. For the spelling with "r" instead of "n," see Note on 21:2.

14. *Declare in Egypt, and proclaim in Migdol, and proclaim in Memphis, and in Tahpanhes say.* The same three imperatives occur in 4:5. See also 50:2. The imperatives are plural, suggesting messengers who will take the message of v 14b to people in the Egyptian cities (Weiser). The LXX lacks "in Egypt, and proclaim," which many commentators omit, but which can be explained as a simple case of haplography (homoeoarcton: *bm . . . bm* or homoeoteleuton: *w . . . w*). A nice poetic structure supports MT (see Rhetoric and Composition). Kimḥi says that Egypt generally is mentioned first, then specific cities are enumerated.

Migdol . . . Memphis . . . Tahpanhes. These three cities also appear together in 44:1, just Memphis and Tahpanhes in 2:16. Migdol and Tahpanhes were

Egyptian border towns where the news of an approaching enemy would be first reported. Memphis, the northern capital, must also get the news.

Migdol. Hebrew *migdôl.* A city or town in the east Delta region of Lower Egypt, usually identified with Tell el-Ḥêr, situated on the coastal road from Asia into Egypt, between Pelusium and Selē (Volz; Gardiner 1920: 107–10; Lambdin, "Migdol," *IDB* K–Q: 377). More recently, Israeli archaeologists from Ben Gurion University have excavated a site one kilometer north of Tell el-Ḥêr, known as T. 21, which they believe to be Migdol of the Saïte period (see Note for 44:1). Israelites camped at a Migdol before crossing the Red Sea (Exod 14:2; Num 33:7), but whether this is the same Migdol as here is not known. Gardiner says that no fewer than four "Migdols" are known to have existed in the eastern Delta, three being forts of smaller size on the road to Palestine (Heb *migdāl* = "tower"), the fourth being a town of some size. The town fits the Migdol mentioned here. From this early period is also a *Ma-ag-da-lí* of unspecified location in the Tell el-Amarna Letters (EA 234: 29). Migdol was one of the places where Judahites settled after the fall of Jerusalem (44:1). The town receives mention also in Ezek 29:10 and 30:6. Herodotus (ii 159) identifies *Magdolus* (probably Migdol) as the place where Neco II met and defeated the Syrians (= Babylonians?), perhaps in the battle of 601–600 B.C. (Lipiński 1972: 235–38). "Magdolus," in any case, is not to be identified with Megiddo, where Neco met and killed King Josiah of Judah. See further Note on 47:1.

Memphis. Hebrew *nōp.* See Note on 2:16.

Tahpanhes. Hebrew *taḥpanḥēs.* Identified with Tell Defneh; see Note on 43:7. The LXX omits and commentators do likewise, but the term is best retained (see Rhetoric and Composition).

'Stand ready, and prepare yourself, for the sword has consumed those around you.' Hebrew *hityaṣṣēb wĕhākēn* ("Stand ready, and prepare") are both infinitive absolutes (Rudolph), not masculine imperatives, even though they function as imperatives. The directive is not a summons to battle, as in vv 3–4 and v 9 (*pace* Giesebrecht and others; cf. T: "arm yourself"), nor a summons to flight (*pace* McKane), but simply a warning for people to be on high alert in light of major casualties round about. The situation sounds like the Babylonian-Egyptian battle in 601–600 B.C. on the Egyptian frontier.

for the sword has consumed those around you. The perfect verb *'ākĕlâ* is to be translated past: "it has consumed" (Cheyne; Peake; NAB; NJV), not future (as in the AV; RSV; NIV; and NRSV). People are being told about battle losses that have already occurred (T: "for the sword has killed your neighbors"). A future tense assumes Babylonian entry into the country, which is not necessarily envisaged in this oracle. The LXX misreads MT *sĕbîbeykā* ("those around you") as "your yew tree," *tēn smilaka sou* (= Heb *subbĕkēk,* "your thicket"); cf. 4:7. For the expression of people all around being consumed, see 21:14 and 50:32.

15. *So why is your mighty bull lying flat?* Hebrew *maddûaʿ nishap 'ab-bîreykā.* This verse has been a problem from earliest times, with two different but not incompatible images having been presupposed. One is that of fleeing warriors (cf. v 21), the other of a fleeing or vanquished bull representing

Egypt's god. The ambiguity is in *'abbîreykā*, lit. "your strong ones," which T takes here to mean "mighty men." This interpretation is carried forward in Rashi, Calvin, and the AV ("valiant men"), and survives most recently in the NIV. The term, however, can also mean "stallions" (8:16; 47:3; 50:11; Judg 5:22) or "mighty bulls" (Isa 34:7; Pss 22:13[Eng 22:12]; 50:13; 68:31[Eng 68:30]). We recall too that *'ăbîr* was an ancient name for Yahweh, the "Mighty One (of Jacob)" (Gen 49:24; Ps 132:5; Isa 49:26; 60:16). The LXX, however, reads *dia ti ephygen ho apis*, "Why has Apis fled?" J. D. Michaelis (1793: 308–9) recognized already that the verb *nishap* ("lying flat") had been divided to read *nās hap*, where *hp* = Apis, the sacred bull of Memphis worshiped as a manifestation of the god Ptah (Herodotus ii 153; Lambdin, "Apis," *IDB* A–D: 157). In Greco-Roman times Apis was closely associated with Osiris (Plutarch, *de Iside* 33), known as Osiris-Apis, or Serapis. The LXX reading has been accepted by many scholars (Giesebrecht; Duhm; Cornill; Peake; Ehrlich 1912: 353; Bright; Thompson; McKane; Holladay; Jones; Keown et al.) and many modern Versions (RSV; NEB; JB; NAB; NSB). Yet the image of a "fleeing" god—particularly a cumbersome bull made of stone—leaves something to be desired. Hyatt gives the standard interpretation. He says that images of a god were frequently carried into battle, and their flight or capture symbolized the defeat of those who worshiped the deity (cf. Isa 46:1–2). Volz, nevertheless, judges the "flight of Apis" to be a strange thought, and he together with others (Hitzig; Rudolph; Weiser; NJV) have opted therefore for the reading of MT, which makes perfectly good sense. The N-stem *nishap* means "lie down, lay down flat" (KB³), or "be prostrated" (BDB), having a close cognate in Akk *saḥāpu*, which means "lay / lie flat, overturn, be overturned," used often of someone lying flat on the stomach or face down (*CAD* 15: 30–36). In the present context *nishap* may be a wordplay on Memphis (Heb *nōp*). What we are talking about, in any case, is a bull image—very likely the bull Apis—that has been knocked down. Jeremiah is being ironic. Hebrew *'abbîreykā* is a plural of majesty, meaning "mighty bull" (Ember 1904–5: 213–14; Rudolph; cf. GKC §124e). D. N. Freedman notes a plural "these are your gods" (*'ēlleh 'ĕlōheykā*) referring to the golden calf in Exod 34:2 as being ironic. The same may be true here. Many MSS read a singular. For a picture of the bull Apis from this period, see *ANEP²* 190 #570; *IDB* A–D: 157.

So why? Hebrew *maddûa'*. The term follows a string of imperatives as it does also in vv 3–5. The sequence is somewhat different in 30:6. Here the "so why?" question expresses incongruity, not surprise as in v 5. Jeremiah imagines a people hearing the call to be on the alert, yet are doing nothing.

it stands not, because Yahweh shoved it. The rhetorical question is answered by Jeremiah himself (*hypophora*). See Note on 49:7. In v 21 it is mercenaries who do not stand (*lō' 'āmādû*), i.e., hold their ground, but here it is Egypt's mighty bull. Yahweh by overturning the bull is seen to be the real enemy of the Egyptians; it is not the Babylonians (cf. v 10). The verb *hdp* means "shove" (KB³; cf. Ezek 34:21). Most modern Versions have Yahweh felling the idol in vigorous combat (e.g., RSV: the LORD thrust him down"); JB: "Yahweh has knocked him flat"—but changed in NJB to "Yahweh has overturned him"). That combat has in fact taken place between the "mighty one of Egypt" and the "Mighty One of Jacob / Israel" is clear enough (Boadt; cf. Isa 19:1), but I would take Yahweh's decisive stroke as being one that required much less effort, giving the colon—together with v 16a—an ironic tone. What Yahweh did was simply give the bull a shove, then another and another, until finally it tottered, stumbled, and fell.

16. *he kept on*. The difficult *hirbâ* is best taken as expressing continued action of the previous verb (see v 11). The idea is that Yahweh kept shoving Egypt's idol until it stumbled and fell. The T has: "They have increased their stumblings, each man has deserted his colleague," but this assumes that *'abbîrîm* in v 15 means "mighty men," that *hirbâ* goes with *kôšēl*, "stumbling" (note the *athnah* under *kôšēl*), that "each person to his fellow" belongs in v 16a (not in 16b, as in BHS), and that the image as a whole is more or less the same as in vv 5–6, 12, and 21. This reading, which fails to distinguish a different image from those in the surrounding verses, is reflected in Rashi, Kimhi, and the AV ("He made many to fall, yea, one fell upon another"). Yahweh, however, is shoving the bull, not making the warriors to stumble. The LXX's reading of *hirbâ*, which is *to plēthos sou* ("your crowd"), offers no help.

stumbling, yes, it fell. Hebrew *kôšēl gam-nāpal*. For these verbs in combination, see vv 6 and 12.

Each person to his fellow, indeed, they said, 'Arise, and let us go back to our people and to the land of our birth, before the oppressive sword.' The *waw* in *wayyō'mĕrû* is emphatic: "indeed, they said." The LXX's *kai ekastos pros plēsion autou elalei* ("and each one to his neighbor said") leads most commentators to relocate the verb or delete the *waw*. Expatriates in Egypt are now heard urging one another to return home in light of the failed war effort, and the possibility of more war with a similar outcome in the future. On the expression "each person to his fellow," compare 9:3–4[Eng 9:4–5].

Arise. Hebrew *qûmâ* is the long form of the imperative. Q^OR have the plural *qûmû*. Either can be read.

'before the oppressive sword.' Or "because of the oppressive sword." Hebrew *mippĕnê hereb hayyônâ*. This Jeremianic phrase recurs in 50:16 and LXX 32:38 [= MT 25:38]. On the grammar, see GKC §126w.

17. *Call the name of Pharaoh, king of Egypt: 'Loud Noise, Who Lets the Deadline Pass.'* This mocking epithet for Egypt's king is the "parting shot" of the expatriates—some being mercenary soldiers—as they leave for home. Compare Egypt's epithet in Isa 30:7 ("Rahab Who Sits Still"); the disparaging name given to Baal in Jer 3:23 ("Noise of the Mountains"); and the name given to Jerusalem in Jer 30:17 ("That Zion Whom No One Cares About"). Here the slur states that Egypt's Pharaoh talks big but acts small. Rashi says he appointed a set time to go forth and wage war, but did not go forth. Hoffmeier (1981: 168) notes also an Egyptian wisdom tradition that labels a loud, boisterous person a fool. Cornill's proposal that *he'ĕbîr* ("he lets pass") contains a wordplay on the name Hophra (*Uah-ab-ra*) has not found much acceptance. Hophra (= Apries) reigned from

589 to 570 B.C., and is mentioned in the Egypt prophecy of 44:30. The LXX here simply transliterates the mocking name, also adding "Neco" after "Pharaoh," which, if accurate, would require for the oracle a date before 594 B.C.

MESSAGE AND AUDIENCE

Yahweh begins this oracle by addressing messengers whom he has chosen to carry his message to cities in Egypt. To Migdol, Memphis, and Tahpanhes goes out the word for people to be on high alert, perhaps even on a war footing, because death and terror have reigned beyond Egypt's borders. Jeremiah then interjects a question of his own, asking the Egyptians why their sacred bull is lying flat on the ground. Has their image been toppled, or has the representative bull in the cult become sick and died, now to be mummified and buried by the priest in solemn ritual? The mighty bull Apis no longer stands because Yahweh gave it a shove, then another, until it tottered, stumbled, and fell. Presumably the audience will know precisely what indignity has come upon Egypt's sacred bull. There are some, however, Greek mercenaries and other expatriates, who realize that the situation is not good and that the better part of wisdom is to avoid further war and get on home. What we hear is them talking this over among themselves, deciding to do just that. The land of their birth seems infinitely better than the present land, which could turn out to be the land of their death. The oracle ends with these foreigners giving a "parting shot" to Egypt, calling its Pharaoh "Loud Noise, Who Lets the Deadline Pass."

While this oracle is ostensibly addressed to an Egyptian audience, the preferred audience is doubtless Jehoiakim and the pro-Egyptian party in Jerusalem. The background is then the years between 604 and 597 B.C., when Judah's foreign policy vacillated between pro-Egyptian and pro-Babylonian factions, changing a second time with disastrous results (2 Kgs 24:1). By 604 both Ashkelon and Ekron were destroyed, and the battle between Babylon and Egypt in 601–600 on the Egyptian frontier left both sides with considerable losses. This was a reversal for Nebuchadnezzar, which complicated Jerusalem foreign policy. One or more of these battles was a fresh memory, explaining the two mentions of a consuming sword in vv 14 and 16. If the bull idol suffered its indignity in battle, then this too recalls an event in the recent past. A date before 594 B.C. would make the LXX mention of Neco in v 17 accurate, for he died in this year. Most important, perhaps, is that this oracle neither predicts nor presupposes an invasion of Egypt, which comes in the later verses and takes place later in time. People here are simply told to be on alert, with invasion being no more than a possibility. Actually, 604 B.C. is a good time for the delivery of this oracle, as the recent Battle of Carchemish is cause enough for Greek mercenaries and other expatriates in Egypt to begin thinking about returning home. Many scholars (Rudolph; Weiser; Hyatt 1956: 282–83; Bright; Thompson), date these verses—and the others in vv 18–24—between 605 and 600 B.C. Some who take vv 14–24 as a single poem opt for a date after the fall of Jerusalem in 586 B.C., but this better suits later verses that speak pointedly about an invasion of Egypt.

3. Invasion, Destruction, and Exile for Egypt (46:18–26)

a) Daughter Egypt Better Start Packing (46:18–19)

46 [18]'As I live'—oracle of the King
  Yahweh of hosts is his name
Indeed like Tabor among the mountains
  and like Carmel by the sea, he will come

[19]Exile baggage prepare for yourself
  sitting daughter Egypt!
Indeed Memphis shall become a desolation
  and burned without inhabitant.

RHETORIC AND COMPOSITION

MT 46:18–19 = LXX 26:18–19. This oracle announcing exile for Egypt is delimited at the top end by an emphatic "oracle of the King" formula, also by content and rhetorical criteria. Its conclusion is marked by a *setumah* in M[L] and M[A] at the end of v 19. The M[P] has no section here. The oracle is the first of three in vv 18–23 having similar length: eight colons. These oracles have each final bicolon beginning with the asseverative particle *kî* ("Indeed"), also a simile prefaced by *kĕ* in each second colon. Oracle III has an additional simile in its first bicolon (v 22a). A poetic fragment in v 24 concludes the grouping, its key word "daughter Egypt" making an inclusio with "daughter Egypt" in v 19a. Verses 25–26 then close out the Egypt collection with a pair of oracles in prose. The poetic grouping in vv 18–24 has the following key word structure:

I	. . . .	. . . .		v 18
	Indeed like	*and like . . . .*	*kî kĕ . . . . ûkĕ*	
	. . . .	*. . . daughter Egypt*	*bat-miṣrāyim*	v 19
	Indeed	. . . .	*kî*	
II	. . . .	. . . .		v 20
	. . . .	*like . . . .*	*kĕ*	v 21
	Indeed	. . . .	*kî*	
	Indeed	. . . .	*kî*	
III	. . . . *like . . . . . .*	*indeed . . . .*	*kĕ . . . . kî*	v 22
	. . . .	*like . . . .*	*kĕ*	
	. . . .	*indeed . . . .*	*kî*	v 23
	Indeed	. . . .	*kî*	
IV	*. . daughter Egypt.*	. . . .	*bat-miṣrāyim*	v 24

Verse 24 speaks of Egypt's shame, which corresponds to the mention of Egypt's "disgrace" at the end of the first grouping of oracles in v 12:

Nations have heard of *your disgrace (qĕlōnēk)*	v 12
Daughter Egypt *has been greatly shamed (hōbîšâ)*	v 24

The present oracle divides into two stanzas, v 18 and v 19. The lines are all bicolons, with the key repetition being an asseverative *kî* beginning 18b and 19b. Yahweh opens the oracle with a self-asseveration, "As I live," after which the prophet extols Yahweh and states that Yahweh, not Nebuchadnezzar, will come. Stanza II (v 19) can either be Yahweh or the prophet speaking. In my view, the oracle gains if Yahweh is the speaker, for then Yahweh is heard picking up from his self-asseveration to provide the divine word with substance, which is a judgment upon Egypt.

Catchwords connecting to the prior oracle in vv 14–17:

v 19	*Memphis*	v 14 *Memphis*

Catchwords connecting to the following oracle in vv 20–21:

v 18	*he will come*	v 20	*came, came*
		v 21	*has come*
vv 18, 19	*Indeed* (2×) *kî . . . kî*		*Indeed* (2×) *kî . . . kî*

NOTES

46:18. *'As I live.'* On Yahweh's self-asseveration, *ḥay-ʾānî* ("As I live"), see Note on 22:24. Only Yahweh can swear by his own name (see Note for 49:13).

oracle of the King, Yahweh of hosts is his name. This unusual and expanded messenger formula occurs also in 48:15 (MT) and 51:57. The LXX has simply "says the Lord God," which many take to be the preferred reading, although it should be noted that the LXX of 28:57 [= MT 51:57] contains the entire phrase including "of hosts." See Appendix VI. Rudolph rightly reads the MT, which accents the greatness and power of Yahweh over against a weak and discredited Pharaoh (Calvin; J. G. Snaith 1971: 27). "Yahweh of hosts is his name" is a recurring doxology in Jeremiah (see Note on 10:16).

Indeed like Tabor among the mountains and like Carmel by the sea, he will come. The AV recognized the initial *kî* as an asseverative, translating it "Surely." The dual comparison to Tabor and Carmel extends Yahweh's honorific title, and as such does not require a verb. Yahweh in his grandeur and majesty compares to Israel's two prominent mountains. The comparison has nothing to do with "he will come" at the end (*pace* T; RSV; NRSV; NIV), other than making Yahweh the subject. Yahweh is the unnamed foe; it is not Nebuchadnezzar (*pace* Duhm; Peake; S. R. Driver; Thompson).

Tabor. A small but prominent mountain in the northeast corner of the Jezreel Valley, ca. 10 kilometers east of Nazareth. Its height is just above 1800 feet, substantially less than Mount Hermon, which joins Tabor in praising Yahweh in Ps 89:13[Eng 89:12]. Tabor is often said to be an isolated peak far from other mountains (e.g., Holladay), but, in fact, there are numerous mountains nearby. Tabor can thus be said to have mountains surrounding it (so Calvin). For a picture of Mount Tabor, see *IDB* R–Z, 509.

Carmel by the sea. The well-known Mount Carmel is situated on the Mediterranean near present-day Haifa. Another mountain of not particularly great height, ca. 1750 feet at maximum elevation, it is nevertheless high within Israel (cf. Amos 9:3). The Carmel range, extending southeast from Haifa ca. 21 kilometers, had rich orchards and vineyards in antiquity.

19. *Exile baggage prepare for yourself.* Daughter Egypt is being addressed. Hebrew *kēlîm* ("baggage") will consist of miscellaneous articles — here probably cooking utensils, clothing, and other provisions carried in a bundle on the trip into exile (Ezek 12:3–4). See Note on 10:17. Josephus (*Ant* x 181–82) reports that Judahites living in Egypt were exiled by Nebuchadnezzar to Babylon sometime after 582 B.C. Egyptians were probably exiled to Babylon at the same time. From the Bīt Murašû archive we know that in the sixth century B.C. Egyptians, together with Jews and other ethnic minorities, were living in Nippur and other Babylonian cities (Eph'al 1978: 74–80).

sitting daughter Egypt. Hebrew *yôšebet bat-miṣrāyim.* An English translation of this phrase is difficult, for "sitting" means not only inhabiting but dwelling securely or occupying a place of high honor (like a "sitting" president). The NRSV translates the phrase "sheltered daughter Egypt," but in 48:18 it has "enthroned daughter Dibon." The image here is one of daughter Egypt dwelling securely, just as daughter Zion dwelt securely in her wood-paneled palaces of Jerusalem (22:23). NJV: "you who dwell secure." Now, however, it will be a migratory existence for many in Egypt. Compare variations of this signature Jeremianic expression in 10:17; 21:13; 48:18–19, 28, 43; and 51:35 (2×). On the "daughter Egypt" metaphor, see v 24 and Note on 46:11.

Indeed Memphis shall become a desolation, and burned without inhabitant. Variations of this curse appear throughout the book of Jeremiah (see Note on 48:9). Hebrew *šammâ* ("desolation") occurs together with the similar *šĕmāmâ* a total of 40 times in the book. On Memphis, see v 14 and Note on 2:16.

and burned without inhabitant. Hebrew *wĕniṣṣĕtâ mē'ên yôšēb.* One variant of a familiar Jeremianic expression; cf. 2:15; 4:7; 9:9, 11[Eng 9:10, 12]. The verb is taken by some as an N-stem of *yṣt*, "be kindled, burned" (BDB; Holladay), although an N-stem of *nṣh* ("be ruined") is also a possibility (KB³; Rudolph; cf. Freedman, Lundbom, "yṣt," *TDOT* 6: 266–69). Neither T nor LXX indicates a burning.

MESSAGE AND AUDIENCE

This brief poem opens with an oath by Yahweh, who alone can swear by the life of himself. Jeremiah then says that this is an oracle by the King, Yahweh of hosts being his name. The extolling of Yahweh continues with a comparison of his majesty to the celebrated mountains of Israel, Tabor and Carmel, which are both familiar to a Jerusalem audience. The prophet concludes his first stanza with "he will come." Who will come? The careful listener will discern that it is Yahweh who will come, although some in the audience may imagine with good reason that it will be Nebuchadnezzar. Clarity of the addressee and the errand on which the coming one embarks is achieved in the second stanza of the oracle, where a nicely-settled daughter Egypt is told pointedly to prepare her bundle for exile, as a destruction of some magnitude will come upon Memphis.

This oracle announces an invasion of Egypt, a destruction of Memphis, and an exile for many Egyptians, all at the hands of the Babylonians, who are the major threat to Egypt after 605 B.C. When the oracle may have been spoken is difficult to say. It could have been after the fall of Jerusalem, when Jeremiah was in Egypt announcing a judgment against the land (43:8–13; 44:30), but since Jeremiah gives most of his Egypt oracles ca. 605 B.C. this date is also a possibility, in which case the prediction is well in advance of its fulfillment. Fulfillment, too, is not known with certainty. There was the incursion into Egypt reported by Josephus in 582 B.C., a 571/0 B.C. campaign reported by Ezekiel (Ezek 29:17), and a 568 campaign in the reign of Pharaoh Amasis, cited in the Babylonian Chronicle. In any case, there is no talk here about Egypt being destroyed and depopulated, as alleged by Duhm and McKane. That claim, made largely to disclaim Jeremianic authorship for the Egypt oracles, is easily dispensed with. Not one of Jeremiah's Egypt oracles envisions such a thing happening. The destruction here comes only upon Memphis, and exile for the Egyptians does not translate into a depopulation of the entire country.

When this oracle is heard in tandem with the previous one, the mocking comments of the departing mercenaries (v 17) are supplemented by the authoritative voice of Yahweh and the extolling voice of the prophet (v 18), affirming Yahweh's kingship over a discredited Pharaoh. Also, with the mercenaries now gone home, the Egyptians are told that they too must prepare for a journey: into exile.

b) A Horsefly from the North on Heifer Egypt (46:20–21)

46 [20]A beautiful, beautiful heifer was Egypt
  a horsefly from the north came, came
[21]Even her hired hands in her midst
  were like stall heifers

Indeed even they, they turned back
  they fled together, they did not stand
Indeed the day of their disaster came upon them
  the time of their reckoning.

RHETORIC AND COMPOSITION

MT 46:20–21 = LXX 26:20–21. This brief poem is delimited mainly by content and rhetorical criteria (see Rhetoric and Composition for 46:18–19, and note demarcations in the RSV, NRSV, and REB). A *setumah* prior to v 20 in M^L and M^A corroborates its upper limit. Its structural integrity is to be seen in the repetitions and key word balance in two stanzas of poetry, including an inclusio made by the verb *bāʾ* ("came"). This inclusio I noted in an earlier analysis (Lundbom 1975: 59–60 [= 1997: 80–81]); another inclusio in Stanza I is made by the repetition "heifer / heifers." The two stanzas then with their key words are structured as follows:

I   *beautiful, beautiful heifer* . . . .   *ʿeglâ yĕpēh-pîyyâ*   v 20
     . . . . *came, came*   *bāʾ bāʾ*
     Even . . . .   *gam*   v 21
     . . . *heifers* . . . .   *ʿeglê*

II   *Indeed even* . . . .   *kî-gam*
     . . . .
     Indeed . . . . *came* . . . . . .   *kî . . . bāʾ*
     . . . .

The doublets in Stanza I, "beautiful, beautiful" and "came, came," are intentional, giving the poetry an echo effect. In my earlier analysis I went with the LXX reading, "came upon her" (= *bāʾ bāh*), but I now think the MT preserves a better text, and is not the victim of scribal error (see Notes).

The speaker here can be either Yahweh or the prophet. If the poem is an oracle, then Yahweh is the speaker, although there is no messenger formula. This omission, also the casting of the poem in the prophetic perfect, suggest a vision by the prophet, in which case Jeremiah is the speaker.

Catchwords connecting to the previous oracle in vv 18–19:

v 20   *came, came*   v 18   *he will come*
v 21   *came*
     Indeed (2×)   *kî . . . kî*   vv 18, 19 *Indeed* (2×)   *kî . . . kî*

Catchwords connecting to the following oracle in vv 22–23:

v 20   *came, came*   v 22   *they are coming*
v 21   *came*   *indeed*   *kî*
     Indeed (2×)   *kî . . . kî*   v 23   *Indeed* (2×)   *kî . . . kî*

NOTES

46:20. *A beautiful, beautiful heifer was Egypt.* Hebrew *ʿeglâ* is a heifer (= young cow), a suitable metaphor for a nation practicing bull worship (cf. Apis discussion in Note on 46:15). The construction *yĕpēh-pîyyâ* is doubtless an ancient superlative meaning "most beautiful," although the meaning of *pîyyâ* remains obscure. Many MSS contain a single word, *yĕpêpîyyâ*, which is explained as a doubling of *yph(y)* for intensification (BDB; KB^3; GKC §84b n.). But compare the superlative *ṣĕbî ṣib'ôt*, "beauty of beauties," in 3:19; also the triple construct chain, *yĕpēh pĕrî-tō'ar*, "beautiful in fruit, in form," in 11:16. Egypt, in any case, was one beauty of a heifer, but, because she was filled with hubris, disaster awaited her. The lovely, delicate daughter Zion was destined for a similar fate (6:2). Giesebrecht sees here a picture painted of strength and cocky spirit, typical of the young (cf. 31:18; 50:11).

a horsefly from the north came, came. Hebrew *qereṣ* is a *hapax legomenon* in the OT, but it is generally taken to mean horsefly or gadfly (*Tabanus bovinus*). Such was the interpretation of Hitzig (*Bremse*), who was anticipated in earlier readings of Aq, Symm, and St. Chrysostom (Field 1875: 708), also the Vg. The verb *qrṣ* most likely means "nip (off)" (BDB), although more common OT usages are "wink (the eye)" (Ps 35:19; Prov 6:13; 10:10) and "compress (the lips)" (Prov 16:30). A Pual in Job 33:6 means "nipped off (from a piece of clay)," a usage attested also in Akk (KB³). Ugaritic *qrṣ* means "gnaw, rip off, bite." Arabic *qāriṣ* means "biting, stinging," said of an insect or even the cold. What we are doubtless talking about here is a fly that nips or stings cattle. Homer in a well-known passage in the *Odyssey* (xxii 299–301) describes frightened individuals, who flee "like a herd of cattle that the darting gadfly (*t' aiolos oistros*) falls upon and drives along in the season of spring, when the long days come" (Loeb). Classical authors refer also to the god Io, who, after being turned into a cow, is pursued by a gadfly all the way to Egypt (Apollodorus, *Lib* ii 1 3; Virgil, *Georgics* iii 146–53). Gershenson (1996) argues that this myth may have been known in Israel before the time of Jeremiah, and could therefore have influenced the portrayal here. In Isa 7:18 it is a fly (*zĕbûb*) representing the Egyptian army and a bee (*dĕbôrâ*) representing the Assyrian army that are summoned by Yahweh to come against Judah. Here a single horsefly representing the Babylonian army has already come from the north against Egypt.

came, came. Hebrew *bā' bā'*. Most everyone (but not Gershenson) goes with the LXX (*ēlthen ep' autēn*), other Versions, and 100+ MSS in reading the second *bā'* as *bāh*, "upon her." This is the *lectio facilior*, and a prosaic alternative to the more vigorous poetry preserved in MT, particularly in light of a repeated "beautiful, beautiful" in the first colon. The repetition in both cases is for emphasis (*geminatio*; compare 4:19: "my innards, my innards"; 23:25: "I have dreamed, I have dreamed"; 51:3: "will bend, will bend"; and see Note for 7:4), driving home the point that an enemy is seen as having come. But here it is Nebuchadnezzar and his army who come, not Yahweh as in v 18.

21. *Even her hired hands in her midst were like stall heifers.* Hebrew *śĕkīreyhā* ("her hired hands") were mercenaries in the Egyptian army (Calvin; McKane), identified as the men of Cush, Put, and Ludim in v 9, and those who were heard from directly prior to leaving Egypt in vv 16–17. See further Note on 46:9. Calvin emphasized the particle *gam*, "*even* her hired hands," as if to say, these mercenaries instead of being fit were living the good life in Egypt. As such they were like "stall heifers" (*'eglê marbēq*), i.e., heifers in the stall who are well-fed, fat, and soon to be slaughtered (Kimhi, following T; also Calvin). Duhm says fat cows are not good war bulls. For the term "stall heifer(s)" elsewhere in the OT,

see 1 Sam 28:24; Mal 3:20[Eng 4:2]; and particularly Amos 6:4, where the translation "stall" for *marbēq* seems to be the right choice (Wolff 1977: 272, 276; Andersen and Freedman 1989: 544; and Paul 1991: 516–17; cf. Ar *rabaqa*, "to tie up, bind tightly"; BDB says *marbēq* is lit. "tying place"; KB³ gives the definition "fattening"). Herodotus (ii 154) locates alien Carians and Ionians on either side of the Nile, also on an arm of the Nile called Pelusian (cf. Ezek 30:15–16) below the town of Bubastis, saying that Pharaoh paid them all that he promised. He goes on to state that Apries (= Hophra) in his sumptuous palace had a bodyguard of 30,000 Carians and Ionians, and that warriors in Egypt were given special privileges, e.g., each bodyguard received an untaxed plot of twelve acres and daily provisions of roast grain, beef, and wine (ii 163, 168).

Indeed even they, they turned back, they fled together, they did not stand. Reading *kî* here and in the next line as asseveratives (cf. Rudolph), with *gam* again emphasizing how *even* the mercenaries, who might be expected to hold their ground and fight, turned and fled when the battle was joined. Soldiers in the Egyptian army did likewise at Carchemish (v 5). The defeat is portrayed as already past, or else as good as already having taken place (thus prophetic perfects).

the day of their disaster. The expression *yôm 'êdām* occurs also in 18:17. Compare 48:16 and 49:32. On the "day of Yahweh" in store for Egypt and other nations, see Note on 46:10.

the time of their reckoning. Hebrew *'ēt pĕquddātām.* A Jeremianic expression; see Note on 6:15.

MESSAGE AND AUDIENCE

This poem begins with the striking image of a horsefly having come from the north to attack one beautiful, beautiful heifer Egypt. The repetition "came, came" nicely echoes "beautiful, beautiful," driving home the point that the uninvited guest did indeed come. The heifer is identified but the horsefly is not. Perhaps some in the audience will recall Isaiah's vision of a fly and a bee coming to attack Judah, and if so, they will discern now a strange turn of events. Isaiah's fly was the army of Egypt. Now that same army has fallen victim to another fly. It will perhaps also be recognized that Babylon is the army currently on the march. Egypt has foreign soldiers in her army, but in living comfortably along the Nile they became something less than fighting bulls. They were more like heifers in the stall—well fed, fat, and ready for slaughter. Whether they were in fact slaughtered is not said, but we are told that Pharaoh's pampered army was fit only to turn and flee the battle, which is pretty much what happened when Egypt faced Babylon at Carchemish. Their day of disaster came.

This poor showing by Egypt and its soft mercenary army—fleeing before a Babylonian foe from the north—points to a battle on Egyptian soil, although the battle in 601–600 b.c. on the Egyptian frontier is perhaps a possibility. The one problem with this latter conflict is that Jeremiah was not speaking publicly during Jehoiakim's last years, which requires for the poem a later date. As for fulfillment, this could come in any of the reported Babylonian incursions into Egypt up until 568 B.C.

c) An Enemy More Numerous than Locusts (46:22–23)

46 ²²Her sound is like a snake going
    indeed with strength they are coming
    yes, with axes they came against her
like those cutting wood

²³They cut down her forest—oracle of Yahweh—
    indeed it was not searched out!
    indeed they were more numerous than locusts
yes, of them there was no number.

RHETORIC AND COMPOSITION

MT 46:22–23 = LXX 26:22–23. This poem is the last of three similarly written and equal in length (four bicolons). It is delimited from the surrounding poetry largely by rhetorical criteria (see Rhetoric and Composition for 46:18–19), although content too points to its original independence. The *nĕ'um yhwh* messenger formula identifies the poem as a divine oracle, making Yahweh the speaker.

The oracle has two nicely balanced stanzas. Both stanzas have the asseverative particle *kî* ("indeed") in the center, with Stanza I repeating also *bĕ* ("with") at the beginning of its center colons. For this repetitional pattern elsewhere in Jeremianic poetry, see Rhetoric and Composition for 6:8–12. Also, in Stanza I the particle *kĕ* ("like") introduces similes at beginning and end, making an inclusio:

I .... *like*	*ka*	v 22
indeed with	*kî bĕ*	
yes, with	*ûbĕ*	
like	*kĕ*	
II		v 23
indeed	*kî*	
indeed	*kî*	
....		

In v 22a the verb *hlk* is repeated, first meaning "go," then "come." Some scholars explain away this repetition, but in doing so they diminish the poetry and create unnecessary problems for interpretation (see Notes). The two stanzas taken together have snake and locust images at beginning and end, and a woodcutter image in the center:

I like a *snake* going	v 22a
with axes ... *those cutting wood*	v 22b

| II | *they cut down her forest* | v 23a |
| | they were more numerous than *locusts* | v 23b |

There is no need with Cornill to relocate 23b in order to go with 22a, which is done simply to bring the snake and locusts together. The oracle is not structured in this fashion.

Catchwords connecting to the prior oracle in vv 20–21:

v 22	*they are coming*		v 20	*came, came*	
	indeed	*kî*	v 21	*came*	
v 23	*Indeed* (2×)	*kî . . . kî*		*indeed* (2×)	*kî . . . kî*

There are no catchwords to the fragment of poetry in v 24.

NOTES

46:22. *Her sound is like a snake going . . . with strength they are coming.* A correct interpretation of this oracle requires a recognition of the play Jeremiah makes on the verb *hlk*, which can mean "to come" (Exod 9:23; 1 Sam 17:41) as well as "to go." One like a snake is going (*yēlēk*), and a host with strength is coming (*yēlēkû*). The two metaphors are thus connected (*pace* Jones). This repetition should not be eliminated with Rudolph and Bright, who defer without reason to an inferior LXX reading. There is, however, a problem with verb tense. The bicolon here has imperfect forms, whereas the rest of the oracle has perfect forms (assuming a Qal perfect at the beginning of v 23, not a future or an imperative, both of which are arguable). The solution adopted is to read the imperfects as timeless presents, setting the stage for what follows. The remainder of the oracle goes on to describe an event that is past or perceived as if it were past (= prophetic perfect).

Her sound is like a snake going. The undeclared subject must be Egypt. Interpretation divides over whether *qôlāh* should be translated "her sound" or "her voice." The LXX reading, *phōnē ōs opheōs surizontos*, "a sound like a hissing snake," almost requires "(her) voice." The idea here would be that a defeated Egypt, perhaps like Jerusalem in Isa 29:4, is heard moaning in a nearly inaudible voice (Cheyne). Calvin says her voice is only a mutter; she is not openly complaining because of fear.

with strength. Hebrew *bĕhayil.* Modern English Versions all have "in force," which is the proper sense. The AV (following T) had "with an army." The LXX has a hissing snake going *en ammō*, "in the sand" (= Heb *bĕḥōl*), a translation that has not been followed.

with axes they came against her. Hebrew *qardummôt* are tools for cutting wood (Judg 9:48; Ps 74:5). The attackers are now seen as having come with axes to do their destructive work in Egypt. They could be pursuing the retreating snake, but their mission may simply be to destroy Egypt's forest. The image could be taken literally, as axes were carried in Assyrian (= Babylonian) chariots of the period (see Note on 4:29). Many MSS read "against you," but MT's "against her" is preferable, assuming that the rest of the oracle continues in the third person (cf. v 23).

like those cutting wood. Hebrew *kĕḥōṭĕbê 'ēṣîm*. Or "like those cutting trees" (cf. NIV; NRSV; REB). The verb *ḥṭb* means to cut or gather firewood.

23. *They cut down her forest.* Reading *kārĕtû* as a Qal perfect, "they cut down" (although both M[L] and M[A] lack the *metheg*), and taking the verb as a prophetic perfect (Kimḥi; Calvin). The LXX has a future, *ekkopsousin*, "they shall cut down," which is adopted in the AV, RSV, JB, NJV, and NIV. Others (J. D. Michaelis 1793: 315; Giesebrecht; Duhm; Cornill; Ehrlich 1912: 355) repoint to a plural imperative, *kirtû*, "Cut down!" (cf. 6:6). This has Yahweh commanding the Babylonians to cut down Egypt's forest. This reading cannot be dismissed out of hand, but the oracle proceeds better if everything is kept in the third person. "Her forest" should probably be interpreted broadly, i.e., referring not only to Egypt's lush growth along the Nile, but to her grand cities with their wood-paneled buildings and the like. The boast of Jerusalem was that its cedar-lined buildings were a "forest of Lebanon" (21:14; 22:6–7, 14–15, 23; cf. 1 Kgs 7:2). Isaiah spoke earlier of Yahweh cutting down forested places on the day of his coming (Isa 2:12–13; 10:18–19, 33–34). For an Egyptian painting showing a man felling a tree with an axe, see *ANEP*[2] 27 #91.

it was not searched out! Hebrew *lō' yēḥāqēr*. The forest was not searched but instead cut down. House to house fighting means more casualties for the attackers, and the Babylonians may well decide to carry out a destruction with less cost to themselves and more cost to Egypt.

they were more numerous than locusts. Hebrew *rabbû mē'arbeh*, which may be a play on words (Carroll). Hebrew *'arbeh* ("locust") is one of twelve words used for "locust" in the OT (cf. Joel 1:4), this particular insect being an adult with wings and thus able to migrate (Exod 10:19). It is a common OT word, often meaning simply "multitudinous." Note the contrast with the one horsefly in v 20. This third image in the oracle then portrays the large number of Babylonian soldiers descending upon Egypt. On locusts in the ancient world and in the OT, including pictures, see Y. Palmoni, "Locust" in *IDB* K–Q, 144–48.

MESSAGE AND AUDIENCE

This oracle begins by comparing the slithering glide of someone going with the strident march of someone coming. The attacked retreats hissing like a snake; the attacker makes its appearance in strength. Neither is identified. A shift is then made to a drama already played out. The attackers are seen as having come with axes, like woodcutters, proceeding to cut down the victim's forest. No search was this! Their numbers were beyond counting, descending like a swarm of locusts.

The oracle makes no mention of Egypt or Babylon, although the audience might see in the images of the snake and the axe-wielding men a drama being played out between these nations. The outcome of the drama is not left in doubt. Wholesale destruction was the goal of the attackers, who are depicted as carrying out something less than selective cutting in a truly grand forest.

Only in the context of the surrounding prophetic utterances are we able to give this oracle any interpretation. Egypt is the one being attacked; the attacker is Nebuchadnezzar and his army. A date for the oracle, as well as a fulfillment, will likely be the same as for the surrounding oracles, i.e., between 605 and 568 B.C., when Babylon first threatened and then actually invaded Egypt. The other Egypt oracles are assigned a date ca. 605 B.C., but the date for this oracle is probably later.

d) Egypt Given Over to a People from the North (46:24–26)

46 [24]Daughter Egypt has been greatly shamed
   she is given into the hand of a people from the north.

[25]Yahweh of hosts, God of Israel, said:
Look I will make a reckoning to Amon of Thebes, and upon Pharaoh, and upon Egypt, and upon her gods, and upon her kings, and upon Pharaoh, and upon those trusting in him. [26]And I will give them into the hand of those who seek their life, and into the hand of Nebuchadrezzar, king of Babylon, and into the hand of his servants.

But afterward she shall dwell as in the days of old—oracle of Yahweh.

RHETORIC AND COMPOSITION

MT 46:24–26 = LXX 26:24–25. The present verses contain a fragment of poetry (v 24) and two oracles in prose (vv 25–26a; v 26b). The poetry closes a group of poems (vv 18–24) delimited on the basis of rhetorical criteria (see Rhetoric and Composition for 46:18–19). Supporting this closure is a *setumah* in M[P] after v 24; there is no section in either M[L] or M[A]. The prose oracles are marked off by messenger formulas, one at the beginning and one at the end. Content too aids in their delimitation. The first oracle is judgment, the second a stereotyped word of restoration. The end of the unit, which is also the end of the Egypt collection, is marked by a *setumah* in M[L], and a *petuḥah* in M[A] and M[P], after v 26.

The fragment of poetry (I) is linked to the first prose oracle (II) by these key words:

I	*she is given into the hand*	*nittĕnâ bĕyad*	v 24
II	*and I will give them into the hand . . .*	*ûnĕtattîm bĕyad . . .*	v 26
	and into the hand . . . and into the hand	*ûbĕyad . . . ûbĕyad*	

Rudolph takes vv 25–26a as later commentary on v 24 (25 = 24a; 26a = 24b), but the verses appear rather to be a divine oracle, beginning as they do with the characteristic "Look I" followed by a participle (see Note on 1:15). The introductory "Yahweh of hosts, God of Israel, said" is not the usual messenger formula; nevertheless it functions here as such and is not a superscription (see Note for 15:11). The LXX omits the formula.

The two oracles, as mentioned, are prose (*pace* NEB and REB), Oracle I being particularly heavy in accumulation. Some scholars (S. R. Driver, Volz, Rudolph, Weiser; Janzen 1973: 118) delete one of the two occurrences of "Pharaoh" as an awkward redundancy, but this may not be necessary. The accumulation looked at as a whole appears to be structured, with the two Pharaohs coming in the second and penultimate positions and Egypt's gods placed climactically at the center:

I   Amon of Thebes   v 25
         and upon *Pharaoh*
            and upon Egypt
               and upon *her gods*
            and upon her kings
         and upon *Pharaoh*
     and upon those trusting in him

Following this sixfold repetition of "upon" (*'al*) is a threefold repetition of "into the hand" (*bĕyad*), which picks up from "into the hand" (*bĕyad*) in v 24:

I   *and upon . . . and upon . . . and upon . . . and upon . . . and upon . . . and upon* v 25
    into the hand . . . and into the hand . . . and into the hand   v 26

Catchwords link the poetry of v 24 to the first Philistine poem in 47:2–5, suggesting that the two were connected before the prose oracles and the salvation oracle for Israel in vv 27–28 were added:

46:24 *the north*   47:2 *from the north*

There are no catchwords connecting back to 46:22–23.

NOTES

46:24. *Daughter Egypt has been greatly shamed*. Hebrew *hōbîšâ* is an internal H-stem: "has been *greatly* shamed." This verb and the one following are prophetic perfects (RSV and NJV translate as future). Egypt's shame (*qālôn*) received mention in v 12. Earlier it was Judah being shamed by Egypt (2:36). On both "shame" in ancient culture and the internal H-stem, see Note for 2:26.

Daughter Egypt. The term occurred earlier in vv 11, 19. For the "daughter" metaphors in Jeremiah, see Kartveit 2001 and Note for 4:11.

she is given into the hand of a people from the north. I.e., Babylon. This may refer to defeat in battle, being taken into exile (v 19), or both. The point is reiterated in the oracle following (v 26a).

25. *Look I will make a reckoning.* Hebrew *hinĕnî pôqēd.* The same Jeremianic expression is used against Babylon in 50:18. The verb *pqd* means "pay a visit, reckon (for the purpose of punishing)" (see Note on 5:9).

Amon of Thebes. Hebrew *'āmôn minnō',* where *nō'* = "Thebes" (cf. Nah 3:8). In Egyptian texts, *niwt 'Imn* means "the city of Amon" (Lambdin, "Thebes" in *IDB* R–Z: 615), suggesting that *nō'* is probably simply "the city." Egypt's god was variously called Amon, Amun, or Amen (meaning "hidden"), and over time was fused with the sun god Rē to become Amon Rē, Amun Rē, or Amen Râ, the imperial god of Egypt. Amon was worshiped primarily at Thebes, which was called "the City of Amon" (*IDB* R–Z: 615–17). The god was usually represented in human form, but sometimes figured with a human body and the head or horns of a ram. Amon survived in classical culture as Jupiter-Ammôn, being equated also with the Greek god Zeus (Herodotus ii 42; LXX of Ezek 30:14, 16). An ancient hymn written to Amen Râ (= Amon Rē) began:

> Praise to Amen Râ!
> To the bull in Heliopolis, to the chief of all the gods
> To the beautiful and beloved god
> Who giveth life by all manner of warmth, by
> All manner of fair cattle
> Hail to thee, Amen Râ, lord of the throne of the two lands
> Dwelling in Thebes
> Husband of his Mother, dwelling in his fields
> Wide-ranging, dwelling in the Land of the South. . . .
> (Wiedemann 1897: 111; cf. *ANET*[3] 365; *CS I* 37–38)

The Versions all had difficulty with "Amon of No." The LXX translated "Amon, her son," which Lambdin says misconstrued *mn'* as *bn'.* The T rendered "noise of Alexandria," where Heb *'āmôn* was read *hāmôn* ("noise, multitude") as in Ezek 30:15, and "No" was taken as Alexandria. The Vg (*tumultum Alexandriae*), AV ("multitude of No"), Rashi, and Calvin all followed T.

Thebes. Hebrew *nō'.* The capital of Upper Egypt from the time of the Middle Kingdom (ca. 2000 B.C.), celebrated in Homer's *Iliad* (ix 381–84) as a city "where treasures in greatest store are laid up . . . a city of a hundred gates from which burst forth through each two hundred warriors with horses and chariots" (Loeb). Thebes was sacked by Assurbanipal in ca. 661 B.C. The impressive monuments surviving at Karnak and Luxor are from ancient Thebes. For pictures, see *IDB* R–Z: 615–16. Ezekiel in one of his Egypt oracles also pronounced judgment on Thebes (Ezek 30:14–16).

and upon Pharaoh, and upon Egypt, and upon her gods, and upon her kings, and upon Pharaoh, and upon those trusting in him. The LXX omission, "and upon Egypt, and upon her gods, and upon her kings, and upon Pharaoh," is not MT expansion (*pace* Bright; Carroll), but very likely more loss due to haplography (whole-word: *wĕʿal . . . wĕʿal;* or two-word: *wĕʿal-parʿōh . . . wĕʿal-parʿōh*).

See Janzen 1973: 118. On the repetition of "Pharaoh," see Rhetoric and Composition.

her gods. Yahweh's punishment of a nation includes the destruction of its idols (43:12–13).

her kings. Hebrew *mĕlākeyhā.* The plural could denote successive kings if the judgment is to be spread out over a period of time; otherwise this is an intensive plural meaning simply "her king" (see Note on 13:13). Calvin takes "kings" as referring to high officials of state: satraps and princes.

those trusting in him. I.e., Pharaoh. Those trusting in the Pharaoh would be first and foremost the Egyptians and expatriates residing in Egypt, but here would include the pro-Egyptian population in Judah (Cornill, Peake, Streane, Weiser, Keown et al.). It is a recurring theme in Isaiah and Jeremiah that Judah's inveterate trust in Pharaoh and the Egyptians is doomed to disappointment (Isa 30:1–7; 31:1; 36:6; Jer 2:18–19, 36; 37:6–10). See also Ezek 29:16.

26. The entire verse is omitted in the LXX, and many regard it as a later insertion (cf. 21:7; 44:30; Janzen 1973: 41–43). But it also could be more loss due to haplography (homoeoarcton: *w . . . w*). Theodotion translates the verse.

And I will give them into the hand of those who seek their life, and into the hand of Nebuchadrezzar, king of Babylon, and into the hand of his servants. Reading the verb as a future. This is a prose version of what is stated in v 24 about Egypt's subjugation, exile, or both.

Nebuchadrezzar. On the spelling, see Note on 21:2. Here it becomes clear, except for what is stated in the superscription of v 13, that Nebuchadrezzar is Egypt's foe from the north.

his servants. I.e., important officials in the employ of the king (see Note for 21:7).

But afterward she shall dwell as in the days of old—oracle of Yahweh. A concluding word about Egypt's restoration once its judgment is past. Compare the restoration oracles for Moab (48:47), Ammon (49:6), and Elam (49:39). Isaiah envisions an Egypt that survives to worship Yahweh and receive—along with Assyria and Israel—Yahweh's blessing (Isa 19:16–25). Ezekiel's restoration word for Egypt is that the nation will not enjoy a return to its former glory, but will remain small and not rule other nations (Ezek 29:13–16). The oracle here is usually taken as an add-on, and it may be, although Dobbs-Allsopp (1993: 92–94, 106–7) has shown how Mesopotamian city laments often contain a concluding word about the city's eventual restoration. The oracle may then be bona fide prophecy, possibly even prophecy spoken by Jeremiah. It is neither compromised nor rendered ingenuine by the claim that Egypt was never depopulated (*pace* McKane, who cites with approval Duhm's gratuitous remark that Egypt was always populated). There will, needless to say, be an exile of some Egyptians.

as in the days of old. Hebrew *kîmê-qedem* (cf. GKC §118u). The term *qedem,* besides its common meaning of "east," can also mean "of old" (BDB, 869; cf. 30:20).

MESSAGE AND AUDIENCE

The fragment of poetry (v 24) is a summary word for the preceding poetry in vv 18–23, stating the end result of an invasion and defeat: Daughter Egypt is shamed, having been given over to a people from the north. The audience will doubtless perceive that the northern people is Babylon, and will know too that with defeat comes death and exile for Egypt's inhabitants (v 19).

Oracle I (vv 25–26a) has Yahweh paying a visit to Egypt and its notables similar to visitations planned for Judah and other nations, including Babylon, the purpose of which is to punish. Amon of Thebes is singled out for special mention, but the list of dignitaries drawn up to meet Yahweh includes Ptah and other gods, Egypt and its royalty, and Pharaoh with all those trusting in him. The Jerusalem audience may detect in the words "all those who put their trust in him" an indirect hit at some within its own ranks who just now are looking for Egyptian help. Calvin thinks too that the emphasis on "Yahweh of hosts" aims the oracle at the prophet's own nation, and is not a threat to the Egyptians.

Read in tandem with the oracles preceding, Oracle I identifies the horsefly from the north (v 24) and the people from the north (v 24) with Nebuchadnezzar and the Babylonians. This oracle also encourages the audience to see in prior oracles the events occurring during the years 609–568 (J. G. Snaith 1971: 30). The present fragment of poetry and two prose oracles fit somewhere within this time frame. Since Jeremiah gave the majority of his Egypt oracles around 605 b.c., an earlier date suggests itself here more than a later date. Oracle II (v 26b) gives a word of hope to Egypt, reminding an early or later audience, or both, that Egypt will once again be inhabited as it was before its inhabitants were killed or carried off into exile (v 19).

4. But Jacob Will Return Home (46:27–28)

46 ^{27}But you, do not you be afraid, Jacob my servant
    and do not you be broken, Israel
For look I will save you from afar
    and your offspring from the land of their captivity
Jacob will return and be undisturbed
    yes, be at ease and none will frighten

^{28}You, do not you be afraid, Jacob my servant
    —oracle of Yahweh—
    for I am with you
For I will make a full end of all the nations
    among which I have dispersed you
But of you I will not make a full end
    Yes, I will correct you justly
        but I will by no means leave you unpunished.

RHETORIC AND COMPOSITION

MT 46:27–28 = LXX 26:27–28. These salvation oracles for Jacob (= Israel) appear with slight variation in 30:10–11, where they answer judgment in a larger liturgical structure. There the LXX omits, as it ocasionally does with duplicated passages in the book. Here the oracles are present in both MT and LXX, and have shown up also in 2QJer. Their independence as a pair is corroborated by section markings at top and bottom. The M^L has *setumahs* before v 27 and after v 28. The M^P has a *petuḥah* before v 27 and a *setumah* after v 28. The M^A in both places has a *petuḥah*. There is also a section in 2QJer after v 28. Dividing the verses at the end of v 27 is a *setumah* in M^L, but this section is absent in M^{A1}, M^P, and 2QJer, as it is also in 30:10–11.

Here the oracles have only one messenger formula in v 28a, whereas in 30:10–11 there are two. But here the beginnings are almost identical:

I   *But you, do not you be afraid, Jacob my servant*   v 27

   . . . .

II   *You, do not you be afraid, Jacob my servant*   v 28

   . . . .

The parallel passage (30:11) lacks the second "You, do not you be afraid, Jacob my servant," but Volz, Rudolph, and Holladay restore the words there. It may be that the longer version with the repetition is more original, but one cannot be sure.

NOTES

46:27–28. See exegesis of 30:10–11.

27. *But you, do not you be afraid, Jacob my servant . . . For look I will save you from afar.* According to Rashi, these words in their present context are addressed to righteous Judahites who have been exiled to Egypt. On this first use of "Jacob my servant" in the OT, see Note for 30:10.

I will save you. Hebrew *môšî'ăkā*. In 2QJer the spelling is *mwšy'kh*, as in 30:10.

28. *You, do not you be afraid, Jacob my servant . . . for I am with you.* This line expands but also differs from the parallel line in 30:11a, which has "for I am with you . . . to save you."

For I will make a full end of all the nations. These words become problematic in the present context because it has just been stated (v 26b) that Egypt will enjoy a future restoration. The same is promised to Moab (48:47), Ammon (49:6), and Elam (49:39), and can be assumed for other nations as well, except Babylon. The problem existed also with respect to Israel, who was brought to a full end, then not brought to a full end. The noun *kālâ* means "(full) end," but not necessarily an absolute end (see Note on 5:10).

---

[1] *HUB* has a *setumah* after v 27, although none exists in M^A.

among which I have dispersed you. Hebrew *'ăšer hiddaḥtîkā šammâ.* In 30:11 the reading is *'ăšer hăpîṣôtîkā šam,* which means the same.

But of you. Hebrew *wĕ'ōtĕkā.* In 30:11 is a stronger *'ak 'ōtĕkā.*

Yes, I will correct you. Hebrew *wĕyissartîkā.* The 2QJer spelling of the suffix is again *kh.*

MESSAGE AND AUDIENCE

These oracles, which speak to questions about return from exile and the end of nations, clear up any ambiguity that might exist in the minds of post-586 B.C. Jewish survivors once they have heard the oracles and other utterances in the Egypt collection, where it is stated that Egypt is destined to fall into the hands of Nebuchadnezzar and its citizens are to be cut down in battle or carried away into exile. Not a few Judahites went to Egypt following the destruction of Jerusalem, Jeremiah himself being one of them. It apparently needed to be affirmed at this juncture that Israel would be saved from exile—whether to Egypt, Babylon, or somewhere else—and as a people would survive. These oracles make such an affirmation. Mercenary soldiers have left Egypt for home, and the Egyptians themselves face involuntary exile to a foreign power. But Jacob, Yahweh's chosen servant, will return home and will survive, whatever happens to other nations whose glory crumbles into dust and ruins.

The date of composition for these oracles could be early, during Josiah's reign even, when Jeremiah was looking for the return of people from Northern Israel who had been exiled to Assyria. But in the post-586 B.C. period, they are addressed to survivors from both Israel and Judah.

C. A DAY FOR YAHWEH AGAINST THE PHILISTINES (47:1–7)

47 ¹What came as the word of Yahweh to Jeremiah the prophet, to the Philistines before Pharaoh struck down Gaza.

²Thus said Yahweh:

Look, waters are rising from the north
  and have become an overflowing torrent
They will overflow the land in its entirety
  the city and those living in it
The people cry out
  everyone living in the land wails

³At the sound of the stamping hoofs of his stallions
  at the clatter of his chariotry, the rumbling of its wheels
Fathers do not turn to children
  for weakness of hands

[4]Because of the day that has come to devastate
   everyone of the Philistines
To cut off for Tyre and for Sidon
   every survivor, helper

For Yahweh is devastating the Philistines
   remnant of the island of Caphtor
[5]Baldness has come to Gaza
   Ashkelon is silenced
   remnant of their strength
How long will you slash yourselves?

[6]Woe! sword of Yahweh!
   how much longer before you are idle?
Gather yourself into[1] your sheath
   rest and be silent

[7]But how can you be idle?
   when Yahweh has commanded it
toward Ashkelon and toward the seacoast
   there he has assigned it.

RHETORIC AND COMPOSITION

MT Chapter 47 = LXX Chapter 29. In this brief chapter are brought together two poems against the Philistines, vv 2–5 and vv 6–7, preceded by a scribal introduction in v 1. Many take the poetry to be a single poem, which it could be. But a break between vv 5 and 6 is indicated by a *setumah* in M[L] and M[P] after v 5, although neither 2QJer nor M[A] has a section here. Whether there are two poems or one poem dividing into two (Carroll), a break cannot be made between 5a and 5b as Holladay does, as this builds on the mistaken notion that v 5b belongs with v 6.

The one messenger formula beginning v 2 suggests that only the first poem is a divine oracle. Verses 6–7 are best taken as a soliloquy by the prophet (Mc-Kane). They may also be a feigned lament (Weiser: "einer bewegten klage"). The pattern is familiar from Jeremiah's utterances against Judah: a divine word from Yahweh, then a response by the prophet. Peake says another dialogue is going on within vv 6–7: a cry of the Philistines in v 6, and an answer from the prophet in v 7. But it seems rather that Jeremiah is the speaker throughout, addressing the sword in v 6 with a question it cannot answer, then in v 7 providing the answer himself. The irony of v 6 is lost if spoken by the Philistines.

The unit as a whole is delimited at the top end by a *setumah* in M[L] and M[P], and a *petuḥah* in M[A], prior to v 1, which is also the chapter break. The lower limit is marked by a *setumah* in M[L] and a *petuḥah* in M[A] and M[P] after v 7,

---

[1]Reading *'el* with many MSS; MT has the negative *'al*.

which is another chapter break. A section after v 7 may also be present in the reconstructed 2QJer, although Baillet fails to mention this in his notes. The introduction is set off in M^L and M^P by a *setumah* after v 1; 2QJer and M^A do not have sections here.

The oracle (vv 2–5) has three stanzas with a line division of 3:4:3. It begins with the familiar Jeremianic *hinnēh* ("Look!"), and concludes with a rhetorical *'ad-mātay*, "How long?" (5b). A reversed *mātay 'ōd*, "how much longer?" concludes a divine speech in 13:27. Commentators are generally agreed that this poetry is Jeremianic. Duhm and Volz denied Jeremianic authorship, but this was part of a larger misapprehension on their part that the Foreign Nation Oracles in the book must come from another source. Even Mowinckel (1914: 66), who shared the view that the Foreign Nation Oracles were largely of anonymous origin, said that Jeremiah may have had a hand in composing this oracle and the one following. Other prophets delivered oracles against the Philistines; see Amos 1:6–8; Isa 14:29–31; Zeph 2:4–7; and Ezek 25:15–17.

Both poems contain repetition and balancing key words. Stanza I of the oracle contains a key word at the end of line 1 that is picked up by a cognate at the beginning of line 2 (*anadiplosis*):

| I | . . . . *an overflowing* torrent | *šôṭēp* | v 2a |
| | *They will overflow* . . . . | *wĕyišṭĕpû* | v 2b |

For other examples of *anadiplosis* in Jeremianic poetry, see Note for 22:20; also Rhetoric and Composition for 51:27–33.

Final lines in the stanza contain this balance:

I	. . . .		v 2b
	the city and those living in it	*'îr wĕyōšĕbê bāh*	
	. . . .		v 2c
	everyone living in the land . . .	*kōl yôšēb hā'āreṣ*	

Stanza II repeats *kōl* at the end of its two final lines:

II	. . . .		v 4a
	everyone of the Philistines	*kol-*	
	. . . .		v 4b
	every survivor, helper	*kōl*	

Stanza III nicely balances its first and last lines:

III	. . . .		v 4c
	remnant of the island of Caphtor	*šĕ'ērît*	
	. . . .		v 5a
	. . . .		
	remnant of their strength	*šĕ'ērît*	v 5b
	. . . .		

In v 5 is also a key word chiasmus (see Notes).

Stanzas I and II are linked together by the substantive *kōl*, "every(one)":

I	*everyone* living in the land	*kōl*	v 2c
II	*everyone* of the Philistines	*kol-*	v 4a
	every survivor, helper	*kōl*	v 4b

Linkage between Stanzas II and III is created by the verb *šdd*, "to devastate":

II	Because of the day that has come *to devastate* everyone of the Philistines	*lišdôd* v 4a
III	For Yahweh *is devastating* the Philistines	*šōdēd* v 4c

The second poem (vv 6–7) is four lines dividing into two stanzas. Stanzas I and II have the following key words in their opening lines, which are also nicely inverted (Condamin):

I	Woe! sword *of Yahweh*		v 6a
	how much longer before *you are idle?*	*tišqōṭî*	
II	But how *can you be idle?*	*tišqōṭî*	v 7a
	when *Yahweh* has commanded it		

The two poems have these key words binding them together:

I	Yahweh		v 4c
	Ashkelon		v 5a
	is silenced	*nidmĕtâ*	
	How *long* will you slash yourselves?	*'ad-mātay*	v 5b
II	Yahweh		v 6a
	how much *longer* before you are idle?	*'ad-'ānâ*	
	be silent	*wādōmmî*	v 6b
	Yahweh		v 7a
	Ashkelon		v 7b

Catchwords connecting 47:2–5 to 46:24, before the Judah poem in 46:27–28 was added, are the following:

47:2 *from the north*	46:24 *the north*

Catchwords connecting to the next poem in 48:1–2 are the following:

47:4 *to devastate . . . is devastating*	48:1 *woe*
47:6 *woe*	*it is devastated*

NOTES

47:1. *What came as the word of Yahweh to Jeremiah the prophet, to the Philistines before Pharaoh struck down Gaza.* A scribal superscription placing the following prophetic utterance in a historical context. The LXX simply has *epi tous allophulous* ("on the other tribes"), which many scholars (Duhm; Volz; Weiser; Rudolph; Janzen 1973: 114; Holladay), consider to be original. Compare "to Egypt" (46:2); "to Moab" (48:1); "to the sons of Ammon" (49:1); etc. However, the LXX omission of *'ăšer hāyâ dĕbar-yhwh 'el-yirmĕyāhû hannābî'* ("What came as the word of Yahweh to Jeremiah, the prophet") can be explained as a loss due to haplography (homoeoarcton: *'aleph . . . 'aleph*). Aquila and Symm have the words. Giesebrecht thought the LXX may have suffered from omission, and more recently the merits of the shorter LXX text as explained by Janzen have been questioned by Soderlund (1985: 208–11). Katzenstein (1983: 250) sees the historical reference as being authentic, adding that it could derive from Baruch ca. 600 B.C. For the longer superscription, see 46:1; 49:34; cf. 14:1.

the Philistines. The LXX has *tous allophulous* ("the other tribes"), which recurs in v 4. As a designation for the Philistines in the LXX, see elsewhere 32:20 [= MT 25:20]; Amos 1:8; and Zeph 2:5.

before Pharaoh struck down Gaza. The subject of much discussion because 1) neither the Bible nor the Babylonian texts record any attack on Gaza by an Egyptian pharaoh at the end of the seventh century or beginning of the sixth century B.C.; and 2) the oracle following describes the Babylonians, the "waters rising from the north" (v 2), who are about to silence Ashkelon and bring mourning to Gaza (v 5). If the historical reference is to be accepted at face value—which not everyone will grant—the mourning of Gaza in the oracle must be disassociated from the attack on Gaza in the superscription, and the latter taken to be a separate event brought in simply for the purpose of establishing relative chronology. Gaza, then, must have come under attack twice—once from the Babylonians and once from Egypt (Kimḥi). This is not unreasonable, as Judah suffered precisely the same fate (in reverse order) between 609 and 597 B.C. Like Jerusalem, Gaza was doubtless forced to shift loyalties during the years Egypt and Babylon struggled for control of the coastal region—indeed for all the territory "from the brook of Egypt to the river Euphrates" (2 Kgs 24:7). Between 604 and 600 B.C. a war between these superpowers took place before Gaza's very eyes. The question then is which Pharaoh might have attacked Gaza, and when could he have done so? Of the various proposals made, the one most convincing envisions Neco II attacking Gaza ca. 600 B.C., when the pharaoh moved to reestablish his authority over the coastal region after a Babylonian show of strength in 604 B.C. (Bright; Katzenstein 1983; 1994: 43). In 604 Nebuchadnezzar destroyed Ashkelon and Ekron. Gaza in all likelihood came under Babylonian control at this time. A cuneiform text lists a "king of Gaza" among Nebuchadnezzar's prisoners in Babylon (ANET³ 308). In 601–600 B.C., however, Neco gained a qualified victory following a pitched battle with Nebuchadnezzar, and the Babylonians were obliged to return home (BM 21946: rev. 6–7; Wiseman 1956: 70–71; Bright 1981: 327). If Gaza had sworn loyalty to Nebuchadnezzar in 604, as Jehoiakim in Judah was required to do (2 Kgs 24:1), it would now be time for Neco—who controlled Gaza at the beginning of his reign—to punish the city for disloyalty and bring it back within Egypt's sphere of influence.

There is also a report in Herodotus (ii 159) that Neco "with his land army met and defeated the Syrians at Magdolus, taking the great Syrian city of Cadytis after the battle" (Loeb). Now, if 1) "the Syrians" refer here to Babylonians and/or their mercenaries (Katzenstein (1983); 2) "Magdolus" is to be equated with the Egyptian border town of "Migdol" (Lipinski 1972; Oren 1984: 34) at the time Gaza was still an Egyptian vassal, and not Megiddo, as argued by many scholars (Hitzig; Cornill; Peake; Malamat 1950: 221; 1950–51: 154–55; Holladay; McKane), who connect the attack on Gaza with the events of 609 B.C.; and 3) Cadytis is equated with Gaza (Hitzig), then we have independent confirmation of an attack by Neco on Gaza ca. 600 B.C. All these identifications have been debated; nevertheless, the reference may still have merit. Elsewhere Herodotus (iii 5) locates Cadytis as a far southern city on the coastal road from Phoenicia to Egypt, saying that it "belongs to the Syrians of Palestine." The statement in 2 Kgs 24:7 that Egypt's pharaoh did not come out of his land once Babylon had established control "from the brook of Egypt to the river Euphrates" refers not to 601–600 B.C., when Egypt sent Babylon home in defeat, but to the Babylonian campaign of 598–597 B.C., when Jerusalem was forced to surrender to Nebuchadnezzar. Jehoiakim's death, occurring in December 598, is mentioned just prior in the biblical text (2 Kgs 24:6). Early in the reign of Zedekiah, when a conspiracy against Babylon was being discussed in Jerusalem (27:3), Philistia was unrepresented. If, then, the poems introduced by this note were spoken *before* Pharaoh attacked Gaza, we can date them without difficulty to ca. 604 B.C.

2. *Thus said Yahweh.* 2QJer has the spelling *kwh* ("thus"); MT: *kōh*.

waters are rising from the north. The T: "peoples are coming from the north" (cf. 6:22). The reference is to Babylon, the foe coming to destroy cities of the Philistines. On the "foe from the north," see Note on 1:14. Jeremiah speaks here a traditional curse on the flooding of a land as punishment for treaty violation. In the Esarhaddon treaty (488–489) is this curse:

May a flood, an irresistible deluge, rise from the
bowels of the earth and devastate you.
                    (*ANET*³ 539; Hillers 1964: 70)

In 51:42 Jeremiah uses sea imagery to describe the judgment slated for Babylon, adding in v 44: "the nations will not *stream* to him [i.e., Nebuchadnezzar] any longer." See Egypt's boast in 46:8, also Amos 5:24; Isa 8:6–8; Nah 1:8; and Ezek 26:19.

and have become an overflowing torrent. Hebrew *wĕhāyû lĕnaḥal šôṭēp*. A *naḥal* is a stream or wadi that becomes a virtual torrent in rainy season. In Isa 30:28 it describes Yahweh's indignation. The "waters rising out of the north" will come and overflow the land of Philistia. The verb *šṭp* is used to describe a horse running headlong into battle in Jer 8:6. Isaiah uses the same verb to describe the "waters of Assyria" coming to overflow Judah (Isa 8:8).

They will overflow the land in its entirety, the city and those living in it. The T again eliminates the flood imagery: "and they shall plunder the land and its fullness." "Land" and "city" (without the definite articles in Hebrew) are poetic correlatives meaning "everything." Giesebrecht takes *'ereṣ* to mean "the whole earth," but this is unwarranted even in light of *hā'ādām* ("the people") in the next line. Weiser and Rudolph have "land." The language echoes 8:16: "the land in its entirety, the city and those living in it." Verbs alternate in the verse between perfect and imperfect, but action is expected in the (near) future.

city. Hebrew *'îr* is singular. Giesebrecht and others take as a collective, i.e., "(the) cities." *Mezudath David* says "every city and its inhabitants." The poet appears to deliberately balance "land" and "city"; in the next bicolon it is "the people" and "the land," both terms having the definite article.

and those living in it. 2QJer appears to spell [*wy*]*w*[*šby*], i.e., with the full *holem* vowel letter; the MT: *wĕyōšĕbê*.

The people cry out; everyone living in the land wails. The two verbs *z'q* and *yll* (H-stem) occur together in 25:34; 48:20, 31, and often elsewhere (see Note for 25:34). The verb *z'q* actually means "cry out for help." Here the loud crying comes from a frightened people anticipating disaster. A letter in diplomatic Aramaic found in 1942 at Saqqârah (Memphis), Egypt, may possibly reflect the real-life panic felt in Philistia as the Babylonian army headed their way in 604 B.C. The letter was written by a certain Adon, who, in the name of a Canaanite deity, Baalshemain, calls for help from the Pharaoh. The Babylonian army, he says, has already reached Aphek (Dupont-Sommer 1948; H. L. Ginsberg 1948; Bright 1949; Porten 1981; Kuhrt 1995: 591). Adon was king of a city on the coastal highway, but the text is broken precisely where we expect the city's name to occur. Albright (1956: 31 n. 14), Ginsberg, and Bright thought the city was probably Ashkelon, although others, e.g., D. W. Thomas (1950), and more recently McKane, have preferred a location in Phoenicia. Of the numerous Apheks in the Bible, there is one city by this name in Phoenicia, east of Byblos (Josh 13:4), and another identified with Tell Ras el-ʿAin in the Sharon Plain, about 32 kilometers north of Ekron (Josh 12:18; 1 Sam 4:1; 29:1). A Philistine location for both Aphek and the city of Adon would put the letter in the period we are dealing with here, i.e., 604, when Nebuchadnezzar came to Philistia and destroyed Ashkelon and Ekron. A Phoenician location for the cities would put it later, i.e., ca. 587, when Nebuchadnezzar appeared in northern Syria on his way to take Jerusalem (D. W. Thomas 1950: 13). Malamat (1950: 222), too, for different reasons, dates the letter in 599–598 B.C. Porten (1981: 43–45) has reexamined the papyrus and found a demotic line on the reverse side written by an Egyptian court official, which is deciphered to read "what the Prince (?) of Ekron gave to (?). . . ." This leads him to conclude that Adon was king of Ekron. If this be the case, then the letter was written as the Babylonians approached Ekron in 604 B.C. Egyptian help apparently did not come, for the city was destroyed. On the text of "King Adon's Appeal to Pharaoh," see also Miller and Hayes 1986: 386.

the people. Hebrew *hā'ādām* requires a meaning broader than "the man." RSV: "men."

3. *At the sound of the stamping hoofs of his stallions, at the clatter of his chariotry, the rumbling of its wheels.* The stanza begins with *miqqôl* ("At the sound"), a common beginning to both poems and stanzas of poems in Jeremiah (see Note for 3:21). Jeremiah shifts here from the figurative to the literal. The northern foe is now a noisy army, the unspecified antecedent of "his" being Nebuchadnezzar. With similar imagery Jeremiah depicts the Babylonian army approaching Judah (4:13, 29; 6:22–23). Compare also Isa 5:28–29. Sounds of galloping horses and rumbling chariot wheels have as modern counterparts the sounds of warplanes overhead and tanks on the ground.

the stamping hoofs of his stallions. Hebrew *'abbîrîm* (lit. "mighty ones") means "stallions," as in 8:16; 50:11; and Judg 5:22. Elsewhere it can mean "mighty men" or "bulls" (see Note for 46:15). The term *ša'ăṭat* is a *hapax legomenon* in the OT, generally taken to mean "stamping." Kimḥi defines the image as one of galloping horses. Calvin similarly.

at the clatter of his chariotry. Hebrew *mēra'aš* ("clatter") is the verb translated "quaking" in 4:24. On chariots of the period, see Note on 4:29.

the rumbling of its wheels. Hebrew *hămōn galgillāyw*. Chariot wheels make a loud noise, creating also a whirlwind of dust with their spin (4:13; Isa 5:28). The term *hāmōn* is used often by the prophets to describe impending chaos.

Fathers do not turn to children. I.e., to help them. Fathers (and mothers) quite naturally help children in a crisis, but not here. In the crisis of a drought, Jeremiah sees a doe forsaking her calf (14:5). Dobbs-Allsopp (1993: 41, 133–34) has shown that fathers and mothers turning away from their children is a common motif in the Mesopotamian laments. Two examples from the "Lament over the Destruction of Ur" (cf. *ANET*[3] 459):

The mother left before her child's eyes	LU 233
The father turned away from his son	LU 234

Other laments bewail parents leaving children, husbands and wives their spouses, and animals their young (M. E. Cohen 1988: 138, 166).

for weakness of hands. Here is the reason for the fathers' inattentiveness to their children. It is not because they are trying to save their own lives, which could be happening, but because they are paralyzed and can do nothing (cf. 6:24; 50:43). Hebrew *mēripyôn yādāyim* is lit. "for the sinking of (their) hands." Hebrew *ripyôn* ("weakness, slackness") is a *hapax legomenon* in the OT, but comes from an attested verb *rph*, meaning "to drop, become limp." Weakness of hands may also signify a loss of courage (cf. 38:4). On "hands becoming weak" and "knees trembling / going to water," see Isa 13:7; Nah 2:11[Eng 2:10]; and Ezek 7:17.

4. *Because of the day that has come to devastate everyone of the Philistines.* A "day of Yahweh" awaits the Philistines, even as one awaits Egypt (46:10, 21),

Moab (48:41), Edom (49:22), Damascus (49:26), and Babylon (50:27, 30, 31). See further the Note on 4:9. Here the day itself is personified as the destroyer.

everyone of the Philistines. 2QJer spells "Philistines" with double *yod.* In 25:20 Yahweh's judgment is said to be determined for "all the kings of the land of the Philistines, that is, Ashkelon, and Gaza, and Ekron, and the remnant of Ashdod." Nebuchadnezzar brought an effective end to the Philistines, who had occupied the coastland west of Judah since the twelfth century B.C. Their tenure in Canaan was roughly the same as that of ancient Israel. Those surviving the onslaught were exiled to Babylon. Babylonian ration texts list the king of Gaza; the king of Ashdod; two sons of Aga', king of Ashkelon; and three mariners, eight officials, and some chief musicians from Ashkelon (Weidner 1939: 928; *ANET*[3] 308).

To cut off for Tyre and for Sidon every survivor, helper. Tyre and Sidon are coastal cities farther north in Phoenicia (modern Lebanon). The sense here is that both cities will be deprived of Philistine help should they need it, because the Philistines will be destroyed. Rashi says the Philistines were aiding Tyre and Sidon; Kimḥi says Tyre and Sidon were aiding the Philistines. It has therefore been assumed that a political alliance of some sort must have existed between Phoenicia and Philistia. There certainly was trade back and forth. American archaeologists digging at Ashkelon found in the destruction level attributed to Nebuchadnezzar numerous Phoenician artifacts, indicating a lively trade between the Philistines and the Phoenicians during the period (Stager 1996: 66–67). Philistia and Tyre are mentioned together in Ps 83:8[Eng 83:7], also in Joel 4:4[Eng 3:4]. The LXX goes even further in the present text, saying, "and I shall obliterate Tyre and Sidon and all those remaining of their allies." T similarly: "to destroy Tyre and Sidon." Graf, Duhm, and others have therefore taken the present oracle to be also against Tyre and Sidon, who are promised judgment in 25:22. Amos, Isaiah, and Ezekiel all deliver judgment oracles against Tyre, or Tyre and Sidon (Amos 1:9–10; Isa 23:1–8; Ezek 28:1–23). Sidon submitted to Nebuchadnezzar before the final destruction of Jerusalem. P. J. King (1993: 34) says it was while Nebuchadnezzar was on the way. The Babylonian king's 13–year siege of Tyre (Josephus, *Ant* x 228; *Against Apion* i 144) is probably to be dated from 585 to 573 ("Tyre" in *ABD* 6: 690; P. J. King 1993: 34), although an earlier date of 603–590 B.C. has also been argued (Wiseman 1985: 27–28). However, both Tyre and Sidon are represented in Jerusalem when a revolt is being planned against Babylon early in Zedekiah's reign, 594 B.C. (27:1–3; cf. 28:1). Nebuchadnezzar, in any event, succeeded finally in capturing all but the island portion of Tyre.

To cut off. The M^L and M^A have *lĕhakrît* ("to cut off"); 2QJer has *whkrty* ("and cut off"), which Baillet says = LXX. The verse with a compound predicate would read:

Because of the day that has come to devastate
   everyone of the Philistines

and cut off for Tyre and for Sidon
    every survivor, helper.

Admittedly, this reading could be interpreted to mean that Tyre and Sidon will
be besieged or in some other way cut off from help in the face of an enemy attack; nevertheless, the MT reading is the *lectio difficilior* and should probably
be accepted.

Tyre. 2QJer spells *ṣwr* (with the full *ḥolem* vowel letter); MT has *ṣōr*.

every survivor, helper. Hebrew *kōl śārîd ʿōzēr.* I.e., there will be no survivor or
helper for Tyre and Sidon once Philistia has been destroyed.

For Yahweh is devastating the Philistines, remnant of the island of Caphtor. In
v 4a it was the "day" coming to destroy the Philistines; now we find out that the
destroyer is Yahweh (cf. Ezek 25:16). In 20:14–18 is a progression from "the
day" to "the man who brought my father the news," to "[Yahweh], who did not
kill [Jeremiah] in the womb" (see discussion there). Here it is important to note
that no reason is given for Yahweh's judgment upon the Philistines (Clements).
The Philistines were not bound to Yahweh by covenant, as was the case with Israel, but neither are they cited here for any wrongdoing. Other nations are
punished because of their wickedness (25:31), pride (50:31–32), violence done
to the covenant people and to Jerusalem (51:35), and because they trusted in
their own gods (50:38; 51:47, 52).

the Philistines. The LXX omits, but the term is translated by Symm and
Theod. This could be a clarifying gloss (so Giesebrecht; Duhm; Janzen 1973:
59, 210 n. 67; Holladay; McKane), although Rudolph, Weiser, and Bright retain. The repetition is not the problem. We have a nonpoetic *nota accusativi,*
although the same is present in an earlier occurrence of the term in 4a.

remnant of the island of Caphtor. Hebrew *ʾî* might also be translated "coastland" (25:22; Isa 20:6). 2QJer has the plural *ʾyy kptor,* "islands of Caphtor"
(cf. 2:10), whereas the LXX (29:4) contains simply "the islands" (*tōn nēsōn* =
hāʾîyîm). "Caphtor" is translated by Aq and Theod. In Deut 2:23 and Amos 9:7
the LXX translates "Caphtor" as "Cappadocia," as do the other Versions in
those passages and also here. Caphtor ("Keftiu" in the Egyptian texts; "Kap-
tara" in the cuneiform tablets), is usually identified with the island of Crete,
which is probably what is meant here. Cretans most likely are the "Cherethites" of the OT (1 Sam 30:14; Ezek 25:16; Zeph 2:5), a people associated in
the Bible with the Philistines but possibly a separate group of Sea Peoples living southeast of Philistia (J. C. Greenfield, "Cherethites and Pelethites" in
IDB A–D: 557; cf. 1 Sam 30:14: "the Negeb of the Cherethites"). Cappadocia
is an inland country in the heart of Asia Minor (modern Turkey), although
Wainwright (1956a; 1956b) argues that when the LXX was translated Greater
Cappadocia, having expanded southward, possessed a coastline. According to
Amos 9:7, Caphtor was the original homeland of the Philistines. See also the
Table of Nations in Gen 10:14 (= 1 Chr 1:12).

5. *Gaza . . . Ashkelon.* Two of originally five principal Philistine cities: Ekron, Ashdod, Ashkelon, Gath, and Gaza. Gath (possibly Tell eṣ-Ṣafi) was de-

stroyed by Sargon II of Assyria in 711 B.C. (*ANET*³ 286; *CS II* 297; cf. "Gath" in *ABD* 2: 909), and is last mentioned in the Bible in Mic 1:10. Only four Philistine cities are listed in Amos 1:6–8 (although see 6:2); Zeph 2:4; Jer 25:20; and Zech 9:5. Ashdod (Tel Ashdod, ca. 6 kilometers south of modern Ashdod) has Iron II destruction, which could be attributed to Josiah's late seventh-century expansion of Judah's borders, at which time he built a fortress at Joppa (Bright 1981: 317), or to the campaign of Nebuchadnezzar when he came to Philistia in 604–600 B.C. (D. N. Freedman 1963c: 139; cf. *NEAEHL* 1: 100). Ekron (Tel Miqne, ca. 35 kilometers southwest of Jerusalem) is known from excavations to have been a large olive oil and textile production center in the seventh century (Gitin 1990: 279–80; 1995: 63–69; 1997: 84–93; *NEAEHL* 3: 1051–59; P. J. King 1993: 20), and was destroyed by Nebuchadnezzar ca. 604 B.C. (Gitin 1998: 276; Gitin and Golani 2001: 30).

Baldness has come to Gaza. Shaving the head and slashing the body (v 5b) are ancient mourning rites, on which see Notes for 7:29 and 16:6. Moab will so mourn in its day of calamity (48:37). The 80 men arriving at Mizpah from Northern Israel after the fall of Jerusalem had beards shaven, clothes torn, and bodies slashed (41:5). The present action on the part of Gaza's inhabitants, anticipated here with a prophetic perfect, is in response to an attack on the city that will leave many people dead. T has: "punishment has come to the inhabitants of Gaza." The actual attack may have come when the Babylonians overran Philistia in 604 B.C. Gaza, however, was not completely destroyed as was Ashkelon and Ekron, for it was retaken by the Egyptians ca. 601–600 B.C. (v 1). Identified with Tell Kharubeh (= Tell ʿAzza), ca. 5 kilometers inland on the coastal highway (P. J. King 1993: 34; *NEAEHL* 2: 464), Gaza was the southernmost city of the Philistine Pentapolis. Nebuchadnezzar eventually made it a Babylonian garrison town, and from cuneiform texts we learn that the king of Gaza was receiving rations along with kings of other coastal cities imprisoned in Babylon (*ANET*³ 308).

Ashkelon is silenced. Hebrew *nidmĕtâ ʾašqĕlôn*. A euphemism for complete destruction or death; see Note on 8:14. The LXX has *aperriphē*, "is cast aside," which appears to have mistaken *resh* for *dalet* and read Hebrew *nirmĕtâ* (from *rmh*). Ashkelon is 19 kilometers north of Gaza and 16 kilometers south of Ashdod on the coastal highway. According to the Babylonian Chronicle, the city was destroyed by Nebuchadnezzar in 604 B.C. (BM 21946: obv. 18–20; Wiseman 1956: 28, 68–69). Babylonian ration lists include as prisoners in Babylon two sons of Agaʾ, king of Ashkelon, and mariners, officials, and chief musicians from Ashkelon (Weidner 1939: 928). The ancient site, which occupies 150 acres, has been excavated since 1985 by Lawrence Stager and a team from Harvard, who have uncovered evidence for a Babylonian destruction in the winter of 604 B.C. (see Note for 25:20).

remnant of their strength. Hebrew *šĕʾērît ʿimqām*. The problematic term here is *ʿimqām*, which the AV translated legitimately enough as "their valley." Some recent translations (NJV; NIV; NJB) have stayed with the same basic rendering, but others (RSV; JB; NSB) and the majority of commentators (Giesebrecht;

Duhm; Peake; Volz; Condamin; Rudolph; Holladay; McKane) emend to
"Anakim" (*Enakim* = giants), the reading of the LXX (Josh 11:22; cf. 2 Sam
21:18–22). This latter reading, however, is rightly abandoned in the NRSV
and NJB. The T reads "the remnant of their strength," which is now the preferred translation (NEB; NAB; NRSV and REB) since ʿmq is known to have
the meaning "strength, force" (G. R. Driver 1950: 61; Dahood 1959: 166;
Bright). Driver cites Akk *emūqu*, "force, strength," and Ug *b-ʿmq*, "with
force, with vigor"; cf. *UT* 457 #1874. Dahood gives the term this meaning
also in 49:4, which is less convincing. The phrase as a whole stands in apposition to Ashkelon (Graf), so the meaning is that Ashkelon is the remnant of
Philistine strength. The phrase is not to be translated as a vocative (as in the
RSV and NJV), which connects it with the second person in the next colon.
The entire verse is a chiasmus: Gaza at the extremes will be shaving the
head and slashing the body; remnant Ashkelon's demise is anticipated in the
center:

> Baldness has come to *Gaza*
> > *Ashkelon* is silenced
> > remnant of their strength (i.e., *Ashkelon*)
> How long will you (i.e., *Gaza*) slash yourselves?

In 25:20 the phrase "remnant of Ashdod" (*šěʾērît ʾašdôd*) occurs, but that does
not justify the insertion of "Ashdod" here (*pace* Condamin; Rudolph; JB;
NAB). NJB rightly abandons the JB reading.

How long will you slash yourselves? The MT has *titgôdādî* ("slash yourselves"); 2QJer has *ttgwrry* (Hithpolel from *grr*, "to whirl about"?), which misreads *resh* for *dalet*, and may also be connecting this colon to v 6a. The break,
however, comes here at the end of v 5 (*pace* Holladay; see Rhetoric and Composition). The MT is to be followed. For *gdd* in the Hithpolel meaning "slash
oneself," see 16:6; 41:5; Deut 14:1; and 1 Kgs 18:28. The slashing here goes
with making the head bald in 5a, and Gaza will be doing both. Jeremiah asks
ironically for how long?

How long? Hebrew ʿad-mátay. A term of lament, on which see Notes for 4:21
and 23:26.

6. *Woe! sword of Yahweh! how much longer before you are idle?* The LXX lacks
"woe" (*hôy*), which could be due to haplography (homoeoteleuton: *y . . . y*).
Aquila and Symm have the term (*ō*). For more sword imagery, see 50:35–37.
Jeremiah begins his speech with apostrophe (Calvin). Blayney thinks the Babylonian king is being addressed (cf. Isa 10:5: "Woe, Assyria, rod of my anger"),
but the prophet is more likely addressing the sword. In 2:12 he speaks directly
to the heavens, and in 22:29 to the land. There is also unmistakable irony here,
for the implication is that the sword is going to be active a good long while. If
the words are taken as a cry from the Philistines (Peake; Boadt), the irony is
lost. On *hôy* ("woe") as as an expression wavering between lament and invective, see Note for 22:13.

sword of Yahweh. Hebrew *ḥereb yhwh*. The expression (with *layhwh*) occurs elsewhere in 12:12 and Judg 7:20. For Yahweh being the ultimate destroyer of the Philistines, see v 4.

how much longer? Or "until when?" Hebrew *'ad-'ānâ*. The more usual expression is *'ad mātay*, occurring in v 5.

Gather yourself into your sheath. The N-stem imperative, *hē'āsĕpî* ("gather yourself"), has the sense here of "withdraw" (Isa 60:20). The LXX has *apokatastēthi eis ton koleon sou* ("Be restored into your sheath"), which is a near-quotation of Ezek 21:35[Eng 21:30]. Elsewhere in Jeremiah *'sp* in the N-stem imperative means "Gather together!" (4:5; 8:14). The MT *'al* ("not") is unexplainable, and should be repointed with many MSS to *'el* ("into").

sheath. Hebrew *ta'ar* has this meaning also in Ezek 21:8–10[Eng 21:3–5], although elsewhere the noun means "razor" or "knife" (Isa 7:20; Jer 36:23; Ps 52:4[Eng 52:2]).

rest and be silent. Hebrew *hērāgĕ'î wādōmmî*. The verb *rg'* in the H-stem occurs in 31:2 and 50:34. The verb *dmm* appeared earlier in v 5, and is a common Jeremianic word. 2QJer has the spelling *wdwmy* (with the full *ḥolem* vowel letter). In one of the Mesopotamian city laments for a city besieged in wartime, the recurring refrain is "When will it be silent?" (M. E. Cohen 1988: 493).

7. *But how can you be idle, when Yahweh has commanded it?* The MT *tišqōtî* ("can you be idle") repeats intentionally from v 6a. It is the *lectio difficilior*, but can nevertheless be read once it becomes clear that the pronoun "it" (*lāh*) in the following colon does not refer to the sword, but to destruction carried out by the sword. Jeremiah is answering his own question (*hypophora*), asking the sword rhetorically how it can stop its reign of terror when Yahweh has commanded the destruction. On *hypophora*, see Note for 49:7. The modern Versions and most all commentators follow the LXX, S, and Vg and emend to the third person, assuming that the third person in the next colon is a reference to the sword. McKane concedes that this shift of person may in fact be "allowable licence," but in the end he joins the consensus and emends.

toward Ashkelon and toward the seacoast. "The seacoast" (*ḥôp hayyām*) refers here to cities on the Philistine coast. See also Ezek 25:16. Mighty Ashkelon will be the great casualty (v 5), but other coastal cities will also suffer destruction and loss of life.

there he has assigned it. Hebrew *šām yĕ'ādāh*. Compare Ezek 21:21[Eng 21:16], where Yahweh's sword is "assigned" (*mū'ādôt*) a bloody work against Jerusalem (M. Greenberg 1997: 426). The LXX in the present verse has a different reading entirely: "toward those remaining, to arouse." For MT *šām* ("there"), 2QJer has the spelling *šmh*.

MESSAGE AND AUDIENCE

Yahweh in the oracle begins with an ominous reference to "waters rising from the north." These will overflow the land to which they come, inundating cities and those inhabiting them. Everything will suffer. Some in the audience will perceive this to be none other than the mighty onrush of the Babylonian army. People will cry for help. Everyone will be wailing loudly. The oracle continues by describing the terrifying sounds of war—stamping hoofs of the stallions, clattering chariots with their rumbling wheels. Fathers will be so weak in their hands that they will not turn to their children, who are frightened and desparately need help. A day is coming to devastate the Philistines, bringing hardship also to Tyre and Sidon, since not a survivor will remain to give them help when they need it. We now learn that it is Yahweh coming to devastate the remnant from Caphtor. No reason for the judgment is given. For Gaza it will be a day of shaven heads and slashed bodies. For Ashkelon, the remnant of Philistine strength, it will be a day of silence. Contrasted at the end of the oracle is the loud mourning at Gaza with the deafening silence in Ashkelon. At the very end Yahweh addresses the unblessed inhabitants of Gaza with a question they will not, indeed they cannot answer: "How long will you slash yourselves?"

In his soliloquy, Jeremiah begins by addressing the sword of Yahweh, asking it a rhetorical question not unlike the one asked to the inhabitants of Gaza: "How much longer before you are idle?" He then feigns compassion, telling the sword to put itself back into the sheath, to rest and be silent. The sword too cannot respond. So Jeremiah answers his own question with another saying, "How can you be idle when Yahweh has commanded (the destruction)?" Toward Ashkelon and other Philistine cities he has assigned destruction. Again no reason for the judgment, and no answer to the "How long?" question.

The oracle and the prophet's sequel can be assigned a date of 604 B.C., just before Nebuchadnezzar attacked Ashkelon in December of that year (Peake; Rudolph; Hyatt 1956: 283; Bright; Holladay). Ashkelon seems to be the main focus of both poems. The superscription, added sometime after 601–600 B.C., dates the poetry in this earlier period *before* Pharaoh retook Gaza.

D. WHAT ABOUT MOAB? (48:1–47)

1. Devastation for the Whole of Moab (48:1–10)

a) Moab the Renowned Is No More (48:1–2)

48 ¹For Moab.
  Thus said Yahweh of hosts, God of Israel:
  Woe to Nebo, for it is devastated
    Kiriathaim is very shamed, is captured
    The Height is very shamed and shattered
  ²The Praise of Moab is no more

  In Heshbon they planned evil against her:
    'Come, and let us cut her off from being a nation'

Even Madmen, you shall be muted
after you the sword shall go.

RHETORIC AND COMPOSITION

MT 48:1–2 = LXX 31:1–2. The beginning of the Moab collection is announced by the superscription "For Moab," which is balanced off by a subscription at the end of the collection:

For *Moab*	v 1
Thus far the judgment on *Moab*	v 47

Before the superscription is a *setumah* in M^L; M^A and M^P both have a *petuḥah*.
There may also be a section prior to v 1 in the reconstructed 2QJer, although
Baillet fails to note one. In addition, we have here a chapter division. From this
point on in the chapter, section markings in the major codices give us little
help in delimiting the units. There are only three remaining sections in M^L
and M^A: following vv 11, 39, and 47, the last-mentioned coinciding with the
end of the chapter. M^P has one more after v 9. Commentators therefore differ
widely in delimiting the units, basing their judgments usually on content and
the few changes between poetry and prose. But we can seek help from rhetorical structures and note characteristic beginnings, e.g., "The sound" (*qôl*) in
v 3, "Look, hereafter, days are coming" in v 12, "How can you say?" (*'êk
tō'mĕrû*) in v 14, "Say, How . . ." (*'imrû 'êkâ . . .*) in v 17b, "To the way,
stand . . ." (*'el-derek 'imdî*) in v 19, and "Look" (*hinnēh*) in v 40. Some of these
are nicely corroborated by poetry and prose changes, by positioned messenger
formulas, or by both.

The opening poem in the collection is introduced by a messenger formula
marking the upper limit and identifying it as a prophetic oracle. The lower
limit is less certain. A unit appears to be indicated in vv 1–2, which is the judgment of Volz, Rudolph, Weiser, and Bright. The RSV and JB also break after
v 2, as do the NRSV and NJB. But is this simply a stanza in a larger poem, or a
self-standing poem in a cluster of other poems? I lean toward the latter, although recognizing that certainty is not assured. The shift to direct address at
the end of v 2 is a characteristic way of Jeremiah bringing closure (see Note on
12:13). Also, the content of vv 1–2, while compatible with the content in vv 3–
9, can also stand alone. The next unit I begin at v 3 with *qôl*, a common opening term in Jeremianic poems and stanzas of poems (see Note on 3:21). The
first poem then, which is a divine oracle, is directed against Nebo and Kiriathaim, cities located on Moab's northern plateau. The second poem is directed
against Horonaim and Luhith, cities further south in the so-called "central plateau" region.

It has been widely noted that the number of Moab oracles in Jeremiah is dis-
proportionately large. Also, after v 29 are numerous overlaps with oracles found
elsewhere in the OT, notably Isaiah 15–16, and 24. Thus we could reasonably

conclude that a Jeremianic collection of oracles has been supplemented with oracles older in date and quarried from elsewhere (Elitzur 1963; Holladay). But in vv 30–47 are two bona fide Jeremiah oracles, vv 38b–39 and 40–41, and there may well be others. On the Jeremianic vocabulary and phraseology in vv 1–28, also in vv 38–45, see Holladay (II: 347–52).

The present oracle has two stanzas: vv 1bc–2a, and v 2bc. Both are double bicolons. Stanza I has a nice repetition of the verb "shame" at the center:

I . . . .   v 1b
       is very shamed . . . .   *hōbîša*
       is very shamed . . . .   *hōbîša*
     . . . .   v 2a

The LXX lacks the first occurrence of this verb, for which reason many commentators delete, but it should be retained (see Notes). For similar repetitions in the Jeremianic double bicolon, see Lundbom 1975: 66–67 [= 1997: 88–89]. Stanza II is distinguished by the introduction of another voice, viz., the voice of the enemy in v 2bβ, also the shift to direct address in v 2c. Except for the other voice brought in, the speaker of the oracle is Yahweh.

Catchwords connecting to the prior poem in 47:2–7 are these:

48:1 *Woe*   47:4 *to devastate . . . is devastating*
      it is devastated   47:6 *woe*

Catchwords connecting this oracle to the unit following are these:

v 1 *is captured*   v 7a *you shall be captured*

These key words in tying the first two poems together make an inclusio.

NOTES

48:1. *For Moab.* On the short introduction, see Note for 46:2. The Bible remains our primary source for information about Moab, although inscriptional evidence does exist. There are Egyptian texts from the reign of Rameses II (ca. 1290–1224 B.C.), Assyrian texts from the eighth and seventh centuries B.C., and most important the celebrated Moabite (Mesha) Stone found in 1868 at Dhibân, which is dated to the mid–ninth century B.C. The last-mentioned contains the most important historical and topographical information about Moab outside the Bible. For a transcription of the text and translation, see C. Ginsburg (1871: 5–7); *ANET*[3] 320–21; *IDB* K–Q, 420; Smelik (1992: 61–66); and *CS II* 137–38. Archaeological work in Moab has been limited, but our knowledge of the country is growing, particularly with regard to the northern plateau region above the River Arnon.

Moab was situated on the high plateau east of the Dead Sea (elev. 3,000 feet; 4,300 feet above the Dead Sea), which continues the Anti-Lebanon Mountain

range. Its reasonably good agricultural land is attested by the biblical story of
Ruth and from 2 Kgs 3:4, where we learn that Moab was also good sheep-
breeding country. Tristram (1873: 314) in travels throughout Moab in the late
nineteenth century said: "The soil of all Moab, and pre-eminently of this
neighbourhood [i.e., around Medeba], is wonderfully rich—a fine, red sandy
loam, which year after year grows successive crops of wheat, without manure,
and into which one can with ease thrust a stick for at least two feet." For much
of its history Moab's northern boundary was the spectacular canyon at the base
of which lies the Wadi al-Mūjib, known as the River Arnon in the Bible (Num
21:13; 22:36; Judg 11:18). Its boundary on the south was the no-less-impressive
canyon containing the Wadi el-Ḥasā, generally identified with the biblical
River Zered (Glueck 1939: 88–89; Van Zyl 1960: 46–49; J. M. Miller 1997:
194; cf. Num 21:11–12). Moab's western boundary was the narrow plain
along the Dead Sea called "the Ghôr" (= ʾArabah); its eastern boundary the
Syrian–Arabian Desert beyond the modern-day Desert Highway.

The Moab heartland had natural boundaries, which on the north, south,
and east were said to have been further secured by a line of fortresses (Glueck
1939: 61–74). More recent archaeological work has established the existence
of some Iron Age fortresses in border areas, but more excavations are needed
to fully substantiate Glueck's claim, which was made largely on the basis of
surface pottery finds. The desert was Moab's greatest point of vulnerability,
opening the country to periodic raids by desert tribes. It was east of Moab, one
may recall, that the Israelites were said to have journeyed on their trek from
Egypt to Canaan (Judg 11:18). At various periods Moab controlled the area
north of the Arnon to Heshbon, which was taken by Israel after Moses defeated
the Amorite king Sihon and assigned the city to the tribes of Reuben and
Gad, who then settled there (Deut 2:24–37; 3:12; Num 32:33–37; cf. Judg
11:21–22). A reference to Gadites living in this area is found on the Moabite
Stone (line 10), which celebrates a return of the territory to Moabite control.
This northern plateau region is called *hammîšōr* ("the tableland") in the
Bible (Deut 3:10; 4:43; Josh 13:9; Jer 48:21; et passim). Lacking natural
boundaries such as central Moab possessed, the northern plateau region
changed hands more than once during the Iron Age, and is believed to have
contained a mixed population. The Ammonites—heirs real or otherwise of
the dispossessed Amorites—claimed early possession of this territory (Judg
11:13). From the eighth century on, following the western campaign of
Tiglath-pileser III in 734–732 B.C., Moab occupied the northern plateau as an
Assyrian vassal (cf. 1 Chr 5:26). Most of the towns mentioned in the Bible and
identified today with reasonable certainty by archaeologists are in this northern region. Down from the northern plateau, in the Jordan Valley near Jericho, is what the Bible calls the "plains of Moab," *ʿarbôt môʾāb* (Num 22:1;
33:48; cf. Deut 1:1–5; 4:44–48). At the time of the Conquest, Moabite cities
on the descent included Kiriathaim, Sibmah, and Zerethshahar (Josh 13:19);
and in the Jordan Valley, Bethharam, Bethnimrah, Succoth, and Zaphon
(Josh 13:27).

Through the center of Moab went the King's Highway (*derek hammelek*), an ancient caravan route and royal road cutting a path through the Transjordan highlands from Damascus to Elath (Aqaba). It is known from Num 20:17; 21:22, and indirectly from Genesis 14. This roadway, probably in use a thousand years before the biblical period, was known as Trajan's Road in Roman times, and is called the Sultan's Road in modern Arabic. On the King's Highway, see further Glueck 1970: 21–22 and Aharoni 1979: 54–57.

Nothing is known of Moab's response to Nineveh's destruction and the collapse of Assyria. After the Battle of Carchemish in 605 B.C., Moab probably swore alliegance to Nebuchadnezzar and stayed loyal when Jehoiakim rebelled, for which reason it was not attacked in 597 B.C. Moab appears to have aided Nebuchadnezzar in his offensive against Judah at this time (2 Kgs 24:2; Lam 1:2; Van Zyl 1960: 155; Bright), yet just a few years later it was represented in Jerusalem when rebellion against Babylon was being discussed (27:3). But the nation was spared in 587–586 B.C., when Jerusalem was laid waste. According to Josephus (*Ant* x 181–82), Moab and Ammon suffered destruction at the hands of Nebuchadnezzar in a campaign of 582 B.C. On the history, archaeology, and geography of Moab, see Van Zyl 1960; J. M. Miller 1989; "Moab" in *ABD* 4: 882–93; *OEANE* 4: 38–39; 1997; and Dearman 1989b; 1997. Jeremiah prophesied judgment on Moab elsewhere in 9:25[Eng 9:26] and 25:21. Other OT prophecies against Moab occur in Amos 2:1–3; Isaiah 15–16; 25:10b–12; Zeph 2:8–11; and Ezek 25:8–11.

Yahweh of hosts, God of Israel. The LXX omits "of hosts, God of Israel," but nevertheless introduces the following as an oracle. On the LXX omission of "of hosts," see Appendix VI.

Woe to Nebo, for it is devastated. Hebrew *hôy 'el-nĕbô kî šuddādâ*. The *hôy* ("woe") has funerary overtones, as it does again in 48:46 (Holladay; Dobbs-Allsopp 1993: 106; cf. 22:18; 34:5), but there is judgment as well in the words (see Note for 22:13). Holladay compares with Jeremiah's anticipatory "woe to us, for we are devastated!" in 4:13. The verb *šdd* (here a Pual: "is devastated") appears often in Jeremiah (26 times), with an (unnamed) enemy being designated "the devastator (of Moab)" in vv 8, 15, and 18. The verbs in this first stanza are best taken as prophetic perfects (Weiser; McKane), referring to a future judgment, the outcome of which has already been decided.

Nebo. Nebo is remembered in the Bible chiefly as the mountain (modern Jebel Neba) from which Moses viewed the Promised Land just prior to his death (Deut 32:49; 34:1). Reference here is to a nearby city of the same name (Num 32:3, 38; Isa 15:2), currently under Moabite rule subsequent to its repossession by Mesha in the mid–ninth century. The Moabite Stone says that Nebo had cultic vessels dedicated to YHWH at the time of its capture (lines 14–18), indicating the existence of a Yahwistic sanctuary there. Eusebius located the city of Nebo 8 Roman miles south of Heshbon (*Onom.* 294–97). Today it is commonly identified with Khirbet Muḫaiyat, a site 8 kilometers southwest of Heshbon that has turned up large quantities of Moabite Iron Age pottery (Kuschke 1961a: 188; Grohman, "Nebo," *IDB* K–Q, 528; Rudolph, 287; Holladay).

Another possibility is Khirbet ʿAyun Musa, a valley site just a few kilometers to the north, where large quantities of Iron I pottery have turned up (Cross 1988: 51–52; Dearman 1997: 207). Cross says only here could a sizable population have been supported.

Kiriathaim is very shamed, is captured. Hebrew *hōbîšâ* is another internal H-stem of *bôš*: "is very shamed" (see 46:24 and Note on 2:26). There is no reason to delete this verb with the LXX (*pace* Cornill, Peake, Rudolph, Weiser, Bright, McKane, Holladay) simply because it repeats in the next colon. The repetition is vintage Jeremianic poetry (see Rhetoric and Composition), and its omission can be due to haplography (homoeoteleuton: *h . . . h*). Shame comes as a matter of course when one is captured by an enemy, as Judah too discovered to her great sorrow (2:36–37). Kiriathaim is said to await future judgment in Ezek 25:9. In Jer 48:21–23 judgment on the city has already occurred.

Kiriathaim. Another city listed on the Moabite Stone (line 10), but whose exact location is unknown. It is mentioned in v 23 as one of Moab's tableland (northern plateau) cities. The site now is commonly identified with Khirbet al-Qureiye, ca. 16 kilometers west of Madeba (Kuschke 1961a: 191–96; 1961b: 28–31; 1967: 105; Dearman 1989b: 176–77; Rudolph, 287), which corroborates the testimony of Eusebius, who said the city lay 10 Roman miles west of Medeba (*Onom.* 250–53). This puts Kiriathaim near Nebo, where one would expect it to be. Earlier scholars placed the city farther south at Khirbet al-Qureiyet, which is about 16 kilometers north of the Arnon, 10 kilometers northwest of Dibon, and 6 kilometers southwest of Jebel ʿAtarus (Tristram 1873: 275–76). But Glueck (1939: 131) in a surface exploration turned up only Nabatean, Roman, and later sherds at this site (Grohman, *IDB* K–Q, 36–37). Khirbet al-Qureiyet has yet to be systematically excavated. The city became Israelite after the conquest of Sihon and was built up by the tribe of Reuben (Num 32:37; Josh 13:19). Earlier it was said to be home to the legendary Emim, one of the giant peoples (Gen 14:5; cf. Deut 2:10–11). On the Emites, see Van Zyl 1960: 106–8. Ezekiel too predicted judgment on this Moabite city (Ezek 25:9).

The Height is very shamed and shattered. Hebrew *hōbîšâ hammiśgāb wāḥātâ.* These verbs occur together in vv 20 and 39, and commonly elsewhere (see Note on 17:18). The difficult *miśgāb* means "a refuge high up," but with feminine verbs, a proper noun is here indicated. "The Height" is best taken as an appellation for Kiriathaim (Blayney). The AV translated a place-name, "Misgab," which survives in the NEB and REB, also in McKane. But no such place is known, although Misgab could certainly play on a place-name, as may be the case with "Madmen" in v 2. The Versions all had difficulty with the term. Most commentators and modern Versions (RSV, JB, NAB, NIV, NJV, NSB) translate "fortress" or the like, but this requires emending the verbs to masculine forms (cf. Rudolph; *BHS*). The point, however, is clear. Lofty, well-fortified Kiriathaim will be brought down by an enemy, the predicted fate also for a lofty Edomite fortress (49:16). Compare Isa 25:12.

2. *The Praise of Moab is no more.* Hebrew *tĕhillat môʾāb* can also be translated "the renown of Moab," or "the glory of Moab." This appears to be another

appellation, probably of Nebo, since Kiriathaim is designated "The Height" in the prior colon. Stanza I with its repeated verbs is then a key word chiasmus:

I   ...... *Nebo* ....
       Kiriathaim is very shamed ....
       The Height is very shamed ......
       The Praise of Moab ....

The stanza declares woe upon Nebo, "The Praise of Moab," because it is devastated and is no more. In 49:25 Damascus, "city of praise," is said to be forsaken; in 51:41 it is Babylon, "the praise of all the land / earth," that has become a desolation. The LXX's *iatreia Mōab* ("healing of Moab") appears to read Heb *tĕ'ālat* (cf. 46:11), and in other ways varies from MT.

   no more. Hebrew *'ên 'ôd*. This expression with *'ên* occurs elsewhere in 10:20; 38:9; and 49:7; usually in Jeremiah it is with the negative *lō'* (2:31; 3:16, 17; 7:32; 11:19; 31:29, 34 [2×], 40; and often). The meaning is the same: "no more" or "no longer."

   In Heshbon they planned evil against her. I.e., against Moab. There is paronomasia in *bĕhešbōn hāšĕbû*, "in Heshbon they planned" (Casanowicz 1893; #149). Eusebius (*Onom*. 192–95) located the city of Heshbon 20 Roman miles east of the Jordan, in the mountains opposite Jericho. Ancient Heshbon has generally been identified with Tell Ḥesbân in modern Ḥisbân, a lofty mound 200 meters above 'Ain Ḥesbân guarding the northern edge of the Moabite Plain, 19 kilometers south of Amman and 8 kilometers northeast of Mount Nebo (*NEAEHL* 2: 626). Questions, however, have been raised about this site (Herr 1993b; 1997: 168–69; Dearman 1997: 206–7) following excavations in the 1960s and 1970s by a consortium of American universities in cooperation with the American Schools of Oriental Research, which turned up a prosperous seventh- to sixth-century B.C. occupation surrounding a fort. Pottery found in a reservoir fill pointed to Ammonite occupation, which appears to have met up with a violent end (*NEAEHL* 2: 628). Heshbon was settled by the Israelite tribe of Reuben following the defeat of Sihon (Num 32:33–37; Josh 13:17), but by the end of the eighth and into the seventh century it was under Moabite control (Isa 15:4; 16:8–9; cf. Jer 48:34). The city was said to be Moabite before Sihon captured it (Num 21:26–30). Heshbon is not mentioned on the Moabite Stone. In Jeremiah's time it is probably an Ammonite city (49:3). Envisioned here is an enemy having come to Heshbon from where it will plan its attack on the northern cities of Moab: Nebo and Kiriathaim. It will be a repeat of the past times about which the ancient ballad-singers sang "a fire went forth from Heshbon" to destroy the cities of Moab (Num 21:27–30; Jer 48:45–46).

   'Come, and let us cut her off from being a nation.' Again the referent is Moab. This is the voice of the enemy (cf. 6:4–5). The quotation ends with "from being a nation," after which a direct word is spoken to "Madmen." The LXX lacks the initial "Come," translating the boast as one celebrating an action already accomplished, or as good as accomplished (Gk *ekopsamen*, "we have cut off"). The Heb has an H-stem imperfect, *nakrîtennâ*. Jeremiah speaks

in 11:19 about enemies who planned (*ḥšb*) an attack on him personally. They said, "Let us cut him off from (*nikrĕtennû mē* . . .) the land of the living, that his name be remembered no more (*lō'* . . . *'ôd*)."

Even Madmen, you shall be muted. We continue with imperfect verbs, but now the oracle addresses "Madmen." Hebrew *madmēn tiddōmî* is more paronomasia (Casanowicz 1893: #84). The verb *dmm*, normally "be silent," is a euphemism here as elsewhere in Jeremiah (see 49:26; 51:6; and Note on 8:14). Dahood (1962b: 70) proposed for *gam* "in a loud voice," a meaning it has in Ug. He translated the colon, "With a loud voice shall Madmen weep." See also Kuschke (1961a: 185). But isn't the point rather that Madmen is going to be silenced? The LXX has *pausin pausetai*, "and she shall be completely silenced," seemingly taking *mdmn* as the infinitive absolute of *dmm*, *dāmôm*—not a particularly good reading, which should be rejected.

Madmen. Rashi said Heb *madmēn* was a place-name, although no such place is known in the OT, nor was it so rendered by the T. The LXX, as we just noted, had a different interpretation. The same is true with the S and Vg. The term seems either to be an appellation for another Moabite city, or else a deliberately distorted city name found suitable for a wordplay. Holladay thinks we may have a cognate of *dōmen*, "dung," noting that *madmēnâ* means "dung pit" (or "dung heap") in Isa 25:10. "Dung Heap" might then be an appellation for some Moabite city. Should the initial *mem* happen to be a result of dittography, which is often suggested, then "Dimon" is a possibility, the waters of which receive mention in the Moabite oracle of Isa 15:9. Dimon (without the *mem*) could also be a shortened form of Madmen (D. N. Freedman). Dimon has been identified with Khirbet Dimneh overlooking Wadi Ibn Ḥammād, four kilometers northwest of Rabbah along the King's Highway in central Moab (Worschech and Knauf 1986: 70–75; Mattingly, "Dimon" in *ABD* 2: 199). Volz took Madmen to be Medeba (Isa 15:2), present-day Madaba, which is another possibility. It does appear, however, that a place-name is intended, which is how the modern Versions translate the term.

after you the sword shall go. For the personified sword, see also 47:6.

MESSAGE AND AUDIENCE

This oracle begins by pronouncing woe on Nebo, which will be assuredly devastated by some unnamed foe. Neighboring Kiriathaim too will be much shamed on its day of capture. "The Praise of Moab," which can mean none other than the city of Nebo, from that day forward will be no more. Destruction will be planned in nearby Heshbon, where the enemy is now heard to say, "Come, let us cut her off from being a nation." The whole of Moab will be brought to nothing! The oracle closes with a warning to a place called Madmen that imagines it will escape. But this city too, whichever it is, will be silenced. After it a sword shall go in relentless pursuit.

Calvin said this oracle and others like it would not necessarily to be heard by the Moabites, but were spoken for the benefit of the Jews so they would know that Moab will not go unpunished. But the delivery may have been more direct than Calvin imagines, since Moab was represented at the Jerusalem conference of 594 B.C., when rebellion against Babylon was under discussion, and Jeremiah could have addressed the Moabite ambassador with these words. It is even possible that Moab heeded these words promising disaster to the nation, for it did not rebel against Nebuchadnezzar as Zedekiah ended up doing. The present oracle and others following could also have as background the events of 604 B.C., after the Battle of Carchemish, when the Babylonian Chronicle states that "all the kings of Hatti came before him [i.e., Nebuchadnezzar] and he received their heavy tribute" (Hyatt 1956: 283; cf. Holladay). Moab's only other involvement in Judah's affairs was in 599–598 B.C. when, at the behest of Nebuchadnezzar, Moab together with other peoples came to harass Judah (2 Kgs 24:2). This too could be background for the Moab oracles. An actual attack on Moab did not take place until 582 B.C., when Nebuchadnezzar, according to Josephus, marched against both Ammon and Moab and subdued them.

b) Moab's Cry Is Heard (48:3–7a)

48 ³The sound of a scream from Horonaim:
   'Destruction and a great shatter!'
   ⁴Moab is shattered
Her young ones¹ make heard a cry

   ⁵Yes, at the Luhith² ascent
     weeping on weeping goes up
Yes, on the Horonaim descent
     a distressful, shattering scream they hear

   ⁶Flee, deliver your own lives³
     and be like Aroer in the desert.

⁷ᵃFor because of your trust in your works and in your treasures, even you, you shall be captured.

RHETORIC AND COMPOSITION

MT 48:3–7a = LXX 31:3–7a. An upper limit for the present unit is marked by *qôl*, "sound, voice," a characteristic opening term in the Jeremianic poetry, and also by content. For the commentators and modern translations that break between vv 2 and 3, see Rhetoric and Composition for 48:1–2. The lower limit is more difficult to determine. A number of scholars (Giesebrecht; Volz; Bardtke 1936: 240; Weiser; Rudolph; Bright), and two of the modern Versions (NJV;

---

¹Reading the Q *ṣĕʿîreyhā* ("her young ones"); cf. 14:3.
²Reading the Q *halluḥît* ("the Luhith") with the Vrs; cf. Isa 15:5.
³Reading the plural "your lives" with the LXX; MT has "your life."

NRSV), make a division after v 6, although this may simply be an internal break in a poem of greater length. In my view, vv 3–6 (or vv 3–5) constitute a self-standing poem in a three-poem cluster. In the first poem of the cluster, vv 1b–2, the northern cities of Nebo and Kiriathaim are addressed. Here in the second poem, vv 3–5/6, it is Horonaim and Luhith, cities farther south in the central Moabite plateau. The directive to flee in v 6 may or may not have been originally connected to vv 3–5; it is the reversal of another ending in 2:25a, where Jeremiah tells a Judahite audience not to "run their feet bare." The third poem in the cluster, delimited on the basis of content and rhetorical structure, is vv 7b–9 (see Rhetoric and Composition for 48:7b–10). If the messenger formula in v 1a means to introduce the first two poems, then this second poem is a divine oracle. The third poem is identified as a divine oracle by the messenger formula in v 8.

The problem is knowing what to do with v 7a. This half-verse is taken by most everyone to be poetry, although Cornill and others since (Janzen 1973: 20; Holladay; McKane) judge the line to be overloaded in view of a shorter LXX text. There is also the change here from plural forms to (second feminine) singular. In my view, v 7a is a prose add-on, offering a reason for the coming judgment. It is also transitional, supplementing the preceding poetry and connecting to the poetry following in v 7b. That it means to expand upon v 7b can be seen by a comparison with 49:3–4 (cf. Jones). There, Daughter Ammon is indicted for "trusting in her treasures" (49:4b); here Moab or a city in Moab is scored for "trusting in her treasures." The words of v 7b, "Chemosh shall go out into exile, his priests and his princes together," are also a variant of 49:3b, "For Milcom into exile shall go, his priests and his princes together." Both verses show an indebtedness to Amos 1:15.

Verse 7a also gives continuity to the first two Moab poems. To begin with, the line makes an inclusio with v 1b, helping to tie the two poems together. The key words:

| I | . . . . *is captured* | *nilkĕdâ* | v 1b |
| II | . . . . *you shall be captured* | *tillākēdî* | v 7a |

These words function also as catchwords. Secondly, v 7a as an add-on to the second poem provides a conclusion like that of the first poem, i.e., having a *gam* clause with a second person imperfect verb:

| I | *even . . . you shall be muted* | *gam . . . tiddōmî* | v 2c |
| II | *even . . . you shall be captured* | *gam . . . tillākēdî* | v 7a |

If v 6 is integral to the present poem, then the poem has three stanzas. But with various text problems in v 6 and the fact that v 6 lacks key word continuity with vv 3–5, it may well be that vv 3–5 constitute the core poetry, with v 6 being a later poetic supplement. We shall nevertheless take all the verses as a three-stanza poem. Stanza I (vv 3–4) is a double bicolon with key word chiasmus (*šĕʿāqâ / wāšeber / nišbĕrâ / zĕʿāqâ*), similar to Stanza I of the previous poem (vv 1b–2a). Stanza II (v 5) is a double bicolon with repetition and an "up and down" contrast in parallelism. Stanza III (v 6) is a single bicolon containing a simile. Stanzas I and II are individually structured and linked together by the following key words:

I	. . . . *a scream from Horonaim*	*ṣĕʿāqâ mēḥōrônāyim*	v 3
	. . . . *and shatter*	*wāšeber*	
	is shattered	*nišbĕrâ*	v 4
	make heard a cry	*hišmîʿû zĕʿāqâ*	

II	*Yes* . . . . *ascent*	*kî maʿălēh*	v 5
	. . . . *on*	*bi*	
	Yes, on the Horonaim descent	*kî bĕmôrad ḥôrōnayim*	
	. . . . . . *shattering scream they hear*	*ṣaʿăqat-šeber šāmēʿû*	

In Stanza I, the words "scream" (*ṣĕʿāqâ*) and "cry" (*zĕʿāqâ*) are a standard asso-nantal pair (25:34, 36), casting doubt on the omission of the latter in the LXX. Oral haplography might here be a possibility. The repetitions and balancing terms giving continuity to Stanzas I and II cast doubt also on the widely held view that v 5 has been quarried from Isa 15:5 (so Duhm; Cornill; Rudolph, Weiser; Holladay; McKane). The verse has admitted similarities to Isa 15:5; nevertheless, each verse needs to be evaluated on its own merits and read in the context where it is found.

Catchwords connecting this oracle to the one preceding, as noted above, are these:

v 7a *you shall be captured*   v 1b *is captured*

Catchwords connecting to the oracle following are these:

v 6 *deliver*   *mallĕṭû*   v 8 *shall not escape*   *lōʾ timmālēṭ*

NOTES

48:3. *The sound of a scream from Horonaim.* Hebrew *qôl ṣĕʿāqâ,* "the sound of a scream," occurs also in 25:36. Compare "the sound of a cry (*qôl zĕʿāqâ*) from Babylon" in 51:54. For poems beginning with *qôl* in Jeremiah, see Note on 3:21.

Horonaim. A Moabite city mentioned again in vv 5 and 34, in Isa 15:5, and also on the Moabite Stone (lines 31–32). The site is unknown, but is generally thought to be in the central highlands between the rivers Arnon and Zered (Cheyne; Duhm; Van Zyl 1960: 65; Dearman 1989b: 188; *ABD* 3: 289). Among the suggested sites are Tell Mēdān west of Kathrabba, which has an Iron Age fortress (Schottroff 1966: 207; cf. Glueck 1939: 94–96), and the summit peak of ed-Deir, which is west of the King's Highway between er-Rabba and Kerak, four kilometers northwest of Rakin (Worschech and Knauf 1986: 80–85; J. M. Miller 1991: 55–56 with photo). The latter site lies on a Roman road descending from er-Rabba to the the Dead Sea (cf. v 5). Dearman (1989b: 188–89; 1997: 211) points out, however, that none of these sites has been excavated and that identifications depend largely on finding ancient road systems and evaluating surface pottery.

'Destruction and a great shatter!' Hebrew *šeber gādôl* ("a great shatter") is a common Jeremianic expression (see Note on 4:6). In the previous oracle we heard a boasting enemy preparing to attack (v 2). Now it is an impassioned cry coming from the people of Horonaim, who bewail the destruction of their city. Compare the alternating voices in 6:4–5.

4. *Moab is shattered, Her young ones make heard a cry.* The verbs are prophetic perfects (Calvin). Hebrew *sĕʿîrîm* means "young ones," either young children (14:3) or young animals (49:20; 50:45). The MT makes perfectly good sense, and is translated by the AV, NJV, and NIV; now also by the NRSV and NJB. But most all commentators and many of the modern Versions (RSV; JB; NEB; NAB; REB; NSB) emend to "a cry is heard as far as Zoar," or the like, assuming that the idea here is the same as that expressed in 49:21. But no ancient Version has this reading, and the alleged parallel in Isa 15:5 speaks rather about fugitives fleeing to Zoar (cf. Gen 19:20–23). The T has "their rulers have uttered a shout," which simply substitutes "their rulers" for "her young ones." The LXX's "proclaim to Zogora [= Zoar]" yields tolerable sense, but does not inspire confidence. It presupposes an imperative *hašmîʿû*, omits the balanced term *zĕʿāqâ*, "cry" (see Rhetoric and Composition), and reads *ṣōʿar* instead of *sĕʿîreyhā* (Q). The idea being expressed here is that Horonaim's cry consists of young children making their scream heard (cf. v 5b). Stanza I is then a chiasmus.

5. *Yes . . . Yes.* These two *kî* particles should be taken as asseveratives; cf. Duhm.

Yes, at the Luhith ascent, weeping on weeping goes up. There is sound accumulation in *kî maʿălēh . . . bibkî yaʿăleh bekî* (cf. Casanowicz 1893; #308), also a play on "upward" imagery (cf. Barthélemy 1986: 777). But this extraordinary poetry is not saying that weeping people are ascending (the mountain), but rather that (their) accumulated weeping is ascending (for all to hear). People may be descending the mountain or simply weeping at locations along the way.

the Luhith ascent. Hebrew *maʿălēh* is "a (steep) path up"; Rashi: "the ascent of a mountain." The Luhith ascent, mentioned also in Isa 15:5, has long been thought to be a road from the Moabite highlands down to the Jordan Valley near the Dead Sea. Mittmann (1982) identified it with a still-visible Roman road just south of the Wadi ʿEsāl / Wadi Sulēmān, descending from Kathrabba to the Jordan Valley (Holladay; Dearman 1997: 211; cf. *ABD* 4: 397). For the city of Luhith, Mittmann suggested Khirbet Mēdan, a promontory just west of Kathrabba in southern Moab. In one of the Bar Kochba Letters (early second century A.D.) mention is made of two En-Gedi residents having come originally from Ha-Luhith in the district of ʿAgaltain (Yadin 1961: 94; 1962b: 250–51). Yadin says this is undoubtedly the ancient Moabite city referred to here.

weeping on weeping goes up. Hebrew *bibkî yaʿăle-bekî.* A difficult phrase because the verb (a third masculine singular, not a third masculine plural as most modern Versions translate) breaks up an idiom expressing the superlative, "weeping on weeping," or "much weeping" (cf. GKC §133k, l). Poetry allows for unconventional word order. Compare for meaning the superlative *mirmâ bĕmirmâ*, "deceit upon deceit," in 9:5[Eng 9:4]. Conveyed here is weeping on a grand scale, probably weeping heard everywhere along the Luhith ascent (Calvin). For another image of human cries "going up" (*ʿlh*), see 14:2. The verb now shifts to an imperfect and should be translated future (Kimḥi). Many commentators (Giesebrecht; Duhm; Ehrlich 1912: 356; Rudolph; Bright; Holladay), with an eye to Isa 15:5, emend—reading *bô* ("on it") for *bekî*, and taking the *kî* as a dittography of the following *kî*. But these emendations have no support in the Versions and should be rejected.

   on the Horonaim descent. Hebrew *môrad* means "descent, slope." This phrase intends to balance "the Luhith ascent," but we have no way of knowing whether two different roads down to the Jordan Valley are indicated, or simply one (Schottroff 1966: 200). See Dearman (1989b: 188–89). The parallelism in Isa 15:5 does not settle the matter. There is more play on the "up and down" in v 15. See also 8:18 and 14:2, and more expansively yet the narrative in 2 Kings 1–2 (Lundbom 1973).

   a distressful, shattering scream they hear. The MT points as a triple construct chain, which is how the Hebrew is translated in the NJV and NRSV. The construct *ṣārê* must then mean "distressful," not "enemies" (Symm: *hoi echthroi*; Vg: *hostes*; cf. AV), and cannot be the subject. It is perhaps an intensive plural (GKC §124e). The colon repeats vv 3–4, saying that screams are coming from Horonaim. The LXX omits *ṣārê*, and many scholars (Hitzig; Giesebrecht; Cornill; Duhm; Ehrlich 1912: 356–57; Rudolph; Bright; Holladay; McKane) delete, again because the term is also absent in Isa 15:5. However, the omission here could be the result of haplography (homoeoarcton: *ṣ . . . ṣ*).

   6. *Flee, deliver your own lives.* Hebrew *nūsû mallĕṭû napšĕkem*. The verb *mlṭ* in the Piel means "to let escape, deliver." See also 51:6, 45. One should also read *napšĕkem* with the LXX and Vg as a plural, "your (own) lives." Compare the directive to Lot in Gen 19:17: "Escape for your life" (*himmālēt ʿal-napšekā*). In the present case, however, the directive is ironic: people fleeing Moabite towns and cities will not save their lives (vv 7a, 8).

   Flee! Hebrew *nūsû*. This imperative occurring also in 49:8, 30; 51:6 and Zech 2:10[Eng 2:6] is taken by some as a formal element in the prophetic preaching (Bach 1962; Christensen 1975). For an envisioned flight from Judah's cities, see 4:29 and 6:1.

   and be like Aroer in the desert. Hebrew *wĕtihyeynâ kaʿărôʿēr bammidbār*. The words are a curse on those taking flight, but precisely what the curse consists of remains unclear. The initial *wĕtihyeynâ* is best explained as a second masculine plural imperfect with energic ending (D. N. Freedman), which can then go with the masculine imperatives and masculine plural ending on *napšĕkem*, "your lives." More problematic is *ʿărôʿēr*, about which interpretation ancient and modern is divided. The MT pointing is the same as on another occurrence of the term in v 19, where the place Aroer is indicated. A place is indicated also in T: "and be like the tower of Aroer, which is situated alone in the wilderness." But Kimḥi identifies *ʿărôʿēr* as a tamarisk or juniper tree, which is the translation of Aq (*myrikē*), the Vg (*myricae*), and the AV ("heath"). This reading is accepted by Giesebrecht, Barthélemy (1986: 780), Holladay, and Keown et al., and draws support from *ʿarʿār* in a similar curse in 17:6. If "juniper" was intended, it could have been a play on the city Aroer (Peake). The LXX's *onos agrios*, "wild ass," apparently reads Heb *ʿārôd* (cf. Job 39:5), and is the choice of some commentators (Cornill; Streane; Thompson; Jones) and a few modern Versions (RSV; JB; NAB). The text may also be corrupt. Duhm, Volz, Weiser, Rudolph, Bright, and McKane delete, emend, or do not translate. Also, in Isa 15:5 a not-entirely-secure *yĕʿōʿerû* ("they keep crying"?) only complicates matters further. Giesebrecht pointed out that Aroer on the Arnon is not exactly a desert location. But possibly another place of the same name is indicated. The NJV reads Aroer. The problem is not in comparing people with a city. The curse on the man bringing the news of Jeremiah's birth to his father in 20:16 states: "Let that man be like the cities, which Yahweh overthrew and did not pity." Aroer could then be a destroyed city like Sodom and Gomorrah, in which case the curse on the people fleeing is that they will suffer a fate similar to the proverbial cities, i.e., they will be destroyed (cf. Gen 19:18–19). On the city of Aroer, see Note for 48:19.

7a. *For because of your trust in your works and in your treasures, even you, you shall be captured.* There is alliteration in the threefold *bi . . . bĕ . . . bĕ*. This add-on line may come from 49:4, where Daughter Ammon is said to be "trusting in her treasures." But there an indictment is made. Here a reason is given for the capture of some unnamed Moabite city (suffixes and verb forms are second feminine singular). Reasons for divine judgment occur now and then in the Foreign Nation Oracles, but they are not common. See, however, Ezekiel's oracle against Tyre for a judgment given to a nation of accumulated wealth (Ezek 28:4–7).

in your works and in your treasures. Hebrew *bĕmaʿăśayik ûbĕʾôṣĕrôtayik*. In 15:13 and 17:3 the expression is "your wealth (*ḥêlĕkā*) . . . your treasures." Here the feminine singular suffixes point to an unnamed city being addressed, otherwise the entire nation of Moab. The T has two nouns ("in your treasures and in your treasure-houses"), but the LXX contains only one, *en ochyrōmasin sou* ("in your strongholds"). The LXX is doubtless rendering *bĕʾôṣĕrôtayik*, which can also mean "in your storehouses" (cf. 10:13 [= 51:16]; 38:11; 50:25). Most commentators assume here an MT plus, but it is possible that *bĕmaʿăśayik*, "in your works," is an LXX omission due to haplography (homoeoteleuton: *k . . . k*, or homoearcton if the *waw* on the following word was not present: *b . . . b*). Aquila and Symm both have *epi tois ergois sou* ("in your works"). The treasures are Moab's material wealth, stored usually in the palace or the temple (see Note on 15:13). The term "your works" means "fruit of one's works," i.e., flocks, herds, handwork, and other such goods in one's possession (Kimḥi; cf. 1 Sam 25:2). A potter's inscription, "the work of my hands" has turned up on a thirteenth-century B.C. jar handle from Sarepta (see Note on 1:16). The expression "work(s) of one's hands" has this same positive meaning in Deuteronomy (Deut 2:7; 14:29; 16:15), but can also refer in Deuteronomy and especially

Jeremiah to idols (Deut 4:28; Jer 1:16; 25:6–7, 14; 32:30; 44:8). Cornill thinks the reference here is to idols since Chemosh, Moab's idol, is mentioned in v 7b. Either idols or accumulated possessions is a possible meaning for the term.

even you, you shall be captured. See 50:24. For the emphatic *gam-'at* ("even you"), see also Nah 3:11 (2×). Baillet identifies a masculine pronoun *'th* on a fragment of 2QJer, which he says is from this line.

MESSAGE AND AUDIENCE

This oracle begins with the report of a sound coming from Horonaim. It is from people screaming at the destruction of their city and others in the Moab highlands. Moab is shattered! It is young children from Horonaim who are making their cries heard. At the well-known Luhith ascent, much weeping is going up. On the Horonaim descent, a shattering scream is heard below and beyond. People are told to flee for their lives, having about as much hope of survival as Lot and his family had when they fled nearby Sodom. These people, in fact, are cursed to become lifeless monuments in the desert—an allusion this time to Lot's wife and what happened to her. At some point the oracle is expanded to include a word to some other city, whose name is not revealed, that it too will be captured. This city has trusted in an accumulation of things that will do it no good in the crisis at hand. The envisioned enemy is doubtless Nebuchadnezzar and the Babylonian army.

A suggested date for this oracle could be 604, otherwise a date between 597 and 594 B.C. See discussion of dates for the Moab oracles in Message and Audience for 48:1–2.

Taken in tandem with the oracle in 48:1b–2, the combined passage is a coming judgment on all of Moab, cities in both the north and south. And the voice of the enemy planning the attack (v 2) is set over against the voices of people who have become the unfortunate victims of this attack (v 3).

c) Exile and Wandering Ahead for Moab (48:7b–10)

48⁷ᵇ Chemosh shall go out into exile
    his priests and his princes together
⁸The devastator shall come to every city
    and the city shall not escape

The valley shall perish
    and the tableland be wrecked
        —as Yahweh said

⁹Make a rosette for Moab
    for ruined she shall go out
Her cities shall become a desolation
    without an inhabitant in them.

[10]Cursed be he who does the work of Yahweh half-heartedly
and cursed be he who holds back his sword from blood.

RHETORIC AND COMPOSITION

MT 48:7b–10 = LXX 31:7b–10. The present verses contain an oracle in poetry
(vv 7b–9), followed by an added comment that could be poetry or prose (v 10).
The NEB, REB, and NSB take v 10 to be poetry, but other modern Versions
and most modern commentators (except McKane) consider it prose. If it were
prose, one would expect one or more of the common prose particles in a reading such as *'ārûr hā'ōśeh 'et-mĕle'ket yhwh (bi)rmiyyâ, wĕ'ārûr hammōnēa'
'et-ḥarbô middām*. This verse, in any event, is to be set off from what precedes.
Although neither M[L] nor M[A] has a section after v 9, M[P] has a *petuḥah* there.
The overly zealous holy-war ideology of the curse, while not out of keeping
with what one finds elsewhere in the OT (Num 31:1–20; Judg 5:23), goes ill
with the Moab oracles and with the Jeremiah sentiments expressed elsewhere.
The vindictiveness exceeds even that which is hurled against Babylon in 50:25.
The poetry in vv 7b–9 is identified as a divine oracle by the unconventional
messenger formula concluding v 8.

The unit then as a whole concludes with v 10. The poetry of v 11 is joined
thematically with the prose oracle in vv 12–13. The upper limit of the present
unit is set by the structural integrity of the poetic oracle in vv 7b–9, and by the
content of the oracle, i.e., a coming exile for Moab. Volz, Rudolph, Weiser,
and Bright take vv 7–9 as a poetic unit. This oracle is the third of three within
vv 1–10. The first (vv 1b–2) announces judgment on Moab's northern cities;
the second (vv 3–5/6) does the same on cities farther south; and now here in the
third oracle (vv 7b–9), it is the northern plateau region again, and with it the
Moabite plains, that will fall prey to the enemy. All of Moab will be destroyed.

The present oracle consists of three stanzas. Yahweh is speaker throughout,
with the unusual messenger formula in v 8 ("as Yahweh said") not marking the
end of divine discourse. Stanza I (vv 7b–8a) is a double bicolon; Stanza II
(v 8b) a single bicolon (the messenger formula is extra-metrical); and Stanza
III (v 9) another double bicolon. The three stanzas are bound together by the
following key word structure:

I . . . .*shall go out*	*yāṣā'*	v 7b
. . . .		
. . . . *every city*	*kol-'îr*	v 8a
the city	*'îr*	
II *The valley*	*hā'ēmeq*	v 8b
the tableland	*hammîšōr*	
III		v 9
. . . . *she shall go out*	*tēṣē'*	
Her cities	*'āreyhā*	
. . . .		

This rhetorical structure has features that occur in other Jeremianic poems. A center stanza half the length of stanzas on either side can be seen also in 2:33–37. Poems with balancing terms in the center, very often repetitions, are particularly common in the Jeremianic poems; see 2:5–9; 5:1–8; 51:34–45; and others listed in Rhetoric and Composition for 49:7–11. Finally, the "(every) city" repetition in v 8a can be compared with the "every city" repetition in 4:29.

Catchwords connecting to the preceding unit:

v 8 *shall not escape*   *lō' timmālēṭ*   v 6 *deliver*   *mallĕṭû*

Catchwords connecting to the following unit:

v 7b *Chemosh*   v 11 *into exile*
      into exile   v 13 *Chemosh*

NOTES

48:7b. *Chemosh shall go out into exile, his priests and his princes together.* This line is a variation on 49:3: "Milcom into exile shall go (*yēlēk*) . . . ," and Amos 1:15: "their king shall go (*hālak*) into exile." Here, with the verb *yṣ'* ("to go out"), the saying is well integrated into its context (see Rhetoric and Composition). The verb should not be emended to an H-stem passive to give better parallelism with the N-stem passive in v 7a (*pace* Holladay). This bicolon begins a new oracle. When an ancient people was exiled, images of its gods together with other booty went along (43:12; 49:3; Amos 5:26–27; Isa 46:1–2). Esarhaddon and Assurbanipal both report carrying off "gods" of conquered peoples (Luckenbill 1927: 207, 209–10, 307–8). In some cases these were later returned. In Ezekiel, Yahweh's glory is said to have departed from Jerusalem in a chariot for Babylon, ca. 591 B.C. (Ezek 8:1–11:25; cf. 1:1–28). There is no evidence of Moabites going into exile when Nebuchadnezzar invaded the land in 582 B.C. (Josephus, *Ant* x 181–82), but some could have. Judahites living in Egypt and in Judah (52:30) were exiled to Babylon in that year. If Chemosh with his priests and princes did go into exile, there was a subsequent return, as Chemosh worship is attested at Kerak in a third-century Aramaic inscription found there (Beyerlin 1978: 244–45).

Chemosh. The Q is *kĕmôš*, as in vv 13, 46, and elsewhere in the OT. But the Kt *kĕmîš* compares with a god now known to have been worshiped at Ebla, *kamiš* (Pettinato 1976: 48; Matthiae 1980: 187), which may mean that what we have in the Kt is simply a variant spelling, not a scribal error (*pace* Rudolph; Carroll; Holladay). The Moabite god Chemosh, well known in the OT (Num 21:29; Judg 11:24; 1 Kgs 11:7, 33; 2 Kgs 23:13; Jer 48:7, 13, 46), has turned up in multiple references on the Moabite Stone (in line 17 with his consort, Ashtart), on the Kerak and Dibon Inscriptions, and is commonly identified with gods of similar name worshiped elsewhere, indicating that this is a not just a deity of the Moabites, who in the Bible are called the "people of Chemosh" (Num 21:29;

Jer 48:46), but a deity worshiped in other Syrian city-states as well. "Carchemish" embodies the name of this god (*karkamiš* = "the city of Kamiš"). Kammuš in the god lists of Assyria and Babylonia is said to be another name for the god Nergal (Lambert, *RLA* 5: 335), but may also be identified with Chemosh (Van Zyl 1960: 38–39). A god of similar name has also turned up in the Ugaritic texts (*kmṯ* in *UT* 420 #1263a). Ashtart is said to be goddess of the morning star (Venus), pointing to an association with astral deities (see Note on 7:18). Solomon built a high place for Chemosh on the mountain east of Jerusalem (1 Kgs 11:7, 33), which stood until it was dismantled along with high places built to other gods in the reform of King Josiah (2 Kgs 23:13). A temple to Kamish is attested at Ebla, and Chemosh temples appear also to have existed at Dibon and Karak. Little is known about the worship of this deity. Chemosh is generally thought to be a god of warfare, and his cult appears to have included child sacrifice (2 Kgs 3:26–27). On Chemosh and the religion of Moab, see Van Zyl (1960: 193–202) and Mattingly (1989; "Chemosh," *ABD* 1: 895–97).

his priests and his princes together. Jeremiah prophesied that the priest Pashhur would be taken into exile (20:6), and it is later reported that priests and princes were among those exiled to Babylon in 597 B.C. (29:1–2).

together. Hebrew *yāḥad* (Kt). The more usual form in these chapters of Jeremiah (46–49) is the Q *yaḥdāyw* (cf. 46:12, 21; 49:3), which appears here in numerous MSS. For other inclusive statements using *yaḥdā(y)w* ("together"), see 6:12, 21; 31:8; and 49:3.

8. *The devastator shall come to every city.* The verb *šdd* ("devastate") occurs often in Jeremiah (26×), denoting particularly "coming devastator(s)" (4:13; 5:6; 6:26; 12:12; 15:8; 25:36; 47:4; 48:8, 15, 18, 20, 32; 49:28; 51:48, 53, 55–56). A devastator coming to Moab is a key theme of the present chapter (Jones). This devastator is not named, but it is doubtless Nebuchadnezzar and the Babylonians (cf. 15:8; 49:28). Elsewhere it is identified as Yahweh (cf. 25:36; 47:4; 51:55–56).

and the city shall not escape. The LXX lacks *wĕʿîr*, which could be a loss due to haplography (whole-word: *ʿyr . . . ʿyr*). See Janzen 1973: 118. The term should be retained (*pace* Giesebrecht; Volz; Rudolph). The point is that the destroying enemy will come to every city, and each city in turn will not escape. The hope being quashed is that while some cities will doubtless suffer destruction, others will be spared (cf. vv 2c and 7a).

The valley shall perish. The valley (*hāʿēmeq*) is the Jordan Valley, down from Moab's northern plateau at the north end of the Dead Sea. The Bible refers to this area as the "plains of Moab." For cities on the descent and in the valley itself, see Note on 48:1.

and the tableland be wrecked. The Heb *wĕnišmad hammîšōr* has assonance. Moab's tableland (*hammîšōr*) is the northern plateau region, from the Arnon River to about Heshbon (see Note on 48:1). The verb *šmd* (here an N-stem) is strong, meaning "made totally useless" when referring to property (Hos 10:8), and "exterminated" when referring to persons (48:42; Ezek 32:12). It appears often in Deuteronomy, particularly in the covenant curses (Deut 28:20, 24, 45,

48, 51, 61, 63). Destruction of the valley and the tableland means that all of northern Moab will be destroyed.

as Yahweh said. An unusual messenger formula with *ʾăšer*, which the LXX translates with *kathōs.* The formula without the relative pronoun occurs in 6:15. J. D. Michaelis (1793: 327) raised the possibity here of dittography (*šr* ends the previous term), and some scholars (Giesebrecht; Ehrlich 1912: 357; Rudolph; Keown et al.; cf. *BHS*) have followed this lead, although it fails to explain the *ʾaleph.* The dittography could also be the sequence *ʾšr ʾmr*, in which the first and last letters are the same (D. N. Freedman). The formula as existing can certainly stand, however, and need not be omitted with Volz and Holladay.

9. *Make a rosette for Moab, for ruined she shall go out.* Hebrew *těnû-ṣîṣ lěmôʾāb kî nāṣōʾ tēṣēʾ.* The paronomasia in *ṣîṣ . . . nāṣōʾ tēṣēʾ* (noted by J. D. Michaelis 1793: 327) doubtless has something to do with the difficulty in translating this line, particularly with respect to the noun *ṣîṣ*, but also with the verb *nāṣōʾ.* Traditional Jewish interpretation departed from T ("Make the crown pass away from Moab, for she shall surely go into captivity") and rendered the line, "Give wings to Moab, for she shall fly away," assuming a collective noun "wings" for *ṣîṣ* and a verb "fly away" for *nāṣōʾ* (Cornill; Barthélemy 1986: 783–84). This reading carried over subsequently into the AV. Both renderings are dubious (although BDB cites an Aramaic *ṣîṣ* meaning "wing" or "fin"), and modern commentators have given up the translation of AV, which survives only in the RSV; NJV; and NJB. The attested Heb word meaning "appendage, what hangs down," is *ṣîṣīt* (thus "lock" of hair in Ezek 8:3, and "tassel" on a priestly garment in Num 15:38). The Gk *sēmeia* ("signs"), in an otherwise undistinguished LXX translation, has led many to emend the Heb to *ṣîyûn*, which means "signpost" in Jer 31:21, and "gravestone" in 2 Kgs 23:17. This gives the translation, "Make a gravestone for Moab," or the like (Volz; Weiser; Rudolph; JB; NAB; NSB), but requires also an emending of the second colon to read, "for she shall surely be destroyed." Otherwise a gravestone is not the proper marker for one consigned to wandering and exile. The translation "warning flash / signal" of NEB and REB builds even less convincingly on the LXX.

Another possible translation to have gained currency (Dahood 1959a: 274; Bright; Thompson; Holladay; Keown et al.; McKane) comes from a suggestion made by W. L. Moran (1958) that *ṣîṣ* means "salt," and that the line calls for Moab's land to be salted to prevent future resettlement; cf. Judg 9:45. Moran translates: "Give salt for Moab," completing the line, "for surely shall she surrender." Salt is then being readied for use after Moab's fall (cf. Zeph 2:9), which becomes an anachronism in the NIV ("Put salt on Moab, for she will be laid waste"), but is remedied in the NRSV ("Set aside salt for Moab, for she will surely fall"). One problem with this solution is that Ug *ṣṣ* means "salt mine, salt field" (*UT* 475 #2187; KB³ *ṣîṣ* II), to be distinguished from the product of the mine, *mlḥ(t)*; cf. Heb *melaḥ*, "salt" (Gen 19:26), and *mikrēh-melaḥ*, "salt pit" (Zeph 2:9). See Dietrich and Loretz 1964–66: 221 n. 60; Heltzer 1968: 357; M. Weippert, *BRL*², 264–65; and Barthélemy 1986: 783. The solution also founders on the translation of verbs in the next colon. It is by no means assured that either verb means "surrender" (see below). Another explanation is thus required.

The attested meaning for Heb *ṣîṣ* is "flower" or "blossom" (BDB; KB³), which survives in Rabbinic Hebrew (*Dict Talm*, 1279). The feminine *ṣîṣâ* is a "flower" in Isa 28:4. Aquila (*anthos*), Symm (*blastēma*), and the Vg (*florem*) all reflect this basic meaning, but what we are surely talking about here is not a real flower, but one that has been crafted as a design. The NRSV correctly translates *ṣîṣ* as "rosette" in Exod 28:36 and 39:30, which gives the proper meaning and also a helpful context for deciding the difficult usage here. The priest wore on his forehead a gold rosette; the engraving, "holy to Yahweh," was said to be like a seal (*ḥōtām*). From here may derive the LXX's "signs." The T rendering "crown" also has an association with the head, and it is worth noting that Lev 8:9 calls the priestly rosette a "holy crown" (*nēzer haqqōdeš*). Compare also *ṣyṣ* in Sir 40:4, which Cowley and Neubauer (1897: 4–5) translate as "(priestly) plate" after Exod 28:36, but which the RSV translates as "crown." We are not, of course, talking here about a priestly rosette on the forehead of Moab. But Moab may be getting the rosette as a sign on its forehead, just as Cain received a sign on the forehead following his judgment, at which time he went out (*yēṣē'*) from Yahweh's presence to wander the earth (Gen 4:15–16). Yahweh promised Cain protection, but here it is unclear whether wandering Moab will get the same (but see 48:47). The tone appears to be ironic. The directive to make a rosette is given to an imaginary craftsman. On Jeremiah's use of apostrophe, see Note for 2:12.

for ruined she shall go out. Hebrew *kî nāṣō' tēṣē'*. The second verb is not in doubt. It is *yṣ'* and means "go out (into exile)," as in v 7b. There Chemosh was said to be going out into exile; here it is Daughter Moab. The meaning of this verb is not "surrender" (*pace* Moran; Keown et al.). The first verb is a *hapax legomenon* in the OT and more difficult to decide. I read it as an infinitive absolute of *nṣ'* (= *nṣh*), thus "ruined." We have then two different verbs in combination, which McKane finds "awkward" but which occurs elsewhere (8:13; 42:10) and is fully in keeping with Jeremiah's discourse style (Holladay). The two make a wordplay that might be translated, "for wrecked she shall trek." Others emend to *tiṣṣeh*, which gives the reading, "she shall surely be ruined" (Volz; Rudolph; Weiser; McKane; JB; NAB; *BHS*). This is supported by the paraphrastic T, but is unnecessary. The idea conveyed is that a much-battered remnant of Moab is left to wander, or make the trip into exile.

Her cities shall become a desolation, without an inhabitant in them. Variations of this land-and-city curse appear throughout the book of Jeremiah, in the poetry (2:15; 4:7, 29; 6:8; 9:10[Eng 9:11]; 10:22; 18:16; 46:19; 48:9; 49:33; 50:3, 13; 51:29, 37, 43) and in the prose (19:8; 25:9, 11, 12, 18; 34:22; 44:6, 22; 49:13, 17–18; 51:62). For a conditional blessing of the same in Judah, see 17:25.

10. *Cursed be he who does the work of Yahweh half-heartedly; and cursed be he who holds back his sword from blood.* The LXX lacks the second "curse," but otherwise retains the basic sense. The second curse is present in Aq and Symm

(. . . *ho kōluōn machairan autou*). The form reflects that of the covenant curses in Deut 27:15–26 and Jer 11:3, as well as curses appearing in Jer 17:5 and 20:14–15, but the maledictions here are of a different sort entirely, brandishing as they do a holy war ideology against Moab that is all out of proportion to judgments elsewhere against that nation (Bach 1962: 88–89 n. 2). The verse is rightly denied to Jeremiah, but may nevertheless owe inspiration to Jeremiah's words about the "sword of Yahweh" in 47:6–7. See also 46:10. Calvin points out how soldiers have to be prodded with such words in war, but says the encouragement to Chaldean severity is done for the benefit of a Jewish audience. He goes on to emphasize that the whole import of the passage is that the destruction being carried out is none other than the work of God. That idea is presented also in 50:25, but not as simplistically as here (Jones). Cornill and others point out that this verse found especial favor with Hildebrand (Pope Gregory VII), but Rudolph adds that such is a classic example of the false use of the OT in the Christian religion.

work of Yahweh. Hebrew *měle'ket yhwh*. See also 50:25.

half-heartedly. Hebrew *rěmiyyâ*. In Proverbs this term refers to "sloth" and "laziness" in work generally (Prov 10:4; 12:24, 27; 19:15; Kartveit, *rmh* in *TWAT* 7: 525). Proverbs 10:4 speaks of a "slack hand" (*kap-rěmiyyâ*), which could apply here in use of the sword. Another noun with the same spelling means "deceit" (Mic 6:12), which appears in T and is carried over into the Vg and AV. The reference, in any case, is to soldiers pretending to do the work of Yahweh in combat, but who are not doing it. Modern soldiers, too, may go through the motions and never fire a gun in actual combat.

from blood. Hebrew *middām*. I.e., from shedding blood (in war).

MESSAGE AND AUDIENCE

This oracle begins with a word about Chemosh, the national god of Moab, having to make the trip into exile. Accompanying him will be his priests and princes. The audience has heard it all before, only with respect to kings and other gods. The devastator is not named, but will be known to people in both Judah and Moab as Nebuchadnezzar and the Babylonians. He will come to every city, and each in turn will not escape. The totality of destruction is not in doubt, with the oracle going on to state that the valley and the tableland will be completely destroyed. This dire situation is ameliorated, but ever so slightly, with a word following about wandering and exile. A craftsman is told to make for Moab a rosette, since a ruined, badly-battered remnant must leave its land for a nomad existence. An emblem on the forehead will perhaps be a sign of grace, as it was for the chastened Cain. Left behind will be desolate cities with no one inhabiting them; nevertheless, Moab may survive.

The added curse (v 10) identifies the destruction on Moab as the work of Yahweh, but by bringing disproportionate support for those carrying out this work, is not in keeping with the prior oracle or any other oracle in the Moab collection.

For the date of this oracle, which is probably no earlier than 604 and no later than 594 B.C., see Message and Audience for 48:1–2. We do not know whether Moabites were exiled to Babylon following Nebuchadnezzar's campaign into the country in 582 B.C. The possibility exists, even though Josephus fails to mention exile when reporting that campaign. Judahites living in Egypt and also in Judah were exiled to Babylon in that year. When the curse of v 10 was added is not known, but the likelihood is that the curse originated from the time when enmity was renewed between Judah and Moab in this same general period, i.e., after Moab joined those sent to ravage Judah in 599–598 B.C. (2 Kgs 24:2), and before Moab itself fell victim to Nebuchadnezzar. It could have been when Moab was actually being attacked by Nebuchadnezzar, being a projection of Judah's own hostility at having suffered at the hands of the same devastator herself.

The three oracles in vv 1–9 form a progression when heard in sequence. In the first oracle, destruction is envisioned for Moab's northern cities. In the second, the same fate awaits cities farther south, where mention is made also of roads down into the Jordan Valley. The third oracle returns to the northern plateau region, combining the judgment on this region with a judgment on the valley at the north end of the Dead Sea. Thus, to all of Moab will come widespread devastation. The third oracle also ends, appropriately enough, with a prediction of exile and wandering. And the final curse—crude though it may be in urging the Babylonians and local allies to be more zealous in wielding the sword—adds something all three of the oracles lack, viz., an attribution of the coming judgment to Yahweh and the work he is carrying out.

2. Look at Moab Settled into His Lees! (48:11–13)

48 [11]Moab has been at ease from his youth
  and settled is he into his lees
He has not been poured from container to container
  and into exile he has not gone
Therefore his flavor has remained in him
  and his fragrance has not changed.

[12]Look, hereafter, days are coming—oracle of Yahweh—when I shall send to him decanters and they will decant him; and his containers they will pour out and his jars[1] they will smash. [13]Then Moab shall be ashamed of Chemosh just as the house of Israel was ashamed of Bethel, their trust.

RHETORIC AND COMPOSITION

MT 48:11–13 = LXX 31:11–13. The present verses combine a fragment of poetry (v 11) with an oracle in prose (vv 12–13). The two are linked thematically

---

[1]Reading the singular suffix "his" with the LXX and Aq; MT has "their jars."

as well by key words containing two inversions: 1) an inversion of balancing words and phrases in the unit as a whole; and 2) an inversion of syntax and vocabulary in the outer phrases of a larger rhetorical structure:

I	*He has not been poured / from container to container*		v 11b
	Therefore	*ʿal-kēn*	v 11c
II	*Hereafter . . . . .*	*lākēn*	v 12a
	and his containers / they will pour out		v 12b

Mirsky (1977: 11–12) calls attention to yet other inversions of normal Hebrew syntax at the end of 11b and 11c, which he says indicate closure:

| I | *and into exile, he has not gone . . .* | *ûbaggôlâ lōʾ hālāk* | v 11b |
| | *and his fragrance, it has not changed* | *wĕrêḥô lōʾ nāmār* | v 11c |

Actually, the entire bicolons in 11b and 11c are syntactic chiasms with verbs at the extremes, a commonplace in the Jeremiah poetry (Lundbom 1975: 62–64 [= 1997: 84–86]; Alter 1985: 16).

The verse of poetry is nevertheless to be distinguished from the prose oracle. A demarcation is indicated by *setumah*s in M^L, M^A, and M^P after v 11. The messenger formula, embellished with a "Look, hereafter, days are coming" introduction, ought not be deleted (*pace* Cornill, Rudolph, and Holladay). Here a divine oracle answers Jeremiah's verse of astonished wonderment. The suggestion has been made by some (Rudolph, Weiser, Bright, Holladay) that v 13 is a later add-on, which it may be. But the verse is not poetry as printed in NEB (but changed in REB), NIV, and in Thompson.

Catchwords connecting to the prior oracle are these:

| v 11 | *into exile* | v 7b | *Chemosh* |
| v 13 | *Chemosh* | | *into exile* |

The only seeming catchwords connecting to the following oracle are these:

| vv 11, 13 | *Moab* (2×) | vv 15, 16 | *Moab* (2×) |

NOTES

48:11–12. Jeremiah's assessment of Moab's fortuitous history and Yahweh's promise of judgment build here on a metaphor derived from wine-making, or vinification. Though not clear in every precise detail, the process is generally understood, thanks largely to Egyptian texts, vintage scenes from Egyptian tombs, and the excavation of actual wineries. The essential operations of wine-making in Egypt—treading, pressing, fermentation, filtration, filling, and storage—were the same as those in Mesopotamia (Singer et al. 1954: 282), and doubtless in Israel and Moab as well. Here, too, the application of a wine-making metaphor is sufficiently aided by an interpretive comment indicating that Moab's exile is ultimately what is at issue.

After harvested grapes are crushed in a vat by treading and pressed in cloth to extract all the remaining juice, the must is collected in earthenware jars or wineskins and left to ferment (the sugar converts to alcohol and carbon dioxide). This takes place naturally, and in warm climates begins almost immediately. Fermentation can take place in vats or in open jars; if the latter were closed, oxidation would cause them to burst, as sometimes happened even after jars or wineskins were sealed (cf. Matt 9:17). Left undisturbed for a time on its lees (= sediment), the wine gains in strength, flavor, and fragrance. When fermentation is nearly complete, the clear wine is separated carefully from its lees, perhaps poured once or more into other containers to make sure that fermentation has stopped (racking). Then it is filtered through linen, after which it is sealed in wineskins or jars with stoppers, and stored in cellars. Pritchard (1964) excavated some 63 wine cellars belonging to an eighth- or seventh-century B.C. winery at Gibeon (P. J. King 1993: 177–78). A wine jar with a clay stopper from Gibeon is pictured in *ANEP*² 344 #787. Wine cannot be left exposed to air or it will turn to vinegar. In the "Instruction of Ankhsheshonq," an Egyptian document probably to be dated to the Ptolemaic period, is this aphorism: "Wine matures as long as one does not open it" (Lichtheim 1980: 174; Lesko 1996: 223). Shelf life of wine was not very long, perhaps two or three years. For more on ancient Egyptian vinification, see Lucas (1934: 13–20), Singer et al. (1954: 281–85), and Lesko (1977: 15–21; 1996). Verse 11 from the present passage has been found inscribed on a wine-jar seal of unknown provenance dating to the early Christian era (Irwin 1931–32).

11. *Moab has been at ease from his youth, and settled is he into his lees.* Calvin notes an often-overlooked point that the initial metaphor portrays Moab as an old man having passed his entire life in security without substantial losses. Moab is here masculine, a shift from being feminine in v 9. The portrayal is a romantic one, to be sure, but so also is Jeremiah's portrayal of Israel's youth in 2:2–3. The metaphor then shifts. Old Man Moab is said to be settled on his lees, an appropriate image of a nation known for its exceptional tableland vineyards (vv 32–33; Isa 16:8–10). The verbs *š'n(n)* Palel, "be quiet, rest easily," and *šqṭ*, "be settled, undisturbed," occur together also in 30:10 (= 46:27).

Moab has been at ease from his youth. I.e., it has lived securely (Prov 1:33). The nation's "youth" could perhaps date from the time it subjugated the legendary Emim (Deut 2:10). Since then it has known no major reversal of fortune, no loss of the central plateau, and no exile by the Assyrians, such as the Israelites living in Transjordan experienced at the hands of Tiglath-pileser III in 733 B.C. (1 Chr 5:26; cf. 2 Kgs 15:29), and all Northern Israel experienced a decade later under Sargon II.

and settled is he into his lees. Hebrew *wĕšōqēṭ hû' 'el-šĕmārāyw*. In English we would say "on his lees." Poetically, the preposition *'el* may balance *'el* in the next line. The lees (or dregs) are sediment that accumulates at the bottom of the wine container during fermentation. Early in the process, wine must be left on its lees, but here complacency is suggested by the parallelism, an interpretation supported by Zeph 1:12 and a nonmetaphorical rendering of the present phrase in T ("and have been quiet along with their possessions"). In Zeph 1:12, however, the wine is ruined, possibly because it has been left too long on its lees. In Isa 25:6 wine settled on its lees is highly refined wine, thus fit for a banquet. It is difficult to know which image is more appropriate here. Moab is certainly not highly prized wine, but neither is it ruined, because at the end of the verse it still retains its taste and fragrance.

He has not been poured from container to container, and into exile he has not gone. Some delete "and into exile he has not gone" (Ehrlich 1912: 357; Volz; McKane), imagining it to be a gloss interpreting the imagery. But what we have here is a familiar Jeremianic construction in the bicolon, where a statement is first made in metaphorical, hyperbolic, or ironic terms, and then restated negatively in literal terms (see Note on 3:3). Here the first colon is metaphorical, continuing what was just said about the nation being settled on its lees. The T does away with the metaphor, going immediately to the application: "neither have they been exiled from place to place." We are talking here about the racking of wine, i.e., the separation of clear wine from its lees by being poured into another container. Again, this is not necessarily a bad thing, even though Kimḥi says it impairs the flavor and fragrance. In the present case, pouring wine from one container to another is a figure for being exiled, which is not a normal, much less happy, event.

and into exile he has not gone. The claim is probably a reasonable one that Moab did not suffer major destruction and exile prior to the Neo-Babylonian period. It is true that battles were fought north of the Arnon all during Moab's history, with land being won and lost, but the central plateau region because of its natural barriers seems to have been left relatively undisturbed. During the Assyrian period Moab was a loyal subject to a line of Assyrian kings, enjoying good relations with them and paying, in many cases, only nominal tribute (Van Zyl 1960: 148–54). Even when Nebuchadnezzar first entered the region, after 605 B.C., Moab appears to have made peace with him and to have begun doing his bidding, to the detriment of Judah (2 Kgs 24:2). Only after its participation in the Jerusalem conference in 594 B.C. was there any reason for the Babylonians to suspect Moabite disloyalty and think about retaliation. Even in 586 when Jerusalem was destroyed, Nebuchadnezzar did not enter Moab. According to Josephus, he arrived on Moabite soil only in 582 B.C., when war was declared also on Moab's northern neighbor, Ammon. The REB, one should note, mistakenly puts this colon before "and settled is he on his lees."

Therefore his flavor has remained in him, and his fragrance has not changed. The Hebrew has a syntactic chiasmus of the type commonly found in Jeremiah, where the verbs are at the extremes (Lundbom 1975: 64 [= 1997: 85]): "Therefore it has remained / his flavor in him // and his fragrance / it has not changed." The faint praise accorded Moab is here completed. Moab is still Moab, unmixed with other nations as a result of not having been exiled. If it be assumed that Jeremiah all along has been meaning to censure Moab, then there is irony in the present words, and the flavor and fragrance can be taken as essentially bad.

and his fragrance has not changed. Hebrew *wĕrêḥô lōʾ nāmār.* The verb is an N-stem of *mûr,* "change"; on the pointing, see GKC §72dd. Moab's national character, whether good or bad, remains basically intact.

12. *Look, hereafter, days are coming—oracle of Yahweh—when I shall send to him decanters and they will decant him.* This beginning compares closely to the beginning of another prose oracle in 16:16: "Look I am sending for plenty of fishers—oracle of Yahweh—and they will fish for them; and after this I will send for hunters aplenty, and they will hunt them down from upon every mountain." There is a wordplay in *ṣōʿîm wĕṣēʿuhû,* "decanters and they will decant him." The verb *ṣʿh,* lit. "tilt (wine jars)," has the obscene meaning of "bend over (backward)" in 2:20. This divine oracle retains the figure of the poetry, depicting Moab's overthrow in terms of uninvited wine stewards who come and pour wine from its present jars into other jars. Decanting is a prediction of exile (Kimḥi). The action here is destructive. Cornill imagines the wine being decanted carelessly, not in the way decanters ordinarily do their work. The T has "plunders . . . and they shall plunder them," carrying forth its interpretation of the undisturbed wine being Moab's possessions. The LXX's *apostelō autō klinontas, kai klinousin auton* is behind the rendering of the AV: "I will send unto him wanderers, that shall cause him to wander." The MT reading, however, is better and should be followed.

Look, hereafter, days are coming. This formulaic phrase, which introduces oracles of divine favor or divine judgment for the future, recurs in 49:2; 51:47, and 52; see Notes on 7:32 and 16:14.

and his containers they will pour out and his jars they will smash. The figure is now extended to cover the actual damage about to occur in Moab. We need not imagine simply jars being emptied and smashed in Moab's wine cellars, although this will doubtless occur in a general destruction. What we are looking at is violent activity on a much greater scale. In Lam 4:2 the (smashed) jars are Zion's sons. Compare also Jeremiah's smashing of the pot in the Valley of Ben Hinnom (19:1–13).

his jars. Hebrew *niblêhem.* These are earthenware jars (Rashi; Cheyne) capable of being smashed. The Vg has *lagunculas* ("flasks"). A *nēbel* can also be a "(wine) skin"; see Note on 13:12.

13. *Then Moab shall be ashamed of Chemosh just as the house of Israel was ashamed of Bethel, their trust.* A comparison using *kaʾăšer,* on which see Note for 7:14. Calvin says this verse shows that Jeremiah's audience consisted of Judahites, not Moabites. Some commentators (Peake; S. R. Driver; Bright; McKane) and some modern Versions (NAB; REB) give *bôš* the meaning "(bitterly) disappointed in, let down" (2:36; 12:13; 20:11; 50:12), the idea being that Moab will feel let down by Chemosh when the expected help does not come, which is precisely what happened to Northern Israel when it relied on a god other than Yahweh. Note also the comparison to Israel made later in v 27.

Chemosh. See Note on 48:7b.

Bethel. Hebrew *bēt 'ēl* is written here and elsewhere as two words, but in some ancient MSS it appears as one word (C. D. Ginsburg 1885 III: xiv). The term is not without difficulty. Reference is usually made to the calf erected at Bethel by Jeroboam I (1 Kgs 12:28–29), a symbol of Yahweh roundly condemned by the prophets Amos and Hosea (Hos 4:15; 5:8; 10:15; Amos 3:14; 4:4; 5:5–6). But here the parallelism would seem to require a deity like Chemosh, and so it is not without interest that "Bethel" has turned up in extrabiblical texts as a divine epithet: 1) in a seventh-century B.C. treaty between Esarhaddon and Baal of Tyre; 2) in names in Neo-Babylonian texts; and 3) in Jewish names (e.g., Bethelnathan, Anathbethel) in the Elephantine Papyri (Cowley 1923: xviii, 54–56, 70–72; Hyatt 1939; Porten 1968: 160–73; cf. *ANET*[3] 491). It has therefore been argued that Bethel was a West-Semitic deity worshiped in Syria, later in Babylonia, and in Egypt by Elephantine Jews (Hyatt). Elsewhere in the OT, Bethel is only a place-name, for which reason some commentators (McKane; Jones) argue that the term must stand for the cult of Bethel. But this presupposes that the parallelism is inexact, which it does not seem to be. It has also been argued that since Bethel is referred to instead of Jerusalem, destruction of the latter has not yet occurred (Cornill; Peake).

their trust. Hebrew *mibṭeḥām.* Sarcasm. Israel's trust should have been in Yahweh (cf. 2:37; and see Note on 7:14 for misplaced trust). The LXX expands to *elpidos autōn pepoithotes ep' autois,* "their hope, having trusted in them," which Janzen (1973: 26) says is a doublet.

MESSAGE AND AUDIENCE

Jeremiah begins the present dialogue by expressing incredulity at Moab's ability to avoid dispersion and exile. One might even call it another of his complaints. Old Man Moab has been at ease from its early years of nationhood; like wine, he is settled on his lees and has not been poured from container into container. Jeremiah explains this to mean that Moab has not experienced exile. Other nations have. Israel has; the Transjordan tribes have; maybe Judah already has. But Moab, perched comfortably on his tableland vineyard, has his taste and sense of smell unchanged.

Yahweh answers by saying that the days are coming when he will send decanters to decant Moab. Jars will be emptied and smashed. The audience will perhaps perceive that Moab's destruction will be complete and its accumulated possessions taken. Then, in an ending perhaps added later, the oracle states that Moab will be ashamed of Chemosh just as Israel was ashamed of Bethel in whom it put its trust. To a Jerusalem audience this will evoke memories of Jeroboam's ill-conceived cultic site in Northern Israel, but some may remember also what Jeremiah said to Judahites about trusting in the deceptive words "The temple of Yahweh, the temple of Yahweh, the temple of Yahweh" (7:4).

When the present oracle is heard following the oracle in vv 7b–9, the theme of exile will get the accent. But we seem to be going backward in time. The present dialogue appears to be earlier than what precedes, for Jeremiah is really questioning Yahweh about Moab avoiding the indignity of exile, and finding out for the first time that Yahweh does indeed have exile planned for Moab in the future. Holladay dates vv 11–12 to 605 B.C., which may be a bit too early. The dialogue in its entirety could date to 597 B.C., when Moab had been harassing Judah and not been troubled itself in the least by Nebuchadnezzar and the Babylonians. Jeremiah could then be giving expression here to a widespread feeling in Judah that Moab deserved punishment and exile, but was not getting it. The answer received was that punishment would be meted out in due course. Nebuchadnezzar's invasion of Moab in 582 is, in any case, a terminus ad quem for the oracle and the dialogue as a whole.

3. The Talk Now and the Talk Later (48:14–24)

a) Warriors Are We! (48:14–17a)

48 ¹⁴How can you say, 'Warriors are we
  and valiant men for war'?
¹⁵The devastator of Moab and her cities has come up
  and the best of his young men have gone down to the slaughter
  — oracle of the King, Yahweh of hosts is his name

¹⁶The disaster of Moab is near to come
  his trouble hastens apace
¹⁷ᵃGive consolation to him, all you round about him
  and all you who know his name.

RHETORIC AND COMPOSITION

MT 48:14–17a = LXX 31:14–17a. In these verses are no section markings, but vv 14–20 can be delimited as poetry framed by prose preceding (vv 12–13) and following (vv 21–24). The poetry divides into three poems (vv 14–17a, 17b–18, 19–20), all containing calls to lament and the first identified as being a divine oracle. These poems share key words, balancing metaphors, and plays on the "up and down," containing also stereotyped openings seen elsewhere in Jeremiah's Judah poems:

I *How can you say . . .*	*'êk tō'měrû*	v 14
The devastator of Moab . . . has come up	*šōdēd¹ mô'āb . . . 'ālâ*	v 15
have gone down	*yārĕdû*	
II *Say, How . . .*	*'imrû 'êkâ*	v 17b
Come down	*rĕdî*	v 18
sitting daughter Dibon	*yōšebet bat-dîbôn*	
For the devastator of Moab has come up	*kî-šōdēd mô'āb 'ālâ*	

---

¹Repointing to the Qal participle (cf. v 18b); see Notes.

III	To the way, stand ... ask ... say	ʾel-derek ʿimdî ... šaʾălî ... ʾimrî	v 19
	sitting one of Aroer	yôšebet ʿărôʿēr	
	Indeed Moab is devastated	kî šuddad môʾāb	v 20b

All contain at the beginning or near the beginning a form of the verb ʾmr, "say," which occurs also in poems and stanzas of poems in the Judah collection, e.g., 2:20, 23, 25b, 35; 8:8 (see Rhetoric and Composition for 2:20–22), and all contain the verb šdd, "devastate," coupled with "Moab." Oracle I begins like 2:23 and 8:8, also Isa 19:11b (Duhm; Holladay); Oracle III has a beginning like 6:16. The break then between Oracle I and Oracle II is after v 17a, not after v 16 (*pace* Cheyne; Volz) and not after v 17b (*pace* Rudolph; Weiser; Bright; Carroll). One may also discern in the three-poem cluster a progression of thought from boasting, to humiliation, to the reaction of neighbors—far and wide—who observe Moab's shame.

That the present poem is an oracle is indicated by the expanded messenger formula in v 15. The LXX omits, but the formula enriches the poem and should be retained. The oracle has two stanzas: vv 14–15, and vv 16–17a, the first a bicolon and a tricolon with the messenger formula, and the second a double bicolon. Yahweh is the speaker in Stanza I, addressing first a band of Moabite soldiers (v 14), then an unidentified audience (v 15). The speaker in Stanza II is either Yahweh or the prophet, who addresses first an unidentified audience (v 16), then Moab's neighbors (v 17a). The two stanzas have this repetition in their closing lines:

| I | .... | his name | šĕmô | v 15 |
| II | .... | his name | šĕmô | v 17a |

The name in v 15 is Yahweh's; in v 17a it is Moab's.

Catchwords connecting to the dialogue preceding are these:

| vv 15, 16 Moab (2×) | vv 11, 13 Moab (2×) |

Catchwords connecting to the next poem are these:

v 14	How can you say	v 17b	Say, How
v 15	the devastator of Moab ...	v 18	Come down
	has come up		the devastator of Moab
	have gone down		has come up

NOTES

48:14. *How can you say, 'Warriors are we, and valiant men for war'?* This is the language of disputation, but with a decidedly Jeremianic flavor as in 2:23 and 8:8. It is meant to be a setup for what follows in v 15, which will show up an incongruity. Verse 15 envisions an enemy coming against Moab's select warriors and leaving them strewn on the battlefield. Boasting before such an eventuality is foolishness, as all Moab will learn to its great sorrow. This boast of military might may derive from the time when Moabites, together with other Babylonian mercenaries, overran Judah in 599–598 B.C. (2 Kgs 24:2).

Warriors. Or "mighty men." Hebrew *gibbôrîm.* Such are David's elite warriors in 2 Sam 23:8. On the term, see further Note for 46:6.

valiant men for war. Hebrew *'anšê-ḥayil lammilḥāmâ.* See 1 Sam 14:52 and 2 Kgs 24:16.

15. *The devastator of Moab and her cities has come up.* This colon as pointed in the MT cannot be read unless one allows a singular verb, "it has come up" (*'ālâ*) to predicate a plural subject, "her cities" (*'āreyhā*). Kimḥi does this by assuming an ellipsis: "(the multitude of) their cities has ended," which Cornill quotes with approval, saying that the cities could also "go up in smoke" (Judg 20:40). This proposal was made earlier by Grotius (cf. Hitzig, 356). We may note in this connection that the verb *'lh* means "go away, be gone" in 8:18 (see Note there). The LXX reads *ōleto Mōab polis autou,* "Moab has been destroyed, [with?] his city," supporting the first part of the verse but omitting "has come up." Janzen (1973: 59) thinks the verb is MT expansion (from v 18), but more likely we have another LXX omission due to haplography (homoeoteleuton: *h . . . h*). Symmachus has the verb (*anebē*). Without this verb there is no play on the "up and down" (see Rhetoric and Composition), which is widely recognized by commentators. The T reads: "The Moabites have been plundered and their cities are a destruction," again showing that the MT has antecedents, however problematic its reading now is. The problem is largely with the initial verb, which the MT points as a Pual perfect, *šuddad,* "(Moab) has been devastated." This verb with the same pointing appears also in v 20b. But in vv 8 and 18 the same verb is pointed as a Qal participle, *šōdēd,* "the devastator," with J. D. Michaelis (1793: 330) suggesting long ago that this should be the pointing here. Support for this reading comes from six MSS that actually contain the participle spelled *šwdd* (Blayney). A much improved rendering of the entire colon, "The devastator of Moab and his cities has come / gone up," has thus been adopted by a majority of commentators and modern Versions. Only the NJV, NIV, and NJB stay with MT, disregarding its subject-verb infelicity. Holladay (with emendations) also reads MT. Repointing avoids a possible anachronism with v 16 where Moab's destruction is envisioned as being imminent. If Moab is already a land in ruins (as the MT presumes), then destruction has occurred. Either way, the verbs in the line are prophetic perfects, envisioning a future reality that has not yet taken place.

The devastator of Moab. On the verb *šdd,* see Note on 48:1.

and her cities. Hebrew *wĕ'āreyhā.* Volz and Holladay emend with the LXX to "his cities," which harmonizes with the masculine suffixes in the following colon. But here, too, MT is better, since elsewhere in the cluster are two other seemingly intentional gender alternations (v 19b; 20a).

come up . . . gone down. For the play on the "up and down," see v 18 and Note on 48:5.

and the best of his young men have gone down to the slaughter. The Heb ûmibḥar baḥûrāyw yārĕdû laṭṭābaḥ has alliteration on the consonants *bḥ* (Casanowicz 1893 #44). A contrast is made with the boasting (young) warriors in v 14. The "best" here are the choicest (*mibḥar*); cf. Exod 15:4.

gone down to the slaughter. Or "to the sacrifice." Hebrew yārĕdû laṭṭābaḥ. The expression "go down / bring down to the slaughter" occurs also in the Babylon oracles (50:27; 51:40). Followed here by an attribution of sovereignty to Yahweh, this sacrifice compares with one carried out by Yahweh against the nations in Isa 34:2, 6. See also Jer 25:34.

oracle of the King, Yahweh of hosts is his name. The "oracle of the King" formula appears also in 46:18 (MT) and 51:57. For other occurrences of "Yahweh of hosts is his name," many of which are climactic shouts in the poetry, see Note on 10:16. This asseveration is to put God's power before the audience. The LXX omits here as elsewhere (Janzen 1973: 79).

16. *The disaster of Moab is near to come.* Hebrew qārôb 'êd-mô'āb lābô'. The LXX has ēmera ("day") for Heb 'êd ("disaster"); cf. Deut 32:35 and Isa 13:22. In the OT, the "day" of a nation or city can be its day of disaster, e.g., "the day of Egypt" (Ezek 30:9) and "the day of Jerusalem" (Ps 137:7). Judah's day of disaster is envisioned in Jer 18:17. The day of Yahweh coming near is a recurring theme in the prophecy of Joel (1:15; 2:1; and 4:14[Eng 3:14]). On the concept of the "day of Yahweh" in the OT, see Note for 4:9. Here we seem to be stepping back a pace, looking at a battle that is imminent, rather than over or nearly over. In v 15, Moab's losses are said to be heavy.

his trouble hastens apace. Hebrew rā'ātô miḥărâ mĕ'ōd, where rā'â is translated "trouble," rather than "evil." In the Bible judgment (as well as salvation) may not come soon (Hab 2:3), but it does come quickly. In v 11 Jeremiah was bothered about a delay in Moab's judgment, specifically its exile. Calvin discusses the matter of delay—and also faith—at some length. On the suddenness theme in Scripture, see Daube 1964 and Note for 4:20.

17a. *Give consolation to him.* Hebrew nūdû lô. Here the verb nûd denotes the show of grief by shaking the head (see 16:5; 18:16; 22:10; 31:18; and Note on 15:5). This is not a call for Moab's neighbors to show genuine sympathy (*pace* Cheyne), but an ironic directive intended to accentuate Moab's misfortune. Compare the calls for mourning in vv 17b and 20.

all you round about him. Hebrew kol-sĕbîbāyw. A circumlocution for Moab's neighbors.

and all you who know his name. I.e., the name of Moab. The irony could be heightened here by an allusion to Moab's name (= reputation). Ehrlich (1912: 357) says the meaning is not "know his name," but "respect his name." That idea is present with regard to Yahweh's name in Isa 52:6.

MESSAGE AND AUDIENCE

This poem begins the way so many of Jeremiah's poems do, by quoting a claim of certain individuals who have no idea how empty their words really are. The boast here is put into the mouths of Moabite soldiers, who were perhaps physically present in Judah in Jehoiakim's latter years (2 Kgs 24:2). They claim to be valiant warriors, but the question is raised as to why they should be so confident. If they are really the soldiers they claim to be, why is a devastating enemy seen coming up against Moab and its select warriors going down to an inglorious slaughter? This may be a vision of something that has not yet happened. But no matter. Moab's crack troops who boast now will be dead later. This word is announced as an oracle of the King, whose name is Yahweh of the army.

We are then told that Moab's devastation is near, its time of arrival hastening to fulfillment, which must mean the nation's demise has not yet occurred. The poem—or oracle—then closes with a call for Moab's neighbors to give the beleaguered country consolation, at which time they can eulogize her great name. But will they? Given the hubris of Moab's soldiers, no one in a Jerusalem audience will likely be moved to tears.

This poem with others in the collection fits into the general period between 604 and 582 B.C. (see Message and Audience for 48:1–2). It reflects sentiments likely to have been widespread in Judah after the Moabite incursion in 599–598 B.C.

When heard with the Moab poems preceding, this poem will not carry forth the theme of exile present in the dialogue of vv 11–13, but will return to the destruction theme in the poetry of vv 1–9, with the difference that now we hear calls for mourning.

b) How the Mighty Scepter Is Broken! (48:17b–18)

48 ^{17b}Say, 'How the mighty scepter is broken
    the most glorious staff!'
¹⁸Come down from glory and sit[1] in thirst
    sitting daughter Dibon
For the devastator of Moab has come up against you
    he has destroyed your fortresses.

RHETORIC AND COMPOSITION

MT 48:17b–18 = LXX 31:17b–18. These verses are delimited within the poetry of vv 14–20 by stereotyped openings in v 17b and v 19 (see Rhetoric and Composition for 48:14–17a). The "Say, How . . ." (*'imrû 'êkâ*) is a deliberate reversal of "How can you say?" (*'êk tō'mĕrû*) in v 14. That v 17b goes with v 18 seems clear, since both contain imagery of royal statehood. Rudolph correctly notes that 17b is a little lament, having all the marks of the *qinah* (dirge) form, on which see Note for 9:9[10]. The meter through to the end of v 20 is *qinah* (3:2); cf. Volz, who begins with v 17a. There is another reversal in this poem from the poem preceding: the "come down–come up" contrast in v 18 reverses

---

[1]Reading the Q *ûšĕbî*, "and sit" (Qal feminine imperative) with many MSS and the Vrs. The Kt *yšby* may simply be a scribal error (Cornill; Holladay).

the "come up–gone down" contrast in v 15. For the integrated structure of a three-poem cluster in vv 14–20, see Rhetoric and Composition for 48:14–17a.

Catchwords connecting to the poem preceding:

v 17b	*Say, How*	v 14	*How can you say*
v 18	*Come down*	v 15	*the devastator of Moab . . .*
	the devastator of Moab		*has come up*
	has come up		*have gone down*

Catchwords connecting to the poem following:

v 17b	*Say*	v 19	*sitting one of Aroer*
v 18	*sitting daughter Dibon*		*say*
	the devastator of Moab	v 20	*Moab is devastated*

NOTES

48:17b. *Say, How . . . !* Hebrew *'imrû 'êkâ*. The K^{OR} have *'êk*. The language continues to be ironic. Moabites are now supplied with a lament to replace the boast made by their soldiers (v 14). Or perhaps the soldiers themselves are being addressed. The imperative "Say!" (*'imrû*) is masculine plural, which is the common form in Jeremianic poetry (see Note on 13:18). Laments typically begin with an impassioned *'êk* or *'êkâ*, "How!" (9:18[Eng 9:19]; 48:17, 39; 49:25; 50:23 [2×]; 51:41 [2×]; Isa 1:21; Mic 2:4; Obad 5, 6; Lam 1:1; 2:1; 4:1).

   mighty scepter. Hebrew *maṭṭēh-'ōz*. A phrase occurring also in Ps 110:2 and Ezek 19:11–12, 14, symbolizing kingly rule. See also Isa 14:29. Lamented here is the loss of rule once exercised by Moab's capital city, Dibon.

   most glorious staff. Hebrew *maqqēl tip'ārâ*. A parallel expression to "mighty scepter," the focus here being on the ornamental character of this wood symbol. The attributive noun, *tip'ārâ*, means "beauty, glory, ornament, honor." Jeremiah, speaking to a situation in Jerusalem similar to the present one, uses *tip'ārâ* to describe the gloriously decorated crowns of Jehoiachin and the queen mother, also the queen's blue-ribbon flock (13:18, 20; cf. Isa 28:5). Here the attribution of power and beauty to Moab's national symbol makes for biting irony, since something once the cause for boasting is now broken. Lamented ultimately is the loss of Moab's pride (*tip'eret* means "arrogance" in Isa 10:12), which comes tumbling in the verse following and is attacked directly in vv 29–30.

   18. *Come down from glory and sit in thirst, sitting daughter Dibon.* Feminine imperatives now address the city of Dibon, personified here as a woman. The imagery is reminiscent of 13:18, where King Jehoiachin and the queen mother are told to come down from their places of honor, sit on the ground, and surrender to the king of Babylon. The same indignity awaits Daughter Babylon later (Isa 47:1). It is supposed here that because Dibon is situated on two hills high above the Arnon with deep wadis surrounding them, a descent of nobility and other citizenry after the city's surrender could occur quite literally (Duhm;

Peake; Cornill). Even so, there will be another coming down from glory. Kimḥi interprets "glory" as meaning a state of wealth and plenty, when nothing was wanting.

and sit in thirst. Hebrew *baṣṣāmāʾ* ("in thirst") occurs elsewhere in the OT in contexts of war (2 Chr 32:11), the aftermath of war (Lam 4:4), and the sending of divine curses (Deut 28:48; Hos 2:5[Eng 2:3]), all of which have application here. Daughter Dibon is being called down from her seat of glory to sit as a (hungry and) thirsty captive. Some commentators, however, revocalize to *baṣṣāmēʾ* to get "in thirsty / parched (ground)" (Cheyne; Thompson; Keown et al.; cf. RSV; NEB; NIV; NJB), while others revocalize (with S) to *baṣṣōʾâ* to get "in dung" or "in filth" (Cornill; Volz; Rudolph; Weiser; Bright; Holladay; McKane; cf. JB; NSB). Cornill, Rudolph, and Holladay prefer the latter reading because the others, they say, do not make a strong enough contrast with "glory." But who says the contrast has to be that sharp? The LXX has *en hugrasia kathēmenē* ("in a wet place"), which Cornill and Peake say may mean "in the mire." The T generalizes with "in desolation." The correct reading is probably "in thirst," which appears in Aq and Symm (*en dipsē*), the Vg (*in siti*), and in the AV and NJV. See also 13:18; Isa 3:26; and 47:1 on exalted nations, cities, and royalty coming down from seats of splendor to sit on the ground. Dobbs-Allsopp (1993: 107 n. 53) refers in this connection to the conventional image in ANE literature of gods or goddesses coming down from their thrones to sit on the ground.

sitting daughter Dibon. Hebrew *yōšebet bat-dîbôn*. The expression is difficult, nevertheless a bona fide Jeremianic signature (see Note for 46:19; on the "daughter" metaphor, see Kartveit 2001 and Note for 4:11). The NRSV renders the phrase "enthroned daughter Dibon," which calls attention to Dibon's status as a capital city; thus Moab's royal seat. Holladay translates: "poor enthroned Dibon!" In the ANE gods and kings were commonly given an epithet such as this one, with Yahweh too being called "the one enthroned in heaven," *yōšēb baššāmayim* (Ps 2:4; cf. Dobbs-Allsopp 1993: 108–9). But not to be overlooked is a play here on the verb *yšb*, "sit": Daughter Dibon has been sitting in regal splendor, but now she will sit in humility and want. The LXX lacks "daughter," which is better explained as LXX haplography (homoeoteleuton: *bt . . . bt*), than MT dittography (*pace* Giesebrecht; Duhm; Janzen 1973: 29; McKane; cf. RSV; NEB; NAB; NSB).

Dibon. This tableland city (v 22) was the Iron Age capital of Moab, its tell now located just north of the modern village of Dhiban. The ancient and modern cities lie on two hills connected by a saddle. Dibon is 64 kilometers south of Amman on the King's Highway, and ca. 3 kilometers north of the Arnon River (*NEAEHL* 1: 350–52; *OEANE* 2: 156–57). After Israel's conquest of the Amorite king Sihon, Dibon was settled by the tribes of Gad (Num 32:34; cf. 21:30) and Reuben (Josh 13:9, 15–17). By the ninth century B.C., the city was in Moabite hands. Mesha's father ruled presumably from Dibon as a vassal of Omri, and Mesha himself ruled from Dibon after repossessing the tableland, although the tableland cities are said to have been destroyed later by Jehoram

(Moabite Stone; 2 Kgs 3:4–27; cf. Dearman 1989b: 171). Excavations carried out at the site by the American School of Oriental Research in Jerusalem, beginning in 1950, came up with evidence of Moabite occupation—possibly as early as Iron Age I—on the summit of the mound (Stratum VI). On the southeast corner was found evidence of Moabite occupation in Iron II—pottery, for the most part—from the mid–ninth century B.C. to the presumed destruction of the city by Nebuchadnezzar in 582 B.C. (Tushingham 1972: 15, 25). The Moabite Stone was found in Dibon in 1868, and from it we learn that Dibon was King Mesha's birthplace. Dibon, too, is mentioned on the Stone (lines 2, 21, 28). On the excavations of ancient Dibon, see Winnett and Reed 1964; Tushingham 1972; OEANE 2: 157–58; and Dearman 1989b: 171–74.

For the devastator of Moab has come up against you. A repeat of v 15. Note again a play in the verse on the "up and down."

he has destroyed your fortresses. The verb *šḥt* ("destroy, ruin") occurs together with *ʿlh* ("come / gone up") also in 5:10 (Holladay).

MESSAGE AND AUDIENCE

This brief poem offers to the people of Moab, or perhaps the boasting soldiers heard from in the preceding poem, a lament they can use when the seat of Moabite prestige and power lies in ruins. Moab's mighty scepter will be broken; its glorious staff will be no more. The city of Dibon, sitting as an elegant woman high above the Arnon, is told to come down from her regal splendor and sit as a thirsty captive. The devastator of Moab will come up against her, to destroy her trusted fortifications. For the date of this and other Moab poems, see Message and Audience for 48:1–2.

c) What Has Happened? (48:19–24)

48 ¹⁹To the way, stand and watch
   sitting one of Aroer!
Ask him who flees and her who escapes
   say: 'What has happened?'

²⁰Moab is very shamed
   indeed she is shattered
     wail and cry out!
Declare by the Arnon:
   'Indeed Moab is devastated.'

²¹Judgment has come to the tableland—to Holon, and to Jahzah, and upon Mephaath, ²²and upon Dibon, and upon Nebo, and upon Beth-diblathaim, ²³and upon Kiriathaim, and upon Beth-gamul, and upon Beth-meon, ²⁴and upon Kerioth, and upon Bozrah, and upon all the cities of the land of Moab, those far and those near.

RHETORIC AND COMPOSITION

MT 48:19–24 = LXX 31:19–24. These verses consist of a concluding poem in a three-poem cluster (vv 19–20), followed by a list of tableland cities affected in the ruinous visitation upon Moab (vv 21–24). This listing is a later addition in prose (*pace* Thompson). On the structure of the three-poem cluster in vv 14–20, see Rhetoric and Composition for 48:14–17a. The poem here is delimited at the top end by a stereotyped opening in v 19, and at the bottom end by the onset of prose in v 21. The prose is delimited by poetry on either side; in v 25 is a brief poetic oracle.

The poem continues the *qinah* (3:2) meter of the preceding poetry (Volz; Rudolph), and has two stanzas. Stanza I (v 19) is a double bicolon, concluding with a question for inhabitants of Aroer to ask refugees fleeing Dibon. Stanza II (v 20) is a tricolon and a bicolon, ending with the answer for those who make it to safety across the Arnon. The *qinah* meter appears to be abandoned in 20b, which otherwise has the tone of a lament. It is unclear who is speaker of the poem. It could be Yahweh or Jeremiah. Stanza II has a repetition of an asseverative *kî*:

II	*indeed* she is shattered	*kî . . .*	v 20
	Indeed Moab is devastated	*kî . . .*	

The listing of cities has this inclusio:

. . . . *the tableland*	*'ereṣ hammîšōr*	v 21
. . . . *the land of Moab*	*'ereṣ mô'āb*	v 24

One should not omit then *'ereṣ* ("land") in v 24 with the LXX, as many commentators do.

Catchwords linking this poem to the poem preceding:

v 19 *sitting one of Aroer*	v 17b *Say*
say	v 18 *sitting daughter Dibon*
v 20 *Moab is devastated*	*the devastator of Moab*

From this point on, all remaining poetic or prose units in chap. 48, except for the prose insertion of v 34, appear to be linked by the catchword "Moab." Five of the units, vv 32–33, 35–39, 40–43, 44, 45–46, have other catchwords as well. The units linked together by "Moab":

48:19–20	poetry	Moab (2×)	v 20
48:21–24	prose	Moab	v 24
48:25	poetry	Moab	v 25
48:26–27	prose	Moab	v 26
48:28	poetry	Moab	v 28
48:29–31	poetry	Moab (3×)	vv 29, 31
48:32–33	poetry	Moab	v 33

48:34	prose	—	—
48:35–38a	poetry	*Moab* (3×)	vv 35, 36, 38a
48:38b–39	poetry	*Moab* (3×)	vv 38b, 39 (2×)
48:40–41	poetry	*Moab* (2×)	vv 40, 41
48:42–43	poetry	*Moab* (2×)	vv 42, 43
48:44	poetry	*Moab*	v 44
48:45–46	poetry	*Moab* (2×)	vv 45, 46
48:47a	prose	*Moab*	v 47a
48:47b	prose	*Moab*	v 47b

NOTES

48:19. *To the way, stand and watch.* Hebrew *'el-derek 'imdî wĕṣappî.* An urgent directive telling the people of Aroer to get out on the road and await news from refugees fleeing Dibon, which lies about five kilometers to the northwest. Aroer is situated on the northern slope of Wadi Mujib (= River Arnon), and it has not yet been attacked. The aged Eli sat similarly by the way watching (*yōšēb . . . yad*[Q] *derek mĕṣappeh*) for news about Israel's battle with the Philistines (1 Sam 4:13). The directive here is similar to the one given in 6:16 ("Stand by the ways . . . and ask"), only there the people of Judah are instructed to seek out the "ancient paths" set forth by the Sinai covenant.

sitting one of Aroer! Hebrew *yōšebet 'ărô'ēr.* Aroer is personified here as a woman (feminine singular imperatives) resting comfortably; cf. "sitting daughter Dibon" in v 18a. On this particular Jeremianic construction, see 21:13; 48:43; 51:35; and Note on 46:19.

Aroer. A Moabite city found elsewhere in the OT and appearing on the Moabite Stone (line 26), generally identified with Khirbet 'Ara'ir (*NEAEHL* 1: 92), about four kilometers west of the King's Highway on the northern slope of Wadi Mujib (River Arnon). The Bible places it on the "edge of the Wadi Arnon" (Deut 2:36; 3:12; 4:48; Josh 12:2; 13:9, 16), perhaps to distinguish it from the Aroer east of Rabbath Ammon (Josh 13:25; Judg 11:33). There was also another Aroer in Judah (1 Sam 30:28). Throughout its history, Aroer on the Arnon was primarily a fortress guarding the King's Highway as it descended to cross the Arnon. Crystal-M. Bennett (1982b: 183) says this fortress also protected Dibon. The Israelites captured Aroer in their campaign against Sihon, after which it was assigned to the Reubenites (Josh 13:15–16). It was built up by the Gadites (Num 32:34) and became the southern boundary of Israel's Transjordan territory. In the mid–ninth century, Aroer was taken by Mesha of Moab, who claimed to have rebuilt it and made a road across the Arnon (Moabite Stone, line 26). During the eighth century it was in Syrian hands (2 Kgs 10:33) until 732 B.C., when Damascus fell to the Assyrians. Excavations in the 1960s by a Spanish team revealed that Aroer was unfortified during the seventh century, and that its pottery showed trade with Assyria and Edom. In the early sixth century a fortress was erected on the highest point of the mound. This fortress appears to have been destroyed by the Babylonians, perhaps when Nebuchadnezzar campaigned against Moab in 582 B.C. See further G. L. Mattingly, *ABD* 1: 399–400.

Ask him who flees and her who escapes. Hebrew *ša'ălî-nās wěnimlāṭâ*. The alternation of gender is intentional and should be retained (Kimḥi; Holladay), done here for the sake of inclusiveness (Calvin; Cornill; Volz; Rudolph; Bright; Carroll). Men are fleeing; women are escaping; all humanity is coming down the road with what little they can carry. Another gender shift comes in the next verse: "Moab (masc.) is very shamed, indeed she is shattered." For other shifts in gender, see 44:25. For a pairing of the verbs *nûs* ("flee") and *mlṭ* ("escape / deliver"), see also 46:6; 48:6; and 51:6.

say: 'What has happened?' The answer comes in v 20b: "Indeed Moab is devastated."

20. *Moab is very shamed, indeed she is shattered.* The first verb *hōbîš* is another internal H-stem: "he is very shamed" (see Note on 2:26). The second verb, *ḥattâ*, is feminine: "she is shattered," and should not be emended to a masculine (Duhm and Volz: gender alternation is possible). A shift in gender occurred in the previous verse, and happens again with the same feminine form, *ḥattâ*, in v 39. Those who emend presume dittography (Blayney; Giesebrecht; Cornill; Ehrlich 1912: 357; Rudolph; Carroll; and Keown et al.), which is possible but unnecessary. Holladay emends the first verb to a feminine (cf. 46:24; 48:1), which is also unnecessary. On the pairing of verbs *bôš* ("be [very] shamed") and *ḥtt* ("be shattered, shatter"), see also 48:1, 39, and Note for 17:18.

wail and cry out! Hebrew *hêlîlî ûzĕ'āqî* (Kt). The Q has masculine plural imperatives, which go with the masculine plural imperative beginning v 20b. The MS evidence is divided; some support the Q, some the Kt (Blayney). The Versions, except for LXX, render both verbs plural. With two other gender changes in 19b and 20a, the Kt is probably the original. The subject does not change; it is still Moab ("Judah" is both masculine and feminine in Lamentations). But the advantage of reading all three imperatives the same is that those who are called upon to wail and cry out are then the same individuals who are instructed to lament in 20b: "Indeed Moab is devastated!" (Giesebrecht; Duhm; McKane). This seems to make more sense than taking the directive in 20b as one issued to Moab's neighbors (Calvin). It is the people of Moab who are called upon to lament the destruction of the tableland. The two verbs occurring here are also paired in 25:34 and 47:2.

Declare by the Arnon: 'Indeed Moab is devastated.' If Dibon has fallen the entire tableland has been overrun (vv 21–24), and the news will be told at the Arnon because people are fleeing in that direction hoping to cross the fords of the river (cf. Isa 16:2). The Arnon is the southern boundary of Moab's tableland. The impassioned declaration answers the "What has happened?" question of v 19. The small but perennial Arnon River, which is mentioned often in the Bible, flows north through the central Moabite mountains, turns westward south of Aroer, and then empties into the Dead Sea.

21. *the tableland.* Hebrew *hammîšōr.* The northern plateau region of Moab, from the Arnon River to about Heshbon. See Note on 48:1.

Holon. A tableland city of unknown location, not to be confused with Holon in the southern Judean hill country (Josh 15:51; 21:15). A first-century A.D. ostracon from Khirbet Qumran turned up in 1996 identifying a slave from the town of Holon (Cross and Eshel 1997). The document is a deed of gift written by a certain Honi, who was passing on an estate and other possessions to his slave, Hisday. Assuming the slave to be a non-Jew, Cross and Eshel suggest a Moabite location for Holon.

Jahzah. Hebrew *yahṣâ.* Spelled *yahaṣ* (Jahaz) in v 34; Isa 15:4; and elsewhere. The town is mentioned on the Moabite Stone as having been annexed by Mesha to Dibon (lines 19–21). Its location is unknown, although Eusebius (*Onom.* 238–39; vid. Jassa) said in his day that it lay between Medeba and Dibon. Jahzah was the site of a battle with Sihon (Num 21:23; Deut 2:32; Judg 11:20), after which it was assigned to Reuben and became a Transjordanian Levitical city (Josh 13:18; 21:36; 1 Chr 6:78). Suggested sites include Umm el-walīd, southwest of Medeba (Bernhardt 1960: 158); Khirbet Libb (Smelik 1992: 74–79); and Khirbet Medeiniyeh (Dearman 1989b: 181–84; *ABD* 3: 612).

Mephaath. Another town originally belonging to the territory of Reuben (Josh 13:18; 21:37; 1 Chr 6:79), but now under Moabite control. Various sites have been proposed, but the location remains unknown (*ABD* 4: 696). Van Zyl (1960: 94) and Kallai (1986: 440) think the site may be Jawa atop a high hill about 10 kilometers south of Amman, which would have been the most northeastern frontier fortress in the Iron Age. Kallai says it has preserved the ancient name in an adjoining site, Khirbet Nēfaʿah. Dearman (1997: 210), on the basis of a recently unearthed dedicatory inscription, says the site is probably farther south, at Umm er-Raṣaṣ (= Kastron Mefaa), east of Dibon.

22. *Dibon.* See Note on 48:18.

Nebo. See Note on 48:1.

Beth-diblathaim. A Moabite settlement of unknown location, mentioned elsewhere only on the Moabite Stone (line 30). The Bible, however, knows of an Almon-diblathaim along the King's Highway between Nebo and Dibon (Num 33:46–47). Suggested sites include Khirbet Libb, 13 kilometers north of Dibon on the King's Highway, and Khirbet Deleilat esh-Sherqiyeh, about 4 kilometers northeast of Khirbet Libb, where Iron Age occupation has been established (Van Zyl 1960: 86; Dearman 1989b: 187; *ABD* 1: 684).

23. *Kiriathaim.* See Note on 48:1.

Beth-gamul. Another tableland settlement of unknown location. Some put the city at Khirbet el-Jemeil, 13 kilometers east of Dibon (Van Zyl 1960: 75–76; Dearman 1989a: 300, 302; *ABD* 1: 686).

Beth-meon. A northern Moabite town also going by the name Baal-meon (Num 32:38), which was settled after the Transjordanian conquest by the tribe of Reuben. The town appears as Baal-meon and Beth-Baal-meon on the Moabite Stone (lines 9, 30), and as Baal-meon in Ezek 25:9, where, together with

Kiriathaim the city is to be given over to an enemy from the east. The probable location of Beth-meon is the modern village of Maʿin, about 6 kilometers southwest of Medeba (Bernhardt 1960: 143 n. 26; Dearman 1989b: 175–76; *ABD* 1: 690).

24. *Kerioth*. Hebrew *qĕrîyyôt* is lit. "cities." A fortified Moabite city according to Amos 2:2. The same Hebrew word appears again in v 41, although there it is usually translated "towns" or "cities." Kerioth is mentioned on the Moabite Stone (line 13), where it appears to be a cult center of Chemosh. Its location is unknown. Suggested sites are in the vicinity of Dibon, one possibility being Khirbet ʿAleiyan, 8 kilometers northeast of Dibon (Bernhardt 1960: 143–52; Dearman 1989b: 178–79).

Bozrah. A Moabite city of unknown location, not to be confused with Bozrah in Edom, on which see Note for 49:13.

and upon all the cities of the land of Moab, those far and those near. The aggregate of cities is only those on the tableland, not cities of the central plateau region between the Arnon and the Zered. On the closing expression "those far and those near," compare 25:26. Kimḥi says the reference here is to cities on the border and those in the interior. *Mezudath David*: (cities) far from and near the Arnon.

MESSAGE AND AUDIENCE

The poem begins with an anxious call for the complacent people of Aroer to go out to the highway and stand watch, where they will see humanity in flight. They are to ask man and woman, "What has happened?" But before they can do so, much less get an answer, it is said that Moab is now very ashamed, shattered beyond description, and the only thing to do is lament in a loud voice. The refugees, being joined by their awakened neighbors from Aroer, are told in conclusion what to say as they descend amidst much wailing to the Arnon: "Indeed Moab is devastated."

This poem envisions the end of a battle wresting the tableland out of Moabite hands, fulfilled finally in the Babylonian campaign against Moab in 582 B.C. But it need not be later than other Moab poems. For the range of possible dates, see Message and Audience for 48:1–2.

The three poems heard in sequence show a progression. The first poem (vv 14–17a) attacks Moabite boasting, saying that the disaster of Moab is near at hand. The second poem (vv 17b–18) offers a lament as replacement for Moab's boasting, calling also for the royal city to relinquish its glory since the enemy has destroyed her defenses. The present poem (vv 19–20) is a wrap-up, calling for people at the Aroer citadel to proceed with all haste to the highway and ask what happened to Dibon, then to join the refugees in lamenting Moab on the banks of the Arnon.

The listing of cities upon whom judgment has fallen (vv 21–24) gives specificity to the claim that Moab is devastated, also making it clear that the loss is only the tableland region, not all of Moab.

4. The Horn of Moab Is Cut Off (48:25–27)

48 ^{25}The horn of Moab is cut off
his arm is broken
—oracle of Yahweh.

^{26}Make him drunk, because against Yahweh he made himself great. Then Moab shall splash in his vomit and become a joke—even he. ^{27}Then surely the joke is for you, Israel, if among thieves he has been found.[1] For more than all your words against him, you will shake your head!

RHETORIC AND COMPOSITION

MT 48:25–27 = LXX 31:25–27. Here is a brief oracle (v 25) followed by a spiteful prose comment of later date (vv 26–27). Rudolph takes v 25 as an answer to the question of v 19b, while Holladay believes the verse continues the quotation of 20b, but both omit the messenger formula to accommodate their views (see Notes). Verse 25 should also not be bracketed out (*pace* Volz). It is simply a one-line oracle like the oracles of similar length in 3:12, and can stand alone.

The NEB, REB, NJV, and NIV take vv 26–27 as poetry, but the consensus otherwise is that the verses are prose (*pace* Thompson). They have all the marks of a later interpolation, and are best attributed to a mind other than Jeremiah's (cf. v 10). Addressed first is Moab's conqueror, doubtless the Babylonians (v 26), and then Israel (v 27). Verse 27 is not addressed (rhetorically) to Moab, as most commentators and the modern Versions assume (see Notes).

The unit as a whole is linked to what precedes and what follows by the catchword "Moab," on which see Rhetoric and Composition for 48:19–24.

NOTES

48:25. *The horn of Moab is cut off, his arm is broken.* The "horn (of an animal)," *qeren,* and the "(human) arm," *zĕrôaʿ,* are common OT metaphors for strength and power (17:5; Lam 2:3, 17; Ps 10:15; cf. Luke 1:69). The horn is used often with these meaning in the Psalms (Pss 18:3[Eng 18:2]; 75:5–6, 11[Eng 75:4–5, 10]; 89:25[Eng 89:24]; 92:11[Eng 92:10]; 112:9). The T has "the kingdom . . . their rulers." Moabite sovereignty is now ended, which is the lament in v 17b.

oracle of Yahweh. 2QJer spells *n[w]ʾm,* which Baillet says occurs in 1QIsa and is pronounced *nûm.* 2QJer has the same spelling again in v 30. The LXX omits the entire formula, which could be attributed to haplography (homoeoteleuton: *h . . . h*).

26. *Make him drunk, because against Yahweh he made himself great.* This intrusive comment is directed at the instrument of divine judgment, presum-

---

[1]Reading with 2QJer the Q *nimṣāʾ* ("he has been found"), which is masculine; Kt form is feminine.

ably Babylon, since reference is made to Yahweh in the third person. It is a common OT motif that Yahweh makes nations imbibe to a shameful drunkenness, at which point they stumble and fall. Foreign nations are thus repaid for the drunkenness they have induced in others. The imagery appears in 13:12–14 with respect to judgment upon Judah, and in 25:15–29 with respect to judgment upon other nations. See also Isa 19:14; Hab 2:15–16; Obad 16; Lam 4:21; Pss 60:5[Eng 60:3]; 75:9[Eng 75:8]; Ezek 23:31–35; Isa 51:17–23; 63:6; Zech 12:2. While it is not stated here that Moab is being made drunk as a prelude to its fall—the object seems merely to let Israel make sport of Moab—a falling (= death) may nevertheless be assumed. In the old Scandinavian legend of Hagband and Signe, the Queen hands Hagband the drinking horn before his hanging and mockingly invites him to drink his departure from life (Olrik 1930: 66).

because. 2QJer here and elsewhere spells *ky'*.

against Yahweh he made himself great. Hebrew *kî 'al-yhwh higdîl*. 2QJer has the feminine *hgdylh*, "she made herself great." The entire phrase has probably been lifted from v 42, where it appears *verbatim*. In Zeph 2:10, divine judgment is said to come upon Moab because it made itself great against the people of Yahweh, which may explain T's paraphrase in this verse ("for they have made themselves great against the people of the Lord").

Then Moab shall splash in his vomit. Hebrew *wĕsāpaq mô'āb bĕqî'ô*. There is no doubt here that Moab will suffer indignity in its vomit, but uncertainty in translating the verb *spq* leaves things less than clear. It is generally agreed that the usual rendering of "wallow" (AV; RSV; JB; NIV; NRSV; NJB) is dubious. This image may derive from Kimḥi, who, in a vivid portrayal envisaged Moab wallowing in vomit like a drunkard who rolls and turns after vomiting wine, then bumping into the ground. From G. R. Driver (1950: 61–62) who cites cognates in Aramaic and Syriac comes the meaning "overflow, emptying oneself out" (cf. BDB; KB³ *spq* II); Driver translates: "and Moab shall overflow with his vomit," which appears as the translation in the NEB and REB, and is accepted by Holladay. The usual meaning of *spq* is "slap, clap," usually of the hands or thighs (31:19; Lam 2:15; Num 24:10; Ezek 21:17[Eng 21:12]). BDB therefore suggests as a meaning here: "fall with a splash." The idea of falling, which accompanys the drunkenness in 25:27, is present in Giesebrecht ("fall loudly") and Cheyne ("fall heavily"). Calvin says Moab shall roll or clap hands in his vomit. A clapping noise with the hand is preserved in readings of the LXX (*epikrousei Mōab en cheiri autou*, "and Moab shall clap with his hand") and the Vg (*et allidet manum Moab in vomitu suo*, "and Moab's hand will be dashed in its vomit").

and become a joke—even he. Hebrew *wĕhāyâ lisḥōq gam-hû'*. Becoming a joke is to be subjected to derisive laughter; see again v 39. The emphatic *gam-hû'* ("even he") assumes that Moab on an earlier occasion had made a joke of Judah, but now he will be the joke. Jeremiah complained of himself being the butt of a joke in 20:7. 2QJer has *lsḥwq* with the full *holem* vowel letter, also the spelling *hw'h* for the masculine pronoun.

27. *Then surely the joke is for you, Israel, if among thieves he has been found.*
The line has caused much difficulty for translators, but can make perfectly
good sense if

1. the initial *wĕ'im lô'* is taken as an asseverative, i.e., meaning "then
   surely" (so 15:11; cf. McKane), and not as an interrogative equivalent
   to *hălō'* (*pace* Giesebrecht; Cornill; and all the modern Versions since
   the AV);
2. the *hē'* on *haśśĕḥōq* is taken as the definite article, not as a *hē'* interrogative; thus "the joke" (McKane);
3. "Israel" is taken as a vocative, not as the subject of the main clause
   (*pace* all modern Versions since the AV); and
4. the second *'im* is taken in the usual sense of "if."

The words are addressed to Israel, not Moab, the point being that Israel is now
in a position to make a joke of Moab. That is the meaning of "the joke is for
you." It all depends upon Moab having been caught among thieves (= being
found guilty of wrongdoing), which presumably has happened, or will happen.
It makes little sense to ask if Israel has been caught among thieves, because it
has (cf. 2:26, 34). 2QJer adding a feminine pronoun reads: "Then surely she,
she is (*hy'h h[yth]*) a joke to you, Israel."

among thieves. Hebrew *bĕgannābîm.* 2QJer has *bgnbk[]*, which Baillet says
may have contained an archaic feminine suffix.

For more than all your words against him, you will shake your head! The LXX
appears to omit all but the initial *kî*, "For," and has simply: *hoti epolemeis auton,*
"because you fought against him." Symmachus translates all of the Hebrew.
The LXX assumes that Israel was a joke to Moab, was the one caught among
thieves, and that this came about because Moab did battle earlier against her.

For more than all your words against him. Hebrew *kî-middê dĕbāreykā bô.*
MT *dĕbāreykā* ("your words") can certainly be read, although most commentators emend with a few MSS and Symm (*elalēsas*) to the verbal form *dab-
berkā*, "your speaking" (cf. 31:20).

you will shake your head. Hebrew *titnôdād.* 2QJer again has the feminine
(with final *yod*). Shaking or wagging the head is a gesture of derision; cf. Ps
64:9[Eng 64:8]; Lam 2:15; and Note on 18:16. In the NT, see Mark 15:29 and
parallels. Israel is thus told it can go beyond disparaging talk to shake its head
derisively at Moab's demise. The T, assuming Moab to be the addressee, interprets the verb to mean "wander (to and fro)," thus exile. The LXX and S both
read "you fought him."

MESSAGE AND AUDIENCE

This brief oracle announces with the use of familiar metaphors the military
and political demise of Moab. If such has not already happened, it may as well

have. This oracle, perhaps at one time following immediately the three-poem cluster portraying Moab's tableland destruction (vv 14–20), repeats what is said in v 17b: "How the mighty scepter is broken, the most glorious staff!"

The prose addition in vv 26–27 interprets Moab's loss of sovereignty as being due to hubris, stating that the nation made itself great before Yahweh. This interprets the poetry just preceding, but brings in an idea from an oracle further on in the collection (v 42). Moab is thus consigned to shame, ridicule, and punishment. The enemy, presumably the Babylonians, is told to make Moab drunk, and in a helpless condition of retching and falling it will become a joke—yes, it too! A post-586 audience may remember when Israel, and then Judah, fell in like manner. But now the joke is for Israel if Moab is found guilty, for that spells destruction of the nation. Then Israel can unleash more than a barrage of demeaning words; it can have the dubious pleasure of shaking its head in derision.

For the date of this oracle and others against Moab, see Rhetoric and Composition for 48:1–2. Cornill thought the prose addition presupposed the fall of Jerusalem since Moab is seen as having escaped calamity. A date close to Babylon's actual punitive campaign in Moab, i.e., 582 B.C., best suits this comment of thirsty revenge.

5. Go Live in a Rock! (48:28)

48 ²⁸Abandon the cities
   and go live in a rock
      sitting ones of Moab!
Become like a dove that nests
   in the sides of an open gorge.

RHETORIC AND COMPOSITION

MT 48:28 = LXX 31:28. This two-line poem concludes the core collection of Jeremiah's Moab utterances (48:1–28). Peake thinks it connects well with v 25; nevertheless, it is self-standing and should be taken as a poetic verse in its own right (so JB; NJB; NSB). A 2-cm space in 2QJer after v 28 may be a section marking (Baillet 1962: 67; Oesch 1979: 272–73). The verse, in any case, is delimited from v 27 by the return to poetry.

The poem is linked to preceding poetry (v 25) and poetry following (v 29) by the catchword "Moab," on which see Rhetoric and Composition for 48:19–24. It appears also that *bĕ'ebrê*, "in the sides of," in v 28, is a catchword connecting to *'ebrātô*, "his insolence," in v 30. A form of this verbal root, *'br*, is also a catchword connecting to vv 32–33 (see Rhetoric and Composition for 48:29–31).

NOTES

48:28. *Abandon the cities and go live in a rock.* A flight from cities to the rocks and other remote places is described in 4:29. See also Isa 2:10, 19, 21. Jeremiah has in mind here the rocky gorge of the Arnon, which is well-suited for fugitives seeking refuge. The LXX has "they abandoned the cities and lived in rocks," but it is better to read the imperatives of MT, which are supported by both Aq and Symm (*katelipete tas poleis kai ōkēsate en petra*, "abandon the cities and live in a rock").

the cities. Hebrew *ʿārîm*. 2QJer has "your (feminine singular) cities."

go live. Hebrew *šiknû*. 2QJer has the feminine singular imperative.

sitting ones of Moab. Hebrew *yōšĕbê môʾāb*. On the "sitting one(s) of _____" idiom, see Note on 46:19. 2QJer has the feminine singular participle *ywšbt* ("inhabitant"), spelling it with the full *holem* vowel letter. The feminine participle is usual in Jeremiah, but 48:43 has a masculine form.

Become like a dove that nests in the sides of an open gorge. Holladay notes a similar construction in 50:8: "become like he-goats." The image here of fugitives becoming like doves escaping to the mountains is present also in Ezek 7:16. Homer (*Iliad* xxi 493–95) likened a fleeing goddess to a dove flying into a hollow rock to escape a pursuing falcon. For other comparisons to doves nesting in caverns and rocky coverts, see Virgil (*Aeneid* v 213–17) and Song 2:14. Tristram (1898: 214–15) identified these birds as nonmigratory rock pigeons (*Columba livia*) who nest in lofty cliffs, caves, and rock fissures of the Arnon gorge.

nests. Hebrew *tĕqannēn*. 2QJer appears to have the second person *tqnn[y]*.

in the sides of an open gorge. Hebrew *bĕʿebrê pî-paḥat*, where *bĕʿebrê* means "in the sides of" (AV; RSV; NJV; cf. Gemser 1952: 351). The phrase *pî-pāḥat* is lit. "opening of a pit," referring here to the deep gorge of the Arnon. The LXX has *en petrais stomati bothunou* ("in rocks, at the opening of a pit"), which interprets "the sides," but expresses the same basic idea.

MESSAGE AND AUDIENCE

This brief poem directs the inhabitants of Moab to flee their cities and find refuge in the rocky gorge of the Arnon. The common image of doves in flight to the very same places is used to hurry the homeless on to safety, at least for a time. This directive carries forth the imagery of vv 19–20, where Moabite people, having abandoned Dibon and other cities, are heading for the Arnon.

For the range of dates assignable to the Moab poems, see Message and Audience for 48:1–2.

6. We Have Heard of the Pride of Moab (48:29–31)

48 ²⁹We have heard of the pride of Moab
   great haughtiness
His loftiness and his pride and his arrogance
   and the highness of his heart

³⁰I, I know—oracle of Yahweh—his insolence
   his boastings are not right
      what they do is not right

³¹Therefore over Moab I will wail
   for all of Moab I will cry out
      for the men of Kirheres I will moan.¹

RHETORIC AND COMPOSITION

MT 48:29–31 = LXX 31:29–31. Here begins a supplemental collection of Moab oracles that expands the core collection of 48:1–28. Many of the verses have close parallels in Isa 15:2–7; 16:6–12; and 24:17–18, with some phrases echoing even earlier poetry in Num 21:28–29 and 24:17. The Isaiah poetry is taken by Holladay (II: 347–48) as being prior, and he agrees with Peake that the Jeremiah verses are no improvement over the original. Ringgren (1949: 50–52) says that differences between the Jeremiah and Isaiah passages can all be explained as a result of oral transmission.

The present verses are a modification of Isa 16:6–7. There is no certainty about delimitation, as vv 32–33 are paralleled by what follows in Isa 16:8–9. Goodspeed's translation (AmT) takes vv 29–31 as a unit, and Volz provides indirect evidence for the delimitation of these verses by bracketing them out as a later interpolation. If Kirheres in v 31 happens to be Kerak, then vv 29–31 focus on the central plateau region between the Arnon and Zered Rivers, whereas in vv 32–33 the focus is on the tableland vineyards of Jazer and Sibmah to the north, in the vicinity of Heshbon. At the top end delimitation is largely determined by the beginning of shared material (with Isaiah) in v 29. 2QJer has a two-centimeter space before v 29 that could be a section marking (Oesch 1979: 272–73). But Baillet (1962: 67) thinks it is not.

Verse 29 is agreed by most everyone (but not Holladay) to be poetry. Verses 30–31 in *BHS*, and v 30 in NJV, are taken as prose, but otherwise commentators and the modern Versions judge these verses to be poetry. The parallel verses in Isaiah are taken by everyone (even *BHS*) as poetry. The poem here divides into two stanzas. Stanza I (v 29) with its accumulation and alliteration is a double bicolon. Stanza II (vv 30–31) having accumulation and repetition is two tricolons.

Despite the similarity between these verses and Isa 16:6–7, a Jeremianic dialogue occurs here that is not in Isaiah. Streane notes that Yahweh in v 30 corroborates the prophet's assertion in v 29:

| I | The prophet says: | *We have heard . . .* | v 29 |
| II | and Yahweh responds: | *I, I know . . .* | v 30 |

There is reason then to retain the messenger formula in v 30, which the LXX omits.

The present poetry is linked to preceding poetry (v 28) and poetry following (vv 32–33) by the catchword "Moab," on which see Rhetoric and Composition

---

¹Reading with one MS and Q^{OR} *'ehgeh* ("I will moan"); MT has *yehgeh* ("he will moan").

for 48:19–24. It is also possible that forms of the verbal root *ʿbr* link three successive units: vv 28, 29–31, and 32–33:

I	in the sides of	*bĕʿebrê*	v 28
II	his insolence	*ʿebrātô*	v 30
III	they extended over	*ʿābĕrû*	v 32

NOTES

48:29. *We have heard of the pride of Moab.* 2QJer has a plural imperative *šmʿw n'* ("Do hear!"); cf. 5:21. The LXX has "I have heard" (cf. Zeph 2:8), but the plural "we have heard" occurs in Isa 16:6, and should be retained here. The prophet is speaking on behalf of Israel (Giesebrecht; Weiser), also other nations (Kimḥi; Holladay). A sample of Moabite boasting appears in v 14.

great haughtiness. Hebrew *gēʾeh mĕʾōd.* This pride is a disaster waiting to happen (Isa 2:12; Ps 94:2; Prov 15:25; Job 40:11–12).

pride . . . haughtiness . . . his loftiness . . . his pride and his arrogance. In the Hebrew is a fivefold alliteration on words beginning with the "g" consonant. The accumulation is for emphasis.

His loftiness and his pride and his arrogance. Hebrew *gābĕhô ûgĕʾônô wĕgaʾăwātô.* The LXX, S, and 2QJer lack *gābĕhô û,* "his loftiness and," which may be another loss due to haplography (homoeoarcton: *g . . . g*), although the term is also absent in Isa 16:6. But Symm translates (*to hypsos autou*). 2QJer curiously adds *wʾynn[w]*, "and he is no more." On the pride of Moab coming in for censure, which is the main theme of these verses, see Isa 25:11 and Zeph 2:8–10. The pride of Edom is censured in 49:16. Yahweh declared his intention earlier to spoil the pride (*gĕʾôn*) of Judah and the great pride (*gĕʾôn . . . hārāb*) of Jerusalem (13:8; cf. Isa 2:6–22). This string of different words for pride sets up the judgment to follow. "Pride (*gāʾôn*) goes before destruction, and a lofty spirit (*gōbah rûaḥ*) before a fall" (Prov 16:18).

his heart. Hebrew *libbô.* 2QJer spells with a double *beth*, i.e., *lbbw.*

30. *I, I know.* This emphatic *ʾănî yādaʿtî* construction answers "we have heard" in v 29.

oracle of Yahweh. On the 2QJer spelling of "oracle," see v 25. The LXX omits, but the formula should be retained because of the divine "I" preceding.

his insolence. Hebrew *ʿebrātô.* The term signifies excess, coming from *ʿbr*, "to pass over" (Calvin). Kimḥi translates "his wrath." The LXX has *erga autou*, "his works," and the T "deeds," which may result from a misreading of *daleth* for *resh*, i.e., *ʿăbōdōtayw*, "his works." However, the verse does go on to condemn false deeds.

his boastings are not right. Hebrew *lōʾ-kēn baddāyw.* It is generally agreed that the *athnaḥ* under *lōʾ-kēn* has to be moved either forward or back (Giesebrecht; Ehrlich 1912: 358; Rudolph; cf. Isa 16:6). Compare "they speak what is not right (*lōʾ-kēn*)" in 8:6. The term *baddîm* is "empty talk, boasting" (BDB;

KB³), having also the meaning "diviners" (= empty talkers) in 50:36 and Isa 44:25. We are concerned here not simply about the impropriety of boasting, for which criticism can certainly be made, but about talk that is empty or false (NEB; JB; NRSV).

what they do is not right. Hebrew *lō'-kēn 'āśû.* 2QJer spells the negative *lw'* (with a full *ḥolem* vowel letter) and has a feminine singular verb: "she does." The LXX has a masculine singular: "he does." Moab's deeds are no better than its words. Isaiah 16:6 censures Moab's false talk, but not its false deeds.

31. *Therefore over Moab I will wail.* In Isa 16:6 Moab is told to join others in bewailing itself, which could help explain the T reading here: "Therefore the Moabites howl, and the Moabites, all of them shout . . . ," also the reading of LXX beginning with an imperative: "Howl you!" In 9:9[Eng 9:10] the LXX similarly has an imperative for MT's "I make weeping." Kimḥi says the prophet is speaking here for the people of Moab, but it is also possible that Yahweh carries on as speaker from v 30. The wailing, in any case, is feigned.

all of Moab. Cheyne thinks this is Moab both north and south of the Arnon, which it would be if Kirheres is located at Kerak or some other site in the central plateau (see below).

for the men of Kirheres I will moan. MT has "for the men of Kirheres he will moan" (cf. v 36). This reading has its defenders (Cheyne; Barthélemy 1986: 786–87), but if *qîr-ḥereś* is to be taken as a place-name, Kirheres, the reading "I moan" of the Q^OR and one MS is virtually required. The modern Versions all adopt this reading. Isaiah 16:7 has *la'ăšîšê qîr-ḥăreśet,* "for the raisin-cakes of Kirheres." See also the parallel expression in Isa 16:11.

Kirheres. Hebrew *qîr-ḥereś.* Literally "potsherd city," which may be an intentional corruption of "new city, *qîr ḥādāš* (Van Zyl 1960: 70–71; Smelik 1992: 88). The spelling here occurs in v 36 and in Isa 16:11, whereas in Isa 16:7; 2 Kgs 3:25; and 2QJer of the present text the spelling is *qîr-ḥăreśet,* Kirhareset. The LXX transliterates with *Kiradas* (misreading *daleth* for *resh*), but neither T ("their strong fortified city") nor Vg (*viros muri fictilis,* "strong wall of clay" or "strong earthenware rim"?) translates a place-name. Kirheres does not appear on the Moabite Stone, but other cities beginning with "Kir" do, e.g., Kirjathaim, Kirjath, and possibly Kirchoh. There is also a Kir-Moab in Isa 15:1, whose identification is unclear (J. M. Miller 1991: 89; 1992: 85–86). Kirheres is thought to have been a capital of ancient Moab (cf. 2 Kgs 3:25), and is most commonly identified with modern Kerak, ca. 26 kilometers south of the Arnon and 18 kilometers east of the Dead Sea. Kerak is ideally situated on the north end of a ridge naturally protected by deep ravines at an intersection where an important east–west road crosses the King's Highway (Van Zyl 1960: 70; *ABD* 4: 84; *OEANE* 3: 280). On the King's Highway, see Note on 48:1. However, the Kerak-Kirheres identification has recently been called into question, with B. C. Jones (1991) and Smelik (1992: 85–89) wanting to place Kirheres north of the Arnon in the vicinity of Heshbon. If this be the case, then its precise location is unknown.

MESSAGE AND AUDIENCE

This dialogue begins by the prophet reporting that he and others have heard of the pride of Moab. It is an exceedingly great pride, as one may infer from the rich biblical vocabulary called forth to embellish the idea. Yahweh then responds with an emphatic "I, I know . . ." Moab is insolent; his boastings are false and so also are his deeds, for which reason Yahweh says he will lament over the whole of Moab, and moan in heavy tones for the men of Kirheres. Now will he really?

This poem carries forth the themes of boasting heard earlier in vv 14 and v 26, and promises a supplement to the lamenting that began in vv 17b and 20b. Now, with the destruction of Moab having occurred, its people having become fugitives, many of them scurrying for safety in the rocky caverns of the Arnon, it is time for a good cry. Yahweh will begin the process, and the unblessed remnant of Moab will continue with laments of its own.

Assuming that this poetry predates Jeremiah, we can simply imagine it finding reuse now that Moab's judgment is awaited. The dates then for this reuse will probably be the same as for Jeremiah's utterances regarding Moab, on which see Message and Audience for 48:1–2.

7. Gladness and Rejoicing Are No More (48:32–34)

48 [32]More than the weeping of Jazer I weep for you
    O vine of Sibmah!
Your branches extended over the sea
    as far as the sea
        Jazer they reached

Upon your summer fruit and upon your vintage
    the devastator has fallen

[33]Gladness and rejoicing are taken away
    from the garden land, from the land of Moab
And wine from the presses I made cease
    no one treads a shout
        the shout is not a shout!

[34]—the cry from Heshbon as far as Elealeh, as far as Jahaz; they raised their voice from Zoar as far as Horonaim, as far as Eglath-shelishiyah. Indeed, even the waters of Nimrim are a desolation.

RHETORIC AND COMPOSITION

MT 48:32–34 = LXX 31:32–34. The present verses are a variation of Isa 16:8–10, but with vocabulary and a structure eminently suitable to the present context. The verses—as in Isaiah—are poetry, except for v 34, which is a prose add-on incorporating portions of Isa 15:4–6. Delimitation here is difficult, but not impossible. The unit ends with the add-on of v 34. Verse 35, also prose, with a messenger formula begins a new oracle. The poetry of vv 32–33 is marked off thematically by its focus on Moab's tableland vineyards (see Rhetoric and Composition for 48:29–31).

The poetry divides into two stanzas. Stanza I (v 32) is a bicolon followed by a tricolon and another bicolon. Stanza II (v 33) is a bicolon and a tricolon. The tricolons in the two stanzas balance one another with these repetitions:

I	. . . . *the sea*	*yām*	v 32
	. . . . *the sea*	*yām*	
II	. . . . *a shout*	*hêdād*	v 33
	the shout is not a shout	*hêdād lōʾ hêdād*	

The first person "I" in both stanzas is the voice of Yahweh. He weeps in v 32 and ends wine-making in v 33 (see Notes).

The poetry is linked to preceding poetry (vv 29–31) and poetry following (vv 35–38a) by the catchword "Moab" (see Rhetoric and Composition for 48:19–24). The following catchwords also connect to the oracle preceding:

v 32 *they extended over* ʿāběrû   v 30 *his insolence* ʿebrātô

The verbal root ʿbr actually links three successive units (see Rhetoric and Composition for 48:29–31).

These catchwords also connect to the oracle following:

v 33 *I made cease*   v 35 *I have made cease*

NOTES

48:32. *More than the weeping of Jazer I weep for you, O vine of Sibmah!* Yahweh is weeping—ironically or otherwise—for Sibmah, metaphorically designated here as the "vine of Sibmah." It is not the prophet (*pace* Giesebrecht). The vine metaphor was used to represent the "remnant of Israel" in 6:9. On the ANE "weeping god" motif, see Roberts 1992. The question here is whether Yahweh is weeping more for Sibmah than for Jazer, or weeping more for Sibmah than Jazer weeps—presumably for itself. If *mibběkî yaʿzēr* is a construct chain, the better translation is "more than the weeping *of* Jazer," although most modern Versions have "more than the weeping *for* Jazer" (RSV; NEB; JB; NAB; NJV). Isaiah 16:9 has "with the weeping (*bibkî*) of Jazer I weep," which is adopted by the AV in the present verse. Also, the LXX reads here, "as (*hōs*) the weeping of Jazer," which is adopted by the NIV. Rashi says that when this prophecy was spoken Jazer had already been destroyed, which would explain its own weeping or Yahweh's weeping in a lesser amount. The emended reading "fountain of Jazer" (based on Ug *nbk* / *mbk*, "spring, fountain") proposed by Landes (1956) and Mansoor (1961–62: 393–94), and accepted by Bright, Thompson, Holladay, and Jones, should be rejected. There is no compelling reason to get rid of the comparative *min*; moreover, the revised translation makes questionable sense for the line as a whole: "Fountain of Jazer I weep for you, O vine of Sibmah."

Jazer. A Transjordanian city originally allotted to Gad after its capture from Sihon, king of the Amorites (Num 21:32; 32:1, 3, 35; Josh 13:25; 21:39; 1 Chr 6:81; 26:31). Jazer was made a Levitical city. Eusebius (*Onom.* 224–25) locates Jazer 10 Roman miles west of Philadelphia (= Rabbath Ammon), and 15 Roman miles north of Heshbon, from where, he says, a large stream breaks out to enter the Jordan. Its exact location is unknown, but most commentators place it in this general area, in southern Gilead near the Ammonite border (LXX of Num 21:24; 1 Chr 26:31: "in Gilead"). It is now thought by many to be a Moabite city, but that cannot be determined. It could be Ammonite, as it was later when taken by Judas Maccabeus (1 Macc 5:8). Various sites have been suggested, among which are 1) the prominent Khirbet es-Ṣār (Peake; Cornill), 16 kilometers north of Heshbon and 11 kilometers west of Rabbath Ammon, where Glueck (1939: 155) later found small quantities of early Iron Age sherds and other evidence of Iron Age occupation; 2) Khirbet Jazzir, located about 4 kilometers south of es-Salt (de Vaux 1941: 25–27; for a picture, see de Vaux 1938: 425 #1; *ABD* 3: 650–51); and 3) Tell ʿArēme, which lies farther south on the Wadi Schita–Wadi Baḥḥāṭ, southwest of Khirbet es-Ṣār (Rendtorff 1960; cf. Rudolph, 286).

O vine of Sibmah! Hebrew *haggepen śibmâ*. The definite article in apposition to a second person pronoun becomes a vocative (GKC §126ef). 2QJer does not have the vocative particle, nor does Isa 16:8 and 9, but see *haggepen* in Jer 2:21. Sibmah, originally an Israelite town assigned to Reuben (Num 32:37–38; Josh 13:17–19), is now Moabite. Some commentators (e.g., S. R. Driver; Jones) connect it with Sebam of Num 32:3. Situated somewhere close to Heshbon (Isa 16:8–9), the actual site is unknown, although some identify it with Khirbet Qarn el-Qibsh (*ABD* 6: 1–2). Sibmah was undoubtedly fine wine country, for its lush vines are also celebrated in Isa 16:8–11. Nineteenth-century travelers reported grapes and raisins of especially good quality being brought from this area to Jerusalem. Sibmah may here represent Moab's entire northern tableland, on which see Note for 48:1.

Your branches extended over the sea. On the "branches" or "tendrils" of a vine, see 5:10. The difficult phrase here (and also in Isa 16:8) is *ʿābĕrû yām*, the usual translation of which is "passed over the sea," or the like. The image is not, however, one of branches crossing the Dead Sea, say, to En-Gedi, where they meet up with vine branches there (Cornill; cf. Song 1:14), much less of branches crossing the Mediterranean, which Keown et al. suppose to be an allusion to Moab's international wine trade. The more reasonable picture is simply branches reaching or overhanging the Dead Sea, which the verb ʿ*br* can convey (Volz; McKane; cf. NEB; NAB; NIV). This allows "as far as the sea" coming next to be the qualifying phrase. The image, so interpreted, is still grand hyperbole.

as far as the sea. Hebrew *'ad yām.* A qualification of what has just been said about Sibmah's branches overhanging the sea. This is a separate colon in a tricolon, precluding the impossible reading "the sea of Jazer" (T; Aq; Symm; AV; NIV). Isaiah 16:8 has "they reached as far as Jazer," which prompts Hitzig and many commentators since, also some of the modern Versions (RSV; NEB; JB; NAB; NSB) to delete this second occurrence of *yām* in the line. But that is too simplistic, even with "sea" wanting in two MSS (probably haplography due to homoeoarcton: *y . . . y*). The term is present in T and Vg, and some LXX MSS have *poleis Iazēr,* "cities of Jazer," which is doubtless a misreading of *'ārîm* for *'ad yām* (Cornill; Barthélemy 1986: 788). The repetition of *yām* is perfectly acceptable in a tricolon; also it is structurally important in the poetry (see Rhetoric and Composition).

Jazer they reached. More hyperbole in a northward direction. Isaiah has them also meandering eastward to the wilderness (Isa 16:8c).

Upon your summer fruit and upon your vintage, the devastator has fallen. Isaiah 16:9 has "upon your summer fruit and upon your harvest (*qĕṣîrēk*), the shout (*hêdād*) has fallen." The choice of "devastator" (*šōdēd*) here is Jeremianic (see Note on 48:1), and "your vintage" (*bĕṣîrēk*) a legitimate alternative term. However, Cornill points out that the Isaiah passage has paronomasia with "your summer fruit" (*qêṣēk*) and "your harvest" (*qĕṣîrēk*). Rashi says the summer fruit is dried figs (cf. NJV). The vintage is the season's grape harvest (see 5:17; 8:13; and Note on 8:20). The attacking army has apparently taken the summer fruit and vintage for itself (see Note on 6:3).

Upon your summer fruit. 2QJer has *w'l* ("and upon"), which could be dittography of the previous *waw* on *ng'w,* otherwise a case of MT haplography.

33. *Gladness and rejoicing are taken away.* Compare Isa 16:10. Not the usual "joy (*śāśôn*) and gladness" phrase of Jeremiah (see Note on 7:34). The verb is actually *'sp,* "to gather," which is particularly riveting here since it indicates a harvest the planters did not intend. There is always much joy at harvest time (see Note on 8:20), but now Moabites are denied their harvest.

from the garden land. Hebrew *mikkarmel.* Jeremiah uses "garden land" in 2:7. The LXX omits, although the word is present in Isa 16:10. The LXX omission could be more haplography (homoeoarcton: *m . . . m,* if the omission includes the next *waw*; homoeoteleuton: *l . . . l,* if it does not). The frequent explanation that the word is an MT plus from Isa 16:10 (Duhm; Cornill; Volz; Janzen 1973: 59; Carroll; Holladay; McKane) should be rejected. A garden land is one well suited for grains, vines, fig and olive trees, and so to praise Moab's tableland only heightens the sense of loss.

And wine from the presses I made cease. Hebrew *wĕyayin mîqābîm hišbattî.* Yahweh continues to be the speaking voice, rendering unnecessary a repointing of the verb to a Hophal, *hošbat,* "it has ceased" (*pace* Rudolph; Bright; Holladay). The first person of the verb is present again in v 35, also earlier in 7:34.

from the presses. Hebrew *mîqābîm.* Ancient wine presses were of many types, but quite typically consisted of two vats, a higher and larger one where the treading of grapes was done, and a lower one of smaller size where the juice was collected. The lower vat of hewn stone (Isa 5:2) was the *yeqeb* (P. J. King 1993: 177). For a picture of wine being pressed and collected in the lower vat, see *ANEP²* 48 #156; and Lesko 1977: 16.

no one treads a shout. I.e., no one treads with a shout because no treading is going on. Hebrew *lō'-yidrōk hêdād*. The term *hêdād* is the shout men make when picking or treading grapes (BDB; KB³; Rashi; Kimḥi), giving rhythm to their labor and also making it pleasurable. See Note on 25:30 for discussion and pictures. Isaiah 16:10 has "the treader does not tread," which also indicates a cessation of wine-pressing. The attempt by de Moor and de Vries (1988) to interpret *hêdād* as a "thunderstorm" (= Canaanite storm god Hadad), and translating it here as "storm troop" must be judged unsuccessful.

the shout is not a shout! Hebrew *hêdād lō' hêdād*. The idiom might also mean "(there is) no shouting"; cf. Isa 16:10: "the shout I have ended." But a better reading has one shout replacing the other. There is silence at the wine-presses, but a loud shout now rises up from those fleeing the sword (Rashi). This idea is carried forward in the expansion of v 34, where it states that Heshbon's outcry is heard in far distant places.

34. — *the cry from Heshbon as far as Elealeh, as far as Jahaz.* The supplement begins, as does the poetry of v 32, with a prefixed *min*, only the construct formation here is a curious one. The *min* governs Heshbon, not the outcry (D. N. Freedman), which means it does not need to be emended away in order to achieve correspondence with Isa 15:4 (*pace* Giesebrecht, Duhm, Rudolph, Weiser, Bright, Holladay, McKane, and others). The present add-on draws upon Isa 15:4–6, its purpose being to explain the shout concluding v 33.

Heshbon. A Moabite tableland city, on which see Note on 48:2.

as far as Elealeh, as far as Jahaz. The former town is to the north, the latter to the south.

Elealeh. A Moabite town belonging earlier to the tribe of Gad following Israel's Transjordan settlement. Always mentioned in the OT together with Heshbon (Num 32:3, 37; Isa 15:4; 16:9), this town has long been identified with Khirbet el-ʿĀl, located two kilometers northeast of Tell Ḥesbân–Heshbon (Tristram 1873: 339; Van Zyl 1960: 93; Dearman 1989a: 300–302; 1997: 207; *ABD* 2: 432).

Jahaz. An alternate spelling of Jahzah, on which see Note for 48:21. The LXX omits. If the LXX's *Vorlage* had the longer spelling, *yhṣh*, then the omission could be explained by haplography (homoeoteleuton: *h . . . h*).

they raised their voice from Zoar as far as Horonaim, as far as Eglath-shelish-iyah. I.e., the people of southern Moab did. The LXX has "their cities" for a subject, which provides clarification. Here the possibility of MT haplography exists if the LXX *Vorlage* had *ʿārêhem* after *qôlām*, i.e., it read *nātĕnû qôlām ʿārêhem miṣṣōʿar*, "their cities raised their voice, from Zoar. . . ."

Zoar. The city to which Lot and his daughters fled (Gen 19:22–23, 30), generally located near the southern end of the Dead Sea (Gen 13:10; Deut 34:3). It is mentioned in Isa 15:5 together with Eglath-shelishiyah. Zoar may be a Moabite city, but one cannot be sure. For the LXX reading of Zoar in 48:4, where it occurs together with Horonaim, see Note there.

Horonaim. A site in southern Moab; see Note on 48:3.

as far as Eglath-shelishiyah. Hebrew *ʿeglat šĕlišîyâ.* 2QJer spells *šlyšyh*, against MT *šlšyh.* The term is a puzzlement, although now generally taken to be a city (RSV; NEB; JB; NAB; NJV; NIV; NSB), the location of which is unknown. Its only other mention is in Isa 15:5, where, as here, it is paired with Horonaim. That would put it somewhere in southern Moab. The AV translated "a heifer of three years old"; Kimḥi the same, assuming it to be an honorific epithet for Horonaim. But as the text currently reads, without a conjunctive *waw* or *ʿad*, Eglath-shelish-iyeh must stand in apposition to Horonaim. Peake therefore translated "the third Eglath," i.e., the one Eglath among three villages of the same name. But an *ʿad* could have been lost by haplography (homoeoarcton: *ʿayin . . . ʿayin*).

Indeed, even the waters of Nimrim are a desolation. Taken with only slight change from Isa 15:6. The *kî* is here translated as an asseverative: "Indeed" (Calvin; Holladay). The imperfect *yihyû*, which occurs also in Isa 15:6, is prob-ably best translated as a present, although the AV and NJV render it a future: "shall become." For the 2QJer spelling *kyʾ*, see v 26. Eusebius and Jerome placed the "waters of Nimrim" (*mē nimrîm*) at "Bennamerium," north of Zoar, with modern scholars concurring only to the extent that the location has to be in southern Moab. Many locate the waters at the Wadi en-Numeirah, which flows into the Dead Sea some 14 kilometers above its southern end (Tristram 1873: 56–57; 1898: 113; Volz; Van Zyl 1960: 55; Rudolph, 287; Holladay; *ABD* 4: 1116). The waters of Nimrim should not be confused with Wadi Nimrin near Tell Nimrim in the Jordan Valley, ca. 11 kilometers north of the Dead Sea and 16 kilometers east of Jericho (*OEANE* 4: 140–41). The latter is identified with the north tableland city of Beth-nimrah (Num 32:36; Josh 13:27).

a desolation. I.e., waterless, perhaps due to a drought, although Peake imag-ines an enemy blocking up the sources (cf. 2 Kgs 3:25).

MESSAGE AND AUDIENCE

In this poem Yahweh says he will weep more for Sibmah than Jazer wept over its own ruined city, thanks to an enemy attack from the north. Does Yahweh really hurt for Sibmah and its lush tableland vineyards? One cannot be sure, although Isaiah, who crafted this poem originally, was a master of verbal irony. Perhaps, then, Yahweh is not weeping at all. Sibmah's branches, in any case, are said to have spread out over the sea, extending also to the northern border city of Jazer. Upon Sibmah's summer fruit and vintage, a cruel enemy has descended. As a result, gladness and rejoicing are missing in this grim harvest of Moab's cele-brated garden land. Yahweh says that he has ended the flow of wine in the presses. No longer does one hear the shout of treaders. The shout now heard is another shout, and the audience can only imagine what that might be.

The supplement interprets the last-mentioned shout to be a wild cry from Heshbon, which reverberates to Elealeh in the north and to Jahaz in the south. To this is added loud voices in south Moab, from Zoar to Horonaim, also one Eglath-shelishiyah. As a final indignity, the sweet waters of Nimrim in the south are now a desolation. Alas, the whole land is under a curse. On the dates for a reuse of this poetry and the supplement in the time of Jeremiah, see Message and Audience for 48:1–2.

8. Lament the End of Moab! (48:35–38a)

48 [35]I have made cease for Moab—oracle of Yahweh
    the one who brings up to the high place
       and the one who burns incense to his gods
[36]Therefore my heart for Moab moans like flutes
    and my heart toward the men of Kirheres moans like flutes
       therefore the rest of what one has made—they are lost!

[37]For every head is shaved
    and every beard cut off
On all hands are slashes
    and on (all) loins sackcloth
[38a]On all the roofs of Moab and in her squares
    —everywhere rites of mourning.

RHETORIC AND COMPOSITION

MT 48:35–38a = LXX 31:35–38a. These verses are a florilegium made from Isa 15:2–3, 7a, and 16:11. Yahweh, in a divine oracle, announces, participates in, and describes a funerary lament for Moab. This oracle is delimited at the top end by a messenger formula in v 35, and by a prose add-on to the preceding oracle (v 34). It is delineated from another oracle in vv 38b–39, which has its own formula and is a bona fide Jeremiah composition (see Rhetoric and Composition for 48:38b–39).

The comparable verses in Isaiah are poetry; nevertheless, most commentators (Volz; Rudolph; Weiser; Boadt; McKane) and most modern Versions (RSV; NEB; JB; NAB; NSB) follow *BHS* and judge the present verses to be prose. Bright separates out v 37 as poetry, with only Thompson and Holladay taking all the verses as poetry. The NJV and NIV also render the whole as poetry. The decision here is to take the verses as poetry, but with the recognition that, like other discourse in chaps. 1–20, this might simply be rhythmic prose. One thing is clear: these verses contain more repetition and balancing key words than the Isaiah verses.

The oracle can be taken as having two stanzas. Stanza I (vv 35–36) is two tricolons; Stanza II (vv 37–38a) three bicolons. The whole is structured by the following key words:

I	. . . . *for Moab*	*lĕmôʾāb*	v 35
	the one who brings up		
	and the one who burns incense		
	Therefore my heart for Moab moans like flutes	*ʿal-kēn . . . lĕmôʾāb*	v 36

and my heart . . . . moans like flutes		
therefore	*'al-kēn . . .*	
II ... every head	*kol . . .*	v 37
and every beard	*wĕkol . . .*	
On all hands	*'al kol . . .*	
and on (all) loins	*wĕ'al (kol) . . .*	
On all the roofs . . . and in her squares	*'al kol . . .*	v 38a
everywhere	*kullōh . . .*	

The messenger formula identifies Yahweh as the speaker throughout (Mc-Kane). In vv 35–36 Yahweh announces judgment on Moab, after which he purports to lament the judgment. The lament—whether Isaiah or a later reviser of Isaiah—must be taken as full-blown irony. The stanza closes with a sober statement that every last vestige of human creativity has been destroyed. In vv 37–38a the lamenting Moabites are themselves portrayed.

The present poetry is linked to the preceding poetry (vv 32–33) and the poetry following (vv 38b–39) by the catchword "Moab"; see Rhetoric and Composition for 48:19–24. The following catchwords also connect to the preceding oracle:

v 35 *I have made cease*   v 33 *I made cease*

NOTES

48:35. *I have made cease.* Delete the *waw* and read *hišbatî* as a prophetic perfect; this begins a new oracle.

the one who brings up to the high place. Hebrew *ma'ăleh* is an H-stem participle meaning "one who brings up (sacrifices)." Compare the usage in 33:18. The T adds "sacrifices," and the modern Versions (except AV and NJV) do likewise. Kimḥi says the worshiper is bringing an animal to the high place for sacrifice. Rudolph and Holladay therefore propose an original *'ōlâ* ("whole burnt offering") as having existed in the text (cf. 33:18), which is possible, as the loss could be explained by haplography (the prior word ends in *'lh*). The MT is also without a preposition before *bāmâ* ("high place"), which is remedied in T and by *epi (ton) bōmon* ("upon the high place") in the LXX, Aq, and Symm. *BHS* suggests an original *'al-habbāmâ* in the text (cf. Isa 16:12), which is favored by G. R. Driver (1937–38: 124). This would make possible a double haplography—a loss of the preposition and definite article, due again to the preceding *'lh*. According to this reconstruction, the same three letters were repeated twice after *m'lh*, producing the reading:

m'lh ['lh 'l h]bmh   the one who brings up a burnt offering upon the high place.

The meaning, in any case, is the same: Yahweh says he has put a stop to worshipers ascending the high place to offer sacrifice.

high place. Hebrew *bāmâ.* A funerary shrine usually—but not always—situated on hills or ridges (Albright 1957c; P. J. King 1993: 110–11). See Note on

7:31. The term "high place" in the OT has associations with Canaanite religion (Num 33:52), although the expression *ba'ălê bāmôt 'arnōn* in Num 21:28 may mean "Baals of the high places of the Arnon." According to the OT, there was sacrificial worship aplenty in Moab, e.g., in the Balaam-Balak stories (Num 22:39–23:6; 23:13–17, 28–30), the report of an Israelite romp at Shittim (Num 25:1–5), and the report of Mesha's sacrificing his son as a whole burnt offering (2 Kgs 3:26–27). See also the Moabite Stone. The first Moabite sanctuary to come to light was excavated at Khirbat al-Mudayna, about 20 kilometers southeast of Madaba. The site revealed Iron II occupation (ca. 900–586 B.C.). In this sanctuary were found animal bones and zoomorphic ceramic figurines, also numerous altars—one painted red—comparable to those found at Megiddo and Tel Miqne–Ekron, except that they were without horns (Daviau and Steiner 2000). On sacrifice and Moabite religion generally, see Van Zyl (1960: 193–202) and Mattingly (1989).

the one who burns incense to his gods. Chemosh was Moab's preeminent god, but other gods were also worshiped in the land (see Note on 48:7b). The practice of burning incense to Baal and other gods came under strong censure in Israel (see Note on 1:16). A Moabite incense stand has turned up at Tell Dhîbân = Dibon (Mattingly 1989: 228–29; picture on p. 320; NEAEHL 1: 332).

36. *Therefore my heart for Moab moans like flutes, and my heart toward the men of Kirheres moans like flutes.* The verb *hmh* here denotes a low-pitched moan (cf. Isa 16:11; Ps 55:18[Eng 55:17]; and see Note on 4:19). Yahweh's "innards" (*mē'ay*) were said also to moan for Ephraim, but in that case with tender compassion (31:20). What we have here is more full-blown irony, not a sympathetic lament (*pace* Peake). The T reading has the Moabites making noises in their own hearts.

flutes . . . flutes. Hebrew *ḥălilîm . . . ḥălîlîm.* The second occurrence in 2QJer is spelled *ḥll[y]m.* The flute, or pipe, is an instrument used for joyous occasions (1 Kgs 1:40; Isa 5:12; 30:29), but here for lament. Both uses are attested in the NT (Matt 9:23; 11:17). Isaiah 16:11 has *kinnôr,* "lyre."

Kirheres. Hebrew *qîr-ḥereś.* The spelling in 2QJer is the same as MT; see Note on 48:31.

therefore the rest of what one has made—they are lost! This colon presents various difficulties in spite of significant duplication in Isa 15:7a. The meanings in their respective contexts are not the same. In Isaiah, the Moabites because of desolation in their land are carrying away what remains of their treasures. Here Moab's remaining treasures are lost. Hebrew *yitrat,* "remnant," is a feminine construct in a shortened relative clause (GKC §130d; Giesebrecht; Duhm); thus: "the rest of what one has made." Reference is to Moab's "hard-earned wealth" (NEB) or, more correctly, the wealth that remained in Moab following an earlier loss (T: "remnant of their possessions"; Calvin: "hidden treasure"). Blayney imagines that Moab's reserves were entirely consumed by Assyrian or Arab plundering. Another problem is MT's *'ābādû,* "they are lost," which has a feminine collective subject. Such a construction can stand, however (cf. Rudolph). Isaiah 15:7 also has a plural verb *yiśśā'ûm,* "they carried them away," so perhaps the MT pointing here is correct. The verb, in any case, must be read as a prophetic perfect. Another option would be to repoint as a Piel plural imperative, *'abbĕdû* ("Destroy!"), which has Yahweh commanding the enemy to destroy Moab's remaining reserves. Finally, the initial "therefore," while appropriate in Isa 15:7, is thought to be less appropriate here, for which reason many commentators (Rashi; Kimḥi; Cheyne; Duhm; Weiser; Bright; McKane) translate *'al-kēn* as "because" (so also AV). But we may not have here a reason for the divine lament.

37. *For every head is shaved, and every beard cut off; On all hands are slashes, and on (all) loins sackcloth.* Compare Isa 15:2b–3a. These are ancient mourning rites (Gaster 1969: 590–602), which are looked upon with disfavor in the OT. Herodotus (ii 36) says the Egyptians too, while otherwise shaven, let their hair and beards grow after a death. On mourning practices of shaving oneself bald and self-mutilation by slashing, see Notes for 7:29 and 16:6. On wearing sackcloth, see Note for 4:8. Mourning rites are portrayed also in 41:5 and 47:5.

is shaved. Hebrew *qorḥâ.* 2QJer spells with a *waw: qwrḥḥ.*

cut off. Hebrew *gĕru'ā.* 2QJer has an imperfect form (with a prefixed *taw*).

on (all) loins. The MT lacks the *kol,* but it exists in many MSS, the LXX, and Vg. Cornill plausably suggests MT haplography (homoeoteleuton: *l . . . l*). Its inclusion makes for better poetry.

38a. *On all the roofs of Moab and in her squares.* Compare Isa 15:3. House roofs and city squares are both public places, so the lamenting is taking place where all may see it (Kimḥi; Calvin). In modern Western society it is more common to lament in private. House roofs (*gaggôt*) in the Near East were flat, used as living space and for acts of worship, such as incense burning; see Note on 19:13. Since Yahweh says in v 35 that he has put an end to the burning of incense in Moab, there is then a shift of activity on the Moabite house roofs: from incense burning to lamentation.

all the roofs. 2QJer spells "all" *kwl.*

—everywhere rites of mourning. Hebrew *kullōh mispēd.* One hears and sees the mourning everywhere. Compare Isa 13:3b. The LXX omits the phrase, which is doubtless more loss due to haplography (homoeoarcton: *k . . . k*).

MESSAGE AND AUDIENCE

Yahweh begins here by saying that he has put an end to well-established Moabite rituals—people bringing animals to sacrifice on the high places, and people burning incense to Chemosh and other gods of the land. With the tone of a consummate dramatist, Yahweh then says that his heart moans for Moab like the low notes of a flute; the same goes for the men of Kirheres. Now does it really? And is Yahweh really distraught because all the remaining Moabite possessions are lost? A lament scene in Moab is then portrayed—heads shaven, beards cut, hands slashed, and sackcloth on all loins. One sees it on house roofs and in the squares—everywhere, rites of mourning!

This oracle heard in tandem with what precedes carries forth the wild shout heard at the end of v 33; it also clarifies that Moab's enemy is none other than Yahweh. The oracle connects well with the Jeremianic oracle in vv 38b–39, which calls for more lamentation. On possible dates for this reworked version of Isaiah poetry in the time of Jeremiah, see Message and Audience for 48:1–2.

9. Moab like a Broken Jar (48:38b–39)

48 ³⁸ᵇFor I have broken Moab
   like a jar in which no one takes delight
    —oracle of Yahweh
³⁹'How it is shattered!' wail
   'How Moab has turned the back ashamedly!'
So Moab shall become a joke and a terror
   to all those round about it.

RHETORIC AND COMPOSITION

MT 48:38b–39 = LXX 31:38b–39. These verses are delimited as a separate oracle by the messenger formula in v 38b, and by *setumah*s in M^L and M^A after v 39. M^P has no section here. A new oracle begins in v 40. The oracle here has characteristic Jeremianic vocabulary and phraseology (Holladay II: 348), and since no parallel exists in Isaiah 15–16, it may be taken as a genuine Jeremiah oracle amidst a collection of oracles predating Jeremiah. Cornill pronounced v 38b genuine because of the broken pot simile, which in 22:28 is used to describe a deposed and exiled King Jehoiachin.

The poetry-prose question raised in connection with vv 35–38a applies also here. *BHS* takes the present verses as prose, and most commentators and modern Versions follow suit (see Rhetoric and Composition for 48:35–38a). The decision here is again to take the verses as poetry, but with the recognition that they may also be rhythmic prose. There is a nice repetition in the center (anaphora), which is seen in other Jeremianic poetry (see Rhetoric and Composition for 49:7–11):

. . . .		v 38b
How	*'êk*	v 39
How	*'êk*	
. . . .		

This poetry is linked to preceding poetry (vv 35–38a) and poetry following (vv 40–41) by the catchword "Moab"; see Rhetoric and Composition for 48:19–24.

NOTES

48:38b. *For I have broken Moab like a jar in which no one takes delight.* The phrase, *kiklî 'ên-ḥēpeṣ bô*, "like a jar in which no one takes delight," appears also in Hos 8:8, from which it may derive. The broken jar is also used meta-phorically with reference to Jehoiachin in Jer 22:28. See also Ps 2:9. In Jer 19:1–13 Jeremiah breaks an earthenware pot in the Valley of Ben Hinnom to accompany his prophecy that Yahweh will break Jerusalem beyond mending. The same will now happen to all of Moab. The verb is a prophetic perfect.

oracle of Yahweh. The LXX has *phēsi Kurios* ("says the Lord") after "I have broken (Moab)," instead of at the end of the verse. A formula then is not lack-ing in the LXX (*pace* Holladay).

39. *'How it is shattered!' wail, 'How Moab has turned the back ashamedly.'* Reading *hêlîlû*, which is lacking in LXX, as an imperative: "wail!" (Rashi; NJV; NJB). The two "How . . ." statements are the actual laments people are to wail (NSB). The AV achieves a similar result by translating the verb as a third plu-ral, which it can be, although it makes the perfect verb into a future: "They shall howl *saying,* 'How it is broken down! how hath Moab turned the back with shame!'" In any case, there are not three "How . . ." statements, such as appear in the RSV, NIV, and NRSV. On the paired verbs *bôš* ("be [very] shamed") and *ḥtt* ("be shattered, shatter"), see 48:1, 20, and Note on 17:18.

How! Hebrew *'êk,* sometimes *'êkâ.* A common Jeremiah word used for dis-putation or to begin a lament. On laments in Jeremiah beginning with "How!" see Note for 48:17b.

How Moab has turned the back ashamedly. On the expression to "turn the back (of the neck)," see Note on 2:27. Hebrew *bôš* is here the infinitive abso-lute having an adverbial function (Volz; Rudolph), thus "ashamedly." One can turn the back as an act of defiance, but here it is done in shame.

has turned. Hebrew *hipnâ.* 2QJer has a third plural: "they turned."

back. Hebrew *'ōrep.* 2QJer spells with a full *holem* vowel letter: *'wrp.*

a joke and a terror. Hebrew *liśḥōq wĕlimḥittâ.* On *śĕḥōq,* which is derisive laughing, joking or mockery, see 20:7; 48:26–27; and Lam 3:14. The term *mĕḥittâ,* "terror, fright," having overtones of ruin, occurs also in 17:17; see in addition Ps 89:41; Prov 10:14–15; 13:3.

MESSAGE AND AUDIENCE

In this oracle, Yahweh says that he has broken Moab like a jar no one desires. The Moabites are then instructed to wail and given actual words they can use. They are to say "How it is shattered!" and "How Moab has turned the back ashamedly!" Moab is indeed shattered, and because it has lost face one sees only its back. The massive destruction will also cause Moab to be looked upon with scorn by its neighbors, one of whom will be an already chastened or soon-to-be chastened Ju-dah, who knows something about mockery from onlooking neighbors.

This oracle carries forth the lament theme of the prior oracle, which was re-worked from the Isaiah tradition. It appears to predate the reuse of that oracle, since Yahweh is here giving people words for a lament. In vv 37–38 people are already engaged in lamenting. On possible dates for this oracle from Jeremiah, see Message and Audience for 48:1–2.

10. Eagles Above and Traps Below (48:40–44)

a) Look Out for the Eagle! (48:40–41)

48 ⁴⁰For thus said Yahweh:
Look, as the eagle he flies
    and he spreads his wings toward Moab
⁴¹The towns are taken
    and seized are the strongholds
And the heart of the warriors of Moab shall be in that day
    as the heart of a woman much distressed.

RHETORIC AND COMPOSITION

MT 48:40–41 = LXX 31:40–41. In 48:40–44 is a cluster of three oracles announcing Moab's capture by an enemy, stressing particularly Moab's inability to make an escape. The enemy is portrayed as threatening Moab from above and below. All three oracles, vv 40–41, 42–43, and 44, have messenger formulas at beginning or end:

I	For thus said Yahweh:	*kî-kōh 'āmar yhwh*	v 40
II	—oracle of Yahweh	*nĕ'ūm yhwh*	v 43
III	—oracle of Yahweh	*nĕ'ūm yhwh*	v 44

The "oracle of Yahweh" formulas in II and III are lacking in the LXX, also in the parallel verses of Isa 24:17–18, which lead some commentators (Cornill; Holladay; McKane) to delete. But they should be retained. Volz suggests omitting "For thus said Yahweh" in Oracle I, which again is unnecessary, particularly since the formula is present in the LXX. These formulas nicely delimit the oracles in the larger grouping. Before v 40 is also a *setumah* in Mᴸ and Mᴬ. That vv 40–41 exist as a separate oracle seems confirmed by a shorter version reappearing against Edom in 49:22. The RSV, NJV, NIV, NRSV, NJB, and NSB all break after v 44, with NJV and NJB taking v 44 as a separate unit.

The present oracle has no parallel in Isaiah, and can confidently be ascribed to Jeremiah. It begins with the familiar *hinnēh*, "Look," on which see Note for 1:9. Jeremianic phraseology is also present in the first and last bicolons, although some commentators (Giesebrecht; Duhm; Peake; Cornill; Rudolph; Holladay; McKane) take vv 40 and 41b as interpolations from 49:22. Since both bicolons are lacking in the LXX, some scholars invoke the *lectio brevior praeferenda est* principle in defense of its reading (cf. McKane, 1194). But Volz argues that the verses are original in the present context. It seems unnecessary here to argue either for or against interpolation. Jeremiah's poetry is simply turning up in two different oracles, one against Moab and one against Edom. One notes in 50:41–43 a Jeremiah oracle against Judah (6:22–24) modified for reuse against Babylon.

This oracle appears to be entirely poetry, although Holladay and the JB (but not NJB) take 41b as prose. The three bicolons are nicely structured into a chiasmus, with similes and a repeated "Moab" occurring in the outer bicolons, and a syntactic chiasmus at the center:

```
. . . . as the eagle . . . . . . . . . . . .        ka . . .                          v 40
. . . . . . . . . . . . . . . . . . . . . . . . . . Moab
     The towns / are taken                                                            v 41
     and seized are / the strongholds
. . . . . . . . . . . . . . . . . . . . Moab . . . . . . .
as the heart of a woman . . . . .                  kĕ . . .
```

This poetic oracle is linked to preceding poetry (vv 38b–39) and poetry following (vv 42–43) by the catchword "Moab"; see Rhetoric and Composition for 48:19–24.

NOTES

48:40. *Look, as the eagle he flies, and he spreads his wings toward Moab.* The "swift-flying eagle" image—here and in 49:22 (against Bozrah in Edom)— may derive from Deut 28:49. Compare also the "two eagle" allegory in Ezekiel 17. Reference here is to Nebuchadnezzar (Kimḥi; Calvin). See further Note on 4:13.

and he spreads his wings. The T has "so a king with his troops shall go up and encamp."

41. *The towns are taken, and seized are the strongholds.* A syntactic chiasmus of the type commonly found in Jeremiah, where the verbs in Hebrew are at the extremes (Lundbom 1975: 64 [= 1997: 85]). On feminine singular verbs predicating plural subjects, see GKC §145k.

the towns. Hebrew *haqqĕrîyôt.* See 49:25 for the singular, *qiryat.* This is not the place named "Kerioth" in v 24 (*pace* LXX [*Akkariōth*]; Vg [Carioth]; Rashi; AV; NJV; NIV). The definite article and parallelism with "the strongholds" make necessary "the towns" (or "the cities").

the strongholds. Hebrew *hammĕṣādôt* are "mountain strongholds" (KB³), to which access is difficult; cf. 51:30. David spent time in a Moabite stronghold when fleeing Saul (1 Sam 22:4–5).

And the heart of the warriors of Moab shall be in that day as the heart of a woman much distressed. Yahweh steps back from his certitude about the future destruction to reflect on what it will be like on that day. This is an ancient curse (see Notes on 4:31 and 6:24). The LXX omits, which can be attributed to haplography (homoeoarcton: *w . . . w*; or homoeoteleuton: *h . . . h*). Aquila and Theod have the words.

in that day. I.e., the day of Yahweh, which comes for all nations; see Note on 46:10.

a woman much distressed. I.e., a woman in labor. Hebrew *'iššâ mĕṣērâ.* The feminine participle is an internal H-stem, which adds intensity; see Note for

2:26. This particular phrase occurs only here and in 49:22, although it varies just slightly a common image in Jeremiah used to describe the distress of war (see Note for 6:24).

MESSAGE AND AUDIENCE

In this brief oracle Yahweh calls his audience to take note. An enemy is approaching Moab like a swift-flying eagle, its wings spread wide over the land. With lightning speed towns are taken and mountain strongholds are seized. Yahweh says the heart of the warriors—referring to their courage and resolve to fight—will be on this fateful day like the heart of a woman in great distress. It is left to the audience to imagine the rest. Is Moab in the throes of birth or death? On possible dates for this oracle, see Message and Audience for 48:1–2.

b) Scare, Pit, and Snare Are before You! (48:42–43)

48 ⁴²Moab shall be exterminated from being a people
  for against Yahweh he made himself great
⁴³Scare, and pit, and snare
  are against you, sitting one of Moab
    —oracle of Yahweh.

RHETORIC AND COMPOSITION

MT 48:42–43 = LXX 31:42–43. This oracle is delimited within a three-oracle cluster by a messenger formula at the end of v 43 (see Rhetoric and Composition for 48:40–41). Although v 42 has no parallel in Isaiah (Jones: "of fresh mintage"), and v 43 does, a break should nevertheless not be made after v 42 (*pace* Bardtke 1936: 249; Rudolph; Bright; Carroll). In the present context, the oracle concludes with v 43 (NJB). Verse 43 has a near-duplication in Isa 24:17, which raises the question of priority, since Isaiah 24–27 are dated by many in the postexilic period (Holladay). It could be that vv 43–44 (v 44 = Isa 24:18) are original to Jeremiah and appear later in Isaiah. We cannot be sure.

This oracle comprises two brief bicolons that can be divided into two stanzas on the basis of a speaker change. The prophet speaks in Stanza I (v 42), where Yahweh is referred to in the third person, and in Stanza II (v 43) Yahweh speaks, threatening Moab but not yet judging it. The stanzas with their repetitions are as follows:

I   *Moab* . . . .   v 42
     . . . . *against Yahweh* . . . .   ʿal-yhwh

II . . . .   v 43
    against you . . . . *Moab*   ʿāleykā

This poetry is linked to preceding poetry (vv 40–41) and poetry following (v 44) by the catchword "Moab"; see Rhetoric and Composition for 48:19–24. These catchwords also connect to the poetry following:

v 43 *Scare, and pit, and snare*   v 44 *scare . . . pit . . . pit . . . snare*

NOTES

48:42. *Moab shall be exterminated from being a people.* Hebrew *nišmad mô'āb mē'ām*. The same point is made somewhat differently in 48:2. On the strong sense of *šmd*, "to be exterminated, made useless," see Note for 48:8.

for against Yahweh he made himself great. See v 26. Moab is not a people of Yahweh; nevertheless, by exalting itself over Israel, which it has done (Zeph 2:10), it exalts itself over Yahweh.

43. *Scare, and pit, and snare.* See Isa 24:17. The Heb has nice alliteration: *paḥad wāpaḥat wāpāḥ*. Hitzig reproduced it in German as "Grauen und Graben und Garn." Streane thinks the saying here may have been a popular proverb. Hebrew *paḥad* is elsewhere translated "terror" (30:5; 49:5), but hunting imagery here makes preferable the translation "scare" (NEB; REB), i.e., what provokes the hunted to begin running. The term *paḥat* was translated "gorge" in v 28, but here it is a "pit" set up as a trap (Lam 3:47). Hebrew *pāḥ*, "snare," is a bird trap (18:22). On the trapping of birds with clap nets, see Note for 5:26.

sitting one of Moab. Hebrew *yōšēb mô'āb*. This translation, used elsewhere in Jeremiah for the more normal feminine, *yōšebet* (see Note for 46:19), is better than "inhabitant of Moab" because a personified nation is being addressed. Isaiah 24:7 has "sitting one / inhabitant of the earth."

MESSAGE AND AUDIENCE

In this oracle, the prophet begins by telling his audience—perhaps a Jerusalem audience—that Moab shall cease from being a people. The reason: it has exalted itself against Yahweh, presumably by exalting itself against Yahweh's people. Yahweh then issues a threat—not yet a judgment—in words that echo the indictment. Against Moab will come first a scare, then a pit, and finally a snare. It remains to be seen what will happen.

Heard in tandem with the previous oracle, this one moves now from a swift-flying eagle to threats facing Moab on the ground and below ground. The total effect is to drive home the point that the enemy is everywhere, with the audience left wondering whether escape is possible. On possible dates for an initial use or later reuse of this oracle in Jeremiah's time, see Message and Audience for 48:1–2.

c) One of Them Will Get You! (48:44)

48 [44]The one who flees[1] from the scare
    shall fall into the pit

---

[1]Reading the Q *hannās* ("the one who flees"); the Kt, if pointed *hannayyās*, could also be "the fleer" (compare *haggannāb*, "the thief").

And the one who comes up from the pit
 shall be taken in the snare
For I will bring to her, to Moab
 the year of their reckoning
  —oracle of Yahweh.

RHETORIC AND COMPOSITION

MT 48:44 = LXX 31:44. The present oracle is the third in a cluster of three, concluding both it and the cluster with an "oracle of Yahweh" messenger formula (see Rhetoric and Composition for 48:40–41). The NJB is thus correct in separating out this verse as a separate unit. One will also note that in the LXX the Moab collection—and the entire Foreign Nation Collection—ends with v 44, after which comes the "cup of wrath" passage appearing in MT 25:15–38. Here in v 44 the LXX lacks the messenger formula, but does have "the year of their reckoning," which is a recognized closing in Jeremiah (11:23; 23:12). The present verse closely reproduces Isa 24:18, but there is uncertainty about authorship and which of the two is prior (see Rhetoric and Composition for 48:42–43).

Catchwords connecting to the poetry preceding:

v 44	*Moab*	vv 42–43	*Moab (2×)*
	scare . . . pit . . . pit . . . snare	v 43	*Scare, and pit, and snare*

Catchwords connecting to the poetry following:

v 44	*The one who flees*	v 45	*those fleeing*
	Moab	vv 45–46	*Moab (2×)*

On "Moab" as a catchword connecting all the oracles in the later part of the chapter, see Rhetoric and Composition for 48:19–24.

NOTES

48:44. *The one who flees from the scare shall fall into the pit, and the one who comes up from the pit shall be taken in the snare.* See Isa 24:18. This imagery derives from the hunt, where the chased animal escapes one danger only to fall headlong into another (Gerleman 1946: 86–87). The point then, as stated elsewhere in the OT (15:2; Amos 5:19; 9:1–4; Joel 1:4; Ps 139:7–12), is that escape with Yahweh in pursuit is impossible. For imagery of the hunt in Jeremiah, see also 16:16.

the scare . . . the pit . . . the snare. See Note for 48:43. The scare (*paḥad*) refers to cries of the beaters who, in the hunt, generate noise so as to drive the game toward the traps.

For I will bring to her, to Moab. The MT can be read (AV), although some commentators (Cornill; Volz; Rudolph; Weiser; Bright; Keown et al.) translate the LXX (*tauta* = *'ēlleh*, "these [things]"), while others (Blayney; Holladay) emend *'ēleyhā* ("to her") to *'ālāh* ("curse"). The Vg deletes *'ēleyhā*, which is the solution of Giesebrecht and McKane. The plural suffix on the following "their reckoning" is awkward in the MT reading, but still possible (Moab becomes a collective).

the year of their reckoning. I.e., their punishment. Hebrew *šěnat pěquddātām.* The phrase recurs in 11:23 and 23:12, and has other variations in Jeremiah (see 46:21; 49:8; and Note for 6:15). On the verb *pqd* in Jeremiah, see Note for 5:9. Calvin gives a particularly good exposition here, speaking about the importance of being patient until God judges the ungodly. Our tendency, he says, is to want God to act in haste. God, however, is slow to anger (Exod 34:6).

MESSAGE AND AUDIENCE

In this oracle Yahweh says that the one fleeing from the scare will fall into the pit, and having climbed out of there will then be caught in the snare. There will be no escape, for Yahweh will bring to Moab the year of its reckoning. The audience, perhaps again one assembled in Jerusalem, realizes that reckoning here means unambiguous punishment.

When this oracle and the previous one are heard in tandem, the image of the hunt is carried through to its expected conclusion. All attempts to escape will be thwarted, and Moab will fall captive to its pursuer. The threat has now become a judgment, and Yahweh is the one bringing it. We see a similar progression in the Temple Oracles of 7:3–14. On possible dates for initial use or later reuse of this oracle in the time of Jeremiah, see Message and Audience for 48:1–2.

11. In the Shadow of Heshbon They Stop (48:45–47)

48 ⁴⁵In the shadow of Heshbon they stopped
    those fleeing without strength
Indeed a fire went forth from Heshbon
    a flame from within Sihon

And it consumed the temples of Moab
    and the crown of the uproarious sons

⁴⁶Woe to you, Moab
    the people of Chemosh has perished
Indeed your sons are taken captive
    and your daughters into captivity.

⁴⁷But I will restore the fortunes of Moab in the days afterward—oracle of Yahweh.
Thus far the judgment on Moab.

RHETORIC AND COMPOSITION

MT 48:45–47 = LXX 0. The present verses contain a judgment poem against Moab (vv 45–46), a salvation oracle in prose for Moab's future (v 47a), and a concluding subscription for the Moab collection as a whole (v 47b). The main judgment poem adapts and expands old poetry in Num 21:28–29 and 24:17, the former drawn from a mocking song celebrating the victory of Sihon, king of the Amorites, over Moab (Num 21:26), and the latter coming from one of the Balaam oracles. This poem is delimited at the top end by the messenger formula concluding the prior oracle in v 44 (see Rhetoric and Composition for 48:41–42). At the bottom end it is demarcated from the salvation oracle in v 47a, which has a messenger formula. The unit—and the whole of chap. 48— concludes with a subscription, section markings after v 47 (*setumahs* in M^L and M^A; a *petuḥah* in M^P), and the chapter divison. All of the present verses are omitted in the LXX. For the Gk reading preserved in Theod, with variations in Aq and Symm, see Field 1875: 716–17.

The subscription and superscription of the Moab collection combine to form an inclusio:

For *Moab*	v 1a
Thus far the judgment on *Moab*	v 47

It appears also that the initial poem in the Moab collection is meant to balance the poem with which the collection concludes. Dobbs-Allsopp (1993: 106) notes the collocation of "woe" in vv 1 and 46, to which should be added the collocation of "in . . . Heshbon" in vv 2 and 45, which is noted in Keown et al. (p. 320). Key words are inverted, making a chiasmus:

Woe	*hôy*	v 1b
. . . .		
In Heshbon	*bĕḥešbôn*	v 2b
. . . .		
In . . . Heshbon	*bĕ . . . ḥešbôn*	v 45a
. . . .		
Woe	*'ôy*	v 46a
. . . .		

The main poem, though a conglomerate, is nevertheless divisible into three stanzas with a 2:1:2 line structure. Stanza I (v 45ab) is a double bicolon, Stanza II (v 45c) a single bicolon, and Stanza III (v 46) another double bicolon. The last bicolon of Stanza I and all of Stanza III are taken from Num 21:28–29. The single line of Stanza II is a variation on Num 24:17b. The whole has these repetitions and balancing key words, two of the latter ("Sihon" / "uproarious") also creating assonance:

I	.... Heshbon		v 45
	.... without	mi. .	
Indeed .... from Heshbon		kî ...... mē ...	
.... from .... Sihon		mi ... sîḥôn	
II	.... Moab		
	.... uproarious sons	bĕnê šā'ôn	
III	.... Moab		v 46
	....		
Indeed .... your sons		kî .... bāneykā	
and your daughters		ûbĕnōteykā ...	

"Moab" is the catchword connecting all the units in the latter part of the chapter; see Rhetoric and Composition for 48:19–24. In addition, these catchwords connect to the preceding oracle:

v 45 *those fleeing*   v 44 *The one who flees*

Catchwords connecting to the first two Ammon oracles in 49:1–2 are these:

48:46 *sons ... daughters*   49:1–2 *sons ... daughters*

NOTES

48:45. *In the shadow of Heshbon they stopped, those fleeing without strength.* This line is not present in Num 21:27–30, so reference must be to the imagined panic in connection with the approach of Nebuchadnezzar in the early sixth century B.C. Perfect forms of the verb here and throughout the poem are to be taken as prophetic perfects. People are seen fleeing to Heshbon at the beginning of the invasion, needing rest and hoping to find security in the city. With Heshbon being on Moab's northern boundary, we are not to imagine fugitives coming from the south, a point that troubled earlier commentators (Cheyne; Peake). If this poem returns to the theme set forth in the first poem of the collection (see Rhetoric and Composition), there is no problem. The enemy is coming from the north, and the first attempt to find respite and refuge will be in "the shadow of Heshbon," where "shadow" (ṣēl) is a symbol for protection (Num 14:9; Pss 17:8; 36:8).

Heshbon. A city in Moab's northern tableland on the King's Highway (see Note for 48:2).

those fleeing without strength. Hebrew mikkōaḥ nāsîm. People fleeing have no strength to proceed farther, for which reason they seek refuge in Heshbon (Rashi).

Indeed a fire went forth from Heshbon, a flame from within Sihon. Words from an old song (Num 21:28a) are recalled in order to say that Heshbon can be no refuge since the city will be set afire. In fact, the fire beginning in Heshbon will spread throughout Moab.

Indeed. Reading *kî* as an asseverative (suggested by Calvin), as there is no causation.

a fire went forth. Hebrew *'ēš yāṣā'*. Many MSS and Num 21:28 have a feminine verb, but *'ēš* ("fire") can take the masculine (Ps 104:4; cf. BDB, 77). Another possibility would be to repoint to an infinitive absolute, *yāṣō'*, which would give the same basic meaning (D. N. Freedman).

from within Sihon. I.e., from within the city of Sihon, king of the Amorites, whose capital was Heshbon (Num 21:26). Hebrew *mibbēn sîḥôn*. 2QJer has *mqryt*, "from the town (of Sihon)," with the *mem* not being absolutely certain (Baillet 1962: 69). This reading corresponds to that in Num 21:28. Theodotion, too, has *poleōs Sēōn* ("from the city of Sihon"). The MT reading, while certainly the *lectio difficilior*, is not impossible (*pace* Bright). Its unusual nature may be explained by the assonance ending 45b and c: *mibbēn sîḥôn . . . bĕnê šā'ôn.*

And it consumed the temples of Moab, and the crown of the uproarious sons. This line is brought in from Num 24:17 to make the point that the Heshbon fire, before it is extinguished, will have consumed the whole of Moab (Calvin).

temples . . . crown. Hebrew *pĕ'at . . . qodqōd.* Assuming here a personified Moab, *pĕ'at* refers to the "temples" or "hair at the side of the head" (9:25[Eng 9:26]; 25:23; 49:32), and *qodqōd* to the "crown" of the head. The fire will be all-consuming. The AV opted for a geographical interpretation, translating *pĕ'at* as the "corners" of Moab (Neh 9:22), which comes out with much the same meaning. Kimḥi, too, took "the corner of Moab" to mean Moab even to the last corner.

uproarious sons. Hebrew *bĕnê šā'ôn* is lit. "sons of uproar." Compare "sons of thunder" in the NT (Mark 3:17), and see Note on 4:11 for other examples of the idiom. The term *šā'ôn* sometimes refers to the tumult of war (25:31; Amos 2:2; Hos 10:14); therefore, the expression here could be a circumlocution for "warriors" (Cheyne). Numbers 24:17 has "sons of Seth" (*bĕnê-šēt*), but, as we just noted, the phrase appearing here creates assonance in the Hebrew with "from within Sihon."

46. *Woe to you, Moab.* Compare "Woe to you, Jerusalem," in 13:27, and "Woe to Nebo" in 48:1. On *hôy* ("woe!") as as an expression wavering between lament and invective, see Note for 22:13. A shift to the second person now has Moab being addressed directly. For a similar audience shift, see 12:13.

the people of Chemosh has perished. The "people of Chemosh" are the Moabites (Num 21:29). On this preeminent Moabite god, see Note for 48:7b. One MS, Theod, T, S, Vg, and Num 21:29 have the second person, *'ābadtā*, "you have perished," which keeps consistency in the verse. However, Num 21:30 (with a different subject) has the third person, as here. Either reading is acceptable.

Indeed your sons are taken captive, and your daughters into captivity. In Num 21:29 Moabite sons were made "fugitives" (*pĕlêṭîm*) and its daughters "captives"—to the Amorite king, Sihon. Now Moabite sons and daughters will be taken by Nebuchadnezzar into exile.

47. *But I will restore the fortunes of Moab in the days afterward—oracle of Yahweh.* The phrase "But I will restore the fortunes" is stereotyped, occurring often in the book with respect to Judah (see Note for 29:14), but applying to Moab, Ammon (49:6), and also Elam (49:39). A different formula conveying the same message is used for Egypt (46:26). While the phrase here may be a later add-on, restoration promises are now recognized as being integral to laments and judgment oracles. Dobbs-Allsopp (1993: 106–7) has shown that a concluding restoration word is common in the ancient Mesopotamian city laments.

in the days afterward. Hebrew *bĕ'aḥărît hayyāmîm*. On this expression, see Note for 23:20. Rudolph points out that the expression is not eschatological (e.g., Kimḥi says that Moab will return to its land in the Messianic Age), but simply has the meaning of "future."

Thus far the judgment on Moab. Hebrew *'ad-hēnnâ mišpaṭ mô'āb*. A similar subscription closes the Jeremiah book in 51:64. Here the term "judgment" (*mišpaṭ*) may be picked up from v 21.

MESSAGE AND AUDIENCE

In this closing poem of the Moab collection, the prophet, as speaker, returns his audience to the opening oracle, envisioning how people at the beginning of the war will be fleeing from the advancing Babylonians to the city of Heshbon. Sapped of their strength, they will hope to find protection in its shadow. But their hope will be in vain, and with a reuse of old words from a familiar mocking song over Moab, the prophet says that a fire will go forth from Heshbon, a flame from within Sihon's city. The audience will doubtless perceive that the "new Sihon" is none other than Nebuchadnezzar.

The poem continues with another familiar line, this one from the celebrated seer, Balaam ben Beor. The Heshbon fire is only the beginning. It will burn until it has consumed the whole of Moab. No longer will one hear boasts such as "Warriors are we, and valiant men for war!"

The poem concludes with more words from the old mocking song. The rhetoric is well suited to a Jeremianic audience, with a shift now being made to the second person: "Woe to you, Moab!" Once again the people of Chemosh are destroyed, their sons and daughters headed this time for a Babylonian exile.

The prophet's word is followed by a closing oracle from Yahweh. But it has a happy turn, for it affirms that Yahweh will restore Moab's fortunes in future days. Then a closing subscription announces to the audience that this overly long judgment on Moab is now finally ended.

The beginning of the main poem will strike a responsive chord in a Judahite—or Jerusalem—audience that will feel no remorse over Moab's losing its land. The latter part of the poem, spoken directly to Moab, has a Judahite audience listening in. Even before the subscription, the audience may well anticipate closure if it has heard the entire Moab collection, for the final woe and flight to Heshbon remind them of the opening oracle. On possible dates for the use of this poem and oracle, see Message and Audience for 48:1–2.

E. WHAT ABOUT THE AMMONITES? (49:1–6)

1. So Why Has Milcom Inherited Gad? (49:1–2)

49 ¹For the Ammonites.
Thus said Yahweh:
Has Israel no sons?
 Has he no inheritor?
So why has Milcom inherited Gad
 and his people live in his cities?

²Look, hereafter, days are coming—oracle of Yahweh:
I will make Rabbah of the Ammonites hear
 the shout of battle
and she shall become a desolate tell
 her daughters burned with fire.
Then Israel shall inherit those who inherited him—said Yahweh.

RHETORIC AND COMPOSITION

MT 49:1–2 = LXX 30:17–18 (Ziegler 30:1–2). Here in chap. 49 are brought together oracles and other prophetic utterances against Ammon, Edom, Damascus, Kedar, and Elam. Oracles against Ammon and Moab in the MT are contiguous, which is reasonable since, according to biblical tradition, the two peoples were fraternal (Gen 19:36–38) and were even jointly discriminated against in the Deuteronomic law denying certain groups entrance to the Temple (Deut 23:3–6).

The Ammon oracles (vv 1–6) have been brought together into a compositional unit demarcated at the top end by the superscription, "For the Ammonites" (v 1), before which come *setumahs* in M^L and M^A. M^P has a *petuḥah*. This is also the chapter division. At the bottom end (v 6), M^L and M^P have a *setumah*, M^A a *petuḥah*. Commentators generally take vv 1–6 as a single oracle with supplements, some (e.g., Condamin; Weiser; Holladay) dividing the oracle into two stanzas: vv 1–2, and vv 3–5. Verse 6 is considered a later add-on. Not infrequently the messenger formulas in vv 2a, 2d, 5a, and 6 are eliminated (Holladay; McKane), even though only one, *'āmar yhwh* at the end of v 2, is completely absent in the LXX. The *BHS* too suggests eliminating "look . . . days are coming" in v 2a, and "oracle of the Lord Yahweh of hosts" in v 5a. If the messenger formulas are retained, we seem then to have not one oracle, but four. The first two (vv 1–2) belong together, as they are linked thematically and connected to the previous oracle by catchwords (see below). The last two also belong together, as they shift thematically to an ironic call for lament and are connected to the oracle following by catchwords (see Rhetoric and Composition for 49:3–6). A break then comes between v 2 and v 3, indicated also by "said Yahweh" concluding v 2.

The two groupings of vv 1–2 and vv 3–6 nevertheless correspond. In each, the second oracle (v 2 and v 5) is the one delivering judgment. Also each second oracle begins with the familiar Jeremianic "Look / Look I," and is framed by messenger formulas:

Look . . .—oracle of Yahweh:	v 2	*Look I . . . .*		v 5
. . . .		*oracle* of the Lord *Yahweh* of hosts		
. . . . said *Yahweh*		. . . . oracle of *Yahweh*		v 6

The final lines of the two oracles, "Then Israel shall inherit those who inherited him—said Yahweh" (v 2), and "But afterward I will restore the fortunes of the Ammonites—oracle of Yahweh" (v 6), may be supplements (Cornill; Peake; Rudolph), the former deriving from Zeph 2:9 and the latter a stereotyped restoration promise similar to those in 46:26; 48:47; and 49:39. Nevertheless, we know now from the Mesopotamian laments that a concluding word regarding the city or country's restoration is commonly present (Dobbs-Allsopp 1993: 92–94, 106–7). Whether the restoration statements here were originally part of the oracles is difficult to say. What is clear is that both are structurally integrated into the oracles as they now appear in the text. And there is certainly no reason to deny either statement to Jeremiah.

The first oracle (v 1) is a double bicolon with the familiar threefold Jeremianic rhetorical question, functioning here as an introduction, as it does in 2:14. The second oracle (v 2) is a double bicolon delivering judgment, framed by a split bicolon containing the messenger formulas. The two oracles are linked by key words making an inclusio:

I	Has *Israel* no *sons?*	*bānîm*	v 1
	Has he no *inheritor?*	*yôrēš*	
II	*her daughters*	*bĕnōteyhā*	v 2
	Then Israel shall inherit those who inherited him	*wĕyāraš . . . yōrĕšāyw*	

McKane denies the Jeremianic authorship of these oracles, citing with approval the earlier views of Giesebrecht and Duhm. Their judgments, and those of others, were based largely on an imagined lateness of the stereotypical phrases—the messenger formulas and summary statements promising later well-being. For Duhm and McKane also, Jeremiah is not a prophet to foreign nations. Whereas the promised hope for Israel and the nations may be later add-ons, though not necessarily postexilic in date, stereotypical phrases such as "look, days are coming" cannot be judged secondary. As for the vocabulary and phraseology in the oracles themselves, what we have is "vintage Jeremiah," e.g., the threefold rhetorical question, "Has . . . has . . . so why . . . ?" (*hĕ . . . 'im . . . maddûaʿ . . .*), "the shout of battle" (*tĕrûʿat milḥāmâ*), "desolation" (*šĕmāmâ*), "wail . . . cry out" (*hêlîlû . . . zāʿăqû*), "wail . . . scream" (*hêlîlî . . . šĕʿaqnâ*), "devastated" (*šuddĕdâ*), "put on sackcloth, beat your chests" (*hăgōrĕnâ śaqqîm sĕpōdĕnâ*), "go back and forth" (*hitšōṭaṭnâ*), "turnable daughter" (*habbat haš-šōbēbâ*), "Look I am bringing" (*hinĕnî mēbî'*), and "from everyone on every side of you" (*mikkol-sĕbîbāyik*).

Giesebrecht correctly perceived that vv 1–6 formed a redactional work, but with Duhm he judged it late because it was "without a clear prophetic thought." McKane remarks, too, about "threadbare" oracles and literature of "low rank." That Jeremiah's Foreign Nation Oracles pale in comparison to his Israel and Judah oracles goes without saying. While certainly not lacking in irony, they nevertheless contain no arguments for breach of covenant, no penetrating critiques of personal and social evil, no attempts to mediate a nation's sin, no personal involvement in suffering and judgment, and no great insights into the character and doings of Yahweh. Yet most commentators take these oracles as genuine, which they undoubtedly are. Jeremiah judges the Ammonites elsewhere in 9:25[Eng 9:26] and 25:21. For other prophecies against the Ammonites, see Amos 1:13–15; Zeph 2:8–11; Ezek 21:33–37[Eng 21:28–32]; and 25:1–7.

Catchwords connecting to the prior oracle in 48:45–47:

49:1–2 *sons . . . her daughters*   48:46 *sons . . . daughters*

Catchwords connecting to the remaining Ammon oracles in vv 3–6:

vv 1–2 *Milcom . . . Rabbah*   vv 3–4 *Rabbah . . . Milcom*
          her daughters   *daughters . . . daughter*

NOTES

49:1. *For the Ammonites.* Hebrew *libnē ʿammôn*. On the short introduction, see Note for 46:2. The Ammonites were a Transjordanian tribal people living to the north of Moab, although the territory immediately east of the Jordan (Gilead) was at various times under Israelite control. The capital city of Ammon was Rabbah, up over the mountains about 40 kilometers east of the Jordan River (see below). Ammonite geography, religion, and culture are well summarized in Herr, *OEANE* 1: 103–5. On ancient Ammonite territory and sites, see MacDonald (1999); on archaeological work of Ammonite sites, see Sauer (1985; 1986), Younker (1999), and Stern (2001: 238–58).

Has Israel no sons? Has he no inheritor? So why has Milcom inherited Gad . . . ? On Jeremiah's threefold rhetorical question in the *hă . . . 'im . . . maddûaʿ* form, see Note for 2:14. Questions one and two could elicit from the prophet's audience the answer: "Of course he has!" Israel most certainly has "sons" to inherit (= take possession of) Gad. And yet, the Gadites were taken away by Tiglath-pileser III to Assyria in 733 B.C. (1 Chr 5:26; cf. 2 Kgs 15:29), which could mean that there are no Gadites to possess their former territory, thus a pained "No" answer, should the audience be willing to give it.

So why has Milcom inherited Gad, and his people live in his cities? Assonance on the *a* sound is noted throughout the bicolon by Watson (1984: 223). Also, a connection to the prior question is made by a wordplay: *yāraš* ("he has inherited") picks up from *yôrēš* ("inheritor"). The verb *yrš* ("inherit") is comonly associated with military action in the OT (Deut 1:8, 21, 39, and often; Mic 1:15; Hab 1:6; Ps 44:4[Eng 44:3]) and in extrabiblical literature, e.g., the Moabite Stone (Haak 1991: 39–40). According to biblical tradition, Israel and Ammon had a running dispute over territory going back at least to the time of the Judges (Judges 11; 1 Samuel 11; 2 Sam 10:1–11:1; 12:26–31). Gad originally settled a portion of the territory east of the Jordan after Israel's defeat of Sihon, king of Heshbon (Josh 13:24–28; cf. Deut 2:24–3:22). But the "men of Gad" are mentioned on the Moabite Stone (line 10) as having been subdued by Mesha, king of Moab (mid–ninth century). From this point on, most of what we know about the Ammonites comes from Assyrian texts; in the Egyptian texts they are not mentioned (*ABD* 1: 194). Israel's Transjordan population was deported by Tiglath-pileser III to Assyria in 733, and when Northern Israel collapsed a few years later, the Ammonites presumably moved into the vacuum, annexing portions of Gad (Kimḥi; Blayney; Bright). See Amos 1:13 about Ammonites enlarging their borders. During the seventh century Ammon prospered as a semiautonomous kingdom within the Assyrian Empire (Landes 1961: 66–86; Stern 2001: 237–38).

Milcom . . . Gad. The LXX reading, *Melchol . . . Galaad* (= Gilead), is adopted by Ziegler (1957: 310); Rahlfs (1971: 708) reads *Melchom . . . Gad*. "Gilead" in Amos's Ammonite oracle (Amos 1:13) is doubtless the same territory, since the Gadites inherited a portion of Gilead (Num 32:29).

Milcom. The patron deity of the Ammonites, correctly revocalized in LXX, S, and Vg, and adopted by all the modern Versions. The MT has *malkām*, "their king," which carried over into T and was the translation of the AV. Calvin too read "their king," wondering why Jerome rendered the term as if it were the name of an idol. Jewish opinion is similarly divided. Rashi interprets the Hebrew as the name of an Ammonite deity; Kimḥi renders it "their king." The term appears again in v 3, which is a quotation from Amos 1:15, where the usual translation is "their king." But "Milcom" is correct—probably in all three texts. A seal impression found at Tell el-ʿUmeiri and dated to the early sixth century B.C. reads, "Belonging to Milkomʾur, servant of Baalyasha" (Aufrecht 1989: 308–9; Herr 1985; 1993a: 31–34). The owner of this seal bears the name of Milcom, and Baalyasha is doubtless the King Baalis mentioned in 40:14. Another excavated sixth-century seal contains the name "Badmilkom" (Aufrecht 1989: 3–5). The MT here and in the Amos passage is probably avoiding the name "Milcom," although the name does occur in 1 Kgs 11:5 and 33. A further complication is presented in 1 Kgs 11:7, where "Molech" is said to be "the abomination of the Ammonites." Molech is mentioned also in Jer 32:35. The suggestion has therefore been made that Milcom and Molech are one and the same deity (Bright), the latter perhaps being a deliberate distortion of the former. Like biblical Topheth and Ashtoreth, Molech contains the vowels of *bōšet* ("shame") for purposes of disparagement (see Note on 7:19). But Herr (*OEANE* 1: 105) says Milcom should not be equated with Molech as 1 Kgs 11:7 appears to do (*mlk* he takes to be a scribal error for *mlkm*). The two deities seem to have separate cult places in 2 Kgs 23:10, 13. On Molech worship, see Note for 7:31. Here the question is why has the Ammonite god dispossessed the Gadites? The audience will probably not answer because it has no answer to give. Compare, however, the "give possession–dispossess" language used with reference to Yahweh and Chemosh in Judg 11:23–24.

2. *Look, hereafter, days are coming.* This phrase recurs in 48:12; 51:47 and 52; see Notes on 7:32 and 16:14. The formula here announces future judgment on the Ammonites, apparently for their dispossession of Gad. No wrongdoing is otherwise indicated. But reasons for a dispossession of Ammon by "the people of the east" are given in Ezek 25:1–7.

I will make Rabbah of the Ammonites hear the shout of battle. Ammon probably submitted to Nebuchadnezzar when the latter came to Palestine in 604, since in 599–598 Ammon and Moab joined a Babylonian-sponsored rampage within Judah (2 Kgs 24:2). Yet in 594 both Moab and Ammon were represented in Jerusalem when a rebellion was being planned against Babylon (27:3). According to Josephus (*Ant* x 181–82), Nebuchadnezzar marched against Ammon and Moab in 582 B.C., bringing both nations into subjection. This, most likely, is the battle predicted here and in Ezek 21:33–37[Eng 21:28–32] and 25:1–7. Ammon was threatened with invasion in 588 B.C., according to Ezek 21:23–32[Eng 21:18–27], but Nebuchadnezzar went instead in the direction of Jerusalem. For an interesting parallel to Nebuchadnezzar's choice of campaign routes in the Mari Letters (ARM 26/2 #404), see Malamat 1991a: 188–90. Ammon, in any case, was punished for its disloyalty in 594 B.C., and then later for the role it played in the assassination of Gedaliah (40:13–41:18), the Babylonian-appointed governor of Judah (Thompson; Herr in *OEANE* 1: 104). In the latter insurrection Babylonian soldiers were also killed (41:3). Gedaliah's assassination can be dated as late as 582 B.C. if it correlates with the third deportation of Judahites to Babylon (52:30). Ammon's destruction, in any event, does not appear to have been total. Recent archaeological evidence shows both Ammon and Moab existing well into the Persian and Hellenistic periods (Herr 1993a: 29; LaBianca and Younker 1995: 411).

Rabbah of the Ammonites. Hebrew *rabbat běnê-ʿammôn.* Literally, "Rabbah, of the sons of Ammon." We know from the Tell Sīrān Bottle Inscription (*CS* II 139) that Ammonite kings referred to themselves as "king of the sons of Ammon (*bn ʿamn*)," indicating that the Ammonites were more a tribe than a nation (Bienkowski and van der Steen 2001: 38–39). The LXX lacks "sons of Ammon." Rabbah was the capital city of ancient Ammon (2 Sam 12:26), today Amman, the capital of Jordan. It lies 40 kilometers east of the Jordan

River, into which the Jabbok River empties. A spring near Rabbah begins the Jabbok. The ancient city survives on a hill in central Amman called el-Qalʿa ("the Citadel"). Excavations of the Citadel show a major urban center in Iron II (900–586 B.C.). On the archaeology of the site, see Zayadine 1973: 28–35; cf. *NEAEHL* 4: 1243–52.

the shout of battle. I.e., the shout of soldiers engaged in battle. Hebrew *tĕrûʿat milḥāmâ.* The expression appears earlier in 4:19. The term *tĕrûʿâ* can also mean simply an "alarm" (20:16).

a desolate tell. Hebrew *tēl šĕmāmâ.* A "tell" is a mound of abandoned city ruins (30:18; Deut 13:17[Eng 13:16]; Josh 8:28; 11:13). The term *šĕmāmâ* ("desolation") occurs often in Jeremiah poetry and prose (4:27; 6:8; 9:10[Eng 9:11]; 10:22; 12:10, 11; 32:43; 34:22; 44:6; 49:2, 33; and 50:13). Hillers (1964: 44) cites this curse from the Sefire Treaties (I A 32–33): "Arpad shall become a *tell*, inhabited only by wild animals."

her daughters. Hebrew *bĕnōteyhā,* i.e., her daughter-villages (Num 21:25; 32:42). The T reads "her villages." The LXX's *bōmoi autēs* ("her altars" = Hebrew *bāmōteyhā*) misreads *mem* for *nun.* Ammon was a small tribal kingdom consisting of Rabbah and surrounding towns, villages, and farmsteads. While its borders were not always clearly defined, archaeology has revealed a common Iron I–II material culture in an area extending from the Jabbok River (Wadi Zerqa) in the north to the hilly region between Wadi Hesban and Madaba in the south, and from the Syrian–Arabian Desert in the east, to the Jordan Valley in the west. The northern and southern boundaries fluctuated; e.g., Moab seems for a time to have controlled the southern edge of this territory. The line of so-called fortresses running north and south of Qasr es-Sar, eight kilometers directly west of Amman (Landes 1961: 69), is no longer taken as a western border since many of the sites are now identified as farmsteads. The area contains mountains and deep valleys.

Then Israel shall inherit those who inherited him. Hebrew *wĕyāraš yiśrāʾēl ʾet-yōrĕšāyw.* The LXX eliminates the wordplay, translating: "and Israel shall take possession of his dominion." Justice in the future will be worked out according to the *lex talionis* principle; cf. Isa 14:1–2; Zeph 2:8–10; Jer 30:16; Obad 15–21; and Ezek 39:10. The present line can certainly derive from Jeremiah, as it is little different from 30:16 (Holladay). Repossession of Ammonite land may be a dream of later Judaism (Rudolph), but nothing precludes the dream from being also contemporary in Judah, which, for over a century now, has steadily seen land and people taken away from Israel and Judah. Did Judah ever repossess this land? Only if Josiah expanded his borders eastward into Ammon and the oracle is to be dated in the Josianic period (Bardtke 1936: 250; Weiser; Landes in *IDB* A–D: 112). But of such an expansion nothing is known, nor also whether Jeremiah would have supported it. It is better to see unfulfillment in the immediate future (Calvin), since the Babylonian attack on Ammon came after the fall of Jerusalem. Blayney sees a second-century B.C. fulfillment when Judas Maccabeus defeated the Ammonites (1 Macc 5:6–8).

MESSAGE AND AUDIENCE

The first oracle sets up an incongruity likely to cause a Jerusalem audience initial discomfort. Regardless of how it answers the first two questions, pain will be felt in answering question three: "Why has the god Milcom inherited territory once settled by Gad, and why do the people of Milcom live in Gadite cities?" This question will be left unanswered, but a second oracle promises a future time when Rabbah will hear the shout of enemy soldiers at its gates and the city will be reduced to a heap of ruins. Daughter villages, too, will be burned with fire. Why we are not told, but Yahweh has so spoken, and the audience will be ever so glad that he has. A concluding word also from Yahweh then states that Israel shall one day inherit those who have now disinherited him.

These oracles could derive from the reign of Zedekiah, perhaps ca. 594 B.C., when Ammon along with Judah and other nations was plotting rebellion against Babylon (27:3). Actual judgment of Ammon is still a way off. But Jeremiah at this time is preaching a future restoration for Israel.

2. Scream, Rabbah's Daughters! (49:3–6)

49 ³Wail, Heshbon, for Ai is devastated
 scream, Rabbah's daughters!
Put on sackcloth, beat your chests
 and run back and forth in the stone enclosures

For Milcom into exile shall go
 his priests and his princes together

 ⁴How you boast in valleys
 your flowing valley
  turnable daughter!
The one trusting in her treasures:
 'Who will come to me?'

⁵Look I am bringing terror against you
  —oracle of the Lord Yahweh of hosts—
 from everyone on every side of you
And you shall be dispersed, each one before him
 and none will gather him who flees.

⁶But afterward I will surely restore the fortunes of the Ammonites
 —oracle of Yahweh.

RHETORIC AND COMPOSITION

MT 49:3–6 = LXX 30:19–21 (Ziegler 30:3–5). The LXX lacks MT 49:6, but the verse is translated in Aq and Theod. These verses contain a call for Heshbon to lament (vv 3–4), a judgment oracle against Rabbat Ammon (v 5), and a restoration word for Ammon concluding the Ammon oracle collection (v 6). The M^L and M^P have a *setumah*, and the M^A a *petuhah*, after v 6. The lament is demarcated from the preceding oracle by a messenger formula concluding the latter (v 2d). The first oracle begins with an embellished messenger formula (v 5a); the restoration oracle has its formula at the end (v 6). For correspondences between the first oracle and the oracle in v 2, see Rhetoric and Composition for 49:1–2.

The call to lament consists of a double bicolon (v 3ab), an inserted bicolon from Amos 1:15 (v 3c), and a tricolon followed by a bicolon (v 4). The whole makes three stanzas. The oracle of judgment is a double bicolon with a lengthy messenger formula (v 5), to which has been added a line that appears not to be poetry (v 6). Jeremiah speaks the call to lament, directly addressing Heshbon, Rabbah's daughters, and Daughter Ammon, then shifting to indirect discourse at the end to bring in a final quote from Ammon herself. Yahweh is the speaker of the oracle (v 5: "I am bringing terror against you"), first addressing Daughter Ammon (feminine singular suffixes in v 5a), then turning to address the men of the army (*niddahtem* in v 5b).

Stanzas I and III of the call to lament are linked by key words balancing sound and meaning:

| I | Wail . . . . | *hêlîlî* | v 3a |
| | . . . . *daughters* | *běnôt* | |

| III | . . . *you boast* . . . . | *tithalělî* | v 4a |
| | . . . . *daughter* | *habbat* | |

The prior oracles in vv 1–2 had as link terms "sons . . . daughters" (see Rhetoric and Composition for 49:1–2).

Linking the call to lament with the oracle are more key words balancing sound and meaning:

| Who will come to me? | *mî yābô' 'ēlāy* | v 4b |
| Look I *am bringing* terror *against you* | *mēbî' 'ālayik* | v 5a |

Catchwords connecting to the prior Ammon oracles in 49:1–2 are these:

| 49:3–4 | Rabbah . . . Milcom | 49:1–2 | Milcom . . . Rabbah |
| | daughters . . . daughter | | her daughters |

The negative *'ên* is a catchword linking the present oracles to those in 49:7–11 and 12–13:

v 5	none	v 7	*is there no*
		v 10	*he is no*
		v 12	*there is no*

NOTES

49:3. *Wail, Heshbon, for Ai is devastated.* This call for Heshbon to lament the destruction of Ai is irony. Calvin says the prophet is triumphing over Ammon. What distinguishes this discourse from Jeremiah's laments over Israel and Judah is that in the latter the prophet was deeply involved in a suffering also his own. There is none of that present here.

Wail. Hebrew *hêlîlî.* See also 25:34; 47:2; 48:20, 39; and 51:8.

Heshbon . . . Ai. This Ai is not the well-known city by that name east of Bethel (Joshua 8). But precisely where in Transjordan there was an Ai near Heshbon is difficult to say. Hebrew *ʿay* simply means "heap of ruins" (26:18 = Mic 3:12). Rashi, Kimhi, and Calvin all assume a neighboring city to Heshbon. Blayney cites Grotius, who said that a city called "Gaia" by Ptolemy lay near Heshbon (the LXX has *Gai*). There is a modern village named ʿAi in the Kerak region ca. two kilometers southeast of Kathrabba (J. M. Miller 1991: 109) that has Iron II remains and may be the site (P. J. King 1993: 39). Commentators since Graf declare the city unknown, and thus emend to "city" or something else. Heshbon is well known, although at the end of the eighth and the beginning of the seventh centuries B.C. it was a Moabite city (48:2, 34, 45). But since it lay near the Moabite–Ammonite frontier, it could have changed hands during Jeremiah's time. On Heshbon, see Note for 48:2.

scream, Rabbah's daughters! Or "Rabbah's daughter-villages" (v 2). Dobbs-Allsopp (1993: 124) says that the image of professional mourners, who are traditionally women in ANE society (cf. 9:16–20[Eng 9:17–21]), is combined here with the personification of the city weeping. Rabbah was the capital city of Ammon; see Note on 49:2. For the "daughter" metaphor, see Kartveit 2001 and Note on 4:11.

Put on sackcloth, beat your chests. Rites of mourning, on which see Notes for 4:8 and 6:26.

run back and forth in the stone enclosures. Hebrew *hitšôṭaṭnâ baggĕdērôt.* The text is difficult. The LXX omits and the T reads: "and make a loud noise in companies." Yet the Hebrew can be translated. A Polel of *šôṭ* occurs in 5:1 with the meaning "go back and forth," and *gĕdērôt* are (small) stone walls (Nah 3:17; Ps 89:41[Eng 89:40]), built to keep out thieves and contain small animals. Kimhi thus translates: "run to and fro within the enclosures (of the villages)." Stone enclosures were commonly "sheepfolds," *gĕdērôt ṣōʾn* (Num 32:16, 24, 36; 1 Sam 24:4[Eng 24:3]; Zeph 2:6), mentioned in Numbers 32 as having been built in Gadite (= Ammonite) territory. The image then seems to be one of people running wildly within sheepfolds or other village enclosures when refuge is not possible in fortified cities. Jones says, "The Ammonites will be like their own frightened sheep." In v 5 people are once again portrayed as running every which way. Emending *baggĕdērôt* to *bigdudôt*, "with gashes" (cf. 48:37), as proposed by Duhm, Rudolph, and McKane and adopted variously in the NEB, JB (but not the NJB), NAB, and NRSV translations, is unnecessary.

For Milcom into exile shall go, his priests and his princes together. This bicolon, adapted from Amos 1:15, interjects exile into the prophecy. The Ammonite god Milcom will go into exile just as Israel's ill-chosen gods did (Amos 5:26–27). In Jer 48:7 the same indignity awaits the Moabite god Chemosh and his entourage. That the present bicolon is an insertion may go some way in explaining why this prophecy, as a word from Jeremiah, does not find fulfillment. Herr (1993a: 35) concludes on the basis of excavations at Tell Hesban and Tell el-'Umeiri that the Ammonites were not destroyed by Nebuchadnezzar, nor were they exiled, but continued living "unscathed" in their homeland into the Persian period. This does not entirely square with the testimony of Josephus in *Ant* x 181–82 (see Note on 49:2), although Josephus says nothing about Ammonites being exiled to Babylon.

his priests and his princes together. On this phrase, see Note for 48:7b.

Milcom. God of the Ammonites; see Note on 49:1. Reading here with the LXX and the Vrs; MT has *malkām*, "their king" (cf. Amos 1:15).

4. *How you boast in valleys, your flowing valley . . . !* Hebrew *'ēmeq* means "valley" (21:13), of which there are many in mountainous Ammon. In one valley of exceptional beauty flows the river Jabbok north of Rabbah, which may be "your flowing valley" (Volz; Holladay). Compare the Rhine Valley in Germany. The LXX has: "why do you exult in the plains of the Anakim?" which misreads the Hebrew, as happens also in 47:5 [LXX 29:5]. Dahood (1959: 166–67) proposes the meaning "strength" for *'mq*. His translation:

Why do you boast of your strength?
Your strength has ebbed, O faithless daughter.

His argument is more convincing in 47:5, where there is support from T for reading *'ēmeq* as "strength." Here *'ămāqîm* is a plural, which means Dahood has to argue additionally for an enclitic *mem*. Although Dahood's suggestion is accepted by Bright and Thompson, also in the translations of NEB, NAB, NJV, NRSV, and NSB, it is unnecessary and should be rejected. The traditional reading, "valleys, your flowing valley," makes good sense (*pace* Bright), and suits the passage well.

How you boast . . . ! Hebrew *mah-tithalělî.* Not "Why do you boast . . . ?" (so RSV; NEB; NAB; NJV; NIV), which translates the interrogative pronoun *ti* of the LXX. If Ammon has beautiful valleys, which she does, she will naturally boast. The pronoun *mah* is here the exclamatory "how . . . !" used ironically (BDB, 553; cf. 2:33, 36): "How you boast . . . !" or "How you take pride in . . . !" NJB: "How you used to glory . . . !" The point is that Daughter Ammon has boasted of beauty and wealth, but she will do so no longer after being humbled by an enemy. On the subject of "boasting," Jeremiah says in 9:22–23[Eng 9:23–24]: "Let not the wise man boast of his wisdom, and let not the strong man boast of his strength, and let not the rich man boast of his riches; but the one who boasts, let him boast of this: that he understands and knows me." See also 4:2.

turnable daughter! Or "rebellious daughter." Hebrew *habbat haššôbēbâ*. A Jeremianic expression occurring one other time, in 31:22, where reference is to "virgin Israel." Many scholars (Duhm; Cornill; Ehrlich 1912: 360; Rudolph; Holladay) think it inappropriate to speak of Ammon as a rebellious daughter, and emend to *haššaʾănannâ*, "complacent / careless (daughter)." The LXX has *thugater itamias* ("reckless daughter"). Gordis (1933b: 161), however, says that the verb *šûb* can mean "be secure, confident," which yields the same basic meaning. He translates: "O over-confident daughter." Overconfidence is indicated in the boast that follows, "Who will come to me?" Nevertheless, "turnable daughter," "rebellious daughter," or "faithless daughter" (Bright) can stand. Ammon has no covenant with Yahweh and therefore cannot be charged with breach of covenant as Israel can; however, the nation was certainly a rebel from the Babylonian point of view, having plotted with other nations against Babylon (27:3) and later having arranged the assassination of Gedaliah, a Babylonian appointee in Judah (40:13–41:15). Elsewhere Ammon is said to be deserving of punishment because it reviled Israel and its territory (Zeph 2:8–10) and was gleeful over the defilement of Judah's Temple, the desolation of its land, and its exile (Ezek 25:1–7).

The one trusting in her treasures: 'Who will come to me?' "Saying" (*hāʾōmĕrâ*) is supplied before the quote in a few MSS and the Versions, but Hebrew discourse, particularly poetry, does not require it (see "Rhetoric and Composition" for 6:1–7). There is a change here to the third person, which can stand. Most modern translations emend to "your treasures." A Moabite city is similarly cited for putting unwarranted trust in its treasures (48:7). The folly of trusting in abundant riches is a common wisdom theme; see Pss 49:6–7[Eng 49:5–6]; 52:9[Eng 52:7]; Prov 11:28; and Job 31:24–28. The day comes when these are taken away, as Jerusalem learned to her sorrow (Lam 1:10). Plundered temple treasure is a common theme in the laments of Mesopotamia (Dobbs-Allsopp 1993: 69). In the NT, see the parable of the rich man in Luke 12:16–21.

her treasures. Hebrew *ʾōṣĕrōteyhā*. Or "her supplies, her storehouses"; see Note on 15:13. Calvin takes the term to mean "her hidden places," i.e., her strongholds.

Who will come to me? I.e., who will come and attack me? (NEB; JB; NJV; NIV; NRSV). This adds to the boast about the valleys, but is more arrogant. For other overconfident boasts, see 21:13; Zeph 2:15; and Obad 3. Compare also Lam 4:12. Jeremiah said of boasts made by worshipers at the Jerusalem Temple that they amounted to "trusting in deceptive words" (7:4).

5. *Look I am bringing terror against you.* Hebrew *hinĕnî mēbîʾ* ("Look I am bringing . . .") is a common Jeremianic construction (5:15; 6:19; 11:11; 19:3; 31:8; 35:17; 45:5). On *hinĕnî* with the participle, see Note on 1:15. It is Yahweh who will bring the terror of war against the Ammonites.

oracle of the Lord Yahweh of hosts. The LXX omits "Yahweh of hosts."

terror . . . from everyone on every side of you. Hebrew *paḥad . . . mikkol-sĕbîbāyik*. A variation of Jeremiah's more usual "terror on every side" (*māgôr missābîb*). See Note on 6:25. Jeremiah uses *paḥad* ("terror") with reference to the war against Judah in 30:5. In 48:43, 44, where hunting imagery is used in the judgment against Moab, *paḥad* will be "scare (tactics)" of the enemy. The term derives from holy war (Exod 15:16; Deut 2:25; 11:25; 1 Sam 11:7).

And you shall be dispersed, each one before him. Hebrew *wĕniddaḥtem 'îš lĕpānāyw.* The verb is second masculine plural. After speaking directly to Daughter Ammon, Yahweh now addresses soldiers in the Ammonite army. Cheyne says "each one before him" means "straight forward" (cf. Amos 4:3), which is still less than transparent. Kimḥi explains it to mean that each one will flee whichever way he is facing; no two will flee together. The expression is doubtless one describing panicked flight (46:5). Calvin says that people will be so terrorized that they will think of nothing but flight, considering not the best or safest way, but whatever way is open to them.

and none will gather him who flees. The verb *qbṣ* in the Piel means "to gather together," often of a dispersed people (31:10). The LXX omits the final "him who flees" and shifts to a second person "you": "and there is none to gather you." This omission, together with the whole of v 6, is likely another loss by haplography (homoeoarcton: *l . . . l*), as pointed out by D. N. Freedman. The Hebrew is clarified by Isa 13:14–16, which shows this to be a curse stating that there will be no one to assemble soldiers of a routed army, who, as a consequence are unprotected and will be caught and killed. In the African savanna, zebras and wildebeests who get separated from the pack fall prey to the lions. See also Nah 3:18. Bright's translation, "with no one to rally the fugitives," found also in the JB, NAB, and REB, has in mind the lack of someone to reassemble a beaten army so it can once again fight.

6. *But afterward I will surely restore the fortunes of the Ammonites.* The LXX accidently omits (see v 5 above). Despite the hopeless state of affairs depicted at the end of the oracle, there is nevertheless hope for Ammon, as for Judah (see Note for 29:14), Moab (48:47), and Elam (49:39). On the genre and its inclusion in ancient Mesopotamian city laments, see Note for 48:47. For the expression on "restoring the fortunes" and the use of an internal H-stem as we have here, see Note for 29:14.

afterward. Hebrew *'aḥărê-kēn.* The expression occurs also in Gen 6:4.

MESSAGE AND AUDIENCE

In this first poem, Jeremiah calls upon Ammonite peoples to mourn and lament. The tone is not one of sympathy (*pace* Hyatt), but is ironic and detached. Ai has been devastated, or else will be, meaning that Heshbon and Rabbah's daughters must now do what is required. Let women wail and beat their breasts; let sackcloth be worn; watch as people run like frightened sheep in the stone enclosures. They will know not where to go. How Daughter Ammon boasts in her valleys, her deep valley through which the Jabbok flows! She trusts also in her other treasures, thinking no one strong enough to seize them from her. But she is a rebellious daughter, having played a reckless game in opposing Babylon, and will come to regret that recklessness. In the center of the poem—whether original or added later—is imagined the Ammonite god Milcom making the journey into exile, and with his image go the priests and princes of Ammon. Did some of those running wildly in the stone enclosures subsequently join the procession?

In the oracle following, Yahweh says he is bringing terror against Daughter Ammon; it will come on every side. Addressing then the soldiers in the army, Yahweh says they shall be dispersed, every last one of them, in panic, and no one will be there to reassemble them. The audience can imagine the rest. It will be their death, but not before they see their houses plundered, their children killed violently, and their wives ravished. Yet after all this horror, Yahweh says he will restore the fortunes of the Ammonites.

These poems are best dated after those in vv 1–2, i.e., when a Babylonian attack on Ammon can actually be anticipated. This could be before the fall of Jerusalem, otherwise after when Ammon is known to have been implicated in the murder of Gedaliah (40:13–41:18). Depending on the date of Gedaliah's murder, this would be sometime between 586 and 582 B.C. The Babylonian army came against Ammon ca. 582 B.C., at which time a third deportation of Judahites to Babylon was also carried out (52:30). The restoration word for Ammon could have been spoken with the judgment, otherwise added as a later supplement.

F. WHAT ABOUT EDOM? (49:7–22)

1. Is There No Longer Wisdom in Teman? (49:7–11)

49 ⁷For Edom.

> Thus said Yahweh of hosts:
> Is there no longer wisdom in Teman?
> > counsel has perished from people of understanding
> > > their wisdom stinks!
> ⁸Flee! Be gone! Go deep to dwell
> > dwellers of Dedan
> For Esau's disaster I have brought upon him
> > at the time I reckoned with him
>
> ⁹If grape-pickers came to you
> > they would surely leave gleanings
> If thieves in the night
> > they would destroy but enough for themselves
>
> ¹⁰But I, I have stripped Esau
> > I have uncovered his hiding places
> > > so the hidden one he cannot be

His offspring is devastated
  also his brothers and his neighbors
    and he is no more
[11]Abandon your orphans
  I, I will keep alive
As for your widows
  put your trust upon me.

RHETORIC AND COMPOSITION

MT 49:7–11 = LXX 30:1–5 (Ziegler 29:8–12). The present verses constitute a single oracle that begins the collection of oracles against Edom. An upper limit is marked by the heading, "For Edom," after which comes a messenger formula introducing the oracle. The lower limit is set by a *setumah* in M^L and M^A, and a *petuḥah* in M^P, after v 11.

Verses 7, 9–10—and also vv 14–16 following—have recognized similarities to Obad 1–8. For comparison and discussion, see Dicou (1988; 1994: 58–70), Raabe (1996: 22–31), and Pagán (1996: 436–40). Dicou concludes after examining vocabulary and motifs in the Jeremiah verses that the "common material" is nevertheless at home in the book of Jeremiah, and not a later insertion. Raabe's view is that Obadiah reused and adapted material from Jeremiah, which, if a judgment on dependence be made one way or the other, seems to be the correct one. Pagán suggests that both Jeremiah and Obadiah could have used earlier cultic preaching, although he thinks it possible that Obadiah may have witnessed the destruction of Jerusalem. Giesebrecht took vv 7–11, with the exception of v 9, to be from Jeremiah; Obad 1–9 he judged postexilic. Obadiah need not be postexilic, but it does appear to postdate Jeremiah's Edom oracles, at least to the extent that Obad 9–14 are a response to Edom's glee at Jerusalem's fall. These verses have no parallel in Jeremiah, nor does Jeremiah allude anywhere to this singular indignity that lived unforgotten in Jewish memory (Lam 4:21; Ps 137:7; Obad 10–11, 13–14; Ezek 25:12–14; 35:15; Joel 4:19[Eng 3:19]; and 1 Esd 4:45). This point, though noted by Cheyne, is missed entirely by more recent commentators, e.g., Hyatt, Bright, Thompson, Boadt, and Clements, who read Jeremiah through the refracted lenses of Obadiah and other OT passages of late date.

The present oracle divides into three stanzas. Stanza I (vv 7–8) is three lines: a tricolon followed by a double bicolon. Stanza II (v 9) is a tidy bicolon. Stanza III (vv 10–11), taken by virtually all commentators to be poetry despite two signs of the direct object in v 10a, divides into two tricolons and a double bicolon. The final double bicolon may, however, be simply a single bicolon (so *BHS*). The main break, in any case, is after *'ăḥayyeh* ("I will keep alive"), which gives the line an 11:11 syllable count. This double bicolon (or single bicolon) also contains verbs (both with imperative force) at beginning and end, and objects with the second masculine singular suffix in the middle.

Yahweh is the speaker throughout, alternating between indirect and direct address. The oracle ends with direct address, a common feature in Jeremianic style (see Note for 12:13). Repetitions and key words (some of similar sound) give internal balance to the stanzas and create an overall chiastic (aba') structure:

I	*Is there no . . . wisdom . . . . ?*	*haʾên . . . ḥokmâ*	v 7
	. . . . their wisdom	*ḥokmātām*	
	For . . . . . . Esau	*kî . . . ʿēśāw*	v 8b
II	*If . . . .*	*ʾim*	v 9
	. . . .		
	If	*ʾim*	
	. . . .		
III	*But I, ... Esau*	*kî-ʾănî . . . ʿēśāw*	v 10
	also his brothers . . .	*wĕʾeḥāyw*	
	and he is no more . . .	*wĕʾênennû*	
	I, I will keep alive . . .	*ʾănî ʾăḥayyeh*	v 11

Verse 9 cannot be taken as an editorial insertion from Obad 5 (*pace* Giesebrecht, Duhm, Rudolph, Weiser, McKane, Holladay, and others). It is tighter poetry than Obad 5, it reverses the imagery of that verse, and it is well integrated into the present oracle structure. Center repetitions of vocabulary and phraseology are common in the Jeremianic oracles, e.g., in 2:5–9, 33–37; 4:19c–21; 5:1–8; 6:1–7, 8–12; 23:18, 21–22; 48:38b–39; 51:34–45, 47–51. Double *ʾim* ("if") clauses are also common in the poetry and prose of Jeremiah, seen elsewhere in 4:1; 5:1; 7:5; 14:18; 15:19; 27:18; and 38:16; the same goes for double *ʾim lōʾ* ("if not / if surely") clauses, which occur elsewhere in 15:11; 49:20; and 50:45 (Dicou 1994: 61–62). In 14:18, two bicolons beginning with *ʾim* are framed by two bicolons beginning with *kî*, the same as here. Perhaps most important, the larger argument of vv 9–10 requires v 9, as Calvin clearly recognized. Arguments used then in support of the secondary nature of v 9: 1) the shift to the second person in v 9; 2) the issue of whether v 9 consists of questions or declarations; and 3) there being continuity between vv 8 and 10 because both mention "Esau"—prove nothing (*pace* McKane, 1217). The entire oracle shifts between second and third person discourse; the value of v 9 for the argument in vv 9–10 is unaffected by whether it contains questions or declarations; and the continuity between v 8 and v 10 amounts simply to a repetition of the term "Esau," nothing more. The oracle reads better with v 9 than without it.

The oracle structure also casts doubt on the view that v 11, which is a concluding word of hope, must be reinterpreted or eliminated (see Notes). This verse is also well integrated into the oracle, even more so than the concluding hope in the Ammon oracles of 49:1–6 (see Rhetoric and Composition for 49:1–2).

The particle *ʾên* is a catchword linking the present oracle to oracles in 49:1–6 and 12–13:

and none	*wĕ'ên*	v 5
is there no	*ha'ên*	v 7
and he is no more	*wĕ'ênennû*	v 10
there is no	*'ên*	v 12

On the rhetorical function of *'ên* elsewhere, see Rhetoric and Composition for 8:13–17.

Catchwords connecting to the next unit are emphatic key words:

| v 10a | *But I* | *kî-'ănî* | | v 13 | *For by myself* | *kî bî* |
| v 11 | *I* | *'ănî* | | | | |

NOTES

49:7. *For Edom.* On the short introduction, see Note for 46:2. Ancient Edom consisted of the high plateau and rugged mountain country straddling the King's Highway below the Dead Sea, from the River Zered (Wadi el-Ḥasā) in the north, 160 kilometers south to the Gulf of Aqaba (Deut 2:8). In the north it is 1,500 meters above sea level (Herr 1997: 173), receiving snow in winter. Edom (= Esau) means "red" (Gen 25:25), and the region (e.g., Petra) is noted for its red soil and red sandstone. The country was bounded on the east by the Syrian–Arabian Desert, and on the west by the ʿArabah Valley. Edom's southern and western borders fluctuated. Some scholars extend the southern border only as far as Ras en-Naqb (Edelman 1995b: 2–3); however, a seventh-century Edomite presence is attested at Tell el-Kheleifeh near the shore of the Gulf of Aqaba (P. J. King 1993: 50–53). According to biblical tradition, Edom at one time occupied territory west of the ʿArabah, in the wilderness of Zin (Josh 15:1–4). The land of Seir, part of which lay west of the ʿArabah, is also identified with Edom (Gen 32:4[Eng 32:3]). In the late seventh or early sixth century B.C., Edomites appear to have moved into the eastern Negeb (Beit-Arieh 1995b: 35), their presence now being attested at Tel ʿIra, Tel Masos, Ḥorvat ʿUza, Ḥorvat Qitmit, and ʿEn Ḥazeva, among other sites (P. J. King 1993: 53). Just how extensive this penetration was is not known. Two Edomite shrines have been discovered at Ḥorvat Qitmit (Beit-Arieh 1987; 1991; 1995a) and ʿEn Ḥazeva (Cohen and Yisrael 1995). Tel Arad and Tel ʿAroer, both Judahite sites, have Edomite finds from this period. One of the Arad ostraca (24.20) warns of an attack by Edom on the Judahite frontier (Aharoni 1981: 46–49; P. J. King 1993: 57). Following the destruction of Jerusalem, Edomites penetrated farther west, and in the Hellenistic period were known in southern Judah by their Greek name, Idumeans (1 Esd 4:50; 1 Macc 5:65; Josephus, *Ant* xi 61). Their territory was called Idumea. By this time the original Edomite homeland had been taken over by Nabatean Arabs. The history and archaeology of Edom are well summarized in Bartlett (1989); Bartlett and MacDonald in *ABD* 2: 287–301; P. J. King (1993: 45–63); and Bartlett in *OEANE* 2: 189–91. See also the essays on Edomite history, culture, and religion in Edelman (1995a).

Yahweh of hosts. The LXX omits "of hosts," as elsewhere (see Appendix VI).

Is there no longer wisdom in Teman? counsel has perished from people of understanding; their wisdom stinks! Most commentators (e.g., Giesebrecht; Condamin; Volz; Rudolph; Weiser; Bright), and virtually all the modern Versions translate the colons as three rhetorical questions, even though only the first colon has the *hē'* interrogative. According to this view, the *hē'* interrogative assumes a triple-duty function for all three colons. Questions in Hebrew can lack the interrogative particle (H. G. Mitchell 1908; GKC §150a; cf. Note on 3:1). The LXX lacks even the first interrogative, which leads Cornill and Holladay to translate as three declarations. Either way, the point is that wisdom no longer resides in Edom. The T has one question and two declarations, which are adopted here. According to this reading, Jeremiah asks a rhetorical question, then not receiving an answer, he gives two answers himself. Classical rhetoricians called the answering of one's own rhetorical question *hypophora* (*ad Herennium* iv 23), other examples of which occur in 25:29; 30:15; 31:20; 46:7–8, 15; and 47:6–7. One should note also in 8:8 the question posed about there being wisdom in Judah, which is followed by immediate condemnation. Calvin read in the present verse two rhetorical questions followed by a declaration. In his view, the rhetorical questions registered astonishment and were intended to awaken a lethargic audience. The declaration following then gave the audience a reason for the astonishment. Whether the verse is read as three rhetorical questions, three declarations, or a combination of question and declaration, Edom's lack of wisdom is unambiguously affirmed (Obad 7d: "there is no understanding [*tĕbûnâ*] in it"), which prepares for the directive in v 8 to flee the place.

Teman. Hebrew *têmān* ("south"). The T translates here and in v 20: "the land of the south." Rashi does similarly, but Kimḥi notes that in Obad 9 the term appears to be a name. Teman was a tribe, the eponymous ancestor of which was the eldest son of Esau (Gen 36:11, 15). Teman also designated a northeast region of Edom, the capital city of which was Bozrah (Giesebrecht; Edelman 1995b: 10–11; cf. Amos 1:12). Appearing here together with Dedan (v 8), a settlement in northwest Arabia, the two locations denote the north and south of Edom's sphere of influence. In Ezek 25:13 is the phrase: "from Teman even to Dedan." Glueck at one stage identified Teman with the modern village of Tawilan, eight kilometers east of Petra, but later gave that up (Glueck 1970: 32; cf. de Vaux 1969). Edom in general (Obad 8), and Teman in particular (Bar 3:22–23), had reputations for being repositories of tribal wisdom. Job's friend Eliphaz was a Temanite (Job 2:11; 4:1). On Edomite wisdom, and the view that selected portions of Proverbs, Psalms 88 and 89, and the entire book of Job reflect Edomite local color, if not being Edomite in origin, see Pfeiffer 1926.

no longer. Hebrew *ha'ên 'ôd.* For this expression without the interrogative, see 48:2.

counsel has perished from people of understanding. Hebrew *'ēṣâ* means "counsel, advice" (18:18). In 7:28, Jeremiah lamented that "truth had perished (*'ābĕdâ ha'ĕmûnâ)*" in Judah. More problematic is *mibbānîm*, which T and Vg translate "from the children," but which in the LXX is translated *ek sunetōn* ("from the intelligent ones"), presupposing a Qal participle *bānîm*, from *bîn* ("to discern, have understanding"). Kimḥi read the participle, citing the cognate term *tĕbûnâ* ("understanding") that occurs in Obad 7–8. Calvin too rendered the participle of *bîn* ("the intelligent"), saying that "sons" was unsuitable. What we are talking about is "people of understanding," from whom good counsel can no longer be had in Edom. Holladay says we may also have a wordplay (cf. Prov 4:1: *bānîm . . . bînâ*), which is a possibility.

their wisdom stinks! Or "their wisdom is excessive." Hebrew *nisrĕḥâ* is the only attested N-stem of *srḥ* in the OT; in the Qal the verb means "go free, overhang." In postbiblical Hebrew *srḥ* carries the meaning of "decompose, smell badly" (*srḥ* III in *Dict Talm*, 1024), which KB[3] gives to a *srḥ* II. The T has "their wisdom has been ruined." Commentators and the modern Versions divide over the translation. "Vanished" in the AV (RSV and NJB) and McKane's "fled and gone" are too paraphrastic. Rashi opts for "spoiled"; Calvin for "overflowing," which he says makes the statement ironical. Jeremiah might then be saying something like what Festus, the Roman governor, said to Paul: "Your great learning is turning you mad!" (Acts 26:24). In any case, the statement here is an answer to the question "Is there no longer wisdom in Teman?" According to the one interpretation, Jeremiah is answering: "Yes, there is wisdom in Teman, and it runs at the mouth"; according to the other interpretation, he is answering: "Yes there is . . . , and it stinks!"

8. *Flee! Be gone! Go deep to dwell, dwellers of Dedan.* A similar directive is issued to the "dwellers of Hazor" in v 30. The rapid-fire verbs are asyndeton (Bardtke 1936: 252; cf. Note on 4:5). There is also wordplay: "to dwell . . . dwellers" (*lāšebet . . . yōšĕbê*). Following an assessment of Edom's wisdom or lack thereof, an urgent directive now tells people to leave Dedan and go hide.

Flee! Hebrew *nūsû*. On the command to flee for one's life, see Note for 48:6. Calvin imagined that people would not want to flee; cf. Gen 19:14–22.

Be gone! Hebrew *hopnû*. Literally, "Be turned back!" Rashi translates "Clear out!" citing Lev 14:36; Bright has "Turn tail!" On the rarity of the Hophal imperative, which occurs only here and in Ezek 32:19, see GKC §46a n. The H-stem active of *pnh*, however, is common in Jeremiah (46:5, 21; 47:3; 48:39; and 49:24).

Go deep to dwell. Hebrew *heʿmîqû lāšebet*. As with the previous verb, so here also is a question whether the verb form is an H-stem perfect or an imperative. It is generally agreed that an imperative is required (Cornill; Volz; Rudolph; McKane). The LXX has *bathunate* ("Deepen!" or "Hollow Out!"). Some commentators and *BHS* suggest repointing to a *pathaḥ* under the *hēʾ*, but that may be unnecessary (GKC §63 o says the MT pointing with the *sĕghôl* is the imperative). The image here seems to be that of finding hiding places deep in the ground or in caves (Judg 6:2; 1 Sam 13:6; Isa 2:10, 19, 21). For the same expression, see 49:30. In the end the advice proves to be unhelpful, for in v 10 Yahweh says he has uncovered Esau's hiding places.

Dedan. Dedan was a caravan center and commercial settlement at a major oasis in northwest Arabia. Dedanites were traders (Isa 21:13), journeying into

Israel, Syria, and Phoenicia with saddle blankets for horses and other goods (Ezek 27:15 [MT], 20). Since 1890 Dedan has been identified with the ruins of al-Khuraybah just north of the modern village of al-ʿUlā (Albright 1953: 1; *OEANE* 2: 133–34; *ABD* 2: 121–23). The place turns up as *Dedanu* in one of the Harran Inscriptions of Nabonidus that records a campaign against it and other towns by Nabonidus (556–539 B.C.) in his Arabian sojourn of ten years (Gadd 1958: 58–59, 79–89; Lambert 1972: 56; Lindsay 1976: 33–39). Mention is also made of a "war against Dedan" in four of the Jabal Ghunayim Inscriptions (#20–23), which are possibly from this same period (Winnett and Reed 1970: 89–92, 102–3). Here, as in Ezek 25:13, Dedan is placed within Edom's sphere of influence. Ezekiel predicts judgment against Dedan; Jeremiah the same in 25:23.

For Esau's disaster I have brought upon him, at the time I reckoned with him. I.e., Edom. The verbs *hēbēʾtî* ("I have brought") and *pĕqadtîw* ("I reckoned with him") are prophetic perfects, which is to say the disaster is as good as accomplished in the mind of Yahweh. The RSV, NEB, JB, NAB, NJV, and NIV all translate the verbs as futures.

Esau's disaster. Hebrew *ʾêd ʿēśāw.* There could be a pun here on *ʾĕdôm* (Edom). The LXX mistranslates "Esau" as "he has done" (*epoiēsen* = Hebrew *ʿāśâ*). While some earlier "disaster of Esau" may exist in Israel's memory and is here being recalled, the important disaster is an unblessed visitation on some future Day of Yahweh. This is the sense in Obad 8. "(Days of) disaster" are also announced for Judah, Egypt, Moab, and Hazor (18:17; 46:21; 48:16; 49:32). For background, see Deut 32:35.

Esau. The brother of Jacob-Israel (Gen 25:19–26), and eponymous ancestor of Edom (Gen 36:1). "Esau" is used exclusively in this oracle to refer to Edom; cf. v 10.

at the time I reckoned with him. On this Jeremianic expression, see Note for 6:15. Calvin says the prophecy will not be immediately fulfilled, which now finds confirmation in recent archaeological work carried out in Edom. See v 10.

9. *If grape-pickers came to you, they would surely leave gleanings.* Reading the *lōʾ* here and in the next bicolon as asseveratives (Nötscher 1953: 374; Sivan and Schniedewind 1993: 224). The T reads two questions; the LXX two declarations. On the asseverative *lōʾ*, see Note for 4:27. The same sense, however, is obtained with a negative. Rashi reads the second colon as a rhetorical question, "would they not leave gleanings?" Answer: "Of course they would!" Kimḥi says this is a proverb (*māšāl*). On the gleaning image, see 6:9 and Obad 5. Ruth is a gleaner in the fields of Boaz (Ruth 2).

grape-pickers. Hebrew *bōṣĕrîm,* which may play on Bozrah, *bāṣĕrâ* (Jones; cf. v 13).

to you. Hebrew *lāk.* The LXX omits, which could as Janzen (1989: 43) points out be due to haplography (homoeoarcton: *l . . . l*).

If thieves in the night, they would destroy but enough for themselves. The verb *bāʾû* ("they came") in 9a does double duty for the first colon here (prostasis). Comparing the line with Obad 5, we note that the image of plundering thieves in Obad 5 is expanded into two lines. Also, the images of grape-pickers and thieves are reversed from here. The point here is that thieves, bad as they are, do not ruin everything; they take only enough for themselves. Hebrew *dayyām* is lit. "their sufficiency." The LXX's "they shall lay their hands upon" appears to reflect a different Hebrew (see *BHS*).

10. *But I, I have stripped Esau*. The verb is *ḥśp*, meaning "strip (bare)"; see the same usage with reference to Judah in 13:26. Again we have a prophetic perfect, as in v 8b, only here the modern Versions (AV; RSV; NEB; NJV; NRSV; REB; NJB) translate as a past. But NAB and NIV: "I . . . will strip Esau." The pronoun *'ănî* ("I") is for emphasis. Yahweh will harvest Esau with a thoroughness unknown among grape-pickers and thieves (cf. Obad 6). Edom is said to be destined for destruction in 9:25[Eng 9:26] and 25:21, 23; other prophets predict the same; see Amos 1:11–12; Isa 34:5–7; Ezek 25:12–14; 35; Joel 4:19[Eng 3:19]; and the book of Obadiah.

Edom apparently escaped punitive action by Nebuchadnezzar when Ammon was threatened (Ezek 21:23–32[Eng 21:18–27]) and Judah was destroyed in 588–586 B.C., and maybe also when other Transjordanian states were attacked in the campaign of 582 B.C., even though Edom was represented in the anti-Babylonoian plot of 594 B.C. (27:3). Jewish tradition was unforgiving of Edom's glee at the destruction of Jerusalem (Lam 4:21; Ps 137:7; Obad 10–11, 13–14; Ezek 25:12–14; 35:15; and Joel 4:19[Eng 3:19]) and alleged help in burning the Temple (1 Esd 4:45), which must mean that Edom had shifted ground and was now aiding the war effort of the Babylonians. The end of the Edomite state is still controverted, but it appears from what evidence there is that upheaval and destruction came in the middle of the sixth century at the hands of Nabonidus (Albright 1941a; Lindsay 1976; Bartlett 1989: 160–61; 1990; cf. *OEANE* 2: 189). Albright argued for a mid-sixth-century date on the basis of an ostracon from Tell el-Kheleifeh, found in 1939, and Lindsay argued for the same date based on a reference in the Nabonidus Chronicle to an apparent attack on Edom: "[Against the town . . . A]dummu they pitched (camp)" (*ANET*[3] 305; Lindsay 1979: 33–34). Excavations by Bennett at Umm el-Biyara (Bennett 1966; Bienkowski 1990a), Tawilan (Bennett 1984; Bienkowski 1990b; Bennett and Bienkowski 1995), and Buseirah [= Bozrah] (Bennett 1973; 1974; 1975; 1977; 1983) show Edomite communities flourishing during a prosperous seventh century when Edom was subject to Assyria, then a settlement gap at the beginning of the sixth century or later (Bienkowski 1995: 60–61). Edom, then, was not emptied of its people; nevertheless, its cities were burned and a destruction of some magnitude did occur (cf. Mal 1:2–5).

I have uncovered his hiding places. The verb *glh*, "uncover," occurs in 13:22 in connection with Judah's anticipated denouement. In v 8, Yahweh sent the Edomites in search of hideaways; but such will avail them not because now he is there to uncover them. Subtle irony. There are no hidden places with Yahweh; see 23:24 and Note on 7:11. Calvin interprets *mistārāyw* ("his hiding places") as places where "treasures" are stored, citing Obad 6 and noting the allusion to thievery in v 9. But hiding places could also be places of concealment for people on the run. The Wadi Daliyah caves 15 kilometers north of ancient Jericho, and the Wadi Murabbaat caves west of Herodium are the sort of hiding places envisioned here, although they are not in Edom. In the former, hundreds of skeletal remains and a cache of possessions were found, dating from the time when Alexander the Great conquered Palestine in 331 B.C. See ABD 2: 3–4; 6: 863–64.

so the hidden one he cannot be. Hebrew *wěnehbâ lōʾ yûkāl.* Reading the N-stem participle of *ḥbʾ.* Many comentators (Giesebrecht; Volz; Rudolph; Holladay; and others) revocalize with the LXX, T, and Vg to the infinitive absolute, *wěnahbōh = wěnahbōʾ:* "so to hide himself he is not able." Either reading is acceptable.

His offspring is devastated, also his brothers and his neighbors. The LXX reads *zěrôaʿ* ("arm") for MT *zarʿô* ("his seed / offspring"), an apparent metathesis (*zrwʿ* for *zrʿw*). Read the MT. The "offspring" doubtless refers to Edom's young warriors who, together with brothers and friends, will be war casualties (cf. 6:21).

and he is no more. I.e., Esau (= Edom) as a nation is no more. Hebrew *wěʾênennû.* The MT reading is carried over into T. Rudolph and Bright, citing Symm (*kai ouk estin hos erei*) and LXX^L, emend to *wěʾên ʾōmēr* ("and there is no one to say: . . ."). Kimḥi reads similarly, so also Holladay, whose emendation comes up with the reading of the JB: "of his neighbors, not one will say: . . ." This has the effect of converting v 11 from being a divine word of consolation to Edom's orphans and widows to one offering them no hope. With kin and neighbors gone, no one will be left to care for them. This interpretation is to be rejected (cf. NJB). It is scarcely better than the interpretation of Calvin, who said that God in v 11 is taunting the Edomites, telling them he will not help their orphans and widows.

11. *Abandon your orphans—I, I will keep alive; As for your widows, put your trust upon me.* Kimḥi says that this word addresses dying Edomites, telling them that Yahweh will care for their orphans and widows because they now have no survivors to do so. It is consistent with Yahweh's gracious and compassionate character (Pss 68:6[Eng 68:5]; 146:9). Yahweh himself will do what he expects the covenant people to do in a similar situation, i.e., care for the orphans and the widows (Exod 22:22–24; Deut 10:18; 14:29; 16:11, 14; 24:19–21; 26:12–13; 27:19; Isa 1:17; Jer 7:6; cf. Job 22:9). Perhaps because of the covenant requirement, Rashi (following T) thinks the present word is addressed to Israel. On favored treatment for Edomites in gaining Temple entrance, see Deut 23:7–8.

Abandon your orphans. The verb *ʿzb* ("leave, forsake, abandon") receives here a new twist. This is not the "abandonment" censured so often in Jeremiah; see 1:16; 2:13; 5:7, 19; 16:11; 17:13; 19:4; 22:9; and elsewhere. The Edomites are told that they can abandon their orphans to Yahweh.

I, I will keep alive. Referring to the orphans and by extension to the widows next mentioned. Hebrew *ʾănî* is the emphatic divine "I," as also in 10a.

put your trust upon me. The verb *tibṭāḥû* is a second masculine plural imperfect, in pausal, having here the force of an imperative: "You, put your trust (in me)!" Such a reading is not "impossible in the context" (*pace* Holladay II,

376), although most commentators and modern translations read a third feminine plural imperfect with jussive force: "let them trust (in me)." GKC (§47k) takes the form as equivalent to the third feminine plural imperfect, *tibṭaḥnâ* (cf. Giesebrecht; Volz; Rudolph; Holladay; and *BHS*), but this is unnecessary. Yahweh is saying here at the end of the oracle that orphans and widows can be entrusted to his care. He will keep them alive; they only need trust in him. Trusting Yahweh assumes great importance in 17:7–8 and 39:18; in the latter verse it is shown by Ebed-melech, a foreigner. Trusting in treasures, however, proved to be a big mistake for both the Moabites and the Ammonites (48:7; 49:4).

MESSAGE AND AUDIENCE

Yahweh begins this oracle by asking, "Is there no longer wisdom in Teman?" An Edomite partisan or perhaps just anyone would likely say, "Of course there is!" But some in the audience might answer "No." Yahweh, however, does not wait for a response and answers the question himself: "Counsel is no longer possible from this people of understanding; the wisdom of Teman stinks!"

Yahweh then turns his attention to the inhabitants of Dedan, an Edomite protectorate in the far south. Dedanites are urged to flee their towns and villages, to go deep into caves or holes in the ground, for an enemy is coming upon them. Yahweh is bringing the disaster. In his own mind it is a *fait accompli*; however, it will not take place until he comes to reckon with Edom.

Precisely how great will this disaster be? If grape-pickers came they would leave gleanings; even thieves coming through would take only enough for themselves. But Yahweh will strip Esau bare. He will uncover any and every hiding place he told the people to seek out. Edom can no longer be the hidden one. Devastation visiting the young warriors, their brothers, and their neighbors will be great. Only orphans and widows will remain, but Yahweh says they can be abandoned to him; he will keep them alive. Emphatically he will.

This oracle likely predates the fall of Jerusalem since there is no trace of bitterness over Edom's behavior toward Judah in 586 B.C. A date prior to 605 B.C. (Bekel 1907: 342) is a bit early; more likely is a date ca. 594 B.C., when Edom was plotting against Babylon (Holladay). The Edomites will be judged along with Judah's other neighbors at a time when Yahweh chooses to reckon with them.

2. Yahweh to Bring the Eagle Down! (49:12–18)

49 [12]For thus said Yahweh:
Look, those for whom there is no judgment to drink the cup must surely drink. Are you then one who will surely go free? You will not go free, for you will surely drink!

[13]For by myself I have sworn—oracle of Yahweh—that a desolation, a reproach, a ruin, and a swearword Bozrah shall become, and all her cities shall become eternal ruins.

¹⁴I have heard a message from Yahweh
   and an envoy is sent among the nations:
'Gather together and go against her!
   Up! To the battle!'
¹⁵For look! I have made you small among the nations
   despised among humankind

¹⁶Your horror!
   the arrogance of your heart
      has deceived you
Inhabitant in the clefts of the rock
   occupier of the top of the hill
For as the eagle, you make high your nest
   from there I will bring you down!
      —oracle of Yahweh.

¹⁷So Edom shall become a desolation; everyone passing by it will be horrified and will hiss at all her blows, ¹⁸just like the overthrow of Sodom and Gomorrah and her neighbors—said Yahweh. No person shall inhabit there, and no human shall sojourn in her.

RHETORIC AND COMPOSITION

MT 49:12–18 = LXX 30:6–12 (Ziegler 29:13–19). The present unit is delimited at the top end by *setumahs* in M^L, M^A, and M^P prior to v 12. The lower limit is less clear. Since the prose of vv 17–18 appears to expand the judgment of v 16b (McKane), and is balanced also by means of key words with the prose of vv 12–13, a break belongs after v 18. Verse 19 begins a new oracle in poetry. The present unit then consists of two prose oracles (vv 12–13), a dialogue oracle in poetry (vv 14–16), and a concluding prose oracle (vv 17–18). Since the last-mentioned could be verses quarried from elsewhere, e.g., 19:8 or 50:40, it may not be an oracle per se, but simply editorial supplement. Yet it does have a "said Yahweh" messenger formula (the parallel in 50:40 has "oracle of Yahweh"). Verse 18, although taken to be poetry in v 33, is here embedded in prose (cf. 50:40). This verse does not connect back to v 11 (*pace* Holladay).

Verses 14–16 are similar to Obad 1–4, which again has generated much discussion on dependence one way or the other. The poetry is of a general nature, i.e., it has no place-names or other clues as to audience, meaning that its application to Edom—in both locations—could be secondary. Here in Jeremiah, prose on either side provides a context: v 13 mentions Bozrah, and v 17 Edom. The usual view (Duhm, Cornill, Peake, Volz, Rudolph, Weiser, Holladay, McKane) is that the Jeremiah verses are a borrowing from Obadiah. Yet the ideas are Jeremianic, so also some of the diction (*pace* Holladay), leading Dicou (1994: 58–70) and Raabe (1996: 22–31) to argue for borrowing in the other direction, i.e., from Jeremiah to Obadiah. The dependency question is perhaps best set aside, except to say that there are no compelling reasons for denying these verses to Jeremiah.

A chiastic structure in Oracle I (v 12) was noted already by Boys (1825: 30):

I   Look, those for whom there is no judgment *to drink the*   *lištôt . . . šātô yištû*
          cup, *must surely drink*
          Are you then one *who will surely go free?*   *nāqōh tinnāqeh*
          You will not go free   *lōʾ tinnāqe*
       for *you will surely drink!*   *šātōh tišteh*

Oracle II (v 13) has stair-like repetition:

II   *For* by myself I have sworn . . .   *kî*
          that a desolation, a reproach . . . Bozrah *shall become*   *kî . . . . tihyeh*
          and all her cities *shall become . . . . . .*   *. . . tihyeynâ*

Oracle III (vv 14–16) here in Jeremiah has good poetic structure, better than in Obad 1–4. It consists of two stanzas, vv 14–15 and v 16. Stanza I consists of three bicolons; Stanza II is a tricolon and two bicolons. Stanza I has alternation of speaker, with the envoy's message from Yahweh to the nations positioned in the center:

Jeremiah: *I have heard a message from Yahweh*   v 14
                    and an envoy is sent among the nations:
Envoy: *'Gather together and go against her!*
                    Up! To the battle!'
Yahweh: *For look! I have made you small among the nations*
                    despised among humankind

In Stanza II the speaking voice is Yahweh addressing the condemned nation directly. The oracle concludes with a messenger formula, although this is lacking in the LXX. The two stanzas taken together have these key word repetitions:

I   . . . .   v 14
          . . . . *among the nations*   *baggôyim*
          . . . .
       For . . . . *among the nations*   *kî . . . baggôyim*   v 15

II   . . . .   v 16
          . . . .
          . . . .
       For . . . .   *kî*

The Obad 1–4 passage repeats *baggôyim* ("among the nations") but lacks the *kî* ("For") repetition.

Oracle I has key word balance with Oracle III:

I   *Look* . . . .   *hinnēh*   v 12
          . . . .

III   . . . .
    Look . . . .   *hinnēh*   v 15

Oracle II has key word balance with Oracle IV:

II	*a desolation* . . . . . . Bozrah *shall become*	*lĕšammâ . . . tihyeh*	v 13
IV	Edom *shall become a desolation*	*wĕhāyĕtâ . . . lĕšammâ*	v 17

The particle *'ên* is a catchword linking Oracle I (v 12) with prior oracles in 49:1–6 and 7–11:

v 12 *there is no*	v 5	*none*
	v 7	*is there no*
	v 10	*he is no*

For the rhetorical function of this negative particle, see also Rhetoric and Composition for 8:13–17.

Catchwords in Oracle II (v 13) connect to the prior oracle in 49:7–11 by emphatic key words:

v 13 *For by myself* *kî bî*	v 10a	*But I*	*kî-'ănî*
	v 11	*I*	*'ănî*

These catchwords in Oracle III connect to the unit ahead in 49:19–22:

v 16 *your heart*	v 22 *as the eagle*
as the eagle	*heart . . . as the heart*

The expansion in vv 17–18 also has a catchword connecting to 49:19–22:

v 17 *he will be horrified*	v 20 *it will be horrified*

NOTES

49:12. *Look, those for whom there is no judgment to drink the cup must surely drink. Are you then one who will surely go free?* Assuming that a judgment does exist against Edom, we have an argument *a minori ad maius*; on which, see Note for 3:1. Without a judgment, the argument is by analogy, as in Obad 16. On the cup of Yahweh's wrath, see Jer 13:12–14 and 25:15–29.

Look. Hebrew *hinnēh*. The LXX omits, which could, as Janzen (1973: 118) points out, be attributed to haplography (homoeoteleuton: *h . . . h*).

those for whom there is no judgment to drink the cup must surely drink. This expresses a general truth regarding other nations, i.e., that punishment on occasion is meted out without a specific judgment having been rendered against them. Reference could thus be to Philistia (47:2–7), Ammon (49:1–6), Damascus (49:23–27), Kedar (49:28–33), or Elam (49:35–38), none of whom received judgment for wrongdoing in the oracles spoken against them, but who nevertheless must drink Yahweh's cup of wrath. Reference cannot be to an innocent Israel, as is often alleged. Calvin read the verse in this manner, although he went on to say that such an idea from Jeremiah was unthinkable. He finally came around to the well-supported theological idea that God first punishes his own, then later punishes others (25:28–29; Deut 32:19–43; Psalms 37; 73; in the NT, see 1 Pet 4:17–18). More recent scholars (e.g., Giesebrecht; Cornill; Duhm; Rudolph; Carroll; and Holladay) have said that while the reference here is to Israel, Jeremiah could scarcely have said such a thing; therefore, the verse must be a nongenuine, postexilic supplement. Actually, it makes no sense at any time to say that Israel was undeserving of the punishment it received. The saying must remain a general maxim regarding Yahweh's sometimes-undeclared reasons for punishing other nations.

there is no judgment. Or "there is no sentence (of judgment)." Hebrew *'ên mišpāṭām.*

drink the cup. I.e., the "cup of wine," given here metaphorically to the nations. Babylon is the nation that will make other nations drink (51:7). Compare the directive to Moab that it drink and become drunk (48:26). On "cup" (*kôs*) and its metaphorical uses, see Note for 25:15.

Are you then one who will surely go free? You will not go free. This could have been spoken when Nebuchadnezzar was carrying out punitive campaigns in Philistia (604 B.C.), in Judah (586 B.C.), or in Transjordan (582 B.C.). All three times Edom appears to have escaped unharmed. But Edom will not go free, and will have to drink the cup later on, as it apparently did under Nabonidus. Recall in this connection Agag's false hope for a reprieve in 1 Sam 15:32–33.

Are you then one. Hebrew *wĕ'attâ hû'.* An emphatic interrogative construction. The LXX and T omit *hû'.* But Aq translates the term with *autos.* See 25:29 for another instance in which the LXX changes a question into an assertion.

For you will surely drink! Hebrew *kî šātōh tišteh.* Some LXX MSS lack *oti pinōn piesai* (Rahlfs includes; Ziegler omits), which could be due to haplography (homoeoarcton: *ky . . . ky,* or homoeoteleuton: *h . . . h*). See Janzen (1973: 118). To Edom the cup of wrath will pass (25:21; Lam 4:21), and it must drink.

13. *For by myself I have sworn.* On Yahweh swearing by his own name, see also 22:5, 24; 44:26; 46:18; 51:14; Deut 32:40; Gen 22:16; and Isa 45:23. In the NT, see Heb 6:13, where it says that there is none greater by whom Yahweh can swear.

a desolation, a reproach, a ruin, and a swearword. *Accumulatio.* The LXX omits *lĕḥōreb,* "(for) a ruin," which could be more loss due to haplography (homoeoarcton: *l . . . l*). Aquila translates with "sword" (*romphaian*). Most commentators (Cornill; Giesebrecht; Duhm; Volz; Rudolph; Holladay) take *lĕḥōreb* as an MT plus. But arguments for dittography from the prior *lĕḥerpâ* (Ehrlich 1912: 361), or *lĕḥorbôt* in the next clause (Bright; Carroll), or that this is a "typical filling out of this series" (Janzen 1973: 59), are unconvincing. On strings of curse words such as the present one in Jeremiah, see Note for 24:9.

Bozrah. Hebrew *boṣrâ.* A major city and natural stronghold in northern Edom, possibly the capital (so Kimḥi; Cheyne). It is mentioned again in v 22 and in Gen 36:33; 1 Chr 1:44; Amos 1:12; Isa 34:6, and 63:1. Not to be confused with Bozrah in Moab (48:24). Bozrah is generally identified with a mountain site near the small town of Buṣeirah in modern Jordan, 22 kilometers south of Tafila and 4 kilometers west of the King's Highway, near Wadi Dana (Bennett 1983: 9; *ABD* 1: 774–75; *NEAEHL* 1: 264–66). On the King's Highway, see Note for 48:2. British excavations in the early 1970s and in 1980 (Bennett 1973; 1974; 1975; 1977; "Busayra" in *BANE*: 61–62) discovered a well-fortified administrative center on the summit, one of its large buildings being similar to a late-seventh- or early-sixth-century B.C. building excavated at Hazor. Evidence was also found of a destruction by fire, possibly dating to the sixth century B.C. and possibly attributable to the Babylonians, after which the site was abandoned (Bennett 1983: 15–17). The LXX translates the city name with *en mesō autēs,* "in the midst of her" (= Heb *btwkh*).

14. *I have heard a message from Yahweh, and an envoy is sent among the nations.* Hebrew *šĕmûʿâ* is not news of an approaching army (6:24; 10:22; 37:5; 49:23; 50:43), much less a "rumor" of the same (Ezek 7:26), but a proclamation from Yahweh, carried by an envoy, that the nations are to assemble for battle (Calvin; cf. Isa 28:9, 19; 53:1). The proclamation is given in 14b. In this paratactic construction the prophet, who is now speaking, says he has heard the divine message and relayed it to an envoy, or else Yahweh has given the message to the envoy directly, and the envoy is on his way to deliver it to the nations. The LXX has the prophet hearing the divine message and Yahweh sending multiple envoys: "I have heard a message from the Lord, and he has sent envoys to the nations." Obadiah 1 reads: "We have heard a message. . . ."

I have heard a message. Hebrew *šĕmûʿâ šāmaʿtî* has assonance and alliteration.

an envoy. Hebrew *ṣîr.* In Prov 13:17 the term is parallel to *malʾāk* ("messenger"). For the plural *ṣîrîm,* see Isa 18:2. Assyrian *ṣîru* means "(foreign) envoy" (*CAD* 16: 213, *ṣîru* A), the plural *ṣîrāni* occurring in the late-eighth-century Assyrian Summary Inscription #8 from Calah (line 21), where Tadmor (1994: 178–79) says these are high-ranking foreign ambassadors, as opposed to individual messengers.

Gather together and go against her! Assuming contextual help from v 13, the nations are called together to fight Bozrah and its cities (Kimḥi). Compare the imagery in Isa 13:4–5. Rudolph notes that Edom will be attacked here by the nations rather than by a single concrete enemy. How this finds fulfillment in Nabonidus's sixth-century campaign against Edom is unclear, but Nabonidus could have rallied local allies in the same way that Nebuchadnezzar did against Judah earlier. On the campaign of Nabonidus, see Note for 49:10.

Up! To the battle! The imperative *qûmû* ("Up!") occurs five times in Jeremiah as a summons to battle (6:4–5; 49:14, 28, 31). Yahweh as commander-in-chief of the army issues the battle orders (Bach 1962: 52; Christensen 1975: 231).

15. *For look! I have made you small among the nations.* Small, if not in size, at least in importance. Hebrew *kî* ("For") could be an asseverative, i.e., "Indeed." The LXX omits *kî-hinnēh* ("For look!"), which is doubtless more loss

due to haplography (homoeoteleuton: *h . . . h*); cf. Obad 2. The term *hinnēh* has a rhetorical function in the poem (see Rhetoric and Composition). The verb *nĕtattîkā* ("I have made you") is a prophetic perfect, with most modern Versions translating as a future.

among the nations, despised among humankind. Alliteration here with three successive words beginning with the *b* consonant: *baggôyīm bāzûy bā'ā-dām.* Obadiah 2 reads "among the nations, you are greatly despised." The psalmist speaks of being "scorned by humankind and despised by people" (Ps 22:7[Eng 22:6]).

16. *Your horror! the arrogance of your heart has deceived you.* Taking Heb *tiplaṣtĕkā* ("Your horror"), which is a *hapax legomenon* in the OT and not present in Obad 3, as an exclamation with a suppressed predicate (GKC §147c). This eliminates the gender problem of a feminine noun preceding a masculine verb. More common translations, "your horrible nature" (NJV), or "the horror you inspire" (RSV), are guided largely by the phrase, "arrogance of your heart," following. This latter phrase seems to have influenced Jerome's Vulgate translation: *arrogantia tua decepit te* ("your arrogance has deceived you"). The T renders *tiplaṣtĕkā* with "your folly," and the LXX with "your game-playing" (*ā paignia sou*). J. D. Michaelis (1793: 360) proposed a connection with *mipleṣet* ("horrible idol") in 1 Kgs 15:13, resulting in a contemptuous term for Edom's god. But the verse does not otherwise disparage Edomite worship, making this explanation unlikely. What we are talking about, essentially, is a manifestation of Edomite hubris, which occupies the rest of the verse and is basically what is stated in Obad 3–4. This people is puffed up with arrogance (*zĕdôn*), unaware that it is headed for a fall (cf. 50:31–32; Prov 11:2).

Inhabitant in the clefts of the rock, occupier of the top of the hill. The description immediately suggests Petra, 80 kilometers south of the Dead Sea and west of the King's Highway in southern Jordan, known from antiquity for its inaccessible dwellings within rock, atop rock, and concealed by rock. Petra achieved prominence as a Nabatean center in the Hellenistic period, but an unfortified Edomite settlement is attested at Umm el-Biyara, a rugged mountain 300 meters up from the valley floor overlooking Petra from the west. Excavation of the site by British archaeologists in 1960–65 showed extensive seventh-century occupation (Bennett 1966; Bienkowski 1990a). One important find of a seal impression of Qos-Gabr, King of Edom, who is known also from Assyrian inscriptions of Esarhaddon and Assurbanipal, confirms the dating of the pottery to the seventh century. On Umm el-Biyara, see Bienkowski in *NEAEHL* 4: 1488–90 and *OEANE* 5: 274–76.

clefts of the rock. Or "clefts of Sela." Hebrew *hassela'* = The Rock. The phrase occurs also in Song 2:14, and in Obad 3 without the article. The LXX translates as *petrōn* (= Petra, according to Eusebius of Caesarea), but it is widely agreed that Umm el-Biyara cannot be the Sela given dubious fame by King Amaziah in the early eighth century (2 Kgs 14:7; 2 Chr 25:12). That Sela is located farther north, perhaps near Bozrah. Among classical writers, Diodorus of Sicily (xix 97.3) mentions a "rock" in connection with the Nabateans, and

Strabo (*Geog.* xvi 4.18, 21) describes the well-fortified Nabatean metropolis of Petra.

Inhabitant . . . occupier. Hebrew *šōkĕnî . . . tōpĕśî.* Two nouns or Qal participles with the old case ending (*ḥireq compaginis*) to emphasize the construct state (GKC §90k–m; cf. Deut 33:16; Obad 3).

For as the eagle, you make high your nest. For the height at which the eagle makes its nest, see also Job 39:27. Here is another description of an inaccessible Edomite dwelling at a height such as one finds at Umm el-Biyara. The nest image symbolizes security; see also in 22:23 and Hab 2:9.

hill . . . you make high. Hebrew *gibʿâ . . . tagbîāḥ* makes a wordplay.

from there I will bring you down! From Yahweh there is no safe retreat; therefore, Edom will be brought down from whatever secure place it inhabits. See also Isa 14:12–15 and Amos 9:2.

17. For variations of this standard curse, see Note on 18:16.

everyone passing by it will be horrified and will hiss at all her blows. See also 19:8. The LXX abbreviates to "everyone who passes by will hiss at her." There appears to be a subtle connection with v 16, where people shuddered in horror (*plṣ*) at Edom's arrogance. Now they will shudder in horror (*šmm*) at Edom's ruin.

18. *just like the overthrow of Sodom and Gomorrah and her neighbors—said Yahweh. No person shall inhabit there, and no human shall sojourn in her.* This verse is repeated with minor change in 50:40. The latter bicolon occurs also in 49:33b, and with variations in 51:43b. For the use of the "Sodom and Gomorrah curse" in Jeremiah, see Notes on 20:16 and 23:14. Bozrah and her cities will become like Sodom and Gomorrah and their neighboring cities. Not only will people not live there, no one will even come to visit.

her neighbors. There were five so-called Cities of the Plain: Sodom, Gomorrah, Admah, Zeboiim, and Zoar (Gen 14:2, 8; Wis 10:6). Admah and Zeboiim were destroyed along with Sodom and Gomorrah (Deut 29:22[Eng 29:23]; Hos 11:8); Zoar was spared (Gen 19:20–23).

said Yahweh. The LXX has *Kurios pantokratōr* ("Lord Almighty"),which it sometimes uses to translate "Yahweh of Hosts." See Appendix VI.

human. Hebrew *ben-ʾādām.* Literally, "son of man" = "man."

MESSAGE AND AUDIENCE

In Oracle I Yahweh tells a nation that thinks others will suffer judgment, but it will not, that such will not in fact be the case. If other nations not given specified judgment are made to drink Yahweh's cup of wrath, why can this nation bank on going free? It will not go free. It too must drink Yahweh's cup of desolation.

In companion Oracle II, Yahweh swears an oath by himself that Bozrah will become a curse, and that her daughter cities will be ruins for all time. The audience now knows that judgment is against Edom.

In dialogue Oracle III, the prophet begins by saying that he has heard a message from Yahweh. An envoy has been dispatched to the nations with the same message. From the envoy we then hear battle orders issued by Yahweh, who is commander-in-chief of the army. The nations are told to gather themselves together and go against a designated foe. The audience presumably knows the identity of the foe. Yahweh then addresses the targeted nation directly, telling it that he has made it small among other nations and rendered it universally despised. Yahweh continues speaking in Stanza II, addressing now the nation's hubris, which had only been hinted at earlier. The nation's horrible arrogance is all a deceit. Although it inhabits clefts in the rock and occupies high hills, Yahweh will bring this lofty eagle down from its nest.

The final oracle, which may be a composite quarried from elsewhere, brings clarity to the oracle that has preceded. It is now clear that Edom shall become a desolation. People will still be horrified, but for a different reason. Before, they were intimidated by Edom's arrogance; now they will shudder at the ruin of Edom. Bozrah and its cities will be like Sodom and Gomorrah and their neighboring cities: a place where no one will live and no one will visit.

These oracles can probably be dated with the other Edom oracles to a time before the fall of Jerusalem, perhaps 594 B.C., when Edom joined the anti-Babylon conspiracy. Philistia at that time had already been destroyed by Nebuchadnezzar. There is no trace here of Judahite bitterness over Edom's behavior toward Jerusalem and the Temple in 586 B.C.

3. As a Lion, as an Eagle against Edom (49:19–22)

49 [19]Look, as a lion goes up
    from the pride of the Jordan to perennial pasture
Indeed I will in a moment chase him from her
    and who is the young man I will appoint over her?
Indeed who is like me?
    and who will summon me?
        and who is this, a shepherd that can stand before me?

[20]Therefore hear the counsel of Yahweh that he counseled toward Edom,
and his plans that he planned toward the inhabitants of Teman:
    Surely they shall drag them away—the little ones of the flock
        surely their pasture shall be horrified over them
[21]At the sound of their fall the land quakes—a scream
    at the Red Sea its sound is heard!

[22]Look, as the eagle he goes up and flies
    and spreads his wings over Bozrah
The heart of the warriors of Edom shall be in that day
    as the heart of a woman greatly distressed.

RHETORIC AND COMPOSITION

MT 49:19–22 = LXX 30:13–16 (Ziegler 29:20–23). In the present verses are three concluding oracles against Edom (v 19, vv 20b–21, and v 22), although none contains the expected messenger formula. Oracle II is preceded by a different sort of introduction (v 20a), and Oracle III, in a longer version against Moab (48:40–41) does have an introductory "Thus said Yahweh." The upper limit of the present unit is determined by the shift to poetry in v 19 (Werner 1988: 160–62). That v 19 is poetry is recognized by *BHS* and most modern Versions, although the RSV, NRSV, NJV, and NSB take the verse as prose. The lower limit of the unit is set after v 22 by a *setumah* in M^L, and *petuḥahs* in M^A and M^P. M^L has another *setumah* after v 19, which coincides with the conclusion of Oracle I. A small space in M^A after v 19 may also be a *setumah*, but *HUB* indicates no section. There is no section after v 19 in M^P. Oracles I and II (vv 19–21) are readapted for use against Babylon in 50:44–46, which aids in confirming their delimitation in the present context; Oracle III (v 22) is a shortened version of the Moab oracle in 48:40–41.

Oracle I (v 19) is two bicolons and a tricolon. Oracle II (vv 20b–21) is a double bicolon with a prose introduction (v 20a). Oracle III (v 22) is another double bicolon. Verse 20a is then prose (*pace BHS*; JB; NAB; NIV; NJB; also Condamin; Volz; and Holladay), just as we have in 49:30b, and vv 20b–22 are poetry (*pace* RSV and NRSV).

Key words balance the oracles internally and with one another:

I	Look as . . . . . . .goes up	*hinnēh kĕ . . . yaʿăleh*	v 19
	. . . . pasture	*nĕwēh*	
	Indeed	*kî*	
	and who	*ûmî*	
	Indeed who	*kî mî*	
	and who	*ûmî*	
	and who	*ûmî*	
II	Surely	*ʾim-lōʾ*	v 20b
	surely . . . . their pasture	*ʾim-lōʾ . . . nĕwēhem*	
	At the sound	*miqqôl*	v 21
	. . . . its sound!	*qôlāh*	
III	Look as . . . . . . he goes up	*hinnēh ka . . . yaʿăleh*	v 22
	. . . .		
	The heart	*lēb*	
	as the heart	*kĕlēb*	

Condamin notes the repeated beginnings of Oracles I and III. The *miqqôl . . . qôlāh* inclusio in Oracle II is not present in the LXX, nor in 50:46 (see Notes). Yahweh with his self-asseverations is identified as the speaker of Oracle I, and presumably he speaks also in Oracles II and III. The introduction of 20a—doubtless a later addition—tells us only that what follows is the "counsel of

Yahweh" (*'ăṣat-yhwh*) and "his plans" (*maḥšĕbôtāyw*). The audience for all three oracles remains unspecified, but is probably the people of Judah and Jerusalem.

Catchwords connecting to the prior unit in 49:12–18 are the following:

v 20 *it shall be horrified*	v 16 *your heart*
v 22 *as the eagle*	*as the eagle*
heart . . . as the heart	v 17 *he will be horrified*

Catchwords connecting ahead to the Damascus oracle appear to be these:

v 22 *as . . . a woman . . . distressed kĕ . . .*   v 24 *like a woman in labor kayyôlēdâ*
      'iššâ mĕṣērâ

NOTES

49:19. *Look.* Hebrew *hinnēh*. Together with *hinĕnî* ("Look I"), the most common beginning to the Jeremianic oracle and stanza in the Jeremianic oracle, occuring elsewhere among the Foreign Nation Oracles in 46:25; 47:2; 48:12, 40; 49:2, 5, 12, 19, 22, 35; 50:9, 18, 31, 41, 44; 51:1, 25, 36, 47, and 52. See further Notes on 1:9 and 1:15.

as a lion goes up. The expression without *kĕ* ("as") occurs in 4:7. NJB's "like a lion he climbs" is gramatically possible, but inadmissible if we assume that Yahweh is speaking and is comparing himself to a lion, the usual interpretation (RSV; NEB; JB; NAB; NJV; NIV) and doubtless the correct one. The problem is the same with T's reading: "a king with his troops shall come up," which renders another metaphor in v 22 and does the same elsewhere (4:13; 5:6; 48:40; 50:44; 51:42). Yahweh, as a lion, will leave his concealed habitation to chase a shepherd from his flock and despoil their pasturage. The same imagery is present in 25:34–38. See also Zech 13:7.

the pride of the Jordan. Hebrew *gĕ'ôn hayyarden*. The expression describes lush areas of the Jordan Valley where lions lived in antiquity. See Note on 12:5.

perennial pasture. Hebrew *'êtān* means "permanent, perennial," referring here probably to pastureland that remains green all year long (NAB: "permanent feeding grounds"; NJV: "a secure pasture"; NIV: "rich pastureland"). For other uses of *'êtān*, see Note for 5:15. Earlier commentators and translators who took *nāweh* to mean "habitation" (23:3; 25:30) came up with the translation of "a strong sheepfold," or the like (Rashi; Kimḥi; Calvin; AV; RSV). The LXX experienced difficulty with *'êtān*, for here and also in 50:44 [LXX 27:44] it simply rendered a place-name: *eis topon Aitham* ("to the place of Aitham"). The T has "a campsite of shepherds." Such a description was said to suit the mountaneous dwellings of the Edomites. Another application would be required in 50:44, however, for Babylon has a different geography (Calvin). The lion then will go either from one lush area to another, or from his covert against a protected habitation. Either way, Edom has no chance of withstanding the attack.

Indeed . . . Indeed. Hebrew *kî* beginning both 19b and 19c is taken as an asseverative. Some commentators (e.g., Duhm, Volz, Rudolph, and Bright) suggest emending to *kēn* in 19b which, together with *kĕ* in 19a, would fill out the comparison as it exists in 2:26 ("as . . . so"), but this is not necessary.

I will in a moment chase him from her. Hebrew *'argî'â 'ărîṣennû mē'āleyhā.* On the coordination of verbal ideas, see GKC §120g. Two imperatives are coordinated in 13:18a. Most commentators and translations simply give *'argî'â* adverbal force; cf. Prov 12:19. The more difficult problem has been the interpretation of "him" and "her." The LXX, T, and 50:44(Q) have "them" instead of "him." An easy solution has been to emend both here and in the next colon, but no emendation is required if we simply recognize that Hebrew discourse often lacks antecedents (see Note on 5:12), with clarification coming in what follows. The "him" is the one who could conceivably be replaced by the "young man" in the next colon and the "shepherd" at the end of the verse (not "Edom," as supplied in the NRSV). He will not be replaced; nevertheless, at present he is the shepherd (= king) of Edom. The "her"—here and in the next colon—is Edom (Calvin). The meaning then is that Yahweh will come with lightning speed to chase away the shepherd from his flock, i.e., the Edomite king from his Edomite subjects. On the suddenness of Yahweh's judgment, see Note on 4:20.

and who is the young man I will appoint over her? Once Yahweh has chased away Edom's shepherd, he considers whom to appoint as a replacement (Calvin). But the question is rhetorical; therefore, the answer is "There is none!" No "young man" (*bāḥûr*) will be appointed over Edom; no "shepherd" is able to stand before Yahweh (v 19c).

over her. Hebrew *'ēleyhā.* It appears that *'el* and *'al* (in the prior *mē'āleyhā*) are here poetic equivalents; cf. BDB, 823 and see Note on 11:2.

Indeed who is like me? On the incomparability of Yahweh, see 10:6–7 and Isaiah 40–48.

and who will summon me? I.e., who will summon me to meet at an appointed time for a challenge of one sort or another? The same expression occurs in Job 9:19, where the imagined summons is for God to appear before a court of law. Rashi thinks the present summons would be for the purpose of waging war. The point is that no one can summon Yahweh, for whatever reason. Yahweh is like no other.

and who is this, a shepherd that can stand before me? "Who is this?" is Hebrew *mî-zeh* (46:7; Job 38:2; Ps 24:8). The question is once again rhetorical. No Edomite shepherd the likes of David can stand before Yahweh. Saul's question after David killed Goliath was "whose son is this?" *ben-mî-zeh* (1 Sam 17:55–56). T again has "king" for "shepherd," which in this case is acceptable (Rashi; Kimḥi; Giesebrecht). On "shepherd" being a general term for rulers in the ANE, see Note on 2:8. The failure of a shepherd to arise in Edom is somewhat compensated for in Isa 63:1, where in language echoing the present passage a watchman inquires about the approaching conqueror from the south (Muilenburg 1956a: 726):

Who is this (*mî-zeh*) coming from Edom
  in red garments from Bozrah
this one adorned in his apparel
  marching in the greatness of his strength?
It is I, announcing deliverance
  mighty to save

20. *counsel of Yahweh that he counseled . . . his plans that he planned.* The construction reappears in 49:30, only there the designs are those of Nebuchadnezzar. "Counsel" (*ʿēṣâ*) is given by the wise (18:18; 49:7), but also by Jeremiah, who claims he could offer counsel to King Zedekiah (38:15). People are known to give themselves bad counsel (7:24 [*mōʿēṣôt*]; 18:23; 19:7), and both they and nations too devise evil plans for others (11:19; 48:2). Yahweh, however, is said to be "great in counsel" (32:19) and to actively "plan" (*ḥšb*) both good and bad for nations of the world (18:8, 11; 26:3; 29:11; 36:3; cf. Lam 2:8). On the Jeremianic coinage "to plan a plan," see Note for 29:11.

Teman. The northeast region of Edom; see Note on 49:7.

Surely . . . surely. Hebrew *'im-lō'* in both cases is a particle of asseveration, otherwise an oath ("I swear that . . ."); cf. GKC §149.

Surely they shall drag them away. Hebrew *'im-lō' yishābûm.* The subject of the verb is indefinite, and the object "them" is "the little ones of the flock." S. R. Driver translates: "Surely they shall drag them, even the smallest of the flock." He says Edom is being compared to the smallest and the helpless of a flock whose enemies, like dogs, will drag them along and treat as they please (cf. 15:3; 2 Kgs 9:35–37). Both the subject and object are plural, but since this is a new oracle there is no need for correspondence to what precedes in v 19, where Yahweh (like a lion) was chasing the shepherd (= king) from its flock (= Edom). Here the multiple enemy will doubtless be people who drag the corpses away (cf. 22:19).

the little ones of the flock. Luther translated *ṣĕʿîrê haṣṣōʾn* as *Hirtenknaben* ("shepherd boys"), which some commentators follow (Duhm; Cornill; Volz; Holladay; McKane). So also the NJV: "Surely the shepherd boys shall drag them away." The reading has some justification. In 14:3(Q) *ṣĕʿîrêhem* means "their young (boys)," and in 48:4(Q) *ṣĕʿîreyhā* refers to "her young (children)." But I doubt whether such a reading can be correct here, for shepherd boys— whoever they are—will not likely be dragging anyone anywhere. Others will drag off the Edomite young.

their pasture shall be horrified over them. Hebrew *yaššîm* is an internal H-stem meaning "to be (deeply) horrified" (GKC §53e; cf. Ehrlich 1912: 361), and need not be emended with Giesebrecht, Cornill, and Volz to a Qal. The picture is one of a personified pasture struck numb with disbelief at what has happened to the little ones of the flock. Again, as in v 19, should *nāweh* be translated "habitation," then it is Edom's sheepfold that will be thoroughly scandalized.

21. *At the sound of their fall the land quakes.* Hebrew *hāʾāreṣ* could also translate here as "the earth." Hyperbole, in either case, although terrestrial convulsions do accompany momentous events (see Note on 51:29). Compare the quaking of the mountains in 4:24, and of the land / earth in 8:16; 10:10; 50:46; and 51:29. Hebrew *miqqōl* ("at the sound") is a familiar Jeremiah word (4:29; 8:16; 47:3; 50:46).

a scream. Hebrew *ṣĕʿāqâ.* This is an agonizing cry from the earth.

at the Red Sea its sound is heard! The corporate cry of Edom, together with a scream from the earth, is heard all the way down at the Red Sea. More hyperbole. Hebrew *yam-sûp,* lit. "sea of reeds," refers here—as in 1 Kgs 9:26 and perhaps also Num 21:4—to the eastern finger of the Red Sea, i.e., the Gulf of Aqaba (Snaith 1965: 396–97; Werner 1988: 165; Batto 1983: 27–28). Snaith thinks the original reading was *sôp* ("end"), making the reference indefinite, i.e., to a sea in the south, the boundaries of which no one knew. The referent, in any case, is not the Nile Delta region—with or without an assumed allusion to the Exodus—or the western finger of the Red Sea (Gulf of Suez). The LXX has "at the sea (of reeds)" (Rahlfs: *en thalassē;* Ziegler: *en thalassē souph*). In 50:46, where the oracle is adapted for use against Babylon, the cry is heard "among the nations." The LXX omits *qôlāh,* "its sound," but the term is not superfluous nor is it a gloss, as many commentators allege. The T includes the term. The balanced terms—*miqqōl* at the beginning of the line and *qôlāh* at the end—perhaps simulate an echo; NJB translates the final colon: "the sound of it echoes to the Sea."

22. See exegesis for 48:40.

Look, as the eagle he goes up and flies, and spreads his wings over Bozrah. Reference is to the mighty Babylonian army. Calvin says the expedition will be quick and ruinous.

Look. Hebrew *hinnēh.* Beginning the oracle as also in v 19.

he goes up. Hebrew *yaʿăleh.* The LXX omits the verb, which does not appear in the Moab oracle of 48:40. This omission can be attributed to haplography (homoeoarcton without the following *waw: y . . . y*). Aquila and Symm have the verb (*anabēsetai*).

and spreads his wings over Bozrah. The T again renders the metaphor "a king with his troops." See v 19 and 48:40. Bozrah was Edom's major city in the north; see Note on 49:13.

in that day. I.e., in the "Day of Yahweh"; see further Note on 46:10.

as the heart of a woman greatly distressed. Hebrew *mĕṣērâ* is an internal H-stem participle (GKC §53de; Giesebrecht), referring here to a woman suffering the distress of childbirth. See 48:41, and Notes on 4:31 and 6:24. The first simile in the verse describes the swiftness of Yahweh's attack; this one, the fright of Edom's dispirited defenders (Holladay). Calvin notes that the Edomites are given no remnant, and that the judgment against them is unmitigated. This may have something to do with the behavior of Edom toward Judah when Jerusalem fell to the Babylonians in 586 B.C.

MESSAGE AND AUDIENCE

In the first oracle (v 19), which could be spoken against any nation, Yahweh compares himself to a lion who leaves a lush thicket in the Jordan Valley for greener pasture. With increased emphasis, but not addressing the nation directly, Yahweh says that in a flash he will chase a certain someone away from it. What young man will he then appoint over it? If he were a conquering king of the usual sort, he would doubtless appoint someone of his own choosing. But who is like me, Yahweh asks, and who will summon me for a challenge? What shepherd can stand before me? Will no one be appointed? The audience, which is probably Judahite, must answer the questions for itself. It learns only what it should already know, that Yahweh is like no other, and his judgment will be like no other king. Still, it does not know at this point to whom the oracle is directed and what the outcome will be.

Oracle II (vv 20–21) is another judgment oracle suitable for delivery against any nation, but the audience here is told at the outset that Yahweh's plans have to do with Edomite people in Teman. The oracle opens by saying that an unspecified attacker will drag away little ones of the flock, and the pasture in which they have grazed or the sheepfold that has given them protection will be stricken with horror at the violence—sounds like Edomite people and Edomite homes are to be laid waste. And it appears too that no shepherd will be appointed by Yahweh over Edom. The collapse of Edom will reach earthquake proportions; its scream will echo down at the Red Sea.

In Oracle III (v 22) the audience is told to take notice. As the eagle ascends, flies swiftly, and spreads its wings over Bozrah, something ominous is about to happen. The audience may or may not know it will be the doing of Yahweh. For the first time in the three oracles, Edom is mentioned, but still not addressed directly. The wings will spread wide not to protect, but to bring a violent presence. The heart of Edom's stout warriors in that day—that awesome Day of Yahweh—will be like the heart of a woman with labor pains. We need hear no more. If the three oracles are heard in tandem, we already know what will happen to Edom's little ones on that terrible day.

These oracles require a date no different from what has been suggested for the other Edom oracles, i.e., perhaps about 594 B.C., when Edom was plotting rebellion against Babylon. And fulfillment will probably come in the mid-sixth-century B.C. campaign of Nabonidus against Edom.

G. What about Damascus? (49:23–27)

49 [23]Concerning Damascus.
   Hamath is shamed, also Arpad
      for an evil report they have heard

They rock
   anxiety in the sea
      they cannot keep quiet

²⁴Damascus went limp
   she turned to flee
      but panic grabbed hold of her
Distress and pangs seized her
   like a woman in labor
²⁵How she is utterly forsaken
   city of praise
      town of my joy!

²⁶Therefore her young men shall fall in her open squares
   and all the men of war shall be silent in that day
    —oracle of Yahweh of hosts
²⁷And I will kindle a fire in the wall of Damascus
   and it will consume the citadels of Ben-hadad.

RHETORIC AND COMPOSITION

MT 49:23–27 = LXX 30:29–33 (Ziegler 30:12–16). This unit is delimited by a *setumah* in M^L before v 23 and after v 27. The M^A and M^P in both places have a *petuḥah*. At the beginning is also an introductory "concerning Damascus," identifying the recipient of the prophetic utterances that follow. These consist of 1) a lament (vv 23–25); and 2) an oracle of judgment (vv 26–27). The speaking voice in the former is the prophet, except at the end, where a resident of Damascus is heard voicing his pain ("town of my joy"). In the latter Yahweh is the speaker, as we see by the expanded messenger formula, "oracle of Yahweh of hosts."

Most modern Versions translate the verses as poetry, although *BHS* (and JB) take v 26 as prose, which it may be. This verse is repeated in 50:30. Assuming the verses to be poetry, the lament can be divided into two stanzas. Stanza I (v 23) is a bicolon and a tricolon; Stanza II (vv 24–25) is a tricolon, a bicolon, and a tricolon. The judgment oracle (vv 26–27) is a double bicolon, not counting the messenger formula. The key word "Damascus" links the lament to the oracle (Condamin).

Jeremianic authorship of these poems is denied by some commentators (Giesebrecht; Cornill; Volz; Rudolph; Bright), one reason being that neither Damascus nor Syria appears in the judgment list of 25:18–26. But Holladay considers them genuine. Amos and Isaiah both spoke judgments against Damascus (Amos 1:3–5; Isa 8:4; 17:1–6), and so also did Zechariah at a later time (Zech 9:1–2).

Catchwords connecting to the Edom oracle preceding are the following:

v 24   *like a woman in labor kayyôlēdâ*   v 22   *as . . . a woman in distress kĕ . . .*
                                                         'iššâ mĕṣērâ

There do not appear to be any catchwords connecting ahead to the Kedar–Hazor oracles.

NOTES

49:23. *Damascus*. The capital of Syria (Isa 7:8), which here represents the entire nation. From Solomon's reign until Assyria's rise in the mid–eighth century, Syria was (Northern) Israel's major antagonist (1 Kgs 11:23–25; 15:18–20; 20; 22; 2 Kings 1–9; 13–14; Isaiah 7–8), and ongoing tension existed between the two. Damascus fell to Tiglath-pileser III in 732 B.C. after a year-long campaign, with the surrounding country suffering complete devastation (2 Kgs 16:9; Calah Annal 23 of Tiglath-pileser; Tadmor 1994: 78–81, cf. *ANET*[3] 283: 205–40; *CS II* 286). After this it became an Assyrian province. Whether it enjoyed a brief independence after the fall of Assyria is not known, but peace with Babylon must have been made quite soon, for by 599–598 B.C. the Syrians had joined a Babylonian-sponsored campaign to raise havoc in Judah (2 Kgs 24:2).

Hamath is shamed, also Arpad, for an evil report they have heard. Hamath is an old city in the central Syrian plains, 214 kilometers north of Damascus. It survives in the modern city of Hama, situated where the main road from the north crosses the Orontes River. Pharaoh Neco occupied "the land of Hamath" before the Battle of Carchemish in 605 B.C. (2 Kgs 23:33), after which it fell heir to the Babylonians (Grayson 1975a: 99; Wiseman 1985: 17; cf. Jer 39:5). Arpad is a north Syrian city, 35 kilometers north of Aleppo and identified with modern Tell Rifaʿat (*OEANE* 4: 427–28; *ABD* 1: 401). Modest archaeological finds at the site show Assyrian occupation in the seventh century and Neo-Babylonian occupation in the sixth century. Arpad, Hamath, and Damascus appear together, both in the Bible (Isa 10:9; 36:19 [= 2 Kgs 18:34]; 37:13 [= 2 Kgs 19:13]) and in Assyrian documents (Luckenbill 1927: 27, 70). Hamath and Arpad are shamed here because of the indignity visited upon Damascus (Rashi). On shame in ancient culture, see Note on 2:26.

They rock, anxiety in the sea. Hebrew *nāmōgû bayyām dĕʾāgâ*. The *athnaḥ* under *nāmōgû*, "they rock (back and forth)," yields a tricolon for the line. This obviates the need to emend MT to *kayyām* ("like the sea") on the basis of Isa 57:20 and a paraphrastic T reading, or to follow Dahood (1980: 18) in taking the *ba* on *bayyām* as a comparative ("they heave more than a troubled sea"). The LXX ("they are astonished, they are angry") is of no help. The metaphor in MT is a stronger reading. Hamath and Arpad are floundering on an "anxious sea," which must refer to the Babylonian advance under Nebuchadnezzar (Peake). In 51:34–45, nautical metaphors describe Babylon and its attacker.

they cannot keep quiet. Hebrew *hašqēṭ lōʾ yûkāl*. The phrase recurs in Isa 57:20.

24. *Damascus went limp*. The verb *rph* means "sink, relax, become feeble," referring usually to the hands; cf. 6:24 and 47:3. Rashi says the hands of Damascus's defenders have become too feeble to wage war. According to Hillers (1965), this fits a literary convention describing the arrival of bad news, where typically the hands fall helpless, labor-like pains come to the loins, and a melting of the heart is felt. See Note on 6:24, and compare Hab 3:16.

she turned to flee. She could not, however, because of her panic (Abarbanel).

but panic grabbed hold of her. Hebrew *wĕreṭeṭ heḥĕzîqâ*. Reading a third feminine suffix in the final *hē'* of the verb (Giesebrecht; GKC §§58g; 91e). The noun *reṭeṭ* ("panic") is an OT *hapax legomenon*, generally taken to be Aramaic.

Distress and pangs seized her, like a woman in labor. The LXX omits, and most commentators delete, but this could be another loss due to haplography (homoeoteleuton: *h . . . h*). Aquila and Theod translate the phrase. The MT should be read (Volz). On the curse of warriors' becoming like (weak) women, see Notes on 4:31 and 6:24.

25. *How she is utterly forsaken!* Hebrew *'êk lō'-'uzzĕbâ*. Reading the *lō'* as asseverative against the LXX (Nötscher 1953: 374; Soggin 1975d; see Note on 4:27). The Vg omits the negative. An inhabitant of Damascus is now speaking. Dobbs-Allsopp (1993: 45–51, 132–33) notes here the theme of divine abandonment so common in the Bible (2:28; 6:8; 8:19; 12:7; Lam 1:1; 5:20; Ezek 8:1–11:23), occurring also in the Mesopotamian laments.

city of praise. Hebrew *'îr tĕhillâ*. On the Q *tĕhillāt*, see GKC §80g. In 48:2, "the Praise of Moab" (*tĕhillat mô'āb*) is no more, and in 51:41 it is Babylon, "the praise of all the land / earth" (*tĕhillat kol-hā'āreṣ*), suffering a similar fate. A native praises the rivers of Damascus in 2 Kgs 5:12, and Ezekiel singles out Damascus for praise because of its wine and wool (Ezek 27:18). Because of its fertile land and produce, Damascus was called "the gateway of the Garden of Eden" in Talmudic literature (*EncJud* 5: 1240).

town of my joy. Hebrew *qiryat mĕśôśî*. No need to emend with the Versions to "joy" without the suffix. An inhabitant of Damascus is lamenting his late, great city (Peake). Rashi said it was the king of Damascus mourning. Calvin too assumed that Jeremiah was assuming the persona of another.

26. *Therefore her young men shall fall in her open squares, and all the men of war shall be silent in that day.* The bicolon repeats in 50:30. The phrase "young men in her open squares" is a wordplay in Hebrew: *baḥûreyhā birḥōbōteyhā*. See on this phrase 9:20[Eng 9:21], and compare 6:11.

and all the men of war shall be silent in that day. I.e., soldiers will lie dead in the coming Day of Yahweh. On the "Day of Yahweh" for all nations, see Note for 46:10. The LXX omits "in that day" here and in 27:30 [= MT 50:30]. The T in both places has "at that time." Read the MT. The euphemistic *dmm*, "be silent," occurs often in Jeremiah; see 25:37; 48:2; 51:6; and Note on 8:14.

oracle of Yahweh of hosts. The LXX omits "of hosts," as elsewhere. See Appendix VI.

27. *And I will kindle a fire in the wall of Damascus, and it will consume the citadels of Ben-hadad.* A formulaic judgment similar to Amos 1:14, but see also Jer 17:27; 21:14; and 50:32.

the citadels of Ben-hadad. For *'armĕnôt* ("citadels, palaces, fortresses") the LXX translates *amphoda* ("streets"), as it does also in 17:27; see Note on 6:5. Ben-hadad = the Syrian royal house.

MESSAGE AND AUDIENCE

The prophet here laments over a Damascus already seen as having fallen. Hamath and Arpad, sister cities in Greater Syria, have heard the bad news and are terror-struck. They rock as if caught in an anxious sea, unable to be still. Damascus in its moment of crisis turned to flee, but could not. Panic grabbed it like a woman in labor. A concluding cry is heard from a stricken citizen, who sees Damascus utterly forsaken, a city much praised, the town of his joy.

What follows is an anticipatory judgment oracle along standard lines. Young men in the city squares and on the battlefield will be killed on this coming Day of Yahweh, for Yahweh will kindle a fire in Damascus's proud wall, and flames will lick up the royal palace.

A natural date for this lament and oracle would be ca. 605 B.C., when Nebuchadnezzar fought and defeated the Egyptians at Carchemish for control of Syria (Peake; Hyatt 1956: 283; Clements). But there is no record of Damascus being attacked by the Babylonians; we simply know that by 599/8 the Syrians were doing Nebuchadnezzar's bidding by joining in the campaign to ravage Judah.

H. WHAT ABOUT KEDAR? (49:28–33)

1. Curtains for the People of the East! (49:28–30)

49 ^{28}To Kedar and to the kings of Hazor whom Nebuchadrezzar, king of Babylon, struck down.
Thus said Yahweh:
Up! advance to Kedar!
  Devastate the people of the east!
^{29}Their tents and their flocks they shall take away
  their curtains and all their gear

Their camels they shall carry off for themselves
  and they shall call out upon them: 'Terror on every side!'
^{30}Flee! Wander all about! Go deep to dwell!
  dwellers of Hazor
    —oracle of Yahweh.
For Nebuchadrezzar, king of Babylon, has counseled against you a counsel and planned against you[1] a plan.

RHETORIC AND COMPOSITION

MT 49:28–30 = LXX 30:23–25 (Ziegler 30:6–8). The upper limit of the present unit is marked by the introductory "To Kedar" in v 28, before which

---

[1]Reading the Q *'ălêkem* ("against you"); Kt *'ălêhem* ("against them").

there is a *setumah* in M^L and a *petuḥah* in M^A and M^P. Delimitation at the lower end is indicated by the prose subscription in v 30b, which together with the prose superscription in v 28 frame the intervening poetry. Modern translations all take v 30b as poetry, as does Bright, though he concedes "it can be rendered metrically only with forcing." Volz and Condamin make the major break between v 30 and v 31. The frame repeats a key phrase, "Nebuchadrezzar, king of Babylon":

> v 28   To Kedar and to the kings of Hazor whom *Nebuchadrezzar, king of Babylon,* struck down.
> v 30b   For *Nebuchadrezzar, king of Babylon,* has counseled against you a counsel and planned against you a plan.

"Nebuchadrezzar" in 30b should not be omitted with the LXX (*pace* Cornill; Volz; Bardtke 1936: 255; McKane; and Holladay). For a parallel to 30b, see the superscription of v 20, where Yahweh carries out planned action against Edom.

The intervening poetry is two brief oracles, both double bicolons and both having messenger formulas. Oracle I (vv 28b–29a) is introduced by "Thus said Yahweh"; Oracle II (vv 29b–30a) has "said Yahweh" at its conclusion. The LXX lacks the latter formula, for which reason Holladay and McKane omit. The formula should be retained. Holladay would not find this text nearly so "baffling" if he retained all the messenger formulas in vv 28–33 and found four oracles in the verses instead of one. Similarly, the exegesis of McKane would not be nearly so labored if he retained the messenger formulas and recognized multiple audiences instead of just one. Bright too eliminates an audience change by rendering the verbs in v 29 as participles. The NEB and REB do the same by continuing in v 29 with two imperatives. Yahweh, who speaks throughout both oracles, alternates direct and indirect speech and shifts his audience in the following manner:

I	**direct speech** to the attacker of Kedar	v 28b
	indirect speech to an unidentified audience	v 29a
II	**indirect speech** to an unidentified audience	v 29b
	direct speech to the attacked people of Hazor	v 30

Speaker and audience changes are common in the Jeremianic oracles. It is the way this prophet carries on prophetic discourse.

The two oracles here have striking continuity with the two oracles following. Key words repeat in the same collocations (Condamin), doubling as catchwords connecting the oracle clusters:

I	*Up! advance to*	*qûmû ʿălû ʾel-*	v 28b
II	*Their camels*	*gĕmallêhem*	v 29b

. . . . *Hazor*	*ḥāṣôr*	v 30a
III *Up! advance to*	*qûmû ʿălû ʾel-*	v 31a
IV *Their camels*	*gĕmallêhem*	v 32a
. . . . . . *Hazor*	*ḥāṣôr*	v 33a

There appear to be no catchwords connecting to the prior Damascus oracle.

NOTES

49:28. *Up! advance to Kedar! Devastate the people of the east!* Asyndeton, on which see Note for 4:5. More asyndeton occurs in 49:30 and 31.

Kedar. Hebrew *qēdār*. A group of North Arabian tribes recorded in the OT as descending from the "sons of Ishmael" (Gen 25:13; 1 Chr 1:29). The Kedarites lived in the Syrian–Arabian Desert east of Edom. They were known for their tents made from black goat hair (Ps 120:5; Song 1:5; *qdr* = "blackness"). The preferred merchants in lambs, rams, and goats (Ezek 27:21; cf. Isa 60:7), they were also good archers (Isa 21:16–17). Jeremiah refers to Kedar on an earlier occasion (2:10). Kedar and its desert neighbors receive mention also in the Assyrian and Babylonian sources—quite often, in fact, because they were attacked and despoiled by a succession of Assyrian and Babylonian armies. Tiglath-pileser III (745–727), Sargon II (721–705), Sennacherib (704–681), and Esarhaddon (680–669) all campaigned against them, carrying off booty as well as their gods (ANET[3] 284, 286, 291–92). Kedar gave Assurbanipal trouble in the general rebellion of 652 B.C., but when things were brought under control, the Assyrian king took punitive measures (Bright 1981: 314; cf. ANET[3] 297–301). Isaiah delivers an oracle against Arabia in Isa 21:13–17.

the kings of Hazor. Hebrew *mamlĕkôt ḥāṣôr*. For *mamlĕkôt* meaning "kings," see Albright 1950–51: 34. The T has "kingdoms of Hazor." The LXX goes a different way, translating "the queen of the courtyard" (*aulē* = Hebrew *ḥāṣēr*). "Hazor" is not here the well-known city in Palestine, and probably not a city at all, but rather the country of the *ḥăṣērîm*, i.e., villages and fortified enclosures of desert-dwelling Arab tribes living east and southeast of Palestine (Gen 25:16; Isa 42:11). S. R. Driver makes a comparison with Ar *ḥāḍir*, which refers to desert people living in settlements near a water source (cf. Lane, 590b). Akkadian *ḥaṣāru* means "enclosure for sheep" (CAD 6: 130; AHw 1: 331). Blayney suggests a connection to the Arabs descended from Hazermaveth (*ḥăṣar-māwet*) in Gen 10:26, identified now with the incense-producing Hadhramaut kingdom in South Arabia that flourished from the seventh to the fifth century B.C. (OEANE 2: 452–53; ABD 3: 85–86).

whom Nebuchadrezzar, king of Babylon, struck down. Kedarites also gave Nebuchadrezzar trouble, for the Babylonian Chronicle (BM 21946: rev. 9–10; Wiseman 1956: 70–71; ANET[3] 564) reports an attack on the Arabs (= Kedar) in the king's western campaign of 599/8 B.C., just prior to subjugating Jerusalem, at which time their desert settlements were raided from a base in Syria (Malamat 1956: 254–55; Wiseman 1956: 31–32; 1981: 30–31). Josephus, quoting Berossus, also mentions this campaign (*Against Apion* i 133, 137). In the list of kings and nations slated to drink Yahweh's cup of wrath in 25:17–26, various desert peoples are mentioned: "Dedan, and Tema, and Buz, and all who crop the hair at the temples; and all the kings of Arabia, and all the kings of the mixed races who dwell in the desert" (vv 23–24).

Nebuchadrezzar. On the spelling, see Note for 21:2.

Up! advance to Kedar! Hebrew *qûmû ʿălû ʾel-qēdār.* Compare the similar idiom, "Up, and let us go / attack" (*qûmû wĕnaʿăleh*) in 6:4–5 and 31:6. Here Yahweh is giving battle orders to Nebuchadrezzar and the Babylonian army (Bach 1962: 53; Christensen 1975: 210).

Devastate the people of the east! The LXX again goes its own way, with "fill (*plēsate*) the sons of Qedem." There is nice assonance in the parallel terms *qēdār* ("Kedar") and *qedem* ("east"). The "people of the east" (*bĕnê-qedem*) is a general OT term for Kedar and other tribes living in the Syrian–Arabian Desert possessing quantities of sheep, goats, camels, oxen, and asses, and enriching nations far and wide with their celebrated store of tribal wisdom (Gen 29:1; 1 Kgs 4:30). Many of the animals were gained by plundering. Job, from the land of Uz, was said to be the greatest of the "people of the east" (Job 1:3). In Judges, the "people of the east" are associated with Midianites and Amalekites (Judg 6:3, 33; 7:12; 8:10), Judg 6:1–6 being a showcase example of the problem these desert raiders posed for Israel during its early settlement years. In the present time, according to Ezekiel, the Ammonites and Moabites will suffer similarly (Ezek 25:1–11). Here, however, the process is going to work in reverse, with the "people of the east" being themselves victims of plunder. The same is promised to them in Isa 11:14. Qedem is mentioned in a twentieth-century B.C. Egyptian classic, "The Story of Si-nuhe" (29–30, 180–84, 219; ANET³ 18–22), although here it denotes simply an area east of Phoenician Byblos. Ephʿal (1982: 10) says this is a region on the western border of the Syrian–Arabian Desert. In any case, during a year-and-a-half sojourn in Qedem, our Egyptian traveler (Sinuhe) reports dispensing wisdom to his host, eating sumptuously the choicest of cattle, engaging in expeditions of plunder, and showing skill with the bow—all activities one expects to find among a desert people of the east.

29. *Their tents and their flocks they shall take away.* For a picture of Assurbanipal's soldiers sacking and burning Arab tents, see Yadin 1963: 451. In Isa 60:7, Kedar's flocks will come to Zion.

their curtains. Or "their tent hangings." Hebrew *yĕrîʿôtêhem.* Judah's destroyed tents and curtains are lamented in 4:20 and 10:20.

all their gear. Hebrew *kĕlî* is a general term meaning "goods" (RSV) or "gear." The Babylonian Chronicle says that Nebuchadnezzar "took much plunder from the Arabs, their possessions, animals and gods" (BM 21946: rev. 10; Wiseman 1956: 70–71).

Their camels they shall carry off for themselves. Reading *lāhem* as a reflexive, "for themselves" (Isa 3:9; cf. GKC §135i). The enemy will plunder Kedar's camels. Tiglath-pileser III (745–727) in one of his campaigns against the Arabs, records as booty: 30,000 camels, 20,000 (heads) of cattle, and 5,000 containers of spices (*ANET*³ 284; *CS II* 288). A relief in the British Museum shows a Bedouin queen surrendering to Tiglath-pileser, bringing her camels with her; for a picture, see Barnett and Falkner 1962: 75. For other pictures of Assyrians carrying away camels as tribute on reliefs of Shalmaneser III (859–825), see *ANEP*² #351, #353, and #355 (pp. 120–22, 291).

and they shall call out upon them: 'Terror on every side!' This colon has given commentators difficulty in spite of the familiar Jeremianic expression "Terror on every side!" Ehrlich (1912: 362) took the subject to be the Kedarites and the suffix "against them" as a reference to the Chaldeans. Thus because of the Chaldeans, Kedar will be screaming, "Terror on every side!" But the shout is better placed in the mouths of the attackers. The NAB has it right: the enemy, riding off on camels they have seized, further terrorize their Kedarite victims by shouting, "Terror on every side!" A relief in the British Museum from the time of Tiglath-pileser III shows an Arab riding off on a camel with Assyrian cavalry in pursuit; for a picture, see Barnett and Falkner 1962: 61.

'Terror on every side!' A favorite Jeremianic expression; see 46:5 and Note on 6:25.

30. *Flee! Wander all about! Go deep to dwell!* Asyndeton, also assonance in *nūsû nūdû* ("Flee! Wander all about!"). The same directive is issued to the Moabites in 48:6 and the people of Dedan in 49:8. There is irony in Yahweh's telling people to seek a refuge that will do them no good.

Wander all about! Hebrew *nūdû mĕ'ōâ*. For this meaning of *nûd*, see 4:1 and 50:3, 8. The T has "Go into exile." The LXX omits, which could be due to haplography (homoeoteleuton: *w . . . w*). This can hardly be a doublet of the previous imperative (*pace* McKane; cf. Janzen 1973: 25).

Go deep to dwell! Hebrew *he'mîqû lāšebet*. Reading here an H-stem imperative with the LXX; see Note on 49:7. The T also reads an imperative but continues thinking of exile; its translation: "Go afar off to dwell." There will be no exile, however, because there will be no escape.

to dwell . . . dwellers. Hebrew *lāšebet yōšĕbê* is a play on words, as also in 49:8.

dwellers of Hazor. On the meaning of "Hazor" and the LXX translation, "you that dwell in the courtyard," see v 28.

For Nebuchadrezzar, king of Babylon, has counseled against you a counsel and planned against you a plan. The construction "counseled . . . a counsel" and "planned . . . a plan" is the same as in 49:20. On the Jeremianic coinage "to plan a plan," see Note for 29:11. "Nebuchadrezzar" is omitted by the LXX, but to its loss (see Rhetoric and Composition). This subscription, which expands upon what is said in the oracles about Yahweh directing the attack on

Kedar, brings to a conclusion what was stated in the superscription about Nebuchadrezzar dealing Kedar a fatal blow.

Nebuchadrezzar. On the spelling, see Note on 21:2.

MESSAGE AND AUDIENCE

Yahweh in the first oracle begins by issuing battle orders to attack Kedar and
bring devastation to the people of the east. Turning to address another audience, he says that the tents and flocks of these desert tribes shall be taken away,
and with them everything else in their possession. In a second oracle, Yahweh
says that the attackers will carry off camels belonging to these people for themselves. Riding away on these "ships of the desert," they will shout, "Terror on
every side!" The oracle ends on an ironic note. Yahweh tells the victims of
plunder to flee, wander hither and yon, dig deep into the ground that they
might escape the enemy. But will these "dwellers of Hazor," who only now are
named, save their lives or become themselves victims?

Because of a final irony stating the judgment in veiled terms, it was necessary
to give this oracle and the one preceding clarification. The prose frame does
that, saying that Nebuchadrezzar both conceived and carried out this judgment against Kedar, Hazor, and the people of the east. But the audience knows
from the oracles that the driving force in this punitive action was Yahweh.

A date just prior to 599 B.C., when Nebuchadrezzar attacked the desert Arabs
before coming to subdue Jerusalem, would suit both oracles (Hyatt 1956: 283).
The superscription and subscription can be dated to that time or later, and can
be judged essentially correct.

2. A Desert Nation to the Winds (49:31–33)

49 [31]Up! advance to a nation at ease
  who dwells in security
    —oracle of Yahweh
No doors and no bars for it
  they dwell alone

[32]And their camels shall be for booty
  and their noisy cattle for spoil

For I will scatter them to every wind
  those who crop the hair at the temples
And from every one of its sides
  I will bring their disaster
    —oracle of Yahweh.

[33]Hazor shall become a den of jackals
  a desolation forever

No person shall inhabit there
and no human shall sojourn in her.

RHETORIC AND COMPOSITION

MT 49:31–33 = LXX 30:26–28 (Ziegler 30:9–11). The upper limit here is set by the prose conclusion to the first two Kedar–Hazor oracles in v 30b. The present verses contain two more Kedar–Hazor oracles, in poetry, which balance the prior oracles (see Rhetoric and Composition for 49:28–30). The lower limit of the unit is set at v 33, where M^L, M^A, and M^P all have a *setumah*. Verse 34 begins a new oracle against Elam.

Oracle I (vv 31–32a) is three bicolons, not counting the messenger formula, which may be divided into stanzas with a 2:1 line division. Oracle II (vv 32b–33) is four bicolons, not counting the messenger formula, and is best divided 2:2. The LXX omits the formula in v 31, leading some commentators (Cornill; Rudolph; Bright; Holladay) to judge it an MT plus. Without the formula Nebuchadnezzar becomes the speaker of v 31, but this mistakenly assumes that 30b introduces 31, when in fact 30b concludes what precedes. Yahweh is then the speaker of both oracles, just as he is speaker of both oracles in vv 28b–30a. The messenger formula in v 31 should therefore be retained. Also, we must not assume with Rudolph that the mesenger formula in v 32 marks the end of an oracle, making v 33 a later add-on. Verse 33 belongs to Oracle II, as a close look at all four Kedar–Hazor oracles makes clear (see Rhetoric and Composition for 49:28–30). Messenger formulas usually begin or end oracles, but sometimes they come in other locations (see Rhetoric and Composition for 6:1–7 and 6:16–21).

Oracle II has balancing phrases in both of its stanzas:

I	*For I will scatter them to every wind*	*wĕzērîtîm lĕkol-rûaḥ*	v 32b
	....		
	And from every one of its sides	*ûmikkol-ʿăbārāyw*	v 32c
	I will bring	*ʾābîʾ*	
II	....		v 33
	....		
	No person shall inhabit there	*lōʾ-yēšēb šām ʾîš*	
	and no human shall sojourn in her	*wĕlōʾ-yāgûr bāh ben-ʾādām*	

Stanza I varies the normal parallelism by alternating the position of the verb in each bicolon.

For catchwords linking to prior Kedar–Hazor oracles, see Rhetoric and Composition for 49:28–30. The connection ahead to the Elam oracles is made with these catchwords:

v 32   *I will scatter them to every wind*   v 36b   *I will scatter them to all these winds*

NOTES

49:31. *Up! advance to a nation at ease.* Asyndeton, but with only two verbs. Yahweh is again shouting out battle orders to an attacker, as in v 28b. To be "at ease" (*šĕlêw*) is to be undisturbed (Job 16:12), to be prosperous (Job 21:23; Ps 73:12). In the postexilic period, Zechariah recalls when Jerusalem was inhabited and "at ease" (Zech 7:7). Desert tribes with their great wealth were sufficiently isolated to live largely undisturbed, but this looks to be a mere holiday march for the Babylonians, as resistance will be impossible (Cheyne).

who dwells in security. Hebrew *yôšēb lābeṭaḥ.* In the divine economy a settled, secure existence can presage danger and destruction (Judg 18:7–10, 27–28; Amos 6:1; Zeph 2:15; Isa 47:8), or else come as a blessing (Deut 33:28; Hos 2:20[Eng 2:18]; Jer 23:6; 32:37; 33:16; Ezek 28:26).

No doors and no bars for it, they dwell alone. Compare the description of Arab settlements in Ezek 38:11. Double doors (dual *dĕlātayim*) used in antiquity needed a horizontal bar (*bĕrîaḥ*) on the inside, anchored in sockets, to keep them from being broken open at the center. On the doors of a city gate, see Yadin 1963: 21–22. The pairing of doors / gates and bars occurs elsewhere in Deut 3:5; 1 Sam 23:7; Lam 2:9; and Sir 49:13. Desert tribes did not need this security, since they lived alone.

32. *And their camels shall be for booty.* See 49:29 on the plundering of camels.

their noisy cattle. Hebrew *hămôn miqnêhem.* The term *hămôn* can be assigned a double-duty function in the bicolon, which is to say, the (large number of) rounded-up camels will also be noisy. Desert Arabs also had cattle, as attested in Assyrian booty lists. Tiglath-pileser III took from the Arabs 20,000 (head) of cattle. A relief in the British Museum shows the cattle captured by Tiglath-pileser; for a picture, see Barnett and Falkner 1962: 79.

For I will scatter them to every wind. A winnowing metaphor (4:11; 15:7; 31:10; 49:32, 36; 51:2), although here, as in v 36, 31:10, and 51:2, the accent is on dispersion rather than separation. The verb *zrh* is a favorite of Ezekiel (see Ezek 5:2, 10, 12; 6:5; 12:14–15; and elsewhere).

those who crop the hair at the temples. See 25:23 and discussion in Note for 9:25[Eng 9:26].

And from every one of its sides. Hebrew *ûmikkol-ʿăbārāyw.* I.e., "from every direction."

their disaster. Hebrew *ʾêdām.* The noun *ʾêd* occurs earlier in 49:8.

33. *Hazor shall become a den of jackals.* A Jeremianic expression embodying a standard curse; see 10:22 and Note on 9:10[Eng 9:11]. On Hazor and the LXX translation "courtyard," see Note for 49:28.

a desolation forever. Hebrew *šĕmāmâ* ("desolation") is a common term in Jeremiah and Ezekiel (see Note on 12:10), appearing elsewhere in the Foreign Nation Oracles in Jer 49:2 and 50:13. According to 25:12; 51:26, and 62, Babylon will become "eternal desolations" (*šimmôt ʿôlām*).

No person shall inhabit there, and no human shall sojourn in her. The bicolon is repeated verbatim in v 18 and 50:40b, and with variations in 51:43b. For land and city curses in the book of Jeremiah, see Note on 48:9.

human. Hebrew *ben-'ādām.* Literally "son of man" = man.

MESSAGE AND AUDIENCE

These oracles cover much the same ground as the first two Kedar–Hazor oracles, with the one difference that they speak in a more straightforward manner about Yahweh's judgment. The first oracle cluster ended on an ironic note (v 30a). Here Yahweh begins Oracle I by once again issuing battle orders to a presumably Babylonian army. It is to march against a nation resting comfortably, dwelling securely without walls, city gates, or bars on the doors. These people live alone, and rarely need worry—as city folk do—about armies coming to attack. But Yahweh tells the attacking band—otherwise another audience—that camels and much cattle will be booty for the victorious host.

Oracle II in its entirety is directed to an unidentified audience. Yahweh says he will scatter these oddly-shaven folk to winds that they know better than anyone. From every side disaster will come. No reason for the judgment is given, but the audience knows that these desert Arabs will receive the very treatment they so mercilessly inflict upon others. Hazor is given the curse of a city: it will become a den of jackals with not a soul living there or passing through.

These oracles can be assigned the same date as the previous Kedar–Hazor oracles, just prior to 599 B.C., when Nebuchadnezzar campaigned against the Arab tribes before going on to Jerusalem.

I. ELAM TOO SHALL BE SCATTERED (49:34–39)

49 [34]What came as the word of Yahweh to Jeremiah the prophet concerning Elam in the beginning of the reign of Zedekiah, king of Judah:
  [35]Thus said Yahweh of hosts:
  Look I am shattering the bow of Elam
    the first line of their strength.
[36]And I will bring to Elam four winds
    from the four corners of the heavens
  And I will scatter them to all these winds, and there shall be no nation
    to which the dispersed of Elam[1] do not come.[2]

[37]And I will break Elam before their enemies
    before those who seek their life
  And I will bring evil upon them

---

[1]Reading the Q *'êlām* ("Elam"); Kt has *'ôlām* ("forever").
[2]Reading with several MSS, Symm, T, and Vg the plural *yābō'û* ("they come").

my burning anger
—oracle of Yahweh.

And I will send after them the sword
    until I have made an end of them
[38]And I will set my throne in Elam
    and I will banish from there king and princes
    —oracle of Yahweh.

[39]But it will happen in the days afterward, I will surely restore the fortunes[3] of Elam—oracle of Yahweh.

RHETORIC AND COMPOSITION

MT 49:34–39 = LXX 25:14–20 (Ziegler 25:14–26:1). The upper limit here is marked by *setumahs* in M[L], M[A], and M[P] before v 34. The lower limit is set by a *setumah* in M[L] and *petuḥahs* in M[A] and M[P] after v 39, which is also the chapter division. The verses contain a superscription (v 34) and four brief oracles (vv 35–36, v 37ab, vv 37c–38, and v 39), the same number spoken against Kedar–Hazor. All have messenger formulas, although the two in vv 37 and 38 are omitted in the LXX. These should be retained (*pace* Cornill and Holladay). Verse 39 is a standard restoration oracle, similar to those concluding the Moabite and Ammonite oracle collections (48:47; 49:6).

The MT superscription appears to have been divided up in the LXX, part of it having been made into a subscription (Lundbom 1975: 27–28 [= 1997: 41–42]). In the LXX, the Elam oracles begin the Foreign Nation Collection in 25:14–20, where they are provided with the following frame:

25:14 What Jeremiah said concerning the nation of *Elam*:

25:20 In the beginning of the reign of Zedekiah the king,
        this word came about *Elam*.

Note how a divine command and its execution by the prophet are similarly broken up to frame two oracles in 36:27–32.

The chief difficulty here is deciding whether the oracles are prose or poetry. Prose particles are frequent (*'et* five times in vv 35, 37, and 39; *'ăšer* once in v 36b); however, most modern Versions follow *BHS* and take vv 35–38 as poetry, some excepting v 36b, which is judged prose expansion (Cornill took all of v 36 as secondary). Commentators generally concur, with Rudolph and Holladay adding v 37c as prose expansion from 9:15b[16b]. The RSV takes these verses as prose, and NJV the same, except for v 38, which it formats as poetry. Oracles I–III are taken here as poetry and Oracle IV as prose, with v 36b of Oracle I judged to be prose expansion. The point is also made quite often that

---

[3]Reading the Q for both *'āšîb* ("I will restore") and *šĕbût* ("fortunes"); cf. 33:26; 48:47; and 49:6.

these oracles are lackluster. Jones says they are without "poetic distinction." Holladay notes a lack of specifics, which might be expected for a nation so far distant from Judah, but having analyzed the vocabulary, Holladay concludes that the material is authentic to Jeremiah, which it does seem to be.

Oracles I and II, both originally double bicolons, have key word repetitions that were noted already with minor change by Condamin:

I ....*Elam*   v 35
  ....
  And I will bring ....   *wĕhēbē'tî*   v 36
  ....

II ....*Elam* ....   v 37ab
  ....
  And I will bring ....   *wĕhēbē'tî*
  ....

Oracle III, another double bicolon, has key word linkage to the hopeful Oracle IV in prose:

III And I will send *after them* the sword   *'aḥărêhem*   v 37c

IV But it will happen *in the days afterward*   *bĕ'aḥărît*   v 39

Catchwords connecting to the prior Kedar–Hazor oracles are the following:

v 36b *I will scatter them to all these winds*   v 32 *I will scatter them to every wind*

No catchwords connect to the Babylon oracles, which constitute a separate collection in chaps. 50–51. One cannot, then, combine the Elam oracle with the Babylon collection (*pace* Dicou 1989, who argues that the historical references to Zedekiah in 49:34 and 51:59 form an inclusio).

NOTES

49:34. *What came as the word of Yahweh to Jeremiah the prophet concerning Elam in the beginning of the reign of Zedekiah, king of Judah.* A superscription of the type found elsewhere in 1:2; 14:1; 46:1; and 47:1.

Elam. During the seventh century the Elamites and Medes occupied what later became Persia and is present-day Iran. Elam was located in the hill country east of the Tigris, opposite southern Babylonia. The nation was ancient (Gen 14:1, 9), with its capital, Susa, attaining later prominence in the postexilic period (Esth 9:6; Dan 8:2). In the table of nations, Elam is listed as one of the sons of Shem (Gen 10:22). Jeremiah alone among the prophets delivers oracles against Elam, and the question is often asked why he should address a nation so far distant. The answer would seem to be that Elam was very much a part of world affairs in the seventh century, and may have survived in some form into the early sixth century, in which case its mention would be a necessity if Yahweh's judgment is to encompass all nations. The kings of Media and Elam are in line for Yahweh's cup of wrath in 25:25. During the seventh century Elam was in continual conflict with the Assyrians. Assurbanipal attacked Elam following the general rebellion of 652 B.C., and after a series of further battles, he destroyed Susa, bringing Elamite independence to an end ca. 640 B.C. (Luckenbill 1927: 355, no. 920; cf. Bright 1981: 314; CAH 3/1: 155). Assyrian triumphs at the river Ulai and at Hamanu are depicted on reliefs in the British Museum; for pictures, see Parrot (1961: 42) and Yadin (1963: 442–49). Exactly what happened to Elam following this defeat until its absorption a century later into the Persian Empire (Ezra 4:9; Neh 1:1) is unclear. The present oracles are the only biblical evidence of a continued Elamite existence into the Neo-Babylonian period, and extrabiblical evidence is scant and somewhat uncertain (see below). Ezekiel has Elam already consigned to the grave (Ezek 32:24–25). But there was a remnant (cf. Isa 11:11), and in the NT Elamites are mentioned as being present at Pentecost (Acts 2:9).

   in the beginning of the reign of Zedekiah, king of Judah. Rudolph takes *rēʾšît malkût* ("beginning of the reign") to mean the accession year, which for Zedekiah would have been from the exile of Jehoiachin to the 1st of Nisan, 597 B.C. But the phrase is probably nontechnical, as in 26:1; 27:1; and 28:1, referring simply to a time early in Zedekiah's reign (see Note for 26:1). A damaged portion of the Babylonian Chronicle says that Nebuchadnezzar marched against an enemy in 596/5 B.C., who panicked and turned back. Wiseman originally read "the king of El[am]" at two critical junctures but later said the restoration, while possible, remained doubtful (BM 21946: rev. 17, 20; Wiseman 1956: 72–73; 1985: 34). Grayson (1975a: 102) retained one of the readings, and Kuhrt (1995: 592) more recently assumes that an action of some sort took place. Malamat (1979: 214) says that Elam did attack Babylonia in this year, and that the present oracle was directed against that action. If a clash did occur between Nebuchadnezzar and Elam in 596/5 B.C., it would nicely corroborate the date given here. *CHI* (2: 23) says that an Elamite pretender seems to have unified the nation after the devastation of 640 B.C., and that Elam had dealings with both Nabopolassar and Nebuchadnezzar during the Neo-Babylonian period.

   Zedekiah. Hebrew *ṣidqîyâ*. This shortened spelling of the king's name is found also in 27:12; 28:1; 29:3; and 1 Chr 3:16.

   35. *Thus said Yahweh of hosts.* The LXX omits "of hosts," as elsewhere. See Appendix VI.

   Look I. The LXX omits this common beginning to the Jeremianic oracle, which occurs elsewhere in the Foreign Nation Oracles in 46:25; 47:2, 5; and 49:5 (see further Note on 1:5). Read the MT. First person divine speech dominates all four of the Elam oracles.

   I am shattering the bow of Elam. The Elamites, particularly those inhabiting the mountainous areas, were known as skillful bowmen (Isa 22:6; Strabo, *Geog.*

xvi 1.18; Livy xxxvii 40.9), making this a particularly apt metaphor for the nation's overthrow. Bow = strength (so T). For the expression "break / shatter the
bow," see also 1 Sam 2:4; Hos 1:5; and 2:20[Eng 2:18].

the first line of their strength. Hebrew *rēʾšît gĕbûrātām.* A number of translations (RSV; NAB; NJV; NIV) render *rēʾšît* as "mainstay," i.e., the best of the
Elamite army. The T and the LXX: "the chief of their power."

36. *And I will bring to Elam four winds from the four corners of the heavens.*
Or "the four quarters of heaven" (RSV; NEB; NJV). The metaphor intends
maximal judgment. The T has "four kings" for "four winds." On "the four
winds of the heavens," see also Ezek 37:9 (maximal restoration in Ezekiel's
"valley of the dry bones" vision); Zech 2:10[Eng 2:6]; 6:5; and Dan 8:8.

And I will scatter them. The verb *zrh* occurs often in Jeremiah and Ezekiel;
see Note on 49:32. Exile is envisioned, as is evident in what follows.

and there shall be no nation to which the dispersed of Elam do not come. Hyperbole for "all the neighboring nations" (Calvin).

37. *And I will break Elam before their enemies.* On the verb *ḥtt*, see Note for
1:17. Yahweh will bring about the collapse of Elam. The perfect form of the
verb presently has a *waw consecutive* for future tense. But since this begins a
new oracle, the *waw* may originally not have been present, in which case the
verb would be a prophetic perfect: "I have broken. . . ."

those who seek their life. Hebrew *mĕbaqšê napšām.* The expression is common in Jeremiah; see 19:7; 21:7; 44:30; and 46:26; cf. 4:30 (poetry).

And I will bring evil upon them. Hebrew *wĕhēbēʾtî ʿălêhem rāʿâ.* For the Jeremianic expression "(Look), I am bringing evil" and discussion on Yahweh as
bringer of evil, see Note on 6:19.

my burning anger. Hebrew *ḥărôn ʾappî.* Another Jeremianic expression, see
Note on 4:8.

And I will send after them the sword until I have made an end of them. A repetition of the judgment promised to Judah in 9:15[Eng 9:16] and 44:27. On a
personified sword under Yahweh's command, see also Amos 9:4.

38. *And I will set my throne in Elam.* Yahweh, the King, will set his throne in
Elam to judge it. Compare 1:15; 39:3; and 43:10–13.

and I will banish from there king and princes. This is what Assurbanipal did
after his victory over Elam in 640 B.C., the Babylonian princes similarly when
they came and sat in Jerusalem's Middle Gate in 586 B.C. — moving immediately to pursue and capture Zedekiah (39:4–7), and what every king does once
victory over the enemy is achieved. In the NT, see Revelation 19–20.

39. *But it will happen in the days afterward, I will surely restore the fortunes of
Elam — oracle of Yahweh.* This formulaic oracle repeats (with reversal) the formulaic oracle ending the Moab oracles in 48:47. See also 46:26 and 49:6. The
verse should not be omitted with Holladay, now that restoration promises are
known to be more integral to judgment oracles and laments than was formerly
imagined. See Note on 49:6.

in the days afterward. Hebrew *bĕʾaḥărît hayyāmîm.* On this expression, see
Note for 23:20.

I will restore the fortunes. Hebrew *ʾāšîb ʾet-šĕbût* (Q). On this phrase and its variants, also the use of an internal H-stem as we have here, see Note for 29:14. On the inclusion of this expression in ancient Mesopotamian city laments, see Note for 48:47.

MESSAGE AND AUDIENCE

Yahweh in Oracle I says that he is shattering the bow of Elam, a people known for skill in wielding this weapon. He will take out their first line of defense. Yahweh will bring all four winds from his storehouse in the heavens, and they will blow Elam away. To this oracle is later added a word the original audience might already have assumed, namely, that Yahweh will scatter Elam among all its neighbors. The hyperbole, however, makes for a more spectacular conclusion.

Oracle II abandons metaphorical language and in discourse sounding almost like prose speaks straightforwardly about Yahweh's breaking Elam and bringing upon the nation evil in the heat of divine anger. Oracle III has Yahweh sending forth his all-consuming sword, after which he says he will himself become King in Elam, destroying the pretender now at the helm of this once-great nation. The princes will go down with him. In Oracle IV Yahweh offers a mitigating word for the future, telling a Judahite audience that he will restore Elam's treasures taken away by a succession of Assyrian and Babylonian armies.

The superscription places these oracles in the beginning of Zedekiah's reign, which would be after Nebuchadnezzar's subjugation of Jerusalem and the exile of Jehoiachin with his royal family in 597 B.C. If the Babylonian king went on to attack Elam in 596/5 B.C., this oracle would be a timely word against a nation that was only a shadow of its former self.

> So be it Lord; thy throne shall never
> Like earth's proud empires, pass away.
> Thy kingdom stands, and grows forever
> Till all thy creatures own thy sway.
> > John Ellerton (1826–93)

J. AND WHAT ABOUT BABYLON? (50:1–51:58)

1. Babylon Is Taken (50:1–3)

50 [1]The word that Yahweh spoke to Babylon, to the land of the Chaldeans, through Jeremiah the prophet.
[2]Declare among the nations and make heard
set up a flag! make heard!
keep it not hidden, say:

Babylon is taken
> Bel is very ashamed
>> Merodach is shattered
Her images are very ashamed
> her idols are shattered

³For a nation from the north has come up upon her
> it, it will make her land a desolation
and an inhabitant will not be in her
> from human to beast
>> they are wandering, they are gone.

RHETORIC AND COMPOSITION

MT 50:1–3 = LXX 27:1–3. The present verses contain the superscription to the entire Babylonian collection in chaps. 50–51 (v 1), followed by a lead poem — most likely a divine oracle — announcing Babylon's doom and a discrediting of its gods (vv 2–3). The judgment of v 2bc is reiterated in 51:56bc, and the judgment of v 3 reiterated in the colophon of 51:62, combining to make an inclusio for the collection as a whole:

50:2bc	Babylon *is taken*	*nilkĕdâ* . . .
	Bel is very ashamed	
	Merodach *is shattered*	*ḥat* . . .
	Her images are very ashamed	
	her idols *are shattered*	*ḥattû* . . .
51:56b	*And* her warriors *have been taken*	*wĕnilkĕdû* . . .
	their bows *shattered*	*ḥittĕtâ* . . .
50:3	it, it will make her land *a desolation*	. . . . *lĕšammâ*
	and an inhabitant will not be in her	*welo'-yihyeh yošeb bah*
	from human to beast	*mē'ādām wĕ'ad-bĕhēmâ*
51:62	. . . *without there being an inhabitant in it,*	. . . *lĕbiltî hĕyôt-bô yôšēb*
	from human to beast;	*lĕmē'ādām wĕ'ad-bĕhēmâ*
	indeed eternal *desolations it shall be*	*kî-šimmôt* . . . . . . *tihyeh*

The directive in 50:2a to proclaim to the nations Babylon's capture makes another inclusio, with a shout celebrating the same at the conclusion of chap. 50 (Aitken 1984: 30):

50:2a	Declare *among the nations and make heard*	. . . *baggôyim wĕhašmî'û.*
	. . . *make heard!* . . . *Babylon is taken*	*hašmî'û* . . . *nilkĕdâ bābel*
50:46	*Babylon is captured!* . . .	*nitpĕśâ bābel*
	. . . *among the nations is heard*	. . . *baggôyim nišmā'*

The lead oracle here is a directive from Yahweh to Jeremiah and others (plural imperatives) to make public the news of Babylon's demise. In the colophon (51:59–64) we are told how this directive was carried out. Jeremiah prepared a scroll of his Babylonian utterances, gave it to Seraiah ben Neriah, who was brother to Baruch, the scribe, and instructed him to read it publicly in Babylon when he arrived there with King Zedekiah in 594/3 B.C. This incident parallels the preparation and public reading by Baruch of Jeremiah's first scroll, which is recorded in chap. 36.

Earlier commentators, e.g., Giesebrecht, Duhm, Peake, and Cornill, took chaps. 50–51 to be one large oracle against Babylon. These chapters, however, are no different from others in the book, including the long chap. 48 against Moab, containing relatively brief oracles and other prophetic utterances joined together by catchwords, theme, and audience. Short poems within 50–51 were recognized already by T. H. Robinson (1917–18), whose form-critical judgments have been reaffirmed and improved upon by Reimer (1993: iv) more recently. Studies by Aitken (1984) and Bellis (1995) that find large compositional units in the chapters (Aitken: six movements with smaller sections; Bellis: six poems, two of which have additions) are unconvincing. Bellis has an opening poem of 19 verses (50:2–20) and a closing poem of 24 verses (51:34–58), both far too long.

A long line of critical scholars from Eichhorn to McKane have judged the entire Babylonian collection to postdate Jeremiah, even though much of the vocabulary and phraseology here is precisely what one finds in bona fide Jeremiah poetry (see Rhetoric and Composition for 46:1). Smelik (1987), who dates the Babylon oracles between 560 and 550 B.C., thinks they compensate for Jeremiah's pro-Babylonian stance in chaps. 27–29, 39–40, intending to show that the prophet was not a friend of Babylon and thus not a traitor. This latter point may have merit, but does not require a midexilic date for the composition, collection, and integration of the Babylon oracles into the rest of the Jeremiah book (cf. 51:59–64). From a theological point of view, it is important to affirm that the prophet who views Babylon as Yahweh's instrument of judgment sees also a Babylon deserving of judgment itself, otherwise the great genius of prophetic theology is reduced to an impoverished and unacceptable prophetic politic. Reinhold Niebuhr (1935: 139) said many years ago:

> In prophetic religion there is a more genuine dialectic in which the movements of history are in one moment the instruments of God and in the next come under his condemnation. Thus Babylon and the king of the Medes are regarded by the prophets as the instruments of vengeance in God's hands. But that does not mean that they are better than others and that they will not be cut down in time. They pronounce doom upon Babylon as well as upon Israel.

This view of Yahweh's working in history is clearly stated in the Song of Moses in Deuteronomy 32.

The position taken here with regard to chaps. 50–51 is essentially the one taken by Holladay, i.e., that these chapters contain a substantial core of Jeremiah utterances to which have been added some non-Jeremianic oracles and supplements of various kinds. The oracles and poems here convey judgment in a very general sense, lacking specific names and places such as we find in oracles against other nations in chaps. 46–49, especially the Moabite oracles of chap. 48. Lacking too is the audience engagement present in other Foreign Nation Oracles, and especially in oracles delivered to Judah. For example, there are no rhetorical questions in the Babylon oracles. Also, simulated battle orders in 50:14, 29, and especially 51:11a, 12, lack the irony present in orders of the same type barked out rapid-fire against Egypt in 46:3–4. And this is to say nothing of the prediction that the Medes would conquer Babylon (51:11, 28), which never materialized. All of this points to a date prior to 594 B.C. for most of the Babylon utterances, corroborating the tradition in 51:59–64 that Seraiah prepared a scroll of Jeremiah's oracles for a symbolic reading in Babylon in 594/3, anticipating Babylon's demise more distantly than what the "peace prophets" envisioned. Diction in the present poem (vv 2–3) is clearly that of Jeremiah—otherwise it has to be that of a skillful imitator, which is an uneconomical hypothesis and one lacking real conviction. For further discussion of the authenticity and provenance of Jeremiah's Foreign Nation Oracles, see Rhetoric and Composition for 46:1.

While the RSV and NRSV take v 3 as prose, other modern Versions and numerous scholars (T. H. Robinson 1917–18; Volz; Weiser; Rudolph; Bright; Thompson; Holladay; Keown et al.; McKane) take both vv 2 and 3 as poetry, which is the better judgment. A new oracle in prose begins v 4 (NEB; REB; NJV; NSB), aiding in the demarcation of the two units. The messenger formula in v 4a signals a new beginning, as does the *setumah* before v 4 in M^P. M^L and M^A have no sections here.

The present poem has two stanzas. Stanza I (v 2) is two tricolons and a bicolon. Stanza II (v 3) is a bicolon and a tricolon. Stanza I has repetition in each of its three lines:

I   . . . . *make heard*   v 2
         . . . . *make heard*
         . . . .
         . . . .
         . . . . *is very ashamed*
         . . . . *is shattered*
         . . . . *are very ashamed*
         . . . . *are shattered*

The LXX omits the second occurrence of "make heard," and the verbs "very ashamed" and "shattered" in the final line. The MT reading is better rhetorically (Kessler 1973: 19–20), and should be retained.

Catchwords connecting to the following oracle:

v 3 *they are gone*   *hālākû*   v 4 *they shall go*   *yēlēkû*

NOTES

50:1. *The word that Yahweh spoke to Babylon, to the land of the Chaldeans, through Jeremiah the prophet.* The LXX omits "to the land of the Chaldeans, through Jeremiah the prophet," which has given rise to the suggestion that the attribution to Jeremiah of the Babylon oracles is a later development. However, attribution is assumed in the colophon (51:59–64), which is present in the LXX [28:59–64]. We need not, in any case, follow Janzen (1973: 60) and Holladay, who propose a quarrying of the common "to the land of the Chaldeans" from somewhere else in the book, nor the taking of "through Jeremiah the prophet" as a gloss from 51:59. The LXX version may simply be a reduction of the longer MT reading (Weiser; Bright). The words are present in Aq.

through Jeremiah the prophet. Hebrew *běyad yirměyāhû hannābî*'. This expression, denoting the prophet's role as divine mediator (*běyad*), occurs also in 37:2. The use of *běyad* (lit. "by the hand of"), is in fact quite common in the OT, appearing often in the Deuteronomic History (e.g., 1 Kgs 8:53, 56; 12:15; 14:18; 15:29; 16:7, 12; 17:16) and elsewhere (Hos 12:11[Eng 12:10]; Hag 1:1, 3; 2:1; and Mal 1:1).

Babylon. The capital city of southern Mesopotamia, situated in antiquity on the Euphrates, ca. 88 kilometers south of modern-day Baghdad, Iraq. Classical writers (Strabo, *Geog.* xvi 1.5; Diodorus Sic. ii 7.3; 8.4) report the Euphrates as running through the center of the city. The ruins, said to extend over 3 square miles, are near the modern town of Hilla. Babylon gave its name also to all of southern Mesopotamia between the Euphrates and the Tigris, from the city of Babylon in the north to the Persian Gulf in the south. Thus in the Neo-Babylonian period the names Babylon (or Babylonia) and Chaldea, the southernmost part of Mesopotamia, become more or less interchangeable. Greater Babylon was bounded on the west by the Arabian Desert, from which it was separated by a narrow strip of fertile land. To the east was a plain below the Elamite mountains. Although Babylon was known at least as early as the middle of the third millennium B.C., and attained prominence during the reign of King Hammurabi (1728–1686 B.C.), its zenith was reached under Nabopolassar and Nebuchadnezzar II, kings of the Neo-Babylonian empire (625–562 B.C.). These kings, particularly Nebuchadnezzar, embarked on an ambitious building program that included a temple to Marduk, a grand palace on the Southern Citadel, a huge outer wall made of burnt brick, a moat in front of the wall, and a finely decorated Ishtar Gate, giving entrance into the city. Babylon and its empire fell to Cyrus the Persian in 539 B.C. But its huge walls and magnificant buildings largely survived into the Persian period. On Babylon's city walls, see Note for 51:58. Strabo and Diodorus say that the Persians only partially ruined the city, carrying off its gold, silver, and precious stones; time and neglect brought ruin to the rest. Classical writers (Herodotus i 178–81; Strabo, *Geog.* xvi 1.5; Diodorus Sic. ii 7–9) were much taken with the size and grandeur of this ancient city, exaggerating their descriptions but also giving details that recent excavations have confirmed. Investigations and early excavations at the site began with the British in 1811. French and British archaeological teams returned in the 1850s, after which a team from the British Museum excavated the site from 1878 to 1889. A group from the German Oriental Society came subsequently to carry out systematic excavations from 1899 to 1917. These were halted by the First World War. Because of a high water table, excavations were largely restricted to the Neo-Babylonian and later periods. On the excavations of ancient Babylon and their results, also Nebuchadnezzar's inscriptions proclaming himself a mighty builder, see L. W. King 1919: 14–86, 278–80; Lane 1923: 177–95; cf. *ANET*³ 307. Babylon's treasures, including texts and portions of the Ishtar Gate, are now housed in the Pergamum Museum of Berlin, the British Museum in London, and the Oriental Institute of the University of Chicago (see further Note on 2:15). On Babylon and the Neo-Babylonian empire, see T. Jacobsen, "Babylon (OT)" in *IDB* A–D, 334–38 (with pictures); Wiseman 1985; Kuhrt 1995: 589–622; and Klengel-Brandt in *OEANE* 1: 251–56. On the city of Babylon and urbanism in ancient Mesopotamia, see Oppenheim 1964: 109–42.

the land of the Chaldeans. Hebrew ʾ*ereṣ kaśdîm*, where *kaśdîm* can mean either "Chaldeans" (50:1, 8, 25, 35, 45; 51:4, 5, 54; 52:7–8, 14, 17) or "Chaldea" (50:10; 51:1, 24, 35). The term *kaśdîm* occurs throughout Jeremiah 21–52 (46 times), as well as elsewhere in the OT. Chaldea (Akk *kaldu*) was the southern portion of ancient Mesopotamia between the Euphrates and the Tigris, known in the early third millennium B.C. as Sumer. In the Bible its inhabitants are first associated with the city of Ur (Gen 11:28, 31; 15:7; Acts 7:4), from which the patriarch Abraham descended. Chaldea, known from ninth-century B.C. Assyrian royal inscriptions, gained prominence in the late eighth and early seventh centuries, when its king, Merodach-baladan (Marduk-apal-iddin), did battle with Tiglath-pileser III, Sargon II, and Sennacherib (cf. 2 Kgs 20:12–19 = Isa 39:1–8). Nabopolassar, founder of the Neo-Babylonian dynasty, is said in Hellenistic sources to have been a native Chaldean (Kuhrt 1995: 621 n. 4), and after the fall of Nineveh (612 B.C.) he and his son Nebuchadnezzar II became the undisputed rulers of a far-reaching Babylonian / Chaldean Empire. Chaldea is used interchangeably with Babylon in the Neo-Babylonian period, as the Bible attests, even replacing Babylon in the reign of Nebuchadnezzar. The Chaldeans are the Babylonian army that brings down the kingdom of Judah (21:4; 22:25; 32:4–5, 24–25, 28–29; 33:5; 2 Kgs 25:4, 5, 10, 13). Chaldean rule effectively ends with Nebuchadnezzar, as his immediate successors, Awel-marduk (= Evil-merodach of 2 Kgs 25:27 = Jer 52:31) and Neriglissar (perhaps Nergal-sharezer of Jer 39:3, 13), reign but briefly, and Nabonidus (556–539 B.C.) comes from different stock entirely, having descended from Aramean nobility in Haran (Bright 1981: 352–53). On Chaldea and the Chaldeans, see further A. L. Oppenheim, "Chaldea" in *IDB* A–D, 549–50; and R. Hess, "Chaldea" in *ABD* 1: 886–87.

2. *Declare among the nations and make heard, set up a flag! make heard! . . . say.* These same plural imperatives begin the foe-lament collection in 4:5–6. Compare also 46:14. Babylon's demise is to be announced to the nations,

which Jeremiah, his scribal associate Seraiah (51:59–64), and a host of others will carry out. Masculine plural imperatives function similarly in Isa 34:1 and 40:1–3.

set up a flag! make heard! The LXX omission of this phrase, as Giesebrecht and Barthélemy (1986: 816) point out, can be attributed to haplography (whole-word: *hašmyʿw . . . hašmyʿw*). The phrase is present in Aq. In 4:6, 21 the raised flag (*nēs*) is a war alert; in 51:12, 27 it is the standard of an attacking army, but here it announces—as also in modern times—a battle fought and won.

keep it not hidden. W. Janzen (1981: 105) points out a tendency with prophets either to shrink from declaring the word entrusted to them or not to tell the whole of it. Yahweh instructs Jeremiah in 26:2: "Do not hold back a word," which he may have done (cf. 20:9). See also 42:4 and 1 Sam 3:17. King Zedekiah instructed Jeremiah in a similar manner, and Jeremiah agreed to tell all on the condition that the king not put him to death (38:14–16). Compare the tactic employed by Micaiah in 1 Kgs 22:13–23, which consisted initially of withholding the divine word so as to unmask the false prophets around him, but then to follow by a full revelation of the truth.

Bel is very ashamed, Merodach is shattered; Her images are very ashamed, her idols are shattered. For a similar repetition, see 14:3–4. The point being stressed is that the Babylonian gods, together with their images, are discredited and broken—their images perhaps being literally broken. Both verbs are common in Jeremiah, singly and in combination: on the internal H-stem of *bôš* ("be very ashamed"), see Note for 2:26; on *ḥtt* ("be shattered"), see Note for 1:17; on the pairing of the two verbs, see Note for 17:18.

Bel. Hebrew *bēl.* Essentially a title meaning "lord" (Akk *bēlu*; CAD 2: 191–99; AHw 1: 118–19), equivalent to Canaanite *baʿal.* In Akk it becomes a divine name or replaces a divine name. In early times Bel was used as an appellation for numerous Sumerian and Babylonian deities, but was chiefly the title given to the Sumerian storm-god Enlil. By the Neo-Babylonian period Marduk (= Merodach) had become Bel Marduk, or just Bel. Bel, then, is not a second god along with Marduk, but simply another name for him (Rudolph). Other mentions of Bel occur in 51:44; Isa 46:1; Ep Jer 40; and Bel and the Dragon. On the last-named apocryphal book, see Note for 51:44.

Merodach. Hebrew *mĕrōdāk.* The biblical pronounciation of the god Marduk, said to have been given the vowels for Heb *ʾădōnāy*, "lord" (Perles 1905: 7–8; Rudolph; Weiser). Marduk, patron deity of Babylon, rose to prominence under Hammurabi, when he replaced Enlil as head of the pantheon (Prologue to Code of Hammurabi i 1–20; ANET[3] 164; CS II 336). His meteoric rise to power is recorded in the Babylonian creation epic, *enuma eliš*, where, after being proclaimed king, he defeats Tiamat, the chaos monster, and goes on to do "artful works" of creation (ANET[3] 62–68; CS I 392–400). Veneration of Marduk reached its zenith during the reign of Nebuchadnezzar II (604–562 B.C.), at which time he was indisputably "king of the gods." But as a result he had also to share in the fate of a humiliated Babylon. Actually, Bel Marduk may have fallen from prominence earlier. Nabonidus left him out of the New Year's procession in his seventh to eleventh years (Nabonidus Chronicle ii; *ANET*[3] 306; cf. Isa 46:1), and is said to have wanted him replaced by the moon god Sin (Bright 1981: 353; *ABD* 4: 522–23). But Kuhrt (1995: 600–601) argues that the latter point may be somewhat exaggerated.

Her images are very ashamed, her idols are shattered. The LXX omits, as it commonly does with repetitions, but the line is better retained (*pace* Duhm; Cornill; Rudolph; McKane) in view of repetitions elsewhere in the stanza (see Rhetoric and Composition). The words are present in Theod. The suggestion of Janzen (1973: 20) and Holladay that a conflate LXX text has been corrected to MT is needless speculation. The terms *ʿăṣabbîm* ("images") and *gillûlîm* ("idols") are used disparagingly in the OT for foreign gods and their representations (C. R. North 1958: 154–55). On the former, see Hos 8:4; 13:2; and Isa 46:1; on the latter, see Deut 29:16[Eng 29:17]; Lev 26:30; and Ezek 16:36. The literal meaning of *gillûlîm* is "dung pellets" (Ezek 4:12, 15; Zeph 1:17), a favorite term of Ezekiel (41 times).

3. *For a nation from the north has come up upon her.* Things have come full circle. In the lead oracle of 4:5–8, the northern foe coming to destroy Judah was Babylon. Now Babylon has its own foe from the north to contend with (cf. 50:9, 41–42; 51:48). The "north" in both contexts has mythological overtones; nevertheless excavations of ancient Babylon indicate that Nebuchadnezzar's fortifications were aimed at strengthening the capital on its northern side, where danger of invasion was always the greatest (L. W. King 1919: 27, 29). On the foe from the north and its mythological overtones, see Note on 1:14. The verb here is a prophetic perfect (Cheyne; McKane); the disaster has not yet happened, but it may as well have. The verbs immediately following are futures; then at the end of the verse are two more prophetic perfects: "they are wandering, they are gone." The sequence has been noted by Reimer 1993: 28. The prophecy here is general, and most likely has no specific enemy in mind. Rashi and Kimḥi, however, foresee a threat from the Persians and the Medes. On the latter, see 51:11, 28; and Isa 13:17.

come up upon her. Hebrew *ʿālâ ʿāleyhā* contains a wordplay (see also 50:21). For a slightly different wordplay with the same verb and preposition, see 8:18.

it, it will make her land a desolation, and an inhabitant will not be in her, from human to beast. For variations on this common land-and-city curse in Jeremiah, see Note for 48:9. The pairing of "human" (*ʾādām*) and "beast" (*běhēmâ*) is common in the Jeremiah prose (see Note for 21:6); this is the only occurrence in poetry.

they are wandering, they are gone. Hebrew *nādû hālākû.* The phrase is absent in the LXX, and numerous commentators take it to be an MT plus adapted from 9:9[10]. However, there the verb is *ndd* ("to flee"); here it is *nûd* ("to wander, be homeless"). The phrase may then be original in the present context, although it is not repeated with the rest of the verse in the colophon (see Rhetoric and Composition). The phrase is present in Aq. The T takes the phrase as a reference to exile.

MESSAGE AND AUDIENCE

In this divine speech Yahweh instructs Jeremiah and certain others to announce to the nations that Babylon is taken, and that its god Bel-Merodach is ashamed and broken. All the images of this celebrated Babylonian deity are in a similar condition, and news of their fall is to be spread by word and by the raising of a flag, signaling victory. Justice has been served. A foe from the north has now come upon Babylon, and will make her land a desolation. No inhabitants of any description will be seen in her, neither humans nor beasts. All are homeless and all are gone.

This oracle was doubtless delivered in the first instance to a Jerusalem audience, possibly at the beginning of Zedekiah's reign after Nebuchadnezzar had brought Judah into humiliating submission and taken away its king, queen mother, leading citizens, and Temple treasures to Babylon. The debate going on at the time centered around Babylon's continued sovereignty in world affairs and Judah's continued servitude, as chaps. 27–29 make clear. The debate achieved sharp focus in the confrontation between Jeremiah and Hananiah, where Hananiah stated that Babylonian sovereignty would last but two more years, and then the exiles and treasures taken to Babylon would return home (28:2–4, 10–11). Jeremiah's position, stated earlier to multiple audiences, was that Judah and the neighboring nations would have to serve Nebuchadnezzar "until the time of his land comes" (27:7), and that the city's wealth now in Babylon would remain there "until the day I [i.e., Yahweh] attend to them," when they will be brought back (27:22). In two passages, 25:11 and 29:10, a round number of 70 years is given (cf. Zimmerli 1995: 428). Jeremiah's bona fide Babylon oracles fit best in the first four years of Zedekiah's reign, i.e., 597–594/3 B.C., at which time he was active in Jerusalem (Lundbom, "Jeremiah [Prophet]" in ABD 3: 689) and can be imagined to have been preaching both about Babylon's future and the future of the covenant people. It is doubtful whether there was any talk at this time about a threat to Babylon from the Medes and the Persians, even though such threats did develop later, and mention is made of the Medes in 51:11 and 28.

In the fourth year of Zedekiah, 594/3 B.C., Jeremiah's scroll of Babylon oracles went to Babylon with Seraiah and was given a reading there (51:59–64), but before what sort of audience we cannot say. This oracle was the lead one in the collection, and would have been read again at that time. The superscription is for a Jewish audience hearing the collection later. All the oracles in the collection predicting judgment on Babylon, as well as all those promising restoration for the covenant people, doubtless took on great importance for Jews during the exile, up until 539 B.C., when Cyrus the Persian took Babylon, and Jews were then given permission to return to their homeland.

2. Israel and Judah Will Ask the Way to Zion (50:4–5)

50 ⁴In those days and at that time—oracle of Yahweh—the children of Israel shall come, they and the children of Judah together.

Weeping continually they shall go
  and Yahweh their God they shall seek
[5]'Zion,' they will ask
  their faces in this direction
'Come!' And they attach themselves to Yahweh!
The eternal covenant will not be forgotten!

RHETORIC AND COMPOSITION

MT 50:4–5 = LXX 27:4–5. The present verses consist of a brief salvation or-acle from Yahweh for the whole people of God—a united Israel and Judah (v 4a)—followed by a salvation word for the same from the prophet (vv 4b–5). Compare 50:33–34. Like the oracle of vv 2–3, this dialogue also has a lead function in chaps. 50–51, since the collection speaks not only about Babylon's demise but about the return of Jews to their homeland (Weiser; Reimer 1993: 31). There is mention as well of the important eternal covenant (= new cove-nant) that will undergird the relationship between Yahweh and his people in future days.

A Qumran fragment, 4QJer[b] (Tov: 4QJer[e]), contains vv 4–6. This fragment has the messenger formula that is lacking in LXX. Janzen (1973: 184) says this is the only instance where 4QJer[b(e)] sides with MT against LXX when the latter has a zero variant. The fragment, however, is small. We should not, in any case, omit the formula with Cornill, Rudolph, Holladay, and McKane, as it helps delimit the top end of the unit and aids in clarifying portions of the unit. The lower limit is marked by a *setumah* in M[L] after v 5, which makes unlikely a unit of vv 4–7 that many commentators assume. The M[A] and M[P] lack this section, as does 4QJer[b[e]] (Tov 1997: 206).

Uncertainty about whether these verses are prose or poetry is reflected in the commentaries and the modern Versions. The problem, basically, is that the in-troductory "In those days and at that time" in v 4a seems to be prose (cf. 33:15; 50:20), whereas vv 4b–5 having inverted syntax of accusatives, subjects preced-ing verbs, and lines dividing nicely into bicolons, read better as poetry (so *BHS*). As a result, some commentators (Rudolph; Weiser; Bright; Thompson; Keown et al.) and some modern Versions (JB; NJB; NAB; NIV) take the whole of vv 4–5 as poetry, while other commentators (Volz; McKane) and other mod-ern Versions (RSV; NEB; REB; NJV; NSB) take the whole as prose. T. H. Rob-inson (1917–18) took v 4 as prose and v 5 as poetry. Holladay has done similarly, taking v 4a as an added introductory formula (in prose?), and vv 4b–5 as poetry. This latter division is made also by Reimer (1993: 29–30), only with the difference that the introduction is not bracketed out. The decision here is to take v 4a as a brief oracle from Yahweh in prose, and vv 4b–5 as a salvation word from the prophet in poetry. Yahweh cannot be the speaker in vv 4b–5 ex-cept, perhaps, with respect to the single word "Come!" (see Notes).

The poetry has a structure made up of key word repetitions and balancing quotations:

II . . . .   v 4b
    Yahweh . . . .
    'Zion' . . . .   v 5
    . . . .
    'Come!' . . . . . . *Yahweh*
    . . . .

The seeking of Yahweh in v 4b balances the attachment made to Yahweh in
v 5b. The double reference to "Yahweh" may in addition be echoed in the double reference to "Yahweh" in v 7b, where the collocations are different, but
nevertheless striking (see Rhetoric and Composition for 50:6–7).

The introductory oracle is linked to the poetry by these key words (Reimer
1993: 31):

I . . . . *shall come*   *yābō'û*   v 4a
II *Come!* . . . .   *bō'û*   v 5b

Catchwords connecting to the previous oracle:

  v 4b *they shall go*   *yēlēkû*   v 3 *they are gone*   *hālākû*

Catchwords connecting to the dialogue following:

  v 4b *they shall go*   *yēlēkû*   v 6 *they went*   *hālākû*
  v 5   *will not be forgotten* *lō' tiššākēaḥ*   *they forgot*   *šākĕḥû*

Reimer (1993: 33) cites the latter verb, *škḥ*, "forgot(ton)," as a link term for the
two units.

NOTES

50:4. *In those days and at that time.* This combined introductory phrase occurs
also in v 20 and 33:15. For the "in those days" and "at that time" introductions,
see Notes for 3:16 and 17. Restoration will take place in the indefinite future,
as stated by the prophet in 27:7 and 22.

    they and the children of Judah together. For the reuniting of Israel and Judah,
see 3:18; 23:6; 30:3; 31:27; 33:7, and 14. Duhm considered reunion a late convention, a view reflected in *BHS*, where deletion of the phrase is urged. Rudolph's judgment (also in his commentary) survives in Holladay. But deletion
is unwarranted, particularly since Rudolph wants to read all of vv 4–5 as poetry
and says the phrase in question disturbs the rhythm.

    Weeping continually they shall go. Hebrew *hālôk ûbākô yēlēkû*. On *hālôk*
with the infinitive absolute meaning "continually," see GKC §113u. Volz and
Rudolph: "immerfort weinend." The T has the people weeping in exile, but
the situation envisaged must rather be the same as it is in 31:9, where people
have mingled tears of contrition and joy on their return to Zion.

Yahweh their God they shall seek. See 29:13 and Hos 3:5. "Seeking (*bqš*) Yahweh" means seeking him in worship (Amos 5:4–6; Zeph 1:6), which will happen on the return from exile.

5. *'Zion,' they will ask.* Hebrew *derek* ("in the direction of") goes with the following colon; the *zaqeph qaton* is over *yiš'ālû* ("they will ask"). Returnees in future days will ask one another the directions to Zion (Kimhi). On the return to Zion, see also 3:14; 31:6, 12; Isa 35:10; 51:11; 62:10–12.

their faces in this direction. Hebrew *derek hēnnâ pěnêhem*. Here *derek* means "in the direction of," not "way," although many of the modern Versions (RSV, JB, NAB, NIV, and REB) include both terms. The readings of NEB, NJV, and NSB are better. Hebrew *hēnnâ* means "here," as in 31:8; the prophet is speaking from Jerusalem (Cornill).

'Come!' And they attach themselves to Yahweh! Hebrew *bō'û wěnilwû 'el-yhwh*. The colon is difficult, there being no agreement on interpretation except in a very general sense. According to the three common readings: 1) people are either being called to attach themselves to Yahweh; 2) they are calling themselves to be attached to Yahweh; or 3) they are said to be actually carrying out attachment at a future time when their rebellion is over. The first verb, *bō'û*, is the plural imperative "Come!" The second verb, *wěnilwû*, is pointed in MT as an N-stem perfect, "and they attach(ed) themselves," which leaves "Come!" a single-word quotation. But this is not the problem, since "Zion" is a single-word quotation in v 5a. It has also been suggested that *wě-nilwû* may be an irregular N-stem imperative (Kimhi; Cornill), which would extend the quotation to at least, "Come and attach yourselves to Yahweh." But doubts are expressed about such a reading, also about the commonly cited parallel of *niqběṣû* in Isa 43:9 and Joel 4:11[Eng 3:11] (GKC §51 o). The LXX goes its own way with *kai hēxousin kai katapheuxontai*, "and they shall come and shall flee for refuge," although it does achieve consistency with the other future verbs in vv 4–5. The T makes both verbs futures: "they shall come and be added to the people of the Lord." Some modern Versions also read both verbs as futures (NEB [but not REB], NJV, NIV, NRSV), but this does away with the quotation "Come!" The preferred solution (AV, RSV [but not NRSV], JB, NAB, REB; cf. *BHS*) has been to emend the second verb with the Syriac to an N-stem imperfect, *wěnillāweh*, "and let us attach ourselves," where the combination "Come, (and) let us" has good parallels in 35:11; 51:10; and Ps 95:6. This also extends the quotation to: "Come and let us attach ourselves to Yahweh." The reading adopted here takes both verbs with their MT pointing, reading the first verb as a "welcome home" imperative to the returnees from exile—perhaps from the prophet, but even better from Yahweh—and the second verb as a statement that the welcome home is happily accepted. Thus:

Welcome to the returnees:	*"Come!"*
Their response reported:	*And they attach themselves to Yahweh!*

The eternal covenant. Hebrew *bĕrît ʿôlām*. The term is not an accusative in relation to what precedes (*pace* Giesebrecht; Duhm). The "eternal covenant" is another name for Jeremiah's "new covenant" (see Note for 32:40).

will not be forgotten! Hebrew *lōʾ tiššākēaḥ*. The same phrase occurs in 20:11 and 23:40, where it is eternal disgrace that will not be forgotten. In the new covenant passage, Yahweh says "I will not remember again" (*lōʾ ʾezkār-ʿôd*) the sins of the people that are now forgiven (31:34). But the point here is that the eternal covenant will not be forgotton by the people, as the Sinai covenant was.

MESSAGE AND AUDIENCE

The prophet in his poem speaks about a band of weeping people going to seek Yahweh their God. They ask after Zion as they walk in the direction of Zion. The prophet—or perhaps, Yahweh—says "Come!" and with a readiness not seen in awhile the returnees are seen attaching themselves to their God. The eternal covenant now binding Yahweh to his people will not be forgotten.

To this poem has been added a brief oracle to serve as introduction. It is a divine word from Yahweh stating that in future days a united Israel and Judah "shall come." Where shall they come? The audience must provide the answer. They shall come from exile, they shall come to Zion, but Yahweh wants even more that they will come and attach themselves to him in the eternal covenant that will never be forgotton. All of this is being affirmed in Jeremiah's salvation word of v 5.

When this dual word of salvation for the covenant people is heard in tandem with the prior word of judgment on Babylon, two main themes of the present collection are put into bold relief: Babylon's destruction, and the return of the covenant people to their homeland. The fall of Babylon, then, is not simply an act of happy revenge, but an occasion for the restoration of the whole people of God to Zion, and an indication that an eternal covenant will undergird the divine-human relationship for all days to come.

This poem and its introductory oracle are not spoken on the eve of Babylon's demise, but well in advance of that event. For probable dates of these and other utterances in the Babylon collection, see Message and Audience for 50:1–3.

3. My People Became Lost Sheep (50:6–7)

50 [6]My people became[1] lost sheep
   their shepherds let them wander off
     mountains led them astray[2]

---

[1]Reading the Q *hāyû* ("they became") to go with the plural *ʾōbĕdôt* ("lost"); Kt has the singular *hāyâ*.

[2]Reading the Q *šôbĕbûm* ("they misled them / they led them astray"), which is a Polel perfect with third plural suffix; Kt is the plural adjective, *šôbēbîm*.

From mountain to hill they went
　they forgot their resting place

[7]All who found them consumed them
　and their foes said, 'We are not guilty'
inasmuch as they sinned against Yahweh
　The Righteous Pasture
　　and Hope of Their Fathers—Yahweh.

RHETORIC AND COMPOSITION

MT 50:6–7 = LXX 27:6–7. The present verses continue the interruption of prophecies against Babylon to give a retrospective word concerning Judah. Following the word about a future salvation for reunited Israel–Judah, we step back briefly to reflect on why Judah's punishment became necessary. Delimitation of the verses is by *setumahs* prior to v 6 and following v 7, although M[A] and M[P] lack the former sections. *BHS* correctly scans the verses as poetry (*pace* RSV, NRSV, NEB, REB, NJV, and NSB), which can be divided into two stanzas (v 6 and v 7). The outer lines of 6a and 7b are tricolons; the center lines of 6b and 7a bicolons. The whole then has an inverted rhythm:

I	tricolon	v 6
	bicolon	
II	bicolon	v 7
	tricolon	

Jeremianic poetry commonly alternates bicolons and tricolons, sometimes resulting in inversions such as we find here. Compare 10:19–20; 14:20–22; and 46:3–5.

The poem appears to be another dialogue between Yahweh and the prophet, inasmuch as "my people" (v 6) in Jeremianic poems usually identifies Yahweh as the speaker (2:10–13, 31–32; 4:22; 5:26–31). The prophet speaks in Stanza II, where Yahweh is twice referred to in the third person. The poem follows then the same sequence as the oracle and poem preceding, where first Yahweh speaks, then the prophet. There is also a similarity to the prior poem in that another voice is again brought in (v 7a: the foes say, "We are not guilty"). In vv 4–5 the people were heard asking for "Zion," and Yahweh (or else the prophet) responded with a welcoming "Come!" There is also the possibility here that the enemy continues speaking in v 7b, giving a reason as to why it is not guilty (see Notes).

Stanza I has a key word repetition in the center:

I	. . . .	v 6
	. . . .	
	mountains	*hārîm*
	From mountain	*mēhar*
	. . . .	

Stanza II concludes with a double occurrence of "Yahweh," which may balance the double occurrence of "Yahweh" strategically positioned in vv 4–5 (see Rhetoric and Composition for 50:4–5).

II . . . . *against Yahweh*	*layhwh*	v 7b
. . . .		
. . . . *Yahweh*	*yhwh*	

The LXX omits the final "Yahweh," but there is good reason to retain it (see Notes).

Catchwords connecting to the prior dialogue:

v 6	*they went*	*hālākû*	v 4b	*they shall go*	*yēlēkû*
	they forgot	*šākēḥû*	v 5	*will not be forgotten*	*lōʾ tiššākēaḥ*

Catchwords connecting to the next oracle:

v 6 *sheep*		v 8 *sheep*

NOTES

50:6. *My people became lost sheep.* The plural *ʾōbĕdôt* ("lost, destroyed") is explained by the collective noun "sheep"; cf. Gen 30:43. The Q adjusts to a plural verb. The Kt, however, is doubtless original. These sheep did not simply lose their way; according to v 7, they perished. So we are talking here not about surviving exiles (Isa 27:13), but about individuals who lost their lives when the nation was overtaken by Babylon. Death is portrayed similarly by a pastoral metaphor in 50:17. In the NT, the portrayal of people as "lost sheep" is made memorable in Jesus' parable of the "Lost Sheep" (Matt 18:12–14; Luke 15:4–7).

their shepherds let them wander off. The term immediately following, *hārîm* ("mountains / hills"), does not belong with this phrase (*pace* McKane, who emends the line to read with the LXX: "their shepherds led them astray in the hills"). The line is a tricolon (see Rhetoric and Composition), and there is no reason to delete *šôbĕbûm* (Q), "they led them astray." "Shepherds" here are probably the kings (Rashi and Kimḥi, following T), as elsewhere (2:8; 3:15; 6:3; 23:1–4; 25:34–36; cf. Zech 11:6), although prophets and priests may certainly be included (Volz). "Shepherd" is a general term for ruler in the ANE (see Note for 2:8). It was prophets who led Northern Israel astray with their prophecies by Baal (23:13). For sweeping judgments on Judah's shepherds, see 23:1–4 and Ezekiel 34. Calvin says that blame is placed on the shepherds, not to absolve the people, but to commend the greatness of God's grace. In the NT, Jesus puts himself forth as the good shepherd (John 10:11–18).

mountains led them astray. Hebrew *hārîm šôbĕbûm* (Q). The Polel of *šûb* also means "lead astray" in Isa 47:10. These are doubtless the mountains on which fertility worship took place (Jer 3:23; 17:2–3; Ezek 6:3–4, 13; 18:6; Hos 4:13; cf. Deut 12:2). A nice figure here of metonymy and personification. The portrayal of people as sheep that have "gone astray" in Matthew's version of the parable of the "Lost Sheep" (Matt 18:12–13) recalls the imagery in this verse (Hultgren 2000: 55).

From mountain to hill they went, they forgot their resting place. A syntactic chiasmus with verbs in the center. For other examples, see 2:36b; 10:11; and 51:38. On their wayward trek the sheep wandered aimlessly from mountain to hill, forgetting the secure pasture from which they had strayed. In their lost state they thus became exposed to grave danger. Compare Ezek 34:6 and Isa 53:6 ("All we like sheep have gone astray"). The point being made is that people wandered to the high places in illegitimate worship (cf. 2:20; 3:6), forgetting proper worship of Yahweh in the Temple. See 3:21–23. Reference then is not to exile, as stated in T.

From mountain to hill. Hebrew *mēhar ʾel-gibʿâ*. In 4QJer[b(e)] Tov (1992: 541) originally read *rm*[*h*], "height," but later (1997: 207) read *gbʿ*[*h*], "hill," agreeing with Janzen (1973: 184).

their resting place. Hebrew *rēbeṣ* is a place of lying down, for sheep a pasture or a fold (Ezek 25:5; Isa 65:10). This resting place is well portrayed in Ps 23:1–3. Reference here is probably to Zion and the Temple. According to Ps 132:14, Zion is Yahweh's resting place (*mĕnûḥâ*).

7. *All who found them consumed them.* The verb *ʾkl* is lit. "to eat." See 5:17 and 30:16. This is precisely what happens when sheep wander from the shepherd and the security of their fold: wild animals get them (Ezek 34:5, 8).

'We are not guilty.' The claim of the enemy, i.e., the Babylonians, in light of the destruction they sponsored and carried out in Judah. It was different in the early days, when Yahweh exercised care over his people. At that time, says Jeremiah, those who consumed Israel became guilty (2:3). The quotation should probably be limited to just these words (Kimḥi, Giesebrecht, Cornill, Volz, Weiser, Rudolph, and Holladay). Calvin extends to ". . . against Yahweh," with Bright and virtually all the modern Versions carrying the quotation to the end of the verse. The NSB, however, limits the quotation to "We are not guilty." It is better to attribute the words about Israel sinning against Yahweh and Yahweh being Israel's true and eternal God to the prophet.

inasmuch as. Hebrew *taḥat ʾăšer*. See 29:19 and Deut 28:47.

The Righteous Pasture. Or "The True Pasture" (NJV, NIV, and NRSV). Hebrew *nĕwēh-ṣedek*. Seemingly the first of two epithets for Yahweh, although this one is strange, since "pasture" normally denotes territory. In 31:23 the same expression is a metaphor for Jerusalem, while in 10:25; 23:3; and 50:19 "pasture" denotes the land of Israel. Similarly, "your holy pasture" (*nĕwēh qodšekā*) in Exod 15:13 refers to the Promised Land. If "righteous pasture" here is territory, then people are being cited for sinning against their land, which was a gift of Yahweh. But Calvin thinks the reference here is to God, and that the prophet is alluding to the tabernacle (T: "the dwelling-place of his truth").

pasture . . . hope. There is assonance in *nĕwēh* and *miqwēh*.

and Hope of Their Fathers—Yahweh. Hebrew *ûmiqwēh ʾăbôtêhem yhwh*. The divine epithet, "Hope of Israel" (*miqwēh yiśrāʾēl*), is used of Yahweh in 14:8 and

17:13. The term *miqweh* also means "pool of water," which may be what the LXX intends with *synagagonti*. The two meanings, "hope" and "pool," are played upon in 17:13. Here the final "Yahweh" is lacking in the LXX, leading numerous commentators (Blayney, Giesebrecht, Peake, Cornill, Bright, Holladay, McKane) to delete the name as an MT plus, while others (Ehrlich 1912: 364; Volz; Weiser; Rudolph; Bright; Holladay) emend it away. But with Aq, Theod, Symm, T, and Vg, it should be retained. It is not a gloss such as we have at the end of 17:13, where the divine name is preceded by the *nota accusativi* and cannot be original because Yahweh is speaker of the line. Cheyne argues plausibly that in the present verse the placement of the divine name at the end of the verse is for emphasis (see Rhetoric and Composition). For other climactic asseverations of the divine name in Jeremiah and in the OT, see Note for 10:16.

MESSAGE AND AUDIENCE

Yahweh begins this dialogue by stating that his covenant people became like so many lost sheep. Their shepherds let them wander, and mountains offering other enticing forms of worship led them astray. The wayward souls went from mountain to hill, forgetting, as sheep do, their resting place. Jeremiah continues the dialogue by stating what most anyone will imagine at this point, namely, that those finding the lost sheep went on to consume them. We now know that the lost sheep were more than lost. They were destroyed. The enemies, however, responded with a "We are not guilty," and the prophet without a pause tells us why. The people sinned against Yahweh, who was their Righteous Pasture and Hope of Their Fathers. The final "Yahweh" forcefully drives the point home.

When this poem is heard in tandem with the one preceding, the focus will be on the covenant people exclusively—their return home, the sin that made their going away necessary, and their true God, who is Yahweh. For a brief moment, then, mighty Babylon is not held responsible for what it did to the covenant people. The disclaimer it makes is not answered. Rather, it is accepted as valid.

This poem could have been spoken any time after 597 B.C., fitting well into the period of Babylon utterances between 597 and 594 B.C. See further Message and Audience for 50:1–3.

4. Wander from the Midst of Babylon! (50:8–10)

50 [8]Wander from the midst of Babylon
  from the land of the Chaldeans, go out[1]
    and become like he-goats before the sheep

[9]For look, I am the one rousing
  and bringing up against Babylon

---

[1]Reading the imperative with Q *ṣ'ēû* ("Go out!").

an assembly of great nations
    from the land of the north
And they shall line up against her
    from there she shall be taken

Its arrows are like those of a successful warrior
    who does not return empty
[10]Yes, the Chaldeans have become spoil
    all who despoil her shall be sated
    —oracle of Yahweh.

RHETORIC AND COMPOSITION

MT 50:8–10 = LXX 27:8–10. The present unit is delimited by a *setumah* in
M^L, M^A, and M^P prior to v 8 and a messenger formula concluding v 10. The
LXX omits the latter, but it should be retained since Yahweh is the speaker of
v 9 ("For look, I am the one rousing and bringing up against Babylon . . ."),
and all of vv 8–10 seems otherwise to be a divine oracle. The verses are generally taken as poetry (Volz: "a very lively poem"), although the RSV and NRSV
print as prose. Keown et al. single out v 9 as prose, and McKane does likewise
for v 10, but all three verses can be read as poetry once the colon structure in
v 9 is clarified. Vocabulary and phraseology are Jeremiah's (Holladay); the
composition is not, as Jones (p. 527) alleges, superficially original, "composed
of borrowed ideas and phrases."

The poem has three stanzas (Volz). Stanza I (v 8) is a tricolon, not a double
bicolon as scanned in *BHS*. Stanza II (v 9abc) is a triple bicolon, and Stanza
III (vv 9d–10) a double bicolon. A structure for the whole is made by these balancing key words:

I		v 8
from the land of the Chaldeans . . .		
and become like	*wihyû kĕ*	
II		v 9a
. . . .		
. . . .		
from the land		
III . . . .*like*.	*kĕ*	v 9d
. . . .		
Yes, the Chaldeans have become . . .	*wĕhāyĕtâ*	v 10
. . . .		

The poem also contains a pattern of inverted syntax, supporting MT in v 9
over against the shorter reading in LXX and revised scansion in *BHS*. These inversions come at the beginning of Stanza I, the beginning and end of Stanza II,

and the end of Stanza III. Stanza I at the beginning has a syntactic chiasmus with verbs at the extremes:

I   *Wander* / from the midst of Babylon   v 8
      from the land of the Chaldeans / *go out*

Stanza II begins with a partial chiasmus: two H-stem participles positioned at the center of a bicolon:

II   For look, I am the one / *rousing*   . . . . . . / *mēʿîr*   v 9a
      and bringing up / against Babylon   *ûmaʿăleh* / . . . .

At the end of Stanza II is another partial chiasmus: verbs coming at the extremes:

II   *And they shall line up* / against her   v 9c
      from there / *she shall be taken*

Concluding Stanza III is a chiasmus with cognate terms at the center and main verbs at the extremes:

III *Yes, she has become*, the Chaldeans / *spoil*   . . . . / *lěšālāl*   v 10
      all *who despoil her* / *shall be sated*   *šōlěleyhā* / . . .

Catchwords connecting to the prior dialogue:

v 8 *sheep*   v 6 *sheep*

Catchwords connecting to following poem:

v 9   *Look*   v 12 *Look*
       nations   *nations*
v 10 *and she has become*   v 13 *and she has become*

NOTES

50:8. *Wander from the midst of Babylon.* On the verb *nûd*, "wander (about), be homeless," see also 4:1; 49:30; and 50:3. The imperative makes this a directive: people are told to leave Babylon and become homeless. The latter adds a touch of irony, in that people are being advised to embark on an uncertain and possibly life-threatening pilgrimage. At the same time they receive fair warning about the danger of staying where they are now, since a hostile army is envisioned as ready to take over the city. The addressee is Israel (Kimhi), although as the end of the verse makes clear, others will follow Israel in the exodus. The directive is even more urgent in 51:6: "Flee (*nūsû*) from the midst of Babylon," and in 51:45: "Go out from her midst, my people!"

from the land of the Chaldeans, go out. On "the land of the Chaldeans," see Note for 50:1. The *athnaḥ* should not be relocated under "Chaldeans" (*pace* Giesebrecht; Duhm; Volz; Rudolph; Weiser; McKane; cf. *BHS*), which is to say, the verb "go out" (Q) belongs with "(and) from the land of the Chaldeans" at the end of line 1 (Reimer 1993: 34–35). This is the reading adopted in all modern Versions except the NEB; JB [but not NJB]; and REB. Compare Isa 48:20.

and become like he-goats before the sheep. Compare the directive in 48:28: "Be as a dove that nests." He-goats are known to push their way ahead of sheep to the front of the flock. They also push aside the she-goats. The Jews then are to be the first out the gate, after which other residents in Babylon will follow. The T embellishes with "and be like princes at the head of the people." The LXX has a quite different reading: "Be as serpents (*drakontes*) before sheep."

9. *For look.* Hebrew *hinnēh* is the most common beginning of the Jeremianic oracle; here it begins the stanza of an oracle (see Notes for 1:9 and 1:15; in the Foreign Nation Oracles, see Note for 49:19).

I am the one rousing and bringing up against Babylon. The second verb, *ûma'ăleh* ("and bringing up"), should not be deleted with the LXX (*pace* Cornill; Rudolph; Holladay; McKane). The two verbs have similar but not identical meanings, which renders less likely the view of Janzen (1973: 20) that MT has conflated synonyms; cf. 33:6; 51:1; Isa 8:7; 13:17; Ezek 23:22; and Joel 4:7[Eng 3:7]. The T has both verbs, and together they fit into a larger scheme of inversions within the oracle (see Rhetoric and Composition). The first verb, *mē'îr*, can also mean "stirring (up)"; cf. Deut 32:11 and Hos 7:4. The pronoun "I" is emphatic: Yahweh is the one rousing and bringing against Babylon a formidable foe (Calvin). In 51:11 and 28 this foe is said to be the kings of Media (cf. Isa 13:17).

an assembly of great nations. Hebrew *qĕhal-gôyīm gĕdōlîm.* In 6:22 Jeremiah told Judah, "a great nation is roused" (*gôy gādôl yē'ôr*) against Daughter Zion, which was later recast for use against Babylon (50:41). Here as there the nations are unnamed, which may be deliberate (Jones) although this could be the coalition referred to in 51:27–28 (Streane). The LXX lacks "great," which can be explained as another loss due to haplography (homoeoteleuton: *ym . . . ym*). The term should not be omitted (*pace* Cornill; Rudolph; Janzen 1973: 60; and McKane). Volz, Weiser, and Holladay retain. Cornill notes that Ezekiel uses *qahal* ("assembly") often to denote a military force (Ezek 17:17; 26:7; 27:27; 32:22–23; 38:4, 7, 13, 15).

from the land of the north. Against Judah and its neighbors, Babylon along with allies was the foe from the north (25:9). Here a multiple foe from the proverbial north will come up against Babylon (cf. 50:3, 41; 51:48). On the foe from the north, see Note for 1:14; on the foe from the north coming against Babylon, see Note for 50:3; on the particular phrase here, see Note for 16:15.

And they shall line up against her. I.e., in battle formation. Compare 6:23; 46:3; and 50:14.

from there she shall be taken. The phrase is less than transparent. Presumably reference is to the place where Babylon will experience defeat—whether in the proverbial north (which could be anywhere), or at a northern location where earlier battles were decided (cf. 46:10).

Its arrows are like those of a successful warrior. I.e., the arrows of the attacking force (*qahal*). An ellipsis makes necessary "those of" to smooth out the analogy. The term of uncertainty is the H-stem participle, *maškîl*, which, as pointed in MT, means "one causing bereavement." This is the meaning in T ("a mighty man who makes people childless"), in Aq (*gigas ateknōn*), and in the Vg (*viri fortis interfectoris*). Another possibility yielding good or even better sense is *maśkîl* (reading a *śin* instead of a *šin*), i.e., "one achieving success." This reading is attested in some MSS, and is reflected in the LXX, Symm (*dynatou synetou*), and the Syriac. Modern Versions beginning with the AV all adopt the latter reading, as do most commentators from Calvin to the present. Holladay, however, departs from the recent consensus and translates, "like those of a bereaving warrior," although he suggests emending to a Piel (participle), for which a meaning of "bereave, make childless" is attested (cf. 15:7). Either reading is possible in the context. In the end it comes down to the warrior's arrows hitting their target, resulting in fatalities and thus bereavement.

who does not return empty. I.e., without having achieved success. Hebrew *lōʾ yāšûb rêqām.* The RSV, NEB, JB, and NIV have "empty-handed," which clarifies the image and anticipates the "spoil" of v 10. Reference has to be to the successful warrior; "arrows" cannot be the antecedent because the verb is singular. The sword is said "not to return empty" in 2 Sam 1:22, and the same is affirmed for Yahweh's word in Isa 55:11. Jeremiah speaks about water jars that do "return empty" (*šābû . . . rêqām*) in a drought (14:3). Here the attacking warrior will shoot his arrows at Babylonian soldiers and not return home without having achieved an unqualified success.

10. *Yes, the Chaldeans have become spoil.* A vigorous prophetic perfect; we might say today, "The Chaldeans are history!" "Chaldeans" is a collective taking a singular verb. This term is also inclusive in the sense that it takes in the nation's many possessions, which are spoil in the strict sense; cf. 49:32. Hebrew *šālāl* is the noun, "spoil, booty" (Volz; Rudolph; Bright; Holladay; Keown et al.), not a verb (*pace* RSV; NEB; JB; NJV; NIV; Thompson; McKane).

all who despoil her shall be sated. The spoil will fill the victors to overflowing. Calvin envisions a completely destroyed Babylon, emptied of all its treasure. Another turnaround from the battle described in 46:10, where Yahweh's sword wielded by the Babylonians becomes sated with Egyptian casualties.

MESSAGE AND AUDIENCE

Yahweh begins this divine word by telling people to wander off from the city of Babylon, becoming as he-goats before the sheep. The addressee is an audience of Jewish exiles, to whom Yahweh is issuing a wake-up call. They are to take the lead in this exodus; the others will follow. Yahweh is rousing an assembly of great nations to bring up against Babylon. They will come from the proverbial north, which may evoke for this audience memories not altogether sanguine.

Never mind; the hope this word contains is sufficient to overcome painful memories. The coming foe will line up against Babylon's celebrated warriors, and in this northland—where an earlier Babylonian army decimated the Assyrians and the Egyptians—the latter will be taken. The arrows now shot will be like those of a successful warrior unaccustomed to returning from battle empty. They will hit their targets. The Chaldeans will therefore become spoil, with the despoilers becoming sated to the full.

The present word is spoken as if Babylon's fall is imminent; nevertheless, the much-awaited event may still be a considerable way off. Jeremiah could have spoken it before 594 B.C.; otherwise at a later date. Despite his repudiation of Hananiah's oracle announcing a return from Babylon in two years (chap. 28), Jeremiah did believe that a return would take place eventually. For suggested dates of this and other discourse in the Babylon collection, see Message and Audience for 50:1–3.

When this poem is heard in tandem with what precedes, the covenant people's wandering off in apostasy (v 6) will be set over against this wandering out of Babylon (v 8). The covenant people were lost sheep; now they become he-goats at the head of the flock. Once they were consumed (v 7); now the consumed one is Babylon (v 10).

5. Babylon Facing Yahweh's Fury (50:11–13)

50 [11]How glad you are! How you exult!
    plunderers of my heritage
How you frisk like a threshing heifer
    and neigh like stallions

[12]Your mother is greatly shamed
    she who bore you is disgraced
Look, the last of nations
    a wilderness of drought and a desert!

[13]At Yahweh's fury she shall not be inhabited
    and she shall become a desolation—all of her
All passing by Babylon shall be horrified
    and shall hiss over all her blows.

RHETORIC AND COMPOSITION

MT 50:11–13 = LXX 27:11–13. Verse 11 is marked off from what precedes by the messenger formula closing a prior oracle in v 10. While the T makes a causal connection between v 10 and v 11 (see Notes), commentators are nearly unanimous in taking v 11 as a new beginning. There are no section markings or messenger formulas until the *setumah* in M[L], M[A], and M[P] at the end of v 16; however, content and different addressees suggest two, perhaps three, separate poems in vv 11–16. Calvin noted a shift at v 14 to address Babylon's enemies. More recent scholars (Holladay; Reimer 1993: 38) note also the string of imperatives beginning v 14, suggesting a break with v 13. Opening imperatives can also be seen in 46:3, 9; 49:28b, 31; and 50:29. With a break established between vv 13 and 14, we find some commentators (Volz, Weiser, Carroll, Holladay) dividing vv 11–16 into two units on the basis of addressee: vv 11–13 addressing Babylon, and vv 14–16 addressing the foe of Babylon. In my view, there appear to be three separate poems, vv 11–13, 14–15, and 16, each announcing the destruction of Babylon. Earlier, T. H. Robinson (1917–18) took vv 14–15 as a unit.

The present poem (vv 11–13) celebrates Babylon's destruction as a *fait accompli*—to the point where passersby are now hissing at the city's ruins. The poem divides into three stanzas, each a double bicolon. There appears also to be a dialogue going on, since Yahweh has to be the speaker in Stanza I (v 11: "my heritage"), and Jeremiah is most likely the speaker in Stanza III (v 13: Yahweh being referred to in the third person). It is unclear who speaks in Stanza II. However, with the generally acknowledged connection between vv 11 and 12, it seems best to have Yahweh as speaker in Stanzas I and II (vv 11–12), and Jeremiah as speaker in Stanza III (v 13).

Stanza I has these repetitions:

I	*How* . . . . *How*	*kî* . . . *kî*	v 11
	. . . .		
	How	*kî*	
	. . . .		

Catchwords connecting to prior oracle:

v 12	*Look*	v 9	*Look*
	nations		*nations*
v 13	*and she has become*	v 10	*and she has become*

Catchwords connecting to the poem following:

v 13	*all . . . Babylon . . . all*	v 14	*Babylon . . . all*

NOTES

50:11. *How glad you are! How you exult! plunderers of my heritage. How you frisk like a threshing heifer, and neigh like stallions.* Reading with the Q second masculine plurals for all four verbs (Kt has feminine singulars), which correspond to the masculine plural "plunderers" and the masculine plural suffixes in v 12a. A multiple audience within Babylon is being addressed. Earlier interpretation of this verse linked it with v 10, translating the threefold *kî* as "because" (so T, followed by AV, NJV, and NIV). This has the effect of making Babylon's judgment in v 10 the result of the (earlier) wanton behavior in v 11. Babylon plundered Yahweh's heritage; therefore, others will plunder Babylon

(30:16). Modern commentators, however, are nearly unanimous in rejecting this interpretation, preferring instead a concessive meaning for *kî*, i.e., "although," or the like (cf. RSV; NEB). This makes v 11 the protasis of v 12, the meaning being that although Babylon frolics amidst vast quantities of plunder—some gained from Judah—she will be reduced to a desert wilderness, with the shame accompanying such a reversal. This latter interpretation is correct in the main, but there is no reason to make the causality so explicit. Bright's translation betters most others with its "Ah, rejoice! Ah, exult . . . Yes, frisk . . . !" The decision here is to go with an emphatic "How!" (cf. Albright 1957b on *kî-ṭôb* in Genesis 1), which reflects Yahweh's astonishment in the verse at what he sees: first a gluttonous and noisy romp, then emptiness and shame. This is a new poem, having no original causal connection with v 10.

glad . . . exult. The verbs *śmḥ* and *ʿlz* occur in close proximity in 15:16–17, and together in Zeph 3:14. The latter can refer to foolish behavior—for example, when one is drunk (51:39). Jeremiah himself shunned the "jolly" behavior of others when accepting his call to become a prophet (15:17). Here the exuberant behavior will be of short duration (Calvin; Cheyne), giving the words an ironic tone. See the ironic usage of "exult" in 11:15, and compare with 48:14–16 and Lam 4:21.

plunderers. The verb is *šsh*; compare 30:16 and 2 Kgs 17:20.

my heritage. Hebrew *naḥălātî*. The term can mean either land or people. Yahweh's heritage is preeminently his people, Israel (see Note on 2:7).

you frisk like a threshing heifer. The verb *pûš* means "leap, frisk (about)" (KB³), the image in Mal 3:20[Eng 4:2] being one of calves leaping forth from the stall. The T in the present verse has "you skip like calves of the threshing team." Rashi took *pûš* as meaning "increase, become fat," which is attested in Late Hebrew (*Dict Talm* 1149) and suits the overall image well enough, but is not the meaning here (*pace* AV). It can be inferred from Hos 10:11 that threshing was something heifers enjoyed (Ehrlich 1912: 364), although Volz (p. 425) disagrees. He says, "'Dreschende Kuh' ist kein Bild hüpfender Freude" ("'a threshing cow' is no image of bounding joy"). But it doubtless surpassed plowing, where the animal had no food to eat (Kimḥi; cf. Deut 25:4). The image then of a young calf frolicking while threshing is a reasonable one. The calf could also eat unrestrained. Daughter Zion's envisioned threshing of its enemies in Mic 4:13 is unlikely to be lackluster activity. This interpretation, in any case, is adopted by Rashi, Kimḥi, Giesebrecht, and McKane, also by the NEB ("like a heifer after threshing"), NJV, NIV, and REB ("like a heifer during the threshing"). The M^L, M^A, and M^P all have *dāšâ*, which is the Qal feminine participle of *dûš*, "one who threshes." But some MSS read *dāšāʾ* (substituting *ʾaleph* for *hēʾ*), which may simply be an alternate spelling (Rosenberg, 384; cf. McKane, 1262; BDB, 190; *BHS* fails to note). These same consonants are those of the noun *dešeʾ*, "grass," which may account for the LXX's *hōs boidia en botanē*, "like calves at grass." The Vg similarly: *sicut vituli super herbam*. Many commentators (Calvin, Duhm, Peake, Streane, Volz, Rudolph, Weiser, Bright, and Holladay) and many modern Versions (AV, RSV, JB, NAB, NJB, NRSV, and NSB) go with the reading of LXX and Vg. Either image—threshing or grazing in the field—adequately describes the act of human plundering, where unrestrained consumption is the point at issue.

threshing heifer. Threshing was done with a single animal or a team hitched together. They commonly pulled a threshing sled, or else were attached to a wheel thresher (Isa 28:27–28). For more on threshing in ancient Israel, see Borowski 1987: 63–65.

and neigh like stallions. The LXX and Vg translate *'ăbbīrîm* (lit. "mighty ones") as "bulls," and the T (also Kimḥi) as "mighty men." Both renderings, while suitable elsewhere (see Note for 46:15), do not fit here. The correct rendering is "stallions," as in 8:16 and 47:3. It is stallions who make a (shrilling) "neigh" sound (*ṣhl*, with cognates in Ar and Syr; cf. KB³; BDB; *Dict Talm* 1264). See also 5:8. Calvin points out rightly that bulls "bellow." The combined images then portray unrestrained eating and shrill noises, an apt description of the revelry associated with plundering armies.

12. *Your mother is greatly shamed.* Hebrew *bôšâ 'immĕkem mĕ'ōd.* The usual view here is that "your mother" personifies the Babylonian nation (Rashi following T; Giesebrecht; Cheyne; Cornill; Streane; Weiser; Rudolph; Bright; cf. Hos 2:4, 7[Eng 2:2, 5]; 4:5; Isa 50:1), although some commentators (Peake, Volz) suggest that Babylon is the "mother city" of other towns and villages (cf. Rabbah and her daughter-villages in 49:2). This mother, in any event, is now enveloped in shame—possibly because of the wanton plundering carried out by her children, but more likely because her children are now assumed to have been cut down in battle; cf. 15:9; 31:15. A stunning contrast to the prior merriment. On the expression "greatly shamed" (with *mĕ'ōd*), see also 20:11.

she who bore you is disgraced. Hebrew *ḥoprâ yôladtĕkem.* The LXX embellishes with "for good" (*ep' agatha*), the idea being that mothers bear children for a good (= successful) end. The similar-meaning verbs *bôš* ("be shamed") and *ḥpr* ("be disgraced") appear together also in 15:9.

Look. Hebrew *hinnēh.* The LXX omits.

the last of nations. Hebrew *'aḥărît* can mean "last" or "end," just as *rē'šît* means "first" or "beginning." Babylon is now characterized as ranking last on the world scene, the opposite of being "first of the nations" (*rē'šît haggôyīm*), a designation ascribed to Israel in Amos 6:1 (Giesebrecht; Holladay). For Israel's return to being "head of the nations" (*rō'š haggôyīm*), see Jer 31:7. Babylon is coming to an inglorious end—a desert, no less (Rashi; Calvin). Compare Num 24:20. Something similar is happening in Russia today, where people—within the country, at least—remember being a lead nation in the world, but now find themselves faced with the reality of a lost empire, shrunken borders, reduced population, and internal unrest leaving them among the lowliest of nations.

a wilderness of drought and a desert! Hebrew *midbār ṣiyyâ wa'ărābâ.* The first two terms form a construct chain. On the phraseology, compare 2:6 and 51:43. The LXX has only one term, *erēmos* ("wilderness").

13. *At Yahweh's fury she shall not be inhabited, and she shall become a desolation—all of her. All passing by Babylon shall be horrified, and shall hiss over*

all her blows. Jeremiah now offers a theological explanation for Babylon's re-duction to a wasteland. The prefixed *min* on *miqqeṣep* could be more explicitly causal, i.e., "because of," but the same basic construction in 10:10 translates "at his [i.e., Yahweh's] fury." The curse language is conventional, found through-out the book of Jeremiah. For variations on the land and city curse in Jere-miah, see Notes for 18:16 and 48:9.

Yahweh's fury. Hebrew *miqqeṣep yhwh.* The related expression "in great fury" (*bĕqeṣep gādôl*) is stereotypical (see Note on 21:5). On Yahweh's "indignation" (*za'am*), see Note for 15:17.

she shall not be inhabited. Hebrew *lō' tēšēb.* See 50:39–40 and 51:29, 37. This curse on Babylon is even stronger in Isa 13:20. For the same curse spoken against Judah, see 6:8; 9:10[Eng 9:11]; and 34:22.

and she shall become a desolation. The term "desolation" (*šĕmāmâ*) appears often in Jeremiah; see Notes on 12:10 and 46:19.

All passing by Babylon shall be horrified, and shall hiss over all her blows. The Hebrew has a nice chiasmus: *kol . . . 'al / 'al-kol.*

and shall hiss over all her blows. Hebrew *wĕyišrōq 'al-kol-makkôteyhā.* Gosse (1998: 79) sees here an answer to the curse of 19:8 against Judah. Compare also 18:16; 25:9; 49:17; and 51:37.

MESSAGE AND AUDIENCE

Yahweh in this poem addresses those who plundered his heritage, noting how like threshing heifers and neighing stallions they enjoyed their revelry. But it was short-lived. Now comes an indictment against these reckless intruders, who as yet remain unnamed. Yahweh says their mother is much shamed and disgraced. Look, they are now the least of the nations, a wilderness, a dry land, and a desert! The audience is left to surmise that this is a nation that once thought of itself as number one. Jeremiah completes the poem by identifying Yahweh's fury and the recipient of that fury: it is Babylon. Yahweh has spoken almost as an onlooker, though not a disinterested one. Jeremiah says that Yah-weh's fury will leave this nation an uninhabited desolation. Those passing by the ruined city will recoil in horror and hiss at the devastation they see.

This poem fits well in the period between 597 to 594 B.C., where the Baby-lonian plunder of Judah is a fresh memory. The judgment on Babylon is couched in stereotypical language, and should not be correlated with Baby-lon's actual fall to Cyrus in 539 B.C.

When the present poem is heard in tandem with the poem immediately pre-ceding, the message is this: Babylon became spoil because she herself plun-dered with abandon the heritage of Yahweh.

6. Babylon Facing Yahweh's Vengeance (50:14–15)

50 [14]Line up against Babylon round about
all who bend the bow

Shoot at her
  spare not an arrow
    (for against Yahweh she has sinned)

[15]Shout against her round about
  she has given her hand
Her towers[1] have fallen
  her walls are overthrown.

For this is the vengeance of Yahweh. Take vengeance against her; as she has done, do to her!

RHETORIC AND COMPOSITION

MT 50:14–15 = LXX 27:14–15. This poem is the second in a cluster of three, delimited largely by content and the one to whom it is addressed (see Rhetoric and Composition for 50:11–13). The addressees here are warriors fighting against Babylon. The concluding word about Yahweh's vengeance in v 15c also aids in delimitation, comparing as it does with a similar add-on in v 28. There is another later supplement at the end of v 14: "for against Yahweh she has sinned." Since both supplements speak of Yahweh in the third person, Yahweh may be the original speaker of the poem. But Jeremiah could also be the speaker in the absence of a clarifying messenger formula.

The original poem has two stanzas (v 14ab, v 15ab), both of which are double bicolons nicely balanced by the following repetitions and key words:

I	. . . . *against Babylon round about*	*'al-bābel sābîb*	v 14
	. . . .		
II	. . . . *against her round about*	*'āleyhā sābîb*	v 15
	. . . .		

Catchwords connecting to the prior poem:

v 14 *Babylon . . . all*   v 13 *all . . . Babylon . . . all*

Catchwords connecting to the poem following:

v 14 *Babylon*   v 16 *from Babylon*

NOTES

50:14. *Line up . . . Shoot at her, spare not an arrow.* Asyndeton, on which see Note for 4:6.

---

[1]Reading the Q '*ošyôteyhā*, "her towers" (see Notes).

Line up against Babylon. I.e., in battle formation. See v 9. Yahweh here and in the next verse is again giving battle orders, a formal element in the prophetic oracles according to Bach (1962: 54) and Christensen (1975: 257). See further Note for 46:3. The actual lineup of Cyrus's army before Babylon is described by Xenophon (*Cyropaedia* vii 5, 3–6).

all who bend the bow. Hebrew *kol-dōrĕkê qešet.* There may be a wordplay in *ʿirkû* ("Line up") and *dōrĕkê* ("who bend"). The composite bow required both the hand and foot to set the arrow; see 46:9; 50:29; and Note for 9:2[Eng 9:3]. The Medes, whether or not they are envisioned here (51:11, 28), are depicted as able archers against the Babylonians in Isa 13:18.

Shoot at her. Hebrew *yĕdû ʾēleyhā.* There is uncertainty about the verb. A few MSS have *yrh*, which also means "to throw, shoot." In either case, we are talking about the shooting of arrows, as the context makes clear. But Rashi imagined here the throwing of stones (cf. Lam 3:53).

spare not an arrow. Hebrew *ʾal-taḥmĕlû ʾel-ḥēṣ.* The verb *ḥml ʾel* means "have compassion, spare" (KB[3]; cf. 50:14). The same construction occurs in 51:3: "Spare not her young men" (*ʾal-taḥmĕlû ʾel-baḥûrehā*). Elsewhere *ḥml* produces the same sense with *ʿal* (2 Sam 12:6; Job 20:13). Kimhi says the meaning here is that one should not worry about arrows not finding their mark, and thus being wasted, for every arrow will surely find its mark. But maybe the point is that one should not worry about wasted arrows because the battle will assuredly be won.

(for against Yahweh she has sinned). The LXX omits, and most commentators take as MT expansion, which it probably is (cf. 50:24). If Yahweh is the original speaker of the poem, then it definitely is expansion. In 50:7 it is stated that the Babylonians were not guilty because it was the covenant people who had sinned (*ḥṭʾ*) against Yahweh. Since Babylon has no covenant with Yahweh, it seems here that a wrong against God's people is a wrong against God himself (Calvin).

15. *Shout against her round about.* The battle orders now rise to a dramatic climax, with a command that the attacking host give an anticipatory victory shout (cf. Josh 6:10, 16; 1 Sam 17:52; Amos 1:14; Isa 42:13). Kimhi says the purpose is to confuse and create chaos. The LXX is poorer for its omission of "round about" (*sābîb*), which repeats in a significant collocation the "round about" of v 14 (see Rhetoric and Composition). This is a well-attested Jeremiah term (1:15; 6:3; 12:9; 25:9; 50:14, 15, 29), not to mention the more familiar *missābîb* (see Note for 6:25). The LXX reading, *katakrotēsate epʾ autēn* ("Strike against her"), should be rejected (Cornill; McKane).

she has given her hand. I.e., she has submitted, surrendered (Kimhi). Hebrew *nātĕnâ yādāh.* See 2 Kgs 10:15; Ezek 17:18; Lam 5:6; 1 Chr 29:24; 2 Chr 30:8; also Virgil's *Aeneid* xii 936–37, where stretching forth the hand indicates surrender to the victor. Compare too Latin *manus dare* ("to give in, surrender"). The LXX's *parelythēsan hai cheires autēs* ("her hands were weakened"), which correctly renders the Hebrew in v 43, is not quite right here.

Her towers have fallen, her walls are overthrown. The Q *ʾošyôteyhā* is a *hapax legomenon* in the OT and does not mean "her foundations," which is the translation in T and the one adopted in the AV. The term is a loanword from Akk *asītu*, which means "tower in a city wall" (*CAD* 1/2: 332–33; KB³: *'ošyâ*). Babylon's city walls—both the inner and outer walls—had many small and large towers. The northeast wall alone contained an estimated 90 towers (L. W. King 1919: 26 n. 2). The correct rendering, "her towers" (NIV; NSB), was anticipated by Hitzig, who, in noting that foundations do not fall, suggested "towers" from LXX's *hai epalxeis autēs*, "her battlements." Giesebrecht proposed the same translation. H. R. Cohen (1978: 46–47) cites an Akkadian text where "tower" and "wall" stand in parallelism as they do here. Once again, the envisioned judgment on Babylon is stereotypical, and need not be correlated with the nation's actual fall to Cyrus. According to Xenophon (*Cyropaedia* vii 5), Cyrus diverted water from a protecting river; then, on a night when the Babylonians were partying, he and his army entered the city without difficulty. Herodotus (i 191) and the Nabonidus Chronicle agree that Babylon fell without a fight (*ANET*³ 306; cf. Bright 1981: 360; Kuhrt 1995: 600–602), but Kuhrt thinks some hard battles were nevertheless fought before Cyrus walked unopposed into the city.

her walls are overthrown. I.e., they are torn down. The verb *hrs* occurs in 1:10. Babylon's wall is also seen as fallen in 51:44 and 58. According to Xenophon (*Cyropaedia* vii 5.1, 7), Cyrus surveyed Babylon's walls upon arrival and decided that they were too massive and too high to attack. On the celebrated walls of Babylon, see further Note on 51:58.

For this is the vengeance of Yahweh. Take vengeance against her; as she has done, do to her! This add-on is post-586 B.C. when Jerusalem's walls had already been torn down by the Babylonians (52:14 = 2 Kgs 25:10). Introduced is a *lex talionis* theme that may come from the poetry in v 29cd. Holladay thinks the vengeance idea, which recurs in v 28, may derive from the poetry in 51:6. See also Ps 137:8. For Yahweh's vengeance (*nqm*) carried out against the nations, see Note for 46:10.

as she has done, do to her! A comparison using *ka'ăšer*; see v 18 and Note on 7:14.

MESSAGE AND AUDIENCE

This poem begins, as many others do, with Yahweh giving battle orders to an army fighting on his behalf. This army, whose identity we do not know, is told to line up against Babylon on all sides. Those bending the bow are to shoot without letup, holding back not a single arrow. The army is simultaneously to raise a deafening shout on all sides, which will remind a Jerusalem audience of the legendary assault on Jericho. The results are once again immediate. Babylon is seen giving her hand in surrender; her mighty towers have fallen and her massive city walls have been hammered down.

In the post-586 B.C. period, when Jerusalem was itself a ruin of fallen walls, some scribe added that Babylon's fate would come about because she had sinned against Yahweh. This same hand, or else another, added also the concluding words about Babylon being the recipient of Yahweh's vengeance. The fall of Babylon had not yet taken place, as the concluding words ask that Babylon be punished in the same manner that Jerusalem was punished. This audience here is expected to link future fallen walls with walls already fallen—the one set of walls in Babylon; the other in Jerusalem.

This poem as a future judgment against Babylon fits well in the period of 597 to 594 B.C. For dates of poems generally in the Babylon collection, see Message and Audience for 50:1–3.

7. Cut Off the Sower from Babylon (50:16)

50 ¹⁶Cut off the one sowing from Babylon
　and the one handling the sickle at harvest time
Before the oppressive sword
　each to his people they turn
　　and each to his land they flee.

RHETORIC AND COMPOSITION

MT 50:16 = LXX 27:16. For the delimitation of this verse as a separate poem, see Rhetoric and Composition for 50:11–13. T. H. Robinson (1917–18) takes it as a fragment added to vv 14–15. The first colon in 16b is repeated in 46:16c, and the two final colons are nearly the same as Isa 13:14b. The poem's lower limit is marked by *setumahs* in M^L, M^A, and M^P after v 16. No speaker is indicated, but we may assume it is Yahweh directing the foe against Babylon as in vv 14–15.

At the end of the poem is this climactic repetition (*anaphora*):

each (person)	*ʾîs*	v 16b
and each (person)	*wĕʾîs*	

Catchwords connecting to the prior poem:

v 16 *from Babylon* 　　　　　 v 14 *Babylon*

Catchwords connecting to the oracles following:

v 16 *his land* 　　　　　 v 18 *his land*

NOTES

50:16. *Cut off the one sowing from Babylon, and the one handling the sickle at harvest time.* The enemy is not sent to open areas in the city but to farming acreage in the country. Giesebrecht says "Babylon" here means Babylonia, which is correct. Destruction will come upon workers at both ends of the agricultural season—sowing and reaping. The verb "cut off" (*kirtû*) does double duty for both colons, making the second word particularly sharp: the one cutting grain will himself be cut down. This prophecy too is stereotypical, Calvin saying that it was not fulfilled by Cyrus.

sickle. The Heb *maggāl* occurs only here and in Joel 4:13[Eng 3:13]. Another tool, *ḥermēš,* was of a similar nature (Deut 16:9; 23:26). Ancient flint sickles (flint pieces attached to handles of wood or bone) continued in use during the Iron Age along with metal sickles. Excavations have turned up both types in quantity, e.g., the fine collection of iron sickles from Hazor (Borowski 1987: 61). A flint sickle (without wooden handle) was found amidst a collection of domestic objects at Tell Hassura, which is in the Mosul region of northern Iraq; for a picture, see Lloyd and Sufar 1945: fig. 37. A painting of an Egyptian harvest (fifteenth century B.C.) survives, in which two men are seen cutting grain with sickles; for a picture, see $ANEP^2$ 27 #91. On reaping in ancient Israel, see Borowski 1987: 57–62; also "Harvests, Harvesting" in *ABD* 3: 63–64.

Before the oppressive sword, each to his people they turn, and each to his land they flee. The scene is that reflected in 46:16: foreigners in the country decide it is time to return home. Among such will be Jews. See also 50:8; 51:9; and especially Isa 13:14. Americans decided to leave Beirut after civil war began there in 1975, and not a few departures were made in great haste. The same happens to foreigners in any region under threat of war or where war has already broken out.

Before the oppressive sword. Hebrew *mippĕnê* can mean either "(from) before" or "because (of)." The same phrase occurs in 46:16c and in LXX 32:38 (= MT 25:38).

MESSAGE AND AUDIENCE

Yahweh in this brief poem addresses once again the unnamed enemy of Babylon, this time focusing not on the defenders of city walls and fortified towers, but upon the defenseless farmers inhabiting the countryside. Occupation of the land will be such that the entire growing season—from planting to harvesting—will be affected. Both sowers of seed and reapers of the harvest will be cut down. Before the oppressive sword, foreigners will return in haste to their homeland.

This poem could fit, along with others in the cluster, into the period prior to 594 B.C. when much of Judah's farmland had been overrun by foreign intruders. Holladay (p. 417) suggests a setting for vv 14–16 in the later part of Jeremiah's career.

When this poem is heard in tandem with the prior poem, judgment will be perceived as taking in both city and country. People everywhere will be cut down. The only survivors will be foreigners, who will flee in haste to their homelands.

8. Israel Back in Its Pasture (50:17–20)

50 ¹⁷Israel is a dispersed sheep
    lions have isolated.

First the king of Assyria consumed him, and lastly Nebuchadrezzar, the king of Babylon, has gnawed his bones.

[18]Therefore thus said Yahweh of hosts, God of Israel:
Look I will make a reckoning to the king of Babylon and to his land, as I made a reckoning to the king of Assyria. [19]And I will restore Israel to his pasture, and he shall graze on Carmel and the Bashan, and on the mountains of Ephraim and Gilead his appetite shall be sated.

[20]In those days and at that time—oracle of Yahweh—the iniquity of Israel shall be sought out and there shall be none, also the sins of Judah, and they shall not be found. For I will forgive those whom I leave remaining.

RHETORIC AND COMPOSITION

MT 50:17–20 = LXX 27:17–20. The present verses are delimited at the top end by the *setumah* in M^L, M^P, and M^A prior to v 17. At the bottom end, M^A has a *petuḥah* and M^P a *setumah* after v 20. One MS in the Cambridge Genizah Collection (NS 282. 18) also has a section after v 20. The M^L has no section here. In M^L and M^P appears also a *setumah*, and in M^A a *petuḥah*, after v 17, separating the poetic fragment and its expansion from the prose oracles following. Both oracles contain messenger formulas, Oracle I an expanded "Therefore thus said Yahweh of hosts, God of Israel," and Oracle II an "oracle of Yahweh" formula after "In those days and at that time." The LXX reduces the first formula, and the second it puts at the end of v 20, where also it reads "on the land" (*epi tēs gēs* = *ʿal-hāʾāreṣ*) after "I leave remaining" (see Notes).

It is widely—though not universally—agreed that v 17a is a genuine fragment of Jeremiah poetry (T. H. Robinson 1917–18; Rudolph; Weiser; Bright; Holladay; cf. *BHS*), with v 17b being later prose expansion. Regarding vv 18–20 opinions of commentators and the modern Versions differ. Cornill found these verses to be metrically cumbersome. Also, they contain common prose particles such as *kaʾăšer* in v 18, *laʾăšer* in v 20, and three occurrences of the *nota accusativi* in vv 19–20 (cf. D. N. Freedman 1982). The verses are then best taken as prose, with a return to poetry coming in v 21. Verses 17b–19 (20) are not all commentary on v 17a (*pace* Bright), still less the work of a later glossator (*pace* Giesebrecht, Volz, and Jones). The commentary is confined to v 17b, with vv 18–20 being two bona fide oracles that announce punishment for Babylon and restoration for Israel. These oracles are consistent with Jeremianic preaching elsewhere in the book, and should be taken as genuine utterances from the prophet (Eissfeldt 1961: 35). We may also have another dialogue here, with Jeremiah speaking in v 17a, and Yahweh responding with two oracles in vv 18–20.

Catchwords connecting to the preceding poem:

v 18 *his land*   v 16 *his land*

Catchwords connecting to the following unit:

v 18	*his land*	v 21–28	*the land* (5×)
v 20	*I leave remaining*	v 26	*remnant*

NOTES

50:17. *Israel is a dispersed sheep, lions have isolated.* A suffix on the second verb appears in the LXX (*auton*) and the Vg (*eum*): "lions have isolated him." Both may take their cue from the masculine pronouns in v 17b. The image in the poetry is of lions attacking sheep, and "sheep" (*śeh*) is feminine. The loss of a *hē'* on the verb could be attributed to haplography (the following *hārī'šôn* begins with *hē'*), but this would have to be the feminine *hā*. A suffix makes for easier reading, but is not absolutely necessary. Like the lost sheep of vv 6–7 (collective *ṣō'n*), a dispersed Israel is isolated and has fallen victim to attackers. Lions on the prowl commonly isolate young, old, weak, and injured animals from the herd, and then make the kill. Hebrew *hiddîḥû* means more precisely in this context "to thrust out of the flock and seize."

sheep. Hebrew *śeh* means "one of a flock," either a sheep or a goat (BDB; KB³). The term is usually taken as a collective (Giesebrecht, Cornill, Duhm, Peake, Bright); however, it cannot denote an entire flock simply because the image here is one of a single sheep — or at most a limited number of sheep — that has become separated from the flock, and as a result vulnerable to enemy attack.

lions. The T expectedly has "kings," which is supported here by the supplementary 17b.

Nebuchadrezzar. The LXX omits; perhaps an MT plus (Cornill; cf. Janzen 1973: 70).

has gnawed his bones. Hebrew *'iṣṣĕmô* appears to be a denominative Piel with suffix from *'eṣem*, "bone." Rashi: "he broke his bones," i.e., in order to suck out the marrow. Envisioned here is progressive destruction: Assyria consumed the flesh, and Babylon gnawed the bones. Reference is to the demise of Northern Israel in 722 B.C. and Judah in 586 B.C.

18. *Yahweh of hosts, God of Israel.* The LXX lacks "of hosts" as elsewhere (see Appendix VI), also "God of Israel."

Look I will make a reckoning . . . as I made a reckoning. A comparison using *ka'ăšer*; on which see v 15 and Note for 7:14. For the verb *pqd* ("pay a visit, reckon") in Jeremiah, see 46:25 and Note for 5:9. The construction here is similar to the one in 44:13. The promised visit will again be to punish. The Babylonian Empire has not yet been overthrown. Nineveh, the capital of Assyria, fell to a coalition of Babylonians and Medes in 612 B.C. (§Introduction: Late Seventh and Early Sixth Centuries B.C.). Here the demise of both is attributed to Yahweh of hosts.

19. *And I will restore Israel to his pasture.* "Pasture" (*nāweh*) denotes the land of Israel, as in 10:25 and 23:3. In 31:23, "righteous pasture" (*nĕwēh-ṣedek*) refers to Jerusalem, and in 50:7 is an epithet for Yahweh. For an expanded version of the present image, see Ezek 34:11–16.

and he shall graze on Carmel and the Bashan, and on the mountains of Ephraim and Gilead his appetite shall be sated. The richest of pastureland is promised to Israel on its return home (cf. Mic 7:14; Deut 32:14; Song 4:1). On "the Bashan" (*habbāšān*), see Note for 22:20. The *bĕ* on *ûbĕhar* ("and on the mountains") does double duty (backward gapping), although in Hebrew poetry the sense can be obtained without the preposition. The LXX omits "and the Bashan," which is probably more loss due to haplography (homoeoarcton: *w . . . w*).

his appetite shall be sated. The basic meaning of *nepeš* is "throat," where the appetite is first sated; cf. 31:14.

20. *In those days and at that time.* This introductory phrase occurs also in v 4 and 33:15; see further Notes for 3:16–17.

the iniquity of Israel shall be sought out and there shall be none, also the sins of Judah, and they shall not be found. Grand hyperbole, anticipating Yahweh's future grace toward Israel. "Iniquity" and "sin(s)" are a stereotyped pair in Jeremiah (see Note for 16:18). Envisioned here is a happy reversal of the judgments in 2:22 and 30:14–15, made possible by Yahweh's forgiveness as stated in the New Covenant passage (31:34), also what follows here. Kimḥi says this condition cannot possibly refer to the Second Temple period, when Jews committed many sins, as they were also doing in his day. Christian interpretation would be somewhat different, not so far as God's renewed people being without sin is concerned, but to the extent that God's promise to forgive sin is seen as having been fulfilled in the death of Jesus (see "New Covenant" in *ABD* 4: 1088–94, also Excursus V in *Jeremiah 21–36*, 474–79).

the iniquity of Israel shall be sought out. For the accusative with a passive form of the verb, see also 35:14 and cf. GKC §121b.

For I will forgive those whom I leave remaining. Hebrew has a wordplay in *la'ăšer 'aš'îr* ("those whom I leave remaining"). In 31:34 and 33:8 forgiveness, as here, is seen as a unilateral act of divine grace. In 36:3 it is conditional on Judah returning from evil. For an unconditional pardon and cleansing of Israel's remnant elsewhere in the Prophets, see Mic 7:18–19 and Ezek 36:25–29. In the NT, Paul talks of a "remnant chosen by grace" (Rom 11:5).

whom I leave remaining. The LXX finishes the sentence with *epi tēs gēs* ("on the land"), after which comes the messenger formula. The MT has the formula earlier in the verse, and *'al-hā'āreṣ* ("against the land") at the beginning of v 21. Both readings make sense.

MESSAGE AND AUDIENCE

A fragment of Jeremianic poetry has been pressed into service here as a foil for two restoration oracles addressed to Israel. The nation is now a dispersed sheep, having been isolated from the flock by lions on the prowl. Another hand assists a later audience by interpreting and expanding the metaphor. Israel, as

it happened, was not simply hunted by hungry foes; Assyria consumed Northern Israel, and what remained of Judah was eaten and gnawed by Nebuchadrezzar and the Babylonians.

The metaphor of a dispersed Israel, without the later embellishment, sets up
admirably two quite extraordinary oracles promising divine visitations to Babylon and Remnant Israel. The first oracle states that Babylon will be paid a visit
by Yahweh, just as Assyria was earlier, and the audience is left to surmise that
judgment will again be the result. The good news for Israel is that it will be restored to its land, and will be sated as in earlier times on the lush mountains
and highlands it knows so well—Carmel, Bashan, Ephraim, and Gilead. For
those hearing the oracle with the expansion in v 17b, a dispersed nation that
was once food for the enemy will now be sated with every good thing in a land
still seen as being its own.

The second oracle is hyperbolic in predicting a future time when Israel's
sins will be sought but not found. The reason: Yahweh will forgive those he
leaves as a remnant. The audience hears in this oracle something no less grand
than what is conveyed in the New Covenant oracle.

Oracle I reflects a time after the demise of Assyria (609 B.C.) and before
judgment comes upon Babylon. The second oracle, so similar to the New
Covenant oracle of 31:31–34, can be dated along with it and other hopeful
prophecies to the days just before Jerusalem's fall. The poetic fragment can be
from any time after the exile of 597 B.C. Thus we can propose for the poetic
fragment and the two oracles in combination a date within the decade between 597 and 586 B.C. The expansion material in v 17b requires a date after
586 B.C.

9. Shattered Is the Hammer of the Whole Land! (50:21–28)

50 ²¹Against the land, Merathaim
   go up against her
And to the inhabitants of Pekod
   slay and devote to destruction the last of them[1]
    —oracle of Yahweh—
   (and do according to all that I have commanded you).

²²The sound of war in the land
   yes, a great shatter!

²³How he is cut off and shattered
   the hammer of the whole land!
How she has become a desolation
   Babylon among the nations!

---

[1]Emending to 'aḥărîtām ("the last of them"), which provides an equivalent to Targum's "their
remnant"; MT has 'aḥărêhem ("after them").

²⁴You set a trap for yourself[2]
and even you were captured, Babylon!
and you, you did not know
You were found, and even you were seized
for with Yahweh you ventured into a struggle

²⁵Yahweh opened his armory
and brought out the weapons of his wrath
For Lord Yahweh of hosts had this work
in the land of the Chaldeans

²⁶Come against her from every side
open her granaries
Pile her up like heaps and devote her to destruction
let there not be for her a remnant!

²⁷Slay all her bulls
let them go down to slaughter
Woe to them for their day has come
the time of their reckoning.

²⁸The sound of escapees and fugitives from the land of Babylon to declare
in Zion: the vengeance of Yahweh our God, the vengeance of his temple.

RHETORIC AND COMPOSITION

MT 50:21–28 = LXX 27:21–28. The present unit consists of three parts: 1) an oracle calling for holy war against Babylon (v 21); 2) a dialogue poem describing that war (vv 22–27); and 3) a later supplement celebrating Babylon's fall from the perspective of Jewish escapees who lived to proclaim Yahweh's vengeance (v 28). The opening oracle is delimited at the top end by a return to poetry in v 21. Its conclusion is marked by the messenger formula concluding 21b, and after the expansion in 21c (see Notes), by *setumahs* in M^L, M^A, and M^P at the end of v 21. The oracle is characterized by singular imperatives, distinguishing it from the poem following, where the imperatives in vv 26–27a are plural. The first oracle is a double bicolon in MT, which begins with "against this land"; in the LXX, where the same words are a conclusion to v 20, the oracle is a tricolon. The MT reading is followed here.

The dialogue poem begins in v 22 and concludes with v 27, after which occur *setumahs* in M^L, M^A, and M^P. The M^P also has a *setumah* after v 24, which could indicate two poems originally in vv 22–24 and vv 25–27. The rhetorical analysis following shows that if at one time there were two separate poems, they

---

[2]Reading MT *yāqōštî* as the archaic second feminine singular, "you set a trap" (2:20; cf. 2:33 and 4:19c), instead of the first singular "I set a trap."

are now well integrated. The probability seems greater that the verses were a single poem to begin with. Closure of the unit comes at v 28 (Rudolph), as the linking words show.

The oracle is linked to the dialogue poem by inverted key words, some of which have been noted by Condamin and Keown et al.:

I	*Pekod = reckoning*	*pĕqôd*	v 21
	slay	*ḥărōb*	
	and devote to destruction	*wĕhaḥărēm*	
II	*and devote her to destruction*	*wĕhaḥărîmûhā*	v 26b
	Slay	*ḥirbû*	v 27
	their reckoning	*pĕquddātām*	

The dialogue poem, assuming it is a single composition, divides into six stanzas. Stanza I (v 22) is an introductory bicolon beginning with the Jeremianic *qôl*, "sound, voice," on which see Note for 3:21. This bicolon should not be deleted with Volz, who takes it as a stereotyped supplement.

Stanza II (v 23) is a double bicolon with the following repetition:

II	*How*	*'êk*	v 23
	. . . .		
	How	*'êk*	
	. . . .		

The lines also alternate masculine and feminine imagery: "How *he* is cut off and shattered" / "How *she* has become a desolation." Both could refer to Babylon, but a better reading has the masculine figure as the Babylonian king, and the feminine figure as Babylon the nation. The T, one will note, has "the king" as subject of the first verb. The alternation of gender, in any case, is intentional.

Stanzas I and II have key word linkage with inversion:

I	. . . . *in the land*	*bā'āreṣ*	v 22
	. . . . *shatter*	*šeber*	
II	. . . . *shattered*	*yiššābēr*	v 23a
	. . . . *the whole land*	*kol-hā'āreṣ*	

Stanza III (v 24) is nicely balanced with this repetition:

III	. . . . *and even*	*wĕgam*	v 24
	. . . .		
	. . . . *and even*	*wĕgam*	
	. . . .		

Stanzas II and III are linked together by these key words:

II	*Babylon*		v 23b
	. . . . *Babylon*		v 24b

In Stanza IV (v 25) internal balance is created with the divine name:

IV *Yahweh*	v 25
. . . .	
. . . Lord Yahweh of hosts	
. . . .	

Stanzas III and IV are also linked by a repetition of the divine name and the particle *kî* ("for"):

III *for with Yahweh*	*kî bayhwh*	v 24b
IV *Yahweh*	*yhwh*	v 25
For . . . . Yahweh	*kî . . . yhwh*	

Stanza V (v 26) has this internal repetition:

V . . . . . *against her*	*lāh*	v 26
. . . . . *for her*	*lāh*	

Stanzas IV and V are linked together by a key word repetition seen earlier in 1:14–15 (see Rhetoric and Composition for 1:13–19):

IV . . . . . . *opened*	*pātaḥ*	v 25
V *open*	*pithû*	v 26

Stanzas V and VI (v 27) are linked by this repetition:

V *Come*	*bō'û*	v 26
VI . . . . *has come*	*bā'*	v 27

The supplement (v 28) links up to the beginning of the dialogue poem with the following key words, which are noted in part by Holladay:

The sound . . . . . . *in the land*	*qôl . . . bā'āreṣ*	v 22
The sound . . . . . . *from the land*	*qôl . . . mē'ereṣ*	v 28

The dialogue poem alternates speakers, although uncertainties remain as to who the speakers are. The prophet may be taken as the speaker in Stanzas I and II (vv 22–23), which makes him the one hearing the din of war (Calvin; Thompson) and the one making an ironic lament. Stanza III (v 24) is a problem, requiring a speaker change at midpoint if we read the opening *yāqōštî* as a first person, "I set a trap." That would make Yahweh the speaker in 24a, and someone else the speaker in 24b, where Yahweh is referred to in the third person (Rudolph). This second speaker could be Jeremiah again. But if v 24a opens with "You set a trap," as the Hebrew is now commonly read (see Notes), then Jeremiah is likely speaker of the entire stanza. He is also the speaker in Stanza IV (v 25), where Yahweh is again referred to in the third person. In

Stanzas V and VI (vv 26–27) either Yahweh or the enemy is issuing orders in the heat of battle and its aftermath.

Assuming a second-person beginning to v 24, I would propose the following sequence of speakers in the unit as a whole:

The oracle:	Yahweh speaking	v 21
The dialogue poem:	Jeremiah speaking	vv 22–25
	Yahweh or Babylon's foe speaking	vv 26–27
Supplement:	Jewish escapees from Babylon speaking	v 28

Catchwords connecting to the prior unit:

v 21–28	the land (5×)	v 18	his land
v 26	remnant	v 20	I leave remaining

Catchwords connecting to the following unit:

v 21	and do according to all that . . .	waʿăśēh kěkōl ʾăšer . . .	v 29c	according to all that she has done, do . . .	kěkōl ʾăšer ʿāśĕtâ ʿăśû . . . .
v 27	their day		v 30	that day	
v 28	escapees	pělēṭîm	v 29b	escape	pělēṭâ

NOTES

50:21. *Against the land, Merathaim, go up against her; And to the inhabitants of Pekod, slay and devote to destruction the last of them.* An unidentified foe is commissioned here to make holy war on two regions of Babylon, which may be regarded as an offensive action against the entire country. Yahweh's command is to kill and devote to destruction every last inhabitant. On the "summons to battle" in the prophetic oracle, see 50:14 and Note for 46:3.

Against the land, Merathaim. Hebrew ʿal-hāʾāreṣ měrātayim cannot be a construct chain (i.e., "against the land of Merathaim") because of the definite article on hāʾāreṣ, "the land" (*pace* NJV; cf. McKane). If the MT is to be read, Merathaim must stand in apposition to "the land" (Volz). The LXX places "on the land" at the end of v 20: "those whom I leave remaining on the land," which is also a viable reading (see Note for 50:20). Most commentators and modern translations (AV; RSV; NEB; JB; NAB; NIV; NSB) redivide the consonants and revocalize to ʿălēh ʾereṣ, a suggestion made by J. D. Michaelis (1793: 378) and adopted by Duhm, Rudolph, and others. This provides the initial colon with a verb and alleviates the construct chain problem: "Go up (against) the land of Merathaim." BHS (citing S) advocates this reading, despite the absence of an ʿal ("against") or ʾel ("to") after the verb. A loss of one particle or the other is said by some commentators (e.g., Bright; McKane) to be attributed to haplography, but if so, it cannot be argued as a case of homoeoarcton or ho-moeoteleuton. The NEB, NAB, and NIV smooth things out with "Attack the land of Merathaim." All these solutions give the same basic meaning, and all in one way or another build on the reading of MT.

Merathaim. Hebrew *mĕrātayim* is lit. "double rebellion," a perjorative name given to Babylon (Rashi; Kimḥi). The dual may express intensity (Cheyne; Peake; cf. discussion in Note on 16:18), although it is frequent in biblical place-names. The term sounds very Jeremianic; see also 17:18. The Versions rendered it as an appellative, but it is now believed to be a wordplay on *mar-ratu*, Akk for a salt-water region in southern Babylonia where the Tigris and Euphrates empty into the Persian Gulf (*CAD* 10/1: 285; KB³).

go up against her. Hebrew *ʿălēh ʿāleyhā* is paronomasia (cf. 50:3). For another paronomasia made from the same verb and preposition, see 8:18.

Pekod. Hebrew *pĕqôd.* An Aramean tribal region in southern Babylonia, situated east of the Tigris between Sealand in the south and the Diyala River in the north (Dalglish, *ABD* 5: 216–17). Pekod also denotes the tribe inhabiting this region (Ezek 23:23). Known as the Pukûdu in Neo-Assyrian and Neo-Babylonian texts, these people are well attested in the Assyrian annals of Tiglath-pileser III (745–727 B.C.), Sargon II (721–705 B.C.), and Sennacherib (704–681 B.C.), being mentioned also in "The Court of Nebuchadnezzar" document (iv; *ANET³* 308; cf. Jacobsen, *IDB* K–Q, 709; Tadmor 1994: 130–31). The name plays on the oft-used Jeremiah verb *pqd*, where the infinitive here would mean "visit or reckon (to punish)." On this verb, see Note for 5:9. Merathaim and Pekod are then chosen for their wordplay possibilities, and in tandem make an implied connection between rebellion and punishment.

slay and devote to destruction the last of them. Poetic artistry continues with a threefold alliteration on the *ḥr* consonants. Yahweh is pressing into service an unidentified agent to carry out holy war against Babylon. The first imperative, *ḥărōb*, is correctly taken by T as a denominative of *ḥereb* ("sword"), meaning "slay (by the sword)." The LXX reads with the prior *pqwd* (MT: Pekod): *ekdikē-son machaira* ("avenge, O sword"); Symm is similar: *episkepsai dia machairas* ("look in upon / visit by the sword"); cf. LXX of 9:25 [MT 9:24] and 11:22, where *episkeptomai* translates Heb *pqd*. Hebrew *haḥărēm* ("devote to destruction") is a term taken from holy war, referring to the ban (*ḥērem*) placed upon a captured city's inhabitants—sometimes also cattle and other spoil—for the purpose of devoting (= destroying) them as a gift to Yahweh (vv 26–27; cf. 25:9; 51:3; Deut 2:34–35; 3:5–6; 13:16–18[Eng 13:15–17]; Josh 6:21).

the last of them. The reading of the NRSV, which emends as Giesebrecht does to achieve "their remnant" of the T (see textual footnote). The NJB has "every last one of them." Kimḥi and the AV read MT *'aḥărêhem*, "after them," with Kimḥi explaining the action as a pursuit of those fleeing. The LXX omits, and numerous scholars (Cornill, Streane, Volz, Jones, McKane) as well as some modern Versions (NEB, NAB, REB) do likewise, assuming MT dittography. But the explanation by Janzen (1973: 118) of an LXX omission here due to haplography (homoeoteleuton: *m . . . m*) is better.

(and do according to all that I have commanded you). A prosaic supplement indicated both by content and the relative pronoun *'ăšer*. Compare the prose of 11:4, 8; 17:22; also more importantly Deut 1:3, 41; 4:5, 13–14; 5:32; et passim, where Yahweh "commands" (*ṣwh*) and people are to "do" (*'śh*). This homiletical prose also commonly contains the relatives *kĕkōl 'ăšer* or *(ka)'ăšer*.

22. *The sound of war in the land, yes, a great shatter!* Compare 48:3 and 51:54. The "land" is Babylon, which is clarified in an expanded and rearranged LXX text. Here and throughout the poem is portrayed a war in progress, but one whose outcome can be taken as a *fait accompli*.

a great shatter! Hebrew *šeber gādôl*. A signature expression of Jeremiah; see Note on 4:6.

23. *How! . . . How!* Hebrew *'êk . . . 'êk*. A stereotypical beginning for a lament, on which see Note for 48:17b. Rashbam, citing this verse and 51:41 in his commentary on Ecclesiastes, says that "How!" always makes a rhetorical statement (Japhet and Salters 1985: 108–9). Calvin says the "How!" expresses the prophet's astonishment that mighty Babylon could be brought low. Weiser calls the entire verse an ironic lament.

How he is cut off and shattered, the hammer of the whole land. A reference not to the nation, as in the next line, but to its king (so T; cf. Rhetoric and Composition). Isaiah 14:4 says, "And you will take up this taunt against the king of Babylon and you will say, How (*'êk*) the tyrant has ceased!" Nebuchadnezzar, who was an indisputable "hammer of the whole land"—where *'āreṣ* really means "earth"—is doubtless being described. In 51:20–24 a war club (*mappēṣ*), which could be Jeremiah or some other divine agent, is ready to break nations— including Babylon—into pieces. One might make a comparison here to Charles Martel ("The Hammer"), a Frankish ruler (A.D. 688–741) who defeated the Arabs at Tours in A.D. 732; or to Edward I of England (A.D. 1239–1307), whose two victories over the Scots earned him the Westminster epitaph "Scottorum malleus" ("Hammer of the Scots").

he is cut off and shattered. Hebrew *nigda' wayyiššābēr*. The verb *gd'* means "hew down, cut off," which can include also the breaking of rock (stone horns of an altar are "cut off" in Amos 3:14). The verb occurs elsewhere in Jer 48:25. The verb *šbr* ("shatter"), like its cognate noun *šeber* in the preceding verse, appears frequently in Jeremiah. Compare Isa 14:5.

hammer. Hebrew *paṭṭîš*. KB³ says this is a blacksmith's hammer (Isa 41:7), corresponding to Ar *fiṭṭîs*. In 23:29 such a hammer is said to break rock in pieces.

How she has become a desolation, Babylon among the nations. The once-powerful king of Babylon now lies cut into pieces, and Babylon herself has been turned into a wasteland. Hebrew *šammâ* ("desolation") is another common Jeremianic term found throughout the book. This line is repeated verbatim in 51:41b.

24. *You set a trap.* Hebrew *yāqōštî*. The archaic second feminine singular, now widely adopted among scholars (G. R. Driver 1940: 168; Rudolph; Weiser; Bright; Thompson; Holladay; McKane) and in the modern Versions (NEB;

NAB; NRSV; REB; NSB), is accepted largely because v 24b—indeed all of vv 22–25—seems to presume a speaking voice other than Yahweh. The first person singular of MT, "I set a trap for you," sounds more like Yahweh speaking (see Rhetoric and Composition). Babylon's entrapment and capture is then its own doing. It ventured into a struggle with Yahweh, which was unwise in the extreme. Verse 25 gives an additional reason: Yahweh then opened his armory, and in the face of this unknown cache of weapons Babylon was overwhelmed.

and even you were captured. I.e., by Yahweh, from whom escape is impossible (see Note on 48:44). Hebrew *wĕgam-nilkadt.* A nearly identical phrase occurs in 48:7. On the collocation of "snared (*yqš*) and captured (*lkd*)," see also Isa 8:15, where Yahweh is acting against his own people.

Babylon. A vocative belonging with "and even you were captured" (*pace* BHS), which should not be omitted (*metri causa*) with certain commentators (e.g., Giesebrecht, Duhm, Cornill, Volz, and Holladay). The JB also omitted, but the NJB has restored. "Babylon" is being intentionally repeated from v 23b (see Rhetoric and Composition).

and you, you did not know. More surprise with the emphatic pronoun *wĕʾat,* "and you." Kimḥi envisions a destruction coming suddenly; if people had known, they could have fled. Jones thinks Babylon did not know that Yahweh was behind its downfall. Either explanation is plausible. It is in the very nature of entrapment that the victim be caught unaware; compare the prophet's own experience in 11:19.

You were found, and even you were seized. The S omits, which can be more haplography (homoeoteleuton: *t . . . t*). Again, Babylon cannot imagine that it will succumb to an enemy, but even the unthinkable can happen. On the impossibility of hiding from God, see Note for 49:10.

for with Yahweh you ventured into a struggle. Hebrew *kî bayhwh hitgārît.* Here a reason is given for Babylon's destruction. Labuschagne (1966: 107) says it is a case of arrogant self-exaltation, here—as in v 29—ascribed to the nation, but in vv 31–32 ascribed to the king of Babylon. The pharaoh of Egypt fell victim to the same trap at the time of the Exodus (Exod 5:2).

25. *Yahweh opened his armory, and brought out the weapons of his wrath.* Yahweh's vented wrath (*zaʿam*) is equivalent to a curse; see 6:11; 10:10; and Note on 15:17. There is paronomasia in *ʾôṣārô wayyôṣēʾ* ("his armory, he brought out"). A possible English rendering: "Yahweh opened his *closet, he disclosed* the weapons of his wrath." On Yahweh's store of weapons, see 1:14 and Deut 32:34–42. Yahweh's wrathful indignation (*zaʿam*) is discussed in Note for 15:17.

Lord Yahweh of hosts. The LXX omits "of hosts," as elsewhere; see Appendix VI.

work. Hebrew *mĕlāʾkâ.* On Yahweh's work (= mission) of judgment, see also 48:10.

the land of the Chaldeans. See Note for 50:1.

26. *Come against her . . . open her granaries . . . Pile her up . . . devote her to destruction.* The imperatives here and in the next verse are masculine plural. If the enemy is the speaker, then the warriors are urging one another on to enter

the city and begin the plundering. Otherwise it is Yahweh urging the foe to do the same. Bach (1962: 55) takes vv 26–27a as another "summons to battle," but the battle seems largely to be over, and the call now is to enter the city, begin the plunder, and devote Lady Babylon to destruction.

from every side. Hebrew *miqqēṣ* (lit. "from the end"), which Rashi took to mean from the end of the city (AV: "from the utmost border"). The term is probably elliptical, meaning "from end (to end)," or "from one end (to the other)" (Blayney; Bright), a function *miqqāṣeh* has in 51:31 (Cornill; Rudolph; cf. KB³). Rudolph cites for support the reading of Symm: *eiselthete eis autēn pantes* ("come in against her on every side"). The point is that the enemy is being summoned from every direction.

open her granaries. Hebrew *maʾăbuseyhā* ("her granaries") builds on a *hapax legomenon* in the OT, but the meaning of the noun is reasonably secure, although T rendered "her gateways." The AV has "her storehouses." The verb *ʾbs* means "to feed, fatten," where in 1 Kgs 5:3[Eng 4:23] and Prov 15:17 reference is to birds and oxen fattened for slaughter. Blayney suggested "her fattening stalls," imagining in Babylon's cities pampered inhabitants like beasts fattened for slaughter (cf. v 17 and Note on 46:21). The NEB thus has "cattle-pens" as a marginal reading. The directive, however, was to open Babylon's granaries and destroy food that had been put into storage. Babylon consumed food when it came against Judah (5:17), only it may have taken what was available on trees and in the field. Granaries of this period were of various types, most commonly stone-lined silos dug into the ground (Kelso 1948: 42 #100). A large circular granary discovered at Megiddo (ca. 780–650 B.C.) had a pair of winding stairs leading to the bottom (for a picture, see *IDB* E–J, 469). The royal stores in Babylon are believed to have been located in Nebuchadnezzar's large citadels (L. W. King 1919: 27).

Pile her up like heaps and devote her to destruction; let there not be for her a remnant. A shift now from plundered granaries to the heaping of bodies and spoil of a personified nation, then devoting the whole to destruction. Hebrew *ʿărēmîm* does not here mean "granaries," but rather "heaps" (*pace* Rashi; KB³), although the difference is slight. "Like heaps" may be a clarifying gloss; on the other hand there is nice assonance in *ʿărēmîm wĕhaḥărîmûhā*. The LXX goes its own way with *ereunēsate autēn hōs spēlaion* ("search her as a cave"). Read the MT.

and devote her to destruction. Hebrew *wĕhaḥărîmûhā*. Here again is holy war terminology such as we had in v 21 (see discussion there). Dead bodies along with other spoil are to be destroyed as a sacred gift—perhaps to Yahweh. Earlier it was a Babylonian-led alliance who, as Yahweh's agent, devoted Judah and surrounding nations to destruction (25:9).

let there not be for her a remnant. A curse. Israel gets a remnant (v 20); Babylon does not.

27. *Slay all her bulls, let them go down to the slaughter*. Hebrew *par* generally denotes a bull calf (BDB; KB³; cf. Péter 1975), though it can be as old as seven years, according to Judg 6:25. The question here is whether "bulls" is to be

taken literally, or is meant to be a metaphor for select warriors (48:15; Ps 22:13[Eng 22:12]) or Babylon's leaders (Isa 34:6–7; Ezek 39:18). The T's "mighty men" is followed by most commentators (Rashi; Kimḥi; Calvin; Giesebrecht; Cheyne; Streane; Volz; Weiser; Rudolph; Bright). P. D. Miller (1970: 184) thinks that the reference is to the nation's leaders. But Duhm says these are actual bulls. Holladay concludes that either a human or animal interpretation is possible. Since we have been talking thus far about captured people and grain, the inclusion of animals here may be the better interpretation (cf. 5:17). The LXX continues the agricultural metaphor with *anaxēranate autēs pantas tous karpous* ("dry up all her produce"), reading *ḥrb* as the verb "dry up." On *ḥrb* as a denominative meaning "slay (by the sword)," see v 21 above.

Woe to them for their day has come, the time of their reckoning. This lament, unlike the one in v 23, is in dead earnest. But it combines mourning with judgment, on which see Note for 22:13. On the "day of Yahweh" for all nations, see Note for 46:10.

the time of their reckoning. Hebrew *ʿēt pĕquddātām*, occurring also in 46:21. On variations of this stereotyped expression in Jeremiah, see v 31 and Note on 6:15.

28. *The sound of escapees and fugitives from the land of Babylon to declare in Zion: the vengeance of Yahweh our God, the vengeance of his temple.* Here liberated Jews (Babylon has no remnant) are heard bringing the news of Babylon's demise to Zion. It is the vengeance of Yahweh, God of Israel, vengeance for his temple. See also 50:15; 51:11; and Isa 47:3. Regarding Yahweh's vengeance upon other nations generally, see Note on 46:10.

the vengeance of his temple. The LXX omits, leading many commentators (Cornill; Duhm; Giesebrecht; Rudolph; Janzen 1973: 60; Holladay; Jones; McKane) and some modern Versions (NEB, JB, and NAB) to delete as an MT plus (cf. 51:11). But the LXX omission is better attributed to haplography (homoeoteleuton: *w . . . w*). The REB and NJB rightly restore the phrase.

MESSAGE AND AUDIENCE

Yahweh in the opening oracle directs an unidentified foe to move against Babylon. Two regions in the country are singled out for mention: Merathaim and Pekod. To the careful listener this will have overtones of rebellion and a reckoning. It will be holy war, with inhabitants of this once-mighty Empire put to the sword and devoted to destruction. No remnant. In a final word added later, the enlisted foe is warned do all that Yahweh has commanded it to do.

Jeremiah begins the poem following, as he often does, by reporting a deafening sound in the land. It is the shattering noise of war. Someone called the world's "hammer" has been shattered, and as for the grand lady of Babylon, well, she has become a desolation. The prophet expresses surprise and sorrow. The audience may believe the former, but scarcely the latter.

Jeremiah then turns to address the victim directly. He tells the nation that it set a trap for itself, and wonder of wonders, it was captured. This came as a surprise to Babylon since the nation was caught completely unaware. The nation is also envisioned as having played a hiding game, but alas, it was found and brought into the enemy's grip. Babylon dared to do battle with Yahweh, and with Yahweh there are no escapes, no hiding places.

Returning to his Jerusalem audience, Jeremiah portrays Yahweh as having opened the armory about which covenant people have some knowledge, even if Babylon does not, and Yahweh is seen as having brought out the weapons needed for his work of wrath. Yahweh is Yahweh of the army, and he had a work to be done in the land of the Chaldeans.

The voice of Yahweh is now heard, and if not his voice, then voices of the foe working on his behalf. Attackers of Babylon are urged to enter the city from every side, break open the granaries, pile up bodies and spoil, and devote the whole to destruction. Will it be a sacred gift to Yahweh? Babylon is further cursed to have no remnant! The rampage continues, with bulls now being brought in for sacrifice. Woe to Babylon. Her day of Pekod has come!

In a final comment, Jewish escapees from Babylon are heard declaring the news in Zion: "The vengeance of Yahweh our God, the vengeance of his temple." The oracle, poem, and added comment have a progression when heard in tandem: a directive for the enemy to engage in holy war against Babylon; a description of that war carried to its completion; and a celebrated vindication in Zion.

The unit in its entirety can be taken as prophecy in advance of Babylon's actual fall, which means a date in the reign of Zedekiah before 594 B.C. is possible.

10. Curtains for Arrogant Babylon! (50:29–30)

50 ²⁹Summon to Babylon a multitude
  all who bend the bow
Encamp against her round about
  let there not be for her[1] an escape

Repay her according to her deed
  according to all that she has done, do to her
For to Yahweh she acted arrogantly
  to the Holy One of Israel

³⁰Therefore her young men shall fall in her open squares
  and all her men of war shall be silent in that day
    —oracle of Yahweh.

---

[1]Adding *lāh* ("for her") with the Q, many MSS, T, and the Vrs; Kt omits.

RHETORIC AND COMPOSITION

MT 50:29–30 = LXX 27:29–30. The present oracle is likely a composite and may not derive in its entirety from Jeremiah; nevertheless, as presently constituted it forms a coherent unit. The upper limit is marked by a return to poetry in v 29, acknowledged by all commentators and all modern Versions except the RSV and NRSV, which scan this verse and v 30 as prose. A return to battle commands after the plundering of Babylon also points to a new beginning (Rudolph; Weiser). The lower limit of the oracle is marked by a messenger formula in v 30, after which comes a *setumah* in M^L and M^P, and a *petuḥah* in M^A.

Verse 30 occurs elsewhere in the Damascus oracle (49:26). It, too, appears to be poetry, although *BHS* takes it in both contexts as prose. The JB and NJB do likewise; however, most of the other modern Versions scan the verse as poetry. The RSV and NRSV render 49:26 as poetry, but the present verse as prose. Verse 30 should be taken as poetry; the bicolon has good parallelism, a syntactic chiasmus, and contains no prose particles.

The oracle as presently constituted may be divided into three stanzas, the first two of which have the following repetitions and balancing key terms:

I	. . . *to Babylon*	*'el-bābel*	v 29
	all	*kol*	
	. . . .		
	. . . . *for her*	*lāh* (Q)	
II	. . . . *her*	*lāh*	
	. . *all* . . . . *to her*	*kōl . . . lāh*	
	. . . *to Yahweh*	*'el-yhwh*	
	to the Holy One of Israel	*'el-qĕdôš yiśrā'ēl*	

This oracle appears to be another dialogue, with Yahweh speaking in Stanzas I and III, and the prophet—or whoever—speaking in Stanza II (Yahweh referred to in the third person).

Catchwords connecting to the prior unit:

v 29c	*according to all that she has done, do* . . .	*kĕkōl 'ăšer 'āśĕtâ 'āśû* . . .	v 21	*and do according to all that* . . .	*wa'ăśēh kĕkōl 'ăšer* . . .
v 29b	*escape*	*pĕlēṭâ*	v 28	*escapees*	*pĕlēṭîm*
v 30	*that day*		v 27	*their day*	

Catchwords connecting to the following oracle:

v 29	*round about*		v 31, 32	*Arrogance* (2×)	*zādôn*
	she acted arrogantly	*zādâ*	v 31	*your day*	
v 30	*that day*		v 32	*round about him*	

NOTES

50:29. *Summon to Babylon a multitude . . . Encamp against her round about.*
More battle orders by Yahweh to a multiple foe of Babylon (Bach 1962: 56;
Christensen 1975: 258). See Note for 46:3. The beginning here is similar to
that in 50:14.

Summon. Hebrew *hašmîʿû* means "call together," as in 51:27; cf. 1 Sam 15:4;
1 Kgs 15:22.

Babylon. The city is meant, as a siege operation is envisioned. Also, v 30
states that young men will fall in the city's open squares (*rĕḥōbōt*).

a multitude. Hebrew *rabbîm.* Most commentators and modern Versions repoint with Rashi to *rōbîm*, "those who shoot," i.e., "archers" (KB³; cf. Gen 21:20,
and perhaps Job 16:13), but the T, LXX (*pollois*), and Vg (*plurimis*) all have
"many, multitude," which is a perfectly acceptable reading.

all who bend the bow. The same expression occurs in 50:14. The composite
bow required both hand and foot to set the arrow. For further discussion on
archery technique in antiquity, see Notes on 9:2[Eng. 3] and 46:3.

Encamp against her round about. The verb *ḥnh*, which is the familiar "encamp" in accounts about the wilderness trek (e.g., Numbers 33), can also
have the military meaning of "besiege." Nebuchadnezzar and his army encamped around Jerusalem to besiege it (52:4; 2 Kgs 25:1), but here Yahweh is
directing a multitude to encamp around the city of Babylon, for the same
purpose.

let there not be for her an escape. Hebrew *ʾal-yĕhî- pĕlēṭâ*, inserting with Q
and other ancient witnesses *lāh* after *yĕhî-*. The text is further complicated by a
masculine verb; for the feminine *tĕhî* in a similar construction, see v 26b. Entrapment is the stated objective in a siege.

Repay her according to her deed, according to all that she has done, do to her.
Judgment according to the *lex talionis.* On repayment to Babylon for the evil
done in Zion, see 51:24.

For to Yahweh she acted arrogantly, to the Holy One of Israel. The reason for
judgment on Babylon. The verb *zyd* means to "boil up, act presumptuously, be
arrogant"; NJV: "For she has acted insolently against the Lord." On Babylon's
arrogant self-exaltation, see also v 24 and Isa 13:11; 14:13–14. The arrogance of
Babylon's king receives mention in vv 31–32. The charge of hubris was similarly leveled against Jerusalem and its king in 21:13–14 and 22:6–23. On the
pride of Moab, see 48:29–30; on Edomite pride and Yahweh's vow to bring it
down, see 49:16.

the Holy One of Israel. Hebrew *qĕdôš yiśrāʾēl.* The expression is characteristic of both First and Second Isaiah (Muilenburg 1956a: 383, 400), although it
does occur one other time in Jeremiah, in 51:5. See also Pss 71:22; 78:41; and
89:19[Eng 89:18]. Yahweh is named "the Holy One" (*qādôš*) in Hab 3:3 and
Hos 11:9.

30. See exegesis for 49:26.

MESSAGE AND AUDIENCE

Yahweh begins this oracle by summoning a mighty host to make war against Babylon. Wanted particularly are crack archers to surround the city. A siege is envisioned, making escape impossible. The voice of the prophet—whether Jeremiah or someone in the tradition of Isaiah—calls for judgment according to the *lex talionis*. May Babylon receive in like measure what she meted out to other nations, particularly Judah! The charge is that Babylon was arrogant to Yahweh, to the Holy One of Israel. The double expression, "*to* Yahweh, *to* the Holy One of Israel," will echo "*to* Babylon," reinforcing the *lex talionis* principle to an audience of Jewish survivors. Yahweh completes the oracle by spelling out his judgment on the city thought to be invincible: its finest warriors will fall on the fateful day of its visitation.

This oracle, depending on its unity and authorship, could date from the reign of Zedekiah, otherwise to a time closer to Babylon's actual fall. The oracle goes better with what follows than with what precedes, unless one sees here a continuation of the holy war motif. In vv 31–32 the hubris is extended to the king of Babylon.

11. A Day for Mr. Arrogance As Well! (50:31–32)

50 ³¹Look, I am against you, Arrogance
   —oracle of Lord Yahweh of hosts
For your day has come
    the time I reckon with you

³²Arrogance shall stumble and fall
    and there will not be one to pick him up
And I will kindle a fire in his cities
    and it will consume everything round about him.

RHETORIC AND COMPOSITION

MT 50:31–32 = LXX 27:31–32. These verses are another divine oracle, as indicated by the expanded messenger formula in v 31a. Yahweh is the speaker throughout. Delimitation at the top is marked by a *setumah* in M^L and M^P, and a *petuḥah* in M^A, prior to v 31. The M^L, M^A, and M^P all have a *setumah* after v 32, which marks the lower limit. In addition, masculine pronouns set off these verses from vv 29–30, where the pronouns are feminine. The oracle may possibly be a reworking of the two oracles in 21:13–14, as the first and last lines are nearly the same. The repeated phraseology is all arguably Jeremianic. Many commentators take vv 29–32 to be a unit, but these verses are in fact two separate oracles joined by catchwords. The larger compositional unit is actually vv 29–34 (see Rhetoric and Composition for 50:33–34).

This oracle has two stanzas nicely balanced by the following repetition:

I . . . . *Arrogance*   *zādôn*   v 31

II *Arrogance* . . . .   *zādôn*   v 32

Catchwords connecting to prior oracle:

v 31, 32	Arrogance (2×)	zādôn	v 29	round about	
v 31	your day			she acted arrogantly	zādâ
v 32	round about him		v 30	that day	

Catchwords connecting to the oracle following:

v 31 *Yahweh of hosts*   v 33, 34 *Yahweh of hosts* (2×)

NOTES

50:31. *Look, I am against you, Arrogance.* A stereotyped beginning for the Jeremiah oracle, found elsewhere with variation in 21:13 and 51:25. Masculine pronouns here and throughout the oracle point to the king as the addressee, not Babylon the nation, although Babylon the city is addressed with masculine pronouns in 51:25. The two terms doubtless overlap and acquire one another's meanings. The T embellishes with "O wicked king." In Jewish tradition vv 29–30 are taken as addressed to the Babylonian nation, and the present verses to the king of Babylon (Rosenberg). This is correct if the former be revised to the city of Babylon. The present oracle is indicting the king of Babylon as arrogance personified. Earlier, Yahweh indicted the king of Assyria for his boastful demeanor, and promised punishment (Isa 10:12; 37:22–29 = 2 Kgs 19:21–28). On Tyre's arrogant king, whom Yahweh also vows to bring down, see Ezek 28:1–19.

against you. Hebrew *'ēleykā*. The preposition *'el* has the adversative meaning of *'al*, as in 21:13; 50:35; 51:1, 25; and elsewhere. For *'el* and *'al* alternating in Jeremiah, see Note on 11:2.

Arrogance. Hebrew *zādôn* is the noun occurring again in v 32 (cf. 49:16). In both instances it is a disparaging title for the Babylonian king (like "Obstinate" in John Bunyan's *Pilgrim's Progress*). Bright: "Sir Pride"; Holladay: "Sir Arrogance." Goodspeed (AmT) has "O Insolence!" The LXX achieves comparable meaning with a participial *tēn hybristrian* ("the insolent one"), only the feminine assumes that Babylon is the referent (Moffatt had "Queen Insolence"). In v 32 is a noun phrase again feminine: *hē hybris sou* ("your insolence"). The masculine gender throughout vv 31–32 must be retained. "(Mr.) Arrogance" is Babylon's king.

Lord Yahweh of hosts. The LXX omits "Lord (*ădōnāy*) . . . of hosts"; see Appendix VI. Read the MT; "Yahweh of hosts" is here a catchphrase to vv 33–34 (see Rhetoric and Composition).

For your day has come, the time I reckon with you. Compare v 27b. On the "day of Yahweh" for all nations, see Note for 46:10.

the time I reckon with you. On this expression, see Note for 6:15. Calvin says that Yahweh's vengeance comes only in due time, not in haste, as is typical with human beings. God is patient and slow to anger (Exod 34:6). Also, the time of the divine reckoning is unknown. And yet, prophetic perfects here and in v 32 make Yahweh's judgment on the king of Babylon a thing of the past.

32. *Arrogance shall stumble and fall.* Pride precedes destruction (cf. Prov 16:18), and pride is one of the reasons why Yahweh judges other nations with whom he has no covenant. For the collocation of *kšl* ("stumble") and *npl* ("fall") in Jeremiah and in the OT, see Note for 46:6.

and there will not be one to pick him up. Hebrew *wĕ'ēn lô mēqîm*. Amos (5:2) envisions the same unhappy circumstance for "virgin Israel," where reference is to the end of nationhood. Jewish interpretation (Abarbanel; *Mezudath David*) takes this to mean that the Babylonian king will have no son to reign in his stead (cf. 22:30).

And I will kindle a fire in his cities, and it will consume everything round about him. A stereotyped judgment with *hiṣṣattî* ("I will kindle"), echoing Amos 1:14 but occurring also in Jer 17:27; 21:14b; and 49:27. This need not be judged an MT plus from 21:14b (*pace* Volz; Rudolph).

in his cities. I.e., the many cities over which the Babylonian king rules, not just Babylon, as in the previous oracle. The LXX has *en tō drymō autēs* ("in her forest"), which is consistent with the feminine imagery adopted in vv 31a and 32a.

MESSAGE AND AUDIENCE

Yahweh himself declares at the outset of this oracle to be dead set against arrogance. The audience knows that arrogance typically has a short life; nevertheless, to what or to whom is Yahweh referring? It appears to be some man of repute, as Yahweh says the day has come when he will reckon with him. This can only mean judgment. And indeed it does, for Yahweh goes on to say that Mr. Arrogance will stumble and fall, and none shall pick him up. Moreover, Yahweh will kindle a fire in his cities, and everything around him will be consumed. Mr. Arrogance sounds as if he were a king. A very generic oracle, with stereotyped indictment and judgment and no particular audience specified.

The oracle takes on specificity only when heard in tandem with the preceding oracle, which was a judgment on the arrogant city of Babylon. "Arrogance" in the present oracle must then be the king of Babylon, who will suffer the same fate as his arrogant capital. And the fall of the capital city is here supplemented by the fall of other cities over which the proud king rules.

The general nature of the oracle suggests a judgment envisoned for a distant and unspecified future—whenever Yahweh in his own time chooses to reckon with the arrogant Babylonian king. A date is thus possible in the reign of Zedekiah, prior to 594 B.C.

12. Their Redeemer Is Strong! (50:33–34)

[33]Thus said Yahweh of hosts:
Oppressed are the children of Israel
   and the children of Judah together
All their captors hold them strongly
   they refuse to let them go

[34]Their Redeemer is strong
   Yahweh of hosts is his name
He'll pleadingly plead their plea
   so as to give the earth rest
      and give unrest to the inhabitants of Babylon.

RHETORIC AND COMPOSITION

MT 50:33–34 = LXX 27:33–34. The present verses are another divine oracle, this one promising salvation to Israel-Judah, whose redeemer is Yahweh. The oracle is demarcated at the top end by a "Thus said Yahweh of hosts" messenger formula in v 33, before which comes a *setumah* in M[L], M[A], and M[P]. The conclusion is at v 34 (*pace* Holladay), with vv 35–38 being a separate oracle containing a messenger formula of its own (v 35a). Content and rhetorical features also distinguish vv 35–38 as a separate oracle (see Rhetoric and Composition for 50:35–38). Three oracles in sequence form an expanded compositional unit in vv 29–34:

I	Judgment on the arrogant city of Babylon	vv 29–30
II	Judgment on Babylon's arrogant king	vv 31–32
III	Salvation for Israel and Judah	vv 33–34

The present oracle compares with oracles in 50:4–5, 6–7 in announcing salvation for a united Israel and Judah, also in combining a divine word with a word from the prophet (see Rhetoric and Composition for 50:4–5 and 50:6–7). The prophet's word here in v 34 is a hymnic affirmation (Weiser; Holladay). The language—despite the Isaiah-sounding "Redeemer"—is definitely Jeremianic, e.g., *ʿăšûqîm* ("oppressed ones") in v 33b, which compares with *ʿšq* ("oppress / oppressor") in 7:6 and 21:12; *ʿōšeq* ("oppression") in 6:6 and 22:17; and *ʿāšôq* ("oppressor") in 22:3; also the familiar *mēʾănû* ("they refused") in v 33c, occurring in 3:3; 5:3 (2×); 8:5; 15:18; and often elsewhere (Giesebrecht; Holladay II: 404). We have in 33c a particularly striking parallel to the bicolon in 8:5b, which is a signature construction of Jeremiah (Lundbom 1975: 151 n. 9 [= 1997: 86–87 n. 9]):

8:5b	They hold fast / strongly to deceit	*heḥĕzîqû battarmît*
	they refuse to return	*mēʾănû lāšûb*
50:33c	All their captors hold them strongly	*kol-šōbêhem heḥĕzîqû bām*
	they refuse to let them go	*mēʾănû šallĕḥām*

Verses 33–34 then ought not be bracketed out with Volz as a later addition.

Both verses are best taken as poetry (so *BHS*), although v 34b is admittedly a long tricolon with two occurences of the *nota accusativi* and a prosaic *lĕma'an* ("so that"). Here is perhaps later editorial revision. Only the RSV and NRSV among the modern Versions print the verses as prose.

The oracle has two stanzas bound together by a key word repetition, not counting the "Yahweh of hosts" that occurs in the messenger formula and in Stanza II of the poem:

I . . . .   v 33
   . . . . *hold them strongly*   *heḥĕzîqû bām*

II . . . . *is strong*   *ḥāzāq*   v 34
    . . . .

Yahweh is the speaker in Stanza I; Jeremiah leads a doxology to Yahweh in Stanza II.

Catchwords connecting to the prior oracle:

v 33, 34 *Yahweh of hosts* (2×)   v 31 *Yahweh of hosts*

Catchwords connecting to the oracle following:

v 34b *the inhabitants of Babylon*   v 35 *the inhabitants of Babylon*

NOTES

50:33. *Thus said Yahweh of hosts.* The LXX omits "of hosts," as elsewhere, but in the next verse it translates the same with *pantokratōr*; see Appendix VI. Retain with MT; "Yahweh of hosts" is a connecting catchphrase to v 31 (see Rhetoric and Composition).

Oppressed are the children of Israel, and the children of Judah together. The Hebrew for "oppressed (ones)" is *'ăšûqîm*. Reference is to the unblessed experience of national defeat and exile for the covenant people, spelled out with specificity in the covenant curses of Deut 28:29, 33.

All their captors hold them strongly, they refuse to let them go. See Isa 14:17. Captors are both the Assyrians and Babylonians. While reference here is to the more recent exiles of Israel and Judah, the language betrays an unmistakable allusion to Israel's defining captivity in Egypt. Moses, directed to deliver nothing less than a divine oracle to Pharaoh, prefaced his condemnation with these words: "Thus said Yahweh, God of the Hebrews: Let my people go (*šallaḥ*) that they may serve me, for if you refuse to let them go (*mā'ēn 'attâ lĕšalleaḥ*) and continue to hold them strongly (*maḥăzîq bām*) . . ." (Exod 9:1–2). See also Exod 4:23; 7:14, 27[Eng 8:2]; 9:13; and 10:3. The covenant people have then had two—or rather three—extraordinary experiences of captors' refusing to let them go.

33–34. *All their captors hold them strongly . . . Their Redeemer is strong.* The Hebrew has a wordplay on *heḥĕzîqû* ("hold strongly") and *ḥāzāq* ("is strong"), creating an implied contrast between the strong Assyrian and Babylonian captors, and Israel's Redeemer, who is strong(er). In 31:11, Jeremiah anticipates a divine redemption (*g'l*) from hands too strong (*ḥzq*) for Jacob. Note another wordplay between *šōbêhem* ("their captors") and *lĕyōšĕbê* ("inhabitants") at the end of v 34.

34. *Their Redeemer is strong.* Hebrew *gō'ălām ḥāzāq*. The phrase is given added vigor with a prior *kai* in the LXX, which can be an adversative: "*But* their Redeemer is strong." The same phrase in Prov 23:11 is preceded by *kî*, giving similar meaning. The *gō'ēl* is a near kinsman who acts as avenger of wrongdoing and redeemer of the debtor or oppressed (Lev 25:25, 47–55; Num 35:21). Titular usage anticipates Second Isaiah, where Yahweh is repeatedly championed as the Redeemer of Israel (Isa 41:14; 43:14; 44:6, 24; 47:4; 48:17; et passim; Muilenburg 1956a: 400–401). But the idea is also present in Jer 31:11. The point here is that even though Assyria and Babylon are strong and able to keep the covenant people captive, their Redeemer, Yahweh, is stronger and will thus be able to free them. Again, with Yahweh depicted here as Israel's *gō'ēl*, we have a clear allusion to the Exodus deliverance (Exod 6:6; 15:13). For the role played by the *gō'ēl* in ancient Israelite family law, and its theological importance in both the OT and NT, see Note on 31:11.

Yahweh of hosts is his name. For this recurring doxology in Jeremiah, see Note on 10:16.

He'll pleadingly plead their plea. Hebrew *rîb yārîb 'et-rîbām*. An attempt to capture the alliteration, wordplay, and threefold repetition in the verb-noun combination from *rîb*, meaning "issue a complaint, accuse" (see Note on 2:9). The phrase is commonly translated, "He will surely plead their case," although the infinitive absolute *rîb* (for *rōb*) is unusual (cf. GKC §73d; also Q/Kt readings for the infinitive construct in Judg 21:22). In Jeremiah, as also in the other Prophets, Yahweh is heard accusing Israel of covenant violation. But here he will litigate for Israel's release, the outcome of which is not in doubt. See also 51:36. According to the LXX, Yahweh "will make a judgment on his adversaries" (*krisin krinei pros tous antidikous autou*), i.e., Babylon (cf. 25:31) in order to bring destruction (not rest) upon the earth. The final colon, which provides unrest for the inhabitants of Babylon, is omitted in the LXX (not noted in BHS). This reading does not inspire confidence, and should be rejected. For the collocation of pleading a case (*rîb*) and bringing about redemption (*g'l*), see also Ps 119:154.

so as to give the earth rest, and give unrest to the inhabitants of Babylon. The verb *rg'* means "rest" (N-stem in 47:6) and "provide rest" (H-stem here and in 31:2; cf. BDB; KB³), although the Qal (of perhaps a *rg'* II) has the more provocative meaning, "stir up, terrify" (31:35 = Isa 51:15). The latter seems to have guided the T ("so as to shatter the wicked ones of the earth"), the LXX (*hopōs exarē tēn gēn*, "so that he may demolish the earth"), and the Vg (*ut exterreat ter-ram*, "so that he may terrify the earth"); however Rashi, Kimḥi, and virtually all modern commentators opt for "give rest," or the like, which makes possible a contrast with the colon following. The AV and other modern Versions (except NEB and REB) translate similarly. The H-stem of *rgz* means "agitate, cause unrest" (KB³; cf. Isa 14:16; 23:11). The point here is that divine litigation will put the remainder of the earth at peace, while bringing upon Babylon unwel-comed agitation. Compare Isa 14:1–8. The terms *hirgîaʿ* and *hirgîz* are close in sound, making a wordplay (Duhm). On their irregular form, see GKC §53 1, and compare 51:33 and 52:3.

the earth. The preferred rendering of *ʾet-hāʾāreṣ*, which is not here the land of one country.

MESSAGE AND AUDIENCE

Yahweh opens here by citing the oppression currently afflicting both Israel and Judah, saying that their captors are holding them with a strong hand and refus-ing to let them go. The message has a familiar ring, with an eerie parallel in Egypt ages ago. A Judahite audience knows the story well, for oppression de-fined its very emergence as a people. Now oppression in Assyria and Babylonia, it says. But Jeremiah counters: "Their Redeemer is strong; Yahweh of hosts is his name!" and assures his audience that Yahweh will surely plead their case, which is all that faithful souls need to know. Yahweh's litigation will in fact give the whole earth rest, and will bring unrest to the nation that has caused so much agitation and now is finally named: Babylon.

This oracle heard in tandem with the two prior oracles on arrogant Babylon and its arrogant king will contrast the judgment awaiting Babylon and the salva-tion promised a united Israel and Judah. All three oracles, vv 29–30, 31–32, and 33–34, speak to a distant future and may therefore be dated in Zedekiah's reign, before 594 B.C.

13. A Sword upon Chaldeans! (50:35–38a)

50 ³⁵A sword upon Chaldeans—oracle of Yahweh—
  and to the inhabitants of Babylon
    and to her princes and to her wise men
³⁶A sword to the diviners, that they become foolish
  a sword to her warriors, that they be broken

³⁷A sword to his horses and to his chariots
  and to all the mixed races who are in her midst
    that they become women
A sword to her treasures, that they become booty
  ³⁸ᵃa drought to her waters, that they be dried up.

RHETORIC AND COMPOSITION

MT 50:35–38a = LXX 27:35–38a. The present verses embody a curse from Yahweh upon Babylon, designated a divine oracle by the messenger formula in v 35a. This formula, which the LXX lacks, delimits the oracle at the top end. Its conclusion is at v 38a (Volz; Rudolph; McKane), with v 38b going better with what follows (see Rhetoric and Composition for 50:38b–40). There are no section markings here, but delimitation is aided by both content and rhetorical structure.

The poem is another showcase example of *anaphora* (Cornill; Kessler 1973: 19), comparable to poetry in 4:23–26; 5:15–17; 31:4–5; and 51:20–23, all Jeremianic. A structure of two stanzas, each consisting of two lines, best accounts for the symmetries in the poem as well as its deviations from symmetry. Stanza I (vv 35–36) and Stanza II (v 37–38a) are then tricolons followed by bicolons. The tendency among commentators has been to make a highly repetitive poem even more consistent by emendation, but this should be resisted. The one questionable colon is at the end of v 37, which has a prosaic *'ăšer*. Jeremiah poetry, however, contains more *'ăšer* particles than early lyric poetry, also a higher percentage than one finds in Psalms, Proverbs, and Job (D. N. Freedman). The two stanzas with their repetitions and balancing key words:

I	A sword upon	*ḥereb 'al-*	v 35
	and to	*wĕ'el-*	
	and to . . . . and to	*wĕ'el-* . . . *wĕ'el-*	
	A sword to	*ḥereb 'el-*	v 36
	a sword to	*ḥereb 'el-*	
II	A sword to . . . . . . and to	*ḥereb 'el-* . . . . *wĕ'el-*	v 37
	and to	*wĕ'el-*	
	. . . .		
	A sword to	*ḥereb 'el-*	
	a drought to	*ḥōreb 'el-*	v 38a

After a fivefold repetition of *ḥereb* ("sword"), which simulates the sense (*onomatopoeia*: the repeated stabbing of the victim), the poet deliberately shifts at the end to the similar-sounding *ḥōreb* ("drought"), a known device within ancient Hebrew rhetoric (Lundbom 1975: 156 n. 75 [= 1997: xlii–xliii; 121 n. 75]). Casanowicz (1893; #142a) sees in this an example of paronomasia; D. N. Freedman (1986b) as a deliberate deviation in a series. It is both. A shift coming at the end of the poem is also climactic. It should be noted in addition that the poet does just the reverse with his prepositions: a beginning *'al* ("upon"), then 10 occurrences of *'el* ("to") to the end. Neither deviation should be emended in the interest of achieving total symmetry (see Notes).

Catchwords connecting to the prior oracle:

v 35 *the inhabitants of Babylon*   v 34b *the inhabitants of Babylon*

Catchwords connecting to the oracle following:

v 35 *inhabitants*   vv 39, 40 *inhabit* (4×)

NOTES

50:35. *A sword upon Chaldeans.* Hebrew *ḥereb ʿal-kaśdîm.* These curses being short and direct, spoken hurriedly and with emotion, require neither verbs (cf. AV: "a sword *is* upon the Chaldeans") nor paraphrasing (cf. T: "those who kill with the sword shall come against the land of the Chaldeans"). We might say today: "A plague upon both your houses!" Also, Yahweh may here be addressing his sword directly (apostrophe; cf. 47:6). In Amos 9:4, Yahweh's sword is personified as an agent acting on its own by divine command. On Chaldea and the Chaldeans, see Note for 50:1.

sword. Here the term can refer to actual swords doing their bloody work on the hapless people of Babylon. When the referents are chariots and treasuries (v 37), "sword" simply means "war" (metonymy).

and to the inhabitants of Babylon. Hebrew *wĕʾel-yōšĕbê bābel.* Reference here is to the inhabitants of the city of Babylon (Calvin), wherein reside the nation's leading citizens and its military force mentioned next. There is no need with Duhm to emend *ʾel* ("to") to *ʿal* ("upon") here and throughout the rest of the poem. The two prepositions can be used interchangeably, and are in Jeremiah (see Note on 11:2), but usage here appears to be intentional (see Rhetoric and Composition).

and to her princes. Hebrew *śāreyhā.* These are royal officials, including military leaders and heirs to the throne; cf. 17:25.

and to her wise men. Hebrew *wĕʾel-ḥăkāmeyhā.* Babylon's political leaders, including counselors to the king (cf. 18:18), astrologers, and diviners of various description (cf. Isa 47:10–13). Jeremiah has some forceful words for Judah's wise men in 8:8–9.

36. *A sword to the diviners, that they become foolish.* Included now in the curse is a consequence of the sword's commissioning work. Because the sought-after end here is foolishness, it is frequently assumed that the individuals being cursed, who are called *baddîm,* are none other than the wise men just mentioned (Calvin; Cheyne). More likely they are associates of wise men (cf. Isa 44:25). The term *baddîm* has been variously interpreted. In 48:30 it denotes "empty talk, boasting" (BDB; KB[3]), which suggests to some that the individuals here and in Isa 44:25 are "empty talkers." Rashi and Kimḥi follow T, which has "diviners," Rashi saying that they are so named because they say false things. The modern Versions all incorporate one or both of these ideas (AV: "liars"; NEB and NIV: "false prophets"; RSV, JB, and NJV: "diviners"). In Akkadian texts a class of *bārû* priests is attested, the *bārû* being a diviner practiced in hepatoscopy, i.e., the inspection of livers (CAD 2: 121–25; AHw 1: 109–10). Haupt (1900: 56–57) therefore proposed emending here and in Isa 44:26 to *bārîm,* a suggestion accepted by certain older commentators (Giesebrecht;

Duhm; Volz). Haupt also compared the present passage to Ezek 21:24–26[Eng 21:19–21] where the Babylonian king, still at his zenith of power, wielded the sword on the advice of liver-consulting diviners who were accompanying him. An Amorite *baddum* is now also attested, who is some sort of functionary at Mari (AHw 1: 95; KB³ *bad* V). This suggests that "diviners" could translate *baddîm* here and in Isa 44:25, although the Amorite term and its context remain obscure. The LXX omits the entire colon, which Giesebrecht, Rudolph, and others plausibly attribute to haplography (two-word haplography: *ḥrb ʾl . . . ḥrb ʾl*).

that they become foolish. The N-stem of *yʾl* means "turn out to be foolish, be without sense," appearing also in 5:4 and Isa 19:13.

a sword to her warriors, that they be broken. The N-stem of *ḥtt* ("be broken") denotes either a physical or psychological condition. Here the end result—whatever condition is indicated—is total defeat (T: "and they shall be shattered"). On this common Jeremiah verb, see Note for 1:17. Babylon's defeated warriors (*gibbôrîm*) are also described in 51:30, 56, and 57.

37. *A sword to his horses and to his chariots.* This beginning curse of the second cluster lacks a consequence, as does the beginning curse of the first cluster (see Rhetoric and Composition). Once again, commentators are unnecessarily troubled about the shift to masculine pronouns (cf. vv 31–32), either emending to the feminine (Blayney; Giesebrecht; Duhm) or omitting the entire colon as an MT plus from 51:21 (Cornill; Volz; Rudolph; Bright; Holladay). Neither alteration is warranted. The horses and chariots belong to the king (Calvin). Also, the colon is not absent from the LXX (*pace* Jones). The LXX and T have "their horses . . . their chariots," which is carried over into the AV.

and to all the mixed races who are in her midst. The people of "mixed race" (*hāʿereb*) are probably mercenary soldiers in the Babylonian army (Duhm; Cornill; Peake; McKane), but according to Kimḥi and Calvin may also include traders and other foreign residents in Babylon. The term means "mixed races" in 25:20 and 24 (KB³ *ʿereb* II; cf. *ʿărābî* = Arab in 3:2; and *ʿărab* = "Arabs / Arabia" in 25:24). The LXX in 32:20 [= MT 25:20] and in the present verse has *symmiktos*, "mingled (ones)." On (Greek) expatriates in Egypt, see 46:9, 16, and 21. The omission of "all" (*kol*) in the LXX can again be attributed to haplography (homoeoteleuton: *l . . . l*), and should not be deleted (*pace* Holladay).

that they become women. One of the standard curses of antiquity was that a defeated people—soldiers particularly—become like (weak) women or like women in labor; see 48:41; 49:22, 24; 50:43; 51:30; and Notes on 4:31 and 6:24. In an ancient Hittite text, entitled "A Soldier's Oath" (*ANET*³ 354; *CS I* 166), the turning of defeated soldiers into women was dramatized in a ritual where women's clothes, a distaff,[1] and mirror were brought in. Any soldier breaking his loyalty oath could look forward to the indignity of being clothed in the dress

---

[1] A rod on which wool or flax is wound in preparation for spinning; commonly held up as a symbol of women's work.

of women, having his weapon broken, and being made to carry the distaff and mirror in his hand. The curse put upon him was the following:

Let them break the bows, arrows (and) clubs in their hands,
and [let them put] in their hands distaff and mirror.

A *sword to her treasures, that they become booty.* Hebrew *ʾôṣĕrōteyhā* ("her treasures, stores") refer to the nation's storehouses of wealth, usually located in special rooms in the palace or the temple (2 Kgs 14:14; 24:13). Babylon's great treasures / stores are mentioned again in 51:13, where *ʾōṣārôt* may mean "store-houses." In Babylon, the royal stores, treasury, and arsenal of weapons were housed in a citadel protecting the royal palace (L. W. King 1919: 27). Now the whole of it will become booty for a victorious enemy (30:16; cf. 15:13). Plun-dered temple treasure is a common theme in the laments of Mesopotamia; see Note on 49:4. That Babylon should be thoroughly despoiled is only fair, for de-spite Nebuchadnezzar's reputation as a builder and as a peace-loving conquerer, he was, in fact, worse than Assyrian kings in devastating conquered lands and leaving them abandoned. The Assyrians, by contrast, quickly rebuilt and re-populated conquered cities. The stated consequence makes it clear that "sword" here means "war" (Rudolph; Weiser).

38a. *a drought to her waters, that they be dried up.* The change here to "drought" (*ḥōreb*) is intentional (Calvin), and should be retained (see Rhetoric and Composition). A nice wordplay is the result. The term is wanting in the main witnesses of the LXX, but is present in T ("scorching heat") and Vg (*siccitas*). A wordplay made from *ḥārēb* ("waste") and *ḥōreb* ("drought") appears in Hag 1:9, 11. Many commentators (Giesebrecht; Cheyne; Duhm; Cornill; Peake; Volz; Rudolph; Weiser; Bright; Thompson; Jones; McKane), and some modern Versions (NEB; REB; JB [but reversed in NJB]; NAB; NSB), emend to *ḥereb* ("sword"), citing the need for consistency or alleging that "drought" is a prosaic substitute by some scribe intent on making the curse on Babylon's wa-ters more literal. The reading "sword" is also supported by S and G^OL, but nevertheless should be rejected.

her waters. Babylon was a land of "many waters" (51:13; Ps 137:1), making this curse particularly grave, and doubtless climactic. The curse is not aimed primarily at the Euphrates, which is not likely to dry up, but at the city's many canals and other waterways (Rudolph; cf. Code of Hammurabi §§53–56; *ANET³* 168; *CS II* 340; Herodotus i 179, 185–86, 191). These will certainly dry up in a drought, which will be curse enough upon the city and the nation.

that they be dried up. Hebrew *wĕyābēšû.* The LXX has "that they be ashamed," translating *bôš* instead of *ybš.* Read the MT.

MESSAGE AND AUDIENCE

Yahweh in this oracle hurls a riveting string of curses upon Babylon, naming first the proud Chaldeans in the south. It is a catalogue poem, citing represen-tatives of the ruling elite, the nation's war machine, and national treasures, and ending with a reference to Babylon's most precious natural resource: its many waters. All this—and more—is under a divine curse, with consequences standard in curses of antiquity: diviners becoming foolish; warriors broken physically and mentally; mercenaries in the Babylonian army faring similarly, becoming weak as women; treasures plundered; and last but not least, Babylon's celebrated canals becoming dry as bone. The repetition of "sword" simulates the repeated stabbing of the victim, a nation known to have done more than its share of the same to Judah and other nations east and west. The concluding shift to "drought" is a poetic flourish sure to awaken anyone lulled by the repetition, bringing the oracle also to a grand climax.

Coming immediately after a promise that Israel's Redeemer will unsettle the nation of Babylon (v 34), this oracle serves to carry the unsettlement theme forward, showing how Yahweh will fight vigorously on Israel's behalf to cut Babylon down (Rudolph). The date of the present oracle can be the same as many of the other Babylon oracles, in Zedekiah's reign, prior to 594 B.C.

14. A Land of Images with New Inhabitants (50:38b–40)

50 [38b]Indeed it is a land of images
  and with terrors they are going mad!

[39]Therefore desert beasts with island beasts shall inhabit, and daughter ostriches shall inhabit her. And she shall not again be inhabited for all time, and she shall not be settled for generation after generation. [40]Just like God's overthrow of Sodom and Gomorrah and her neighbors—oracle of Yahweh. No person shall inhabit there, and no son of man shall sojourn in her.

RHETORIC AND COMPOSITION

MT 50:38b–40 = LXX 27:38b–40. The present verses contain a poetic fragment (v 38b) followed by a divine oracle in prose (vv 39–40). The oracle as presently constituted concludes at v 40, where a messenger formula occurs mid-verse. This formula is probably not an MT plus (*pace* Rudolph), as the LXX has it and a variant formula exists in the parallel verse of 49:18. The three major medieval codices have no section after v 40, but one MS in the Cambridge Genizah Collection (A 14.3) does. Demarcation at the top end is determined by the separate integrity of the prior oracle, on which see Rhetoric and Composition for 50:35–38a.

Verse 38b is judged secondary by Volz and Rudolph, but their concern is mainly to separate it from the oracle in vv 35–38a, to which it does not belong. The line is Jeremianic (Holladay), and is best taken as an opening indictment after which comes a judgment beginning with *lākēn*, "therefore" (v 39a). There is an implied connection between an idol-filled land (v 38b) and the wilderness creatures destined to inhabit that land (v 39). The judgment comprises all of vv 39–40. Verse 40 is repeated in 49:18, but since it is well integrated into the present context, there is little likelihood of its being a later supplement. Parallels have been drawn between vv 39–40 and Isa 13:19–22, but these are imprecise, and the relationship between the two passages — considering also the LXX omission of Jer 50:39b — is unclear (cf. Janzen 1973: 60–61). On the face of it, vv 39–40 seem to be an abridged and contrived imitation of a more vigorous Isaiah oracle, in which are included fragments of Jeremiah poetry quarried from elsewhere.

A decision regarding poetry or prose for all of the verses is difficult, as a look at *BHS*, the modern Versions, and the commentaries makes clear. This may be due to the composite nature of the unit. The indictment in v 38b I take to be a bicolon of poetry. The oracle in vv 39–40 I take with the RSV and NEB to be prose, although it may be a type of free verse. The parallels to v 40b have been rendered inconsistently in the contexts where they occur (49:18 is taken as prose; 49:33b as poetry). The decision here in favor of prose is based on the thrice-repeated *yšb* ("inhabit") in v 39, which troubled Cornill and does seem prosaic, also three occurrences of the *nota accusativi* in v 40. Moreover, in v 40 the divine name *ʾĕlōhîm* ("God") as subject is awkward with a *nĕʾūm yhwh* ("oracle of Yahweh") formula ending the verse. The divine name fits well in Isa 13:19, but not here. In Jer 49:18 it is absent. The same also makes for a confusion of speaker (cf. 17:13), although one will likely conclude that with an oracle formula the speaker has to be Yahweh. The whole appears to be a dialogue, with Jeremiah speaking the indictment and Yahweh following with an oracle of judgment.

The oracle in v 40 has an inclusio with balancing circumlocutions:

daughter ostriches	*bĕnôt yaʿănâ*	v 39
son of man	*ben-ʾādām*	v 40

Internal balance is achieved by paired repetitions — first positive and then negative — of the verb "inhabit" (*yšb*):

. . . they shall inhabit . . . and they shall inhabit . . .	*yēšĕbû . . . wĕyāšĕbû . . .*	v 39
And she shall not again be inhabited . . .	*wĕlōʾ-tēšēb . . .*	
No person shall inhabit . . .	*lōʾ-yēšēb . . . .*	v 40

This same verb doubles as a catchword to the prior oracle:

vv 39, 40 *inhabit* (4x)	v 35 *inhabitants*

Catchwords connecting to the oracle following:

v 39 *daughter ostriches* *bĕnôt yaʿănâ*   v 42 *daughter Babylon* *bat-bābel*

NOTES

50:38b. *Indeed it is a land of images.* Images, or idols (*pĕsîlîm*), are human and animal likenesses sculptured from wood, stone, or metal; see 10:14 [= 51:17] and Note on 8:19. Babylon's images come under judgment again in 51:47 and 52. See also Isa 21:9. The *kî* is taken here as an asseverative: "Indeed."

and with terrors they are going mad! Hebrew: *ûbāʾêmîm yithōlālû*. The "terrors" (*ʾêmîm*) are Babylon's images, given this name presumably because of the fear gripping those who worship them (Kimḥi). Indigenous African religions might be characterized today as fear-oriented. The verb *hll* in the Hithpolel means "go mad /act madly" (25:16; 46:9; 50:38b; 51:7), although two MSS and the Vrs (LXX, Aq, Symm, T, S, and Vg) presuppose the Hithpael "boast" (*hll* II KB³). The difference is but a small change in pointing (*yithallālû*). The latter verb occurs in Ps 97:7: "All those serving images are shamed, who boast (*hammithallîm*) in worthless idols." Calvin says either meaning is suitable here, although he prefers "boast, glory in." Either way, the statement is pejorative (Rudolph). People are intoxicated with their terrorizing images! In the NT, see Rom 1:20–23. The LXX translation of the phrase is otherwise corrupt, misreading *ʾêmîm* as "islands" (*nēsois*).

39. *desert beasts with island beasts.* Hebrew *ṣiyyîm ʾet-ʾîyyîm*. The straightforward and paraphrastic rendering of the AV ("the wild beasts of the desert with the wild beasts of the islands") may be about as close as we get to an adequate translation here, since both terms remain uncertain. Wilderness creatures of some sort are indicated (Kimḥi), who make their habitat in abandoned ruins (Rashi). These two types of animals are similarly joined in Isa 34:14, and appear in wider company in Isa 13:21–22. The first term is cognate to *ṣîyyâ*, "(land of) drought, dryness" (KB³; BDB; cf. 2:6), thus the common rendering, "inhabitants of the wilderness" or "wild beasts" (Isa 23:13; Ps 74:14). The T in the present text has "(wild) beasts." The second term is not the plural of *ʾi*, "island" (*pace* LXX), but another noun with a meaning similar to its paired term, thus "(wild) island beasts." Islands are not typically imagined within Palestine, much less in Transjordan or the desert areas farther east, but they were common enough in Babylon, which had lakes, canals, a marshy delta region where the Tigris joined the Euphrates, and the Persian Gulf to the south, which had—and still does have—islands off the coast. In 51:13 Babylon is called a place of "many waters." See also 50:38a and Ps 137:1. The term "island beasts" is therefore suitable here—as in Isa 13:22 (Babylon), and probably also Isa 34:14 (Edom). Wolves and other wild animals live today on Isle Royale in Lake Superior, as well as on sparsely inhabited islands elsewhere in the world. The two terms in the present verse were chosen to create paronomasia. Cornill rendered them "Fuchs und Luchs" ("fox and lynx"). Whether either or both might denote specific animals is uncertain, despite the various naming attempts (e.g., jackals, [wild] cats, owls, hyenas, wolves, martens, marmots [= prairie dogs]) in the ancient and modern Versions. Ancient and modern Versions also, in some cases, render one or both terms by monstrous beings (e.g., demons, goblins, ghouls), a view given impetus in the last century by C. C. Torrey (1928: 289–91; cf. Ps 74:14). Torrey believed the *ṣîyyîm* of Isa 34:14 were the jinn, i.e., demons of the desert (cf. Matt 12:43). Bright and Holladay have followed this line of interpretation. Since both

terms occur here with "ostriches," and the Isaiah passages similarly contain identifiable wild beasts and birds, the question is whether the same can be combined with demons and other monstrous beings. T. H. Gaster was unsure when discussing Isa 13:21 and 34:14 (*IDB* A–D, 818), but Torrey sees no diffi-culty in doing this, at least in Isa 13:21–22, where he envisions beasts and de-mons paired together family style—entertaining one another, dancing side by side, and howling in friendly chorus. In Isa 34:14 Torrey thinks all are from the demon tribe. J. Pedersen (1964 I–II: 455–56) in Isa 34:13–15 envisions a mix of beasts and otherworldly creatures. In the present verse I think we best keep the creatures simply as wild beasts, although otherworldly creatures can-not be completely ruled out (cf. Bar 4:35; Rev 18:2). Belief in demons inhabit-ing the desert is well known among Bedouin people today. That ruined cities become haunts for wild beasts and birds is a standard curse of antiquity; see Note on 9:10[Eng 9:11].

and daughter ostriches shall inhabit her. The expression "daughter ostriches," *běnôt yaʿănâ*, here as elsewhere in the OT (Isa 13:21; 34:13; 43:20; Mic 1:8), is a periphrasis meaning simply "ostriches." Compare "son of man" in v 40, and see Note on 4:11 for the various daughter metaphors in Jeremiah. In antiquity, the ostrich (*Struthio camelus*) was found in the eastern plains of Moab, the Ti-gris-Euphrates region, and in central Arabia (Xenophon, *Anab* i 5, 2–3; cf. Tris-tram 1884: 139; 1898: 233–39), where it inhabited desert areas (Lam 4:3[Q]; Isa 43:20) and abandoned ruins (Isa 13:21; 34:13). In the modern day it is never seen in settled areas, and only rarely in cultivated land. Like the jackal, it was known for its howling noises (Mic 1:8). The LXX in the present text contains "daughters of the sirens" (*thygateres seirēnōn*), but the T has "ostriches." The AV translated "owls." The ostrich has exceptional overland speed; Xenophon says it outran their horses and could not be captured. Modern Arabs capture them only after a wild chase. An Assyrian seal impression has turned up show-ing an ostrich being pursued in a hunt; for a picture, see *IDB* K–Q, 611.

And she shall not again be inhabited for all time, and she shall not be settled for generation after generation. Hebrew *lāneṣaḥ* ("for all time") is a parallel ex-pression to *ʿad-dôr wādôr* ("for generation after generation"), both meaning "forever." The term *lāneṣaḥ* appears in 3:5, but *dôr wādôr* occurs nowhere else in Jeremiah, where *ʿôlām* and other expressions are used to convey perpetuity. The LXX lacks "and she shall not be settled for generation after generation," which could be whole-word haplography if this colon and the previous one were written in block poetry (see Appendix V). This curse on Babylon, which may derive ultimately from Isaiah, is more severe than the one laid upon Egypt (46:26). In actual fact, Babylon was not thoroughly depopulated, but contin-ued to be inhabited all during the reign of Cyrus.

40. See exegesis for 49:18, and compare Isa 13:19.

God. Hebrew *ʾĕlōhîm.* Here the subject, as in Isa 13:19; the term is lacking in Jer 49:18.

her neighbors. Hebrew *šěkēneyhā.* A wordplay is perhaps intended with *tiškôn* ("she shall [not] be settled") in the prior line. The neighboring cities to Sodom and Gomorrah were Admah and Zeboiim; cf. Gen 10:19; 14:2; Deut 29:22[Eng 29:23].

son of man. Hebrew *ben-'ādām.* I.e., "man" or "human (being)." The usage is standard, but the translation here highlights what may be intentional balance with "daughter ostriches" in v 39 (see Rhetoric and Composition).

MESSAGE AND AUDIENCE

In this dialogue, Jeremiah is heard first exclaiming about an image-filled land and a people mad over images. Ironically these handmade wonders are called "terrors," reflecting the fear people have in worshiping them, while conveying at the same time a mocking disregard of such fear. The audience is expected to know that Babylon is being described, but specification is lacking. In the following oracle Yahweh is heard delivering stock curses on Babylon's land. Wild beasts and birds will inhabit the ruins, and the land will lie uninhabited for all time. A final comparison is made to God's celebrated overthrow of Sodom and Gomorrah and their neighboring cities. Once again it is said that no person will live there, which reinforces the comparison with nonhumans who will.

When this oracle is heard in tandem with the curse of the sword, Babylon's identity will be clarified and a reason will be given for its destruction: idolatry and people's behavior regarding their idols (Calvin; Holladay; McKane).

The stock nature of the curses suggests a date for the oracle well before Babylon's actual destruction, which could be prior to 594 B.C. The Jeremiah poetry is similarly general, and could be dated any time.

15. A People from the North against Babylon! (50:41–43)

50 [41]Look! a people comes
    from the north
A great nation and many kings are roused
    from remote parts of the earth

[42]Bow and sword they seize
    cruel are they, they have no mercy
Their sound makes a roar like the sea
    on horses they ride
Lined up like one man for battle
    against you, daughter Babylon!

[43]The king of Babylon has heard the report of them
    his hands are weakened
Distress seizes him
    pain like a woman in labor.

RHETORIC AND COMPOSITION

MT 50:41–43 = LXX 27:41–43. The present poem adapts the opening portion of a Judah oracle (6:22–24) for use against Babylon (Rudolph; Weiser; Gosse 1998). The earlier version had a "Thus said Yahweh" messenger formula (6:22), but here there is no formula; nevertheless, a divine oracle can be assumed. The text here is also without section markings, but the duplication elsewhere makes delimitation reasonably secure. The poetry is unquestionably Jeremiah's, notably v 41, which, besides the duplication in 6:22, occurs with only slight variation in 25:32; 31:8; and 50:9.

The rhetorical structure of the present oracle represents no advance over its earlier version; in fact, the omission here of two stanzas in the original results in a loss of certain key word repetitions (see Rhetoric and Composition for 6:22–26). In the original is also a lively dialogue between Yahweh and the prophet: the beginning messenger formula identifies Yahweh as the speaker (6:22); the shift to "we" discourse in Stanza III (6:24) brings in the voice of Jeremiah. The present version lacks both features, which means either Yahweh or Jeremiah can be the speaker throughout.

Catchwords connecting to the prior oracle:

v 42 *daughter Babylon*   *bat-bābel*   v 39 *daughter ostriches*   *běnôt yaʿănâ*

Catchwords connecting to the following unit:

v 4 *Look*   v 44 *Look*

NOTES

50:41–43. See exegesis for 6:22–24.

41. *from the north*. Compare "from the land of the north" in 6:22. On a "foe from the north" that is to come against Babylon, see Note for 50:3.

A great nation and many kings. The earlier version lacks "and many kings." Anticipated here is a coalition army coming against Babylon.

42. *sword*. The spelling *kîdōn* is the same as in the Qumran *War Scroll* (Yadin 1962: 124); elsewhere in the OT it is *kîdôn*. On this small, double-edged sword, see Note for 6:23.

daughter Babylon. Replacing "daughter Zion" in 6:23. The "daughter Babylon" metaphor occurs again in 51:33.

43. *The king of Babylon has heard the report of them, his hands are weakened. Distress seizes him*. Here the king is rendered helpless by the report of war; in 6:24 it was Jeremiah and all Judah.

MESSAGE AND AUDIENCE

A Judahite audience may recognize this as an older oracle recycled for use against Babylon. Yahweh will bring a foe from the north against the nation that was itself a foe from the north against Judah. On swift horses, crack archers and sword-wielding warriors will ride. Woe to the mighty king of Babylon, who will now be rendered helpless as a woman in labor. Will this audience appreciate the irony that what Babylon has done to others will now come to Babylon itself?

16. As a Lion from the Jordan against Babylon! (50:44–46)

50 ⁴⁴Look, as a lion goes up
    from the pride of the Jordan to perennial pasture
Indeed I will in a moment chase them[1] from her
    and who is the young man I will appoint over her?
Indeed who is like me?
    and who will summon me?
      and who is this one, a shepherd that can stand before me?

⁴⁵Therefore hear the counsel of Yahweh that he counseled toward Babylon, and his plans that he planned toward the land of the Chaldeans:
    Surely they shall drag them away—the little ones of the flock
      surely the pasture shall be horrified over them
⁴⁶At the sound 'Babylon is captured!' the land quakes
    and a cry among the nations is heard.

RHETORIC AND COMPOSITION

MT 50:44–46 = LXX 27:44–46. The present verses adapt two Edom oracles (49:19–21) for use against Babylon (v 44; vv 45b–46). In the Edom collection they appear in a cluster of three oracles. Here, as there, no messenger formulas are present, but since Yahweh is speaker throughout (the self-asseverations in v 44), we may assume these to be divine oracles. The prose introduction to Oracle II (v 45a) is also present in the Edom collection (49:20a). Again, duplication elsewhere clarifies delimitation, although both M^L and M^A have a *setumah* after v 46 (M^P lacks the section). This lower limit is also the chapter division.

The shout announcing Babylon's fall at the end of Oracle II, which has no parallel in the Edom oracle, makes an inclusio with the directive to proclaim the event at the beginning of the chapter (Aitken 1984: 30; Carroll):

50:2a Declare *among the nations and make heard*   ... *baggôyim wĕhašmîʿû.*
    ... *make heard ... Babylon is taken!*   *hašmîʿû ... nilkĕdâ bābel*

50:46 *Babylon is captured! ...*   *nitpĕśâ bābel*
    ... *among the nations is heard*   ... *baggôyim nišmāʿ*

---

[1]Reading the H-stem of the Q, *ʾărîṣēm*, "I will chase them" (cf. 49:19); the Kt is the Qal *ʾărûṣēm*, "I will run (?) them."

The rhetorical structure of these oracles differs little from the Edom versions, except for the last line in Oracle II. Here the cry over Babylon's fall is heard "among the nations" (making possible the inclusio), whereas in 49:21 Edom's own scream is heard "at the Red Sea." But the Edom oracle has a *miqqôl . . . qôlāh* ("at the sound . . . its sound") inclusio in 49:21, which is not present here. On structure and prose-poetry issues in the two sets of oracles, see Rhetoric and Composition for 49:19–22.

Catchwords connecting to the prior oracle:

v 44 *Look*   v 41 *Look*

Catchwords connecting to the following oracle:

v 44 *Look*   51:1 *Look I*
v 45 *the land of the Chaldeans*   51:4 *the land of the Chaldeans*

NOTES

50:44–46. See exegesis for 49:19–21.

44. *to perennial pasture.* The LXX reads "to the place of Aitham," as in 49:19.

45. *toward Babylon . . . the land of the Chaldeans.* In 49:20 it is "toward Edom . . . inhabitants of Teman."

the pasture. Hebrew *nāweh.* The T, S, and Vg read *nĕwēhem* ("their pasture"), which is the reading in 49:20. Cornill and Rudolph are probably correct in attributing the loss of a *mem* in MT to haplography (next word begins with *mem*).

46. *the land quakes.* Hebrew *nirʿăšâ hāʾāreṣ.* The N-stem has the same meaning as the Qal in 4:24; 8:16; 10:10; 49:21; and 51:29. On the land / earth quaking, see Note on 51:29.

Babylon is captured. A victory shout. The Edom oracle has simply "their [i.e., Edom's] fall."

MESSAGE AND AUDIENCE

As with the previous oracle, so here too, Jeremiah's audience may well recognize oracles spoken on other occasions against other nations that are here recycled for use against Babylon. Oracle I is general, and could have been spoken against any nation. Its image of Yahweh coming as a lion out of the Jordan thicket is not particularly apt for a war destined to be fought in the Tigris-Euphrates region, nor, for that matter, is it suitable for an audience of Jewish exiles in faraway Babylon. It makes sense only if spoken to a Jerusalem audience (Jones), which means a date can be assigned prior to 594 B.C., when the bulk of Jeremiah's Babylon oracles were spoken. The central point of the oracle will not be missed. Yahweh, as the main mover in world affairs, will chase other predators from Babylon and select for that nation a ruler of his own choosing. The audience is then confronted with questions it has heard before.

Yahweh says, "Indeed who is like me? and who will summon me? and who is this one, a shepherd that can stand before me?" It knows the answer.

Oracle II has an introduction telling its audience in advance that Yahweh has plans concerning Babylon, whose name occurs in the oracle. Unspecified attackers will drag away the little ones in Babylon's flock, and the pasture in which they have grazed will be numb with horror at the violence. At the end comes a shout, "Babylon is captured!" With this tumultuous sound the earth quakes, and a cry of unrestrained joy is heard reverberating among the nations. For an audience hearing the entire Babylon collection of chap. 50 recited at one time, if such a recitation ever took place, this shout will be what it had been waiting for from the beginning.

17. I Am Rousing a Destroying Wind (51:1–5)

51 [1]Thus said Yahweh:
Look I am rousing against Babylon
　　and against the inhabitants of Leb-qamai
　　　　a destroying wind
[2]And I will send to Babylon
　　strangers who will scatter her
　　　　and empty her land
Because they were against her round about
　　in the day of evil

[3]God will bend, will bend[1]
　　the bender his bow
　　　　and God[2] will rise in his scale armor!
Spare not her young men
　　devote to destruction all her host!
[4]The slain have fallen in the land of the Chaldeans
　　and those pierced in her streets

[5]But Israel is not widowed, nor Judah
　　before his God, before Yahweh of hosts
But their land is filled with guilt
　　before the Holy One of Israel.

RHETORIC AND COMPOSITION

MT 51:1–5 = LXX 28:1–5. The present verses constitute a divine oracle whose upper limit is indicated by the messenger formula in v 1, prior to which is a

---

[1]Repointing MT ʾel ("to") to ʾēl ("God") and reading the unpointed Kt ydrk the same as the preceding yidrōk, "(he) will bend"; see Notes.
[2]Repointing MT ʾel ("to") to ʾēl ("God").

setumah in M^L and M^A. M^P has no section here. This break is also a chapter division. There are no subsequent section markings until v 10 (M^A only), for which reason opinions differ as to where the lower limit is to be placed. In my earlier work (1975: 155 n. 73 [= 1997: 121 n. 73]), I took vv 1–10 as a single poem. Cheyne and Giesebrecht take vv 1–4 as the unit; Jones vv 1–5; Volz and Holladay vv 1–6. Verse 5 shifts the focus to Israel and Judah after a judgment on Babylon, which, in this particular case, points not to the independence of the verse, but to its being a conclusion, since a similar-type verse concludes the next unit at 51:10. Verse 6 begins "Flee from the midst of Babylon," which has its closest parallel in the beginning verse of 50:8: "Wander from the midst of Babylon." The decision, then, is to take v 5 as a conclusion and v 6 as a new beginning (see further Rhetoric and Composition for 51:6–10).

The oracle is three stanzas of well-balanced poetry. Stanza I (vv 1–2) consists of two tricolons and a bicolon. Scanning the first line as a tricolon obviates the need to delete "against Babylon" *metri causa* with Volz, Rudolph, and Holladay. Stanza II (vv 3–4) is a tricolon followed by two bicolons. Stanza III (v 5) is shorter, only two lines, both of which are bicolons. The rhetorical structure for the whole contains the following repetitions and balancing key words:

I	. . . . *Babylon*	. . . . . . *bābel*	v 1
	. . . . *Leb-qamai*	. . . *lēb qāmāy*	
	. . . . *Babylon*	. . . . . . *bābel*	v 2
	. . . . *her land*	. . . . . *'arṣāh*	
II	. . . . *her host*	. . . *ṣĕbā'āh*	v 3
	. . . . . *in the land of the Chaldeans*	. . . *bĕ'ereṣ kaśdîm*	v 4
III	But . . . . . *Israel*	*kî* . . . . . . *yiśrā'ēl* . . .	v 5
	before . . . . *before* . . . . *hosts*	*mē* . . *mē* . . . . . *ṣĕbā'ôt*	
	But their land	*kî 'arṣām*	
	before . . . . *Israel*	*mi* . . . . *yiśrā'ēl*	

Stanzas I and III have their own internal balance. Stanza II contains link terms—in inverted order—to both I and III: "her host" (v 3) to "hosts" (v 5); and "Chaldeans" (v 4) to "Leb-qamai" (v 1), the latter a cipher for "Chaldeans" (see Notes). All three stanzas have the key word "land."

The oracle—with a clarified v 3a—appears to be another dialogue poem between Yahweh and the prophet. Yahweh speaks in Stanza I, announcing his resolve to dispatch a ruinous enemy against Babylon. Jeremiah speaks in Stanzas II and III, where God is referred to in the third person (see Note on v 3a). In II, there is rapid movement from prediction to fulfillment: Jeremiah predicts divine readiness for war (v 3a), issues a command to annihilate the foe (v 3b), and then describes the Babylonian defeat (v 4). In III the prophet turns to speak a contrasting word of hope to Israel and Judah, despite guilt in their own land before the Holy One, Yahweh (v 5).

Catchwords connecting to the oracles in the prior unit:

51:1 *Look I*	50:44 *Look*
51:4 *the land of the Chaldeans*	50:45 *the land of the Chaldeans*

Catchwords connecting to the poem following:

vv 1–2 *Babylon* (2×)	vv 6–9 *Babylon* (4×)
v 4 *have fallen*	v 8 *is fallen*

NOTES

51:1. *Look I am rousing against Babylon.* Hebrew *hinĕnî mē'îr 'al-bābel.* The wording is similar to that in 50:9. Babylon at an earlier time was roused against Judah (6:22), but now Yahweh has another work to carry out (50:41). The Medes are named as Yahweh's current punishing agent in the inserted prose of 51:11b and in 51:28 (cf. Isa 13:17). The initial *hinĕnî* ("Look I"), as also *hinnēh* ("Look"), are signatures of the Jeremianic oracle (see Notes for 1:9, 15; and 49:19).

against . . . against. The prepositions *'al* and *'el* are both adversative, as in 21:13; 50:35; and elsewhere; for their frequent alternation in Jeremiah, see Note on 11:2. A few MSS here have *wĕ'al* for *wĕ'el.*

Leb-qamai. Transliterating the term here with the NRSV (JB, NJV, NIV, REB: "Leb-kamai"). Hebrew *lēb qāmāy* is a cipher (Heb *atbash*) for Chaldea / Chaldeans (Rashi; LXX: *Chaldaious*). The same type of cipher for Babylon ("Sheshak") occurs in v 41 and 25:26. On the *atbash,* see Note for 25:26. The origin of the cipher—assuming it is a cipher—is unknown; there certainly is no need to be cryptic, as Babylon is twice mentioned in vv 1–2. Noegel (1996) thinks the *atbash* is simply a wordplay. Cornill took the term to be a later invention, citing the LXX's "Chaldeans" as original. But it is questionable whether any sense can be made of the resulting Hebrew (Kimhi: "heart of my adversaries"; cf. T; Rudolph; Weiser; McKane), although the Masoretic pointing and division into two words may give indirect support to this having once been the case.

a destroying wind. Hebrew *rûaḥ mašḥît.* "Wind" rather than "spirit" is better retained here as a metaphor for the coming enemy (Calvin; Bright; Holladay; McKane; cf. AV; NEB; NAB; NJV; NRSV; REB; NJB; NSB: "storm"). The LXX has *anemon kausōna diaphtheironta,* "a scorching, destructive wind," which is the desert wind of 4:11–12 (cf. 18:17). This is not a gentle wind for winnowing, making unlikely the reading "winnowers" in v 2. The translation "destroying spirit" or "spirit of a destroyer" (T; Rashi; Giesebrecht; Duhm; and others; RSV; JB), depends largely on the secondary 51:11b, where "spirit" is a better rendering for *rûaḥ.* For the idiom of "Yahweh arousing the spirit" of someone to carry out work on his behalf, see Hag 1:14; 1 Chr 5:26; 2 Chr 21:16; 36:22; Ezra 1:1, 5. Reference has also been made here to "the destroyer" (*hammašḥît*) active at Passover (Exod 12:23), although Volz rightly rules out a demonic figure in the present verse (cf. 2 Sam 24:16). Forms of the verb "destroy" (*šḥt*) occur throughout the prose and poetry of Jeremiah (23x), being particularly frequent in the present chapter (2:30; 4:7; 5:10, 26; 6:5, 28; 11:19; 12:10; 13:7, 9, 14; 15:3, 6; 18:4; 22:7; 36:29; 48:18; 49:9; 51:1, 11, 20, 25 [2×]). Jones compares *mašḥît* with the other oft-used participle in Jeremiah, *šōdēd* ("devastator"), saying that the former in chaps. 50–51 substitutes for the latter in chaps. 46–49, and may argue literarily for the independence of the Babylonian collection. It is not quite that simple. Both participles occur in chaps. 50–51 (*šōdēd* and *šōdĕdîm* in 51:48, 53, 55–56). For more on the verb *šdd* in Jeremiah, see Note on 48:8.

2. *And I will send to Babylon strangers who will scatter her.* Another Jeremianic expression (16:16; 23:4; 48:12), but here embellished with an implied play on *zārîm* ("strangers") and *zōrîm* ("scatterers / winnowers"). The verb *zrh* more precisely means "to winnow." In 15:7 the winnowing metaphor accents a separation process: some warriors have fallen in battle, others not, at least not yet (15:9c). Elsewhere (31:10; 49:32, 36) the metaphor accents dispersion, thus the translation "scatter." In the present case exile is doubtless indicated; the land will be emptied. Yahweh is portrayed here not as acting in direct fashion, but rather through intermediaries.

strangers. Hebrew *zārîm*. A case can also be made for repointing to *zōrîm*, "winnowers," which is presupposed by Aq and Symm (*likmētas*), the Vg (*ventilatores*), and numerous commentators (J. D. Michaelis 1793: 385; Giesebrecht; Duhm; Cornill; Volz; Rudolph; Weiser; Holladay; McKane) and some modern Versions (AV; RSV; NEB; JB; NAB). In other occurrences of this expression in Jeremiah, the verbal root is repeated. That would give the reading here: "And I will send to Babylon winnowers who will winnow her." The LXX and T both have nonmetaphorical renderings that keep the verb constant. The T: "And I will send against Babylon plunderers, and they shall plunder it"; the LXX: "And I will send to Babylon vandals (*hybristas*), and they will vandalize (*kathybrisousin*) her." One wonders then if the winnowing image is quite right. A "destroying wind" (v 1) would seem to preclude winnowing, where a gentle wind is required (4:11–12). A violent scattering is more to the point (31:10; 49:32, 36), and "strangers"—who elsewhere in Jeremiah (5:19; 30:8; 51:51) and in Ezekiel (Ezek 28:7; 30:12; 31:12) are enemies—can suitably carry out such an activity. "Strangers" is thus read by Rashi; Calvin; Cheyne; NJV; NIV; and NSB ("främlingar"). Note the similar problem of pointing *rbym* in 50:29: Is it *rabbîm* ("multitude"), or *rōbîm* ("those who shoot")?

and empty her land. The verb *bqq* in the Qal occurs in 19:7, where a play is made in vv 1 and 10 with *baqbuq* ("decanter"). The Polel here has the same basic meaning, "to empty, lay waste." See also Isa 24:1 and Nah 2:3[Eng 2:2]. Reference is to dispersion; cf. 50:8, 16, 28; 51:6, 9, 45.

Because they were against her round about. The verb *hāyû* is perfect, and the tense is past: "they were" (so T). The subject then is not "strangers" in v 2a, but the Babylonians themselves, who, on an earlier occasion surrounded Jerusalem (Ehrlich 1912: 367–68). The *kî* should thus be translated "because," since a reason is being given for Babylon's judgment. The same phrase, except for *kî*, occurs verbatim in 4:17. The LXX has *ouai epi Babylōna kyklothen* ("Woe to Babylon round about"), where *ouai* appears to be a misreading of Heb *hyw* (metathesis). All attempts to get a future verb (Volz; Rudolph; Bright; McKane), which modern Versions since the AV contain, should be rejected.

in the day of evil. I.e., Jerusalem's evil day, perhaps in 597 B.C. On the "day of evil" (*yôm rā'â*) in Jeremiah, which is a familiar concept also from the Psalms, see Note on 17:17.

3. *God will bend, will bend, the bender his bow, and God will rise in his scale armor.* The text here is difficult, and cannot be read, according to Cornill, except as a "violent ellipsis": "To him who bends, I say: Let him bend his bow; and to him who envelopes himself in his coat of mail: Spare not." Rashi's explanation of the first part is also elliptical: "To wherever I say, there the archer shall bend his bow" (Rosenberg). There are two problems: the double occurrence of *'l* and *w'l*, which are pointed in MT as *'el* and *wě'el* ("to . . . and to"), and the double occurrence of *ydrk*, the first of which is pointed *yidrōk* ("he will bend"), and the second of which is left unpointed (a note in the margin says "written but not read"). Blayney noted that some 94 MSS—perhaps 95—do not have the repeated term (perhaps due to haplography). The two occurrences of *'el* are repointed by some to the negative *'al*, which is done for the first occurrence of the particle in T, S, and Vg (cf. *lō'-yidrōk* in 48:33). The T has: "He who bends his bow, let him not bend it." The result is a directive (with the jussive) that Babylonian soldiers not use their bows nor stand up in their coats of mail (cf. RSV; JB; NIV); they are an army already defeated and need not take up the fight. Some commentators accept this reading (Rudolph, Weiser, Holladay, Keown et al., Jones), but others do not (Cornill, Peake, Streane, Volz, Bright, Thompson, McKane), the main reason being that the enemies of Babylon are the preferred addressee. Also, the LXX omits the negatives (cf. NAB and NJV). Another way to get a positive reading would be to take *'al* in both cases as an asseverative (see Note on 5:10). But a better solution, in my opinion, is to repoint both occurrences to *'ēl* ("God"), which makes God the subject and Jeremiah the speaker of the verse (see Rhetoric and Composition). The *'ělōhāyw* in v 5 may be a balancing term. There is another occurrence of *'ēl* in 51:56, and the prose of 32:18 has *hā'ēl* ("O God"). In 10:1 *'el* should also be repointed to *'ēl* (see Note there). This form of the divine name is nevertheless uncommon in Jeremiah, whereas in Isaiah—both First and Second—it occurs often (Isa 8:8, 10; 9:5[Eng 9:6]; 10:21; 40:18; 45:14, 15; 46:9; et passim). The MT repointing can be explained as an attempt to get rid of a bold anthropomorphism. But for Yahweh to bend the bow and put on a coat of mail is not to be wondered at, since Yahweh is seen bringing out weapons from his armory in 50:25. As for the repetition of *ydrk*, this need not be taken as dittography (*pace* Holladay), but rather as a deliberate repetition for emphasis (*geminatio*), of which there are many fine examples in Jeremiah: "my innards, my innards" in 4:19; "temple of Yahweh, temple of Yahweh, temple of Yahweh" in 7:4; "land, land, land" in 22:29; "I have dreamed, I have dreamed" in 23:25; and especially "came, came" in 46:20. See further Note for 7:4. The unpointed *ydrk*

can be pointed the same as *yidrōk* preceding. On the verb *drk* and the bending of the composite bow, see Notes on 9:2[Eng 9:3] and 46:9.

in his scale armor. Hebrew *bĕsiryōnô*. This is a coat of mail, on which see Note for 46:4.

Spare not her young men. Jeremiah now addresses Babylon's appointed enemy, which may be another "summons to battle" so-called (Bach 1962: 56). The verb *ḥml* with *'el* means "spare, have compassion" (50:14: "spare not an arrow"). The T: "Do not have pity on her young men" (cf. NJV).

devote to destruction. Hebrew *haḥărîmû*. The holy war ban, on which see Note for 50:21.

all her host. The T: "all her possessions." Captured people will also become victims.

4. *The slain have fallen in the land of the Chaldeans, and those pierced in her streets.* The battle was predicted, ordered to commence, and now is over. Babylon's warriors and others lie fallen in the country and on city streets (cf. 6:11; 49:26; 50:30).

The slain. Hebrew *ḥălālîm* are "those pierced (by the sword), struck dead" (8:23[Eng 9:1]; 14:18; 25:33; 51:4, 47, 49, 52; cf. Ezek 28:23).

and those pierced in her streets. Here "those pierced" (*mĕduqqārîm*) may be only wounded (so T; cf. 37:10). The mention of "streets" locates the fighting in the city of Babylon.

5. *But . . . But.* Hebrew *kî . . . kî* introduces two qualifying remarks: first, that Israel and Judah are spared the total judgment visited upon Babylon, and second, that judgment is carried out despite Israel's guilt before the Holy One of Israel.

But Israel is not widowed, nor Judah, before his God, before Yahweh of hosts. A repudiation of the idea that Israel—also Judah—has been abandoned by its God, despite difficulties in language and metaphor. The "divine abandonment" motif is common in the Mesopotamian city laments (Dobbs-Allsopp 1993: 51), and present also in Lam 1:1. Hebrew *'almān* is a *hapax legomenon* in the OT, apparently being the adjective "widowed." Masculine in form, it goes with "his God," precluding any "Yahweh as husband, Israel as wife" imagery. Duhm thus repoints to *'almōn*, "widowhood" (Isa 47:9). For the widowhood metaphor and its ultimate rejection in the case of Israel, see Isa 54:4–8. In the present verse T has: "For the house of Israel and Judah have not been forsaken of their God," which carries over into the AV, RSV, and NRSV. Kimḥi says: "[Israel] is not like a widow whose husband is dead . . . for her husband is alive" (Rosenberg, 395).

Yahweh of hosts. The LXX translates *ṣĕbā'ôt* ("of hosts") with *pantokratoros*, which it does occasionally in Jeremiah. More often the term is omitted. See Appendix VI.

But their land is filled with guilt. I.e., Israel's land, not the Chaldean land mentioned in v 4 (and v 1). The latter interpretation is made by Rashi, Kimḥi, Calvin, and others, some of whom cite for support the Babylonian offense in 50:29. However, in 50:7 the Babylonians absolve themselves of guilt. The NRSV rightly returns to "their land" of the AV, reversing the interpretive RSV reading. The REB similarly abandons the interpretive reading of the NEB (but

McKane does not). The notion that "their land" refers to Chaldean land has led some commentators (Cornill; Condamin; Rudolph; Holladay; Keown et al.) to transpose 5a and 5b, which is to be rejected. The JB took the same line, but that too has been reversed in the NJB. The point being made is that Israel and Judah are not forsaken by their God despite the fact that their land is filled with guilt before the One called Holy.

before the Holy One of Israel. The divine name, "Holy One of Israel," is common to both First and Second Isaiah, but it occurs elsewhere in Jeremiah (see Note on 50:29).

MESSAGE AND AUDIENCE

This oracle begins with Yahweh vowing to rouse against Babylon a wind of destroying proportions. Strangers will scatter the nation's people and the land will be left empty. The reason: Babylon surrounded an unnamed place in its day of evil. Will the audience know the place? Will it remember Nebuchadnezzar's encirclement and capture of Jerusalem? More than likely it will.

The discourse is then picked up by Jeremiah, who recounts in rapid fashion the judgment just announced. God will carry out the promised action, bending his bow and rising up in a full coat of mail. Battle commands follow. Holy war is being declared. Young men will not be spared; everyone and everything is to be devoted to destruction. The curtain falls quickly in the land of the Chaldeans. Dead fill the country and wounded lie helpless on the city streets. The oracle contrasts this scenario with others that a chastened Israel and Judah know well. Such are not mentioned, but what is said is that Israel has not been left widowed, nor has Judah, by Yahweh of the army—even though the land of promise is filled with guilt, which is repugnant before the "Holy One of Israel." The oracle thus ends with hope for the covenant people, but a reminder too of imputed sin and implied judgment.

This oracle, like others against Babylon, is general and spoken to an unspecified future. If Israel's "day of evil" (v 2) is Nebuchadnezzar's capture of Jerusalem in 597 B.C., then the oracle can be dated prior to 594 B.C., perhaps when that unblessed event was still fresh in everyone's mind.

18. A Golden Cup Was Babylon (51:6–10)

51 ⁶Flee from the midst of Babylon
    and deliver each his own life
        be not silenced in her iniquity
For this is Yahweh's time of vengeance
    a requital he is repaying her

⁷A golden cup was Babylon
    in the hand of Yahweh
        making drunk all the earth

From her wine drank the nations
　therefore went mad the nations

[8]Suddenly Babylon is fallen and shattered
　wail madly over her!
Get balm for her pain
　perhaps she can be treated

[9]We treated Babylon, but she could not be treated
　forsake her, and let us go each to his land
For her judgment reaches to the heavens
　and is lifted up to the clouds

[10]Yahweh has brought forth our vindication
　come, and let us recount in Zion
　the work of Yahweh our God.

RHETORIC AND COMPOSITION

MT 51:6–10 = LXX 28:6–10. The present unit is delimited at the lower end by a *setumah* in M[A] after v 10. M[L] has a *setumah* (ס) written *manu* in the margin opposite v 10 (reproduced in *BHS*); M[P] has no section after the verse. The upper limit is set at v 6 on the basis of the phrase "Flee (*nūsû*) from the midst of Babylon," which closely parallels the opening phrase in 50:8: "Wander (*nūdû*) from the midst of Babylon." This parallel outweighs other occurrences of *nūsû*, "flee!" in poems where location is not at the beginning (48:6; 49:8, 30). A break between vv 5 and 6 yields two consecutive poems concluding with a hopeful word for Israel (and Judah)—about their covenant with Yahweh, and Yahweh's vindication on their behalf:

I　　But Israel is not widowed, nor Judah　　　v 5
　　　　before his God, before Yahweh of hosts
　　　But their land is filled with guilt
　　　　before *the Holy One of Israel*

II　　*Yahweh* has brought forth our vindication　　v 10
　　　come, and let us recount in Zion
　　　　the work of *Yahweh our God*

　　The present poem divides into five stanzas. Stanzas I (v 6) and II (v 7) are tricolons followed by bicolons; Stanzas III (v 8) and IV (v 9) are double bicolons; and Stanza V (v 10) is another tricolon. Scanning the first lines of I and II as tricolons renders unnecessary the deletions *metri causa* of "and deliver each his own life" (v 6a) and "in the hand of Yahweh" (v 7a). There is no textual basis for either deletion; both phrases should be retained (see Notes). The poem begins by declaring Yahweh's vengeance on Babylon (v 6), and concludes by celebrating Yahweh's vindication of Israel (v 10).

The rhetorical structure comprises repetitions, balancing key words, and sound links:

I . . . . *Babylon*		v 6
. . . . *each*	*'îš*	
. . . .		
. . . . *this* . . . *(to) Yahweh*	*hî' layhwh*	
. . . . *he* . . . . *(to) her*	*hû' . . . lāh*	
II . . . . *Babylon*		v 7
. . . . *Yahweh*		
. . . .		
. . . . *the nations*	*gôyīm*	
. . . . *went mad the nations*	*yithōlĕlû gôyīm*	
III . . . . *Babylon*		v 8
wail madly	*hêlîlû*	
. . . . *she can be treated*	*tērāpē'*	
IV *We treated Babylon, but she could not be treated*	*rippi'nû . . . wĕlō' nirpātâ*	v 9
. . . . *each*	*'îš*	
V *Yahweh*		v 10
. . . . *Yahweh*		

Stanzas I–IV all contain the term "Babylon" in the same collocation (the third term in every first colon). "Yahweh" balances in Stanzas I and II, and another double recurrence of "Yahweh" in Stanza V makes an inclusio for the poem as a whole. Stanzas I and IV are balanced by the key word "each (person)." Stanzas II and III have a sound link in "went mad" (*yithōlĕlû*) and "wail madly" (*hêlîlû*), whereas III and IV are linked by a repetition of the verb *rp'* ("heal, treat to heal"). Stanzas I and II also have nice balance in their second lines, with the repeated "nations" (7b) being an example of *epiphora* (Kessler 1973: 20). The LXX omission of the second "nations" has led many commentators to delete (see Notes), but the term should be retained. Note an *anaphora* with "nations" in 5:15.

Jeremiah is the speaking voice in the poem, although other voices are brought in at the close (vv 9–10). In v 8a the call is for mourners to bewail a fallen, shattered Babylon, and in v 8b imaginary bystanders are dispatched to get balm for the not-yet deceased (apostrophe and irony). In v 9 the latter answer, saying that treatment has been attempted, but Babylon is beyond treatment. They then repeat for themselves Jeremiah's directive about fleeing for home. The poem closes with the Jewish escapees celebrating Yahweh's vindication of Israel, and anticipating a reporting of the news in Zion. Verse 10 should not be deleted with Volz and Rudolph; it is anticipatory and also the climax of the poem.

Catchwords connecting to the oracle preceding:

| vv 6–9 | *Babylon* (4×) | | vv 1–2 | *Babylon* (2×) |
| v 8 | *is fallen* | | v 4 | *have fallen* |

Catchwords connecting to the unit following:

| v 6 | *this is Yahweh's . . . vengeance* | v 11 | *this is the vengeance of Yahweh,* |
| | | | *the vengeance . . .* |

NOTES

51:6. *Flee from the midst of Babylon.* This directive could be to all foreigners currently residing in Babylon (Kimḥi; Calvin), although Rashi imagines it addressed only to Israel (cf. 50:8, 28; 51:45, 50; Isa 48:20). The echo in v 9a has a broad referent ("each to his land"), with the focus narrowing to Jews only in v 10.

and deliver each his own life. There is no textual support for judging this a secondary addition from 51:45 (*pace* Cornill; Rudolph; Carroll). The line is a tricolon, thus accommodating the phrase nicely (see Rhetoric and Composition). The same basic expression occurs in 48:6 and 51:45. Also, here is another example of asyndeton in Jeremianic poetry: "Flee . . . and deliver . . . be not silenced." See elsewhere 46:3–4; 49:8, 28, 30–31; 50:14; 51:11–12, 27; and Note for 4:6.

be not silenced in her iniquity. I.e., do not die in the punishment coming to Babylon. On the euphemistic *dmm*, "be silent," see 48:2 and Note for 8:14. Hebrew *ʿāwôn* can mean punishment for iniquity or the iniquity itself (Gen 4:13; 1 Sam 28:10; Ezek 14:10). There may be an allusion here to the punishment (*ʿāwôn*) that awaited Sodom (Gen 19:15). The point is that foreigners should not remain in Babylon lest they die (with others) in the city's overthrow. In the NT, see Rev 18:4.

For this is Yahweh's time of vengeance. On Yahweh's vengeance (*nqm*) with respect to the nations, see Note on 46:10. Vengeance is promised upon Babylon elsewhere in 50:15, 28; 51:11, and 36. It will take place in Yahweh's time (*ʿēt*), which is not yet, but in some indefinite nevertheless certain future.

a requital he is repaying her. Hebrew *gĕmûl hûʾ mĕšallēm lāh*. The two roots occur together again in 51:56. The noun *gĕmûl* can mean "benefit, reward" in a positive sense (cf. T; JB), which in this case would add a note of irony: "a benefit he is repaying her." We speak today of "getting one's just reward," meaning that one is getting due punishment. See 50:15 and 29 for other applications of the *lex talionis* principle to Babylon; compare also Rev 18:6. For this nation, which brought Judahite nationhood to an end, is reserved the strongest, unmitigated judgment in the book of Jeremiah.

7. *A golden cup was Babylon in the hand of Yahweh, making drunk all the earth.* The "gold(en) cup" metaphor is thought here to signify wealth (cf. Job 37:22), which for Babylon would have been considerable given its many conquests and years of world-power status. Elsewhere in the book (25:15, 17, 28;

49:12) reference is simply to "a cup." Aeschylus (*Persians* 52–53) refers to "Babylon . . . teeming with gold" (*Babulōn . . . hē polychrysos*). Babylon's splendor is attested also in 51:13, and played upon in even grander detail when "Babylon redivivus" comes up for review in Revelation 17–18, where also the "golden cup" turns up (17:4), this time signifying wealth and the impurity accruing from wealth (17:4–6; 18:3, 11–19). The "golden" epithet adds in both cases a touch of irony, as something once glorious is now said to be destined for the very indignity it brought upon others. The point made here is that Babylon's exaltation derived from being in Yahweh's service—nothing more, nothing less—in which capacity it carried out judgment on nations of the world. In Isa 10:5, Yahweh called Assyria "the rod of my anger, the staff of my fury." The cup-of-wrath vision in Jer 25:15–28 also invites comparison, although there Jeremiah serves the nations Yahweh's cup via the prophetic word. Kimḥi and Ehrlich (1912: 368) interpret *kôs-zāhāb* as "a goblet of golden wine," but this is doubtful even though the cup does contain wine. The cup is made of gold (Rashi), or else of some other substance overlaid with gold. The latter should be considered if the cup is being shattered (v 8). Assyrian annals include in their booty lists items (from Egypt) overlaid with gold (*ANET*[3] 293). Jehu's tribute to Shalmaneser III included a golden bowl, a golden pointed-bottom vase, golden tumblers (= cups), and golden buckets (*ANET*[3] 281). On the "cup" (*kôs*) as a drinking vessel and its metaphorical uses, see Note for 25:15.

in the hand of Yahweh. Many commentators (Giesebrecht; Duhm; Peake; Cornill; Weiser; Rudolph; Holladay) delete the phrase as an addition based on 25:15, some for metrical reasons, others because of uneasiness about Yahweh using Babylon against the nations and then turning on Babylon itself. Both reasons lack merit, and the phrase should be retained (Rashi; Kimḥi; Volz; Bright). The line can be read as a tricolon (see Rhetoric and Composition). As for theology, taking Babylon as Yahweh's instrument of wrath and then as the object of his wrath raises no problems (*pace* Carroll, 843). This is precisely the point being made. Compare the theology in 27:6–7, and earlier with respect to Assyria in Isa 10:12, 15.

making drunk all the earth. See 25:16, 27; and compare Rev 18:3. The image is one of inebriation, not of drinking a poisonous brew (*pace* McKane; Carroll). Once drunkenness ensues, madness follows and the hapless victim can then be slain (25:15–16, 27; cf. 51:57).

therefore went mad the nations. This madness is predicted in 25:16. The verb *hll* in the Hithpolel (BDB; KB[3] *hll* III) means "go mad / act madly" (25:16; 46:9; 50:38b; 51:7). The LXX, S, and Vg omit "nations," and many commentators delete (Giesebrecht; Duhm; Cornill; Volz; Rudolph; Bright; Holladay; McKane). But the repetition is good poetry (*epiphora*), and the word is best retained (see Rhetoric and Composition).

8. *Suddenly Babylon is fallen.* Hebrew *pit'ōm nāpĕlâ bābel*. Compare Isa 21:9: "Fallen, fallen is Babylon" (*nāpĕlâ nāpĕlâ bābel*), which again is picked up in Rev 18:2. Collapse comes not soon, but suddenly (*pit'ōm*), a recurrent theme regarding divine visitation in Jeremiah (4:20; 6:26; 15:8; 18:22) and in all of

Scripture (cf. Matt 24; 25:1–12; Luke 12:35–46; Rev 22:12, 20 AV). See also Note on 4:20. Plagues will come to Babylon-Rome in "a single day" (Rev 18:8), and judgment "in one hour" (v 10). More recently, in November of 1989, the world witnessed the fall of the DDR (East Germany), which only months before was anticipated by no one.

and shattered. Hebrew *watiššābēr.* The question here is whether the golden cup image carries over into the present verse; if so, the cup must be made of a breakable substance. A cup of pure gold does not fit this description. The metaphor, however, could be restricted to v 7. McKane connects the shattering to the medical vocabulary in v 8b, saying that Babylon's brokenness is a sickness that cannot be cured. This is possible (cf. 8:22; 14:19). On the other hand, if the cup is simply overlaid with gold, and not pure gold, a fall could leave it broken into pieces. Also, the "cup" could be hurled away by Yahweh and shatter on landing. Compare the "smashed-pot" metaphor used for King Jehoiachin in 22:28.

wail madly over her. This begins Jeremiah's dramatic appeal for sympathetic mourners, which continues throughout the verse. More examples of apostrophe and irony (*epitrope*). The wailing here is anticipatory, as the victim is not yet deceased. Who will wail over Babylon, unless it be foreign mercenaries, merchants, or other self-interested allies? Revelation 18:9–19 envisions a distraught company of (allied) kings and individuals busy in various aspects of foreign commerce.

Get balm for her pain, perhaps she can be treated. The metaphor now shifts to someone gravely ill. Imagined bystanders are directed to go for medicine, although one knows it will do no good. The prognosis for Babylon is the same as for Judah (30:12–15) and Egypt (46:11). The point is not that balm is unavailable (*pace* Jones); rather, that balm exists in great quantity but will not bring healing. On balm (*ṣorî*), see Note for 8:22.

perhaps she can be treated. Hebrew *'ûlay tērāpē'.* Full-blown irony. There is no chance she can be treated. The verb *rp'* can also mean "treat to heal" (6:14; 8:11).

9. *We treated Babylon, but she could not be treated.* The response from the would-be medical team is that treatment has already been tried, but Babylon's condition was found to be untreatable. Giesebrecht takes the respondents to be the nations. Have they sought to shore up a faltering ally as Egypt did when Assyria collapsed in 609 B.C., or as the United States and other Western nations did in the 1990s when the Russian empire fell apart, making considerable outlays to keep Russia from total collapse? More likely, this is Babylon's foreign population speaking, since what follows is a decision to give the nation up for lost and return each to his own country.

forsake her, and let us go each to his land. This has to be the voice of Babylon's foreign population (Calvin: foreign mercenaries), whose resolve now to return home echoes Jeremiah's directive at the beginning of the poem (v 6). The phrase "each to his land" occurs also in 50:16b, but that is scant reason for judging it secondary here (*pace* Volz and Holladay). The LXX has "let us forsake her" (*egkatalipōmen autēn*), the reading also of S and Vg.

For her judgment reaches to the heavens. The problematic term here is *mišpāṭāh* (lit. "her judgment, justice"); we expect something more like "her evil" (cf. *ḥaṭṭāʾtām*, "their sin," in Gen 18:20), since one imagines that it is Babylon's evil being adjudicated. But Berkovitz (1969: 188) says that *mišpaṭ* here is the measure of Babylon's punishment, which will be the maximum. The term *baššāmāyim* (lit. "into the heaven") is a superlative meaning "to (or beyond) the maximum" (Deut 1:28). On justice and judgment in the OT, see Note for 21:12.

and is lifted up to the clouds. The LXX has "to the stars."

10. *Yahweh has brought forth our vindication.* We hear now from the Jewish contingent of evacuees who break forth in a hymn of deliverance (cf. Weiser). The verse continues the prophetic perfect. Babylon's fall will make possible Israel's salvation. Compare again in the NT, Rev 18:20.

our vindication. Hebrew *ṣidqōtênû*. The term here denotes Israel's deliverance (Isa 62:1–2), there being no strict sense of righteousness per se. "Our righteousness" in the AV is not right, as the Jews even in elation are not celebrating their own righteous deeds (*pace* T; Rashi), but, as the verse goes on to say, a mighty deed of Yahweh. NEB's "our innocence" is also not correct (REB changes to "our victory"). The LXX appears to have experienced difficulty with the term as well, rendering the entire phrase *exēnegken kyrios to krima autou*, "the Lord has carried out his judgment." Compare Aq: *exēnegke kyrios tēn dikaiosynēn autou*, "the Lord has carried out his righteousness."

come, and let us recount in Zion the work of Yahweh our God. See 50:28. The deliverance of Israel will be another mighty act of God. On this important motif in Scripture, see G. E. Wright 1952. The verb *spr* ("tell, recount") occurs frequently in the Psalms, often in connection with recounting (to the next generation) Yahweh's mighty acts (see Pss 26:7; 40:6[Eng 40:5]; 44:2[Eng 44:1]; 73:28; 75:2[Eng 75:1] 78:3–4; 118:17).

MESSAGE AND AUDIENCE

Jeremiah begins once again with an echo of the Sodom and Gomorrah story, pointing people ahead to the day when the evacuated city will be Babylon. His audience has heard it before. It will be a matter of life and death; if they fail to exit, they will be silenced in Babylon's iniquity. Yahweh's day of vengeance will be just payment for the excesses Babylon carried out against other nations. If this poem was recited prior to 594 B.C., which it may well have been, a Jerusalem audience would nod with approval, remembering Babylon's subjugation of its capital a short time earlier. Exiles in Babylon would respond similarly, some of them entertaining the false hope that Yahweh's day will come soon. Later audiences, having lived through Jerusalem's destruction, will take any hope they can get.

The poem goes on to recall Babylon as once the golden cup in Yahweh's hand, the nation that made other nations drunk from the wine it served up. Those listening—whether in Jerusalem or in exile—will know something of this madness, and so will peoples of neighboring nations. But now Babylon's time is imagined as having come suddenly, as it typically does when Yahweh acts. Once Yahweh's agent of judgment, Babylon must now itself face judgment. The golden cup lies fallen and shattered, and Jeremiah asks for mourners to come and wail on her behalf. Others are told to get balm. "Perhaps she can be treated," he says. But can she?

The response comes back that the attempt was made, but Babylon could not be treated. Those administering the treatment—presumably foreigners in the country acting in self-interest—decide therefore to forsake their terminally ill host and return home. Babylon's judgment, they admit, will reach to highest heaven. The poem ends with the Jewish evacuees breaking forth into song. For them this is Yahweh's vindication of Israel, and they vow a return to Zion where, once again, they can recount another mighty act of Yahweh their God.

This poem lies behind the great lament of Revelation 18, where Babylon becomes the symbol of another proud city abounding in wickedness and ripe for divine judgment: Rome. The people there awaiting vindication are the saints, the apostles, and the prophets (Rev 18:20).

19. You Who Dwell by Many Waters (51:11–14)

51 [11]Sharpen the arrows!
fill the quivers!
Yahweh has roused the spirit of the kings of Media, for his purpose against Babylon is to destroy it; for this is the vengeance of Yahweh, the vengeance of his temple.
   [12]To the walls of Babylon!
     set up a flag!
       strengthen the watch!
       station watchmen!
     prepare men in ambush!
For Yahweh both planned and did what he said to the inhabitants of Babylon.

   [13]You who dwell[1] by many waters
     by manifold treasures
   Your end has come
     your cutoff measure
   [14]Yahweh of hosts has sworn by himself:
     Surely I have filled you
       humanity like the locust
         and they shall raise a shout over you.

---

[1]Reading the feminine singular participle of the Q, *šōkant* ("you who dwell"), which appears to be a mixed form (GKC §90n); the Kt is the archaic second feminine singular, *šākanty* ("you have dwelt"); cf. 2:33; 10:17; and 22:23.

RHETORIC AND COMPOSITION

MT 51:11–14 = LXX 28:11–14. The present verses contain a poem with two—perhaps three—later prose expansions. The unit as a whole is delimited at the top end by a *setumah* in M^A before v 11 (no sections occur in M^L and M^P). Delimitation at the bottom end is by a *setumah* in M^L, M^A, and M^P after v 14. The core poem, having two stanzas, is further seen to be self-contained by an inclusio made from the verb *mlʾ*, "fill" (Condamin; Lundbom 1975: 50–51 [= 1997: 69–71]):

I   . . . .   v 11
        fill the quivers   *milʾû . . .*

II   Surely *I have filled you*   *. . . millēʾtîk*   v 14
        . . . .

In my earlier analysis I took all the verses as poetry, but now I believe a poem of shorter length has been theologically embellished with at least two prose expansions, which are the following:

v 11bc *Yahweh has roused the spirit of the kings of Media, for his purpose against Babylon is to destroy it; for this is the vengeance of Yahweh, the vengeance of his temple*
v 12c *For Yahweh both planned and did what he said to the inhabitants of Babylon*

The first expansion (v 11bc), which interrupts a string of battle commands to state that Yahweh is the prime mover in Babylon's demise, is judged secondary in full or in part by Volz, Rudolph, Weiser, Bright, Thompson, Carroll, Holladay, Jones, and Keown et al., also by the RSV, NRSV, JB, NJB, and NSB. It may borrow theology from "I am rousing . . . a destroying wind / spirit" in 51:1, and "the kings of Media" in 51:28. The "vengeance of Yahweh" and "vengeance of his temple" themes appear elsewhere in secondary additions (50:15c, 28b; cf. 51:6).

The second expansion (v 12c) avers that Yahweh did indeed what he planned to Babylon, thus fulfilling the prophecy contained in the first interpolation. This expansion is judged secondary in full or in part by Volz, Holladay, Jones, and Keown et al., also by the JB and NJB.

The following may also be expansion slightly modified from Amos 6:8a (Volz; Holladay):

v 14a *Yahweh of hosts has sworn by himself*

This could qualify as a clarifying gloss, informing the hearer that Yahweh is delivering the following curse on Babylon. It is otherwise not indicated that Yahweh is the speaking voice in the poem.

When the interpolations are stripped away, particularly the first two, we have a tight two-stanza poem similar in form and content to the first two stanzas of the Egypt oracle in 46:3–6. Stanza I (vv 11a, 12ab) is a three-line string of battle commands (asyndeton): a bicolon, a tricolon, and a bicolon; Stanza II (vv 13, 14b) is a three-line word of divine judgment: two bicolons and a tricolon. The speaker throughout is Yahweh, who elsewhere issues the battle commands (46:3–4; 50:14, and 29) and in v 14 is the one announcing judgment and delivering the curse.

The end of Stanza I and beginning of Stanza II contain cognate repetitions:

| I | . . . . *the watch* | *hammišmār* | v 12b |
| | . . . . *watchmen* | *šōmĕrîm* | |

| II | . . . . *many* | *rabbîm* | v 13a |
| | *manifold* . . . . | *rabbat* | |

Catchwords connecting to the unit preceding:

> v 11   *this is the vengeance of Yahweh,*   v 6   *this is Yahweh's . . . vengeance*
> *the vengeance . . .*

Catchwords connecting to the unit following:

v 11	*spirit*	*rûaḥ*			
v 12	*he did*	*'āśâ*	v 15	*the maker*	*'ōśēh*
			v 16	*he made*	*'āśâ*
v 13	*treasures*	*'ōṣārōt*		*his storehouses*	*'ōṣĕrōtāyw*
			vv 16–17	*wind / breath* (2×)	*rûaḥ*
v 14	*Yahweh of hosts*		v 17	*human*	*'ādām*
	humanity	*'ādām*	v 19	*Yahweh of hosts*	

NOTES

51:11. *Sharpen the arrows.* Hebrew *hābērû*, an H-stem imperative, means "clean, polish, sharpen" (BDB; KB³ *brr* II), used often of arrows (cf. Qal in Isa 49:2). The T has "sharpen"; so also the Vg (*acuite*). Burnished arrows penetrate more easily. Here begin more rapid-fire orders to an assembled army (Bach 1962: 56–57; Christensen 1975: 270), simulating a commander who is readying his troops for battle (Volz; cf. 46:3–4; 50:14, 29). Calvin says the words could be addressed to either Babylon's attackers or defenders. If the latter, they would be a taunt as in 46:3–4. But Kimḥi says Yahweh is addressing Babylon's attackers, which appears to be the correct interpretation.

fill the quivers! Hebrew *mil'û haššĕlāṭîm.* The war accessory here indicated has long been in question, with *šĕlāṭîm* denoting "shields" elsewhere in the OT, and both LXX (*tas pharetras*) and Vg (*pharetras*) translating "quivers" in the present text. Rashi translated "quivers"; Kimḥi (following T) stayed with "shields." The singular *šeleṭ* is now attested at Qumran, but with uncertain meaning (Yadin 1962: 133–35). The problem with "shields" is that it does not go well with *ml'*, and everyone adopting it has to depart from the verb's usual meaning of "fill" (see AV; RSV; NIV). The matter appears now settled, however, with an Aramaic loanword having turned up in Akkadian, *šalṭu*, meaning "bow (and arrow) case," or a case for other weapons (Borger 1972; *CAD* 17/1: 271–72; AHw 3: 1151). This may then make "quivers," which is widely adopted by the modern Versions (NEB, JB, NAB, NJV, NRSV, REB, NJB, NSB), the correct reading after all. The meaning "spear cases" for *šĕlāṭîm* could possibly fit in 2 Kgs 11:10, but not in the parallel text of 2 Chr 23:9.

Yahweh has roused the spirit. See 50:9 and 51:1.

the kings of Media. The term is perhaps a cliché, as in 25:25 (MT only) and 51:28. An independent Median attack on Babylon never materialized. In Esth 10:2 and Dan 8:20 it is "the kings of Media and Persia." Both here and in 51:28 the LXX and S have "king" singular (cf. NEB; REB; JB—but not NJB), which Duhm thinks refers to Cyrus. Such may later have been the case. The T has "kings" plural. "Kings" (plural) is used often in the Judah oracles (1:18; 13:13; 17:24; 22:4), and may here be another intensive plural (see Note on 13:13). On Media and the Medes, see Note for 51:28.

his purpose. Hebrew *mĕzimmātô*. On the purposes of Yahweh's mind, see 23:20 (= 30:24).

for this is the vengeance of Yahweh, the vengeance of his temple. Compare 50:15, 28; and 51:36. On Yahweh's vengeance with respect to other nations, see Note for 46:10. The LXX has "vengeance of his people" instead of "vengeance of his temple."

12. *To the walls of Babylon.* Hebrew *'el-ḥômōt bābel*. The commands of v 11a continue, the call here being for the attacking army to advance toward the city walls. Babylon's brick walls were legendary (see Note on 51:58). When Cyrus saw them he decided they were too formidable, and that the city must be taken in some other way. He thus diverted a canal to gain entrance (Xenophon, *Cyropaedia* vii 5.1, 7). The fact that the capture of Babylon did not correspond to prediction only goes to show that prophecies such as the present one were uttered well in advance of their fulfillment, not on the eve of battle or even when a battle seemed imminent.

set up a flag. Hebrew *śĕ'û-nēs*. The raised flag (or standard) functioned in wartime to lead attacking armies (51:12, 27), guide people to safe haven (4:6), signal distress (4:21), or announce a victory already achieved (50:2). On the flag itself, which was hoisted atop a pole, see Note for 4:6. The flag here is envisioned as going before the attacking army to give it direction and keep the soldiers together (Cheyne). Its modern peacetime counterpart is the raised flag of the tour guide. Xenophon (*Cyropaedia* vi 3.4; vii 1.4) reports a soldier leading Cyrus's army with a raised standard (*sēmeion*). But Kimḥi thinks the flag here is one that will be raised on the wall once the city has been conquered, showing that it now belongs to the attackers. The T and LXX both have a flag lifted upon Babylon's walls (cf. AV), but it is not clear whether such is held by the victors or by those defending the city.

strengthen the watch! station watchmen! Hebrew *haḥăzîqû hammišmār hāqîmû šōmĕrîm*. Both call for tightened security in blockading the city. Inhabitants must not be allowed to leave, and defensive maneuvers by the besieged must be guarded against (2 Sam 11:16–17). In Jer 4:17, the Babylonian besiegers of Jerusalem were likened to "watchers / keepers of a field" (*šōmĕrê śāday*). For the first of these commands, the LXX curiously has *epistēsate pharetras* ("attend to the quivers").

prepare men in ambush! This directive anticipates a possible onrush by city defenders, which is best countered by ambush (cf. Josh 8:14–21; Judg 20:29–37). Xenophon (*Cyropaedia* vii 1.36) reports a rearguard action of this type by Cyrus, and in modern times, MacArthur used the same ploy with paratroopers to turn the Korean War around. The LXX again has a different reading: *hetoimasate hopla* ("prepare the weapons").

For Yahweh both planned and did what he said to the inhabitants of Babylon. The *gam . . . wĕgam* construction, meaning "both . . . and . . ." (GKC §154c), serves to strengthen associations. Yahweh both planned Babylon's destruction and carried it out. The same point is made regarding Jerusalem in Lam 2:17.

13. *You who dwell by many waters, by manifold treasures.* Or "by great waters . . . by great treasures." Hebrew *rabbîm / rabbat* will also admit alternate or double meanings. Calvin says "many waters" (= a good defense), and "much treasure" are setups for God's destructive work to come. The city of Babylon is here personified as a woman; in Rev 17:1 she becomes "the great whore . . . seated upon many waters" (NRSV). Compare personified Jerusalem in 4:30–31.

many waters. Hebrew *mayyim rabbîm*. This expression, nicely sonorous in Hebrew, occurs often in the OT (Hab 3:15; Isa 17:13; Jer 51:13, 55; Ezek 32:13; Pss 29:3; 32:6; and Song 8:7), in some cases with mythological overtones, i.e., referring to the great subterranean ocean and chaotic forces associated with it (May 1955). "Many waters" may represent chaos in 51:55, but not here, where it simply denotes the Euphrates together with lakes, streams, and canals around Babylon (see Note on 50:38a, and compare Isa 8:7). Canals were dug for defense, although Cyrus diverted one to capture the city (Xenophon, *Cyropaedia* vii 5).

by manifold treasures. The preposition *ʿal* ("by") does double duty in the line. The Hebrew word *ʾôṣārôt* ("treasures") represents Babylon's stored wealth and here may mean "storehouses" (see Notes for 15:13 and 50:37). Kimḥi says reference is being made to stored grain, or else silver and gold. In 51:7, Babylon is represented as a "golden cup" (= wealth).

Your end has come, your cutoff measure. Hebrew *bāʾ qiṣṣēk ʾammat biṣʿēk*, with *qiṣṣēk . . . biṣʿēk* again nicely sonorous. The second phrase is taken here as a construct chain containing the noun *beṣaʿ*, "cut(off), severing" (KB³). Thus: "the measure (lit. cubit) of your cutoff." If the infinitive is to be read (Rudolph), the translation would be "the measure (cubit) of your cutting." The expression, in any case, is a technical one deriving from the weaving industry, referring to the last cubit (*ʾammat*) of (warp) threads on a loom before the completed work is cut off (Isa 38:12; Job 6:9; cf. Matt 6:27; J. D. Michaelis 1793: 389–90). Babylon's life thread is about to be cut off. The translation of the LXX (*hēkei to peras sou alēthōs eis ta splangcha sou*, "your end has come truly into your innards") simply compounds misreadings: *ʾĕmet*, "in truth" for *ʾammat*, "cubit"; and *bĕmēʿayik*, "into your innards" for *biṣʿēk*, "your cutoff" (cf. Cornill). For a conversion of cubits to modern measures, see Appendix IV.

Your end has come. Hebrew *bāʾ qiṣṣēk.* See *bāʾ haqqēṣ* ("the end has come") in Amos 8:2, also in Ezek 7:2–6, which has multiple occurrences and playful variations on the expression.

14. *Yahweh of hosts has sworn by himself.* Compare Amos 6:8, which is similar. Yahweh alone can swear by his own name; see Note on 49:13. The LXX has "The Lord has sworn by his arm" (cf. Isa 62:8a). It also omits "of hosts," as elsewhere (see Appendix VI), but here the term is possibly a catchword connecting to the next unit (see Rhetoric and Composition).

Surely I have filled you, humanity like the locust. The verb is a prophetic perfect (Kimḥi), depicting a future day as one already past. Yahweh anticipates the day when he will have filled Babylon with enemy soldiers as numerous as locusts (T: "troops of nations who are as many as the locust"). For more locust imagery, some of which remembers the plague in Egypt prior to the Exodus, see Nah 3:15–17; Joel 1:4; 2:25; and Ps 105:34–35. The OT has no fewer than twelve words for "locust." This locust (*yeleq*) is in the early (non-winged) stage, which means it cannot yet migrate but will have more destructive capability. The term recurs in 51:27. See also the Keret Legend for a comparison of troops to locusts (KRT A ii 104–5; iv 192; ANET[3] 144; CS I 334). For locusts in the ancient world and in the OT, including pictures, see Palmoni, "Locust" in *IDB* K–Q, 144–48.

Surely. Or "in truth" (Rashi). Hebrew *kî ʾim* is an oath-related expression (Kimḥi), giving emphatic assurance (§GKC 163d). In 2 Kgs 5:20 it follows the oath formula.

humanity like the locust. Hebrew *ʾādām kayyeleq.* Both terms are collectives.

and they shall raise a shout over you. Hebrew *hêdād* is the shout heard from men picking or treading grapes (see Notes for 25:30 and 48:33); here it will come from the victorious invaders.

MESSAGE AND AUDIENCE

Yahweh begins the present poem as commander of an army poised to attack Babylon. Soldiers are told rapid-fire to clean and sharpen arrows, fill their quivers, and march toward the walls of the mighty city. Hoisted flags will guide them, guards must assume positions, and others must make sure that security is tight. Men must also be ready for an ambush, should one be needed.

Yahweh then turns to address Daughter Babylon, sitting comfortably by many waters and manifold treasures. Her end has come; her life thread is about to be cut off. According to Yahweh's measure of time, the city has already been filled with enemies in enormous quantity—like locusts they have appeared—and their loud shouts of victory can already be heard. The city is theirs. This filling of the city with enemy soldiers brings to completion the earlier filling of the quivers, serving to press home the point that fullness belongs to the enemy; no, rather to Almighty Yahweh.

This poem can be assigned to Zedekiah's reign, prior to 594 B.C. It anticipates, as the other Babylon poems do, the fall of a now-mighty Empire at some future time. Interpolations in vv 11bc and 12c are post-586 B.C. In the first, an editor imagines a Median attack upon Babylon, which will be Yahweh's vengeance for Nebuchadnezzar's destruction of Judah and the Jerusalem Temple. In the second, which has to be post-539 B.C., Babylon has already been brought down, and the editor wants to confirm to his audience that Yahweh assuredly carries out what he plans, even if the fulfillment did not correspond exactly to what was predicted. A later editor at some point may also have added "Yahweh of hosts has sworn by himself" in v 14a, clarifying the *kî* *'im* expression following, and making it explicit that Yahweh was the one delivering the curse.

When this poem is heard in tandem with the one preceding (vv 6–10), the emphasis will fall upon Babylon's wealth and the calamity consuming it. It will also be recognized at some point that the calamity was Yahweh-directed, and was Yahweh's vengeance for the destruction Babylon carried out earlier on the Jerusalem Temple. In 51:24 it will be for all the evil Babylon did in Zion.

20. Yahweh the God of Creation! (51:15–19)

51 ¹⁵The Maker of the earth by his strength
    the Establisher of the world by his wisdom
        and by his understanding he stretched out the heavens

¹⁶When he utters his voice—a roar in heavens' waters
    clouds come up from the ends of the earth[1]
Lightning bolts for rain he made
    and he brought forth the wind from his storehouses

¹⁷Every human is stupid without knowledge
    every smith is very shamed because of the idol
For his cast image is a lie
    and no breath is in them
¹⁸They are nothing—a laughable work!
    at the time of their reckoning they shall perish

¹⁹Not like these is the Portion of Jacob
    for the one forming everything is he
And Israel is his tribal heritage[2]
    Yahweh of hosts is his name!

---

[1] Reading *hā'āreṣ* with the LXX and Q of 10:13.
[2] MT lacks "Israel," though it does appear in many MSS; cf. 10:16.

RHETORIC AND COMPOSITION

MT 51:15–19 = LXX 28:15–19. This hymn celebrating Yahweh's greatness is duplicated with only minor change in 10:12–16, an indication that it is a self-standing composition. In the present context it is delimited by a *setumah* in M[L], M[A], and M[P] prior to v 15, and a *setumah* in M[L] and M[P] after v 19. The M[A] has a *petuḥah* after v 19.

The hymn may have been placed here by the same editor responsible for the two—perhaps three—"Yahweh" embellished supplements in the previous poem. If so, it is an expanded "Blessed be he" interpolation following a divinely planned and executed judgment upon Babylon. The hymn puts the accent on Yahweh's power to create, which is indicated directly or indirectly by the catchwords "do, make" (*'śh*) in vv 12, 15–16. The emphasis is not upon idols (the hymn disparages the foolish men who make idols), which will come up for censure later in the chapter (vv 47–49 and vv 52–53).

Variations from 10:12–16 are all orthographic except for MT's lack of "Israel" in v 19, which does appear, however, in some MSS and in the Versions. "Israel" belongs and should be read. The present passage—like 30:23–24—is represented in the LXX. Other doublets in the book, the LXX often omits in their second occurrence. For the hymn's stanza formation and rhetorical features, see Rhetoric and Composition for 10:12–16.

Catchwords connecting to the preceding unit:

			v 11	*spirit*	*rûaḥ*
v 15	*the Maker*	*'ōśēh*	v 12	*he did*	*'āśâ*
v 16	*he made*	*'āśâ*			
	his storehouses	*'ōṣĕrōtāyw*	v 13	*treasures*	*'ôṣārōt*
vv 16–17	*wind / breath* (2×)	*rûaḥ*			
v 17	*human*	*'ādām*	v 14	*Yahweh of hosts*	
v 19	*Yahweh of hosts*			*humanity*	*'ādām*

There are no catchwords connecting to the unit following.

NOTES

51:15–19. See exegesis for 10:12–16.

MESSAGE AND AUDIENCE

This hymn builds on the "Yahweh" interpolations of the previous poem, celebrating with a post-539 B.C. audience that Babylon's demise was brought about by the God of all creation and the one known simultaneously as the Portion of Jacob: Yahweh of hosts.

21. You Were a Club for Me, Weapons of War (51:20–24)

51 ²⁰You were a club for me
    weapons of war:

And with you I smashed nations and with you I destroyed kingdoms
    ²¹and with you I smashed horse and its rider
        and with you I smashed chariot and its rider

        ²²and with you I smashed man and woman
            and with you I smashed old and young
            and with you I smashed young man and maiden

        ²³and with you I smashed shepherd and his flock
    and with you I smashed farmer and his team
and with you I smashed governors and commanders.

²⁴But I will repay to Babylon and to all the inhabitants of Chaldea all their evil that they did in Zion before your eyes—oracle of Yahweh.

RHETORIC AND COMPOSITION

MT 51:20–24 = LXX 28:20–24. The present unit consists of a well-crafted poem (vv 20–23), followed by a brief prose oracle (v 24). In the latter Yahweh promises a Judahite audience ("before your eyes") that he will repay Babylon for all it did to Zion. Yahweh speaks judgment in the poem as well, but the addressee there is not specified. The unit as a whole is delimited at the top end by the prior hymn in vv 15–19, which is self-standing, and by a *setumah* in M^L and M^P, and a *petuḥah* in M^A, before v 20. At the bottom end delimitation is by a concluding "oracle of Yahweh" formula in v 24, after which is a *setumah* in M^L, M^A, and M^P.

BHS scans v 24 as poetry, and is followed by the NEB, NAB, NJV, REB, and NSB. The RSV, JB, NIV, NRSV, and NJB render the verse as prose. Its sentence-like quality—also the *nota accusativi* and relative pronoun *'ăšer* in 24b—point to the verse's being prose, which is how it is taken here. Holladay takes 24a as the climax of the poem and 24b (including the messenger formula) as secondary prose, but a division of the verse does not seem possible.

The main question regarding the poem has to do with the addressee. To whom is Yahweh speaking? I expressed the view earlier (Lundbom 1975: 91 [= 1997: 121]) that Jeremiah was being addressed as Yahweh's weapon of war, but now I am not so sure. Jeremiah is the bearer of Yahweh's word, which in 23:29 is described as a hammer breaking rocks into pieces. Also, in his call to be a prophet, Jeremiah is designated as one who will break down "nations and kingdoms" (1:10), which eminently qualifies him to be the addressee here. But the more widely-held view is that the war club was, is, or shall in the future be Babylon. There is uncertainty in assigning tense to the verbs, which are all perfects, but the main difficulty with Babylon being the addressee—and thus Yahweh's punishing agent against other nations—is that the poem stands now in a collection of utterances *against* Babylon. Another is that the pronoun "you" (*'attâ*) in v 20a is masculine, whereas Babylon the nation would be feminine. But perhaps the king of Babylon is meant, in which case the masculine pronoun would be correct (cf. Nah 2:2: *ʿālâ mēpîṣ* . . . , "The Clubber has come up . . ."). Other proposals for an addressee include Cyrus (Cunliffe-Jones), Israel (Holladay), or an unknown nation (Thompson; Boadt), none of which is very convincing.

If the poem is to be taken as addressed to Babylon or the king of Babylon, and sense is to be achieved in the context where the poem now exists: 1) a past tense must be assigned to v 20a, which has no verb; 2) the perfect verbs in vv 20b–23 must all be translated past; and 3) the poem as a whole must be seen as a setup for the oracle in v 24, which states that Yahweh will now repay Babylon for the evil it did in Zion. All of this is possible, and is discussed further in the Notes. So understood, the poem is a word telling Babylon that once indeed it was Yahweh's punishing agent against the nations, but now, as the subsequent oracle relates, Babylon itself faces Yahweh's judgment. Left open is the question of whether at some earlier time the poem was a judgment against (Israel and) the nations, and is here being recycled—with little or no change—for another purpose entirely.

The poem is a catalogue poem, and has been analyzed fully in my earlier work (Lundbom 1975: 91–92 [= 1997: 120–22]). Like other Jeremianic poems, particularly the sword poem of 50:35–38a, it contains an elaborate anaphora with onomatopoeia, where, in this case, the latter simulates repeated smashings of a war club. On anaphora in the Jeremianic poems, see further Rhetoric and Composition for 50:35–38a. This poem additionally has a carefully-crafted chiasmus enumerating objects of the divine wrath, making it similar to the structured enumeration in 5:17. If the poem is to be assigned stanzas, it seems best to take v 20a as introductory (like 2:14 and 20a), and divide what remains according to key word clusters. The result is then an introductory stanza (v 20a), followed by three stanzas each having three lines (vv 20b–21, 22, 23), making four stanzas in all:

I   You were a club for me   v 20
         weapons of war:

II   *And with you I smashed **nations and . . . kingdoms***
         *and with you I smashed **horse and its rider***   v 21
            *and with you I smashed **chariot and its rider***

III   *and with you I smashed **man and woman***   v 22
                 *and with you I smashed **old and young***
               *and with you I smashed **young man and maiden***

IV   *and with you I smashed **shepherd and his flock***   v 23
    *and with you I smashed **farmer and his team***
    *and with you I smashed **governors and commanders***

The first line in Stanza II has extended length because of a second verb "I destroyed." This could be what D. N. Freedman (1986b) calls a deliberate deviation in a series, or it could be secondary expansion, the purpose of which is to provide a catchword that connects to the unit following (see below). The LXX omits the center line in III, but that can be attributed to haplography (see Notes). It is the pivot point of the poem as a whole and of Stanza III in particular, with key words *zāqēn* ("old") and *nāʿar* ("young") distinguishing *ʾîš* ("man") from *bāḥûr* ("young man") and *ʾiššâ* ("woman") from *bĕtûlâ* ("maiden"). But taken together, the terms mean "everybody" (merismus). The LXX also transposes lines 1 and 3 of this stanza, but with no net loss. Stanzas II and IV have inversion, with the human figures in II—the rider of the horse and the rider of the chariot—coming second in the pairings, and the human figures in IV—the shepherd and the farmer—coming first. The opening line of II and closing line of IV make an inclusio for the body of the poem: "governors and commanders" are rulers of "nations and kingdoms." Here also is more inversion, with Jeremiah choosing terms that form their plurals with *îm* and *ôt* suffixes, and then switching them around. The final line of IV should not be deleted as an MT plus (*pace* Rudolph; cf. *BHS*). It is an integral part of an extremely well-balanced poem.

Other ancient poetry shows repetition and balanced predications such as we have here. In a Mesopotamian lament is this description of a merciless storm of Enlil (M. E. Cohen 1988: 36):

Storm which has no regard for a mother!
Storm which has no regard for a father!
Storm which has no regard for a spouse!
Storm which has no regard for a child!
Storm which has no regard for a sister!
Storm which has no regard for a brother!
Storm which has no regard for a friend!
Storm which has no regard for a companion!

Here the terms providing inclusiveness in the poem come in pairs—mother / father; spouse / child; sister / brother; and friend / companion—and there are no inversions.

The present unit has no catchwords connecting to the hymn preceding. Catchwords connecting to the unit following are these (Condamin):

v 20b *I destroyed*   v 25 *destroying* (2×)

NOTES

51:20. *You were a club for me, weapons of war.* This opening word of address has no verb in the Hebrew, and is most commonly translated present tense. But Kimḥi and Calvin translated it past, which is correct in a context where the poem sets up the oracle following (v 24). The perfect verbs beginning in 20b must also be past, although they are commonly translated present or future by commentators and the modern Versions. Babylon *was* Yahweh's war club (Moffatt, JB, NJB), but is no longer (cf. 50:23). If the poem had a prior use against Judah and other nations, this introductory word could be rendered present or future tense. It could be rendered present or future also if Jeremiah, by virtue of his preaching the divine word, was understood as being Yahweh's weapon of war (see Rhetoric and Composition). Yahweh, in any case, possesses a weapon-stocked armory (50:25) and employs punishing agents at will to carry out his judgments (Isa 10:5). The LXX ("you scatter for me the weapons of war") and T ("you scatter before me the fortified city in which are weapons of war") both translate *mappēṣ* as a verb meaning "scatter, disperse" (presumably the H-stem participle *mēpîṣ* from *pûṣ*), which give different and less-convincing prose equivalents.

club. Hebrew *mappēṣ* is a war club knobbed at one end (NJV, NIV, NRSV), or a mace (JB, NJB), not a "battle axe," as rendered by the AV and carried over into the NEB and REB. The term is cognate to the verb following, *npṣ* ("smash, shatter"), and may be simply another spelling for *mēpîṣ* (Nah 2:2[Eng 2:1]; Prov 25:18), which is also a club. Kimḥi took this weapon to be a sledgehammer (RSV and NAB: "hammer"). In Nah 2:2 the king of Babylon is a clubber that has come up against Nineveh. The mace was in common use among the Assyrians and Babylonians. The Assyrian kings Ashurnasirpal II (884–860 B.C.) and Shamshi-adad V (824–812 B.C.) are both portrayed holding a mace in the left hand; for pictures and drawings, see *ANEP*[2] 152–53 #439, #442; cf. 299–300; Yadin 1963: 11. In the NT, clubs are carried by those coming to arrest Jesus (Mark 14:43, 48 [= Matt 26:47, 55]).

weapons of war. The MT construct plural, *kĕlê* ("weapons"), may owe its existence to the reading of T, in which case it should be repointed with numerous commentators (Giesebrecht; Duhm; Cornill; Peake; Rudolph; Bright; Holladay; McKane) to *kĕlî* ("weapon"), a more exact parallel to the singular "club." On the other hand, figures of speech do not require exact parallels, and the plural may be correct. In actual fact, an entire nation—king, army, and countless ordinary citizens—functioned as "war weapons" when Babylon was at its zenith of power. Compare "his weapon of smashing" (*kĕlî mappāṣô*) in Ezek 9:2, and "his weapons of war" (*kĕlê milḥamtô*) in Deut 1:41.

And with you I smashed nations and . . . kingdoms. The verb *npṣ* means "to smash, break in pieces," and is used often for the smashing of pottery (22:28; 48:12; KB[3] *npṣ* I). It denotes the smashing together of people in 13:14. The LXX translates with *kai diaskorpiō*, "and I will scatter," which reads *npṣ* II (KB[3]) and takes the prefixed *waw* as a *waw consecutive* (cf. AV; NEB; REB; Holladay; McKane). I prefer to read the verbs here and throughout the poem as ordinary perfects, rendering them past tense since Babylon is being remembered as Yahweh's once-feared war club against the nations (cf. Moffatt, JB, NJV, NJB). Calvin says that all these destructive acts are stated by way of concession, the main point being that Babylon itself will be destroyed. If the poem is assigned an earlier use, and/or Jeremiah is taken as Yahweh's weapon of war, then a present or prophetic perfect (= future) rendering is appropriate.

nations . . . kingdoms. See 1:10 and 51:27 for the same pairing.

21. *horse and its rider . . . chariot and its rider.* Duhm's repointing to *wĕrakkābô*, "and his charioteer," which is adopted by many commentators and numerous modern Versions (RSV, JB, NAB, NJV, NIV, NRSV, and REB), is made to avoid a repetition and should be rejected. The MT and LXX both have "its rider" (T: "their riders"). English "charioteer" does have an advantage, however, in that you cannot ride a chariot in the way you ride a horse. Compare "her horses . . . her chariots" in the similarly-written "sword" poem (50:37).

22. *man and woman.* Hebrew *'îš wĕ'iššâ*. Or "husband and wife."

and with you I smashed old and young. Hebrew *zāqēn wānā'ar* are more precisely "old man and boy" (on the latter, see Note for 1:6), but here at the center of the poem the accent is on "old and young," which means everybody (see Rhetoric and Composition). The LXX omission of this line can be due to haplography, as Janzen (1973: 118) has already noted (two-word: *wnpsty bk . . . wnpsty bk*).

young man and maiden. Hebrew *bāḥûr ûbĕtûlâ* are fully grown, unmarried adolescents, with *bĕtûlâ* also meaning "virgin" (see Note for 31:13).

23. *shepherd and his flock . . . farmer and his team.* See the pairing in 31:24, which looks ahead to national restoration. The farmer's team (*ṣemed*) will be a (yoked) pair of oxen.

governors and commanders. Hebrew *paḥôt ûsĕgānîm*. Both terms, which occur again in vv 28 and 57, are Akkadian loanwords with technical meaning. In the OT, the title *peḥâ* ("governor") is given to Nehemiah (Neh 5:14) and Zerubbabel (Hag 1:1), with the corresponding *pāḫatu* or *bēl pāḫāti / piḫāti* in Akk meaning "(lord) governor of a region" (*bēlu* CAD 2: 191–98; AHw 1: 120 §18; 2: 862; *peḥâ* KB³; Petit 1988). Akkadian *šaknu* was a low-ranking military or civic official—a commander in charge of troops, a military administrator, or a subordinate to the king in some other capacity (*šaknu* CAD 17/1: 180–92; AHw 3: 1141; *segen / sāgān* KB³). In the OT, however, the two terms are used more or less interchangeably. Reference is made in Ezek 23:6, 12, and 23 to governors and commanders associated in some way or other with the Assyrian and Babylonian armies.

24. *But I will repay to Babylon.* Hebrew *wĕšillamtî lĕbābel*. Taking the *waw* here as an adversative (Giesebrecht; Volz; Rudolph; Weiser; McKane; cf. NEB) and as a *waw consecutive*. Babylon's judgment is yet to come (Rashi; Calvin).

On repayment (*šlm*) to Babylon for violent action done in times past, which in no way compromises Babylon's prior role as Yahweh's punishing agent (*pace* Carroll, 843), see also 25:14; 50:29; 51:6, and 56. The same point is made in Isa 10:5–19; 37:22–29; and especially Jer 27:5–7 (referring to Nebuchadnezzar).

the inhabitants of Chaldea. For *kaśdîm* meaning "Chaldea" or "Chaldeans," see Note on 50:1.

before your eyes. These words are addressed to a Judahite audience, but when and where? Is this a Jerusalem audience that has witnessed a recent Babylonian violence to its city, or an exilic audience a decade or so before Cyrus, which can expect to witness a repayment to Babylon for the violence it carried out earlier? Many commentators (Giesebrecht; Peake; Cornill; Ehrlich 1912: 369; Volz; Rudolph; Bright; Jones) connect these words with "I will repay" at the beginning of the verse, which would imagine an exilic audience seeing a repayment to Babylon (cf. Ps 91:8; Matt 24:33–34). But if the oracle is delivered in 594 B.C. or before, then Jeremiah promises to a Jerusalem audience a future repayment to Babylon for the recent violence it did in Zion. The same basic interpretation is possible even if the oracle is spoken after 594, though only to a Jerusalem or Judahite audience.

MESSAGE AND AUDIENCE

Yahweh in this poem presents no argument, no indictment, no reasons—giving only a single-minded judgment via some unspecified agent to the nations and kingdoms of the world. By means of extraordinary repetition and patterned variation, this single idea is stated and embellished: Yahweh in his fury has, is, or will in the future smash people on a broad scale, regardless of age, sex, or social status. Even the animals will be destroyed. While the addressee of the poem is unnamed, the power and might of Babylon will be readily perceived. With Babylon as Yahweh's punishing agent, the poem can be dated early, i.e., ca. 605 B.C. or so, when Nebuchadnezzar and his army were on the march and Judah together with other nations—including the mighty Assyria—were the objects of Yahweh's wrath.

The audience hearing the poem in its present context, where it is followed by a divine oracle, will recognize that Babylon was indeed Yahweh's club against the nations, but no longer. Now this nation must itself be punished. The oracle (v 24) gives a reason for the divine judgment: Babylon has to pay for what it did in Zion. The poem and oracle in tandem could therefore date anytime after 597 B.C.; otherwise after 586 B.C. The evil done by Babylon "before your eyes" would seem to indicate an aggression of recent memory.

This poem and oracle, primarily the poem, will be heard as a powerful follow-up to the hymn of Yahweh's greatness immediately preceding. In that hymn the might and power of Yahweh in creation are lifted up; here is lifted up the mighty doings of Yahweh in history.

22. From Destroying Mountain to Burned-Out Mountain (51:25–26)

51 ²⁵Look, I am against you, O Destroying Mountain
—oracle of Yahweh—
the one destroying all the land!
So I will stretch out my hand against you
and I will roll you down from the cliffs
and make you a burned-out mountain.

²⁶They shall not take from you stone for a corner or stone for foundations;
indeed eternal desolations you shall be—oracle of Yahweh.

RHETORIC AND COMPOSITION

MT 51:25–26 = LXX 28:25–26. The present verses are delimited at the top by
a *setumah* in M^L, M^A, and M^P prior to v 25. There is no section at the end of
v 26, but an "oracle of Yahweh" formula there marks the unit's conclusion.
Another "oracle of Yahweh" formula in v 25 raises the question as to whether
we have, in fact, two oracles—one in v 25, and one in v 26—or simply a single
oracle with two formulas, one at the beginning and one at the end. The latter
is not common in the Jeremiah oracles, but does occur (e.g., 2:2–3, 5–9;
30:18–21). The decision here is to take the verses as two oracles combined
(like 51:52–53), at the same time recognizing that what we may have is two
stanzas of a single oracle. Content is indecisive. The stone imagery of v 26 is
compatible with the mountain and rock imagery of v 25, but the two do not
necessarily go together. On the other hand, the oracles together have a parallel in an oracle found in Ezek 35:3–4. The LXX lacks the formula in v 25, but
this need not be deleted with Cornill, Volz, and Holladay. It is present in T,
and both Rudolph and Weiser retain.

There is also a question whether v 26 is poetry or prose. All the modern Versions render the verse as poetry, but the words just prior to the closing messenger formula, "indeed eternal desolations you [it] shall be," recur in v 62 as
prose. Taking the verse here as prose, as we do, reinforces the decision that two
oracles have been combined.

Oracle I contains this key word inclusio:

I	. . . . *mountain*	*har*	v 25
	. . . . *mountain*	*lĕhar*	

Catchwords connecting to the previous unit:

v 25 *destroying* (2×)   v 20b *I destroyed*

Catchwords connecting to the unit following:

v 25	*against you (2×)* *'ēleykā . . . 'āleykā*	v 27–28	*in the land / all land*
	all the land		*against her (4×)* *'āleyhā*
		v 29	*(the) land (2×)*

NOTES

51:25. *Look, I am against you, O Destroying Mountain.* A stereotypical beginning found elsewhere in 21:13 and 50:31. See also Ezek 35:3: "Look, I am against you, Mount Seir." On *hinnēh* ("Look") and *hinĕnî* + participle ("Look I . . .") beginning the Jeremiah oracle, see Notes on 1:9 and 15.

against you. Hebrew *'ēleykā* alternates with *'āleka* in the next line, both in this case having adversative meaning. On the alternation of *'el* and *'al* in Jeremiah, see Note on 11:2.

O Destroying Mountain. Hebrew *har hammašḥît* is lit. "(O) Mountain of the Destroyer," here a metaphor for the city of Babylon (T: "O destroying city"), despite the fact that Babylon is situated not on mountainous terrain but on level ground beside a great river (cf. *biq'â* in Gen 11:2). Compare the NT prophecy concerning Harmagedon (= Mount Megiddo) in Rev 16:16, which is similar. Ezekiel's oracle against Mount Seir (Ezek 35:3), by contrast, presupposes mountainous Edom. This depiction of Babylon has been variously interpreted. Reference could be to the city's high walls and tall buildings (Kimḥi; Calvin), most notably the celebrated temple (= ziggurat) of Marduk, which was a replica of the mountain of the gods and symbolic of the nation (cf. Gen 11:1–9). Others aver that a "destroying mountain" ending up as a "burned-out mountain" is suggestive of a volcano (J. D. Michaelis 1793: 392; Cheyne), supported further by the stones unsuitable for reuse in v 26. Michaelis cited for comparison the burning mountain imagery in Rev 8:8. The expression *har hammašḥît* is found one other time in the OT, in 2 Kgs 23:13, where it appears to be a play on the Mount of Olives (*har hammišḥâ*), east of Jerusalem (Weiser). Whether the usage there has any connection to the present usage is unclear. Morgenstern (1961: 70) has proposed a mythological interpretation for both texts, translating *har hammašḥît* as the "Mountain of the Destroyer," where Yahweh is depicted as a God rising from death and the nether world. This is unconvincing. Holladay's emended reading for both texts, "Mount of (Sesame) Oil," is also unconvincing—doubly so here because with Volz and Rudolph he deletes the following phrase, "the one destroying all the land." Forms of the verb *šḥt* ("destroy") occur often in the chapter (51:1, 11, 20, 25 [2×]), arguing in favor of the term being retained. The point here seems to be that Babylon, for a time, has been a destroying force over all nations, but now Yahweh will take action to destroy it.

the one destroying all the land. More precisely, "the whole earth." Volz, Rudolph, and Holladay delete, which is unjustified. Both LXX and T have the expression.

So I will stretch out my hand against you. On Yahweh "stretching out the hand" in judgment, see Note on 6:12.

and I will roll you down from the cliffs. Hebrew *wĕgilgaltîkā min-hassēlā'îm.* This colon has given commentators difficulty, mainly because the image shifts from Babylon as a mountain to Babylon rolling down a mountain. The solution is not to delete "from the cliffs" (*pace* Rudolph, Holladay), for which there is no textual support. We simply have to allow for a shift in metaphor, which poses no problem in Hebrew rhetoric. In Ezek 35:7–8 Yahweh calls Edom "Mount Seir," and then goes on to say that he will fill its mountains with the slain.

the cliffs. Hebrew *hassēlā'îm* are high rocks (48:28; Isa 33:16). Kimḥi, following T, sees these as representative of Babylon's strength.

and make you a burned-out mountain. Hebrew *ûnĕtattîkā lĕhar śĕrēpâ.* The metaphor changes again, only here if a volcano is envisioned continuity is possible with the "destroying mountain" beginning the verse. It has been pointed out that a volcano is an inappropriate image for low-lying Babylon, which may explain the change to a simile in the LXX: *hōs oros empepyrismenon,* "as a burned-out mountain" (Luria 1975–76). Giesebrecht notes that cities are commonly burned by fire (38:23; 43:12–13). In Jewish tradition a comparison was made here with Sodom and Gomorrah, which in Deut 29:22[Eng 29:23] is described as *śĕrēpâ,* "a burned-out (place)." See also Amos 4:11. As it turned out, Cyrus did not put Babylon to the torch when he took the city.

26. *They shall not take from you stone for a corner or stone for foundations.* The question must be asked again just how suitable such a description is for Babylon, which, as Calvin noted, was a city of brick, not stone. See further Note on 51:58. The image would have currency in Palestine, however, where it was common practice to quarry stones from a destroyed city and then use them in rebuilding. The T has: "And they will not appoint from you a king for a kingdom, nor a ruler for rulership." The point may be that Babylon's envisioned fiery end will render its largest and best stones unfit for reuse. Calvin says there will be no hope of restoration for the city. This will be in contrast to Jerusalem, which will be rebuilt (31:38–40; cf. Isa 28:16).

indeed eternal desolations you shall be. Hebrew *kî-šimmôt 'ôlām tihyeh.* Reading the *kî* as an asseverative: "indeed." This curse is repeated verbatim in 51:62, although there *tihyeh* has to be a third feminine singular, "it [fem.] shall be." The plural *šimmôt* ("desolations"), which occurs also in 25:12 and Ezek 35:9, is an intensive plural (GKC §124e). More common to both Jeremiah and Ezekiel is the singular *šĕmāmâ,* "desolation" (see Notes on 12:10 and 49:2). Here and elsewhere the Versions translate the intensive plural as a singular.

MESSAGE AND AUDIENCE

Yahweh in the first oracle declares himself to be against a certain "Destroying Mountain." It is left to the audience to decide what mountain that might be. It is one that has destroyed the entire land, which suggests Babylon. Yahweh then says he has stretched out his hand against this destroyer, and promises it a violent tumble from its perch of exaltation. In a final image, Yahweh says he will leave behind a burned-out mountain. A follow-up oracle affirms that so complete will the destruction of this monolith be that stones from it will be unavailable for a future rebuilding, and that ruins will exist on the spot for all time.

This judgment of near apocalyptic proportions, highly stereotyped, and cast in imagery more suitable to Palestine than to Babylon, is another general word of judgment against Babylon for some future time. It bears little resemblance to Babylon's actual fall. Thus a date prior to 594 B.C. for these oracles is reasonable, and the audience will be Judahites living in Jerusalem and Judah.

The idea that a mighty power known for carrying out widespread destruction will now itself be destroyed repeats the point made in the prior unit. When the two passages are heard in tandem, there may also be discerned an implicit contrast between (Mount) Zion, which is Yahweh's bastion of strength ultimately not to be forsaken, and Mount Babylon—once Destroying Mountain but now Burned-Out Mountain—which Yahweh will make unusable for all time (Boadt).

23. Sanctify the Nations against Her! (51:27–33)

51 ^{27}Set up a flag in the land
  blow the trumpet in the nations
Sanctify the nations against her
  summon the kingdoms against her
    —Ararat, Minni, and Ashkenaz

Appoint the marshal against her
  bring up the horse like a bristling locust
^{28}Sanctify the nations against her
  —the kings of Media
her governors and all her commanders
  and all land under his rule

^{29}Thus the land quakes and writhes
  for it rises up against Babylon
    —the plans of Yahweh to make the land of Babylon
  a desolation without inhabitant

^{30}The warriors of Babylon cease to fight
  they sit in the strongholds
Their strength is sapped
  they have become women!
They have set her dwellings on fire
  her bars are broken

^{31}Runner runs to meet runner
  and herald to meet herald

To herald the news to the king of Babylon
 that his city is taken from every side
[32]also the fords have been seized
 and the marshes they have burned with fire
 and the men of war are terrified.

[33]For thus said Yahweh of hosts, God of Israel:
Daughter Babylon is like a threshing floor at the time one treads her. Just a
little while, and the harvest time will come upon her.

RHETORIC AND COMPOSITION

MT 51:27–33 = LXX 28:27–33. The present unit contains a rather lengthy
judgment poem against Babylon (vv 27–32), followed by a brief judgment
oracle against the same in prose (v 33). Yahweh is the speaking voice in both
(compare v 27a with 4:5b–6; "the plans of Yahweh" in v 29b is a later addition).

The unit is delimited at the top by 1) the formula concluding the prior oracle (v 26b); 2) the return to poetry in v 27; and 3) the feminine genders for
Babylon in v 27 after masculine genders in the preceding verses (Duhm). The
end of the poem is marked by a shift to prose in v 33 and confirmed by the formula beginning the oracle in that verse. Also, a *setumah* is present in M^L, M^A,
and M^P after v 32. The conclusion of the prose oracle and the unit as a whole
(v 33) is indicated by a change back to poetry in v 34, and a self-standing poem
in vv 34–45 (see Rhetoric and Composition there). Most commentators take
vv 27–33 as the literary unit. McKane puts v 33 with vv 34–35, but concedes
that the result is not particularly convincing.

Some commentators see later expansion in the poetry, suggested initially by
occurrences of the *nota accusativi* in vv 28, 29, and 32. The statement in v 29b
about Yahweh's plans to put Babylon under a land curse is doubtless supplementary, having parallels elsewhere that are supplementary (see Notes). "Ararat,
Minni, and Ashkenaz" in v 27b, however, are not later embellishment (*pace*
Volz, Rudolph, Carroll, and Holladay), nor is "Sanctify the nations against
her" in v 28 a gloss from v 27b (*pace* Volz, Rudolph, Bright, Carroll, and Holladay). The former balances "the kings of Media" in the v 28, and the latter is
simply good repetition. We note also in v 28 a balancing of "nations . . . kings"
with "(her) governors and (her) commanders," which compares to the intentional balancing of "nations . . . kingdoms" with "governors and commanders"
in 51:20–23.

Allowing then for expansion only in v 29b, the poem is seen to be five stanzas with a near-symmetrical line structure:

I	one bicolon and a tricolon	v 27ab
II	three bicolons	vv 27c–28
III	one bicolon (expanded)	v 29
IV	three bicolons	v 30
V	two bicolons and a tricolon	vv 31–32

The stanzas contain these repetitions and balancing key words:

I   . . . . *in the land*   v 27ab
     . . . . *in the nations*
     Sanctify the nations against her
     . . . . *the kingdoms against her*
     . . . .

II   . . . . *against her*   v 27c

     . . . .   v 28
     Sanctify the nations against her
     . . . .
     her governors and all her commanders
     and all land . . . .

III *the land* . . . .   v 29
     . . . . *against Babylon*
     (. . . . . *the land of Babylon*
     . . . .)

IV   . . . . *Babylon* . . . .   v 30

V   . . . .   v 31
     herald to meet *herald*
     To herald . . . . *Babylon*
     . . . .

Kessler (1973: 20) points out that "herald . . . herald," followed by "To herald,"
is *anadiplosis* (Latin: *conduplicatio; ad Herennium iv* 28), i.e., a word (or
words) in one colon repeating at the beginning of a subsequent colon. For
other examples of this rhetorical figure in Jeremiah, see Note for 22:20.

Stanza II also has this key word inclusio helping to clarify the antecedent of
the masculine singular suffix in v 28b:

II   Appoint *the marshal* against her   v 27c
     . . . .
     and all land under *his rule*   v 28b

Catchwords connecting to the prior unit:

vv 27–29 *in the land / all land /*   v 25   *against you* (2×) ʾēleykā . . . ʿāleykā
          the land (2×)
          against her (4×)   ʿāleyhā   *all the land*

Catchwords connecting to the poem following:

vv 27–29 *in the land / all land / the land* (2×) v 34   *king of Babylon*
vv 27–28 *the nations* (3×)   vv 35–44 *Babylon* (6×)

v 29	*desolation*	vv 37, 41, 43	*desolation* (3×)
vv 29–33	*Babylon* (4×)	vv 41, 43	*all the land / land*
v 31	*the king of Babylon*	vv 41, 44	*the nations* (2×)
v 32	*his city*	v 43	*her cities*

NOTES

51:27. *Set up a flag . . . blow the trumpet.* Hebrew *śĕʾû-nēs . . . tiqʿû šôpār.* A familiar Jeremiah introduction (cf. 4:5–6, where the commands are reversed), summoning here a coalition army (plural imperatives) to prepare for war against Babylon. More asyndeton. Flags will lead the attacking armies (51:12; cf. Isa 13:2). In 4:5–6, 19, and 21, trumpets and flags are warning Judahites of imminent attack and leading them to safe haven; in 50:2 the flag is informing nations of the world that the war against Babylon has been won. McKane thinks the addressees here are divine envoys of undisclosed identity, a view expressed also by P. D. Miller (1968: 104–5). More battle orders, in any case, of the type noted by Bach (1962: 57) and Christensen (1975: 271). On the flag and trumpet, see further Notes on 4:5–6 and 51:12.

in the land. Hebrew *bāʾāreṣ* can be taken here as a collective, i.e., "in every land" (cf. AV; NEB; NIV; NRSV), since war preparations are called for in many nations, not just one. Many modern English Versions translate "throughout the earth," or the like (cf. Moffatt; AmT; RSV; JB; NAB; NJV; REB). In 4:5 the term denotes the land of Judah.

nations . . . kingdoms. This pairing occurs elsewhere in 1:10 and 51:20.

Sanctify the nations against her. Hebrew *qaddĕšû ʿāleyhā gôyĭm.* This is a holy war shout accompanied by religious rites and sacrifice; compare the shouts heard from Babylonian soldiers when they were besieging Jerusalem (6:4). On Yahweh's holy war against Babylon, see also Isa 13:3.

summon the kingdoms against her. The verb *hašmîʿû* means "call together," as in 50:29. This summoning will precede the consecration rites. For other examples of sequence reversal in Hebrew poetry and rhetoric, see Note on 1:15.

Ararat, Minni, and Ashkenaz. Three northern nations of military reputation envisioned here as joining a coalition with the Medes against Babylon (note the plural, "kings of Media," in v 28). All were political powers in Jeremiah's day, during which time also they became subjected to the Medes following the collapse of the Assyrian Empire.

Ararat. A highland and mountainous region north of Assyria, cited in the OT in connection with the Flood story (Gen 8:4), and in reference to an internal Assyrian struggle ending the reign of Sennacherib in 681 B.C. (2 Kgs 19:37 = Isa 37:38; cf. Tob 1:21). The territory is also known from Assyrian cuneiform texts, where it is called *Uraṛṭu*, and from recovered records of its own. Ararat was earlier inhabited by Hurrians (Bright 1981: 61–62), and later became Armenia, the name by which it is known in classical sources (Luke 1992: 186). In the LXX of Isa 37:38, "land of Ararat" is translated as *Armenian* (= Armenia); cf. AV. Ararat centered around Lake Van in present-day southeastern Turkey, but at its zenith its boundaries extended well into modern Iran, Iraq, Azerbaijan, and Armenia. Ararat was warring with Assyria already in the time of Shalmaneser I (ca. 1265–1235 B.C.), but did not emerge as a political power until the ninth century, when Assyria was weak. The nation suffered defeats at the hands of Tiglath-pileser III (745–727 B.C.) and Sargon II (721–705 B.C.), the latter receiving help from the Cimmerians (Bright 1981: 254–56, 270, 280; Luke 1992: 186–87). Independence ended for Ararat when the Medes annexed the country ca. 585 B.C. (cf. 25:26). The Median empire was then in turn defeated by Cyrus in the mid–sixth century. Xenophon (*Cyropaedia* ii 4, 31–iii 2, 31) reports that Armenians (= Ararat) formed part of Cyrus's army against Babylon. On Russian archaeological finds in ancient Urartu, including royal inscriptions, expedition reports, religious texts, and remains of an extensive building program, also for an Urartian king list, see "Ararat" in *IDB* A-D, 194–95; in *ABD* 1: 351–53; and Luke 1992: 185–92. Some artifacts from Urartu are housed in the Museum of Fine Arts, Boston.

Minni. A minor power north of the Assyrian border during the ninth to seventh centuries B.C., centered south of Lake Urmia in present-day northwest Iran. Mentioned only here in the OT, the region and its inhabitants are generally identified with the Manneans, known from Assyrian texts as the *Mannai*. Minni was a buffer state between Assyria and Urartu from the reign of Shalmaneser III (859–825 B.C.) to the fall of the Assyrian Empire, at which time it was defeated and absorbed into Media (cf. 25:26), and after that into the Persian Empire. Minni was Assyria's ally when Nineveh fell in 612 B.C. (BM 21901: obv. 5; Wiseman 1956: 12, 54–55). The LXX in the present text did not recognize the term as a proper noun, translating *par' emou* ("by me"). Mannean depictions can be found in the University Museum, University of Pennsylvania. On Minni, see further *IDB* K–Q, 392; *ABD* 4: 482; and Luke 1992: 192–94.

Ashkenaz. Not the medieval and early modern Jewish name for eastern Germany (Saxony), but an ancient territory and its inhabitants situated north of Ararat and Minni, between the Black and Caspian Seas. Inhabitants were the *Ashguzas / Ishkuzas* of Assyrian cuneiform texts, known in classical sources as the Scythians (Herodotus iv; CAH 3: 82; Cazelles 1967: 30–31 [= 1984: 135–36]; and Luke 1992: 194). Ashkenaz is mentioned in the Table of Nations as one of the sons of Gomer (Gen 10:3; cf. 1 Chr 1:6). These people were absorbed along with Ararat and Minni into the Median Empire in the early sixth century (cf. 25:26), and afterward into the Persian Empire. However, a Scythian identity survived into the Greek and Roman periods, lasting until A.D. 400 (Luke 1992: 201). For more on the Ashkenaz / Ashguzas / Scythians, see CAH 3: 187–205; Yamauchi 1983; and Luke 1992: 194–205. The Hermitage in St. Petersburg contains a fine collection of Scythian relics.

Appoint the marshal against her. Hebrew *ṭipsār* is a "clerk, scribe" (Nah 3:17), here a high-ranking military official with writing skills who will accompany the attacking force (cf. Ezek 9:2). Note the scribal person (*sōpēr*) accompanying

Deborah's army in Judg 5:14. The Hebrew term, which was misunderstood in both T ("those who make war") and LXX ("engines of war"), is a loanword from Akk *ṭupšarru*, meaning "tablet writer" (AHw 3: 1395–96; KB³). The term here is a collective, i.e., "marshals" (Cheyne; Cornill; cf. Nah 3:17). Reference is not to Cyrus (*pace* Calvin).

bring up the horse like a bristling locust. The terms *sûs* and *yeleq* are also collectives, i.e., "horses" and "locusts." Locusts are brought in to emphasize the number (cf. Joel 2:4; Rev 9:7). Hebrew *sāmār* is a *hapax legomenon* in the OT, usually translated "bristling" or "bristly" (Rashi citing Job 4:15; BDB; KB³). Its meaning, however, is uncertain, although the verb in the Qal means "to tremble" and in the Piel means "to make the hair stand on end." Kimḥi translates "trembling locusts." The LXX has *plēthos* ("a great number"), which could indicate an original *mispār*, "number, quantity" (cf. BHS), or otherwise be a misreading. The NJV translates "swarming locusts." The S omits.

locust. Hebrew *yeleq* is one of many OT words for "locust," denoting the insect in in its early, nonwinged stage; see Note for 51:14.

28. *Sanctify the nations against her.* The phrase is not a dittography from v 27 (*pace* Holladay and others; see Rhetoric and Composition).

the kings of Media. See also 25:25 and 51:11. Here and in 51:11 the LXX and S have "king" singular, which is perhaps a (later) reference to Cyrus (Duhm; Streane). The T has "kings." Babylon is envisioned here as coming under attack from a coalition army that will include Ararat, Minni, and Ashkenaz (v 27); therefore, "kings" could include the leaders of these (and other) nations, or simply be an intensive plural, on which see Note for 51:11. Media was an ancient kingdom in what is today northwest Iran, eastern Turkey, and Azerbaijan. In the Table of Nations it appears as Madai (Gen 10:2). Its capital was Ecbatana, and from mountains farther north and west came the tributaries of the Tigris. An Assyrian vassal in the mid–ninth century, Media rose to power in the late seventh century, joining forces with Babylon in the overthrow of Assyria in 612 B.C. (BM 21901: obv. 23–24, 28; Wiseman 1956: 13–17, 56–57; cf. Herodotus i 96–103). Media was then itself conquered by Cyrus in 550 B.C. (Bright 1981: 354), after which it became assimilated into the Achaemenid (Persian) Empire. Thereafter, the Medes and Persians were closely identified (Esth 1:3, 14, 18–19; Dan 5:28; 6:9, 13, 16[Eng 6:8, 12, 15]), a later Persian king having the name (but only in Daniel) of "Darius the Mede" (Dan 6:1[Eng 5:31]; 9:1; 11:1). Though the Medes were a force to be reckoned with after Nineveh's fall, an independent Median attack on Babylon, such as predicted here, in 51:11, and in Isa 13:17, never materialized. Present-day Kurds claim descent from the ancient Medes (P. J. King 1993: 42). For more on Media and the Medes, see *IDB* K–Q, 319–20 and *ABD* 4: 658–59.

her governors and all her commanders. On these Akkadian loanwords, see Note for 51:23. The feminine suffixes refer to Media and can stand (Rudolph). Giesebrecht, Duhm, Cornill, Volz, Bright, Holladay, and McKane all read masculine suffixes following LXX and S, which refer back to a singular "king."

and all land. Hebrew *kol-'ereṣ* can also be "every land." The LXX places these words after "the king of Media" (for discussion, see Janzen 1973: 62). Read the MT. Land too will be sanctified in the upcoming war against Babylon.

under his rule. I.e., the rule of the marshal mentioned in v 27c (see Rhetoric and Composition). The masculine singular suffix does not derive from (a singular) "king" in the LXX (*pace* Blayney). The LXX with its different word order omits the term. Also, the suggestion that *memšaltô* is an MT addition from 1 Kgs 9:19 (Janzen 1973: 62; Holladay) is arbitrary, and should be rejected.

29. *Thus the land quakes and writhes.* Hebrew *wattir'aš hā'āreṣ wattāḥōl*. Compare the quaking of the mountains in 4:24, and of the land / earth in 8:16; 10:10; 49:21; and 50:46. Terrestrial convulsions accompany momentous world events, particularly events guided by the divine hand. At Yahweh's wrath, the earth quakes (10:10). The earth was said to quake when Jesus died, and to quake once again on Easter morning (Matt 27:51; 28:2). Divine activity is attested here in the added line about terrestrial unrest being the result of Yahweh's plans. Compare the earth's writhing before Yahweh in Pss 96:9; 97:4; and 114:7, also Jeremiah's wartime writhing in 4:19.

for it rises up against Babylon. It is the land rising up (*qāmâ*) against Babylon, not plans of Yahweh rising up or being confirmed, as is often alleged (Q^{Or} has a plural verb, *qāmû*, "they arise / are confirmed"). The seemingly self-destructive land activity is the result of Yahweh's plans to make Babylon an uninhabitable wasteland.

the plans of Yahweh. Hebrew *maḥšĕbôt yhwh*. Some MSS, LXX, S, and Vg have "plan" singular, which supports the interpretation that a plan of Yahweh is being confirmed. But 29b is a later addition (like 49:20a; 50:45a; and 51:11b), providing a theological explanation for the destructive land activity. In 49:20–21 and 50:45–46 Yahweh's plans are associated with earthquakes, as here.

to make the land of Babylon a desolation without inhabitant. On land-and-city curses in the book of Jeremiah, see Note for 48:9. For the curse as applied specifically to Babylon, see also 50:3, 13; 51:37, 43, and 62. Earlier, it was Babylon making desolate the land of Judah (4:7).

30. *The warriors of Babylon cease to fight, they sit in the strongholds.* Babylon's warriors (LXX: "warrior") are under a curse, portrayed here as lacking the will to fight. See also 48:41.

Their strength is sapped. The verb *nšt* means "dry up, be exhausted" (KB^3; cf. Isa 41:17). Hebrew *gĕbûrātām* ("their strength") makes a wordplay with *gibbôrê* ("warriors") in the prior line.

they have become women. Hebrew *hāyû lĕnāšîm*. On this standard curse of antiquity, see Notes on 4:31; 6:24; and 50:37.

They have set her dwellings on fire. Holladay emends to a Hophal verb in order to get the passive readings of LXX, T, and Vg (which additionally achieves parallelism with the next colon); however, this form of the verb is unattested (the passive is embodied in the N-stem), and a change is not required. Use of the Hiphil simply requires an indefinite subject, which is perfectly acceptable

(Kimḥi). Enemies here are envisioned as having set Babylonian dwellings on fire.

her bars are broken. These could be bars on the dwellings just mentioned, otherwise bars securing Babylon's city gates (Cheyne; cf. 49:31; Amos 1:5; Nah 3:13; Lam 2:9; and Isa 45:2). The latter is more likely in view of what follows, where couriers are seen running from the outer limits of the city to inform the king at the city center. Perhaps all the protective bars in the city are broken.

31. *Runner runs to meet runner, and herald to meet herald.* Babylonian runners coming from all corners of the city are meeting one another on their way to tell the king, who resides in the city center, the news of enemy invasion at the city limits. The king is certain to be demoralized, as he is depicted in 50:43. Compare the runners bearing bad news in Job 1:13–19.

that his city is taken from every side. Hebrew *miqqāṣeh* is lit. "from the end," here meaning "from every side" (cf. *miqqēṣ* in 50:26). With Babylon's outer limits having been overrun, it is just a matter of time until the enemy has control of the entire city.

32. *also the fords have been seized.* Hebrew *wĕhammaʿbārôt nitpāśû*. We learn more about Babylon's capture at its outer limits. The enemy has successfully negotiated shallow water crossings on the Euphrates, or irrigation canals, or the moat surrounding Babylon's outer wall.

and the marshes they have burned with fire. Hebrew *ʾăgammîm* is now widely taken to mean "marshes" (Ullendorff 1953: 157), which is supported by T ("marshlands"), Vg (*paludes*, "swamps"), and certain modern Versions (AV: "reeds"; NJV: "swamp thickets"; NIV and NRSV: "marshes"). The Akk *agammu* means "swamp of reeds" (AHw 1: 15). Diodorus of Sicily (ii 7) says Babylon was surrounded by swamps, for which reason fortified towers were not built there, the swamps themselves offering a sufficient natural defense. Cane grew in these swamps (Oppenheim 1964: 42). The burning then is of the marsh grass, which is either a purely offensive action by the attackers (Kimḥi), or a defensive move to cut off escape from the city (Bright; Holladay). Kimḥi notes that the medieval commentator Ibn Janah suggested on the basis of Ar *ʾujum* a meaning of "fortresses" for *ʾăgammîm* (Rosenberg; McKane; Holladay). This has led to a rendering of "bulwarks," or the like (Condamin; Rudolph; McKane; Jones; RSV [but not NRSV]; NEB; JB; NAB; NSB). But the Heb nowhere has this meaning. The LXX offers no help with *ta systemata autōn* ("their assemblies").

and the men of war are terrified. We may conclude as much in light of the portrayal in v 30. The N-stem of *bhl* is strong, meaning "to be terrified, horrified, out of one's senses" (Isa 13:8; KB³).

33. *For thus said Yahweh of hosts, God of Israel.* The LXX has simply, "For thus says the Lord"; see Appendix VI on the usual LXX omission of *ṣĕbāʾôt* ("of hosts") in Jeremiah.

Daughter Babylon is like a threshing floor at the time one treads her. Since this is a simile, the pronominal suffix "her" can refer to both feminine nouns, "Babylon" and the "threshing floor." In the Bible judgment and salvation are commonly described as a harvest. The harvest here will bring judgment. The threshing floor is not used for nine or ten months out of the year, only during harvest, when it is smoothed and hardened by tamping. Babylon's day of judgment will consist of a trampling by the enemy, at which time she will be like a threshing floor at harvest time. Compare the tamping imagery in Amos 2:7.

Daughter Babylon. The term appears also in 50:42, which reworks an earlier Jeremiah oracle. On the various "daughter" metaphors in Jeremiah and the OT, see Kartveit 2001 and Note for 4:11. The LXX's "houses of the king of Babylon" appears to embellish a misreading of the underlying Hebrew text (*bāttê,* "houses," for *bat,* "daughter").

one treads her. Hebrew *hidrîkāh* is an irregular H-stem infinitive with suffix (GKC §53 1; cf. 50:34; 52:3).

Just a little while, and the harvest time will come upon her. Babylon's harvest is not yet, but will come shortly (Calvin: "in God's time"). On the expression *'ôd mĕ'aṭ* ("just a little while"), see also Exod 17:4; Isa 10:25; Hos 1:4; and Ps 37:10. The LXX omits *'ēt* ("time"), reading "her harvest will come." Read the MT (cf. 50:16).

MESSAGE AND AUDIENCE

This poem, like so many others in the book, is permeated from beginning to end with a sense of immediacy, portraying events leading up to battle and then the subsequent outcome as if both were happening before our very eyes. As with the oracle against Egypt in 46:3–6, there is no report of an actual battle, or, if there was a battle, it quickly turned into a rout. Orders are given to raise flags in the land, to sound trumpets among the nations. A coalition is being summoned to attack the mighty Babylon. Everything must be properly sanctified, as this is holy war carried on in Yahweh's name. The fighting force will include Ararat, Minni, and Ashkenaz, peoples from the distant north who are no strangers to war, and who will join the fray with enthusiasm. The appointment of marshals is called for, also horses are to be brought like consuming locusts into the field. Again, nations are to carry out consecration rites, sanctifying kings of the coalition, governors, commanders, and the land.

Next comes a description not of the battle, but what will accompany the battle. The land will quake and writhe in its own uprising against Babylon. The striking image is later qualified, but also given a theological dimension by some later editor who hastens to add that these terrestrial convulsions stem from Yahweh's plans to make Babylon's land an uninhabitable desolation.

The field of vision now shifts to the desperate situation inside the targeted city, and we see a Babylon on the brink of defeat. Its warriors sit motionless in the strongholds, their strength sapped, rendering them weak as women. The audience is expected to imagine women in labor. The enemy has set afire Babylon's dwellings, and the bars securing city gates and buildings are now broken. The city is wide open, awaiting violation by an intoxicated and intemperate enemy.

With the gates now open, couriers are seen running frantically toward the city center, meeting others en route who are in a similar state of panic. All are rushing to inform the king that his city has been invaded on every side. Defenses on the city's perimeter have been overrun—fords have been seized, and the enemy has burned the reeded marshy areas with fire. The poem ends by saying that Babylon's fighting men are terrified. Small wonder. The battle is lost, and the audience is left to imagine what sort of frenzied activity will take place next.

The oracle following is a terse judgment on Daughter Babylon—the irony of this endearing term not likely to be missed. The once-mighty nation will be a virtual threshing floor when enemy soldiers come to tread upon her. Yahweh adds that the harvest is not yet, but will come soon.

Taken in tandem with the preceding poem, this oracle puts the imagined war scene in proper perspective. The urgent battle preparations and a war already over have not happened yet. But they will happen, in just a little while. The poem then is general in nature, applicable to the situation when it arises (Rudolph; Jones). It need not have been uttered close in time to Babylon's actual fall (*pace* Cazelles 1984: 136), nor should the poem be denied to Jeremiah any more than other poems depicting Babylon's fall as being imminent. There is no mention here of the Persians; destruction is expected at the hands of the Medes and peoples farther north. Calvin, for his part, believed that Cyrus was not yet born when this prophecy was spoken. Reflected is a period when Media controlled the territory north and east of Mesopotamia, including Ararat, Minni, and Ashkenaz, which is a reference to the years following Assyria's demise but before Media's fall to Cyrus in the mid–sixth century. Bright therefore suggested a date of 550 B.C., prior to Cyrus's overthrow of the Median king Astyages (cf. CAH 3: 183). But the poem could be earlier—from the 590s, when the northern nations had been defeated by the Medes and brought under their control. A date prior to 594 B.C. for both the poem and the prose oracle is thus eminently possible, and actually to be preferred over a later date (Holladay; Keown et al.).

24. Bel No Longer King in Babylon (51:34–45)

51 [34]He consumed me[1], he shook me up[2]
    Nebuchadrezzar, king of Babylon
        he set me down[3] an empty jar
    Like a monster he swallowed me[4]
        he filled his belly with my delicacies
        he rinsed me out[5]

---

[1]Reading the Q *ʾăkālanî*; Kt here and in the next four verbs has a first-person plural suffix.
[2]Reading the Q *hămāmanî*.
[3]Reading the Q *hiṣṣîganî*.
[4]Reading the Q *bĕlāʿanî*.
[5]Reading the Q *hĕdîḥānî*.

³⁵'My violated flesh be upon Babylon'
   let the inhabitant of Zion say
'My blood be upon the inhabitants of Chaldea'
   let Jerusalem say

³⁶Therefore thus said Yahweh:
Look I have pled your plea
   and I have avenged your avenging
I have drained her sea
   and I have dried up her fountain
³⁷And Babylon will become heaps
   a den of jackals
a desolation and an object of hissing
   without inhabitant

³⁸Together like lions they roar
   they growl like lion cubs
³⁹When they are heated I will set out their drinks
   and make them drunk so they become silly
They shall sleep an eternal sleep
   and not waken—oracle of Yahweh
⁴⁰I will bring them down like lambs to the slaughter
   like rams with he-goats

⁴¹How Sheshak is taken
   and the praise of all the land occupied!
How she has become a desolation
   Babylon among the nations!
⁴²The sea has come up upon Babylon
   with its roaring heaps she is covered
⁴³Her cities have become a desolation
   a land of drought and desert
   (a land in which any person shall not dwell
   and a human shall not pass through)

⁴⁴So I have reckoned with Bel in Babylon
   and taken out what he swallowed from his mouth
And nations will not stream to him any longer
   even the wall of Babylon has fallen!
⁴⁵'Go out from her midst, my people!
   and deliver each his own life
     from the burning anger of Yahweh!'

RHETORIC AND COMPOSITION

MT 51:34–45 = LXX 28:34–44a. Verses 44b–45 are wanting in the LXX, being part of a larger omission extending through to v 49a. DeWette (1843: 398–401) argued that because of the omission the passage in question was "probably spurious"; however, the loss can be attributed to haplography (see Notes). As for for vocabulary and phraseology, Holladay says quite rightly that there are "reminiscences of [Jeremianic] phrasing everywhere."

The verses constitute a 20-line poem (excluding the formula in 36a and the add-on in 43b), in which Jerusalem laments its treatment by Nebuchadnezzar and calls for curses by its citizens upon Babylon (vv 34–35), which is followed by Yahweh's response that he will mete out similar treatment to Babylon and will send forth the exiled people before his savage anger erupts (vv 36–45). If v 43b is taken as a later supplement, which it appears to be, then the poem has five stanzas with an original line division of 4:4:4:4:4. The poem begins with two tricolons (v 34) and ends with two tricolons (vv 44b, 45); the intervening lines are all bicolons.

The poem combines in rare fashion images of land and sea (vv 36–37, 42–43, 44), also sea monsters and an array of land animals—jackals, lions, lion cubs, lambs, rams, and he-goats (vv 34, 37–38, 40). Balancing terms within and between stanzas are the following:

I		v 34
Nebuchadrezzar, king of Babylon		
he swallowed me	*bělā'anî* (Q)	
....		
.... *Babylon*		v 35
let the inhabitant of Zion say	*yōšebet* ...	
.... *inhabitants*	*yōšěbê*	
let Jerusalem say		
II		v 36
.... *her sea*	*yammāh*	
.... *will become heaps*	*wěhāyětâ gallîm*	v 37
a desolation	*šammâ*	
.... *inhabitant*	*yôšēb*	
III .... *like lions*	*ka*	v 38
.... *like lion cubs*	*kě*	
		v 39
.... *like lambs*	*kě* ...	v 40
like rams	*kě* ...	
IV *How Sheshak*	*'êk*	v 41
.... *all the land*	*kol-hā'āreṣ*	
How she has become a desolation	*'êk háyětâ lěšammâ*	
Babylon among the nations	... *baggôyīm*	

The sea . . . . Babylon	hayyām . . .	v 42
. . . . its heaps	gallāyw	
. . . . . . have become a desolation	hāyû . . . lĕšamma	v 43
a land	ʾ ereṣ	

V . . . . Bel in Babylon		v 44
and taken out what he swallowed	wĕhōṣēʾtî ʾet-bilʿô	
. . . . the nations	gôyīm	
. . . . Babylon		
Go out	ṣĕʾû	v 45
. . . .		

The poem was analyzed earlier as having a large key word chiasmus with balancing terms at the center, making it structurally similar to the Jeremiah poems in 2:5–9; 5:1–8; and 8:13–17 (Lundbom 1975: 92–95 [= 1997: 123–26]). Key words making the chiasmus:

I	Nebuchadrezzar . . . . . . Babylon		v 34
	he swallowed me	bĕlāʿanî (Q)	

II	. . . . her sea	yammāh	v 36
	. . . . and will become heaps	wĕhāyĕtâ gallîm	v 37
	a desolation	šammâ	

III	. . . . like lions	ka	v 38
	. . . . like lion cubs	kĕ	
	. . . . like lambs . . .	kĕ . . .	v 40
	like rams	kĕ . . .	

IV	. . . . a desolation	lĕšammâ	v 41
	The sea	hayyām	v 42
	. . . . its heaps	gallāyw	
	. . . . have become a desolation	hāyû . . . lĕšamma	v 43

V	. . . . Bel in Babylon		v 44
	. . . . he swallowed . . .	bilʿô	

The poem is further delimited by prose preceding (v 33) and following (v 46). The M^L, M^A, and M^P all have a *setumah* after v 35, which is doubtless guided by the messenger formula beginning v 36a. This section appears to be lacking in one MS in the Cambridge Genizah Collection (A 14.13). The messenger formula may be secondary. If so, the "oracle of Yahweh" formula at the center of the poem (v 39) was originally the sole indicator that vv 36–45 constituted a divine word. Otherwise we must take the divine word portion of the poem as having two formulas, which is possible (cf. 2:2b–3, 5–9). But one should not divide between v 35 and v 36 to make two poems, even though the oracle portion begins with the common "Look I" (*hinĕnî*). Other divisions, e.g., the break

made by Bright and Jones between v 40 and v 41, should be rejected. Jones
begs the question by saying that not a single new idea appears in vv 41–45/46.
This poem, like so many others, builds on repetition, and here the chiasmus
functions to highlight the main point, i.e., that Babylon will receive the very
treatment it meted out to Jerusalem. The only real question is whether to include v 45. Some commentators (Boadt; Carroll; Holladay; Keown et al.) take
vv 34–44 as the unit, presumably wanting the exodus directive (v 45) at the beginning of a new unit. Holladay judges v 45 secondary, but on the spurious
grounds that it has conventional language. It is not necessary that directives to
flee come at the beginning of a unit. They do begin units in 50:8 and 51:6, but
not in 48:6 and 49:30, where they come at the end. Moreover, if the exodus directive is separated from vv 34–44, it is left an isolated fragment of poetry (v 46
is a prose introduction to the poetry of vv 47–49). It is best then to include v 45
with what precedes and delimit the poem to vv 34–45.

Catchwords connecting to the prior poem:

v 34	*king of Babylon*	vv 27–29	*in the land / all land / the land (2x)*
vv 35–44	*Babylon (6x)*	vv 27–28	*the nations (3x)*
vv 37, 41, 43	*desolation (3x)*	v 29	*desolation*
vv 41, 43	*all the land / land*	vv 29–33	*Babylon (4x)*
vv 41, 44	*the nations (2x)*	v 31	*the king of Babylon*
v 43	*her cities*	v 32	*his city*

Catchwords connecting to the poem following:

vv 34–44	*Babylon (7x)*	v 47	*when I will reckon*
v 35	*Jerusalem*	vv 47–49	*Babylon (4x)*
v 44	*So I have reckoned*	v 51	*Jerusalem*

NOTES

51:34. *He consumed me, he shook me up . . . he set me down . . . he swallowed
me . . . he rinsed me out.* The Q with a first singular "me" brings all these verbs
into line with "my delicacies." A personified Jerusalem is speaking (T prefaces
the verse with "Jerusalem said"). The Kt readings, "he consumed us, he shook
us up," etc., simply make it clearer that Jerusalem is speaking on behalf of its
citizens, who are given curses to utter in v 35. Most Versions ancient and modern, also a majority of commentators, go with the Q. The NIV reads the Kt, but
then has to emend to "our delicacies."

He consumed me. The verb *ʾkl* is frequent in Jeremiah (2:30; 5:14, 17; 46:10,
14; 50:17; et passim); in this verse it parallels *blʿ* ("to swallow"). Babylon was in
the prophet's mind when he stated in 5:17 that a distant nation would consume
everything in Judah. Here the consuming agent is named: It is Babylon's king,
Nebuchadrezzar.

he shook me up. Hebrew *hămāmanî* (Q). This verb is difficult, and attempts to render it rely heavily on the context. The T has "he destroyed me," and the LXX *emerisato me* ("he divided me, cut me up"), which survives in Calvin's "(he has) broken me in pieces" (cf. Isa 28:28). Calvin envisions a breaking of bones, as a wild animal does after he has eaten the flesh (50:17). Compare AV, RSV, and NRSV: "he crushed me." The Vg chose a synonym of "consume": *devoravit me* ("he devoured me, gulped me down"), and is followed by Bright, JB, and NJB. Rudolph, however, looks ahead to the third colon ("he set me down an empty jug") for a parallel, and proposes the meaning "suck dry" for *hmm* (KB³ *hmm* II; cf. Ar *hamma*, "to exhaust"). He is followed by the NEB and REB, also McKane. But one can translate the lexical meaning of *hmm*, i.e., "bring into motion and confusion" (KB³). See renderings of the NAB and NJV. This verb commonly denotes the routing of armies (Exod 14:24; Josh 10:10; 1 Sam 7:10), but here we are talking about an interior condition. It is a personified Jerusalem that has been thrown into confusion. Compare Jonah's interior distress after being consumed by the great fish (Jonah 2).

Nebuchadrezzar, king of Babylon. Some commentators (Cornill; Volz; Rudolph; Weiser; Holladay) delete "Nebuchadrezzar" on metrical grounds, although the name is present in the LXX and T. I agreed earlier to the deletion (Lundbom 1975: 94 [= 1997: 125]), suggesting that the subject—originally Bel—was not revealed until v 44. But Nebuchadrezzar could be original, in which case the subject is named at the outset and a coalescence with the Babylonian god, Bel, occurs in v 44. The line in either case is a tricolon, as is the (shorter) line of v 34b.

he set me down an empty jar. Jerusalem laments the plundering of its land and wealth, also the robbery of inhabitants taken into exile.

empty jar. Hebrew *kĕlî rîq* is a construct chain, lit. "jar of emptiness."

Like a monster he swallowed me. An image like the first one, but not exactly the same. Compare *Pss. Sol.* 2:25(29), where the dragon is Pompey (*OTP II*: 653; *APOT II*: 633). Calvin notes that dragons (= monsters) devour animals whole; cf. Jonah, who was consumed whole. In Ezek 29:3 and 32:2, Egypt's Pharaoh is a self-satisfied sea or river monster (reading *hattannîn* for MT *hattannîm*) whom Yahweh will pluck from the water and cast into the open field as food for the birds and beasts. According to Gunkel (1895: 84), the most destructive aspect of the chaos dragon was his arrogant self-exaltation (cf. Labuschagne 1966; 107). Cheyne and others see an allusion here to the Babylonian creation epic (*enuma eliš*), in which Marduk defeats Tiamat, the chaos monster, and then rends asunder her belly (see Note on 50:2). There are also (non-creation) parallels in the Ugaritic texts, where Baal does battle with the sea god Yam, the goddess Anat, and an array of serpents and sea monsters (J. Day 1985: 61, 109–11; "Dragon and Sea, God's Conflict with" in *ABD* 2: 228–31). These parallels suit the Ezekiel texts where Yahweh readies himself to overcome the monster, but not the present text where the monster itself does the devouring and fills its own belly.

monster. Hebrew *tannîn* is a serpent, dragon, or sea monster, usually of mythical character or having mythical overtones (Isa 27:1; 51:9; Ezek 29:3;

32:2; Ps 74:13; Job 7:12). A demythologized chaos monster appears simply as *tĕhôm* ("the deep") in Gen 1:2. Compare also Ps 104:6 and Isa 51:9–10. For a discussion of otherworldly beings, see also Note on 50:39.

he filled his belly with my delicacies. Repointing MT *mē'ădānāy,* "from my delights" to *ma'ădannāy,* "my delicacies" (cf. Lam 4:5), with Giesebrecht and others, and reading a double accusative for *m'l* , "to fill" (cf. Gen 21:19; GKC §117cc). The monster of Babylon became sated with Jerusalem's treasured possessions, both in 597 B.C and in 586 B.C. (2 Kgs 24:13; 25:13–17; cf. Jer 52:17–23).

belly. Hebrew *kārēś* is a *hapax legomenon* in the OT, but is well supported in the cognate languages (KB³). Akkadian *karšu(m)* has the meaning "belly" (AHw 1: 450–51).

he rinsed me out. Or "he cleansed me." Hebrew *hĕdîḥānî* (Q). The verb *dûaḥ* means "rinse, cleanse" (Isa 4:4; Ezek 40:38; 2 Chr 4:6), and if it be the right verb here, then the rinsing or cleansing must take place in the mouth of Nebuchadrezzar. This image, like the "empty jar" image in the prior line, refers again to depopulation and a loss of Jerusalem's material wealth. But many commentators (Hitzig; Giesebrecht; Duhm; Peake; Jones; Keown et al.; Holladay; McKane), and most of the modern Versions (AV; NEB; NAB; REB; NIV; NJB; NSB), follow the (otherwise problematic) LXX (*exōsen me,* "thrust me out") and the Vg (*eiecit me,* "cast me out, vomited me up"), which convey an image of disgorging (cf. v 44) and point unambiguously to exile. Presupposed here is a different pointing of the Hebrew, *hiddîḥānî* (Q), which is from *ndḥ* ("scatter, drive away"), occurring often in Jeremiah (8:3; 16:15; 23:8; 24:9; 46:28; 50:17; et passim), and is here the *lectio facilior.* The T says plainly, "he has taken me into exile." Either reading is possible.

35. *My violated flesh be upon Babylon.* A hendiadys; lit. "my violence and my flesh." The first of two curses addressed to an unspecified audience, although God can be expected to hear and does hear, as we see from the divine response immediately following. In 10:25 the call was put out for Yahweh to pour out wrath upon the nations because they had consumed Jacob. Some take "my flesh" (*šĕ'ērî*) to mean "my kin," or the like (RSV [abandoned in NRSV]; NJV), but this only introduces ambiguity. Who is Jerusalem's kin? There is similarly no compelling need with Duhm, Volz, Rudolph, and others to emend away "my flesh," which suits the context fine (*pace* Holladay). Violated flesh is torn or eaten flesh (cf. Mic 3:2–3). Weiser notes here a liturgical style such as we find in Pss 118:2–4; 124:1; and 129:1.

My blood be upon the inhabitants of Chaldea. Compare the curse formulas in Lev 20:9, 11–13, 16, and 27. Hebrew *'el* alternates here with *'al*; see Note on 11:2.

inhabitant of Zion . . . inhabitants of Chaldea. Or "sitting one of Zion . . . sitting ones of Chaldea"; see Note on 46:19. The expression "inhabitant of Zion" occurs only here and in Isa 12:6.

36. *Look I have pled your plea, and I have avenged your avenging.* Yahweh now speaks. He has heard the complaints and maledictions, and says he will

plead Jerusalem's case (*rîb*) and then do its avenging for it (cf. Deut 32:35–36). The verbs in the verse are all prophetic perfects. Yahweh does this because he is Israel's *gō'ēl*, "redeemer" (50:34). On Yahweh's vengeance with respect to the nations, see Note for 46:10.

I have drained her sea, and I have dried up her fountain. The punishment will suit the crime: Yahweh will drain Babylon as Babylon drained Jerusalem. But now the imagery cuts more deeply. To say that Babylon's "sea will be drained" and her "fountain dried up" is to attack frontally a proud city situated amidst "many waters" (v 13), something Jerusalem was not. Babylon was situated on the bank of the Euphrates, surrounded by a network of canals, and even boasted an artificial lake, the building of which was attributed by Herodotus (i 185) to the legendary Queen Nitocris. But the lake is known now to have been the design of Nebuchadnezzar (Wiseman 1985: 57). Some commentators (Cheyne, Peake, Rudolph, McKane) believe that "her sea" may refer simply to the Euphrates (JB and REB: "her river"; "the sea" = the Nile in Isa 18:2; 19:5). Similarly, "her fountain" (*mĕqōrāh*) could refer collectively to Babylon's system of canals and lakes (Cheyne; McKane, citing Vg *venam*, "water course"). But specificity for either image is not required. Hosea 13:15 says that at the coming of Yahweh's east wind "(Ephraim's) fountain will dry up" (*wĕyēbôš mĕqōrô*). If reference there is to Samaria (cf. 14:1[Eng 13:16]), then we have a targeted city with a deep well but no natural water supply. Yahweh, nevertheless, formed the seas at Creation (Gen 1:9–10; Ps 95:5) and, according to a more ancient cosmology, subdued hostile forces with awesome might to bring the sea under his control (Pss 74:13–14; 89:9–10; Job 26:12; Jer 5:22; cf. Matt 8:27). More importantly for Israel, Yahweh rolled back the sea to make the Exodus from Egypt possible (Exod 14:16, 21–22, 29; 15:8; Isa 51:10). After Yahweh's final eschatological battle is waged (Isa 27:1; Revelation 20), and the new creation takes place, the sea will be no more (Rev 21:1).

37. *And Babylon will become heaps, a den of jackals, a desolation and an object of hissing, without inhabitant.* These curses on a now dry and ruined land are stereotyped; see Note for 48:9. For similar curses on Babylon, see 50:3, 13; 51:29, 43 and 62. The LXX lacks "a den of jackals, a desolation and an object of hissing," which Janzen (1973: 63) and Holladay take to be MT expansion from 9:10[Eng 9:11]. The expansion theory is unnecessary; the LXX omission is probably another loss due to haplography (homoeoarcton: *m . . . m*).

heaps. Hebrew *gallîm*. Here heaps of ruins (T: "heaps of stones"); in vv 42 and 55 heaps of water, i.e., waves.

a desolation. Hebrew *šammâ*. A very common term in the poetry and prose of Jeremiah, occurring often in strings of curse words such as the present one (see Note for 24:9).

an object of hissing. Hebrew *šĕrēqâ*. Another common Jeremiah curse word (see Note for 25:9), occurring often in curse-word strings (see Note for 24:9).

den of jackals. Hebrew *mĕ'ôn-tannîm*. For this phrase elsewhere in Jeremiah, also for extrabiblical parallels on cursed cities that are left as haunts for wild animals, see Note on 9:10[Eng 9:11]). The AV's "dwelling place for dragons" is a mistranslation (reading *tannîn* for *tannîm*). The T is also wide of the mark with its "dwelling place of wild asses."

38. *Together like lions they roar, they growl like lion cubs.* A syntactic chiasmus in the Hebrew with verbs here in the center; compare 51:12a. The Babylonians are still alive and hungry; here they roar in chorus, anticipating yet more prey to devour (Amos 3:4; Pss 22:14[Eng 22:13]; 104:21). They will have one last feast, but it will end in an eternal sleep (v 39). Weiser sees a "harsh humor" in these verses. The LXX lacks "they roar," but readings are attested in Aq and Theod (*ereuxontai*), also in Symm (*ōrusontai*). On lions and lion sphinxes that once guarded entrances to the Babylonian temples and palaces, also lions on stone reliefs and glazed tiles in ancient Babylon, see Note on 2:15.

they growl. Hebrew *nā'ărû*. The verb with this meaning (KB³ *n'r* I) is a *hapax legomenon* in the OT, but has a cognate in Ar *na'ara*, "to roar, snore, be very angry."

39. *When they are heated I will set out their drinks, amd make them drunk so they become silly.* Another reversal: earlier Babylon was Yahweh's golden cup making all nations drunk (51:7). Here the table is set differently. To appetite-driven Babylon, Yahweh will serve drinks that will make it drunk (cf. 51:57). The verb *ḥmm* means "become hot," referring here (as in Hos 7:7) to a display of passion. The Babylonian passion is seen in the pre-feast growling. Most modern Versions render accordingly, e.g., the NRSV: "When they are inflamed, I will set out their drink." The Babylonians are heated not because of wine and subsequent drunkenness (*pace* Calvin and Kimḥi), but because they come to the table in that condition. The NEB and REB thus have it wrong (REB: "I shall cause their drinking bouts to end in fever"). Here the prophet's words were indeed prophetic. When Babylon did fall to Cyrus and the Persians, the city was caught unaware because, as Herodotus (i 191) says, it "was dancing and making merry at a festival"; see Note on 50:15.

their drinks. Hebrew *mištêhem*. Some translate "their feast (with drinks)."

they become silly. Hebrew *ya'ălōzû*. Here the verb *'lz* means "be merry, jolly" in a foolish manner, a meaning it may also have in 15:17. Drunkenness leads to just such behavior (cf. 51:7).

They shall sleep an eternal sleep, and not waken. The same words occur again in v 57. Whereas banqueters usually sleep off their drunkenness and wake up sober, that will not happen here. This sleep will be the sleep of death (cf. Herodotus i 211).

40. *I will bring them down like lambs to the slaughter, like rams with he-goats.* If proud Babylon was like a lion, drunken Babylon will be like a lamb ready for slaughter (cf. Hos 4:11, 14c; Lundbom 1979: 304). This verse should not be treated as a gloss (*pace* Volz), nor should it be placed before v 39b so the slaughter precedes the eternal sleep (*pace* Rudolph; Holladay). Poetry does not require strict sequentiality. A sober but unsuspecting Jeremiah, after discovering a plot on his life, likened himself to a trusting lamb led to the slaughter (11:19). In the Keret Legend is the expression, "bring down for Baal your sacrifice" (Rin 1963: 30).

lambs . . . rams with he-goats. Hebrew *kārîm* are young he-lambs (= rams); *'êlîm* are full-grown male sheep (= rams), and *'attûdîm* are "he-goats." All three are cited as (choice) animals for slaughter in Deut 32:14.

41. *How! . . . How!* Hebrew *'êk . . . 'êk.* On this rhetorical doublet, see Note for 50:23.

How Sheshak is taken, and the praise of all the land occupied! An ironic lament (Weiser), similar to the lament over Damascus in 49:25. The verb *wattitāpēś* ("and it is occupied") is placed in the second colon (so RSV; NEB; NJV; and NIV), in conformity with the *zaqeph* accent over *šēšak* ("Sheshak"). BHS puts it in the first colon, presumably because of the *ṭiphḥa* accent under *wattitāpēś*. In the similar verse of 50:23a, both verbs appear in the first colon.

Sheshak. Hebrew *šēšak* is a cipher (Heb *atbash*) for "Babylon," occurring also in 25:26 (see Note there). A cipher for "Chaldea / Chaldeans" appears in 51:1. The LXX lacks the present cipher, as it does the cipher in a larger omission at 32:26 (= MT 25:26). Symmachus has *Sēsach*.

occupied. Hebrew *tittāpēś.* Babylon is now in the firm grip of the enemy.

the praise of all the land. Better here "all the earth." Hebrew *tĕhillat kolhā'āreṣ.* "The Praise of Moab" (= Mt. Nebo) and "city of praise" (= Damascus) were also brought down (48:2; 49:25). Yahweh wanted the covenant people to be for him a "praise" (13:11).

How she has become a desolation, Babylon among the nations! A repeat of the line in 50:23b.

42. *The sea has come up upon Babylon, with its roaring heaps she is covered.* Earlier it was Babylon's sea drying up (v 36). Here the sea roars in upon Babylon as a chaotic force. The image will not be lost on either the Babylonians or the Judahites. Lutz (1939: 5–7) points out how water was considered a malevolent tyrant in Babylonian thought, having grand ambitions to reduce an orderly world to desolation. Annual floodings of the Tigris and the Euphrates, along with the heavy winter rains, were seen as visitations from heaven, acts of Enlil, which left people lamenting in their temples and shrines. Such a prediction as the one here, while it would surely cause people to be afraid, would not be unexpected in nature. In Israelite thought, the memory of all memories was of Yahweh causing the sea to cover Pharaoh and his hosts as they pursued Israel out of Egypt (Exod 14:27–28; 15:1, 4, 10). This prediction, then, will suggest to a Judahite audience another mighty act of Yahweh against an oppressor as bad or worse than the pharaoh of Egypt. See also 47:2 and Isa 8:7–8. Some scholars (Blayney; Cheyne; Duhm) think the "sea" again refers specifically to the Euphrates (cf. v 64; and see Note on v 36), but this seems too restrictive. Rashi and Kimḥi follow the T, which eliminates the metaphor but does capture the sense: "a king with his troops who are as many as the waters of the sea has come up against Babylon." On the annual spring floodings of both the Tigris and Euphrates, see Oppenheim 1964: 40–42.

with its roaring heaps. Hebrew *bahămôn gallāyw.* The "heaps" (*gallîm*) here are waves or billows that will inundate Babylon (cf. v 55). In v 37 Babylon was to be left heaps of dry, dusty ruins. The image of a sea in tumult echoes the

Song of the Sea, where a "heap" (*nēd*) of water saved the Israelites but then covered the Egyptians (Exod 15:8–10).

43. *Her cities have become a desolation, a land of drought and desert.* The image changes again to desolate land. Like v 37, the present verse is a stereotyped curse. But these are daughter cities of Babylon, not Babylon itself. On the land-and-city curse in Jeremiah, see Note on 48:9.

desolation. Hebrew *lĕšammâ.* The LXX omits; Holladay and Janzen (1973: 63) take the MT as expanded from vv 37, 41, but the omission is better explained as another LXX loss due to haplography (homoeoteleuton: *h . . . h*).

a land of drought and desert. Hebrew *'ereṣ ṣiyyâ wa'ărābâ.* Compare 2:6 and 50:12. The former passage is a liturgy recalling Yahweh's gracious leading during Israel's wilderness trek.

(*a land in which any person shall not dwell, and a human shall not pass through*). This is almost certainly a later add-on, not simply because it enlarges the stanza (Rhetoric and Composition), but because its awkward Hebrew reproduces poorly the standard curse as found in 49:18, 33b; and 50:40b. The LXX and S omit "land," which goes ill both with what precedes and what follows. The phraseology has some affinity with 2:6c, which is not a curse but words out of a confession. My earlier conclusion (Lundbom 1975: 152 n. 25, 156 n. 85 [= 1997: 95 n. 25, 125 n. 85]) was that both 2:6 and the present verse show signs of expansion, which I still believe to be the case.

44. *So I have reckoned with Bel in Babylon.* Hebrew *bēl . . . bĕbābel . . . bil'ô* has alliteration and paronomasia (Casanowicz 1893: #49). The LXX omits "Bel in," which can be explained as a loss due to haplography (homoeoarcton: *b . . . b*). This explanation is given also by Janzen (1973: 119). On the verb *pqd* ("reckon, pay a visit"), see vv 47, 52, and Note on 5:9. Yahweh here is asserting his superiority over the Babylonian god (or his idol), now seen to be the powerless deity he really is.

Bel. A shortened title (= "lord") for the Babylonian deity, Bel Marduk. See Note for 50:2.

and taken out what he swallowed from his mouth. Bel is now said to be the devouring monster; in v 34 it was Nebuchadrezzar. In either case, what has been swallowed, viz., Jerusalem, its Temple treasures, and a good deal more, will now be reclaimed by Yahweh. The same point is made with regard to the wicked in Job 20:15. Nebuchadrezzar, it will be recalled, placed Jerusalem's treasures in the temple of his god (Ezra 1:7; Dan 1:2). Again, too, the Jonah tale comes to mind. There Yahweh commanded the great fish to swallow Jonah, after which he commanded the fish to vomit him up (Jonah 2:1, 11[Eng 1:17; 2:10]). A late second-century B.C. (apocryphal) addition to Daniel, "Bel and the Dragon," contains two tales ridiculing idolatry and cultic practices in Babylon. The first (vv 1–22) is a polemic against the image of Bel; the second (vv 23–42) inveighs against a (live) dragon worshiped by the Babylonians.

And nations will not stream to him any longer. The verb *nhr* ("stream, flow") with "nations" as subject makes an *abusio* (rivers normally stream or flow), on which see Note for 4:4. The same figure occurs in Isa 2:2 and Mic 4:1. Wiklander (1978) prefers translating "rejoice, shine" (KB³ *nhr* II), which is possible (cf. 31:12), but does away with the rhetorical language. The better reading is "stream." The point, in any case, is that nations will no longer be sending embassies to Bel and the land of Bel (cf. 2:18), for both will cease to be of any importance.

even the wall of Babylon has fallen. Another prophetic perfect, anticipating ahead of its time an event as great or greater than the fall of the Berlin wall on November 9, 1989. The point is restated climactically at the end of the Babylon oracle collection, in v 58. One will note that the rebuilding of Jerusalem's wall occupies in similar fashion a climactic position at the end of the first Book of Restoration, in 31:38–40. Babylon's walls were reputedly huge (see Note for 51:58), and were not toppled by Cyrus when he took the city in 539 B.C. The LXX omits all of vv 44b–49a, which is generally recognized as being due to haplography (whole-word: *gm . . . gm*).

45. *Go out from her midst, my people.* Hebrew *ṣĕ'û* ("Go out") may play intentionally on *hōṣē'tî* ("I have taken out") in v 44. The covenant people are now told to make a new Exodus, this time from Babylon. A similar directive is issued in 50:8, and one more broadly to all foreigners in 51:6. Compare also Isa 48:20 and 52:11–12.

and deliver each his own life. The same expression occurs in 51:6.

from the burning anger of Yahweh. Yahweh speaks of his own burning anger. This same expression occurs in 12:13. On Jeremiah's varied expressions regarding "(Yahweh's) burning anger," see Note on 4:8.

MESSAGE AND AUDIENCE

This poem begins with a lament by Lady Jerusalem who says that Nebuchadrezzar, Babylon's king, consumed her, gave her great internal distress, and then set her down an empty jar. The metaphors continue, but the message does not change. He swallowed her like a monster, filling his belly with all her good things, and then rinsed her out. All the rich imagery is to portray a loss of Jerusalem's population, Temple treasures, and much, much more. Lady Jerusalem then calls for the inhabitants who remain to curse the nation that carried out this violence: "May Jerusalem's violated flesh and blood be upon Babylon!"

Yahweh, having heard the plaint and the curses, responds with an oracle of judgment. The fall of Babylon is still a way off, but there are indications here that it may as well have already happened. No need for Jerusalem to plead her case; Yahweh has already done that for her. Yahweh will also do her avenging for her. Whereas Babylon was once a water wonderland, Yahweh says he will make her dusty ruin heaps where jackals come to live. The place will be desolate with no one living there, and people passing by will whistle in derision at the ruins of this once-proud city.

But the end is not yet. Babylon's mighty ones are roaring like lions, growling like lion cubs, awaiting another victim to devour. Yahweh, nevertheless, is ready. When passions are elevated and apetitites have peaked, he will set out drinks and make them so drunk they will behave like silly fools. It is an old ploy, but it still works. It will definitely work here. The hapless souls will then fall asleep, but it will be a sleep from which they will not awaken. Yahweh has spoken. Babylon's crack troops will now be easy prey, brought down like lambs to the slaughter. The climax of the oracle has been reached. It remains only to repeat and spell out the details of this spectactular turn of events.

Yahweh now utters a lament that an attentive audience will perceive to be laden with irony. What a pity that Babylon—mentioned now in cipher—is captured, a nation that was once the praise of all the earth! What a pity that she should become a desolation! If Babylon's own sea has become dry, another sea is now about to roll in upon her, its roaring waves waiting to make her disappear from view. The curse is repeated, only now upon the daughter cities: they too will be a desolation.

Yahweh has visited Bel in Babylon. The god—now the monster rather than Nebuchadrezzar—must give up what he has swallowed. Respect and tribute money will no longer flow to him from nations of the world. Even the celebrated wall of Babylon lies flat on the ground. In closing, Yahweh tells his own people to flee the city, save their lives, and escape the outpouring of his burning anger.

If the opening lament is hyperbole, which it may well be, then the poem as a whole could be dated after Nebuchadrezzar's subjugation of Jerusalem in 597 B.C., when many—but not all—of the city's inhabitants were taken along with Jerusalem's treasures to Babylon (2 Kgs 24:10–16). This date is more likely than 586 B.C., because there are still *inhabitants* of Zion remaining to speak their curse on this much-hated nation (v 35).

25. Look! A Reckoning for Babylon and Its Images (51:46–51)

51 [46]Now lest your heart be weakened and you become afraid at the rumor heard in the land, as the rumor comes in this year and after it the rumor in the next year, and violence is in the land, and ruler is against ruler:
[47]Look, hereafter, days are coming
   when I will reckon with the images of Babylon
And all her land shall be shamed
   and all her slain shall fall in her midst

[48]They shall cry for joy concerning Babylon
   sky and land
      and all that is in them
For from the north they shall come[1] to her
   the devastators!—oracle of Yahweh

[49]Yes, Babylon is to fall, O slain of Israel!
Yes, to Babylon fell the slain of all the land!

---

[1]Reading the plural *yabō'û* with *sebir* notation, a few MSS, and the Vrs; cf. v 53.

⁵⁰You who have escaped from the sword:
    Go, don't just stand there!
Remember Yahweh from afar
    and let Jerusalem come to your mind

⁵¹We are shamed, for we have heard the reproach
    disgrace covers our faces
For strangers have come
    against the holy places of Yahweh's house.

RHETORIC AND COMPOSITION

MT 51:46–51 = LXX 28:49b–51. The present verses contain a Yahweh / the people–Jeremiah dialogue in poetry (vv 47–51), preceded by a later prose introduction to Yahweh's opening oracle (v 46). Some modern Versions (RSV, NEB, NJV, NIV, NRSV, REB) take the introductory v 46 as poetry, but *BHS* rightly scans it as prose (Holladay: "secondary prose"). The NAB mistakenly takes all of vv 46–49 as prose (cf. Volz, who eliminates vv 45–48, 50–51 as secondary prose). Verses 46–49a are part of a larger LXX omission attributable to haplography (see Note on 51:44). Dialogue is created by an oracle emanating from Yahweh (vv 47–48), a retributive shout from the people (v 49), and a word-lament from Jeremiah (vv 50–51). In v 50 Jeremiah exhorts and gives hope to those leaving Jerusalem for Babylonian exile; in v 51 he laments the enemy intrusion into Jerusalem on behalf of those leaving and those who are left behind.

The unit is delimited at the top end by a shift to prose in v 46, before which comes the long self-contained poem in vv 34–45. At the bottom delimitation is by a *setumah* in M^L and a *petuḥah* in M^A after v 51. Some commentators (Duhm, Condamin, Weiser, Rudolph, Thompson, Holladay, McKane) begin a new unit with v 49, which has validity only if the oracle in vv 47–48 is taken to be originally self-standing, which it may have been. At its conclusion is an "oracle of Yahweh" formula (v 48b). But in the present text this oracle is integrated into a dialogue with Jeremiah and the people.

The oracle has striking similarities in form and content to the oracle(s) in vv 52–53 following:

51:47–48

I   *Look, hereafter, days are coming*   v 47
     when I will reckon with the images of Babylon
    And all her land . . . .
     and all her slain . . . .

II . . . . *Babylon*   v 48
    sky . . . .
    . . . .

For . . . . *they shall come to her*
    the devastators!—*oracle of Yahweh*

                    51:52–53
I   *Look, hereafter, days are coming*   v 52
        . . . .
        when I will reckon with her images
            and in all her land the slain . . . .

II   *For* . . . . . . *Babylon* . . . . *the sky*   v 53
        . . . .
        . . . . *devastators shall come to her*
        —*oracle of Yahweh*

The present oracle (vv 47–48) is two stanzas of the larger dialogue with these
repetitions and balancing key words:

I   . . . . *are coming*   v 47
        . . . . *Babylon*
        And all her land . . . .
            and all her slain . . . .

II   . . . . *Babylon*   v 48
        . . . . *land* . . . .
        and all that is in them . . . .
        . . . . *they shall come* . . . .
        . . . .

Stanza III (v 49) is the center of the dialogue, and like the center of the prior
poem and centers of numerous other Jeremianic poems, it has an internal
structure of its own created by repetition and balancing key words (see Rhetoric and Composition for 49:7–11):

III   *Yes, Babylon is to fall, O slain of Israel!*   v 49
        Yes, to Babylon fell the slain of all the land!

In this double bicolon is also a wordplay resulting from the repeated use (12
times) of the letter *lamed*. See earlier the poems in 6:1–7 and 6:8–12 (Rhetoric
and Composition for 6:1–7).
    Stanzas IV and V of the dialogue (vv 50–51) are spoken by Jeremiah. Here
we see alternate collocations of the name "Yahweh" in each final bicolon:

IV   . . . . *Yahweh* . . . .   v 50b
        . . . .

V   . . . .   v 51b
        . . . . *Yahweh*

The dialogue is then five stanzas structured by these repetitions and key words:

I	. . . . . *are coming*	*bāʾîm*	v 47
	. . . . . *shall be shamed*	*tēbôš*	
II	*For . . . they shall come*	*kî . . . yābôʾ*	v 48
III	*Yes, Babylon is to fall, O slain*	*gam-bābel linpōl ḥalĕlê . . .*	v 49
	Yes, to Babylon fell the slain	*gam-lĕbābel nāpĕlû ḥalĕlê . . .*	
V	*We are shamed*	*bōšĕnû*	v 51
	For . . . have come	*kî bāʾû*	

The following key words link the oracle to the people's climactic shout:

I	*And all her land* . . .	*wĕkol-ʾarṣāh . . .*	v 47
	and all her slain shall fall . . .	*wĕkol-ḥălāleyhā yippĕlû . . .*	
III	. . . *to fall* . . . *O slain of Israel*	. . . *linpōl* . . . *ḥalĕlê yiśrāʾēl*	v 49
	. . . *the slain of all the land*	. . . *ḥalĕlê kol-hāʾāreṣ*	

Key words also link the oracle to its prose introduction:

v 46 *the land* (2×)	v 47 *are coming*
it comes	*her land*
	v 48 *land*
	they shall come

And key words link vv 50–51 of the poetry to the prose introduction:

v 46 *the rumor heard šĕmûʿâ hannišmaʿat*	v 50 *your mind lĕbabkem*
your heart lĕbabkem	v 51 *we have heard šāmaʿnû*

Catchwords connecting to the prior poem:

v 47	*when I will reckon*	vv 34–44	*Babylon* (7×)
vv 47–49	*Babylon* (4×)	v 35	*Jerusalem*
v 50	*Jerusalem*	v 44	*So I have reckoned*

Catchwords connecting to the unit following:

v 46 *in the land* . . . *in the land*	
comes	
v 47 *Look, hereafter, days are coming*	v 52 *Look, hereafter, days are coming. . .*
when I will reckon with	*when I will reckon with*
the images of Babylon	*her images*
And all her land	*and in all her land*
her slain	*the slain*

v 48	*Babylon*	v 53	*Babylon*
	sky and land		*the sky*
	they shall come		*[they] shall come*
	the devastators		*devastators*
v 49	*Babylon* (2×)	v 54–55	*Babylon* (2×)
	slain . . . slain	v 55	*is devastating*
	all the land	v 56	*it has come*
v 51	*have come*		*Babylon*
			the devastator

NOTES

51:46. *Now lest your heart be weakened and you become afraid at the rumor heard in the land, as the rumor comes in this year and after it the rumor in the next year, and violence is in the land, and ruler is against ruler.* This is a word to Judah's dispirited remnant on the verge of losing courage and hope in a world rapidly breaking up. People must remember the oracle following, which promises judgment on Babylon and its idols, and will cause them with all creation to break forth into song.

Now lest your heart be weakened. Hebrew *ûpen-yērak lĕbabkem.* The verb *rkk* ("be weak, tender") with *lēb* ("heart") means "be fainthearted" (Deut 20:3). NEB: "beware of losing heart."

and you become afraid. Kimḥi says that people need not fear the enemy coming against Babylon for it will not harm the Jewish exiles.

the rumor. Hebrew *haššĕmûʿâ* here and following is a collective noun. Elsewhere *šĕmûʿâ* is "news" good or bad (10:22; 49:14, 23; Prov 15:30). In the NT, compare Matt 24:6.

as the rumor comes in this year and after it the rumor in the next year. The Hebrew is difficult, but the meaning is clear. In unsettled times war rumors circulate one year and again the next. For *haššānâ* meaning "this year," see 28:16. Rashi says *wĕʾaḥărāyw baššānâ* means "in the second year."

comes. Hebrew *bāʾ.* A masculine singular verb can predicate a feminine singular noun, here *haššĕmûʿâ*, "(the) rumor"; cf. GKC §145 o. Incongruence with a following plural occurs in v 48.

and violence is in the land. For violence (*ḥāmās*) earlier in Jerusalem, see 6:7 and 20:8.

and ruler is against ruler. Josephus, quoting Berosus (*Against Apion* i 145–49), reports of violence and civil disorder occurring in Babylon after Nebuchadnezzar's death in 562 B.C. Evil-merodach, Nebuchadnezzar's son, was murdered after reigning two years. The usurper, Neriglissar, and after him a young son, Labashi-Marduk, each reigned only briefly before Nabonidus seized the throne in 556 B.C. (Bright 1981: 352–53). Labashi-Marduk was reportedly beaten to death by friends. The verse then need not be taken as eschatological (*pace* Volz and Rudolph, who cite Matt 24:6–7), but can be an actual portrayal of Babylon's seven-year period of instability three decades after the fall of Jerusalem (Weiser; Bright; Holladay).

47. *Look, hereafter, days are coming.* This stereotyped phrase introduces Foreign Nation Oracles in 48:12; 49:2; 51:47, and 52; see also Notes on 7:32 and 16:14.

when I will reckon with the images of Babylon. I.e., for the purpose of doing away with them. The verb *pqd*, which recurs in vv 44 and 52 (see also Note on 5:9), is a prophetic perfect. Babylon's "images" (*pĕsilîm*) are mentioned elsewhere in 50:38b and 51:52 (see also Note on 8:19). One of these images will be of Bel cited in v 44. On the fall of Babylon's images, see also Isa 21:9.

And all her land shall be shamed. I.e., everyone and everything in the land; cf. v 48a.

and all her slain shall fall in her midst. I.e., no one will escape; all will die in the city. The "slain" (*ḥălālîm*) are lit. "those pierced (by the sword)," who will die as a result. See Note on 51:4.

48. *They shall cry for joy concerning Babylon, sky and land, and all that is in them.* Hebrew *šāmayim wā'āreṣ* can also be translated "heaven and earth." All creation will rejoice over Babylon's fall (cf. Isa 14:7). Calvin says "all that is in them" means to include the stars, humans, trees, fishes, birds, fields, stones, and rivers. Creation will also sing at Yahweh's future redemption of Israel (Isa 44:23; 49:13). It sings on other occasions simply in praise of Yahweh (Psalm 148). See also Ps 19:2–5[Eng 19:1–4].

For from the north they shall come to her, the devastators. This northern foe being readied by Yahweh against Babylon is mentioned also in 50:3, 9, and 41. On the proverbial "foe from the north," see Note on 1:14. It should be noted, however, that Babylon, like Jerusalem, was fortified in the Neo-Babylonian period against anticipated attacks from the north, the side on which the city was most vulnerable (see Note on 50:3). The "devastator" motif is common in Jeremiah; see Note on 48:8.

they shall come. The MT has the singular *yābô'* ("it shall come"), but a *sebir* marginal note calls for the plural (see footnote). Compare the plural in v 53. The MT reading here may simply be the result of metathesis, in which case the original reading was a plural. However, a masculine singular verb can stand with a plural subject following, here *haššôdĕdîm* ("the devastators"). See GKC §145 o, and another incongruence with the same verb and a subsequent feminine in v 46.

49. *Yes, Babylon is to fall, O slain of Israel.* If all creation is to break forth into song over the demise of Babylon, the covenant people can rightly shout about the same. On the "fall (*npl*) of Babylon," see 51:8 and especially Isa 21:9. It is generally agreed that the construct chain, *ḥălĕlê yiśrā'ēl*, should be read as a vocative: "O slain (ones) of Israel," but few commentators and modern Versions translate it so (Holladay does), wanting better parallelism in the lines and a clearer expression of the *lex talionis*. The usual solution is to insert a prefixed *lamed* before "slain" (Cornill; Volz; Rudolph; Bright), where the suggestion is sometimes made that this letter may have fallen out by haplography. The line would then read: "Yes, Babylon is to fall for the slain of Israel" (cf. NJV). But the line can express the *lex talionis* even with-

out close parallelism, and the vocative can be read as apostrophe, of which there are other examples in Jeremiah (see Note on 2:12). Bernard of Cluny's twelfth-century hymn "Jerusalem the Golden" speaks as follows to the faithful dead:

> Exult, O dust and ashes!
>   The Lord shall be thy part
> His only, his forever
>   Thou shalt be, and thou art!
>   (tr. John Mason Neale, 1818–66, *NEH* #381)

Here Israel's slain, over whom Jeremiah wept in 8:23[Eng 9:1], are being told the good news of Babylon's fall.

to fall. Hebrew *linpōl*. On the infinitive with *lĕ*, see GKC §114i.

Yes, to Babylon fell the slain of all the land. This line and the one preceding expresses the *lex talionis*, which occurs elsewhere in the Babylon oracles (50:29; 51:24, 35). Since to Babylon fell the slain of many lands, the phrase may better be rendered, "the slain of all the earth."

50. *You who have escaped from the sword: Go, don't just stand there!* This line has been widely misunderstood as a directive, like 50:8 and 51:45, bidding Jewish exiles to flee a doomed Babylon and return to Jerusalem (Kimḥi, Calvin, and others since, who cite for comparison 44:28). But that is not its meaning. The directive is rather to survivors of Nebuchadnezzar's attack on Jerusalem, perhaps in 597 B.C., telling them to get on their way into exile as instructed, and not to linger lest they meet up with new danger. The LXX's *anasōzomenoi ek gēs, poreuesthe kai mē histasthe*, "Go forth out of the land, you who escape, and do not stay," may convey this meaning. The T reading is more transparent: "Go into exile, do not hold back" (Hayward 1987: 188). The verse has its closest affinity with 10:17 and 31:21, conveying also the general sentiments of Jeremiah's letter to the exiles in 29:4–28. Compare in addition 31:2, where reference is to those who escaped the sword of Assyria some years earlier. The imperative *hilkû* ("Go!") is unusual (normally *lĕkû*), but can be taken as a strong formation of the verb *hlk*, rare and occurring late (KB³). There is thus no need to emend (*pace* Giesebrecht; Duhm) or redivide and repoint to get the reading "her sword" (*pace* Blayney; Volz; Rudolph; Holladay; and others; similarly NEB [but not REB]; JB; and NJB).

don't just stand there. Hebrew *'al-taʿămōdû*. A Jeremianic expression; see 4:6a. For a similar call to action, see 8:14. But note how Jeremiah himself just stands there after being released (40:5).

Remember Yahweh from afar. Hebrew *mērāḥôq* ("from afar") is a measure of distance (LXX: *oi makrothen*), not time. The meaning then is not "remember (Yahweh) from seventy years ago" (*pace* Kimḥi). Captives leaving Jerusalem are told to remember Yahweh from the distant land of Babylon (Abarbanel; *Mezudath* David). Yahweh will be there (31:2–3), and save his people from there (30:10).

and let Jerusalem come to your mind. Hebrew *wîrûsālayim taʿăleh ʿal-lĕbabkem.* The exiles did precisely this (Ps 137:5–6). In 3:16–17 people are told that in future days the ark of the covenant will not come to mind (*wĕloʾ yaʿăleh ʿal-lēb*), and people will not remember it (*wĕloʾ yizkĕrû-bô*). But Jerusalem will be remembered, since it will then be called "The Throne of Yahweh."

51. *We are shamed, for we have heard the reproach.* The "reproach" (*ḥerpâ*) is from enemies (cf. 15:15; 20:8; Ps 44:16–17[Eng 44:15–16]). On this very common word in Jeremiah, see Note for 24:9. The speaking voice continues to be that of Jeremiah, who laments now the indignities brought upon Jerusalem's inhabitants after the city capitulated to Nebuchadnezzar, probably in 597 B.C. This lament does not come from exiles in Babylon (*pace* Cheyne), nor does the reproach necessarily result from the Temple already having been destroyed (*pace* Rashi; Weiser).

disgrace covers our faces. Hebrew *kĕlimmâ* is another noun meaning "disgrace, dishonor." The same phrase, except for a singular suffix, occurs in Ps 69:8[Eng 69:7]. In Ps 44:16[Eng 44:15] shame is said to cover the face. "Reproach" and "disgrace" are promised to people feeding on false prophecy in 23:40; in 3:25 the entire community confesses dishonor because of their sin.

For strangers have come against the holy places of Yahweh's house. The "strangers" are the Babylonians, and the "holy places" are portions of the Temple complex. Hebrew *miqdĕšê* ("holy places") could be an intensive plural (Ember 1904–5: 212; cf. GKC §124e), i.e., meaning simply "sanctuary," which is how the term is translated in S, T, and Vg. The LXX too reads "our sanctuary." Possibly multiple buildings are referred to (cf. 7:4: "The temple of Yahweh, the temple of Yahweh, the temple of Yahweh are these"). Note also "holy places" plural in Ps 84:2[Eng 84:1] and 2 Chr 8:11. Kimḥi explains the plural as referring to three parts of the Temple: the porch, the Temple, and the Holy of Holies, each regarded as a sanctuary. Calvin similarly. Many believe that reference here is to a Temple already destroyed, which elsewhere in the OT is a bitter memory (Pss 74:1–8; 79:1) and a sacrilege, for which vengeance must be taken (50:28; 51:11). This would give a date for the verse subsequent to 586 B.C. But such a date is not required, even though the possibility cannot be ruled out. Jones compares the present indignity to later Temple profanations occurring in the second century B.C. by Antiochus Epiphanes (2 Macc 5:15–21), and in the first century B.C. by Pompey (*Pss. Sol.* 1:8–2:1–3; 7:2; 8:12–13; cf. *OTP II*: 640–41; *APOT II*: 629), neither of which was a destruction. But Nebuchadnezzar (or his army) entered the Temple and made off with some of its treasures in 597 B.C. (2 Kgs 24:13; 2 Chr 36:7, 10), which could be the profanation alluded to here.

MESSAGE AND AUDIENCE

Yahweh in the present oracle says that in future days he will reckon with Babylon's images. Indeed, the whole land will be shamed, and all of Babylon's slain will fall within the city. None will escape. The whole of creation will then break forth into song, as devastators from the proverbial north come and do their work. In anticipation of this event, the covenant people then add their own sure word that Babylon will fall, addressing it to those of their own number who fell to the Babylonians. If all creation can sing, so can the covenant people make a climactic shout. The slain of Israel, in any case, are given the good news that Babylon will fall, just as they and many, many others fell to Babylon in earlier times. A Judahite audience will view it as retributive justice.

Jeremiah then picks up the discourse, turning to the here and now. First he addresses those who survived Nebuchadnezzar's attack on Jerusalem and are singled out for exile. They are survivors to be sure; nevertheless, they stand in shock at the prospect of taking the long walk to Babylon. Jeremiah tells them to go, and not just stand there. When they get to Babylon they are to remember Yahweh and the beloved Jerusalem. Jeremiah then speaks more somberly for himself and everyone else when he says that all have been shamed by taunts from the enemy. What is more, strangers came into Yahweh's temple. What they did to profane the holy places the audience is left to ponder.

The introduction addresses a dispirited Judahite remnant now in a foreign land. These souls, however, are told not to lose courage even though rumors of war circulate from one year to the next, with violence again rife, and ruler fighting against ruler. But now just when things seem to be getting worse and worse, the frightened exiles are told to remember a word of judgment spoken by Jeremiah against Babylon. Yahweh will visit this once-dreaded nation with its empty idols and render a just punishment, and a joyful creation will then celebrate a fall for which it has long waited.

When the present oracle is heard in tandem with the oracle preceding, a connection will be made back to the monster Bel (v 44), who is now one of many Babylonian idols that Yahweh will punish. Jeremiah's word to Jerusalem's survivors to get on the road to exile (v 50a) will also connect to the word being readied for exiles to leave Babylon when Yahweh vents holy anger on that nation (v 45).

The oracle portion of this dialogue can be dated along with other Babylon oracles to the period prior to 594 B.C. The same goes for the climactic shout of v 49. If profanation of the Temple does not include its destruction, then the word from Jeremiah can also be dated just after Nebuchadnezzar's capture of Jerusalem in 597 B.C. But if the Temple's profanation includes its actual destruction, then the Jeremiah word must be given a date after 586 B.C. The prose introduction to the oracle requires a date after Nebuchadnezzar's death in 562 B.C.

26. Look Again! A Reckoning for Babylon and Its Images (51:52–57)

51 ^{52}Look, hereafter, days are coming
   —oracle of Yahweh—
when I will reckon with her images
   and in all her land the slain shall groan

[53]If Babylon should climb to the sky
    and if she should make inaccessible her fortified height
From me devastators shall come to her
    —oracle of Yahweh.

[54]The sound of a cry from Babylon
    and a great shatter from the land of the Chaldeans
[55]For Yahweh is devastating Babylon
    and killing in her a great sound

Yes, their waves roar like many waters
    their crashing sound is uttered
[56]For it has come upon her
    upon Babylon—the devastator!

And her warriors have been taken
    their bows shattered
For a God of requital is Yahweh
    he will surely repay.

[57]And I will make drunk her princes and her wise men, her governors and
her commanders, and her warriors. And they shall sleep an eternal sleep,
and not waken—oracle of the King, Yahweh of hosts is his name!

RHETORIC AND COMPOSITION

MT 51:52–57 = LXX 28:52–57. The present verses contain an oracle (or oracles)
in poetry from Yahweh (vv 52–53), a balancing word in poetry from Jeremiah
(vv 54–56), and another oracle in prose from Yahweh (v 57). Verses 52–53 have a
messenger formula each, which could point to two separate oracles (as in 51:25–
26); otherwise a single oracle with two formulas, one at the beginning and one at
the end. Since we are near the end of a collection in which smaller units are often combined, a group of multiple oracles is here a distinct possibility. Yet, the
comparable oracle in vv 47–48 has just one formula at the end, which leads one
to believe that the present verses are also just one oracle. For similarities between
the oracle here, assuming there is just one, and the oracle in vv 47–48, see Rhetoric and Composition for 51:46–49. The oracle here and Jeremiah's word following combine to create a dialogue, like the dialogue in the whole of vv 47–51.
    The prose oracle in v 57 contains terminology from the surrounding poetry,
viz., 50:35 ("her princes and . . . her wise men"), 51:23 and 28 ("[her] governors and [all her] commanders"), and 51:39 ("they shall sleep an eternal sleep,
and not waken"), which has led some commentators (Duhm, Volz, Rudolph,
Holladay) to take the verse as a pastiche supplementing what precedes. This is
unnecessary. The verse is an oracle in its own right with a climactic messenger
formula at the end.

The larger unit is delimited at the top end by a *setumah* in M^L and a *petuḥah* in M^A before v 52. At the bottom end delimitation is made on the basis of the climactic "oracle of the King, Yahweh of hosts is his name!" in v 57, after which comes a *setumah* in M^L, M^A, and M^P. A break between the opening oracle and the prophet's own word is marked by a closing messenger formula at the end of v 53, after which comes a *setumah* in M^L, M^A, and M^P.

The oracle (vv 52–53) has two stanzas with these repetitions and balancing key words:

I	. . . . *are coming*	*bā'îm*	v 52
	. . . . *her land*	*'arṣāh*	
II	. . . . *the sky*	*haššāmayim*	v 53
	. . . . *shall come*	*yābō'û*	

Jeremiah's word (vv 54–56) comprises three stanzas with these repetitions and balancing key words:

I	*The sound* . . . . *from Babylon*	*qôl* . . .	v 54
	a great . . . *from the land of the Chaldeans*	. . . *gādôl* . . .	
	For Yahweh is devastating Babylon	*kî šōdēd* . . .	v 55
	. . . . *great sound*	. . . *qôl gādôl*	
II	. . . .		
	their sound	*qôlām*	
	For . . . . *upon her*	*kî* . . .	v 56
	upon Babylon—the devastator!	. . . *šôdēd*	
III	. . . .		
	. . . .		
	For . . . . *Yahweh*	*kî* . . .	
	. . . .		

While the majority of repetitions are in Stanzas I and II, all three stanzas begin their final line with *kî* ("For"). In the preceding oracle is also a double occurrence of *kî* (v 53a).

The concluding prose oracle (v 57) is structured by complementary verbs of punishment and death that frame an enumeration of victims in the center:

And I will make drunk
  her princes and her wise men
  her governors and her commanders
  and her warriors
And they shall sleep an eternal sleep, and not waken

Stanza III of Jeremiah's word provides this key word linkage to the prose oracle:

gibbôreyhâ	*her warriors*	v 56b
gibbôreyhâ	*her warriors*	v 57

Catchwords connecting to the unit preceding:

		v 46	*in the land . . . in the land*
			comes
v 52	*Look, hereafter, days are coming . . .*	v 47	*Look, hereafter, days are coming*
	when I will reckon with		*when I will reckon with*
	her images		*the images of Babylon*
	and in all her land		*And all her land*
	the slain		*her slain*
v 53	*Babylon*	v 48	*Babylon*
	the sky		*sky and land*
	they shall come		*they shall come*
	devastators		*the devastators*
v 54–55	*Babylon* (2×)	v 49	*Babylon* (2×)
v 55	*is devastating*		*slain . . . slain*
v 56	*it has come*		*all the land*
	Babylon	v 51	*have come*
	the devastator		

Catchwords connecting to the oracle following:

v 53–56	*Babylon* (4×)	v 58	*Yahweh of hosts*
v 57	*Yahweh of hosts*		*Babylon*

A grand key word inclusio ties together the entire Babylon collection, a portion of which builds on repeated verbs in 50:2bc and 51:56b (see Rhetoric and Composition for 50:1–3).

NOTES

51:52. See exegesis for 51:47.

Look, hereafter, days are coming. The *lākēn* in this stereotyped opening takes on the meaning of "therefore" when the oracle becomes a divine answer to the people's lament in v 51. When the oracle was self-standing, *lākēn* meant simply "hereafter," indicating that the promised judgment would take place in later days (see Notes on 7:32 and 16:14). Calvin, who reads the text sequentially, says that the people are confounded, but God now gives them reason to glorify him and hope for the future. Compare the exhortation in v 46 and the discussion there of community despair and divine promise.

her images. In v 47 it is "the images of Babylon."

the slain shall groan. I.e., those pierced (by the sword) who are dying (Rashi; Kimḥi). See the discussion on *ḥălālîm* in Note for 51:4. In v 47 the expression is the more usual "her slain shall fall" (cf. 51:4, 49; Ezek 28:23). The Versions avoid a possible problem of fallen dead said to be heard still groaning (LXX: *pesountai traumatiai*, "the wounded shall fall"; T: "the slain shall be cast out"). Here the groans of Babylon's fallen may anticipate the sounds heard coming out of Babylon in vv 54–55a. Compare Ezek 26:15, where a groaning of Tyre's "slain" is predicted.

53. *If Babylon should climb to the sky, and if she should make inaccessible her fortified height.* The line is different from v 48a. There land and sky sing together over Babylon's fall; here Babylon has climbed to the sky and made inaccessible her fortified height. In the OT, nations metaphorically and individuals literally ascend high places to escape their enemies, or else to fulfill ambitious desires; the two often occur simultaneously (cf. Amos 9:2; Isa 14:12–15; Jer 49:16; Obad 3; Hab 2:9). Both are present here: an expression of national ambition, and a desire for protection from the enemy (cf. Gen 11:4). The metaphor of the first colon is clarified by a nonmetaphorical equivalent in the second, which is a common rhetorical construction in Jeremiah poetry (see Note on 3:3). Here, as elsewhere, the T to avoid a metaphor translates the line, "Even though Babylon should build buildings which are as high as the top of heaven, and though she should fortify strong fortified cities up to the height . . ." (Hayward 1987: 188).

climb to the sky. Or "ascend to the heavens." Hebrew *taʿăleh . . . haššāmayim* See Amos 9:2.

make inaccessible her fortified height. Hebrew *tĕbaṣṣēr mĕrôm ʿuzzāh.* Commentators generally interpret here along the lines of the T paraphrase, taking "fortified height" to refer to Babylon's celebrated buildings, whether temples, palace buildings, defense towers, or the city's massive walls. Babylon's "strong / fortified height" cannot be a mountain stronghold like the one occupied by the Edomites (49:16), since the city lies on a plain. KB[3] and BDB take *mĕrôm* to mean "mountain top," which can only have metaphorical meaning and is possible (cf. 51:25). The verb *bṣr* in the Piel means "make inaccessible, fortify," referring here to Babylon's making massive its city walls. The meaning then is that Babylon rests secure in lofty buildings protected by huge walls. These walls are cited by classical writers, and their remains have been seen more recently by excavators of the site (see Note for 51:58).

From me devastators shall come to her. In v 48 the "devastators" come from the proverbial north; here they come from Yahweh, and emphatically so (Heb *mēʾttî,* "from [with] me," begins the line in the Hebrew). Rashi sees here a play on height. From Yahweh—i.e., from a heavens higher than the heavens into which proud Babylon has climbed with its lofty temples, palace buildings, and defense towers—will come the judgment. An echo, certainly, of the Tower of Babel story (Gen 11:1–8), where Rashi notes how the descending judgment of Yahweh deliberately imitates the ascending hubris of humankind (cf. Lundbom 1983: 205).

54. *The sound of a cry from Babylon, and a great shatter from the land of the Chaldeans.* The prophet follows now with a report of loud noises coming from Babylon—human cries, barking dogs, crashing buildings, and other sounds accompanying the destruction of a great city (cf. Isa 22:2, 5).

The sound of a cry. Hebrew *qôl zĕʿāqâ.* Similar expressions, *qôl ṣaʿăqat* and *qôl ṣĕʿāqâ,* occur in 25:36 and 48:3. Jeremianic poems often begin with *qôl,* "sound / voice" (see Note for 3:21).

a great shatter. Hebrew *šeber gādôl.* A common Jeremianic expression; see Note for 4:6.

the land of the Chaldeans. On Chaldea and the Chaldeans, see Note for 50:1.

55. *For Yahweh is devastating Babylon.* The reason for the loud noises (Calvin).

and killing in her a great sound. Hebrew *wĕʾibbad mimmennā qôl gādôl.* The verb *ʾbd* in the Piel means "cause to perish, kill" (cf. 15:7), and the prefixed *min* in *mimmennā* is read here as "in" (see Note for 20:17). While Yahweh is responsible for the current tumult in Babylon, he intends finally to become the great silencer of the city, much as he was with Jerusalem when he made cease the cries of children in the streets and happy talk of young men in the squares (9:20[Eng 9:21]), "the voice of joy and the voice of gladness, the voice of the groom and the voice of the bride," the sound of [grinding] millstones (7:34; 16:9; 25:10), and the lowing of cattle on Judah's hillsides (9:9[Eng 9:10]). Silencing city sounds is a curse. One of Esarhaddon's vassal-treaty curses (437–39; ANET³ 538) was that nurses would miss the cries of babies; see also Note on 25:10 for a Mesopotamian lament bewailing the loss of happy sounds in the city. Compare in the NT, Rev 18:21–23.

Yes, their waves roar like many waters, their crashing sound is uttered. The line is difficult, one problem being the lack of an antecedent for "their waves," the other being whether "their crashing sound" repeats and has the same referent as "the sound of a cry" in v 54 and "a great sound" in v 55a, both of which refer to the tumult in Babylon. The question then is whether the present image carries over from vv 54–55a, describing further a city in panic where buildings are crashing to the ground, or whether there is now a description of the enemy coming in waves to inundate Babylon. The latter view can also be deduced from the context, since v 55a speaks about Yahweh devastating Babylon, and v 55b could be repeating this, only with the difference that human agents are now doing the job. The LXX connects with what precedes, taking the "great voice sounding as many waters" (*phōnēn megalēn ēchousan hōs hydata polla*) to be Babylon's voice that Yahweh is cutting off. G°, Aq, and Symm interpret similarly with *ta kumata autēs,* "her waves," eliminating the antecedent problem (cf. AV; JB; NAB; Volz; Rudolph). Kimḥi, too, takes the crashing waves to refer to Babylon's noisy populace (cf. NJV). But T sees enemy troops in the metaphor ("and the troops of many nations shall be gathered against her, and they shall lift up their voice with roaring"), and along these lines most commentators since Calvin make their interpretation, assuming that foes are rolling in like mighty waves to inundate Babylon (NIV: "waves of enemies"). This is doubtless the correct view. In 6:23 Babylon's invasion of Judah is compared to a roaring sea, and more to the point, sea imagery has just been used in 51:42 to describe the enemy coming against Babylon. The lack of an antecedent for "their waves" is no problem, as pronouns in Hebrew often lack antecedents, e.g., in Jeremiah: 5:12; 8:16; 10:3; 11:4; 18:18; 46:5; and 49:19. "Their waves" then refer to waves of attacking foes. We speak even today about "waves" of advancing troops.

Yes, their waves roar like many waters. Hebrew *wĕhāmû gallêhem kĕmayim rabbîm.* Jeremiah refers to the low-pitched roaring of waves or the sea in 5:22; 6:23; 31:35; and 50:42. There is an irony here, as Babylon itself dwells by "many waters" (see Note on 51:13). The term may also have mythological overtones, i.e., "many waters" could have reference to the chaotic forces of the great subterranean ocean (May 1955; cf. Isa 17:12–13).

their crashing sound is uttered. Hebrew *nittan šĕ'ôn qôlām*, where *šĕ'ôn qôlām* is read as a construct chain: "their crashing sound" (Dimant 1973: 95). Here again is *qôl* ("sound") repeating from vv 54–55a, reinforcing the irony that one loud sound is drowning out another.

56. *For it has come upon her, upon Babylon—the devastator.* Again we see how Jeremiah's rhetoric moves from the figurative to the literal. This line states straightforwardly what the previous line conveyed by metaphor, viz., that a devastator has come upon Babylon (Calvin). The line then is not an MT plus (*pace* Rudolph; Holladay), for which there is no textual support. The repetition from v 55a is good poetry, creating also structure in the poem (see Rhetoric and Composition). The line achieves emphasis by the repetition, "upon her, upon Babylon," and by positioning "the devastator" at the end, where it becomes climactic. The LXX lacks *'āleyhā*, "upon her," which should not be taken as an MT plus or the result of a conflate text (*pace* Giesebrecht, Duhm, Volz; Condamin; Janzen 1973: 20; Holladay; McKane). The omission can be attributed to haplography (homoeoarcton: *'l . . . 'l*). The T has "upon her," and so also does the Vg. The LXX also contains "suffering" (*talaipōria* = Heb *šōd*) for "devastator" (*šôdēd*), which should be rejected as an inferior reading (*pace* Bright), as it does away with another repetition: *šōdēd* from v 55a. This too could be another loss due to haplography: *dd* reduced to *d*. The longer reading of MT is better, and should be retained.

And her warriors have been taken. I.e., captured (Heb *nilkĕdû*). Compare 46:5–6, 12; 51:30.

their bows shattered. Hebrew *hittĕtâ qaššĕtôtām.* The verb is an intransitive Piel, where we would normally expect a Pual (cf. GKC §52k). Both LXX and Vg have "their bow" singular, which is commonly explained as a feminine singular verb sometimes predicating a plural subject (GKC §145k). The T has "their bows" plural. D. N. Freedman suggests the possibility of haplography, where the scribe's eye skipped from the first *taw* to the second *taw*, leaving out *tw*. The result would then be "their bow" singular. Reading either a singular or a plural, the "bow(s)" are representative of Babylon's entire arsenal (synecdoche), as in 49:35 (Calvin; Holladay).

For a God of requital is Yahweh. Hebrew *kî 'ēl gĕmūlôt yhwh.* The term *gĕmūlôt* can mean "benefits" in a positive sense (Ps 103:2), but here the meaning is "requital, recompense." The point seems to be that it is Yahweh's very nature to seek compensation (Calvin; cf. Isa 59:18). In Jer 51:6 it says pointedly that Yahweh is repaying (*šlm*) Babylon a requital (*gĕmûl*).

he will surely repay. More than that, he will repay in full. Hebrew *šallēm yĕšallēm.* It is definitely in God's nature to repay evil and enmity toward him

(Deut 7:10; 32:35; Jer 32:18; Isa 59:18). This he will now do with Babylon (25:14; 50:29; 51:6, 24, 56). Yahweh repaid (in full) Judah (16:18), and he repays any nation acting with enmity toward him (Deut 32:41).

57. *And I will make drunk.* Hebrew *wĕhiškartî*. Reading the verb as a converted perfect (so T). The verb following is an imperfect. The LXX has an impersonal third person: "and he will make drink a strong drink" (*kai methysei methē*). In either case, Babylon will drink Yahweh's cup of wrath, which is the repayment (25:14–29; 51:39).

her princes and her wise men, her governors and her commanders, and her warriors. This rhetoric of *accumulatio* occurs often in the prose and poetry of Jeremiah (1:18; 5:15–17; 50:35–38; and 51:20–23; §Introduction: Rhetoric and Preaching: Accumulation). The LXX has only three of the five terms (*tous hēgemonas autēs kai tous sophous autēs kai tous stratēgous autēs,* "her leaders, and her wise men, and her commanders"), appearing to omit "her governors" (Heb *paḥôteyhā*), also "and her warriors" (Heb *wĕgibbôreyhā*). The loss of both can be attributed to haplography (the first term by homoeoteleuton: *yh . . . yh*; the second by either homoeoarcton: *w . . . w,* or homoeoteleuton: *yh . . . yh*). The T has all five terms, and both Aq and Symm supply *kai tous apchontas (autēs),* "and (her) rulers." "Governors and commanders" are Akkadian loanwords, occurring elsewhere in the Babylon oracles as a fixed pair (see Note for 51:23).

And they shall sleep an eternal sleep, and not waken. The LXX omits, but the phrase is present in Aq and Theod. Sleep normally follows drunkenness, but here those drinking Yahweh's cup will not waken. The phrase recurs in the poetry of v 39. The T reads: "and they shall die the second death and not live for the world to come."

oracle of the King, Yahweh of hosts is his name. The LXX includes (see Appendix VI). This embellished messenger formula celebrates Yahweh as King (cf. 46:18 and 48:15). The confessional, "Yahweh of hosts is his name," occurs numerous times in Jeremiah (see Note on 10:16).

MESSAGE AND AUDIENCE

In the opening oracle, which is spoken to a Jerusalem audience, Yahweh says again that he will reckon at some unspecified time with some unspecified images, and throughout the land where they exist groans will be heard from the dying. Babylon is now mentioned, and Yahweh says should this city of grand aspiration climb into the sky, which it has, and protect all its buildings of great height from him whose dwelling is higher, which it has, devastators shall come upon her. Will a Jerusalem audience and audiences in surrounding areas hearing this judgment give any thought to what Yahweh might also do about idol worship in Jerusalem and throughout Judah?

Jeremiah follows with a description of the havoc these devastators will wreak. Ominous sounds are coming from Babylon—anguished cries, calls for help, the collapse of buildings, the howl of frightened animals, and crackling sounds of fires burning out of control. Yahweh is devastating Babylon, and in the end an eerie silence will envelop the city. But the silence is not yet. Enveloping the city now is a chaos of cosmic proportions: waves of the enemy roar in, breaking with a deafening crash. Jeremiah repeats what has now become a virtual refrain in Yahweh's word and his own: "Upon her, upon Babylon, has come the devastator!" Warriors have been captured, their bows shattered, and other weapons rendered useless. Jeremiah closes by saying that Yahweh is a God of recompense, and will surely repay. Repayment will come to Babylon. Will it also come to Jerusalem?

In the oracle that follows, Yahweh declares his intention to make drunk Babylon's princes, wise men, governors, commanders, and fighting men. They will drink his cup of wrath and not awaken as drunkards ordinarily do. These hapless souls will sleep an eternal sleep. The oracle ends by identifying its speaker as the King, whose name is Yahweh of hosts.

When the opening oracle, the word from Jeremiah, and second oracle are heard sequentially, the word from Jeremiah describing Babylon's destruction will come as an explication of what was stated summarily in the oracle. The final oracle makes a connection between Jeremiah's concluding word about Yahweh repaying enemies (v 56c), and Yahweh's resolve to give Babylon his cup of wrath, which will cause drunkenness and finally death. This oracle then gives substance to Yahweh's repayment, which is spelled out in 25:14–29.

When the first oracle is heard in tandem with what precedes, its judgment will come as a confirming word to what the languishing souls are saying in v 51. The "hereafter" beginning v 52 will then become "therefore." This dynamic of human cry and divine answer is similar to what is created in the previous unit, when v 46 is made the introduction to a parallel oracle in vv 47–48.

The two oracles and Jeremiah's intervening word can all be dated prior to 594 B.C.—singly, and in combination. We need not assume with Calvin that the Temple has already been destroyed. It is possible that some or all of the material was composed post-586 B.C., but none of it need be.

27. The Walls of Grand Babylon Demolished! (51:58)

51 ⁵⁸Thus said Yahweh of hosts:
The walls of grand Babylon
   shall be totally demolished!
And her high gates
   with fire they shall burn

So peoples labor for nothing
and nations for fire, so they tire themselves.

RHETORIC AND COMPOSITION

MT 51:58 = LXX 28:58. The present oracle is delimited in M^L, M^A, and M^P by *setumahs* before and after v 58. The oracle is poetry, presently two stanzas with a final bicolon that may be an add-on (cf. Hab 2:13). The two stanzas have this balancing repetition:

I	*with fire*	*bā'ēš*	v 58b
II	. . . . *for fire* . . .	*bĕdê-'ēš*	v 58c

This oracle concludes the Babylon collection, and in MT the entire Foreign Nation Collection. In MT it hearkens back to a divine word in chap. 1 concerning the fate of Jerusalem, the two verses making an inclusio for a book of 51 chapters. The key words forming the inclusio are "gates" and "walls," which in typical fashion are inverted the second time they appear:

> 1:15 Yahweh says: A foe shall come against *Jerusalem's gates and walls*
> *ša'ărê yĕrûšālayim . . . ḥômōteyhā*
> 51:58 Yahweh says: [A foe] shall demolish *Babylon's walls and gates*
> *ḥômôt bābel . . . ûšĕ'āreyhâ*

In the collection of Babylon oracles, which is of considerable length, it should be noted that the judgment against Babylon is unmitigated—no word of restoration, no talk of a remnant, not even a hint that the sword might cease its bloody rampage before everyone is killed. Egypt, Moab, Ammon, and Elam are all given a final word of restoration (46:26; 48:47; 49:6, 39); Yahweh promises Edom that its orphans and widows will be kept alive (49:11); one lone individual survives to lament the fallen Damascus (49:25); the inhabitants of Kedar are told to flee for their lives (49:30); and in the case of the Philistines, there is uncertainty over how long it will be until Yahweh's sword is silent (47:6–7); but Babylon is given no hope, no grace, no future. Commands to flee its destruction are given only to Jewish exiles and other expatriates, not to the Babylonians (50:8, 28; 51:6, 9, 45). Salvation, too, is reserved exclusively for the remnant of Israel (50:4–5, 18–20, 33–34; 51:5, 10, 50). The suggestion that Babylon might possibly be healed in 51:8 is full-blown irony, as the next verse makes clear. Even the ancient Mesopotamian city laments contain concluding words about restoration and a return of the gods (Dobbs-Allsopp 1993: 92–94), making it all the more remarkable that some mitigating word for Babylon is not present in these oracles.

Catchwords connecting to the unit preceding:

v 58	*Yahweh of hosts*	vv 53–56 *Babylon* (4×)
	Babylon	v 57 *Yahweh of hosts*

Catchwords connecting to the colophon following:

v 58	*so they tire themselves* *wĕyā'ēpû*	v 64 *so they tire themselves* *wĕyā'ēpû*

NOTES

51:58. *Yahweh of hosts*. The LXX omits "of hosts" as elsewhere; see Appendix VI.

The walls of grand Babylon shall be totally demolished! And her high gates with fire shall be burned. Again the imagined destruction of Babylon is Jeremiah's projection of Jerusalem's anticipated destruction. When Cyrus took Babylon in 539 B.C., he did not demolish the city walls or burn its high gates with fire (see Note on 50:15).

The walls of grand Babylon shall be totally demolished. Hebrew *ḥōmôt bābel hārĕḥābâ arʿēr titʿarʿār*. The MT pointing of *ḥmwt* (*ḥōmôt* = "walls") follows T, which reads "the walls of broad Babylon" (cf. 50:15). The feminine singular *hārĕḥābâ* ("the broad, spacious") is taken here as an adjective modifying "Babylon," which is the better reading. Many MSS have the singular construct, *ḥōmat* ("wall"), which appears also to lie behind the readings of LXX and Vg (cf. v 44). The double construct chain then translates: "the broad wall of Babylon." Modern Versions divide, some reading "the broad wall" (RSV; NJV; NIV; NRSV; NSB), others reading "broad Babylon," or the like (NEB; NAB; REB; NJB). Most commentators opt for "the broad wall," with Volz getting a singular meaning for *ḥōmôt* by taking it as an intensive plural, as in 1:18 (cf. GKC §124e). Its meaning is then "a thick wall." As for the singular predicate following, feminine singular verbs can have plural subjects (GKC §145k). Other examples of this in Jeremiah occur in 4:14b; 48:41; and 51:56. Either reading is then possible, with nothing really at stake other than our knowing the precise meaning of the Hebrew. Both portrayals—Babylon as a grand city, and Babylon as a city of broad walls—correspond to tradition and the facts as we know them. Babylon's wall(s) will in any case be completely brought down.

The walls. Babylon had an inner and outer wall, both of which were very large. Rich clay was a natural resource of the area, so wall construction was of brick, not stone as in Palestine. The Babylonians did not even have the soft limestone available farther north in Assyria, which builders there used to line their mud brick. Babylon's inner wall, which predates the Neo-Babylonian period, was made of crude mud brick. Nebuchadnezzar built a new outer city wall of kiln-burnt brick, digging clay from outside the wall and then filling the trench with water to make a protective moat (Herodotus i 179; for a picture of its reconstruction, see *IDB* A–D, 336). Bitumen, another natural resource, was heated and used for mortar (cf. Gen 11:3). Nebuchadnezzar's palace walls and the famous Ishtar Gate were also of burnt brick, enameled in brilliant blue, and decorated with animals in white and yellow. This outer wall with its reported 250 towers was massive. Strabo (*Geog* xvi 1.5) says it was wide enough that four-horse chariots could pass one another. He puts its height at 50 cubits, and the height of the towers at 60 cubits, which are 75 and 90 feet respectively (a cubit = ca. 18 inches). Herodotus (i 178) exaggerates the height to over 300 feet! Excavations have shown the outer wall to be about seven meters in thickness. The inner wall was about the same thickness. Both walls with rubble in between formed an elevated roadway nearly 20 meters wide (L. W. King 1919: 25–26). Inside the city and also outside were other walls, e.g., a wall 20+ meters wide in the bed of the Euphrates, and a high wall surrounding the grand palace. On Babylon's walls and towers, see L. W. King 1919: 19–46;

Lane 1923: 177–95; and T. Jacobsen, "Babylon (OT)" in *IDB* A–D, 335–37. For the conversion of cubits to feet, also meters to feet and feet to meters, see Appendix IV.

grand Babylon. Herodotus (i 178) says the city was square, its distance around the outer wall being 480 stadia (ca. 55 miles). Strabo (*Geog* xvi 1.5) puts the circumference somewhat less, at 385 stadia (ca. 48 miles), and Diodorus (ii 7.3) at 360 stadia (ca. 42.5 miles). Excavation of the outer wall east of the Euphrates, and an estimated equal portion of the city west of the Euphrates, of which there is now no trace, suggests a distance around the city of about 11 miles (L. W. King 1919: 24). By comparison, the distance around the present-day walled city of Old Jerusalem is only about 2.5 miles. Oppenheim (1964: 140–41) says that in the Chaldean period Babylon was a huge city of 2500 acres. Jacobsen (*IDB* A–D, 335) puts the area of a smaller, rectangular Babylon, with a western portion half the size of its eastern portion, at about 1000 acres. Nebuchadnezzar's Babylon was nevertheless grand; see further Note for 50:1. For the conversion of miles to kilometers, see Appendix IV.

shall be totally demolished. More intensification. Babylon's walls will lie flat on the ground. Hebrew *'ar'ēr tit'ar'ār* is lit. "shall be utterly laid bare." The infinitive is a Pilpel from *'rr* ("to strip, lay bare"), the imperfect verb a Hithpalpel from the same root (BDB; KB³).

And her high gates. A reckoning of 100 gates in Babylon by Herodotus (i 179) is perhaps excessive; nevertheless, there were multiple gates into the city and within the city. Most important was the imposing and finely decorated Ishtar Gate, Babylon's main entrance on the northeast corner (L. W. King 1919: 51–60). It was a double gateway, flanked by massive twin towers, with an arched opening perhaps 30 feet in height (Jacobsen, *IDB* A–D, 336). For museum reconstructions of the Ishtar Gate and pictures, see Notes on 2:15 and 50:1.

with fire they shall burn. The LXX omits "with fire"; the NJV adds it at the end of v 64.

So peoples labor for nothing, and nations for fire, so they tire themselves. The line is repeated with minor alterations in Hab 2:13, where "they tire themselves" (*yi'āpû* without the initial *waw*) makes better parallelism. In both contexts the line is a syntactic chiasmus with verbs at the extremes. Here *wĕyā'ēpû* ("so they tire themselves") corresponds to the same verb (with *waw*) in v 64, where the two appear to be catchwords linking the oracle to Seraiah's colophon (see Rhetoric and Composition). Duplication of the line in Habakkuk and Jeremiah suggests that this may be a quotation from elsewhere (Graf; Andersen 2001: 245). If it is an old proverb (Streane; Boadt), which seems likely, the verbs (alternating imperfect and perfect forms) are better translated present tense (RSV; JB; NAB; NIV). The T translates future tense, Calvin past tense. It is a truism that people labor for nought in building grand cities with massive walls and high gates when, in the end, an enemy comes and burns them. Compare 3:24. The LXX misses the point entirely, reading: "and peoples shall not grow weary in vain, nor nations in [their] dominion cease."

for nothing. Hebrew *bĕdê-rîq*. Or "for no purpose."

nations. Hebrew *lĕ'ummîm* is an archaic parallel to *gôyim* (KB³ quoting Albright; Isa 34:1).

MESSAGE AND AUDIENCE

In this closing oracle of the Babylonian collection, Yahweh says that the walls of grand Babylon shall be brought to the ground, her high gates burned with fire. A climactic and finishing word for Nebuchadnezzar, whose military exploits abroad were exceeded only by his ambitious building program at home. A reflective word follows. What good is such a vast outlay of human energy when in the end an enemy puts it all to the torch? The sweat and ruined human bodies have been for nought.

A Jerusalem audience prior to 594 B.C. will give such a prophecy a nervous welcome. It is all well and good to hear about Nebuchadnezzar's celebrated city being reduced to rubble, but what about Jerusalem? Could the same happen here with Nebuchadnezzar directing the demolition? These people know what happened three years ago. For a later post-586 B.C. audience hearing a near-complete (51 chapters of the) Jeremiah book, the connection between Jerusalem and Babyon has become explicit, with Jerusalem's destruction now a matter of record. The closing oracle about judgment on Babylon's walls and gates will for them hearken back to Yahweh's earlier word about a foe coming against the walls and gates of Jerusalem. At this point Babylon is perceived as getting the punishment it deserves.

When this oracle is heard following the oracle in vv 52–53, grand Babylon with its huge walls and lofty gates will aid in clarifying the "fortified height" of v 53.

K. SERIAH'S COLOPHON (51:59–64)

51 ⁵⁹The word that Jeremiah the prophet commanded Seraiah son of Neriah, son of Mahseiah, when he went with Zedekiah, king of Judah, to Babylon in the fourth year of his reign. Now Seraiah was caravan prince. ⁶⁰And Jeremiah wrote all the evil that would come to Babylon in one scroll, all these words that are written toward Babylon. ⁶¹And Jeremiah said to Seraiah: 'When you come to Babylon, then you shall see to it that you read aloud all these words.
⁶²And you shall say:

> Yahweh, you, yourself have spoken toward this place, to cut it off without there being an inhabitant in it, from human to beast; indeed eternal desolations it shall be.

⁶³And when you have finished reading this scroll aloud, you shall tie a stone to it, and you shall throw it into the middle of the Euphrates. ⁶⁴Then you shall say:

> Even so shall Babylon sink and not rise, because of the evil that I am bringing upon it.'

so they tire themselves

Thus far the legacy of Jeremiah.

RHETORIC AND COMPOSITION

MT 51:59–64 = LXX 28:59–64. The present verses are delimited at the top end by a *setumah* in M^L, M^A, and M^P before v 59. At the bottom end is a *setumah* in M^L and M^P, and a *petuḥah* in M^A, after v 64. In v 59 is also a shift from poetry to prose, and after v 64 is the chapter division. Content, too, virtually assures the verses' independence, as does a rhetorical structure in the narrative between the superscription and subscription. The inner narrative contains this inclusio:

> Jeremiah wrote *all the evil that would come (tābô᾽) toward Babylon*   v 60
> . . . because of *the evil that I am bringing (mēbî᾽) upon it*   v 64

Compare the inclusio holding together Huldah's oracles in 2 Kgs 22:16–20 (§Introduction: The Method of Rhetorical Criticism: Discerning the Structure).

The verses are familiar Jeremianic prose not requiring the label of a "symbolic act" genre (*pace* K. W. Schmidt 1982: 213), even though a symbolic act is being reported. Based both on location and content, the verses show themselves to be a colophon, or more precisely an expanded colophon, which belongs generically with the expanded colophons similarly written in 36:1–8 and chap. 45 (Lundbom 1986b). Those in 36:1–8 and 45 name Baruch ben Neriah as the scribe of record (cf. 36:26, 32); the present colophon names Seraiah ben Neriah, who is Baruch's brother, as the scribe of record. Both individuals belong to the scribal family of Mahseiah (32:12; 51:59).

Evaluated according to the colophon criteria set forth by Leichty in his important study of ancient colophons (1964), the present colophon is seen to contain the following elements:

1. name of the scribe (with double patronym) making the copy: "Seraiah son of Neriah, son of Mahseiah"
2. date: the fourth year of Zedekiah
3. the source for the copy: "all these words that are written [by Jeremiah] toward Babylon" (= 50:1–51:58)
4. reason for making the copy: a public reading in Babylon
5. the disposition of the text: "the middle of the Euphrates"
6. the curse: "Even so shall Babylon sink and not rise, because of the evil that I am bringing upon it"
7. the catch-line: "so they tire themselves" (vv 58, 64).

It is not said that Seraiah copied the Jeremiah scroll, but we can assume he did and that it was this copy he took to Babylon, read aloud upon arrival, and sank in the Euphrates. The original, after all, has survived for our reading. Earlier I identified in this colophon six of the ten Leichty criteria (Lundbom 1986b), not recognizing "so they tire themselves" as a catch-line. Catch-lines occur commonly in extrabiblical texts, where the last line of one tablet is written also as the first line on the next (§Introduction: Rhetoric and Composition: Catch-words). Now we see that seven of the Leichty criteria are met, making even more reasonable the claim that this prose was indeed meant to function as a colophon. In addition, we note the obvious but nevertheless important fact that location in both the MT and LXX is at the end of the Babylon collection, and in the MT at the end of a once-complete book of Jeremiah (chaps. 1–51), another indication that we have here a bona fide scribal colophon.

If we compare key events, related happenings, and other details associated with the dates in the colophons of 36:1–8 and chap. 45, i.e., the fourth year of Jehoiakim (605 B.C.), to key events, related happenings, and other details associated with the date in the colophon of 51:59–64, i.e., the fourth year of Zedekiah (594/3 B.C.), some striking parallels emerge:

605	594/3
1. Political unrest on the international scene (war at Carchemish)	1. Political unrest on the international scene (rebellion in Babylon)
2. Decision is made to prepare a scroll of Jeremiah's Judah prophecies	2. Decision is made to prepare a scroll of Jeremiah's Babylon prophecies
3. A member of a scribal family writes a scroll from the prophet's dictation, viz., Baruch ben Neriah	3. A member of a scribal family copies a scroll written by him or by the prophet, viz., Seraiah ben Neriah
4. This scribe (Baruch) later makes a public reading of the scroll	4. This scribe (Seraiah) later makes a public reading of the scroll
5. After the reading, the scroll is not deposited in the Temple, but rather burned in the fire	5. After the reading, the scroll is not deposited in the Temple, but rather sunk in the Euphrates
6. Jeremiah disappears from public view for a time	6. Jeremiah disappears from public view for a time

The authenticity of these verses we are here calling a colophon have been much discussed, largely because of their relationship to oracles and other utterances in chaps. 50–51 that many judge to be inauthentic (see Rhetoric and Composition for 46:1). Duhm, Volz, and McKane, for example, take the verses as late midrash. McKane cannot ascribe them to Jeremiah because, in prophesying doom for Babylon, they conflict with passages such as chap. 29, where submission to Nebuchadnezzar is advocated and the exiles in Babylon are advised to settle in for a long stay. But other scholars believe that the passage as a whole inspires confidence, featuring as it does Seraiah, brother of Baruch, and reporting an otherwise credible embassy going to Babylon in 594/3 B.C. (Peake; Cornill; Streane; Rudolph; Bright; Holladay; Zimmerli 1995: 428). The problematic line is said only to be "all these words that are written toward Babylon" in v 60b, which is taken as an add-on, its purpose being to associate at a later time Seraiah's embassy with the oracle(s) in chaps. 50–51 (Budde 1878: 551–52; 1906: 20–21). Originally, so the argument goes, the judgment against Babylon was brief and consisted only of what was written on a piece of papyrus that Seraiah carried with him (Budde: v 62). Bright therefore translates *sēper* in 60a as "sheet," not "scroll," placing also the present verses with those containing Jeremiah's letters to the exiles (chap. 29). Holladay, however, keeps these verses together with 50:1–51:58, assuming also a scroll of genuine material from the Babylonian collection. With the Babylon oracles now seen as emanating largely from Jeremiah, this is the more reasonable view. And if the present verses are a colophon, then a scroll must have existed to which this colophon was attached. That scroll would have to be the collected utterances in chaps. 50–51, or "all these words" referred to in vv 60 and 61.

The colophons in chap. 45 and here in 51:59–64 are similar in form, content, and function. Budde (1878: 553) called them "Zwillingsbruder," and more recently the two have been compared by Wanke (1971: 140–43) and others. The former concludes a Jeremiah book roughly equivalent to our 51 chapters that Baruch presumably completed in Egypt. This book, to which chap. 52 was later added, became the prototype of the LXX. The present colophon concludes a corresponding book of roughly 51 chapters that ended up in Babylon, presumably completed by Seraiah. This book, to which chap. 52 was later added, became the prototype of the MT. Here the Foreign Nation Oracles were relocated to the end (chaps. 46–51), with the Babylon oracles appropriately placed last (Lundbom 1986b: 108–9). Baruch's composition was otherwise left intact, his colophon now immediately preceding the Foreign Nation Collection in chap. 45. Gosse (1986) has argued plausibly that the earlier (LXX) version puts the accent on the curses spoken against Jerusalem, while the later (MT) version puts the accent on the curses spoken against Babylon. For more discussion on Seraiah's compilation of chaps. 1–51, see Rhetoric and Composition for 1:1–3.

The final words of the colophon make an inclusio in MT with the opening words of the book (Lundbom 1975: 25–27 [= 1997: 39–41]; 1986b: 101–4):

| 51:64 (MT) | . . . the legacy of Jeremiah | . . . *dibrê yirmĕyāhû* |
| 1:1 | The legacy of Jeremiah . . . | *dibrê yirmĕyāhû* . . . |

This subscript is lacking in the LXX, which can be explained if Seraiah is the one who added it after relocating the Foreign Nation Oracles (with his colophon) to the end of his book. The subscript also excludes chap. 52 from the prophetic book of Jeremiah per se, which might otherwise be concluded from the fact that chap. 52 largely repeats 2 Kgs 24:18–25:34. Some commentators (Rudolph; Bright; Carroll) suggest that originally this subscript came at the end of v 58, which is not impossible, particularly in light of a similar subscript concluding the Moab oracles in 48:47. But this proposal is not compelling. Carroll thinks that its position at the end of v 64 indicates that Jeremiah stopped speaking in the fourth year of Zedekiah, which is not at all implied. Calvin correctly states that the subscript need not apply only to the Babylon oracles, but to all Jeremiah's prophecies written thus far. There is also a grand inclusio tying together the entire Babylon collection, a portion of which is created by repeated key words in 50:3 and 51:62 (see Rhetoric and Composition for 50:1–3).

The two commands in the colophon show that an element of drama is being introduced into the river bank performance. Seraiah will address two different audiences:

Seraiah is to address Yahweh	v 62
Seraiah is to address a Babylonian audience	v 64

Some believe that the Babylonian audience will comprise Jewish exiles (Amesz 1997; Friebel 1999: 157–58); others say that any doom pronounced on Babylon would have to be spoken secretly (Peake; Bright), or else before no audience at all (Calvin; Rabinowitz 1966: 323). Rabinowitz says it is important only that the word get out to unleash its power in the world, not that it be communicated to an audience. Seraiah, in his view, may simply apostrophize.

Seraiah's curse on Babylon does not have an accompanying messenger formula, which is noteworthy since it concludes with Yahweh speaking in the first person ("because of the evil that I am bringing upon it"). Also, other occurrences of the *kākâ* ("even so") form in the book, 13:9; 19:11; and 28:11, all begin divine oracles that have messenger formulas. The absence here of a messenger formula could be attributed to Seraiah's lack of prophetic standing.

Catchwords connecting to the oracle preceding:

v 64 *so they tire themselves*   *wĕyā'ēpû*   v 58 *so they tire themselves*   *wĕyā'ēpû*

NOTES

51:59. *The word that Jeremiah the prophet commanded Seraiah.* A formula similar to the one in 45:1, only there the verb is "spoke to" (*dbr 'el*); here it is "commanded" (*ṣwh*). Keown et al. (p. 372) state incorrectly that nowhere else in the book does Jeremiah "command." But in a passage very similar to the present one, Jeremiah "commands" (*ṣwh*) Baruch to read a newly written scroll in the Temple (36:5, 8), and on a later occasion he "commands" (*ṣwh*) Baruch to commit to safe-keeping deeds for a newly purchased field (32:13). Jeremiah also "commands" (*ṣwh*) envoys attending the Jerusalem conference to give messages to their masters (27:4). The LXX in the present verse reads: "The word that the Lord commanded Jeremiah the prophet to say to Seraiah." The T supports MT, which should be read.

Seraiah son of Neriah, son of Mahseiah. The double patronym identifies Seraiah as a brother of Baruch (32:12), the two belonging to the Mahseiah scribal
family. Scribal families are known to have existed from earliest times, being
attested in the Old Babylonian period (Lambert 1957: 2–3) and also at Uga-
rit (Rainey 1969: 128; cf. Lundbom 1986b: 102). Seraiah was a high-ranking official in Zedekiah's government. A late-seventh-century seal impression has
turned up with the inscription "Belonging to Seraiah (ben) Neriah," which
doubtless belonged to this individual (Avigad 1978a: 56; 1978b; Shiloh and
Tarler 1986: 204; *AHI* 230 [100.780]; "Seraiah," *ABD* 5: 1104–5). "Seraiah" is a
common name, occurring elsewhere in the Bible and known also from contemporary extrabiblical inscriptions (see Appendix I). The spelling on the inscription is *sryhw*, a long form of *sryh*, which is the spelling here. Orthographic
differences of a similar nature occur with the name "Jeremiah" (see Note on
1:1). More significantly, Seraiah's seal does not contain "the scribe," which is
present on the seal impression found with Baruch's name on it (see Note on
36:4), and is the title supplied in 36:26 and 32. This indirectly corroborates Seraiah's title here of "caravan prince." Seraiah, nevertheless, is a professionally
trained scribe capable of executing a range of scribal functions. His role here
as Jeremiah's amanuensis parallels Baruch's amanuensis role on behalf of the
prophet in chap. 36.

*when he went with Zedekiah, king of Judah, to Babylon in the fourth year of
his reign.* An embassy went to Babylon soon after the exile of Jehoiachin, i.e.,
597 B.C., and with it went a hand-carried letter from Jeremiah to the exiles
(chap. 29). The present embassy goes three or four years later. The two embassies, then, are not one and the same (Sarna 1978: 93–95; *pace* Althann 1991).

with Zedekiah. Hebrew *'et-ṣidqîyāhû*. The LXX has *para sedekiou*, "from
Zedekiah," which presupposes Heb *mē'ēt*, although Althann (1991) argues on
the basis of Akkadian, Phoenician, and Ugaritic that *'et* can mean "from." But
his OT examples (Gen 6:13; Isa 7:17; 53:8) are unconvincing. Something substantive is at stake. If we read *'et* as "with," which is standard Biblical Hebrew
and has support from the Vg (*cum*) and Midrash Seder Olam 25 (Rosenberg),
then Seraiah accompanies Zedekiah on the trip to Babylon. But if we read
"from," which has the support of T (so Kimḥi), then Seraiah is sent by Zedekiah, and the king stays home. Either scenario is possible. Calvin, being dismissive of Seder Olam, adopts the LXX reading; so also Volz; Holladay; and
Keown et al. Others (Bright; Thompson; McKane) follow the MT and imagine
Zedekiah making the trip. There was seditious talk in Jerusalem sometime
early in Zedekiah's reign (chaps. 27–28; cf. Sarna 1978), and actual rebellion
in Babylon in 595/4, as we know from the Babylonian Chronicle (BM 21946:
rev. 21–22; Wiseman 1956: 36–37, 48, 72–73; D. N. Freedman 1956: 58), which
means that Zedekiah could have been summoned to Babylon to reaffirm loyalty to Nebuchadnezzar (Bright 1981: 329). With Zedekiah absent from Jerusalem for six months or more, we have a reason for Jeremiah's disappearance
from public view. If Jerusalem had a fragile existence with Zedekiah present,
and it did, how much more would it be tottering on the brink of chaos with the

king gone? It makes good sense then for Seraiah to have made the trip with Zedekiah to Babylon, but whether he actually did or not, we cannot say.

in the fourth year of his reign. I.e., in 594/3 B.C.

caravan prince. Hebrew *śar měnûḥâ* is lit. "prince of the resting place," a term occurring only here in the OT. The modern Versions commonly translate as "quartermaster" (§*měnûḥâ* in KB³), which in the U.S. Army is a commissioned officer responsible for providing the troops with quarters, storage, clothing, and transportation. Seraiah was in charge of the royal caravan, i.e., arranging for stopping places on the trip to Babylon (Hitzig; Cheyne; Cornill; Volz; and others). The term does not mean "quiet prince," i.e., a man of quiet disposition (*pace* Calvin; AV), nor "prince of rest" (*pace* Kimḥi, who imagined a companion for the king while at leisure—like Billy Graham golfing with American presidents). The T and LXX both presuppose Heb *minḥâh* ("gift, tribute"), which gives the reading, "tribute officer." In this view, Seraiah carries the tribute Zedekiah was obliged to pay the Babylonian king (Rashi; Blayney; Holladay; cf. 2 Kgs 17:3–4; Hos 10:6). The LXX reading is a possibility, although it may be tied to the view in both LXX and T that Seraiah went to Babylon as Zedekiah's representative, and that the king himself did not go.

60. *And Jeremiah wrote all the evil that would come to Babylon in one scroll, all these words that are written toward Babylon.* Peake makes the point that while Jeremiah would hardly have fanned the flame of fanatical patriotism, he certainly could have looked forward to the ultimate overthrow of Babylon. This would show his circle of followers, as well as those wanting to discredit him, that he had not lost faith. The conflict between him and Hananiah (chap. 28) was not that Hananiah believed in Babylon's overthrow while Jeremiah did not, but that Hananiah proclaimed an overthrow in two years, while Jeremiah knew it was on the other side of a painful defeat, thus a good way off. In 29:10 a round number of 70 years is given before restoration will occur, which is not likely to alarm Nebuchadnezzar or anyone else in Babylon (cf. Isa 39:5–8).

Jeremiah wrote . . . in one scroll. Jeremiah had writing capability (30:2; 32:10), as did other prophets (Isa 8:1; 30:8; Hab 2:2; cf. R. T. Anderson 1960; Zimmerli 1995: 422–31), and could have written this scroll himself. But more likely this is shorthand for a dictation to Seraiah, who did the actual writing. In the view expressed here the verses are an expanded colophon, which would make Seraiah the scribe of record.

one scroll. Hebrew *sēper 'eḥād* does not mean "a single sheet" (*pace* Bright); rather, "one particular scroll" (cf. Ehrlich 1912: 372). This is the scroll of oracles and other utterances against Babylon in 50:1–51:58, referred to also in 25:13, after which came originally the Foreign Nation collection. The LXX lacks "one" (Heb *'eḥād*), which can be attributed to haplography (homoeoarcton: *'aleph . . . 'aleph*).

all these words that are written toward Babylon. Reference is to the words on the Babylon scroll of chaps. 50–51. Budde (1878: 551–52) believed the verb "and he [i.e., Jeremiah] wrote" originally had but one object, "all the evil that would come to Babylon," and that the present phrase was a later "staple"

(Klammer) binding vv 59–64 together with 50:2–51:58, a view that survived in Peake, Cornill, S. R. Driver, and Bright, among others. But the phrase is taken here as being original, specifying what has been said about Jeremiah writing on a scroll all the evil that would come upon Babylon. .

61. *'When you come.'* Hebrew *kĕbō'ăkā*. The prefixed *kĕ* can have a temporal meaning of "when" (many MSS have *bĕ*). Compare *kĕkallōtĕkā*, "when you have finished," in v 63.

then you shall see to it that you read aloud all these words. Hebrew *wĕrā'îtā wĕqārā'tā 'ēt kol-haddĕbārîm hā'ēlleh*. The verb "see (to it)" is auxiliary to "read aloud." Seraiah must be sure to read aloud this scroll when he arrives in Babylon. His brother Baruch was directed earlier to read aloud words on a scroll from Jeremiah in the Jerusalem Temple, which he did (36:4, 8).

62. *And you shall say.* Hebrew *wĕ'āmartā*. The word Seraiah is instructed to address to Yahweh will be spoken before the reading of the scroll; the curse upon Babylon will be spoken after.

Yahweh. The LXX has *Kyrie, Kyrie* ("Lord, Lord"), which could indicate MT (whole-word) haplography. But the T also has only one "Lord."

this place. On the frequent use of this expression in the Temple Oracles and elsewhere, see Note on 7:3. Here "this place" refers to Babylon.

without there being an inhabitant in it, from human to beast; indeed eternal desolations it shall be. For this curse applied elsewhere to Babylon, see Note on 51:29. On land-and-city curses throughout the book of Jeremiah, see Note for 48:9. On the pairing of "human and beast," see Note for 21:6.

indeed eternal desolations it shall be. This portion of the curse is repeated verbatim in 51:26, although there *tihyeh* translates "you [masc.] shall be." See also 25:12. On the intensive plural, see Note for 51:26.

63. *And when you have finished reading this scroll aloud, you shall tie a stone to it, and you shall throw it into the middle of the Euphrates.* This symbolic act, like so many others the prophet himself performed, is not "sympathetic magic," but a natural extension of the preached word (Zimmerli 1995: 427–28; Amesz 1997; cf. Note on 13:1; §Introduction: Prophetic Symbolism: Act and Being). King Jehoiakim cast Jeremiah's first scroll into the fire (36:23), but that symbolic act came to nothing because Yahweh was not behind it. In the Vassal Treaties of Esarhaddon (410–411 *ANET*[3] 538), there is a solemn warning not to throw the tablet containing the treaty stipulations into the water, or destroy it by any other means. Herodotus (i 165) reports too how the Phocaeans, having cursed any of their number who should stay at Phocaea and not sail with them, symbolically sank a mass of iron in the sea. Haran (1982–83; 1984) argues that the present scroll must have been of papyrus, in that a stone is needed to make it sink. Scrolls made of skin will sink on their own. Normally, scrolls are deposited in the Temple (Deut 31:26; 2 Kgs 22:8), as we learn from colophons elsewhere (see Rhetoric and Composition), but this one is cast into the river.

when you have finished. The verb is *klh*, the same verb bringing closure in 10:25 and 20:18.

you shall tie a stone to it, and you shall throw it into the middle of the Euphrates. In the NT, see Rev 18:21.

the middle of the Euphrates. According to T. Jacobsen ("Euphrates" in *IDB* E–J, 181), this was a branch of the Lower Euphrates called Arachtu, which flowed through the center of Babylon and from the beginning of the first millennium B.C. was the river's main course.

64. *Then you shall say: 'Even so shall Babylon sink and not rise, because of the evil that I am bringing upon it.'* For the *kākâ* ("even so") construction used to interpret a symbolic action, see Note on 13:9. Elsewhere the construction occurs in divine oracles, where in each case it is preceded by a messenger formula (13:9; 19:11; 28:11). Here there is no messenger formula; hence, no clear indication of a divine oracle, but as we have said, this is probably because Seraiah lacks status as a prophet. The pronouncement, nevertheless, is a curse.

because of the evil that I am bringing upon it. For this Jeremianic expression, see Note on 6:19. Rudolph and McKane take the phrase as a later addition; however, as part of an inclusio (see Rhetoric and Composition), it is more likely original.

so they tire themselves. A catchphrase to the final oracle of the collection, v 58 (see Rhetoric and Composition). It is neither part of the preceding curse (*pace* T; Vg; AV; NIV) nor the subscript that follows (*pace* NAB). Most commentators and modern Versions omit with the LXX.

Thus far the legacy of Jeremiah. Hebrew *'ad-hēnnâ dibrê yirmĕyāhû*. This too is omitted in the LXX, while in the MT it forms an inclusio with 1:1 (see Rhetoric and Composition). The phrase is present in Aq (*eōs entautha hoi logoi Ieremiou*).

MESSAGE AND AUDIENCE

This colophon, written we may imagine by Seraiah as a conclusion to the Babylonian collection of oracles he has also put into writing, addresses a Judahite audience in both Judah and Babylon. Seraiah writes in the third person, as does Baruch in his colophon of chap. 45. Seraiah states that Jeremiah gave him a word before he (Seraiah) left with Zedekiah on a trip to Babylon in the fourth year of the king's reign, a word he is now reporting. Seraiah says he was caravan prince for the trip. The scroll announced all the evil that would come eventually to Babylon. Upon arrival, he is to read it aloud, but before the reading he is to address Yahweh, confirming that it is Yahweh who will cut off Babylon from the surrounding world, make the land devoid of humans and beasts, and leave it a desolation forever. After the scroll is read, Seraiah is to tie a stone to it and cast it ceremoniously into the middle of the Euphrates. Then he is to speak a curse on Babylon. Like the scroll that is now consigned to the bottom of the Euphrates, Babylon will sink and not rise. Seraiah's concluding word repeats what was said at the beginning about evil coming upon Babylon, but with the one difference that now the divine "I" is employed. The Jerusalem and

Babylon audiences will doubtless know whether Seraiah carried out this directive. We assume that he did.

Sometime later, when the Foreign Nation Oracles were relocated to the end of the Jeremiah book, Seraiah, we may imagine, added to the Babylon scroll and colophon a final subscript, "Thus far the legacy of Jeremiah," which tied the end of the book in with the beginning.

This colophon can be dated any time after the scroll of Babylon oracles was compiled in 594/3 B.C. The final MT subscript dates to after the Foreign Nation Oracle relocation, when the colophon had become a colophon for an entire book. This subscript does not presuppose the attachment of chap. 52, and as a result does not require a post-550 B.C. date (*pace* Delamarter 1999: 39).

IX. POSTSCRIPT (52:1–34)

◆

A. ZEDEKIAH MEETS THE KING AND GOES TO PRISON (52:1–11)

1. Summary of Zedekiah's Reign (52:1–3)

52 ¹Zedekiah was twenty-one years old when he became king, and he reigned eleven years in Jerusalem. His mother's name was Hamutal[1] daughter of Jeremiah from Libnah. ²And he did what was evil in the eyes of Yahweh, just like everything that Jehoiakim had done. ³Indeed, concerning the anger of Yahweh—it came against Jerusalem and Judah until he cast them away from his presence. So Zedekiah rebelled against the king of Babylon.

2. Capture of Jerusalem and Zedekiah (52:4–11)

⁴And it happened in the ninth year of his reign, in the tenth month, on the tenth of the month, Nebuchadrezzar, king of Babylon, came—he and all his army—against Jerusalem. And they encamped against it and built a siege wall against it all around. ⁵So the city came under siege until the eleventh year of King Zedekiah. ⁶In the fourth month, on the ninth of the month, the famine in the city became severe, and there was not any bread for the people of the land. ⁷Then the city was breached, and all the fighting men fled, and they went out from the city by night in the direction of the gate between the double walls, which was by the king's garden, though the Chaldeans were against the city all around. So they went in the direction of the Arabah. ⁸But the army of the Chaldeans pursued after the king and overtook Zedekiah in the desert regions of Jericho. And all his army was scattered from him. ⁹So they captured the king and brought him up to the king of Babylon at Riblah in the land of Hamath, and he spoke judgments against him. ¹⁰And the king of Babylon slaughtered Zedekiah's sons before his eyes, and also all the princes of Judah he slaughtered at Riblah. ¹¹Then the eyes of Zedekiah he blinded, and he bound him in bronze chains. And the king of Babylon brought him to Babylon and put him in the detention house[2] until the day of his death.

---

[1] Reading the Q with T; Kt spelling is "Hamital" (cf. LXX and Vg).

[2] Reading the Kt *bĕbêt-happĕqūdōt* ("in the detention house"); Q lacks the preposition *bĕ* ("in").

RHETORIC AND COMPOSITION

MT 52:1–11 = LXX 52:1–11. The present chapter is largely—but not entirely—a repetition of 2 Kgs 24:18–25:30, which was added to the Jeremiah book at a later time. The book of Jeremiah proper ends with 51:64: "Thus far the legacy of Jeremiah." Something similar exists in First Isaiah, where chaps. 36–39 are a later add-on repeating portions of 2 Kings 18–20. The main difference here between the parallel accounts is that chap. 52 omits the Gedaliah material of 2 Kgs 25:22–26, probably because it is covered in greater detail in chaps. 40–43. In its place is substituted (in MT only) the deportation summary of vv 28–30, which occurs nowhere else. The Chronicler's account of these events (2 Chr 36:11–21) is a later recasting, making the point that Jeremiah's prophetic word went unheeded. This account is repeated for the most part in 1 Esd 1:46b–58. Nebuzaradan's destruction of Jerusalem, his carrying away of the Temple treasures, and his exiling of priests and other citizens are recounted also in summary fashion in the Qumran *Apocryphon of Jeremiah* ($4Q385^b$ i 4–6), dated ca. 50–25 B.C. (Dimant 1994). Josephus reports Jerusalem's fall in *Ant* x 108–50.

Chapter 52, despite its similarity to 2 Kings, has an integrity of its own (G. Fischer 1998; 2001b). Inclusion of the deportation summary results in a rhetorical compilation of four unequal segments that report: 1) Jerusalem's fall and Zedekiah's capture (vv 1–11); 2) destruction, looting, and death following Jerusalem's fall (vv 12–27); 3) three Judahite deportations to Babylon (vv 28–30); and 4) Jehoiachin's leaving prison for a seat at the king's table (vv 31–34), which doubles as the concluding postscript to the Primary History. These four segments are held together by key word repetitions ending or beginning each segment, the whole of which forms a chiasmus:

I	*until the day of his death*	ʿad-yôm môtô	v 11
II	*so it went into exile*	wayyigel	v 27
III	*exiled*	heglâ	v 28
IV	*until the day of his death*	ʿad-yôm môtô	v 34

A similar structure, although not chiastic, exists in 37:1–40:6 (see Rhetoric and Composition for 37:1–16). One should note that the structure here does not exist in 2 Kings 24–25, which lacks the phrase "and put him in the detention house until the day of his death" in v 11 (cf. 2 Kgs 25:7), the phrase "took into exile" in v 28, and the phrase "until the day of his death" in v 34 (cf. 2 Kgs 25:30). The whole of chap. 52 then, in its final form, has been given a rhetorical structure. Duhm, Montgomery (1951: 559), and Gray (1970: 768–69) think "So Judah went into exile from its land" in 2 Kgs 25:21 (= Jer 52:27) was once the end of 2 Kings, and that what follows are later postscripts. This finds corroboration in chap. 52, which appears at one time to have ended at v 27 (see Rhetoric and Composition for 52:12–27). The two final segments in vv 28–30 and vv 31–34 are postscripts added later to complete the chapter and the entire Jeremiah book.

The present narrative segment consists of two parts: 1) the stereotyped summary of Zedekiah's reign (vv 1–3); and 2) a report of Jerusalem's fall and Zedekiah's capture (vv 4–11). The whole follows closely 2 Kgs 24:18–25:7, and the second part repeats with minor changes Jer 39:1–7. The segment is delimited at the top end by a *setumah* in M^L and M^P, and a *petuḥah* in M^A, prior to v 1, which is also the chapter division. At the bottom end is a *setumah* in M^P after v 11. M^L and M^A have no sections there. That v 11 ends the segment is indicated also by the phrase "until the day of his death," as was noted above. M^P has an additional *setumah* after v 3, and another *setumah* after v 5, where again there are no sections in either M^L or M^A. The section after v 3 sets off Zedekiah's years of reign from Jerusalem's fall and Zedekiah's capture, which in 2 Kings is marked by a chapter division. Jeremiah 39 corroborates the division by reporting only Jerusalem's fall and Zedekiah's capture (39:1–7). The section after v 5 has no obvious explanation.

NOTES

52:1. *Zedekiah was twenty-one years old when he became king, and he reigned eleven years in Jerusalem.* An eleven-year reign for Zedekiah, beginning in 597 and ending in 586 B.C., is the standard reckoning (1:3; 52:5; 2 Kgs 24:18; 2 Chr 36:11; 1 Esd 1:46), but Zedekiah's age at accession appears to be too low (Streane; Rudolph). He was older than his predecessor, Jehoahaz (= Shallum of 1 Chr 3:15; cf. Jer 22:11), and Jehoahaz became king at twenty-three (2 Kgs 23:31; 2 Chr 36:2).

twenty-one years old. The Hebrew expression is *ben-ʿeśrîm wěʾaḥat šānâ*, lit. "son of twenty and one years," where "son" in expressions of age takes on the meaning "aged / old" (KB^3).

His mother's name was Hamutal daughter of Jeremiah from Libnah. Hamutal was also the mother of Jehoahaz (2 Kgs 23:31; 24:18); Jehoiakim had a different mother (2 Kgs 23:36).

Libnah. A Levitical city in the Shephelah (Num 26:58; Josh 10:31–32), whose precise location is unknown. Referred to often in the OT, Libnah was doubtless an important city (Josh 15:42; 2 Kgs 8:22), located perhaps on the Judah–Philistia border. Whereas earlier the site was thought to be Tell eṣ-Ṣâfi, now it is commonly identified with Tell Bornāṭ, about eight kilometers northeast of Lachish (Albright 1924: 9; Elliger 1934: 63; Naʾaman 1991: 17–18; J. Peterson, *ABD* 4: 322–23).

2–3. Lacking in the LXX, very likely the result of haplography (homoeoarcton: *wy* . . . *wy*). The verses are present in 2 Kgs 24:19–20.

2. *And he did what was evil in the eyes of Yahweh.* A standard Deuteronomic formula (1 Kgs 11:6; 14:22; 15:26, 34; 16:25; et passim). In 2 Chr 36:12 and 1 Esd 1:47 it is added that Zedekiah paid no heed to Jeremiah, who spoke "from the mouth of Yahweh."

just like everything that Jehoiakim had done. See the Jehoiakim summary in 2 Kgs 23:37.

3. *Indeed, concerning the anger of Yahweh.* Taking *kî* as an asseverative: "Indeed" (cf. RSV; NAB; NJV; NRSV). A connection between Zedekiah—and also Jehoiakim's—evil deeds and the divine anger is not explicitly made; hence, the problem in interpretation. Evildoing in Jerusalem and Judah cannot be attributed to the divine anger (*pace* JB; NIV; NJB). The present verse is simply stating that Yahweh's anger against Jerusalem and Judah built up to the point where Yahweh had to cast the nation out from his presence.

until he cast them away from his presence. It was so promised in 7:15. Hebrew *hišlîkô* (lit. "his casting") is another irregular H-stem infinitive with suffix (cf. 50:34; 51:33; and GKC §53 l).

So Zedekiah rebelled against the king of Babylon. Rebellion here means breaking the loyalty oath sworn by Zedekiah—in the name of Yahweh—to the king of Babylon (Ezek 17:11–21; 2 Chr 36:13). It would have been carried out by nonpayment or nondelivery of the annual tribute at the appointed time. Again, without explicit connection to what has preceded, the narrator is attributing Yahweh's outpouring of anger to Zedekiah's unfaithfulness (Montgomery 1951: 560). In the book of Kings it is dogma that the nation suffers on account of the sins of its kings (1 Kgs 14:16; cf. M. Greenberg 1983: 322). Precisely when Zedekiah's rebellion occurred is not known. Malamat (1975: 142) places it in 589 B.C., after the accession of Pharaoh Apries in Egypt. But Greenberg (1957b; 1983: 323), in connecting the rebellion to Ezekiel's allegory of the two eagles of Ezekiel 17, says the beginning could have been under Psammetichus II, as early then as 591 B.C. See also Cogan and Tadmor 1988: 323. On the accession of the ambitious Apries (= Hophra) in Egypt, see Note on 39:1.

4–11. See exegesis for 39:1–7.

4. *in the tenth month.* This is also the MT reading in 39:1 and 2 Kgs 25:1. G^BS have "in the ninth month," G^A "in the seventh month." Compare defective Gk readings in LXX 46:1 [= MT 39:1].

on the tenth of the month. The day is included in 2 Kgs 25:1 and Ezek 24:1, but not in Jer 39:1.

he and all his army. Hebrew *hû' wěkol-ḥêlô.* Here, as in 2 Kgs 25:1, it is emphasized that Nebuchadrezzar did accompany his army to Jerusalem. The pronoun *hû'* ("he") is lacking in 39:1.

And they encamped against it and built a siege wall against it all around. In 2 Kgs 25:1 the reading is "and he encamped . . . and they built." In Jer 39:1 it is simply "and they besieged it." An encampment against Jerusalem by the Babylonians is anticipated in 6:3. At a later time, however, an enemy will set up camp around Babylon (50:29).

siege wall. Hebrew *dāyēq.* Besides 2 Kgs 25:1, this somewhat uncertain term occurs four times in Ezekiel (Ezek 4:2; 17:17; 21:27[Eng 21:22]; 26:8), where in every case it stands in parallelism with "siege ramp" (*sōlělâ*). Elsewhere in Jeremiah mention is made only of siege ramps (6:6; 32:24; and 33:4—the last mentioned being defense ramps inside the city). An Assyrian cognate *dāiqu* occurs in an Esarhaddon text, where reference is to [troops] climbing over a "siege wall" (*CAD* 3: 27). Josephus (*Ant* x 131) says Nebuchadnezzar built earthworks (*chōmata*) equal in height to the walls.

6. *In the fourth month, on the ninth of the month, the famine in the city became severe, and there was not any bread for the people of the land.* Lacking in 39:2, but present in 2 Kgs 25:3.

In the fourth month. Hebrew *baḥōdeš hārĕbîʿî*. The LXX omits, which can be attributed to haplography (homoeoarcton: *b* . . . *b*), although 2 Kgs 25:3 also omits (*pace* RSV). In LXX 46:2 [= MT 39:2] "in the fourth month" is present.

the famine in the city became severe. Nothing is said about famine in 39:2, but a hint comes in 37:21, where it is said that bread in the city finally ran out. Famine in Jerusalem's last days was sorely lamented (Lam 1:19; 2:11–12, 20; 4:3–5, 8–10), and earlier had been a recurrent theme in Jeremiah's preaching (see Note for 5:12; cf. 8:20; 14:11–18; and 15:2). Ezekiel acted out a parable on the present siege and famine (Ezekiel 4, particularly vv 16–17; cf. 5:16–17). It is pointed out by Gray (1970: 764–65) that this famine was intensified because the Babylonians had been present in the land for two harvest seasons, eating up existing crops and not allowing produce from surrounding areas into the city. Even today, one sees farm women from various locales outside Jerusalem sitting at the gates of Old City, or along its narrow inner streets, selling seasonal fruits and vegetables—greens, olives, grapes, grapeleaves, bananas, eggplant, figs, also spices—sage and mint. On Ben-hadad's siege of Samaria, which led finally to a severe famine, see 2 Kgs 6:24–31.

the people of the land. The term is general, denoting not a special class but simply ordinary folk in the population (Rudolph; Holladay; Carroll; McKane). In 37:2 it means everyone other than Zedekiah and his servants. The meaning in 44:21 is similar. See further Note for 1:18.

7. *and all the fighting men fled.* The verb *yibrĕḥû* is imperfect but must be read as a past tense (Rashi). The LXX lacks "fled and," which could be more loss due to haplography (homoeoarcton: *w* . . . *w*). The MT of 2 Kgs 25:4 lacks a predicate and is unreadable, omitting "fled, and they went out from the city."

though the Chaldeans were against the city all around. Lacking in 39:4, but present in 2 Kgs 25:4. The initial *waw* must be read as a qualifying "(al)though" (NRSV). The point here is that the king and his entourage somehow managed to exit the city, even though the Babylonians had it surrounded.

10. *the princes of Judah.* Hebrew *śārê yĕhûdâ*. On this phrase, see Note for 24:1.

11. *and put him in the detention house until the day of his death.* Lacking in 39:7 and 2 Kgs 25:7. This addition has a larger rhetorical function in the present chapter and in 39:1–40:6 (see Rhetoric and Composition above, and Rhetoric and Composition for 39:1–14).

in the detention house. Hebrew *bĕbêt-happĕqūdōt.* The term occurs nowhere else in the OT, but its meaning is not in doubt. This is a house of confinement, i.e., a prison (Rashi; T: "prison house"). The LXX has an interesting variant: *eis oikian mulōnos,* "in the millhouse," suggesting not only confinement but forced labor of a type well known in antiquity (Feigin 1933–34: 224; Oppenheim 1967: 91; cf. Exod 11:5; Job 31:10). Mesopotamian sources show hand-milling to be a common punishment for prisoners of war (van der Toorn 1986). Even young men in Judah found themselves doing this degrading activity—usually reserved for women—after the war was over (Lam 5:13). If this LXX interpretation of the Hebrew is correct, then Zedekiah's captors put him to the grinding wheel, which is what the Philistines did to Samson after blinding him (Judg 16:21).

MESSAGE AND AUDIENCE

The summary of Zedekiah's reign is immediately recognizable as conforming to a standard type in the book of Kings, and it will not go unnoticed to the audience that this king gets the same negative wrap-up as Manasseh, Amon, Jehoahaz, and Jehoiakim—a succession of kings unworthy of royal office and morally bankrupt as far as Yahweh is concerned (2 Kgs 21:1–2, 19–20; 23:31–32, 36–37). Zedekiah's immediate predecessor, Jehoiakim, is singled out for particular censure. The audience is then told that Yahweh's anger built to the point where he had no choice but to cast the nation from his presence. Mention of Zedekiah's rebellion is a final indictment against this last Judahite king. The larger message here is that rebellion against Nebuchadrezzar added up to rebellion against Yahweh, and that as a king goes, so goes the nation. The audience will likely understand the latter point, but will it understand the former?

The next portion of narrative recounts Jerusalem's fall and the capture of Zedekiah. For an audience that has heard the narrative in chap. 39, this account will cover familiar ground. In chaps. 39–40 Zedekiah's capture is juxtaposed to the promise of salvation for Ebed-melech and Jeremiah's actual deliverance. Here, at the chapter's end, Zedekiah's imprisonment is contrasted to Jehoiachin's release from prison. But the very attachment of this account to the Jeremiah book makes implicit a connection between the life and preaching of Jeremiah and what happened ultimately to the nation (Ackroyd 1968: 42). Details of Jerusalem's fall are reported in laconic fashion: the date when Nebuchadnezzar came to Jerusalem, that he besieged the city from Zedekiah's ninth to eleventh year, that a severe famine ensued, and that the city was finally breached, at which time soldiers fled in darkness and headed for the Arabah. Then, somewhat belatedly, we learn that the king was with them. We more or less knew it. The chase was on, with the Babylonians catching the king near Jericho and his army scattering in every direction. The king was then given the dubious distinction of being personally escorted into Nebuchadnezzar's presence at Riblah, only to hear multiple judgments read out against him. Zedekiah's sons, and after them Judah's princes, were slaughtered before the king's eyes. The king was then blinded, enchained, and brought to Babylon. There he was put in a detention facility, where he remained until he died. If this facility was a millhouse, the audience will know to what a humiliating end this king came, and they will remember Samson, only Samson lived to bring one final indignity upon his captors. This king, who gave no thought as to how things might end, died shamefully in a foreign land.

While the present narrative segment can be dated along with 39:1–7 to a time soon after the fall of Jerusalem, the chapter as a whole, because of its similarity to 2 Kgs 24:18–25:30 and also because of its own rhetorical structure, must date to when the final postscript (52:31–34) was added to the book of Jeremiah and the Primary History, i.e., ca. 560 B.C., or soon after. Holladay says after the death of Jehoiachin, which is the same time.

B. JERUSALEM: DESTRUCTION, REMNANT, LOOTING, AND DEATH (52:12–27)

1. Destruction, yet a Remnant (52:12–16)

[12]In the fifth month, on the tenth of the month (it was the nineteenth year of King Nebuchadrezzar, king of Babylon), Nebuzaradan the Rab-tabahim came. He stood before the king of Babylon in Jerusalem. [13]And he burned the house of Yahweh, and the house of the king, and all the houses of Jerusalem, yes, every great house he burned with fire. [14]And all the walls of Jerusalem round about, the entire army of the Chaldeans who were with the Rab-tabahim broke down. [15]But some of the poor people, and the rest of the people who were left in the city, and the deserters who had deserted to the king of Babylon, and the rest of the craftsmen, Nebuzaradan the Rab-tabahim exiled. [16]And some of the poor of the land Nebuzaradan the Rab-tabahim left for vinedressers and for plowmen.

2. Temple Treasures Go to Babylon (52:17–23)

[17]And the bronze pillars that belonged to Yahweh's house, the stands and the bronze sea that were in Yahweh's house, the Chaldeans broke in pieces, and they carried away all their bronze to Babylon. [18]And the pots, the shovels, the snuffers, the sprinkling bowls, the incense dishes, and all the vessels of bronze with which they served, they took. [19]And the small bowls, the fire pans, the sprinkling bowls, the pots, the lampstands, the incense dishes, and the libation bowls—whatever was gold for gold, and whatever was silver for silver, the Rab-tabahim took. [20]The two pillars, the one sea and the twelve bronze bulls that were underneath the sea,[1] and the stands that King Solomon made for Yahweh's house—there was no weight to the bronze from all these vessels. [21]Regarding the pillars: eighteen cubits high the one pillar, and a thread of twelve cubits would encircle it; its thickness four fingers—it was hollow. [22]And a capital of bronze was above it, and the height of the one capital five cubits; also latticework

---

[1] Adding "the sea" with the LXX and 1 Kgs 7:44 (see Notes).

and pomegranates were above the capital round about—all of it bronze. And likewise for the second pillar and pomegranates. [23]So there were ninety-six pomegranates to a side; all the pomegranates: one hundred above the latticework round about.

3. Death to Jerusalem's Great and Small (52:24–27)

[24]And the Rab-tabahim took Seraiah the head priest, Zephaniah the associate priest, and the three keepers of the threshold, [25]and from the city he took one eunuch who was an overseer of the fighting men, seven men from those seeing the king's face who were found in the city, the scribe of the prince of the army who conscripted the people of the land, and sixty men from the people of the land who were found amidst the city. [26]And Nebuzaradan the Rab-tabahim took them and brought them to the king of Babylon at Riblah. [27]And the king of Babylon beat them and put them to death at Riblah in the land of Hamath. So Judah went into exile from its land.

RHETORIC AND COMPOSITION

MT 52:12–27 = LXX 52:12–27. The present narrative segment follows closely 2 Kgs 25:8–21, with vv 13–16 repeating also, with some variation, Jer 39:8–10. Here the segment fits into a rhetorical structure comprising all of chap. 52; hence, the delimitation of vv 12–27 (see Rhetoric and Composition for 52:1–11). In this structure, "So Judah went into exile from its land" balances "the people whom Nebuchadrezzar exiled" in v 28. Rudolph, Bright, and NJV take "So Judah went into exile from its land" as an introduction to the deportation summary, which it is not. The phrase concludes the prior narrative segment (Rofé 1995: 166), also an early edition of the chapter, even as the same phrase at one time concluded an early edition of 2 Kings (Duhm; Montgomery 1951: 559, 564; Gray 1970: 768–69). In both texts, what follows are later postscripts. The segment here is further delimited at the top by a *setumah* in M^P before v 12 (M^L and M^A have no sections here). At the bottom is a *setumah* in M^A after v 27 (M^L and M^P have no sections here).

This narrative segment divides into three parts: 1) a report of Jerusalem's destruction but Judah being left a remnant (vv 12–16); 2) a summary of Temple treasures carried off to Babylon (vv 17–23); and 3) a report of death for select representatives of Jerusalem's population, great and small (vv 24–27). Josiah's reform is similarly reported. Following the destruction of cult objects in the Temple is a destruction of cultic sites around Jerusalem and further distant, after which priests of the high places are put to death (2 Kgs 23:4–20). The division between parts II and III of the segment here is marked by a *setumah* in M^A (only) after v 23. Parts I and III balance the fate of Jerusalem's inhabitants. Part II, which is the center, has intentional framing. This narrative begins and ends with the pillars, sea, and stands; in between cult objects in bronze, silver, and gold are listed:

I	Nebuzaradan exiled some people, left others in the land	vv 15–16

	a pillars, stands, and sea	v 17
	b pots, shovels, snuffers, sprinkling bowls, incense dishes	v 18
II	b′ small bowls, fire pans, sprinkling bowls, pots, lampstands,	
	incense bowls, libation bowls	v 19
	a′ pillars, sea, stands	v 20
	a″ pillars, capitals, and decoration on capitals	v 21–23

III	Nebuchadrezzar put to death Jerusalem's great and small	vv 24–27

Embellishment in II occurs as the narrative progresses. In the return to the pillars, sea, and stands (a′ and a″) are added capitals to the pillars and their decorations. Similarly, the listing of Temple vessels in silver and gold (b′) expands the number of vessels listed in bronze (b). All of this occurs in 2 Kgs 25:13–17 as well, which is to say the structure here is "Deuteronomistic." This comes as no surprise, since narrative is framed in precisely the same way in Deuteronomy, 2 Kings 22–23 (Lundbom 1976; 1990; 1996a), and elsewhere in the Deuteronomic History. There is no reason then with Volz and Rudolph to take vv 20–23 as a secondary supplement. It is integral to the whole of vv 17–23.

In the larger chapter, the report of death coming to Jerusalem's great and small (vv 24–27) returns to balance Zedekiah's capture and the death sentences carried out on those fleeing with the king (vv 4–11). This gives added support to the view that v 27 ended an earlier version of the chapter and that vv 28–30 and vv 31–34 are two later postscripts.

NOTES

52:12. *In the fifth month, on the tenth of the month . . . Nebuzaradan the Rabtabahim came.* Nebuzaradan's arrival in Jerusalem, the destruction of the city and Temple, and an exile in the fifth month (of Zedekiah's eleventh year) correlates with 1:3 and 2 Kgs 25:8. However, 2 Kgs 25:8 has "the seventh of the month," a difference of three days. Baruch 1:2 puts the burning of Jerusalem on "the seventh day of the month." The Rabbis handled this discrepancy by spreading the event out. The destruction of the Temple was set at 7 Ab (see below), and a day of national mourning for 9 Ab (Cogan and Tadmor 1988: 318; cf. Josephus, *Ant* x 135).

it was the nineteenth year of King Nebuchadrezzar. Babylonian chronology is provided in Jer 25:1 and 32:1, also in 2 Kgs 24:12 and 25:8. Here and in Jer 25:1 the LXX omits, but not in 32:1. Some scholars (Giesebrecht; Duhm; Janzen 1973: 100; Holladay; McKane) take the Babylonian date in the present verse to be an MT plus, which is doubtful since it occurs in 2 Kgs 25:8. Nebuchadrezzar's first year corresponds to the fourth year of Jehoiakim, i.e., 605 B.C. (25:1). Dating the exile in Nebuchadrezzar's nineteenth year conflicts with v 28 of the deportation summary, which puts it in the king's eighteenth year. On the *šĕnat . . . šānâ* ("year . . . year") repetition in compound numbers, see 32:1 and GKC §134 o.

He stood before the king of Babylon in Jerusalem. The verb *ʿmd* means here "to stand (with respect) before," i.e., "serve" (see Note for 15:19). Today we might say that Nebuzaradan "had standing with the king of Babylon," which allowed him to act on the king's behalf. In 2 Kgs 25:8 Nebuzaradan is said to be a "servant" (*ʿebed*) of the Babylonian king. Some commentators (Giesebrecht; Duhm; Cornill, Volz; Rudolph; Holladay) in the interest of getting a better reading with the prior verb "came," emend *ʿāmad* ("He stood before") with LXX and Vg to the participle *ʿōmēd* ("who stood before"). The meaning is the same. Nebuzaradan came to Jerusalem on the date given, and he is the one who served the king of Babylon there. The idiom here should not be interpreted to mean that Nebuzaradan literally stood before Nebuchadrezzar in Jerusalem, since the king was now up at Riblah. On this officer in the Babylonian army and his title, see Note for 39:9.

13–16. See exegesis for 39:8–10.

13. *And he burned the house of Yahweh, and the house of the king, and all the houses of Jerusalem, yes, every great house he burned with fire.* The narrative follows 2 Kgs 25:9. The burning of the Temple goes unmentioned in 39:8, where the phraseology is different (see Note there). Jeremiah's prediction of this crowning indignity in a Temple Oracle (7:14) was cause for his having to stand trial (26:1–19). Tadmor (1956: 230) and Malamat (1968: 156) date the burning of the Temple to 7 Ab, which would be August 14, 586 B.C. Bright's date is a year earlier (see Note for 39:1). Jeremiah anticipated a burning of Jerusalem's houses in 32:29. Kenyon (1967: 78–104) found meager evidence of destroyed private houses in Jerusalem; these were small, roughly built, and generally unimpressive. More-recent excavations have turned up clear evidence of the 586 B.C. destruction, e.g., the "Burnt Room" in the so-called "House of Ahiel." Here also on the border between Ophel and the Upper City is the "House of the Bullae," which yielded the collection of 51 seal impressions, one belonging to Gemariah son of Shaphan, in whose chamber Baruch read the Jeremiah scroll in 604 B.C. (36:10–12). This building may have been an archive or public office. Alongside a defense tower was a thick ash layer in which arrowheads were found. Among the finds were also large quantities of pottery, fragments of carved wood, metal and stone vessels, and implements of bone (Shiloh, "Jerusalem" in *NEAEHL* 2: 708–9).

yes, every great house he burned with fire. This is a summary statement emphasizing that every last one of Jerusalem's great houses was set ablaze by Nebuzaradan. The translation is aided by taking the initial *waw* as an asseverative, "yes!" or "indeed!" not "and," which makes a redundancy (Blayney). Bright solves the problem by making the phrase parenthetical, although it is not, as he says, a gloss qualifying "every house of Jerusalem." Bright imagines that the Chaldeans set fire only to important buildings and that the flames then spread to consume all houses in the city. There is good rhetorical prose here: a fourfold repetition of "house"; the first and last clauses repeating and inverting the position of the verb, also expanding upon the verb at the end; and a repetition in the last two clauses of *kol* ("all, every"), which points up a shift at midpoint from the specific to the inclusive:

And he burned the house of Yahweh	*wayyiśrōp ᵓet-bêt*
and the house of the king	*wĕᵓet-bêt*
and all the houses of Jerusalem	*wĕᵓēt kol-bātê*
yes, every great *house he burned with fire*	*wĕᵓet-kol-bêt . . . śārap bāᵓēš*

The net result was that every building in Jerusalem was set ablaze by Nebuzaradan. In the British Museum is a relief showing the city of Khazanu ablaze after its capture by Shalmaneser III (859–825 B.C.). For a picture, see Parrot 1961: 122, panel D.

15. The verse is lacking in the LXX, and a good case can be made here not only for textual loss due to haplography (whole-word plus: *wmdlwt h . . . wmdlwt h* or two-word: *rb-tbhym . . . rb-tbhym*), but for scholarly predisposition to favor the shorter LXX text and dispense with repetitions, the repetition here being *ûmiddallôt* ("But some of the poor") beginning vv 15 and 16. Giesebrecht suggests haplography, but Duhm, Janzen (1973: 20–21, 119), and McKane have their doubts. It is true that the opening phrase is lacking in 39:9 and 2 Kgs 25:11, but that bears little or not at all on the present omission, which consists of an entire verse. Moreover, the lack of *ûmiddallôt hāʿām* ("But some of the poor people") in 2 Kgs 25:11 is very likely a case of MT haplography (see below). Rofé (1995) argues that since this verse and vv 27b–30 refer to exile, the two texts could point to a systematic abridgment in the Hebrew *Vorlage* to the LXX. But the omission in vv 27b–30 is another arguable haplography (see Note there), and Zedekiah's exile in v 11 the LXX retains. Rofé therefore cannot say that according to the LXX there was no exile of Judah after the revolt of Zedekiah, only destruction and execution. However, the MT of chap. 52 is better and likely more original than the LXX (*pace* Bogaert 1991). On omissions outnumbering additions in the ancient scrolls, based on evidence from Qumran, see §Introduction: MT and LXX.

But some of the poor people . . . Nebuzaradan the Rab-tabahim exiled. The majority of modern commentators follow Giesebrecht, Cornill, Volz, and others in omitting the phrase *ûmiddallôt hāʿām* ("But some of the poor people"), some saying it is erroneously placed here from v 16. The words are omitted in 39:9 and 2 Kgs 25:11, and an exile of the poor may seem to be precluded by what is said in 2 Kgs 24:14, although it is not. It is certainly possible that some poor people were taken into exile; in fact, it would be remarkable if such were not the case, since there had to be some of Judah's poor that the Babylonians did not want left in the land, e.g., if they were hostile to Babylonian occupation, or were perceived as being potential troublemakers once the Babylonians had returned home. Verses 15 and 16 make it clear that some of the poor were exiled and some of the poor were left in the land. The *middallôt* repetition, where the prefixed *min* is a partitive genitive (GKC §119w), gives a meaning of "from among the poor people," "some of the poor people," or the like. Interpretation here seems to founder on the mistaken notion that none of the poor went to Babylon, and that the only people left in the land were the poor. Neither was the case. The text here is simply saying that some of the poor were taken into exile. This reading is to be preferred over the reading in 2 Kgs 25:11, where a lack of the phrase is easily explained as MT haplography (homoeoarcton: *w . . . w*, or homoeoteleuton: *m . . . m*).

and the rest of the craftsmen. Hebrew *wĕ'ēt yeter hā'āmôn.* Presumably those craftsmen not exiled to Babylon in 597 B.C. (29:2; 2 Kgs 24:14, 16). In 2 Kgs 25:11 the phrase is "and the rest of the multitude (*wĕ'ēt yeter hehāmôn*)," and in 39:9, "and the rest of the people who were left." In the famous cuneiform text listing rations for the king of Judah (= Jehoiachin) in his Babylonian prison are listed also rations for imprisoned craftsmen from many nations (Albright 1942: 51; cf. ANET³ 308§c).

16. *Nebuzaradan.* The LXX and 2 Kgs 25:12 omit. Possible MT expansion.

for vinedressers and for plowmen. Hebrew *lĕkōrĕmîm ûlĕyōgĕbîm.* Compare *'ikkārêkem wĕkōrĕmêkem* ("your farmers and your vinedressers") in Isa 61:5. In 39:10, Nebuzaradan gives poor people "vineyards and fields" (*kĕrāmîm wîgēbîm*), where the latter term is no more etymologically certain than *yōgĕbîm* here. But LXX *geōrgous* and Vg *agricolas* support the translation "plowmen," or the like, which is doubtless the meaning intended. The hill country of Judah being what it is, we are probably to think here of terrace farmers, as suggested by de Geus (1975: 73), since most of the orchards, vineyards, and gardens were on irrigated terraces (see also Note for 5:10). Graham (1984) thinks these plowmen would not be self-employed, but rather workers on organized terrace estates. He cites the admonition of Gedaliah to serve the king of Babylon by harvesting wine, summer fruit, and oil in 40:10, and notes also a report by Josephus (*Ant* x 155) that Gedaliah imposed upon the people tribute payment to the king of Babylon that was to come from cultivation of the soil. In the Talmud, Rabbi Joseph is quoted as saying that these vinedressers and plowmen were "balsam gatherers from En-Gedi to Ramah" (Shabbath 26a). Balsam oil (*bōśem*) was used to make perfume.

17. Temple furnishings in bronze, silver, and gold not seized by Nebuchadrezzar in his first visit to Jerusalem (2 Kgs 24:13) were this time stripped from the building prior to its destruction and taken to Babylon. Jeremiah—to the horror of other prophets—said this would happen (27:19–22). The pillars, stands, and bronze sea, because of their size and worth as precious metal, were broken up and carried off in pieces. Once in Babylon, they could be melted down and reused. For a listing of the accoutrements of Solomon's newly-built Temple, some but not all of which are mentioned here, see 1 Kgs 7:13–51. According to Ezra 1:7–11, Nebuchadrezzar enriched his own temple with the loot, and it remained there until Cyrus restored it to Jewish exiles who returned it to Jerusalem.

the bronze pillars. Hebrew *'ammûdê hannĕḥōšet.* These are the two pillars named Jachin and Boaz that stood on either side of the Temple entrance

(1 Kgs 7:15–22, 41–42; 2 Kgs 25:13, 17; Ezek 40:49; 2 Chr 3:15–17; 4:12, 13). Most likely they were freestanding. These pillars with other large and small furnishings of bronze were cast under the supervision of Hiram, king of Tyre (1 Kgs 7:13–14, 40–46). Temple entrances with decorative columns on each side are known from excavations and surviving artifacts to have been a common architectural design in antiquity, being attested in Egypt, Mesopotamia, Phoenicia, Cyprus, Syria, and Canaan, before and after the Israelite period. Temples at Khorsabad dedicated to Sin, Shamash, and Nabu had decorative "trees" flanking their entrances—the Sin temple had cedar trees encased in bronze, and the Shamash temple trees wrapped in bronze bands (Loud et al. 1936: 97–98, 104–5; Scott *IDB* E–J, 780–81 with a picture). Egyptian temples at Heliopolis, Thebes, Karnak, and elsewhere had tall red granite obelisks flanking their entrances (see Note for 43:13). Basalt pillar bases found *in situ* on either side of the main entrance to a Canaanite temple at Hazor are believed to have supported freestanding pillars (Yadin et al. 1989: 246–47; 1961: pl. 127, #1, #3; Ottosson 1980: 29–31, 112; *NEAEHL* 2: 598). Albright (1969: 138–44), following Robertson Smith, took the pillars to be lofty cressets (= fire altars), but this view has not won much favor, largely because of the seeming impracticability of attending altars at such a great height (J. L. Myres 1948: 29). The pillars could just as well have been decorative, or symbolic, or both. For a reconstructed Solomonic Temple with its outer pillars, see G. E. Wright (1957: 138), and for the survival of these or other Temple pillars on coins and artifacts from a later time, see Parrot (1957: 28–30); S. Yeivin (1959: 20); and Gray (1970: 186).

the stands. Hebrew *hammĕkōnôt*. These were freestanding bronze pieces on which lavers, or wash basins, rested (1 Kgs 7:38; 2 Chr 4:14). The lavers were used for cleansing purposes after bloody burnt offerings (2 Chr 4:6). King Ahaz in his eighth-century Temple renovation (2 Kgs 16:17) removed the lavers from their stands, and we hear of them no more. Perhaps they went as tribute to Tiglath-pileser III. Originally there were ten stands (and ten lavers) in the Temple courtyard, the stands being bronze openwork with animals and other decorations, having also wheels and axles of bronze (1 Kgs 7:27–37; cf. Josephus, *Ant* viii 81–86). They may have looked something like the miniature eleventh-century wheeled stand found at Megiddo (May 1935: 19–20, pl. 18; Lamon and Shipton 1939: pl. 89; *ANEP*² 195, #587). From Ras Shamra in Syria has come a one-piece tripod laver, made of bronze, with pomegranates hanging from the brim (Schaeffer 1929: 295–96 + pl. 60/1; G. E. Wright 1941: 29; 1957: 142; *ANEP*² 195, #588). Other stands of similar description have turned up at Enkomi and Larnaka in Cyprus (Parrot 1957: 49 with drawings; Gray 1970: 192–93; Paul and Dever 1973: 258–59).

the bronze sea. Or "the molten sea." Hebrew *yām hannĕḥōšet*. A large round tank over seven feet high and fifteen feet in diameter with an estimated capacity of 10,000 gallons of water (Wylie 1949: 90). Used for priestly washings (2 Chr 4:6), the bronze sea stood in the southeast corner of the Temple courtyard (1 Kgs 7:39). Designed originally with a base of twelve ornamental oxen

(1 Kgs 7:23–26), the oxen were removed by Ahaz and the tank remounted on a slab of stone (2 Kgs 16:17). For reconstructed drawings, see G. E. Wright 1941: 17; 1957: 139; Parrot 1957: 46; P. J. King 1993: 117; and *IDB R–Z*, 253. An Assyrian relief from Sargon II (721–705 B.C.) has two large cauldrons at the temple entrance resting on legs in the shape of bulls' feet. A large stone basin found at Amathus in Cyprus, now in the Louvre, is also frequently compared with Solomon's bronze sea. Decorated with bulls' heads, it stands just under six feet high. See J. L. Myres 1948: 37–38; Gray 1970: 189–90; Paul and Dever 1973: 257–58. This sea—also the pillars—were made from bronze that David took home as booty from a successful Aramean campaign (1 Chr 18:8); now it goes as booty to the Babylonians.

18. *And the pots, the shovels, the snuffers, the sprinkling bowls, the incense dishes, and all the vessels of bronze with which they served, they took.* Listed here are cultic objects taken for their bronze. Hebrew syntax is reversed: the objects come first and the verb last. The narrator wishes to emphasize the various assemblages of Temple vessels that Nebuzaradan carried off. All had been used by the priests in performing their ritual service at the courtyard altar. The LXX specifies only three items: "the crowns" (*tēn stephanēn*), presumably on the laver stands (cf. 1 Kgs 7:31); "the bowls" (*tas phialas*); and "the meat-forks" (*tas kreagras*).

the pots. Hebrew *hassîrôt*. Large, wide-mouth pots with handles, broad and shallow, used for cooking sacrificial meat (Honeyman 1939: 85; Kelso 1948: 27, #63; Paul and Dever 1973: 259), and also for carrying ashes from the altar (Exod 27:3). Elijah used a pot of this type to cook vegetables (2 Kgs 4:38–41), and Jeremiah, in his commissioning vision, saw a pot of this type over fire (1:13).

the shovels. Hebrew *hayyā'îm*. With their long handles, these were to remove ashes from the altar. Examples have turned up at Megiddo and Beth-shemesh (Loud 1948: pl. 283, #2; G. E. Wright 1941: 29–30; 1957: 141–42 with a drawing).

the snuffers. Hebrew *hamĕzammĕrôt*. An instrument of uncertain description used to trim lampwicks (Exod 25:37–38). Not like the snuffers used to extinguish modern candlewicks. Guided by the root *zmr*, meaning "to trim, prune," some commentators (Giesebrecht; Cornill; Volz; cf. KB^3) translate the term "knives." A type of scissors has also been suggested (C. Meyers, *ABD* 6: 75). Snuffers made of gold, which are not mentioned in v 19, were also among the Temple furnishings (1 Kgs 7:50; 2 Chr 4:22). Rashi's rendering of "musical instruments," which appears also in the Vg (*psalteria*), builds on another root *zmr*, and cannot in the present context be correct.

the sprinkling bowls. Hebrew *hammizrāqôt*. These are medium-sized bowls said to have been used for sprinkling sacrificial blood on the altar (Lev 1:5, 11; 3:2; Milgrom 1991: 155 says only in Priestly texts, e.g., Exod 38:3; Num 4:14). They had other—if not entirely proper—uses (Amos 6:6). Identification has been made with the ceramic ring-burnished four-handled banquet bowls known from Iron II excavations (Honeyman 1939: 83–84; Kelso 1948: 22–23 #50). Paul and Dever (1973: 261) cite gold-colored brass bowls of this description from the Israelite period found at Tell Ziklag.

the incense dishes. Hebrew *hakkappôt.* These are smaller dishes (or cups or spoons) in the shape of a hand (Heb *kap* = "hollow of the hand"), used for burning frankincense in connection with the Bread of the Presence offering (Exod 25:29–30; Num 7:14, 86). Numerous vessels of this general description—hands crafted on the back, with hollow tubes opening into the dish to facilitate use as censers—have been found in Syria and Palestine, two very nice specimens from eighth–seventh-century Megiddo (May 1935: 18–19; pl. 17; G. E. Wright 1941: 30; 1957: 142 with drawings). For incense dishes/spoons from Tell Beit Mirsim in the form of a lion's jaw, with other decorations, see *ANEP*[2] 196 #592; cf. 320.

19. Listed here are cultic vessels of silver or gold, taken because of their precious metal but also because of their continued usefulness. The LXX has six items, one fewer than the MT. When the Egyptians looted the Jewish temple at Elephantine in 410 B.C., they carried off cultic vessels of silver and gold (*AP* 30.12–13; *ANET*[3] 492).

the small bowls. Hebrew *hassippîm;* LXX transliterates with *saphphôth,* which presupposes a feminine plural ending; cf. *sippôt* in 1 Kgs 7:50. Rashi is uncertain about the identification of these vessels, deciding finally that they were basins to receive sacrificial blood for sprinkling on the altar (cf. Exod 12:22). If so, they have the same use as the "sprinkling bowls" (*mizrāqōt*). Kimḥi says they are wine vessels, or else Temple vessels in general. The Vg has *hydrias,* "jugs." Kelso (1948: 27 #64) says the *sap* is probably about soup-bowl size. The "bowl of reeling" (*sap-raʿal*) in Zech 12:2 holds a sufficient amount of wine to bring about drunkenness.

the fire pans. Hebrew *hammaḥtôt.* The LXX has *masmarōth,* which appears to transliterate Heb *mĕzammĕrôt* ("snuffers"), an item it did not include in v 18 (1 Kgs 7:50 lists snuffers of gold). These were used as censers or for carrying burning coals off the altar (Lev 16:12; Rashi; Kelso 1948: 23 #52), e.g., in the offering of incense (Lev 10:1). They were also used for removing ashes (Exod 27:3; Milgrom 1991: 596–97), and doubtless had other functions (Snaith 1967: 75: "any utensil which can be used for carrying what is too hot to be held in the hand"). Their precise shape is not known, but they are believed to have been shallow with long handles (Milgrom 1991: 1024–25).

the sprinkling bowls. The same as in v 18, only these are silver or gold. The LXX has *tous hypochutēras,* "vessels to pour oil into a lamp."

the pots. The same as in v 18, only of silver or gold. The LXX omits, as it did also in v 18.

the lampstands. Hebrew *hammĕnōrôt.* The LXX: *tas luchnias* ("the lampstands"). The Temple lampstand (= menorah) was a stand branching at the top into seven lamps (Exod 25:31–37; 37:17–24; cf. Zechariah 4). It was all one piece: a base, a shaft, and seven branches, tall enough to light an otherwise dark place (cf. Matt 5:15). Ten golden lampstands stood in the main nave (*hēkāl*) of the Temple, five on the south side and five on the north (1 Kgs 7:49). Bronze stands with flat tops from Megiddo (May 1935: pl. 17; Guy 1938: pl. 119 #1) and Beth Shan (James 1966: 13–14, fig. 103 #1) may also have been lampstands, the latter found in a house, however, not in a temple. See further Paul and Dever 1973: 252–55; and Tombs, *IDB* K–Q, 64–66.

the incense dishes. The same as in v 18, only these are silver or gold. The LXX has *tas thuiskas*, "the censers"; in v 18 it did not translate the items.

the libation bowls. Hebrew *hammĕnaqqîyôt*. The M^L lacks a *dagesh forte* in the *qop* and the *yod*, but they are present in M^A and other MSS. These items of uncertain identification, not listed in 1 Kings 7 or 2 Kings 25, were used in connection with drink offerings (= libations). Kelso (1948: 24, #54) says they appear to have been bowls, although they may also have been dippers used to draw wine out of bowls (LXX: *tous kuathos*; Vg: *cyathos*). Chalices have also been suggested (KB^3). Placed on the table of the Bread of the Presence, they were used together with wine pitchers (Exod 25:29; 37:16; Num 4:7). Rashi, however, thinks the items in question were the gold frames on the table of the Bread of the Presence (Exod 25:25), but this does not fit the assemblage. For pictures of libations being poured into vessels, see $ANEP^2$ 197 #597 (into a large chalice); 200 #611 (into a large jug).

whatever was gold for gold, and whatever was silver for silver, the Rab-tabahim took. Again Hebrew syntax is reversed in the verse to emphasize the vessels taken. The verb comes at the end. The *'ăšer zāhāb zāhāb wa'ăšer-kesep kāsep* idioms are similar to those in 15:2, with the one difference being that the latter have a prefixed *lamed*. The phrases here are elliptical: "whatever (was) gold (was taken for its) gold, and whatever (was) silver (was taken for its) silver." The repetition is not to express superfine quality (*pace* §GKC 123e). For reports in Strabo and Diodorus of the Persians carrying off Babylon's gold and silver at a later time, see Note on 50:1.

20. *The two pillars, the one sea . . . and the stands*. Resuming from v 17.

the twelve bronze bulls that were underneath the sea. See 1 Kgs 7:25. This phrase is in the LXX, but not in 2 Kgs 25:16, which leads some to question whether the decorative base was still in the Temple. According to 2 Kgs 16:17, the bronze sea was taken off the twelve bulls when Ahaz carried out his Temple renovations, and remounted on a stone base. Some scholars therefore assume that the twelve bulls went as tribute to Tiglath-pileser III a century-and-a-half earlier, and that the narrator has simply forgotten this fact (Cornill; Rudolph; Gray 1970: 767; Thompson; Boadt; Carroll; Holladay; Cogan and Tadmor 1988: 320; Jones). However, 2 Kgs 16:8 says only that Ahaz gave the Assyrian king silver and gold (not bronze!), and that the bronze sea was taken off its decorative base in the renovations—perhaps at the Assyrian king's request (vv 17–18). It does not say that the base went to Assyria. It may simply have been put to another use, or placed in storage. Also, the omission of the present phrase in 2 Kgs 25:16 could well be attributable to haplography (homoeoarcton: *h . . . h*).

that were underneath the sea. Hebrew *hayyām* ("the sea") has fallen out of MT by haplography (homoeoarcton: *h . . . h*), and needs to be restored with the LXX and 1 Kgs 7:44 (Volz; Rudolph; Bright; Janzen 1973: 111; Holladay; Keown et al.; also RSV; NAB; NSB). Otherwise one gets a nonsensical reading of bulls being under the stands (AV: "twelve brazen bulls that were under the bases" is not correct). Rashi avoids the problem by translating "beside the bases," which will not do. Kimḥi says the phrase is elliptical. The MT has to be emended.

there was no weight to the bronze from all these vessels. I.e., the bronze was too much to be weighed. A similar rhetorical statement occurs in 1 Kgs 7:47. The LXX lacks "all these vessels," ending simply with "their bronze" (*tou chalkou autōn*). But the omitted words are present in Aq and Symm (*pantōn tōn skeuōn toutōn*). Giesebrecht deletes the suffix in light of 2 Kgs 25:16. To retain the MT, which has probably been expanded, one had best redivide, attaching the *mem* on *něḥuštām* to *kol*, giving the reading: "to the bronze from all these vessels" (Blayney).

21. *eighteen cubits high the one pillar.* A cubit is ca. 18 inches, making the height of the pillar some 27 feet (see Appendix IV for a precise conversion of measures). The decorative column of the Sin temple at Khorsabad (see v 17) was estimated at 10 or 11 meters, roughly the same height. The LXX has 35 cubits (cf. 2 Chr 3:15), which cannot be right. The Temple itself was only 30 cubits high (1 Kgs 6:2). Perhaps the erroneous dimension is the total height of both pillars (Blayney; S. Yeivin 1959: 6).

and a thread of twelve cubits would encircle it; its thickness four fingers—it was hollow. These dimensions are omitted in 2 Kgs 25:17, possibly due to haplography (homoeoarcton: *w . . . w*). A circumference (only) is given in 1 Kgs 7:15 (*pace* RSV).

and a thread of twelve cubits would encircle it. I.e., it had a circumference of 12 cubits (Rashi), which is about 18 feet. The diameter would then be about six feet.

its thickness four fingers—it was hollow. The bronze was three inches thick, the center being hollow (*nābûb*). This dimension and a mention of the pillar being hollow are omitted in 1 Kgs 7:15, due to haplography (Cogan 2001: 262). The suggestion has thus been made that the original pillars of Solomon's Temple were cast solid, but in a subsequent renovation were replaced by hollow pillars (S. Yeivin 1959: 7–8; Paul and Dever 1973: 255–56). Yeivin argues that the "molten bronze" (*mûṣaq něḥōšeh*) capitals of 1 Kgs 7:16 were solid, and that the pillars were similarly cast solid (although *mûṣaq* is never used to describe the pillars, as Yeivin claims). The argument is unconvincing and said by Cogan to be unnecessary if one accepts a loss by haplography in MT 1 Kgs 7:15. Also, one is forced to ask how pillars of such size (6 feet in diameter and 27 feet in length), to say nothing of their weight, could be transported up to Jerusalem from the Jordan Valley where they were allegedly made (1 Kgs 7:46). It seems more likely that the pillars were cast hollow from the beginning, and that these pillars are the ones now being broken up by the Babylonians and carried off.

22. *And a capital of bronze was above it . . . also latticework and pomegranates were above the capital round about—all of it bronze.* The capital, richly decorated and also made of bronze, stood atop the pillar (1 Kgs 7:16–20, 41–42). The latticework (*śěbākâ*) was delicate ornamental open work, here of

twisted bronze. The pomegranates (*rimmônîm*)—a common fertility symbol throughout the ANE because of their many seeds (Parrot 1957: 52–53; *ABD* 2: 808)—were also of bronze, and probably hung suspended from the capital (Josephus, *Ant* viii 78; Montgomery 1951: 171), somewhat like the bronze pomegranates suspended from the brim of the Ras Shamra laver (see v 17). Pomegranates decorated the robe of the high priest (Exod 28:33–34). A small thumb-sized ivory pomegranate has turned up with the inscription: "Belonging to the House[of Yahwe]h, something holy for the priests." It is believed to derive from Solomon's Temple and was possibly the decorated top of a scepter (Avigad 1989; P. J. King 1993: 149–50; *CS II* 173). A pomegranate of the same size, only in bronze, was found earlier at Megiddo (May 1935: 20 with picture).

the height of the one capital five cubits. This dimension agrees with 1 Kgs 7:16; in 2 Kgs 25:17 the height is "three cubits," which may be the capital less the latticework above it.

and pomegranates. The text here is uncertain, with the LXX and MT of 1 Kgs 7:18 and 2 Kgs 25:17 all reading differently. Some commentators want to read "also latticework and pomegranates," as in v 22, which would indicate a loss of "also latticework" in MT due to haplography (homoeoarcton: *w . . . w*).

23. *So there were ninety-six pomegranates to a side; all the pomegranates: one hundred above the latticework round about*. This verse is omitted in 2 Kings 25. Rashi and Kimhi take *rûḥâ* as meaning "to each side, with Rashi adding that only 96 of the 100 pomegranates were visible. In 1 Kgs 7:42 and 2 Chr 4:13 are 400 pomegranates total: 200 on each pillar, arranged in two rows of 100 (cf. Josephus, *Ant* viii 78).

24. *And the Rab-tabahim took Seraiah the head priest, Zephaniah the associate priest, and the three keepers of the threshold*. Resuming from v 11, where we now hear about the city roundup of select individuals who did not flee with Zedekiah or manage an exit in some other manner. These three high priestly offices—head priest, associate priest, and keeper of the threshold—are the same ones represented in 2 Kgs 23:4, where King Josiah is beginning his cleansing of the Temple. The LXX omits the names of the priests, but they are present in 2 Kgs 25:18 and not likely to be secondary (*pace* Janzen 1973: 71; Holladay). Second Kings commonly supplies names of priests, scribes, and other Temple functionaries, e.g., Shaphan the scribe in 22:3; Hilkiah the high priest in 22:4; and so on throughout chaps. 22–23.

Seraiah the head priest. The title *kōhēn hārō'š* ("head priest, chief priest") occurs for the first time in 2 Kgs 25:18. About the individual here, who stands in a distinguished priestly line in Judah, we hear nothing prior in the book of Jeremiah. His grandfather was Hilkiah the high priest (*hakkōhēn haggādôl*) who found the Temple lawbook that sparked the Josianic Reform (2 Kgs 22:8), and his father Azariah was head priest before him. Seraiah's son, Jehozadak, was exiled to Babylon (1 Chr 5:39–41[Eng 6:13–15]), and the latter's son, Joshua, became high priest after the exile (Hag 1:1; Zech 3:1; 6:11). This head priest, however, must go to meet the king of Babylon. The name "Seraiah" was a common one in the period, belonging to other individuals in the book of

Jeremiah (36:26; 40:8; 51:59, 61) and in the OT, and known also from contemporary seals and seal impressions (see Appendix I).

Zephaniah the associate priest. Hebrew *kōhēn hammišneh* is lit. "the second priest." Most likely this is Zephaniah son of Maaseiah, whose father was "keeper of the threshold" (35:4). We know rather little about the duties of the associate priest. It seems that Zephaniah assisted the head priest (21:1; 37:3) and was responsible for maintaining Temple order (29:25–29). In the latter capacity he was roundly criticized in a letter from Babylon for not disciplining Jeremiah when the prophet was announcing a long exile. Zephaniah's father Maaseiah gave Jeremiah Temple access when he came there with the Rechabites. But now, along with the head priest and others, Zephaniah must go to meet the king of Babylon (cf. 2 Kgs 25:18–21). On this Zephaniah the priest, see further Note for 21:1.

the three keepers of the threshold. AV: "the three keepers of the door." Hebrew *wĕʾet-šĕlōšet šōmĕrê hassap*. These priests kept watch over entrances to the Temple, allowing or disallowing access to its sacred areas and adjacent rooms. Rashi says these priests kept the keys to the Temple. They also had custody of the cultic vessels (2 Kgs 23:4) and collected offerings from people entering the Temple (2 Kgs 12:10[Eng 12:9]; 22:4).

25. *and from the city he took.* Lacking in the LXX, and perhaps unnecessary with "city" occurring twice more in the verse (Duhm). The point, in any case, is that those named here were taken from the city at large, as opposed to the priests of v 24, who were taken from the Temple (Kimhi).

one eunuch who was an overseer of the fighting men. Hebrew *sārîs* ("eunuch") can denote a "state official" (29:2; 34:19), being here a highly-placed official (*pāqîd*) in the military. Compare *Rab-saris* ("chief of the eunuchs") in 39:3. Ebed-melech, a domestic eunuch in Zedekiah's employ (38:7), was likely spared in view of the oracle given him by Jeremiah (39:17–18).

fighting men. Hebrew *ʾanšê hammilḥāmâ* is lit. "the men of war."

seven men from those seeing the king's face. I.e., those having personal access to the king (Exod 10:28–29; 2 Sam 3:13; 14:24, 28; Esth 1:14). Hebrew *mērōʾê pĕnê-hammelek*. In Akk the idiom "to see the face" means "have an audience with" (Oppenheim 1941: 258). Second Kings 25:19 has five men, but Josephus (*Ant* x 149) has seven, as here. There were actually more than five or seven of such individuals; these were simply the ones who suffered the misfortune of being found in the city. It is somewhat ironic in that they must now go "to see the face" of the king of Babylon (cf. 32:4; 34:3).

the scribe of the prince of the army who conscripted the people of the land. This scribe who served the prince of the armed forces (*śar haṣṣābāʾ*) was in charge of conscription (Rashi). Bright calls him head of the Selective Service. Scribes marched in Barak's army (Judg 5:14), and later commanded troops in the army of Judas Maccabeus (1 Macc 5:42).

the prince of the army. Or "the commander of the army"; cf. 1 Sam 17:55 (Abner); 1 Kgs 11:15 (Joab). Hebrew *śar haṣṣābā*. Jeremiah prose has the term *śārê haḥăyalîm*, "princes of the troops" (40:7, 13; 41:11, 13, 16; 42:1, 8;

43:4, 5). The LXX here omits *śar* ("prince"), which should be retained (*pace* Holladay); the omission is possibly due to haplography (homoeoteleuton: *r . . . r*).

who conscripted. Hebrew *hammaṣbî'*. A denominative H-stem from *ṣābā'* ("army, hosts"), lit. "the one who raised the army."

the people of the land. Hebrew *'am hā'āreṣ*. This term appearing twice in the verse refers in both cases to ordinary city people pulled out for what is possibly selective punishment (Cornill; Volz; Bright). These are not landowners or other elite citizens (*pace* Rudolph; Jones; Holladay). On the term *'am hā'āreṣ*, see Note for 1:18. The entire section wants to emphasize that both great and small were represented in Nebuzaradan's roundup, which becomes a chilling sequel to Jeremiah's preaching in 5:4–6. In 2 Kgs 25:26, which concludes the section not found Jeremiah 52, reference is made to "all the people, from the least to the greatest," who fled to Egypt. This is the way of war, and the implication here is that harsh treatment was also meted out to Jerusalem's poor (*pace* Keown et al.).

26. *Riblah.* The city in central Syria where Zedekiah was taken; see v 9 and Note for 39:5.

27. *And the king of Babylon beat them and put them to death.* The double verb probably indicates that the king of Babylon had his prisoners beaten before killing them (Rudolph). The verb *nkh* can mean either "beat (savagely)" (2:30; 37:15) or "beat to death." Bright has "put to the sword and killed," though he concedes that the men were doubtless beaten before being put to death. The LXX, perhaps sensing a redundancy, omits the second verb.

So Judah went into exile from its land. This sentence and all of vv 28–30 are lacking in the LXX, most likely another loss due to haplography (homoeoteleuton: *t . . . t* or homoeoarcton: *wy . . . wy*). The sentence, which is integral to the final structure of the chapter (see Rhetoric and Composition for 52:1–11), is definitely not a secondary MT addition (*pace* McKane). For a reading of the omitted sentence and vv 28–30 in Theod, see Field 1875: 739–40.

MESSAGE AND AUDIENCE

This narrative segment begins with the precise date on which Nebuzaradan came to Jerusalem. The audience is told that he arrived as Nebuchadrezzar's representative. In briefest fashion possible, it is then reported that Nebuzaradan burned the Temple, the king's house, indeed every great house in Jerusalem, after which the Chaldean army took to breaking down the city walls. The first portion of narrative ends by reporting that some of the poor, some left in the city, some deserters, and the rest of the craftsmen were exiled by Nebuzaradan. Then in a parting gesture, this man of violence gave land to the poor who remained, enabling them to be vinedressers and plowmen. Nothing is said about prophecies of Jeremiah, but what is said confirms an entire ministry of this brave man. The audience may even now remember his Shiloh Oracle, which caused such a stir at the time it was spoken.

The Temple having been destroyed, the audience is now told what was stripped away before Nebuzaradan set the building afire. The mighty Jachin and Boaz pillars were brought down, broken in pieces, and readied for shipment to Babylon. The same with the bronze sea and ten bronze stands gracing the Temple courtyard. What follows is then an inventory—perhaps not complete, but certainly representative—of Temple vessels in bronze, silver, and gold that were looted by the Babylonians. They took them all. There was no need to break these up, as they could be used or kept for display in the temple of Marduk. Following this survey, the audience is brought back once more to the pillars, sea, and stands of bronze. With the sea went also the twelve bronze bulls that once served as a base. In connection with the stands, the name of King Solomon is invoked. About the pillars, more needed to be said regarding their size and the capitals on the top, complete with latticework and pomegranates. Did the audience know that so many pomegranates—all of them bronze—hung at the top of the capitals? And will anyone wonder about the ark of the covenant, overlaid as it was in pure gold within and without and the Temple's most valuable possession (Exod 37:1–5)?

In the third portion of narrative, the audience is told about Nebuzaradan's roundup in the city. It too took place before the Temple was burned and the city walls were pulled down. The audience heard earlier what happened to Zedekiah and those making their escape with him. Now back in the city we learn that Nebuzaradan found in the Temple precinct Seraiah, the head priest, Zephaniah, the associate priest, and three keepers of the threshold. From the city at large—perhaps in the royal complex—were taken a high-placed eunuch who directed the city's defense, seven men from the king's privy council, the army commander's scribe in charge of conscription, and sixty men without title who were wandering or hiding in the city. It was a selective roundup, some highly placed people, some very ordinary citizens. All were brought by Nebuzaradan to the king of Babylon at Riblah, where the other captives had been taken. Nebuchadrezzar lost no time in flogging them and putting them to death. On a less violent note, the audience is then told again that Judah went into exile from its land.

Will the audience now remember Jeremiah preaching that both small and great who knew not Yahweh's way would suffer an inglorious end? And will it remember, now about forty years ago, how Josiah dismantled the high places, cleansed the Temple of vessels to Baal, and killed the idolatrous priests to make Jerusalem the single sanctuary? And could it believe that something so all-consuming had now happened to the Jerusalem Temple and its priesthood, leaving the nation without any place of worship?

The present narrative segment can be dated to a period soon after the fall of Jerusalem. An expanded compilation of vv 4–27, or else vv 1–27, can be dated at the same time or later. The chapter as a whole is to be given a date of ca. 560 B.C., or soon after.

C. DEPORTATION SUMMARY (52:28–30)

52 [28]This is the people that Nebuchadrezzar exiled in the seventh year: 3,023 Judahites. [29]In the eighteenth year of Nebuchadrezzar, from Jerusalem: 832 persons. [30]In the twenty-third year of Nebuchadrezzar, Nebuzaradan the Rab-tabahim exiled 745 Judahite persons. Total persons: 4,600.

RHETORIC AND COMPOSITION

MT 52:28–30 = LXX 0. This deportation summary occurs nowhere else in the OT. Its omission in the LXX can be explained by haplography (see Note for 52:27); it is present in Theod, T, and Vg. Its absence in 2 Kings results possibly from the inclusion there of a summary of Gedaliah's governorship (2 Kgs 25:22–26), which is lacking in the present chapter (see Rhetoric and Composition for 52:1–11). This summary is then an independent account, the first of two supplements to a narrative that originally concluded at v 27 (see Rhetoric and Composition for 52:12–27). Delimitation of the unit is possible here on content alone, but is indicated also at the top end by a *setumah* in M^A (only) before v 28. At the bottom end is a *petuḥah* in M^L and M^P, and a *setumah* in M^A, after v 30. M^P has another *setumah* after v 29, which may point to v 30 being a later addition.

The omission of this summary in 2 Kings is important in light of the numbers it contains; 2 Kgs 24:14 and 16 give significantly higher totals for the 597 exile: 10,000, then 7,000 and 1,000. Here the number is only 3,023. Some suggest that the smaller number is a count only of adult males, and that the small numbers of the two subsequent exiles are likewise only adult males. Others think the totals in 2 Kings are inflated. Both possibilities must be considered. The present summary, being an independent account and one that is not included in 2 Kings 25, need not correlate with the numbers in 2 Kings 24. So far as the book of Jeremiah is concerned, the problem of correlation is nonexistent since there are no other figures. The different totals in the two books must simply be allowed to stand. Also, the provenance of the summary—v 30 at least—must be Babylon, since a count and reporting of the third deportation could be made nowhere else. After 582, Jeremiah and Baruch were in Egypt, others were among the Ammonites, and the Mizpah community was history. The numbers then of the summary doubtless represent those who actually arrived in Babylon, which may go some—though not necessarily all the—way in explaining their low totals. Not everyone leaving Judah completed the trip.

Key words "he exiled" in v 28 and "so it went into exile" in v 27 are part of a rhetorical structure for the entire chapter (see Rhetoric and Composition for 52:1–11). Smit (1969: 112) sees a connection made by "the people" in v 28 and "Judah" in v 27.

NOTES

52:28. *in the seventh year.* I.e., of Nebuchadrezzar, which corresponds to the chronological reckoning in the Babylonian Chronicle (BM 21946: rev. 11–12; Wiseman 1956: 72–73). In 2 Kgs 24:12 it says "in the eighth year." For the one-year discrepancy between biblical chronology and chronology in the Babylonian Chronicle, see Note on 46:2. The year, in any case, is 597 B.C. when Nebuchadrezzar captured Jerusalem and took the first group of exiles to Babylon. Many emend with Ewald and Graf to "in the seventeenth year," but this is simply a way around the number discrepancy between the present summary and 2 Kgs 24:14–16, and should be rejected (Hyatt; Bright).

3,023 Judahites. In 2 Kgs 24:14, 16 the totals are 10,000, 7,000, and 1,000, which may include women and children. The present count may be only adult males (cf. Num 1:2–3). Differences still exist, which result from this being an independent prisoner list (see Rhetoric and Composition).

29. *In the eighteenth year of Nebuchadrezzar.* Again, a one-year discrepancy with 52:12 and 2 Kgs 25:8, which have "nineteenth year." This is the exile after the fall of Jerusalem in 586 B.C.

from Jerusalem: 832 persons. The number would doubtless be larger if people from outside Jerusalem were included. Rashi, in fact, explains the number differences in 2 Kgs 24:14 and 16, and the discrepancy with the total here in v 28, as a result of the 10,000 figure referring to *all* Judahites. However, 2 Kgs 24:14 gives the 10,000 figure in connection with an exile of "all Jerusalem."

30. *In the twenty-third year of Nebuchadrezzar, Nebuzaradan the Rab-tabahim exiled 745 Judahite persons.* This was the exile of 582 B.C., which probably came in response to Gedaliah's murder and a subsequent disintegration of the Mizpah community. Josephus (*Ant* x 182) reports that Nebuchadrezzar, in his twenty-third year, campaigned against Syria, Ammon, Moab, and Egypt, after which more Jews were exiled to Babylon. En-Gedi (Tell Goren) on the Dead Sea shows a complete destruction by fire about this time (Stratum V), and the excavator, Benjamin Mazar, suggested that this was carried out by Nebuchadnezzar in 582/1 B.C. (*NEAEHL* 2: 402; Stern 2001: 136). According to the Talmud, En-Gedi was made a balsam-producing center by Nebuchadnezzar after the destruction of Jerusalem (see Note for 52:16). Perhaps then some of the Judahites exiled to Babylon in 582 B.C. were from En-Gedi. During the seventh century B.C. there was extensive cultivation along the west coast of the Dead Sea. Stager in a study of the area (1975: 225) says: "There the fresh-water springs provided environments with fairly lush tropical vegetation and a setting for a very specialized kind of oasis agriculture, where date-palms and rare spices were cultivated." Cross and Milik did minor excavations at three Israelite sites in the Buqê'ah Valley west of Khirbet Qumran: Khirbet Abu Tabaq (Middin), Khirbet es-Samrah (Secacah), and Khirbet el-Maqari (Nibshan). All are known from Josh 15:61–62. Iron II occupation appears to end there in the early sixth century, probably as a result of Nebuchadnezzar's destruction (Cross

1956: 14; idem, *NEAEHL* 1: 267–69; Cross and Milik 1956; 8, 14–15). Stager (1975: 257) puts the first permanent settlements in the Buqêʿah in Josiah's reign.

MESSAGE AND AUDIENCE

This deportation summary reports to a Babylonian audience of expatriate Jews the number of persons exiled to Babylon in 597, 586, and 582 B.C. As such, it expands upon the closing statement of v 27b, "So Judah went into exile from its land." The date of composition for vv 28–29 could be any time after 586 B.C.; the date for all of vv 28–30 would have to be after 582 B.C.

D. JEHOIACHIN LEAVES PRISON FOR THE KING'S TABLE (52:31–34)

52 [31]And it happened in the thirty-seventh year of the exile of Jehoiachin, king of Judah, in the twelfth month, on the twenty-fifth of the month, Evil-merodach, king of Babylon, in the year he became king,[1] lifted up the head of Jehoiachin, king of Judah, and brought him out from the prison house. [32]And he spoke good things to him, and he put his seat above the seat of the kings[2] who were with him in Babylon. [33]So he changed his prison clothes and ate food in his presence regularly all the days of his life. [34]On his allowance: a regular allowance was given to him from the king of Babylon, a day's portion each day, until the day of his death, all the days of his life.

RHETORIC AND COMPOSITION

MT 52:31–34 = LXX 52:31–34. These verses repeat in 2 Kgs 25:27–30, where they serve as a final postscript to the Primary History (= Genesis to 2 Kings; cf. D. N. Freedman 1983a). Here they are a final postscript to the Jeremiah book. The addition in each case occurs in Babylon after the death of Nebuchadnezzar and the accession of Evil-merodach, which is 562 B.C. The verses are delimited at the top end by the independent nature of vv 28–30 (see Rhetoric and Composition there), by a rhetorical structure encompassing the entire chapter (see Rhetoric and Composition for 52:1–11), and by a *setumah* in M^A and a *petuḥah* in M^L and M^P before v 31.

NOTES

52:31. *the thirty-seventh year of the exile of Jehoiachin, king of Judah, in the twelfth month, on the twenty-fifth of the month.* Chronological reckoning by day

---

[1]Reading the infinitive *molkô* ("he became king") with the LXX and 2 Kgs 25:27. MT has *malkūtô* ("his reign").

[2]Reading the Q, *hammĕlākîm*, "the kings" (cf. LXX and 2 Kgs 25:28); Kt has *mlkym* ("kings").

and month, beginning also from the exile of Jehoiachin, occurs in Ezek 1:2. The thirty-seventh year of Jehoiachin's exile was 561/560 B.C. The LXX has "the twenty-fourth" of the month; 2 Kgs 25:27 has "twenty-seventh. Also, the LXX has *Iōakim* (= Jehoiakim), which is wrong. The error could stem from 2 Chr 36:6, where it says that Jehoiakim was taken prisoner to Babylon.

Evil-merodach, king of Babylon, in the year he became king, lifted up the head of Jehoiachin, king of Judah, and brought him out from the prison house. An act of amnesty, which kings could carry out upon accession to the throne. Engnell (1943: 77) cites evidence of kings' freeing prisoners on such occasions in Mari. More contemporary is a letter addressed to Assurbanipal wishing him a happy reign and rejoicing that now with the new king in Assyria

> Whom his crime has condemned to death
>   the king my lord has let live
> [who] was held prisoner many [ye]ars
>   is set free.
>
> (*ANET*³ 627)

The Jehoiachin incident revives memories of the Joseph story. Joseph was released from prison and given a seat of honor in the court of Pharaoh, and the idiom "to lift up the head" appears in that story with reference to the butler who was earlier freed from the same prison (Gen 40:13). Speiser (1964: 305) translates this idiom in Gen 40:13 as "pardon," the translation of Cogan and Tadmor (1988: 328) in 2 Kgs 25:27 and the translation of Becking (1990: 287) here. We also see in this incident a reversal of the phrase "And there arose a new king over Egypt who knew not Joseph" (Exod 1:8; Carroll). In Babylon there arose a new king who knew not (or chose to know not) the charge against Jehoiachin.

Evil-merodach. Hebrew *ʾĕwîl mĕrōdak.* Literally, "Foolish Merodach," a disparagement of Amel-marduk, king of Babylon, who succeeded his father, Nebuchadnezzar, in 562 B.C. On the succession of Babylonian kings following the death of Nebuchadnezzar, see Note for 50:1.

in the year he became king. This reading of the LXX and 2 Kgs 25:27 is preferred by most all commentators. Reference is to the king's accession year (before the first calendar year), at which time this gracious act and perhaps others were carried out.

lifted up the head of Jehoiachin. G^B adds "and shaved him," which appears to follow the account of Joseph's release from prison (Gen 41:14).

the prison house. On the Q-Kt spellings for "prison," see Note for 37:4. This appears to be the more general term for a prison (cf. 37:15).

32. *And he spoke good things to him.* Hebrew *wayĕdabbēr ʾittô ṭōbôt.* This is in sharp contrast to what Zedekiah heard from Nebuchadrezzar (v 9), where the text says *wayĕdabbēr ʾittô mišpāṭîm,* "and he spoke judgments to him" (Becking 1990: 287). A similar expression, "to speak good things" (*dbr* + *dĕbārîm ṭôbîm*), occurs 1 Kgs 12:7b. All modern English Versions and some scholars (Gray 1970: 774; Cogan and Tadmor 1988: 328; Holladay) continue to

follow the AV in translating *ṭōbôt* adverbally: "he spoke kindly to him," or the like; however, something more than a manner of speaking is required. Aramaic *ṭbt* means "good things" in the eighth-century Sefire Treaties (Moran 1963c), referring specifically to "friendship" and "good relations" established by the treaty. Akkadian *ṭābūtu* similarly means "close frendship, brotherhood" in a formal alliance (AHw 3: 1378). However, to say with Levenson (1984: 356–58) that there is treaty language in the present text is outrunning the evidence. Evil-merodach did not make a treaty with Jehoiachin. We are talking here about an act of amnesty and pardon extended to Jehoiachin by the Babylonian king, nothing more.

and he put his seat above the seat of the kings who were with him in Babylon. There were other kings in Babylonian captivity besides Jehoiachin. The "Court of Nebuchadnezzar" document (ANET³ 308) mentions the king of Tyre, the king of Gaza, the king of Sidon, the king of Arvad, the king of Ashdod, and other kings, some or all of whom may still have been there in 561/560 B.C. Compare in this connection the reflection of the captured Canaanite king, Adonibezek, in Judg 1:7.

33. *So he changed his prison clothes.* Putting on clean clothes at the end of an imprisonment was a general ANE custom. In ancient Sumer it signified acquittal, and was accompanied by ritual cleansing. See also Zech 3:3–5. In the Nungal hymn from Nippur, a prisoner still in confinement complains of not having been given clean clothes (Frymer 1977: 85–87). Joseph changed his clothes upon release from prison, as he now had to appear before Pharaoh (Gen 41:14). The same show of respect operates here, as Jehoiachin is now to eat at the king's table. In the NT, compare Luke 15:22.

and ate food in his presence regularly all the days of his life. Commentators generally take this to mean that Jehoiachin was now elevated to eat at the king's table, or else in the presence of the king. The key phrase is *lĕpānāyw tāmîd*, which NJV translates "regularly in his presence." Mephibosheth when restored by David was invited to sit "regularly" at the king's table (*tāmîd* three times in 2 Sam 9:7, 10, 13). But Kimḥi says the present expression is not to be taken literally, i.e., Jehoiachin did not eat with the king, because the next verse states that he received meals from the king. But v 34 deals only with rations for him and his family. Kimḥi's view has been adopted more recently by Cogan and Tadmor (1988: 328–29), who translate *lĕpānāyw* "by his favor." But this makes little sense in the context. What does it mean to say that Jehoiachin ate by favor of the Babylonian king? By whose favor did he eat before in prison? The translation here has to be "in his presence."

all the days of his life. I.e., Jehoiachin's life, not Evil-merodach's (*pace* Cornill; Rudolph).

34. *a regular allowance was given to him from the king of Babylon, a day's portion each day, until the day of his death.* A cuneiform text discovered a century ago in Babylon mentions rations allocated for Jehoiachin and his family (ANET³ 308). The text is dated to 592 B.C., and according to Albright, Jehoiachin at the time was enjoying freedom of movement in Babylon (Albright

1942: 52). When Jehoiachin was imprisoned and for what reason, no one seems to know. Cogan and Tadmor (1988: 329), who subscribe to this view, say that the ration here is a new ration, not the one reported in the Babylonian text. This reconstruction is unnecessarily complex, since the Babylonian text says nothing about Jehoiachin's status, only that he and his family were receiving state pension. Jehoiachin was probably in prison, where he was put by Nebuchadnezzar after being brought to Babylon in 597 B.C. and where he remained until Evil-merodach released him after Nebuchadnezzar's death.

a regular allowance. Hebrew *'ărūḥat tāmîd.* The term *'ărūḥâ* here and in 40:5 appears to mean "food allowance," although its etymology is uncertain. The LXX translates here with *suntaxis,* "quota," and in 2 Kgs 25:30 with *hestiatoria,* "feast."

a day's portion each day. Hebrew *dĕbar-yôm bĕyômô.* Literally: "a day's (some)thing in its day." The idiom occurs also in Exod 5:13; 16:4; and Dan 1:5. The RSV translates in Exod 16:4: "a day's portion every day"; and in 2 Kgs 25:30: "every day a portion." A new twist on the idiom may occur in the well-known NT proverb, *arketon tē hēmera hē kakia autēs,* "Sufficient to the day the evil of it" (Matt 6:34). Here for Jehoiachin and his family, the day's sufficiency is something good.

until the day of his death, all the days of his life. This redundancy has been much discussed, since "all the days of his life" is lacking in the LXX, whereas in 2 Kgs 25:30 "all the days of his life" is the sole conclusion. The following explanation of these variant readings is the most reasonable. In the present verse, the original reading was "until the day of his death," since the rhetorical structure in the chapter has this phrase balancing the exact same phrase in v 11 (see Rhetoric and Composition for 52:1–11). Also, in the LXX this phrase is the sole conclusion to the verse. The conclusion "all the days of his life" in 2 Kgs 25:30 is original to the passage there, which is to say, the two passages did not end the same way. What happened here in Jeremiah 52 is that the ending of 2 Kgs 25:30, "all the days of his life," was later added to its ending, "until the day of his death," thus the redundancy (or conflation; Bright; Janzen 1973: 21). Or the words could just as easily have been taken from the end of v 33. It is also possible that LXX suffers in the present verse from haplography (homoeoteleuton: *w . . . w*), and if so, this must have occurred after the conflation. The most reasonable explanation for tacking on the 2 Kgs 25:30 ending, which has often been stated, is that the book of Jeremiah would not then conclude on a negative note, viz., the word "his death" (Streane; Montgomery 1951: 569). We know later Jewish tradition required a rereading of the penultimate verse in Isaiah so that book would not end on a negative note (Liebreich 1955–56: 277); the same was true with Malachi, which has as a final word "curse" (Dentan 1956: 1144).

MESSAGE AND AUDIENCE

The exilic audience hearing this postscript is told that time now is being reckoned not according to the reigning years of a Judahite king, nor even the reigning years of Nebuchadnezzar, but according to the number of years Jehoiachin has spent in exile. They add up to 37. But something good has happened in Babylon. King Evil-merodach, however infelicitous his name be in Hebrew, saw fit in his accession year to release Jehoiachin from prison. What is more, the king spoke good things to him and elevated him above other kings who were living out their days in Babylonian captivity. Jehoiachin thus exchanged his clothes for something less prison-like, and for the rest of his days was permitted to eat at the king's table. For himself and his family, Jehoiachin received a daily food allowance until the day of his death, the date of which we are not told.

This final postscript to both the Primary History and the book of Jeremiah will likely lift the spirits of Jewish exiles after hearing a prior word that has such finality to it. Deuteronomy made no provisions for a people having to witness the covenant curses come to pass, and the Deuteronomic History, with its past and present focus, its pessimism about the working out of sacred history, and its lack of hope for the future (Noth 1981: 12, 97–99), could scarcely have foreseen what now is being said in a later supplement to its work. The word here is cautiously optimistic. It says nothing about a restored Israel or a continuance of the Davidic line; nevertheless, it does report the dawning of a new day, and one is simply left to imagine what this unexpected event will mean for future days (cf. von Rad 1962: 343). The audience may perhaps recall that Jeremiah was given an allowance of food by Nebuzaradan upon his release, and that this was confirmation to the writer of the Jeremiah narrative that Yahweh's word was sure, and that Jeremiah was indeed rescued as promised, though the nation tumbled headlong into ruin. Will the release of Jehoiachin from prison cause this audience to wonder if Yahweh's promise to David (2 Samuel 7) will continue in the future? It is difficult to say. Jeremiah gave no hope for the Davidic line continuing through Jehoiachin (22:20). Still, this final word may kindle the imagination of weary exiles and raise in their breasts a hope that this will not be the end of it all, that there will be a tomorrow in which Yahweh will show favor in a way that will make his present goodness pale by comparison.

This postscript is to be dated following the accession of Evil-merodach in 562 B.C., but not necessarily subsequent to the death of Jehoiachin (*pace* Gray 1970: 773). Jehoiachin's allocation is simply "until the day of his death," which may still be in the future. If he had already died, that would have been explicitly stated. About this time also the Deuteronomic History is brought to completion (Noth 1981: 12; Cross 1973a: 287; D. N. Freedman 1983a). Neither work gives any hint of the rise of Cyrus the Persian two decades later.

ILLUSTRATIONS FROM THE DEAD SEA SCROLLS

◆

4QJer^a: Jer 9:7–15 on left; Jer 7:29–8:10 on right with 7:30–31 inserted horizontally in small letters, and 7:31–8:3 inserted vertically in small letters between the columns.

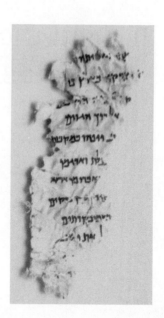

4QJer^b: Jer 9:22–10:18

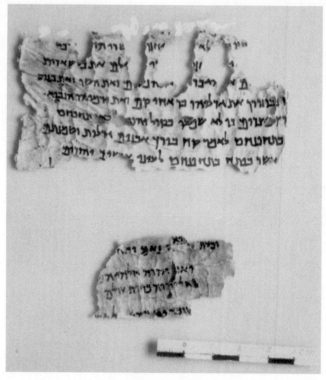

4QJer^d: Jer 43:3–9; 4QJer^e: Jer 50:4–6

4QJer^c: Jer 20:2–5 on right; Jer 20:7–9 on left

4QJer^c: Jer 22:17–28

4QJer^c: Jer 22:11–15

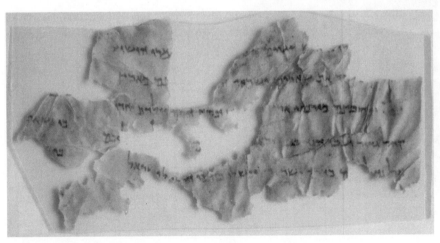

4QJer^c: Jer 31:7–9

APPENDIXES

◆

APPENDIX IV

◆

CONVERSION TABLES OF WEIGHTS, MEASURES, AND DISTANCES

a) Shekels to Grams and Ounces

The shekel was a unit of weight for payments in gold and silver. In preexilic Judah the light Babylonian system was in use, in which one shekel weighed 11.0–11.5 grams (*EncJud* 14: 1347). Archaeological finds (inscribed stone weights) show that the Judahite shekel in the seventh century B.C. weighed 11.4 grams (Meshorer 1978: 131–33).

SHEKELS	GRAMS	OUNCES
1	11.4	.40
17	193.8	6.78
22.7	259.4	9.08

b) Cubits to Inches, Feet, Meters, and Yards

The cubit is an ancient biblical measure for length, extending from the elbow to the tip of the middle finger. This works out to be roughly 18 inches, or 0.457 meters. A list of equivalents:

CUBITS	INCHES	FEET	METERS	YARDS
1	18		.46	
1.5	27		.69	
2	36	3	.91	
3		4.5	1.37	
4		6	1.83	
5		7.5	2.29	
12		18	5.48	
18		27	8.27	
30		45	13.71	
35		52.5	16	
50		75	22.9	25
60		90	27.42	30

200	300	91.4	100
400	600	182.8	200

c) Centimeters to Inches

One centimeter equals 0.03937 inches. A list of equivalents:

CENTIMETERS	INCHES
8	3.15

d) Feet to Meters

A foot equals 0.305 meters. A list of equivalents:

FEET	METERS	FEET	METERS
1	.31	30	9.15
4.5	1.37	75	22.88
5	1.53	90	27.45
6	1.83	100	30.50
7	2.14	300	91.50
10	3.05	1750	533.75
15	4.58	1800	549
18	5.49	3000	915
20	6.10	4300	1311.50
27	8.24	6000	1830

e) Meters to Feet

A meter equals 3.282 feet. A list of equivalents:

METERS	FEET	METERS	FEET
1	3.28	9	29.54
2	6.56	10	32.82
3	9.85	11	36.10
4	13.13	20	65.64
5	16.41	32.77	107.55
6	19.69	300	984.60
7	22.97	800	2625.60
7.3	23.96	900	2953.80
8	26.26	1500	4923

f) Miles to Kilometers

One English mile is equivalent to 1.609 kilometers. Conversions are as follows:

MILES	KILOMETERS	MILES	KILOMETERS
1	1.61	10	16.09
2	3.22	11	17.70
3	4.83	12	19.31
4	6.44	18	28.96
5	8.05	20	32.18
5.5	8.85	23	37.00
6	9.65	42.5	68.38
7	11.26	48	77.23
8	12.87	55	88.50
9	14.48	700	1126.30

g) Kilometers to Miles

One kilometer is equivalent to 0.621 English miles. Conversions are as follows:

KILOMETERS	MILES	KILOMETERS	MILES
1	.62	20	12.42
2	1.24	21	13.04
3	1.86	22	13.66
4	2.48	23	14.28
5	3.11	24	14.90
6	3.73	25	15.53
7	4.35	26	16.15
8	4.97	30	18.63
9	5.59	32	19.87
10	6.21	35	21.74
11	6.83	40	24.84
12	7.45	50	31.05
13	8.07	58	36.02
14	8.69	64	39.74
15	9.32	80	49.68
16	9.94	88	54.65
17	10.56	100	62.10
18	11.18	160	99.36
19	11.80	214	132.89

h) Roman Miles to English Miles and Kilometers

The Roman mile equals 1,000 paces, which comes out to about 0.919 English miles, or 1.480 kilometers.

ROMAN MILES	ENGLISH MILES	KILOMETERS
1	.92	1.48
2	1.84	2.96
3	2.76	4.44
4	3.68	5.92
8	7.35	11.84
10	9.19	14.80
15	13.79	22.20
20	18.38	29.60

i) Dunams to Acres

The dunam is a land measure equal to 1,000 square meters, or about 1/4 of an acre.

DUNAMS	ACRES
44	11
130	32.5
180	45
500	125
600	150

APPENDIX V

◆

HAPLOGRAPHY IN JEREMIAH 21–52

21:4   LXX omits *'ăšer bĕyedkem*, "that are in your hand" (whole-word: *'šr* . . . *'šr*).

       LXX omits *'et-melek bābel wĕ*, "the king of Babylon and" (whole-word: *'t* . . . *'t*).

21:5   LXX omits *ûbĕ'ap*, "yes, in anger" (homoeoarcton: *wb* . . . *wb*).

21:7   LXX omits *bĕyad nĕbûkadre'ṣṣar melek-bābel û*, "into the hand of Nebuchadrezzar, king of Babylon, and" (whole-word: *byd* . . . *byd*).

       LXX omits *wĕlō' yaḥmōl*, "and he will not pity" (whole-word: *wl'* . . . *wl'*).

21:9   LXX omits *ûbaddāber*, "and by pestilence" (homoeoarcton: *w* . . . *w*).

21:10   LXX omits *nĕ'ūm-yhwh*, "oracle of Yahweh" (homoeoteleuton: *h* . . . *h*).

21:12   MT omits *ûṣĕdāqâ*, "and righteousness" after *mišpāṭ*, "justice"; LXX has *krinate . . . krima kai kateuthunate*, "Judge a judgment . . . and act rightly" (homoeoarcton: *w* . . . *w*).

21:14   LXX omits *ûpāqadtî 'ălêkem kiprî ma'allêkem nĕum-yhwh*, "But I will reckon upon you according to the fruit of your doings—oracle of Yahweh" (homoeoarcton: *w* . . . *w*).

22:8   LXX omits *rabbîm*, "many" (homoeoteleuton: *ym* . . . *ym*).

22:11   LXX omits *melek yĕhûdâ*, "king of Judah," which could be haplography if the prior "Josiah" was spelled without the final *waw* (*y'šyh*), as it is in 4QJer[a] (homoeoteleuton: *h* . . . *h*).

22:18   MT may omit *hôy 'al-hā'îš hazzeh*, "Woe upon this man," after *melek yĕhûdâ*, "the king of Judah," since LXX adds *ouai epi ton andra touton* (homoeoteleuton: *h* . . . *h*).

22:25   LXX omits *ûbĕyad nĕbûkadre'ṣṣar melek-bābel*, "and into the hand of Nebuchadrezzar, king of Babylon" (whole-word: *wbyd* . . . *wbyd*).

22:26   LXX omits *'aḥeret*, "another" (homoeoarcton: *'aleph* . . . *'aleph*).

22:27   LXX omits *lāšûb šām šammâ*, "to return there, there" (homoeoarcton: *l* . . . *l*).

22:28   LXX omits *nāpûṣ hā'îš hazzeh*, "smashed, this man" (homoeoteleuton: *zh* . . . *zh*).

       LXX omits *hû' wĕzar'ô*, "he and his offspring" (homoeoteleuton: *w* . . . *w*).

22:29   LXX omits one of three successive occurrences of *'ereṣ*, "land" (whole-word).

22:30   LXX omits *kōh 'āmar yhwh*, "Thus said Yahweh" (homoeoarcton: *k . . . k* or whole-word: *yhwh . . . yhwh*).

23:2   LXX omits the first *hārō'îm* in the expression *hārō'îm hārō'îm*, "the shepherds who shepherd" (whole-word).

23:4   LXX omits *wĕlō' yippāqēdû*, "and they shall not be reckoned with" (homoeoteleuton: *w . . . w*).

23:7-8   LXX omits two entire verses (homoeoarcton: *l . . . l*).

23:8   LXX omits *he'ĕlâ wa'ăšer*, "who brought up and who" in its supplement at the end of the chapter (homoeoarcton: *h . . . h*, or whole-word: *'šr . . . 'šr*).

23:10   LXX omits *kî mĕnā'ăpîm mālĕ'â hā'āreṣ*, "Indeed of adulterers the land is full" (whole-word plus: *ky-m . . . ky-m*).

23:16   LXX omits *hannibbĕ'îm lākem*, "who prophesy to you" (homoeoteleuton: *m . . . m*).

23:17   Some LXX MSS omit *'āmĕrû*, "they say" (homoeoteleuton: *w . . . w*).

23:19[= 30:23]   LXX omits *rō'š*, "head" (homoeoarcton: *r . . . r*).

23:20   LXX omits the cognate accusative, *bînâ*, "understanding / meaning" (homoeoteleuton: *h . . . h*).

23:22   LXX omits *m middarkām hārā' û*, "them from their evil way and" (homoeoarcton: *m . . . m*).

23:28   MT omits final *waw* on second *ḥălôm*, "dream," in the verse; LXX has *to enupnion autou*, "his dream" (following word begins with *waw*).

23:36-37   LXX omits *wahăpaktem 'et-dibrê . . . meh-'ānāk yhwh*, "and you pervert the words . . . 'What has Yahweh answered you?'" (homoeoarcton: *w . . . w*).

23:38   LXX omits *wĕ'im-maśśā' yhwh tō'mērû*, "But if 'the burden of Yahweh' you say" (homoeoteleuton: *w . . . w*), since the end of LXX v 37 has *ho theos hymōn* ("our God"), presupposing Heb *'ĕlōhênû*.

24:1   LXX omits *wĕhinnēh*, "and there!" (homoeoteleuton: *h . . . h*).
         MT omits *wĕ'et-he'āšîr*, "and the rich," after "and the smiths"; LXX has *tous plousious*, "the wealthy" (homoeoteleuton: *r . . . r*).

24:3   LXX omits one of two occurrences of *tĕ'ēnîm*, "figs" (whole-word).

24:8   LXX omits *kî*, "indeed," prior to the messenger formula (homoeoarcton: *k . . . k*).

24:9   LXX omits *lĕrā'â*, "(for) a calamity" (homoeoarcton: *l . . . l*, or homoeoteleuton: *h . . . h*).

24:10   LXX omits *wĕla'ăbôtêhem*, "and to their fathers" (homoeoteleuton: *hm . . . hm*).

25:2   LXX omits *kol*, "all," in the phrase "and to all the inhabitants of Jerusalem" (homoeoteleuton: *l . . . l*).

25:3   LXX omits *wĕlō' šĕma'tem*, "but you have not listened" (homoeoarcton: *w . . . w*).

25:4   LXX omits *lišmōa'*, "to listen" (homoeoarcton: *l . . . l*).

25:7   LXX omits *lĕma'an hak'îsēnî bĕma'ăśēh yĕdêkem lĕra' lākem*, "so as to provoke me to anger with the work of your hands, to your own hurt," assuming that "oracle of Yahweh," also omitted, was lacking in the LXX's *Vorlage* (homoeoarcton: *l* . . . *l*).

25:9   LXX omits *wě'el-něbûkadre'ṣṣar melek-bābel 'abdî*, "also to Nebucha-drezzar, king of Babylon, my servant," assuming that "oracle of Yah-weh," also omitted, was lacking in the LXX's *Vorlage* (homoeoarcton: *w* . . . *w*).

25:12   LXX omits *'al-melek-bābel wě*, "against the king of Babylon and" (whole-word: *ʿl* . . . *ʿl*).

25:14   LXX omits entire verse (homoeoarcton: *k* . . . *k* with *kōh*, not *kî*, or ho-moeoteleuton: *m* . . . *m*).
       MT omits *yod* on *ya'abdû*, "(they) shall make . . . serve" (prior word ends with *yod*).

25:15   LXX omits initial *kî*, "For" (homoeoarcton: *k* . . . *k*).
       LXX omits *'ōtô*, "it," after the verb "(you) make . . . drink" (homoeoarc-ton: *'t* . . . *'t*).

25:16   Some LXX MSS omit *wěšātû*, "And they shall drink" (homoeoarcton: *w* . . . *w*).

25:18   LXX omits *wěliqlālâ kayyôm hazzeh*, "and a swearword, as at this day" (homoeoteleuton: *h* . . . *h*).

25:20   LXX omits *wě'ēt kol-malkê 'ereṣ hā'ûṣ*, "and all the kings of the land of Uz" (four-word: *w't kl-mlky 'rṣ* . . . *w't kl-mlky 'rṣ*).

25:24   LXX omits *wě'ēt kol-malkê 'ărāb*, "and all the kings of Arabia" (three-word: *w't kl-mlky* . . . *w't kl-mlky*).

25:25   LXX omits *wě'ēt kol-malkê zimrî*, "and all the kings of Zimri" (three-word: *w't kl-mlky* . . . *w't kl-mlky*).

25:26   LXX omits *ûmelek šēšak yišteh 'aḥărêhem*, "And the king of Sheshak shall drink after them" (homoeoarcton: *w* . . . *w*).

25:29   LXX omits *lō' tinnāqû*, "You shall not go unpunished" (whole-word: *tnqw* . . . *tnqw*).

25:33   LXX omits *lō' yissāpědû wělō' yē'āsěpû wě*, "They shall not be la-mented, and they shall not be gathered, and" (whole-word: *l'* . . . *l'*).

25:34   LXX omits anomalous *ûtěpôṣôtîkem*, "and you will be scattered" (ho-moeoarcton: *w* . . . *w*).

26:4   LXX omits "to them" (*pros autous*) after "And you shall say" (*ereis*), which is an inner-Greek haplography; MT has *wě'āmartā 'ălêhem* (ho-moeoteleuton: *s* . . . *s*).

26:12   LXX omits *kol*, "all," before "the princes" (homoeoteleuton: *l* . . . *l*).

26:20   LXX omits *'al-hā'îr hazzō't wě*, "against this city and" (whole-word: *ʿl* . . . *ʿl*).

26:21   LXX omits *wěkol-gibbôrāyw*, "also all his officers" (whole-word: *wkl* . . . *wkl*).
       LXX omits *hammelek*, "the king," after the verb "and he sought" (ho-moeoarcton: *hm* . . . *hm*).
       LXX omits *wayyirā' wayyibraḥ*, "and he was afraid and fled" (homoeo-arcton: *wy* . . . *wy*).

26:22 LXX omits *'ēt 'elnātān ben-ʿakbôr waʾănāšîm 'ittô 'el-miṣrāyim*, "El-
nathan son of Achbor and men with him to Egypt" (whole-word: *mṣrym*
... *mṣrym*).

27:3 MT appears to omit *liqrāʾtām*, "to meet them," after *habbāʾîm*, "who
are coming," since LXX supplements MT with *eis apantēsin autōn*, "to
meet them" (homoeoteleuton: *m ... m*).

27:5 LXX omits *'et-hāʾādām wĕ'et-habbĕhēmâ 'ăšer ʿal-pĕnê hāʾāreṣ*, "human and beast that are on the face of the earth" (whole-word: *h'rṣ*
... *h'rṣ*).

27:6 LXX omits *wĕʿattâ 'ānōkî*, "And now, I" (homoeoteleuton: *y ... y*).

27:7 LXX omits entire verse (homoeoarcton: *w ... w*).

27:8 LXX omits the initial *hāyâ* (without *waw*), "And it shall be" (homoeoarcton: *h ... h*).
LXX omits *yaʿabdû 'ōtô 'et-nĕbûkadneʾṣṣar melek-bābel wĕ'ēt 'ăšer lōʾ*,
"serve him, that is, Nebuchadnezzar, king of Babylon, and who will
not" (two-word: *'šr l' ... 'šr l'*).

27:9 LXX omits *'ălêkem*, "to you" (homoeoteleuton: *m ... m*).

27:10 LXX omits *wĕhiddaḥtî 'etkem waʾăbadtem*, "for I will disperse you
and you will perish" (homoeoarcton: *wh ... wh*, or homoeoteleuton:
m ... m).

27:12b–14 LXX omits part of three verses: *'ōtô wĕʿammô wiḥyû ... lōʾ*
taʿabdû, "him and his people, and live! ... You shall not serve" (whole-
word: *ʿbdw ... ʿbdw*).

27:16 LXX omits *ʿattâ mĕhērâ*, "now shortly" (homoeoteleuton: *h ... h*).
MT omits *lōʾ šĕlaḥtîm*, "I did not send them," at the end of the verse,
which is present in the LXX's *ouk apesteila autous* (homoeoteleuton:
m ... m).

27:17–18a LXX omits all of v 17 and the *waw* beginning v 18: *'al-tišmĕʿû*
ʿălêhem ... lāmmâ tihyeh hāʿîr hazzō't ḥorbâ wĕ, "Do not listen to
them ... Why should this city become a ruin? And" (homoeoarcton:
'aleph ... 'aleph).

27:18 MT omits *yod* on an original imperfect *yābōʾû*, "they go" (prior word
ends in *yod*).

27:19 LXX omits *'el-hāʿammûdîm wĕʿal-hayyām wĕʿal-hammĕkōnôt*, "concerning the pillars, and concerning the sea, and concerning the stands"
(homoeoteleuton: *wt ... wt*).

27:20a LXX omits *ben-yĕhôyāqîm melek-yĕhûdâ*, "son of Jehoiakim, king of Judah" (homoeoteleuton: *h ... h*).

27:20b–22a LXX omits a portion of three verses: *wĕ'ēt kol-ḥōrê yĕhûdâ wîrûšālāyim ... ûbêt melek-yĕhûdâ wîrûšālāyim bābelâ*, "also all the nobles of
Judah and Jerusalem ... and the house of the king of Judah, and Jerusalem: To Babylon" (four-word: *mlk-yhwdh myrwšlm bblh ... mlk-
yhwdh wyrwšlm bblh*).

27:22 LXX omits *wěhaʿălîtîm wahăšîbōtîm ʾel-hammāqôm hazzeh*, "and I bring them out and bring them back to this place" (homoeoarcton: *w . . . w*, or homoeoteleuton: *h . . . h*).

28:3 LXX omits *kol*, "all," in the phrase "all the vessels" (whole-word: *kl . . . kl*).

LXX omits *ʾăšer lāqaḥ nĕbûkadneʾṣṣar melek-bābel min-hammāqôm hazzeh wayĕbîʾēm bābel*, "that Nebuchadnezzar, king of Babylon, took from this place and brought to Babylon," which could be haplography if the final *bābel*, "Babylon," was originally the expected *bābelâ*, "to Babylon" (homoeoteleuton: *h . . . h*).

28:4 LXX omits *ben-yĕhôyāqîm melek-yĕhûdâ*, "son of Jehoiakim, king of Judah" (homoeoteleuton: *h . . . h*).

LXX omits *habbāʾîm bābelâ ʾănî mēšîb ʾel-hammāqôm hazzeh nĕʾūm-yhwh*, "who came to Babylon, I will bring back to this place—oracle of Yahweh" (homoeoteleuton: *h . . . h*).

28:14 LXX omits *waʿăbādûhû wĕgam ʾet-ḥayyat haśśādeh nātattî lô*, "and they shall serve him; even the beasts of the field I have given to him" (homoeoarcton: *w . . . w*).

28:15 LXX omits *hannābîʾ šĕmaʿ-nāʾ ḥănanyâ*, "the prophet: 'Do listen Hananiah" (whole-word: *ḥnnyh . . . ḥnnyh*).

29:1 LXX omits *ʾăšer heglâ nĕbûkadneʾṣṣar mîrûšālayim bābelâ*, "whom Nebuchadnezzar exiled from Jerusalem to Babylon" (homoeoarcton: *ʾaleph . . . ʾaleph*).

29:2 LXX omits *(wě)śārê yĕhûdâ wîrûšālayim*, "(and) the princes of Judah and Jerusalem," where several MSS and the Vrs contain an initial *waw* (homoeoarcton: *w . . . w*).

29:4 LXX omits *kol*, "all" (homoeoteleuton: *l . . . l*).

LXX omits *bābelâ*, "to Babylon" (homoeoarcton: *b . . . b*).

29:6 LXX omits *wĕtēladnâ bānîm ûbānôt*, "and let them bear sons and daughters" (homoeoarcton: *w . . . w*).

29:11 LXX omits *yādaʿtî ʾet-hammaḥăšābōt ʾăšer ʾānōkî*, "I know the plans that I" (whole-word: *ʾnky . . . ʾnky*).

29:12 LXX omits *ûqĕrāʾtem ʾōtî wahălaktem*, "And you will call me and will come" (homoeoarcton: *w . . . w*).

29:14 LXX omits most of the verse: *nĕʾūm yhwh wěšabtî ʾet-šĕbûtĕkem . . . ʾăšer-higlêtî etkem miššām*, "oracle of Yahweh—and I will restore your fortunes . . . from which I exiled you" (homoeoteleuton: *m . . . m*).

29:16–20 LXX omits five whole verses: *kî-kōh ʾāmar yhwh . . . mîrûšālayim bābelâ*, "For thus said Yahweh . . . from Jerusalem to Babylon" (homoeoarcton: *k . . . k*, or whole-word plus: *m bblh . . . m bblh*).

29:21 LXX omits *hannibbĕʾîm lākem bišmî šāqer*, "who are prophesying a lie to you in my name" (homoeoarcton: *hn . . . hn*).

29:24 LXX omits *lēʾmōr*, "saying" (homoeoteleuton: *ʾmr . . . ʾmr*).

29:25 LXX omits *koh-ʾāmar yhwh ṣĕbāʾôt ʾĕlōhê yiśrāʾēl lēʾmōr*, "Thus said
       Yahweh of hosts, God of Israel (saying)" (whole-word: *lʾmr . . . lʾmr*).
       LXX omits *ʾel-kol-hāʿām ʾăšer bîrûšālayim wĕ*, "to all the people who
       are in Jerusalem, and" (whole-word: *ʾl . . . ʾl*).

29:31 LXX omits *kol*, "all" in the phrase "Send to all the exiles" (ho-
       moeoteleuton: *l . . . l*).

29:32 LXX omits *kî-sārâ dibber ʿal-yhwh*, "for he has spoken rebellion against
       Yahweh," assuming that the prior *nĕum yhwh*, "oracle of Yahweh," was
       present in the LXX's *Vorlage* (whole-word: *yhwh . . . yhwh*).

30:5   LXX omits initial *kî*, "for" (homoeoarcton: *k . . . k*); this could also be
       an inner-Greek haplography since Aq, Symm, and Theod have *hoti*
       houtōs (homoeoarcton: *ho . . . ho*).

30:8   LXX omits *bô*, "him," after "they shall not make serve" (homoeoteleu-
       ton: *w . . . w*).

30:14 LXX omits *ʾōtāk*, "you" (homoeoteleuton: *k . . . k*).

30:15 LXX omits entire verse (homoeoteleuton: *k . . . k*).

30:19 LXX omits *wĕhikbadtîm wĕlōʾ yiṣʿārû*, "I will give them honor, and they
       shall not be insignificant" (homoeoarcton: *w . . . w*, or homoeoteleu-
       ton: *w . . . w*).

30:20 LXX omits *kol*, "all" (homoeoteleuton: *l . . . l*).

30:22–23 LXX omits all of v 22 and *hinnēh*, "Look," beginning v 23 (ho-
       moeoteleuton: *h . . . h*).

30:23 See LXX omission in 23:19.

30:24 MT omits *bînâ*, "understanding," after *titbônĕnû bāh*, "you will under-
       stand it"; cf. 23:20 (homoeoteleuton: *h . . . h*).

31:1   LXX omits *kōl*, "all," in "all the tribes" (homoeoteleuton: *l . . . l*).

31:13 LXX omits *wĕniḥamtîm*, "and I will comfort them" (homoeoarcton: *w*
       . . . w).
       LXX omits *mîgônām*, "their sorrow" (homoeoteleuton: *m . . . m*).

31:15 LXX omits the first *ʿal-bāneyhā*, "over her sons" (homoeoteleuton: *h*
       . . . h).

31:17 LXX omits *wĕyēš-tiqwâ lĕʾaḥărîtēk nĕʾūm-yhwh*, "And there is hope for
       your future—oracle of Yahweh" (homoeoarcton: *w . . . w*).

31:20 LXX omits the interrogative *ʾim* preceding "the child of delight" (ho-
       moeoteleuton: *m . . . m*).
       LXX omits *ʿôd*, "still" (homoeoarcton: *ʿayin . . . ʿayin*).

31:23 LXX omits *nĕwēh*, "pasture" (homoeoteleuton: *h . . . h*).

31:28 LXX omits *lintôš wĕlintôṣ wĕ*, "to uproot and to break down, and" (ho-
       moeoarcton: *l . . . l*).
       LXX omits *ûlĕhaʾăbîd*, "and to destroy" (homoeoarcton: *wlh . . . wlh*).

31:38 MT omits *bāʾîm*, "are coming" (homoeoteleuton: *ym . . . ym*).
       MT omits prefixed *lamed* on *šaʿar*, "gate" (double *lamed* in succession).

31:39 LXX omits *wĕnāsab gōʿātâ*, "and turn to Goah" (homoeoarcton:
       w . . . w).

31:40 LXX omits *wĕkol-hāʿēmeq happĕgārîm wĕhaddešen*, "And all the valley land, the corpses and the ashes" (whole-word plus: *wkl-h . . . wkl-h*).

32:2 LXX omits *hannābîʾ*, "the prophet" (homoeoarcton: *h . . . h*).

32:5–6 LXX omits *ʿad-poqdî ʾōtô nĕʾūm-yhwh kî tillāḥămû ʾet-hakkaśdîm lōʾ taṣlîḥû wayyōʾmer yirmĕyāh*, "'until I reckon with him—oracle of Yahweh—for though you fight the Chaldeans, you shall not succeed' And Jeremia(h) said" (homoeoteleuton: *h . . . h*).

32:8 LXX omits *kidbar yhwh*, "according to the word of Yahweh," which is an inner-Greek haplography (homoeoteleuton: *patros mou kata ton logon kuriou*).

32:11 LXX omits *hammiṣwâ wĕhaḥuqqîm*, "the contract and the conditions" (homoeoteleuton: *m . . . m*).

32:12 LXX omits *hayyōšĕbîm*, "who were sitting" (homoeoteleuton: *ym . . . ym*).

32:14 LXX omits *ʾet-hassĕpārîm hāʾelleh*, "these deeds" (whole word: *ʾt . . . ʾt*).
LXX omits *wĕʾēt heḥātûm*, "sealed" (whole-word: *wʾt . . . wʾt*).

32:17 LXX omits *hinnēh*, "Look" (homoeoteleuton: *h . . . h*).

32:19 LXX omits *kol*, "all" in "all the ways" (homoeoteleuton: *l . . . l*).
LXX omits *wĕkiprî maʿălālāyw*, "and according to the fruit of his doings" (homoeoteleuton: *yw . . . yw*).

32:22 LXX omits *lātēt lāhem*, "to give to them" (homoeoteleuton: *m . . . m*).

32:23 LXX omits *laʿăśôt*, "to do" before "they did not do" (homoeoarcton: *l . . . l*).

32:24 LXX omits *wĕhaddāber*, "and the pestilence" (homoeoarcton: *w . . . w*).
LXX omits *wĕhinnĕkā rōʾeh*, "So look, you are watching!" (homoeoarcton: *w . . . w*, or homoeoteleuton: *h . . . h*).

32:25 LXX omits *ʾădōnāy yhwh*, "O Lord Yahweh," which is an inner-Greek haplography (homoeoteleuton: *me . . . kurie*).

32:30 LXX omits *kî bĕnê-yiśrāʾēl ʾak makʿisîm ʾōtî bĕmaʿăśēh yĕdêhem nĕʾūm-yhwh*, "Indeed, the children of Israel have only provoked me to anger with the work of their hands—oracle of Yahweh" (whole-word: *ky . . . ky*).

32:35 MT omits terminal *ʾaleph* on Kt *haḥăṭîʾ*, "make to sin"; corrected by Q (double consonants in succession).

32:40 LXX omits *lĕhêṭîbî ʾôtām*, "to do good to them" (homoeoteleuton: *m . . . m*).

32:43 LXX omits *hēʾ* ("the") before *śādeh*, "field" (double consonants in succession).

33:2 LXX omits second occurrence of *yhwh* in the verse (homoeoarcton: *y . . . y* or homoeoteleuton: *h . . . h*).

33:9 LXX omits *lî*, "to me" (homoeoarcton: *l . . . l*).
LXX omits *šēm*, "name" (homoeoarcton: *š . . . š*).

33:10 LXX omits *ûmēʾên yôšēb*, "and without inhabitant" (whole-word: *wmʾyn . . . wmʾyn*).

33:11   MT omits conjunctive *waw* on *mĕbî'îm*, "those bringing," which is present in LXX, S, and Vg (double *waw* in succession).

33:16   MT omits *šĕmāh*, "her name," which is present in T and suggested also by parallel verse in 23:6 (homoeoteleuton: *h . . . h*).

33:14–26   LXX omits entire 13 verses (homoeoarcton: *h . . . h*).

34:2   MT omits *ûlĕkādāh*, "and he will take it," after "Babylon," which is present in LXX (homoeoarcton: *w . . . w*).

34:3   LXX omits *ûpîhû 'et-pîkā yĕdabbēr*, "and his mouth shall speak to your mouth" (homoeoarcton: *w . . . w*).

34:7   LXX omits *kol*, "all," before the first "cities of Judah" (homoeoteleuton: *l . . . l*).

34:8   LXX omits *'ăšer bîrûšālayim*, "who were in Jerusalem" (homoeoteleuton: *m . . . m*).

34:10   LXX omits *ḥopšîm lĕbiltî 'ăbād-bām 'ôd wayyišmĕ'û wayĕšallēḥû*, "free . . . so that he should not make them serve again; and they gave heed and sent them away" (homoeoteleuton: *w . . . w*).

34:11   LXX omits *wayyāšûbû 'aḥărē-kēn wayyāšîbû 'et-hā'ăbādîm wĕ'et-haš-šĕpāḥôt 'ăšer šillēḥû ḥopšîm*, "Then they turned around after this and took back the male slaves and female slaves that they had sent away free" (homoeoarcton: *wy . . . wy*).

34:13   LXX omits *'ĕlōhê yiśrā'ēl*, "God of Israel" (homoeoarcton: *'aleph . . . 'aleph*).

34:14   LXX omits *'ăbôtêkem*, "your fathers" (homoeoarcton: *'aleph . . . 'aleph*).

34:16   LXX omits *wattikbĕšû 'ōtām*, "and you subjugated them" (homoeoteleuton: *m . . . m*).
        LXX omits *lihyôt*, "to be" (homoeoarcton: *l . . . l*).

34:17   LXX omits *'îš lĕ'āḥîw wĕ*, "each person to his kin" (whole-word plus: *'yš l . . . 'yš l*).

34:19   LXX omits *wĕśārê yĕrûšālayim*, "and the princes of Jerusalem," which is an inner-Greek haplography, since in the LXX the word immediately following the omission is *kai* (whole-word: *kai . . . kai*).

34:20   LXX omits *ûbĕyad mĕbaqšê napšām*, "and into the hand of those who seek their life" (homoeoarcton: *w . . . w* or homoeoteleuton: *m . . . m*).

34:21   LXX omits *ûbĕyad mĕbaqšê napšām*, "and into the hand of those who seek their life" (whole-word: *wbyd . . . wbyd* or homoeoteleuton: *m . . . m*).

35:2   LXX omits *wĕdibbartā 'ôtām*, "and you shall speak to them" (homoeoarcton: *w . . . w* or homoeoteleuton: *m . . . m*).

35:5   LXX omits *mĕlē'îm*, "full" (homoeoteleuton: *ym . . . ym*).

35:7   LXX omits *lō'-tiṭṭā'û wĕ*, "you shall not plant, nor" (whole word: *l' . . . l'*).

35:8   LXX omits *ben-rēkāb*, "son of Rechab" (homoeoteleuton: *b . . . b*).
        LXX omits *lĕkōl 'ăšer ṣiwwānû*, "in all that he commanded us" (homoeoteleuton: *nw . . . nw*).

35:16 LXX omits *'ăšer ṣiwwām*, "which he commanded them" (homoeoteleu-ton: *m . . . m*).

35:18 LXX omits *ûlĕbêt hārēkābîm 'āmar yirmĕyāhû*, "But to the house of the Rechabites Jeremiah said" (homoeoteleuton: *w . . . w*).
LXX omits *wattišmĕrû 'et-kol-miṣôtāyw*, "and you have kept all his com-mands" (homoeoarcton: *wt . . . wt*).

35:19 LXX omits *lākēn kōh 'āmar yhwh ṣĕbā'ôt 'ĕlōhê yiśrā'ēl*, "Therefore thus said Yahweh of hosts, God of Israel" (homoeoarcton: *l . . . l*).

36:6 LXX omits *ûbā'tā 'attâ*, "So you, you shall enter" (homoeoarcton: *w . . . w*, or homoeoteleuton: *h . . . h*).
LXX omits *'ăšer-kātabtā-mippî 'et-dibrê yhwh*, "that you have written from my dictation the words of Yahweh" (homoeoteleuton: *h . . . h*).

36:9 LXX omits *ben-yō'šîyāhû melek-yĕhûdâ*, "son of Josiah, king of Judah" (homoeoarcton: *b . . . b*).
LXX omits *wĕkol-hā'ām habbā'îm mē'ārê yĕhûdâ bîrûšālāyim*, "and all the people who had come in from the cities of Judah—in Jerusalem" (whole word: *byrwšlm . . . byrwšlm* or homoeoarcton: *w . . . w*).

36:13 LXX omits *bassēper*, "aloud the scroll" (homoeoarcton: *b . . . b*).

36:25 LXX omits *ûgĕmaryāhû*, "and Gemariah" (homoeoteleuton: *yhw . . . yhw*).
LXX omits *wĕlō' šāma' 'ălēhem*, "but he did not listen to them" (ho-moeoarcton: *w . . . w*).

36:26 LXX omits *wĕ'et-šelemĕyāhû ben-'abdĕ'ēl*, "and Shelemiah son of Ab-deel" (homoeoteleuton: *'l . . . 'l*).

36:28 LXX omits *hārī'šōnîm*, "the former," after "all the words" (ho-moeoteleuton: *ym . . . ym*).
LXX omits *hārī'šōnâ*, "the first," after "the roll" (homoeoteleuton: *m . . . m*).

36:29 LXX omits *wĕ'al-yĕhôyāqîm melek-yĕhûdâ*, "And concerning Jehoiakim, king of Judah" (three-word: *yhwyqym mlk-yhwdh . . . yhwyqym mlk-yhwdh*).

36:32 LXX omits *wayyittĕnāh 'el-bārûk ben-nērîyāhû hassōpēr*, "and gave it to Baruch son of Neriah, the scribe" (homoeoarcton: *wy . . . wy*).

37:1 LXX omits first occurrence of *melek*, "king" (homoeoteleuton: *mlk . . . mlk*).
LXX omits an original *yĕhôyāqîn ben*, "Jehoiachin son of" (LXX^A: *iechoniou uiou*) (homoeoarcton: *y . . . y*).

37:5 LXX omits *haṣṣārîm 'al-yĕrûšālayim*, "who were beseiging Jerusalem" (homoeoteleuton: *m . . . m*, or *ym . . . ym* if "Jerusalem" had the dual ending *-ayim*).

37:12 MT omits *'el*, "to," before *'ereṣ*, "land"—a few MSS contain; T has *lĕ'ereṣ*—(homoeoarcton: *aleph . . . aleph*).

37:15 LXX omits *bêt hā'ēsûr*, "in the stockhouse" (whole-word: *byt . . . byt*).

37:16 LXX omits *yirmĕyāhû*, "Jeremiah" (homoeoarcton: *y . . . y*).

37:19 LXX omits *'ălêkem wĕ*, "against you and" (homoeoarcton: *'l . . . 'l*).

38:1   LXX omits *ûpašḥûr ben-malkîyyāh*[*û*], "and Pashhur son of Malchiah," assuming the preexilic spelling -*yhw* in the patronym (homoeoteleuton: *yhw* . . . *yh*[*w*]).

38:2   LXX omits *ûbaddāber*, "and by pestilence" (homoeoarcton: *w* . . . *w*).

38:6   LXX omits *wayyiqḥû ʾet-yirmĕyāhû*, "And they took Jeremiah" (homoeoarcton: *wy* . . . *wy*).

       LXX omits *baḥăbālîm û*, "with ropes. And" (homoeoarcton: *b* . . . *b*, or homoeoteleuton: *w* . . . *w*).

39:4–13   LXX omits entire ten verses: *wayĕhî kaʾăšer rāʾām ṣidqîyāhû melek-yĕhûdâ* . . . *wĕkōl rabbê melek-bābel*, "And it happened when Zedekiah, king of Judah, saw them . . . and all the chief officers of the king of Babylon" (homoeoarcton: *wy* . . . *wy* or two-word: *mlk-bbl* . . . *mlk-bbl*).

39:15   LXX omits *bihyōtô ʿāṣûr*, "when he was confined" (homoeoarcton: *b* . . . *b*).

39:16   MT omits ʾ*aleph* on *mēbî*, "bringing" (double ʾ*aleph* in succession).
       LXX omits *wĕhāyû lĕpāneykā bayyôm hahûʾ*, "and they shall come to pass before you in that day" (homoeoarcton: *wh* . . . *wh*).

40:1   LXX omits *yĕrûšālayim w*, "Jerusalem and" (homoeoarcton: *y* . . . *y*).

40:3   LXX omits *wayyābēʾ*, "So he brought it about" (homoeoarcton: *wy* . . . *wy*).

       LXX omits *kaʾăšer dibbēr*, "according to what he spoke" (homoeoarcton: *k* . . . *k*).

       LXX omits *wĕhāyâ lākem (had)dābār hazzeh*, "so this thing happened to you" (homoeoarcton: *w* . . . *w*).

40:4   LXX omits *wĕʿattâ*, "But now" (homoeoteleuton: *h* . . . *h*).

40:5   LXX omits *wĕʿôdennû lōʾ-yāšûb*, "And still he did not turn" (homoeoarcton: *w* . . . *w*).

40:7   LXX omits *wāṭāp ûmiddallat hāʾāreṣ mē*, "and small children, and some of the poor of the land—from those" (homoeoteleuton: *m* . . . *m*).

40:8   LXX omits *wĕyônātān*, "and Jonathan" (homoeoteleuton: *n* . . . *n*).

40:12   LXX omits *wayyāšūbû kol-hayyĕhûdîm mikkol-hammĕqōmôt ʾăšer niddĕḥû-šām*, "So all the Judahites returned from all the places where they had been dispersed" (homoeoarcton: *wy* . . . *wy*).

40:14   MT omits ʾ*ēleykā*, "to you" after the verb "has sent" (homoeoarcton: ʾ*aleph* . . . ʾ*aleph*).

41:1   LXX omits *wĕrabbê hammelek*, "and one of the chief officers of the king" (homoeoarcton: *w* . . . *w*).

41:2   LXX omits *ben-ʾăḥîqām ben-šāpān baḥereb wayyāmet ʾōtô*, "son of Ahikam, son of Shaphan, with the sword. So he killed him" (homoeoteleuton: *w* . . . *w*).

41:3   LXX omits ʾ*et-gĕdalyāhû*, "that is, Gedaliah" (homoeoteleuton: *w* . . . *w*).

41:6   LXX omits *wayĕhî kipgōš ʾōtām*, "And it happened as he met them" (homoeoarcton: *wy* . . . *wy*).

41:10   LXX omits *wayyišbēm yišmāʿēʾl ben-nĕtanyâ*, "And Ishmael son of Nethaniah took them captive" (homoeoarcton *wy* . . . *wy*).

41:13–14 LXX omits *wayyiśmāḥû wayyāsōbû kol-hā'ām 'ăšer-šābâ yišmā'ē'l min-hammiṣpâ*, "that they were glad. So all the people whom Ishmael had taken captive from Mizpah turned about" (homoeoarcton: *wyš . . . wyš*).

LXX omits *wayyēlĕkû*, "and they went over" (homoeoteleuton: *w . . . w*).

42:4 LXX omits *'etkem*, "you" (homoeoarcton: *'aleph . . . 'aleph*).

42:9 LXX omits *'ĕlōhê yiśrā'ēl 'ăšer šĕlaḥtem 'ōtî 'ēlāyw lĕhappîl tĕḥinnatkem lĕpānāyw*, "God of Israel, to whom you sent me to lay your request before him" (homoeoarcton: *'aleph . . . 'aleph*).

42:15 LXX omits *šĕ'ērît yĕhûdâ*, "Remnant of Judah" (homoeoteleuton: *h . . . h*).

42:17 MT omits *wĕkol-hazzārîm*, "and all the foreigners," which is present in the LXX after "all the men" (homoeoteleuton: *ym . . . ym*).

LXX omits *ûbaddāber*, "and by pestilence" (homoeoarcton: *w . . . w*).

42:18 LXX may have lacked *waḥămātî*, "and my wrath" in its *Vorlage* (homoeoteleuton: *y . . . y*).

42:19 LXX omits *kî-ha'îdōtî bākem hayyôm*, "that I have warned you today" (whole-word plus: *ky h . . . ky h*).

42:20 LXX omits *'el-yhwh 'ĕlōhêkem*, "to Yahweh your God" (repetition of the letters *'aleph* and *lamed*: *'l . . . 'l . . . l' . . .*).

LXX omits *kēn hagged-lānû*, "so tell us" (homoeoteleuton: *nw . . . nw*).

42:21 LXX omits *wā'aggid lākem hayyôm*, "And I told you today" (homoeoarcton: *w . . . w*).

LXX omits *'ĕlōhêkem ûlĕkōl*, "your God regarding all" (homoeoarcton: *'aleph . . . 'aleph*).

43:1 LXX omits *kol*, "all," in the phrase "to all the people" (homoeoteleuton: *l . . . l*).

43:2 LXX omits *hazzēdîm*, "the insolent men" (homoeoteleuton: *ym . . . ym*).

LXX omits *'attâ mĕdabbēr*, "You are telling" (homoeoteleuton: *r . . . r*).

LXX omits *'ĕlōhênû*, "our God" before a probable *ēlênû*, "to us," in its *Vorlage*—it contains *pros hēmas* (homoeoarcton: *'l . . . 'l*).

MT omits *ēlênû*, "to us" (LXX: *pros hēmas*) after *'ĕlōhênû*, "our God" (homoeoteleuton: *ynw . . . ynw*)

43:9 LXX omits *bammeleṭ bammalbēn 'ăšer*, "with mortar in the pavement that" (homoeoarcton: *b . . . b*).

44:1 LXX omits *ûbĕnōp*, "and in Memphis" (homoeoarcton: *wb . . . wb*).

44:2 LXX omits *hayyôm hazzeh*, "this day" (homoeoteleuton: *h . . . h*).

44:3 LXX omits *la'ăbōd*, "to serve" (homoeoarcton: *l . . . l*).

LXX omits *hēmmâ 'attem wa'ăbōtêkem*, "they, you, and your fathers" (homoeoteleuton: *m . . . m*).

44:9 LXX omits *wĕ'et rā'ōtēkem*, "and your evils" (two-word: *w't r't . . . w't r't*).

44:10 LXX omits *wĕlō' yārĕ'û*, "And they are not afraid" (whole-word: *wl'* . . . *wl'*).

LXX omits *bĕtôrātî û*, "in my law and" (homoeoarcton: *b* . . . *b*, or homoeoteleuton: *w* . . . *w*, with the sequence *wb* repeating).

44:13 LXX omits *ûbaddāber*, "and by pestilence" (homoeoarcton: *w* . . . *w*).

44:18 LXX omits *wĕhassēk-lāh nĕsākîm*, "and pouring out drink offerings to her" (homoeoteleuton: *ym* . . . *ym*).

44:19 MT omits *wĕhannāšîm 'āmĕrû*, "And the women said," which is present in G^L at the beginning of the verse (homoeoarcton: *w* . . . *w*, or homoeoteleuton: *w* . . . *w*).

44:24 LXX omits *kol-yĕhûdâ 'ăšer bĕ'ereṣ miṣrāyim*, "all Judah who are in the land of Egypt" (homoeoarcton: *k* . . . *k*).

44:28 LXX omits *mimmennî ûmēhem*, "mine or theirs" (homoeoteleuton: *m* . . . *m*).

44:29 LXX omits *bammāqôm hazzeh lĕma'an tēdĕ'û kî qôm yāqûmû dĕbāray 'ălêkem* "in this place so that you may know that my words will be fully confirmed against you" (whole-word: *'lykm* . . . *'lykm*).

45:3 MT has one occurrence of *'ôy*, "woe," where LXX has *oimmoi, oimmoi* ("woe, woe"), which could indicate MT (whole-word) haplography; T, however, has only one "woe."

45:4 LXX omits *wĕ'et-kol-hā'āreṣ hî'*, "and that is the whole earth" (homoeoarcton: *w't* . . . *w't*).

46:1 MT omits *kol*, "all," before "the nations" (homoeoteleuton: *l* . . . *l*).

46:8aβ LXX omits *wĕkannĕhārôt yitgō'ăšû māyim*, "and like the great river, the waters are swollen" (homoeoarcton: *w* . . . *w*).

46:14 LXX omits *bĕmiṣrayim wĕhašmî'û*, "in Egypt, and proclaim" (homoeoarcton: *bm* . . . *bm*, or homoeoteleuton: *w* . . . *w*).

46:25 LXX omits *wĕ'al-miṣrayim wĕ'al-'ĕlōheyhā wĕ'al-mĕlākeyhā wĕ'al-par'ōh*, "and upon Egypt, and upon her gods, and upon her kings, and upon Pharaoh" (whole-word: *w'l* . . . *w'l*, or two-word: *w'l-pr'h* . . . *w'l-pr'h*).

46:26 LXX omits entire verse (homoeoarcton: *w* . . . *w*).

47:1 LXX omits *'ăšer hāyâ dĕbar-yhwh 'el-yirmĕyāhû hannābî'*, "What came as the word of Yahweh to Jeremiah the prophet" (homoeoarcton: *'aleph* . . . *'aleph*).

47:6 LXX omits *hôy*, "Woe" (homoeoteleuton: *y* . . . *y*).

48:1 LXX omits first occurrence of *hōbîšâ*, "is very shamed" (homoeoteleuton: *h* . . . *h*).

48:5 LXX omits *ṣārê*, "distressful" (homoeoarcton: *ṣ* . . . *ṣ*).

48:7a LXX omits *bĕma'ăśayik*, "in your works" (homoeoteleuton: *k* . . . *k*, or homoeoarcton if the *waw* on the following word was not present: *b* . . . *b*).

48:8 LXX omits *wĕ'îr*, "and the city" after "every city" (whole-word: *'yr* . . . *'yr*).

48:15 LXX omits *'ālâ*, "has come up" (homoeoteleuton: *h* . . . *h*).

48:18   LXX omits *bat*, "daughter" (homoeoteleuton: *bt . . . bt*).

48:25   LXX omits *něʾūm yhwh*, "oracle of Yahweh" (homoeoteleuton: *h . . . h*).

48:33   LXX omits *mikkarmel (û)*, "from the garden land (and)" (homoeoarcton: *m . . . m*, if the omission includes the next *waw*; homoeoteleuton: *l . . . l*, if it does not).

48:34   LXX omits *ʿad-yaḥaṣ*, "as far as Jahaz," whose *Vorlage* could have had the longer spelling, *yḥṣh* (homoeoteleuton: *h . . . h*).
            MT omits *ʿārêhem* if the LXX *Vorlage* read *naténû qôlam ʿarêhem miṣṣoʿar*, "their cities raised their voice, from Zoar . . ." (homoeoteleuton: *m . . . m*).
            MT omits *ʿad*, "as far as," before *ʿeglat sélisîyâ*, "Eglath-shelishiyah" (homoeoarcton: *ʿayin . . . ʿayin*).

48:35   MT omits *ʿolâ*, "whole burnt offering," and *ʿal ha*, "to the" in the phrase *ʿal-habbamâ*, "to the high place" (double haplography due to the prior *ʿlh*).

48:37   MT omits *kol*, "all," in the phrase "on all loins," which is present in many MSS, the LXX, and the Vg (homoeoteleuton: *l . . . l*).

48:38a   LXX omits *kullōh mispēd*, "everywhere rites of mourning" (homoeoarcton: *k . . . k*).

48:41   LXX omits *wěhayâ leb gibbôrê môʾāb bayyôm hahûʾ kěleb ʿissâ měṣerâ*, "And the heart of the warriors of Moab shall be in that day as the heart of a woman much distressed" (homoeoarcton: *w . . . w*; or homoeoteleuton: *h . . . h*).

49:5–6   LXX omits *lannōdēd wěʾaḥǎrê-kēn ʾāšîb ʾet-šěbût běnê-ʿammôn něʾūm-yhwh*, "him who flees. But afterward I will surely restore the fortunes of the Ammonites—oracle of Yahweh" (homoeoarcton: *l . . . l*).

49:9   LXX omits *lāk*, "to you" (homoeoarcton: *l . . . l*).

49:12   LXX omits *hinnēh*, "Look" (homoeoteleuton: *h . . . h*).
            Some LXX MSS omit *kî šātōh tišteh*, "for you will surely drink" (homoeoarcton: *ky . . . ky*, or homoeoteleuton: *h . . . h*).

49:13   LXX omits *lěḥōreb*, "(for) a ruin" (homoeoarcton: *l . . . l*).

49:15   LXX omits *kî-hinnēh*, "For look!" (homoeoteleuton: *h . . . h*).

49:22   LXX omits *yaʿǎleh wě*, "he goes up and" (homoeoarcton without *waw*: *y . . . y*).

49:24   LXX omits *ṣārâ waḥǎbālîm ʾǎḥāzattâ kayyôlēdâ*, "Distress and pangs seized her, like a woman in labor" (homoeoteleuton: *h . . . h*).

49:30   LXX omits *nūdû*, "Wander all about" (homoeoteleuton: *w . . . w*).

50:2   LXX omits *ûśěʾû-nēs hašmîʿû*, "set up a flag! make heard!" (whole-word: *hšmyʿw . . . . hšmyʿw*).

50:9   LXX omits *gědōlîm*, "great" (homoeoteleuton: *ym . . . ym*).

50:19   LXX omits *wěhabbāšān*, "and the Bashan" (homoeoarcton: *w . . . w*).

50:21   LXX omits *ʾaḥǎrêhem*, "the last of them" (homoeoteleuton: *m . . . m*).

50:28   LXX omits *niqmat hêkālô*, "the vengeance of his temple" (homoeoteleuton: *w . . . w*).

50:36   LXX omits *ḥereb ʾel-habbadîm wĕnōʾālû*, "A sword to the diviners, that
        they become foolish" (two-word: *ḥrb ʾl . . . ḥrb ʾl*).
50:37   LXX omits *kol*, "all" (homoeoteleuton: *l . . . l*).
50:39   LXX omits *wĕlōʾ tiškôn ʿad-dôr wādôr*, "and she shall not be settled for
        generation after generation" (whole-word if this and the previous colon
        were written in block poetry: *wlʾ . . . wlʾ*).
50:45   MT omits the *mem* in *nĕwēhem*, "their pasture," which is present in the
        Vrs and the parallel passage of 49:20 (the next word begins with *mem*).
51:22   LXX omits *wĕnippaṣtî bĕkā zāqēn wānāʿar*, "and with you I smashed
        old and young" (two-word: *wnpṣty bk . . . wnpṣty bk*).
51:37   LXX omits *mĕʿôn-tannîm šammâ ûšĕrēqâ*, "a den of jackals, a desola-
        tion and an object of hissing" (homoeoarcton: *m . . . m*).
51:43   LXX omits *lĕšammâ*, "(for) a desolation" (homoeoteleuton: *h . . . h*).
51:44a LXX omits *bēl bĕ*, "Bel in" (homoeoarcton: *b . . . b*).
51:44c–49a   LXX omits *gam-ḥômat bābel nāpālâ . . . ḥalĕlê yiśrāʾēl*, "even
        the wall of Babylon has fallen! . . . O slain of Israel!" (whole-word:
        gm . . . gm).
51:56   LXX omits *ʿāleyhā*, "upon her" (homoeoarcton: *ʿl . . . ʿl*).
        LXX omits *dalet* on *šôdēd*, "(the) devastator," reading instead *talaipōria*
        = Heb *šôd*, "suffering" (double *dalet* in succession).
51:57   LXX omits *paḥôteyhā*, "her governors" (homoeoteleuton: *yh . . . yh*).
        LXX omits *wĕgibbôreyhā*, "and her warriors" (homoeoarcton: *w . . . w*,
        or homoeoteleuton: *yh . . . yh*).
51:60   LXX omits *ʾeḥād*, "one" (homoeoarcton: *ʾaleph . . . ʾaleph*).
51:62   MT has one occurrence of "Yahweh" where LXX has *Kyrie, Kyrie*
        ("Lord, Lord"), which could indicate MT (whole-word) haplography;
        T, however, has only one "Lord."
52:2–3 LXX omits *wayyaʿaś hāraʿ bĕʿênê yhwh . . . bĕmelek bābel*, "And he
        did what was evil in the eyes of Yahweh . . . against the king of Baby-
        lon" (homoeoarcton: *wy . . . wy*).
52:6   LXX omits *baḥōdeš hārĕbîʿî*, "In the fourth month" (homoeoarcton: *b
        . . . b*).
52:7   LXX omits *yibrĕḥû wa*, "fled, and" (homoeoarcton: *w . . . w*).
52:15   LXX omits entire verse (whole-word plus: *wmdlwt h . . . wmdlwt h* or
        two-word: *rb-tbhym . . . rb-tbhym*).
52:20   MT lacks *hayyām*, "the sea," after *taḥat*, "underneath," which is present
        in the LXX and 1 Kgs 7:44 (homoeoarcton: *h . . . h*)
52:22   MT may omit *ûśĕbākâ*, "also lattice-work" before "and pomegranates"
        at the end of the verse in light of 2 Kgs 25:17 (homoeoarcton: *w . . . w*).
52:25   LXX omits *śar*, "prince" (homoeoteleuton: *r . . . r*).
52:27b–30   LXX omits two and a half verses: *wayyigel yĕhûdâ mēʿal ʾadmātô
        . . . ʾarbaʿat ʾălāpîm wĕšēš mēʾôt*, "So Judah went into exile from its
        land . . . four thousand and six hundred" (homoeoarcton: *wy . . . wy* or
        homoeoteleuton: *t . . . t*).

52:34 LXX omits *kōl yĕmê hayyāyw,* "all the days of his life" (homoeoteleuton: *w . . . w*).

Summary for Jeremiah 21–52

	LXX	MT
Haplographies by homoeoarcton, homoeoteleuton, or whole-word repetition	263[a]	17
Haplographies by double consonants in succession	2	6
Inner-Greek haplographies	4 (26:4; 32:8, 25; 34:19)	
Other possible haplographies	9 (21:11; 23:36–37, 38; 25:7, 9; 28:3; 42:18, 20; 48:34)	9 (22:18; 27:3; 45:3; 48:34 [2×]; 48:35 [2×] 51:62; 52:22)
Total	278	32

[a]The haplography listed for 30:5 could also be inner-Greek, and is therefore not listed a second time among the inner-Greek haplographies below.

Combined Summary for Jeremiah 1–52

(See haplography tally for chaps, 1–20 in Appendix III of *Jeremiah 1–20*).

	LXX	MT
Haplographies by homoeoarcton, homoeoteleuton, or whole-word repetition	312	23
Haplographies by double consonants in succession	2	6
Inner-Greek haplographies	4	
Other possible haplographies	12	10
Total	330	39

The number of Hebrew words arguably lost by haplography in the LXX totals 1715, which is 7.8% of the Jeremiah MT word count (21,835). The number of Hebrew words arguably lost by haplography in MT totals 39 (8 words in chaps. 1–20; 31 words in chaps. 21–52).

APPENDIX VI

◆

MT AND LXX COMPARED ON NAMES
WITH TITLES IN JEREMIAH 1–52

A. MT and LXX on "Yahweh of Hosts"

	MT	LXX	
2:19	ṣĕbā'ôt ("Hosts")		—
5:14	ṣĕbā'ôt		pantokratōr ("Almighty")
6:6	ṣĕbā'ôt		—
6:9	ṣĕbā'ôt		—
7:3	ṣĕbā'ôt		—
7:21	ṣĕbā'ôt		—
8:3	ṣĕbā'ôt		—
9:6[7]	ṣĕbā'ôt		—
9:14[15]	ṣĕbā'ôt		—
9:16[17]	ṣĕbā'ôt		—
10:16	ṣĕbā'ôt		—
11:17	ṣĕbā'ôt		—
11:20	ṣĕbā'ôt		—
11:22	ṣĕbā'ôt		—
15:16	ṣĕbā'ôt		pantokratōr
16:9	ṣĕbā'ôt		—
19:3	ṣĕbā'ôt		—
19:11	ṣĕbā'ôt		—
19:15	ṣĕbā'ôt		—
20:12	ṣĕbā'ôt		—
23:15	ṣĕbā'ôt		—
23:16	ṣĕbā'ôt		pantokratōr
23:36	ṣĕbā'ôt		—
25:8	ṣĕbā'ôt		—
25:27	ṣĕbā'ôt	32:27	pantokratōr
25:28	ṣĕbā'ôt	32:28	—
25:29	ṣĕbā'ôt	32:29	—
25:32	ṣĕbā'ôt	32:32	—
26:18	ṣĕbā'ôt	33:18	—
27:4	ṣĕbā'ôt	34:4	—
27:18	ṣĕbā'ôt	34:18	—
27:19	ṣĕbā'ôt	34:19	—
27:21	ṣĕbā'ôt	34:21	—

28:2	ṣĕbā'ôt	35:2	—
28:14	ṣĕbā'ôt	35:14	—
29:4	ṣĕbā'ôt	36:4	—
29:8	ṣĕbā'ôt	36:8	—
29:17	ṣĕbā'ôt	36:17	—
29:21	ṣĕbā'ôt	36:21	—
29:25	ṣĕbā'ôt	36:25	—
30:8	ṣĕbā'ôt	37:8	—
31:23	ṣĕbā'ôt	38:23	—
31:35	ṣĕbā'ôt	38:36	*pantokratōr*
32:14	ṣĕbā'ôt	39:14	*pantokratōr*
32:15	ṣĕbā'ôt	39:15	—
32:18	ṣĕbā'ôt	39:18	—
33:11	ṣĕbā'ôt	40:11	*pantokratori*
33:12	ṣĕbā'ôt	40:12	*tōn dunameōn* ("The Power")
35:13	ṣĕbā'ôt	42:13	—
35:17	ṣĕbā'ôt	42:17	—
35:18	ṣĕbā'ôt	42:18	—
35:19	ṣĕbā'ôt	42:19	—
38:17	ṣĕbā'ôt	45:17	—
39:16	ṣĕbā'ôt	46:16	—
42:15	ṣĕbā'ôt	49:15	—
42:18	ṣĕbā'ôt	49:18	—
43:10	ṣĕbā'ôt	50:10	—
44:2	ṣĕbā'ôt	51:2	—
44:7	ṣĕbā'ôt	51:7	*pantokratōr*
44:11	ṣĕbā'ôt	51:11	—
44:25	ṣĕbā'ôt	51:25	—
46:10	ṣĕbā'ôt	26:10	—
	ṣĕbā'ôt		*sabaōth* ("Hosts")
46:18	ṣĕbā'ôt	26:18	—
46:25	ṣĕbā'ôt	26:25	—
48:1	ṣĕbā'ôt	31:1	—
48:15	ṣĕbā'ôt	31:15	—
49:5	ṣĕbā'ôt	30:21	—
49:7	ṣĕbā'ôt	30:1	—
49:26	ṣĕbā'ôt	30:32	—
49:35	ṣĕbā'ôt	25:15	—
50:18	ṣĕbā'ôt	27:18	—
50:25	ṣĕbā'ôt	27:25	—
50:31	ṣĕbā'ôt	27:31	—
50:33	ṣĕbā'ôt	27:33	—
50:34	ṣĕbā'ôt	27:34	*pantokratōr*
51:5	ṣĕbā'ôt	28:5	*pantokratoros*
51:14	ṣĕbā'ôt	28:14	—
51:19	ṣĕbā'ôt	28:19	—
51:33	ṣĕbā'ôt	28:33	—

| 51:57 | *ṣĕbāʾôt* | 28:57 | *pantokratōr* |
| 51:58 | *ṣĕbāʾôt* | 28:58 | — |

Total occurrences of *ṣĕbāʾôt* in the MT of Jeremiah   82
Texts in which LXX translates with *pantokratōr/os*   11
Texts in which LXX translates with *tōn dunameōn*   1
Texts in which LXX translates with *sabaōth*   1
Texts in which LXX omits   69

B. MT and LXX on "Jeremiah" + Title

	MT	LXX
1:1	Jeremiah son of Hilkiah	Jeremiah of Hilkiah
25:2	Jeremiah the prophet	—
28:5	Jeremiah the prophet	Jeremiah
28:10	Jeremiah the prophet	Jeremiah
28:11	Jeremiah the prophet	Jeremiah
28:12	Jeremiah the prophet	—
28:15	Jeremiah the prophet	Jeremiah
29:1	Jeremiah the prophet	Jeremiah
29:27	Jeremiah the Anathothite	Jeremiah the Anathothite
29:29	Jeremiah the prophet	Jeremiah
32:2	Jeremiah the prophet	Jeremiah
34:6	Jeremiah the prophet	Jeremiah
36:8	Jeremiah the prophet	Jeremiah
36:26	Jeremiah the prophet	Jeremiah
37:2	Jeremiah the prophet	Jeremiah
37:3	Jeremiah the prophet	Jeremiah
37:6	Jeremiah the prophet	Jeremiah
37:13	Jeremiah the prophet	Jeremiah
38:9	Jeremiah the prophet	—
38:10	Jeremiah the prophet	—
38:14	Jeremiah the prophet	—
42:2	Jeremiah the prophet	Jeremiah the prophet
42:4	Jeremiah the prophet	Jeremiah
43:6	Jeremiah the prophet	Jeremiah
45:1	Jeremiah the prophet	Jeremiah the prophet
46:1	Jeremiah the prophet	—
46:13	Jeremiah the prophet	Jeremiah
47:1	Jeremiah the prophet	—
49:34	Jeremiah the prophet	Jeremiah
50:1	Jeremiah the prophet	—
51:59	Jeremiah the prophet	Jeremiah the prophet

C. MT and LXX on "Nebuchadrezzar (king of Babylon)"

	MT	LXX
	MT	LXX
21:2	Nebuchadrezzar, king of Babylon	king of Babylon

21:7	Nebuchadrezzar, king of Babylon	—
22:25	Nebuchadrezzar, king of Babylon	—
24:1	Nebuchadrezzar, king of Babylon	Nebuchadnezzar, king of Babylon
25:1	Nebuchadrezzar, king of Babylon	—
25:9	Nebuchadrezzar, king of Babylon	—
27:6	Nebuchadnezzar, king of Babylon	Nebuchadnezzar, king of Babylon
27:8	Nebuchadnezzar, king of Babylon	king of Babylon
27:20	Nebuchadnezzar, king of Babylon	king of Babylon
28:3	Nebuchadnezzar, king of Babylon	—
28:11	Nebuchadnezzar, king of Babylon	king of Babylon
28:14	Nebuchadnezzar, king of Babylon	king of Babylon
29:1	Nebuchadnezzar	—
29:3	Nebuchadnezzar, king of Babylon	king of Babylon
29:21	Nebuchadrezzar, king of Babylon	king of Babylon
32:1	Nebuchadrezzar	Nebuchadnezzar, king of Babylon
32:28	Nebuchadrezzar, king of Babylon	king of Babylon
34:1	Nebuchadrezzar, king of Babylon	Nebuchadnezzar, king of Babylon
35:11	Nebuchadrezzar, king of Babylon	Nebuchadnezzar
37:1	Nebuchadrezzar, king of Babylon	Nebuchadnezzar
39:1	Nebuchadrezzar, king of Babylon	Nebuchadnezzar, king of Babylon
39:5	Nebuchadrezzar, king of Babylon	—
39:11	Nebuchadrezzar, king of Babylon	—
43:10	Nebuchadrezzar, king of Babylon	Nebuchadnezzar, king of Babylon
44:30	Nebuchadrezzar, king of Babylon	Nebuchadnezzar, king of Babylon
46:2	Nebuchadrezzar, king of Babylon	Nebuchadnezzar, king of Babylon
46:13	Nebuchadrezzar, king of Babylon	king of Babylon
46:26	Nebuchadrezzar, king of Babylon	—
49:28	Nebuchadrezzar, king of Babylon	Nebuchadnezzar, king of Babylon
49:30	Nebuchadrezzar, king of Babylon	king of Babylon
50:17	Nebuchadrezzar, king of Babylon	king of Babylon
51:34	Nebuchadrezzar, king of Babylon (poetry)	Nebuchadnezzar, king of Babylon
52:4	Nebuchadrezzar, king of Babylon	Nebuchadnezzar, king of Babylon
52:12	Nebuchadrezzar, king of Babylon	Nebuchadnezzar
52:28	Nebuchadrezzar	—

APPENDIX VII

♦

SECTION MARKINGS IN JEREMIAH 1–52

Section markings in Jeremiah are at least as old as 200 B.C., since they appear in 4QJerᵃ. In this and other Jeremiah fragments from Khirbet Qumran (Dead Sea Scrolls), and in the oldest extant medieval manuscripts of the Hebrew Bible (Mᴾ, Mᴬ, and Mᴸ), sections are marked by blank spaces at the beginning, middle, and end of lines, or between lines. The sigla, ס (*setumah*) for a closed section and פ (*petuḥah*) for an open section, were written in the blank spaces as early as A.D. 1492, where they appear in an edition of Isaiah and Jeremiah published in Lisbon (C. D. Ginsburg 1885 III: xvi).

Listed below are the sections appearing in the Qumran fragments (2QJer; 4QJerᵃ; 4QJerᵇ⁽ᵈ,ᵉ⁾; and 4QJerᶜ) and major medieval manuscripts (Mᴬ = Aleppo Codex; Mᴸ = Leningrad Codex; Mᴾ = St. Petersburg Codex of the Prophets) of Jeremiah. Sections or lack of the same in square brackets are reconstructed determinations in the Qumran fragments:

	2QJer	4QJerᵃ	4QJerᵇ⁽ᵈ,ᵉ⁾	4QJerᶜ	Mᴬ	Mᴸ	Mᴾ
1:3					פ	ס	ס
1:6					ס	פ	—
1:10					פ	פ	פ
1:12					ס	פ	פ
1:19					פ	פ	פ
2:3					פ	פ	פ
2:28					ס	ס	ס
3:5					פ	פ	פ
3:10					ס	פ	—
3:17					ס	ס	פ
3:25					פ	ס	—
4:2					ס	ס	ס
4:8					פ	פ	פ
4:13			[פ]		—	—	—
4:18					פ	ס	פ
4:21					פ	ס	פ
4:26					ס	ס	ס
4:31					פ	פ	פ
5:9					ס	ס	ס
5:13					ס	ס	ס
5:19					פ	ס	ס

5:29			ס	ס	פ
6:5			פ	ס	ס
6:8			פ	פ	פ
6:15			ס	ס	ס
6:20			—	ס	—
6:21			פ	פ	ס
6:30			פ	פ	פ
7:2			ס	ס	ס
7:11			—	ס	ס
7:15	ס		פ	ס	פ
7:19	[section]		—	ס	—
7:20			פ	ס	ס
7:28	[ס]		ס	ס	ס
7:29	פ		—	—	—
7:31	[—]		פ	ס	ס
8:3		[ס?]	ס	ס	—
8:5	[ס]		—	—	—
8:7	פ		—	—	—
8:9	פ		—	ס	ס
8:12	[section]		פ	ס	פ
8:16	[—]		פ	ס	ס
8:17	[section]		ס	ס	ס
8:18	[section]		—	—	—
8:22	[—]	[פ]	ס	—	ס
8:23	[—]	[—]	ס	—	—
9:2	[—]	—	—	ס	—
9:5			ס	ס	ס
9:8	[פ]		ס	ס	פ
9:10	[פ]		ס	ס	—
9:11	[—]		ס	ס	ס
9:13	[פ][1]		פ	ס	ס
9:15	[פ]		פ	פ	פ
9:18			ס	ס	ס
9:21			ס	ס	ס
9:23			ס	ס	ס
9:25			פ	ס	פ
10:5			פ	ס	ס
10:10	[פ]		פ	ס	ס
10:11	פ		ס	ס	ס
10:16			ס	ס	ס
10:17			ס	ס	—
10:18			ס	ס	ס
10:21			פ	ס	פ

---

[1] Tov (1997: 148) mistakenly lists this section as concluding 9:12.

10:22		ס	ס	ס
10:25		פ	פ	פ
11:5	[−]	פ	ס	ס
11:8		ס	ס	פ
11:10		ס	ס	פ
11:13		ס	ס	פ
11:14		ס	ס	ס
11:17		פ	ס	ס
11:19	[ס]	—	—	ס
11:20		ס	ס	פ
11:21		פ	ס	פ
11:23		ס	ס	—
12:3	[−]	פ	ס	ס
12:6	[−]	ס	ס	פ
12:12		ס	ס	—
12:13	[פ]	פ	ס	פ
12:17	[פ]	פ	ס	פ
13:2	—	פ	ס	פ
13:7		פ	פ	פ
13:10		ס	—	ס
13:12		ס	ס	ס
13:14		—	ס	—
13:17		ס	ס	ס
13:19		ס	ס	פ
13:27		ס	פ	ס
14:9		ס	ס	—
14:10		פ	ס	ס
14:12		ס	ס	—
14:13		ס	ס	פ
14:14		ס	ס	ס
14:18		ס	ס	ס
14:22		פ	פ	ס
15:9		ס	ס	—
15:10		ס	ס	ס
15:14		ס	ס	ס
15:16		ס	ס	—
15:17		—	ס	—
15:18		ס	ס	ס
15:21		ס[2]	פ	פ
16:2		ס	—	—
16:4		ס	ס	ס
16:8		פ	ס	ס
16:13		פ	ס	ס

[2] HUB has a *petuḥah*, but M[A] has a *setumah*.

	A	B	C	D	E
16:15			פ	ס	ס
16:18			פ	ס	פ
16:21			ס	ס	ס
17:4			ס	ס	ס
17:6			ס	ס	ס
17:8	[ס]		—	—	—
17:10	ס		ס	ס	ס
17:11	ס		—	—	—
17:13	ס		פ	ס	פ
17:16	[פ]		—	—	—
17:18 middle	ס		—	—	—
17:18 end	פ		ס	ס	—
17:20	—		—	ס	—
17:27			פ	פ	פ
18:4			ס	פ	ס
18:6			ס	ס	ס
18:8			ס	ס	ס
18:10			ס	ס	ס
18:12			פ	ס	פ
18:17	פ		ס	ס	ס
18:23	פ		ס	ס	ס
19:5			פ	פ	ס
19:13			פ	פ	ס
19:14			ס	ס	ס
20:3		פ	ס	פ	ס
20:6			פ	ס	פ
20:9		פ	—	—	—
20:12			ס	ס	פ
20:13	פ		ס	ס	ס
20:18	[פ]³		פ	פ	פ
21:2			—	ס	—
21:3			ס	—	—
21:10			ס	ס	ס
21:14			—	ס	—
22:2			—	ס	ס
22:4	[—]	[ס?]	—	—	—
22:5	[—]	פ	פ	ס	ס
22:9	פ		ס	ס	פ
22:10	[—]	[פ]	—	ס	ס
22:12	[—]	[פ]	ס	ס	ס
22:17		[ס]	ס	ס	פ
22:19		[פ]	ס	ס	—
22:27		—	פ	ס	פ

³ Tov (1997: 148) mistakenly lists this verse as 20:26, which does not exist.

Verse				
22:29		—	ס	ס
22:30		פ	—	ס
23:1		ס	—	—
23:4		ס	ס	—
23:6		פ	ס	ס
23:8		פ	ס	ס
23:13		—	ס	—
23:14		פ	ס	פ
23:15		פ	פ	—
23:18		ס	ס	ס
23:22		ס	ס	—
23:29		ס	ס	—
23:30		—	—	ס
23:38		—	—	פ
23:40		פ	ס	פ
24:2		פ	ס	פ
24:3		פ	פ	ס
24:7		ס[4]	ס	ס
24:10		פ	פ	פ
25:7	[פ]	פ	ס	פ
25:14		פ	ס	ס
25:26	section?	—	—	—
25:27		פ	ס	—
25:31		ס	ס	ס
25:38		פ	פ	פ
26:6		פ	ס	ס
26:9		—	—	ס
26:10	[—]	ס	ס	—
26:15		ס	ס	ס
26:24		פ	פ	פ
27:18		—	פ	—
27:20		—	ס	ס
27:22		פ	פ	פ
28:11		פ	פ	ס
28:17		פ	פ	ס
29:3		—	ס	—
29:7		—	פ	—
29:9			ס	ס
29:15			ס	פ
29:17			—	ס
29:19			—	פ
29:20			ס	פ
29:23			ס	פ

[4] HUB has a *petuḥah*, but M^A has a *setumah*.

29:29			פ	פ
29:31			—	ס
29:32			ס	פ
30:3			פ	פ
30:7	פ		—	—
30:9	[—]		ס	פ
30:11	[פ]		פ	פ
30:17		פ	ס	פ
30:19 middle	פ		—	—
30:22	פ		ס	פ
31:1	פ		ס	ס
31:6	[ס]		פ	ס
31:9	פ		ס	פ
31:10	[ס]		—	—
31:14	פ		ס	פ
31:15 middle	[פ]			
31:15 end	[פ]		ס	פ
31:17	[—]		ס	—
31:20	ס		ס	פ
31:22	פ		ס	ס
31:26	פ		ס	ס
31:30			ס	פ[5]
31:34			ס	פ
31:36		ס	ס	פ
31:37		ס	ס	ס
31:40		פ	ס	ס
32:5		פ	פ	פ
32:6		—	—	ס
32:14			ס	פ
32:15			פ	פ
32:25		ס	—	ס
32:27		—	—	ס
32:35		ס	ס	—
32:41		ס	ס	פ
32:42		—	—	פ
32:44		פ	פ	פ
33:3		פ	ס	ס
33:9		ס	ס	פ
33:11		ס	ס	פ
33:13		ס	ס	פ
33:14		—	—	פ
33:16	[ס]	ס	ס	ס
33:18	[פ]	פ	ס	פ

---

[5] Text uncertain; omitted words are written into open section in small writing.

33:22	ס	ס	פ
33:24	ס	ס	פ
33:26	פ	ס	פ
34:5	ס	ס	פ
34:7	פ	פ	פ
34:11	פ	ס	פ
34:16	ס	ס	ס
34:22	פ	פ	פ
35:11	פ	פ	פ
35:16	—	ס	ס
35:18	—	ס	—
35:19	פ	פ	ס
36:3	ס	ס	פ
36:8	פ	ס	פ
36:18	ס	פ	פ
36:26	ס	ס	פ
36:29	ס	ס	ס
36:31	—	ס	ס
36:32	פ	ס	פ
37:2	—	—	פ
37:5	פ	פ	פ
37:8	פ	ס	פ
37:11	ס	ס	ס
37:16	—	פ	—
37:17	—	ס	—
38:1	—	ס	פ
38:2	ס	ס	ס
38:6	ס	ס	פ
38:13	ס	ס	פ
38:16	ס	ס	פ
38:17 middle	ס	—	—
38:18	ס	ס	פ
38:19	—	פ	—
38:23	ס	פ	ס
38:26	פ	פ	ס
38:27	—	פ	—
38:28 middle	—	ס	—
38:28 end	ס	פ	ס
39:1	—	ס	ס
39:14	ס	ס	פ
39:18	פ	ס	ס
40:6	פ	ס	פ
40:12	ס	פ	פ
40:16	פ	ס	פ
41:6	—	ס	—

Verse					
41:10			ס	ס	פ
41:15			ס	ס	ס
41:18			פ	ס	פ
42:6	section		פ	ס	ס
42:17			—	ס	—
42:22			ס	ס	ס
43:1			ס	ס	ס
43:4		section	—	—	—
43:7		—	ס	ס	ס
43:9		section?	—	—	—
43:13			פ	ס	פ
44:1	—		—	ס	—
44:6			ס	ס	ס
44:10			ס	ס	ס
44:14			פ	ס	ס
44:19			ס	פ	ס
44:23			ס	ס	פ
44:24			—	ס	—
44:25			ס	פ	ס
44:29			פ	ס	פ
44:30			ס	ס	ס
45:1			—	ס	—
45:3			—	ס	—
45:5			פ	ס	ס
46:12			פ	פ	ס
46:19			ס	ס	—
46:24			—	—	ס
46:26			פ	ס	פ
46:27	—		—	ס	—
46:28	[section]		פ	ס	ס
47:1	—		—	ס	ס
47:5		—	—	ס	ס
47:7	[section]		פ	ס	פ
48:9			—	—	פ
48:11			ס	ס	ס
48:28	[section]		—	—	—
48:39			ס	ס	—
48:47			ס	ס	פ
49:6			פ	ס	ס
49:11			ס	ס	פ
49:19			ס	ס	—
49:22			פ	ס	פ
49:27			פ	ס	פ
49:33			ס	ס	ס
49:39			פ	ס	פ

50:3		—	—	ס
50:5	[−]	—	ס	—
50:7		ס	ס	ס
50:16		ס	ס	ס
50:17		פ	ס	ס
50:20		פ	—	ס
50:21		ס	ס	ס
50:24		—	—	ס
50:27		ס	ס	ס
50:30		פ	ס	ס
50:32		ס	ס	ס
50:46		ס	ס	—
51:10		ס	—	—
51:14		ס	ס	ס
51:19		פ	ס	ס
51:24		ס	ס	ס
51:32		ס	ס	ס
51:35		ס	ס	ס
51:51		פ	ס	—
51:53		ס	ס	ס
51:57		ס	ס	ס
51:58		ס	ס	ס
51:64		פ	ס	ס
52:3		—	—	ס
52:5		—	—	ס
52:11		—	—	ס
52:23		ס	—	—
52:27		ס	—	—
52:29		—	—	ס
52:30		ס	פ	פ

APPENDIX VIII

◆

TABLE OF ARCHAEOLOGICAL
PERIODS IN PALESTINE

This table of archaeological periods in Palestine follows with minor changes the designations and divisions given in *The Anchor Bible Dictionary* 1: inside cover (1992), which revises slightly downward the chronology given in *The Interpreter's Dictionary of the Bible*, A–D: 207 (1962).

Neolithic	8000–3800 B.C.	Late Bronze (LB)	
Chalcolithic	3800–3400 B.C.	LB I	1500–1400 B.C.
Early Bronze (EB)		LB II	1400–1200 B.C.
EB I	3400–3100 B.C.	Iron Age	
EB II	3100–2650 B.C.	Iron I	1200–900 B.C.
EB III	2650–2350 B.C.	Iron II	900–586 B.C.
EB IV	2350–2000 B.C.	Iron III	586–539 B.C.
Middle Bronze (MB)		Persian Period	539–323 B.C.
MB I	2000–1800 B.C.	Hellenistic Period	323–37 B.C.
MB II	1800–1650 B.C.	Roman Period	37 B.C.–A.D. 324
MB III	1650–1500 B.C.	Byzantine Period	A.D. 324–640

APPENDIX IX

◆

NAMES OF MONTHS IN THE JEWISH CALENDAR

This list of the names of months in the Jewish calendar, which follows the Babylonian (Nisan) calendar, is taken from Hayes and Hooker (1988: 101). In the older Israelite calendar, the New Year began in the fall with Tishri (see Note for 39:1).

1.	Nisan	March / April
2.	Iyyar	April / May
3.	Sivan	May / June
4.	Tammuz	June / July
5.	Ab	July / August
6.	Elul	August / September
7.	Tishri	September / October
8.	Marheshvan	October / November
9.	Kislev	November / December
10.	Tebet	December / January
11.	Shebat	January / February
12.	Adar	February / March

APPENDIX X

◆

JEREMIAH CHRONOLOGY

This chronology builds on the chronologies of Bright (1981: 471–72); Tadmor (1956); and Fried and Freedman (2001), which correlate biblical material with the Babylonian Chronicle and information gained from other extrabiblical sources.

664 B.C. Psammetichus I becomes king in Egypt; beginning of Saïte Restoration, 26th Dynasty

655 Psammetichus declares independence from Assyria

642 Manasseh's reign in Judah ends; Amon becomes king

640 King Assurbanipal of Assyria regains control over his Empire
Amon's reign in Judah ends; Josiah enthroned at eight years of age
Jeremiah born at Anathoth

632 Josiah, according to the Chronicler, begins in the eighth year of his reign to seek Yahweh

628 Chronicler reports a reform beginning under Josiah; purge of worship sites

627 Ashurbanipal, king of Assyria, dies; Babylon in open revolt
The boy Jeremiah receives call to be a prophet; call awaits acceptance and ratification

626 Nabopolassar defeats Assyrian army outside Babylon; becomes king of Babylon

622 Assyria has retreated from Palestine; Judah's subservience to Assyria ended
Lawbook found by Hilkiah in the Temple
Covenant renewal ceremony; purge of worship sites; grand Passover celebration
Jeremiah accepts call to be Yahweh's prophet
Jeremiah receives divine commission to begin public ministry

614–612 Jeremiah begins preaching about a foe from the north

612 Nineveh falls to a coalition of Babylonians and Medes

610 Assyrian refugee government dislodged at Haran by allies

609 Egypt goes to the aid of Assyria in attempt to retake Haran
Josiah killed at Megiddo by Neco II of Egypt; attempt to retake Haran fails
Jeremiah utters a public lament for Josiah
Jehoahaz made king; reigns three months

609/8   Neco deposes Jehoahaz on return from Mesopotamia and deports him to Egypt
          Jeremiah utters a public lament for Jehoahaz
          Jehoiakim made king by Neco; Judah under Egyptian domination
          Jeremiah delivers Temple Oracles; some confessions also from 609–605
605   Jeremiah delivers oracles against Egypt
          Nebuchadnezzar and Babylonians defeat Egyptians in Battle of Carchemish
          Babylonian victory at Hamath; Nebuchadnezzar takes over Egyptian base at Riblah
          First scroll of Jeremiah's prophecies prepared by Jeremiah and Baruch; Jeremiah currently debarred from Temple
          Jeremiah gives personal word to Baruch, which becomes scribal colophon for First Edition of the Book of Jeremiah
604   Nebuchadnezzar becomes king of Babylon; late in the year he campaigns in Philistine Plain, destroying Ashkelon and Ekron[1]
          Jehoiakim transfers allegiance to Nebuchadnezzar
          Jehoiakim proclaims fast in Jerusalem
          Scroll read by Baruch in Temple; heard by King Jehoiakim, who consigns it to the fire
          Jeremiah and Baruch go into hiding; Jeremiah out of public view until ca. 597
601   Nebuchadnezzar at war with Egypt on Egyptian frontier; battle indecisive
          Jehoiakim declares independence from Babylon
599/8   Nebuchadnezzar raids desert camps of Arabs from base in Syria
          Arameans, Moabites, Ammonites, and Babylonians ravage Judah
598   Babylonian army begins westward march
          Jeremiah again active
          Jeremiah utters a non-lament for Jehoiakim
          Jehoiakim dies, probably December, 598
          Jehoiachin made king; rules 3 months and 10 days
          Babylonian army enters Judah; besieges Jerusalem
597   2 Adar (March 16); Jerusalem surrenders to Nebuchadnezzar; Jehoiachin captured
          Jehoiachin, queen mother, and leading citizens deported to Babylon
          Jeremiah utters a lament for Jehoiachin
          Nisan 1 (April 13); Zedekiah made king by Nebuchadnezzar
597/6   First embassy to Babylon; Jeremiah sends letter to exiles
          Letters sent by Jeremiah to Babylon in subsequent embassies
596/5   Possible battle between Elam and Babylon

---

[1] In *Jeremiah 1–20* (p. 104), the date of Ekron's destruction was put at 603 B.C. Seymour Gitin (1998: 276) has since revised the date upward to 604 B.C. (see Note for 47:5).

595/4	Rebellion in Babylon; put down by Nebuchadnezzar
594	Psammetichus II becomes pharaoh in Egypt
594/3	Regional revolt against Babylon discussed in Jerusalem; Jeremiah wears yoke
	Jeremiah's encounter with the prophet Hananiah
	Embassy to Babylon by (Zedekiah and) Seraiah; Jeremiah sends scroll with Seraiah
	Scroll of Babylon oracles read by Seraiah in Babylon, then sunk in the Euphrates
	Jeremiah retires from public life for 5 or 6 years, until ca. 588
593	Call of the prophet Ezekiel in Babylon
591	Psammetichus II seeks support in Syria and Palestine for revolt against Babylon
589	Psammetichus II dies; Apries (Hophra) becomes pharaoh in Egypt
	Zedekiah withholds tribute from Babylon
	Babylonian army begins westward march
588	Jeremiah again active
	Tebet 10 (January 15); Nebuchadnezzar begins siege of Jerusalem
	Manumission of slaves by Zedekiah and all slave owners
587	Siege lifted due to Egyptian advance
	Slaves recaptured; Jeremiah imprisoned after attempting to visit Anathoth
	I Adar 1 (February 24); siege resumed
	Jeremiah visited by cousin Hanamel (summer); buys field at Anthoth
586	Tammuz 9 (July) Jerusalem falls; city and Temple destroyed a month later
	Second deportation of exiles to Babylon
	Community reconstituted at Mizpah; Gedaliah appointed governor
582	Gedaliah murdered in plot instigated by king of Ammon
	Jeremiah and Baruch taken to Egypt in group led by Johanan son of Kareah
	Nebuchadnezzar campaigns in Moab, Ammon, Judah, and Egypt
	Third deportation of exiles from Judah and Egypt to Babylon
570	Apries (Hophra) dies; Amasis becomes king in Egypt
568	Nebuchadnezzar invades Egypt
562	Nebuchadnezzar dies; Amel-marduk (Evil-merodach) becomes king in Babylon
	Jehoiachin released from prison and given preferential treatment
560	Postscript (Jer 52:31–34) added to a completed Primary History, recast from 2 Kings; completes Book of Jeremiah
556	Nabonidus seizes throne in Babylon
539	Cyrus the Persian captures Babylonia
	Edict by Cyrus allowing Jews to return to Palestine
525	Cambyses the Persian conquers Egypt; end of Saïte period and 26th Dynasty

APPENDIX XI

◆

ASSIGNED DATES TO TEXTS IN
THE BOOK OF JEREMIAH

The listing below is an attempt to correlate texts in the book of Jeremiah with known events in Judah and elsewhere between 627 B.C. and 560 B.C., also events in the life of Jeremiah spanning a shorter number of years. These dates should not be taken as the time when the texts were committed to writing. According to chap. 36, the first Jeremiah scroll was prepared in 605 B.C., at which time many of the Jeremianic utterances and narrative accounts were presumably written down for the first time. For texts assigned a date after 605 B.C., the dates can be taken as a terminus a quo for when the texts were written down. Needless to say, the writing of any given text may have occurred some years after its public proclamation or, in the case of narratives, some years after the event took place.

Josiah's Reign (627–609 B.C.)

1:4–12	5:14–17	14:10–16
1:13–19	6:16–19	14:20–22
2:1–3	6:27–30	16:1–9
2:4–9	7:3–7	17:1ab
2:10–13	8:4–7	17:5–8
2:15–19	8:8–9	17:19–23
2:20–22	9:2–5[3–6]	17:24–27
2:23–25a	9:6–8[7–9]	18:1–10
2:25b–17ab	10:1–10	18:11–12
2:31–32	10:12–16 [= 51:15–19]	18:13–17
2:33–37	11:1–5	31:2–6
3:1–5	11:6–8	31:7–9
3:6–11	11:18–23	31:10–14
3:19–20	12:1–3, 5–6	31:15
3:21–22	13:1–11	31:16–17
4:1–2	13:26–27	31:18–19
4:3–4	14:1–6	31:20
4:23–28	14:7–9	

Jehoiakim's Early Reign (609–604 B.C.)

2:14	18:19–23	46:11–12
5:20–25	19:1–13	46:13–17
5:26–31	19:14–20:6	46:18–19
6:8–12	20:7–10	46:20–21
6:13–15 [= 8:10b–12]	20:11–13	46:22–23
6:20–21	20:14–18	46:24–26
7:1–2	21:11–14	47:2–7
7:8–11	22:1–5	48:1–2
7:12–15	22:6–9	48:3–7a
7:16–20	22:10–11	48:7b–10
7:21–28	22:13–17	48:17b–18 (604 or later)
7:29	22:18–19	48:19–24 (604 or later)
7:30–31	23:9–12	48:25 (604 or later)
7:32–34	25:1–14	48:28 (604 or later)
8:1–3	25:15–29	48:29–31 (604 or later)
11:9–13	25:30–31 (605 or later)	48:32–34 (604 or later)
11:14–17	25:32–33 (605 or later)	48:35–38a (604 or later)
13:12–14	25:34–38 (605 or later)	48:38b–39 (604 or later)
15:15–18	26:1–24	48:40–41 (604 or later)
15:19–21	35:1–19 (or 597)	48:42–43 (604 or later)
17:1c–3a	36:1–32	48:44 (604 or later)
17:9–10	45:1–5	48:45–47 (604 or later)
17:11	46:2–6	49:23–27
17:12	46:7–8	51:20–24
18:18	46:9–10	

Around Jerusalem's Capture in 597 B.C.

2:29–30	9:19–21[20–22]	15:1–4
3:12–13	9:22–25[23–26]	15:5–9
3:14–16a	10:11	15:10–12
4:5–8	10:17–18	15:13–14
4:13–17	10:19–21	16:10–13
4:19–21	10:22	17:3b–4
4:22	10:23–24	17:13–16a
4:29–31	12:4	17:16b–18
5:1–9	12:7–11	22:20–23
6:1–7	12:13	22:24–27
6:22–26	13:15–17	47:1
8:13–17	13:18–20	48:11–13
8:18–21	13:21–23	48:14–17a
8:22–9:1[2]	13:24–25	49:28–30
9:9–10[10–11]	14:17–19b	49:31–32
9:16–18[17–19]	14:19c	49:34–39

After Jerusalem's Capture and
First Judahite Exile in 597 B.C.

2:27c–28	16:16–18	29:1–23
3:24–25	16:19–21	29:24–32
9:11–15[12–16]	22:28–30	31:21–22
12:12	23:1–4	
16:14–15	24:1–10	

Zedekiah's Early Reign (597–594 B.C.)

4:9–10	49:3–6	50:33–34
5:10–13	49:7–11	50:35–38a
12:14–17	49:12–18	50:38b–40
23:5–6	49:19–22	50:41–43
23:7–8	50:1–3	50:44–46
23:13–15	50:4–5	51:1–5
23:16–17	50:6–7	51:6–10
23:18, 21–22	50:8–10	51:11a, 12ab, 13–14
23:23–24	50:11–13	51:25–26
23:25–32	50:14–15	51:27–33
23:33–40	50:16	51:34–45
27:1–22	50:17a, 18–20	51:47–51
28:1–17	50:21–28	51:52–57
37:1–2	50:29–30	51:58
49:1–2	50:31–32	51:59–64a

Around the Fall of Jerusalem in 586 B.C.

3:16b–18	30:12–15	37:3–11
4:11–12, 18	30:16–17	37:12–16
21:1–7	31:31–34	37:17–21
21:8–10	32:1–44	38:1–6
23:19–20 [= 30:23–24]	33:1–3	38:7–13
30:5–7	33:4–9	38:14–28
30:10–11 [= 46:27–28]	34:1–22	39:15–18

After the Fall of Jerusalem and
Second Judahite Exile in 586 B.C.

1:1–3	31:1	31:38–40
5:18–19	31:23–26	33:10–11
10:25	31:27–30	33:12–13
30:18–21	31:35–37	33:14–16

33:17–18	39:11–14	51:64b
33:19–22	40:1–6	51:11bc
33:23–26	46:1	52:1–11
39:1–10	50:17b	52:12–27

Mizpah Sojourn (586–582 B.C.)

30:1–3	40:13–16	41:7–10
30:8–9	41:1–3	41:11–15
40:7–12	41:4–6	48:26–27

Geruth Chimham Sojourn (after 582 B.C.)

41:16–18
42:1–6
42:7–22
43:1–4
52:28–30

Among Judahite Exiles in Egypt (after 582 B.C.)

43:5–7
43:8–13
44:1–25
44:26–30

After Nebuchadrezzar's Death (562 B.C.)

51:46
52:31–34

After Cyrus Captures Babylonia (539 B.C.)

51:12c

APPENDIX XII

◆

Glossary of Rhetorical Terms

In the absence of Hebrew names for rhetorical devices appearing in ancient Hebrew discourse, Greek and Latin terms from the classical handbooks, viz., Aristotle's *Rhetoric*, the *ad Herennium*, and Quintilian's *Institutes*, are here used. Among the modern works discussing rhetorical devices, one may consult Brandt (1970), Corbett (1971), Lanham (1968), and *The Encyclopedia of Rhetoric* (2001).

a minori ad maius An argument from the lesser to the greater; also called in Latin an argument **a fortiori**; Hillel: qal weḥomer. In 12:5 are two of these arguments in sequence: "If with men on foot you have run and they have wearied you, how then will you fare in a heat with horses? And (if) in a peaceful land you have fallen down, how then will you do in the pride of the Jordan?"

abusio Latin (*ad Herennium* iv 33); Greek: κατάχρησις. An implied metaphor involving a base term and a figurative one (Brandt 1970: 139). Jeremiah speaks of "each man for his neighbor's wife, they *neighed*" (5:8), and admonishes people to "remove the foreskins of your *hearts*" (4:4).

accumulatio The heaping up of nouns or verbs in twos, threes, and fours, also the balancing of longer phrases in parallelism (16:4: "they shall not be lamented and they shall not be buried; for dung upon the surface of the ground they shall become, and by sword and by famine they shall come to an end; their dead bodies shall be food for the birds of the skies and for the beasts of the earth").

allegory An extended metaphor in which a series of actions are symbolic of other actions and where the symbolism frequently—but not always—involves personification. See Jeremiah's allegory of the Fallen Sisters in 3:6–11.

alliteration The repetition of consonants in succession, usually at the beginning of two or more consecutive words, or of words near one other.

anadiplosis	Greek. A repetition of one or more words for the purpose of amplification or an appeal to pity (*ad Herennium* iv 28: *conduplicatio*; Quintilian, *Institutes* ix 3.28: *adiectione*). One common type is a word or phrase in one colon repeating at the beginning of a subsequent colon (2:10; 25:30).
anaphora	Or Greek ἐπαναφορά; Latin: *repetitio* (*ad Herennium* iv 13). The repetition of a word or words at the beginning of two or more successive colons, lines, or poetic verses (4:23–26; 5:15–17; 50:35–38; 51:20–23), which can heighten pity, disdain, fear, joyful anticipation, or other emotional states. See also **epiphora**.
antiphony	The alternation of speaking voices in discourse (6:4–5; 8:18–21); not a musical response, as in the Greek *antiphon*.
antithesis	Greek; Latin: *contentio* (*ad Herennium* iv 15, 45); *contrapositum* (Quintilian, *Institutes* ix 3.81). An opposition created by contrasting words, phrases, or ideas. Opposing discourse elements that apportion form a **distributio**.
apodosis	The consequent clause in a conditional ("If . . . then") sentence, as distinguished from **protasis**, the clause expressing the condition (4:1–2; 12:16).
aposiopesis	Greek; Latin: *praecisio* (*ad Herennium* iv 30). A sudden and intentional breaking off of discourse in midsentence (10:18; 46:5).
apostrophe	A turning away from one's audience to address a person, city, nation, or other inanimate object directly in order to emphasize a point, heighten grief, or express indignation before that audience (*ad Herennium* iv 15; Quintilian, *Institutes* ix 2.38–39. The person may be dead (Rachel in 31:16–17), absent (Jeremiah's mother in 15:10), or purely imaginary (a scribe in 22:30), and the object incapable of hearing (the heavens in 2:12; the sword in 47:6). See also **personification**.
assonance	Repetition of vowel sounds anywhere in a word or words, which occurs very frequently in Hebrew; near-rhyme (2:10, 12; 3:14).
asyndeton	A rapid accumulation of verbs, with or without connectives, in both poetry and prose (4:5; 7:9; 25:27; 31:7b;

46:3–4). Used to heap up blame, press home the message of divine judgment, or emphasize the joy of future salvation.

authority

In Hebrew rhetoric the driving force behind assertive discourse carried on by one who is speaking for God.

chiasmus

Greek: "a placing crosswise"; Latin: *commutatio* (*ad Herennium* iv 28). An inversion of repeated or paired words, syntactical forms, sounds, or speaking voices in small or large segments of poetry and prose, sometimes connecting the segments. Used largely to vary parallelism or give structure to discourse, but functioning in some cases to develop prophetic arguments.

comparison

Greek: παραβολή; Latin: *similitudo* (*ad Herennium* iv 45–48). Speech that carries over elements of likeness from one thing to another thing, used to clarify or prove. More general and less vivid than a **simile**. Appearing frequently in Jeremianic discourse in *kĕ . . . kēn* and *'ākēn . . . kēn* constructions (2:26; 3:20; 7:14; 18:6), also in *(ka) 'ăšer . . . kēn* prose constructions (13:11; 31:28; 33:22).

conduplicatio

See **anadiplosis**.

correctio

A climactic figure that intentionally corrects what has just been said, replacing it or improving upon it with something more suitable (*ad Herennium* iv 26.36).

descriptio

Latin; derived from Greek διατύπωσις (*ad Herennium* iv 39). An argumentative figure used by the prosecution or defense to describe adverse consequences of possible court action (26:15: "Only know for sure that if you put me to death, then you will bring innocent blood upon yourselves and to this city and to its inhabitants; for in truth, Yahweh sent me against you to speak in your ears all these words").

dialogue

Direct speech—real or imagined—between oneself and others, others among themselves, or individuals and God, introduced into discourse to reflect the character of the participants and to add animation (*ad Herennium* iv 43, 52; Quintilian, *Institutes* ix 2.29–37).

distributio

Latin (*ad Herennium* iv 35); Greek: διαίρεσις, μερισμός. An argumentative figure that divides a concept and apportions its parts (Brandt 1970: 133–35). Jeremiah says to his opponent, Hananiah: "The prophets who were before me and before you . . . prophesied . . . war and evil and pestilence. The prophet who prophesies peace, when the word of the prophet comes to be, the prophet whom Yahweh has truly sent will be known" (28:8–9). The division is heightened in the **exaggerated contrast** to make the point more forcibly.

ellipsis

The omission of a word in an expression, usually a prefixed preposition ("to, in, for"), or a pronominal suffix (17:21; 24:1).

enthymeme

A syllogism with one premise implied, but not stated. The major premise is usually the omitted one. Most all prophetic indictments are enthymemes, in which the omitted premise is a statement in the Law that Israel or individuals within the nation in violation of the Sinai covenant will be punished (Deuteronomy 28). The full syllogism would be:

> [An Israel in violation of the covenant will be punished]
>
> Israel has violated the covenant
>
> Israel will therefore be punished.

In Jeremiah the enthymeme more often takes the form:

> [A Judah not listening to Yahweh's word will be punished]
>
> Judah—or its king, priests, prophets—have not listened to Yahweh's word
>
> Judah—or its king, priests, prophets—will therefore be punished.

epiphora

Or Greek ἀντιστροφή; Latin *conversio* (*ad Herennium* iv 13). The repetition of a word or words at the end of two or more successive colons, lines, or poetic verses (4:19; 8:22–23[9:1]). See also **anaphora**.

epithet

An honorific or disparaging title giving character to a name. Jeremiah uses a disparaging epithet for Pharaoh in 46:17 ("Loud Noise, Who Lets the Deadline Pass"), and honorific epithets for Yahweh in 17:13 ("The Hope of Israel"), and in 50:7 ("The Righteous Pasture" and "Hope of Their Fathers").

epitrope   Greek; Latin *permissio* (*ad Herennium* iv 29). The granting of permission for an action of which one disapproves (7:21; 15:2; 22:20; 44:25). See also **surrender**.

ethos   In Greek rhetoric, an appeal to the speaker's character; in Hebrew rhetoric replaced largely by **authority**. But see Jeremiah's confessions to Yahweh: 8:6; 12:3; 15:10; and 18:20.

euphemism   The substitution of a milder term or one with adjunct meaning to avoid saying something too harsh or too explicit (3:13: "your ways" for "your sexual acts"; 13:22: "your skirts" for "your private parts"). Expression by circumlocution is **periphrasis**.

exaggerated contrast   Antithetical statements juxtaposed solely to emphasize the one appearing second (see **distributio**, also *Jeremiah 1–20*, 488–89).

exclamation   Latin: *exclamatio*. A figure showing strong emotion, often combined with **apostrophe** (*ad Herennium* iv 25.22) and most suitable for use in conclusions (13:27: "Woe to you, Jerusalem; you are not clean—for how much longer?").

exergasia   Greek; Latin: *expolitio* (*ad Herennium* iv 42). A repetition that "refines" or "polishes" (1:5: "Before I formed you in the belly I knew you, and before you came forth from the womb I declared you holy; a prophet to the nations I made you"; 5:6: "Therefore a lion from the forest has struck them down, and a wolf of the steppes will destroy them. A leopard is prowling around their cities"). See also **parallelism**.

expolitio   See **exergasia**.

geminatio   Repetition of a word of phrase for emphasis (4:19; 7:4; 22:29; 23:25; 46:20).

hyperbole   A deliberate exaggeration of the truth in which something is represented as greater or less, better or worse, than is possible. Its purpose is to magnify or minimize before an audience disinclined to listen (*ad Herennium* iv 33), also to shock (4:13, 23–26) or heighten a divine affirmation (1:5). Used often with **irony**.

hypophora	The answering of one's own rhetorical question, commonly stating what an adversary ought or ought not to have said (*ad Herennium* iv 23–24). In Jeremiah, see 46:7–8 and 49:7.
inclusio	A repetition of opening words, word cognates, or phrases at the conclusion of smaller and larger segments of poetry and prose, serving to structure discourse, give emphasis, show up incongruities, strengthen arguments, and effect closure.
irony	Feigned ignorance or agreement aimed at provoking one's antagonist ("socratic irony"); more commonly, saying with subtlety or ambiguity the opposite of what one means when straight talk is deemed inadequate (verbal irony). Irony addresses a double audience, one that hears but does not understand; another that perceives more than what meets the ear as well as the outsider's incomprehension. An example of so-called "socratic irony" is Jeremiah's feigned agreement with the false prophecy of Hananiah (28:6); examples of verbal irony occur throughout the Jeremianic discourse, e.g., in 2:28a, 33; 10:4; and 11:15. See also **hyperbole**.
litotes	An understatement for rhetorical effect (8:14: "let us be silent" for "let us die"; 18:23: "their counsel" meaning "their murderous plots").
logos	In Greek rhetoric, the appeal to reason (Aristotle).
merismus	Latin; derived from Greek μερισμός. A form of **synecdoche** in which a totality is expressed by contrasting parts or extremes (51:22: "old and young" meaning "everyone").
metaphor	A trope in which figurative terms or descriptions are superimposed over literal terms or descriptions, creating a vivid mental likeness of objects or ideas. Jeremiah's discourse teems with familial, animal, sexual, wilderness, agricultural, and military metaphors. Jeremiah frequently uses metaphors in combination with similes and literal equivalents, tending to weaken the figure.
metonymy	The substitution of one word for another it suggests, commonly the abstract for the concrete (4:29: "*every city* is fleeing" means "the people of every city are fleeing"; 26:2 "*all the cities of Judah* who come to worship

in the house of Yahweh" means "all the people of the cities of Judah who come to worship." See also **synecdoche**.

multiclinatum   Double occurrence of a root in succession (11:18: "Yahweh made me know and I knew"; 17:14: "Heal me, Yahweh, and I shall be healed").

onomatopoeia   The sound of a word or its repetition imititating natural sounds or simulating the sense (*ad Herennium* iv 31). In Jeremiah, see 5:17 (the fourfold "it/they shall consume" simulates an enemy eating without stopping); 50:35–38 (the fivefold "sword" simulates a repeated stabbing of the victim); and 51:20–23 (the ninefold "with you I smashed" simulates the sound of a hammering club).

oxymoron   Incongruous or contradictory terms placed in juxtaposition to one another (25:9 and 27:6: Yahweh speaks of "Nebuchadrezzar . . . my servant").

parallelism   Two or three successive colons of poetry, less often successive lines of prose, where the same thing is repeated in similar terms, or where an antithesis is created by contrasting terms. See also **exergasia**.

paronomasia   A play on multiple meanings of identical or cognate words, or else a play on different words similar in sound (*ad Herennium* iv 21–22). In Jer 50:35–37: *ḥereb* ("sword") and *ḥōreb* ("drought"). See also **pun** and **wordplay**.

pathos   In Greek rhetoric, an emotional appeal to awaken feelings of pity and sorrow. In Jeremiah, see 3:19–20; 20:14–15; and 31:15–20.

periphrasis   Greek; Latin: *circumitio* (*ad Herennium* iv 32). Embellishment of a simple idea by means of circumlocution (4:11: "daughter of my people" for "my people"). The avoidance of an indelicate word is **euphemism**.

permissio   See **epitrope** and **surrender**.

personification   Greek; Latin: *conformatio* (*ad Herennium* iv 53). Representing an absent or dead person as being present; also the representation of inanimate objects or abstract ideas as having personality, or as being endowed with personal attributes (9:20[21]: "Death has come up through our windows"; 10:17: the city of Jerusalem is told to "Gather up from the land your bundle"). The dead Rachel is heard lamenting her lost children in 31:15. See also **apostrophe**.

protasis   The conditional clause in an"If . . . then" sentence, as distinguished from **apodosis**, the clause expressing the consequence (4:1–2; 12:16).

pun   A play on words having the same sound but different meanings, or on different applications of a word (1:11–12: *šāqēd*, "almond branch," and *šōqēd*, "watching"). Used interchangeably with **paronomasia**.

repetition   Latin: *repetitio*. The repetition of words, cognates, and phrases is the single most important feature of ancient Hebrew rhetoric, used for emphasis, wordplays, expressing the superlative, creating pathos, and structuring prophetic discourse.

rhetorical question   A question posed for which there is only one answer, but because the answer is self-evident or self-condemnatory, the addressee will not give it. Rhetorical questions thus function as emphatic statements, and are used often to intimidate. The prophets use rhetorical questions in arguments as foils for final statements or questions meant to get the emphasis. Jeremiah uses rhetorical questions as "set-ups" for indictment (2:23), more often double and triple questions to contrast the regularity in nature or human life generally with the irregularity in (sinful) human behavior (2:32), or to highlight a vexation or incongruity (2:31).

simile   Greek: εἰκών; Latin: *imago*. A metaphor preceded by "as" or "like," resulting in an imaginative comparison. The wayward individual is "*like* a horse plunging headlong into battle" (8:6); when judgment comes upon the nation, the anguish will be "*like* a woman in labor" (6:24). Jeremiah frequently uses metaphors and similes in combination.

surrender   Greek ἐπιτροπή; Latin: *permissio* (*ad Herennium* iv 29). A veiled argument, in which one yields the matter to the will of another (26:14: "But I, look I am in your hands. Do to me as seems good and right in your eyes"). See also **epitrope**.

synecdoche   A type of metonymy, in which a part is substituted for the whole or the whole for a part (*ad Herennium* iv 33;

Quintilian, *Institutes* viii 6.19–22). In 4:20: "suddenly my tents are devastated; in a moment *my curtains*," where "my curtains" represents all of one's home furnishings; in 14:2: "[Judah's] *gates* languish" for "[Judah's] cities languish." See also **metonymy**.

trope   The use of a word or expression to mean something other than what it normally means, yet with a connectedness to normal meanings—sometimes through a link term—so as to give an idea freshness or emphasis (Brandt 1970: 135–37; cf. Quintilian, *Institutes* viii 6.1; *ad Herennium* iv 31). Common tropes are metaphor, simile, allegory, metonymy, synecdoche, abusio, epithet, and irony, all of which are amply represented in Jeremiah.

wordplay   The more general term for **pun** or **paronomasia**.

INDEX OF AUTHORS

◆

A

Abarbanel, Isaac   60, 350, 413, 487
Abrego, José Maria   52, 98, 128
Ackroyd, Peter R.   516
Aeschylus   440
Aharoni, Yohanan   71, 86, 110, 117, 246, 327
Aitken, Kenneth T.   365, 366, 428
Albright, W. F.   56, 67, 103, 121, 235, 297,
    330, 331, 353, 387, 501, 513, 522, 523, 536
Alexander, J. E.   150
Alonso-Schökel, L.   130, 131, 134
Alt, Albrecht   144
Alter, Robert   264
Althann, Robert   506
Amesz, J. G.   145, 505, 508
Andersen, Francis I.   132, 194, 219, 500
Apollodorus   218
Aquila   56, 58, 59, 66, 68, 76, 77, 78, 81, 98,
    100, 101, 103, 110, 112, 113, 117, 120, 121,
    122, 129, 133, 134, 135, 136, 140, 145, 146,
    147, 148, 158, 159, 160, 165, 167, 168, 175,
    176, 200, 208, 218, 233, 238, 240, 246, 255,
    261, 263, 275, 286, 293, 297, 303, 308, 318,
    337, 346, 350, 368, 370, 371, 380, 384, 424,
    433, 442, 477, 494, 496, 509, 527, 554
Avigad, Nahman   84, 86, 116, 506, 528
Avi-Yonah, M.   58

B

Bach, Robert   187, 190, 198, 201, 254, 262,
    338, 354, 391, 406, 410, 435, 445, 463
Badè, William F.   103, 112
Baillet, M.   132, 154, 157, 231, 237, 243, 256,
    282, 284, 285, 287, 310
Bardtke, Hans   250, 304, 317, 329, 352
Barkay, Gabriel   116
Barnett, R. D.   188, 355, 358
Barthélemy, Dominique   116, 253, 255, 260,
    289, 293, 370
Bartlett, John R.   327, 331
Becking, Bob   535
Begg, Christopher T.   103, 115, 116, 128

Beit-Arieh, Itzhaq   327
Bellis, Alice Ogden   366
Bennett, Crystal-M.   278, 331, 338, 339
Bentzen, Aage   183
Berkovitz, Eliezer   442
Berlin, Adele   480
Bernard of Cluny   487
Bernhardt, Karl-Heinz   280, 281
Berridge, John Maclennan   133, 134
Bewer, Julius A.   85
Beyerlin, Walter   159, 258
Bieberstein, Klaus   84
Bienkowski, Piotr   316, 331, 339
Blayney, Benjamin   66, 84, 96, 133, 146, 147,
    148, 159, 186, 197, 200, 208, 240, 247, 271,
    279, 298, 307, 315, 317, 320, 353, 380, 406,
    420, 434, 466, 478, 487, 507, 520, 527
Bloedhorn, Hanswulf   84
Boadt, Lawrence   115, 116, 148, 162, 165,
    182, 196, 211, 240, 296, 325, 452, 460, 473,
    500, 526
Boer, P. A. de   177
Bogaert, Pierre-Maurice   84, 521
Bonhoeffer, Dietrich   179
Borger, Riekele   446
Borowski, Oded   388, 394
Bowers, John E.   170
Boys, Thomas   155, 335
Brandt, William J.   369, 586, 589, 594
Bright, John   51, 54, 56, 60, 66, 71, 75, 81, 83,
    85, 90, 97, 98, 99, 102, 109, 117, 118, 119,
    120, 122, 127, 129, 130, 133, 145, 147, 148,
    157, 158, 161, 164, 165, 174, 175, 176, 182,
    186, 189, 190, 191, 192, 194, 196, 197, 200,
    201, 204, 206, 208, 210, 212, 221, 225, 233,
    235, 238, 239, 240, 242, 243, 246, 247, 250,
    254, 255, 257, 260, 264, 267, 270, 275, 279,
    292, 293, 294, 296, 299, 304, 306, 310, 315,
    316, 321, 322, 323, 325, 328, 329, 332, 337,
    344, 348, 352, 353, 357, 362, 367, 368, 369,
    371, 373, 379, 380, 384, 387, 388, 392, 395,

396, 402, 404, 406, 407, 412, 420, 421,
424, 432, 434, 440, 444, 454, 456, 461,
463, 464, 465, 467, 469, 473, 474, 485,
486, 495, 504, 505, 506, 507, 508, 518,
520, 526, 529, 530, 533, 537, 579
Brueggemann, Walter   198
Budde, Karl   76, 182, 183, 504, 507
Budge, E. A. Wallis   150
Bunyan, John   412

C

Calvin, John   63, 72, 77, 83, 90, 101, 111,
118, 119, 130, 131, 133, 141, 143, 146,
147, 148, 162, 166, 175, 191, 192, 195,
198, 201, 204, 210, 214, 215, 218, 221,
222, 225, 226, 227, 236, 240, 249, 250,
253, 254, 262, 265, 267, 272, 279, 283,
288, 295, 298, 299, 303, 307, 310, 315,
317, 320, 322, 323, 326, 328, 329, 330,
331, 332, 337, 338, 343, 344, 346, 350,
363, 378, 379, 383, 384, 386, 387, 388,
391, 394, 401, 404, 407, 413, 419, 420,
421, 424, 426, 432, 433, 435, 439, 441,
445, 447, 454, 455, 458, 459, 465, 468,
469, 474, 477, 486, 487, 488, 492, 494,
495, 497, 500, 505, 506, 507
Carr, A.   164
Carroll, Robert P.   50, 71, 97, 98, 99, 103,
109, 117, 174, 181, 182, 190, 192, 200,
204, 206, 222, 225, 230, 258, 270, 279,
293, 304, 337, 386, 428, 439, 440, 444,
456, 461, 473, 504, 505, 515, 526, 535
Casanowicz, Immanuel M.   248, 249, 253,
272, 418, 479
Cassuto, Umberto   182
Cazelles, Henri   464, 469
Charlesworth, James H.   178
Cheyne, T. K.   58, 62, 66, 77, 84, 98, 99,
113, 117, 130, 133, 159, 162, 193, 194,
200, 209, 221, 252, 267, 270, 272, 275,
283, 289, 299, 309, 310, 323, 325, 337,
358, 371, 380, 387, 388, 403, 407, 419,
421, 431, 433, 446, 458, 465, 467, 474,
476, 478, 488, 507
Childs, Brevard S.   182
Chotzner, Joseph   203
Christensen, Duane L.   185, 187, 189, 190,
198, 201, 206, 254, 338, 354, 391, 410,
445, 463
Clements, Ronald E.   238, 325, 351
Clines, David J.   189
Cogan, M.   67, 83, 88, 89, 514, 519, 526,
527, 535, 536, 537

Cohen, Mark E.   236, 241, 327, 392, 453
Condamin, A.   148, 163, 176, 182, 232, 240,
312, 342, 348, 352, 361, 400, 436, 444,
453, 467, 482, 495
Copher, Charles B.   143
Cornill, D. Carl Heinrich   57, 70, 71, 75,
76, 80, 97, 98, 99, 102, 111, 117, 119, 120,
122, 127, 128, 129, 133, 136, 140, 145,
148, 159, 164, 167, 168, 171, 174, 175,
176, 182, 191, 192, 196, 198, 201, 204,
207, 210, 211, 221, 222, 226, 234, 247,
251, 252, 254, 255, 256, 260, 262, 264,
267, 268, 271, 273, 275, 279, 284, 285,
292, 293, 299, 300, 302, 306, 313, 322,
328, 329, 334, 337, 345, 348, 352, 357,
360, 366, 371, 373, 375, 379, 380, 383,
388, 391, 395, 396, 403, 405, 406, 407,
418, 420, 421, 423, 424, 429, 432, 433,
434, 436, 439, 440, 448, 454, 456, 457,
465, 474, 486, 504, 507, 508, 520, 521,
524, 526, 530, 536
Cowley, A. E.   268
Crenshaw, James L.   163
Cross, Frank M.   114, 247, 280, 533, 534,
538
Crown, A. D.   192
Cunliffe-Jones, H.   452

D

Dahood, Mitchell   120, 240, 249, 260, 321,
349
Daube, David   272
Daviau, Michèle   298
Day, J.   474
de Moor, Johannes C.   294
Dearman, J. Andrew   246, 247, 248, 252,
253, 254, 276, 280, 281, 294
Delamarter, Steve   510
Dentan, Robert C.   537
Dever, William G.   523, 524, 526, 527
Di Vito, R. A.   56
Dicou, A.   325, 326, 334, 361
Dietrich, E. L.   260
Dimant, Devorah   128, 495, 512
Diodorus   83, 148, 167, 339, 368, 467, 500,
526
Diringer, David   83, 92
Dobbs-Allsopp, F. W.   203, 205, 226, 236,
246, 275, 308, 311, 313, 320, 322, 350,
435, 498
Driver, G. R.   87, 145, 240, 283, 297, 404
Driver, S. R.   127, 191, 214, 224, 267, 292,
345, 353, 508

Duhm, D. Bernhard   57, 66, 70, 75, 76, 81,
    84, 97, 98, 109, 113, 117, 127, 128, 129,
    132, 133, 134, 139, 140, 142, 143, 158,
    159, 162, 164, 165, 167, 171, 174, 176,
    177, 181, 182, 191, 192, 194, 195, 196,
    200, 201, 204, 210, 214, 216, 218, 222,
    226, 231, 233, 237, 238, 240, 252, 253,
    254, 255, 270, 274, 275, 279, 293, 294,
    298, 299, 302, 313, 314, 320, 322, 326,
    334, 337, 344, 345, 366, 371, 374, 376,
    383, 387, 396, 402, 405, 407, 417, 419,
    420, 421, 432, 433, 435, 440, 446, 454,
    455, 461, 465, 475, 478, 482, 487, 490,
    495, 503, 512, 518, 519, 520, 521, 529

E

Edelman, Diana Vikander   327, 328
Ehrlich, Ernst Ludwig   54, 72, 78, 141, 148,
    191, 197, 210, 222, 254, 260, 266, 272,
    279, 288, 322, 337, 345, 355, 380, 387,
    433, 440, 456, 507
Eissfeldt, Otto   50, 182, 395
Elat, Moshe   208
Elitzur, Yehuda   244
Ellerton, John   364
Elliger, K.   513
Ember, Aaron   210, 488
Engnell, Ivan   535
Eph'al, Israel   83, 215, 354
Erman, Adolf   190, 192
Eshel, Esther   280
Eusebius   246, 247, 248, 280, 292, 295, 339
Everson, A. Joseph   187
Ewald, Georg Heinrich August   533

F

Falkner, M.   355, 358
Feigin, Samuel   515
Field, Frederick   81, 218, 308, 530
Fischer, Georg   512
Fitzmyer, Joseph A.   163
Fohrer, Georg   187
Freedman, David Noel   54, 56, 57, 68, 83,
    114, 132, 136, 188, 194, 197, 215, 219,
    239, 249, 254, 260, 294, 310, 323, 395,
    418, 453, 495, 506, 534, 538, 579
Freedy, K. S.   56, 57
Friebel, Kelvin G.   505
Fried, Lisbeth S.   56, 57, 83, 579
Frykman, Nils   179
Frymer, Tikva Simone   59, 60, 536

G

Gadd, C. J.   177, 330
Gardiner, Alan H.   201, 208, 209

Gaster, Theodor H.   299, 425
Gelb, I. J.   70, 88
Gerleman, Gillis   306
Gershenson, Daniel E.   218
de Geus, C. H.   91, 522
Giesebrecht, Friedrich   50, 52, 75, 76, 81,
    85, 98, 100, 102, 116, 117, 118, 119, 121,
    127, 129, 132, 133, 134, 140, 141, 146,
    148, 150, 157, 158, 159, 165, 167, 171,
    174, 175, 176, 182, 186, 192, 197, 200,
    208, 209, 210, 218, 222, 233, 235, 238,
    239, 250, 254, 255, 259, 260, 275, 279,
    283, 284, 288, 291, 294, 298, 302, 307,
    313, 314, 325, 328, 332, 333, 337, 344,
    345, 346, 348, 350, 366, 370, 376, 379,
    380, 383, 387, 388, 392, 393, 395, 396,
    403, 405, 407, 414, 419, 420, 421, 431,
    432, 433, 440, 441, 454, 455, 456, 459,
    465, 475, 487, 495, 519, 520, 521, 524, 527
Ginsberg, H. L.   83, 235
Ginsburg, C. D.   244, 268
Gitin, Seymour   239, 580
Glueck, Nelson   245, 246, 247, 252, 292,
    328
Golani, Amir   239
Gonen, Rivka   190, 191, 192
Gordis, Robert   164, 322
Gorringe, Henry H.   150
Gosse, Bernard   181, 427
Grätz, Heinrich   115
Graf, Karl Heinrich   58, 59, 71, 81, 159,
    182, 237, 240, 320, 500, 533
Graham, J. N.   522
Graupner, Axel   172
Gray, John   83, 512, 515, 518, 523, 524, 526,
    535, 538
Grayson, A. Kirk   349, 362
Greenberg, Gillian   164
Greenberg, Moshe   241, 514
Greenfield, Jonas C.   163, 238
Grintz, Y. M.   178
Grohman   246, 247
Grotius, Hugo   271, 320
Gunkel, Hermann   474
Guy, P. L.   525

H

Haak, Robert D.   315
Habachi, Labib   149, 150
Haddad, George   67, 71
Haran, Menahem   188, 190, 369, 508, 579
Haupt, Paul   76, 419, 420
Hayes, John H.   57, 115, 182, 235, 578

Hayward, Robert   130, 487, 493

Heltzer, Michael L.   260

Herodotus   83, 144, 147, 149, 157, 167, 200, 201, 209, 210, 219, 225, 234, 299, 368, 421, 464, 465, 476, 477, 499, 500, 508

Herr, Larry G.   114, 248, 314, 315, 316, 321, 327

Hess, Richard S.   369

Hillers, Delbert R.   234, 317, 349

Hitzig, F.   70, 71, 122, 159, 167, 182, 210, 218, 234, 254, 271, 293, 305, 392, 475, 507

Hoffmeier, James K.   211

Hogarth, D. G.   188

Holladay, William L.   50, 51, 52, 54, 59, 66, 81, 85, 89, 92, 97, 102, 103, 109, 110, 111, 114, 115, 117, 119, 120, 121, 127, 129, 132, 133, 134, 135, 136, 140, 143, 145, 148, 155, 157, 158, 160, 161, 163, 164, 165, 167, 176, 178, 182, 186, 187, 189, 191, 192, 193, 196, 198, 200, 203, 204, 206, 210, 215, 228, 230, 233, 234, 238, 240, 242, 244, 246, 247, 249, 250, 251, 252, 253, 254, 255, 258, 260, 261, 264, 269, 270, 271, 273, 275, 276, 279, 282, 283, 286, 287, 288, 292, 293, 294, 295, 296, 297, 300, 301, 302, 303, 304, 307, 312, 317, 321, 322, 326, 328, 329, 332, 333, 334, 337, 342, 345, 346, 348, 352, 357, 360, 361, 363, 367, 368, 371, 373, 374, 379, 380, 381, 383, 384, 386, 387, 388, 392, 394, 395, 401, 404, 405, 407, 412, 414, 420, 422, 424, 426, 431, 432, 433, 434, 436, 440, 441, 444, 451, 452, 455, 457, 458, 459, 461, 465, 466, 467, 469, 471, 473, 474, 475, 476, 477, 479, 482, 485, 486, 487, 490, 495, 504, 506, 507, 515, 517, 519, 520, 526, 528, 530, 535

Homer   204, 218, 225

Honeyman, A. M.   524

Hooker, Paul K.   115, 578

Huddlestun, John R.   196

Hultgren, Arland J.   130, 379

Hyatt, J. Philip   50, 68, 81, 97, 109, 115, 117, 121, 128, 130, 142, 145, 168, 171, 176, 182, 208, 210, 212, 242, 250, 268, 323, 325, 351, 356, 533

J

Jacobsen, Thorkild   188, 369, 403, 500, 509

Jahnow, Hedwig   76

James, Frances   525

Janzen, Waldemar   54, 56, 57, 59, 63, 66,

70, 81, 101, 103, 110, 111, 113, 120, 127, 128, 129, 130, 132, 135, 136, 142, 143, 145, 155, 157, 160, 161, 164, 167, 168, 174, 175, 181, 189, 192, 224, 226, 233, 238, 251, 259, 268, 271, 272, 275, 293, 330, 336, 337, 355, 368, 370, 371, 373, 379, 383, 396, 403, 407, 423, 455, 466, 476, 479, 495, 519, 521, 526, 528, 537

Japhet, Sara   404

Jerome   295, 315, 339

de Jong, C.   187

Jones, Douglas   51, 66, 67, 70, 75, 81, 85, 100, 109, 115, 118, 121, 127, 131, 148, 176, 182, 185, 192, 200, 210, 221, 251, 255, 259, 262, 268, 289, 292, 304, 320, 330, 361, 381, 383, 395, 403, 405, 407, 420, 421, 429, 431, 433, 434, 441, 444, 456, 467, 469, 473, 475, 488, 526, 530

Josephus   83, 84, 85, 86, 88, 103, 114, 116, 117, 118, 120, 147, 167, 188, 200, 208, 215, 216, 237, 246, 250, 258, 263, 266, 316, 321, 327, 354, 485, 512, 515, 519, 522, 523, 528, 529, 533

K

Kallai, Zecharia   280

Kartveit, Magnar   204, 224, 262, 275, 320, 468

Katzenstein, H. J.   233, 234

Kegler, Jürgen   192, 207

Kelso, James L.   145, 406, 524, 525, 526

Kenyon, Kathleen M.   520

Keown, Gerald L.   50, 54, 75, 133, 148, 192, 197, 206, 210, 226, 255, 260, 261, 275, 279, 292, 306, 308, 367, 373, 381, 384, 400, 434, 436, 444, 469, 473, 475, 505, 506, 526, 530

Kessler, Martin   367, 418, 438, 462

Kimḫi   54, 63, 70, 72, 77, 84, 85, 86, 89, 90, 93, 99, 110, 118, 119, 121, 139, 145, 146, 148, 159, 165, 166, 174, 189, 192, 193, 194, 201, 205, 208, 211, 218, 222, 233, 236, 237, 254, 255, 266, 267, 271, 275, 279, 281, 283, 288, 289, 294, 295, 297, 299, 303, 310, 311, 315, 320, 323, 328, 329, 330, 332, 337, 338, 343, 344, 371, 375, 378, 379, 382, 387, 388, 391, 397, 403, 405, 407, 417, 419, 420, 424, 432, 435, 439, 440, 445, 446, 447, 448, 454, 458, 459, 465, 467, 477, 478, 485, 487, 488, 492, 494, 506, 507, 525, 527, 528, 529, 536

King, L. W. 369, 371, 392, 406, 421, 499, 500
King, P. J. 68, 119, 237, 239, 265, 294, 297, 320, 327, 465, 524, 528
Kletter, Raz 163
Knauf, E. A. 249, 252
Köhler, Ludwig 84
Kraft, Robert A. 73, 178
Kremers, Heinz 51
Kuenen, A. 164
Kuhrt, Amélie 91, 235, 362, 369, 371, 392
Kuschke, Arnulf 246, 247, 249

L

LaBianca, Øystein S. 316
Labuschagne, C. J. 405, 474
Lambdin, Thomas O. 200, 209, 210, 225
Lambert, W. G. 91, 177, 259, 330, 506
Lamon, Robert S. 523
Landes, George M. 291, 315, 317
Landsberger, Franz 90
Lane, W. H. 353, 369, 500
Layton, Scott 134, 161
Leichty, Erle 172, 502, 503
Lesko, Leonard H. 265, 294
Levenson, Jon D. 536
Levin, Christoph 116
Licht, J. 73
Liebreich, Leon J. 537
Lindblom, Johannes 187
Lindsay, John 330, 331
Lipiński, Edward 209, 234
Lipschits, Oded 56, 110, 112, 113, 115, 130
Livy 363
Loretz, Oswald 260
Loud, Gordon 206, 212, 523, 524
Lucas, Alfred 265
Luckenbill, Daniel David 258, 349, 362
Luke, K. 463, 464
Lund, Nils W. 444, 493
Lundbom, Jack R. 52, 172, 174, 181, 182, 207, 215, 217, 244, 254, 264, 266, 303, 360, 372, 414, 418, 451, 452, 472, 474, 477, 479, 502, 503, 504, 506, 519
Luria, Ben-Zion 459

M

MacDonald, J. 314, 327
Machinist, Peter 88
Mackay, Ernest 149
Malamat, Abraham 83, 84, 90, 116, 164, 183, 188, 189, 234, 235, 316, 354, 362, 514, 520

Mansoor, Menahem 292
Maspero, G. 88, 145
Matthiae, Paulo 258
Mattingly, Gerald 249, 259, 279, 298
May, Herbert G. 112, 196, 447, 495, 523, 525, 528
Mazar, Benjamin 112, 533
McCown, Chester Charlton 103, 112
McKane, William 50, 52, 57, 59, 66, 76, 85, 87, 99, 102, 109, 113, 117, 119, 127, 128, 129, 132, 133, 134, 136, 140, 143, 145, 148, 155, 157, 158, 160, 161, 164, 167, 168, 175, 176, 182, 185, 191, 192, 196, 200, 201, 202, 204, 209, 210, 216, 218, 226, 230, 234, 235, 238, 240, 241, 246, 247, 251, 252, 254, 255, 257, 260, 261, 266, 267, 268, 275, 279, 284, 292, 293, 294, 296, 297, 299, 302, 307, 312, 313, 314, 320, 326, 329, 334, 345, 352, 355, 366, 367, 371, 373, 378, 380, 381, 383, 384, 387, 391, 402, 403, 404, 407, 418, 420, 421, 426, 432, 433, 434, 436, 440, 441, 454, 455, 461, 463, 465, 467, 474, 475, 476, 482, 495, 503, 506, 509, 515, 519, 530
Mellink, M. J. 201
Mendenhall, George E. 201
Meshorer, Ya'akov 545
Meyers, Carol L. 524
Michaelis, J. D. 210, 222, 260, 271, 339, 402, 433, 447, 458
Milgrom, Jacob 83, 84, 88, 90, 117, 118, 164, 524, 525
Milik, J. T. 163, 533, 534
Miller, J. M. 235, 245, 246, 252, 289, 320
Miller, Patrick D. 407, 463
Mirsky, Aaron 264
Mitchell, Hinckley G. 131, 142, 176, 328
Mittmann, Siegfried 253
Montgomery, James A. 81, 83, 512, 514, 518, 528, 537
Moran, William L. 260, 261, 536
Morgenstern, Julian 458
Moss, Rosalind L. B. 149
Mowinckel, Sigmund 50, 173, 182, 231
Muilenburg, James 103, 118, 121, 172, 173, 174, 175, 177, 178, 199, 410, 416
Myres, John L. 523, 524

N

Na'aman, Nadav 513
Niebuhr, Reinhold 366

Noegel, Scott B.   432
Nötscher, F.   330, 350
North, Christopher R.   90, 371, 398
Noth, Martin   86, 538

O

Oesch, Josef M.   285, 287
Olrik, Axel   283
Oppenheim, A. Leo   59, 369, 467, 478, 500, 515, 529
Oren, Eliezer D.   157, 234
Ottosson, Magnus   523

P

Pagán, Samuel   325
Palmoni, Y.   222, 448
Parrot, André   362, 521, 523, 524, 528
Paton, Lewis Bayles   84
Paul, Shalom M.   219, 523, 524, 526, 527
Peake, A. S.   50, 54, 71, 75, 78, 97, 99, 101, 102, 111, 115, 120, 122, 130, 132, 133, 159, 163, 175, 176, 182, 191, 192, 198, 200, 204, 209, 210, 214, 226, 230, 234, 240, 242, 247, 255, 267, 268, 274, 275, 285, 287, 292, 295, 298, 302, 309, 313, 334, 349, 350, 351, 366, 380, 387, 388, 396, 403, 420, 421, 434, 440, 454, 456, 475, 476, 504, 505, 507, 508
Pedersen, Johannes   57, 425
Pericles   58
Perles, Felix   370
Péter, René   406
Peterson, John L.   513
Petit, Thierry   455
Petrie, W. Flinders   143, 144, 145, 149
Pettinato, Giovanni   258
Pfeiffer, Robert H.   328
Pohlmann, Karl-Friedrich   50
Porten, Bezalel   157, 163, 235, 268
Porter, Bertha   149
Pritchard, James B.   119, 121
Purintun, Ann-Elizabeth   73, 178

R

Raabe, Paul R.   77, 325, 334
Rabinowitz, Isaac   505
von Rad, Gerhard   538
Rahlfs, Alfred   122, 181, 315, 337, 346
Rainey, A. F.   177, 506
Rashi   70, 72, 77, 78, 91, 99, 100, 121, 145, 146, 148, 159, 177, 190, 192, 202, 205, 208, 210, 211, 225, 228, 237, 249, 253, 267, 291, 293, 294, 299, 301, 303, 309, 315, 320, 328, 329, 330, 332, 343, 344,

349, 350, 371, 378, 387, 388, 391, 396, 403, 406, 407, 410, 417, 419, 424, 432, 433, 434, 435, 439, 440, 442, 445, 448, 455, 465, 478, 485, 488, 492, 493, 507, 515, 524, 525, 526, 527, 528, 529, 533
Rast, Walter E.   164
Redford, D. B.   57
Reed, William L.   276, 330
Reimer, David J.   366, 371, 373, 374, 383, 386
Rendtorff, Rolf   292
Rice, Gene   68, 97
Riemschneider, Kaspar K.   59, 60
Rietzschel, Claus   172
Rin, Svi   120, 477
Ringgren, Helmer   287
Roberts, J. M.   291
Robinson, Edward   100, 103
Robinson, T. H.   366, 367, 373, 386, 393, 395
Rofé, Alexander   518, 521
Rogers, John B. Jr.   83
Rosenberg, A. J.   130, 387, 412, 434, 435, 467, 506
Ruben, Paul   193
Rudolph, W.   52, 54, 62, 63, 75, 77, 81, 84, 85, 99, 102, 109, 111, 115, 119, 122, 127, 129, 131, 133, 140, 141, 143, 145, 146, 148, 157, 164, 165, 171, 174, 175, 176, 182, 185, 187, 189, 191, 192, 195, 196, 200, 203, 206, 207, 209, 210, 212, 214, 215, 219, 221, 223, 224, 228, 233, 235, 238, 240, 242, 243, 246, 247, 250, 252, 254, 255, 257, 258, 259, 260, 261, 262, 264, 270, 273, 275, 277, 279, 282, 288, 292, 293, 294, 295, 296, 297, 298, 301, 302, 304, 306, 311, 313, 317, 320, 322, 326, 328, 329, 332, 333, 334, 337, 338, 344, 348, 357, 360, 362, 367, 370, 371, 373, 374, 379, 380, 383, 384, 387, 388, 395, 400, 401, 402, 404, 406, 407, 413, 418, 420, 421, 422, 424, 427, 429, 431, 432, 433, 434, 436, 438, 439, 440, 444, 447, 453, 454, 455, 456, 457, 458, 459, 461, 465, 467, 469, 474, 475, 476, 477, 482, 485, 486, 487, 490, 494, 495, 504, 509, 513, 515, 518, 519, 520, 526, 530, 536

S

Saggs, H. W.   87
Saleh, Abdel-Aziz   149
Salters, Robert B.   404

Sarna, Nahum M.   506
Sasson, Jack M.   59
Sauer, James A.   314
Schaeffer, Claude F.-A.   523
Schmidt, Kenneth W.   502
Schmidt, Nathaniel   109
Schniedewind, William   330
Schottroff, Willy   252, 254
Schwally, Friedrich   182, 196
Scott, R. B. Y.   523
Seitz, Christopher R.   51, 173, 181
Shiloh, Yigal   506, 520
Shipton, Geoffrey M.   523
Simons, J.   200
Sivan, Daniel   330
Skinner, John   51, 76, 131, 133, 156, 163, 174
Smelik, Klaas A.   244, 280, 289, 366
Smit, E. J.   532
Smith, Morton   163
Smith, Robertson   523
Snaith, John G.   185, 187, 195, 198, 201, 203, 214, 227, 346, 525
Soderlund, Sven   233
Soggin, J. Alberto   350
Sommer, Benjamin D.   235
Speiser, E. A.   535
Stager, Larry   103, 208, 237, 239, 533, 534
van der Steen, Eveline   316
Steiner, Richard C.   298
Stern, Ephraim   114, 157, 163, 201, 314, 315, 533
Stipp, Hermann-Josef   101
Strabo   148, 149, 340, 362, 368, 499, 500, 526
Streane, A. W.   57, 130, 133, 145, 146, 163, 175, 192, 199, 226, 255, 287, 305, 383, 387, 388, 403, 407, 434, 465, 500, 504, 513, 537
Swete, Henry Barclay   81
Symmachus   58, 59, 66, 68, 76, 77, 78, 81, 100, 103, 110, 112, 117, 121, 122, 129, 134, 135, 136, 140, 143, 145, 146, 147, 148, 158, 159, 164, 175, 176, 200, 218, 233, 238, 240, 254, 255, 261, 275, 284, 286, 288, 293, 297, 308, 332, 346, 359, 380, 384, 403, 406, 424, 433, 477, 494, 496, 527, 554

T
Tadmor, H.   83, 88, 89, 189, 338, 349, 403, 514, 519, 520, 526, 535, 536, 537, 579

Tarler, David   506
Thelle, Rannfrid I.   55
Theodotion   56, 58, 59, 66, 68, 71, 81, 91, 98, 101, 110, 132, 134, 136, 145, 148, 158, 159, 160, 161, 165, 167, 168, 226, 238, 303, 308, 310, 318, 350, 371, 380, 477, 496, 530, 532, 554
Thiel, Winfried   101, 109, 128, 173
Thiele, Edwin R.   83, 84
Thomas, D. Winton   56, 67, 235
Thompson, J. A.   52, 75, 98, 127, 133, 148, 192, 210, 212, 214, 255, 260, 264, 275, 277, 282, 292, 296, 316, 321, 325, 367, 373, 384, 401, 404, 421, 434, 444, 452, 482, 506, 526
Tombs, L. E.   526
Toorn, K. van der   516
Torczyner (Tur-Sinai), Harry   56, 67
Torrey, Charles C.   116, 424, 425
Tov, Emanuel   139, 142, 143, 145, 178, 181, 373, 379
Tristram, H. B.   245, 247, 286, 294, 295, 425
Tufnell, Olga   83, 92
Tushingham, A. D.   276
U
Ussishkin, David   190, 191
V
Van Zyl, A. H.   245, 246, 247, 252, 259, 266, 280, 289, 294, 295, 298
de Vaux, Roland   67, 292, 328
Virgil   218, 286, 391
Volz, D. Paul   52, 62, 63, 71, 75, 76, 101, 109, 111, 113, 115, 117, 121, 122, 127, 128, 129, 130, 131, 133, 134, 140, 143, 146, 148, 157, 159, 165, 171, 174, 175, 182, 187, 189, 192, 196, 199, 204, 206, 209, 210, 224, 228, 231, 233, 240, 243, 249, 250, 255, 257, 259, 260, 261, 266, 270, 271, 273, 275, 277, 279, 282, 287, 292, 293, 295, 296, 301, 302, 306, 321, 328, 329, 332, 333, 334, 337, 342, 344, 345, 348, 350, 352, 367, 373, 374, 378, 379, 380, 381, 383, 384, 386, 387, 388, 395, 400, 402, 403, 405, 407, 413, 415, 418, 420, 421, 422, 431, 432, 433, 434, 438, 440, 441, 444, 445, 455, 456, 457, 458, 461, 465, 474, 475, 477, 482, 485, 486, 487, 490, 494, 495, 499, 503, 506, 507, 519, 520, 521, 524, 526, 530
de Vries, Herman F.   294

W

Wainwright, G. A.   238
Wanke, Gunther   50, 51, 52, 173, 174, 504
Watson, Wilfred G.   185, 187, 315
Weidner, Ernst F.   237, 239
Weippert, Manfred   260
Weiser, Artur   52, 62, 66, 75, 77, 109, 127,
    128, 129, 133, 140, 143, 148, 157, 159,
    163, 174, 177, 182, 185, 192, 195, 196,
    199, 203, 204, 206, 208, 210, 212, 224,
    226, 230, 233, 235, 238, 243, 246, 247,
    250, 252, 255, 257, 260, 261, 264, 270,
    275, 288, 294, 296, 299, 306, 312, 317,
    326, 328, 334, 367, 368, 370, 373, 379,
    380, 383, 386, 387, 388, 395, 404, 407,
    409, 414, 421, 427, 432, 433, 434, 440,
    442, 444, 455, 457, 458, 474, 475, 477,
    478, 482, 485, 488
Weissbach, F. H.   83
van der Westhuizen, J. P.   186, 197
deWette, Wilhelm Martin   471, 182
Wevers, J. W.   190
Wiedemann, Alfred   225
Wilkinson, J. Gardner   86
Wilson, John A.   150
Winnett, Fred V.   276, 330
Wiseman, Donald J.   85, 188, 190, 193, 197,
    208, 233, 237, 239, 349, 353, 354, 362,
    369, 464, 465, 476, 506, 533

Wolff, Hans W.   219
Woolley, C. Leonard   188, 190
Worschech, Udo   249, 252
Wright, G. Ernest   92, 103, 104, 178, 442,
    523, 524, 525
Wylie, C. C.   523

X

Xenophon   391, 392, 425, 446, 447, 464

Y

Yadin, Yigael   89, 190, 191, 192, 200, 253,
    354, 358, 362, 427, 445, 454, 523
Yamauchi, Edwin   464
Yaron, Reuven   58
Yeivin, S.   523, 527
Yisrael, Yigal   327
Younker, Randall W.   114, 314, 316

Z

Zayadine, Fawzi   317
Ziegler, Joseph   181, 312, 315, 318, 325,
    334, 337, 342, 346, 348, 351, 357, 360
Zimmerli, Walther   50, 171, 176, 372, 504,
    507, 508
Zorn, J.   103
Zorn, Jeffrey Ralph   103

INDEX OF SCRIPTURE

◆

OLD TESTAMENT
Genesis
1   387
1:2   475
1:9–10   476
1:16   148
2:14   188
4:13   439
4:15–16   261
6:4   323
6:12   177
6:13   177, 506
8:4   463
10   200
10:2   465
10:3   464
10:6   200
10:13   200, 201
10:13–14   201
10:14   157, 238
10:19   426
10:22   200, 361
10:26   353
11:1–8   493
11:1–9   458
11:2   458
11:3   499
11:4   493
11:28   369
11:31   369
13:9   102
13:10   294
14   246
14:1[Eng 13:16]   361, 476
14:2   340, 426
14:5   247
15:7   369
15:18   188
16:15–16   111
18:5   67
18:20   442
18:22   102
19:7–8   116

19:14–22   329
19:15   439
19:17   254
19:18–19   255
19:20–23   253, 340
19:22–23   294
19:26   260
19:30   294
19:36–38   312
21:19   475
21:20   410
22:16   337
22:24   112
25:13   353
25:16   353
25:19–26   330
25:25   327
27:45   115
28:18   149
28:22   149
29:1   354
30:43   378
31:13   149
32:4[Eng 32:3]   327
35:20   149
36:1   330
36:11   328
36:15   328
36:33   338
37:21   114
37:36   91
39:1   91
40:13   535
41:1–3   196
41:14   535, 536
41:45   149
41:50   149
43:16   92
43:25   116
43:32   116
43:34   103
46:20   149
49:24   210

Exodus
1:7   130
1:8   535
2:5   194
4:21   100
4:23   100, 415
5:1   100
5:2   405
5:13   537
6:6   416
7:14[Eng 8:2]   415
7:27   415
9:1–2   415
9:23   221
10:19   222
10:28–29   529
11:5   515
12:22   525
12:23   432
14:2   209
14:6   190
14:16   476
14:21–22   476
14:24   474
14:27–28   478
14:29   476
15:1   478
15:4   272, 478
15:8   476
15:8–10   479
15:10   478
15:13   379, 416
15:16   323
16:2–3   134
16:4   537
16:29   71
17:4   468
19:8   131
19:18   165
22:22–24   332
23:5   78
23:16   115
24:3   131

24:7   131
25:25   526
25:29   526
25:29–30   525
25:31–37   525
25:37–38   524
27:3   524, 525
28:33–34   528
28:36   261
32:7   130
32:11–14   133
32:32   192
34:2   210
34:6   307, 413
37:1–5   531
37:16   526
37:17–24   525
38:3   524
39:30   261

Leviticus
1:5   524
1:11   524
3:2   524
8:9   261
10:1   525
14:36   329
16:12   525
19:27–28   118
20:5   134
20:9   475
21:5   118
25:25   416
26:30   371
26:36–37   57
26:37   205

Numbers
1:2–3   533
3:12   278
4:7   526
4:14   524
7:14   525
11:4–6   163
11:26   175
11:33   102
13:29   194
14:2–3   134
14:9   309
14:22   136
15:38   260
20:17   246
21:4   346
21:11–12   245
21:13   245
21:22   246

21:23   280
21:24   292
21:25   317
21:26   308, 310
21:26–30   248
21:27–30   248, 309
21:28   298, 309, 310
21:28–29   287, 308
21:29   258, 310
21:30   275, 310
21:32   292
22:1   245
22:5   188
22:36   245
22:39–23:6   298
23:13–17   298
23:28–30   298
24:10   283
24:17   287, 308, 310
24:20   388
25:1–5   298
26:58   513
30:2   163
30:6–15   164
30:12   163
31:1–20   257
32   320
32:1   292
32:3   246, 292, 294
32:16   320
32:24   320
32:29   315
32:33–37   245, 248
32:34   275, 278
32:35   292
32:36   295, 320
32:37   247
32:37–38   292
32:38   280
32:42   317
33   410
33:7   209
33:46–47   280
33:48   245
33:52   298
35:21   416

Deuteronomy
1:1   86
1:1–5   245
1:3   404
1:8   102, 315
1:28   442
1:41   404, 454
2:7   255

2:8   86, 327
2:10   265
2:10–11   247
2:23   238
2:24–3:22   315
2:24–37   245
2:25   323
2:32   280
2:34–35   403
2:36   278
2:37   194
3:5   358
3:5–6   403
3:10   245
3:12–37   245
3:14   112
3:17   86
4:1   160
4:5   404
4:8   160
4:13–14   404
4:28   256
4:43   245
4:44–48   245
4:48   278
4:49   86
5:32   404
6:1–2   160
7:10   496
8:11   160
8:18–20   134
10:18   332
10:21   177
11:24   188
11:25   323
11:32   160
12:2   378
12:3   149
13:1[Eng 12:32]   52
13:7[Eng 13:6]   158
13:16–18[Eng 13:15–
    17]   403
13:17[Eng 13:16]   317
14:1   118, 240
14:29   255, 332
16:9   394
16:11   332
16:13–15   115
16:14   332
16:15   255
16:22   149
17:16   130
18:21–22   167
20:3   485

22:25   110
23:3–6   312
23:7–8   332
23:24[Eng 23:23]   163
23:26   394
24:19–21   332
25:4   387
26:5   130
26:12–13   332
27:15–26   262
27:19   332
28:15   134
28:20   259
28:24   259
28:29   415
28:38   260
28:45   134, 259
28:47   379
28:48   275
28:49   303
28:51   260
28:61   260
28:62   134
28:63   260
28:68   130
28:69[Eng 29:1]   52
29:16[Eng 29:17]   371
29:22[Eng 29:23]   340,
    426, 459
30:15–20   68, 77, 134
31:26   508
31:29   165
32   366
32:11   383
32:14   397, 478
32:16   158
32:19–43   337
32:21   158
32:34–42   183, 201, 405
32:35   272, 330, 496
32:35–36   476
32:40   337
32:41   496
32:41–42   202
32:49   246
33:16   340
33:28   358
34:1   102, 246
34:3   294

Joshua
4:13   87
5:10   87
6:10   391
6:21   403

7:11   113
8   320
8:14–21   447
8:28   317
10:10   474
10:31–32   513
11:13   317
11:22   240
12:2   278
12:5   112
12:18   235
13:4   235
13:7   58
13:9   245, 275, 278
13:11   112
13:13   112
13:15–16   278
13:16   278
13:17   248
13:17–19   292
13:18   280
13:19   245, 247
13:24–28   315
13:25   278, 292
13:27   245, 295
14:5   58
15:1–4   327
15:5–7   86
15:38   103
15:42   513
15:51   280
15:61–62   533
18:2   58
18:10   58
18:16–18   86
21:15   280
21:36   280
21:37   280
21:39   292
24:3   188

Judges
1:7   536
4:5   100
5:8   191
5:14   465, 529
5:22   210, 236
5:23   257
6:1–6   354
6:2   329
6:3   354
6:25   406
6:33   354
7:12   354
7:20   202, 241

8:10   354
9:45   260
9:48   221
10:17   103
11   315
11:13   245
11:18   245
11:20   280
11:21–22   245
11:23–24   316
11:24   258
11:29   103
11:33   278
16:21   88, 89, 516
16:22   78
18:7–10   358
18:27–28   358
19:23   116
20:29–37   447
20:40   271
21:22   416

Ruth
2   330

1 Samuel
1:12   204
1:19   100
2:4   192, 363
2:36   63
3:17   370
4   90
4:1   235
4:13   278
6   150
7:10   474
7:15–16   103
7:17   100
10:17–24   103
11   315
11:2   88
11:7   323
13:6   329
13:7   102
14   111
14:52   271
15:2–3   182
15:4   410
15:32–33   337
17:5   191
17:41   221
17:52   391
17:55   529
17:55–56   344
19:33[Eng 19:32]   122
21:7   111

22:3   103
22:4–5   303
22:6   117
23:7   358
24   86
24:4[Eng 24:3]   320
25:2   255
28:10   439
28:24   219
29:1   235
30:14   238
30:28   278

2 Samuel
1:11   117
1:21   190
1:22   384
2:12–17   121
2:23   71
3:13   529
3:33–34   76
3:34   89
5:6   57
5:16   116
7   538
9:7   536
10:1–11:1   315
11:3   111
11:16–17   447
12:6   391
12:26   316
12:26–31   315
14:11   204
14:24   529
14:28   529
15–17   76
15:2–6   71
15:18   70
15:23–16:14   86
17:12   117
17:22–29   86
18:18   149
18:21–32   70
19:38–41[Eng 19:37–40]   122
21:18–22   240
23:8   271
24:16   432

1 Kings
1:40   298
2:7   122
4:30   354
5:3[Eng 4:23]   406
6:2   527
7   526

7:2   222
7:13–14   523
7:13–51   522
7:15   527
7:15–22   523
7:16   527, 528
7:16–20   527
7:18   528
7:23–26   524
7:25   526
7:27–37   523
7:31   524
7:38   523
7:39   523
7:40–46   523
7:41–42   523, 527
7:42   528
7:44   517, 526
7:46   527
7:47   527
7:49   525
7:50   524, 525
8:15   165
8:53   368
8:56   368
9:19   466
9:26   346
10:16–17   190
11:4   159
11:5   315
11:6   513
11:7   258, 259, 315, 316
11:15   529
11:23–25   349
12:2   102
12:7   535
12:15   368
12:28–29   268
14:16   514
14:18   368
14:22   513
15:13   339
15:18–20   349
15:22   103, 120, 410
15:26   513
15:29   368
15:34   513
16:7   368
16:12   368
16:25   513
17:16   368
18:3   92
18:28   191, 240
20   349

20:13–14   182
20:34   63
22   130, 183, 349
22:13–23   370
22:15   194

2 Kings
1–9   349
3:2   149
3:4   245
3:4–27   276
3:16–19   182
3:25   289, 295
3:26–27   259, 298
4:38–41   524
5:12   350
5:20   448
5:30   512
6:24–31   515
8:4   177
8:22   513
9:12   59
9:20   199
9:35–37   345
10:15   391
10:22   72
10:27   149
10:33   278
11:10   446
11:19   76
12:10[Eng 12:9]   529
13–14   349
14:7   339
14:13   58
14:14   421
15:29   90, 265, 314
16:8   526
16:9   349
16:17   523, 524, 526
16:18   76
17:1–6   90
17:3–4   507
17:5   84
17:20   387
18–20   512
18:13   90
18:19–25   101
18:34   349
19:4   55
19:13   349
19:21–28   412
19:37   463
20:12–19   369
21:1–2   516
21:19–20   516

22–23   519
22:3–14   92
22:4   529
22:8   508, 528
22:12   70
22:16–20   502
23:4   528, 529
23:4–20   518
23:5   148
23:8   103
23:10   316
23:13   258, 259, 458
23:14   149
23:17   260
23:19–20   117
23:20   202
23:31   513
23:31–32   516
23:33   87, 349
23:36   513
23:36–37   516
23:37   513
24   532
24:1   212, 233
24:2   246, 250, 263, 266,
    271, 273, 316, 349
24:6   234
24:7   188, 233, 234
24:10–16   481
24:12   189, 519, 533
24:13   421, 475, 488, 522
24:14   91, 521, 522, 532,
    533
24:14–16   533
24:16   91, 271, 522
24:17–20   53
24:18   68, 513
24:18–25:7   513
24:18–25:30   512, 517
24:18–25:34   504
24:19   54
24:19–20   513
24–25   512
25   526, 528, 532
25:1   82, 83, 410, 514
25:1–2   51
25:1–12   81
25:3   83, 84, 515
25:4   85, 369, 515
25:5   77, 87, 369
25:6   87, 88
25:7   88, 89, 512, 515
25:8   189, 519, 520, 533
25:8–21   518

25:9   89, 90, 520
25:10   369, 392
25:11   90, 521, 522
25:12   91, 522
25:13   369, 523
25:13–17   475, 519
25:16   526, 527
25:17   523, 527, 528
25:18   528
25:18–21   529
25:19   529
25:21   512
25:22–25   103
25:22–26   512, 532
25:23   111
25:23–25   109
25:24   112
25:24–25   115
25:25   51, 115, 116, 117,
    122
25:26   127, 530
25:27   56, 369, 534, 535
25:27–30   54, 534
25:28   534
25:30   537
52:1–11   532

1 Chronicles
1:6   464
1:11   201
1:11–12   201
1:12   157, 238
1:29   353
1:44   338
2:34–41   116
2:54   111
3:8   116
3:15   513
3:16   362
5:26   245, 265, 314, 432
5:39–41[Eng 6:13–15]   528
6:78   280
6:79   280
6:81   292
9:16   111
18:8   524
26:31   292
29:24   391

2 Chronicles
3:15   527
3:15–17   523
4:6   475, 523
4:12   523
4:13   523, 528
4:14   523

4:22   524
8:11   488
9:15–16   190
14:8–14[Eng 14:9–15]   70
20:19   111
21:16   432
23:9   446
25:12   339
26:14   190, 191
30:8   391
32:3–5   86
32:11   275
33:14   84
34:6–7   117
35:20–24   201
35:22   100
36:2   513
36:6   535
36:7   488
36:11   513
36:11–21   512
36:12   54, 513
36:13   88, 514
36:22   432

Ezra
1   70
1:1   432
1:7   479
1:7–11   522
3:1–6   118
4:9   362

Nehemiah
1:1   362
2:14   86
3:1–3   84
3:15   86
3:25   63
3:31   58
3:32   58
5:14   455
7:26   111
8:16   58
9:22   310
12:28   111
12:39   84
13:5   118
13:9   118

Esther
1:3   465
1:14   529
9:6   361
10:2   446

Job
1:3   354

1:13–19   467
2:11   328
4:1   328
4:15   465
6:9   447
7:12   475
8:4   120
9:19   344
16:12   358
16:13   410
20:13   391
20:15   479
21:23   358
22:9   332
26:12   476
26:13   146
31:10   515
31:24–28   322
33:6   218
37:22   439
38:2   344
39:5   255
39:27   340
40:11–12   288

Psalms
2:4   275
2:9   301
6:7[Eng 6:6]   175
6:10[Eng 6:9]   129
10:15   282
17:8   309
18:3[Eng 18:2]   282
19:2–5[Eng 19:1–4]   486
22:7[Eng 22:6]   339
22:13[Eng 22:12]   210, 407
22:14[Eng 22:13]   477
23:1–3   379
23:6   132
24:8   344
26:7   442
27:2   194
28:2   129
28:6   129
29:3   447
31:23[Eng 31:22]   129
32:6   447
34:17[Eng 34:16]   161
35:19   218
36:8   309
37   337
37:10   468
37:11   91
40:3[Eng 40:2]   68
40:6[Eng 40:5]   442

42   111
44:2[Eng 44:1]   442
44:4[Eng 44:3]   315
44:16[Eng 44:15]   488
44:16–17[Eng 44:15–
   16]   488
49:6–7[Eng 49:5–6]   322
50:13   210
52:4[Eng 52:2]   241
52:9[Eng 52:7]   322
55:2[Eng 55:1]   129
55:18[Eng 55:17]   298
60:5[Eng 60:3]   283
64:9[Eng 64:8]   284
66:13–14   163
68:6[Eng 68:6]   332
68:31[Eng 68:30]   210
69:8[Eng 69:7]   488
71:9   68
71:19   177
71:22   410
73:12   358
73:28   442
74:1–8   488
74:5   221
74:13   475
74:13–14   476
74:14   424
75:2[Eng 75:1]   442
75:5–6[Eng 75:4–5]   282
75:9[Eng 75:8]   283
75:11[Eng 75:10]   282
78:3–4   442
78:41   410
79:1   488
80:13[Eng 80:12]   89
83:8[Eng 83:7]   237
84:2[Eng 84:1]   488
88   328
89   328
89:9–10   476
89:13[Eng 89:12]   215
89:19[Eng 89:18]   410
89:25[Eng 89:24]   282
89:41[Eng 89:40]   89, 301,
   320
91:8   456
92:11[Eng 92:10]   282
94:2   288
95:5   476
95:6   375
96:9   466
97:4   466
97:7   424

103:2   495
104:4   310
104:6   475
104:21   477
105:15   67
105:18   89
105:34–35   448
106:21   177
110:2   274
112:9   282
114:7   466
116:1   129
118:2–4   475
118:17   442
119:70   129
119:154   416
120:5   353
124:1   475
129:1   475
130:2   129
131:1   177
132:5   210
132:14   379
137:1   421, 424
137:5–6   488
137:7   114, 272, 325, 331
137:8   392
139:7–12   306
140:7[Eng 140:6]   129
143:1   129
143:3   159
146:9   332
148   486
149:8   89

Proverbs
1:33   265
4:1   329
6:13   218
6:26   63
10:4   262
10:10   218
10:14–15   301
11:2   339
11:28   322
12:19   344
12:24   262
12:27   262
13:3   301
13:17   338
14:5   131
15:17   406
15:25   288
15:30   485
16:18   288,   413

16:30   218
19:15   262
23:11   416
25:18   454

Song of Songs
1:5   353
1:14   292
2:14   286, 339
3:6–7   197
4:1   397
8:5–7   197
8:7   447

Isaiah
1:17   332
1:21   274
1:24   202
2:2   479
2:6–22   288
2:10   285, 329
2:12   201, 288
2:12–13   222
2:15   89
2:19   285
2:21   285
3:9   355
3:26   275
4:4   475
5:2   294
5:5   89
5:12   298
5:28   236
5:28–29   236
7–8   349
7:8   349
7:10–17   167
7:17   506
7:18   218
7:20   241
8:1   507
8:4   348
8:6–8   196, 234
8:7   383, 447
8:7–8   478
8:8   234, 434
8:10   434
8:15   194, 405
8:18   167
9:5[Eng 9:6]   434
10:5   240, 440, 454
10:5–19   456
10:9   349
10:12   274, 412, 440
10:15   440
10:18–19   222

10:21   434
10:25   468
10:33–34   222
11:11   157, 362
11:14   354
12:6   475
13:2   463
13:3   299, 463
13:4–5   338
13:6   201
13:7   236
13:8   467
13:9   201
13:11   410
13:14   393, 394
13:14–16   323
13:17   371, 383, 432, 465
13:18   391
13:19   423, 425
13:19–22   423
13:20   389
13:21   425
13:21–22   424, 425
13:22   272, 424
13–23   181
14:1–2   317
14:1–8   417
14:4   404
14:5   404
14:7   486
14:12–15   340, 493
14:13–14   197, 410
14:16   417
14:17   415
14:29   274
14:29–31   231
15–16   243, 246, 300
15:1   289
15:2   246, 249
15:2–3   296, 299
15:2–7   287
15:3   299
15:4   248, 280, 294
15:4–6   291, 294
15:5   250, 252, 253, 254,
     255, 294, 295
15:6   295
15:7   296, 298, 299
15:9   249
16:2   279
16:6   288, 289
16:6–7   287
16:6–12   287
16:7   289

16:8   292, 293
16:8–9   248, 287, 292
16:8–10   265, 290
16:8–11   292
16:9   291, 293, 294
16:10   293, 294
16:11   289, 296, 298
16:12   297
17:1–6   348
17:12–13   495
17:13   447
18:2   338, 476
19–20   188
19:1   211
19:5   476
19:6–8   196
19:10   159
19:11   270
19:13   420
19:14   283
19:16–25   226
19:18   149
19:20   167
20:3   167
20:6   238
21:5   190
21:9   424, 440, 486
21:13   329
21:13–17   353
21:16–17   353
21:17   166
22:2   493
22:6   362
22:9–11   86
22:12   118
22:15   92
22:17   148
23:1–8   237
23:11   417
23:12   204
23:13   424
24   243
24–27   304
24:1   433
24:7   305
24:11   205
24:12   193
24:17   304, 305
24:17–18   287, 302
24:18   304, 306
25:6   266
25:10   249
25:10–12   246
25:11   288

25:12   247
27:1   202, 474, 476
27:13   378
28:4   261
28:5   274
28:9   338
28:16   459
28:19   338
28:27–28   388
28:28   474
29:4   221
30:1–7   57, 226
30:7   211
30:8   507
30:28   234
30:29   298
31:1   226
31:1–3   191, 195
31:3   194
31:8   202
33:16   459
34:1   370, 501
34:2   272
34:5–6   202
34:5–7   202, 331
34:6   338
34:6–7   407
34:7   210
34:8   201
34:13   425
34:13–15   425
34:14   424, 425
35:10   375
36:4–10   101
36:6   226
36:19   349
37:4   55
37:13   349
37:22–29   412, 456
37:30   167
37:38   463
38:7   167
38:12   447
39:1–8   369
39:5–8   507
40–48   344
40:1–3   370
40:18   434
41:7   404
41:14   416
41:17   466
42:11   353
42:13   391
43:9   375

43:14   416
43:20   425
43:23   118
44:6   416
44:23   486
44:24   416
44:25   289, 419, 420
44:26   419
44:28   70
45:1–8   70
45:2   467
45:14   434
45:15   434
45:23   337
46:1   85, 370, 371
46:1–2   210, 258
46:2   147
46:9   434
47:1   204, 274, 275
47:3   407
47:4   416
47:8   358
47:9   435
47:10   378
47:10–13   419
48:17   416
48:20   383, 439, 480
49:2   445
49:13   486
49:26   210
50:1   388
51:9   474
51:9–10   475
51:10   476
51:11   375
51:15   416
51:17–23   283
52:6   272
52:11–12   480
53:1   338
53:3–4   175
53:6   379
53:8   506
54:4–8   435
55:11   384
57:15   159
57:20   349
59:18   495, 496
60:7   353, 354
60:16   210
60:20   241
61:5   522
62:1–2   442
62:8   448

62:10–12   375
63:1   338, 344
63:4   201
63:6   283
64:6[Eng 64:7]   120
65:10   379
66:3   118
66:16   202
66:19   200, 201

Jeremiah
1   109, 172, 498
1–20   183, 296
1–29   109
1–39   81
1–51   503, 504
1–52   563
1:1   58, 504, 509
1:1–3   81, 109
1:2   184, 361
1:3   54, 513, 519
1:5   71, 183
1:5–20:18   172
1:7   175
1:8   133, 177
1:9   175
1:10   176, 183, 392, 451, 455, 463
1:11–12   167
1:12   166, 175
1:13   524
1:14   175, 234, 405
1:14–15   401
1:14–19   98
1:15   84, 89, 363, 391, 498
1:15–16   146, 173
1:16   87, 88, 164, 256, 332
1:17   192
1:18   446, 496, 499
1:18–19   173
1:19   99, 133, 177
2:1   308, 357
2:2   357
2:2–3   265, 457, 472
2:3   379
2:5   159
2:5–9   258, 326, 457, 472
2:6   87, 388, 479
2:7   293
2:8   378
2:10   238, 353
2:10–13   377
2:12   240
2:13   332
2:14   313, 452

2:15   215, 261
2:16   143, 156, 157, 208
2:18   188, 195, 196, 480
2:18–19   57, 226
2:20   202, 267, 270, 379, 399, 452
2:21   292
2:22   397
2:23   270
2:25   162, 251, 270
2:26   284, 344
2:27   149
2:28   63, 350
2:30   204, 433, 473, 530
2:31   77, 248
2:31–32   377
2:33   321, 399, 443
2:33–37   258, 326
2:34   284
2:35   270
2:36   224, 226, 267, 321, 379
2:36–37   247
2:37   99, 268
3:1   176
3:2   76, 273, 277, 420
3:3   414
3:4   231
3:5   425
3:6   379
3:9   149
3:12   282
3:13   158
3:14   375
3:15   378
3:16   165, 248
3:16–17   488
3:17   248
3:18   374
3:19   218
3:21–23   379
3:23   211, 378
3:24   500
3:25   159, 488
4–6   182
4:1   326, 355, 382
4:1–2   166
4:2   321
4:5   207, 208, 241, 463
4:5–6   369, 461, 463
4:5–8   371
4:6   102, 370, 446, 487
4:7   209, 215, 261, 343, 433, 466

4:9   91
4:11   358
4:11–12   432, 433
4:12   87, 88
4:13   187, 194, 236, 246, 259, 343
4:14   499
4:17   434, 447
4:19   218, 317, 399, 434, 463, 466
4:19–21   326
4:20   354, 440
4:21   370, 446, 463
4:22   377
4:23   418
4:24   236, 346, 429, 466
4:27   317
4:29   236, 254, 258, 261, 285, 346
4:30   204, 363
4:30–31   447
4:31   174
5:1   207, 320, 326
5:1–8   258, 326, 472
5:2   166
5:3   414
5:4   420
5:4–6   530
5:6   259, 343
5:7   166, 332
5:8   388
5:10   113, 276, 292, 433
5:12   494
5:14   473
5:15   98, 322, 438
5:15–17   418, 496
5:17   99, 293, 379, 406, 407, 452, 473
5:19   332, 433
5:21   288
5:22   196, 476, 495
5:26   433
5:26–31   377
6:1   58, 254
6:1–7   186, 326, 483
6:2   218
6:3   378, 391, 514
6:4   463
6:4–5   164, 248, 253, 338, 354
6:4–6   189
6:5   67, 89, 433
6:6   67, 222, 414, 514
6:7   485

6:8   261, 317, 350, 389
6:8–12   186, 326, 483
6:9   291, 330
6:10   136
6:11   159, 350, 405, 435
6:12   259
6:14   441
6:15   194, 260
6:16   270, 278
6:19   322
6:21   194, 259, 332
6:22   234, 383, 427, 432
6:22–23   236
6:22–24   302, 427
6:22–26   187
6:23   189, 383, 427, 494, 495
6:24   236, 338, 349, 427
6:26   259, 440
6:28   433
6:29   204
7:3–14   307
7:4   99, 268, 322, 434, 488
7:5   326
7:6   332, 414
7:9   166
7:14   520
7:15   514
7:16   56, 129
7:17   163
7:18   162, 165
7:18–20   168
7:20   158
7:23   131
7:24   345
7:24–26   136
7:25–26   159
7:28   328
7:31   165
7:32   248
7:34   293, 494
8:2   148
8:3   72, 113, 475
8:5   414
8:6   234, 288
8:8   270, 328
8:8–9   419
8:11   441
8:12   194
8:13   113, 132, 261, 293
8:13–17   472
8:14   102, 241, 487
8:16   210, 235, 236, 346, 388, 429, 466, 494

8:18   175, 254, 271, 371,
   403
8:19   192, 350
8:20   515
8:21   175
8:22   441
8:23[Eng 9:1]   435, 487
9:1[Eng 9:2]   58
9:3[Eng 9:4]   99
9:3–4[Eng 9:4–5]   211
9:5[Eng 9:4]   254
9:9[Eng 9:10]   215, 289,
   371, 494
9:10[Eng 9:11]   261, 317,
   389, 476
9:11[Eng 9:12]   215
9:12[Eng 9:13]   158, 160
9:13[Eng 9:14]   159, 415
9:15[Eng 9:16]   166, 360
   363
9:16–20[Eng 9:17–21]   320
9:18[Eng 9:19]   274
9:20[Eng 9:21]   350, 494
9:22–23[Eng 9:23–24]   321
9:23[Eng 9:24]   136
9:24[Eng 9:25]   403
9:24–25[Eng 9:25–26]   183
9:25[Eng 9:26]   187, 246,
   310, 314, 331
9:25 (LXX)   403
10:1   434
10:3   415, 494
10:6–7   344
10:10   346, 389, 405, 429,
   466
10:11   379
10:12–16   450
10:13   449
10:13 (LXX)   255
10:14   423
10:16   449
10:17   215, 443, 487
10:18   192
10:19   174
10:19–20   377
10:20   146, 248, 354
10:22   261, 317, 338, 358,
   485
10:25   183, 379, 396, 475,
   508
11–20   51
11:3   262
11:4   404, 494
11:7–8   159

11:8   158, 404
11:10   159
11:11   98, 322, 325
11:14   56, 129
11:15   387
11:16   218
11:18–20   186
11:19   248, 249, 345, 405,
   433, 477
11:22   403
11:23   306, 307
12:1   88
12:1–3   186
12:5   58
12:7   350
12:9   391
12:10   317, 433
12:11   317
12:12   202, 241, 259
12:13   267, 310, 480
12:14–17   176
12:16   166
13:4   144
13:6   144, 175
13:7   433
13:8   288
13:9   433, 505, 509
13:11   146, 158, 478
13:12–14   283, 336
13:13   446
13:14   433, 454
13:18   274, 275, 344
13:20   63, 274
13:21   77
13:22   331
13:25   99
13:26   204, 331
13:27   231, 310
14:1   184, 233, 361
14:2   205, 254
14:3   250, 253, 345, 384
14:3–4   370
14:5   236
14:8   379
14:11   56, 129, 175
14:11–18   515
14:14   175
14:18   326, 435
14:19   441
14:20   159
14:20–22   377
15:2   147, 306, 515, 526
15:3   345, 433
15:6   433

15:7   358, 384, 433, 494
15:8   259, 440
15:9   388, 433
15:10   174
15:11   284, 326
15:13   255, 421
15:15   488
15:16–17   387
15:17   387, 405, 477
15:18   414
15:19   326
15:20   99, 133
15:20–21   177
16:5   272
16:6   117, 240
16:9   494
16:11   332
16:11–12   159
16:14–15   113
16:15   113, 475
16:16   87, 267, 306, 433
16:18   496
16:19   159, 193
16:19–20   183
17:2–3   378
17:3   255
17:4   440
17:4–6   440
17:5   99, 262, 282
17:6   255
17:7–8   333
17:13   332, 380, 423
17:15   63
17:17   301
17:18   403
17:19   58
17:22   404
17:24   446
17:25   261, 419
17:26   118
17:27   89, 147, 350, 413
18:1–5   131
18:3   440
18:4   433
18:7–9   176
18:7–10   183
18:8   345
18:11   345
18:11–19   440
18:13   204
18:15   194, 204
18:16   261, 272, 389
18:17   219, 272, 330, 432
18:18   76, 328, 345, 419,

494
18:20   129
18:21   147
18:22   305, 440
18:23   194, 345
19:1–13   267, 301
19:3   98, 322
19:4   332
19:4–5   159
19:7   345, 363, 433
19:8   261, 334, 340, 389
19:10   145
19:11   505, 509
19:13   158, 164
19:15   98, 158
20   172
20:1–2   55
20:1–3   65
20:2   58, 59
20:4   88
20:4–6   174
20:6   259
20:7   283, 301
20:8   485, 488
20:8–9   162
20:9   370
20:10   77
20:11   194, 267, 376, 388
20:14–15   262
20:14–18   238
20:16   255, 317
20:18   172, 175, 508
21–45   97
21–52   369
21:1   55, 529
21:1–2   56
21:1–10   53
21:2   55, 56, 129, 177
21:4   84, 369
21:7   64, 226, 363
21:8–9   77, 134
21:8–10   65, 66
21:9   58, 64, 66, 90, 99,
    177, 194
21:10   66, 89, 98, 134, 166
21:11   187
21:12   414
21:13   215, 278, 321, 322,
    412, 432, 458
21:13–14   410, 411
21:14   89, 147, 209, 222,
    350, 413
22–23   528
22:3   414, 528

22:4   446, 528
22:5   337
22:6–7   222
22:6–23   410
22:7   89, 433
22:9   332
22:10   272
22:11   513
22:14–15   222
22:17   414
22:18   246
22:19   345
22:20   204, 538
22:23   215, 222, 340, 443
22:24   337
22:25   99, 369
22:27   162
22:28   300, 301, 441, 454
22:29   240, 434
22:30   54, 413
23:1–4   378
23:3   113, 343, 379, 396
23:4   433
23:5   54
23:6   358, 374
23:7–8   113
23:8   113, 475
23:9   187
23:12   306, 307
23:13   378
23:14   140
23:17   118
23:18   77, 326
23:20   446
23:21   140
23:21–22   326
23:24   331
23:25   218, 434
23:26   140
23:27   159
23:29   404, 451
23:32   140
23:40   376, 488
24   59
24:5–7   130
24:6   92, 132, 176
24:8   156
24:9   113, 475
25   182, 189
25:1   156, 189, 519
25:1–38   174, 183
25:3   54, 158
25:6–7   256
25:9   70, 112, 146, 261,

383, 389, 391, 403, 406
25:10   494
25:11   261, 372
25:12   261, 358, 459, 508
25:13   181, 184, 507
25:13 (LXX)   181
25:14   256, 360, 456, 496
25:14–20   360
25:14–29   496, 497
25:15   144, 439, 440
25:15–16   440
25:15–28   440
25:15–29   183, 283, 336
25:15–38   306
25:16   424, 440
25:17   439
25:17–26   354
25:18   261
25:18–26   348
25:19   188
25:19–26   181
25:20   233, 237, 239, 240,
    360, 420
25:21   246, 314, 331, 337
25:22   237, 238
25:23   310, 330, 331, 358
25:24   420
25:25   362, 446, 465
25:26   281, 432, 464, 478
25:27   283, 440
25:28   439
25:28–29   337
25:29   328, 337
25:30   343
25:31   183, 238, 310, 416
25:32   427
25:33   91, 435
25:34   202, 235, 252, 272,
    279, 320
25:34–36   378
25:34–38   343
25:36   252, 259, 493
25:37   350
25:38   211, 394
26   116
26:1   362
26:1–19   520
26:2   370
26:3   345
26:3–6   134
26:4   160
26:7–11   55
26:8–9   162
26:10   76

26:10–16   59
26:11   66
26:12–16   140
26:15   67, 135
26:18   320
26:19   159
26:20–23   56
26:22   117
26:24   59, 92
27   182
27–28   506
27–29   366, 372
27:1   362
27:1–3   237
27:2–11   114
27:3   114, 234, 246, 316,
    318, 322, 331
27:4   505
27:5–7   133, 176, 456
27:6   112, 146
27:6–7   440
27:7   372, 374
27:10   140
27:11   91
27:12   362
27:13 (LXX)   101
27:14   140
27:15   140
27:16   140, 162
27:18   326
27:19–22   522
27:22   372, 374
27:30 (LXX)   350
27:44 (LXX)   343
28   385, 507
28:1   145, 237, 362
28:2–4   63, 372
28:3–4   162
28:5   145
28:8   183
28:8–9   167
28:10–11   372
28:11   63, 145, 505, 509
28:12   131, 176
28:15   99, 140
28:16   485
28:57 (LXX)   214
28:59–64   181
28:59–64 (LXX)   368
29   503, 504, 506
29:1–2   259
29:2   91, 522, 529
29:3   92, 362
29:4 (LXX)   238

29:4–28   487
29:5   132
29:5 (LXX)   321
29:5–7   112
29:6   130, 144
29:10   372, 507
29:10–14   130
29:11   345
29:13   375
29:14   113
29:18   113
29:19   379
29:21   88
29:23   140
29:24–32   55
29:25–29   529
29:28   67, 132
29:31   99, 140
30:2   507
30:3   374
30:5   305, 323
30:6   192, 210
30:8   433
30:10   228, 265, 487
30:10–11   184, 228
30:11   113, 228, 229
30:12–15   441
30:13   204
30:14–15   397
30:15   175, 197, 328
30:16   317, 379, 387, 421
30:17   211
30:18   317
30:18–21   457
30:19   204
30:20   226
30:23–24   450
30:24   446
31   353
31:2   241, 416, 487
31:2–3   487
31:4–5   418
31:6   354, 375
31:7   388
31:8   98, 259, 322, 375, 427
31:9   194, 374
31:10   323, 358, 433
31:11   416
31:12   375, 480
31:14   397
31:15   100, 187, 388
31:18   218, 272
31:19   283
31:20   197, 284, 298, 328

31:21   260, 487
31:22   322
31:23   379, 396
31:24   455
31:27   374
31:28   132, 166, 176
31:29   248
31:31–34   398
31:34   248, 376, 397
31:35   148, 416, 495
31:38–40   176, 459, 480
31:40   248
32   53, 104
32:1   519
32:1–15   56, 63
32:2   63
32:3   63, 66
32:4   62, 88, 529
32:4–5   369
32:5   89
32:6–8   131
32:6–15   57
32:10   507
32:12   145, 172, 502, 506
32:13   505
32:14   144
32:15   114, 167
32:18   434, 496
32:19   345
32:20 (LXX)   233, 420
32:20–21   167
32:23   160, 165
32:24   514
32:24–25   369
32:26 (LXX)   478
32:28   66
32:28–29   369
32:29   89, 147, 520
32:30   256
32:35   315
32:37   113, 358
32:38 (LXX)   211, 394
32:43   317
33:1   102
33:3   177
33:4   90, 514
33:5   369
33:6   383
33:7   374
33:8   397
33:10   158
33:14   374
33:15   373, 374, 397
33:16   358

33:18 297
33:26 360
34 53
34:1–7 55
34:2 66, 89
34:3 62, 87, 88, 529
34:4–5 89
34:5 246
34:14 159
34:17 158
34:18–20 88
34:19 529
34:21 87
34:21–22 57
34:22 66, 89, 103, 261, 317, 389
35:3 112, 129
35:4 55, 529
35:7 143
35:11 54, 375
35:14 397
35:14–16 158
35:14–18 158
35:17 98, 322
36 54, 61, 116, 173, 189, 366, 506
36–39 512
36:1 174
36:1–8 172, 174, 176, 502, 503
36:2 144, 183
36:3 345, 397
36:4 172, 174, 508
36:5 505
36:7 63
36:8 505, 508
36:10 92
36:10–12 520
36:11–19 59
36:12 116
36:14 111
36:19 78, 175
36:20 116
36:23 241, 508
36:25 61
36:26 175, 502, 506, 529
36:27–23 360
36:27–28 172
36:28 144
36:29 433
36:30 54
36:31 54, 158
36:32 172, 174, 502, 506
36:45 502

37 54, 61
37–38 50, 53, 72, 94
37–44 50, 80, 97, 115, 173, 174
37:1 52, 81
37:1–2 52, 53
37:1–16 52, 53, 81
37:1–17 52
37:1–40:6 51, 52, 61, 64, 69, 73, 79, 81, 82, 94, 512
37:2 50, 52, 53, 63, 158, 368, 515
37:3 50, 54, 57, 65, 129, 529
37:3–5 51
37:3–11 53
37:3–16 52
37:5 52, 55, 84, 168, 338
37:6 53, 54
37:6–10 226
37:7 57
37:7–8 57
37:8 66, 89
37:9 53
37:10 89, 435
37:11 52, 84
37:11–12 52
37:12 53
37:12–16 53, 73
37:12–21 51
37:13 54, 90, 194
37:14 141, 194
37:15 56, 63, 530, 535
37:16 52, 68
37:17 62, 76, 87
37:17–21 52, 73, 75
37:19 62
37:20 60
37:21 51, 56, 62, 65, 515
38 51, 54, 81, 97, 383
38:1 51, 55, 67, 68, 82, 92, 98
38:1–2 75
38:1–3 63
38:1–6 52
38:1–10 81, 82
38:1–13 51
38:2 65, 90, 99, 177
38:3 81
38:4 65, 66, 85, 236
38:4–6 59
38:4–10 81
38:4–13 81
38:5 62

38:6 52, 60, 65, 66, 78, 119
38:7 58, 70, 122, 529
38:7–13 52
38:9 99, 248
38:11 70
38:11 (LXX) 68, 255
38:11–14 82
38:13 69, 70, 75, 98
38:14 75, 82
38:14–16 370
38:14–28 52
38:15 76, 345
38:16 99, 326
38:17 75
38:17–18 76, 89, 134
38:17–22 83
38:18 66, 87, 99
38:19 58, 194
38:22 68, 76, 192
38:22–23 70
38:23 66, 77, 87, 89, 459
38:24–27 59, 73
38:26 63
38:27 75
38:28 75, 82
39 54, 79, 80, 81, 513, 516
39–40 366, 516
39:1 51, 75, 83, 87, 92, 514
39:1–2 51
39:1–7 513, 514, 517
39:1–10 81, 109
39:1–14 51, 52
39:1–40:6 81, 515
39:2 68, 115, 515
39:2–3 98, 100
39:3 75, 77, 83, 92, 363, 369, 529
39:3 (LXX) 101
39:4 87, 92, 100, 515
39:4–7 363
39:5 83, 87, 100, 101, 103, 188, 349
39:6 98, 102
39:7 515
39:8 520
39:8–10 518, 520
39:9 58, 194, 521, 522
39:9–14 85
39:10 522
39:11–14 51, 97, 100
39:11–15 91
39:12 102
39:12 (LXX) 101
39:12–24 101

39:13   84, 85
39:14   97, 100, 102
39:15   97
39:15–18   51, 56, 72, 73,
    97, 174, 176
39:15–40:6   52, 94
39:16   91, 97
39:17   99
39:17–18   91, 122, 529
39:18   66, 97, 99, 177, 333
39:28   51
40   81
40–41   103
40–42   100
40–43   52, 100, 512
40:1   91, 97, 98
40:1–6   51, 97, 98
40:3   122, 158
40:4   89, 92, 98
40:5   91, 119, 487, 537
40:6   52, 81, 93, 97, 115
40:7   110, 117, 119, 122,
    143, 529
40:7–9   109
40:7–41:18   109, 126, 127
40:7–43:7   109
40:8   115, 119, 120, 129,
    529
40:9   131, 133
40:10   110, 117, 522
40:11   117, 120
40:11–12   142
40:12   109, 113, 115
40:13   109, 529
40:13–41:15   322
40:13–41:18   316, 324
40:14   86, 122, 315
40:15   114, 117, 121
40:16   117
40:17   121
41:1   51, 111, 121
41:1–3   109, 110
41:3   110, 316
41:4–5   115
41:5   118, 239, 240, 299
41:6   109
41:7   88
41:8   113
41:10   111, 113
41:11   132, 529
41:13   529
41:14   129, 146
41:15   86, 114
41:16   70, 111, 132, 143,

529
41:17   129, 130, 136, 146
41:17–18   133
41:18   110
42   108, 109, 127, 139
42–44   54
42:1   112, 127, 529
42:1–2   132, 146
42:1–3   56
42:1–6   120, 127, 128
42:1–43:7   127
42:2   63, 127
42:4   127, 370
42:4–5   131
42:5   130, 136
42:6   127, 134, 136
42:7   176
42:7–9   128
42:7–22   127
42:8   129, 529
42:8–9   129
42:9   63
42:9–11   128
42:10   127, 133, 176, 261
42:10–12   128
42:10–19   134
42:11 (LXX)   54
42:11–12   128
42:12   132, 146
42:13   134, 136
42:13–15   128
42:14   128, 130, 131, 134
42:15   127, 128, 134, 135,
    143
42:15–17   128, 130
42:15–18   128, 135
42:15–19   128
42:16   116
42:17   127, 136, 143, 162
42:18   127, 128, 158, 159
42:19   127, 128, 134
42:19–21   131
42:19–22   127, 128
42:20   127, 130, 159
42:20–21   129
42:20–22   137
42:21   158
42:22   128, 135, 143
43   126, 169, 182
43–44   173, 181
43:1   139
43:1–3   127
43:1–4   139
43:1–7   140

43:2   129, 143
43:2–3   115
43:2–4   139, 140
43:3   103, 120, 139, 140,
    141
43:3–9   139
43:4   136, 139, 141, 158,
    530
43:4–5   141
43:5   113, 141, 142, 143,
    530
43:5–7   139
43:6   111, 120, 122, 142
43:7   136, 139, 158
43:8–13   127, 139, 140,
    188, 206, 208, 216
43:9   139, 143
43:9–12   169
43:10   112, 133, 144, 146,
    147
43:10–12   140
43:10–13   363
43:12   133, 146, 150, 258
43:12–13   226, 459
43:13   139, 169
43:19–22   141
44   52, 126, 135, 173
44:1   144, 154, 162, 208,
    209
44:1–25   154
44:3   157, 159
44:4   158
44:5   54, 158, 162
44:6   157, 165, 261, 317
44:7–9   155
44:8   143, 158, 161, 165,
    256
44:9   159, 163
44:10   165
44:11   158
44:11–12   134
44:12   143, 156, 159, 161,
    165
44:13   158, 168, 396
44:14   135, 143, 161, 166
44:15–19   159
44:16   54, 158
44:17   159, 164, 165
44:19   164
44:20   122
44:20–23   155
44:21   159, 163, 515
44:22   157, 158, 159, 161,
    165, 261

44:23   136, 158, 160, 165
44:25   156, 163, 165, 279
44:26   154, 337
44:26–30   154, 188, 206
44:27   98, 166, 363
44:27–29   154
44:28   143, 161, 162, 169, 487
44:29   142, 162, 166
44:30   56, 83, 156, 161, 167, 173, 208, 212, 216, 226, 363
45   50, 97, 104, 156, 171, 172, 173, 174, 181, 187, 189, 502, 503, 504, 509
45:1   171, 175, 187, 189, 208, 505
45:2   171, 176
45:2–3   171, 175
45:3   171, 176
45:4   172, 173, 174, 176
45:4–5   98, 171, 174, 176
45:5   66, 98, 99, 171, 322
46   156, 173, 182
46–49   182, 259, 367, 433
46–51   181, 182, 184, 504
46:1   181, 189, 233, 361
46:1 (LXX)   514
46:2   167, 181, 185, 186, 187, 194, 196, 208, 233
46:2 (LXX)   515
46:2–12   174, 185, 186
46:3   383, 386
46:3–4   185, 187, 189, 192, 195, 198, 199, 207, 209, 367, 439, 445
46:3–5   210, 377
46:3–6   185, 186, 198, 207, 444, 468
46:3–12   185, 196, 198, 199, 203
46:5   78, 185, 187, 189, 193, 196, 198, 210, 219, 323, 329, 355, 494
46:5–6   187, 195, 207, 211, 495
46:5–12   495
46:6   185, 186, 187, 194, 195, 211, 279
46:7   195, 344
46:7–8   185, 195, 328
46:7–10   185
46:8   186, 196, 199, 234
46:9   185, 190, 191, 193,

198, 199, 202, 204, 209, 218, 386, 391, 420, 424, 440
46:9–10   196
46:10   185, 186, 194, 199, 210, 236, 262, 384, 473
46:11   185, 203, 211, 224, 248, 441
46:11–12   185, 199, 207
46:12   185, 186, 193, 194, 203, 211, 214, 224, 259
46:13   185, 187, 189, 203, 206, 226
46:13–26   185
46:14   156, 157, 194, 206, 207, 208, 212, 215, 369, 473
46:14–15   191, 192
46:14–17   203, 206, 214
46:14–24   206, 212
46:14–26   208
46:15   211, 328
46:15–16   206
46:16   194, 204, 206, 207, 211, 212, 393, 394, 420
46:16–17   218
46:17   167, 206, 207, 212, 216
46:18   214, 216, 218, 272, 337, 496
46:18–19   206, 217
46:18–23   199, 206, 213, 227
46:18–24   212, 213, 223
46:19   204, 206, 213, 214, 224, 227, 261
46:20   206, 217, 221, 222, 434
46:20–21   214, 221
46:20–24   206
46:21   193, 200, 201, 209, 210, 211, 221, 236, 259, 307, 329, 330, 407, 420
46:22   213, 220, 221
46:22–23   217, 224
46:23   221, 222
46:24   204, 206, 213, 214, 215, 221, 223, 224, 226, 227, 232, 247, 279
46:25   343, 362, 396
46:25–26   206, 213, 223, 227
46:26   185, 187, 223, 224, 227, 228, 311, 313, 363,

425, 498
46:27   228, 265
46:27–28   184, 224, 232
46:28   113, 228, 475
46:32   181
47   182
47:1   184, 189, 230, 231, 239, 361
47:2   196, 205, 224, 230, 232, 233, 279, 320, 343, 362, 478
47:2–5   224, 230, 231, 232
47:2–7   244, 336
47:3   193, 210, 329, 346, 349, 388
47:4   201, 232, 233, 238, 241, 244, 259
47:5   117, 230, 232, 233, 239, 240, 241, 299, 321, 362
47:6   202, 230, 232, 240, 241, 244, 249, 416, 419
47:6–7   230, 232, 262, 328, 498
47:7   230, 231
48   277, 308, 366, 367
48:1   187, 232, 233, 243, 244, 251, 279, 301, 308, 310
48:1–2   232, 243, 244, 251, 256, 257
48:1–9   263, 273
48:1–10   257
48:1–28   244, 285, 287
48:2   243, 244, 247, 250, 253, 256, 259, 305, 308, 320, 328, 345, 350, 439, 478
48:3   243, 250, 256, 404, 493
48:3–4   251, 254
48:3–5   251, 257
48:3–6   251
48:3–9   243
48:4   345
48:4 (LXX)   294
48:5   251, 252, 253
48:6   251, 252, 279, 355, 437, 439, 473
48:7   147, 251, 254, 256, 258, 259, 261, 321, 322, 333, 405
48:7–8   257
48:7–9   251, 257, 268

48:8 246, 251, 254, 257, 258, 259, 271
48:9 132, 243, 257, 261, 265
48:10 257, 262, 263, 282, 405
48:11 243, 257, 263, 264, 265, 272
48:11–12 269
48:11–13 273
48:12 243, 316, 343, 433, 454, 486
48:12–13 257, 263, 269
48:13 258, 264
48:14 243, 270, 272, 273, 274, 288, 290
48:14–15 270
48:14–16 387
48:14–17 269, 281
48:14–20 269, 273, 274, 277, 285
48:15 214, 246, 254, 259, 270, 272, 274, 276, 407, 496
48:16 219, 270, 271, 330
48:16–17 270
48:17 243, 270, 272, 273, 274, 282, 285, 290
48:17–18 269, 281
48:18 215, 246, 259, 269, 271, 273, 278, 433
48:18–19 215
48:19 243, 254, 271, 273, 277, 279, 282
48:19–20 269, 277, 281, 286
48:20 235, 247, 259, 271, 272, 273, 277, 279, 282, 301, 320
48:21 245, 277, 311
48:21–23 247
48:21–24 269, 277, 279, 281
48:22 275
48:23 247
48:24 277, 303, 338
48:25 277, 282, 285, 288, 404
48:26 282, 290, 295, 305, 337
48:26–27 277, 282, 285, 301
48:27 267, 282, 285
48:28 215, 277, 285, 287,

288, 305, 383, 459
48:29 243, 285, 287, 288
48:29–30 274, 410
48:29–31 277, 287, 288, 291
48:30 282, 285, 287, 289, 419
48:30–31 287
48:30–47 244
48:31 235, 287
48:32 113, 259, 291, 294
48:32–33 265, 277, 285, 287, 288, 291, 297
48:33 291, 294, 300, 434
48:34 248, 252, 277, 278, 280, 291, 294, 296, 320
48:35 291, 293, 296, 299
48:35–36 296, 297
48:35–38 278, 291, 300
48:35–39 277
48:36 289
48:37 117, 239, 296, 320
48:37–38 296, 297, 301
48:38 300
48:38–39 244, 278, 296, 297, 300, 303, 326
48:38–45 244
48:39 193, 243, 247, 274, 279, 283, 300, 320, 329
48:40 243, 300, 302, 343, 346
48:40–21 278
48:40–41 244, 300, 302, 305, 342
48:40–43 277
48:40–44 302
48:41 91, 201, 237, 281, 302, 346, 420, 466, 499
48:42 259, 283, 285, 304
48:42–43 278, 302, 303
48:43 215, 278, 286, 304, 323
48:43–44 304
48:44 277, 278, 302, 305, 306, 308, 323
48:45 308, 320
48:45–46 248, 277, 278, 308
48:45–47 314
48:46 246, 258, 259, 308, 309, 314
48:47 226, 228, 243, 261, 278, 308, 313, 323, 360, 363, 498, 505

49 312
49:1 187, 233, 312, 313
49:1–2 309, 312, 313, 314, 319, 324
49:1–6 312, 314, 326, 336
49:2 267, 312, 313, 317, 319, 320, 343, 358, 388, 486
49:3 248, 251, 258, 259, 313, 315, 319
49:3–4 251, 319
49:3–5 312
49:3–6 313, 314
49:4 240, 251, 255, 319, 333
49:5 98, 305, 312, 313, 319, 320, 323, 343, 362
49:6 226, 228, 311, 312, 313, 319, 323, 360, 363, 498
49:7 187, 248, 325, 345
49:7–8 325
49:7–10 77
49:7–11 319, 325, 336
49:8 254, 307, 326, 328, 331, 355, 358, 437, 439
49:9 325, 326, 331, 433
49:9–10 325, 326
49:10 325, 326, 329, 330
49:10–11 325
49:11 325, 326, 332, 334, 498
49:12 334, 335, 336, 343, 440
49:12–13 326, 334
49:12–18 343
49:13 261, 330, 334, 335, 336, 338
49:14 207, 338, 485
49:14–15 335
49:14–16 325, 334, 335
49:16 247, 288, 334, 335, 340, 410, 412, 493
49:17 334, 389
49:17–18 261, 334, 336
49:18 334, 359, 422, 423, 425, 479
49:19 196, 334, 342, 343, 344, 345, 346, 347, 428, 494
49:19 (LXX) 429
49:19–21 342, 428
49:19–22 336
49:20 253, 326, 328, 342,

352, 355, 428, 429, 466
49:20–21   342, 347, 466
49:20–22   342
49:21   253, 429, 466
49:22   91, 201, 237, 302,
   303, 304, 337, 342, 343,
   347, 420
49:23   187, 338, 348, 485
49:23–24   354
49:23–25   348
49:23–27   336
49:24   193, 329, 420
49:24–25   348
49:25   248, 274, 303, 478,
   498
49:26   91, 201, 237, 249,
   348, 409, 410, 435
49:26–27   348
49:27   147, 348, 413
49:28   187, 204, 259, 338,
   351, 352, 355, 358, 386,
   439
49:28–29   352
49:28–30   357
49:28–33   336, 352
49:29   193, 352, 358
49:29–30   352
49:30   254, 329, 342, 345,
   352, 353, 357, 359, 382,
   437, 473, 498
49:30–31   439
49:31   338, 352. 357, 386,
   467
49:31–32   357
49:32   219, 310, 330, 357,
   358, 384, 433
49:32–33   357
49:33   189, 261, 317, 334,
   340, 357, 423, 479
49:34   184, 189, 233, 357,
   360, 361
49:35   343, 360, 495
49:35–36   360
49:35–38   336, 360
49:36   358, 360, 433
49:37   166, 202, 360
49:37–38   360
49:38   146, 360
49:39   226, 228, 311, 313,
   323, 360, 498
50   365, 430
50–51   182, 361, 365, 366,
   367, 373, 433, 503, 507
50:1   208, 365, 369, 384

50:1–51:58   502, 504, 507
50:2   76, 207, 208, 365, 367,
   428, 446, 463, 492
50:2–3   365, 367, 373
50:2–20   366
50:2–51:58   508
50:3   261, 355, 365, 367,
   382, 383, 403, 466, 476,
   486, 505
50:4   367, 373, 374, 397
50:4–5   373, 374, 375, 377,
   378, 414, 498
50:4–6   373
50:4–7   373
50:5   373, 374, 375, 376
50:6   377, 385
50:6–7   396, 414
50:7   374, 377, 378, 385,
   391, 397, 435
50:8   286, 355, 369, 381,
   385, 394, 431, 433, 437,
   439, 473, 480, 487, 498
50:8–10   381
50:9   343, 371, 381, 391,
   427, 432, 446, 486
50:9–10   381
50:10   369, 381, 385, 386,
   387
50:11   210, 218, 236, 385,
   386, 387
50:11–12   386
50:11–13   386
50:11–16   386
50:12   267, 386, 387, 479
50:13   261, 317, 358, 386,
   466, 476
50:14   189, 190, 200, 367,
   383, 386, 390, 391, 402,
   410, 435, 439, 445
50:14–15   386, 393
50:14–16   386, 394
50:15   201, 390, 391, 396,
   407, 439, 444, 446, 499
50:16   193, 211, 385, 386,
   393, 433, 441, 468
50:17   378, 395, 396, 398,
   406, 473, 474, 475
50:17–20   182
50:18   162, 225, 343, 392,
   395
50:18–20   395, 498
50:19   379
50:19–20   395
50:20   373, 374, 395, 399,

402, 406
50:21   190, 371, 395, 397,
   399, 406, 407
50:22   399, 400
50:22–23   401
50:22–24   399
50:22–25   405
50:22–27   399
50:23   274, 400, 405, 407,
   454, 478
50:24   256, 391, 399, 400,
   401, 402, 405, 410
50:25   201, 257, 262, 369,
   401, 405, 434, 454
50:25 (LXX)   255
50:25–27   399
50:26   410, 467
50:26–27   399, 402, 403,
   406
50:27   201, 237, 272, 399,
   401, 413
50:28   201, 390, 392, 399,
   400, 401, 433, 439, 442,
   444, 446, 488, 498
50:29   200, 367, 386, 391,
   392, 405, 409, 433, 435,
   445, 456, 463, 487, 496,
   514
50:29–30   190, 411, 412,
   417
50:29–32   411
50:29–34   411, 414
50:30   91, 201, 237, 348,
   350, 409, 410, 435
50:31   201, 237, 343, 407,
   411, 413, 415, 458
50:31–32   183, 238, 339,
   405, 410, 411, 412, 417,
   420
50:32   147, 194, 209, 350,
   411, 412, 413
50:33   414
50:33–34   412, 415, 417,
   498
50:34   241, 414, 415, 416,
   422, 468, 476, 514
50:35   369, 412, 414, 418,
   432, 490
50:35–36   418
50:35–37   240
50:35–38   414, 422, 452,
   496
50:36   289
50:37   418, 419, 455

50:37–38   418
50:38   183, 238, 418, 422,
    423, 424, 440, 486
50:39   422, 423, 426
50:39–40   389, 422, 423
50:40   334, 340, 359, 422,
    423, 425, 479
50:41   343, 383, 427, 432,
    486
50:41–42   371
50:41–43   302
50:42   189, 468, 495
50:43   236, 338, 391, 420,
    467
50:44   343, 344, 428, 432
50:44–46   342
50:45   253, 326, 428, 432,
    466
50:45–46   428, 466
50:46   342, 346, 365, 428,
    46651:34–45   258
51:1   343, 369, 383, 412,
    429, 430, 431, 432, 433,
    435, 444, 446, 458, 478
51:1–2   431, 432
51:1–4   431
51:1–5   431
51:1–6   431
51:1–10   431
51:1–22   479
51:2   358, 432, 433, 436
51:3   190, 192, 200, 218,
    391, 403, 431
51:3–4   431
51:4   57, 369, 429, 431,
    432, 435, 492
51:5   369, 410, 431, 434,
    437, 498
51:6   201, 249, 254, 279,
    350, 382, 392, 431, 433,
    437, 438, 441, 444, 456,
    473, 480, 495, 496, 498
51:6–10   449
51:7   337, 424, 437, 440,
    441, 447, 477
51:8   203, 320, 437, 438,
    440, 441, 486, 498
51:9   394, 433, 437, 438,
    439, 498
51:9–10   438
51:10   375, 431, 433, 437,
    438, 439, 441, 498
51:11   190, 191, 201, 367,
    371, 372, 383, 391, 407,

432, 433, 439, 444, 446,
    449, 458, 465, 466, 488
51:11–12   439
51:12   367, 370, 444, 446,
    449, 450, 463, 477
51:13   421, 424, 440, 445,
    447, 476
51:14   337, 444, 445, 449
51:15   450
51:15–16   450
51:15–19   451
51:16 (LXX)   255
51:17   423
51:19   450
51:20   183, 433, 451, 452,
    458, 463
51:20–21   452
51:20–23   418, 451, 452,
    461, 496
51:20–24   404
51:21   420
51:22   452
51:23   452, 490
51:23–42   479
51:24   369, 410, 449, 451,
    452, 454, 456, 487, 496
51:25   343, 412, 433, 457,
    458, 493
51:25–26   490
51:26   358, 457, 458, 461,
    508
51:27   370, 410, 439, 446,
    448, 455, 461, 465, 466
51:27–28   383
51:27–33   461
51:28   367, 371, 372, 391,
    432, 444, 446, 455, 461,
    462, 463, 490
51:28 (LXX)   446
51:29   261, 346, 389, 429,
    461, 476
51:30   147, 303, 420, 467,
    495
51:30 (LXX)   173
51:31   406
51:31 (LXX)   189
51:31–35 (LXX)   50, 181
51:32   461
51:33   417, 427, 461, 472,
    514
51:34   461, 471, 474, 479
51:34–35   461, 471
51:34–44   473
51:34–45   326, 349, 461,

473, 482
51:34–58   366
51:35   215, 238, 278, 369,
    472, 473, 481, 487
51:36   201, 343, 416, 439,
    446, 472, 478
51:36–37   471
51:36–45   471, 472
51:37   261, 389, 466, 478,
    479
51:37–38   471
51:38   379
51:39   387, 472, 477, 490,
    496
51:40   272, 471, 473
51:41   248, 274, 350, 404,
    432, 473, 479
51:41–45   473
51:42   234, 343, 476, 494
51:42–43   471
51:43   261, 340, 359, 388,
    466, 471, 476
51:44   234, 370, 392, 471,
    474, 475, 480, 486, 489,
    499
51:44–49   480
51:45   181, 254, 382, 433,
    439, 471, 473, 487, 489,
    498
51:45–48   482
51:46   472, 473, 482, 486,
    497
51:46–49   482
51:47   183, 238, 267, 316,
    343, 424, 435, 479, 482,
    486, 492
51:47–48   482, 483, 490,
    497
51:47–49   450, 473
51:47–51   326, 482, 490
51:48   259, 371, 383, 433,
    482, 485, 486, 493
51:49   435, 471, 482, 483,
    489, 492
51:50   102, 439, 482, 489,
    498
51:50–51   482, 483, 484,
    504
51:51   433, 482, 492, 497
51:52   183, 238, 316, 343,
    435, 479, 486, 491, 497
51:52–53   450, 457, 482,
    483, 490, 491, 501
51:53   259, 433, 486, 491,

501

51:54 252, 369, 404, 494
51:54–55 493, 494, 495
51:54–56 490, 491
51:55 447, 478, 494, 495
51:55–56 259, 433
51:56 365, 420, 434, 439,
  456, 492, 496, 497, 499
51:57 214, 272, 440, 455,
  477, 490, 491
51:58 147, 480, 497, 498,
  502, 505, 509
51:59 172, 173, 177, 208,
  361, 368, 502, 529
51:59–54 172
51:59–64 172, 173, 181,
  366, 367, 368, 370, 372,
  503, 508
51:59–65 504
51:60 504
51:61 504, 529
51:61–64 145
51:62 261, 358, 365, 457,
  459, 466, 476, 504, 505
51:63 508
51:64 311, 478, 500, 502,
  504, 505, 512
52 81, 104, 504, 510, 512,
  518, 521, 530, 537
52:1 513
52:1–3 513
52:1–11 512, 532
52:1–27 531
52:3 417, 468, 513
52:4 82, 83, 410
52:4–11 513, 519
52:4–16 81
52:4–27 531
52:5 513
52:6 71, 83, 84
52:7 85, 86
52:7–8 369
52:8 87
52:9 82, 88, 188, 530, 535
52:9 (LXX) 87
52:10 88
52:11 89, 512, 513, 521,
  528, 537
52:12 518, 533
52:12–16 518
52:12–27 512, 518
52:13 89, 90
52:13–16 518
52:14 369, 392

52:15 58, 90, 91, 521
52:16 91, 521
52:17 369, 526, 527, 528
52:17–18 526
52:17–23 475, 518, 519
52:18 525, 526
52:19 524
52:20–23 519
52:22 528
52:23 518
52:24 55, 529
52:24–27 518, 519
52:25 110
52:27 59, 188, 512, 518,
  519, 532, 534
52:27–30 521
52:28 512, 518, 519, 532,
  533
52:28–29 189, 534
52:28–30 512, 519, 530,
  534
52:29 91, 532
52:30 109, 115, 130, 133,
  167, 208, 258, 316, 324,
  532
52:31 56, 369, 534
52:31–34 54, 512, 517, 519
52:33 116, 537
52:34 103, 512, 536

Lamentations
1:1 274, 350, 435
1:2 246
1:4 90
1:7 90
1:10 322
1:11 90
1:19 90, 515
2:1 274
2:2 89
2:3 282
2:5–9 89
2:8 345
2:9 358, 467
2:11–12 90, 159, 515
2:11–20 515
2:15 283, 284
2:17 282, 447
2:19–22 90
3:14 301
3:47 305
3:53 391
4:1 274
4:2 267
4:3 425

4:3–5 515
4:4 275
4:4–5 90
4:5 475
4:7–10 90
4:8–10 515
4:9 57
4:12 84, 322
4:14–15 90
4:17 57
4:21 283, 325, 331, 337,
  387
5:6 391
5:11–14 90
5:12 88
5:13 516
5:20 350

Ezekiel
1:1–28 258
1:2 535
4 83, 515
4:2 514
4:12 371
4:15 371
4:16–17 515
5:2 358
5:8 88
5:10 88, 358
5:12 358
5:15 88
5:16–17 515
6:3–4 378
6:5 358
6:13 378
7:2–6 448
7:16 286
7:17 236
7:18 118
7:26 338
8:1–11:23 350
8:1–11:25 258
8:3 260
9:2 454, 464
12:1–12 86
12:3–4 215
12:4 86
12:7 145
12:13 89
12:13–16 87
12:14–15 358
12:16 166
14:8 134
14:10 439
15:7 134

16:5   68
16:36   371
17   514
17:11–21   514
17:15   56
17:15–17   57
17:16   88
17:17   383, 514
17:18   88, 391
18:6   378
19:11–12   274
21:8–10[Eng 21:3–5]   241
21:17[Eng 21:12]   283
21:21[Eng 21:16]   241
21:23–32[Eng 21:18–
    27]   114, 316, 331
21:24–26[Eng 21:19–
    21]   420
21:27[Eng 21:22]   514
21:33–37[Eng 21:28–
    32]   314, 316
21:35[Eng 21:30]   241
23:6   455
23:22   383
23:23   403
23:31–35   283
24:1   82, 514
25–32   181
25:1–7   314, 316, 322
25:1–11   354
25:5   379
25:8–11   246
25:9   247, 280
25:12–14   114, 325, 331
25:13   328, 330
25:15–17   231
25:16   238, 241
26:7   383
26:8   514
26:15   493
26:19   234
27:10   200
27:15   330
27:18   350
27:21   353
27:27   383
28:1–19   412
28:1–23   237
28:4–7   255
28:7   433
28:23   435, 492
28:26   358
29–32   147, 188, 208
29:1–12   57

29:3   474
29:10   157, 209
29:13–16   226
29:14   157
29:16   226
29:17   208, 216
29:19–20   148
30:5   200
30:6   157, 209
30:9   272
30:12   433
30:14   157, 225
30:14–16   225
30:15   225
30:15–16   219
30:17   149
30:18   143, 147
30:20–26   57, 204
31:1–18   57
31:12   433
32:2   474, 475
32:12   259
32:13   447
32:19   329
32:22–23   383
32:24–25   362
34   378
34:5   379
34:6   379
34:8   379
34:11–16   397
34:21   210
35:3   458
35:3–4   457
35:7–8   459
35:9   459
35:15   114, 325, 331
36:25–29   397
37:9   363
38:4   383
38:5   200
38:7   383
38:11   197, 358
38:13   383
38:15   383
39:10   317
39:17–20   202
39:18   4076
40:38   475
40:49   523

Daniel
1:2   479
1:5   537
5:28   465

6:1[Eng 5:31]   465
6:9[Eng 6:8]   465
6:13[Eng 6:12]   465
6:16[Eng 6:15]   465
6:22   63
8:2   361
8:8   363
8:20   446
9:1   465
11:1   465
11:19   194

Hosea
1:4   468
1:5   363
2:4[Eng 2:2]   388
2:5[Eng 2:3]   275
2:7[Eng 2:5]   163, 388
2:20[Eng 2:18]   358, 363
3:4   149
3:5   375
4:5   388
4:11   477
4:13   378
4:15   268
5:8   268
6:6   72
7:4   383
7:7   477
8:4   371
8:8   301
8:13   130
10:1–2   149
10:6   507
10:8   259
10:11   387
10:14   310
10:15   268
11:8   340
11:9   410
12:11[Eng 12:10]   368
13:2   371
13:15   476

Joel
1:4   222, 306, 448
1:15   272
2:1   272
2:4   465
2:25   448
4:4[Eng 3:4]   237
4:7[Eng 3:7]   383
4:10[Eng 3:10]   191
4:11[Eng 3:11]   375
4:13[Eng 3:13]   394
4:14[Eng 3:14]   272

4:19[Eng 3:19]   325, 331

Amos
1:2–2:16   183
1:3–5   348
1:5   467
1:6–8   231, 239
1:8   233
1:9–10   237
1:11–12   331
1:12   328, 338
1:13   315
1:13–15   314
1:14   147, 350, 391, 413
1:15   251, 258, 315, 319, 321
2:1–3   246
2:2   281, 310
2:7   468
2:14–16   194, 195
3:4   477
3:14   268, 404
4:3   323
4:4   268
4:6–11   160
4:11   459
5:2   204, 413
5:4–6   375
5:5–6   268
5:19   306
5:24   234
5:26–27   147, 258, 321
6:1   358, 388
6:2   239
6:4   219
6:6   524
6:8   444, 448
7:3   133
8:2   448
8:8   196
8:10   118
8:13   166
9:1–4   306
9:2   340, 493
9:3   215
9:4   92, 363, 419
9:5   196
9:7   201, 238

Obadiah
1   338
1–4   334, 335
1–8   77, 325
1–9   325
2   339
3   322, 339, 340, 493

3–4   339
5   274, 326, 330, 331
6   331
7   77
7–8   329
8   328, 330
9   328
9–14   114, 325
10–11   325, 331
15–21   317
16   283, 336

Jonah
2   474
2:1[Eng 1:17]   479
2:11[Eng 2:10]   479

Micah
1:7   193
1:8   425
1:10   239
1:15   315
1:16   118
2:4   58, 274
3:2–3   475
3:12   320
4:1   479
4:13   387
6:12   262
7:1   113
7:14   397
7:18–19   397

Nahum
1:8   234
2:2[Eng 2:1]   452, 454
2:3[2:2]   433
2:4–9[Eng 2:3–8]   195
2:5[Eng 2:4]   193, 199
2:9[Eng 2:8]   193
2:11[Eng 2:10]   236
3:2–3   199
3:5   193, 195, 204
3:8   225
3:9   200
3:11   256
3:13   467
3:15–17   448
3:17   320, 464, 465
3:18   323

Habakkuk
1:6   315
1:8–9   194
2:2   507
2:3   272
2:9   340, 493
2:13   498, 500

2:15–16   283
3:3   410
3:15   447
3:16   350

Zephaniah
1:6   375
1:7   202
1:10   84
1:12   266
1:17   371
2:4   239
2:4–7   231
2:5   233, 238
2:6   320
2:8   288
2:8–10   288, 317, 322
2:8–11   246, 314
2:9   260, 313
2:10   283, 305
2:15   322, 358
3:14   387

Haggai
1:1   368, 455, 528
1:3   368
1:9   421
1:14   432
2:1   368

Zechariah
2:10[Eng 2:6]   254, 363
3:1   528
3:3–5   536
4   525
6:5   363
6:11   528
7:3   90
7:5   90, 117
7:7   358
8:19   83, 84, 90, 117
9:1–2   348
9:5   239
11:6   378
12:2   283, 525
13:7   202, 343
14:10   58

Malachi
1:1   368
1:2–5   331
3:20[Eng 4:2]   219, 387

APOCRYPHA
Baruch
1:2   519
3:22–23   328
4:35   425

1 Esdras
  1:46   513
  1:46–58   512
  1:47   54, 513
  4:45   325, 331
  4:50   327
Epistle of Jeremiah
  40   370
Judith
  12:10–13:10   116
1 Maccabees
  5:6–8   317
  5:8   292
  5:42   529
  5:65   327
  7:19   119
2 Maccabees
  2:1–3   128
  5:15–21   488
Sirach
  40:4   261
  49:13   358
Tobit
  1:21   463
Wisdom of Solomon
  10:6   340

OLD TESTAMENT
PSEUDEPIGRAPHA
Psalms of Solomon
  1:8–2:1–3   488
  2:25   474
  7:2   488
  8:12–13   488

NEW TESTAMENT
Matthew
  1:11–12   54
  5:5   91

  5:15   525
  6:27   447
  6:34   537
  8:27   476
  9:17   265
  9:23   298
  10:24   177
  11:17   298
  12:43   424
  18:12–13   379
  18:12–14   378
  24   441
  24:6   485
  24:6–7   485
  24:33–34   456
  25:1–12   441
  26:47   454
  26:72–74   131
  27:24   67
  27:51   466
  28:2   466
Mark
  3:17   310
  14:43   454
  15:29   284
Luke
  1:69   282
  6:40   177
  9:51   134
  10:29–37   70
  12:16–21   322
  12:35–46   441
  15:4–7   378
  15:22   536
  15:30   130
John
  10:11–18   378
Acts
  2:9   362

  7:4   369
  26:24   329
Romans
  1:20–23   424
  11:5   397
2 Timothy
  2:9   66
Hebrews
  6:13   337
1 Peter
  4:17–18   337
Revelation
  8:8   458
  9:7   465
  16:16   458
  17–18   440
  17:1   447
  18   443
  18:2   425, 440
  18:3   440
  18:4   439
  18:6   439
  18:8   441
  18:9–19   441
  18:20   442, 443
  18:21   509
  18:21–23   494
  19–20   363
  20   476
  21:1   476
  22:12   441
  22:20   441

THE ANCHOR BIBLE

Commentaries (C) and Reference Library (RL) volumes on the Old and New
Testaments and Apocrypha

THE CONTRIBUTORS

Susan Ackerman, Dartmouth College. RL17

William F. Albright, Johns Hopkins
University. C26

Francis I. Andersen, Professorial Fellow,
Classics and Archaeology, University of
Melbourne. C24, C24A, C24E

Markus Barth, University of Basel. C34,
C34A, C34B

Adele Berlin, University of Maryland. C25A

Helmut Blanke, Doctor of Theology from
the University of Basel. C34B

Joseph Blenkinsopp, University of Notre
Dame. C19, C19A, C19B, RL5

Robert G. Boling, McCormick Theological
Seminary. C6, C6A

Raymond E. Brown, S.S., Union
Theological Seminary, New York
(Emeritus). C29, C29A, C30, RL1, RL7,
RL15, RL22

George W. Buchanan, Wesley Theological
Seminary. C36

Edward F. Campbell, Jr., McCormick
Theological Seminary. C7

James H. Charlesworth, Princeton
Theological Seminary. RL4, RL13, RL14

Mordechai Cogan, Hebrew University,
Jerusalem. C10, C11

John J. Collins, University of Chicago. RL10

James L. Crenshaw, Duke Divinity School.
C24C, RL16

Mitchell Dahood, S.J., The Pontifical
Biblical Institute. C16, C17, C17A

Alexander A. Di Lella, O.F.M., Catholic
University of America. C23, C39

David L. Dungan, University of Tennessee,
Knoxville. RL18

John H. Elliott, University of San Francisco.
C37B

Joseph A. Fitzmyer, S.J., Catholic University
of America. C28, C28A, C31, C33, C34C

J. Massyngberde Ford, University of Notre
Dame. C38

Michael V. Fox, University of Wisconsin,
Madison. C18A

David Noel Freedman, University of
Michigan (Emeritus) and University of
California, San Diego. General Editor.
C24, C24A, C24E

Victor P. Furnish, Perkins School of
Theology, Southern Methodist University.
C32A

Jonathan A. Goldstein, University of Iowa.
C41, C41A, RL21

Moshe Greenberg, Hebrew University,
Jerusalem. C22, C22A

Louis F. Hartman, C.SS.R., Catholic
University of America. C23

Andrew E. Hill, Wheaton College. C25D

Delbert R. Hillers, Johns Hopkins
University. C7A

Luke Timothy Johnson, Candler School of
Theology, Emory University. C35A, C37A

Gary Knoppers, Penn State University. C12

Craig R. Koester, Luther Seminary. C36

Bentley Layton, Yale University. RL11

Baruch A. Levine, New York University. C4,
C4A

Jack R. Lundbom, Clare Hall, Cambridge
University. C21A, C21B

P. Kyle McCarter, Jr., Johns Hopkins
University. C8, C9

John L. McKenzie, De Paul University. C20

Abraham J. Malherbe, Yale University
(Emeritus). C32B

C. S. Mann, formerly Coppin State
College. C26

Joel Marcus, Boston University. C27

J. Louis Martyn, Union Theological
Seminary, New York. C33A

Amihai Mazar, Institute of Archaeology of
Hebrew University, Jerusalem. RL2

John P. Meier, Catholic University of
America. RL3, RL9, RL20

Carol L. Meyers, Duke University. C25B,
C25C

Eric M. Meyers, Duke University. C25B,
C25C

Jacob Milgrom, University of California, Berkeley (Emeritus). C3, C3A, C3B

Carey A. Moore, Gettysburg College. C7B, C40, C40A, C44

Jacob M. Myers, Lutheran Theological Seminary, Gettysburg. C12, C13, C14, C42

Jacob Neusner, University of South Florida at Tampa. RL8

Jerome H. Neyrey, University of Notre Dame. C37C

William F. Orr, Pittsburgh Theological Seminary. C32

Brian Peckham, Regis College, Toronto University. RL6

Marvin H. Pope, Yale University (Emeritus). C7C, C15

William H. C. Propp, University of California, San Diego. C2

Jerome D. Quinn, St. Paul Seminary. C35

Paul R. Raabe, Concordia Seminary, St. Louis. C24D

Bo Ivar Reicke, University of Basel. C37

Jack M. Sasson, University of North Carolina at Chapel Hill. C24B

Lawrence H. Schiffman, New York University. RL12

R. B. Y. Scott, Princeton University. C18

Choon-Leong Seow, Princeton Theological Seminary. C18C

Patrick W. Skehan, Catholic University of America. C39

Ephraim A. Speiser, University of Pennsylvania. C1

Ephraim Stern, Hebrew University, Jerusalem. RL19

Hayim Tadmor, Hebrew University, Jerusalem. C11

James Arthur Walther, Pittsburgh Theological Seminary (Emeritus). C32

Moshe Weinfeld, Hebrew University, Jerusalem. C5

David Winston, Graduate Theological Union, Berkeley (Emeritus). C43

G. Ernest Wright, Semitic Museum, Harvard University. C6